DATE DUE

PRINTED IN U.S.A.

Literature Criticism from 1400 to 1800

Guide to Gale Literary Criticism Series

When you need to review criticism of literary works, these are the Gale series to use:

If the author's death date is:

You should turn to:

After Dec. 31, 1959
(or author is still living)

CONTEMPORARY LITERARY CRITICISM

for example: Jorge Luis Borges, Anthony Burgess,
William Faulkner, Mary Gordon,
Ernest Hemingway, Iris Murdoch

1900 through 1959

TWENTIETH-CENTURY LITERARY CRITICISM

for example: Willa Cather, F. Scott Fitzgerald,
Henry James, Mark Twain, Virginia Woolf

1800 through 1899

NINETEENTH-CENTURY LITERATURE CRITICISM

for example: Fedor Dostoevski, Nathaniel Hawthorne,
George Sand, William Wordsworth

1400 through 1799

LITERATURE CRITICISM FROM 1400 TO 1800
(excluding Shakespeare)

for example: Anne Bradstreet, Daniel Defoe,
Alexander Pope, François Rabelais,
Jonathan Swift, Phillis Wheatley

SHAKESPEAREAN CRITICISM

Shakespeare's plays and poetry

Antiquity through 1399

CLASSICAL AND MEDIEVAL LITERATURE CRITICISM

for example: Dante, Homer, Plato, Sophocles, Vergil,
the Beowulf Poet

Gale also publishes related criticism series:

CHILDREN'S LITERATURE REVIEW

This series covers authors of all eras who write for the preschool through high school audience.

SHORT STORY CRITICISM

This series covers the major short fiction writers of all nationalities and periods of literary history.

ISSN 0740-2880

Volume 9

Literature Criticism from 1400 to 1800

Excerpts from Criticism of the Works
of Fifteenth-, Sixteenth-, Seventeenth-, and
Eighteenth-Century Novelists, Poets, Playwrights,
Philosophers, and Other Creative Writers, from
the First Published Critical Appraisals
to Current Evaluations

James E. Person, Jr.
Editor

Robin DuBlanc
Associate Editor

Gale Research Inc.
Book Tower • Detroit, Michigan 48226

STAFF

James E. Person, Jr., *Editor*

Robin DuBlanc, *Associate Editor*

James P. Draper, Jay P. Pederson, *Senior Assistant Editors*

Claudia Loomis, Shannon J. Young, *Assistant Editors*

Jeanne A. Gough, *Permissions and Production Manager*

Lizbeth A. Purdy, *Production Supervisor*
Kathleen M. Cook, *Assistant Production Coordinator*
Cathy Beranek, Suzanne Powers, Kristine Tipton, Lee Ann Welsh, *Editorial Assistants*

Linda M. Pugliese, *Manuscript Coordinator*
Maureen A. Poole, *Senior Manuscript Assistant*
Donna Craft, Jennifer E. Gale, *Manuscript Assistants*

Victoria B. Cariappa, *Research Supervisor*
Maureen R. Richards, *Research Coordinator*
Mary D. Wise, *Senior Research Assistant*
Joyce E. Doyle, Kevin B. Hillstrom, Karen D. Kaus, Eric Priehs,
Filomena Sgambati, Laura B. Standley, *Research Assistants*

Janice M. Mach, *Text Permissions Supervisor*
Kathy Grell, *Text Permissions Coordinator*
Mabel E. Gurney, *Research Permissions Coordinator,*
Josephine M. Keene, *Senior Permissions Assistant*
Eileen H. Baehr, H. Diane Cooper, Lorraine Ransom, Kimberly F. Smilay, *Permissions Assistants*
Melissa A. Kamuyu, Denise M. Singleton, Sharon D. Valentine, Lisa M. Wimmer, *Permissions Clerks*

Patricia A. Seefelt, *Picture Permissions Supervisor*
Margaret A. Chamberlain, *Picture Permissions Coordinator*
Pamela A. Hayes, Lillian Tyus, *Permissions Clerks*

Mary Beth Trimper, *Production Manager*
Patricia Farley, *Production Assistant*

Arthur Chartow, *Art Director*
Linda A. Davis, *Production Assistant*

Laura Bryant, *Production Supervisor*
Louise Gagne, *Internal Production Associate*
Jean Rushlow, *Internal Production Assistant*

Library of Congress Catalog Card Number 83-20504
ISBN 0-8103-6108-6
ISSN 0740-2880

Printed in the United States of America

10 9 8 7 6 5 4 3 2

Contents

Preface   vii

Authors to Appear in Future Volumes   xi

Appendix   450

Preface

"If I have seen farther," wrote Sir Isaac Newton, echoing Fulbert of Chartres and commenting on his own indebtedness to the sages who preceded him, "it is by standing on the shoulders of giants"; this is a statement as applicable to ourselves today as it was to Newton and his world. Many of the political and intellectual foundations of the modern world can be found in the art and thought of the fifteenth through eighteenth centuries. During this time the modern nation-state was born, the sciences grew tremendously, and many of the political, social, economic, and moral philosophies that are influential today were formulated. The literature of these centuries reflects this turbulent time of radical change: the period saw the rise of drama equal in critical stature to that of classical Greece, the birth of the novel and personal essay forms, the emergence of newspapers and periodicals, and significant achievements in poetry and philosophy. Much of modern literature reflects the influence of these centuries' developments. Thus the literature of this period provides insight into the universal nature of human experience, as well as into the life and thought of the past.

Literary criticism can also give us insight into the human condition, as well as into the specific moral and intellectual atmosphere of an era, for the criteria by which a work of art is judged reflect contemporary philosophical and social attitudes. Literary criticism takes many forms: the traditional essay, the book or play review, even the parodic poem. Criticism can also be of several kinds, including descriptive, interpretive, textual, appreciative, and generic, among others. Collectively, the range of critical response helps us understand a work of art, an author, an era.

Scope of the Series

Literature Criticism from 1400 to 1800 (LC) is designed to serve as an introduction to the authors of the fifteenth through eighteenth centuries and to the most significant commentators on these authors. The works of the great poets, dramatists, novelists, essayists, and philosophers of those years are considered classics in every secondary school and college or university curriculum. Because criticism of this literature spans a period of up to six hundred years, an overwhelming amount of critical material confronts the student. To help students locate and select criticism on the works of authors who died between 1400 and 1800, *LC* presents significant passages from the most noteworthy published criticism on authors of these centuries. Each volume of *LC* is carefully compiled to represent the critical heritage of the most important writers from a variety of nationalities. In addition to major authors, *LC* also presents criticism on lesser-known writers whose significant contributions to literary history are reflected in continuing critical assessments of their works.

The need for *LC* among students and teachers of literature of the fifteenth through eighteenth centuries was suggested by the proven usefulness of Gale's *Contemporary Literary Criticism (CLC)*, *Twentieth-Century Literary Criticism (TCLC)*, and *Nineteenth-Century Literature Criticism (NCLC)*, which excerpt criticism of creative writing from the nineteenth and twentieth centuries. Because of the different time periods covered, there is no duplication of authors or critical material among any of Gale's literary criticism series. For further information about these series, readers should consult the Guide to Gale Literary Criticism Series preceding the title page of this volume. Here, the reader will note that there is a separate Gale reference series devoted to Shakespearean studies. For though belonging properly to the literary period covered in *LC*, William Shakespeare has inspired such a tremendous and ever-growing corpus of secondary material that the editors have deemed it best to give his works the extensive critical coverage best served by a separate series, *Shakespearean Criticism*.

Each author entry in *LC* provides an overview of major criticism on an author. Therefore, the editors include approximately twelve authors in each 550-page volume (compared with approximately forty authors in a *CLC* volume of similar size) so that more attention may be given each author. Each author entry presents a historical survey of the critical response to an author's work: early criticism is offered to indicate initial responses, later selections document any rise or decline in the author's literary reputation and describe the effects of social or historical forces on the work of an author, and retrospective analyses provide students with a modern view. The length of an author entry is intended to present the author's critical reception in English or foreign criticism in translation. Articles and books that have not been translated into English are therefore excluded. Every attempt has been made to identify and include excerpts from the seminal essays on each author's work and to include recent critical commentary providing modern perspectives on the writer. An author may appear more than once in the series because of the great quantity of critical material available, or because of a resurgence of criticism generated by such events as an author's anniversary celebration, the republication of an author's works, or the publication of a newly translated work.

Organization of the Book

An author entry consists of the following elements: author heading, biographical and critical introduction, list of principal works, excerpts of criticism (each followed by a bibliographical citation), and a bibliography of further reading. Also, most author entries reproduce author portraits and other illustrations pertinent to the author's life and career.

- The *author heading* consists of the author's full name, followed by birth and death dates. The portion of the name not parenthesized denotes the form under which the author most commonly wrote. If an author wrote consistently under a pseudonym, the pseudonym will be used in the author heading, with the real name given in parentheses on the first line of the biographical and critical introduction. Also located at the beginning of the introduction to the author entry are any name variations under which an author wrote, including transliterated forms for authors whose native languages use nonroman alphabets. Uncertain birth or death dates are indicated by question marks.

- The *biographical and critical introduction* contains background information designed to introduce the reader to an author and to the critical discussion surrounding his or her work. Parenthetical material following many of the introductions provides references to biographical and critical reference series published by Gale, including *Children's Literature Review, Dictionary of Literary Biography, Something about the Author,* and *Yesterday's Authors of Books for Children.*

- Most *LC* entries include *portraits* of the author. Many entries also contain illustrations of materials pertinent to an author's career, including selected author holographs, title pages, letters, or representations of important people, places, and events in an author's life.

- The *list of principal works* is chronological by date of first book publication and identifies the genre of each work. In the case of foreign authors whose works have been translated into English, the title and date of the first English-language edition are given in brackets following the foreign-language listing. Unless otherwise indicated, dramas are dated by first performance, not first publication.

- *Criticism* is arranged chronologically in each author entry to provide a useful perspective on changes in critical evaluation over the years. All titles by the author featured in the critical entry are printed in boldface type to enable the user to ascertain without difficulty the works being discussed. Also for purposes of easier identification, the critic's name and the composition or publication date of the critical work are given at the beginning of each excerpt. Unsigned criticism is preceded by the title of the source in which it appeared. When an anonymous essay has been attributed to a critic, the critic's name appears in brackets at the beginning of the excerpt and in the bibliographical citation. Publication information (such as publisher names and book prices) and parenthetical numerical references (such as footnotes or page and line references to specific editions of works) have been deleted at the editor's discretion to provide smoother reading of the text.

- Critical essays are prefaced by *explanatory notes* as an additional aid to students using *LC*. The explanatory notes may provide several types of useful information, including: the reputation of a critic, the importance of a work of criticism, the specific type of criticism (biographical, psychoanalytic, structuralist, etc.), the intent of the criticism, and the growth of critical controversy or changes in critical trends regarding an author's work. In some cases, these notes cross-reference the work of critics who agree or disagree with each other. Dates in parentheses within the explanatory notes refer to a book publication date when they follow a book title and to the date of an essay excerpted and reprinted elsewhere in the author entry when they follow a critic's name.

- A complete *bibliographical citation* designed to facilitate location of the original essay or book by the reader follows each piece of criticism.

- The *additional bibliography* appearing at the end of each author entry suggests further reading on the author. In a few rare cases it includes essays for which the editors could not obtain reprint rights.

An appendix lists the sources from which material in each volume has been reprinted. It does not, however, list every book and periodical consulted in the preparation of the volume.

Cumulative Indexes

Each volume of *LC* includes a cumulative index to authors listing all the authors that have appeared in *Contemporary Literary Criticism, Twentieth-Century Literary Criticism, Nineteenth-Century Literature Criticism, Literature Criticism from 1400 to 1800,* and *Classical and Medieval Literature Criticism,* along with cross-references to the Gale series *Short Story Criticism, Children's Literature Review, Authors in the News, Contemporary Authors, Contemporary Authors Autobiography Series, Contemporary Authors Bibliographical Series, Dictionary of Literary Biography, Concise Dictionary of Literary Biography, Something about the Author, Something about the Author Autobiography Series,* and *Yesterday's Authors of Books for Children.* Readers will welcome this cumulative author index as a useful tool for locating an author within the various series. The index, which includes authors' birth and death dates, is particularly valuable for those authors who are identified with a certain period but whose death dates cause them to be placed in another, or for those authors whose careers span two periods. For example, F. Scott Fitzgerald is found in *TCLC,* yet a writer often associated with him, Ernest Hemingway, is found in *CLC.*

Each volume of *LC* also includes a cumulative nationality index, in which authors' names are arranged alphabetically under their respective nationalities and followed by the numbers of the volumes in which they appear. In addition, each volume of *LC* includes a cumulative index to titles, an alphabetical listing of the literary works discussed in the series since its inception. Each title listing includes the corresponding volume and page numbers where criticism may be located. Foreign-language titles that have been translated are followed by the titles of the translations—for example, *El ingenioso hidalgo Don Quixote de la Mancha (Don Quixote).* Page numbers following these translated titles refer to all pages on which any form of the titles, either foreign-language or translated, appear. Titles of novels, dramas, nonfiction books, and poetry, short story, or essay collections are printed in italics, while all individual poems, short stories, and essays are printed in roman type within quotation marks. In cases where the same title is used by different authors, the author's surname is given in parentheses after the title, e.g., *Poems* (Bradstreet) and *Poems* (Killigrew).

Acknowledgments

No work of this scope can be accomplished without the cooperation of many people. The editors especially wish to thank the copyright holders of the excerpts included in this volume, the permissions managers of many book and magazine publishing companies for assisting us in locating copyright holders, and Anthony Bogucki for assistance with copyright research. We are also grateful to the staffs of the Detroit Public Library, the Library of Congress, University of Detroit Library, University of Michigan Library, and Wayne State University Library for making their resources available to us.

Suggestions Are Welcome

Readers who wish to suggest authors to appear in future volumes, or who have other suggestions, are cordially invited to write the editor.

Authors to Appear in Future Volumes

Abravenel, Isaac 1437-1508
Abravenel, Judah 1460-1535
Addison, Joseph 1672-1719
Agricola, Johannes 1494?-1566
Akenside, Mark 1721-1770
Alabaster, William 1567-1640
Alarcón y Mendoza, Juan Rúiz
    1581-1634
Alberti, Leon Battista 1404-1472
Alembert, Jean Le Rond d' 1717-1783
Amory, Thomas 1691?-1788
Anton Ulrich, Duke of Brunswick
    1633-1714
Aretino, Pietro 1492-1556
Ascham, Roger 1515-1568
Aubigne, Théodore Agrippa d'
    1552-1630
Aubrey, John 1620-1697
Bâbur 1483-1530
Bacon, Sir Francis 1561-1626
Bale, John 1495-1563
Barber, Mary 1690-1757
Baretti, Giuseppi 1719-1789
Barker, Jane 1652-1727?
Bartas, Guillaume de Salluste du
    1544-1590
Baxter, Richard 1615-1691
Bayle, Pierre 1647-1706
Beaumarchais, Pierre-Augustin Caron
    de 1732-1799
Beaumont, Francis 1584-1616
Belleau, Rémy 1528-1577
Berkeley, George 1685-1753
Bessarion, Johannes 1403-1472
Bijns, Anna 1493-1575
Bisticci, Vespasiano da 1421-1498
Blackmore, Sir Richard 1650-1729
Boccalini, Traiano 1556-1613
Bodin, Jean 1530-1596
Bolingbroke, Henry St. John
    1678-1751
Boyle, Roger 1621-1679
Bradford, William 1590-1657
Brant, Sebastian 1457-1521
Bredero, Gerbrand Adriaanszoon
    1585-1618
Breitinger, Johann Jakob 1701-1776
Breton, Nicholas 1545-1626
Broome, William 1689-1745
Brown, Thomas 1663-1704
Browne, Sir Thomas 1605-1682
Bruni, Leonardo 1370-1444
Bruno, Giordano 1548-1600
Buffon, George-Louis Leclerc, Comte
    de 1707-1788
Burgoyne, John 1722-1792

Burnet, Gilbert 1643-1715
Burton, Robert 1577-1640
Butler, Samuel 1612-1680
Byrd, William, II 1674-1744
Byrom, John 1692-1763
Calderón de la Barca, Pedro 1600-1681
Camden, William 1551-1623
Campion, Thomas 1567-1620
Carew, Richard 1555-1620
Carew, Thomas 1594-1640
Carver, Jonathan 1710-1780
Casanova di Seingalt, Giacomo
    Girolamo 1725-1798
Castiglione, Baldassare 1478-1529
Castillejo, Cristobalde 1492-1550
Cavendish, William 1592-1676
Caxton, William 1421?-1491
Centlivre, Susanna 1667?-1723
Chapman, George 1560-1634
Chartier, Alain 1390-1440
Chaucer, Geoffrey 1340?-1400
Cibber, Colley 1671-1757
Cleveland, John 1613-1658
Collyer, Mary 1716?-1763?
Colonna, Vittoria 1490-1547
Commynes, Philippe de 1445-1511
Condillac, Etienne Bonnot, Abbé de
    1714?-1780
Cook, James 1728-1779
Corneille, Pierre 1606-1684
Cortés, Hernán 1485-1547
Cotton, John 1584-1652
Courtilz de Sandras, Gatiende
    1644-1712
Cowley, Abraham 1618-1667
Cranmer, Thomas 1489-1556
Crashaw, Richard 1612-1649
Crébillon, Prosper Jolyot de 1674-1762
Cruden, Alexander 1701-1770
Curll, Edmund 1675-1747
Dampier, William 1653-1715
Daniel, Samuel 1562-1619
Davenant, Sir William 1606-1668
Davidson, John 1549?-1603
Da Vinci, Leonardo 1452-1519
Day, John 1574-1640
Dekker, Thomas 1572-1632
Delany, Mary Pendarves 1700-1788
Denham, Sir John 1615-1669
Dennis, John 1657-1734
Deloney, Thomas 1543?-1600?
Descartes, René 1596-1650
Desfontaines, Pierre François Guyot,
    Abbé 1685-1745
Diaz del Castillo, Bernal 1492?-1584
Diderot, Denis 1713-1784
Donne, John 1572-1631

Drummond, William 1585-1649
Du Guillet, Pernette 1520?-1545
Dunbar, William 1460?-1520?
Elyot, Thomas 1490-1546
Emin, Fedor ?-1770
Erasmus, Desiderius 1466-1536
Etherege, Sir George 1635-1691
Eusden, Laurence 1688-1730
Evelyn, John 1620-1706
Fabyan, Robert ?-1513
Fairfax, Thomas 1621-1671
Fanshawe, Lady Anne 1625-1680
Fanshawe, Sir Richard 1608-1666
Farquhar, George 1678-1707
Fénelon, François 1651-1715
Fergusson, Robert 1750-1774
Ficino, Marsillo 1433-1499
Fletcher, John 1579-1625
Florian, Jean Pierre Claris de
    1755-1794
Florio, John 1553?-1625
Fontaine, Charles 1514-1565
Fontenelle, Bernard Le Bovier de
    1657-1757
Fonvizin, Denis Ivanovich 1745-1792
Ford, John 1586-1640
Foxe, John 1517-1587
Franklin, Benjamin 1706-1790
Froissart, Jean 1337-1404?
Fuller, Thomas 1608-1661
Galilei, Galileo 1564-1642
Garrick, David 1717-1779
Gascoigne, George 1530?-1577
Gay, John 1685-1732
Gibbon, Edward 1737-1794
Gildon, Charles 1665-1724
Glanvill, Joseph 1636-1680
Góngora y Argote, Luis de 1561-1627
Gosson, Stephen 1554-1624
Gottsched, Johann Christoph
    1700-1766
Gower, John 1330?-1408
Gracian y Morales, Baltasar 1601-1658
Graham, Dougal 1724-1779
Greene, Robert 1558?-1592
Griffith, Elizabeth 1727?-1793
Guarini, Giambattista 1538-1612
Hakluyt, Richard 1553-1616
Hall, Edward 1498-1547
Harrington, James 1611-1677
Hartley, David 1705-1757
Helvetius, Claude Arien 1715-1771
Henry VIII 1491-1547
Henslowe, Philip ?-1616
Herbert, George 1593-1633
Herrick, Robert 1591-1674
Heywood, Thomas 1574-1641

Hobbes, Thomas 1588-1679
Hogarth, William 1697-1764
Holbach, Paul Heinrich Dietrich 1723-1789
Holinshed, Raphael ?-1582?
Hooker, Richard 1544-1600
Hooker, Thomas 1586-1647
Howard, Henry, Earl of Surrey 1517-1547
Hung Sheng 1646-1704
Hutcheson, Francis 1694-1746
Ibn Khaldun, Abd al-Rahman ibn Muhammad 1332-1406
Iriarte, Tomas de 1750-1791
Isla y Rojo, José Francisco de 1703-1781
James I, King of Scotland 1394-1437
Johnson, Samuel 1709-1784
King, William 1662-1712
Knox, John 1514?-1572
Kochanowski, Jan 1530-1584
Kyd, Thomas 1558-1594
La Bruyére, Jean de 1645-1696
La Fontaine, Jean de 1621-1695
Langland, William 1330?-1400
Lanyer, Aemilia 1569-1645
La Rochefoucauld, Francois de 1613-1680
Law, William 1686-1761
L'Estrange, Sir Roger 1616-1704
Let-we Thon-dara 1752-1783
Lipsius, Justus 1547-1606
Littleton, Sir Thomas 1422-1481
Lo Kuan-chung c.1400
Lodge, Thomas 1558-1625
Lope de Vega 1562-1635
Lopez de Ayala, Pero 1332-1407?
Lovelace, Richard 1618-1657
Loyola, Ignacio de 1491-1556
Lydgate, John 1370?-1452
Lyly, John 1554-1606
Lyttelton, George 1709-1773
MacDomhnaill, Sean Clarach 1691-1754
Macpherson, James 1736-1796
Maitland, Sir Richard 1496-1586
Malory, Sir Thomas ?-1471
Mandeville, Bernard de 1670-1733
Marat, Jean Paul 1743-1793
Marie de l'Incarnation 1599-1672
Marlowe, Christopher 1564-1593
Marston, John 1576-1634
Massinger, Philip 1583-1640
Mather, Cotton 1663-1728
Mather, Increase 1639-1723
Metastasio, Pietro 1698-1782
Michelangelo Buonarrotti 1475-1564

Middleton, Thomas 1580-1627
Molière 1622-1673
Montfort, Hugo von 1357-1423
More, Sir Thomas 1478-1535
Morton, Thomas 1575-1647
Muret, Marc-Antoine de 1526-1585
Nashe, Thomas 1567-1601
Nawa i 1441-1501
Newton, Sir Isaac 1642-1727
North, Sir Thomas 1535?-1601?
Norton, Thomas 1532-1584
Oldham, John 1653-1683
Otway, Thomas 1652-1685
Pade-tha-ya-za 1684-1754
Painter, William 1540?-1594
Paracelsus 1493-1541
Parr, Catharine 1512-1548
Pascal, Blaise 1623-1662
Pasek, Jan Chryzostom 1636-1701
Peele, George 1556-1596
Pembroke, Mary Sidney, Countess of 1561-1621
Penn, William 1644-1718
Pepys, Samuel 1633-1703
Pico della Mirandola, Giovanni 1463-1494
Poliziano, Angelo 1454-1494
Quarles, Francis 1592-1644
Quevedo y Villegas, Francisco Gomez de 1580-1645
Racine, Jean 1639-1699
Raleigh, Sir Walter 1552-1618
Reuter, Christian 1665-1712
Revius, Jacobus 1586-1658
Reynolds, Sir Joshua 1723-1792
Rochester, John Wilmot, Earl of 1648-1680
Rojas Zorilla, Francisco de 1607-1648
Roper, William 1498-1578
Rousseau, Jean-Jacques 1712-1788
Rowe, Elizabeth 1674-1737
Rutherford, Samuel 1600?-1661
Sackville, Thomas 1536-1608
Saint-Simon, Louis de Rouvroy 1675-1755
Santeuil, Jean Baptiste de 1630-1697
Savage, Richard 1696-1742
Savonarola, Girolamo 1452-1498
Scarron, Paul 1610-1660
Scott, Sarah 1723-1795
Selden, John 1584-1654
Sévigné, Madame de 1626-1696
Sewall, Samuel 1652-1730
Shadwell, Thomas 1642-1692
Shaftesbury, Anthony Ashley Cooper, Earl of 1671-1713

Shenstone, William 1714-1763
Shirley, James 1596-1666
Sidney, Sir Philip 1554-1586
Skelton, John 1464?-1529
Smith, Adam 1723-1790
Spee, Friedrich von 1591-1635
Sprat, Thomas 1635-1713
Stanhope, Philip 1694-1773
Steele, Sir Richard 1672-1729
Suckling, Sir John 1609-1642
Swedenborg, Emanuel 1688-1772
Takeda Izumo 1690-1756
Tasso, Bernardo 1494-1569
Taylor, Edward 1645-1729
Taylor, Jeremy 1613-1667
Temple, Sir William 1629-1699
Tencin, Madame de 1682-1749
Teresa de Jesús 1515-1582
Testi, Fulvio 1593-1646
Thomas à Kempis 1380?-1471
Thomson, James 1700-1748
Tourneur, Cyril 1570-1626
Traherne, Thomas 1637-1674
Trai, Nguyen 1380-1442
Tristan 1601-1655
Tyndale, William 1494?-1536
Urquhart, Sir Thomas 1611-1660
Ussher, James 1581-1656
Vasari, Giorgio 1511-1574
Vaughan, Henry 1621-1695
Vaughan, Thomas 1622-1666
Vico, Giambattista 1668-1744
Villiers, George 1628-1687
Villon, François 1431-1463
Voltaire 1694-1778
Waller, Edmund 1606-1687
Walton, Izaak 1593-1683
Warburton, William 1698-1779
Warner, William 1558-1609
Warton, Thomas 1728-1790
Webster, John 1580-1638
Weise, Christian 1642-1708
Wesley, Charles 1701?-1788
Wesley, John 1703-1791
Whetstone, George 1544?-1587?
White, Gilbert 1720-1793
Wigglesworth, Michael 1631-1705
Williams, Roger 1603-1683
Winckelman, Johann Joachim 1717-1768
Winthrop, John 1588-1649
Wyatt, Sir Thomas 1503-1542
Yuan Mei 1716-1797
Zólkiewski, Stanislaw 1547-1620
Zrinyi, Miklos 1620-1664

Readers are cordially invited to suggest additional authors to the editors.

Penelope Aubin

1685-1731?

English novelist, translator, dramatist, poet, and editor.

Aubin exemplifies the resourceful, successful woman writer of the eighteenth century. Though neither a pioneer among female litterateurs nor a flawless exemplar of one, she astutely gauged public taste and created novels ingeniously integrating the type of travel narrative popularized by Daniel Defoe's *Robinson Crusoe* (1719) and the strain of amatory tale evolved by Eliza Haywood, tempering the whole with stern morality. She thereby created, to the delight of her readers, eventful romance in which virtue triumphs over staggering odds. Although Aubin's works were quite popular at first, they received virtually no critical attention before the twentieth century. Modern commentators have cited such works as *The Noble Slaves; or, The Lives and Adventures of Two Lords and Two Ladies* as direct precursors of more widely known novels treating beleaguered innocence, most notably Samuel Richardson's *Pamela; or, Virtue Rewarded* (1740). While debated, this claim, coupled with a rising interest in women writers, has nonetheless served to revive the reputation of an author until recently relegated to obscurity.

Almost all of what is known of Aubin's life is contained in Abbé Antoine François Prévost d'Exiles's caustic portrait of her, written in 1734. Born in London, Aubin was the daughter of French émigrées who were probably part of a mass Huguenot exodus. While the religious persuasion of her parents remains undertermined—whether Roman Catholic, Protestant, or an amalgam of the two—Aubin reflected in the mixed ancestry of her fictional characters not only the influence of rival cultures but of opposing faiths as well, the latter evidenced particularly in a sympathetic portrayal of Catholics unusual in her time. Of her early years little is known, but documents record the inauguration in 1707 and 1708 of her literary career with three topical poems. One of them, celebrating an English military victory over French forces, is entitled "The Exstasy: A Pindarique Ode to Her Majesty the Queen," and was presented to Queen Anne by the Duchess of Ormonde, who is believed to have been a patron of the author at this time. Aubin's initial flurry of activity was followed by better than a decade of literary quietude, during which she married and apparently became preoccupied with domestic duties. According to Prévost, she also published a few anonymous tracts and pamphlets. At any rate, it is very likely that financial necessity compelled Aubin, as it had other women authors of the day, to join the fraternity of Grub Street hacks in writing novels, a popular and enormously marketable commodity. In 1721 and 1722 she published four novels (among them *The Strange Adventures of the Count de Vinevil and His Family* and *The Noble Slaves*), translated two French novels, and edited a previously unpublished French conduct book.

Aubin's success was immediate and her activity prodigious. Her first works were followed over the next several years by more translations (including a rendering of Robert de Challes's acclaimed *The Illustrious French Lovers*) and other novels. She also wrote a dramatic comedy, *The Merry Masqueraders; or, The Humorous Cuckold,* a piece employing typically Restoration elements but one which, found lacking in the funda-

mental wit of competing plays, was aborted after only two performances. Indeed, all of Aubin's later efforts met with rather less warmth than her previous endeavors. In 1729, she established her own oratory near Charing Cross, a brief enterprise that enjoyed some favorable response. Her death, while not precisely dated, probably occurred in 1731, not many months after the final performance of *The Merry Masqueraders.*

Aubin's fiction is notably and avowedly didactic. In a preface to *The Strange Adventures of the Count de Vinevil and His Family,* she proclaimed that readers might find in the ensuing pages "a Story, where Divine Providence manifests itself in every Transaction, where Vertue is try'd with Misfortunes, and rewarded with Blessings: In fine, where Men behave themselves like Christians, and Women are really vertuous, and such as we ought to imitate." Constructed of pell-mell, adventurous episodes, each of Aubin's novels follows a distinct pattern, despite variance of individual incident. Central to the plot are lovers "whose good birth, good sense, and beauty," according to Frans De Bruyn, "are exceeded only by their virtue." Having exchanged vows of eternal fidelity, the lovers are inevitably separated by a host of misfortunes ranging from natural disasters to slavery at the hands of lustful foreign interlopers—all designed to test their faith in one another and in Providence. Much of Aubin's work bears resemblance to that of Defoe: her frequent use of the travel motif, shipwrecks, and castaways on desert islands indicates the extent of her indebtedness. Aubin, like Defoe, tried innocence in exotic and even savage settings, but departed from precedent in her characters' uncompromising adherence to and emphasis upon a traditional Christian sexual moral code. Haphazard in the application of realistic detail, Aubin's narratives, unlike Defoe's, are basically window dressing for didactic message.

Though eschewing the voluptuous indulgence prominent in the novels of her female contemporaries, Aubin gilded her instructional fiction with amatory appeal. Virtue (generally in the guise of chastity) reigns triumphant at the conclusion of tale after tale, having surmounted countless—many of them life-threatening—obstacles, and been rewarded at last with the reunion of faithful lovers. Even more vividly than that of her colleagues, Aubin's work dramatizes an increasing tendency in the period to assign moral values by gender. And it is upon the shoulders of women that the greatest burden of rectitude rests. Nowhere is this distinction made more palpable than in the injunction Ardelisa's husband delivers to his young wife, about to be snatched from him by a lecherous Turk, in *The Strange Adventures of the Count de Vinevil and His Family:* "Remember both your Duty to yourself and me. Permit not a vile Infidel to dishonour you, resist to Death, and let me not be so completely curs'd, to hear you live, and are debauch'd." And, again, when Maria is importuned by a heathen emperor in *The Noble Slaves,* she answers his ungovernable lust by wrenching her eyeballs from their sockets, determined, at least, not to bear witness to impending shame when she can no longer obstruct it. April London has affirmed that Aubin "sees femaleness as a covert invitation to violation. Maria thus achieves moral stature within the novel not by asserting a separate self in opposition to threat, but by mutilating the guilty source of sin: her own body.'' Since Aubin's heroines remain paragons of virtue throughout, John J. Richetti has found them ''improbable stereotypes,'' but adds that ''this woodenness is entirely appropriate to [Aubin's] polemical appeal: absolute and unremitting evil such as defines the troubled world she describes can only be endured and defeated by absolute and unwavering goodness.'' Jerry C. Beasley has further proclaimed that Aubin's ''ambitious and sophisticated didacticism requires that . . . [she endow] her females in particular with a kind of moral energy that foreshadows what the author of *Pamela* and *Clarissa* would achieve with his heroines.''

Some commentators have argued that, in such works as *Pamela* and *Clarissa; or, The History of a Young Lady* (1747-48), Richardson relied exclusively on those delineations of persecuted innocence and passive but persuasive feminine virtue that dominate Aubin's fiction. Other critics, though conceding Richardson's probable acquaintance with Aubin's novels, have questioned the likelihood of any deeper familiarity or dependence. The extent of Aubin's direct influence on Richardson must therefore remain conjectural. Her decided contributions to the development of fiction and to the novel, however, are clear, illumined by the unmistakable hallmark distinguishing all of her work. As Richetti has summarized: ''In the person of Mrs. Aubin, we can see the lady novelist acquiring a new *persona*, one which is to become more important as the century wears on and to linger through the nineteenth century as a powerful and formative public image: moral censor of the age.''

(See also *Dictionary of Literary Biography*, Vol. 39: *British Novelists, 1660-1800*.)

PRINCIPAL WORKS

The Stuarts: A Pindarique Ode (poetry) 1707
The Exstasy: A Pindarique Ode to Her Majesty the Queen (poetry) 1708
The Welcome: A Poem to His Grace the Duke of Marlborough (poetry) 1708
The Doctrine of Morality; or, A View of Human Life, According to the Stoich Philosophy [editor] (treatise) 1721; also published as *Moral Virtue Delineated*, 1726
The Life of Madam de Beaumount, a French Lady Who lived in a Cave in Wales above fourteen years undiscovered, being forced to fly France for her Religion; and of the cruel Usage she had there. Also Her Lord's Adventures in Muscovy, where he was a Prisoner some Years. With An Account of his returning to France, and her being discover'd by a Welsh Gentleman, who fetch'd her Lord to Wales: And of many strange Accidents which befel them, and their daughter Belinda, who was stolen away from them; and of their Return to France in the Year 1718 (novel) 1721
The Strange Adventures of the Count de Vinevil and His Family. Being an Account of What Happen'd to Them Whilst They Resided at Constantinople (novel) 1721
The Adventures of the Prince of Clermont, and Madame de Ravezan [translator] (novel) 1722
The History of Genghizcan the Great, First Emperor of the Antient Moguls and Tartars [translator] (history) 1722
The Life and Amorous Adventures of Lucinda, an English Lady (novel) 1722
The Noble Slaves; or, The Lives and Adventures of Two Lords and Two Ladies Who Were Shipwreck'd upon a desolate Island (novel) 1722; also published as *The Noble Slaves.*

Being an Entertaining History of the Surprising Adventures, and Remarkable Deliverances, from Algerine Slavery, of Several Spanish Noblemen and Ladies of Quality, 1800
The Life of Charlotta du Pont, an English Lady (novel) 1723; also published as *The Life, Adventures and Distresses of Charlotte Du Pont, and Her Lover Belanger, Who . . . Underwent a Greater Variety of Real Misfortunes, and Miraculous Adventures, than any Couple That Ever Existed . . .* , 1800
The Life and Adventures of the Lady Lucy, the Daughter of an Irish Lord (novel) 1726
The Illustrious French Lovers: Being the True Histories of the Amours of Several French Persons of Quality [translator] (novel) 1727
The Life and Adventures of the Young Count Albertus, the Son of Count Lewis Augustus, by the Lady Lucy (novel) 1728
The Life of the Countess de Gondez [translator] (novel) 1729
The Merry Masqueraders; or, The Humorous Cuckold (drama) 1730
A Collection of Entertaining Histories and Novels. 3 vols. (novels) 1739

PENELOPE AUBIN (essay date 1721)

[*In the following preface to the 1721 edition of* The Strange Adventures of the Count de Vinevil, *Aubin expresses her hope that the novel may bolster declining morality.*]

Since serious things are, in a manner, altogether neglected, by what we call the Gay and Fashionable Part of Mankind, and Religious Treatises grow mouldy on the Booksellers Shelves in the Back-Shops; when Ingenuity is, for want of Encouragement, starv'd into Silence, and *Toland's* abominable Writings sell ten times better than the inimitable Mr. *Pope's Homer;* when *Dacier's* Works are attempted to be translated by a Hackney-Writer, and *Horace's* Odes turn'd into Prose and Nonsense; the few that honour Virtue, and wish well to our Nation, ought to study to reclaim our Giddy Youth; and since Reprehensions fail, try to win them to Vertue, by Methods where Delight and Instruction may go together. With this Design I present this Book to the Publick, in which you will find a Story, where Divine Providence manifests itself in every Transaction, where Vertue is try'd with Misfortunes, and rewarded with Blessings: In fine, where Men behave themselves like Christians, and Women are really vertuòus, and such as we ought to imitate.

As for the Truth of what this Narrative contains, since *Robinson Cruso* has been so well receiv'd, which is more improbable, I know no reason why this should be thought a Fiction. I hope the World is not grown so abandon'd to Vice, as to believe that there is no such Ladies to be found, as would prefer Death to Infamy; or a Man that, for Remorse of Conscience, would quit a plentiful Fortune, retire, and chuse to die in a dismal Cell. This Age has convinc'd us, that Guilt is so dreadful a thing, that some Men have hasten'd their own Ends, and done Justice on themselves. Would Men trust in Providence, and act according to Reason and common Justice, they need not to fear any thing; but whilst they defy God, and wrong others, they must be Cowards, and their Ends such as they deserve, surprizing and infamous. I heartily wish Prosperity to my Country, and that the English would be again (as they were heretofore) remarkable for Vertue and Bravery, and our Nobility make themselves distinguish'd from the Crowd, by shining Qualities, for which their Ancestors became so honour'd, and for Reward of which obtain'd those Titles they inherit. I hardly dare hope for Encouragement, after having discover'd, that my Design is to persuade you to be vertuous; but if I fail in this, I shall not in reaping that inward Satisfaction of Mind, that ever accompanies good Actions. If this Trifle sells, I conclude it takes, and you may be sure to hear from me again; so you may be innocently diverted, and I employ'd to my Satisfaction. (pp. 5-8)

> Penelope Aubin, "Preface to the Reader," in her
> The Life of Madam de Beaumount, a French Lady,
> *and* The Strange Adventures of the Count de Vinevil
> and His Family, *1721. Reprint by Garland Publish-*
> *ing, Inc., 1973, pp. 5-8.*

B. G. MacCARTHY (essay date 1944)

[*In the following excerpt, MacCarthy surveys Aubin's fiction, noting especially her didacticism and her blending of romance and realism.*]

[Penelope Aubin] was didactic, but she had the idea of enlivening her stories with unusual backgrounds. Obviously she was much influenced by Defoe and by records of travel. As a result, her narratives bring a new note of adventure into the novel. She was not an advocate of genteel morality. A staunch Catholic, it was her object to win her readers towards the Catholic point of view. She uses her stories to show that the vicissitudes and miseries of this world matter little if one's gaze is fixed on eternity: "The virtuous shall look dangers in the face unmoved, and putting their whole trust in the Divine Providence, shall be delivered, even by miraculous means; or dying with comfort be freed from the miseries of this life, and go to taste an eternal repose." So that her characters may be sufficiently tried Mrs. Aubin subjects them to the most extraordinary occurrences, of which one gains a sufficient idea from the long titles of her stories. For example: *The Life of Madam de Beaumont, a French Lady; who lived in a Cave in Wales about fourteen years undiscovered, being forced to fly France for her religion, and of the cruel usage she had there. Also her Lord's Adventures in Muscovy where he was a prisoner some years, with an Account of his returning to France, and her being discovered by a Welsh Gentleman who fetches her Lord to Wales, and of many strange accidents which befel them, and their daughter Belinda, who was stolen away from them and of their Return to France in the year 1718.*

In 1721, when this tale was published, there also appeared: *The Strange Adventures of the Count de Vinevil and his Family. Being an account of what happened to them whilst they resided at Constantinople. And of Mlle. Ardelisia, his daughter's being shipwrecked on the uninhabited Island Delos in the Return to France, with Violetta, a Venetian Lady, the Captain of the Ship, a Priest, and five Sailors. The Manner of their living. Their . . . Strange Deliverance . . .* This echo of *Robinson Crusoe* was followed a year later by another tale of shipwreck: *The Noble Slaves: or, The Lives and Adventures of Two Lords and Two Ladies upon a desolate Island.* Mrs. Aubin made a determined attempt to imitate Defoe's realism, and in her best story, *The Life and Adventures of the Lady Lucy,* she creates the impression of having been an eye-witness to certain happenings in the Williamite wars in Ireland, such as the sack of a castle after the battle of the Boyne.

As a translator Mrs. Aubin's choice lay with the wonderful. In 1726, before writing *Adventures of the Lady Lucy* she had rendered into English Pétis de la Croix's *History of Genghizcan The Great, First Emperor of the Antient Moguls and Tartars.* She also translated *The Illustrious French Lovers; being the True Histories of the Amours of Several French Persons of Quality.* That interest in the Oriental which led to the translation of *The History of Genghizcan* is very evident in her last original work, a picaresque novel. *The Life and Adventures of the Young Count Albertus, The Son of Count Lewis Augustus, by the Lady Lucy.* The young Count, overwhelmed by his wife's death, tries by foreign travel to divert his mind from his grief. He encounters many people who narrate their lifestories. Some of these inset stories are good, particularly the story of the old miser in Madrid, which is told with dramatic realism. Eventually the young Count becomes a Benedictine and goes as a missionary to China, where martyrdom awaits him.

Mrs. Aubin is worthy of remembrance despite her obvious didacticism, in that she endeavoured to weave together romance and realism, and was, in however slight a degree, one of the early contributors to Oriental fiction. She is notable also in her adherence to the popular theme of the virtuous maiden pursued by the charming rake. Finally, she was one of the very few women who essayed the picaresque. (pp. 253-54)

> B. G. MacCarthy, "From 1689 to 1744," in her
> Women Writers: Their Contribution to the English
> Novel, 1621-1744, *Cork University Press, 1944, pp.*
> *214-62.*

WILLIAM H. McBURNEY (essay date 1957)

[*In the following excerpt, McBurney surveys Aubin's career.*]

As the boldest and most productive imitator of Defoe's works, particularly of *Robinson Crusoe,* [Mrs. Aubin] contributed to the first important cycle of eighteenth-century English fictional publication which reached its peak in 1727. Her original novels helped to fuse the native tradition of Defoe with continental fictional genres. Her translations are in themselves interesting studies in the divergences of English and French tastes, and through both original and derivative works Mrs. Aubin, surprisingly enough, exerted an influence upon the novels of the condescending Abbé [Prévost] and perhaps upon Samuel Richardson, whose vogue in France Prévost was later to initiate as translator.

Although they cannot be classified as historical novels, Mrs. Aubin's works take place against the exciting political and religious background of the great Anglo-French population exchanges of the late seventeenth century—the emigration of the Huguenots after the revocation of the Edict of Nantes in 1685 and the flight of the Jacobites to France with the last Stuart king and after the battle of the Boyne. With the Huguenots Mrs. Aubin was undoubtedly familiar, possibly through family ties, for, according to Prévost [see Additional Bibliography], she was born in London, the daughter of an impoverished French officer. Because of her religion and her friends, she showed a definite sympathy with the English exiles, and her heroines tend to be born, with autobiographical convenience, in the late 1680's of French parents, who are often of different religious faiths. If Mrs. Aubin is her own Belinda de Beaumont or Charlotta Du Pont (in everything but beauty), she too was a Catholic, by birth or conversion, for Huguenots fare as poorly in her fiction as Turks, Italians, Dutch, and Irish.

To this xenophobic catalogue Mrs. Aubin also added "lustful Londoners" in order to exalt Wales, which she praised as the home of the "true-born *English* and *Antient Britons* to whom I wish Increase of Sense and Virtue, Plenty of Money, good Governours, and endless Prosperity." It may be conjectured from this praise and from brief but circumstantial references to Southampton, Pool, Swansea, Bristol, Salisbury Plain, and the Wye that her early life was spent in the south and west of England, where she cultivated her bucolic preferences and perhaps met the Duchess of Ormonde, who in 1708 presented one of Mrs. Aubin's first literary efforts, **"The Ecstacy, A Pindarick Ode,"** to Queen Anne. This poem, which celebrated a victory of "my native Isle" over the French (at Oudenarde?), was preceded by **"The Stuarts. A Pindarick Ode"** in 1707 and followed by **"The Wellcome: A Poem to his Grace the Duke of Marlborough."** The latter, a fourteen-page effusion in the manner of the following triplet:

> Bravest, of Bravest Men, and best if we
> May dare to think that ought can Mortal be,
> That is so Exquisitely Good, and Great as thee,

is fortunately her last—or last surviving—poetic effort. (pp. 246-48)

Mrs. Aubin's method of composition was simple and undoubtedly explains her ability to produce lengthy novels rapidly, by slight variations on a basic pattern. From fictional and dramatic sources she borrowed a group of stereotyped characters, who differ from novel to novel only in nationality. Her heroine, whether English, Welsh, Irish, French, or Spanish, is invariably endowed with good birth, beauty, inviolable honor, and "solid sense." The hero, a male counterpart of the heroine in beauty, is an ardent lover and often an erring husband; the villain is a lustful pirate, Turk, Moor, or Londoner. Among the minor characters are the female confidante, who, like Violetta in *The Count de Vinevil*, may lack unwavering virtue and thus serve as a foil to the heroine; the blackamoor slave, who is always named Domingo; and the benevolent Catholic hermit, who is usually a noble and repentant sinner. As stereotyped as the characters are the ecstasies of love, scorn, hate, jealousy, contrition, and joy which are expressed in highly conventional language and to the usual accompaniment of tears and swoons. Structurally, all the novels are episodic, complicated and prolonged by numerous inserted *récits,* and with one exception—*The Life and Amorous Adventures of Lucinda*—all employ the third person narrative technique. However familiar her characters and her style may have been to readers of diluted Scuderian intrigues, the hazards which Mrs. Aubin places in the paths of the heroines of her first five novels are often purely Defoesque, as are certain backgrounds and descriptive details.

After a brisk introduction Mrs. Aubin separates her lovers or newly married couples. They set out at carefully specified times from familiar ports (Bristol, St. Malo) on ships precisely named (the *Bon Avanture,* the *Entreprenant*) but suddenly find themselves cast up on shores where the maps of Hakluyt, Dampier, Selkirk, and Knox are hardly more useful than a carefully studied "Carte du Pays de Tendre" ["Map of Love"]. Indeed, not since the marvelous geography of the chivalric romance and the *romans de longue haleine* ["long-winded novels"], which were still being read in chapbook condensations in the 1720's, had the world been so confusingly and delightfully disarranged. Don Lopez, in *The Noble Slaves,* tells Teresa that in Spain he had "procured a ship and visited all the Coast of *Peru* and *Canada.* Missing you there, I determined to go to *Japan.*" And in the same novel, the Count de Hautville follows

the abducted Emilia from Rochelle to Quebec only to learn that she is in Panama, to which place he immediately proceeds "with Horses which I hired." She is finally overtaken in New Mexico; they sail for Japan but are shipwrecked on an island where they discover a ruined pagan temple. This they "concluded . . . to be the Work of some *Chinese* or *Peruvians,* who had inhabited that Place in Antient Times."

Seldom, too, had characters revealed such polyglot abilities as do those of Mrs. Aubin. A heroine and her slave wash up on an island where "an old *Indian* came down towards them . . . who proved a *Japanese* cast on shore there, with his Wife and three Children; in the *Chinese* language he invited them to his Home: the *Moor* understood him." Elsewhere, Spanish and French heroes, having escaped from captivity in Barbary, disguise themselves as Greek merchants, for "both speaking *Greek,* they doubted not to pass for such if questioned."

It is fortunate for her noble lords and ladies that they are so hardy and polylingual, for, once shipwrecked, they—and the reader, who to read must run—are swept through an average of fifteen chapters of hairbreadth escapes with vertiginous rapidity. Not only *Hic sunt Leones* ["Here are Lions"] but also *raptores* ["ravishers"]: Mrs. Aubin is as fond of "wild Beasts" as Defoe, and much more so of handsome rakes, preferably Turks or Christian renegadoes. Lacking a lion to provide a fine distress, she may resort to breaking a leg. The only pauses are illusory, for hermits' cottages provide less shelter than excuse for equally exciting stories recounted by the host. Having survived perils and fatigues, however, the indomitable travelers escape, usually disguised *à la Turque,* their borrowed "Turbants" providentially ornamented with diamonds and their pantaloons with ruby and emerald buttons. In a sudden slowing of pace, they arrive home prosaically on May 2, 1718. To assure the reader that solid ground has been reached once more, Mrs. Aubin may then provide one heroine with a son, born on August 10, 1719, and another with twins on September 3 of the same year. As far as the first and last pages of her works are concerned, she was indeed justified in saying that *Robinson Crusoe* is "no more improbable" [see essay dated 1721].

Financially affluent, or exhausted by her initial burst of literary effort which terminated in the Daedalian adventures of *Charlotta Du Pont,* a work claiming with considerable accuracy to be "A History that contains the greatest Variety of Events that ever was publish'd," Mrs. Aubin produced nothing for four years. In 1727 [she] . . . issued a novel, *The Life and Adventures of the Lady Lucy, the Daughter of an Irish Lord, who marry'd a German Officer,* and a two-volume translation from the French of Robert Challes entitled *The Illustrious French Lovers.* The story of the injured Lady Lucy is less various than the earlier works and has the unifying didactic aim of showing the consequences of unreasoning jealousy. It was dedicated, with more point than tact, to Lord Coleraine, who in 1720 had separated from his wife. Lady Coleraine had received Mrs. Aubin's earlier homage in the dedication of *The Noble Slaves.*

Lady Lucy was followed in 1728 by a sequel which recounted *The Life and Adventures of the Young Count Albertus, the Son of Count Lewis Augustus by the Lady Lucy.* . . . Outwardly this final novel regains the expected Aubin scope, for Count Albertus ranges over Germany, France, Spain, and Barbary before his martyrdom as a Jesuit missionary in an outer province of China. The wanderings of the titular hero, however, are merely a framework for six unrelated *novelle* in the manner of Mrs. Haywood or of her popular translation, *La Belle Assemblée, or the Adventures of Six Days* (1724).

Both of these later novels show the effect of the particular temptation of excessive and unintegrated variety against which eighteenth-century fiction was to struggle until Richardson and Fielding showed what a novel might mean in the way of sustained and concentrated effort. Richardson, however, was still only a prosperous printer, and Fielding's first play, *Love in Several Masques,* under the sponsorship of his cousin Lady Mary Wortley Montagu, was just being readied for presentation at Drury Lane. Even Defoe had abandoned the novel after *The Fortunate Mistress* for short "Newgate biographies" and semi-fictional travel literature. His earlier works, however, had provided a model for matter and methods which Mrs. Aubin had followed with gusto and varying fidelity.

In her seven novels she shows a predilection for certain types of adventures—particularly slavery, shipwreck, and piracy. All of these figure in the works of Defoe, but Mrs. Aubin lends a crusading fervor to her anti-slavery propaganda which goes beyond Crusoe's capture by a Turkish rover of Sallee and which predicts the oratory in the York Buildings. In the preface to *The Noble Slaves* she declares:

> We cannot think without Horror of the Miseries that attend those who in Countries where the Monarchs are absolute, and standing Armies awe the People, are made Slaves to others . . . Let us proceed to reflect on the great Deliverance of these Noble Slaves: You will find that Chains could not hold them; Want, Sickness, Grief, nor the merciless Seas destroy them; because they trusted in God, and swerv'd not from their Duty.

And in her last novel, a hermit in Barbary reflects "on the profuse Manner in which Christians live in *Europe* and how unconcerned great and rich Men sit down to their Tables to feast on the costliest Delicacies, whilst thousands of poor Christians perish in loathsome Prisons and the Streets for want of Bread." The subject of Moorish captivity had, of course, been exploited by Cervantes and in many other fictional and dramatic works. It was also present in such serious or sensational publications as Busnot's *The History of the Reign of Muley Ishmael, the Present King of Morocco,* translated in 1715, and Francis Brook's *Barbarian Cruelties; Being a True History of the distressed Conditions of the Christian Captives under the Tyranny of Mully Ishmael, Emperor of Morocco and King of Fez* (1693). (pp. 253-57)

In addition to her noble European slaves in Moslem bondage, Mrs. Aubin also depicted briefly several Negro slaves, such as Domingo (*The Noble Slaves*) who dies confessing his love for Teresa with the statement, "I was born as free as you." Another Domingo, in *Charlotta Du Pont,* succeeds in abducting his mistress, Isabinda, and lives with her and their child in a cave. "Chance made me a Slave," he declares. In this aspect of her work the authoress may have been influenced by Mrs. Aphra Behn's *Royal Slave* or by Dryden's Almanzor. The denunciation of slavery in *Charlotta Du Pont,* however, seems too sharp to be merely a literary echo: "The selling of human Creatures is a Crime my Soul abhors; and wealth so got ne'er thrives." Defoe had also touched upon the problem of racial intermarriage in the *Serious Reflections of Robinson Crusoe.*

The more specific borrowings from Defoe came in the numerous episodes of shipwreck. Ardelisa and her companions in *The Count de Vinevil* live on a goat and two kids which they find on their desert island until other provisions are washed ashore. The castaways on "the barbarous coasts of the great River Oroonoko" subsist on dried grapes, raw turtle, bird eggs,

goat meat, and grape juice. The Indian who rescues Teresa in *The Noble Slaves* resembles Crusoe in his costume of "Beast Skins, a Hat of Canes, and Sandals of Wood upon his Feet," as does the man "pursued by the Tyger" in *Charlotta Du Pont*:

> He had a drawn Sword in his Hand, and a strange fashion'd Coat made of Beasts Skins; he had no Shoes or Stockings, but pieces of Bears Skins ty'd about his Legs with Twigs; his Head had a strange Fur cap on.

The cave of Madam de Beaumont, the rocky refuge of Domingo and Isabinda, several hermitages, and the hut on the Summer Islands, which was "a Place where they saw some Trees growing very close together, in the midst of which they perceived a sort of Hut or Cottage made of a few Boards and Branches of Trees," all owe something to the ingenuity of Defoe. There are references to cannibalistic disposal of war prisoners by certain Indian tribes and to the effects of starvation upon drifting survivors in *Charlotta Du Pont.* Perhaps more coincidental are the similar encounters with lions, tigers, leopards, and "other furious creatures"; the escapes in pleasure fishing boats of Moorish captors; and the resemblance of Crusoe's Tartar idol to the supernatural Oriental statue found by the noble slaves in a subterranean chamber surrounded by grisly ornaments much like those which were later to bedeck the Gothic fiction of Horace Walpole and others.

Usually Mrs. Aubin is too intent upon getting her characters into Turkish captivity to devote much space to a realistic depiction of English life. The first section of *Charlotta Du Pont,* however, does include a sketch of the heroine's villainous stepmother which might have been found in *Moll Flanders.* Dorinda is seduced by an officer of the Guards and becomes a prostitute. Unlike her friend, Miranda, who is "no ways addicted to Vice, but reduced to it by Misfortune and Necessity," she refuses to reform, even when discovered by her family. By the time she meets Mr. Du Pont at a playhouse, she has "laid up a thousand Pounds, besides a great Stock of rich Clothes, a Watch, Necklace, Rings, and some Plate." There are, too, occasional attempts at imitation of common speech, but these glimpses of native realism are rare.

In addition to specific details, Mrs. Aubin also borrowed, or found congenial, several basic ideas and devices which occur in Defoe's works: catastrophe occasioned by disobedience of parental will, necessity as a cause of sin, prudent conservation of money and the economic rewarding of virtue, and warning of approaching danger by dreams and visions. There are also general resemblances of style and structure. Her use of circumstantial detail has been noted earlier; she also employs moralizing digression, the episodic form in which interest is sustained by rapid succession of events (as in the second part of *Robinson Crusoe*), and frequently a final and anti-climactic "surprising adventure." The rapidity with which she wrote probably explains her failure to achieve Defoe's excellence in verisimilitude which makes the island episode of his most famous work so enthralling. To Mrs. Aubin's credit it might be pointed out, however, that this section of *Robinson Crusoe* is a case of unpremeditated art, for, seen in relation to the overall episodic structure of the novel, its great length is obviously the result of the author's personal interest but lack of artistic control.

Even more completely than Defoe, Mrs. Aubin avoids the devices of inserted poems, apt quotations, and learned or luscious allusions which are prominent in the works of Mrs. Jane Barker and Mrs. Haywood. This complete lack of embellishment may be attributed to her strict religious aims, her lack of education, or a desire to avoid the ''Style careless and loose'' of her contemporaries. Certainly her novels are unusual in their high moral tone. Nowhere is the reader allowed to linger over scenes of vice as in the works of Mrs. Manley, Mrs. Hearne, or even Defoe himself in *The Fortunate Mistress.* Her heroines, instead, handle would-be ravishers with dispatch, as did Charlotta Du Pont who, captured by a pirate, ''taking a sharp Bodkin out of her Hair, stabbed him in the Belly so dangerously that he fell senseless on the Bed.'' This promptness is perhaps as much a necessity as a virtue, for Mrs. Aubin had no time to waste on any one incident when the world was so full of a number of lustful bashaws and Irishmen, lurking parties of Indians in ''the Apalattean Mountains,'' and renegade Spaniards; and when there were tempests so obligingly available to precipitate her heroines into the arms of these perils. Perhaps she felt, in accordance with the precept, if not the practice, of Mrs. Manley, that ''Detail discourages Persons of good Taste.''

In the course of these accelerated Defoesque itineraries, Mrs. Aubin showed evidence of considerable reading of seventeenth-century and contemporary French novels, on which she modeled many of her inserted *récits* and three of which she put into English dress. This dress at times assumed proportions of a disguise, for she used the typical freedom of translators of the day as she pursued her ''Design of recommending Virtue and Piety to the World.''

In 1722 her publishers issued anonymously *The Adventures of the Prince of Clermont and Madam de Ravezan: A Novel in Four Parts by a Person of Quality, Done from the French by the Author of Ildegerte.* Prefaced by a quotation from Lansdowne's *Heroick Love,* this work was all that could be desired by what Defoe called ''the airy nice peruser of novels and romances, neatly bound and timely gilt.'' Mrs. Aubin had followed the general practice of her fellow translators. In their attempts to adapt works of the court of Louis XIV and the regent to the tastes of the middle-class public of Queen Anne and George I, the literary hacks were at pains to render more explicit gallant and emotional passages, to poeticize names of characters, and to expand moralizing sections—all of which, in the competitive atmosphere of Grubstreet, had to be done with greatest rapidity. To the task Mrs. Aubin brought the *élan* of her novels and she skilfully gilded over with virtuous passion the dilemmas of Madam de Ravezan. . . . Her characters, too, are rechristened with more elegant Otavian or pastoral names. Madame Rose becomes Monimia; Chavanne, Polydor; de Reling, Albertus; Vineuil, Melissa; and Nevilian, Florinda. Mrs. Aubin's evident fondness for the name Albertus may be recalled, as well as the declaration of one of her heroines: ''I delighted most in reading Plays, and Love Stories and . . . I was wonderfully pleased that my Mother had happened to have given me the Name of *Lucinda*; it sounded in my Thoughts Poetick and Romantick, and would much better become a Song than *Joan* or *Dorothy.*''

Penelope, no doubt also wonderfully pleased with her own mother's choice, continued her liberties in *The Illustrious French Lovers,* issued in 1727 with a signed preface. Here she says that she has ''endeavour'd to translate it both faithfully and in good language, and a familiar Style.'' . . . And the work that follows is handled as might be expected—with expanded moralizing passages, occasional abridgment or excision of erotic passages, and a general increase of sentimental voltage. If the novel had not come into the hands of the Abbé Prévost, it might be dismissed along with her final translation, *The Life of the Countess of Gondez.*

What caused Mrs. Aubin to cease fictional production at this time is unknown—as, indeed, are the reasons for a general fictional decline after the accession of George II. According to Prévost, she was piqued by the cold reception of her later novels and swore to write no more. (pp. 257-62)

Mrs. Aubin had repeatedly urged her readers ''to make Virtue the Rule of all our Actions, and eternal Happiness our only Aim'' and there is nothing particularly surprising in her turning, as Defoe had done, from fictional to more specifically moralistic and speculative fields. Her appearance in public as an oratrix, however, attracted the attention of the Town and of the visiting ecclesiastic [Prévost] who, in the course of a life as varied and exciting as that of an Aubin hero, had recently come to London from France. (pp. 262-63)

Mrs. Manley, Mrs. Mary Davys, and Mrs. Haywood had, within Mrs. Aubin's lifetime, set a pattern of unsuccessfully attempting dramatic writing before turning to fiction. Perhaps the heady success of her oratory, however, inspired her to seek larger audiences in the theater itself. The result of this new venture was *The Merry Masqueraders: or, the Humorous Cuckold,* a comedy in five acts which has as its only merit its relative purity (when compared with *A Wife to be Lett,* in which Mrs. Haywood appropriately acted the role of her own heroine). All elements of the play—the intrigues of two military rakes in the country house of a hypochondriac judge, multiple disguises as ghosts, and the antics of Squire Clumsey who echoes Farquhar's Bonniface by interlarding every remark with ''as they say''—only too clearly reveal Mrs. Aubin's indebtedness to *The Beaux' Stratagem* and its Restoration predecessors. She tried to bring Farquhar up to date with allusions to her favorite abominations such as the Sinking Fund, the South Sea Bubble, Heidegger's masquerades, the free-thinkers, but the play did not take. Even the spectacle of the authoress herself, who delivered a new epilogue on the second night, could not redeem the play's lack of wit or humor. The Town—or the part of it that frequented the Little Theater in the Haymarket—could not forgive such an omission, after the brilliance of Fielding's *Tom Thumb,* then running at the same house. And even a female orator was no attraction to a jaded public who had recently seen mad Samuel Johnson of Cheshire fiddle and walk the stage on stilts as he delivered a rodomontade in his extravagant tragedy, *Hurlothrumbo, or the Supernatural.* The play and Mrs. Aubin's career as actress-dramatist closed with the new epilogue on December 11, 1730.

This final phase of her strange and surprising adventures was apparently cut short by her death. Her novels, however, merited a collected edition in 1739 with an elaborate preface which declared them exponents of the five fictional essentials—probability, purity of style and manners, universal benevolence, punishment of guilt, and reward (here or hereafter) of virtue and innocence. The appearance of the great mid-century novelists relegated her works to deserved obscurity, but she was still a salable copyright commodity in 1764. Mrs. Elizabeth Griffith rescued *The Noble Slaves* once again, for her *Collection of Novels* (1777), from which were evidently taken a surprising number of editions in Boston, Danbury, New Haven, and New York between 1790 and 1815. *Charlotte Du Pont* reappeared in London in 1800, her ''Life, Adventures, and Distresses . . . a greater variety of real misfortunes and miraculous adventures than any couple that ever existed'' crammed into forty-eight sextodecimo pages—a feat that might have inspired the giddy pace of young Jane Austen's *Love and Freindship.*

Whatever the understandable appeal in the 1790's of Mrs. Aubin's heroines to American readers, then poring over the sorrows of Mrs. Susanna Rowson's *Charlotte Temple,* and whatever the mysterious reason for the republication of her *Genghizcan the Great* in Calcutta in 1816, Mrs. Aubin must be consigned to the comparative oblivion of the pre-Richardsonian period, one decade of which she embellished in such profuse and bizarre fashion. Defoe had attempted to graft the devices of fiction and religious teaching to factual travel literature in *Robinson Crusoe.* Mrs. Aubin reversed this procedure by attempting to add Defoe's factual realism to the characters and structure of the short Continental novel. Artistically she had little success, but her works—like those of her great model—added to the growing stockpile of realistic devices and increased the number of middle-class readers. She may also have directly influenced the more talented masters of the novel who succeeded her. And even today her ''Variety of Accidents and strange Deliverances . . . cannot fail to divert the most splenetick Reader, silence the Profane, and delight the Ingenious at a time when we have so much Occasion for something new, to make us forget our own Misfortunes.'' (pp. 266-67)

> *William H. McBurney, ''Mrs. Penelope Aubin and*
> *the Early Eighteenth-Century English Novel,'' in* The
> Huntington Library Quarterly, *Vol. XX, No. 3, May,*
> *1957, pp. 245-67.*

ROGER B. DOOLEY (essay date 1959)

[*Dooley is an American educator and author of fiction who has contributed short stories and articles to such periodicals as* American Literature *and the* Saturday Review, *and whose special interests are reflected in* A Study Guide to Modern British and Irish Drama (1964). *In the following excerpt, he focuses on the pro-Catholic sentiment in Aubin's work.*]

To us who, more than a century after the Oxford Movement, have so long taken for granted its fruits in the Catholic revival as a natural part of our heritage that we readily turn to England for some of the best examples of Catholic writing in every form, the religious situation in the England of two centuries ago may seem well nigh incredible. To be sure, we have all heard of the Penal Laws, not fully abolished until the Emancipation Act of 1829, under which the tiny minority of English Catholics (about one per cent of the population) were barred from Parliament, from the universities, the armed services, and the learned professions; but perhaps less generally known is the full extent to which the anti-Popery of the day affected every branch of English literature.

Venomous attacks were by no means confined to Grub Street hacks, paid to grind out pamphlets with titles like *Popery and Slavery Displayed.* Indeed, it would be difficult to find any writer of the eighteenth century, major or minor, poet or historian, Whig or Tory, from Dean Swift to Monk Lewis, whose works do not at some point show traces of anti-Catholic indoctrination. Whatever their attitudes in private social relationships, this seemed a taboo which seldom, if ever, permitted relaxation when writing for publication. (p. 65)

Small wonder, then, that the average novelist, who just as in our own day lived by pleasing the public, not by trying to reform it, was content to follow obediently where his (or more often, *her*) acknowledged betters had repeatedly pointed the way. Since by mid-century most readers and a large number of writers were women, anti-Popery was less likely to take the coarse forms of Smollett and Sterne than to follow a daintier

variation inspired by Marivaux in his *Vie de Marianne.* Out of the many-volumed sagas of suffering sensibility with which these long-forgotten Elizas, Annes, Charlottes, and Marias supplied the circulating library trade, a whole religious community might well be made up of genteel Protestant heroines tricked by some Popish villain into a French convent and relentlessly urged by some smooth-tongued abbess to take the veil, until rescued by devices even more improbable than the ones which put them there. Even as late as 1791, Mrs. Elizabeth Inchbald, a popular actress and accepted figure in London literary circles, was so cautious in her Catholicism that her best-known novel, *A Simple Story,* though it touches gingerly on religious materials, might as well have been written by a neutral Protestant.

Thus it is truly astonishing to find early in the century, in the thirty-year interim between the Jacobite risings of 1715 and 1745, when popular dread of Popery could at any moment be whipped to fever pitch, a woman who was not only a Catholic and a novelist but who dared to write as a Catholic novelist. (pp. 66-7)

To the modern reader, indeed, the novels of Penelope Aubin, with their long interpolated narratives in which new characters relate the histories of their lives, their shipwrecks on distant shores and captures by infidels, would seem very far from any contemporary ideal of a good novel, but they must be judged in the light of the period that produced them. Certainly they compare more than favorably with the works of many of her contemporaries such as Eliza Haywood, and Mary Manley de la Rivière, who are usually given detailed analysis in standard histories of the novel.

Described by one recent critic, B. G. MacCarthy, as a staunch Catholic whose object was to win her readers to the same faith [see excerpt dated 1944], Penelope nevertheless was discreet enough never to let this design become too palpable. To judge by the dedicatory prefaces of her novels . . . , she and her husband enjoyed the patronage, if not the friendship, of several highly placed aristocrats. Perhaps, however, the real secret of her success in the apparently impossible task of pleasing an anti-Catholic public with pro-Catholic novels was that she steered clear of any vexed contemporary religious issues. Using Turks or other ''infidels'' for her villains, she embodied all the most attractive Christian virtues in her Continental Catholics, usually Italian or French, who, unlike Defoe's, are simply presented as good people without any apology or defense.

The Life of Madame de Beaumount, A French Lady, to be sure, seems to be the earliest piece of eighteenth-century English fiction to use what came to be the stock situation of the heroine detained behind convent walls, but this was apparently no more than a device to win the confidence of Protestant readers. Mrs. Aubin makes it quite clear that her Belinda's stay in a ''Monestary of the Poor Clares'' was the work of wicked guardians, of whose real designs the nuns were quite innocent. Her later imprisonment by her French father-in-law, supposedly as punishment for her refusal to turn Catholic, is discovered and strongly deplored by a wise and humble friar. ''God forbid, said he, our Faith should be propagated by such detestable means as these.'' With the aid of a heroic colleague, he not only frees Belinda but arranges for her reunion with her long-missing husband—surely a surprising end for a story that ostensibly started out to tell of a Protestant lady persecuted by Catholics.

In her second novel, *The Strange Adventures of the Count de Vinevil and His Family,* Mrs. Aubin makes no such compro-

The Strange

ADVENTURES

OF THE

Count *de Vinevil*

And his Family.

Being an Account of what happen'd to them whilft they refided at *Conftantinople.*

And of Madamoifelle ARDELISA, his Daughter's being fhipwreck'd on the Uninhabited Ifland *Delos,* in her Return to *France,* with VIOLETTA a *Venetian* Lady, the Captain of the Ship, a Prieft, and five Sailors. The Manner of their living there, and ftrange Deliverance by the Arrival of a Ship commanded by VIOLETTA's Father.

ARDELISA's Entertainment at *Venice,* and fafe Return to *France.*

By Mrs. *AUBIN.*

Si Genus Humanum, & mortalia temnitis Arma,
At fperate Deos memores fandi atque nefandi.
VIRGIL.

LONDON,

Printed for E. BELL, J..DARBY, A.BETTESWORTH, F. FAYRAM, J. PEMBERTON, J. HOOKE, C. RIVINGTON, F. CLAY, J. BATLEY, and E.SYMON. M. DCC. XXI.

Title page of the first edition of The Strange Adventures of the Count de Vinevil and His Family *(1721).*

mise. Father Francis, a French missionary to Japan, though similar to Defoe's Benedictine in *Robinson Crusoe,* is given a much wider scope in which to display his admirable character. He hears the confession of a dying stranger, he eases the conscience of a lady troubled by her enforced stay in a harem, and when his party is shipwrecked on the isle of Delos he rises to new heights of cheerful selflessness, unobtrusively going without food that others may eat and offering wise counsel (never expressed pompously) on every occasion.

The Noble Slaves, or the Lives and Adventures of Two Lords and Two Ladies contains an almost identical priest, Father Augustine, but in one of the inset narratives Mrs. Aubin attempts a somewhat more complex religious character, M. de Chateau-Roial, a priest who has violated his vows by eloping with Clorinda, a girl destined by her family for the convent. The author is careful to detail the peculiar social factor which might tend to explain, if it cannot condone, such a lapse: the French custom of maintaining great estates intact by placing younger sons and daughters in the religious life without any regard to their inclinations.

Of all fictional uses of this situation, this novel seems the only one in which the lovers are neither sentimentally glorified nor smirkingly exposed as examples of Popish hypocrisy. They are, in fact, punished soon enough for their transgression when capture by Algerian pirates subjects them to a whole train of humiliating experiences terminated only by the influence of still another benevolent priest, a hermit named Clementine, who secretly ministers to Christian captives. By this time both Chateau-Roial and Clorinda are so deeply penitent that, though married, they agree to part if a proper religious dispensation cannot be obtained. Returned at last to Venice, he dies, but not before receiving the last sacraments and offering much belated advice to Clorinda, who now voluntarily retires to a convent. However melodramatized, this unhappy affair ends on a note of almost tragic dignity that must have come as a distinct novelty to English readers nurtured on nunnery tales of a far more lurid sort.

Undoubtedly the best-constructed of Penelope Aubin's novels, if only because it contains the fewest inset narratives, is *The Life and Adventures of the Lady Lucy,* in which the Ulster estate of the heroine's family (apparently the first Jacobites to appear in English fiction) is seized by victorious British troops after the Battle of the Boyne. Fortunately, Lucy soon wins the heart of Count Albertus, a German captain who serves William III but is nonetheless "a very fine Gentleman, a Man nobly born, a Roman Catholick, as the Lady Lucy and her Mother also were." After several years of happy married life at Heidelberg, Albertus, by villainous contrivances too complicated to summarize, is led to believe Lucy unfaithful. Though she is expecting her third child, the outraged husband takes her to a distant wood, stabs her and leaves her for dead. She is saved by a miracle (surely the only seriously presented miracle in any eighteenth-century novel); a mysterious voice announces her plight to a saintly Franciscan in a nearby monastery.

This excellent friar, Father Joseph, has Lucy carefully conveyed to the monastery for first aid, but at once arranges for her permanent care by a neighboring abbess, "it being altogether improper, and against the Rules of that Order, for her to remain in the other Convent, because of her Sex and Condition." No doubt Mrs. Aubin was only too well aware of what use had been made of similar situations in the more scandalous nunnery tales then current. Aided by kindly religious of both sexes, Lucy remains here to bear and rear her son, while Albertus goes off for an eventful career as a mercenary soldier in Flanders.

Years later, when he has learned the truth and repented his rashness, he retires from the world to live as a hermit, not far from the Franciscan monastery, and thus Father Joseph, aided by the long arm of coincidence, is able to reunite the parted pair. Lucy, thinking Albertus dead, had long since forgiven him and even has Masses said for his soul. Besides all these religious motifs, Albertus meanwhile has placed some illegitimate offspring in a "Convent of the Jesuits," and Lucy's cousin, widower of the wicked woman who caused all the trouble, has joined the Benedictines. Needless to say, the reunited couple give "large gifts to the Convent and Monastery where Lady Lucy and her Son had been so generously preserved and entertained."

Lady Lucy's adventures were so well received that, according to Mrs. Aubin's preface to her next novel, she was urged by a noble patroness, a duchess too exalted even to be named, to write a sequel. In *The Life and Adventures of the Young Count Albertus,* the hero's religious bent begins to manifest itself early in the story. Not until near the end of the book, however, after a variety of experiences has disillusioned him with worldly satisfactions, does young Albertus become not only a priest but a missionary to China: "Four Jesuits being ordered on the

Mission . . . Lord Albertus obtained Leave to accompany them, being very desirous to share their Labours, and bear a Part in their Sufferings, to propagate the Christian Faith. Thus the divine Wisdom does often direct us by secret Inspiration to the glorious Ends designed for those who follow its Dictates, and obey the divine Call: and he who loves his Saviour's Honor, and Mankind's Good before his own, shall not fail of a happy End.''

It should be pointed out that the young man's motives are soundly religious, and though he lost his beloved wife some time before he does not, like more sentimental heroes, turn to the cloister as balm for a broken heart. As if to answer directly a charge made by Defoe in *Robinson Crusoe* that most Catholic missionaries were interested in visiting only the wealthiest heathen countries, Mrs. Aubin makes clear that Albertus and his companion, as soon as they have mastered the Chinese language, set out from Pekin for a remote frontier ''on the confines of China next Tartary.'' Here, in a town called Cumchem, ''he preached, exhorted, confessed, and baptized all who were willing, or could be drawn to embrace the Christian Faith, and performed all the Duties of an Apostle and Christian Pastor.'' Captured by Tartars, he secretly converts the son and two daughters of a general and, when this becomes known, is stoned to death, suffering martyrdom ''with such Faith and constancy, that even his Murderers were filled with Admiration.'' Thus Mrs. Aubin created the only character in all eighteenth-century fiction who took religion seriously enough to die for it—a denouement more ''enlightened'' novelists would have shunned as the last extreme of that ''enthusiasm'' they abhorred.

Equally significant are the many Catholic elements in *The Life of Charlotta Dupont, an English Lady,* which may have been meant as a companion piece to *Madam de Beaumont* but which survives only in the posthumous collection of 1739. In an immensely complicated network of loosely connected narratives, one story is told by a man who confesses the murder of his wife to a Franciscan, described as ''a Man of great Wisdom and Piety.'' As in *Lady Lucy,* however, Shakespeare's device of *A Winter's Tale* is borrowed, and the wife has secretly been rescued by another good priest, who keeps her sage in a convent until the husband has suffered sufficient remorse.

Still another plot line finds the hero, Beranger, marooned among South American Indians, among whom he finds an exceptionally good Spanish Benedictine missionary, who has built a chapel (where he keeps his vestments in a vault under the altar), administers Baptism and ''blessed Eucharist'' to the savages whom he has converted, and generally lives up to the frequently applied phrases ''good monk'' and ''humble priest.'' The most singular circumstance in this novel, however, is the unique religious history of Charlotta herself. At one point in her eventful career, thinking Beranger lost to her forever, she marries the son of the Spanish governor of San Domingo and out of sheer necessity becomes a Catholic. Yet long after her husband's death, when she meets the Benedictine, we find that ''Charlotta, who was now a sincere Roman Catholick, prevailed with the Monk to be her Chaplain, and to promise to continue with her the Rest of his days.'' He marries Charlotta to Beranger, who is presently ''persuaded by his wife and the Monk to be a Roman Catholick, which he had been bred at first.'' This is certainly the only English novel of the entire eighteenth century in which either hero or heroine is converted, or won back, *to* Catholicism; in all other cases the process is reversed.

In view of the status of English Catholics in the 1720's, when vicious attacks like Conyers Middleton's *Letter from Rome,* which professed to show ''an exact conformity between Popery and Paganism,'' went into several editions and were applauded from every fashionable pulpit, it surely took more than ordinary independence of mind for this forgotten writer to present Catholic themes with honesty and understanding. Not only do her works contain the only favorably depicted conversions, the only miracle, and the only martyr, but all her heroes and heroines, except Mme. de Beaumont and one other, are active Catholics whose lives are at some point influenced by their faith. Most notable are her many good religious. Whether Franciscans, Benedictines, or Jesuits, they are good, not merely on the humanitarian level of Defoe but specifically as Catholic priests. The only one to violate his vows, Chateau-Roial, is seen as a tragic figure who bitterly repents his transgression. The others baptize, preach, celebrate Mass, convert heathens, hear confessions, give Extreme Unction to the dying, all as if this were no more than was to be expected of them, unqualified by patronizing, grudging editorial comments of the sort that almost negate the few other attempts during the century at sympathetic depiction of priests. Except for Richardson's two in *Grandison,* Penelope Aubin's were the last admirable priests to appear in the English novel for more than fifty years. If her literary skill as a novelist was no more than average for her day, her moral courage as a Catholic was to remain unmatched among English writers for the remainder of the eighteenth century. (pp. 67-71)

Roger B. Dooley, ''Penelope Aubin: Forgotten Catholic Novelist,'' in Renascence, *Vol. XI, No. 2, Winter, 1959, pp. 65-71.*

JOHN J. RICHETTI (essay date 1969)

[*Richetti is an American educator and author whose particular interest in the literature of the early eighteenth century is evidenced in his* Popular Fiction before Richardson: Narrative Patterns, 1700-1739 *(1969). In the following excerpt from that work, he explores Aubin's didacticism in her themes of imperiled virtue and Christian fortitude.*]

Many narratives may accurately be described as miscellanies, in the obvious sense that they contain the digressions, poems, songs, and interpolated stories traditional to narrative, but also in the special sense that they often include several . . . fictional paradigms. . . . Travel narratives are complemented by love stories, and persecuted maidens are sometimes found on desert islands; pirates and highwaymen abduct and sometimes ravish love-sick innocents, and glittering and depraved aristocrats appear in narratives with little real claim to be scandal chronicles. One approach usually dominates, however, and the other type characters may simply be making brief guest appearances.

Successful combination of several of the paradigms is possible. Some well-known examples are Defoe's combination of whore or rogue biography with the exotic travelogue in *Moll Flanders, Captain Singleton,* and *Colonel Jacque.* (p. 211)

Mrs. Aubin's novels were presented to her public as an undisguised attempt to seduce them into virtue through the familiar diversions of popular narrative. Actually, as W. H. McBurney has pointed out, she was quite thorough in fashioning her lures for the frivolous but potentially virtuous and tried to combine 'Defoe's subject matter and method with those of Mrs. Eliza Haywood and of continental fiction'. McBurney finds the stock characters of French amatory fiction in her novels but sees the hazards which she places in the paths of her heroines and certain backgrounds and descriptive details as 'purely Defoesque' [see excerpt dated 1957].

Leaving aside the vexing question this raises of proving literary influences, we can accept this as a fair speculation but translate it into our terminology. Mrs. Aubin's novels, deliberately and consistently, extend the range and significance of the story of persecuted innocence by grafting it to the delightful disasters of travel narrative. This combination is not, as McBurney's literary genealogy implies, an opportunistic and unnatural cross-breeding but a natural and logical union. Innocence, instead of being hounded from country house to city bagnio or brothel, is pursued by lust literally around the world. The artificial and stylized milieu of love and seduction is replaced by the exotic and appalling dangers of the high seas, filled with pirates, lustful Oriental potentates, and ferocious wild animals. There is a loss in erotic 'intensity' but a gain in ideological coherence, for the 'world' through which innocence now moves is the world itself, presented in geographical fullness.

These dangers on which innocence thrives (i.e. asserts itself as innocence in the middle of potentially destructive experience) are, consequently, increased in volume, variety, and authenticity. The hero-traveller, so attractive but ambiguous a figure for the eighteenth century, is concealed under the passive innocent, swept along by events, protected only by God's extraordinary providences and not at all by his (more often her, of course) own ingenuity and resourcefulness. As a result, the pleasures of travel through the exotic and the marvellous and of observing providential deliverance from the huge disasters attendant upon such rare experience are delivered free of disturbing secular implications; the heroes and heroines of Mrs. Aubin's novels are untainted by the daemonic secular spirit to survive and prosper . . . which we admire so much in Defoe's protagonists.

Of course, Mrs. Aubin's innocents are improbable stereotypes, but this woodenness is entirely appropriate to her polemical appeal: absolute and unremitting evil such as defines the troubled world she describes can only be endured and defeated by absolute and unwavering goodness. Mrs. Aubin had not Defoe's gifts, but did not miss them to accomplish her purposes. The guarded individuality, the complex and mature self-knowledge, which Defoe grants some of his great characters, would have been, in this context of didactic efficiency, positively distracting elements.

Mrs. Aubin's first two novels were published in 1721: *The Life of Madam de Beaumont, a French Lady; Who lived in a Cave in Wales above fourteen Years undiscovered, being forced to fly France for her Religion: and of the Cruel Usage she had there;* and *The Strange Adventures of the Count de Vinevil And his Family. Being an Account of what happen'd to them whilst they resided at Constantinople.* Both of these begin with aggressive prefaces bewailing the times as depraved. Mrs. Aubin, later a successful lay preacher, knows how to pitch her appeal and slides carefully into an *O tempora! O mores!* passage with a smoothness which Mrs. Manley's or Mrs. Haywood's automatic indignation was incapable of:

> The Story I here present the Public withal, is very extraordinary, but not quite so incredible as these [i.e. the times]. This is an Age of Wonders, and certainly we can doubt of nothing after what we have seen in our Days: yet there is one thing in the Story of Madam de Beaumont very strange; which is, that she, and her Daughter, are very religious, and virtuous, and that there were two honest Clergymen

living at one time. In the Lord de Beaumont's Story, there is yet something more surprising; which is, that he loved an absent Wife so well, that he obstinately refused a pretty Lady a Favour.

There is a tacit admission here that the events to be narrated are not literally true; Mrs. Aubin's novels are signed, and she appears as an authoress rather than an editor, observer, or compiler. She is claiming a moral truth, a Christian 'realism' in the strict philosophical sense of the word. This point is made even clearer at the end of the preface to *Count de Vinevil* [see essay dated 1721], where Mrs. Aubin asks her readers to believe not so much in the wild series of calamities to be presented as in the perfect rectitude of her good characters:

> As for the Truth of what this Narrative contains, since *Robinson Cruso* [sic] has been so well receiv'd, which is more improbable, I know no reason why this should be thought a Fiction. I hope the World is not grown so abandon'd to Vice, as to believe that there is no such Ladies to be found, as would prefer Death to Infamy; or a Man that, for Remorse of Conscience, would quit a plentiful Fortune, retire, and chuse to die in a dismal Cell. . . . Would Men trust in Providence, and act according to Reason and common Justice, they need not to fear any thing; but whilst they defy God and wrong others, they must be Cowards, and their Ends such as they deserve, surprizing and infamous.

Mrs. Aubin is never violent; she does not fulminate, but tells us gently that she hopes to reform by pleasing: 'In this Story [*Madame de Beaumont*] I have aim'd at pleasing, and at the same time encouraging Virtue in my Readers. I wish Men would, like Belinda, confide in Providence, and look upon Death with the same Indifference that she did'. She is even more explicit in the *Count de Vinevil,* where she begins by describing her effort as a deliberate attempt to rescue didacticism for literature. Her novel, she makes clear, is a systematic counter-statement against the fashionable novels of palpitating passion. Mrs. Aubin tries to substitute a positively exemplary Christian 'realism' for the erotic cautionary tales of Mrs. Haywood and others.

> Since serious things are, in a manner, altogether neglected, by what we call the Gay and Fashionable Part of Mankind, and Religious Treatises grow mouldy on the Booksellers Shelves in the Back Shops . . .
>
> I present this Book to the Publick, in which you will find a Story, where Divine Providence manifests itself in every Transaction, where Vertue is try'd with Misfortunes, and rewarded with Blessings: In fine, where Men behave themselves like Christians, and Women are really vertuous, and such as we ought to imitate.

The prefatory pitch of the amatory novella claimed to warn the innocent of the dangers of emotional experience: this is what happens to the innocents who naïvely follow their hearts in a heartless world. Mrs. Aubin goes much further than this: see, she tells us, how impervious real innocence is to all that the evil world can do, see how effective virtue and resignation to Providence and death are in overcoming any and all obstacles. We are being asked . . . to reject the erotic-pathetic tragedy which dominates the amatory novella for the melodrama of innocence narrowly preserved again and again by the power of faith and Providence. Mrs. Aubin's heroines are not torn asunder by a conflict between inclination and the demands of formal morality. They embody in a thoroughgoing way a purity and innocence which rules out moral ambiguity; they fight only against lust, cunning, and avarice, never against themselves. Read my stories, says Mrs. Aubin to her eighteenth-century readers, for emotional confirmation of that which you affirm rationally; celebrate again and again the victory of faith and virtue against an unbelieving world.

And there is indeed very little cause to accuse Mrs. Aubin of double-dealing and providing erotic bonuses with her ritualistic celebrations of the victory of innocence. Her novels are free of . . . lubricious facility . . . ; she cares very little for the precise psychological-physiological symptoms of passion and declines numberless opportunities for erotic-pathetic fantasy.

But perhaps the most important and certainly the most obvious sign of her integrity (or better, since I wish to avoid ethical judgements, her homiletic efficiency) is the alacrity with which her protagonists are married, or, at least, linked by legal and proper desire, right at the very beginning of the chaos of events which makes up the novel. This marriage or commitment to marriage remains throughout the tangle of disasters a guiding and saving simplification, like the protagonists' faith in Providence.

In *Madame de Beaumont,* for example, one of the heroines has been married for many years when the novel opens. When we meet her she has been living in a cave in Wales for fourteen years with her daughter, Belinda, separated from her husband by the standard machinations of the standard greedy world which always separates lovers. She has a familiarly harrowing story: shut up in a convent by relatives who wish to keep her marriage portion, she escapes from there with her lover and marries him. Mrs. Aubin does not stop there, even though from the point of view of Mrs. Haywood she has already gone too far. Madame de Beaumont is faced with specifically religious dangers and asked to play the role of Protestant champion.

When her husband is ordered to the wars, her father-in-law demands that she turn Catholic (we are in France); and when her husband decides to send her to England while he is away she is offered a large settlement to turn Catholic and stay in France. She refuses. Her virtue is requited by a storm which blows her ship aground on the Welsh coast. There she has remained, not unhappy; since, as Mrs. Aubin has emphasized in her preface, 'He that would keep his Integrity, must dwell in a Cell; and Belinda had never been so virtuous, had she not been bred in a Cave, and never seen a Court'.

Madame de Beaumont and Belinda are the first of many hermits Mrs. Aubin's readers were to meet in her novels. Here, to be sure, the hermitage is a bower of virtue, richly furnished and cleverly lit by a skylight, a freely chosen retreat from the vile world. Other hermits we shall meet will live less splendidly and in more inaccessible places than Wales, but Mrs. Aubin will always make their retreat a deliberate rejection of the world or a self-imposed penitential exile. Her insistence on this point is, in a sense, a counter-statement to the reluctant pilgrimage and spiritual ambiguity of the most famous fictional hermit of the early eighteenth century. Just as she rejects the heroine's internal struggle between passion and moral convention, she modifies instinctively (or perhaps simply through incompetence) Crusoe's internal struggle between acceptance of the penitential fitness of his situation and his daemonic energy to survive and escape.

Madame de Beaumont has left her hermitage only once, to find her husband in France, where she finds that he has presumed her dead and gone off in his grief to fight for the King of Sweden (a Protestant champion). Forays into the world to

obtain justice can only lead to fresh calamity for suffering virtue such as Madame de Beaumont possesses. Not only does she fail to find her husband, but her father-in-law has her thrown into prison. The resulting heroic pose, as evoked for us by Madame de Beaumont's own narration, is the sort of set-piece that Mrs. Aubin resolves her whirling disasters into again and again. There are highly erotic dangers throughout her stories, but they invariably lead to purely devotional set-pieces such as this one. The purpose of all this suffering is to test the virtuous and enable them to practice their fortitude. Madame de Beaumont's description of her reaction to suffering is thus a subdued prelude to the fully orchestrated pathos to be developed later on in the novel: 'Thus, Sir, I experienced that great Truth, That we have nothing more to do, to be happy and secure from all the Miseries of Life, but to resign our Wills to the Divine Being; nor does Providence ever appear more conspicuously than on such Occasions'.

She is telling her story to a Welsh gentleman who has stumbled upon their grotto by accident. He is no intruder, for his credentials are impeccable, a male equivalent of the female recluses. This Mr. Lluelling has 'wisely prefer'd a Country Retirement before noisy Courts, and Business'. He sees Belinda and proposes marriage immediately. Harbouring no designs, he seeks her properly by asking her mother. Unmarried until now, he has been no heretic to love and devotee of lust but simply virtuous and indifferent to women. His perfect qualifications are completed by his proposal, which shows the requisite awareness of the spiritual implications of love; his rhetoric establishes the connection between marriage and beatitude that is unknown to the world of power and property:

> May I be hated by Heaven and you, and may she scorn me, when I cease to love, to honour, and take care of you and her. Madam, till now, I never loved, my Heart has been indifferent to all the Sex; but from the moment I first look'd on that Angel's Face, where so much Innocence and Beauty shines, I have not asked a Blessing in which she was not comprehended; make her mine, and I shall have all I wish on Earth.

They marry, after a few modest hesitations by Belinda. Happiness is achieved, but Mrs. Aubin's homily demands that happiness be earned by patient endurance of hardship and even disaster. So, the secure rural world of secluded virtue is invaded very clearly by the outside world. The ideological collision is obvious to us, but not to the protagonists, when Mr. Lluelling's cousin arrives from London:

> . . . a young Gentleman who was his Cousin-German, and had long wish'd his Death, no doubt because he was his Heir, if he died without Issue. This young Man, Mr. Lluelling had always lov'd and bred up as his Son, having bought him Chambers in the Temple, where he, like most Gentlemen of this Age, had forgot the noble Principles, and virtuous Precepts, he brought to Town with him, and acquir'd all the fashionable Vices that give a Man the Title of a fine Gentleman: he was a Contemner of Marriage, cou'd drink, dissemble, and deceive to Perfection; had a very handsome Person, an excellent Wit, and was most happy in expressing his Thoughts elegantly: these Talents he always employ'd in seducing the Fair, or engaging the Affection of his Companions, who doated upon him, because he was cunning and daring, could always lead them on to Pleasures, or bring them nicely off, if frustrated in any vicious Designs.

We should pause to remind ourselves what the amatory novella as practiced by Mrs. Haywood would have done with such a situation. In one of her novellas, Belinda would be married (or the city rake would be), but either union would be the usual joyless and profitable alliance. She would, as a properly virtuous but sensitive heroine, see Glandore for the wolf in resplendent garments that he is, but feel nevertheless an instant compelling sexual attraction to him. She would be torn between duty and passion, and the dialectic of persecuted innocence would make us see the tragic (and exciting) necessity of such a conflict in a corrupt masculine world.

Here, however, the dialectic of popular prose she-tragedy is discarded for the polemical simplifications of the simple battle between good and evil. All of the familiar moral antitheses of the early eighteenth century are present: country versus city, love-marriage versus lust-seduction, simple rural trust versus urban cunning and duplicity, and aristocratic wit and scintillating surface versus plain-spoken and simply eloquent virtue. The conflict which develops is simple. Belinda loves Lluelling and he her. His cousin seeks his death, his estate, and his wife without a shade of remorse or hesitation.

Lluelling volunteers to go to France to find his father-in-law, and since he is, above all, open and trusting, leaves his cousin in charge. When Glandore quickly declares his passion and threatens to force Belinda if she does not comply, her reply is unequivocal:

> 'By Heaven, I'll never give Consent, and if you force me like a Brute, what Satisfaction will you reap? I shall then hate and scorn you, loath your Embraces, and if I ever escape your hands again, sure Vengeance will o'ertake you; nay, you shall drag me sooner to my Grave, than to your Bed; I will resist to Death, and curse you with my last Breath: but if you spare me, my Prayers and Blessings shall attend you, nay, I will pity and forgive you.' 'I'm deaf to all that you can plead against my Love, he cry'd, yield or I'll force you hence.' 'No, says she, I'll rather die; now, Villain, I will hate you: help and defend me Heaven.'

This speech and the scene which contains it have a simplicity totally lacking in the lush erotic tangles of the amatory novella. Belinda's heroism lacks both the extravagant rhetoric and the erotic suggestion of Mrs. Haywood's cornered ladies. We will, indeed, pass rapidly from this point of the novel to the end from one near-disaster to another; the basic pattern of persecuted innocence remains the same. But each near-climax is much closer to simple fatal violence than to the violent sensuality which threatens to engulf the wandering innocent of the ordinary novella. Mrs. Aubin's heroines, like Belinda, convince us that they will either die or survive with their genuine honour intact; Mrs. Haywood's heroines exist in a moral and psychological world where honour cannot be achieved, where the only alternatives (until the god of love descends to grant exceptions at the end) are fidelity to duty (with the 'spiritual' poverty that involves) or self-immolation in illicit passion. In either case, only some kind of disreputable and unsatisfactory survival is possible.

Belinda, on the other hand, is supremely confident of her virtue and absolute inner purity. She faces disaster with all the equanimity of the intrepid traveller and makes speeches at destiny with an imperturbable confidence in providential wisdom. Death, she reasons, is as much a deliverance as any other rescue. (pp. 216-25)

The rest of **Madame de Beaumont** is simply a series of nearly identical trials for innocence to pass through. Belinda is saved at the point of 'ruin' several times. (p. 226)

[A number of] marvellous coincidences and deliverances justify Mrs. Aubin's concluding summary. Unlike Mrs. Haywood's half-hearted attempts to stick on a moral tag, this is a legitimate gloss, a *moralitas* which fits Mrs. Aubin's purpose and, in an eighteenth-century context, describes the moral uplift and ideological coherence which her works provided for the willing reader:

> Thus Providence does, with unexpected Accidents, try Men's Faith, frustrate their Designs, and lead them thro a Series of Misfortunes, to manifest its Power in their Deliverance; confounding the Atheist, and convincing the Libertine, that there is a just God, so boundless is his Power, that none ought to despair that believe in him. You see he can give Food upon the barren Mountain, and prevent the bold Ravisher from accomplishing his wicked Design: the virtuous Belinda was safe in the hands of a Man who was desperately in love with her, and whose desperate Circumstance made him dare to do almost any thing; but Virtue was her Armour, and Providence her Defender: these Tryals did but improve her Vertues, and encrease her Faith.

Obviously, we might object, very few atheists and libertines were routed by Mrs. Aubin's novels; just as very few heiresses were prevented from eloping by Mrs. Haywood's novellas. Both of them are preaching to the converted, and Mrs. Aubin, especially, is providing the anticipated discovery of pattern and significance in a welter of incredible confusion. Each deliverance and outrageous coincidence is an example, on the popular religious level that Mrs. Aubin is working at, of that simultaneous unity of plot and theme which Northrop Frye calls *dianoia*. Mrs. Aubin's willing readers, in Frye's terminology, see each event or incident as 'a manifestation of some underlying unity', for her plots have their effect not simply in terms of suspense and linear progression but as a series of events which 'regroup themselves around another center of attention'. What McBurney calls 'the particular temptation of excessive and unintegrated variety against which eighteenth-century fiction was to struggle until Richardson and Fielding', was in Mrs. Aubin's case an appropriate failure, for the unity which her homiletic purpose seeks thrives on a disorderly succession of calamities through which the providence of God and the virtue of her heroes can shine.

Mrs. Aubin may have realized the specific value of variety, or she may simply have been imitating the attractive exotic miscellany which made the pseudo-authentic travel narrative so popular. Whatever her reasons, her novels became more and more clotted with interlocking disasters and coincidences, stretching sometimes right around the world. (pp. 227-29)

[Most] of Mrs. Aubin's novels end with a parade. We exult as Christian heroes and heroines march in triumph to their country seats to live safely and virtuously for ever, and we watch approvingly as Mrs. Aubin ends with an aggressively polemical Q.E.D.

> Since Religion is no Jest, Death and a future State certain; let us strive to improve the noble Sentiments such Histories as these will inspire in us; avoid the loose Writings which debauch the Mind; and since our Heroes and Heroines have done nothing but what is possible, let us resolve to act like them, make Virtue the Rule of all our Actions, and eternal Happiness our only Aim.

In the person of Mrs. Aubin, we can see the lady novelist acquiring a new *persona*, one which is to become more important as the century wears on and to linger through the nineteenth century as a powerful and formative public image: moral censor of the age. (p. 229)

John J. Richetti, "The Novel as Pious Polemic," in his Popular Fiction before Richardson: Narrative Patterns, 1700-1739, *Oxford at the Clarendon Press, Oxford, 1969, pp. 211-61.*

JOSEPHINE GRIEDER   (essay date 1973)

[*In the following excerpt, Grieder comments on Aubin's mixture of instruction and delight in* The Life of Madam de Beaumount *and* The Strange Adventures of the Count de Vinevil.]

To introduce Mrs. Aubin and her authorial intentions . . . , one can do no better than to cite the preface to **The Strange Adventures of the Count de Vinevil and His Family** [see essay dated 1721]. "Since serious thing are, in a manner, altogether neglected, by what we call the Gay and Fashionable Part of Mankind, and Religious Treatises grow mouldy on the Booksellers Shelves," she observes sternly, "the few that honour Virtue, and wish well to our Nation, ought to study to reclaim our Giddy Youth; and since Reprehensions fail, try to win them to Vertue, by Methods where Delight and Instruction may go together." Thus, she presents this story, "where Divine Providence manifests itself in every Transaction, where Vertue is try'd with Misfortunes, and rewarded with Blessings: In fine, where Men behave themselves like Christians, and Women are really vertuous, and such as we ought to imitate." How she keeps her promise in this novel and in **The Life of Madam de Beaumount** is easily demonstrable.

The "delight" she speaks of proceeds from her observant use of elements from various genres of popular fiction, as modern scholars have pointed out. Both novels share the geographical variety of tales of travel and adventure. Mme de Beaumount voyages twice from France to England, her daughter wanders around Wales, and her husband goes to serve the King of Sweden against the Czar and returns to France only after having undergone captivity in the wastelands of Russia and in robber-infested Tartary. The Vinevil family sails to Constantinople, where they become separated; before Ardelisa can rejoin her father and her husband, she must endure a long Robinson-Crusoe-like stay on Delos with her fellow castaways and passage through Italy to France. Elements typical of romantic love stories are also to be remarked. Heroes and heroines are forcibly parted, sometimes by chance, sometimes by parental opposition, sometimes by villains' designs. Each sex undergoes those trials suitable to it, the men demonstrating courage and constancy, the women patience and virtue.

But the operative word in Mrs. Aubin's preface is "instruction." Unlike female contemporaries such as Mrs. Manley and Mrs. Haywood, who used the trials of virtue as a pretext for lasciviousness, Mrs. Aubin resolutely banishes any hint of the erotic from the persecutions of her heroines and shows, rather, that though virtue must indeed be tried, it must always, with the proper faith, triumph over those who would seek to sully it. Belinda in **Madam de Beaumount** is perhaps the most beleaguered maiden, dragged from pillar to post by would-be ravishers. Yet she always manages to escape: "the Almighty try'd her Faith and Patience, but design'd not she, who fled from Sin, should perish."

In their misfortunes, Mrs. Aubin's heroes and heroines depend at all times on God and divine providence. Mme de Beaumount,

Frontispiece of The Strange Adventures of the Count de Vinevil and His Family *(1721)*.

incarcerated in a gloomy castle by her wicked father-in-law, prays for help and protection, "after which I grew calm, found my Faith encrease, my Fears abate, and my Soul seem'd arm'd for all Events''; she realizes "That we have nothing more to do, to be happy and secure from all the Miseries of Life, but to resign our Wills to the Divine Being; nor does Providence every appear more conspicuously than on such Occasions." The happy outcome of each couple's adventures proves, of course, that their faith has not been misplaced.

A particular proof of providence's direct action is provided by the story of Don Fernando de Cardiole in **The Count de Vinevil.** Father Francis arrives just in time to aid the dying man and, after burying him, reads his confession. Don Fernando had been a thorough villain: he had his mistress' suitor assassinated, flew to Turkey, and enlisted with the pirates against the Venetians. "There, with the Fleet, I did all the Mischief I was able, enter'd and plunder'd the Churches, deflower'd noble Virgins, and returned much commended." But such a scoundrel could not be left to riot in evil luxury, according to Mrs. Aubin's dictates, and "God . . . awak'd my Conscience, and I felt such bitter Remorse in my Soul, that I could take no Rest or Pleasure." In his solitary rustic retreat he has expiated his crimes, and he bequeathes the testament Father Francis reads to the sincere Christian, that "he may be warn'd of sinning, as I have done."

The relationship between God and man is easily preached and its good effects readily demonstrated in fiction; the relationship between man and woman requires more scrutiny because it involves more difficult considerations. It is clear, however, that Mrs. Aubin views marriage as the paramount component of this relationship: an essential bond which ratifies innocent affection, legitimizes all demands, and drives away any desire or capacity to love elsewhere. The authoress is, in fact, overtly scrupulous about wedding her lovers before their difficulties begin. Ardelisa marries Longueville, and though the union is not (evidently) consummated before they separate, the vows bind her as though they had endured for years. Belinda and Mr. Lhuelling are married before he leaves for France, and the ceremony steels her innocent heart against tender impressions, like the sight of the lovesick young Hide. M. de Beaumount, despondent but steadfastly true to his wife, whom he believes dead, actually causes the death of two ladies who discover they can make no impression on his faithful heart.

The sacredness of marriage—or at least of the first carnal bond between man and woman—allows Mrs. Aubin to resolve a very delicate problem she sets up in *The Count de Vinevil.* Violetta, the lovely Venetian, confesses her despair at having been the mistress of the Turk Osmin and wishes only to retire to a convent "to weep for a Sin, of which"—Mrs. Aubin immediately interjects—"she was in reality altogether innocent." The distraught girl wishes that she had had the courage of Ardelisa, who vowed to die defending her virtue. But Father Francis extricates Violetta neatly from her moral dilemma. Had Ardelisa submitted out of necessity to Osmin's embraces, she would indeed have committed "a horrid Crime," because she was married; "but as you were single, a Virgin, and made his by the Chance of War, it was no Sin in you to yield to him." Moreover, the father warns her of the gravity of the union she had so unwittingly entered into. He counsels her sternly that it would have been "a Sin not to have been faithful to his Bed, whilst he is living you ought not to marry, you might have been a means of his Conversion; you ought to pray for him, and consider he acted according to his Knowledge and Education." Violetta, listening attentively, finds herself "much reviv'd," and Mrs. Aubin saves a heroine who, by the strictest morality, might have been damned.

Though certainly Mrs. Aubin's view of the sanctity of marriage is laudable, her wedded heroes' sentiments regarding their wives' chastity and constancy are insufferably priggish. Lhuelling, reunited with Belinda, whose trials have harrowed her (and us) for pages, can think of nothing else to ask but "Has no vile Ravisher usurped my Right, and forced you to his hated Bed? Has not that lovely Body been polluted with his curs'd Embraces?" Longueville enjoins his new bride before their separation, "Permit not a vile Infidel to dishonour you, resist to death, and let me not be so compleatly curs'd, to hear you live, and are debauch'd. . . . Forgive me, *Ardelisa,*"—he adds somewhat sheepishly—"I know your Vertue's strong, tho you are weak, but Force does oft prevail." Perhaps the only excuse for this male lack of trust is furnished by Mrs. Aubin's portraits of the vile seducers—there are a few—whose designs on the heroines are made devastatingly clear. Glandore crudely offers Belinda the choice of submitting to him quietly in the summerhouse or being kidnapped and living forever in degradation. Mahomet, the amorous infidel in *The Count de Vinevil,* shows his villainy even more dramatically: "'Slaves!'" he commands in front of Ardelisa's aged father, "go, search the Chambers, and bring her naked from her Bed, that I may ravish her before the Dotard's Face, and then send his Soul to Hell'."

It is somewhat unjust perhaps to quote Mrs. Aubin's characters out of context, for the melodramatic language evident here forms a very minor part of the general narrative, in which speech tends to be morally uplifting or consoling, and simple in tone. In fact, Mrs. Aubin succeeds in mixing drama and moralizing as well as she mixes instruction and delight—that is, with a good deal of skill, variety, and brevity. One could never praise her characters for being true to life; but one cannot fault their impeccable behavior and fail to be entertained by their adventures. (pp. 5-10)

> *Josephine Grieder, in an introduction to* The Life of Madam de Beaumount, a French Lady *and* The Strange Adventures of the Count de Vinevil and His Family *by Penelope Aubin, Garland Publishing, Inc., 1973, pp. 5-10.*

JOSEPHINE GRIEDER (essay date 1973)

[*In the following excerpt, Grieder briefly compares* The Life and Adventures of the Lady Lucy *with Eliza Haywood's* The Rash Resolve *(1724).*]

Mrs. Eliza Haywood won her literary reputation for entertaining tales of intrigue and passion, dramatically displayed in narrative and dialogue, and *The Rash Resolve: or, the Untimely Discovery* is a typical example of her novelistic talents. Squarely in the camp of virtue, Mrs. Penelope Aubin demonstrated to her audience that unswerving fidelity and purity of heart were worth the painful sacrifices that Providence imposed before it rewarded; *The Life and Adventures of the Lady Lucy* does not deviate from this message.

Although the difference between the two authoresses' conceptions of fiction is clear, their means are remarkably similar. Mrs. Haywood, to enlist the sympathies of her reader, cannot avoid choosing a heroine who is a veritable paragon of innocence and virtue, betrayed by the perfidious creatures she comes into contact with. Mrs. Aubin, to make her moral point, must contrive difficult or licentious situations for her good characters to triumph over. The foundations of the two works thus bear a family resemblance, and only Mrs. Aubin's overt moralizing converts her fiction into something more edifying.

Of the two, *The Rash Resolve* is technically the better novel. The reader makes the acquaintance of the virtuous but inexperienced Emanuella in Porto Rico, where her knavish guardian robs and imprisons her, only to lose his prey to his compassionate son, who rescues the damsel; he follows her to Madrid, where she recovers her fortune, falls in love with Emilius, is betrayed by Berillia, is once again impoverished, and retreats in shame to a convent. Interest is temporarily diverted during Part II to Emilius himself, who proves his inconstant nature by wooing and marrying Julia; but Emanuella's story is soon taken up again as, pregnant, she escapes from the convent, attempts to support herself and her infant son as a lady's companion, is rediscovered by Emilius and his wife, and dies. This brief plot summary necessarily omits many piquant details of Emanuella's adventures but serves, at least, to show that Mrs. Haywood keeps fairly consistently to a single story line focused on one character.

The Life and Adventures of the Lady Lucy, in comparison, resembles a group of short stories hung loosely on the narrative clothesline of Lucy's marriage to Albertus. When a new character enters, he promptly relates his life; thereafter he may disappear entirely, like the hermit who dies or the couple who shelters Albertus, his story told and his lesson taught. Moreover, Lucy retires, like Emanuella, to a convent in mid-novel, while the focus shifts to Albertus and his progress from debauchery to repentance to saintly benevolence. Lucy and Albertus are, of course, suitably reunited at the end, after their eighteen-day separation.

Emanuella and Lucy are, if not twins, at least sisters whose fates are remarkably similar. Each falls in love with a man who proves himself unworthy of her devotion; each is betrayed by a perfidious, dissembling female friend, motivated by spite and jealousy. Both are deserted, when pregnant, by the child's father, and the babies become the only source of their mothers' hope and joy. Mrs. Haywood's appeal for respect for her heroine on the grounds of Emanuella's maternal devotion is perhaps somewhat specious, since the child is illegitimate; on the other hand, Mrs. Aubin's reader is asked to accept that Lucy, even though Albertus deliberately attempted to murder her, can remain loving and forgiving towards her husband until they are reunited.

Resemblances exist between secondary characters also. The treacherous friends, Henrietta in *Lady Lucy* and Berillia in *The Rash Resolve,* are both ladies of loose morals; Mrs. Aubin makes clear, even, that it is Henrietta's irregular life that is responsible for her perfidy, it having accustomed her so much to deception that she has no scruples about dishonoring her friend. Both heroes, Mrs. Haywood's Emilius and Mrs. Aubin's Albertus, are credulous enough to believe stories which malign their beloved, though the details contradict all they know of the ladies' character; each promptly begins another amour to solace himself; each repents his behavior, though Albertus displays his remorse in a somewhat more flamboyant manner by becoming a hermit and mortifying the flesh.

Whether these resemblances are purely coincidental is impossible to say, although Mrs. Aubin's novel did appear two years after *The Rash Resolve.* The moral use she makes of *Lady Lucy* is, however, considerably different from Mrs. Haywood's desire to entertain. Eschewing dialogue for straight description in dramatic situations and frequently stepping in herself to comment, Mrs. Aubin makes it perfectly clear to her reader that innocent virtue will always triumph (like Lucy), that vice will die painfully (like Henrietta), and that even the most hardened sinner can repent and successfully reform (like Albertus).

Vice's conversion to virtue is, in fact, a favorite topic with Mrs. Aubin, and instances are numerous in *Lady Lucy.* Typical is the hermit's story, which may have been introduced to prefigure Albertus' own reformation. Happily married, the man experiences a violent passion for his wife's sister: "I, who had all my Life long before liv'd a good and virtuous Life, and had the most awful Sense of God and Religion that a Christian ought to have, was in an Instant converted into one of the vilest Wretches on Earth, and grew capable of forming, and at length of acting, the most villainous Designs." And he does not exaggerate his behavior: he poisons the sister's legitimate suitor, rapes her, lives in sin for some months, and, on finding her pregnant, poisons her also. But the dreadful apparition of his dead mistress in a dream terrifies him into repentance; and he retreats to the wood where he has struggled "by the strictest Penance, and continual Prayer to endeavour to reconcile myself to the Almighty, and thro' my Saviour's Merits obtain Pardon of my great and heinous Sins." His story is a succinct demonstration of Mrs. Aubin's wish, as expressed in the novel's last sentence, that the vicious may be "touch'd to the inmost

Recesses of their Soul, at the reading of this History, and amend, that they may have pardon, and God be glorify'd."

Both authoresses were at the height of their literary power and reputation when these works were produced. Mrs. Haywood, as yet untainted by Pope's brush in *The Dunciad,* was proving a veritable golden-egg-laying goose for her publishers; Mrs. Aubin had published four previous novels, all with the same tendentious morality and most achieving at least a second edition. Though even the most charitable critic must rank them as second-rate writers, they deserve some admiration for having developed a formula and adhered to it, thereby succeeding in a precarious profession. (pp. 5-9)

> *Josephine Grieder, in an introduction to* The Rash Resolve *by Eliza Haywood and* The Life and Adventures of the Lady Lucy *by Penelope Aubin, Garland Publishing, Inc., 1973, pp. 5-9.*

APRIL LONDON   (essay date 1986)

[*In the following excerpt from a study of the Edenic garden metaphor in early eighteenth-century novels, London discusses the sexual victimization of Aubin's heroines.*]

In one of the most perceptive analyses of pre-1740 narrative, John J. Richetti traces the contemporary rendering of experience as "secular" or "religious." While this distinction clarifies the psychological appeals made by fiction and the authors' concern with reader response, it to a degree obscures the shared concern of amatory and pious novels with the fundamental issue of authority. Secular and religious can, in fact, be seen not as contrary, but complementary, responses to a world envisioned as ineluctably hierarchical. Although in each genre the chosen code fixes the limits of the fictional world, both structure experience to admit exclusive adherence to the favored model of dominance. This, in turn, delimits possible action as characters exist largely in order to yield control to a superior divine or sexual force. The subordination of character thus works both structurally and thematically; the predominantly female protagonists are bound by the interchangeable codes of gender and genre to realize their subject status.

This generic congruity extends to a shared vocabulary which supplements intellectual and emotional dependence through a recurrent pattern of physical enclosure. Both amatory and pious narratives employ metaphors informed by the myth of the garden and directed toward ratifying the source of significance of power. In the development of circumscribed structures of time, ethics, and action, the garden thus serves as a metonymy within the text for the world the text signifies. Contemporary authors drew upon the multiple meanings of the garden in their evocation of a world of necessary subordination: a place of Edenic innocence or transgression, of the intercession of a benevolent providence or of chaotic possibility, of divine presence or human skill, of natural passion or concealed sin, and of sacred or secular time. Coexistent with these moral and aesthetic perspectives, the garden retains its material status as property, with the attendant issues of ownership, consumption, productivity, and improvement. Within narratives that are often rambling, digressive, and of wavering didactic intent, the sure grasp of the garden image stands in sharp relief. To the early eighteenth-century writer, it was an accessible and often exploited metaphor; to the twentieth-century reader its variable functions provide a key to the ideological assumptions that underlie the rise of the novel. The attempted seduction of Pamela in the garden, then, works within a formulaic tradition of heroines set in apposition to an enclosed "natural" world. Granting the individual will a measure of integrity in accordance with Puritan doctrine involves for Richardson, however, the transposition of intellectual for physical subordination. Pre-1740 narratives rarely make such a distinction. Women writing about women—Mary Delariviere Manley, Eliza Haywood, Penelope Aubin—adapt the actual and symbolic terrain of the garden to stand analogically for the condition of their heroines and their relation to the world beyond. (pp. 101-02)

Pious novels of the period . . . claimed to excise eroticism in the interests of admonitory didacticism. But authors like Penelope Aubin, in fact, adapt the basic premise of the amatory novel as the paradigm of relationships. Innocence persecuted is a persistent motif, and in her pursuit of it, she far exceeds Haywood in imagining possible varieties of degradation. The localized danger of the seducer is thus supplanted in Aubin's world by endemic catastrophe. Victimization is no longer tied to individual aggression, but has become a social reflex directed against the heroine as exemplar of piety and virginity. The conflation of the two contemporary myths of the victimized female and the infidel heathen fuels this view of the beleaguered Christian. Innocence threatened was a staple of romance narratives, and the addition of infidel barbarians to the crowd of besiegers was a sensational twist. Together the two provide a powerful context for the victory of innocence; the heroines emerge spiritually unscathed from captivity in Barbary, while a number of minor characters present the stark alternative of submission of brutal lust and conversion to Mohammedism.

Like Defoe's narratives, Aubin's works depend on the figuration of the world as a play of hostile forces. They differ radically, however, in the forms of defensive opposition permitted the protagonist. Comparison of two responses to adversity—Maria's in *The Noble Slaves* and Moll Flanders' in Defoe's novel—epitomizes this divergence. Moll's narrative chronicles survival through exploitation. By adopting the strategems of the enemy—"to Deceive the Deceiver"—she opposes and ultimately surmounts the penalties of gender and position. A lurid retelling of the St. Lucy story in *The Noble Slaves* represents a more characteristic female response. Maria, importuned by the heathen emperor, answers his lust by declaiming, "My eyes shall never see my shame, said I nor more inflame mankind; these I offer up to virtue, and they shall weep no more in aught but blood. At these words I tore my eye balls out and threw them at him." Her action graphically mimics the ethic of renunciation that shapes the pious novel. To be a woman in the Aubin world involves constant sexual intimidation: a punishment so perfectly instilled, and by implication justified, that the protagonists answer it with self-destruction. Aubin, like Manley in the Diana de Bedamore episode from *The New Atalantis,* sees femaleness as a covert invitation to violation. Maria thus achieves moral stature within the novel not by asserting a separate self in opposition to threat, but by mutilating the guilty source of sin: her own body.

Mrs. Aubin was a successful polemicist, keenly aware of the commercial aspects of novel writing. She records rather plaintively and with heavy irony in the Preface to *The Strange Adventures of the Count de Vinevil* [see essay dated 1721]:

> As for the Truth of what this Narrative contains, since *Robinson Cruso* has been so well receiv'd, which is more improbable, I know no reason why this should be thought a Fiction. I hope the World is not grown so abandon'd to Vice, as to believe that there is no such Ladies to be found, as would prefer Death to Infamy; or a Man that, for Remorse of Conscience,

would quit a plentiful Fortune, retire, and chuse to die in a dismal cell.

But having observed Defoe's popularity, she grafted elements of the travel narrative on to her romances. In *The Noble Slaves,* for example, the boat carrying Teresa and her slave is blown off the coast of Mexico. Three days later they are "cast on a desolate Island" where they are discovered by a Japanese man with his wife and three children who speak Chinese. Subsequent explorations of the island turn up a French man and his wife, a Spaniard, and two Persians living in a hill. This flagrant distortion of geography and the train of marvelous coincidences that provide the semblance of narrative coherence clearly undermine Aubin's claim to verisimilitude. But read on the level of a near-allegorical projection of Christian endurance and providential design, the novels could be seen as models of desirable emotional responses to adversity. The problem in assessing Aubin's didacticism becomes apparent with any attempt to balance such an interpretation against the hysterically defensive tone of her works. Ultimately, the allegorical reading invited by the reliance on providential intercession is defeated by the sheer weight of the impossibly complicated plots and the eagerness with which her heroines embrace martyrdom. Reading the novels as an expression of hierarchical power structures yields, in fact, a grotesquely warped parody of their putative didacticism.

In the novels of Manley and Haywood, the relation of eroticism to enclosure depends upon the presentation of the garden as a displaced image of the susceptible female. To the Aubin heroine like Maria, even this nominal acknowledgment of subjectivity is denied: she is enclosed within, defined by, and perceived as, an erotic object. The only means of grace or escape from this intrinsic identity is mutilation of self *qua* object. (pp. 112-13)

> April London, "Placing the Female: The Metonymic Garden in Amatory and Pious Narrative, 1700-1740," in Fetter'd or Free?: British Women Novelists, 1670-1815, *edited by Mary Anne Schofield and Cecilia Macheski, Ohio University Press, 1986, pp. 101-23.*

JERRY C. BEASLEY (essay date 1986)

[*Beasley is an American educator and author who is best known for his work on eighteenth-century English fiction, particularly the writings of Tobias Smollett. In the following excerpt, he addresses the topical relevance of Aubin's novels.*]

It is a commonplace of English literary history that women novelists of the Restoration and eighteenth century—from Aphra Behn to Jane Austen—were interested mainly in telling stories of domestic conflict featuring blushing virginal maidens whose happiness is threatened by their own social innocence, by avaricious fathers and brothers, by treacherous sisters, rakish seducers, and all manner of hostile people and circumstances. Like most commonplaces of its kind, this one is only partially grounded in the truth. Women did indeed write such stories by the dozens, particularly during the earlier years of the eighteenth century. But, as a quantity of recent feminist scholarship has shown, they did not always do so merely for the diversion or titillation of their readers. It is clear that many women writers actually used their works to give urgent and meaningful expression to a female consciousness, much as the Brontë sisters were to do in the nineteenth century, though not with the same degree of bold sophistication and—it is probable—only rarely with the same deliberate awareness of purpose. There can be no doubt that even the most trite and conventional of eighteenth-century novels by women often dramatize a subversive affirmation of the dominant value of the female as the active embodiment of emotional sensitivity and moral integrity and as the chief force for domestic stability. The popularity of prose fiction, among female readers at least, may be in part attributed to this kind of affirmation, whose importance otherwise to the development of the novel as a literature of common life can hardly be emphasized too much.

What has not yet been sufficiently noticed, even by feminist scholars and critics, is the political content and appeal, and sometimes the explicit political value, of a great many of the early stories by women. The relationships between political circumstances and the rise of the novel during the first several decades of the eighteenth century were both close and important. Works of prose fiction regularly addressed political issues and events, frequently in an emphatically topical manner; and even when they were neither overtly topical nor very direct in their approach to politics, the writers of popular narrative tended to center on moral and social concerns that were deeply affected by the political atmosphere of the period. We may find a singular example of just this kind of thing in Samuel Richardson's hugely successful first novel, *Pamela*. The moralizing heroine of this apparently apolitical work makes an unmistakably political proclamation of the value of the individual life when she writes to Parson Williams, ''But, O Sir! my Soul is of equal Importance with the Soul of a Princess; though my Quality is inferior to that of the meanest Slave.''

The author of *Pamela* was by no means the first novelist to put such a political sentiment in the mouth of a female character, or to project a domestic heroine as the exemplar of all virtue—public as well as private. Most of those who had done so before him were women who, not surprisingly, wrote about females in a social and moral environment. In their stories, as in Richardson's, the example of female virtue typically prevails in the end over all the hostility that a wicked society can fling against it, with the result that harmony is at last wrought out of disharmony and the domestic world is made stable and safe. The female character, it must be admitted, is often presented as a hackneyed expression of a sentimental cliché. But in the best works she is more than that. She is the formal representation of an ideal of order, set against a reality made dangerous by the anarchic forces of power-mongering, lasciviousness, and corruption of all kinds in all realms of human endeavor. We should not underestimate the political relevance of such characters, and the stories told about them, in an anxious age constantly worried over perceived threats of arbitrary power and continually preoccupied with Lockean ideals of moral government, with the controversies and scandals of the Walpole regime, and with repeated rumors of Jacobite uprisings. (pp. 216-17)

The portraits of female character painted by women novelists are often abstract and condescending; and the heroine of a typical fable looks limp and passive as her tender beauty is seen against all the sordid bustling hostility and violence she must endure before enjoying—which she usually does—her triumph in domestic bliss when the world at last becomes transformed into a reflection of what she represents. But even at their most passive, such heroines regularly succeed as rhetorically effective creations because of the contrast they provide to the wicked society that beleaguers them. And besides, they are not always soft and frail. Eliza Haywood's more interesting

ladies sometimes behave with an erotic aggressiveness that comes close to challenging the usual (often complacent) ideal of chaste femininity, and when they prevail it is as much by their energy as by their will or the force of their moral example. Penelope Aubin's women are in many instances similarly firm and lively, though never erotic. (p. 220)

[No] doubt Penelope Aubin wrote her tales of piety in action as responses to the more raffish author of *Love in Excess* [Eliza Haywood]. The public outcry against the supposed lasciviousness of Haywood seems to have prompted such works as *The Life of Madam de Beaumont, The Strange Adventures of the Count de Vinevil and His Family, The Life and Amorous Adventures of Lucinda, The Noble Slaves,* and *The Life of Charlotta Du Pont.* In these narratives of moral adventures on a worldwide scale, Aubin repeats Haywood's successful formula of amorous intrigue, but without the slightest hint of the erotic. Her stories reveal an optimistic faith affirming that those who are strong in pursuit of the Christian life, though they suffer the torments of isolation and persecution in a viciously antagonistic and chaotic world, will always emerge triumphant to enjoy the happiness that is their due. Aubin's characters, while they are never portrayed with the skill or sensitivity of a Richardson, prove more interesting than those of [Jane] Barker or Haywood; her more ambitious and sophisticated didacticism requires that she display something of their interior lives as they struggle to resist temptation and fend off threats, and she endows her females in particular with a kind of moral energy that foreshadows what the author of *Pamela* and *Clarissa* would achieve with his heroines. This she manages partly by keeping everyone in almost constant motion through plots that show goodness and innocence tested everywhere—in France, Wales, Virginia, Madagascar, and the West Indies; on the Spanish Main, up the river Oroonoko, at Constantinople, in Gibraltar, and on board the vessels of marauding pirates.

Aubin's books certainly register the influence of Defoe's currently popular tales of travel and adventure, but they pursue their purposes of edification and censure with a single-minded vigilance. In these novels it is not only England, but all the known world that is corrupted by bad men, bad politics, bad institutions. Against such a dark backdrop of universal villainy, the goodness of a Belinda (in *Madam de Beaumont*) looks bright indeed; and this heroine's wholesome beauty is again and again thrown into the terrifying shadows of evil until at last Providence relieves her and rewards her with the hand of the noble-hearted Mr. Lhuelling, a Welshman by birth. The same pattern of experience is repeated many times over in Aubin's popular stories, so that the whole corpus of her work looks like a comprehensive picture of global amorality, corruption, and disorder—the whole made bearable (the resemblance to Barker's *Exilius* is striking) by the final successes of the genuinely saintly characters, most of them female, whose lives of courage and faith we are admonished to emulate.

The stories themselves are moral fables, or moral histories of private virtue given great public visibility. Aubin obviously conceived them in this way, and since her first object is always the vigorous abrasion of archetypal representations of good and evil against one another in a context of timeless conflict, she does not appear to comment very specifically upon the actual conditions of English life. And yet her novels reverberate with the same criticisms of the contemporary environment that characterize the works of Behn, Manley, Haywood, and Barker. . . . A strong hint of Aubin's immediate preoccupation with the felt moral and political reality she and her readers knew may be found in the Preface to **Madam de Beaumont**. In the present age, the author says, ''Men are grown very doubtful, even in those Things that concern them most''—that is, in the eternal truths that support faith and the Christian life. She follows with a comparison decidedly to the disadvantage of her fellow countrymen: ''Wales being a Place not extremely populous in many Parts, is certainly more rich in Virtue than England, which is now improved in Vice only. . . .'' This jab is sharp and cutting, for Welshmen, like the Scots, were at the time popularly regarded as a species of romantic barbarians. And here Aubin is more than just vaguely topical, for a common charge against the Whig government turned upon its manner of sinking the nation into vice and infamy. But another remark is even more pointed. ''He that would keep his Integrity,'' Aubin complains with some bitterness, ''must dwell in a Cell; and Belinda had never been so virtuous, had she not been bred in a Cave, and never seen a Court.'' (pp. 229-31)

In reacting to the political climate as it seemed to affect the possibilities of a fulfilling moral life, early women novelists were rarely explicit or specific; but they appear to have been sharply aware of the contexts within which their works would be read, and their consciousness of the popular obsession with widespread corruption in the halls of government and in the other critical domains of power helped to dictate what they wrote. They were intensely political people, these novelists, writing in an age during which, as H. T. Dickinson has put it, the ''relationship between politics and literature'' was closer than ever before or since. The polemical effectiveness of the actual fictions by women is usually difficult to gauge. But it is hardly worthwhile attempting to gauge it, for few of their authors—Manley and Haywood excepted—were controversialists anyway. Instead, they were storytellers intent upon enforcing a moral point of view which was sometimes also a political point of view, though rarely identified with any party dogma. The important thing is to note the depth of these female writers' sensitivity to the contemporary scene, and the insistence with which they pursued some kind of reciprocal relationship between the real world they knew and the imaginary worlds they created. Their works vastly extended the reading audience for fiction, and, by responding with such urgency to anxieties over broad social and moral issues as they were touched by political circumstance, they did much to form and then sustain current ideals of public virtue—this is true even of Eliza Haywood's panting tales of tender passion. And all of the important narratives by women, including the scandal chronicles of Manley and Haywood, participated influentially in the cultivation of the popular taste for characters, plots, and themes drawn at least indirectly from the materials of familiar life. Without timely reader acceptance of such subject matter, and of its moralized treatment in a context of imaginative fable, the emergence of the novel as we know it today would not have occurred as it did, and when it did, with the sudden brilliant achievement of Samuel Richardson and Henry Fielding. (p. 234)

Jerry C. Beasley, "Politics and Moral Idealism: The Achievement of Some Early Women Novelists," in Fetter'd or Free?: British Women Novelists, 1670-1815, *edited by Mary Anne Schofield and Cecilia Macheski, Ohio University Press, 1986, pp. 216-36.*

JANE SPENCER   (essay date 1986)

[In the following excerpt, Spencer notes Aubin's pivotal role in the rise of the moral novel.]

In the early decades of the [eighteenth] century the novel was still a 'low' genre, associated with immorality. Penelope Aubin did much to change this, and she pointed the way forward for the moral novelists of the next generation. (p. 86)

Her works share some similarities with the travel narratives popular in the early eighteenth century. Shipwrecks, persecutions, imprisonments, escapes, separations and reunions follow in rapid and bewildering succession as her heroes and heroines move around the globe. Their experiences serve to test their virtue. Her heroines preserve their Christianity and their chastity in all circumstances, and the narrator points the moral: their 'Examples should convince us how possible it is for us to behave ourselves as we ought in our Conditions, since Ladies, whose Sex, and tender Manner of Breeding, render them much less able than Men to support such Hardships, bravely endured Shipwrecks, Want, Cold, Slavery, and every Ill that Human Nature could be tried withal'.

Aubin's didactic fiction differs from [Elizabeth] Rowe's in using more elements from popular fiction of the time, and having a much more sustained (if breathless) flow of narrative: in short, she allows more romance into her moral lessons. In this way her fiction goes further than Rowe's towards making morality compatible with the novel tradition. (p. 87)

Morality for her was here the proper aim of fiction, and she found the society of her time in particular need of moral advice: 'the few that honour Virtue, and wish well to our Nation, ought to study to reclaim our Giddy Youth; and since Reprehensions fail, try to win them by Vertue, and by Methods where Delight and Instruction may go together' [see essay dated 1721]. She declared herself opposed to contemporary trends in the novel, which she associated with an age of loose living generally, and with particular depravity among women writers. In her preface to **Charlotta du Pont** she explains that she has been encouraged 'to write more modishly, that is, less like a Christian, and in a Style careless and loose, as the Custom of the present Age is to live. But I leave that to the other female Authors my Contemporaries, whose Lives and Writings have, I fear, too great a resemblance'.

She does not name these other female authors, but it is very probable she has Eliza Haywood in mind. Haywood's fiction was popular in the early 1720s, the time of Aubin's entry into fiction. This was the beginning of a decade of ideological struggle between the two kinds of novel, and of woman novelist, represented by these two prolific writers. Haywood moralizes, but her didactic tone is used to convey some very permissive comments on the inevitable effects of passion, whereas Aubin's work is intended to demonstrate that the passions can be controlled by virtue.

Despite certain narrative crudities Aubin's novels, with their combination of fast-moving adventures and a plain didactic message, became very popular. Her example seems to have turned the tide in favour of moralized fiction, and her works were praised for not being like Haywood's. The preface to the 1739 collection of her novels contends that novels should be pure in style and manners, should punish the guilty characters, and should not allow the innocent to suffer. Unfortunately, the writer adds, most novels are not like this:

> And we are still more sorry to have Reason to say, That those of the *Sex,* who have generally wrote on these Subjects, have been far from preserving that Purity of Style and Manners, which is the greatest Glory of a fine Writer on any Subject; but, like the *fallen Angels,* having lost their own Innocence, seem,

as one would think by their Writings, to make it their Study to corrupt the minds of others. . . . Mrs. *AU-BIN* had a far happier Manner of Thinking and Acting.

It has been suggested that the author of this preface was Samuel Richardson, who was soon afterwards to follow its precepts in his first novel, *Pamela: or, Virtue Rewarded,* published late in 1740. Certainly Penelope Aubin's determined efforts to moralize fiction provided Richardson with a precedent for his 'new species of writing', intended 'to promote the cause of religion and virtue'. (pp. 87-8)

> *Jane Spencer, "The Terms of Acceptance," in her* The Rise of the Woman Novelist from Aphra Behn to Jane Austen, *Basil Blackwell, 1986, pp. 75-103.*

ADDITIONAL BIBLIOGRAPHY

Baker, Ernest A. "The Followers of Mrs Behn." In his *The History of the English Novel: The Later Romances and the Establishment of Realism,* pp. 107-29. London: H. F. & G. Witherby, 1929.
   Synopsis of Aubin's career and major literary concerns.

Foster, James R. "Sentiment from Afra Behn to Marivaux." In his *History of the Pre-Romantic Novel in England,* pp. 19-44. New York: Modern Language Association of America, 1949.
   Biographical and critical sketch highlighting Aubin's use of sentimentality in her fiction.

Kern, Jean B. "The Fallen Woman, from the Perspective of Five Early Eighteenth-Century Women Novelists." *Studies in Eighteenth-Century Fiction* 10 (1981): 457-68.
   Compares Aubin's perspective of "women as the real guardians of sexual morality in society" with those of four contemporaries: Mary Delariviere Manley, Eliza Haywood, Mary Hearne, and the anonymous "M. A."

Morgan, Charlotte E. "The Novel (1700-1740)." In her *The Rise of the Novel of Manners: A Study of English Prose Fiction between 1600 and 1740,* pp. 89-114. 1939. Reprint. New York: Russell & Russell, 1963.
   Brief but balanced assessment of Aubin's work as contributory to advancing the novel.

Novak, Maximillian E. "Some Notes Toward a History of Fictional Forms: From Aphra Behn to Daniel Defoe." *Novel: A Forum on Fiction* 6, No. 2 (Winter 1973): 120-33.
   Includes a brief comparison of Aubin's and Defoe's realistic techniques.

Prévost d'Exiles, Antoine François. *Le pour et le contre, ouvrage périodique d'un goût nouveau* 4 (1734): 294-97.
   Sketch of Aubin's life and career. Prévost's highly unflattering portrait, to date untranslated, is the primary source of Aubin's biography.

Shugrue, Michael F. "The Sincerest Form of Flattery: Imitation in the Early Eighteenth-Century Novel." *South Atlantic Quarterly* LXX, No. 2 (Spring 1971): 248-55.
   Posits Aubin's scrupulous employment of Daniel Defoe's literary techniques.

Zach, Wolfgang. "Mrs. Aubin and Richardson's Earliest Literary Manifesto (1739)." *English Studies* 62, No. 3 (June 1981): 271-85.
   Admits certain common denominators between the literary creeds of Aubin and Samuel Richardson, but discounts the former's substantial influence on the latter.

Christine de Pizan

1364-1430?

(Also Pisan) Italian-born French poet, essayist, historian, and biographer.

One of the most popular and respected authors of her time, Christine was the first French woman of letters and her nation's first female humanist of note. She composed a tremendous body of work in a variety of genres—lyric poetry, military and political treatises, history, biography, allegory, educational guidebooks, and didactic prose—using her position as her country's only female writer to educate individuals and influence national political affairs. Christine envisioned herself as her nation's conscience, writing works she hoped would inspire her countrymen to lead more peaceful, virtuous lives. Imbued as they are with a feminine perspective, her writings provide valuable insight into life in the Middle Ages. While not a feminist by modern standards, she was one of the first women to write in praise of women. Today, Christine's personal and literary achievements are considered exceptional; scholars rank her among the most important and influential writers of the fifteenth century.

Born in Venice, Christine moved at age four with her family to Paris, where her father served as an astrologer and personal physician to Charles V. In her account of her childhood in the autobiographical allegory *Lavision-Christine,* she explained that despite the widespread belief that learning was dangerous to women, her father encouraged her studies. Her formal education ended at age fifteen, however, when she married Etienne du Castel, a young nobleman and graduate student from Picardy. Their ten-year union was one of deep love, and as a result of their happiness, Christine considered marriage the ideal state between the sexes. Soon after her wedding, though, her family's fortunes began to change. Upon the death of Charles V in 1380, her father lost favor and his position at court—which left the family without much money—and then died, sometime between 1385 and 1389. Later, while on state business as secretary to Charles VI, Etienne died as well, thus leaving Christine to support her mother, two children, two brothers, a niece, and possibly other "poor relations." Etienne's untimely death marked the major turning point in Christine's life, as she was both unprotected and impoverished for the first time. Ignorant of both her husband's and father's financial affairs, she tried to claim her small but much-needed inheritances, only to be ridiculed and misled by corrupt lawyers. As she later noted, had she not had several dependents, she might have given up fighting the men who forced her to pay taxes on her father's land while preventing her from claiming the property titles. Instead, she persevered for almost fifteen years, eventually winning her battles and repeatedly urging all women, in her writing, to become familiar with their household finances.

Throughout Christine's struggles, the wealthy friends she had made at court failed to help her financially, though they did offer excellent advice. Several convinced her to write about her experiences, and the resulting twenty ballades, mainly autobiographical and considered among her finest, provided an important outlet for her grief. The decision to continue experimenting with poetry was most likely inspired by *L'art dicteur,* a treatise on the various forms of courtly poetry, written by

The Bettmann Archive

her close friend, the great poet Eustache Deschamps. Christine's own ballades, rondeaux, and virelays were instantly popular. Having gained confidence in her skills, she pursued what was to her a more compelling subject than any she had yet treated, the role and status of women, in her first "feminist" work, *L'epistre au dieu d'amours (The Letter of Cupid).* Although only a mild attack on negative literary portrayals of women, the poem involved Christine in one of the most famous literary quarrels of the Middle Ages, that surrounding *Le roman de la rose.*

In *Dieu d'amours* and in an extensive correspondence with important religious and political figures, Christine denounced Jean de Meung's 18,000-line section of *Le roman de la rose* as one-sided and slanderous from both a feminine and a moral standpoint. Supporting her in the debate was Jean Gerson, then chancellor of the University of Paris, who agreed that de Meung had portrayed women unfairly and who had already written laudatory essays on the achievements of women. Christine's main opponents Jean de Montreuil—a royal secretary with whom Christine had conversed and whose treatise in praise of *Le roman de la rose* instigated the initial controversy—and brothers Gontier and Pierre Col ridiculed her publicly, claiming that she was incapable of understanding the complex and insightful ideas put forth by de Meung. Gontier, also a royal secretary, in an attempt to slander Christine, claimed she was merely being used as a mouthpiece for the opinions of others. Brother Pierre, a canon of Notre Dame, admonished her for what he saw as inexcusable audacity: ''O most foolish presumption! O word too soon issued and lightly spoken from the mouth of a woman to condemn a man of such high understanding . . . [who] has written such a noble book . . . which surpasses all others. . . .'' With some outside support, including a treatise written by Gerson regarding *Le roman de la rose,* Christine debated with her opponents for almost three years before realizing that the quarrel would never be satisfactorily resolved. Despite her failure to alter her opponents' views, Christine produced numerous arguments and illustrations which are generally perceived as successful refutations of certain ideas espoused by de Meung. Christine's bold criticism of what was then hailed as the greatest French poem, while not entirely successful, introduced her as a serious writer and an important new force in the literary world.

As the quarrel began to abate, Christine returned to her studies. Interested as she was in current political issues, she looked to the past to discover ways to improve the present. Later she wrote: ''I betook my self to ancient histories from the commencement of the world . . . then to the problems of the sciences . . . finally to the book of the poets.'' The first work to result from her extensive studies was *L'epitre d'Othéa (The Epistle of Othea to Hector),* a poem of moral instruction issued in 1400 and most likely intended for her son, Jean du Castel. The poem comprises one hundred ''story-moments'' of mythological legends, each of which includes a moral accompanied by a famous saying or Biblical verse. In *Othea,* Christine utilized the works of such authors as Boccaccio, Dante, Guillaume de Machaut, Thomas Hibernicus, and Guillaume de Tignonville. Although generally considered the least appealing of her works today, *Othea* was very popular in the early years of the fifteenth century. As a result of Christine's growing literary reputation, Philip, Duke of Burgundy, commissioned her in 1404 to write a history of his brother, Charles V. Relying chiefly on her personal memories and accounts of people close to the king, Christine focused her biography on what she considered Charles's three main attributes: nobility of heart, chivalry, and wisdom. The resulting work, *Le livre des fais et bonnes meurs du sage roy Charles V,* while not a particularly accurate historical account, provides valuable anecdotes and personal information about the king which no court biographer would have thought appropriate to include. Although Philip did not live to see the completed work, his daring selection of a female writer resulted in what is considered a unique, strikingly personal portrayal of a late-medieval ruler. From this time forward, Christine's reputation was firmly established, and she envisioned a new role for herself as the conscience of her nation. Continuing to write in a voice of mediation and morality, she produced works on contemporary moral, political, and educational issues until 1418, when, realizing the potential danger of remaining in Paris, a city then torn by civil war, she joined her only daughter at Poissy Abbey, presumably where she died sometime after 1429.

During her career, Christine wrote numerous political, military, and educational works designed to improve the state of national affairs and to ensure the security of her countrymen. In her quest to serve France, Christine wrote personal appeals to influential acquaintances suggesting moderation and compromise as means of resolving political differences. In 1405, for example, she wrote *Une epistre à Isabeau de Bavière* (''Letter to Isabelle of Bavaria''), an impassioned plea to the queen to reconcile the feuding houses of Burgundy and Orléans. After communicating unsuccessfully with Isabeau, Christine shifted focus to address the problem of national organization and security. Wanting both to prevent civil war and to prepare France for potential foreign invasion, she composed *Le livre du corps de policie (The Body of Policye)* in 1406, an instructional piece in which she used the human body as a mirror of the differing political and military roles rulers, noblemen, and the general public perform in society. While Christine did not originate the idea of using the body to describe social and political structures, taken together her commentary on universal justice and interest in reaching the common people provide an important perspective on a poorly documented facet of French society. Continuing her efforts to restore national unity, in 1410 she wrote a military companion piece to *Corps de policie* entitled *Le livre des faits d'armes et de chevalerie (The Book of Fayttes of Armes and of Chyvalrye),* a compiled history of the art of war. *Fayttes of Armes,* one of Christine's most ambitious texts, includes not only examples of successful military campaigns, but also emphasizes the laws and ethics of honorable warfare. Her main historical sources were the fourth century Latin text by Vegetius Renatus, *De re militaris (On Military Affairs),* which, as Charity Cannon Willard notes, has been called ''the most influential military treatise in the western world from Roman times to the nineteenth century,'' and Honoré Bonet's *Larbe des batailles (Tree of Battles),* an important fourteenth-century work on the laws of warfare. Acknowledging her extensive use of other writers' ideas, Christine directed the treatise at the average practitioner, not the military commander or expert already familiar with the works cited in her text. Having treated the organization and education of the masses, Christine turned her attention in 1413 to the edification and education of the Dauphin, Louis de Guyenne. The attendant work, *Le livre de la paix,* reflects the turbulent events and emotions surrounding the eighteen-year-old king's attempt to reestablish order and peace in France. As Paris was threatened not only by civil war but by invasion as well, Christine sought to help Louis find a means of strengthening the much-weakened French state.

Concurrent with her political interests, Christine dedicated herself to changing the image of women. In 1405, she wrote another didactic ''feminist'' work, *Le livre de la cité des dames (The Book of the City of Ladies),* in which she argued convincingly yet lightheartedly for the recognition of the merits of women. Included are several stories adapted from Boccaccio's *De claris mulieribus* and *Decameron,* Ovid's *Metamorphoses,* and Jacobus de Voragine's *Legenda aurea. The City of Ladies* is among the first works written by a woman championing women. In the same year, she completed a companion piece, *Le trésor de la cité des dames; ou, Le livre des trois vertus (The Treasure of the City of Ladies; or, The Book of the Three Virtues),* a guide to conduct intended for women of all classes who wished to enter her virtuous city. Wanting to help all women, she chose to address the middle classes in *The Three Virtues* at a time when secular literature of this kind was almost exclusively the province of the aristocracy. In both pieces, Christine worked to destroy myths that insisted women were either totally evil or divinely good. She wanted men to trust and accept women as human beings and to stop perpetuating the stereotypes commonly advanced by many authors.

During her lifetime, Christine achieved remarkable literary success; her works were eagerly accepted by her patrons and she was well-known and respected not only in France, but in England and Italy as well. Both Henry IV of England and Prince

Gian Galeazzo, Duke of Milan, offered her court appointments, the former using means as extreme as holding her son hostage to force her acquiescence. Such English authors as Thomas Hoccleve, William Worcester, and the anonymous author of *Assembly of Gods* borrowed heavily from her, and Henry IV, Henry VII, Edward IV, Lord Salisbury, and Earl Rivers all had her works copied and translated. In France, Christine's influence was apparent in the poetry Charles d'Orléans wrote during his English imprisonment. Deschamps, praising her scholarly pursuits and professional skills, called her the "handmaiden of learning." Opponents of Christine during her lifetime were mainly men who either believed women were incapable of scholarship or who thought that educating them was unnecessary or even harmful. Such men as Pierre and Gontier Col were appalled that she had had the audacity to criticize *Le roman de la rose* as morally reprehensible in places, when they considered it a work of perfection. Critics with similar views refused to believe that a woman could write works of such quality and accused Christine of plagiarism. At the same time, however, she had some noteworthy supporters as well, including Martin Le-Franc, secretary to Pope Nicolas V and himself a great defender of women who, soon after Christine's death, recognized her value by complimenting her arguments supporting women in his *Champion des dames.*

Christine's influence and popularity continued through the middle of the sixteenth century. Her works were in such demand that four of her most important pieces, *The Epistle of Othea to Hector, The Book of the City of Ladies, The Book of Fayttes of Armes and of Chyvalrye,* and *The Body of Policy* were translated into English within a century of her death. After the middle of the sixteenth century, however, interest in Christine waned, and she was practically forgotten for almost three centuries. Scholars in the eighteenth and nineteenth centuries occasionally took note of her, but almost always by way of minor comparisons between her, Deschamps, Jean Froissart, and Orléans. In general, early critics deemed her less talented than her peers and lacking in originality. Recent critical opinion of Christine has been favorable, however, with scholars emphasizing the relation of her achievements to the time in which she lived. She is regarded as a woman of "firsts" among medieval women, receiving credit for crossing boundaries to write from a completely feminine point of view on subjects that were traditionally pursued only by men. Most scholars agree that while her political and military treatises are not particularly innovative, her writing in general is valuable as a reflection of medieval life. As a result mainly of the twentieth-century feminist movement, interest in Christine has been renewed, although disagreement continues regarding Christine and feminism. Critical opinion in this area can be grouped into two general categories, one containing critics who regard her as one of the forerunners of feminism, the other containing commentators who believe she was not a "feminist" but rather a writer of anti-antifeminist literature. In either case, scholars agree that she furthered the cause of women by defending them at a time when demeaning stereotypes were prevalent. As Earl Jeffrey Richards notes, Christine was a "highly respected and widely disseminated voice on the status of women."

Christine de Pizan was one of the most influential female literary figures of the Middle Ages. In an age when most women were trapped in illiteracy, Christine actively pursued a scholarly career. Many of her ideas on women, while widely accepted today, were revolutionary in the fifteenth century. No female writer (or even many male writers) had ever experimented with so many diverse subjects or written with such boldness on topics certain to evoke harsh personal criticism. Despite the factual errors and repetitiveness of some of her writing, Christine's serious compositions reveal a determination to communicate the necessity of working towards a peaceful, virtuous France. And her defenses of women—today deemed creative and original in argumentative tactics—have, as Richards states, earned her a position as a "writer and a scholar, welding together an enormous creative drive and a deep love of learning," a woman of letters "whose works belong among literary masterpieces."

*PRINCIPAL WORKS

Les cent balades   (poetry)   1399
L'epistre au dieu d'amours   (letter)   1399
  †[*The Letter of Cupid,* 1721]
Le debat de deux amans   (poetry)   1400
L'epitre d'Othéa   (poetry)   1400
  [*The Epistle of Othea to Hector; or, The Boke of Knyghthode,* 1470]
Le livre des trois jugements   (poetry)   1402
Prouverbes moraux   (poetry)   1402
  [*The Morale Proverbes of Cristyne,* 1477]
Le livre de la mutacion de fortune   (allegory)   1403
Le livre du chemin de long estude   (allegory)   1403
Le livre des fais et bonnes meurs du sage roy Charles V (biography)   1404
Le livre de la cité des dames   (allegory)   1404-05
  [*The Boke of the Cyte of Ladyes,* 1521; also translated as *The Book of the City of Ladies,* 1982]
Lavision-Christine   (allegory)   1405
Une epistre à Isabeau de Bavière   (letter)   1405
Le livre du duc des vrais amans   (poetry)   1405
  [*The Book of the Duke of True Lovers,* 1908]
Le trésor de la cité des dames; ou, Le livre des trois vertus   (prose)   1405
  [*The Treasure of the City of Ladies; or, The Book of the Three Virtues,* 1985]
Le livre du corps de policie   (prose)   1406-07
  [*The Body of Polycye,* 1521]
Le livre des faits d'armes et de chevalerie   (prose)   1410
  [*The Book of Fayttes of Armes and of Chyvalrye,* 1489]
Le livre de la paix   (prose)   1412-13
Le dittie sur Jeanne d'Arc   (poetry)   1429

*Christine's works were originally circulated in manuscript form. The dates listed reflect the approximate years in which the manuscripts began circulating.

†This work is a reorganized expansion by Thomas Hoccleve of Christine's poem. While *The Letter of Cupid* is not a literal translation, it does closely follow *L'epistre au dieu d'amours.*

W. MINTO   (essay date 1886)

[*Minto was a Scottish critic, novelist, and educator whose works include* A Manual of English Prose Literature (1872) *and* Characteristics of English Poets from Chaucer to Shirley (1874). *He is perhaps best known for his ability to approach established literary theories from a fresh perspective. In the following excerpt, Minto extols Christine's literary accomplishments in light of her epoch.*]

[There is an aboriginal] ''woman's rights person'' of the fifteenth century, whose claims to this high honour rest on the substantial foundation that she not merely acquired fame as a writer in man's most peculiar fields, composing the best mediæval manual of military tactics and international law, but also wrote a formal treatise on the disabilities of women, in which she defended her sex against the aspersions of monks and men of the world, and anticipated most of the arguments familiar to the present generation.

This mediæval paragon, who has to her credit more than fifteen thousand verses besides her prose works, was Christine de Pisan. She is mostly known to historians as the author of the **Livre des Fais et Bonnes Meurs du sage Roy Charles V.**, a vivid picture of the court and the policy of that monarch; but this was only a small part of her literary work. There was no kind of composition known in her day which she did not attempt, from *ballades* and *virelays* to moral and scientific treatises. (p. 264)

[Christine's work **La Cité des Dames**] is a surprisingly modern book in spite of its antiquated allegorical dress, and its quaint pre-Renaissance notions of history, in accordance with which Minerva, Medea, and Sappho figure, as shining examples of female capacity and virtue, side by side with Christian martyrs and noble ladies of the Middle Ages. Mediæval allegories are often condemned as tedious . . . [but they] were the novels of the Middle Ages; most of them novels with a very obvious purpose, yet often brilliantly written, and as full of action and lively circumstance as if the leading characters had borne the names of a common humanity instead of those of abstract qualities. (p. 265)

Christine's **City of Ladies** is not a conspicuously brilliant example of the allegory. Its allegorical setting is, in fact, slight and conventional, and affords hardly any artistic protection to the mass of facts arranged in support of her argument. Yet the book opens with a brightness and animation that must surprise those who expect to find dullness or inartistic clumsiness in pre-Renaissance literature. (p. 265)

[In **La Cité des Dames,** all] the gibes of monastic cynicism are triumphantly refuted by examples. The work runs to considerable length, as Christine has gathered into it all the materials she used in her numerous battles on behalf of her sex. We dare say it will be news to many of the modern advocates of the cause that it found so eager and thorough a champion nearly five hundred years ago. Christine's city is a large and rambling range of building, with many quaint towers and turrets, but though time has undermined some of its argumentative defences, one is astonished to find how much of it is still suited for modern habitation.

Another of Christine's works enjoyed a still greater reputation in its day. The manual of military tactics and international law is perhaps the most surprising of her achievements. It is the book known to antiquaries in Caxton's translation as **The Boke of Fayttes of Armes and Chyvalrye.** The importance and authority attached to the work may be judged from the fact that it was at the desire of Henry the Seventh that Caxton undertook the translation. To describe it as a manual of military tactics and international law is strictly correct. The productions of Caxton's press are oftener referred to than read, and the common impression about the **Boke of Fayttes,** derived from a fanciful construction of the title, is that it is a collection of stories of chivalrous exploits. It is a grave, solid, systematic treatise, handling many topics of the highest policy, from the

manners of a good general and the minutiæ of siege operations to the wager of battle, safe-conducts, and letters of marque.

For a woman to attempt the compilation of a soldier's manual was such an extraordinary undertaking that Christine felt bound to make an apology before she went beyond her prologue. She appealed again for her main justification to Minerva, the goddess of war, ''the inventor of iron and of all manner of harness.'' A woman might fairly write about the laws of war when it was a woman that invented its chief implements. But Christine did not profess to be original. She trusted partly to recognised authorities and partly to the kind offices of knightly friends. Indeed, when she was half through her work, it seems to have occurred to her that she might be accused of plagiarism, and she prepared an ingenious defence, in which the vexed question how far an author may help himself from the works of others is solved with great plausibility. One evening after she had completed the second of the four parts of the book she fell asleep, and a venerable figure appeared to her in her dreams which she recognised as the impersonation of her master Study. ''Dear love, Christine,'' he said to her, ''I am hither to come to be thy help in the performing of this present book. It is good that thou take and gather of the Tree of Batailles that is in my garden, some fruits of which thou shalt use.'' This was the master's figurative way of saying that Christine was now to have recourse, for that part of her work which dealt with political questions arising out of war, to Honoré Bonnet's *Arbre des Batailles*. Hitherto she had been chiefly indebted to Vegetius and Frontin. ''But, my master,'' she objected, ''I beg you to say whether any rebuke will be cast at me for using the said fruit.'' ''By no means,'' Study replied. ''It is a common use among my disciples to give and impart one to other of the flowers that they take diversely out of my gardens. And all those that help themselves were not the first that have gathered them. Did not Maister Jean de Meun help himself in his Book of the Rose of the sayings of Lorris, and semblably of others? It is, then, no rebuke, but it is laud and praising, when well and properly they be applucked and set by order. And there lieth the maistrie thereof. And it is better to have seen and visited many books.''

To the statement of this theory of literary communism it ought to be added that Christine not only shows her ''maistrie'' in ''applucking'' skilfully, but is most explicit in the acknowledgement of her obligations. (pp. 268-69)

Christine shows not only great skill in the handling of her materials, but unmistakable evidence of businesslike industry in the accumulation of them. When she had bravely made up her mind to subsist by her pen, Anthony Trollope himself did not go to work with steadier energy and purpose than Christine de Pisan. She reminds us frequently of Trollope in her precise enumerations of the quantity of work accomplished in a given time. Her first six years of authorship, begun after the above elaborate preparation, were especially prolific. ''Between the year 1399,'' she says, ''and the year 1405, during all which time I never ceased, I compiled fifteen principal works, without counting other occasional little writings, amounting altogether to about seventy quires of large size.'' This period of vigorous industry was distracted by the death of her husband in 1402, by lawsuits following thereupon, and by the death of her most munificient patron, Philip of Burgundy, in 1404: but misfortunes only stimulated the courageous woman to increased exertions. (p. 272)

[At that time, an] author's only chance of obtaining remuneration for his labours was to present his work to a powerful patron with a flattering dedication, leaving it to the patron to make such a return as his generosity dictated. (p. 273)

[In her dedications Christine flattered] the Duke of Orleans, the Duke of Burgundy, the Duke of Berry, Isabella of Bavaria, the queen, but she did not attach herself to any party, and she maintained a lofty tone both in morality and in politics. There was nothing base in her flattery. She credited the objects of it with virtues that they did not possess, but the virtues were such as they would have been much the better for possessing. Praise for any quality that was really virtuous, even though the recipient of the praise did not deserve it, was a wholesome influence in a generation when the corruption of the chivalrous ideal had reached its worst, when courtly magnificence of living was disgraced by shameless orgies, and public honours were sought by the vilest intrigues and the most treacherous assassinations. (pp. 273-74)

[In 1405 she wrote a] *plourable requeste des loyaulx Francoys* to the queen, a touching appeal to Isabella of Bavaria to remember the danger to the realm incurred by these dissensions. Again and again in the course of the next ten years she addressed similar appeals to the royal family and the leaders of the factions. She was the mouthpiece of the moderate party in the state, and her writings give a vivid idea of the horror and shame with which they looked on helplessly while the kingdom was being torn in pieces. After the battle of Agincourt, which verified her gloomiest anticipations, Christine disappeared into a convent, and nothing reached the public from her pen till she was able, in 1429, to celebrate the triumphs of Joan of Arc.

The life of this champion of her sex, so denominated by herself, and thoroughly worthy of the title, would furnish occasion for a complete picture of the position of women in the Middle Ages. The various mediæval conceptions of woman as she is and woman as she ought to be are shown in Christine's writings in full argumentative conflict; and practical illustrations of the best and the worst are to be found in plenty in the court of Charles the Sixth. Christine herself is cast after the noblest type of mediæval womanhood, and a certain stage of feudal society is mirrored in her works as it is nowhere else. (p. 275)

> W. Minto, "A Champion of Her Sex," in Macmillan's Magazine, *Vol. LIII, No. 316, February, 1886, pp. 264-75.*

FREDERICK P. HENRY (essay date 1904)

[*In the following excerpt, Henry provides a thorough overview of Christine's literary career.*]

In 1399, when thirty-five years of age, [Christine] began to write systematically. Six years later she published one of her best known and most interesting works, *La Vision de Christine*; one of the most interesting, because from it and from *Le Livre de Mutacion de Fortune* has been obtained most of the materials of her biography. For example, in the *Vision* she tells us that from 1399, when, as above stated, she began to write, until 1405, the date of the publication of the *Vision*, she had written fifteen volumes, not counting many small ditties. (p. 649)

Her most important works in prose and verse appeared in rapid succession between the years 1403 and 1406. *Le Livre du Chemin de long estude* was completed on March 20, 1403, and dedicated to the Duke de Berry. It is an allegorical poem of more than 6,000 stanzas, and is essentially a panegyric upon the wisdom of the lunatic, Charles VI. Its chief interest to-day is found in the lines which contain references to Christine's happy mar-

riage, the death of her husband, and other autobiographical facts.

On November 14 of the same year (1403) *Le Livre de la Mutacion de Fortune* was finished, and on January 1, 1404, it was presented as a new year's gift to Philip, Duke of Burgundy. This extraordinary allegory, the chief design of which seems to have been to disclose Christine's historical and classical learning, closes with a reference to events and persons of contemporary interest, among which are the misfortunes of the late King John, and the malady of his grandson, Charles VI., the reigning monarch.

It was the perusal of this work that induced Philippe le Hardi, Duke of Burgundy, to entrust Christine with the most honorable commission of writing the life of his brother, the late King of France, Charles V.

Christine lost no time in beginning her history of Charles V., a work which, both from the nature of its subject and the original manner in which it is composed, deservedly ranks as a French classic. . . . [*Le Livre des Faits et Bonnes Mœurs du sage Roy, Charge V*] is the first of Christine's prose compositions, and probably the best known of all her works. It is divided into three parts, of which the first was completed in less than four months from the time of its inception.

Christine's history of Charles V. is rather a eulogium than a history. She can scarcely be said to have fulfilled the duty of the historian as defined by Cicero. . . . Nevertheless her work is of the greatest value and interest to students of the reign of Charles the Wise. As he was a good king and his reign a great one, Christine, in praising both, does not depart to any great extent from the path of truth. She possessed a great advantage over most biographers of kings in that she was well acquainted with Charles and his court. According to the criticism of to-day, the work is marred by long digressions which display, as they were doubtless intended to do, her acquaintance with classical writers such as Aristotle, Vegetius, and many others. Yet as De Julleville remarks, no one has better described the attractive grace of the Duke of Orleans, brother of Charles VI., or depicted more clearly the appearance and manners of his father, Charles V.

This history of Charles V. was the first of a series of prose compositions of which *La Vision de Christine* . . . was the second. This remarkable work is in the form of an allegory, the characters being personified abstractions, such as Chaos, Fortune, Opinion, Fraud, and Philosophy. France is prominent among them under the name of Libera. Apart from the autobiographical fragments, which are to us of the greatest importance, there are two passages which seem to the writer worthy of special mention. The first is that in which Christine traces the origin of the French nation through Pharamond to Priam, King of Troy. This genealogical descent was generally accepted in Christine's day and continued so to be until the early part of the eighteenth century, when it was completely refuted by Fréret. What penalty Christine would have undergone for supporting a different opinion it is impossible to conjecture, but it would probably have been severe; for Fréret, in what we regard as a much more enlightened age, was immured in the Bastile for about four months for destroying this historical delusion.

The second passage above referred to is that in which Christine predicts her posthumous fame. "Opinion" tells her that she (Christine) was born at an unpropitious time; *i.e.*, at a time when the sciences were like things out of season. . . . The date of this posthumous fame was vastly more distant than Christine supposed, for it is only now, after the lapse of five hundred years, that full recognition is being accorded to her remarkable merit.

The next two works of Christine . . . are complementary to each other. They are *Le Livre des Faits d'Armes et de Chevalerie* and *Le Livre du Corps de Pollicie.* The first of these is probably the most extraordinary book ever written by a woman. It is a treatise, so to speak, upon the jurisprudence of war and the manner of conducting it. The work is a complete manual for the officer and soldier, and is chiefly derived from the writings of Vegetius and Frontinus. The writer enters into the minutest details concerning the provisioning and defence of a garrison, the overcoming of obstacles to the march of an army, and lays great stress upon the importance of maps of the country which it is traversing. In the fourth and last part of the work truces, safe-conducts, and letters of marque are discussed, and the question is raised whether a safe-conduct given by a Christian prince to a Saracen should be respected by other Christian princes. To this Christine replies ''no,'' and ''because the Saracens are enemies of all Christians.'' This opinion is in complete accord with the prevalent views of the period, but in condemning letters of marque she was many centuries ahead of her time.

The literary style of this work is inferior to Christine's other prose compositions. As she herself confesses, its subject was distasteful to her. Nevertheless, it was a most timely publication, for the French were demoralized by dissensions and civil strife, and their army was in urgent need of the discipline she inculcates. Had her precepts been put into immediate practice, it is possible that France might have been spared the disgraceful and disastrous defeat of Agincourt.

Le Livre du Corps de Pollicie, which was written immediately after the last-mentioned work, is a treatise on morals addressed to the three great classes into which the French nation was then divided, namely, the princes, the nobles, and the people at large. In this treatise Christine has, through her precepts, inferentially described the internal life, the life of the mind and soul, of the people of her day. It may, therefore, be regarded, as far as it goes, as the antithesis, or, rather, the complement, of the work of Froissart, who concerned himself almost exclusively with the external world, its fêtes, tournaments, and battles. Froissart is objective, Christine subjective.

The two most striking features of this treatise are, first, a scathing denunciation of the disorders of the secular clergy; and, secondly, the suggestion that taxation should not be limited to those least able to endure it. This last suggestion was truly revolutionary, and must have been highly displeasing to the governing classes.

One cannot estimate too highly the courage which inspired Christine to strike such a blow at the very root of the feudal system. It was ineffective, it is true, and could only have recoiled upon herself, for the people whom she befriended were blind and deaf, so far as her writings were concerned.

There is a sequence in the works of Christine, the clew to which is to be found in the fact that she had ever in mind the uplifting of her sex and its vindication from the aspersions which, during the reign and through the example of Isabel de Bavière, were only too well merited. This statement as to the design of her work applies particularly to her poems, although it attains its highest development in the two prose compositions: *La Cité des Dames* and *Le Livre des Trois Vertus,* or, as it is also called, *Le Trésor de la Cité des Dames.* Just as *Le Livre des Faits d'Armes et de Chevalerie* and *Le Livre du Corps de Pollicie* were inspired by and complementary to the history of Charles V., so were *La Cité des Dames* and *Le Livre des Trois Vertus* inspired by and complementary to the poems called *l'Épitre au Dieu d'Amour* and *Le Dit de la Rose.*

La Cité des Dames and *Le Livre des Trois Vertus* are addressed particularly to women, and both, in accordance with the taste of the age, are allegorical. The first is, for the most part, a compilation of the heroic deeds of women recorded in fable and history, whether these deeds relate to bravery, virtue, patience, or self-abnegation. The heroines of antiquity are too well known at the present day to excite the interest which they doubtless aroused in the earliest readers of the work. It is in Christine's contemporaries that we are most interested, and, fortunately, she refers to many of them. She does not limit her praises to the princesses of the court and to other women of rank, but takes account of the heroism and talent of the lowly. For example, she extols the talent of a skilful female artist named Anastaise, who could illustrate a book better than any living man and to whom we are doubtless indebted for some of the superb manuscripts of Christine's compositions.

The *Trésor de la Cité des Dames* is a treatise upon the duties of women in all stations of life. The work abounds in valuable information concerning the domestic life and the morality of the time, and contains numerous details which are scarcely to be found elsewhere, and are conspicuously absent from the chronicles of Froissart. The morality of the book is pure, its counsels wise and practical. The ideal which Christine sets before women is not an impossible, or even a discouraging one. It is to maintain, outside of the household, the spirit of peace, sweetness, and indulgence, and, within it, good order, harmony, dignity of manner, and wise economy. Christine, herself a student, advises women to study, but with the object of developing their intelligence and elevating their sentiments; not with the ambitious and absurd idea of dethroning man and reigning in his place.

Just after the two last-mentioned works were completed Christine, in the name of her sex, made a passionate assault upon *Le Roman de la Rose* of Jean de Meun, which was also attacked at the same time by the celebrated Gerson, chancellor of Notre Dame, because of its abuse of the clergy.

The civil war, which continued without intermission after the assassination of the Duke or Orleans (1407), seems to have suppressed Christine's literary enthusiasm. Nevertheless, in the midst of this uproar Christine endeavored to make herself heard. She wrote a lamentation upon the evils of the civil war and *Le Livre de la Paix,* a pathetic pleading for peace. Then France became engulfed in a sea of troubles, and, after the publication of a poem entitled *l'Oraison Notre Dame,* which is virtually a farewell to the world, Christine was no more heard until after the lapse of fifteen years. The invasion of the English, the defeat of Agincourt (October 25, 1415), the occupation of Paris by the English and Burgundians, and the massacre or flight of all her friends and protectors, were enough misfortunes to discourage a much greater genius than she possessed. She fled from Paris and took refuge in a convent—probably that of Poissy, which her daughter had entered many years before, and the year of Christine's admission was 1418. This is established beyond a doubt by one of those autobiographical references which are so frequent in her works, whether in prose or verse. The one now alluded to occurs in a poem dated July 31, 1429. It is a song of triumph over the successes of the immortal Maid who, about two months before, had compelled the English to abandon the siege of Orleans. The news of the reviving fortunes of the French and their miraculous deliverance reached Christine in her cloister and inspired her last poem. (pp. 652-57)

That she was highly esteemed by contemporary opinion is proved, not by that lowest of all standards, the monetary value of her compositions, but by her invitations to foreign courts and the admiration of such a competent judge as the Earl of Salisbury. In addition we have the testimony of Eustache Deschamps, a contemporary poet and the satirist of his time, who addressed laudatory lines to Christine. (p. 657)

The latter-day critics of the works of Christine de Pisan are practically in accord with regard to her standing among the writers of her time. Robineau assigns her a place, as poet, between Charles d'Orleans and Eustache Deschamps, and side by side with Froissart. He draws a striking analogy between her poems and those of the great French chronicler. In both there is the same tendency to allegory, but Christine, while displaying less of art in the form of her poems, is more simple in style than Froissart, more tender and elevated in her sentiments. As historians these two writers are rather to be contrasted than compared. Froissart is an inimitable narrator of facts, whether obtained directly or at second-hand, while with Christine facts are subordinate to the morals to be drawn from them. She is first and foremost a moralist, the first of her own, and one of the most remarkable of any age. She was a writer with a purpose—that of reproving, exhorting, and elevating the people, high and low. If Froissart had any moral purpose in his writings, he sedulously kept it subordinate to the entertainment of his readers, whom he leaves to draw their own conclusions from the facts he narrates. This is perhaps one of the reasons of his continued popularity and, conversely, explains the neglect of the more pedagogical writer. Another reason for the latter fact may be found in the more complicated style of Christine's prose compositions. Simpler in her poetry, she is much more complex than Froissart in her prose. Her more studied works abound in learned and involved phrases which are apparently imitations of the Ciceronian style of eloquence. . . . [At] that time every one conversant with Latin was anxious to display his learning by the employment, in his vernacular, of the words and phrases alluded to above. Christine is somewhat dominated by this pedantry. As already stated, she is at her best in her most spontaneous compositions, such as the ballads in which she deplores her unhappy fate and bewails her misfortunes. (pp. 658-59)

> *Frederick P. Henry, "Christine de Pisan: Her Life and Writings," in* The Catholic World, *Vol. LXXVIII, No. 467, February, 1904, pp. 647-61.*

ALICE KEMP-WELCH (essay date 1913)

[*In the following excerpt, Kemp-Welch surveys Christine's career, emphasizing the unique aspects of Christine's interpretations and use of works by such authors as Dante, Boccaccio and Aristotle.*]

[Christine de Pisan] may be regarded not merely as a forerunner of true feminism, but also as one of its greatest champions, seeing that in her judgment of the sexes she endeavours to hold the scales evenly. Possessed of profound common sense and of a generous-hearted nature, she is wholly free from that want of fairness in urging woman's claims which is so fatally prejudicial to their just consideration. Although, strictly speaking, Christine was not original, she was representative, and interests

us for that very reason. She was perhaps one of the most complete exponents of the finer strain of thought of her time. She stands before us, at the dawn of the fifteenth century, Janus-headed, looking to the past and to the future, a woman typical of a time of transition, on the one hand showing, in her writings, a clinging to old beliefs, and on the other hand asserting, in her contact with real life, independence of thought in the discussion of still unsolved questions. (p. 116)

Endowed with an extraordinary gift of versification, she began by writing short poems, chiefly on the joys and sorrows of love, expressing sometimes her own sentiments, sometimes those of others for whom she wrote. But she tells us that often when she made merry she would fain have wept. How many a one adown the centuries has re-echoed the same sad note!

"Men must work and women must weep." So says the poet. But life shows us that men and women alike must needs do both. And so the sad Christine set to work to fit herself, by the study of the best ancient and modern writers, to produce more serious matter than love-ballads, turning, in her saddest moments, to Boëthius and Dante for inspiration and solace. "I betook myself," she says, "like the child who at first is set to learn its A B C, to ancient histories from the beginning of the world—histories of the Hebrews and the Assyrians, of the Romans, the French, the Bretons, and diverse others—and then to the deductions of such sciences as I had time to give heed to, as well as to a study of the poets." Her master was Aristotle, and she made his ethics her gospel. (pp. 121-22)

Although Christine's reading was very varied and extensive, there were two subjects—the amelioration of her war-distraught country, then in the throes of the Hundred Years' War, and the championship of the cause of womankind—which specially appealed to her as a patriot and a woman, and for which she strove with unceasing ardour. In all her writings she so interweaves these two causes that it is only by approaching them in the same way that we can understand her view of their psychological unity. To Christine these interests were essentially identical, for she recognised how paramount is woman's influence in the making or marring of the world—how, in truth, in woman's hand lies a key which can unlock a Heaven or a Hell.

There was sore need of a patriot, and in Christine one was found. . . . France was in a sorry plight. There was war in the land, there was war in the palace. The sick King suffered more and more from attacks of madness, and during these periods the Dukes of Orleans and Burgundy fought for the regency. Christine began her patriotic work by fervent appeals to Isabella, the Queen . . . , to use her influence to put an end to these dissensions which so greatly added to the troubles of the kingdom. She also lost no opportunity of proclaiming in her various writings the duties and responsibilities of kings and nobles to the people, and the necessity, if there was ever to be peace and prosperity, of winning their regard. At the command of Philip le Hardi, Duke of Burgundy, and uncle of the King, she wrote in prose, from chronicles of the time and from information obtained from many connected with the King's household, *Le Livre des faits et bonnes mœurs du roi Charles V*, recounting his virtuous life and deeds and their advantage to the realm, and introducing a remarkable dissertation on the benefit to a country of a strong middle-class. She, of course, reasoned from Aristotle. The subject is a commonplace one now, but in the case of any one living at the beginning of the fifteenth century, and brought up, as Christine had been, at a magnificent Court, it shows rare independence and breadth of thought to have grasped and proclaimed with such firmness and clearness as is displayed in her treatise the germ of the policy of all modern civilised nations—that a middle-class is essential to bring into touch those placed at the opposite extremes, the rich and the poor. (pp. 123-25)

Although, as regards profundity, her conception of the world and of life cannot be compared with that of her great prototype [Dante], or even with that of such an one as St. Hildegarde, still she had read with unflagging diligence a vast number of profane and ecclesiastical writers, and seems to have been well versed in the varied knowledge of her time, especially history. But whilst it is possible to criticise her learning, tempered as this was by her character and the needs of her day, it is at the same time possible to acknowledge that in spite of flaws and an often over-elaborated setting, moral truth sparkles gemlike throughout her writings. (pp. 125-26)

In her poem *Le Chemin de long Estude*—a title taken from Dante's appeal to Virgil at the opening of the *Inferno*—Christine begins by acknowledging her debt to the immortal poet, saying that much that she has to tell has already been told by "Dante of Florence in his book." Virgil as guide is replaced by the Cumean Sibyl, who appears to Christine in a dream, and offers to conduct her to another and a more perfect world, one where there is no pain and misery. . . . The Sibyl . . . promises to reveal to her . . . in what manner misfortune came upon earth, whilst at the same time showing her on the way all that is worth seeing in this world, from the Pillars of Hercules, "the end of the world," to distant Cathay. However exhausting this programme may appear to us, Christine, knowing the real passion of the late Middle Ages for travel—for even those who could not travel in reality did so in imagination,—makes use of it as a setting for the introduction of a discussion on the qualities most necessary to good government. This she does, even at the risk of incurring displeasure in high quarters, recalling how Dante's patriotism led to banishment and death in exile, but she adds, "Qui bien ayme, tout endure." She pours forth her classical examples in a chaotic stream, but when she leaves earth, and ascends to the celestial regions, she not only shows herself versed in the astronomy of the time, but also expresses some beauty of thought. The order of the firmament, where all obey law without ceasing, so that harmony ensues "like sweet melody," reminds her of Pythagoras and Plato, and suggests to her what life on earth might be if good laws were made and observed. In furtherance of her idea, she appeals to Reason, who presides over the Virtues or Divine Powers, to interrogate the three earthly disputants, Nobility, Riches, and Wisdom. In the end Reason awards the prize to Wisdom, condemning Riches as the great enemy of mankind. Thereupon Wisdom appeals to the verdicts of Juvenal, Boëthius, St. Jerome, and others to establish that it is Virtue alone that is of worth, and ennobles a man, and then sets forth the qualities of a good sovereign. But as this leads to some difference of opinion, Christine, who was withal a courtly lady, descends to earth in order to ask the King, Charles the Sixth, to decide the matter. This dream-poem she dedicates to her royal master for his diversion in his saner moments, and thus once again introduces into high places the subject so near to her heart. She lets it be seen that she herself, like Dante, did not believe in the blending of the spiritual and the temporal powers. And as regards temporal power she adds—perhaps borrowing the idea from Dante's *De Monarchia*, and anticipating Napoleon's dream—that in order to ensure peace on earth, it is necessary that one supreme ruler should reign over the whole world. (pp. 126-28)

Though she laboured so unceasingly for the good of her country, she also did her utmost to defend her sex from the indiscriminate censure which had been heaped upon it, for the evil spoken seemed to her far to outweigh the good. . . . Christine set herself the task of trying to remedy this evil, not by shouting in the market-place, but by studying men and women as God made them and as she found them. Before she began her work, a new day seemed to be dawning. Just as, when classicism was in full decadence, Plutarch wrote *De mulierum virtutibus* (of the virtue of women), so, in the fourteenth century, Boccaccio gave to the world *De claris mulieribus* (of right-renowned women). We do not expect to find woman treated on a very high plane by Boccaccio, but we recognise that, in a way, this work forms a fresh starting-point in the eternal controversy. (pp. 128-30)

[Whilst] love problems could be treated as a pastime [as they are frequently so in Chaucer's writing], they also had their serious side. Of this there is an example in Christine's story of *The Duke of True Lovers*. Although much in its narration is evidently the mere invention of the poetess, it is quite possible, nay even probable, that it has some historical basis. . . . It has been suggested, with much likelihood, that this is in truth the love-story of Jean, Duc de Bourbon, and of Marie, Duchesse de Berri, daughter of the famous Jean, Duc de Berri. . . . Christine, with her womanly sympathy and psychological insight, makes all so intensely real that we are quite carried away in imagination to the courtly life of the fifteenth century. We read . . . a most comprehensive and remarkable treatise on feminine morality, the dangers of illicit love, and the satisfaction of simple wifely duty. . . . [As] we finish the story, we cannot help feeling that even if Christine's setting is fiction, she yet gives us a glance of real life.

When Christine turned to her serious work in the cause of womankind, she began by attacking two books, Ovid's *Art of Love,* and *The Romance of the Rose,* both of which, in the Middle Ages, it was deemed wellnigh sacrilegious to decry. Her challenge, *L'Epistre au Dieu d'Amours,* took the form of an address to the God of Love, professing to come from women of all conditions, imploring Cupid's aid against disloyal and deceitful lovers, whose base behaviour she largely attributes to the false teaching of these two books. . . . Her position was considerably strengthened by the alliance and co-operation of her staunch friend Gerson, the Chancellor, who himself, in the name of the clergy, took up arms against the flagrant scurrility to be found in the portion of *The Romance of the Rose* contributed by Jean de Meun. Other powerful allies joined the cause, and, to help to crystallise their efforts, species of "Courts of Love" were instituted, not alone for discourse on love, as heretofore, but also in the defence of women. All who united in this meritorious fellowship undertook to wear a distinctive badge, and thus proclaim their confession of faith. Among these Orders one was styled "L'Escu vert à la dame blanche," another, "L'Ordre de la Rose," and so on, suggestive of their purport. . . . Of the Order of the Rose and its foundation, Christine, in one of her poems, gives most picturesque and interesting particulars, interesting because they are evidently taken from an actual scene, though Christine, in her rôle as poetess, feels it necessary to add touches suggestive of fairyland rather than of real life. A numerous assembly, with goodwill at heart, has met together in the magnificent dwelling of Louis, Duke of Orleans, the King's brother, Christine being one of the number. Suddenly there comes into their midst one personifying the Goddess Venus, surrounded by maidens garlanded with roses and carrying golden bowls filled with them. The bowls placed on the table, the Goddess proceeds to announce the rules of the Order, above all enjoining those present to avoid envy, and in no way to perjure themselves, since this would be a most heinous and hateful sin. . . . The charter is given by the Goddess into the safe-keeping of Christine. . . . This moral and literary contest is perhaps the most brilliant of the many discussions that took place in the Middle Ages in honour of women. The highest and the wisest in the land joined in it, but all the honour must be given to Christine for having, by her brave and reasonable attitude, caused the problem, which henceforth was to evolve like truth itself, to be treated on a rational basis. (pp. 131-36)

L'Epistre au Dieu d'Amours is an extraordinary product of worldly wisdom and common sense, seasoned with satire. (p. 136)

Christine's line of argument is that the many must not be condemned for the shortcomings of the few, and that even when God made the angels, some were bad. To the charge that books are full of the condemnation of women, she replies with the simple remark that books were not written by women. (p. 137)

Later, Christine, with Boccaccio's *De claris mulieribus* before her, writes **La Cité des Dames**, an account of the building of an imaginary city which is to shelter within its strong ramparts the women of all times and all countries who have distinguished themselves by good and heroic deeds. This has been aptly called "The Golden Book of Heroines." It may certainly be considered her masterpiece on her favourite subject. She urges that philosophers and poets, with one accord, have defamed women, and she appeals to God, asking why such a thing should be, seeing that He Himself made them and gave them such inclinations as seemed good to Him, and that in no way could He err. She maintains that God created the soul, and made it as good in woman as in man, and that it is not the sex, but the perfection of virtue, that is material. Combating the suggestion that women are not fit to plead in Court because they have not sufficient intelligence to apply the law when they have learnt it, she refers to history to prove that women who have had the management of affairs have shown that, far from lacking intelligence and judgment, they have possessed both in large measure. At the same time, whilst defending their capability when necessity arises, she does not think it necessary for women to interfere in matters which seem essentially man's business. Her remarks on the subject of marriage are certainly practical, and at the same time disclose a strange unloveliness in contemporary manners. . . . In truth, her wonderful sense of justice, and her enlightened opinions generally, make it a marvellous résumé of statesmanship as far as it goes. It is a real Utopia. Perhaps to Christine it was a glimpse of the Promised Land! As we read her views on the education of boys and girls together, in this happy city, we feel that she might be discussing with us the problems of to-day. She says that if boys and girls are taught the same subjects, girls can, as a rule, learn just as well, and just as intelligently, as boys, and so on. In this conclusion she forestalls the learned Cornelius Agrippa, a doctor and philosopher of the sixteenth century, and one of the most original and remarkable men of his time, who boldly asserts that sex is merely physical, and does not extend to soul or rational power. She sums up by strongly advocating study and learning, both for self-improvement and as a consolation and possession for all time.

Of her poetical writings on love and the sexes, perhaps the most enchanting is **Le Livre du Dit de Poissy.** In it she takes

us, on a bright spring morning, with a joyous company, from Paris to the royal convent of Poissy, where her child is at school. She describes all the beauties of the country. . . . [And as] the day wanes, they bid farewell to the nuns . . . [and] return to the inn where they are to spend the night. . . . The ride back to Paris in the morning, during which a discussion on love matters is introduced, is painted with the same impressionist touch, and it is with real regret that we take leave of these happy folk as they alight in Paris city from their stout nags.

Another similar discourse, **Le Débat de deux amants,** has for setting a gala entertainment, taking place, like the founding of the "Order of the Rose," under the auspices of Louis, Duke of Orleans, who ever extended a princely protection to Christine. Louis had married Valentine Visconti. . . . It is on a day in May, the garden gay with gallants and fair ladies. . . . Christine is seated in a tapestried hall with one or two esquires who prefer to discourse of love to joining in the jollity. After a time the talk turns on fickle men, and Christine brings forth from her vast storehouse of knowledge classical and mediæval examples. As she mentions Theseus, and recalls his baseness to Ariadne, she points to the tapestry on the wall before them, where the story is woven. This little touch makes the scene very real to us, for the record of the purchase of this tapestry, with the price of twelve hundred francs paid for it, may still be found amongst the royal inventories.

There is such a volume and variety of works from Christine's pen that it is no easy task to make a fair selection. One of the most significant, since it deals with a subject which permeated mediæval thought, and on which she was wont to dwell, is **La Mutation de fortune,** "Fortune more inconstant than the moon," says Christine. In it she writes with her heart in her hand, as it were, telling first of the sore havoc Fortune has wrought amongst those most dear to her. Yet though her own heart has been torn on the Wheel of Fortune, she stands before her fellow sufferers like some figure of Hope pointing upward, where, she says, wrong is surely righted. And thus she turns to the world in general, not in the spirit of the pessimist, but rather in that of the philosopher. She well knows that Fortune is no blindfolded goddess turning writhing humanity on a wheel, but a something rooted in ourselves, and she has pity for "la povre fragilité humaine." Though so independent and advanced in thought, she is still found clinging in her writings to mediæval forms. As a setting for her thoughts on Fortune's changes, she makes use of the favourite simile of a castle—here the Castle of Fortune—as representing the world, wherein the rich and the poor, the strong and the weak, jostle one another. She criticises all men, from the prince to the pauper, but not women, since these have been sufficiently criticised and decried. It is like the prelude to a *Dance of Death.* Then she tells of the paintings on the walls of this imaginary castle, and uses this mediæval fancy, itself borrowed from the classics, to give what is really a history of the world as she knew it, written to demonstrate the instability of all earthly conditions.

Once again, with her versatile gifts, she turns from philosophy to a treatise on military tactics and justice, **Le Livre des faits d'armes et de chevalerie.** However devoid of interest, except as a landmark in the history of military strategy and customs, this work may be to-day, it was thought of sufficient importance in the reign of our Henry the Seventh for the king to command Caxton to translate and print it (1489) with the title of **The Book of Faytes of Arms,** a book still sought after by our bibliophiles. It was further honoured by being quoted as an authority in the reign of Henry the Eighth. Considering the nature of its contents, this seems quite an extraordinary tribute to the judgment and ability of the writer. (pp. 138-43)

Alice Kemp-Welch, ''A Fifteenth-Century Feministe, Christine de Pisan,'' in her Of Six Mediaeval Women, Macmillan and Co., Limited, 1913, pp. 116-45.

A. T. P. BYLES   (essay date 1932)

[*Byles was an English editor, essayist, and educator. In the following excerpt, he discusses Christine's use of historical treatises on war in her* The Book of Fayttes of Armes and of Chyvalrye.]

Although the greater part of [*Le Livre des Faits d'Armes et du Chevalerie*] is a compilation from the works of Vegetius, Frontinus, Valerius Maximus, Honoré Bonet, and a contemporary anonymous authority on sieges, yet Christine deserves credit not only for the skill with which she marshals such a mass of most unfeminine material, but also for the numerous original passages which she inserts. (p. xi)

Christine's works show a keen interest in both the political and the literary life of France. A French critic has well remarked that ''though born a woman and an Italian, she alone at the court of France seemed to have manly qualities and French sentiments.'' She lived through one of the unhappiest periods of French history: the latter stages of the Hundred Years' War, the Great Schism, the madness of Charles VI, the civil wars of Orleans and Burgundy, the catastrophe of Agincourt. She refrained consistently from taking sides in the political strife which divided the court, and invoked patriotism as the cure for civil war. The troubles of the times are clearly reflected in *Les Faits d'Armes*. . . . (p. xii)

Vegetius' treatise on the art of war was well known in the Middle Ages, and is used by Christine as the source of the greater part of Book I, and of chs. xiv to xix and xxxiv to xxxix in Book II, of the *Fayttes of Armes*. (p. xxxvi)

[Christine] freely adapts Vegetius' maxims to the warfare of her own times, selecting, transposing, and commenting with great skill and understanding. (p. xxxvi)

Her main purpose is to draw the character of the ideal commander, selecting passages from various parts of Vegetius' Books I and III to illustrate his gifts and functions. (p. xxxvii)

When Christine is using classical authorities, the value of her work as a treatise on mediæval warfare is greatly diminished. In the first seven chapters of Book I, however, her outlook is entirely mediæval and her remarks apparently original. They are of great interest in illustrating the mediæval attitude towards war. (p. xlii)

In Book I, ch. v, after describing the careful deliberations and calculations that should precede a declaration of war, she alludes to the events leading to the recommencement of the Hundred Years' War in 1369. This is her longest allusion to the history of her own times, but it is full of inaccuracies, due partly to her bias against the English and her desire to represent Charles V in the most favourable light. Modern historians consider that Charles deliberately took advantage of technical difficulties presented by the Treaty of Brétigny to pick a quarrel with the Black Prince in 1369, when he felt himself strong enough to recommence the struggle. Both Christine and Froissart, however, represent him as recommencing the war with the greatest reluctance. (p. xliii)

Les Faits d'Armes belongs to a period when the pure ideals of chivalry had given place to ceremonial observances and extravagant display. ''The auncient noble men,'' says Christine reproachfully, ''made not theyre children to be norisshed in the kyngis and prynces courtes for to lerne pryde, lechery, nor to were wanton clothing.'' Like Ramon Lull, in *L'Ordre de Chevalerie*, she advocates a strict education for youths who aspire to knighthood. Her portrait of the good Constable (Book I, ch. vii) presents her ideal of knighthood; while in Book I, ch. xxi, she shows him in action on the day of battle, and puts into his mouth a rousing speech of encouragement to his men. Courage is the greatest asset to men in sore straits; Christine enthusiastically elaborates Vegetius' description of the desperate resistance offered by the besieged as the enemy break into their city.

It would be too much to expect a fifteenth-century writer to visualise a time when war would be no longer necessary, ''for by that is the fredom of the contrey surely kept.'' But Christine de Pisan consistently presents a conception of warfare that is both honourable and, as far as is possible, humane. (pp. xlv-xlvi)

A. T. P. Byles, in an introduction to The Book of Fayttes of Armes and of Chyvalrye by Christine de Pisan, edited by A. T. P. Byles, translated by William Caxton, Humphrey Milford, Oxford University Press, 1932, pp. xi-lvi.

ROSEMOND TUVE   (essay date 1966)

[*An American essayist and educator, Tuve was a leading scholar on the Renaissance and one of the world's foremost authorities on Renaissance imagery. In the following excerpt, she refutes the argument that* L'epitre d'Othéa *is structurally fragmented, illustrating the theory that Christine borrowed from* Ovide Moralisé *to create ''story-moments'' utilizing classical figures as symbols of moral doctrines usually reserved for Christian allegory.*]

Christine de Pisan uses, with the unusual addition of explicit theoretical comment on her own method, materials which had not been read allegorically, or even read ''morally,'' to convey points of Christian dogma; if we look carefully at some of her attempts, we may observe whether there are any reasons for success and failure. The attempt was a widespread habit which influenced the functions of classical images in authors who did not practice it (as I think Spenser and Milton did not) and varied with authors and with times. Since the examples are diffused in numerous fifteenth- and sixteenth-century works, an examination of the one most explicit text, the *Ovide moralisé,* will lead us only to outstanding principles, to be applied with qualifications to other practitioners. But Christine, who declares what she is doing, was popular and unforgotten, was read, was available in print in illustrated editions, and was translated. The combination is understandably unique, for theory and practice are usually separated, but sixteenth-century availability confirms its value for our purposes.

Christine, like many allegorizing readers, embarks on a far simpler endeavor than did [Jean] Molinet. She will escape his most dreadful flaw, of shattering into fragments the unified work being allegorized, because she had no great work to shatter. It will be recalled that she takes up one hundred separate figures, selected from the general stock of classical myth and story, and also that contrary to the title later given her, **''Cent histoires,''** she does not tell one hundred stories but interprets one hundred personages or story-moments. That keeping of decorum, at which Molinet failed so lugubriously, and which is so fundamental in making material carry an imposed meaning, is hence a simpler task; there is seldom a whole stubborn fiction to be read through the glass of a new symbolical import in the personage. More than this, her book takes its basic structure from elsewhere, a familiar Christian organization shared for historical reasons with many other works. It has been noticed, but the aesthetic significance thereof not to my knowledge pointed out, that she handles the Seven Virtues, Twelve Articles of the Faith, Ten Commandments, sins and so on, giving us a classical image which may be read as signifying each. Her **Othéa** thus joins the large group of earlier *sommes* which were produced and were popular . . . ; it is an ingenious little classical *Somme le roi* with adornments.

It has therefore an ordo and purpose which give to its artificially created symbols a kind of witty usefulness and point which is fulfilled with an unexpected success. Its purpose is only half-seriously a mnemonic one, for the book was ostensibly written for a boy of fifteen, possibly Christine's son, possibly the young Prince; and were it not a mediaeval work, we would attend more to these facts of audience and narrator. This "Hector" knew his creed by this time, and the book is no confession manual except as those too attempted to remind one of all the unnoticed ways one could commit the sins and forget the faith. But it is a revealing demonstration of the fact that authors were not deceived about the didactic force of such images to go through any of these well-known sets of Christian essentials, making the mind concentrate upon the new relations that accrue with the new images. Suppose we follow Christine's lead and think simultaneously about Ceres' significances and the Second Article, "Jesus Christ his only Son Our Lord," about Isis and the Virgin's conception, Midas' false judgment and Pontius Pilate's, Hercules' descent into hell and the Harrowing—and the rest of the Twelve. Despite their alien birth, they not only come remarkably near becoming symbols, but also accomplish what this kind of image-making had as a purpose: they deepen and extend our grasp of the mystery supposedly "symbolized." The difference is immediately apparent to us when, with Fable 45, we leave the most common sevens and twelves and go on to sets not so readily recognized. I think it extremely likely that it was recognized by early readers; Christine ought to continue either with the Seven Gifts and their virtues and elaborations or with some order related to the familiar branches of sins. The sense *we* have that the work is going to pieces, that it is becoming the mere series of little fritters of haphazard didacticism—as it usually is treated—may not have been felt by readers who found themselves unexpectedly rehearsing the old lessons by setting them to all these gay new tunes.

It will be remembered that Christine differentiates allegorie from glose by a distinction which quite clearly descends from the well-worn definitions of religious exegesis. Roughly and over-simply, the second interpretation persistently conceives of man as a soul to be saved, and as always in strict allegory, the singleness and simplicity of the redemptive doctrine which is usually signified made a few great symbolic images the recurrent ones: the soul as spouse, wooed or nuptially united with or ravished by evil or rescued from it; the pilgrim; the castle besieged or delivered; humankind liberated from an enemy, or the recipient of some inexpressible beneficence, symbolically expressed. As she turns from Glose to Allegorie, she seems simply to have thought, "How does this touch man in his relation to the Deity?" Temperance (Fable 2) is to be loved and reasons are given, but in the allegorie, Temperance restrains that *basic* Concupiscentia (Augustine is quoted) which makes us faithless to God's new covenant with us. The pursuit

of riches, of which Juno is goddess (Fable 29), will turn a young knight from Honour; but in the allegorie, the son of Adam, not seeing that riches are neither "vraies ne vostres," loses the kingdom of heaven. As we proceed through the one hundred fables, this constant turn from the temporal world to the eternal one silently builds up a quite spacious definition of the chevalier Jesus Christ whom Christine's allegories instruct.

One other principle differentiates her two interpretations. It may be stressed because it is of considerable help in apprehending the quality of Spenser's obscurely felt difference from authors who simply moralize images. When both her interpretations enjoin some virtue, an attempt is made in the Allegorie to present the virtue simply as an adornment of the bon esprit which is Christ's knight. This beauty of the spirit suiting with its heavenly destination and origin is indicated as the reason for allegory's concern with the virtues (in Christine's Prologue to the Allegory); and images displaying it will be different in effect from those portraying the strenuous battle to conquer vices and achieve heaven.

Christine tries valiantly to make her interpretations show this distinction, usually by some quick attempt to see the thing discussed sub specie aeternitatis through an anagogical reference. Warnings that greedy ambitions may lead one to death (Fable 85; Hector was killed as he stooped to seize Patroclus' fair arms) are diverted to concern "la mort espirituelle" (cf. Fable 92); or from the advice not to trust Fortune's promises (Fable 74), the allegorie turns to a differentiation between her false delights and eternal felicity. Christine has not Spenser's genius to persuade us through the very beauty of virtue seen and the ugliness of vice, but her attempts, even though they fall short, often teach us as much about the way an allegory ought to work as if they had succeeded; and she obviously tried consistently to turn from the good knight's struggle to achieve virtue, to virtue as a divine condition or a beauty which man as chevalier Jesus Christ approximates here and enjoys hereafter.

The laurel crown in the Daphne story (Fable 87) is that New Testament crown which those who attempt the highest virtue will wear, perseverantia (named) understood as we read of it in the *Somme le roi*, Christ's virtue. The basic distinction between the two chivalries, in her piece as in others, involves these two motivations to virtuous conduct. She makes outright reference to the militancy of the faithful, here below, and their state when victorious; "la vie presente et appelle guerriant," when perfected, "appelle triumphant." She does not explicitly use Dante's terms of these two allegories, the poet's and the theologian's, used in the *Convivio* and so much discussed, but seems at any rate to differentiate between the pagan or Christian grammarian's figurative explanation of a fiction, and the allegorist's portrayal of types fulfilled or things in their essence, beautiful to contemplate. (pp. 284-89)

One reason for Christine's lesser success [than Edmund Spenser's] in obtaining our sympathetic concurrence as to where lie moral beauty and ugliness, is in her ineptitudes touching a literary quality which we extoled in Jean de Meun: careful government of the decorum of details. Instead of magnifications or diminutions tending unobtrusively but irresistibly in one direction, our approval or rejection of a figure will depend all on some one intellectually grasped attribute which we must be instructed to select. We are entirely prepared to find Cassandra a diminishing figure because of her faithful worship in their pagan *loy* (Fable 32), when behold she is magnified for "haunting the temple" as the knight should do; she figures to us that article of the Creed which binds our faith to the Holy Catholic Church, the Communion of Saints. (pp. 290-91)

I am certainly not interested in drawing any lines of source-relation between Spenser and Christine on this matter of an inherited differentiation between moral and allegorical reading, or between virtues in conflict in a psychomachia, and virtues as ineffably beautiful universals or ideas, seen fully only by the perfected citizens of the Heavenly City when they shall have returned home after their exile. Christine's book is proof that the inheritance was not forgotten; if we overmoralize Spenser it is partly because we have forgotten it. . . . Many explanations of Christine's method have been given; even the best students of the *Othéa* do not make the connection between it and the ancient distinctions of religious exegesis. Accordingly and as always, much criticism at her expense derives from expecting her to do what she is not doing. She glosses her *texte*, not the full ancient story; she is providing ways to read, not substitutions, and they are sketches of illuminating extensions, not ways to get rid of the pagan story by whitewashing it. (pp. 292-93)

Although Christine shares with Spenser a kind of residue left from the centuries of theological theory and practice, which gave her an idea of how allegory's deeper reach ought to differ from tropology's moral usefulness, we must add to her far inferior imaginative powers the disadvantages of her more direct claim that Christian doctrine informs classical images. Most of her examples in which it is claimed that a classical personage or narrative event can declare the mystery of the Incarnation, the Passion, or the nature of the Christian deity, are taken by her from the *Ovide moralisé*. Campbell has proven that in her frequent allusions to "Ovid," she refers to the metrical *Ovide moralisé* of the first years of the fourteenth century, a rare restriction of dependence even in vernacular belles-lettres. As we noted, she had an easier task than the author she plunders, in that the structure of her book as an ingenious little *Somme* of Christian rudiments gave a kind of rationale to her parallels; thus she had no need to embark on the transformation of whole stories still in their context in a total narrative work, the *Metamorphoses*. (pp.293-94)

Christine's success or failure, like that of other Christianizers of classical images (in literature at least), seems to depend on the *truth of the underlying similarity of import* which has led her to offer a classical figure as capable of symbolizing the mystery or doctrine for which we usually use a Christian symbol or name. Only if the same drift of meaning, a similar burden of feeling, is already *that which seeks signification* through the Christian symbol, does the offered classical synonym really succeed in providing a new usable symbol for us: Orpheus has become an acceptable Good Shepherd, for example, while for all the implications held within the words "the Baptism," only the familiar pictured Christian event suffices, to my knowledge. I will exemplify, after we look at some half-successes.

If there chances to be something of real moment in a classical figure's story which admits, say, of parabolic likeness to Christ's acts, the image will have some chances of Christian life. It is told of Hercules in *Othéa* (Fable 27) that he went down into Hades to rescue Pirotheus and Theseus, his friends; this sufficiently resembles in import Christ's descent into Limbo to deliver his lieges and supporters, the patriarchs and prophets and faithful precursors, that it can take on the mystical import of the Christian event: divine power conquering Death (Cerberus), eternal faithfulness between lord and subject, the quality of love braving the abyss of destruction and evil so as to

save, and so on. We might come to see, quite unconsciously and effortlessly, in the valiant and courteous deliverer pictured in the Laud misc. 570 Hercules, the very qualities and love-linesses which make the faithful action of the Christian Hercules so fair. . . . (p. 295)

When Penthesilea (Fable 15), out of pure loving admiration for Hector, seeks him out and grieves finding him dead and revenges his death, she becomes, with no sense of dislocation or strain, a figure for Christian *caritas*. But the similarity lies too completely in the mere exemplification of a quality to form a sufficient basis for Penthesilea to become a symbol carrying the meanings of Love's descent in the Incarnation to rescue man from death. And revenge does not rescue. Thus, it seems to be necessary that meanings coincide in true identity if the image of one is to bear the symbolic burden of the other.

Whole groups of images offered as symbols newly endowed with Christian meaning have this basis of a typified quality which the chevalier celestien is to wonder at and set his thoughts upon "mire"—an adornment of the questing soul. "Les proprietez des vii. planets" were so well known that all of this group already had symbolic power, and Christine leans much on convention, not least on the commonplaces of astrology. With only one, Mars, does she attempt the sort of artificial typology which results from emptying out the old symbolic force and putting in new. . . . She does this by thinking of the "mars" in one's soul as being the Christ within us who is god of the only battle she admits into these allegorical interpretations—that against Satan, fought by Christ literally and also *in* the Christian spirit as it achieves the supreme victory, self-conquest (Fable 11). Despite a certain thought-provoking ingeniousness, such an image has no chance of permanence; we can imagine no literary work centered on the new symbolic Mars; and Spenser did well to make his champion, the exponent of Christian grace who makes the soul's last stand in every battle, a mediaeval knight. With the other six planets, Christine merely gives Christian force to the planetary properties of conditions: pité or misericorde (Jove), light or truth (Apollo), gravity (Saturn), slowness in judging, for judgment is God's, and so on. The grace and benignity of Jupiter's action as he sprinkles balm upon his needy followers easily translates into the grateful sense of grace received from a Christian deity from whom we prayerfully ask it (in Fable 3 . . .). Indeed, pité and misericorde are the very names of the Fifth and Second Gifts of the Holy Ghost. Christine uses symbolic deepening that is already half-conventional for her most successful translations. Venus and Phebe are pejorative (inordinate love and change-ableness), but they do not become the Great Adversary; nor do the sins, when we come to that group. Nor do they become before our shocked eyes evil in essence, but simply sum up conditions of spirit. Christine had no space to create a Mammon or an Acrasia, who go beyond this to become embodiments of satanic force able to inhabit and possess the human spirit and turn it into itself; neither does she point to this extension of significance. She at least attempts in both glose and allegorie to keep her distinction between the bon chevalier's struggle against these personified single vices and the bon esprit's heavenly destiny when, "perfect" in virtue like a Christ, he fights only as a god fights and is victor over the source of evil as well as its manifestations the vices. She invents no symbols as Spenser does; at most she strengthens the symbolic power of old images by attaching them to Christian truth. (pp. 296-99)

Christine's best novel symbol for Christ's gift to men is Ceres, and the translation is based on the similarity seen in their free gift of "a life more abundant"; their largesse was "abandoned," complete, and motivated by love not merit in the recipient. It is this, the condition of Ceres which the bon esprit is to resemble; Christine ties it to the Second Article of the Creed ("and in Jesus Christ his Son"), and the connection with Ceres who discovered an art to sow in ploughed ground calls on other ancient metaphors (both the sower and the buried seed). The spiritualization of the meanings is effortless, not obstructed. (p. 299)

Christine's bad or weak images do not result inescapably from her poetic theory (a chief difficulty with the *Ovide moralisé*), which is coherent and clear. She is as impressed as all her fellows with the necessity of looking under "lescorce" for more important meanings; though she explains that "la matiere damours" [the usual husk] "est plus delictable a ouir *que* autre" (Fable 82), she does not try to throw out all such idle meanings for profitable ones. In this I think her to have represented a common attitude based on a real acceptance of multiple meanings as the author's own—often stated in ways very congenial to the modern critical welcoming of all the images possible, except for the more careful protection of the last point, now not so regarded. Thus she speaks of the loy of the pagans without condescension as the frame of reference necessarily of their interpretations (Fable 33); it is neither pitied nor ridiculed. She constantly recognizes the fact that images can be understood "en plusieurs manieres" and often herself gives "maintes exposicions"; her commonest words are "*povons* entendre" or "*peut* notter." That is, she knows allegory is a way of *reading* significances in materials, not an author's stunt in which he can say the same thing two ways by cleverly stringing variant sets of equivalents together in parallel order. Although she is not entirely clear on what kind of truth an allegory has, she never claims that it alone was the author's real meaning, or substitutes it for his ostensible meanings.

When Christine talks of poets speaking "en maniere de fable" or "soubz couverture," this generally precedes some rationalization of a figure, euhemeristic or cosmological. In other words, she thinks of the moral glose as the poet's type of figure, but she does not explicitly mention Dante's "allegory of the theologians," though the distinction she laboriously attempts to maintain is based on the difference in aim in these two groups. She explains to her young Hector the sense in which all knights are sons of Minerva, though he knows his mother was Hecuba; that is, just as the illuminations are briefly explained, so also an elementary explanation of how universals can be in particulars, in figurative language, is embarked on; just so Faith, another arms-bestower, is "mere au bon esperit" (Fable 13).

Though Christine is often solemnly pious, the small amount of prudery in these texts should remind us that there is little to support the idea, frequently still stated, that this sort of imagery results from a kind of clerkly movement to bowdlerize the classics and thus to save them. That at least is no part of the meaning of the debated phrase, "the allegory of the theologians"; I incline to accept Christine's own insecurely kept but accurate differentiation. (pp. 302-04)

When Christine's images are weak and dead, the reasons lie in her having chosen a Texte with no clear salient point, or in the bad logic of her application, or in there being no true link between the classical story and the announced Christian significance—as when Pasiphae is "taken" as the penitent soul returning to God, seemingly for no reason except her superlative dissoluteness, though that reason is theologically inad-

missible. Christine shares this flaw with the *Ovide moralisé* searchers for parallels, but she does not egregiously multiply its paralyzing effects by introducing crowds of tiny equations for inessential accompanying details, each weak and thoughtless at its link—as when the metamorphosis of Cygnus is to encourage us to cover ourselves by confession with the plumes of chaste conversation, to have the black feet of humility and the long neck of discretion. . . . (pp. 306-07)

Molinet, typical in this of fundamentally unserious allegory, uses images which cannot adumbrate any Christian idea profoundly because they are mere hasty applications, taken for granted (Virginia is daughter of God in that she is *anima*, yet must be beheaded by her helpless father if he is to keep her from the World); or because when Christianized the images get the author into disastrous contradictions (as when Christ must be Vulcan because he is the Spouse, in the Mars-Venus story); or because they turn morals upside down if accommodated within the original text (the Lover is advised to get all the funds he can out of some unsuspicious Friend, which must equate with Christ's giving all to poor indigent Man, simply because Molinet cannot resist the cliché of Christ as par excellence the Friend). These absurdities do not represent the natural results of imposition of alien meanings in a forced type of parallel and an injudicious mode of figurative thinking, but show the misuse of allegory by writers insufficiently intellectually endowed. They exhibit a bad and foolish theory, not the proper traditional theory on which allegory is based. It is worth noting that Christine, with all her faults and though of a date to promote them, sufficiently avoids this one. She uses ancient commonplaces when they suit (in Narcissus' idolatrous pride, which transforms the figure into a true vision of man's littleness, or in her Actaeon, who as *cerf* figures the true penitent and is moving in his suffering). But she shows restraint in keeping free of familiar identifications when they would have such results as we have noted. This is a principle as applicable in reading allegorically as it is in writing allegory; as critics, we are to notice and follow authors in their tacit demands for restraint in the extension of meanings. (p. 308)

The fault of the Ovidian allegorizers lay not in making wild connections, but in failing to make any. All the inadequacies we have noted, working toward this nullification of figurative sense in the supposed figure, result from mistaking a mere statement of a likeness seen for the "translation" of meaning. . . . All the vehicles in allegorical images are in a way unsuitable; they are grossly disproportionately trivial to carry their great tenor, and an inescapable radical distance characterizes the relations between terms. This observation does not turn the surprises in Christine or *Ovide* into valuable literary achievements, but it is well to recognize time and again that it is not the bizarrerie or lack of common sense in the relations seen which is the factor deserving rebuke. This remains, irrevocably, the uselessness of the figure, its failure to function and hence to live. (pp. 309-10)

Rosemond Tuve, "Imposed Allegory," in her Allegorical Imagery: Some Mediaeval Books and Their Posterity, *Princeton University Press, 1966, pp. 219-334.*

SUSAN GROAG BELL   (essay date 1976)

[*Czechoslavakian-born Bell is an American essayist and educator who has written several works on the history of women. In the following excerpt, she identifies the personal experiences that influenced Christine in her advice to women concerning scholarship in* The Book of the Three Virtues.]

The works of Christine de Pizan are filled with her love of learning and the satisfaction she experienced during her journeys into the world of knowledge. Yet in *Le Livre des Trois Vertus,* concerned specifically with the education and behavior of women, Christine failed to recommend learning and knowledge to the women of her world. She wrote during the Hundred Years' War, for a generation constantly on the brink of civil and international strife, a generation attempting to recover from the ravages of the Black Death. Women were essential to repopulation, economic production, and the judicial stability of French society. *Le Livre des Trois Vertus* was aimed at this goal. But Christine also lived at a time when "learning" for women itself became a matter of discussion within humanism. (p. 173)

Christine de Pizan was born within the decade after Boccaccio began writing *Concerning Famous Women.* By the time Leonardo Bruni wrote his treatise on the education of girls (c. 1405), Christine had become an established writer and poet. She emerges as a strong link in the chain of humanistic thought during the late fourteenth century. (p. 174)

The love of study became the great love of Christine's life. It permeates the entire body of her writing. The most moving example of this love is in *L'Avision:*

> Knowledge has sweet savory, honeyed things which precede in value all other treasures as sovereign; how happy are those who have savored thee to the full; and still since, I cannot judge of this save haphazardly, as if of a thing of which I do not know the whole, nevertheless that knowledge most gives me the delectable taste and savor of it which I find only in the little interconnections and parts of learning (since I cannot attain to anything higher). . . . Ah childhood and youth, if you knew the bliss which resides in the taste of knowledge, and the evil and ugliness that lies in ignorance, how well you are advised to little complain of the pain and labor of learning. Did not Aristotle say that the educated man was the natural master of the ignorant? Thus we see that the soul governs the body, and what thing is more beautiful than knowledge, and what more ugly than ignorance which is unbecoming to mankind; as once I replied to a man who reproved my desire for knowledge, saying that it does not suit a woman to have learning. . . .

She explained in humanistic terms as did Bruni, Erasmus, and Vives, that the pursuit of learning and knowledge must lead to virtue and the love of God. But she also loved learning because it offered an escape from the loneliness of widowhood and the discomforts of her physical existence, beset as it was by debts and creditors. She discovered in learning a rich new world that led to her spiritual and practical independence. (p. 175)

Many of Christine's works concern education. Two books deal specifically with the history and education of women. They are: *Le Livre de la Cité des Dames* and its sequel *Le Livre des Trois Vertus.* It is an interesting comment on the priorities of scholarship that to date the only major works of Christine that have not been awarded a critical edition are these two books on women. They differ vastly in style and approach to the subject. The *Cité des Dames,* written as a response to such misogynistic literary salvos as de Meun's *Roman de la Rose* and especially Matheolus' *Lamentations,* is an allegorical city in which great and independent women can live, safe from the slanders of men. Christine peopled her city with the classical figures collected by Boccaccio, female saints, and some contemporary female figures. She grouped her heroines carefully so as to drive home specific talents, capabilities, and virtues exhibited by these models. As a history of women her book is thus one of the earliest, and like Boccaccio's *Concerning Famous Women,* the *Cité des Dames* uses hundreds of biographical sketches to illustrate Christine's three-fold aim: to prove women's capabilities, to educate other women by example, and to write women's history. The book was inspired by her urgent need to defend and encourage women. It exudes her admiration of literate and studious women including such examples as Sappho, poet and philosopher; Nicostrata, the mythical inventor of the Latin alphabet and of grammar; Cornificia, a Roman girl who was sent to school with her brother, whom she surpassed in learning and as a writer of scholarly books. Christine quoted Boccaccio by name in many passages in her book. She knew that she owed him a great debt; but she used him merely as a source and provided her own interpretation of his material.

It is tempting to indulge in detailed comparisons and contrasts between these two humanist authors who attacked the same subject from their widely different perspectives. Here I must limit myself to a brief highlighting of the outstanding points of difference in general, and to the authors' treatment of studious women in particular. Boccaccio aimed to amuse, while Christine was entirely serious. He could not resist embroidering his material with stories of love and sexual prowess, especially that exhibited by women. Christine on the other hand aimed only to teach by example. She was concerned mainly with demonstrating women's intellect, courage, and moral virtue. Whatever extraneous, lascivious material Boccaccio included, she ignored. Yet she also invented backgrounds for her subjects that were not part of Boccaccio's book. For example, in the story of Cornificia Boccaccio suggested that Cornificia's poetic genius was such that she probably hailed from Greece (the country of true poets in Renaissance admiration) rather than Italy. Christine ignored this entirely, and instead wrote firmly, and with some bitterness, that Cornificia's parents had sent her to school with her brother "as a mockery or a joke" when both were children. "But the little girl frequented the school with such marvelous talent that she soon felt the sweet taste of knowledge." In time she became a "right sovereign poet, learned in philosophy and all manner of knowledge," so much so that she "passed her brother." Boccaccio contented himself with claiming that Cornificia was "equal in glory to her brother."

Boccaccio could not subdue frequent references to the "inherent inferiority" of women, references that Christine invariably ignored in her use of his material. For example, he wrote that Cornificia "rose above her sex" through her genius, and labor, and that "if women through genius, industry and God's grace reach such diversity and sanctity, what must one think of men who have greater aptitude for everything?"

Notable also is the fact that while Christine praised and emphasized women's intellectual pursuits in the *Cité des Dames,* she did so without belittling women's customary occupations. Boccaccio, however, constantly belittled those occupations. In his portrait of Cornificia, she "rejected the distaff and turned her hands skilled in the use of the quill to writing Heliconian verses. . . . She brought honor to womankind for she scorned womanly concerns and turned her mind to the study of the great poets." Christine paraphrased Boccaccio but simply spoke of the praise he had for the woman who leaves her customary work to apply her wit to study and learning. . . . It appears that Christine strengthened her propaganda for women's learning by her constant references to Boccaccio's praise of this. She quoted him not merely to give him his due as an author, but also because as a male advocate he would carry more weight in an area that she knew to be unpopular.

In the interstitial chapters of the *Cité des Dames* Christine made brief suggestions concerning the education of women which place her squarely into the forefront of humanist thinking on this subject. She proposed, for example, that girls should at an early age be sent to school with their brothers; and that school might be of greater benefit to them than to boys because while "their bodies are softer than boys' their understanding is freer and sharper."

In the *Cité des Dames* Christine was also much concerned to explain the reasons for the lack of female scholars and for women's ignorance generally. She drew an analogy of differences between country people and city folk, showing that while the former often seemed like "beasts" this was due merely to a lack of education and manners. Nature had endowed them with the same perfection of body and of understanding as city dwellers. It was simply a question of "learning" and so was the apparent intellectual difference between women and men. Another point she was anxious to establish—and here she paralleled Boccaccio, but surpassed later humanist writers on women's education—was that women were able to produce original creative work. Not only are they good for "taking men about the neck and bearing and nourishing children," she wrote quoting Boccaccio, but like Nicostrata, they are able to invent and create new "crafts and sciences."

Both the *Cité des Dames* and *Le Livre des Trois Vertus* demonstrate Christine's original and humanistic views, as well as her pertinent commentary on the lives of women of her time. The strongest suggestions concerning the education of women, however, are asides amid the histories of the *Cité des Dames*. *Le Livre des Trois Vertus,* a specific guide on how women should behave and what they should learn to suit their station in life, does not spell out humanistic rules regarding the learning of Latin, reading of classical literature, cultivating an interest in poetry or in style, except that young ladies of the nobility should be taught to read in order to study devotional literature.

Both Boccaccio and Leonardo Bruni emphasized that women should learn and read about subjects other than those of a purely religious nature, because in the course of a broader range of learning they would develop their minds, grapple with the truth, and thereby acquire the virtues that enoble humanity. Boccaccio told his female readers: "If at times you find wantonness intermingled with purity, as accuracy has compelled me to do, do not pass over it and do not be terrified. Rather persevere, just as on entering a garden you put out your ivory hands for the flowers after moving the thorns aside. . . ." And Bruni: "All sources of profitable learning will in due proportion claim your study. None have more urgent claim than the subjects and authors which treat of Religion and of our duties in the world; and it is because they assist and illustrate these supreme studies that I press upon your attention the words of the most approved poets, historians and orators of the past." In contrast, Christine recommended only moral literature for a woman of good reputation. Citing Augustine she wrote: "Such a lady will voluntarily read books of moral instruction and sometimes of devotion, but those of dishonesty and lubricity, she will despise and will not have them at her court, nor allow them

to be brought to her daughters or the women about her." Nevertheless she was close at one point to recommending the humanist formula that virtue increased proportionally to learning and knowledge: "as says the Philosopher—he is not wise who knows not part of everything." The context in which this passage appears applies however to a noblewoman's management of her estate, and although it takes in administrative and judicial capabilities, does not deal with the intellectual pursuits recommended by Bruni, and admired and exemplified by Christine.

While the characteristic humanist goals of learning are implicit in Christine's praise of her classical heroines in the *Cité des Dames,* in *Le Livre des Trois Vertus* she concentrates on the underlying characteristic of Christian humanism—moral virtue in this life. Whereas the *Cité des Dames* is constructed around the three virtues, reason, justice, and integrity, the advice given to the inhabitants of the city in *Le Livre des Trois Virtus* is inspired by "Dame Prudence." It is pertinent to compare Christine's approach to instructing women how to live with contemporary Florentine humanist Collucio Salutati's concern with prudence as the crucial ingredient for a life of wisdom.

In Le Livre des Trois Vertus Christine told women how to spend their everyday lives and how best they might fulfill their roles, whether they be queens, aristocrats, merchant wives, or peasants; whether single, married, or widowed. Christine's social stratification of women is very thorough. It recalls John of Salisbury's *Policraticus,* with which she was familiar, and it is most valuable to historians interested in breaking down the nebulous specification of "women" in the fifteenth century into socioeconomic and geographic groups. Although the greater part of her advice was addressed to ladies of royal status, she repeatedly emphasized that much of this applied also to women of lower strata of society. An important consequence of the preeminence of social status was that "woman's place" became merely another such stratification and was accepted as "natural." Christine documented this point in the *Cité des Dames.* She asked Reason, why if women have the potential to learn everything, do they not learn more? Reason replied that there is no need for women to meddle in that which has been relegated to men—it is sufficient if women do that to which they are ordained. Five years earlier in the *Livre de la Mutacion de Fortune* Christine declared that women had lost their right to education to all-powerful social custom. . . . (pp. 176-79)

In a sense, *Le Livre des Trois Vertus* belongs to the long line of behavioral guidebooks culminating in Machiavelli's *Prince.* Its author can also be viewed as an earlier, female Machiavelli. Like the sixteenth-century Florentine humanist, Christine analyzed the realities of life and did not hesitate to write plainly about uncomfortable matters of conscience. But while Machiavelli and the earlier authors of guidebooks for princes dealt with the behavior of men, or when about women concentrated on keeping them in their place, *Le Livre des Trois Vertus,* written by a woman for women, adds a new dimension to this genre.

For example, in discussing the greatest honor commonly ascribed to women, that of loyalty to their husbands, Christine suggested that wives who did not love their husbands should pretend to do so and that this would constitute loyalty. Writing at a time when many marriages were contracted in order to bring families, land, fortunes, or workers together it was extremely likely that the marriage partners suffered from a lack of affection for each other. Although mutual affection often developed, Christine had presumably seen enough loveless marriages to prompt her ideas on this subject. Her advice was strictly practical and concerned with explaining to wives where their best self-interest lay. A wife who openly showed her dislike of her husband diminished him in the eyes of the world and thus undermined her own position. Moreover she suggested that however badly husbands treated their wives, the latter should keep the peace of the marriage and do their duty in all things. For, she maintained there are three benefits to be derived: "(1) doing one's duty is good for the soul; (2) good wifely behavior is honored by the world; and (3) rich husbands who have mistreated their dutiful wives are usually conscience stricken on their deathbeds and direct their wills to their widows' future well-being." Christine obviously considered this matter of simulated wifely affection very important for she discussed it first in her chapter on suggested behavior for royal women and women of the court, and returned to it in her advice to urban and country women of the middle class.

A second example concerns Christine's advice to women forced to defend their domain in the absence of their husbands. They must be able to deal with any emergency, they must be able to advise on laws and customs, they must be able to command their men, both in attack and defense. Moreover, women in such a leadership position must be especially "careful not to let their men be defeated since this inspires hatred" toward women as leaders. This passage in *Le Livre des Trois Vertus* is well taken. It explains why Christine wrote *The Book of Faytes of Arms and of Chivalrie,* a work on the military arts. She knew well that these arts also were an essential part of women's education in the midst of the Hundred Years' War. (pp. 179-80)

That not all women were eager to be prepared to fight military or legal battles in France is evident from Christine's frequent urging that women should be courageous and bold in these areas. In this regard, she frequently used the phrase "coeur d'homme" (heart of a man), utilizing this image to the extent of claiming in the *Livre de la Mutacion de Fortune* that she herself had turned into a man when widowed, and remained so ever since in order to brave the elements of the world. Her reading of the early Church Fathers may well have fostered this recurring image in her oeuvre. The image was a conventional one on which to draw at that time; for example, it can be seen in the Italian renaissance term "virago" applied to staunch women like Caterina Sforza, and in Elizabeth of England's famous rallying speech before the Armada: "I know I have the body of a weak and feeble woman; but I have the heart and stomach of a king."

Yet despite this advice to women to embark on all manner of practical, even dangerous undertakings in the worldly sphere, there is in this book of instruction for women no suggestion that they might interest themselves in intellectual pursuits in order to develop their minds. Why is it that Christine never explicitly recommended that women should study and concern themselves with literary pursuits? Why did she not consider for others a life that she had found so satisfying throughout her long widowhood? Why did she not suggest this occupation in her chapters on widowhood in *Le Livre des Trois Vertus*?

No criticism of Christine as a woman meddling in scholarly pursuits has been traced to her contemporaries. Such criticism might have made her hesitate to recommend the scholarly life to women and to confine her ideas regarding women's pursuit of knowledge to historical and poetical asides. But in fact even her opponents in the debate over the *Roman de la Rose* praised

her mental ability and did not indicate any aversion to women's involvement with scholarship. Thus one of her opponents, Bontier Col, wrote: "Woman of great and elevated understanding, worthy of honor and great commendation, I have heard said by many notable clerics, that among your other studies and virtuous works there is much to praise. . . ." (pp. 180-81)

Just as Christine would not go along with Boccaccio in "scorning" or "despising" women's work so she understood that it was "women's work" that kept the fabric of society intact.

Thus one reason for Christine's failure to recommend a life of scholarship to other women may have been her appreciation of society's need of conventional female work, including administrative work, by those women literate enough to indulge in scholarly pursuits. Another reason was her personal position in society. (p. 181)

Writing at a time when woman's work was urgently needed, Christine felt more justified in endorsing companionable productive work, for example needlework, in preference to the luxury of reading in solitude. (p. 182)

One must distinguish clearly between the pleasure of solitary study which brought Christine de Pizan great rewards, the same rewards reaped by men throughout history, and her painful estrangement from society resulting from the fact that she was not merely a scholar, but a female scholar; not merely studious, but a studious woman. (p. 183)

> *Susan Groag Bell, "Christine de Pizan (1364-1430): Humanism and the Problem of a Studious Woman," in* Feminist Studies, *Vol. 3, Spring-Summer, 1976, pp. 173-84.*

ENID McLEOD   (essay date 1976)

[*An English translator and author, McLeod is best known for her biographies* Heloise *(1935) and* Charles of Orleans *(1969). In the following excerpt from her 1976 biography of Christine, she explicates* Lavision-Christine, *illustrating how Christine's by-now (1405) improved self-image and literary position are reflected stylistically in the text.*]

On February 10th, 1404, only a month after she had begun work on her book on Charles V, Christine did a curious thing. She wrote a letter, in the form of a long poem in her favourite rhymed couplets, to the most famous of contemporary poets, Eustache Deschamps, whom she addressed by his proper name of Eustache Morel and by his title, the bailiff of Senlis. The theme of her letter was the corruption of all classes of society at that time in France, which she describes in great detail. (p. 108)

Whatever Deschamps thought of Christine's letter, he was worldly-wise enough not to be drawn by it into a discussion of the subject she had raised, especially as he was by then an elderly man now retired into the country. So in his reply he did not refer to her complaints at all, but contented himself with praising her in terms which are of great interest as showing the high reputation she had already gained in her adopted country, in a profession that no other woman of her time had entered. 'Handmaid of learning', he called her and, praising her valiant pursuit of her occupation, he signed himself her disciple and well-wisher.

Although she may have been disappointed at his failure to express any opinion on her views, she could not but have been gratified by his warm praise, which might indeed be taken to convey approval of them since he would hardly have lavished it on someone with whom he profoundly disagreed. So it seems not impossible that his eulogy, coming from so illustrious a fellow-writer, played some part in encouraging her to write what is the most original and personal of all her books, on which she embarked in 1405, as soon as she had finished her life of Charles V. She called it *Lavision Christine,* lavision (which she writes all in one word) because she adopted for its framework the favourite medieval convention of a vision or dream which she says she had in sleep, when various allegorical figures appeared and had with her those discussions which form the subject-matter of the book. But she added her own name to the title, as if to underline that this was no mere fantasy of general import but a very personal account of her life and thoughts now that she was, she said, 'more than half-way along the road of my pilgrimage'.

The book was written in her accustomed three parts, in the first of which her aim was obviously to suggest that she had been destined from before her birth to use her gifts in the service of her adopted country, France. She begins in her usual allegorical way, by relating how one day when she felt the need of a rest 'after eating', the drowsiness of sleep came over her senses and she saw in a vision a *Dame Couronnée,* who subsequently turns out to be France. This Crowned Lady was busy making a mixture, which she poured into little moulds 'like those used in Paris to make waffles', and then put into the furnace of Chaos until they were done. Out of them came little bodies, one of which, a feminine one, turned out to be Christine herself. She grew quickly and, as she longed to see again the powerful Crowned Lady, she set out over strange lands until she came to 'the second Athens', Paris. It took her some time to learn the ways and tongue of this country but she got on so well that she met *Dame Renommée,* who asked her to write prayers and songs and the life of Charles V, whereupon the Crowned Lady, saying that God and nature had given her a love of study beyond the common run of women, bade her take parchment, ink and pen and write what she will tell her.

The Crowned Lady then gave her a very brief history of France from its mythical beginnings, remarking that although more than a thousand years had passed since she was born, Christine would be astonished that she should have remained so beautiful if she knew all she has had to suffer not only from her own people but from foreign invaders. (pp. 109-10)

Then asking her not to be taken in by the beauty of her face, she showed her her bruised and wounded limbs and entered into a long account of all the current vices in France in the form of an allegory in which three great ladies, Truth, Justice and Chivalry, are thrown into prison under the guardianship of a hag called Fraud, while in their stead reigns a pale, thin old lady with huge bloody nails whose name is Voluptuousness. The vices are described with a wealth of biblical instances and much lamentation, in the course of which the Crowned Lady cries: 'Oh, what a pleasure and relief it is to talk to a loyal friend and disclose to her the heaviness of one's thoughts!' She thanks Christine for her love and begs that, although she has been invited to go elsewhere—an obvious reference to those invitations from Henry IV of England and the Duke of Milan—and 'from me and mine you receive but meagre emoluments', 'your good heart will not let you forget the nourishment you received in childhood' and thus she will remain true to her and go on with her writings 'which will give ever greater pleasure to me and my children'.

Coming from Christine who, in dedicating her books, was accustomed, as we know, to speak of them in humble and even self-deprecatory terms as the work of a self-educated, feminine mind, that last sentence strikes a new note of self-confidence, even perhaps of self-importance. Had some people perhaps wondered why the task of writing the life of a great French king had been entrusted to a woman and a foreigner at that? And if so was this her reply to them, giving reasons why she had been chosen? A likelier supposition is that that book had gained for her such unusual recognition and praise that she could now claim an established position. Such a position, in fact, that thenceforth, instead of writing privately to a friend she would be able to refer openly to those social evils from which the country was suffering, and which were soon to preoccupy her even more.

In the second part of the book she turned abruptly to what seems quite a different subject, but is perhaps connected with the first part in that it arose from her expressed desire to enlarge her mind, presumably to qualify for the further work that the Crowned Lady had hoped she would write. She went, she says, to the university to join the students disputing in the different faculties. Hanging over them she saw a huge shade, more like a spiritual presence than an actual form. She then noticed that it was made up of millions of smaller shades, which came and went from it, fluttering round the heads of the disputing students, and whispering in their ears.

The 'great shadowy creature' spoke to her and told her she was Dame Opinion, the daughter of Ignorance and born of the desire for knowledge. She was surprised that Christine did not know her already and explained to her how she works. As soon as a human being is born and his mind starts feebly to work, she sends one of those smaller shades, who are her daughters, to help him develop his ideas, whether good, bad or merely foolish, as they were helping the disputing students. There is none so wise that he cannot have a false opinion and the shades do nothing to change these. For Opinion never deliberately influences people, because she herself is never certain; her task is merely to foster the views men hold. At the same time she rather confusingly says that her ultimate aim is to enable the truth to be found, with the aid of Dame Philosophy, after which she will disappear, for there is no place for her in paradise. (pp. 110-12)

There is only one matter on which she suddenly speaks with complete certainty and that concerns those nobles who follow arms and think that the greatest fulfilment in life is military glory. She lays down detailed rules as to when fighting is lawful and when it is not. The sudden intrusion of this matter in the discourse of Dame Opinion is important because it is a first mention of Christine's interest in this age-old question, an unusual subject for a woman and one which she was to treat later in a way that brought her unexpected posthumous fame.

The great shade then asked Christine if she had said enough to convince her of her power and explain who she is. Christine understandably replied that she had found her contradictory actions rather confusing whereupon Opinion, to help her by means of another personal instance, told her that it was she who had stirred up the debate on the *Roman de la Rose,* by encouraging conflicting beliefs in the minds of the participants. This finally so convinced Christine that she asked Opinion whether she had engendered any errors in her writing, for if so she would like to emend them. Dame Opinion reassured her on this with a curious prophecy, saying 'after your death a prince full of valour and visions will come who, hearing of your volumes, will wish that you had lived in his time and will greatly desire that he might have seen you'.

Thus not only reassured but given hope for her future as a writer even beyond what the Crowned Lady had promised, Christine ended her meeting with Dame Opinion. It had certainly been fruitful for this, the most original, imaginative, penetrating and subtle of all her allegories, surpassing in psychological maturity anything she had previously written, is enough to prove how amply Dame Opinion had helped her to achieve her professed aim of enlarging her mind. Another development now awaited her, this time of the spirit rather than the mind, and this she achieved through her meeting with a third lady, which she described in the third and last part of her *Lavision.*

On leaving the schools she went to a convent whose abbess was Philosophy. This time it was Christine who opened the interview by telling Philosophy the story of her life, apologising for the prolixity of her account, which covered not only her own development but what we know of her parents and children. (pp. 112-13)

Christine ended her *Lavision* by likening its three parts to three precious stones, of which this last section resembles a glowing and flawless ruby which, she says, pleases one the more every time one looks at it. The allegory here is clear, that the more she thought about Philosophy's lesson, the more she realised the truth of what she had said (and Dame Opinion had implied): that hitherto her attitude to her life had been all wrong and that she should look at it differently. She had been too ready to pity herself and feel herself persecuted. The change of heart that this lesson induced was moral rather than religious, for there is no evidence that Christine ever had more than the normal piety of the age. But a change of heart it certainly was, for she ceased from then on from her customary complaints. To have admitted it thus publicly, even through her story of the vision or dream which brought it about, was an undeniable act of courage and showed, as much as the second part of her book had done, how much she had matured now that she had reached the age of forty-two and was, she thought, more than half-way along the road of her pilgrimage. (p. 115)

Enid McLeod, in her The Order of the Rose: The Life and Ideas of Christine de Pizan, *Rowman and Littlefield, 1976, 185 p.*

MARY ANN IGNATIUS (essay date 1979)

[*In the following excerpt, Ignatius traces the critical history of Christine's* The Epistle of Othea to Hector.]

Christine wrote the *Othea* early in her career; it was apparently her first attempt to go beyond the courtly genres on which she had built her reputation but which she also considered frivolous. In her *Avision,* Christine refers to a concept of poetry that is akin to theology and philosophy. . . . In the *Epistre Othea* Christine is experimenting not only with a concept of what a book should be, but with an attempt to develop a literary form that might adapt itself to this particularly lofty concept of poetry toward which her serious muse urged her to turn. (p. 137)

Christine, who had already read and admired Dante, was trying to produce a work of art, an object of contemplation, and not a didactic treatise. Her subject is the highest aim of allegory, the portrayal of "things in their essence, beautiful to contemplate." Christine's understanding of allegory in this *visually* contemplative sense is explicitly stated at the end of *Lavision-*

Christine, where the author gives a metaphorical description of her method, in which the three levels of discourse are likened to three stones, each with its individually precious properties. (p. 138)

Each of these stones, the diamond, the cameo, and the ruby, gives its own reflection of reality. Christine had inherited from her cultural tradition a concept of reality as a closed and formally perfect system, containing many levels of truth, all of which reflect the same ultimate Truth. Within this vast edifice of reality, seemingly irreconcilable forms of truth can be elucidated and reconciled. Like the Gothic cathedral, the ideal work of art should aim for the synthetic totality of the scholastic *summa,* whose formal perfection it emulates. The humanist in Christine would make her work man-centered (hence its appearance as a compendium of advice) without sacrificing its universality. What Christine has attempted in the *Othea* is a global synthesis of reality as her culture perceived it, a single universal reality reflected in various modes of investigating or expressing truth: classical literary tradition, poetry, art, science, the social ethic of chivalry, the consoling discipline of philosophy, and the all-encompassing revealed truth of the Church. These modalities of truth are addressed to man on different levels of his being: through myth, poetry, and the art of the illuminator, Christine touches our esthetic sense; our intellect through science and philosophy; our moral and social being through exploration of historical roots and in the ethic of chivalry; and finally our spiritual being, our soul, through her use of allegory. Only a complex multiple structure could convey the author's synthetic vision of interrelated levels of truth, all subordinated to ultimate metaphysical reality. Christine has often been accused of prolixity; we cannot help but admire in the *Othea* how her use of multiple structure has allowed her to be so universally inclusive within such a miniature form.

Christine has created in the *Othea* a tiny mirror of the medieval world view, by means of which young "Hector" may be initiated into the totality of his extraordinary cultural heritage: from its ancient origins to its artistic, scientific, and social thought, from its personal and social ethic to its eschatology, its total vision of human destiny. In this context, Hector may be identified with Christine herself, a relative newcomer to the "chemin de long estude," having just devoted the recent years of her life to a courageous attempt to assimilate all the intellectual riches her civilization had to offer. (pp. 138-39)

It is by concentrating on the formal structure of the *Othea* that we can begin to appreciate the importance of Christine's esthetic intentions, and understand the appeal of the work to readers of the fifteenth and sixteenth centuries, without disparaging either the book or its readers. We can assess the worth of the *Othea,* and the originality of its author more generously, assigning to the book a more appropriate place in literary history, not only as a very important transmitter of medieval culture and its classical origins, but as a remarkable experiment in literary form. Its flaws, hesitations, and uncertainties are those of any pioneering effort: Christine's effort occurs at a point in her career where she is casting about for a new and more authentic mode of serious personal expression, and coincides with the emergence of the popular book, whose nature and impact are not yet fully realized. She developed for the *Othea* an original and sophisticated structure intended to reflect and communicate a personal and cultural experience of the structure of reality. The book is *poetic* rather than didactic: Christine does not claim to impose a definitive interpretation of the metaphors through which she investigates reality, but tries rather to suggest, to open the eyes of her readers to the myriad secret relationships that exist. (p. 140)

> Mary Ann Ignatius, "Christine de Pizan's 'Epistre Othea': An Experiment in Literary Form," in Medievalia et Humanistica: Studies in Medieval and Renaissance Culture, No. 9, 1979, pp. 127-42.

LESLIE ALTMAN   (essay date 1980)

[*Altman is an American essayist and educator who has written studies on such subjects as images of women in medieval romances and eighteenth-century satire. In the following excerpt, she traces the history of Christine's powerful rebuttals of works she deemed disparaging to the role and status of women, written by such authors as Ovid and Jean de Meung.*]

One writer stands out [among the female writers of the Middle Ages] because she supported herself and her family by her pen: Christine de Pisan, one of the most prolific secular writers of the period and the unique professional woman writer...

Christine's works provide fresh insight from a uniquely female perspective into the actual social position of women in France at the end of the fourteenth century; both *La Cité des Dames* and *Le Livre des Trois Vertus* deserve attention as sources of specific and practical information about the lives of women of all classes. Her success as a professional writer is also testimony to the possibilities open to a woman of ability.

Christine's writings, unlike those of most medieval writers, provide a substantial amount of information about her own life. Two works, *Le Livre de la Mutacion de Fortune* and *La Vision-Christine,* provide autobiographical accounts, probably designed in part to inform patrons of her background. (p. 7)

The experience of being a woman in a man's world seems to have affected Christine's attitudes about the role of women in society. During [her] period of domestic, legal, and financial difficulties, she turned to writing; her earliest poems are written during the period following her husband's death. In a long poem (23,636 lines) begun in 1400 and finished in 1403, *Le Livre de la Mutacion de Fortune,* Christine describes how her happiness ended with her husband's death and how Fortune turned her into a man so that she could fend for herself.... That Christine believed her ability to survive depended upon a "mutation" from woman to man testifies to the prevailing social attitudes about women, particularly the view that women were physically weak and subordinate to men, an assumption Christine shared.

Le Livre de la Mutacion de Fortune also provides evidence that Christine had embarked on a wide-ranging program of self-education. After an autobiographical introduction, *Le Livre* becomes a compendium of information, beginning with a description of the castle of Fortune and its inhabitants, a description which includes the famous men of the period, among them Richard II of England and the nobility of France. The poem then considers the branches of learning and the history of the world from the Creation to the present, concluding with descriptions of Edward III of England, Charles V and Charles VI of France, and her patron, Louis, Duke of Orléans, brother of Charles VI. Christine emphasizes the instability of Fortune and the error of men who put their faith in things of this world, repeating a theme that runs through medieval literature. Her suggestion, however, that Fortune can alter one's sexual identity seems unique. (pp. 11-12)

Her earliest work specifically concerned with women is a poem entitled *L'Epistre du Dieu d'Amour.* ... The poem is an attack on antifeminist writers, written in the form of a king's reply to a public request—a form Christine would have known from direct experience. Cupid, King of Love, in response to a request from all gentle ladies, admonishes the writers who speak ill of women. The two antifeminist writers Christine specifically attacks are Ovid for the *Ars Amatoria* and Jean de Meun for *Le Roman de la Rose. L'Epistre du Dieu d'Amour* chooses a middle ground between the exaggerated attacks and defenses that are typical of the period. Basing her discussion on logic and common sense, Christine makes a series of valid and clever points. She begins by arguing that it is ignorant, rude, and ungrateful to condemn women, as all men are given birth, nourished, and buried by women. She insists that one should not generalize that all women are evil because a few are: because Satan fell, are all angels evil? Arguing against the antifeminist writers, she says that Ovid's *Art of Love* should be called the "Art of Deception." She points out that if women are weak-willed and unstable of affection, as Ovid suggests, then it should not have been necessary for him to write an entire book instructing men on how to deceive them. Regarding *Le Roman de la Rose* and other antifeminist works she says:

> . . . les livres ne firent
> Pas les femmes, ne les choses n'i mirent
> Que l'en y list contre elles et leurs meurs;
> . . .
> Mais se femmes eussent les livres fait
> Je scay de vray qu'autrement fust du tait.
>
> [Women did not write the books
> Nor put the things in them
> That one reads there against them and their morals;
> . . .
> but if women had written the books
> I truly know they would have done otherwise.]

Like Geoffrey Chaucer, who portrayed the Wife of Bath as making the same observation, Christine is aware that men do not always present a reliable view of the other sex.

Christine is equally eloquent when she describes the role of women in Christian history. She notes that women did not betray Christ, as the Apostles did, that Christ himself was born of woman, and that Mary sits on the left hand of God, next to her Son. She also writes a lawyerlike brief for the defense of Eve, arguing that Eve did not deceive Adam because she did not intend to deceive Adam; rather she disobeyed God, as Adam did, as nearly all of us do daily. The learned Isotta Nogarola of Verona was later to take up the same issue in the fifteenth century. (pp. 15-16)

In 1405 Christine produced the two works that are of particular interest to the modern reader: *Le Livre de la Cité des Dames* and *Le Trésor de la Cité des Dames* or *Le Livre des Trois Vertus.* (p. 17)

The first book, *Le Livre de la Cité des Dames,* is a dream vision: the poet herself is reading the *Lamentations of Matheolus,* an antifeminist tract, and wondering why clerks write evil of women. Christine falls into a reverie which is interrupted by three allegorical ladies, who appear to her in a ray of light and command her to help them build a city for women who are without defense and without champions. The three figures are Reason, Righteousness (or Integrity), and Justice. Reason will build the foundations and the walls; Integrity will build the houses, palaces, and temples; and Justice will build the towers, battlements, and gates: that is, the City of Ladies will be built by

Reason, peopled by Integrity, and defended by Justice. The book has three sections, each ostensibly concerned with building parts of the city, but actually consisting of Christine's conversations with each of the three allegorical personages in turn. In each section Christine asks questions about women, and the allegorical figure responds with explanations and illustrative *exempla*. Christine begins, for example, by asking Reason how men and women differ. Reason's answer is, as one might expect, logical: women have weaker bodies, but nature compensates them for their physical weakness by making their spirits, and therefore their moral sensibilities, more refined than those of men. The body is not the source of virtue; reason is. Some of God's creatures are more inclined to reason and thence to virtue than others. Christine pursues this issue and asks Reason if God ever made a woman so noble as to achieve a higher understanding of philosophical matters. Reason responds that experience of diverse things is the greatest teacher and that because women have almost exclusively domestic experience, they have little knowledge of higher or abstract learning. Learning is difficult; some are quicker than others, but sex is *not* determinative.

The first section of *La Cité des Dames* argues for women's natural capabilities; the second attempts to educate women by means of examples of righteousness; the third is essentially a history of famous women and their contributions to society. The bulk of all three sections is devoted to retelling the stories of famous women and in this respect *La Cité des Dames* resembles Boccaccio's *De claris mulieribus* and Chaucer's *Legend of Good Women;* from the former many of the stories are drawn. Christine uses two contemporary women as prime examples of women's capabilities: Novella of Bologna and Anastaise. The first of these was the daughter of Johannes Andrea, a teacher at the University of Bologna. Novella was so learned that she taught her father's students in his absence, but she did so behind a veil, so that her beauty would not distract the students. The second, Anastaise, was a skillful illuminator of manuscripts, the most successful at her craft in her time. Christine mentions that she herself used Anastaise's talents, paying a high price for her illuminations. *La Cité des Dames* also includes mythological examples of women's learning and craftmanship, among others Nichostrate, inventor of the Latin alphabet and grammar, and Minerva, inventor of armor.

Christine's conviction that women should be educated, already mentioned in *Le Livre de la Mutacion de Fortune,* is reiterated in *La Cité des Dames.* Here she insists that women are as capable of being taught as men and therefore have an equal right to be taught. If one customarily put girls in school and taught them the arts and sciences, as one does with boys, she writes, then they would learn as well as boys. Their bodies may be weaker, but their attention is greater when it is applied. *La Cité des Dames,* however, is not feminist propaganda. Christine's "feminism" is grounded in medieval philosophy: women are different from men. Each sex has its task and performs its duties according to its nature and its inclination as well as according to custom. She believes that because men are more powerful than women, they alone have the strength to execute the laws. Since by custom women cannot appear in public except discreetly, women have no role in government nor in public life; both custom and nature forbid it. Even so, Christine acknowledges that the work of men and women is not always distinguishable and goes so far as to praise women who do men's work better than men do.

Le Trésor de la Cité des Dames, or *Le Livre des Trois Vertus,* the second of the books devoted to women, is divided into three sections, but in this case the division follows a social hierarchy: the first book is devoted to the high aristocracy, princesses and noble ladies; the second, to women who live at court; the third, to women of the towns, bourgeoisie, commons, and laboring classes. The first section forms more than half of the book. Since *Le Livre des Trois Vertus* is dedicated to the Dauphine, its emphasis on the aristocracy is logical, but its inclusion of all classes seems to be unique. Rather than considering the rights of the husband, Christine is concerned with those of wives. Her advice to a wife married to a bad husband is to be quiet about her problem in order to avoid injury to the husband's reputation and thence to the wife's. If the husband is unfaithful, the wife should ignore the infidelity and try to make herself more attractive to him, for the sake of his soul and his reputation, and especially for the good name of the children. She stresses as well the importance of a woman learning to function as the head of the household in the case of the temporary absence or death of her husband. Her own bitter experience following her husband's death had taught her the dangers of ignorance of worldly affairs.

Because *Le Livre des Trois Vertus* is a didactic work of practical advice, the education of women is discussed as a practical matter. She insists that it is vital to teach women to calculate so that they can keep their household accounts properly. The experience of virtually uninterrupted warfare during her lifetime had demonstrated the importance of a woman learning as much as possible about defending the manor in the case of attack. The education of a woman should teach her feudal law, estate management, household management and budgeting, medicine, farming, crop management, marketing and labor relations. Although women might have neither public rights nor responsibilities, *Le Livre des Trois Vertus* suggests that in practice women of all classes were often equally responsible with men for the operations of daily life.

In her last known work, *Le Dittié de Jehanne d'Arc,* Christine returns to the subject of women. Composed in 1429, the year of Joan's triumph over the English, the poem is religious in tone, praising God for having provided a sixteen-year-old girl from Arc as an instrument to deliver France from its enemies and its internal political problems. In its concern for the political situation of France and in its obvious delight that France was destined to be saved by a woman, *Le Dittié de Jehanne d'Arc* is a fitting conclusion to the work of Christine de Pisan. . . . (pp. 17-20)

In spite of the admiration, even pride, this medieval woman experienced at the achievement of Joan of Arc, her works remain products of the medieval world, based on assumptions regarding differences between the sexes which do not readily lend themselves to a revival by modern feminists. The works of Christine de Pisan assume that each individual has a purpose, a social and political destiny determined by sex. Her contemporary Eustache Deschamps praised her "virility," and a modern French critic has even called her the first female "man of letters." Significantly, and perhaps ironically, she either saw her own career as dependent on her "mutation" from woman to man or realized the necessity of presenting it in this light to her contemporaries. Christine's works and her success as a writer, nevertheless, suggest that the experience of medieval women may have been different from the images derived from literature and theology, and for this reason reexamination of her works should be of value. (p. 20)

Leslie Altman, "Christine de Pisan: First Professional Woman of Letters (French, 1364-1430?)," in

Female Scholars: A Tradition of Learned Women before 1800, *edited by J. R. Brink, Eden Press Women's Publications, 1980, pp. 7-23.*

PAOLA MALPEZZI PRICE   (essay date 1980)

[*Price is an essayist and educator. In the following excerpt, she compares Christine's love poetry to that of her male counterparts and contrasts the use of masculine and feminine personas within Christine's own works.*]

Critic Pierre Le Gentil describes Christine de Pisan as one of the more likable writers in French literary history. Most students of French literature agree with him but offer different explanations for her widespread popularity. Some claim that she is the first and only female poet to treat the theme of the inconsolable widow; others have written that she is not merely "... a forerunner of true feminism but one of its greatest champions" and that she is "the precursor of the learned women of the French Renaissance." It is indisputable that she stands alone, as a female poet, in the fourteenth- and fifteenth-century literary scene. (p. 37)

Men have dominated the European literary scene since the time of the first troubadours and the role of female poetry has always been minimal. The female poets of the twelfth and thirteenth centuries, the *trobairitz,* were influenced and inspired by the male poets, but their poetry was less sophisticated and less literary than the male poetry. As a consequence, they have only recently attracted the attention of the critics. Meg Bogin, in her study of the women troubadours, notes that they "were doing something unique in medieval art: they were writing in a true first person singular at a time when almost all artistic endeavor was collective." They could afford to be subjective because unlike the troubadours they were not writing for professional reasons, and Christine may have chosen to follow the men's literary examples as a better guarantee of success.

Christine de Pisan chose the most famous male poets of her time as the models for her love poetry: Machaut, Deschamps, and Froissart. Like them she favored the ballad and the rondeau as the best vehicles of much of her lyric work and within the frame of these fixed forms she exploited her technical ability by experimenting with line, stanza length, and rhyme scheme. She particularly helped popularize the rondeau by shortening its refrain, a practice that was widely followed by the fifteenth-century poets.

Her poetry has been acclaimed because of its originality and "sincerity" and because it is representative of the literary canons of the period. Her sincerity is expressed in the poems concerning the grief for her husband's death, while the remainder of her lyric work follows the poetic standards and conventions established by tradition and utilized by her male contemporaries. Her lyric opus consists of several love stories recounted by different "voices" rather than a collection of poems with a single speaker. The distance created between the poet and her audience by the plurality of narrators is accentuated by the frequent correspondence of the speaker to a masculine persona. (pp. 37-8)

By analyzing the topos of the eyes and of vision and other aspects of Christine's lyric work we can learn how the speaker's sex determines the treatment of literary topoi. Poets, or more precisely male poets, since as Christine says, "books were not written by women," had exploited this topos for centuries and had canonized its vocabulary and its imagery. Christine re-

peatedly uses this literary cliché in her poems and Daniel Poirion has written that "Christine's feelings are determined by the metamorphosis of the gaze."

Typical of Christine's short poems is a group of ballads in which a young woman recounts her first experience of love. This theme is found in . . . *Cent Balades,* a collection of one hundred ballads. In a few of Christine's longer poems, or *dits,* our poet assumes the role of voyeur, who by chance witnesses behavior and events related to love. The role of voyeur and that of the inconsolable widow who carries "the sad memory / of the man . . . / who left me so lonely" within her heart seem to correspond more intimately to Christine's personal experience and to be her most "sincere" persona.

Christine begins her **Cent Balades** with twenty poems bemoaning the loss of her husband, after which she abruptly changes tone and subject. Putting aside her personal sorrow, deemed improper as the topic of "court" or public poetry, she places her poetry in the stream of tradition and sings of love as poets had done since the twelfth century. Her most sincere tone is found, however, in the poems expressing her reluctance to write love poems when her real interest lay in philosophical and moral issues; a reluctance which shows how deeply she was caught "between the need to write in the tradition of joy and the tendency to yield to feelings of sadness which she experiences more than the other poets and which finally triumph in the fifteenth century." Both her personal grief and her learned, intellectual aspirations had to yield to literary conformism and to the princes' demands of a poetry which revolves mainly around love, the feeling "which best pleases everybody." Perhaps Christine became a court poet despite herself and started writing on command those love poems which constitute the bulk of her lyric opus.

In the poet's treatment of the first phase of the love play, the falling in love, we find a slight difference in the way the masculine and the feminine personae describe the event and their feelings. The male persona confirms the tradition of love at first sight:

> (although) I never saw you
> before now . . .
> you have stolen my heart
> forever . . .

and of the mythic intervention of Cupid's arrows:

> the arrow which has wounded me through the look
> of your beautiful eyes . . .

(pp. 38-9)

Christine's feminine persona, on the other hand, accentuates the sweetness which the first amorous look arouses in the Lover's heart, rather than the immediacy or violence of the gaze. The young Lady lover emphasizes that the Beloved's "sweet behavior . . . / and . . . the sweet, loving and beautiful eyes" have conquered her completely. The poet exploits the traditional formula *dous regart* [sweet look] whenever the motif of the gaze is introduced; nonetheless her insistent use of the adjective *sweet* efficiently conveys the overwhelming sweetness felt by the Lady on this occasion. In the ballad the adjective *sweet* is repeated five times and the word *sweetness* is placed in the first line introducing the theme of the poem: "you have used your sweetness so well, / my dear friend, that you have conquered me." In a rondel the refrain accentuates the power of the Beloved's sweet look on the Lady lover: "your sweetness charms my heart," together with the lethal consequences it brings: "sweet friend, . . . / . . . Cupid is wounding me through your eyes." (p. 40)

In the long poem *Le Dit de Poissy* [*The Debate of Poissy*] a young Lady gives a full description of the physical qualities of the Beloved's eyes together with the troubling effects they provoke in her psyche:

> no man ever had sweeter eyes,
> brown, merry, pensive, warm,
> and his gaze was so filled with sweetness
> that he gave me the illness which makes me grieve.

This mixture of sweetness and cruelty seems to be Cupid's first gift to the new lovers.

The sweetness exemplifying the birth of love through the loving gaze for the feminine persona is also part of the *joye* [joy], the effect of love celebrated by poets and approved by medieval societies because of its social virtues. At the end of the twelfth century the troubadour Arnaut de Mareuil is quoted as singing the praise of joy:

> Without joy there is no worth, nor without worth
> honor, for love brings joy and a gay lady brings
> love and gaiety solace and solace courtesy.

Christine dutifully sings that "rightful is he who lives joyfully," because he or she will be a better person and a better member of society, willing to interact and to share this joy. The female "I" often repeats that only the sight of the Beloved can produce this exhilarating effect in her heart and body: "Now . . . that I see you in front of me . . . / nobody else gives me joy" (*Autres Balades*) and she indicates the Beloved as the only person who "can make her totally happy."

The analysis of the treatment of joy in Christine's poems shows, however, more numerous examples of the masculine voice celebrating its effects than the feminine counterpart. This fact can be ascribed on one hand to the literary tradition in which we find male poets constantly using this motif and, on the other hand, to a suspicion on the part of the woman who fears to threaten this joy through its mere expression in words. The hope of seeing his beloved lady makes the male Lover sing happily and the mere thought of her beauty pleases him so that he is "merrier than a bird on a tree branch." The actual sight of the Beloved, however, triggers his most enthusiastic exclamations of joy. In a rondel the Lover's happiness is accentuated twice: by the repetition of the pronoun *I* in a verse which recurs as a refrain three times in the twelve-line poem: "I am joyful and I ought to be"; and by the precise description of his state as heavenly: "I am in earthly paradise / and not in hell." The final verse (excluding the refrain) best summarizes the cause of this joy: "I look at her appearance and her body."

The Lady lover expresses her "pleasure" at the Beloved's sight more frequently than her joy: "my friend, whenever I can see you vis à vis / I am very pleased that you are totally mine." When she wishes to thank him for his love, she calls the Beloved "my only friend, my heaven on earth / and the most perfect pleasure of my sight," in which the combination heaven-pleasure confirms the link between sacred and erotic loves created by poetry. This is one of the few examples of Christine's homage to this topos, which was widely used by some of her male counterparts, such as Machaut. (pp. 41-2)

Christine de Pisan earned her livelihood writing poems more like the troubadours and *trouvères* than the *trobairitz*, but her poetry, especially the part with the feminine voice, is closer to the opus of the female poets. As in the poetry of the *tro-*

bairitz, the main subject of Christine's feminine poems is the disappointment rather than the joy or pleasure of love, and like their poems, Christine's feminine lyrics show a more marked tone of sensuality than men's poetry or her own masculine poems. For instance, in the first ballad on the young Lady's love she confesses that it is the young man's "so pleasant behavior" and his "such . . . handsome body and sweet face" which mostly impress the Lady, accompanied by his savoir faire: "he begs me so sweetly," and the fame surrounding him: "I have heard such good things about him . . .'. Besides appealing to the Lover's sight and hearing, the word "tant" [such, so much], repeated seven times, also affects the tactile sense by giving consistency and volume to the Beloved's virtues. Furthermore the young Lady encloses the Beloved's "handsome body" in her heart together with his portrait, while another Lady affirms with impatience that "Monday always comes too late / because only then will I see my friend." She longs to see "his handsome body" and the reason she gives for her impatience is that she will then hold him in her arms.

The male lover in Christine's poems hides his request for sensual or sexual gratification behind appeals for the Lady's favors and he often asks to be looked at as a means of obtaining the Lady's attention. This plea, common in the poetry of the male writers, is justified by the situation created by courtly love which requires the Lady to be superior to her lover in social status and worth and the Lover to continually remind the Lady of his existence and his needs. He may also ask her to grant him a kind expression whenever he approaches her, so that, encouraged by her "sweet look," he will overcome his fears. The Lover's fear of the Lady is another recurrent theme in masculine love poetry while it is rarely expressed by Christine's female lover or by the preceding female lovers. One of the *trobairitz* explicitly tells a potential lover whose meekness annoys her that

> . . . fear should not keep
> a courtly lover from
> experiencing joy . . .

In Christine's poetry the future of the lovers' relationship depends on the Lady's answer to the Beloved's requests. The young Lady's initial reaction is typical of a woman who does not want to do

> in deeds, in words, in ways
> what any lady who holds her honor dearly
> would not do.

This attitude translated a rule of feminine common sense besides expressing one of the principles of courtly love which dictated that

> a lady faults
> against honor and nobility
> when she grants at once that which she values so much.

Since the Lady is a teacher of *mesura* [self-discipline, restraint], she responds to the Beloved's requests with this advice:

> May a warm reception suffice you,
> lord, you are asking too much of me,
> you shall lose all if you demand all.

The Lady faces a painful dilemma when she is confronted by the Beloved's insistence and her own feelings. Is she to yield to his requests and show, by so doing, that she is a normal human being who needs love and tenderness, or is she to keep the image of cold inspirer of virtue and joy, untouched by and detached from human weaknesses? Christine chooses to show her Lady as a creature of flesh and blood who follows the laws of her heart rather than those of her reason. The young Lady lover becomes, therefore, so sensitive to the Beloved's tears as to consider his friendship a sufficient reason to grant him her love: "I yield to your prayers: / I wish whatever you wish." Once she has admitted her feelings, the Lady lover expresses her affection in more passionate terms than the male lover. After stating her compliance to the Beloved's requests, the young Lady throws herself into his arms: "Sweet friend / now embrace me / I am your beloved lady." Another example of the Lady's acceptance of love shows the role of her eyes in the decision: "For a long time I have noticed / the love disease of which you complain," and her plan for their future use:

> . . . I will see you often;
> never will my body be so enclosed as
> to prevent me from seeing you . . .

The Lady lover descends from the pedestal of unblemished virtue on which courtly love has placed her as soon as she proves herself to be a normal human being; she enters the game of love and agrees to take part in all the tricks which secret love requires for its survival. The logic of courtly love allows no compromise: once the Lady becomes attainable, she gradually loses her influence on her lover and she ends up alone. She realizes then that she cannot achieve happiness playing the role of the merciful, just as she has realized that she cannot achieve it by denying her favors. Whichever role she decides to play, she is the ultimate loser in the love relationship created by courtly love. Christine has unequivocally denounced this situation.

The stages of falling in love and of the happiness of love are described in only five of the twenty-eight poems concerning the young Lady's story. The topoi of the love martyr and of the amorous suffering, on the other hand, predominate and are analyzed in all their facets. Although not original in Western love literature, the type of the female love martyr had not been extensively analyzed by French poets, since the predominantly male writers were more interested in the male counterpart. Furthermore, according to the principles of courtly love, the amorous spark is supposed to issue exclusively from the woman's heart while "love is important only for men. They love and the women let themselves be adored, and respond to their love". The fact that Christine writes about women actively in love and makes them speak about their love feelings is her implicit denial of such tenets of courtly love. Against the traditional image of love as "a temporary phase of life, as a period of fantasy" for the young man in search of individual harmony, she presents the image of love as a total experience for the woman who believes in its promising beginning and is shattered by its "pitiful ending" (*Debat de deux Amans*).

One of the first obstacles the Lady finds in her path of love is represented by the *losengiers* [talebearers]. These obscure figures are an indefinite "somebody" mentioned by all the troubadours and *trouvères* but described by none. They are the "invisible eyes (which) observed the lover's every movement, malevolent tongues (which) whispered everywhere." The danger of the *mesdisans* [gossips], as Christine calls them, is mentioned mainly in her poems with the female *I* and their mysterious presence becomes an obsessive shadow reviled in many of her feminine poems. Of the twenty-eight ballads forming the young Lady's love story, three have the Lady's revilement of the gossips as their main subject, and at least two mention them in derogatory terms. Love becomes the young Lady's teacher of deception since it advises her to mislead people, and especially the talebearers, about her true feelings. In a poem

she warns the Beloved that her cheerful appearance and impudent behavior are not caused by inconstancy but they aim at "deceiving / the gossips who wish to know everything".

The obscure danger represented by the gossips materializes in the difficulty they create for the lovers to carry on a normal, intimate relationship. The Lady cannot speak to her Beloved nor see him because she fears the watchful eyes, which make her cry out that they "make me end my days / without seeing you, in whom is all my joy". She rebels, however, at this situation and decides that "in spite of everyone . . . / I will do everything possible . . . / to see you." Rebellion is the initial theme of another ballad in which the Lady mentions a more terrible threat to her love. The false gossips have in fact the power to send away the Beloved by spreading the news of their relationship "throughout the town". Secrecy about the amorous relationship was "the conditio sine qua non of true love" and the Lady knows that the gossips' tales can damage the strongest relationship. The poet concludes this ballad by expressing the Lady's deep feeling of frustration at this situation which she is unable to change: "Because of their tongues which say no truth . . . / they prevent me from seeing my friend".

In the *Dit du Duc des Vrais Amans* [*Poem of the Duke of the True Lovers*] a friend of the Lady lover suggests a drastic solution to silence forever the gossips: avoid having any love relation at all. In the shorter poems the Lady's revenge against the gossips takes the form of verbal abuse. Using an impersonal and neutral voice, the poet wishes that they may be tormented by the worst woes of love and in the refrain of a ballad she accuses their envy as the primary cause of their evil behavior: "You speak like people full of envy". If we look at the etymology of the Latin word *envier* we find *invidere*, which means "to look closely." Envy is therefore a degeneration of the act of seeing, and the gossips' original fault is their curious and insistent look at other people's intimate lives. Christine's lovers avoid this envy by acting deveptively and eluding their curiosity whenever possible. For example, a Lady advises her Beloved that since

> gossips are on the watch,
> my friend, in order to spy on us,
> so take another path
> when it is time to come and see me.

Their role is similar to that of the mythic Argus who, because of his hundred eyes, was entrusted by Juno to guard Io, transformed into a cow, from Jupiter's amorous advances. His hundred eyes, however, do not prevent the lovers' reunion attained through deception. The moral drawn from this mythic episode is that all lovers are justified in using any means available to them in order to see one another.

Absence and separation are more defined and terrible dangers than even the fear of the talebearers since they totally deprive the lovers of the most elementary means of communication provided by sight and initiate them to grief and suffering. The young Lady's happiness is suddenly clouded by the news that her Beloved may have to go to Germany for a three- or four-month period. At once she predicts that her heart will split in half if she is unable to see him daily. When the time to say goodbye comes, the Lover is transformed into a mask of sorrow; in response to the Beloved's comforting words she opposes her stubborn pessimism and she insists that she will die when she is prevented from seeing him.

Ten of the twenty-eight poems which present the young Lady's story have as their main theme the grief of love endured by the Lady because of the Beloved's absence. The celebration of Mayday and the return of spring, which invite people to love and be merry, mark more poignantly the contrast between external events and the Lover's feelings. The absent Beloved is described as the "spring" of her happiness and the Lover's unreciprocated love for him as an arid and futile sentiment which consumes her with passion. The sexual image presented here illustrates the contrast between present sterile despair and past luxuriant happiness.

The hope and the joyous anticipation of seeing the Beloved bitterly dissolve when the Lover realizes that the deadline for his return has passed, and he is not back. The first doubts of his loyalty are translated into the Lover's fear that he might be tired of being "seen" by her. She interprets his behavior as an explicit rejection of her love since for Christine's ladies, as for Eluard's lovers, "the gaze is the means par excellence of communicating and of loving." The knowledge that everyone can see that she is suffering except the person who should care most increases the pain caused by his delay. She sees the Beloved's blindness as no physical handicap but as a spiritual default which prevents him from understanding how his prolonged absence hurts the Lover's sensitivity and her faith in him and love.

Deception and disillusionment become two of the most recurrent themes in Christine's feminine poems. Besides the young Lady's painful initiation to the woes of love, we hear the complaints of a more experienced lady, who is able to go beyond the simple appearance and unmask the Beloved's falsehood:

> I see very well
> that whatever is your appearance,
> your heart does not love me at all;
> he who does not see it is truly blind.

She realizes that he does not love her any longer since he has not shown any desire to see her for a whole month. The same realization, and for the same reason, comes to another lady who finally opens her eyes on the Beloved's supposed loyalty: "I see very well that he does not care much / to see me . . .". The young Lady lover experiences humiliation and jealousy when she suspects that her beauty is insufficient to retain the Beloved's love:

> . . . perhaps he loves a lady more beautiful
> than I am, so he does not care much
> to come back . . .

When she has proof of his unfaithfulness, the Lady expresses her bitterness and her disappointment with these words: "Dieux! que j'ai esté deçeüe!" [God! How I have been deceived!] and she regrets that "a tart me suis aperçeüe!" [too late have I perceived it!] (*Virelay*). The past participles of *decevoir* [to deceive] and apercevoir [to perceive] express the Lover's deception through the Beloved's abuse of the *veoir,* or truth, and her going beyond the mere act of *veoir,* or seeing, in order to learn the painful truth. Although the Lover accuses herself for having opened her eyes too late on the Beloved's true behavior, she declares that it is a definitive awakening since

> neither the looks,
> nor the behavior that he may display,
> . . .
> will ever make me believe him again.

The school of love is not only a school of deception and of cynicism but also a breeding ground for hostile feelings since

the statement "he whom I loved truly / wants to marry" equates to the declaration "he becomes my enemy" (*Vir.*).

Christine deals in two ways with the situation resulting from the Beloved's absence. For the male lover a long separation inevitably brings the love relationship to an end, as the squire of the *Dit de Poissy* explicitly says: "out of sight, out of heart." The ladies in Christine's short poems deny the truth of this statement and one of them says: "she who loves well does not forget / her good friend because he is far away." Although the idea of the union of hearts despite the separation of the bodies attracts and charms Christine's female lovers, they realize that its actualization is limited to men's and women's power to endure suffering and that often this love becomes a destructive experience. At the beginning of the separation the Beloved's portrait is enclosed in the young Lady's heart "as in a strong tower," but as time passes the tower walls start crumbling under the pressure of jealousy, doubt, and grief and the indefinable patina which time leaves in its passing. After a year and a half of waiting for the Beloved's return or for his news, the Lady rebels against this situation:

> it is not right that I should
> love him when he loves me not;
> nor when he cares not that I see him.

The pains of separation become unbearable if they are suffered alone.

Most of the examples of this love in absentia in Christine's poems end with the Lady lover completely disillusioned with love in general and the Beloved in particular since they both put her heart in *nonchaloir. Nonchaloir,* the opposite of joy, is acute melancholy and despondency. Christine ascribes the Lady's repudiation and accusation of love, which promised so much and granted so little, to this state of mind. Love is reviled in an impersonal tone which makes the accusations more universal: "(Love,) your warm appearance deceives everyone" and again: "At the end everyone can see that / your actions are nothing but tricks." The last poem on the young Lady's love indicates that the Lady's rejection of Cupid's service is total and irrevocable: "I do not wish to serve you any longer / Love, I fare thee well."

The use of the masculine and feminine personae in Christine's poetry illustrates that there are differences related to the sex of the speaker in the treatment of similar literary motifs. (pp. 43-50)

Besides the differences within Christine's poetry between the masculine and the feminine personae concerning particular topoi, we can also detect more general differences between certain aspects of her poetry and the lyrics of the male poets preceding or contemporary to her. In their poetry men present women either as the devil incarnate, placed on earth to ensnare men in a trap of sexuality, or, at the other extreme, they depict her as the most perfect of creatures, endowed with every virtue and detached from human passion. Christine, instead, presents women of flesh and blood who love and hate, suffer and rejoice. These women are sensual and totally human since they need the reassurance of a tender gesture or touch and are active protagonists of the love relationship, but they are also "spiritual" because they can keep their love alive despite separation and other obstacles. This avoidance of extremes is revealed in her language, which is fresher, more candid, and less sophisticated than the men's diction. This characteristic of her poetry constitutes another link between Christine's work and the *tro-*

bairitz's lyrics, whose language is described by Bogin as being "subjective and refreshing in its spontaneity."

Both female and male poets ultimately write about their disillusionment with love and with the Beloved. The male poet usually accuses the woman of causing the end of the relationship and he depicts the lady, formerly seen as the worthiest creature to be loved, as a fickle and unjust monster when she refuses his advances. At times he maligns the entire female sex as the cause of his misery. In Christine's poems, on the other hand, the female lover does not condemn the male lover for her suffering caused by his disloyalty or his absence or for the end of their relationship. She may blame herself and her lack of discernment which led her into a painful situation or she may accuse a superior force such as Fortune and its attempts to destroy the little happiness allowed to humans. Although she does not openly accuse men of cruelty and insensitivity, the poet's subtle and discreet skill leads the reader to question the ethics of a relationship which allows the woman to become the victim and the man the villain of love.

The importance of Christine's lyric work is not her alleged "sincerity" or the fact that she was a feminist in her everyday life, but instead that she lent the women of her time a convincing voice to express their feelings and that she was able to bring the feminine perspective into the realm of the poetics of courtly love, traditionally reserved for male writers. (pp. 50-1)

> *Paola Malpezzi Price, "Masculine and Feminine Personae in the Love Poetry of Christine de Pisan," in* Gender and Literary Voice, *edited by Janet Todd, Holmes & Meier Publishers, Inc., 1980, pp. 37-53.*

MARINA WARNER   (essay date 1982)

[*Warner is an English novelist, biographer, and short story writer whose works include* All Alone of Her Sex: The Myth and Cult of the Virgin Mary *(1976) and* Joan of Arc *(1981). In the following excerpt, she illustrates how Christine's* Book of the City of Ladies *refutes attacks made on her sex by male scholars throughout the ages.*]

Although *The Book of the City of Ladies* was written more than half a millenium ago, it is filled with potent observations for our times. The *querelle des femmes*—the woman question in late fourteenth- and fifteenth-century France—articulated its arguments in much the same way as today's debate about the equality of women. Here, in *The Book of the City of Ladies*, Christine intersperses her tales of formidable and exemplary heroines of the past with down-to-earth remarks about the wrongs done to women by society's attitudes and opinions. Her tone is not shrill, but forbearing; her comments trenchant; she never whines. She indicts men, Portia-like, from a position of superior benevolence, enacting the drama of women's greater moral qualities by refusing the line of violence or suppliant weakness. Christine de Pizan was born in a court and she was an adept of courtly ways; her strategy in her attack is courteous, and her courtesy, with its appearance of frankness, even artlessness, conceals a fair bit of cunning, and a deal of rage.

Recurring themes with resonance for today provoke in her a controlled indignation. She returns again and again, for instance, to the lack of access women have to education. She praises her own father generously for giving her an education against the conventional objections of her mother, and interjects defiantly that women's minds are "freer and sharper" than men's. She laments the disappointment women of her day felt at the birth of daughters: she gives as its cause the need to provide young women with dowries. Yet today, when the economic reason has failed, the arrival of a girl baby is often greeted with less enthusiasm by grandparents, in-laws. Yet another barbarism that has not been modified in the long interval separating us from Christine appears in her pages: the accusation that women invite rape. Christine exonerates women from this suspicion with a fierce, felt regret, and ends by approving the supreme penalty for rapists. Elsewhere, touching what appears to be a personal note, she also pleads that women can be pretty and enjoy fine clothes without forfeiting their title to chastity. Her anger at the double standard, by which men, raping women, then blame women for allowing them to do so, still rings loud and clear today. She also paints a devastating and unchanged picture of violence in marriage, of drunken beatings and spendthrift husbands.

The Book of the City of Ladies uses a popular medieval convention, of an author's conversation with allegorical figures. In this book, Christine talks to the figures of Reason and Justice, familiar then from iconography as well as theology, but she also creates her own allegorical maiden, *Droiture*, Rectitude, "Right-thinking," "Right-doing." Christine's introduction of this figure into the pageant of the regular female Virtues, Liberal Arts, Heavenly Beatitudes, and other personifications found in the sculpture programs of cathedrals, reveals her mental and emotional bent. In a book like *The City of Ladies*, Christine de Pizan is casting herself as a moral tutor rather than a poet; she is writing to instruct us, to shape our thinking and so incline us to right-thinking and right-doing. When she pleads for education for women, she gives as her reason education's close correlation with good conduct.

The contemporary reader might be unfamiliar with the medieval convention of allegory. Yet the appearance of Reason, Rectitude, and Justice as women reflects the entire purpose of Christine's *Book of the City of Ladies:* to bring back to memory the lives and deeds of virtuous women embodying those qualities, who have been neglected and forgotten by history. She is restoring speech to the silent portion of the past—one of the principal tasks of all historians. *The Book of the City of Ladies* resembles a visit to the shades of the dead, claiming their right to be remembered. Christine, drawing from her reading of classical and Renaissance sources, adds them to our store of knowledge and breaks the narrow molds of female stereotypes. To achieve her vindication of women, Christine alters her source material in the most surprising ways, sometimes refreshing, sometimes bizarre.

Christine praises Medea for her herbal arts and her command of the elements—an interesting and justifiable example of reassessing witchcraft from a positive viewpoint. She thus frees a historical personality from the fears of ignorance and prejudice. But later, when Medea appears again among Christine's stories of women's constancy in love, it is a trifle peculiar to find her story told without a mention of the demented dimension of her despair, with the murder of her children overlooked. Christine actually describes the great prototype of the wronged first wife turning merely "despondent" after Jason leaves her. Similarly, Xanthippe, Socrates' proverbial shrew of a wife, emerges from Christine's pages as loyal and devoted and wise. Modesty also inspires Christine to change the famous story of "Roman charity." The dying old man who is suckled by a young woman is transformed into a female, the girl's mother moreover. Christine's redress of history's judgment can be enterprising and refreshing (it had never occurred to me that Xanthippe might indeed have been maligned), but often the new, virtuous portrait strays toward a stereotype. Christine here is at her best as a storyteller when she writes from personal truth and emotion, and her rebukes rise from within the sting of lived experience.

Christine herself does not seem to distinguish between the levels of reality she seizes with her pen: her own life's lessons merge without interruption into the examples of heroines, legendary and historical. Reading *The Book of the City of Ladies* involves an odd trick of perception, for the circle enclosing Christine, Medusa, the goddess Ops, and Queen Blanche is one and the same without difference of degree, authenticity, or even time scale. Human experience is universal, Christine is telling us, and distance in time constitutes no effective barrier. But it is arresting—and charming—to find that Uranus was "an extremely powerful man in Greece" married to a wife called Vesta, that Minerva figured in Christine's mind as the historical inventor of shorthand, arithmetic, weaving and spinning, the cultivation of the olive, and the forging of armor, and was not just the protagonist in a pagan myth of origin or a symbolic tutelary goddess of specific skills and arts. Christine was a devout Christian woman who saw Minerva as one of her predecessors in wisdom and industry; in the invocation with which she closes *The Book of Feats of Arms and Chivalry,* Christine asks Minerva to preside over her undertaking, as she is a *"femme Italienne"* like herself. For Christine de Pizan, the centuries that had elapsed since Italy was part of Magna Graecia were but the winking of an eye; Minerva was her inspiration, her ally, and her compatriot.

The Book of the City of Ladies represents a determined and clear-headed woman's attempt to take apart the structure of her contemporaries' prejudices; a reasoned but fierce counter-assault against baiting by the male. Christine was not a moderate; she believed deeply in sexual difference and she diagnosed, in this book and in other works, the nature and causes of sexual antagonism. She was always alive to injustice. Yet Christine, who herself resolved to remain a widow and sang of her decision in a famous *ballade "Seulete suy et seulete vueil estre"* ["Alone I am, alone I wish to be"], showed an admirable open mind when she counselled other women not to seek too much independence (even though her words sound like equivocation to our ears), for usually moralists command people to greatness they themselves cannot achieve. But she believed in the possibility of reconciliation: it was largely a matter of the right education leading to moral enlightenment. In this way, *The Book of the City of Ladies* is a work of optimism that is still by no means entirely justified by events. The task Christine de Pizan set herself has still to be done. (pp. xiii-xvii)

Marina Warner, in a foreword to The Book of the City of Ladies *by Christine de Pisan, translated by Earl Jeffrey Richards, Persea Books, 1982, pp. xiii-xvii.*

CHARITY CANNON WILLARD　　(essay date 1984)

[*Willard is an American essayist, editor, biographer, and educator. In the following excerpt, she discusses Christine's educational ideas outlined in such works as* Moral Proverbs, The Book of the Three Virtues, *and* The Body of Policy.]

Like the early Italian humanists, Christine was concerning herself with the *moral* education of the young. In her son's case, she knew it was the only real treasure she could give him. She began her *Moral Teachings* with the explanation:

> Son, I have here no great treasure
> To make you rich, but a measure

> Of good advice which you may need;
> I give it hoping you'll take heed. . . .

> Study carefully to inquire
> How best you may Prudence acquire.

> Mother she is of every virtue,
> Who Fortune's treasons can undo.

Although these quatrains are addressed first of all to her son, Christine eventually shows her concern for the various undertakings of other young men, be they rulers, soldiers, churchmen, or merchants. She admonishes them all to be kind and generous:

> Great Pity have for all the poor
> Whom you find starving at your door;

> Help you can give them don't deny—
> Remember someday you must die.

But in addition to striving to follow virtuous ways, one should also cultivate his mind:

> Willingly read fine books of tales
> Whenever you can, for it never fails

> That examples such books comprise
> Can help you to become more wise.

The *Moral Proverbs* are obviously patterned after the *Distics of Cato,* a popular school text, yet Christine's two little books were popular, too, the proverbs being published by Caxton in an English translation. Christine had a sufficiently good understanding of children to know that verse helps the youthful memory to retain useful precepts. Indeed, a number of her pedagogical ideas seem to have been in advance of her times.

In the program of education she proposes for a young princess in the first part of *The Book of the Three Virtues,* Christine suggests that the governess should tell the child stories to engage her attention and then make use of them to teach her the behavior that is expected of her. She should also play games with the little girl and sometimes give her small, attractive trinkets to win her confidence and affection, so that she can correct her when the need arises without bringing about rebellion. Although Christine had obviously had considerable experience from the upbringing of her own children, it is extraordinary to find her advocating these methods just at the time they were being incorporated into the first humanistic educational programs in Italy. *The Book of the Three Virtues* is contemporary with both Giovanni Dominici's *La Regola del Governo di Cura Familiare (Rule for the Government of Family Care)* and the influential treatise by Petrus Paulus Vergerius entitled *De ingenuis moribus,* written for the Carrera family of Padua. Christine was ten years older than the early humanist educator Guarino da Verona, and she wrote *The Book of the Three Virtues* ten years before Francesco Barbaro's *De Re Uxoria (On Wifely Duties).* One must suspect that Christine's advanced educational ideas were a part of her Italian heritage. Although she was not sufficiently well educated to advocate a program of classical reading as advanced as those developed by the Italian humanists, she nevertheless insisted on the importance of a moral education for civic responsibility based on the lessons of history, mythology, and the example of famous people. Obviously, Christine was familiar with some of Boccaccio's works, but Venice may have been the common bond she shared with the early educators. (pp. 173-75)

After the book for the duke's [John the Fearless's] daughter, Christine's interest turned—or perhaps was directed—toward the education of his son-in-law Louis of Guyenne, the dauphin.

The formation of the "perfect prince" was another favorite concern of humanist writers, who stressed the importance of moral values and civic duty based on a study of the Latin classics. There was no doubt that the dauphin had need of guidance and that Christine's interest in his future was shared by many others. . . . (p. 175)

Christine's first mention of the young dauphin is in a prayer that forms a passage in *Oryson Notre Dame* (*Prayer for Our Lady*), probably written around 1403, where she asks a blessing for his future responsibilities:

> Peace, a good life and a good end
> To my lord, the young dauphin, pray send,
> With wisdom to rule in good fame
> Over the people whose love extends
> To him loyally, and so to such ends
> Like his father, long may he reign.

It is possible to see in these verses the ideal that Christine was to develop at considerable length in *Le Livre du Corps de Policie* (*The Book of the Body Politic*). (p. 177)

Once more following the pattern of dividing the work into three parts, Christine devotes the first to the education of princes, the second to knights and noblemen, and the third to the rest of the social order in which she includes scholars at the University of Paris, merchants, artisans, and laborers.

The idea of the human body as an analogy for the organization of society, the basic concept of the work, is not original with Christine. It had been used by Egidio Colonna, who cited as his source a supposed letter written by Plutarch to the emperor Trajan. It had been repeated by Philippe de Mézières in *The Dream of the Old Pilgrim,* written for the instruction of Charles VI in his youth. Indeed, in his version it is Dame Prudence's attendant Droiture (Rectitude), no doubt the inspiration for Christine's Virtue of the same name, who recounts the story of King Nebuchadnezzar's statue to illustrate the parallel between the structure of society and the human body. Nor was it the first time Christine had made use of the comparison herself. In *The Long Road of Learning* she had written:

> Plutarch said, and leaves the record
> Telling us that civil concord
> Is like a body vivified,
> And as God's gift is sanctified,
> But governed is by Temperance
> From Reason in good ordinance,
> Of which body is the prince the head,
> By which all members will be led,
> For as the head is over all,
> The members must await his call
> Which governs all the rest at will
> Giving commands which then fulfill
> The senses which control the rest.

More recently, the comparison had been used by Gerson in his sermon *"Vivat Rex,"* delivered in November 1405, and it seems probable that Christine was immediately inspired by Gerson, for there are other similarities between his sermon and the first part of *The Book of the Body Politic:* the representation of a king as the good shepherd of his flock, reference to the need to pay French armies so that they do not plunder the population they are supposed to protect, and, especially, a concern for the lot of poor peasants. As in Gerson's sermon, *The Body Politic* contains numerous illustrative examples drawn from the pages of Valerius Maximus. (pp. 177-78)

In common with other treatises on the education of princes, Christine insists on virtue as the only proper basis for ruling

a country. She outlines the qualities he must cultivate in order to prepare for his future responsibilities, but she insists somewhat more than others on his early instruction, saying that it is essential to provide the child with a tutor of excellent character who is capable of instructing him with kindness as well as firmness, teaching him above all to recognize the difference between good and evil, and, if he shows any aptitude, opening for him "the way of philosophy" by introducing him to the pleasure that can come from learning.

At the same time, the young prince should be exposed to more than theory, and as soon as he is capable of understanding what is going on he should be present at meetings of the royal council to hear discussions of the affairs of state. He should also be given the opportunity to learn about other countries and their customs, especially about their governments, and from his contacts with the royal counselors he should learn about the needs of various groups among his subjects. He should learn to appreciate the merits of various social classes, since the welfare of the whole body politic is essential to the well-being of the state. Throughout these instructions reminiscences of Charles V are mingled with examples drawn from Valerius Maximus selected to demonstrate that merit is more important in society than nobility of birth.

After devotion to God and a concern for his subjects untainted by personal interest, the good prince should love justice. In ruling he should be assisted by advisers of high moral character as well as of observable competence. Cicero is quoted to call attention to the fact that such men as these would be inclined to defend the rights of all subjects. Christine also recommends Cicero's advice that young men be excluded from the high councils in favor of more seasoned and experienced counselors.

In her insistence that justice apply to everyone, Christine takes up the cause of the poor and the humble, pointing out with noteworthy courage that it is a disgrace that they should be burdened with heavy taxes from which the rich and powerful are too often exempt. She also speaks out against dishonest tax collectors who feather their own nests at the expense of the poor, citing the superiority of Rome over France in methods of managing such problems.

Of particular interest is the importance accorded to eloquence and oratorical skill in a future ruler, essential for convincing his subjects to do his will. Here Christine cites the talents of Charles V, adding that both Louis of Orleans and Philip of Burgundy had developed oratorical skill to good purpose. This quality was also highly regarded by humanists.

Christine's concept of the perfect prince varies only in detail from the long series of treatises on the subject beginning with Xenophon's *Cyropedia,* written in the fourth century B.C. for the education of Cyrus, the king of Persia. In common with most other writers on the subject, she asserts that the personal moral virtues of the prince affect the prosperity of the land and that Christian goodness can be a cure for human woes.

At the beginning of her book, Christine speaks of the nobles and knights as the arms and hands of the body politic. Turning to these in part two, she bases their value on six principles that she illustrates liberally with examples of Roman leaders drawn from Valerius Maximus and occasionally from Livy. In the first place, knights should love the profession of arms and be willing to devote themselves wholeheartedly to perfecting their skill. In the second place, they should be brave and of such constant courage that they would neither flee from battle nor sacrifice their country to save their own blood. The third condition is that they be prepared to encourage each other and urge their companions on to do their best; the fourth is that they be truthful and faithful to their given word; the fifth that they cherish honor above all worldly things; and the sixth that they be wise and wary not only where the enemy is concerned but in all other military undertakings as well. The ideal that Christine holds out to the knights is not too far removed from the one that would be set forth by Baldassare Castiglione for his courtiers slightly more than a century later. His courtier, too, was to be first of all a good military man.

The second part of **The Book of the Body Politic** would also provide the basis for **Le Livre des Fais d'Armes et de Chevalerie** (**Feats of Arms and of Chivalry**), which Christine wrote two or three years later, and one may well ask what inspired her to write as she did in 1406. (pp. 178-80)

In many respects, the third part of the treatise is the most interesting of all dealing as it does with the common people, about whom so little history has been recorded. They are called the stomach, the legs, and the feet of the body politic, and Christine makes a great point of their importance to the general welfare, dwelling on the necessity of all parts of the body to function harmoniously together. She therefore insists that it is important for all subjects to remain loyal to their rulers and especially to avoid revolting against them. Clearly, the possibility of a civil war is present in her thinking.

Turning to the University of Paris, Christine shifts her attention to the intellectual life of the city, one of its most exhilarating aspects. These chapters underscore once more Christine's genuine devotion to learning and to those who give their lives to the pursuit of knowledge. On the rewards of such a life she comments: ''There is nothing more perfect than to know the truth and the explanation of all things, which is the purpose of knowledge.'' (pp. 180-81)

Focusing her attention next on the merchants, Christine insists on the distinction between wealthy merchants, those who were considered nobles in certain Italian cities, and small businessmen. Her description of the first category quite obviously refers to the Italian merchants and bankers who had established themselves in Paris and with whose life she was familiar, (she had described their wives in **The Book of the Three Virtues**). Here, as elsewhere, she makes it clear that she considers these prosperous merchants a particularly stable and useful element in society because they are able to underwrite the projects of the nobility and even the royalty (they were well known as moneylenders), and at the same time they exercised a calming influence on the volatile nature of artisans and workers. Thus, their cooperation is particularly important to the health of the body politic, and their presence should be welcome, a situation that was not invariably appreciated by the Parisians.

Finally, Christine turns her attention to artisans and agricultural workers. She expresses great respect for the latter, although her sympathy for them is less obvious than for their female counterparts. She honors the dignity of their work, recalling that the common ancestors of all members of society were farmers and shepherds. As for artisans, she praises the quality of their work but expresses considerable reservation about their morals, in particular, their fondness for frequenting taverns. She had already admonished their wives in **The Book of the Three Virtues** against encouraging them in this bad habit. It would appear that bohemian life was already in full flower in Paris at least a generation before François Villon arrived on the scene to immortalize it in his poetry.

In contrast to her disapproval of this undisciplined sort of existence, Christine sees a possibility for contentment in the lives of the poor, perhaps an echo of Boccaccio's *Fates of Illustrious Men*. She points out that they have no reason to fear treason, poison, or robbery.

She ends the book, rather surprisingly, by quoting Ptolemy's *Almagest* to the effect that the happy man is the one who does not care in whose hands the world finds itself, no doubt a consoling thought for anyone living in Paris during the troubled years of 1406 and 1407. More important than prescribing an education that will turn a self-indulged youth into a philosopher-king, Christine is speaking in **The Book of the Body Politic** of the necessity of a society to confront its problems as a unified body, a lesson her contemporaries unfortunately did not heed. (pp. 181-82)

> *Charity Cannon Willard, in her* Christine de Pizan: Her Life and Works, *Persea Books, 1984, 266 p.*

EDITH YENAL (essay date 1988)

[*Yenal is an American literary researcher and bibliographer who is the author of* Charles d'Orléans: A Bibliography of Primary and Secondary Sources (1984). *She is also the first bibliographer of Christine de Pizan. In the following essay from her* Christine de Pizan: Second Edition (1988), *Yenal offers a complete survey of the life and work of Christine, noting her importance not only as a creative writer, but as a cultural teacher and moral influence.*]

As is often noted, Christine de Pizan was one of the best-known and most celebrated literary figures in 15th century France and perhaps in all of late medieval Europe. Her long and illustrious career spanned more than three decades during which she was actively involved in worldly affairs addressing herself to the crucial problems of her time.

Educator of princes, social and political commentator, royal historian . . . Christine spoke with a forceful voice on important issues earning respect in aristocratic and learned circles alike. She occupies a unique place in French letters both as a writer and intellectual arbiter. Largely self-educated and possessed of an invincible spirit, she managed to rise above exceptionally difficult circumstances to become a versatile and highly accomplished lyric poet, a prolific nonfiction writer, and a productive scholar who won renown additionally for her feminism and participation in the quarrel over the *Roman de la Rose* (c. 1236-1276). Her pivotal role in that literary dispute placed her at the center of controversy and debate at a time when women were scarcely allowed to have an opinion let alone express it openly in public. As an author of verse and prose Christine wrote on a variety of subjects, in different genres, making contributions not only to her contemporaries but to the history of ideas.

Born in Venice, Italy c. 1365 into a Bolognese family of academic background, Christine de Pizan was reared near the court of Charles V in Paris where her father, Tommaso di Benvenuto da Pizzano, held a post as an astrologer-physician. He was at the same time a practicing alchemist suspected of having accidentally poisoned members of the royal family. In 1380 at age fifteen Christine was married to a young court notary from Picardy named Etienne de Castel. At twenty-five she was suddenly widowed and left alas with an aging mother, a niece, and several small children to support: a daughter born in 1381 and two sons one of whom seems to have died in infancy, the other being born around 1385. Christine's two brothers, Paolo and Aghinolfo, had in the meantime returned to their native Italy to claim a family inheritance.

Her husband's untimely death (in 1390 during an epidemic) proved to be the turning point of Christine's life. For, as we have learned from her autobiographical writings, this tragic event led not only to her literary career but to a life of study and learning. She would apply herself to both with a singular passion becoming the very model of erudition and scholarship.

Christine turned to writing for personal as well as economic reasons. Other than being left a small sum of money from her late husband's estate—which she was unable to collect for years and then only after prolonged litigation—no financial provisions had been made for her. Neither by her father, who had died on the verge of poverty between 1388 and 1389, nor by her husband. Not able to live by her pen alone Christine is believed to have found employment as a copyist in the medieval booktrade. Her familiarity with manuscripts and bookmaking enabled her later on to supervise the production and illustration of her own manuscripts.

Her career began a few years after Etienne's death, probably around 1393, with a series of poems lamenting her widowhood. These form part of a collection entitled *Cent ballades, Virelais, Rondeaux.* Rueful and melancholy, they tell of the loneliness she suffered as a despondent young widow. After composing her so-called ballades of widowhood Christine wrote on chivalry and courtly love. With the courtly love poems she immediately attracted the attention of the nobility at the French court and became what her biographer, Charity Cannon Willard, has called a "society poet." Her admirers included not only such ducal benefactors as Philip and John of Burgundy, Louis of Orleans, and that renowned collector of illuminated manuscripts, Jean of Berry, but the king of France, Charles VI and his consort, queen Isabeau of Bavaria.

From 1399 to 1405 Christine brought out several love debates among them the *Débat de deux amans* (c. 1400) and the *Livre des trois jugemens* (c. 1400); a pastourelle, the *Dit de la pastoure* (1403); and a long courtly romance, the *Livre du duc des vrais amans* (1404-1405), in which she upholds marriage and cautions women about the "dangers" of courtly love. Viewing courtly love from a uniquely feminine perspective, Christine often portrayed it as disillusioning if not traumatic experience for women.

After 1403 she seems less interested in courtly themes turning instead toward larger and more serious subjects, and increasingly toward prose and didactic writing. The earliest compositions signaling this change are the *Livre du chemin de long estude* (1402-1403) and the *Livre de la mutacion de Fortune* (1403). These two encyclopedic works, though still in verse, contain social criticism and reveal Christine's considerable knowledge of history and geography. In the *Chemin de long estude* she undertakes an allegorical voyage that has been likened to Dante's journey in the *Divine Comedy*. In the *Mutacion de Fortune* she presents a universal history and introduces the theme of poverty, a theme not very extensively treated in French literature prior to Christine.

It was with long philosophical compositions like the *Mutacion* and *Long estude*—as well as with her autobiographical *Avision* (1405) and the treatises on government, peace, and military strategy—that Christine acquired a reputation as a scholar and came to be compared to Boethius whose *Consolatione Philosophiae* she had read and drawn inspiration from. On the basis (presumably) of her learned *Mutacion*, which she presented to

the regent Philip of Burgundy in January 1404, he commissioned her to write the official biography of his later brother, king Charles V. Completed on 30 November 1404, the *Livre des fais et bonnes meurs du sage roy Charles V* chronicles well-known figures and events from Charles's reign. It is the only history Christine ever wrote.

As stated earlier, Christine was both successful and prolific. By 1406 she had already written close to a dozen major pieces and by the end of her career filled scores of manuscripts. Altogether she left some three hundred ballades, over sixty-three rondeaux, six virelais, two lais, and a collection of seventy jeux à vendre, not to mention the allegories, epistolary works and didactic treatises cited below. Her collected writings are preserved at the British Library, London in MS Harley 4431, the Queen's (Isabeau) manuscript. Famed for its frontispiece and outstanding miniatures, of which there are 130, Harley is codicologically important having been identified as an autograph manuscript.

Following the conventions of her day Christine often placed her ideas in an archaic allegorical framework. However her message was always timely. She tried above all to imbue her aristocratic patrons with a sense of justice and appeal to their nobler instincts. In an age where courtly love was the dominant literary theme Christine offered her readers a series of moral precepts, the *Enseignemens moraux* (1400-1401). In the *Livre du chemin de long estude* (1402-03) she set out to popularize science; in the *Livre de la paix* (1412-1413), politics. The *Livre de la prod'hommie de l'homme* (c. 1405-1406) deals with virtue and vice; the *Epistre d'Othea* (1400) with the ideals of knighthood.

In the *Epistre d'Othea* as in other didactic works Christine uses models from mythology and the classics. Her attempt to revive the spirit of antiquity is what linked her to the movement of humanism. Because her writings were among the earliest in France to embrace a humanistic philosophy, modern scholars have come to view Christine as one of the first humanists of the French Renaissance. Her humanistic thinking is especially evident in the political treatise the *Livre du corps de policie* (1406-1407), which falls into the same class of didactic works as Erasmus's *The Education of a Christian Prince* (1516). But as the late Diane Bornstein has pointed out, *Policie* is ironically more often associated with chivalric idealism than with humanism.

As we know, Christine had occasion to correspond with the early French humanists at the beginning of the 15th century when she became involved in a literary dispute over the most popular work of the Middle Ages, the *Roman de la Rose* (c. 1236-1276). Backed by Jean Gerson, the influential Chancellor of the University of Paris, Guillaume de Tignonville, the Provost of Paris, and the Marshal Boucicaut, she accused the author of the second part of the *Roman*, Jean de Meun, of misogyny and immorality. De Meun's apologists—the Provost of Lille, Jean de Montreuil and two royal secretaries named Pierre and Gontier Col—tried, unsuccessfully, to get Christine to recant. They wrote rude letters to her but she replied with irony and wit. Refusing steadfastly to let these eminent humanists convert or intimidate her, she would continue to denounce the sexist writings of Jean de Meun to the very end.

It was under these somewhat unusual circumstances that Christine de Pizan became the first woman of her age to come forward and defend her sex, publicly and in writing, against the foremost intellectuals in France; and further, to raise questions about women that would be debated for the next five centuries starting with the *querelle des femmes* in the Renaissance and going right up to our own day.

Christine presents her eloquent defense of women in four different works: in the *Epistre au dieu d'Amours* (1399), an epistle in verse in which she attacks clerics and misogynic authors; in the *Dit de la Rose* (1402), a poem defending women's honor and condemning the practice of defaming them; in the *Epistres sur le Roman de la Rose* (1401-1403), a collection of polemical letters issuing from the above quarrel; and in the *Livre de la cité des dames* (1405), her most explicit feminist piece. The latter has probably contributed more to Christine's reputation as a feminist than any other single work. Besides being one of the first histories of women, it is the only writing in which she specifically asks for the right of an education for women. In the *Livre des trois vertus* (1405), a follow-up to the *Cité,* Christine does not, oddly, attempt to justify or rehabilitate women. Instead she outlines their roles and responsibilities in society.

Although the two latter works differ in style and content, the notion that women can and have made contributions to the world is implicit in both. Acutely aware of women's low status in medieval society, Christine was determined to redefine the feminine image and help women gain greater self-esteem.

Yet not all of Christine's ideas on women were progressive, as critics who charge her with conservatism are quick to point out. Even in the *Cité des dames,* a book whose aim it is to affirm and celebrate women, instances of feminine subservience can be found. A case in point is the Griselda tale which appears in Part II, chaps. 11.1 and 50.1-4 of the *Cité.* In none of Christine's writings are women urged to abandon their traditional roles or strike out in new directions. Christine did not recommend for women to enter "men's" professions as she had done; nor did she ever propose equal rights for women. To claim that she was a feminist in any modern sense would therefore be misleading.

Still, whether one regards Christine de Pizan as a feminist trailblazer or as a defender of the status quo, her views on women were entirely consistent with her humanistic attitudes and beliefs. For in the end Christine was both a humanist and a humanitarian concerned with the dignity and worth of all human beings, and that included women.

While Christine's final work still pays homage to a woman, she would devote the latter part of her career to the causes of her adopted country rather than her sex. Her writings on the political affairs of France—with which she deals in the *Epistre à la reine* (1405), the *Lamentacion sur les maux de la France* (1410), and again in the *Livre de la paix* (1412-1413)—these compositions form an important genre within the body of her work. They not only reflect the political realities of 15th century France but chart her literary development, showing how her writings evolved from the first love lyrics penned for her patrons' diversion to the later prose works in which she analyzes French society.

After writing the *Epistre de la prison de vie humaine* (1414-1418), a consolatory letter destined for her friend the duchess Marie of Berry, she composed a religious piece based on the Scriptures, the *Heures de contemplation sur la Passion de Nostre Seigneur* (c. 1420-1424). Christine's career came to a close with a tribute to France's national heroine, Joan of Arc. Her lengthy poem, the *Ditié de Jehanne d'Arc,* is said to have been the only work in French to appear before Joan's condemnation and burning at the stake in 1431. Written in exile from the

Poissy convent to which she had fled a decade earlier to escape the bloody French civil war, the *Ditié* is Christine's last-known work. Upon its completion on 31 July 1429 she vanishes from sight never to be heard from again. It is thought that she died sometime around 1430 at the age of sixty-five but her actual date of death has really never been confirmed.

During her own lifetime and in the century after her death Christine de Pizan was held in high esteem. In England the advent of printing created a vogue for her work resulting in the translation and publication of five of her books: *The Epistle of Othea to Hector, or, the Boke of Knyghthode* (c. 1440-1459), *The Morale Proverbes of Cristyne* (1478), *The Book of Fayttes of Armes and of Chyualrye* (1489 or 1490), *The Boke of the Cyte of Ladyes* (between 1509 and 1521), the *The Body of Polycye* (1521). William Caxton himself had translated one and printed two of these volumes at his Westminster Abbey press in London in the final years of the 15th century. Among other Englishmen expressing an interest in Christine were the Earl of Salisbury and kings Henry IV, Edward IV, and Henry VII, as well as the English writers William Worcester and Thomas Hoccleve; in short, many of the notables of the day. Nor was her fame solely confined to France or England, as already indicated. In Flanders, Italy, Spain and Portugal too her works were copied and translated.

After the 16th century however when literary tastes began to change Christine finally fell out of favor. The majority of her writings remained thus in manuscript for over three hundred years. It was not until the 18th century that a handful of French scholars such as Boivin le Cadet, the abbé Lebeuf, and Mlle. de Kéralio rediscovered Christine and published extracts of her works. In the 19th century Raimon Thomassy and his *Essai sur les écrits politiques de Christine de Pisan* (1838) contributed significantly to the revival of interest in Christine, as did the work of her first modern editor, Maurice Roy, whose three-volume edition of the *Oeuvres poétiques de Christine de Pisan* was published in Paris from 1886 to 1896.

During the first quarter of the 20th century there appeared a number of feminist studies on Christine by the French and German scholars Rose Rigaud, Dora Melegari, and Mathilde Kastenberg; as well as surveys of her writings by Fred P. Henry, Carl Baerwolff, and the noted Belgian jurist Ernest Nys. These publications were to be followed in 1927 by Marie-Josèphe Pinet's *Christine de Pisan . . . étude biographique et littéraire,* a pioneering work of 463 pages which despite its flaws has now become a classic.

While it is true that Christine de Pizan has always enjoyed a certain international following, she did not really attract a sizable audience until the women's movement began calling attention to her in the 1960s. By the early seventies her name was appearing regularly in women's literature and latter-day feminists were eager to claim Christine and make her into one of their "mothers to think back through"—a phrase borrowed from Virginia Woolf but more recently taken up by the Canadian scholar Sheila Delany who considers Christine too conservative to be a role model for modern women authors. Just the same, feminist critics view this medieval writer as part of their literary heritage and as a major figure in women's history.

Aside from being indebted to contemporary feminism Christine's current popularity owes something too to interdisciplinary scholarship and its present fascination with the later Middle Ages. This resurging interest in the medieval period has in effect helped further the cause of Pizan Studies, bringing Christine de Pizan critical attention not only from feminists or traditional students of French language and literature but from scholars in every field: medievalists, literary and cultural historians, art historians (for the illuminated manuscripts), political scientists and, not least, bibliographers.

Old-school French critics like Gustave Lanson, who once dismissed Christine as an ''insufferable bluestocking'' but whose views have since lost credibility, seem clearly to have been overruled by modern scholarship.

For today, Christine de Pizan is recognized as an important writer of world literature. Her writings, half a millennium after her death, continue thus to be read, edited, translated, and anthologized. If some of her works seem dated now—those on chivalry and courtly love especially—others, with more universal themes, appear surprisingly modern. What Christine had to say about the human condition (in the **Mutacion,** the **Avision, Vie humaine**) is still relevant. As are her observations on ethics and morality, good and bad rulers, loss and bereavement, misogyny, the eternal battle of the sexes, and a host of other subjects.

In grappling with these basic questions Christine de Pizan has shown herself as an imaginative and critical thinker. History will remember her not only as France's ''first women of letters'' but as a committed writer whose teachings and moral influence were perhaps as significant as her literary achievement.

Edith Yenal, ''Introduction, Part II,'' in her Christine de Pizan: Second Edition, *to be published by Scarecrow Press, Inc., Metuchen, N.J., 1989.*

ADDITIONAL BIBLIOGRAPHY

Bornstein, Diane. Introduction to *The Middle English Translation of Christine de Pisan's Livre du Corps de Policie*, by Christine de Pizan, edited by Diane Bornstein, pp. 8-38. Heidelberg: Carl Winter Universitatsverlag, 1977.
    Explicates *The Body of Policye*, analyzing and comparing French and Middle English manuscripts of the work.

Buhler, Curt F. Introduction to *The Epistle of Othea*, by Christine de Pisan, translated by Stephen Scrope, pp. xi-xxxii. London: Oxford University Press, 1970.
    Detailed account in which Buhler examines the numerous French manuscripts of *The Epistle of Othea*.

Davis, Natalie Zemon. ''Gender and Genre: Women as Historical Writers, 1400-1820.'' In *Beyond Their Sex: Women of the European Past*, edited by Patricia H. Labalme, pp. 153-82. New York: New York University Press, 1980.
    Briefly discusses Christine's roles as historical writer and defender of women's inherent abilities.

Delaney, Sheila. ''Rewriting Woman Good: Gender and the Anxiety of Influence in Two Late-Medieval Texts.'' In *Chaucer in the Eighties*, edited by Julian N. Wasserman and Robert J. Blanch, pp. 75-92. Syracuse: Syracuse University Press, 1986.
    Compares Chaucer's and Christine's literary attempts to portray women favorably, opposing negative portrayals by other writers.

Gabriel, Astrik L. ''The Educational Ideas of Christine de Pizan.'' *Journal of the History of Ideas* XVI, No. 1 (January 1955): 3-21.
    Discusses Christine's educational philosophy for women, describing her as ''one of the great moralists in Christian literature.''

Hindman, Sandra L. ''With Ink and Mortar: Christine de Pizan's *Cite des Dames* (An Art Essay).'' *Feminist Studies* 10, No. 3 (Fall 1984): 457-84.
    Questions Christine's part in the artistic aspects of her manuscripts and debates whether the ''female'' features of her work actually extend to the production and illustration of manuscripts.

Kelly, F. Douglas. ''Reflections on the Role of Christine de Pisan as a Feminist Writer.'' *Sub Stance,* No. 3 (Winter 1972): 63-71.
    Considers how Christine came to be labelled a feminist, concluding that she was not a true feminist, but instead, a woman who improved the image of her sex by writing anti-antifeminist literature.

Kemp-Welch, Alice. Translators's note to *The Book of the Duke of True Lovers,* by Christian de Pizan, edited by Alice Kemp-Welch, pp. ix-xv. New York: Cooper Square Publishers, Inc., 1966.
    Examines the probable historical sources of Christine's tale.

Laidlaw, J. C. ''Christine de Pizan—An Author's Progress.'' *The Modern Language Review* 78, No. 3 (July 1983): 532-50.
    Analyzes the textual revisions made by Christine in manuscripts presented to Queen Isabelle, wife of Charles VI.

———. ''Christine de Pizan—A Publisher's Progress.'' *The Modern Language Review* 82, No. 1 (January 1987): 35-75.
    Reveals the importance of Christine's role in planning and preparing copies of her manuscripts intended for wealthy patrons.

Lawson, Sarah. Introduction to *The Treasure of the City of Ladies or The Book of the Three Virtues*, by Christine de Pizan, pp. 15-26. Hammondsworth, England: Penguin Books, 1985.
    In-depth explication of Christine's *The Treasure of the City of Ladies*.

Margolis, Nadia. ''The Human Prison: The Metamorphoses of Misery in the Poetry of Christine de Pizan, Charles d'Orleans, and François Villon.'' In *Fifteenth Century Studies*, Vol. 1, edited by Guy R. Mermier and Edelgard E. DuBruck, pp. 185-92. Ann Arbor, Michigan: University Microfilms International, 1978.
    Examines Christine's use of prison imagery in her poetry.

———. ''Christine de Pizan: The Poetess as Historian.'' *Journal of the History of Ideas* 47, No. 3 (July-September 1986): 361-75.
    Discusses Christine's feminine perspective in her works, comparing her writings with those of several male historians and philosophers.

Phillippy, Patricia A. ''Establishing Authority: Boccaccio's *De Claris Mulieribus* and Christine de Pizan's *Le Livre de la Cité des Dames*.'' *Romanic Review* LXXVII, No. 3 (May 1986): 167-94.
    Compares Christine's and Boccaccio's works and examines the problem of her quoting a male authority when attempting to prove the misrepresentation of women by male authors.

Power, Eileen. *Medieval Women*, pp. 12ff. London: Cambridge University Press, 1975.
    Study of medieval women which includes interesting biographical and comparative material about Christine.

Richards, Earl Jeffrey. ''Christine de Pizan and Dante: A Reexamination.'' *Archiv für das Studium der Neueren Sprachen und Literaturen* 222, No. 1 (1985): 100-11.
    Reexamines the critical opinion that Christine had only a limited understanding of Dante's work and was unimaginative in her use of his *Commedia*.

Toynbee, Paget. ''Christine de Pisan and Sir John Maundeville.'' *Romania* XXI (1892): 228-39.
    Examines Christine's apparent use of the *Travels of Sir John Maundeville* in her *Le Livre du Chemin de Long Estude*.

Wilkins, Nigel. ''The Structure of Ballades, Rondeaux and Virelais in Froissart and in Christine de Pisan.'' *French Studies* XXIII, No. 4 (October 1969): 337-48.
    Attempts to determine the influence of musical formats on Jean Froissart's and Christine's ballades, rondeaux, and virelais to dis-

cern whether the fourteenth- and fifteenth-century verse patterns were rigidly fixed.

Willard, Charity Cannon. *The ''Livre de la paix'' of Christine de Pisan*. The Hague: Mouton & Co., 1958, 219 p.

   Provides critical insight into the historical events and people that influenced Christine's decision to write *Le livre de la paix*. The essay includes an explanation of the text and notes Christine's literary sources.

———. ''Christine de Pisan's 'Clock of Temperance'.'' *L'Esprit Createur* II, No. 3 (Fall 1962): 149-54.

   Discusses Christine's original concept of the clock as a moral symbol of the cardinal virtues.

———. ''The Manuscript Tradition of the *Livre des Trois Vertus* and Christine de Pizan's Audience.'' *Journal of the History of Ideas* XXVII, No. 3 (July-September 1966): 433-44.

   Traces the book's manuscript history and questions for whom the work was intended.

Nur ud-din 'Abd-ur-raḥman ibn Aḥmad Jami

1414-1492

(Also known as al-Mawlá 'Abd al-Rahmán al-Jámí, Mullá Núru' d-Dín 'Abdu'r-Rahmán Jámí, Mauláná 'Abdu'r-rahmán Jami, and Nur al-Din 'Abd al-Rahman Jami) Persian poet, essayist, critic, and biographer.

Jami is considered the last eminent figure of the classical age of Persian literature, a period that encompasses the ninth through fifteenth centuries in an area roughly the equivalent of present-day Iran. He wrote on a wide variety of subjects in both verse and prose: astronomy, mysticism, grammar, and rhetoric are but a few of the topics he treated in his nonfiction works, and he was a prolific verse adapter of traditional Islamic tales and legends. He was also a scholar and theologian of the first order, and his erudite works—including numerous short biographies and much criticism of Persian scholarship—are deemed among the best examples of classical Persian learning.

Jami's life spanned almost the entire fifteenth century and is well documented. He was born in Kharjird, a town in the district of Jam, in 1414. As a boy he was instructed by Junayd al-Usuli, a celebrated rhetorician, at the Nizamiyah School in Herat. Jami excelled in his studies, assimilating the knowledge of Junayd and other masters and learning to confute his teachers in argument. To pursue further education, Jami went to Samarqand to study under the astronomer Qáḍí-Zádah al-Rúmí. Here again he excelled, causing Qáḍí-Zádah to claim that no equal of Jami had ever crossed the river Oxus into Samarqand since its founding. Around this time Jami began the serious study of Sufism, or Muslim mysticism, and was initiated into the ascetic Naqshbandí order of mystics. He devoted the following years to intense study, associating himself with the most esteemed Sufi thinkers of the age. Although he had yet to write his greatest works, Jami was highly regarded at this time among Persian intellectuals for both his correspondence and conversation.

Jami's later life was spent mainly in Herat at the court of Sultan Husayn Báyqará, the Timurid ruler of Khurásán. As one of many scholars and poets at the court, Jami was exposed to Persian culture more deeply than before and developed a serious interest in writing literature. He produced little at first, but after age sixty he increasingly devoted himself to writing and soon acquired fame throughout the Islamic world. In 1474 he began a pilgrimage to Mecca. On the way he was accused of expressing hostility toward the Shi'ites in one of his works, but, by showing that the offending passage had, in fact, been slipped into Jami's manuscript by a malicious enemy, he publicly demonstrated the falseness of the charge and thereby achieved even greater renown than he had been accorded before. Back in Herat after completing the pilgrimage, Jami apparently wrote assiduously, producing most of his greatest poetry during the last decade of his life. He wrote what is probably his best-known work, the poetry cycle *Haft Aurang* ("Seven Thrones"), composed important works on Sufism, and, at the bidding of Ottoman sultan Mohammed II, wrote *al-Durrah al-Fákhirah (The Precious Pearl)*, a treatise on contemporary philosophy and mysticism. He died in Herat in 1492 and was buried alongside his spiritual guide, Sa'd al-Dín al-Káshgharí.

Jami wrote in two languages, employing Persian for nearly all his poetry and Arabic for much of his prose. Early estimates of the number of his works range from thirty-seven to ninety-nine; contemporary scholars put the number in the forties, although a few of the known works are no longer extant. Most of Jami's writings are concerned to some degree with Sufism; indeed, some of them, especially the prose pieces, treat the subject directly and at length. Jami's chief prose works are *Nafaḥát al-Uns* ("Breaths of Familiarity") and *Lawá' ih*, the former a collection of 616 biographies of noteworthy scholars, saints, and poets considered mystics, the latter a lengthy treatise on the life of the Sufi. In *Lawá'ih* Jami argues, as had others before him, that God's presence in the soul is possible only when the supplicant acknowledges the self to be a delusion. This is the principal teaching of the Sufis and a theme that occurs throughout Jami's works. It is the subject, for example, of *The Precious Pearl*, which treats the respective intellectual merits and faults of the Sufis, the theologians, and the philosophers. Jami is also noted as the author of other prose, including a study of Arabic grammar, a treatise on rhyme and poetry, exegeses of the Koran, a commentary on Iraqi's *Lama' át*, a study of the prophet Mohammed entitled *Shawáhidu'n-Nubuwwat* ("Evidences of Prophethood"), and *Baháristán (Abode of Spring)*, an eight-book composition in prose and verse written in imitation of the *Gulistán* of Sa'di. These works, however, are not generally considered as important as *Nafaḥát al-Uns* and *Lawá' ih* and have not been discussed at length by critics writing in English.

Although Jami is noted for his prose, it is as a poet that he has achieved his greatest reputation. His principal work in this field is *Haft Aurang*, a collection of seven *masnaví*, or idylls, composed between 1468 and 1485 in emulation of the *Khamsa* of Niẓámí. As in Jami's prose, the undercurrent here is one of Sufism, but the idylls are more self-consciously artistic than the prose and are deemed the best examples of Jami's literary ability. Two of the seven poems stand out as Jami's finest work in the genre: *Salámán u Absál (Salámán and Absál)* and *Yúsuf u Zulaikhá (Yúsuf and Zulaikha)*. *Salámán and Absál* is believed to be based on Túsí's summary of the Hellenistic romance of the same name in which a youth becomes the passionate lover of his nurse. Jami's version is longer and more elaborate but, like Túsí's, is an allegory of how the soul can be made independent of sensual lusts. Most readings of the poem see Salámán's love of Absál as that of the rational soul for physical pleasure, with Salámán's emergence alone from the fire in which the despairing lovers have cast themselves as evidence of his liberation from bondage to Absál. Similarly, *Yúsuf and Zulaikha* treats pure and impure love. The story is based on the tale of Joseph and Potiphar's wife as told in the Koran—a favorite theme among Persian authors before Jami. It tells of noble Zulaikha's impure love for Joseph, a slave boy of extraordinary beauty, virtue, and purity. Joseph resists Zulaikha's advances and rises to become the king's chief advisor. Meanwhile, Zulaikha's circumstances are much reduced: she becomes a ragged widow, obsessed with fondling a statue she has had made of Joseph. In time, however, Zulaikha's fleshly love is transformed into a spiritual one and, in a passage noted for its intense mysticism, her beauty is restored, she weds Joseph, and devotes herself to religion. The message of the work—that the life of the soul is infinitely superior to the life of the flesh—is carried over to the remaining five idylls of *Haft Aurang: Silsilatu'dh-Dhabab* ("Chain of Gold") discusses the unity of God and the teachings of the Prophet; *Tuhfat al-Ahrár* ("Gift of the Free") is a collection of didactic eulogies and discourses on the well-lived life; *Subhat al-Abrár* ("Rosary of the Pious") is addressed to Jami's five-year-old son and is strongly moralistic and pedagogical; *Lailá u Majnún* ("Lailá and Majnún") is an adaptation of a desert love story marked by its didactic intent; and *Khirad-náma-yi Iskandarí* ("Wisdom of Alexander") sententiously treats the ancient legend of Alexander the Great. In addition to the seven idylls of *Haft Aurang*, Jami wrote three lyrical *díváns*, or collections of minor verse, notable for their almost mathematical refinement. The *díváns* are comprised mainly of *ghazals*—short lyrical exercises usually on the theme of love—and are extremely ornate. These works, like Jami's major writings and much other Persian literature of the period, are often derivative, but critics note that Jami's handling of the material is almost always original.

In his day Jami was esteemed as one of the greatest living writers of Persia. He was plied with gifts and favors by persons of every rank and class and elaborately entertained at sumptuous banquets given in his honor. As a Sufi, however, he was uncomfortable with such worldly displays of affection, and his early biographers note that he did nothing to promote himself. Nevertheless, his reputation spread, and by the time of his death he was apparently already the subject of several short biographies. The next fifty years saw a proliferation of manuscripts of Jami's writings as well as a steady stream of praise for the author's achievements in prose and poetry alike. With the passage of time, however, new writers gradually supplanted Jami in popularity, and the dissemination of his works decreased. Outside the Islamic world, interest in Jami began almost with the commencement of regular Western contact; the celebrated eighteenth-century English orientalist Sir William Jones, for example, ranked Jami as one of the best Persian poets. Jones's successors have generally concurred with this assessment and have labored to introduce Jami to a wide audience, translating several of the major works into English and commenting on them. But with the exception of a decade or so during the nineteenth century when the English poet and translator Edward FitzGerald actively promoted Jami's writings, the audience for the works has been confined mostly to specialists and ardent students of Sufism. Still, a few of Jami's minor poems have been anthologized in translation during the present century, and the major works have been discussed in several short studies in English. Today Jami is considered a significant Persian poet and an important exponent of Islamic thought, but not one of the preeminent figures of Near-Eastern literature.

Praised by a contemporary as "unrivalled in his day for esoteric and exoteric learning," Jami is now known as an important witness of the literary and cultural life of his age. He wrote enduring scholarly works on subjects of interest to academics and students of Sufism alike, and his major poetry—hugely popular in its day—continues to entertain and instruct a small but discerning group of English-speaking readers. According to Edward G. Browne, these achievements make Jami a polymath of uncommon distinction, for "though he may have been equalled or even surpassed by others in each of the numerous realms of literature which he cultivated, no other Persian poet or writer has been so successful in so many different

fields, and the enthusiastic admiration of his most eminent contemporaries is justified by his prolific and many-sided genius.''

*PRINCIPAL WORKS

Naqdu'n Nuşúş (criticism) 1458-59
Naqd al-Nuşúş fí Sharh Naqsh al-Fuşúş (essay) 1460
Nafahát al-Uns min Hadarát al-Quds (biographical sketches) 1476-78
†*Fátihat al-Shabáb* (poetry) 1479
‡*Salámán u Absál* (poetry) 1479-80
  [*Salámán and Absál: An Allegory*, 1856]
Shawáhidu'n-Nubuwwat (essay) 1480
Ashi''atu'l-Lama'át (criticism) 1480-81
§*al-Durrah al-Fákhirah* (essay) 1481
  [*The Precious Pearl*, 1979]
‡*Tuhfat al-Ahrár* (poetry) 1481
‡*Subhat al-Abrár* (poetry) 1482
‡*Yúsuf u Zulaikhá* (poetry) 1483
  [*Analysis and Specimens of the "Joseph and Zulaikha"* [partial translation], 1873; also published as *Yúsuf and Zulaikha*, 1882; and *The Book of Joseph and Zuleika*, 1892]
‡*Lailá u Majnún* (poetry) 1484
‡*Khirad-náma-yi Iskandarí* (poetry) 1485
‡*Silsilatu'dh-Dhahab* (poetry) 1485
‖*Baháristán* (essay) 1486-87
  [*Persian Wit and Humour: Being the Sixth Book of the Baháristán* [partial translation], 1883; also published as *The Beháristán (Abode of Spring)*, 1887]
†*Wásitat al-Iqd* (poetry) 1489
al-Fawá'id al-Diyá'íyah (essay) 1491
†*Khátimat al-Hayát* (poetry) 1491
Lawámi (criticism) 1491
#*Lawá'ih* (essay) 1906
Jami: The Persian Mystic (poetry) 1907
The Persian Mystics: Jami (poetry and prose) 1908
Divan (poetry) 1938
#"*Al-Jámí's Treatise on Existence*" (essay) 1979; published in *Islamic Philosophical Theology*

*Jami's works were originally disseminated in manuscript form, and many of them remain unpublished today. Jami appears to have given titles only to his major works, and no complete, authoritative list of his writings has yet been compiled. Titles of minor works therefore often differ from copy to copy. Jami often recorded the date for the completion of a work; where he did not do so, scholars have tentatively assigned dates according to the available evidence. With the exception of translations and modern editions, the dates given here are therefore composition dates, not publication dates.

†These works are known collectively as *Divans*.

‡These works are known collectively as *Sab'a* ("Septet") and *Haft Aurang* ("Seven Thrones").

§This work is also known as *Risálah fí Tahqíq Madhhab al-Şufíyah wa-al-Mutakallimín wa-al-Hukamá* and *Risálat al-Muhákamát*.

‖This work is also transliterated as *Beháristán*.

#The composition dates of these works are uncertain.

MULLÁ NÚRU'D-DÍN 'ABDU'R-RAHMÁN JÁMÍ   (poem date 1479)

[*In the following excerpt from Edward FitzGerald's translation of* Salámán and Absál, *Jami looks back on his literary career, lamenting his present old age and feebleness.*]

> And yet, how long, O Jámí, stringing Verse,
> Pearl after pearl, on that old Harp of thine?
> Year after year attuning some new Song,
> The breath of some old Story? Life is gone,
> And that last song is not the last; my Soul
> Is spent—and still a Story to be told!
> And I, whose back is crooked as the Harp
> I still keep tuning through the Night till Day!
> That harp untuned by Time—the harper's hand
> Shaking with Age—how shall the harper's hand
> Repair its cunning, and the sweet old harp
> Be modulated as of old? Methinks
> 'Twere time to break and cast it in the fire;
> The vain old harp, that, breathing from its strings
> No music more to charm the ears of men,
> May, from its scented ashes, as it burns,
> Breathe resignation to the Harper's soul,
> Now that his body looks to dissolution.
> My teeth fall out—my two eyes see no more
> Till by Feringhí glasses turn'd to four;
> Pain sits with me sitting behind my knees,
> From which I hardly rise unhelpt of hand;
> I bow down to my root, and like a Child
> Yearn, as is likely, to my Mother Earth,
> Upon whose bosom I shall cease to weep,
> And on my Mother's bosom fall asleep.

> *Mullá Núru'd-Dín 'Abdu'r-Rahmán Jámí, "Jámí Laments His Old Age and Feebleness," translated by Edward FitzGerald, in* The Asiatic Review, *Vol. XLIII, October, 1947, p. 347.*

MULLÁ NÚRU'D-DÍN 'ABDU'R-RAHMÁN JÁMÍ   (essay date 1480)

[*In the following excerpt from the preface to* Ashi''atu'l-Lama'át, *Jami explains how he came to write the work.*]

It is represented that at the time when the learned, practising, gnostic lover, the author of excellent prose and admirable verse, that cup-bearer of the bowl of generosity to men of high aspirations, Fakhru'd-Dín Ibráhím of Hamadán, commonly known as 'Iráqí, attained to the society of that Exemplar of learned seekers after Truth and that Model of Unitarian Gnostics Abu'l-Ma'álí Ṣadru'l-Ḥaqq Wa'l-Millat wa'd-Dín Muḥammad of Qúnya (may God most High sanctify their secrets!), and heard from him the truths contained in the *Fuṣúṣu'l-Ḥikam*, he compiled a short manual, which, inasmuch as it comprised several "flashes" from the lightnings of these truths, he entitled *Lama'át*. Therein, in pleasant phrases and with charming allusions, he flung together jewels of verse and prose and mingled aphorisms Arabic and Persian, from which the signs of learning and wisdom were apparent, and in which the lights of taste and ecstasy were manifest, such as might awaken the sleeper, render him who is awakened cognizant of the mysteries, kindle the fire of Love and put in motion the chain of longing.

But since the author ['Iráqí] had become the target of the tongues of '*the vilifiers of sundry men of good repute*,' and had suffered at the hands of '*certain ill-conditioned wanderers from the path*,' the blindly orthodox have imposed on him the stigma of repudiation, and withdrawn from him the skirt of acceptance. This humble writer also, in view of this rejection

and repudiation, abstained from preoccupying himself therewith; until the most illustrious of the 'Brethren of Purity' in this country, and the most glorious of the friends of constancy (may God cause him to walk in the ways of His adept servants!), whose auspicious name has been enunciated in the course of this prayer in the best form of enigma and allusion between God and His servants, requested me to collate and correct the text thereof; which request could only be met with obedience. When I entered on this business, and ran over the details of its component parts, I saw in every leaf thereof a 'Flash' from the lights of Truths, and perceived in every page a gust of the declaration of Divine Wisdom. The heart was attracted to the understanding of its subtleties, and the mind was troubled at the difficulty of comprehending its purport. Manuscripts of the text differed, and some of them appeared to be perverted from the path of accuracy. In certain cases of concision and passages of difficulty reference was made to the commentaries on it; but neither was any difficulty solved thereby, nor in any of them was any concise statement properly amplified. As a necessary consequence, this thought passed through a heart disposed to the understanding of subtleties, and this wish established itself in a mind regardful of the essence of truths, that, to correct its sentences and elucidate its hints, a commentary should be compiled gleaned from the sayings of the elders of the Path and leaders in the Truth, especially those two great Shaykhs Muḥyi'd-Dín Muḥammad ibnu'l-'Arabí and his disciple and pupil Ṣadru'd-Dín Muḥammad of Qúnya and their followers (may God most High sanctify their secrets!). So, in consequence of these promptings, the mind decided on undertaking this difficult task, which it brought to a conclusion, by the assistance of God's Grace, in the shortest time. And since most of the statements which are included in this commentary are of the kind which have shone forth upon the heart from the consideration of the luminous words of the text, it is proper that it should be named **Rays of the "Flashes,"** and should be represented to the eyes of students by this description. It is hoped of such as regard justly, though not of scoffers characterized by obstinacy, that when they take this manual into their consideration, and devote their thoughts to its perusal, wherever they see aught of goodness and perfection they will account it the gift of God (Glory be to Him and exalted is He!), whilst wherever they find any fault or defect they will attribute it to the impotence and shortcomings of humanity; and that they will not specially make the humble author a target for the arrows of reproach, nor cast themselves into the vortex of evil-seeking and evil-saying. *We ask aid from God, to whom be glory!* (pp. 445-47)

> *Mullá Núru'd-Dín 'Abdu'r-Rahmán Jámí, in an extract in* A Literary History of Persia: The Tartar Dominion (1265-1502), *Vol. III by Edward G. Browne, 1929. Reprint by Cambridge at the University Press, 1956, pp. 445-47.*

ZAHIRU'D-DÍN MUHAMMAD BÁBUR PÁDSHÁH GHÁZÍ (essay date 1505)

[*Zahíru'd-dín Muhammad, commonly known by his Mongol nickname Bábur (literally, "Tiger"), was the founder of the Mogul dynasty of India and a prolific poet and autobiographer. His greatest literary work is held to be* Bábur-náma, *a long autobiography written in Chaghatay Turkish in which he vividly recorded the stormy events of his daily life. In the following excerpt from a passage in this work dated 1505-06, he praises Jami for his literary and intellectual accomplishments.*]

[Included among the Herī celebrities of the day] were Sl. Ḥusain Mīrza's retainers and followers. His was a wonderful Age; in it Khurāsān, and Herī above all, was full of learned and matchless men. Whatever the work a man took up, he aimed and aspired at bringing that work to perfection. One such man was Maulānā 'Abdu'r-raḥmān *Jāmī*, who was unrivalled in his day for esoteric and exoteric knowledge. Famous indeed are his poems! The Mulla's dignity it is out of my power to describe; it has occurred to me merely to mention his honoured name and one atom of his excellence, as a benediction and good omen for this part of my humble book.

> *Zahiru'd-dīn Muhammad Bābur Pādshāh Ghāzī, in a memoir of 1505 to 1506, in his* The Bābur-nāma *in English (Memoirs of Bābur), Vol. I, translated by Annette Susannah Beveridge, 1922. Reprint by AMS Press, Inc., 1971, p. 283.*

'ABD AL-GHAFŪR AL-LÁRÍ   (essay date 1506?)

[*'Abd al-Ghafūr al-Lárí was both a disciple and student of Jami. He is credited with the authorship of an authoritative biography of his master and wrote at least five commentaries on his works. In the following excerpt from his commentary on* The Precious Pearl, *he closely analyzes selected sections of the treatise, elucidating Jami's theological and philosophical intentions and noting the strengths and weaknesses of the argument. In the text of the commentary, italics are used to indicate words and phrases quoted from* The Precious Pearl *or from its glosses; numerals at the head of sections refer to the corresponding paragraphs of* The Precious Pearl *as edited and translated by Nicholas Heer (1979); and numerals within square brackets at the head of sections refer to the corresponding glosses.*]

1. *Praise be to God, Who became manifest through His essence to His essence:* that is, Who knew His essence through His essence rather than through a knowledge superadded to His essence. This is knowledge in a universal and general manner (*'alā wajh kullī jumlī*) and by it the author has alluded to the first individuation (*al-ta'ayyun al-awwal*).

Became individuated in His inner knowledge: that is, became individuated after that as fixed essences (*ta'ayyana ta'ayyunan thubūtīyan*) in His inner knowledge. This is knowledge of particulars (*'ilm tafṣīlī*) and by it the author has alluded to the second individuation (*al-ta'ayyun al-thānī*).

The effects of these manifestations being then reflected: that is, His existence was dyed with the qualities (*ahkām*) and effects (*āthār*) of these manifestations. This is an allusion to the plane of contingency (*martabat al-imkān*), that is, the existence of contingents in the concrete world (*fī al-'ayn*). (p. 115)

4. *Both in the mind and externally:* that is, mental existence (*al-wujūd al-dhihnī*) is identical with the mental existent (*al-mawjūd al-dhihnī*) and external existence (*al-wujūd al-khārijī*) is identical with the external existent (*al-mawjūd al-khārijī*), as has been transmitted from them.

This implies that existence is common to proper existences in name only, rather than in meaning, etc.: This calls for further investigation, however, because it is possible for the proper existences of things to be identical with those things, so that each of those things, in this respect, would be a singular of absolute existence (*al-wujūd al-muṭlaq*) and absolute existence would be common in meaning to the proper existences, which are identical with those things.

It might also be imagined that if the existence of a thing were identical with that very thing, this would require that it be necessarily existent on the basis of [the argument] that if the existence of a thing is identical with that thing, then that thing is self-existent (*mawjūd bi-dhātihi*), and that what is self-existent is necessarily existent. Such is not the case, however, because if what is meant by self-existent is something whose essence requires its existence and realization, then we should not admit that if the existence of a thing were identical with that thing it would be self-existent in that sense. On the other hand, if what is meant [by self-existent] is something whose essence is a source of its effects (*mabda' lil-āthār*), then it is admitted [that it is self-existent]. We should not admit, however, that what is self-existent is necessarily existent, because it is possible that its being a source of its effects is the creation of an agent (*maj'ūl li-fā'il*), just as its being qualified by existence is the creation of an agent if it is assumed that existence is superadded (*zā'id*).

Belief concerning something in an absolute sense endures: that is, existence in an absolute sense. *Even though belief as to its particular characteristic ceases:* that is, the particular characteristic of existence. In other words we may believe something to exist but, nevertheless, be uncertain as to whether it is necessarily existent, or is a substance or an accident. The combination of this belief with that uncertainty indicates that existence is a common term with respect to meaning.

And because [*existence*] *is subject to division in meaning:* in that we can say existence is either necessary (*wājibī*) or contingent (*mumkinī*). Other methods of demonstrating the falsity of this position may be found in works dealing with this subject, and one who wishes to examine this question in detail may refer to them.

What they meant by identity was indistinguishability in the external world: He restricted the statement to external existence, although the previous discussion included mental existence as well, since there is no difference between the two existences in what has been mentioned so far. He therefore left the case of mental existence to determination by analogy (*al-muqāyasah*).

5. *The existences of things are these portions:* that is, all existent things including the Necessary Existent. In objection it may be said (*wa-fīhi*) that attributed existence (*al-wujūd al-muḍāf*), insofar as it is attributed [to something], is dependent on that thing's being [already] qualified by existence and being existent. Thus if that thing existed through that existence attributed [to it], a circle would result. Furthermore, attributed [existence] is a purely mental entity (*amr ma'qūl maḥḍ*), and mental entities in their opinion are nonexistent. Qualification (*al-ittiṣāf*), however, is a relation (*nisbah*) whose realization in actuality depends on the realization of its two terms (*al-ṭara-fayn*). This would also imply that the existence of the Necessary Existent depended on its apprehension (*al-ta'aqqul*) [by minds]. Furthermore, if the proper existence of a thing consisted of absolute existence together with attribution, then it would have to subsist in that thing, although it is obvious that such a concept does not subsist in that thing, for the meaning of existent is that which has existence, not that which has the existence of that thing.

To all of these [objections] it can be answered that if the cause of the existence of a thing is realized, then that thing becomes such that the intellect (*al-'aql*) abstracts (*yantazi'*) from it the concept of existence during apprehension (*al-ta'aqqul*), not that

that concept subsists in it in actuality. Thus the meaning of an existent is that which has existence in this sense, that is, that from which existence is abstracted during apprehension. And since this implies the validity of attributing existence to the thing, the [term] attributed existence (*al-wujūd al-muḍāf*) was used as an expression for the thing's existence. This should be considered carefully (*fa-ta'ammal*). (pp. 116-18)

9. *That existence is predicated by analogy, etc.*: The philosophers used as proof for their position that this concept was accidental with respect to its singulars of dissimilar realities the fact that it was an analogous term (*mushakhik*). This is therefore an answer to them.

This [argument], however, is refuted by the case of the accident: Furthermore, with respect to their statement: "nor is their essential attribute one" if what is meant by essential attribute (*al-dhātī*) is the absolute attribute (*al-muṭlaq*) which is sometimes qualified by strength (*al-qūwah*) and sometimes by weakness (*al-ḍu'ʾf*), then it is certainly one as well as essential. However, if what is meant by it is the attribute conditioned (*al-muqayyad*) by strength or weakness, then the multiplicity is admitted. This, however, does not imply the multiplicity of the aforementioned absolute essential attribute (*al-dhātī al-muṭlaq*).

The source of the error here is in imagining that the strong attribute (*al-qawī*) insofar as it is qualified by strength is an essential attribute or that the weak attribute (*al-ḍa'īf*) insofar as it is qualified by weakness is an essential attribute. On the contrary strength is an accidental quality inhering in the essential attribute after its realization within some of its singulars. Similarly weakness is an accidental quality inhering in it in some of its other singulars. Even if it were admitted [that the strong or weak attribute was essential], the unity of the absolute attribute is not inconsistent with its being essential also, for what is essential to an essential attribute is also essential. (pp. 120-21)

18. *Moreover, if it is absolute, then the thesis is proven*: Should you say: What is absolute in this sense is a natural universal. Therefore, if the thesis is proven that the Source of Existents (*Mabda' al-Mawjūdāt*) is this absolute, then the Necessary Existent (*al-Wājib*) must, in their opinion, be a natural universal, although this is not their position. We should answer: We do not admit that, considered as an absolute, it is a natural universal. On the contrary, it is possible for it to be an existent which is individuated in itself in such a way as to be consistent with (*yujāmi'*) all individuations and not reject any specific individuation, as the author substantiated below where he said: "It is evident, etc.," and in the appended gloss where he said: "Consequently, what is meant, etc." (p. 124)

21. *Consider this by analogy with the rational soul which pervades the parts of the body*: For example, with respect to its connection with [the organ of] sight, it is manifest in its form and is imbued with its effects and qualities, and with respect to its connection with [the organ of] hearing is imbued with the qualities of hearing. Similarly, with respect to its relationship to the physical faculty (*al-qūwah al-ṭabī'īyah*), it takes nourishment, digests, grows, reproduces, and so forth, and with respect to the physical faculty (*al-qūwah al-nafsānī-yah*), it perceives and moves. Further analogies can be drawn from this, for it is a model for the aforementioned absolute essence.

Or even better by analogy with the perfectional rational soul: that is, the perfect (*kāmilah*) [soul]. Choosing the relative ad-

jective (*al-nisbah*) with its suffixed *yā'* is a constant practice of this group because of the elegance and novelty associated with it. The progression implied by the use of the expression "or even better" has several aspects. The first is that the rational soul does not really become manifest in the forms of the parts and faculties of the body, but rather is qualified with a different attribute with respect to each one of them. The second is that the body with all of its parts and faculties is like a single thing, whereas spiritualized bodies (*al-abdān al-mu-tarawḥinah*) are entities each one of which is separate from the other. The third aspect is that the effects of each one of these [spiritualized bodies] are different from and contrary to the effects of any other. All of these are aspects of the similarity [of the perfectional rational soul] to what is being considered, [namely, the aforementioned absolute essence]. This is thus a closer and more perfect similarity. (pp. 125-26)

28. *As for the Ṣūfīs, they took the position that God's attributes were identical with His essence with respect to existence but other than it with respect to intellection*: It might be imagined from the literal meaning of this expression that there is no difference between the position of the philosophers and that of the Ṣūfīs, since it would appear that to differ (*al-ta-ghāyur*) with respect to concept (*bi-ḥasab al-mafhūm*) and to differ with respect to intellection (*bi-ḥisab al-ta'aqqul*) are one and the same. Upon examination, however, the distinction between them is verified, because the difference between essence and attribute with respect to concept is that the two concepts are different, but what they are true of is one and the same, whereas what is meant by difference with respect to intellection in the doctrine of the Ṣūfīs is that just as the concept of the attribute differs from that of the essence, so also does what the attribute is true of differ from what the essence is true of. However, this difference is with respect to intellection and individuational cognitive existence (*al-wujūd al-'ilmī al-ta'ay-yunī*). Thus, God's knowledge is one of the individuations of His essence in exactly the same way and without any difference as are separate entities (*al-umūr al-munfaṣilah*), for everything which is other than He is one of His individuations. There is no difference in this respect between attributes and separate entities, for an attribute is only distinguished from other things by a relationship (*nis-bah*) and some other characteristic (*khuṣūṣī-yah*). Effectuation (*al-ta'thīr*), however, pertains to the essence rather than to the attributes. Thus the source of revelation (*mabda' al-inkishāf*) is His essence, not His attribute. Let this be pondered. God, in respect to being the source of revelation (*mabda'īyat al-inkishāf*), is knowledge (*'ilm*), and in respect to that knowledge He is knowing (*'ālim*). However, every respect relating to knowledge is realized only in knowledge. Thus, what knowledge is really true of is not His essence but rather His essence in a certain respect, and that is a separate entity (*ghayr*) and contingent. Similarly what "necessary" (*al-wājib*) is true of is not His essence itself but His essence in a certain respect, namely, [in respect to] the attribution of necessity. Thus His essence is the denotation (*miṣdāq*) of "necessary," not what "necessary" is true of. All the other attributes and respects which are predicated of His essence are analogous, for in themselves, and in the plane in which they are themselves, they are neither attribute (*na't*), nor name (*ism*), nor description (*rasm*). This should be remembered. The author stated this clearly in the gloss, where he said: "Thus His attributes are relations, respects, and attributions which attach to the transcendent essence with respect to its connections." (pp. 127-29)

33. *The commentator then indicated, etc.*: The gist of his position is that His knowledge of His essence and of the first

effect is not by means of a form distinct [from Him], whereas His knowledge of other things is by means of forms impressed (*ṣuwar munṭabi'ah*) in the first effect and in the other intellectual substances (*al-jawāhir al-'aqlīyah*).

Other than the form of his own essence through which he is what he is: The word "form" is sometimes applied to an entity resembling the source of revelation (*mabda' al-inkishāf*), by which I mean knowledge, or it may be applied to the thing itself at the time it is perceived, and by this I mean the thing known (*al-ma'lūm*). It is this second meaning which is intended here, as is indicated by his saying: "through which he is what he is." It should be understood that the commentator's thesis here is that the knowledge of the First is not by means of the occurrence of a form in Him, and that it is possible for Him, on the contrary, to know a thing either by means of that very thing or through the occurrence of a form not inhering in Him. He supports this with apparently presumptive premises (*muqaddimāt ẓannīyah ẓāhirīyah*) which conclude with his saying: "The foregoing have been presented." He then specifies the thesis and presents it in detail by stating that God knows His essence through His essence and knows the first effect through the essence of the first effect and by means of its presence (*ḥuḍūr*) and occurrence (*ḥuṣūl*) to Him. He knows all other existents through the occurrence of their forms in the intellects (*al-'uqūl*). This, however, is also a rhetorical rather than a demonstrative method producing, as it were, a certain conviction (*iqnā'*). It should be known that the word "form" in construct [with "his own essence"] gives the illusion of duality (*tuwahhim al-ithnaynīyah*) as between essence and form, and, if the matter were not obvious, it would have been better and clearer to say: Just as an apprehender in perceiving his own essence does not require a form other than his own essence, but on the contrary apprehends his essence through his essence. . . . (p. 131)

40. *This is analogous to what has been said, etc.:* Genus and difference exist through one existence at the level of the specific quiddity (*al-māhīyah al-naw'īyah*), and knowledge of the quiddity is in reality knowledge of the genus and difference but of a sort in which the genus is not distinguished from the difference and neither of them is distinguished from the species. Nevertheless the relation of this knowledge, as it exists in the mind, to the species, genus and difference is [one] reality without differentiation (*min ghayr tafāwut*). Both [genus and difference] have another existence, also in the mind, of a different sort, in which the genus and difference are distinguished. Their two existences are then different from the existence of the species. The foregoing is a perfect analogy (*naẓīr tāmm*) to the essence of the Truth in the doctrine of the unitarian Ṣūfīs (*al-ṣūfīyah al-muwaḥḥidah*), according to which His effects are His modes (*shu'ūnāt*) and aspects (*i'tibārāt*) which are fused (*al-mundamijah*) in His essence without being distinguished at the level of His essential unity. This is contrary to the position of the philosophers, according to which the Truth's effects are really separate entities (*aghyār*) and substances distinct from His essence, may He be praised and exalted above what does not befit Him. The analogy is thus not entirely applicable to their position. (pp. 135-36)

50a. *All of the religionists:* that is, those who believe in one of the divine religions or creeds.

[38] *That is, both of them are proper for Him in accordance with varying motives, etc.:* What is to be understood from the totality of his argument is that the difference between the position of the theologian and that of the philosopher is that in the view of the philosopher action is a concomitant (*lāzim*) of the Creator's essence. This is based on its being a concomitant of His volition (*al-mashī'ah*), which, in turn, is a concomitant of His essence, for the concomitant of a concomitant is a concomitant. Such is not the case in the view of the theologian, for he does not make the basis (*mustanad*) of action a concomitant of His essence. This presents a difficulty, however, because, in the view of the theologians His action is a concomitant of His will (*al-irādah*), for they said: If He wills, He acts, and His will must be concomitant with Him, for it is an attribute of perfection (*ṣifat kamāl*), and its nonexistence would be an imperfection (*naqṣ*). Therefore, if it were possible for will be be separated from Him, imperfection would be possible [for Him]. This, however, is absurd (*muḥāl*), for just as imperfection is absurd with respect to Him, so also is the possibility of imperfection absurd. Thus, if will is concomitant, then the action concomitant with it is also concomitant. Therefore, the nonexistence of the action is impossible in the thing itself (*fī nafs al-amr*). It is apparent, then, that the difference between the theologian and the philosopher consists solely in affirming or not affirming will [of God]. Should it be said that God's action is not concomitant with His will, because His will is eternal, but is rather concomitant with the connection of His will (*ta'alluq al-irādah*), so that the meaning of "if He wills" is "if His will connects"; we should answer by shifting the argument to the connection of His will and asking whether it is a perfection or an imperfection. It cannot be an imperfection, nor, if it is a perfection, can there by any possibility of its not existing. Moreover, one cannot say that it is possible for it to be neither a perfection nor an imperfection, because we should then say that if it were not a perfection then God's action would of necessity be vanity (*'abath*), for if His action were good, then its source would be a perfection. Thus, clearly stated, the real difference between the three positions is that in the view of the theologian both the occurrence of the action from God and its nonoccurrence are proper in the thing itself, whereas in the view of the philosopher and the Ṣūfīs the nonexistence of God's action is not proper in the thing itself. (pp. 139-40)

84. *Its intellect:* that is, the intellect of some sphere, namely, the second sphere from the [First] Principle. It is possible that the possessive pronouns qualifying "matter" and "soul" similarly [refer to some sphere] in order to be in agreement with the pronoun qualifying "intellect." On the other hand it is possible that they convey [a sense of] specificity as [would be the case] with the pronoun [in the expression] "its level," that is, the level of that thing. We have brought this up only because the first intellect brought into existence the form, matter, and soul of the first sphere but not, however, its intellect, since it itself is its intellect. On the contrary, according to their doctrine, it brought into existence the intellect of the second sphere. It should be known that they said that God brought the first intellect into existence, and that the first intellect brought the first sphere into existence along with its matter, its form and its rational soul, which directs it, as well as the second intellect. Then the second intellect brought its sphere into existence both materially and formally, as well as the soul of its sphere and the intellect of the third sphere, and so on up to the tenth intellect. Then the tenth intellect created the four elements and the three generations (*al-mawālīd al-thalāthah*) with all their many species, souls, and faculties, and so on as God willed.

This is what they said, and most people have interpreted their words literally to the effect that there is an agent and cause other than God, may He be exalted above what does not befit

Him. However, al-Muḥaqqiq al-Dawwānī has demonstrated in an essay he wrote to explain the meaning of the following verse by al-Ḥāfiz al-Shīrāzī:

> Said our Pīr: On the pen of creation passed no error.
> On his pure, error-covering sight praise be.

that their real position is that there is no agent in existence except God. He has explained this clearly and whoever desires certainty [on this point] should refer to this essay. Indeed, what they meant by the intellect's bringing something into existence was its having a role (*madkhalīyah*) in bringing that thing into existence. The author's words, however, cannot be restricted to either interpretation and are valid in any case. This should be considered carefully. Nevertheless, some of his expressions towards the end of what he has to say indicate what the substantiation [of this] is. (pp. 150-51)

> *'Abd al-Ghafūr al-Lārí, "The Translation of al-Lārī's 'Commentary' on 'al-Durrah al-Fākhirah'," in* The Precious Pearl: Al-Jāmī's al-Durrah al-Fākhirah *by al-Jāmī, edited and translated by Nicholas Heer, State University of New York Press, 1979, pp. 113-51.*

'IṢĀM AL-DĪN AḤMAD IBN MUṢṬAFĀ ṬĀSHKUBRĪZĀDAH (essay date 1558)

[*Tāshkubrizadah was a distinguished Ottoman encyclopedist and biographer whose* al-Shaqā'iq al-Numaníyah, *a collection of 522 biographies of notable individuals who lived during the reigns of ten Ottoman sultans, is considered the main source for the intellectual history of the period. In the following excerpt from his 1558 biography of Jami, he describes the circumstances of composition of* The Precious Pearl *and accounts for the existence of short and long versions of the text.*]

Al-Mawlā al-A'ẓam Sayyidī Muḥyī al-Dīn al-Fanārī related that his father, al-Mawlā 'Alī al-Fanārī, who was *qāḍī* in al-'Askar al-Manṣūr under Sulṭān Muḥammad Khān, said, "The Sulṭān said to me one day that there was need for an adjudication (*muḥākamah*) between those groups investigating the sciences of reality (*'ulūm al-ḥaqīqah*), namely, the theologians, the Ṣūfīs, and the philosophers." My father replied, "I said to the Sulṭān that no one was more capable of such an adjudication between these groups than al-Mawlā 'Abd al-Raḥmān al-Jāmī." He then said, "Sulṭān Muḥammad Khān accordingly sent an envoy with precious gifts to him and requested of him the aforementioned adjudication. Al-Jāmī thereupon wrote a treatise [**The Precious Pearl**] in which he adjudicated between those groups with respect to six questions, including the question of existence. He sent it to Sulṭān Muḥammad Khān stating that should the treatise prove acceptable, he would supplement it with an explanation of the remaining questions. Otherwise there would be nothing to gain in his wasting his time further. The treatise, however, arrived in Constantinople after the death of Sulṭān Muḥammad Khān." Al-Mawlā Muḥyī al-Dīn al-Fanārī said furthermore that this treatise remained with his father, and I believe he said that it is still with him.

> *'Iṣām al-Dīn Aḥmad ibn Muṣṭafā Ṭāshkubrīzādah, in an extract from an introduction to* The Precious Pearl: Al-Jāmī's al-Durrah al-Fākhirah *by al-Jāmī, edited and translated by Nicholas Heer, State University of New York Press, 1979, p. 5.*

LOUISA STUART COSTELLO (essay date 1845)

[*Costello was a nineteenth-century English essayist, poet, novelist, and travel writer. In the following excerpt from a work originally published in 1845, she describes what she considers Jami's achievement as a poet.*]

The favourite subject of the Loves of Yussuf and Zuleika, which every Persian poet has touched with more or less success, has never found one who so thoroughly entered into it, and rendered it so beautiful, as Jami. He entirely remodelled the poem of Ferdusi, and gave it so many new graces that his composition completely superseded that of his master, and his name is always peculiarly associated with those of the lovers whose "well-sung woes" he has so eloquently sung. (p. 137)

He was a Sufi, and preferred, like many of his fellow-poets, the meditations and ecstasies of mysticism to the pleasures of a court. He became, however, a friend of princes.

One of the great aims of the philosophic and benevolent Jami was to instruct and improve his auditors; and in order to do so effectually, particularly as regarded the common people, he was accustomed to come frequently to the great mosque of Hérât, and there converse familiarly with all whom he met.

His eloquence was great, his manner persuasive, and his doctrine pure; and like St. Aldelm, the friend of King Athelstan, he succeeded in attracting and riveting the attention of his hearers. (pp. 137-38)

An illumination from a late-sixteenth-century manuscript of Haft Aurang, *illustrating the story about how a treasure was found.*

His writings are very voluminous; at Oxford twenty-two volumes are preserved of his works, of which he composed nearly forty, all of great length. The greater part treat of the theology of the Mussulmans, or are written in the mystic style. He collected the most interesting under the name of *Haft-Aurenk,* or **"The Seven Stars of the Bear, or the Seven Brothers"**; and amongst these is the famous poem of Yussuf and Zuleika.

The tale extends in the original to four thousand couplets. Sir William Jones pronounces it to be "the *finest* poem he ever read"; and nothing can exceed the admiration which it inspires in the East. (pp. 138-39)

> *Louisa Stuart Costello, "Jami," in her* The Rose Garden of Persia, *1845. Reprint by T. N. Foulis, 1913, pp. 137-56.*

EDWARD FITZGERALD (essay date 1856)

[*FitzGerald was a nineteenth-century English man of letters who is best known as the translator of the* Rubáiyát of Omar Khayyám, Astronomer Poet of Persia *(1859). A keen student of Persian, he is believed to have taken up the study of the language in 1853 under the direction of his friend Professor E. B. Cowell, with whom he met and corresponded often while translating* Salámán and Absál. *In the following excerpt from the dedication to Professor Cowell in his 1856 translation of the poem, FitzGerald describes his version of the work, noting the formal characteristics of the Persian original and asserting the excellence of the work as literature.*]

Two years ago, when we began (I for the first time) to read this Poem [*Salámán and Absál*] together, I wanted you to translate it, as something that should interest a few who are worth interesting. You, however, did not see the way clear then, and had Aristotle pulling you by one Shoulder and Prakrit Vararuchi by the other, so as indeed to have hindered you up to this time completing a Version of Hafiz' best Odes which you had then happily begun. So, continuing to like old Jámí more and more, I must try my hand upon him; and here is my reduced Version of a small Original. What Scholarship it has is yours, my Master in Persian, and so much beside; who are no further answerable for *all* than by well liking and wishing publisht what you may scarce have Leisure to find due fault with.

Had all the Poem been like Parts, it would have been all translated, and in such Prose lines as you measure Hafiz in, and such as any one should adopt who does not feel himself so much of a Poet as him he translates and some he translates for—before whom it is best to lay the raw material as genuine as may be, to work up to their own better Fancies. But, unlike Hafiz' best—(whose Sonnets are sometimes as close packt as Shakespeare's, which they resemble in more ways than one)—Jámí, you know, like his Countrymen generally, is very diffuse in what he tells and his way of telling it. The very structure of the Persian Couplet—(here, like people on the Stage, I am repeating to you what you know, with an Eye to the small Audience beyond)—so often ending with the same Word, or Two Words, if but the foregoing Syllable secure a lawful Rhyme, so often makes the Second Line but a slightly varied Repetition, or Modification of the First, and gets slowly over Ground often hardly worth gaining. This iteration is common indeed to the Hebrew Psalms and Proverbs—where, however, the Value of the Repetition is different. In your Hafiz also, not Two only, but Eight or Ten Lines perhaps are tied to the same Close of Two—or *Three*—words; a verbal Ingenuity as much valued in the East as better Thought. And how many of all the Odes called his, more and fewer in various Copies, do you yourself

care to deal with?—And in the better ones how often some lines, as I think for this reason, unworthy of the Rest—interpolated perhaps from the Mouths of his many Devotees, Mystical and Sensual—or crept into Manuscripts of which he never arranged or corrected one from the First?

This, together with the confined Action of Persian Grammar, whose organic simplicity seems to me its difficulty when applied, makes the Line by Line Translation of a Poem not line by line precious tedious in proportion to its length. Especially—(what the Sonnet does not feel)—in the Narrative; which I found when once eased in its Collar, and yet missing somewhat of rhythmical Amble, somehow, and not without resistance on my part, swerved into that "easy road" of Verse—easiest as unbeset with any exigencies of Rhyme. Those little Stories, too, which you thought untractable, but which have their Use as well as Humour by way of quaint Interlude Music between the little Acts, felt ill at ease in solemn Lowth-Isaiah Prose, and had learn'd their tune, you know, before even Hiawatha came to teach people to quarrel about it. Till, one part drawing on another, the Whole grew to the present form. As for the much bodily omitted—it may be readily guessed that an Asiatic of the 15th Century might say much on such a subject that an Englishman of the 19th would not care to read. Not that our Jámí is ever *licentious* like his Contemporary Chaucer, nor like Chaucer's Posterity in Times that called themselves more Civil. But better Men will not now endure a simplicity of Speech that Worse men abuse. Then the many more, and foolisher, Stories—preliminary Te Deums to Allah and Allah's-shadow Sháh—very much about Alef Noses, Eyebrows like inverted Núns, drunken Narcissus Eyes—and that eternal Moon Face which never wanes from Persia—of all which there is surely enough in this Glimpse of the Original. No doubt some Oriental character escapes—the Story sometimes becomes too Skin and Bone without due interval of even Stupid and Bad. Of the two Evils?—At least what I have chosen is least in point of bulk; scarcely in proportion with the length of its Apology which, as usual, probably discharges one's own Conscience at too great a Price; people at once turning against you the Arms they might have wanted had you not laid them down. However it may be with this, I am sure a complete Translation—even in Prose—would not have been a readable one—which, after all, is a useful property of most Books, even of Poetry. (pp. 21-5)

But to turn from you Two to a Public—nearly as numerous—(with whom, by the way, this Letter may die without a name that *you* know very well how to supply),—here is the best I could make of Jámí's Poem—"Ouvrage de peu d'étendue" ["A little-known work"], says the "Biographie Universelle," and, whatever that means, here collapsed into a nutshell Epic indeed; whose Story however, if nothing else, may interest some Scholars as one of Persian Mysticism—perhaps the grand Mystery of all Religions—an Allegory fairly devised and carried out—dramatically culminating as it goes on; and told as to this day the East loves to tell her Story, illustrated by Fables and Tales, so often (as we read in the latest Travels) at the expense of the poor Arab of the Desert. (pp. 26-7)

> *Edward FitzGerald, "Letter to Professor Cowell,"* in Salámán and Absál: An Allegory by Jámí, *edited by Nathan Haskell Dole, translated by Edward FitzGerald, L. C. Page and Company, Incorporated, 1899, pp. 21-8.*

STANLEY LANE-POOLE (essay date 1882)

[*Lane-Poole was an English orientalist and historian who wrote extensively on Arabic philology and social life in the East. In the following excerpt, he examines Jami's version of* Yúsuf and Zulaikha.]

[Jami] was a Persian poet of the first rank, though not the foremost in that rank. We cannot place him quite by the side of Ferdaus or Hafiz; but his verse is exceedingly beautiful, and, perhaps, it was rather the diversity of his genius than any inherent weakness that withheld him from the highest place. He was at any rate the last great poet of Persia, and the procession of the classics closes with no unworthy name. (p. 122)

The story of Yusuf and Zulaikha, or, to put it into scriptural English, of Joseph and Potiphar's wife, has always been a favourite theme in the East, but [in *Yúsuf and Zulaikha*] Jami invests it with a dignity and an inner meaning which raises it to a different level from that we might naturally expect. After the usual introductory cantos which Mohammedan canons of style prescribe—concerning the Creator and the Prophet—Jami tells the power of beauty and of love, and announces the purpose of his poem.

> Love stood beside me when my life was new,
> And from my mother's breast Love's milk I drew.
> White as that milk are now my hairs, but still
> Sweet thoughts of Love my aged bosom thrill.
> Still in my heart the youthful warmth I feel,
> While in mine ear re-echoes Love's appeal:—
> 'In love, O Jami, have thy days been passed;
> Die in that love gay-hearted to the last.
> Some tale of love's adventure that may win
> Thy name remembrance in the world, begin:
> Some picture with thy finest pen assay
> Which still may live when thou art gone away.'

Then follow cantos on ''Speech'' and ''The Vision of Adam,'' wherein Yusuf is foreseen, and then the beautiful Canaanite youth is described in befitting terms. The next fourteen cantos are devoted to Zulaikha, a daughter of the ''King of the West,'' a peerless maiden of the true Oriental type, but purified and ennobled by the poet's fine instinct. Three times she sees in her sleep a vision of a beautiful youth, who tells her he is Vizir of the King of Egypt. She pines and sickens, and her nurse finds out the cause. Suitors come from all parts of the world to seek her hand, but all are rejected.

> The soft wind blowing from Egypt's sand
> Bringing dust to mine eyes from that happy land
> Sweeter a hundredfold would be
> Than the musk-laden breezes of Tartary.

So the King, her father, sends to the Vizir of Egypt, and the marriage is arranged. The damsel journeys in state to Memphis, and is met by the Vizir, and then she discovers that he is not Yusuf, the beautiful youth of her dreams. Her despair is frantic, but an angel tells her that the only way to Yusuf is through wedding the Vizir; and in that hope she consents. How she pines and droops in a false magnificence, and longs for the promised love, is told in some of the best cantos in the work. . . .

The story of Joseph is . . . [related] much as in the Biblical narrative, with certain transpositions and amplifications. He arrives in Memphis, and is bought by Zulaikha in the slave-market. Then come a series of twelve cantos in which the wooing love of the woman and the passionless purity of the man are finely treated. Yusuf is released from the false accusation on the testimony of a sucking child, and eventually comes to be, what he foretold in the vision, Grand Vizir of Egypt. Meanwhile, Zulaikha has become a widow, her beauty

A manuscript page from Lawá'ih, *one of Jami's chief prose works.*

is gone for sorrow, and she is old and blind with grief. She leads a hermit life, and comes from her hut only to hear the sound of Yusuf riding by. At last she comes before him and tells her story; and he prays, and her sight and beauty are restored as of old; and, when Yusuf still hesitates, the voice of Gabriel the Archangel is heard:

> From the Lord Almighty a message I bring.
> 'Mine eyes have seen her in humble mood,
> I heard her prayer when to thee she sued;
> At the sight of her labours, her prayers, and sighs
> The waves of the sea of My pity rise.
> Her soul from the sword of despair I free
> And here from My throne I betroth her to thee.'

The real meaning of the poem is seen in the canto which tells of the other damsel who fell in love with Yusuf, and to whom the youth preached a mystical Sufi sermon, whereby her love was diverted to the true channel; ''She folded love's carpet and laid it aside,'' and devoted herself in austerity to good works and the building of mosques. The moral is, in fact, the great philosophic doctrine of the Neoplatonists: the universal unity towards which all yearns, and into which all is resolved.

> —Form is manifold, truth is one.
> In number trouble and error lie:

To unity then for sure refuge fly.
If the might of the foeman oppress thee sore,
Fly to the fortress, and fear no more.

(p. 123)

Stanley Lane-Poole, in a review of "Yusuf and Zulaikha: A Poem," in The Academy, *Vol. XXI, No. 511, February 18, 1882, pp. 122-23.*

[E. REHATSEK] (essay date 1887)

[*In the following excerpt, Rehatsek outlines the principal incidents in* Baháristán.]

[Jâmi] has been generally called the last great poet and mystic of Persia, and is said to have combined the moral tone of Sa'di with the lofty aspirations of Jalal-uddin Rumi; the graceful ease of Hafiz with the deep pathos of Nizami. He devoted his whole life to literature, and was endowed with such extensive learning that he was supposed to be a complete master of the Persian language, in which he was certainly one of the most gifted and productive of writers. He was the author of many works, not only in poetry, but also in prose. The total number is said to amount to forty-five or fifty. (p. vi)

The **Behâristân,** or *Abode of Spring,* is divided into eight chapters, called gardens, which, the author states, he had composed, in the first instance, for the instruction of his own son. The beginning is written entirely in the style of the mysticism of the Sûfis, and from it some slight ideas may be gathered about their tenets; gradually, however, anecdotes are introduced on a variety of subjects, but in the third garden they are mostly about kings, and some of these are excellent. The fourth garden deals with the praises of liberality, embodied in little stories, several of which appear to be founded on actual events, like those of the preceding chapter, and may also, on that score, be considered interesting. The fifth garden is entirely on love affairs, from which something may be learned of the customs and opinions in vogue among the people concerning such matters, and there is scarcely anything which will greatly shock the taste of European readers. The sixth garden has been already done into English by Mr. C. G. Wilson, under the title of "Persian Wit and Humour." . . . The seventh garden may be called a brief anthology of thirty-five poets, containing specimens of their compositions, and will, perhaps, be one of the most pleasing portions of this little book, but the eighth, or last garden, has also its attractions, and consists entirely of animal fables, twenty-three in number. (pp. 1-2)

[*E. Rehatsek*], *in an introduction and preface to* The Behâristân (Abode of Spring) *by Jâmi, translated by E. Rehatsek, Benares, 1887, pp. v-vi, 1-2.*

E. H. WHINFIELD (essay date 1906)

[*Whinfield was a nineteenth-century English man of letters who is recognized for his exacting and scholarly translations of Persian poetry. In the following excerpt from an essay originally published in 1906, he studies what he considers the Neoplatonic foundation of* Lawá'ih.]

The **Lawá'ih** is a treatise on Ṣūfī theology or theosophy, as distinguished from the religious emotions experienced by all Ṣūfīs, learned and unlearned alike. Catholic authorities have drawn this distinction between "experimental" and "doctrinal" mysticism, and it is a great help towards clear thinking on this subject. The religious emotion common to all mankind is, so to speak, raised to its highest power in the mystics. They are overwhelmed by the sense of the Divine omnipresence and of their own dependence on God. They are dominated and intoxicated by their vivid sense of the close relation subsisting between the soul and God. They conceive themselves as being in touch with God, feeling His motions in their souls, and at times rising to the beatific vision and blinded by excess of light. These religious experiences were the rough material out of which the doctrinal reasoned system, set out in treatises like the **Lawá'ih,** was built up. Psychologists have advanced various theories as to the genesis of these experiences. With these we are not at present concerned. But as to the origin of the philosophical ideas and terms employed in the **Lawá'ih** and similar works to formulate the Ṣūfī theology, there can be little doubt. The source of Ṣūfī theology was Neoplatonism.

The title of the book, **Lawá'ih,** or **"Flashes of Light",** suggests the philosophy employed to systematize and give a reasoned basis for the unreasoned "experiences" of unlearned Ṣūfīs. It of course refers to the "inner light". The Platonists were called *Ishráqín* or *Illuminati,* because they regarded intellectual intuition or intuitive reason (*Nous*) as the main source of knowledge, whereas the Peripatetics (*Mashshá'în*) recognized no sources of knowledge except the senses and the discursive reason (*Dianoia*). The word *Ishráq,* or "Lights", is often met with in this connexion. Thus Shams-ud-dín Muḥammad ash-Shahrazúrí is called by Haji Khalfa "a metaphysician learned in the inner lights" (*Ishráq*). Shihâb-ud-din as Suhrawardí, who was put to death at Aleppo in 587 A.H. by advice of that valiant defender of the Faith, Sulṭán Ṣaláḥ-ud-dín, wrote a book entitled *Ḥikmat-ul-Ishráq,* or "Philosophy of Inner Light". The author of the *Dabistán* says that the belief of the pure Ṣūfīs is the same as that of the *Ishráqín* or Platonists, and also that Ṣūfīs were classed as orthodox (*Mutasharri'*) and Platonists. Haji Khalfa, in his article on Ṣūfism (*Tasawwuf*), says that anyone who reads Ṣūfī books cannot fail to remark that their terminology is borrowed from the Platonists (*Ishráqín*), and more especially from the later ones—i.e. the Neoplatonists. Let any reader who has even a slight acquaintance with the terms used by the Greek philosophers look over treatises like the **Lawá'ih** and the *Gulshan i Ráz* and on almost every page he will recognize some familiar Greek term. Schmölders in his *Documenta Philosophiæ Arabum* gives a list of nearly one hundred such terms employed by Avicena (Ibn Sína) and other writers on philosophy in the fifth century of the Hijira.

It was probably at about the end of the fifth century A.H. that Neoplatonic *gnōsis* began to influence and modify Ṣūfī doctrine. Up to that date the doctrine had been expounded in short precepts, parables (*mithál*), and similes like those in the Koran. But educated Moslems had outgrown these primitive methods of instruction. They wanted something more systematic. Jalál-ud-dín Rúmí tells us how his critics assailed him for dealing in trivial examples and parables instead of giving a systematic account of the stages of the soul's ascent to God. Ibn Khaldûn mentions Muḥásibí and the great Imám Ghazálí as among the first who wrote systematic treatises on the doctrines of the Ṣūfīs. We have Ghazálí's own account of the way in which he was attracted to Ṣūfism, and other passages in his writings prove that he used the forms of Greek thought to explain Ṣūfī principles. If it be asked how Greek philosophy reached Ghazálí, who was a native of Khurásán, the answer is easy. When Justinian closed the schools at Athens, Damascius and his Neoplatonist brethren fled to the court of Nushirvân. They only remained there about a year, and left in 533 A.D.; but Nushirvân had some translations of Neoplatonist books made at the time, and these were followed by many others, made two centuries and a half later, under the Abbasides at Baghdad.

Greek philosophy was expounded by the so-called Arabian, but really Persian, philosophers, Al Farābī and Avicena, and afterwards in the *Ikhwān-uṣ-Ṣafā.* Shahrastānī, a contemporary of Ghazālī, gave accounts of all the chief Greek philosophers, including the "Shaikh of the Greeks" or Plotinus, his editor Porphyry, and Proclus. The so-called "Theology of Aristotle", which is a summary of the "Enneads" of Plotinus, appeared probably soon afterwards. The result was that Neoplatonism, mainly in the form expounded by Plotinus, was used by all the more learned Ṣūfīs to explain and justify the simple emotional sayings of the early Ṣūfīs. Henceforward Neoplatonism pervades all systematic treatises on Ṣūfism, such as the *Faṣūṣ-ul-Ḥikam,* the *Maqṣad-ul-Aqṣā,* the *Gulshan i Rāz,* and the *Lawā'ih.* Even the poets use the Greek terminology. Thus Hakīm Sanā'ī, who lived at the same time as Ghazālī, introduces "Universal Reason" and "Universal Soul", the second and third hypostases of the Trinity of Plotinus, and the principal later poets follow suit. (pp. vii-x)

> *E. H. Whinfield, in a preface to* Lawā'ih: A Treatise on Ṣūfism *by Nūr-Ud-Dīn 'Abd-Ur-Raḥmān Jāmī, translated by E. H. Whinfield, 1906. Reprint by Royal Asiatic Society, 1928, pp. vii-xviii.*

F. HADLAND DAVIS (essay date 1908)

[*Davis was an English essayist and critic who wrote widely on Japanese and Persian life and literature. In the following excerpt, he comments on the literary merits of* Lawá'ih, Yúsuf and Zulaikha, *and* Baháristán, *noting as well the mystical character of the two former works and the author's stated objective in the latter.*]

The *Lawá'ih,* or **"Flashes of Light,"** is a theological treatise based on Súfíism, and is a book of immense importance to the student of Mysticism. It will afford him a very interesting and striking parallel to Neo-Platonism (Plotinus in particular), and also to some of the Buddhistic teachings. (p. 25)

The keynote to the *Lawá'ih* is to be found in Jámí's preface. He describes the work as "Explanatory of the intuitions and verities displayed on the pages of the hearts and minds of men of insight and divine knowledge." After a request to his readers to refrain from "cavilling and animadversion," he continues, this time in verse:

> Believe me, I am naught—yea, less than naught.
> By naught and less than naught what can be taught?
>
> I tell the mysteries of truth, but know
> Naught save the telling to this task I brought.

> • • • • •

> With men of light I sought these pearls to string,
> The drift of mystics' sayings forth to bring.

The *Lawá'ih* expounds some very beautiful and very ennobling truths. In "Flash II." Jámí pleads for the love of One and the abandonment of all little earthly loves that distract the attention of the lover for his Beloved—precisely the same theme as that expressed in *Salámán and Absál.* The poet loudly condemns "Hell-born vanity" and the accumulation of worldly wisdom, even all learning except "The lore of God." It would be a strange theme for a poet to so persistently choose were not Jámí a mystic. With the "Inner light" of the true mystic he sets aside the things of the world as being unsatisfactory. He

does not, however, merely pull down the fading, ever vanishing vanities of the world, but with the strong clear voice of the poet-prophet, he sings:

> The fleeting phantoms you admire to-day
> Will soon at Heaven's behest be swept away.
> O give your heart to Him who never fails,
> Who, ever with you, and will ever stay.

Jámí advocates, as others have done before him, the destruction of self in order to gain knowledge of Very Being, "Until He mingles Himself with thy soul, and thine own individual existence passes out of thy sight." The poet also discusses the question of matter being *maya*—delusion, the ceaseless round of "Accidents," the ever coming and vanishing media for the revelations of the Beloved.

The *Lawá'ih* should be studied in conjunction with Mahmud Shabistari's *Gulshan-i-Raz,* or "The Mystic Rose Garden." The main teaching of both these books is that the indwelling of God in the soul can only take place when that soul realises that self is a delusion, that things of this world are but phantom-pictures coming and going, as it were, upon the surface of a mirror:

> Go, sweep out the chamber of your heart,
> Make it ready to be the dwelling-place of the Beloved.
> When you depart out, He will enter in,
> In you, void of your*self,* will He display His beauty.

The phenomenal world to the Súfí was nothing more than an ever-recurring process of genesis and end: union with the Divine, annihilation of that process. The *Lawá'ih* is deeply spiritual throughout, and full of an almost pathetic pity for those who delight in worldly pleasures and find no joy in contemplating Union with the Beloved.

Jámí, after having spent considerable care on his *Lawá'ih,* and after his reader has made a strenuous effort to catch a momentary glimpse of his visionary meaning, concludes:

> Jámí, leave polishing of phrases, cease
> Writing and chanting fables, hold thy peace;
> Dream not that "Truth" can be revealed by words:
> From this fond dream, O dreamer, find release!

> • • • • •

> How long wilt thou keep clanging like a bell?
> Thou'lt never come to hold the pearl of "Truth"
> Till thou art made all ear, as is the shell.

And here we see the great mystical poet sitting, like a little child listening to a tale that is told, quelled into reverential silence by the greatness of the theme. It is in silence, in the quiet places of our hearts, rather than on the housetops of much controversy, that we can hear the sweet call of the Beloved and forget the clanging of the world in the Great Peace which He alone can give. (pp. 25-8)

[*Yúsuf and Zulaikha*] belongs to the series of poems known as the *Haft Aurang.* Jámí heralds his poem with a good deal of laudacious singing on the Prophet, Beauty, Love, and concludes by remarking that the loves of Majnún and Laila "have had their day," and makes this excuse for weaving another love poem on another theme. But this scheme was scarcely original, Firdawsí and Ansari having previously composed poems on a similar subject. However, the tongue of the critic is surely silenced by these humble lines:

> If here and there a slip or fault you see,
> May he not lay the blame of all on me.
> May he correct my errors, or befriend
> With generous silence faults he cannot mend.

If the work be regarded as a love poem, without its mystical interpretation, Yúsuf may well be regarded as a cold, statuesque young man of the St. Anthony type, but cast in a more beautiful mould. While we may equally well regard Zulaikha as a passionate young lady sadly lacking in worldly wisdom. The coldness of Yúsuf would probably irritate us were we not frequently reminded of the way in which poor Zulaikha plagues him with her too constant attentions. Neither strike us as being very ordinary human people for precisely reverse reasons. (pp. 29-30)

The *Baháristán,* or **"Abode of Spring,"** is admitted by Jámí to be an imitation of Sa'di's *Gulistán,* or "Rose Garden." The idea of arranging a book of verse and prose into a series of "Gardens" was a very beautiful one. Two other books compiled on similar lines are Sa'di's *Bústán,* or "Orchard," and the *Nigaristán,* or "Picture Gallery," by Mu'in-uddin Jawini, which appeared in 1334 A.D. Sir Edwin Arnold's *With Sa'di in a Garden* gives the Westerner some idea of the beauty of Eastern gardens, and this particular garden is rendered all the more delectable because it holds a greater beauty than the loveliest garden, the Taj Mahal itself. Sir Edwin transfers Persian poetry to an Indian garden, which is not very dissimilar to the beautiful gardens of Shíráz. Professor A. V. Williams Jackson decribes the *Bagh-i-Takht,* "Garden of the Throne," thus: "Terrace rises above terrace, and fountain, channel, and stream pour their waters in cascades over slabs of marble into reservoirs faced with stone—the walks bordered with cypress and orange trees." It would be interesting to know if the terraces in any way corresponded with the idea of naming and numbering the "Gardens" in Jámí's *Baháristán.* A beautiful mosque, a bower of roses, running water; might not these things alone have suggested to the poet's mind "The pavilion of Excellency, Love, and Laughter?"

The *Baháristán* has a distinct interest apart from its literary merit. It appears to have been written by Jámí for the instruction of his "darling and beloved son Ziá-uddin-Yúsuf." The poet-father goes on to say, "That young boys and inexperienced youths become very disheartened and unhappy when they receive instruction in idiomatic expressions they are not accustomed to." Although Jámí allowed his son to read the *Gulistán,* he evidently thought the last word had not yet been written in the interests of instructing the young, and thus conceived the idea of writing the *Baháristán.*

One is so apt to see printed requests in the public gardens of England that it seems a little ironical to come across the following in the literary "Gardens" of Jámí: "It is requested that the promenaders in these gardens—which contain no thorns to give offence, nor rubbish displayed for interested purposes,—walking through them with sympathetic steps and looking at them carefully, will bestow their good wishes, and rejoice with praise the gardener who has spent much trouble and great exertions in planning and cultivating these gardens." In regard to the statement that the *Gardens* "contain no Thorns to give offence," I, for one, must beg to differ. One ugly weed there is which the gardener would have done well to destroy in his otherwise very beautiful garden.

The *Baháristán* is divided into eight "Gardens." The *First* deals with the sayings and doings of the saintly, wise, and those "who occupy the chief seats in the pavilion of Excellency." The *Second* with philosophical subtleties. The *Third* with Justice, Equity, Government, and Administration, and in general "to show the wisdom of Sultáns." The *Fourth* with Liberality and Generosity. The *Fifth* with Love. The *Sixth* with

"Blowing of the zephyrs of wit, and the breezes of jocular sallies, which cause the buds of the lips to laugh and the flowers of the hearts to bloom." The *Seventh* with a selection from the work of Persian poets. The *Eighth,* and last, with animal stories. (pp. 36-8)

F. Hadland Davis, in his The Persian Mystics: Jámí, *John Murray, 1908, 107 p.*

REYNOLD A. NICHOLSON   (essay date 1914)

[*Nicholson was a twentieth-century English scholar who wrote important studies of Islamic mysticism. In the following excerpt, he discusses Jami as an exponent of Sufism.*]

Both Moslem and Súfí declare that God is One, but the statement bears a different meaning in each instance. The Moslem means that God is unique in His essence, qualities, and acts; that He is absolutely unlike all other beings. The Súfí means that God is the One Real Being which underlies all phenomena. This principle is carried to its extreme consequences, as we shall see. If nothing except God exists, then the whole universe, including man, is essentially one with God, whether it is regarded as an emanation which proceeds from Him, without impairing His unity, like sunbeams from the sun, or whether it is conceived as a mirror in which the divine attributes are reflected. But surely a God who is all in all can have no reason for thus revealing Himself: why should the One pass over into the Many? The Súfís answer—a philosopher would say that they evade the difficulty—by quoting the famous Tradition: "I was a hidden treasure and I desired to be known; therefore I created the creation in order that I might be known." In other words, God is the eternal Beauty, and it lies in the nature of beauty to desire love. The mystic poets have described the self-manifestation of the One with a profusion of splendid imagery. Jámí says, for example:

> From all eternity the Beloved unveiled His beauty in
>   the solitude of the unseen;
> He held up the mirror to His own face, He displayed
>   His loveliness to Himself.
> He was both the spectator and the spectacle; no eye
>   but His had surveyed the Universe.
> All was One, there was no duality, no pretence of
>   'mine' or 'thine.'
> The vast orb of Heaven, with its myriad incomings and
>   outgoings, was concealed in a single point.
> The Creation lay cradled in the sleep of non-existence,
>   like a child ere it has breathed.
> The eye of the Beloved, seeing what was not, regarded
>   nonentity as existent.
> Although He beheld His attributes and qualities as a
>   perfect whole in His own essence,
> Yet He desired that they should be displayed to Him
>   in another mirror,
> And that each one of His eternal attributes should become
>   manifest accordingly in a diverse form.
> Therefore He created the verdant fields of Time and
>   Space and the life-giving garden of the world,
> That every branch and leaf and fruit might show forth
>   His various perfections.
> The cypress gave a hint of His comely stature, the rose
>   gave tidings of His beauteous countenance.
> Wherever Beauty peeped out, Love appeared beside it;
>   wherever Beauty shone in a rosy cheek, Love lit
>   his torch from that flame.
> Wherever Beauty dwelt in dark tresses, Love came and
>   found a heart entangled in their coils.
> Beauty and Love are as body and soul; Beauty is the
>   mine and Love the precious stone.
> They have always been together from the very first;
>   never have they travelled but in each other's
>   company.

In another work Jāmī sets forth the relation of God to the world more philosophically, as follows:

> The unique Substance, viewed as absolute and void of all phenomena, all limitations and all multiplicity, is the Real (*al-Haqq*). On the other hand, viewed in His aspect of multiplicity and plurality, under which He displays Himself when clothed with phenomena, He is the whole created universe. Therefore the universe is the outward visible expression of the Real, and the Real is the inner unseen reality of the universe. The universe before it was evolved to outward view was identical with the Real; and the Real after this evolution is identical with the universe.

Phenomena, as such, are not-being and only derive a contingent existence from the qualities of Absolute Being by which they are irradiated. The sensible world resembles the fiery circle made by a single spark whirling round rapidly.

Man is the crown and final cause of the universe. Though last in the order of creation he is first in the process of divine thought, for the essential part of him is the primal Intelligence or universal Reason which emanates immediately from the Godhead. This corresponds to the Logos—the animating principle of all things—and is identified with the Prophet Mohammed. An interesting parallel might be drawn here between the Christian and Sūfī doctrines. The same expressions are applied to the founder of Islam which are used by St. John, St. Paul, and later mystical theologians concerning Christ. Thus, Mohammed is called the Light of God, he is said to have existed before the creation of the world, he is adored as the source of all life, actual and possible, he is the Perfect Man in whom all the divine attributes are manifested, and a Sūfī tradition ascribes to him the saying, "He that hath seen me hath seen Allah." In the Moslem scheme, however, the Logos doctrine occupies a subordinate place, as it obviously must when the whole duty of man is believed to consist in realising the unity of God. The most distinctive feature of Oriental as opposed to European mysticism is its profound consciousness of an omnipresent, all-pervading unity in which every vestige of individuality is swallowed up. Not to become *like* God or *personally* to participate in the divine nature is the Sūfī's aim, but to escape from the bondage of his unreal selfhood and thereby to be reunited with the One infinite Being.

According to Jāmī, Unification consists in making the heart single—that is, in purifying and divesting it of attachment to aught except God, both in respect of desire and will and also as regards knowledge and gnosis. The mystic's desire and will should be severed from all things which are desired and willed; all objects of knowledge and understanding should be removed from his intellectual vision. His thoughts should be directed solely towards God, he should not be conscious of anything besides. (pp. 79-83)

> *Reynold A. Nicholson, "The Gnosis," in his* The Mystics of Islam, *1914. Reprint by Routledge and Kegan Paul Ltd., 1963, pp. 68-101.*

EDWARD G. BROWNE (essay date 1920)

[*Browne is recognized as one of the leading experts on Persia. He wrote a monumental history of Persian literature, closely studied Persian mystics and dervishes, and composed a work considered a classic of English travel literature,* A Year amongst the Persians *(1893). In the following excerpt from a work originally published in 1920, he examines the form, content, and sources of Jami's major poetry and describes the range and character of selected prose works.*]

Mullā Núru'd-Dín 'Abdu'r-Raḥmán Jámí . . . was one of the most remarkable geniuses whom Persia ever produced, for he was at once a great poet, a great scholar, and a great mystic. Besides his poetry, which, apart from minor productions, consisted of three *Díwáns* of lyrical poetry and seven romantic or didactic *mathnawís,* he wrote on the exegesis of the *Qur'án,* the evidence of the Divine Mission of the Prophet Muḥammad, traditions, lives of the Saints, Mysticism, Arabic grammar, Rhyme, Prosody, Music, acrostics (*mu'ammá*) and other matters. In the *Tuḥfa-i-Sámí* forty-six of his works are enumerated, and I do not think this list is exhaustive. He was held in the highest honour by his contemporaries, not only by his fellow-countrymen, but . . . even by the Ottoman Sulṭán, who vainly endeavoured to induce him to visit his court. By his most illustrious contemporaries he was regarded as so eminent as to be beyond praise and so well known as to need no detailed biography. Thus Bábur, after observing that "in exoteric and esoteric learning there was none equal to him in that time," says that he is "too exalted for there to be any need for praising him," and that he only introduces his name "for luck and for a blessing" [see excerpt dated 1505]. Sám Mírzá, the son of Sháh Isma'íl the Ṣafawí, places him first in the fifth section (*Ṣaḥífa*) of his *Tuḥfa-i-Sámí,* and says "by reason of the extreme elevation of his genius . . . there is no need to describe his condition or set forth any account of him, since the rays of his virtues have reached from the East to the uttermost parts of the West, while the bountiful table of his excellencies is spread from shore to shore." (pp. 507-08)

Of Jámí's minor works I have noted some two dozen, included by Sám Mírzá in the list of forty-six which he gives in his *Tuḥfa-i-Sámí,* but this latter number is more than doubled by the *Mirátu'l-Khayal,* which states that Jámí left behind him some ninety works. These minor works include commentaries on portions of the *Qur'án, e.g.* the *Súratu'l-Fátiḥa;* commentaries on Forty Traditions and on the Traditions of Abú Dharr; theological tracts on the Divine Unity (*Risála-i-Tahlíliyya* and *Lá iláha illa 'lláh*), the Rites of the Pilgrimage (*Manásik-i-Ḥajj*) and the like; monographs on the lives or sayings of various eminent mystics, such as Jalálu'd-Dín Rúmí, Khwája Pársá and 'Abdu'lláh Anṣárí; tracts on Ṣúfí ethics and practice (*e.g.* the *Ṭaríq-i-Ṣúfíyán* and *Taḥqíq-i-Madhhab-i-Ṣúfíyán*); and commentaries on Arabic and Persian mystical verses, such as the *Tá'iyya* and *Mímiyya* (or *Khamriyya*) of 'Umar ibnu'l-Fáriḍ, the opening verses of the *Mathnawí* (also known as the *Nay-náma,* or "Reed-book" from its subject), a couplet of Amír Khusraw of Dihlí, and a commentary of some of his own quatrains. Besides all these Jámí wrote treatises on prosody, rhyme and music, a commentary on the *Miftáḥu'l-Ghayb,* and another for his son Ḍiyá'u'd-Dín on the well-known Arabic grammar of Ibnu'l-Ḥájib known as the *Káfiya.* There is also a collection of Jámí's letters (*Munshá'át*), and five treatises on the *Mu'ammá,* or Acrostic, which was so popular at this period.

Last, but not least, amongst Jámí's prose works is the ***Bahár-istán,*** or **"Spring land,"** a book similar in character and arrangement to the more celebrated *Gulistán* of Sa'dí, composed in 892/1487. It comprises eight chapters (each called *Rawḍa,* "Garden"), the first containing anecdotes about Saints and Ṣúfís; the second sayings of Philosophers and Wise Men; the third on the Justice of Kings; the fourth on Generosity; the fifth on Love; the sixth on Jokes and Witticisms; the seventh on

Poets; and the eighth on dumb animals. The work is written in mixed prose and verse, the proportion of verse being very considerable. (pp. 514-15)

It is as a poet, however, that Jámí is best known, and it is of his poetical works that we must now speak. These comprise seven *mathnawí* poems, known collectively as the *Sab'a* ("Septet") or *Haft Awrang* ("Seven Thrones," one of the names by which the constellation of the Great Bear is known in Persia), and three separate *Díwáns*, or collections of lyrical poetry, known respectively as the *Fátihatu'sh-Shabáb* ("Opening of Youth"), compiled in 884/1479-1480; the *Wásitatu'l-'Iqd* ("Middle of the Necklace"), compiled in 894/1489; and the *Khátimatu'l-Hayát* ("End of Life"), compiled in 896/1490-1, only two years before the author's death. (pp. 515-16)

[The *Silsilatu'dh-Dhahab,* or "Chain of Gold,"] discusses various philosophical, ethical and religious subjects with illustrative anecdotes and comprises some 7200 couplets. A certain incoherence and scrappiness, combined with a not very pleasing metre, seem to have rendered it less popular than the remaining poems of the "Septet." . . . (pp. 516-17)

The *Silsilatu'dh-Dhabab* is divided into three books or *daftars,* whereof the first ends with an *I'tiqád-náma,* or Confession of Faith, which exhibits Jámí, in spite of his mysticism, as a thoroughly orthodox Sunní. This is sufficiently shown by the sectional headings, which run as follows: Necessary Existence;

The son seeks counsel from his father. From a mid-sixteenth-century manuscript of Silsilatu'dh-Dhahab.

Unity of God; the Attributes of God, *viz.* Life, Knowledge, Will, Power, Hearing, Seeing, Speech; Divine Actions; existence of the Angels; belief in all the Prophets; superiority of Muhammad over all other prophets; finality of Muhammad's mission; the Prophet's Law; his Night-Ascent to Heaven; his miracles; God's Scriptures; eternal pre-existence of God's Word; superiority of the people of Muhammad over all other peoples; unlawfulness of regarding as infidels any of the "people of the *Qibla*"; the Angels of the Tomb, Munkir and Nakír; the two blasts of the trumpet; the distribution of the books kept by the recording angels; the Balance; the Bridge of Sirát; the fifty stations of 'Arasát; indicating that the infidels shall remain in Hell-fire for ever, while sinners shall escape therefrom by the intercession of the virtuous and the pious; Paradise and its degrees.

The second book of the "Chain of Gold" consists chiefly of dissertations on the different kinds and phases of Love, "metaphorical" and "real," and anecdotes of saints and lovers. The third contains for the most part anecdotes of kings, and towards the end several about physicians. Amongst the latter it is interesting to find two borrowed from the fourth Discourse of the *Chahár Maqála* of Nizámí-i-'Arúdí of Samarqand, one related by Avicenna concerning a certain physician at the Sámánid Court who healed a maidservant by psychical treatment, and the other describing how Avicenna himself cured a prince of the House of Buwayh of melancholic delusions. These are followed by a disquisition on the two opposite kinds of poetry, the one "a comfort to the soul" and the other "a diminution of the heart"; and an interesting dissertation on poets of old time who rewarded their royal patrons by immortalizing their names, which would otherwise have passed into oblivion. The poets of whom mention is here made are Rúdakí, 'Unsurí, Saná'í, Nizámí, Mu'izzí, Anwarí, Kháqání, Zahír, Sa'dí, Kamál and Salmán of Sáwa. Another anecdote from the *Chahár Maqála* about one of 'Unsurí's happy improvisations is also introduced in this place. The book ends somewhat abruptly with a short conclusion which, one cannot help feeling, would have seemed almost equally appropriate at any other point in the text. In a word, the "Chain of Gold" could bear the withdrawal of many of its component links without suffering much detriment. It contains some excellent matter, but is too long, and lacks artistic unity of conception.

The character and scope of the curious allegorical poem of *Salámán and Absál* may be readily apprehended by the English reader from Edward FitzGerald's rather free and somewhat abridged translation. His rendering in blank verse is generally graceful and sometimes eloquent; but the employment of the metre of *Hiawatha* for the illustrative anecdotes (which, as is generally the case in poems of this class, frequently interrupt the continuity of the text) is a less happy experiment. The story is of the slenderest kind, the *dramatis personæ* being a King of Greece, a Wise Man who is his constant mentor and adviser, his beautiful and dearly beloved son Salámán, Absál the fair nurse of the boy, and Zuhra (the planet Venus), representing the heavenly Beauty which finally expels the memory of Absál from Salámán's mind. Amongst the somewhat grotesque features of the story are the birth of Salámán without a mother to bear him (the poet's misogyny holding marriage in abhorrence, though he was himself married), and the seniority by some twenty years of the charming Absál over her nursling, whom, when he reached maturity, she entangles in an attachment highly distasteful to the king and the sage. The latter, by a kind of mesmeric power, compels Salámán in the earthly paradise whither he has fled with Absál to build and kindle a great pyre of brushwood, into which the two lovers cast themselves, with the result that, while poor Absál is burned to ashes, Salámán emerges unhurt, purified from all earthly desires, and fit to receive the crown and throne which his father hastens to confer upon him. The allegory, transparent enough without commentary, is fully explained in the Epilogue. (pp. 521-23)

The *Tuḥfatu'l-Aḥrár,* or **"Gift of the Free,"** is a didactic and moral poem of theological and ethical contents comprising, besides doxologies, eulogies of the Prophet, and Supplications to God (*Munáját*), twenty *Maqálát* or Discourses, of which the last is addressed to the poet's little son Yúsuf Ḍiyá'u'd-Dín, who was then only four years of age, while his father was sixty. Each discourse is, as a rule, followed by one or more illustrative anecdotes. In a short prose preface prefixed to the poem Jámí implies that it was inspired by the *Makhzanu'l-Asrár* ("Treasury of Mysteries") of Niẓámí and the *Maṭla'u'l-Anwár* ("Dayspring of Lights") of Amír Khusraw of Dihlí. The poem is on the whole dull and monotonous, and cannot be regarded as a favourable specimen of Jámí's work. (pp. 526-27)

The *Subḥatu'l-Abrár,* or **"Rosary of the Pious"** is a didactic poem of theological, mystical and ethical contents very similar to the last, equally lacking in coherence and even less attractive in form and matter. (pp. 528-29)

The story and the moral are admirable, but most Persian scholars will, I think, prefer Sa'dí's older to Jámí's later version.

The fifth of the **"Seven Thrones,"** the *Romance of Yúsuf (Joseph) and Zulaykhá (Potiphar's wife),* is by far the most celebrated and popular. . . . (p. 531)

The story itself, based on the *Súratu Yúsuf (Qur'án* xii), which describes it as "the most beautiful of stories," is one of the most popular themes of romantic poetry in Persia and Turkey, and engaged the attention of the great Firdawsí after he had finished the *Sháh-náma,* and after him of a whole series of Persian poets. (p. 532)

As the *Sab'a* ("Septet") of Jámí was admittedly inspired by and modelled on the *Khamsa* ("Quintet") of Niẓámí, some comparison of their respective styles and methods may fairly be demanded. As I consider that in questions of literary taste it is very difficult for a foreigner to judge, I requested my Persian colleague, Mírzá Bihrúz, son of the distinguished physician and writer Mírzá Abu'l-Faḍl of Sáwa, a young man of great promise and ability, well read in both Arabic and Persian literature, to write a short essay on this point, and I here reproduce in English the gist of his opinions.

Jámí's verses, writes Mírzá Bihrúz, rival, and perhaps even excel, those of Niẓámí in poetical form, sweetness and simplicity, being unlaboured and altogether free from artificiality; but they fall far short of them in strength (*matánat*), poetic imagination and eloquence. To appreciate and enjoy Niẓámí a profound knowledge of the Persian language is required, while Jámí can be read with pleasure by all, whence his greater fame and popularity, especially in India, Turkey and other lands where Persian literature is an exotic. Moreover Niẓámí was a man of far-reaching attainments, not only in the language and history of his country, but in the sciences, especially the mathematical sciences, of his time, so that often he cannot be understood except by a reader similarly gifted. Such an one, however, will find in him depths and subtleties for which he would seek in vain in Jámí's poetry. (pp. 540-41)

Jámí, though a mystic, was essentially an orthodox Muhammadan, and shows little of the enthusiasm for pre-Islamic Persia which inspired Firdawsí, and, in a lesser degree, Niẓámí. Of his indebtedness to the latter he makes no secret, and, indeed, follows his footsteps with extraordinary closeness, though here and there he introduces topics and dissertations entirely his own. Not only does he imitate Niẓámí in the titles, metres and subdivisions of his poems, but even in minute personal details. Thus each poet addresses himself and gives advice to a seven-year-old son, the only difference being that while Niẓámí encourages his son to study Medicine, Jámí recommends Theology. The parallelism is especially apparent in the sections dealing with the "cause of the versification of the tale" of [*Laylá and Manjún*] in the respective versions of the two poets. . . . (pp. 541-42)

Of Jámí's lyric poetry, embodied . . . in three separate *Díwáns,* it is impossible to give an adequate account [here]. . . . (p. 542)

Of the great Persian lyrical poets who preceded Jámí the influence of Sa'dí and Ḥáfiẓ is most noticeable; and in the verses sometimes known collectively as the *Nay-náma,* or **"Book of the Reed,"** he has skilfully imitated the style and lucidly developed the idea of the Prologue to Jalálu'd-Dín Rúmí's great Mystical *Mathnawí.* To conclude and epitomize in one sentence this wholly inadequate account of one who, though I decline to regard him as the last great classical poet of Persia, was certainly one of the most talented, versatile and prolific. In Jámí the mystical and pantheistic thought of Persia may be said to find its most complete and vivid expression; while, though he may have been equalled or even surpassed by others in each of the numerous realms of literature which he cultivated, no other Persian poet or writer has been so successful in so many different fields, and the enthusiastic admiration of his most eminent contemporaries is justified by his prolific and many-sided genius. (p. 548)

> *Edward G. Browne, "Poets of the Later Tímúrid Period," in his* A Literary History of Persia: The Tartar Dominion (1265-1502), *Vol. III, 1929. Reprint by Cambridge at the University Press, 1956, pp. 461-548.*

REUBEN LEVY (essay date 1923)

> [*Levy was an English authority on Eastern languages, Islamic culture, and the Muslim Middle Ages. In the following excerpt, he surveys Jami's major works, maintaining that while Jami ranks high among Persian poets, he was not "the last great classical poet of Persia."*]

The greatest of Mír Alí Shír's clients and the most versatile writer of the Tímúrid period, namely, Mullá Núru 'l Dín Abdu 'l Raḥmán Jámí, was born in the village of Jám in Khurásán in A.D. 1414, and from it took the pen-name of 'Jámí', one of the most notable in Persian literature. . . . [The] Persians consider their seven greatest poets to be Firdawsí for epic poetry, Niẓámí for romances, Rúmí for mystical poetry, Sa'dí for his verses on ethical subjects, Ḥáfiẓ for lyrics, and Jámí for general excellence in all these forms. Though such generalization must be treated with caution, it is a near approximation to the truth. As for Jámí himself, though he is not, as is often said, 'the last great classical poet of Persia', yet he ranks highest amongst the more recent poets of modern Persia. His versatility was astonishing, for his prose works are as valuable as his poetry is good. In addition to three *díwáns* of lyrical poetry, many of which are after the style of Ḥáfiẓ, Jámí composed seven *maṣ-*

nawí poems commonly grouped together, on the analogy of Niẕámí's *Khamsa* (Quintet) under the Arabic title of the *Saba'* *(Septet),* or of the Persian *Haft Awrang (The Seven Thrones).* The themes which the *Septet* employs are ethical, mystical, allegorical, or romantic; they are not always original, and sometimes bear evident traces of the influence of Niẕámí, but the freshness of treatment which is their special characteristic has gained for them an enormous popularity. The occasional defects of Jámí's style, due to decadent influences, are displayed in his treatment of the best known *maṣnawí* of the seven, namely the *Yúsuf u Zulaykhá.* The story, that of Joseph and Potiphar's wife, was first used in verse by Firdawsí, and by comparisons with the work of the master, Jámí's appears marred by much bombast and hyperbole and, most of all, by the predominant mysticism which entirely overshadows the story. It nevertheless has this advantage over Firdawsí's version, that it confines itself to the story of Yúsuf and Zulaykhá without detailing at great length the early history of Jacob, Joseph (Yúsuf) and the brothers.

For purposes of comparison each poet's version of the same incident (Zulaykhá's first approaches to Yúsuf) is appended. Firdawsí, who is the author of the first extract, describes how Yúsuf is distracted by grief at being separated from his father and how Zulaykhá attempts to console him by recounting all the possibilities of diversion open to him. Finally she declares her love:

> If thy heart desires a loving heart,
> A mistress that will be as thine own soul and as the whole
>   world to thee,
> Take me; for behold, I am thine.
> I am thy worshipper and thy lover.
> My heart, night and day, is the home of love for thee.
> Day and night, mine eyes are upon thee:
> Thou art the light in mine eyes,
> Thou hast proved thyself the soul in my body,
> For thee only I employ mind and reason,
> For thine ends only do I work.
>
> A pure body I keep everlastingly for thee,
> Bound to thee I keep a loving heart.
> Thine every command
> I would carry out as a slave.

• • • • •

> Thus softly she spoke, and took him within her arms;
> That she might take a kiss from his red lips.
> But Yúsuf at this leapt to his feet
> And took his hand from Zulaykhá's grasp.
> And with shame his cheeks were blood-red.

• • • • •

> Then finally Yúsuf unloosed his tongue
> And spoke thus: 'Gracious lady,
> What corrupt thought and baseless plan do you entertain
> In your unprofitable and unworthy words?
> What wicked fancy hath possessed you?

• • • • •

Jámí begins by generalizing:

> When a beholder enters a garden
> In his love for the rose his heart is charred like a tulip's.
> First he is intoxicated at sight of the rose,
> And, seeing, puts out his hand to pluck it.
> Thus Zulaykhá sought means for her wooing,
> But Yúsuf drew aside from her.
> Zulaykhá's eyes shed tears of blood,
> But Yúsuf fled from her.

> Zulaykhá's soul was seared with pain,
> But Yúsuf's heart was free from care.
> Zulaykhá gazed in rapture upon his beauteous face,
> But Yúsuf's glances were downward cast.
> Zulaykhá burned with every glance,
> But Yúsuf turned to avoid her eyes;
> From fear of temptation he regarded not her face,
> Nor looked upon her with temptation's eye.

Of Jámí's many prose works his *Ash'i'atu 'l Lama'át (Rays of the Flashes)* is a commentary on the mystical *Lama'át* of 'Irákí. . . . Amongst the best known of the others is a great dictionary of biographies of the Ṣúfí Saints, known as *Nafaḥátu 'l 'Uns (The Breaths of Fellowship),* and a further work connected with Ṣúfíism is his *Lawá'iḥ,* a short treatise on Ṣúfí doctrines with illustrative sections in verse. His *Baháristán (Abode of Spring)* is perhaps the most popular of all his prose works, though from its large proportion of verse in it it may almost be called an anthology of poems. It was admittedly written in imitation of Sa'dí's *Gulistán,* and though, like its prototype, it was meant to amuse, it contains a number of serious biographies of the poets with quotations from their works. The *Baháristán* does not in its style achieve the simplicity of the *Gulistán.* Particularly in the prose introductions to the various chapters there are visible the faults of overloaded rhetoric and ornate wording which were characteristic of most of the writings of the later Tímúrid period. These faults have been traced to foreign influence, and it is true that they appear at their worst, not in the writings of native Persians, but in those of Turks, Indians, and others to whom Persian was the language of literature rather than of everyday use. Foreign elements in Persia were important even under Tímúr, and multiplied enormously after his death. (pp. 83-6)

Reuben Levy, "The Mongol Domination," in his Persian Literature: An Introduction, *Oxford University Press, London, 1923, pp. 53-86.*

A. J. ARBERRY   (essay date 1958)

[*Arberry was a renowned English authority on Eastern life and literature. In the following excerpt, he examines Jami's major prose and closely analyzes the form, content, and intellectual background of* Haft Aurang.]

The most ancient catalogue of the works of Jāmī is the list given by Sām Mīrzā, amounting to 45 separate titles. A very great part of these has survived, but only the most important books will be reviewed here; it will be convenient to glance at the prose compositions first. The *Nafaḥāt al-uns,* comprising 582 biographies of Muslim saints . . . , is an important source for the history of Ṣūfism, especially in the later period; written in a simple and straightforward style, it abounds in interesting and informative anecdotes and is among the finest specimens, as Dr. Ḥikmat affirms [in his 1942 monograph, *Jami*], of fifteenth-century prose. (pp. 427-28)

[Jāmī wrote] *Commentary on the "Lama'āt"* of 'Irāqī at Navā'ī's invitation, completing it in 1481; some years earlier he had composed the *Lavā'iḥ* in emulation of that work, offering it to the 'Shāh of Hamadān.' E. H. Whinfield, who published the text of this book in facsimile with an excellent translation, in which he was assisted by Mīrzā Muḥammad Qazvīnī, suggested that 'the person referred to is probably Shāh Manuchahr, Governor of Hamadān, who paid much attention to Jāmī when he visited the town in A.H. 877'; Ḥikmat however prefers to believe that the veiled reference is to Jahan-Shāh whose name was either omitted or subsequently excised because of the evil reputation he enjoyed in Harāt. The *Lavā'iḥ* is divided into thirty 'Flashes'; the metaphysical prose, following the tradition beginning with Aḥmad Ghazālī in his *Savāniḥ*, is interspersed with quatrains. (p. 428)

As Sa'dī's *Gulistān* is divided into eight chapters, so the *Baháristān* is set out in eight 'gardens.' While Jāmī carefully imitates Sa'dī's rhyming and rhythmical prose and his interspersion of verses, the contents of his book are somewhat different; in particular the seventh 'garden' is a miniature anthology of Persian poets bringing in some pointed criticisms. 'He was much addictd to incoherent expressions' is Jāmī's verdict on the minor poet Ādharī; Kātibī 'used many expressions peculiar to himself in a peculiar manner'; Ḥāfiẓ himself 'wrote exquisite poetry, and his Ghazals are superior in fluency and elegance, but some contain errors in their versification.' The sixth book is advertised as a 'blowing of the zephirs of wit, and the breezes of jocular sallies, which cause the buds of the lips to laugh and the flowers of the hearts to bloom'; some of the anecdotes retailed are of an indecency unexpected in a man famous for his piety. . . . (p. 431)

Considerable as Jāmī's achievements were in prose, it is far more through his poetry that he has dwarfed all who have come after him. Coming so late in the classical tradition, he inevitably had little new to add to what the great figures of the past had said; Persia would need a new contact and a fresh and abundant source of inspiration from outside before her writers could recover the old creativeness. Jāmī's verse testifies to the thoroughness with which he had studied Anvarī and Khāqānī, Sa'dī and Ḥāfiẓ, Niẓāmī and Amīr Khusrau, all the acknowledged masters of ode, lyric, idyll. Yet he fused together these diverse elements and produced out of the amalgam an individual style of great fluency and brilliance, a diction permeated above all else by the language and the ideas of mysticism.

Amīr Khusrau had published five *Dīvāns* representing different phases of his literary activity; Jāmī did not quite rival this productivity, but for all that he put together three separate collections of odes and lyrics. The first, called *Fātiḥat al-shabāb*, was issued in 1479, the second, *Wāsiṭat al-'iqd*, in 1489, the third *Khātimat al-ḥayāt*, in 1491; each is preceded by an elegant preface written by the poet himself. (p. 433)

Jāmī was not ambitious only to emulate Anvarī and Ḥāfiẓ; he also aimed at matching the work of Niẓāmī in the field of more extended composition. Niẓāmī had written five epics (or idylls, as it seems preferable to call the shorter epic); Jāmī composed seven, known collectively as the *Haft Aurang* ('**Seven Thrones**'). It appears that Jāmī himself was responsible for publishing the seven together, for some manuscripts of the collection are introduced by an editorial preface, presumably (as Dr. Ḥikmat believes) from his pen. (p. 437)

Noticing that certain very ancient copies lack this preface, Ḥikmat concludes that Jāmī originally composed only five idylls in emulation of the *Khamsa* of Niẓāmī and of Amīr Khusrau, but afterwards decided to add two more. This conjecture is strengthened by the fact that in the *Khirad-nāma-yi Iskandarī*, the last of the seven, Jāmī expressly states that it was his first intention to write five *mathnavīs* in the same metres as those of Niẓāmī, but that he augmented this total by writing the *Silsilat al-dhahab* and the *Subḥat al-abrār*. We shall now consider these seven poems in the order in which they occur in the manuscripts.

First, the *Silsilat al-dhahab*, written in the *khafīf* metre after the fashion of Sanā'ī's *Ḥadīqat al-ḥaqīqa* and Auḥadī's *Jām-*

i Jam, is dedicated to Sulṭān Ḥusain Bāiqarā and must have been completed between 1468 and 1472. The *terminus a quo* is fixed by the date of that Sultan's accession; the *terminus ad quem* is determined by a more interesting historical argument, for it was in 1472 that Jāmī set out on the pilgrimage to Mecca, and on his way back ran into a storm of protest at Baghdad on account of certain verses from the poem of an allegedly anti-Shī'ite complexion which were already in circulation in that city. A fairly detailed account of the contents of this didactic poem is given by E. G. Browne, who inexplicably assigns its composition to the year 1485; he assesses its length at about 7,200 couplets, speaks of 'a certain incoherence and scrappiness' and declares that 'it contains some excellent matter, but is too long, and lacks artistic unity of conception' [see excerpt dated 1920]. (pp. 437-38)

Second, the *Salāmān u Absāl* was composed for Sulṭān Ya'qūb of the 'White Sheep,' evidently in 1479 or 1480, for Ya'qūb succeeded Uzun Ḥasan in 1478 and the poem was intended as a kind of coronation present. In it Jāmī complains of his advancing years and the necessity to wear 'Frankish spectacles' [see excerpt dated 1479]. (p. 440)

Third, the *Tuḥfat al-ahrār* is a didactic poem in the *sarī'* metre, modelled on the *Makhzan al-asrār* of Niẓāmī and Amīr Khusrau's *Maṭla' al-anwār*. This work makes no mention of any prince and was seemingly intended as a tribute to all the saints; in particular Jāmī blesses the memory of Bahā' al-Dīn Muḥammad Bukhārī the founder of the Naqshbandī order, and prays for the welfare of his friend and contemporary Nāṣir al-Dīn 'Ubaid Allāh called Khvāja Aḥrār. In the twentieth and concluding discourse the poet addresses his son Ḍiyā' al-Dīn Yūsuf, born after his father had reached sixty and at the time of writing four years old. The educational programme outlined for the little boy harks back to the famous *ars longa vita brevis* [''art is long, life is short'']. After recommending a thorough study of the Koran as laying the surest foundations of a religious life, Jāmī proceeds:

> Thereafter put your back into manners and customs
> and turn your face to the acquisition of learning;
> commit to heart a digest of every subject—
> gather a fragrant blossom from every garden.
> Whatever lesson you set yourself, be certain
> not to pass on until you know it completely.
> Science has ways so many and multifarious:
> see you do not transgress the essential limits.
> Life is short: long is learning and virtue—
> only acquire what is absolutely essential.

Fourth, the *Subḥat al-abrār,* yet a third didactic poem, composed in a rare variety of the *ramal* metre otherwise employed in a section of the *Nuh sipihr* of Amīr Khusrau, is dedicated to Sulṭān Ḥusain Bāiqarā and again mentions Jāmī's son Yūsuf. Since the boy is now stated to be five, and since he is known to have been born in 1477, it is possible to date the *Tuḥfat al-ahrār* as completed in 1481 and the *Subḥat al-abrār* in 1482; both poems are preceded by prefaces in elaborately artificial prose. How differently this work has impressed different readers is well seen by comparing verdicts: 'The *Subḥatu'l-Abrār,* or "**Rosary of the Pious**" is a didactic poem of theological, mystical and ethical contents very similar to the last, equally lacking in coherence and even less attractive in form and matter' (E. G. Browne [see excerpt dated 1920]); 'This is a very charming and eloquent poem embracing lofty topics and written in a delightful metre never employed in any work after Jāmī' ('Alī Aṣghar Ḥikmat).

The shah's hunt, as illustrated in a mid-sixteenth-century manuscript of Silsilatu'dh-Dhahab.

Fifth, the *Yūsuf u Zulaikhā* was composed in 1483 in the *hazaj* metre, like the *Vīs u Rāmīn* of Fakhr al-Dīn Gurgānī and the *Khusrau u Shīrīn* of Niẓāmī. Jāmī again commemorates the revered Khvāja 'Ubaid Allāh Naqshband, and eulogizes Sulṭān Ḥusain Bāiqarā; at the end he remembers his good friend and patron Mīr 'Alī Shīr. The poem is based on the story of Joseph and Potiphar's wife as told in Sūra XII of the Koran, a romantic theme (Jāmī gives it a mystical twist) which was a favourite with Persian authors; an idyll on this topic is attributed to Firdausī's old age, and among others who wrote on the same subject were Shihāb al-Dīn 'Am'aq and Mas'ūd of Qum; many Turkish poets also took it up. (pp. 441-42)

Sixth, the *Lailā u Majnūn,* composed in 1484, was a direct challenge to comparison with the poems written on the same theme by Niẓāmī and Amīr Khusrau, for Jāmī chose exactly the same metre, a jaunty variety of the *hazaj.* The poet obligingly gives us the total of the verses as coming to 3,860 and states that the poem took him 'fourteen months, more or less' to complete; he again mentions Khvāja 'Ubaid Allāh and applauds the 'Sulṭān of the Age,' without however naming him more precisely. It may be added that Jāmī's nephew Hātifī, himself a noted poet who died in 1521, also composed a *Lailā u Majnūn;* it was his version of the old desert love-story that Sir William Jones chose to publish (Calcutta, 1788), assigning whatever income might accrue from the sales to 'the poor in the Supreme Court, in trust for the miserable persons under execution for debt in the prison of *Calcutta.*' Jāmī's version has not even attracted that much attention, though it contains many fine descriptions and exhibits to the full his rhetorical virtuosity. Here is a picture of a sandstorm in the summer desert.

> One day the simoom that blows at noontide
> rose scorching the mountain and the plain;
> the desert, with its flying sand and pebbles,
> was a chafing-dish full of sparking embers;
> serpents thrashed about in all directions
> like hairs that have been flung in a fire.
> If any wild ass had ventured in that plain
> and set its foot on that burning surface,
> its sole would have broken into blisters
> like the hoof of a travel-worn mule.
> The whole world ailed of the great heat
> panting like a furnace charged with fire;
> into that furnace the mighty mountains
> ran melting like an unguent of quicklime;
> the mountain springs noisily bubbling
> were stone cauldrons of boiling water.

Seventh, the *Khirad-nāma-yi Iskandarī* ('Wisdom of Alexander'), imitating in *mutaqārib* metre and subject-matter the *Iskandar-nāma* of Niẓāmī and Amīr Khusrau, enabled Jāmī in the guise of the ancient legend of Alexander to write what is virtually a fourth didactic idyll. The poet again addresses Khvāja 'Ubaid Allāh Aḥrār, Sulṭān Ḥusain Bāiqarā, and his own son; since the Khvāja died in 1490, Dr. Ḥikmat concludes that this poem must have been composed about the year 1485, certainly after the *Lailā u Majnūn.* Jāmī repeatedly complains of the increasing weariness of old age; towards the end of the work he speaks of it as the last of his *Khamsa,* and he praises the Turkish *Khamsa* which his old friend Nāvā'ī had written. The wise counsel which he imparts with all of an old man's sententious repetitiveness as his final offering to the world is conveniently if improbably put into the mouths of such famous sages as Aristotle, Plato, Socrates, Hippocrates, Pythagoras, Aesculapius and Hermes. The narrative drags slowy to its close with the death of Alexander and the letter of condolence sup-

posedly sent by Aristotle to the great conqueror's mother. . . . (pp. 447-49)

We have now come to the end of this necessarily incomplete and partial review of classical Persian literature. Jāmī's death marks the conclusion of the golden age; the silver period sets in with the beginning of the sixteenth century. (pp. 449-50)

> *A. J. Arberry, ''Jāmī,'' in his* Classical Persian Literature, *George Allen & Unwin Ltd., 1958, pp. 425-50.*

IDRIES SHAH (essay date 1964)

[*Known as The Sayed as was his father before him, Shah traces his descent from the Prophet Mohammed and the emperors of Persia through the Caliph Musa al-Kasim. Following a centuries-old tradition, Shah became leader of the Sufis, or Islamic mystics, upon his father's death in 1969. He is now widely recognized in academic and religious circles as the world's foremost expert on and proponent of the Sufi philosophy. In the following excerpt, he describes what he considers Jami's achievement as a Sufi.*]

Mulla Nurudin Abdarahman Jami (literally Master Light of Faith, Servant of the Merciful, of Jam) was born in Khurasan in 1414 and died in Herat in 1492. Jami was spiritualized by the glance of the great Master Mohammed Parsa, who passed through his birthplace when the poet was a small boy, according to his own belief. He was a teacher of the Naqshbandi Order. His Sufi teachings are sometimes displayed, sometimes concealed, in his extraordinary poetical and other works. Among these are the romances of Salaman and Absal and the epic of Joseph and Zuleikha, allegorical tales which are among the greatest pieces of Persian literature ever written. His *Abode of Spring* contains the most important initiatory material. Jami was a great traveler, theologian, hagiographer, grammarian and prosodist, as well as a musical theorist. His intellectual powers were such that after studying under the Master Ali of Samarkand he was soon recognized by the great doctor Rum as superior to him. Addressing a great assembly, he said, ''Since the building of this city none equal in mind and the use of it to this youth Jami has ever crossed the Oxus to Samarkand.'' Jami chose his place-name as a pseudonym because it decodes to the numbers 54, reencodable to the letters ND. This combination of letters in Arabic stands for a group of ideas—idol, opponent, running, compounded perfume—all Sufi poetic concepts connected with the ''state'' or ''movement'' of the Sufi. (pp. 377-78)

> *Idries Shah, ''Annotations: Jami,'' in his* The Sufis, *The Octagon Press, 1964, pp. 377-78.*

JAN RYPKA (essay date 1968)

[*Rypka was a Vienna-born Czechoslovakian translator and critic of Persian literature. In the following excerpt, he surveys Jami's major works, noting both the author's originality and indebtedness to earlier writers.*]

Maulānā Nūru'd-dīn ᶜAbdu'r-Raḥmān Jāmī . . . was an outstanding man and poet. Close relations with the court at Herat and the sincere friendship of the vizier ᶜAlī-Shīr Navā'ī did not affect his independence. His object was neither wealth nor success, though the general respect paid him at home and abroad did perhaps stir his vanity. His attachment to the order of Naqshbandīs was genuine; a dervish without pose, he did not live aloof from the world and its tumult. On the other hand he gave the title *Tuḥfatu'l-aḥrār,* 'Gift of [or 'to'] the Free', to one of his didactic *mathnavīs* in honour of the Naqshbandī Shaykh ᶜUbaydu'llāh-Aḥrār, and professed the faith of the Order in another, called **Silsilatu'dh-dhahab, 'The Golden Chain'**, taking the title from the terminology of the Order. Though an orthodox Sunnite, he supplemented his philosophical views from those of Muḥyi'd-dīn ibn al-ᶜArabī. He thus grew into an unusually prolific poet and scholar in both movements. Whereas ᶜA. A. Ḥikmat enumerates only 45 authenticated works, earlier biographers recorded as many as 99. There is no genre of classical poetry in which he was not at one time or another engaged. He even turned his attention to the logigraph. In addition we find erudite works on theology, mysticism, biography, poetics and rhetoric, grammar, epistolography, literary exegesis and music, some of them written in Arabic. The most famous is the group containing his poetical works: (a) three lyrical *dīvāns* composed in youth, middle age, and old age; (b) **Haft aurang, 'Seven Thrones'** (also **'The Constellation of the Great Bear'**) containing three themes taken from Niẓāmī's *Khamsa* (**Tuḥfatu'l-aḥrār, 'Gift of [or 'to'] the Free'**, *Laylī u Majnūn, Khirad-nāma-i Sikandarī*, **'The Book of the Wisdom of Alexander'**). Neither these nor two other poems of religious, mystical and ethical nature found a wide circulation, although, contrary to the opinion of E. G. Browne [see excerpt dated 1920], native critics considered **Subḥatu'l-abrār, 'The Rosary of the Pious'**, to be one of the best works of its kind. But **Yūsuf u Zalīkhā** is one of the most widely read *mathnavīs*, and rightly so, for it is the best of all the epic poems of this name. The mystical allegory **Salāmān u Absāl** takes its subject from the commentary of Naṣīru'd-dīn Ṭūsī . . . on Avicenna's *Ishārāt*, 'Hints', a story presumably of Greek origin and in the Arabic version obviously of a hermetic nature that Avicenna himself had already made use of in a separate allegory of the same name. In relation to Naṣīru'd-dīn, Jāmī—or maybe already his unknown source—exhibits some variations, but without depriving the fable of its grotesqueness (the motherless birth of the boy Salāmān, on the contrary, appealed to Jāmī in view of his misogyny, just as did the fact that Absāl, Salāmān's nurse, gets burned while the boy emerges from the same fire unharmed); (c) The **Bahāristān, 'The Spring Garden'**, a masterly but affected imitation of the *Gulistān* with an excellent chapter (the seventh) on the history of literature. Among his learned prose works mention should be made of **Nafaḥatu'l-uns, 'Breaths of Familiarity'**, which consists of biographies of 616 scholars, saints and poets regarded as mystics (of which Ḥāfiẓ was one), and is a revision and continuation of Anṣārī's *Ṭabaqātu'ṣ-ṣūfiyya*, 'Classes of the Ṣūfīs'. . . . (pp. 286-87)

This universality must be understood correctly: "It was not by chance that Jāmī tried his skill at all genres of poetry, but in order to prove his basic theory that a work lives not by its form, as was commonly thought at that time, but by the profundity of its content. Jāmī demonstrated that not a single one of the classical forms has died out definitively but that it was possible to revive them if the poet were capable of lending them a deep and significant meaning. Instead of bringing superfastidious forms into play, his *qaṣīdas* speak of the urgency of acting justly and further insist that those in power have not the right to indulge in the joys of life while the masses are obliged to beg and suffer violence." He took Ḥāfiẓ and Niẓāmī (sometimes Amīr Khusrau) as his models, though without equalling them on their own grounds. To quote his own words, he "put old stories to new tunes", but he was nevertheless accused of having more likely stolen old and new verses from Saᶜdī, Anvarī, and Khusrau. His main virtues are a relative lucidity and simplicity as compared with the pomposity and perverseness of the 9th/15th century. Yet Jāmī too knows when

to open all the registers of an extravagant style. As a brilliant epigone he knows how to bring the available material elegantly into harmony with the demands of the period. Through his great genius he was able to influence the literature of Central Asia and Persia, Turkey and India, besides the Chaghatay poetry, embodied at that time in ᶜAlī-Shīr Navā'ī (b. 844/1441, d. 906/1501), the admirable vizier and Jāmī's friend and patron.

It only remains to add that the vast fame enjoyed by Jāmī in his homeland and abroad during his lifetime faded considerably later on, especially in the Shīᶜite Persia of the Safavids, and that it ultimately became confined to a few of his works. (pp. 287-88)

Jan Rypka with Otakar Klíma and others, "Tīmūr and his Successors," in their History of Iranian Literature, *edited by Karl Jahn, D. Reidel Publishing Company, 1968, pp. 279-90.*

IRAJ DEHGHAN (essay date 1971)

[*In the following excerpt, Dehghan enumerates the sources of* Salámán and Absál *and offers his view of the aesthetic merits and faults of the poem.*]

Jāmī's **Salāmān and Absāl**, in 1,131 couplets, is based, beyond a doubt, on Ṭūsī's summary of the Hellenistic romance. In several places the literal translation from Ṭūsī's summary is obvious. Moreover, wherever Ṭūsī's omission seems to have damaged the logical progression of the story, Jāmī, who had probably not seen Ḥunayn's text, is at a loss.

However, Jāmī has made several alterations in Ṭūsī's version. According to his version:

(1) The king rules only over Greece.

(2) There is no mention of the king's unwillingness to cohabit with women. Rather it is the Sage who criticizes women and physical pleasure.

(3) It is Absāl who, seeing the infant, falls in love with him and then, when he reaches maturity, tries to make him fall in love with her.

(4) The "instrument" in Ṭūsī's summary appears as *ā'īna-yi gītī-numāy*.

(5) The two lovers build a huge fire and jump into it, while in Ṭūsī's text they throw themselves into the water.

(6) There is no mention of the two pyramids, the Greek origin of the story, and its translation into Arabic.

In the way of detail and elaboration, Jāmī has made a few additions. These include descriptions of Absāl's beauty, her love for him, Salāmān's beauty, his intelligence, his bravery, his generosity, the description of the ocean, the island, etc. Jāmī also introduces a number of extraneous stories upsetting the lineal progression of the tale. Jalāl al-Dīn Rūmī's *Maṣnavī*, more than any other classical work, contains these kinds of stories and, as we shall see, Jāmī seems to have assimilated this particular poem to Rūmī's literary style.

Jāmī's choice of *masnavī* as the form seems quite natural. Traditionally this form, among all other forms of poetry, is the vehicle used for long stories. All surviving Persian romances, as well as Firdausī's *Shah-nāma*, are written in *masnavī*.

The meter chosen for the poem, *Salāmān and Absāl,* is *ramal musaddas maḥẕūf/maqṣūr* (-u--/-u--/-u-), used also by Rūmī in his monumental masterpiece.

The poem opens in a more or less mystic fashion with the praises of God and the Prophet, followed by panegyrics on Sulṭān Yaʿqūb, Beg of Āq Quinlū, ''The White Sheep,'' (d. 896/1490), his brother Amīr Yusef, and his father Ūsūn Ḥasan. Then, as the poem was composed in the last period of Jāmī's life (1479 or 1480), the poet speaks of his old age. When these preliminaries, which occupy many pages, have been completed the story begins without even a mention of its source. While outwardly a romance the story, as we know and as is confessed at the end of the poem, is a pure allegory designed to show how the soul can be freed from the lusts of the flesh. Here also Jāmī, with little modification, is merely translating Ṭūsī's interpretation of Ḥunayn's version. The king represents the Active Intellect, the Sage that Emanation which comes from above, and Salāmān is a symbol for the Rational Soul. Salā-mān's being born without a mother is an allusion to his detachment from material things. Absāl is the symbol of animal physical power. The love of Salāmān and Absāl for each other shows the love of the Rational Soul for physical pleasure. The Western Ocean is their indulgence in transitory affairs, remote from the Truth. Their yearning for and deprivation from one another are due to old age when, despite the inclination of the soul, the physical powers can no longer perform their functions. The return of Salāmān to his father refers to his awareness of perfection. *Zuhra* represents the rational perfection. The book ends with a prayer for the long life of the Sulṭān. (pp. 121-22)

Jāmī is one of the most versatile and prolific writers of Persian. His great fame could have been based on his profound knowledge of the Islamic sciences, Arabic language and grammar, poetics and prosody, music, and riddles as well as his mystical life, but he is best known as a poet. However, though he definitely is the greatest of his contemporaries, Jāmī cannot compete with any of the great classical poets. Therefore most . . . complimentary descriptions of him are questionable. This is certainly the case with *Salāmān and Absāl* which is considered one of Jāmī's best poetical works.

Jāmī in this poem seems little more than an industrious translator of no very remarkable poetic power. His artistic achievement does not seem to equal his industry. It takes the greatest stretch of the imagination to equate Jāmī in ''poetical form, sweetness and simplicity'' [see the excerpt by Edward G. Browne dated 1920] with Niẓāmī or any other great poet of the earlier classical poetry.

In ''poetical form'' Jāmī is only an imitator and almost always unsuccessful. In his *ghazal*'s, like most of his contemporaries, Jāmī largely imitates Ḥāfiẓ and Saʿdī. Of course it is quite legitimate for a poet to take the rhyme, the form, and even the general sense from a great predecessor or contemporary and try to improve the work by expressing it in a more attractive way. Ḥāfiẓ also imitated several *ghazal*'s of Khwājū of Kirmān, Salmān of Sāva, and even of Saʿdī. But in each instance he tremendously improved the *ghazal* and added to its beauty in a multitude of ways. Jāmī, although he has some good *ghazal*'s, was unable to approach the heights attained by the two great masters whom he imitated. In *masnavī*, Jāmī, like most of his contemporaries, imitates Niẓāmī, Amīr Khusrau of Dilhi and, in a lesser degree, Firdausī and others. Niẓāmī, although to some extent an imitator of Firdausī, and in a lesser degree, of Sanā'ī, is recognized as the all-time master of story telling. Many poets have imitated at least one or two *masnavī*'s

of his *Khamsa*. Nevertheless, no one has been able to excel Niẓāmī. Even Amīr Khusrau, the best imitator of the entire *Khamsa*, fell short of it, as he frankly admitted in the opening of his *Qarān al-Saʿdain*.

Jāmī's *Sabʿa* is an imitation of Niẓāmī, and he makes no secret of it. But, as admitted by Browne and his colleague, although ''here and there he introduces topics and dissertations entirely his own,'' he imitates ''Niẓāmī in the titles, meters, and subdivisions'' and ''even in minute personal details.'' In *Salāmān and Absāl,* since no one has treated the subject in Persian poetry before, he is at a loss. Thus, while still impressed by Niẓāmī, Jāmī rather unsuccessfully imitated Jalāl al-Dīn Rūmī. Besides the meter and the short didactic anecdotes, there are references to and quotations from that poet.

That his poetry is [according to Browne and his colleague] simple, ''unlaboured, and altogether free from artificiality'' appears to be a great misjudgment. Jāmī's poems, although not as artificial as those of some of his contemporaries, definitely rank as examples of labored and artificial Persian poetry. *Iʿnāt* or *iltizām*, ''supererogation,'' also called *luzūm-i mā lā yalzam*, ''making necessary the unnecessary,'' is characteristic of extremely elaborate and artificial poetry. Jāmī's *ghazal*, in which he used the word *ashk*, ''tear,'' in every couplet, or his *qaṣīda* in each couplet of which he has used the word *zar*, ''gold,'' are not the only poems where he has employed *iʿnāt*.

Another example of labored poetry is the choice of extremely difficult rhymes in *ghazal* or *qaṣīda*. Jāmī seems to enjoy employing difficult rhymes in which he can show off his poetical skill. Here are the rhymes of a few of his *maṭlaʿ*'s: *naṣ(ṣ)* and *qafaṣ*, *ʿivaż* and *ʿaraż*, *murtāż* and *iʿrāż*, *maṭlaʿ* and *maqṭaʿ*, *khaṭ(ṭ)* and *nuqaṭ*, *inqiṭāʿ* and *vidāʿ*. Another example of his artificiality in rhyme is a *ghazal* with the following double-rhymes which is definitely a *luzūm-i mā lā yalzam*: *zabān/ zabūn*, *-barān/burūn*, *kunān/kunūn*, *darān/darūn*, *ʿayān/ʿuyūn*, *-sitān/sutūn*, etc.

The choice of difficult *radīf*'s is another example of labored poetry. Jāmī seems to enjoy it as can be seen in the following: *mi-khānamash*, *az firāq*, *tu yābam*, *rā chi kunam*, *nist laẕiẕ*, *nīmī rāst nīmī kaj.* In fact no other poet of his age, perhaps with the exception of Bābā Faghānī, has employed so many and so difficult compound *radīf*'s as Jāmī. One wonders how any poet, no matter how talented, can express his own feeling and ideas when he has to repeat the phrase *nīmī rāst nīmī kaj,* ''one half straight, one half crooked,'' every six or seven words!

Fortunately *Salāmān and Absāl,* as compared with Jāmī's *ghazal*'s, contains far fewer decorative devices. With the exception of the occasional employment of *tajnīs*, ''homonymy,'' *zū-qāfiyatain*, ''double-rhymes,'' *tażādd*, ''antithesis,'' *murāʿāt al-naẓir*, ''parallelism,'' and *mubālagha*, ''hyperbole,'' the poem is not too artificial.

While it contains several passages of beauty, *Salāmān and Absāl* is somewhat uncouth in language. The occasional grammatical mistakes, the employment of incorrect word forms, and the use of certain everyday expressions and phrases render the language of the poem defective.

Lofty thoughts and subtle ideas expressed with lively and vigorous diction which were the characteristics of earlier poetry are often replaced in this poem by commonplace ideas expressed in clumsy and immature language. Although displaying some of the marks of the great classical poets, the descriptions in *Salāmān and Absāl* lack the vividness, originality, and directness of the earlier works. They are characterized not only by ingenuities of fancy, an excessively subjective interpretation of reality, and curiosities of expression, but also by conventional patterns of similies and metaphors. The descriptions of Absāl, Salāmān, and the ocean, thus appear as patch-works of worn-out clichés.

Communication of the poet's own thoughts and feelings does not seem to be the main concern anymore. This is perhaps partly due to the censorship of ideas and beliefs which was the result of the great power wielded by the *fuqahā'*, "legalists," and *mullā*'s throughout the fifteenth century—a trend which lasted even into the Qājar period. There is not one single *ghazal* in Jāmī's entire *Dīvān* which could be considered an indication of his real feelings and ideas.

Another characteristic of Jāmī's poetry, as well as that of his contemporaries, is the lack of an independent poetical style. It is almost impossible for a connoisseur of Persian poetry to identify Jāmī's works.

It is these same contagious characteristics in Jāmī's age which later appeared in Deccan and in Delhi and which brought about the so-called "Indian Style" in Persian poetry.

It has often been said that Jāmī was indifferent to the favor of rulers and prices. This assertion is based on one of his *qiṭ'a*'s in which he says:

> . . . If you examine them [*i.e.*, his *dīvān*'s]
> from end to end.
> turn them a hundred ways, and then return,
> you will not light, in all these panegyrics,
> upon a single thought of selfish greed. . . .

That this, however, is not the case is borne out by the several panegyrics scattered throughout his works, especially the descriptions of Salāmān's generosity in this poem. Here, after a highly hyperbolical panegyric on Salāmān and after relating the story of how the poet Qaṭrān fled from the excessive bounty of his patron, he quotes one of the most beautiful couplets of Rūmī:

> Sweeter it is that the description of
> sweethearts
> should be spoken in the story of others, . . .

> . . . my object in this panegyric is another king
> who now wears on his head the crown of prosperity.

(pp. 124-26)

Iraj Dehghan, "Jāmī's 'Salāmān and Absāl'," in Journal of Near Eastern Studies, *Vol. 30, No. 2, April, 1971, pp. 118-26.*

NICHOLAS HEER (essay date 1979)

[*Heer is an American scholar of Arabic and Islamic literature who has translated several works by Jami. In the following excerpt, he considers Jami's method of adjudication in* The Precious Pearl *and comments on the sources of the work.*]

In making his *muḥākamah*, or adjudication, between the theologians, philosophers, and Ṣūfīs, al-Jāmī takes up eleven questions [in *al-Durrah al-Fākhira*], all of which the theologians and the philosophers had debated for centuries. These questions, listed in the order in which they are taken up, are:

1. The nature of God's existence and its relation to His essence, that is, is it superadded to His essence or identical with it?

2. God's unity and the necessity of demonstrating it.

3. The nature of God's attributes and their relation to His essence, that is, are they superadded to his essence or identical with it?

4. The nature of God's knowledge and the problem of attributing knowledge to God without compromising His unity or necessary existence.

5. God's knowledge of particulars and the problems encountered in attributing this type of knowledge to God.

6. The nature of God's will and whether His will is an attribute distinct from His knowledge.

7. The nature of God's power and the related question of whether God is a free agent or a necessary agent.

8. The question of whether the universe is eternal or originated together with the question of whether an eternal universe can result from a free agent or not.

9. The nature of God's speech and the question of whether the Qur'an is eternal or created.

10. The voluntary acts of humans and whether they occur through the power of God or man.

11. The emanation of the universe from God and the question of whether it is possible for multiple effects to result from a single cause.

In general al-Jāmī first presents the opposing positions of the theologians and the philosophers and then the Ṣūfī position. He presents the Ṣūfī position not merely as a rationally possible alternative to the theological and philosophical positions but as a clearly superior position, either because it reconciles the opposing views of the theologians and philosophers on a particular question, or because it avoids problems necessarily resulting from positions the theologians or the philosophers hold.

For example, the Ṣūfī position that God's attributes are identical with His essence externally but superadded to it in the mind represents a position midway between the theologians' position that God's attributes are superadded to His essence and that of the philosophers who assert that His attributes are identical with His essence. The Ṣūfī position that the universe is eternal even though God is a free agent reconciles the philosophers' assertion that because God is a necessary agent, the universe is eternal, with the theologians' assertion that because the universe is originated, God is a free agent.

However, on the question of whether God's existence is superadded to His essence or identical with it, the Ṣūfīs maintain an entirely different position. Instead of considering God as composed of essence and existence, they equate Him with absolute existence. They thus not only avoid the problem of determining the relation of His existence to His essence, but in addition do not have to prove God's unity, as the theologians and philosophers must do, since it is impossible to imagine multiplicity in an absolute concept.

In presenting the respective positions of the theologians, the philosophers, and the Ṣūfīs, al-Jāmī has relied heavily on a number of standard and well-known works. In fact much of the material presented in *al-Durrah al-Fākhirah,* and in the *Glosses* as well, consists of passages quoted or paraphrased from these works. Sometimes al-Jāmī acknowledges these passages as quotations and indicates their source, but often he simply incorporates them into his text as if he had written them himself. The principal theological works from which al-Jāmī quotes are al-Jurjānī's *Sharḥ al-Mawāqif* and al-Taftāzānī's

Sharḥ al-Maqāṣid. Extensive passages from al-Ṭūsī's *Sharḥ al-Ishārāt* and his *Risālah* written in answer to Ṣadr al-Dīn al-Qūnawī's questions are quoted in presenting some of the positions of the philosophers.

As might be expected, al-Jāmī's sources for the Ṣūfī position are both numerous and varied. Among the works he quotes extensively are al-Fanārī's *Miṣbāḥ al-Uns*, al-Qayṣarī's *Maṭla' Khuṣūṣ al-Kilam*, al-Hamadhānī's *Zubdat al-Ḥaqā'iq*, Ibn 'Arabī's *al-Futūḥāt al-Makkīyah*, and al-Qūnawī's *Kitāb al-Nuṣūṣ* as well as his *I'jāz al-Bayān*. (pp. 6-8)

> *Nicholas Heer, in an introduction to* The Precious Pearl: Al-Jāmī's al-Durrah al-Fākhirah *by al-Jāmī, edited and translated by Nicholas Heer, State University of New York Press, 1979, pp. 1-22.*

ADDITIONAL BIBLIOGRAPHY

Ashrafi, Mukadimma, ed. *Sixteenth-Century Miniatures Illustrating Manuscript Copies of the Works of Jami from the USSR Collections.* Moscow: Sovetskii Hudoznik, 1966, 92 p.
  Reproduces numerous miniature paintings from early manuscripts of Jami's works, with brief commentary in Russian and English on selected stories.

Dole, Nathan Haskell, and Walker, Belle M. "Jami." In their *Flowers from Persian Poets*, Vol. II, pp. 388-90. New York: Thomas Y. Crowell, 1901.
  Short biography of Jami, with commentary on *Yúsuf and Zulaika* and *Haft Aurang*.

FitzGerald, Edward. Letter to C. E. Norton and letter to H. Schütz Wilson. In his *Letters and Literary Remains of Edward FitzGerald*, Vol. IV, edited by W. Aldis Wright, pp. 55-58, 242-44. 1902-03. Reprint. New York: AMS Press, 1966.
  Reprints 1879 and 1882 letters in which FitzGerald describes the difficulty of translating *Salámán and Absál* into English verse.

Hekmat, A. A. "FitzGerald's Translation of Jami, or the Allegory of Salaman and Absal." *The Asiatic Review* XLIII (October 1947): 343-51.
  Estimates Edward FitzGerald's role in the promotion of Jami's works.

Nicholson, Reynold A. "Jami." In his *Translations of Eastern Poetry and Prose*, pp. 185-88. Cambridge: Cambridge University Press, 1922.
  Biographical sketch, with brief selections from Jami's works.

Rice, Cyprian, O.P. "The Seven Stages: Poverty (Faqr)." In his *The Persian Ṣūfis*, pp. 42-7. London: George Allen & Unwin, 1964.
  Briefly notices Jami's interest in poverty as a feature of Sufism.

Ross, Sir E. Denison. "Persia's Contribution to Literature." *Open Court* XLVII, No. 1 (January 1933): 21-7.
  Mentions Jami as an exponent of the Persian romantic epic.

Santesson, H. Stefan. "Some Lesser Known Timuride and Afghan Poets." *The Moslem World* XXXII, No. 1 (January 1942): 31-42.
  Recounts Jami's extemporaneous composition of a poem using the words "light," "sieve," "staircase," and "orange" when ordered to do so by Sultan Husain Mirza-i-Baikara.

Smith, Margaret. *Studies in Early Mysticism in the Near and Middle East*, pp. 158ff. London: Sheldon Press, 1931.
  Approaches Jami as a Sufi, noting his contemporary reputation and influence on later writers.

——. "Abd Al-Rahmān Jāmī (898/1492)." In her *Readings from the Mystics of Islam: Translations from the Arabic and Persian, Together with a Short Account of the History and Doctrines of Sufism*, pp. 121-25. London: Luzac & Company, 1950.
  Brief biography of Jami, with selections from his mystical works.

——. *The Sufi Path of Love: An Anthology of Sufism*, pp. 48ff. London: Luzac & Company, 1954.
  Contains scattered brief references to Jami, locating him within the tradition of Sufi mysticism.

Sykes, Sir Percy. "Literature and Architecture under the Moguls." In his *A History of Persia*, 3d ed., Vol. II, pp. 144-57. London: Macmillan, 1930.
  Compares Jami's moral philosophy and mysticism with that of Jalal-u-Din.

Martin Luther

1483-1546

German theologian, essayist, translator, homilist, and hymn writer.

Luther was the principal catalyst of the Protestant Reformation. In 1517 he altered the course of Western history by issuing his *Disputatio pro declaratione virtutia indulgentiarum (The Ninety-Five Theses),* which signaled the beginning of the European religious reform movement that culminated in the establishment of Protestantism. Many believe that Luther's emphasis on the primacy of personal faith, his reliance on the authority of Scripture rather than on that of Rome, and his advocacy of an essentially "democratic" church signified the collapse of the medieval world and the dawn of the modern age, influencing not only religion but the social and political spheres as well. Further, his monumental translation into German of both the Old and New Testaments had an unparalleled impact on the future course of the German language, while his sermons and hymns form an integral part of German culture. As a man of towering historical significance and profound literary influence, Luther invites critical superlatives such as George F. Will's judgment: "He was perhaps the most potent opinion-shaper since Christ."

Luther was born at Eisleben in Saxony to peasant parents who eventually prospered after moving to the copper-mining center of Mansfeld. After attending schools in Mansfeld, Magdeburg, and Eisenach during his early years, Luther enrolled in the University of Erfurt, one of the most respected institutions of higher education in the realm. Performing well in a rigorous curriculum which stressed the separation of faith and reason in contradistinction to the teachings of Thomas Aquinas, Luther received his bachelor's degree in 1502 and his master's degree in 1505. He then entered Erfurt Law School in compliance with his father's wish that he pursue a legal career but abruptly quit his studies two months later to join the local Augustinian monastery. (According to one of the ubiquitous legendary anecdotes told of Luther's life, the unusual severity of a thunderstorm one day so alarmed him that he vowed on the spot to become a monk.) Here he met Johann von Staupitz, vicar of the German Augustinians, who became his spiritual mentor. He was ordained in 1507 and, at the urging of Staupitz, obtained his doctorate in 1512 at the newly established University of Wittenberg, also accepting the chair of biblical theology there. For the next few years Luther taught courses and delivered lectures on the Psalms and the Pauline Epistles to the Romans and Galatians.

Meanwhile, Luther wrestled with an intense spiritual crisis: beset by a sense of alienation from God, he was (as he later recorded) painfully aware that his depravity and sinfulness could not be mitigated by irreproachable behavior, confession, or priestly absolution. His despair centered on the meaning of the phrase "the justice of God" in the Epistle to the Romans, which he at first interpreted as the strict and forbidding justice of a God of righteousness alone. Luther's insight, by which he established the central tenet of his theology, came in his Tower Experience (so called because it took place in the tower of the Black Cloister in Wittenberg): "Then I grasped that the justice of God is that righteousness by which through grace

and sheer mercy God justifies us through faith. . . . If you have a true faith that Christ is your Saviour, then at once you have a gracious God, for faith leads you in and opens up God's heart and will, that you should see pure grace and overflowing love." Thus was the Lutheran doctrine of justification by faith alone established. Luther's Wittenberg colleagues soon came to share his evolving theology, which he disseminated through his lectures and preaching. Consequently Luther began to develop new curricula and standards at the university, stressing the importance of Augustine and the early Church Fathers as opposed to Aristotelian and scholastic learning.

The decisive first step in Luther's break with Roman Catholicism came in 1517, prompted by the Church practice of selling papal indulgences. The practice, which allowed penitent Christians to purchase partial or complete remission from purgatorial punishment for their sins, had become corrupt during the reign of Pope Leo X, when it became chiefly a fundraising ploy; to Luther, such activity was antithetical to Scripture, the teachings of the Apostolic fathers, and divine will. Provoked by the words and activities of Johann Tetzel, a Dominican selling indulgences near Wittenberg, Luther wrote a series of propositions and proofs supporting his denunciation of the sale of indulgences. He posted this document—his famous *Ninety-Five*

Theses—on the door of Castle Church in Wittenberg on October 31. Although such an action was typical at the time for anyone who wished to initiate public debate of ecclesiastical matters, and although *Ninety-Five Theses* is actually one of Luther's least polemical works—its ideas are set forth as proposals for debate, not as dogmatic conclusions—the posting of the theses incited immediate and fierce controversy. Copies of the *Theses* were printed and widely distributed; many disputants, for and against Luther, jumped into the fray; and Luther himself aggravated the issue by publishing *Eyn Sermon von Ablass und Gnade* ("Sermon on Indulgence and Grace") in which he stated more forcefully his burgeoning dissatisfaction with Rome and questioned the very validity of papal authority. Word of Luther's challenges to Church authority quickly spread to Rome, and there ensued during the next few years a series of official debates involving Luther, his followers, and papal representatives. In 1520, Leo X issued the bull *Exsurge domine,* wherein he condemned articles of Luther's teaching and required Luther to recant within sixty days under threat of excommunication. Luther responded with a flurry of literary activity, writing that same year several treatises that are together regarded as the foundation of his Reformation theology, including: *An den Christlichen Adel deutscher Nation: Von des Christlichen Standes Besserung (Address to the Nobility of the German Nation), De captivitate Babylonica ecclesiæ præludium (On the Babylonian Captivity of the Church),* and *Von der Freyheyt eynes Christen Menschen (The Freedom of a Christian Man).* By now, the tentative questioning of the ecclesiastical status quo that had characterized Luther's earlier works had solidified into the firm doctrines of Lutheranism: ultimate spiritual authority lies not with the pope, but with Scripture; the laity is as well qualified as the pope to interpret the word of God; justification is made possible by faith in Christ alone, not by good works. In December of 1520, Luther publicly burned *Exsurge domine.*

In January 1521, Leo officially excommunicated Luther. Later that year Luther was summoned by Holy Roman Emperor Charles V to appear before the secular authority at the Diet of Worms and was asked to recant his heresies. He refused. Whether Luther actually spoke the words attributed to him at this moment is debatable, but the dramatic impact they have had on generations of Protestant sympathizers is hardly lessened by their apocryphal nature: "Here I stand; I can do no other. God help me. Amen." The resulting Edict of Worms proscribed Luther's writings and forbade the propagation of his doctrines. Returning to Wittenberg, Luther was "kidnapped" by friends operating under the authority of the territorial ruler, Elector Frederick of Saxony, who feared for Luther's safety, and placed in hiding near Eisenach. While thus sequestered Luther wrote tirelessly, producing anti-papal tracts, devotional commentaries, and sermons. However, his most significant project was his translation of the New Testament into German: a task completed in only eleven weeks. Luther returned to Wittenberg in 1522 in an effort to combat what he deemed the ill-advised radicalism of reformist leaders who had arisen in his absence. He now enjoyed broad and ardent popular support and it soon became apparent that the Edict of Worms would not be strictly enforced. He continued writing sermons, lectures, and polemical works, spearheading a tremendous surge of publishing activity in Germany and inspiring a widespread literate consciousness.

In 1525 Luther married, apparently motivated more by a desire to demonstrate his thesis that the clergy should not remain celibate than by personal reasons. Nonetheless, his union with Katherine von Bora, a former nun, and the six children that

resulted from it, proved an unexpected source of happiness for Luther, as he frequently stated. Ever in financial difficulties, Luther augmented his income and his household by taking in student boarders. Some of these took notes of Luther's conversation at the dinner table, which were later published as *Tischreden (Table Talk).* Luther continued to write, lecture, preach, and compose hymns throughout his life, producing several works of enduring importance to Protestant Christianity, including his *Deudsch Catechismus (Larger Catechism)* and *Der kleine Catechismus (Small Catechism),* textbook synopses of Lutheran belief for adults and children. In 1530 the Diet of Augsburg was held in an attempt to reconcile Catholics and the reformists. In Luther's stead, Philipp Melanchthon articulated the chief tenets of Lutheranism in one of the most notable documents of the Reformation, the Augsburg Confession. During his last ten years, Luther accomplished what is commonly considered one of his greatest achievements, a comprehensive, meticulous series of lectures on the book of Genesis. In 1545, Luther worked on, among other things, final revisions of his complete Bible translation. The following year he died in Eisleben and was interred in the Church of All Saints, Wittenberg.

The lasting import of Luther's thought would not have been possible without his indefatigable literary activity. He virtually dominated publishing activity in sixteenth-century Germany, writing sometimes in Latin and sometimes in German (and frequently translating his own works from one language to the other for greater accessibility) for an audience encompassing all strata of society. Central to his astonishingly large canon— he wrote more than 450 essays, 3000 sermons, and 2600 letters—are what have been termed the core works of his theology, the so-called *Reformationsschriften (Reformation Writings),* all published during the watershed year of 1520. *The Freedom of a Christian Man* is a rarity among Luther's works in its gentle, joyful tone. An exposition of the gifts given to and the responsibilities required of a Christian, the treatise is free from Luther's usual polemics and abuse. (Luther once wrote of himself: "I am rough, boisterous, stormy, and altogether warlike." These qualities are readily apparent in his writings, most of which were written in response to particular situations, usually in haste, and often in anger. As a result, few of Luther's works are free of polemics. Many, indeed, are masterpieces of invective, as Luther was wont to batter at his opponents with whatever weapon came to hand. Critics often comment also upon Luther's crudity of language, though they are quick to point out that such coarseness was a more commonly accepted polemical method then than now.) His *Von den guten Wercken/Treatyse on Good Works* sets forth his vital doctrine that faith, rather than good works, makes the Christian. Without faith, no action can be truly good; with it, all works are good, for they are done in faith: "Good works do not make a man good, but a good man does good works." *Address to the Nobility* is an overt appeal to the civil authority to resist Rome's exercises of secular power. Here Luther sought as well to undercut the Church's claims to spiritual authority and laid out myriad proposals for practical reforms, including a sharp reduction in German money destined for Roman coffers and the abolition of celibacy for the clergy. The highly controversial, indeed radical, *Babylonian Captivity of the Church* outlines Luther's views on the sacraments. Of the seven Catholic sacraments—baptism, confirmation, the Eucharist, marriage, ordination, penance, and extreme unction—Luther accepted as valid only baptism, the Eucharist, and penance (the last-named of which he later rejected). Further, he denied the doctrine of transubstantion in the Eucharist, asserting that the eucharistic elements retain their essential qualities as bread and wine while they simultaneously become the body and blood of Christ. In advancing these heretical views (which inspired a furious rebuttal from no less a personage than Henry VIII of England), Luther struck hard at the doctrinal authority of the Church, with telling results. Walther Von Loewenich explains it: "With the writing of the *Babylonian Captivity* a whole world crumbled; it was Luther's farewell to medieval piety."

Although Luther is a figure of worldwide importance, he has a special significance for his native land. Concerned not only with the abstractions of theology but with the practical, quotidian aspects of religion as well, he exerted a tremendous influence on German language and culture. Foremost among his contributions to Germany is his translation of the Bible into the vernacular. He broke with tradition by basing his work on the Greek and Hebrew texts rather than the Latin Vulgate. Critical superlatives have been applied to this work, for two reasons: the unparalleled influence of Luther's Bible on German language and religion, and its intrinsic beauty. Writing in an era of linguistic disunity within Germany, he chose for this translation the language he deemed most accessible to all Germans—the language of the Saxon chancellory. Luther's Bible, the extraordinary popularity of which was apparent from its first publication and which has continued to this day, was instrumental in effecting the unity and standardization of the German literary language. Henry Zecher writes that "its phrasing became the people's phrasing, its speech patterns their speech patterns. So universal was its appeal, and so thoroughly did it embrace the entire range of the German tongue, that it formed a linguistic rallying point for the formation of the modern German language." Moreover, critics attest to the outstanding aesthetic merit of Luther's translations. Judged to be something between a literal and a free rendition, the work shows Luther's poetic as well as his scholarly talent. The richness and beauty of the language, couched in a rhythmically musical style, is enlivened on occasion by spicy dialectical idioms, proverbial expressions, and flashes of wit. Critics also note Luther's unusually broad vocabulary and his painstaking accuracy (much of the latter the result of rather unorthodox research; for example, he inspected the court jewels of the elector of Saxony in order to describe accurately the precious stones mentioned in the twenty-first chapter of Revelation). Luther's translation is not altogether free of doctrinal bias. His Old Testament is to some extent Christianized, and there is a telling addition of the word "alone" following the phrase of the original "a man is justified by faith" in Romans 3:28. A music lover, Luther also wrote many hymns, several of which are traditional favorites, including the famous "Ein' feste Burg ist unser Gott" ("A Mighty Fortress Is Our God").

The canon of Luther scholarship is incredibly large and complex and the commentary available in English, though voluminous, does not always adequately reflect the German-language critical history. (This is particularly true of pre-twentieth-century criticism.) In general, Luther's is in large measure the critical history of the evolving Western religious climate; Luther criticism has traditionally been colored by the religious perspectives peculiar to individual critics. In his own day, Luther was hailed as a prophet by some and denounced as a heretic by others: to Melanchthon he was "a blessed instrument of God"; to Pope Leo X, "the slave of a depraved mind." Some, like the Dutch humanist Desiderius Erasmus, initially supported his efforts at Church reform but were later alarmed

and repelled by the combative violence of his polemics, the increasing intransigence of his views. Others, of a more radical temperament, felt that his reforms were not far-reaching enough. Eric W. Gritsch, in his *Martin—God's Court Jester: Luther in Retrospect* (1983), has succinctly outlined critical trends in Luther scholarship: the sixteenth-century polarization of Luther-as-saint and Luther-as-demon; Luther as the standard-bearer of seventeenth-century Protestant orthodoxy and Pietism; his emergence in the eighteenth century as an Enlightenment ideal of spiritual individualism and independence; the use made of Luther and his writings by nineteenth-century critics to support or illustrate causes ranging from pantheism to Marxism. Throughout the centuries there ran a consistent thread of Catholic vilification of Luther, who was portrayed as actively evil, or, at best, misguided and mentally unbalanced. Thus the battle has raged along sectarian lines; it is really only in the present century that Luther criticism has freed itself—insofar as this is possible—of overt partisanship. Modern scholars of all denominations and beliefs have assessed Luther, affirming—regardless of doctrinal differences—the importance of his thought and his impact on world history.

"[Luther] is in the full sense a genius," according to Roman Catholic scholar Joseph Lortz, "a man of massive power in things religious and a giant as well in theological interpretation. Because of this, he has in many respects shaped the history of the world." As catalyst of the Protestant Reformation, Luther has indeed had an incalculable impact on the world. His successful challenges to the authority of Rome prompted other such challenges, so that every Protestant sect, no matter how doctrinally divergent from Lutheran theology, is indebted to Luther for its inception. Further, his influence is often cited as a major factor in bringing about the Counter-Reformation, the Catholic Church's own internal reform movement. One of the most powerful aspects of Luther's legacy is also the most nebulous: his influence, indirect but persuasive, in the realm of ideas. The same iconoclasm that shattered Christendom shattered also the prevalent notion that stasis is desirable, that any institution—religious, political, or social—is or should be inviolable. Thus, to many, Luther's break with Rome symbolizes Europe's transition from medievalism to the modern world. In rejecting the hierarchical authority of the Church as a mediator between the individual and God, in asserting the primacy of a personal covenant of faith with God, in viewing the church community as a priesthood of believers, Luther paved the way—though unwittingly—for feudal hierarchical social and political structures to be abolished and for concepts of individualism and equality to emerge. (It must be remembered, though, that Luther himself was no proto-democrat, holding to the Pauline doctrine that the state is divinely ordained and that the people must submit—under all but the most radical circumstances—to civil authority, however unjust.) Beyond his towering historical stature, Luther is remembered as a man of magnetic personality, great literary talent, considerable musical ability, and irrepressible creative energy. That he was conversant with a wide variety of aesthetic fields is attested to by his German Bible, essays, sermons, lectures, hymns, and *Table Talk*. Summarizing Luther's importance, Gerhard Ritter has written: "The depth of meaning in his writings is unfathomable and inexhaustible. He will always continue to fertilise Christian theology from one generation to another. For not only his theological thinking, but everything, the power of his character and the creative achievement of his thought, has its root in the same mysterious depths: in the encounter of the believer with God."

PRINCIPAL WORKS

Disputatio pro declaratione virtutia indulgentiarum (theses) 1517

[*The Ninety-Five Theses* published in *The Origins and Results of the Ninety-Five Theses of Dr. M. Luther*, 1873]

Die Sieben busspsalm mit deutscher au-siegung nach dem schrifftlichen synne tzu Christi und gottes gnaden, neben seynes selben, ware erkentniss grundlich gerichtet (psalms) 1517

[*The Seven Penitential Psalms* published in Vol. 14 of *Luther's Works*, 1958]

Eyn Sermon von dem Ablasz und Gnade (sermon) 1518

†*Epistola Lutheriana ad Leonem decimum summum pontificem. Dissertatio de libertate christiana per autorem recognita* (letter and essay) 1519; also published as *Von der Freyheyt eynes Christen Menschen* [abridged translation], 1520

[*A Treatise, Touching the Libertie of a Christian*, 1579; also published as *The Freedom of a Christian Man*, 1901]

In epistolam Pauli ad Galatus (lecture) 1519; revised edition, 1535

[*A Commentarie of M. Doctor Martin Luther upon the Epistle of S. Paul to the Galatians*, 1575]

†*An den Christlichen Adel deutscher Nation: Von des Christlichen Standes Besserung* (essay) 1520

[*Address to the Nobility of the German Nation* published in *First Principles of the Reformation*, 1883]

†*De captivitate Babylonica ecclesiæ præludium* (essay) 1520; also published as *Von der babylonischen Gerfencknues der Kirchen*, 1520

[*On the Babylonian Captivity of the Church* published in *First Principles of the Reformation*, 1833]

†*Von den guten Wercken* (sermon) 1520

[*Here after Ensueth a Propre Treatyse of Good Workes*, 1535?]

Warumb des Babits und feuner Jungernn bucher von Doct. Martino Luther vorbrant jeunn (essay) 1520

[*On the Papacy in Rome against the Most Celebrated Romanist in Leipzig* published in Vol. 39 of *Luther's Works*, 1970]

De votis monasticis Martini Lutheri judicium (essay) 1521

[*The Judgment of Martin Luther on Monastic Vows* published in Vol. 44 of *Luther's Works*, 1966]

Enarrationes epistolarum et evangeliorum quas postillas vocant (sermons) 1521

Contra Henricum regem Angliae (letter) 1522

[*A Copy of the Letters, wherin . . . Kyng Henry the Eight . . . made Answere unto a Certayne Letter of Martyn Luther, Sent unto Him by the Same, and also the Copy of the Foresaid Luthers Letter*, 1526]

Das newe Testament Deutzsch [translator] (bible) 1522

Eyn Sermon tzu Sant Michael gethan, tzu Erffordt auff den Tag der XI tausent Juchfrawe vom Glauben und Wercken (sermon) 1522

Praefatio methodica totius scripturæ in Epistolam Pauli ad Romanos (essay) 1524

[*A Methodociall Preface Prefixed before the Epistle of S. Paul to the Romanes*, 1590?]

De servo arbitrio (essay) 1525; also published as *Das der freie Will nicht sey*, 1526

[*Martin Luther on the Bondage of the Will*, 1823]

Wider die morderischen und reubischen Rotten der Bawern (essay) 1525

[*Against the Robbing and Murdering Hordes of Peasants* published in Vol. 46 of *Luther's Works*, 1967]

Deudsche Messe und Ordnung Gott is Diensts (mass) 1526

Dom abendmal Christi, Bekendnis (essay) 1528

[*Short Confessions concerning Christ's Supper* published in Vol. 37 of *Luther's Works*, 1961]

Deudsch Catechismus (catechsims) 1529; revised edition, 1533

[*Larger Catechsim* published in *Luther's Primary Works, Together with His Shorter and Larger Catechisms*, 1896]

Enchiridion. Der kleine Catechismus (catechism) 1529

[*Luther's Small Catechism*, 1855]

Warnung D. Martini Luther an seine lieben Deudschen (essay) 1531

[*Dr. Martin Luther's Warning to His Dear German People* published in *Luther: Selected Political Writings*, 1974]

‡*Biblia; das ist, Die gantze heilige Schrifft Deudsch* [translator, with others] (bible) 1534; revised editions 1539, 1540, 1541, 1545, 1546

†*Artickel, so da hetten sollen auffs Concilion zu Mantua, oder wo es wurde sein, uberantwortet werden von unsere Teils wegen* (essay) 1538; also published as *Die Heubtartikel des Christlichen Glaubens, wider den Babst, und der Hellen Pforten zu erhalten* [enlarged edition], 1543

[*The Last Wil and Last Confession of Martyn Luthers Faith concernng the Principal Articles of Religion Which Are in Controversy, Which He Wil Defend . . . until His Death, agaynst the Pope and the Gates of Hell. . .*, 1543]

Von den Conciliis und Kirchen (essay) 1539

[*Martin Luther's Authority of Councils and Churches*, 1847]

Geistliche Lieder (hymns) 1543

[*Hymns of the Reformation*, 1845]

Kurtz Bekentnis D. Mart. Luthers, vom heiligen Sakrament (essay) 1544

[*Brief Confession concerning the Holy Sacrament* published in Vol. 38 of *Luther's Works*, 1971]

Tischreden; oder, Colloquia. . . (conversations) 1566

[*Dris. Martini Lutheri Colloquia Mensalia; or, Dr. Martin Luther's Divine Discourses at His Table. . .*, 1652; also published as *The Table Talk or Familiar Discourse of Martin Luther*, 1846]

§*D. Martin Luthers Werke: Kritische Gesammtausgabe.* 58 vols. (essays, sermons, lectures, hymns, catechisms, letters, and grammar) 1883—

‖*Luthers Vorlesung über den Romerbrief* (lectures) 1908

[*Lectures on Romans*, 1961]

Luther's Correspondence and Other Contemporary Letters. 2 vols. (letters) 1913-18

Luther's Works. 56 vols. (essays, sermons, lectures, catechism, theses, conversations, letters, and songs) 1955—

*This work is usually referred to as *95 Thesen*.

†These works are collectively referred to as *Die Reformationsschriften (The Reformation Writings)*. The German version of *Dissertatio de libertate christiana per autorem recognita* does not include the letter *Epistola Lutheriana ad Leonem decimum summum pontificem*. The English translations cited contain both works.

‡This work contains a revised version of the earlier *Das newe Testament Deutzsch*.

§Known as the Weimar Edition, this definitive collection is considered indispensible for advanced Luther studies.

‖This work comprises lectures delivered between 1515 and 1516 at the University of Wittenburg.

DESIDERIUS ERASMUS   (letter date 1519)

[*A Dutch humanist, Erasmus exerted a tremendous influence on European Renaissance thought through such works as the religious satire* Encomium Moriae *(1511;* The Praise of Folie, *1549) and the compendium of classical proverbs and Renaissance wisdom entitled* Adagiorum collectanea *(1500;* Proverbes or Adagies, *1539). He was both a classical and biblical scholar, combining the rationalism, tolerance, and skepticism toward established doctrine of humanistic philosophy with an emphasis on personal, keenly felt Christian pietism. Like Luther, Erasmus was an Augustinian monk who left the order yet remained closely involved with Church affairs, biblical study, and doctrinal analysis. Although many believe his early humanist writings were instrumental in helping to launch the Reformation, Erasmus approached Luther and his teachings cautiously, believing moderation in theological disputes and veneration of the Holy See essential to the continued health of the Church. He feared that Luther's polemics encouraged dissention in the Church instead of promoting real reform. Erasmus eventually attacked Luther's views on humanity's innate sinfulness and absolute dependence on divine grace in* De libero arbitrio *(1524;* Concerning Free Will). *Luther replied with* On the Bondage of the Will. *In the following excerpt from a letter to Luther written before this controversy developed, Erasmus describes the turbulent reception of Luther's work among prominent theologians.*]

Greetings, dearest brother in Christ. Your letter gave me great pleasure: it displayed the brilliance of your mind and breathed the spirit of a Christian. No words of mine could describe the storm raised here [Louvain, Belgium] by your books. Even now it is impossible to root out from men's minds the most groundless suspicion that your work is written with assistance from me and that I am, as they call it, a standard-bearer of this new movement. They supposed that this gave them an opening to suppress both humane studies—for which they have a burning hatred, as likely to stand in the way of her majesty queen Theology, whom they value much more than they do Christ—and myself at the same time, under the impression that I contribute something of importance towards this outburst of zeal. In the whole business their weapons are clamour, audacity, subterfuge, misinterpretation, innuendo; if I had not seen it with my own eyes—felt it, rather—I would never have believed theologians could be such maniacs. One would think it was some disastrous infection. And yet this poisonous virus, starting in a small circle, spread to a larger number, so that a great part of this university was carried away by the spreading contagion of this epidemic paranoia.

I assured them that you were quite unknown to me; that I had not yet read your books and could therefore neither disapprove nor approve anything. I merely told them not to make such an offensive uproar in public before they had even read what you have written, and that this was in their own interests, since their judgment ought to carry great weight. I also advised them to consider whether it was a good plan to produce before a casual audience of laymen a distorted account of views which it would be more proper to refute in print or discuss among specialists, especially since all with one voice speak highly of the author's manner of life. I did no good at all: they are so blinded by their own jaundiced, indeed slanderous, disputations. When I think how often we have agreed terms of peace, and how often on some trifling and rash suspicion they have stirred up fresh trouble! And they regard themselves as theologians. Theologians in this part of the world are unpopular at court; and this too they think is my fault. All the bishops are cordially on my side. These men have no confidence in the printed word; their hope of victory lies entirely in malicious gossip. This I despise, for my conscience is clear. Their attitude

to you has softened somewhat. They are afraid of my pen, knowing their own record; and, my word, I would paint them in their true colours, as they deserve, did not Christ's teaching and Christ's example point in quite another direction. Fierce wild beasts are tamed by kindness; these men are driven wild if you do anything for them.

You have people in England who think well of what you write, and they are in high place. There are some here too, the bishop of Liège among them, who favour your views. As for me, I keep myself uncommitted, so far as I can, in hopes of being able to do more for the revival of good literature. And I think one gets further by courtesy and moderation than by clamour. That was how Christ brought the world under his sway; that was how Paul did away with the Jewish law, by reducing everything to allegory. It is more expedient to protest against those who misuse the authority of the bishops than against the bishops themselves; and I think one should do the same with kings. The universities are not so much to be despised as recalled to more serious studies. Things which are of such wide acceptance that they cannot be torn out of men's minds all at once should be met with argument, close-reasoned forcible argument, rather than bare assertion. Some people's poisonous propaganda is better ignored than refuted. Everywhere we must take pains to do and say nothing out of arrogance or faction; for I think the spirit of Christ would have it so. Meanwhile we must keep our minds above the corruption of anger or hatred, or of ambition; for it is this that lies in wait for us when our religious zeal is in full course.

I am not instructing you to do this, only to do what you do always. I have dipped into your *Commentary on the Psalms*; I like the look of it particularly and hope that it will be of great service. There is a man in Antwerp, the prior of the monastery there, a genuine Christian, who is most devoted to you and was once your pupil, or so he says. He is almost the only one among them all who preaches Christ; the others as a rule preach the inventions of men or their own advantage. I have written to Melanchthon. May the Lord Jesus ever more richly endue you with his spirit every day, for his own glory and the good of mankind. (pp. 391-93)

> *Desiderius Erasmus, in a letter to Martin Luther on May 30, 1519, in his* The Correspondence of Erasmus: Letters 842 to 992, 1518 to 1519, *translated by R. A. B. Mynors and D. F. S. Thomson, University of Toronto Press, 1982, pp. 391-93.*

DESIDERIUS ERASMUS   (letter date 1521)

[*The following excerpt is taken from a letter to Jodocus Jonas, an admirer of Luther whom Erasmus hoped to prevent from becoming a full-fledged Lutheran disciple. (His purpose was not achieved, for Jonas eventually became Luther's close associate.) Here, Erasmus warns of Luther's lack of diplomacy and moderation, noting also his pique over the frequent coupling of his name and philosophy with Luther's.*]

There is a rumor persistent here for a long time now, dear Jonas, that at Worms you were with Martin Luther continuously; nor do I doubt that your sense of duty prompted this, as I should have urged if it happened that I were present, so that this tragedy might be so settled on reasonable grounds that in the future it could not erupt again with greater evil for the world. For my part I wonder that that was not accomplished, since this achievement would have been very agreeable to the best men, who, as is worthy of souls truly Christian, desired that the tranquility of the Church be taken into account, the name "church" being lost if concord is not joined to it. For what else is our religion than peace in the Holy Spirit? Furthermore, the orthodox Fathers testify that in former times the church of Christ was afflicted with great vices, because thus far it embraces good fish and bad in the same net and is forced to endure the cockle mixed with the wheat; and they repeatedly lamented the most corrupt morals of those orders from whom it was proper that examples of an inherent piety proceed. Moreover, when the Roman church in times gone by departed from a devotion to evangelical purity, this was made clear enough either by Jerome, who calls it the Babylon of the Apocalypse, or by Saint Bernard in the books which he entitled *De consideratione*—although there have not been wanting also among modern authors, men of celebrated name, who have demanded the public renewal of ecclesiastical discipline.

Yet I do not know whether the princes of the Church have ever coveted the privileges of this world, which Christ taught should be despised, with so much zeal and so openly as we see today. Nor had the study of Sacred Scripture sunk lower than morals themselves. Divine literature was forced to be the servant of human ambition, the credulity of the people was turned to the profit of the few. Pious minds, to whom nothing is more important than the glory of Christ, groaned at the sight of this. And the result was that in the beginning Luther had as much approbation on all sides as, I believe, has come to any mortal for several centuries past. For, as we easily believe what we ardently desire, they thought that a man had arisen who, free from all the attachments of this world, could bring some remedy for such great evils. Nor was I entirely without hope, except that immediately at the first sampling of the tracts which had begun to appear under Luther's name I was quite afraid that the matter might end in tumult and general dissidence throughout the world. And so through my letters I at one time warned Luther himself, then friends of his whose authority I thought would have force with him. I do not know what advice they gave him; in any event the matter was handled in such a way that there is the danger that because of the attempt to apply remedies improperly, the evil for us may be doubled.

And I greatly wonder, my dear Jonas, what god has stirred up the heart of Luther, in so far as he assails with such license of pen the Roman pontiff, all the universities, philosophy, and the mendicant orders. Even if all were true, which those who undertake to judge Luther's writings say is by no means the case, what other outcome could be expected, because of the provocation of so many, than this which we see? Up to now I have not had the time to read Luther's books, but on the basis of those which I have sampled and what in passing I have sometimes gathered from the report of others, although it was not within my competence, perhaps, to pronounce on the truth of the opinions which were advanced, certainly the manner and method of going about the business were by no means approved by me. For when in itself an issue is a matter of bitter truth to very many, and when in itself a turbulent issue usually leads, by long experience, to violent upheaval, it were better to mitigate through courteous treatment an issue sharp by its very nature than to add ill will to ill will.

What purpose did it serve, therefore, to act in a contrary way and to expose certain matters in such a way that at first sight they were even more offensive than when seen at closer and steadier range? For some things even in deliberate obscurity, as it were, are troublesome. What was achieved by raging with such fierce outcries? If it was against those he desired to cor-

rect, his method must be attributed to imprudence; but if it was against those he wished to provoke to evil everywhere, his method should be attributed to impiety. Moreover, although it is the part of the experienced steward to dispense the truth, that is, to bring it forth when the occasion demands, and to bring forth enough of it, and to bring forth what is suitable for each, he poured out everything at the same time in so many pamphlets cast forth headlong, divulging everything and making public even to cobblers what is usually treated among the learned as mysterious and secret; and frequently by some unbridled impulse, in my opinion, at least, he is carried beyond what is just. For example, he calls the whole philosophy of Aristotle the death of the soul when it was sufficient to remind theologians that they are too entangled in Peripatetic, or rather sophist, philosophy. (pp. 151-53)

I do not deny that God sometimes corrects his flock by war, pestilence, and suffering; it is not for the pious, however, to cause war and wicked torment, if God at times turns the misfortune of others into a good for his own. The cross of Christ brought salvation to the world, and yet we execrate those who brought Him to the cross. The death of the martyrs adorned and at the same time strengthened the church of God; nevertheless, the wickedness of those through whom this good has come to us has been condemned. Many would be less wicked if they were deprived of their riches. It is not for the upright man, however, to despoil anyone of his possessions in order to make him better. Moreover, since everything new and unusual gives rise to a disturbance, even when there is a call to better things, if anything differs from what is customary, it must be proposed in such a way that it appears to differ as little as possible.

Yet it is said that Luther, although he teaches the same doctrine as others, several times endeavors by the very language he uses, so it would seem, to make it appear that he asserts the most dissimilar views. Moreover, as men's behavior is inclined to the worse, their vices must be so corrected that the occasion for sinning more freely is not offered to others. Paul preaches evangelical liberty as against the ruinous servitude of the law, but he adds, "Only do not use liberty as an occasion for sensuality." He exhorts against the cold works of the law so that he may incessantly encourage to works of charity. Perhaps there were some who out of honest zeal favored calling the orders and princes of the Church to better things. But I do not know if they are those who under this pretext covet the wealth of the churchmen. I judge nothing to be more wicked and destructive of public tranquility than this. For if they believe it is right to seize the property of priests because some consume their wealth in extravagant living or otherwise spend it for purposes not too honorable, not many good citizens or magnates will find the possession of their goods sufficiently secure. This certainly is a fine turn of affairs, if property is wickedly taken away from priests so that soldiers may make use of it in worse fashion; and the latter squander their own wealth, and sometimes that of others, so that no one benefits.

I do not agree with those men, my dear Jonas, who say that Luther, provoked by the intolerable shamelessness of his adversaries, could not maintain a Christian moderation. Regardless of how others conduct themselves, he who had undertaken such a role ought to be faithful to himself and disregard all other matters. Finally, a way out should have been provided before he descended into that pit, lest there occur what happened to the goat in the fable. Even in pious matters it is foolish to begin what you cannot finish, especially if a not too fortunate attempt brings the greatest misfortune instead of the advantages that were desired. We see the affair brought to that point that I reasonably see no good outcome, unless Christ through His own skill turn the rashness of these men into a public good.

Some excuse Luther because, forced by the incitement of others, he first wrote more violently and then did not intrust himself to the judgment of most clement Leo and of Emperor Charles, by far the noblest and most gentle prince of the faith. But why was he more disposed to give ear to these inciters than to other friends, neither unlearned nor inexperienced in affairs, urging him along different paths? With what kind of defense, I ask , did a great many who favored him attempt to protect him? With ridiculous little books and with empty threats. As if, in fact, this type of nonsense either frightens his adversaries or attracts good men, to whose judgment the whole affair should have been made to conform, provided that they wished their stories to mark a fruitful turning point. How great a swarm of evils this foolhardiness now yields! And ill will greatly weighs down the study of letters as well as many good men who in the beginning were not particularly hostile to Luther, either because they hoped he would handle the matter differently or on account of the enemies they had in common. For it happened by some chance that those who at the outset made trouble for Luther were enemies of learning, and on this account the devotees of letters were less hostile to Luther lest by supporting the ranks of his adversaries they strengthen the power of their own enemies. Although, whatever the case may be, the care of religion must take precedence over that of studies.

And here, my dear Jonas, I have been forced at times to wish for evidence of the evangelical spirit when I saw Luther, but especially his supporters, strive with skill, as it were, to involve others in a hateful and dangerous affair. For what did it avail to have Reuchlin, burdened enough thus far, weighed down with heavier ill will? What was the need to make mention, so often invidious, of my name, when the case by no means demanded it? I have advised Luther in private and sealed letter [see excerpt dated 1517]; it was soon printed at Leipzig. I had advised the Cardinal of Mainz in a sealed letter lest he rashly surrender Luther, whose cause thus far was praiseworthy to most good men, to the wanton pleasure of certain ones. It was published before it was delivered. Pirckheimer complains in his letter to me that certain letters are circulating in printed form which no one ever delivered to him. In these they urge him to continue steadfastly in what he had begun, so that it is clear that they drag him, whether he wishes or not, into the fellowship of that faction.

They extracted certain offensive passages which seemed to have a relationship to some of Luther's tenets from books I wrote before I dreamed that Luther would arise, and they published them in German. And those who do this wish to be considered friends, although a mortal enemy could do nothing more hostile. The men who wish me the most ill have not had as much ingenuity in injuring me. They have presented this weapon to my enemies so that now in public sermons they might proclaim where I agree with Luther. As if, indeed, falsehood may not be the neighbor on both sides of truth, if you go beyond the mark! I somewhere warn, perhaps, that vows should not rashly be made, and I disapprove of those who run off to the shrine of St. James or to Jerusalem, where they had no business, and leave at home their wife and children, whose life and virtue should have been their chief concern. I warn that young men should not be enticed into the bonds of the

religious life before they know themselves and know what the religious life is. Luther, so they say, totally condemns all vows. I complain somewhere that the burden of confession has been made heavier by the subtleties of certain men. Luther, so they say, teaches that all confession should be rejected as a dangerous institution. I have taught somewhere that the best authors should be read first, adding that as much profit may not be gained from the books of Dionysius as their titles appear to promise. Luther calls the man absurd, I hear, and unworthy of being read at all.

This is indeed a fine state of agreement, if, going beyond the limit of my words, another distorts what I have properly written at a favorable time and with moderation. The laws, however, would be most unjust to me if I should be held responsible lest anyone in the future also abuse my writings. This fate did not even befall the Apostle Paul, if we are to believe his colleague Peter! Nevertheless, to speak frankly, if I had foreseen that an age such as this would arise, either I would not have written certain things which I did write, or I would have written them in a different way. For I desire to be of service to all in such a way that no one is injured, if that is possible. Little books composed by conspirators, in which Erasmus also is portrayed, are circulated. However, no name is more hateful to me than that of conspiracy or schism or faction. (pp. 156-60)

Luther could have taught the evangelical philosophy with great profit to the Christian flock, he could have benefited the world by bringing forth books, if he had restrained from those things which could only end in disturbance. He has also taken away from my works a good part of the profit they contained. Not even the disputations in the universities, which used to be most frank, are free. If it is right to hate anyone because of personal offences, the Lutherans have injured no one more than me. And yet I would desire, in spite of that, that this discord, by far the most dangerous, be adjusted, and be adjusted in such a way that it does not break out later with more serious peril, as an ulcer often does that has been badly treated. (pp. 161-62)

Above all, I am of the opinion that discord, ruinous for all, must be avoided. And that thus by what I might call a holy artfulness the needs of the time must be served, that by no means the treasury of the Gospel truth be betrayed, whence can come the reformation of corrupt public morals. Perhaps someone will ask whether I have another mind regarding Luther than I had formerly. No, indeed, I have the same mind. I have always wished that, with changes made of certain things which were displeasing to me, he discuss purely the Gospel philosophy, from which the morals of our age have departed, alas, too far. I have always preferred that he be corrected rather than suppressed. I desired him to carry on the work of Christ in such a way that the leaders of the Church either approved or certainly not disapproved. I desired that Luther be loved openly and without danger. Nor do I have a different mind about my wrangling critics than about him. If they should preach Christ as piously as they rage against me impiously, I would forget what they accomplish in my case, and I will admire their zeal in Christ. I will not detest those babblers, if they begin to herald Christ. Farewell. (pp. 162-63)

> *Desiderius Erasmus, in a letter to Jodocus Jonas on May 10, 1521, in his* Christian Humanism and the Reformation: Selected Writings, *edited by John C. Olin, Harper & Row, Publishers, 1965, pp. 150-63.*

HENRY VIII   (essay date 1521)

[*Henry was king of England from 1509 to 1547. Always keenly interested in theology, he was a staunch supporter of the Catholic*

*Church and of papal authority during the early years of his reign.
He wrote* Assertio septem sacramentorum *(1521; An Assertion
of the Seven Sacraments, 1687) in refutation of Luther's* Babylonian Captivity of the Church. *For this work, in which he defended the validity of the seven Catholic sacraments and strongly
upheld the pope's position as supreme and rightful spiritual leader,
Henry was awarded the title of* Fidei Defensor, *or Defender of
the Faith, by Pope Leo X. Years later, faced with Pope Clement
VII's refusal to sanction Henry's divorce from Catherine of Ar-
agon to allow him to marry Anne Boleyn, the king denied papal
jurisdiction in the matter, broke with Rome, and established himself as Supreme Head of the church in England, thus paving the
way for the Protestantism England eventually embraced. In the
following excerpt from a concluding address to the reader of* An
Assertion, *Henry harangues against what he views as the dangerous heresy and willful intractability of Luther. Luther's pur-
posely rude and dismissive retort,* Contra Henricum regem Angliae *(1522), angered Henry, who commissioned Thomas More
to reply (see excerpt dated 1523).]*

[It] is evident to all men what sacrilegious opinions [Luther]
has of the Sacrament of Our Lord's Body, from which the
sanctity of all the other Sacraments flow. Who would have
doubted . . . how unworthily, without scruple, he treats all the
rest of the Sacraments? which . . . , he has handled in such sort
that he abolishes and destroys them all except Baptism alone;
& that too he abused & deprived of all grace, leaving if for
no other end than in a contumely of Penance; in some denying
the sign, in others the matter itself; neither proves he anything
in this so great a matter, nor brings he anything in confirmation
of his doctrine, contenting himself in only denying whatever
the Church admits. What everybody believes, he alone by his
vain reason laughs at, denouncing himself to admit nothing but
clear & evident Scriptures: and these too, if alleged by any
against him, he either evades by some private exposition of
his own or else denies them to belong to their own authors.
None of the doctors are so ancient, none so holy, none of so
great authority in treating of holy writ; but this new doctor,
this little saint, this man of learning rejects with great authority.
Seeing therefore he despiseth all men and believes none, he
ought not to take it ill if everybody discredit him again. I am
so far from holding any further dispute with him that I almost
repent myself of what I have already argued against him. For
what avails it to dispute against one who disagrees with everyone, even with himself? who affirms in one place what he
denies in another, denying what he presently affirms; who, if
you object faith, combats by reason; if you touch him with
reason, pretends faith. If you allege philosophers, he flies to
Scripture; if you propound Scripture, he trifles with sophistry;
who is ashamed of nothing, fears none, and thinks himself
under no law. Who condemns the ancient doctors of the Church,
& derides the new ones in the highest degree; loads with reproaches the chief bishop of the Church. Finally, he so un-
dervalues the customs, doctrine, manners, laws, decrees, and
faith of the Church; yea, the whole Church itself, that he almost
denies there is any such thing as a Church, except perhaps
such a one as himself makes up of two or three heretics, of
whom himself is chief. Wherefore since he is such a one as
will have no solid or certain principle betwixt himself and his
adversary, but requires to be free in whatever pleases him, &
as often as it pleases him, lawfully to assert or deny, when
neither reason, scripture, custom, laws, human or divine authority binds him, I thought it not fit to dispute any longer with
him, nor to contend by painful reason against his heresies which
he confirms by no reason. But I rather advise all Christians
that as the most exterminating of plagues they shun him, who
endeavours to bring into the Church of Christ such foul prodi-

gies, being the very doctrine of Antichrist. For if he who studies
to move a schism in any one thing is to be extripated with all
care, with what great endeavours is he to be rooted out who
not only goes about to sow dissension, to stir up the people
against the chief bishop, children against their parents, Christians against the Vicar of Christ; finally, who endeavours to
dissolve by his tumults, brawls and contentions the whole Church
of Christ, which he in the time of his precious death has bound
together by the bond of charity and love; and also to destroy,
profane & pollute with a most execrable mind, filthy tongue,
and detestable touch what is most sacred therein? Who if he
did but give any hopes of cure in himself, or any sign of
amendment, would thereby move all people to regard his disposition and to endeavour by all good means possible to heal
him, and to restore him to soundness of mind, that he might
again revoke the heresies he has broached. But indeed, as yet
I see in him all the signs that precede death; I am not so much
moved to think thus by reason of his disease, though never so
mortal, as by his admitting of no medicine, nor of any manual
operation of the chirurgeon; for how can he be cured who will
not suffer himself to be handled? Or in what manner is he to
be dealt withal who, if you teach him, trifles with you? if you
advise him, is angry? if you exhort him, resists? if in anything
you would appease him, is incensed? if you resist him, is mad?
Otherwise, if he could be cured, what has the pious Vicar of
Christ omitted, who following the example of a good shepherd,
would seek, find, take on his shoulders and bring home to the
fold this lost sheep? But, alas, the most greedy wolf of hell
has surprised him, devoured & swallowed him down into the
lowest part of his belly, where he lies half alive and half dead
in death: and whilst the pious pastor calls him and bewails his
loss, he belches out of the filthy mouth of the hellish wolf
these foul inveighings, which the ears of the whole flock do
detest, disdain and abhor.

For first of all, being unprovoked in any kind, he proposed
some **Articles of Indulgences,** in which (under pretence of Godliness) he most impiously defamed the chief bishop; afterwards,
that he might under pretence of honour and duty cast on the
Pope the greater aspersion, he transmitted them to Rome, as
if submitting himself to the Pope's judgment; but he augmented
them with declarations much worse than they were themselves,
that it might appear to all men the Pope not be counselled by
a good and pious man, but derided by a knavish little brother,
as if so stupid as to hold for an honour such a contumely as
the like thereof had never before been heard. If the Pope deserved no ill, why has this degenerate son cast a false and
undeserving scandal on his father? But if anything had been
done at Rome which needed reforming, yet if Luther had been
(as he would be accounted) an honest man & zealous Christian,
he should not have preferred his own private glory before the
public good of all others, nor have desired to have had the
credit of a scorner amongst the wicked, laughing at the nakedness of his sleeping father, uncovering and pointing thereto
with his finger; but contrariwise would have covered the same
& would have more secretly advised him in his own person
by letters, following the example of the Apostle, who commands us not to deride or reproach our superiors, but to seek
of them. Which if Luther had done, I doubt not but the more
holy Pope (so well is his great benignity known to all men)
being awakened, should have blessed his son Japhet, would
have rendered him thanks for his piety, and would not have
cursed him in his anger, who has forborn to curse him when
he was mocked by him; but pitying the miserable, and more
tender of a son than mindful of a scoffer, has dealt with him
by most honourable men, in whose presence he was not worthy

Frontispiece of Johann Cochläus's anti-Lutheran 1529 polemic Septiceps Lutherus *("Seven-headed Luther"). The illustration and the book attack mutually contradictory statements in Luther's doctrine.*

to appear, that he might desist from his iniquity. To which pious and wholesome counsel he was so far from obeying that he not only derided the Legate, careful for his salvation, but also immediately published another book, in which he endeavoured to overthrow the Pope's power; after which he was summoned to Rome, that he might either render reasons of his writings or recant what he had inconsiderately written, having any security imaginable offered him not to undergo the punishment he deserved, with sufficient expenses offered him for his journey; yet for all this, this silly brother, to shew his great modesty and obedience to the pope, refused to go unless in the equipage of a king and guarded by a warlike army; but this wary man made his appeal to a general council, yet not to every council, but to such as should next meet in the Holy Ghost, that in whatsoever council he was condemned he might deny the Holy Ghost to be present therein; for this holy and spiritual man denies him to be anywhere but in his own bosom: wherefore, being oftentimes advised to repent of his impiety, he as often adds impiety to impiety. So that the Good Shepherd was at last forced to cast away from the fold this scabbed & incurable sheep, fearing lest by its touch it might infect the whole flock; and to bewail his Absalom's death, whose life he could not save; whilst he beheld him hang in the tree by his comely hair, of which he was foolishly proud. Luther therefore finding himself cast out from the fellowship of the faithful, began to do like the deplorable impious, who contemn the gulf they are ready to be plunged into. He has not sighed, he has not lamented his fall, in which, like exalted Lucifer, he has been cast down & broken even as a flash of lightning; but imitating the Devil in despair he becomes like the Devil himself; that is, a slanderer, beginning to break out into blas-

phemies and contumelies against the Pope, and envying all the rest of the faithful. Like the old serpent he begins to spread abroad the snares of infidelity, that by tasting of the forbidden fruit of hurtful knowledge, he might procure their expulsion out of the paradise of the Church (from which he had fallen himself) into a land of thorns and thistles. I am indeed heartily sorry for his so great madness and miserable fall; and I wish that as yet, by the inspiration of God's grace, he may repent, be converted, & live. Nor do I so much desire this for his sake alone (although for him also, as wishing the salvation of every man possible) as that he being at last converted, and like the prodigal son returning to the mercy of so bountiful a Father, and confessing his error, may recall again into the right way those whom he has misled. But now if he has so deeply plunged himself that the pit of wickedness & despair has gorged him into its mouth, he rails, he blasphemes, he slanders, he rages, and he who is filthy becomes more filthy still.

But I beseech all the rest of Christians, and beg of them through the bowels of Christ (whose faith we profess) to shut their ears against his impious words, & not to entertain any schisms or discords amongst them, especially at this time, when all Christians ought however to agree together against the enemies of Christ; also let them not give ear to opprobrious detractions against the vicar of Christ, thrown upon him by this wicked brother; neither let them contaminate their hearts consecrated to Christ, with impious heresies sown by him who is void of charity, swelled with pride, in reason cold, but hot in envy. Finally, let them stand up against this puny brother, weak in power, but in mind more pernicious than either Turk, Saracen, or Infidel: let them, I say, resist him with the same mind & resolution that they would the Turks, Saracens, and worst of Infidels. (pp. 149-54)

Henry VIII, "The Assertion of the Seven Sacraments: To the Reader," in his Miscellaneous Writings of Henry the Eighth, *edited by Francis Macnamara, The Golden Cockerel Press, 1924, pp. 149-54.*

PHILIP MELANCHTHON   (essay date 1521)

[*A German humanist, Melanchthon (the name is a grecized version of his original, Schwarzert or Schwarzerd) was Luther's friend and colleague at the University of Wittenberg. He faithfully supported Luther's theological views and greatly contributed to his translation of the Old Testament. Luther thought very highly of Melanchthon as a biblical scholar, remarking in* Table Talk *that in order to become a good theologian one must first master the Bible and then "read diligently and well" Melanchthon's* Loci communes *(1521). "There's no book under the sun in which the whole of theology is so compactly presented. . . . No better book has been written after the Holy Scriptures than Philip's." The work is still considered a seminal text of Protestant doctrine. Melanchthon wrote the essay from which the following excerpt is taken in 1521 in response to a denunciation of Luther issued by the theological faculty of the Sorbonne. Here, he spiritedly defends Luther from the Sorbonne's charges.*]

See, Christian reader, what monstrous theologians Europe spawns, for last year the Sophists at Cologne and Louvain condemned the Gospel by setting forth bare statements which were confirmed neither by valid reasons nor by Scripture. The madness of these has been exceeded by the Parisians who have condemned Luther [in *Determinatio thelogorum Parisiensium super doctrina Lutheriana* (1521)], whoever finally they are (for they cannot bring me to believe that this affair was done by unanimous vote of the theological order).

In addition to the fact that in the former instance comparatively few things were condemned, how much more harshly and severely is Luther treated by the Parisians. In the first place, a bloody letter has been ascribed to him, and then there have been added wicked and atrocious annotations upon individual opinions of Luther. Many of his views have been distorted even in a sinister fashion. And from this source it can also be deduced what spirit and what madness move the authors of the decree, since the Spirit of God operates honestly. In general, the book is of such a nature that it would not be easy for any man to believe that it could have been written in Paris, since indeed it is commonly believed that in that school, as in some sort of fortress, the Scriptures hold sway. (p. 69)

The apostle orders that the Gospel must not be given up to those who are corrupting it, not even if they are angels. Shall we give it up to those insipid ones and to our thoroughly stupid masters, who have not even learned correctly their own little *Logicalia*? Neither powers nor principalities wrenched the apostle from the Gospel. Should these ghosts of men separate us from it? For what are they but ghosts? Let the name of our masters have strength, let the name of the Parisians have strength, but only in their own schools. In the Christian state let nothing have strength besides the voice of Christ, which, if any man does not hear, he is none of Christ's.

It was not of any consequence to answer wholly, since nothing is being opposed to Luther except some bare propositions. For Luther has so strongly fortified his positions on every side with Scripture (especially in that little book which he inscribed *Declaration of the Articles Condemned by Leo X*) that they cannot be judged wicked except by the wicked. Nevertheless, I should like to point out in a few words one or two topics from which you can more freely evaluate the rest and judge the whole decree.

In the first place, if the letter which they have prefixed to the decree is not that of some hired rhetorician, then that theologian who did write the letter, which contains nothing but some ravings of a woman, is exceedingly foolish. For what, I ask you, are these statements like? "He alone pretends to be wise, he hates us, he is Manichaeus, he is Montanus, he is crazy. Let him be coerced by fire and flame because his wrath has not allowed him to speak consistently."

Moreover, in this particular also the people will greatly wish for common sense in that false faculty which says that Luther must be destroyed by fire rather than conquered by reason. At this point, who would not laugh at this feminine and plainly monkish impotence? And with evidence I should be permitted to warn the admirable Lord Dean: "Forbear, Lord Dean, you are already enraged. Do you not know what the poet said, 'Fury and rage cast down the mind'?" Never have those at Cologne or Louvain talked trifles so freely, so that I almost believe that certain of the ancients were not speaking altogether rashly when they said that the Gauls were without understanding.

They accuse Luther of heresy, not because he disagrees with Scripture, but with the universities, the holy fathers, and the councils. And then they call the opinions of the universities, of the holy fathers, and of the councils the primary principles of faith. At this point I could contend with you about your decree also, if the matter is obscure. But what is clearer than the fact that neither the universities, nor the holy fathers, nor the councils can establish articles of faith, since it can happen that not only the universities err, but the holy fathers and the councils likewise? (pp. 71-2)

Why, therefore, do you call the opinions of men principles of faith? Who is ignorant of Paul's statement, "No other foundation can be laid save that which has been laid"? For he is speaking of doctrine. What new articles of faith will our Parisian masters add except perhaps their own stinking articles, concocted in their own cook-shops? Now since there are no articles of faith except those which have been prescribed by sacred Scripture, why is it wicked for us to differ either with the councils or the universities, provided we do not differ with Scripture? But Luther does not differ with Scripture even according to your judgment. Why then is he accused of impiety? He disagrees with the interpretation of Scripture which up to this time has been received through the fathers, the councils, and the schools. This is, as I see it, the sum of the controversy. And here I ask you, my masters, has Scripture come forth in such a manner that its certain meaning can be established without the interpretation of the councils, the fathers, and of the schools, or not? If you will deny that the meaning of Scripture by itself is certain without glosses, I do not see why it was necessary that Scripture be produced if the Holy Spirit was unwilling to establish with certainty what he wants us to think. Or why do the apostles invite us at all to the study of Scripture, if its meaning is uncertain? What of the fact that to the extent to which the fathers want us to believe them, to that same extent they fortified their positions by the evidences of Scripture? What of the fact that even the ancient councils made no decree without the Scripture? It is by this plan that we discern the true and the false in the councils, because these councils evidently concur with Scripture while those differ from Scripture. Therefore, you will grant me that the meaning of Scripture is certain and clear, so that if any passage anywhere is rather obscure, Scripture itself explains itself.

Especially is this true with reference to those things which the Holy Spirit has willed to be known and believed. Moreover, he willed that the Law be known in no doubtful manner inasmuch as he has ordered it to be inscribed upon the doors of houses and to be engraved on the fringes of garments. Likewise he has willed that the Gospel be known, that is, the plan of righteousness bestowed through Christ. For since the Word of God should be a rock on which the soul rests itself, I ask you, what will one think of the Word if it is not certain what the meaning of the Spirit of God is?

Now, since the meaning of Scripture is certain through itself, it ought to be preferred, not only to the schools or the fathers, but also to the councils which have opposing judgments. As the apostle says in Galatians: "If an angel from heaven preaches another gospel than the one we have preached, let him be anathema." Therefore, let Luther be permitted to place the certain meaning of Scripture over against the councils, the father, and the schools.

What will you say here in reply, you Sophists? What glosses will you oppose to us at this point? What little *Logicalia*? What obligations will you devise? Either deny that the meaning of Scripture is sure or else permit Luther to place Scripture over against any persons whatsoever who think differently.

Nor shall we now grant to you that Luther is opposed either to the fathers or to the councils. And indeed, to speak first of the fathers, is not Luther's view on free will and grace the whole view of Augustine, if you rightly judge the matter? And besides, Luther follows him throughout in his *Commentary on Galatians*. The commentaries of both are extant. If you compare them, you will observe an agreement between them on the sum of the matter. (pp. 72-4)

[Our] masters say that they are following the example of the apostles when they set forth certain bare opinions without the authority of the Scriptures. But I would that they brought forth the apostles for our consideration not only in this one respect! Christ cites the authority of the Scriptures, wanted himself to be believed because of the support of Scripture. Paul voiced almost nothing but the words of another, that is to say, the words of the Old Testament Scriptures. And what are the sermons of the apostles but testimonies about Christ from the Old Testament? Shall we believe the Sorbonne alone, without the Scriptures?

Come forth from your Sorbonnic cave, our masters, into the light so that we may see whether such foolish men have any eyes or face. Doubtless the apostolic office was instituted to produce dogma without testimonies although not even Christ wanted himself to be believed without the Scriptures! Indeed we are comparing the work of the apostles with that of the Sorbonne! The question of the rites of the law was set forth as is recorded in the Book of Acts, Chapter 15. In that place when the divine Spirit had signified by various testimonies of Scripture and clear arguments and signs that the Gentiles were not to be burdened with Jewish ceremonies, a decree was made about liberty. At this point I ask you, masters, by what signs, by what evidences of Scripture were you forced to make a pronouncement about Luther? But it goes without saying that we shall not be so rash as to believe even in signs; Scripture alone we believe. In the next instance, they say they are chosen to bring the commands of the apostles with a living voice and to strengthen the faith of the churches. Whom do you send to the churches to set forth to them the reason of your view? Finally, they add an epistle in which they allege the witness of the Holy Spirit when they say: "It seemed good to the Holy Spirit and to us." What spirit do you allege?

Hear, you deaf vipers, what spirit do you allege to the world as a witness of your doctrine? The apostles alleged the Spirit of God and they were certainly assured through Scripture of the will of the divine Spirit. Presently even the churches were assured of the apostolic spirit. But what shall we think about your spirit? What if someone should say to you what that one said in Acts: "Jesus and Paul I know, but who are you"? What of the fact that the apostles, although they cited the testimony of the Spirit, did not write in such a manner as to think they gave satisfaction in such a case by a bare epistle, but added messengers to confirm the churches by a full message. The churches need this message and not dogmas. And Peter wishes Christians to be prepared to give a reason for their faith.

The whole world demands this of you also, our masters. Already before this it was clear in the schools what Paris was thinking. For your commentaries and your scholastic arguments are extant. Now the reason for that doctrine of yours is being sought. For those articles against Luther could have been gathered up from Gabriel or Scotus by some little boy in the middle of Germany. It is not so obscure what Paris teaches, but it is obscure why she teaches so. Luther demands the reason for your doctrine, not dogmas. For beyond question he would not condemn what he did not know. And would that you return to your mind and think about the greater things to be done by Luther rather than about those things which ought or can be entrusted either to the Parisian school or to Luther without the witness of Scripture. Those who favor Luther favor him in such a way because he has rejected human falsehoods, and they see that he teaches nothing but what the Scriptures themselves have produced. These same persons will believe you if they understand that you agree with Scripture, since they seek Christ both from Luther and from you.

You think that you possess the talent to sing a song like David's, for thus the prophet speaks, but you are singing only for yourselves and that which is within you. Luther sings his own song, that is, he proves his doctrine to the whole Christian world by the supports of Scripture. You hold that to Christians these Scriptural supports are nothing. "We are our own masters," you say, "we are Parisians, we are Sorbonnics, we are the parents of all diatribes." Vain are the names to which Germany now has almost become deaf. Wherefore I urge that if you want to atone for the reproach of wickedness, you set forth the reason for your judgment about Luther. Consult together with the Lutherans not about dogma but about the arguments for your dogmas, unless you do not want to be regarded as Christians. Declare sometime by what spirit Luther has been condemned by the apostles of the Sorbonne. Not only is the Christian world now waiting for this, but it even demands by the right of Christian duty that you show in what respect and why you have condemned him.

And in order that I may finish up sometime, it seems good to show in one or two places just what unfamiliarity with sacred matters and what wickedness there are at the Sorbonne. For from these the rest can easily be estimated. Luther has written thus on free will: "Without grace, it cannot do anything but sin." The thing is well known and plain if you but consider Scripture. For thus speaks the Apostle Paul: "The mind of the flesh is enmity against God. For it is not subject to the law of God, neither indeed can be. Those who are in the flesh cannot please God." And John I: "Who have been born not of blood nor of the will of the flesh, nor of the will of man, but of God." And Augustine, following Scripture, deals the same way with the Pelagians, that is, the Sorbonne Sophists, not merely in one place.

In this matter those at the Sorbonne conceal Scripture and dispense with Augustine with a Sorbonnic falsehood, in which alone you will apprehend Sorbonnic blindness. And if it has ever been doubted in what kind of literature or arts Paris was engaged, it would now be made known in respect to this topic, in which it is clearly apparent that there is no one on that whole Sorbonne faculty who has come in contact with Augustine. What their ability is in Scripture itself can be easily estimated when they have not even seen Augustine, a common and well-known writer among theologians. O theologians! O Sorbonne! When Augustine in his dispute about grace says that free will cannot do good works without grace, they say that he is not talking about grace doing something pleasing. Blindness of blindnesses and blindness in all things!

Finally, what kind of grace does that illustrious man discuss? When so often he writes that Pelagius makes different uses of the word grace, he declares that he himself demands a grace that justifies or the Holy Spirit diffused into the hearts of those justified. Gifts of nature he plainly rejects, and he is ignorant of the special Sorbonnic aid. How, therefore, can it be that he is not speaking of justifying grace? And in order that we may evaluate the matter itself, I ask you, Sorbonnic Sorbonners, from what source have you secured the phrase, "grace doing that which is pleasing"? Is it not from the fact that it alone conciliates God? Since this is so, why do you imagine that something has been accepted without grace that does what is pleasing to God? Your words and your dogmas fight among themselves. You accept the phrase, "grace doing what is pleasing," but you do not accept the force of the phrase.

But let us see in what respect Augustine used the word grace. I could include his whole book on *The Spirit and the Letter*, since there is no page on which some mention is not made of grace. But these are his words in Chapter 4: "But when the Holy Spirit does not aid us by inspiring a good longing in place of an evil desire, that is, by diffusing love in our hearts, actually that law, 'Thou shalt not covet,' however good it may be, actually increases evil desire by forbidding it." Now what kind of grace is he here talking about when he plainly says that you cannot do anything without grace except sin? Does he not call grace the love of the Holy Spirit diffused in our hearts?

Now, you Sorbonners, what else do you call grace but love? Allow me to ask, not that you re-read Augustine, but that you simply look into him. For there is no page that does not clearly demonstrate your error. In the ninth chapter on grace he introduces the apostle, who says: "The righteousness of God through faith in Jesus Christ for all who believe." Can these words be twisted into the gratuitous gifts of nature or to special aid? O you rude and truly Sorbonnic masters of ours, who then will believe that you have either eyes or a mind or a brain when in such clear light you are so obscurely blind in everything and under such hallucinations? And at this point there is nothing I so freely wonder at as the fact that there is no one on the whole Sorbonne faculty who has discovered the view of Augustine and, if you please, it is by this argument that a book was edited by one or two Sophists under the fabricated name of the faculty.

Nor with any greater trustworthiness do those French Sorbonners judge the view of Ambrose, since it is agreed that in the entire disputation the author of the book *On the Calling of the Gentiles*, whoever he is, says that those things which are done without grace are sins. When declaring what kind of grace he is talking about, he produces among other witnesses this one also which has been quoted in the Epistle to the Hebrews from Jeremiah: "I will give my law in their inward parts and will write it upon their hearts." It is so far from being the case that these words can be twisted, either into special Sorbonnic aid or into gratuitous gifts, that scarcely any other passage of Scripture describes more suitably the grace given through Christ which you call the grace that makes one pleasing to God.

It is not still obscure, is it, both in what manner Luther has quoted Augustine and Ambrose and what the Sorbonne resembles, which we perceive here is so crassly in error that those at Louvain and Cologne have never been more crassly foolish? O wretched France, to have been polluted by such censors and judges of sacred matters, who are really more worthy to deal with sewers than to treat sacred letters!

From this view on free will follow those things which Luther has written about contrition and therefore about repentance in general. But, oh, how wretched are we who now for almost four hundred years have had no writer in the church to set forth the right and proper form of repentance! Feigned contritions have been imposed upon some, and the consciences of others have been tormented by satisfactions. Now, finally, the mercy of God has looked down upon us and has revealed the Gospel to his people and has raised up the consciences of those whom he has called.

If you ask what Luther has conferred upon the church, you have right here the sum of the matter. He has taught the true way of repentance, and likewise he has shown the use of the sacraments. And as witnesses in this matter I have the consciences of many. But I do not here wish to dispute about the

forms of repentance or about the Sacraments, since those Sorbonners have only condemned Luther, but indeed have not conquered him either by reason or by Scripture.

But the truth of Lutheran doctrine stands unshaken and immovable not only against those Sorbonners but also against the rulers of darkness. If they will use the judgments of Scripture in opposing the things Luther has taught, we shall in no way hesitate to defend his teachings. For this doctrine of Luther about repentance will never be wrested from my heart or from the heart of any of the faithful by any force, not even Sorbonnic or papal. (pp. 82-6)

Christian reader, I have wanted to warn you of these things lest you be frightened away from the Lutheran doctrine by the authority of the Sorbonne, the wisdom of whose position you have already learned from various passages discussed here. And from those passages which I have noted, you will evaluate the rest. For the Sorbonne is like unto itself. And you may find Christ among the carpenters far more quickly than in that class of men. In the meantime, it is your duty to demand along with me that Paris give the reason for its judgment. When it has published that, we shall give a fuller discussion of our own views. Farewell. (p. 87)

> *Philip Melanchthon, "Luther and the Paris Theologians," in his* Selected Writings, *edited by Elmer Ellsworth Flack and Lowell J. Satre, translated by Charles Leander Hill, Augsburg Publishing House, 1962, pp. 69-87.*

GUILIELMUS ROSSEUS [PSEUDONYM OF] **THOMAS MORE** (essay date 1523)

[*An English humanist best known in literary circles for his* Utopia *(1516), an imaginative depiction of an ideal society, More was also a statesman who served Henry VIII in various political capacities. He was a staunch Catholic apologist, which the king also seemed to be in 1521 when he wrote* Assertio septem sacramentorum *(An Assertion of the Seven Sacraments, 1687; see excerpt dated 1521), a refutation of Luther's reduction of the seven sacraments to only three in* The Babylonian Captivity of the Church. *Luther's angry and disrespectful response,* Contra Henricum regem Angliae *(1522), prompted More to defend his sovereign in 1523 in an uncharacteristically scurrilous and scatalogical polemic against Luther written under the pseudonym Guilielmus Rosseus (or, anglicized, William Ross) and from which the following excerpt is taken. In later years, More's relationship with Henry became increasingly stormy due to his opposition to Henry's own subsequent break with Rome. When he refused to swear an oath upholding Henry's supplanting of the pope as head of the Church in England, More was executed for treason in 1535. He was canonized by the Catholic Church in 1935. Here, he condemns Luther's beliefs and methods of argumentation.*]

Luther laments that, despite the books he has published, his mad heresies have been so overwhelmed and refuted that he never hears himself acclaimed as victor among his own followers without at the same time being inwardly rent by the consciousness of his own disgrace. He knows that all peoples everywhere, by comparing the books from either side, perceive with utter clarity how shamefully overthrown and prostrate he lies. Wearied at last, and shrinking from a public trial, yet intending to fight, he challenges his foes cock-like to his own dung hill, where he may crow before his hens.

But I think no one is so senseless as to enter the place to which his enemy summons him for a fight, since there cannot be a more level plain for the struggle, or one less exposed to ambush, than a controversy carried on by means of published books, in which neither side can pretend, either that any point was falsely kept from the record by the secretaries, or later corrupted by forgers, or that anything had escaped him unforeseen in the heat of a hurried disputation. Rather, what he will have brought forward in the most ordered fashion—whatever he is able to bring forward at his leisure in accordance with the merits of the case—that will with honest fidelity appear in public. From these considerations, it is now most clearly evident, and from day to day will become more evident, how the glorious conqueror and victor, Luther, lies prostrate in foul filth, smeared with mud, coated with dung. (pp. 45-7)

[Luther] thought he would doubtless exasperate the king exceedingly if he pretended not to believe that the book published by the king was the king's own, but clearly Lee's, or some phlegmatic sophist's, as he calls him. As if anyone were so phlegmatic, Luther, as not to prefer the phlegm of any person whatever who is not completely raving to your raving bile.

This scoundrel is painfully tormented by the fact that the royal majesty's learning in almost all disciplines and especially in theology is too well known and, in other lands besides Britain, too celebrated for the dolt to be able to persuade anyone that the most wise king wished to seek renown through another man's book at the expense of a frenzied friarlet. I think the king would rather consider it inglorious to contend with him than glorious to conquer him, especially in such a contest as, while it would always be intrinsically noteworthy, he yet knew would be rendered notorious by the folly of his opponent. Nor, I think, would the prince have written anything at all against such a buffoon except that for the honor of Christ he considered nothing a dishonor to himself; but just as for the honor of Christ's name he would not decline to fight against the basest of infidels, if that were his fortune, so for the faith of Christ he deigned to fight with his pen against the most foolish of heretics. (p. 57)

In order to exonerate himself of [the King's charge of inconsistency]. . ., as though with a profound awareness of his innocence, [Luther] pompously reviews the catalogue of his published books, lest anyone be ignorant of the names of those poisons with which the poison-maker has tried to infect the Christian people. Anyone who carefully examines these same books will find so many, such evident, such absurd contradictions that he will think Luther has done nothing else by this review of his books than if he had slit the throat of a man in the sight of the people, and then, when summoned to trial, produced as witnesses of his innocence all those people who had been the spectators of his crime. (p. 63)

Now, since Luther had said in the **Babylonian Captivity** that everyone was commanded to receive the eucharist under both kinds, and not much later on the same page said that neither kind at all was a matter of precept, his royal majesty in the words which follow touches on the signal madness of a man so at odds with himself.

> But please observe how Luther wavers and contradicts himself: in one place he says that at the supper Christ said to each and every one of the faithful, not by way of permission but by way of command: "All of you drink of this." But afterwards, fearing to offend the laity, whom he flatters into hating the priests, he adds these words: "Not that they who use one kind sin against Christ, since He did not command the use of any kind but left it to the choice of each individual, saying: 'As often as you do these things you do them in remembrance of me.' But they

sin who forbid both kinds to be given to persons who desire to exercise this choice. The fault is not in the laity but in the priests." You see clearly that first he said it was commanded, then he says it was not commanded but left to the choice of each individual. What need is there, then, for us to contradict him who so often contradicts himself?

By your raving madness I ask you, "What do you have to say here, friend Luther?" Will you argue here that you are not inconsistent, and will you be so shameless or stupid as to defend as one and the same thing the statement that both kinds were commanded to all and the statement that neither kind was commanded to anyone? But if you were so shameless as to seek this, or if anyone were so senseless as to grant what you seek, yet you could not any the better escape from the snares of your own most deceitful trickery. When you write that the king produces none of your inconsistencies by way of example, lest you be given the opportunity of clearing yourself, it is plain that what you desire is not at all the kind of example which cannot be explained away, but that kind which your opponent at any rate terms a contradiction, in which case you would have the opportunity of clearing yourself of the reproach of that fault by some trick, if you could.

Behold one passage produced by the king; it was the first which occurred to me from among many as I read the book; in it you are so clearly convicted of contradicting yourself that, shameless as you are, you, who conceal by a foolish silence a passage commonly known; you, wicked liar, who in the case of this passage which everyone is reading and which you yourself have read with such torment that you cannot forget it thus read, contended that this passage had never been written; you have yet not been able, by putting on a bold front, to summon up enough audacity to defend the passage as not contradictory. But if you could do precisely this, although you would thus escape being considered inconsistent on the grounds of that one passage, still you would not any the more avoid being convicted of the basest dishonesty clearly fitting a real scoundrel, since you have boasted with so much arrogance that the king had not produced even one passage, even for the sake of example, lest an opportunity be given you of clearing yourself.

Therefore, honest reader—to return to you after disposing of the scoundrel—this one passage suffices to convict Luther, as I said, of the most shameless dishonesty, since he says that the king has produced no example of his inconsistency lest he be given the opportunity of clearing himself. But in order that the fellow's deceitfulness may come to light still more clearly, listen, reader, to yet another passage.

Luther wrote in his **Babylon** that the sacrament of orders was something new, and unknown to the church of Christ; that it has been recently invented by the church of the pope; and yet he admits that this same sacrament is mentioned by Saint Dionysius, who he does not deny is very ancient. The prince did not pass over this most stupid contradiction on the fellow's part, but he censured it very sharply in the following words: "If Dionysius were the only ancient father who wrote that orders is a sacrament, even this would be enough to overthrow Luther, who would have us think that the invention of that sacrament is something new. For its being new contradicts his admission that it is included in the writings of a man he admits is ancient."

See what lies this fellow will dare to tell, reader; he is not ashamed to pretend that the prince has produced no passage in which he may say that Luther contradicts himself, whereas this single passage is such a contradiction that by producing it the prince has overthrown the rascal's whole foundation in almost three lines. I think no one is so given over to Luther as not to admit that either of these passages will suffice to expose the shamelessness of the man who was not ashamed to boast with such great pomposity that the king had produced no passage, even for the sake of example, in which he might say that Luther contradicted himself. Nevertheless, so that on this point there may be a superfluity rather than the slightest lack, we will add still a third passage. We are ready to add more than ten, except that we would be ashamed to dwell so long in this way on an evident matter.

Since Luther perceived himself to be hard pressed by the perfectly clear words from the epistle of James, not only in the matter of the sacrament of extreme unction, but also in that the apostle portrayed precisely the fellow's abusive tongue and poisonous heart, when the most wise prince caught this point very shrewdly and touched on it very skillfully, Luther began to boil with fury, and, desiring to avenge himself, he first contemned the epistle, then treated the apostle as not worth a straw. You will read about this later, when you wish, in the king's book itself. But first we will touch on his remark about the epistle, which he contemned so much that he said it was probably not an apostle's because it contained nothing worthy of the apostolic spirit. I will set down the very words of the king on this matter so that you can see whether the king has brought forward no passage at all in which he might say that Luther contradicts himself. These, then, are the words of the king.

> Surely, if Luther had brought forward reasons why the epistle was not James', but still that of someone else who spoke in the same spirit, it could have been endured somehow. But now he says that it is probably not, because it is unworthy of the apostolic spirit. In which case I bring no other objection against Luther than Luther himself, for hardly anyone contradicts Luther more often or more forcefully than Luther. He, then, in speaking of the sacrament of orders, says that the church has the power of distinguishing the words of God from the words of man. How then does he now say that an epistle is unworthy of the apostolic spirit which the church, whose judgment as he says cannot err in this matter, has judged to be full of the apostolic spirit? Consequently, he has now so hemmed himself in on all sides by his own wisdom that he must either necessarily acknowledge that the epistle is the apostle's, and he has said that the contrary is probable; or he must say that the church can be deceived in determing the sacred scriptures; this possibility he has denied.

What is clearer than this passage, reader? What impudence the scoundrel has who is not ashamed to deny such clear evidence! What does he need to hear from these men who, after comparing these passages with the fellow's shameless lying, may consider the buffoonish words of the most deceitful buffoon when he plays the buffoon as follows?

> Seeing that he was pleased to play behind a mask with masked words in a matter so serious and sacred, a thing without precedent, I say, without a mask and openly, that this King Henry of England is clearly lying and that by his lies he resembles a most frivolous buffoon more than a king. I, Luther, publicly accuse this virulent Thomist of this crime and, with my books as well as my readers as witnesses, convict him throughout the world. In this contest, let me be done with the distinction between his royal majesty and my lowly estate; I am speaking with a lying buffoon veiled by kingly titles concerning divine matters which it is the duty of every Christian to defend against the injury of lies. If the foolish king so forgets his royal majesty that he dares to come out in public with manifest lies, and that while discussing sacred matters, why is it not fair for me to cast his lies back into his mouth, so that, if he has derived any pleasure from lying against the divine majesty, he may lose it by hearing the truth against his own majesty.

Please consider carefully, reader, the very just causes for which this venerable father judges it lawful for him, as if in his own right, to play the buffoon against the king. Because the king has dared to say that Luther contradicts himself, Luther divides his statement into two charges, both very capital. The one charge is that the king made this statement without producing any passage, not even for the sake of example, lest Luther have an opportunity of defending himself. How deceitful and shameless the venerable father is in this matter you see at least from the third passage just presented.

The other charge is that by his statement the king lies against the divine majesty. But since the king has said nothing else but what he has already proved many times; namely, that Luther is stark mad and that he constantly contradicts himself, you necessarily see, reader, that if the prince is lying against the majesty of God in this matter, then that majesty of God is the majesty of Luther. The king has not spoken of any other god; and so you see clearly how this reverend father is openly proclaimed to us as a god, and with his own mouth trumpets his apotheosis.

In the future, therefore, we must avoid arousing this easily aroused new god of the underworld, but by casting honeyed cakes into his Cerberean mouth let us try to pacify him with pastries, and by singing a palinode in the Stesichorean manner let the king soothe him as follows: "The divine Luther is not contradictory, not inconsistent, not a liar, not wicked, not virulent, not a blasphemer against God, not a raving madman, not a scoundrel, not a heretic; but he is more faithful than faith itself, more honorable than honor itself, more prudent than prudence itself, more reverent toward God than the saints themselves, more sincere than sincerity itself, more upright than uprightness itself, more modest than modesty itself, more constant than constancy itself, and more truthful than truth itself." Sufficient proof of which is given even by the fact that he has dared to boast with such bombast that the king did not produce any contradictory passage of his, not even for the sake of example, lest he be given the opportunity of defending himself. Since he knows it is clearly evident to everyone that the king has produced many passages, he is forced, being powerless to defend any of them, to dissemble all of them most shamelessly and to deny that they have been produced. By this most stupid denial he is refuted much more shamefully than he could ever have been refuted by any confession. Therefore, reader, as Luther for his part seeks to have you appraise the trustworthiness of the king in dealing with him from the fact that the king supposedly produces no example of Luther's inconsistency, so now I beg of you in turn that you judge the utterly worthless trustworthiness of Luther from such wicked dishonesty, such proven deceitfulness, such shameful shamelessness. I am utterly convinced that no matter what aspect of the man you examine, you will find him in every respect as you have perceived him to be in this one respect. (pp. 65-75)

[Luther writes:]

The sum of the matter is this: The whole of Henry's book relies upon the words of men and the usage of the ages, not on the words of God or on the usage of the Spirit, as he himself is forced to admit. On the other hand, the sum of my arguments is this, that the words of men and the usage of the ages, although they can be maintained and preserved wherever they do not contradict the sacred scriptures, still do not constitute articles of faith or make for a necessary observance. And so, if King Henry, by the conjoined forces and efforts of all Thomists, papists, demons and men, can show the necessary observance of human words, then Luther is conquered by his own judgment and confession. For then I will finally hold as articles of faith whatever even the Thomists will command. If he cannot do this, Luther is the victor. For what else do they want? Not even if they have written a million books against me, will they be able to ask anything else from me.

The sum of the matter is this: The whole book of Luther is nothing else but a sheer conglomeration of buffoonish words, with distortion of the words of God, contempt of all the saints, and blasphemy against the Holy Spirit, as he himself is forced to admit. On the other hand, the sum of the prince's arguments is the defense of the sacraments, which he has proved more clearly than light to be, not the traditions of men, but the traditions of God, and he has proved this by reason, by the scriptures, and by the confession of Luther himself. And so, if Luther with all his pot-fellows combined, with all his buffoons and rascals combined, with all his spectres and cacodaemons (the inspirers of his blasphemies) combined, if he can, I say, show that the buffoonery of impious scoundrels has more validity than the traditions of God, then Luther is the victor. If he cannot, then Luther is conquered by the confession of Luther himself. For what else does he want? If those who write against him should write even a million books they will be demanding nothing else from him than that he listen to what is said to him and remember what he himself has said. Up till now no one has been able to gain either of these aims from him. (pp. 671-73)

[Luther] testifies that he has absolutely refrained from lies and invective, the very person in whose pen there is nothing but calumnies, lies and deceptions; in whose spirit there is nothing but venom, bombast and ill will; who conceives nothing in his mind but folly, madness, and insanity; who has nothing in his mouth but privies, filth and dung, with which he plays the buffoon more foully and impurely than any buffoon, of whom none has ever been found besides this one such a stupid butt of men's scorn that he would cast into his mouth the dung which other men would spit out into a basin. Therefore, since he is this sort of person, I am not at all surprised if he is now considered unworthy for anyone to dispute with him. Surely, since he has devoted himself totally to hell, and has persisted in schism, and has determined never to retract his heresies, he still ought to resolve on showing some regard at least for public dignity, by which he might claim for himself the authority of a teacher of dogma rather than that of a worthless heretical buffoon. If he will ever be willing to do this, if he will carry on his disputation in a serious manner, if he will retract his lies and deceptions, if he will leave off the folly and rage and the till now too familiar mad ravings, if he will swallow down his filth and lick up the dung with which he has so foully defiled his tongue and his pen, there will not be lacking those who, as is fitting, will discuss serious matters in a serious way. But if he proceeds to play the buffoon in the manner in which he has begun, and to rave madly, if he proceeds to rage with

calumny, to mouth trifling nonsense, to act like a raging madman, to make sport with buffoonery, and to carry nothing in his mouth but bilge-water, sewers, privies, filth and dung, then let others do what they will; we will take timely counsel, whether we wish to deal with the fellow thus ranting according to his virtues and to paint with his colors, or to leave this mad friarlet and privy-minded rascal with his ragings and ravings, with his filth and dung, shitting and beshitted. (p. 683)

Guilielmus Rosseus [pseudonym of Thomas More], "Response to Luther," in his The Complete Works of St. Thomas More, Vol. 5, Part I, *edited by John M. Headley, translated by Sister Scholastica Mandeville, Yale University Press, 1969, pp. 1-683.*

HULDRYCH ZWINGLI   (essay date 1527)

[*The leader of the Reformation in Switzerland, Zwingli shared many beliefs with Luther but strongly disagreed with him regarding the issue of the consubstantiation of the Eucharist. Luther and Zwingli met at the Colloquy of Marburg in 1529 in an unsuccessful attempt to resolve their doctrinal differences and unite their movements. In the following excerpt from a tribute to Luther written in 1527, Zwingli praises Luther's pioneering break with the Church but regrets that his reform does not extend far enough.*]

[There] were not a few who knew just as well as you [Luther] what religion was about, or even better (though you do not admit it). Indeed, there are some people whom I have known for the last twelve years who gave this business attention and moved me to activity. Yet there was no one in all the camps of Israel who dared to throw himself zealously into the combat; they were so afraid of that monster Goliath, so feared the menace of so many armed men.

Here indeed you were the only faithful David anointed hereto by the Lord and furnished likewise with arms. At first you started to argue with them according to their rules and set out your paradoxes [i.e. Luther's ninety-five theses] to cut the Gordian knot. Soon, however, casting aside these hindrances, you picked suitable stones from the heavenly river and flung them so skilfully that you stretched that great body flat on the open field. Hence faithful souls should never cease energetically singing 'Saul has slain his thousands but David his ten thousands.' You were that one Hercules who dealt with any trouble that arose anywhere. You slew the Roman boar and crushed Anteus the son of earth. Who has set forth more clearly and plainly than you from apostolic sources the hostility of body and soul? You dragged out Cacus who drove not only oxen [backwards] but also pulled widows' huts into his cave. What more? You would have cleansed the Augean stable, if you had had the images removed, if you had not taught that the body of Christ was supposed to be eaten in the bread, if you had perceived, by the light of the gospel, that purgatory is a net for collecting money whereas absolution (what the gospel calls 'keys') signifies faith, there being but one God with his Son Christ Jesus as mediator between God and man. If you had done all this, not only would you have effected a thorough cleansing but you would have taken heaven itself on your shoulders. (pp. 100-01)

Huldrych Zwingli, "Tribute to Luther: 'A Friendly Explanation'," translated by G. R. Potter, in Huldrych Zwingli, *edited by G. R. Potter, St. Martin's Press, 1978, pp. 100-01.*

JOHN CALVIN   (letter date 1544)

[*A French theologian and younger contemporary of Luther, Calvin held some theological tenets in common with Luther, including his disbelief in special priestly authority and his rejection of all sacraments save baptism and the Eucharist, but he is best known for a doctrine he did not share with Luther: predestination. As promulgator of this doctrine, which posits a stern God who has foreordained that a few of the elect of humanity will attain salvation while the majority will be damned regardless of their faith or their moral behavior, Calvin has had an immense impact on Western religious thought. Their differences notwithstanding, Calvin respected Luther's piety and church reforms. The following excerpt is taken from a letter to Swiss reformer Heinrich Bullinger, one of the targets of Luther's 1544* Kurtz Bekentnis vom heiligen Sacrament (Brief Confession concerning the Holy Sacrament), *in which he inveighed harshly against the doctrines of other reformers. Here, Calvin distinguishes Luther as a great servant of Christ, though one who too often directs his invective against the wrong objects.*]

I hear that Luther has at length broken forth in fierce invective [in **Brief Confession concerning the Holy Sacrament**], not so much against you as against the whole of us. On the present occasion, I dare scarce venture to ask you to keep silence, because it is neither just that innocent persons should thus be harassed, nor that they should be denied the opportunity of clearing themselves; neither, on the other hand, is it easy to determine whether it would be prudent for them to do so. But of this I do earnestly desire to put you in mind, in the first place, that you would consider how eminent a man Luther is, and the excellent endowments wherewith he is gifted, with what strength of mind and resolute constancy, with how great skill, with what efficiency and power of doctrinal statement, he hath hitherto devoted his whole energy to overthrow the reign of Antichrist, and at the same time to diffuse far and near the doctrine of salvation. Often have I been wont to declare, that even although he were to call me a devil, I should still not the less hold him in such honour that I must acknowledge him to be an illustrious servant of God. But while he is endued with rare and excellent virtues, he labours at the same time under serious faults. Would that he had rather studied to curb this restless, uneasy temperament which is so apt to boil over in every direction. I wish, moreover, that he had always bestowed the fruits of that vehemence of natural temperament upon the enemies of the truth, and that he had not flashed his lightning sometimes also upon the servants of the Lord. Would that he had been more observant and careful in the acknowledgment of his own vices. Flatterers have done him much mischief, since he is naturally too prone to be over-indulgent to himself. It is our part, however, so to reprove whatsoever evil qualities may beset him, as that we may make some allowance for him at the same time on the score of these remarkable endowments with which he has been gifted. This, therefore, I would beseech you to consider first of all, along with your colleagues, that you have to do with a most distinguished servant of Christ, to whom we are all of us largely indebted; that, besides, you will do yourselves no good by quarrelling, except that you may afford some sport to the wicked, so that they may triumph not so much over us as over the Evangel. If they see us rending each other asunder, they then give full credit to what we say, but when with one consent and with one voice we preach Christ, they avail themselves unwarrantably of our inherent weakness to cast reproach upon our faith. I wish, therefore, that you would consider and reflect on these things rather than on what Luther has deserved by his violence; lest that may happen to you which Paul threatens,

that by biting and devouring one another, ye be consumed one of another. (pp. 432-34)

> *John Calvin, in a letter to Henry Bullinger on November 25, 1544, in his* Letters of John Calvin, Vol. I *edited by Jules Bonnet, translated by David Constable, 1855. Reprint by Burt Franklin Reprints, 1973, pp. 429-34.*

MARTIN LUTHER   (essay date 1545)

[*In the following excerpt from an essay written in 1545, the year before his death, Luther comments on his work and recalls his spiritual growth, describing his discovery of the doctrine of justification by faith alone.*]

Martin Luther wishes the sincere reader salvation!

For a long time I strenuously resisted those who wanted my books, or more correctly my confused lucubrations, published. I did not want the labors of the ancients to be buried by my new works and the reader kept from reading them. Then, too, by God's grace a great many systematic books now exist, among which the *Loci communes* of Philip [Melanchthon] excel, with which a theologian and a bishop can be beautifully and abundantly prepared to be mighty in preaching the doctrine of piety, especially since the Holy Bible itself can now be had in nearly every language. But my books, as it happened, yes, as the lack of order in which the events transpired made it necessary, are accordingly crude and disordered chaos, which is now not easy to arrange even for me.

Persuaded by these reasons, I wished that all my books were buried in perpetual oblivion, so that there might be room for better ones. But the boldness and bothersome perseverance of others daily filled my ears with complaints that it would come to pass, that if I did not permit their publication in my lifetime, men wholly ignorant of the causes and the time of the events would nevertheless most certainly publish them, and so out of one confusion many would arise. Their boldness, I say, prevailed and so I permitted them to be published. At the same time the wish and command of our most illustrious Prince, Elector, etc., John Frederick was added. He commanded, yes, compelled the printers not only to print, but to speed up the publication.

But above all else, I beg the sincere reader, and I beg for the sake of our Lord Jesus Christ himself, to read those things judiciously, yes, with great commiseration. May he be mindful of the fact that I was once a monk and a most enthusiastic papist when I began that cause. I was so drunk, yes, submerged in the pope's dogmas, that I would have been ready to murder all, if I could have, or to co-operate willingly with the murderers of all who would take but a syllable from obedience to the pope. So great a Saul was I, as are many to this day. I was not such a lump of frigid ice in defending the papacy as Eck and his like were, who appeared to me actually to defend the pope more for their own belly's sake than to pursue the matter seriously. To me, indeed, they seem to laugh at the pope to this day, like Epicureans! I pursued the matter with all seriousness, as one, who in dread of the last day, nevertheless from the depth of my heart wanted to be saved.

So you will find how much and what important matters I humbly conceded to the pope in my earlier writings, which I later and now hold and execrate as the worst blasphemies and abomination. You will, therefore, sincere reader, ascribe this error, or, as they slander, contradiction, to the time and my inexperience. At first I was all alone and certainly very inept and unskilled in conducting such great affairs. For I got into these turmoils by accident and not by will or intention. I call upon God himself as witness.

Hence, when in the year 1517 indulgences were sold (I wanted to say promoted) in these regions for most shameful gain—I was then a preacher, a young doctor of theology, so to speak—and I began to dissuade the people and to urge them not to listen to the clamors of the indulgence hawkers; they had better things to do. I certainly thought that in this case I should have a protector in the pope, on whose trustworthiness I then leaned strongly, for in his decrees he most clearly damned the immoderation of the quaestors, as he called the indulgence preachers.

Soon afterward I wrote two letters, one to Albrecht, the archbishop of Mainz, who got half of the money from the indulgences, the pope the other half—something I did not know at the time—the other to the ordinary (as they call them) Jerome, the bishop of Brandenburg. I begged them to stop the shameless blasphemy of the quaestors. But the poor little brother was despised. Despised, I published the *Theses* and at the same time a German *Sermon on Indulgences,* shortly thereafter also the *Explanations* [*of the Ninety-five Theses*], in which, to the pope's honor, I developed the idea that indulgences should indeed not be condemned, but that good works of love should be preferred to them.

AMORE ET STVDIO ELVCIDANDAE
ueritatis hæc subscripta disputabunt Vuittenbergæ, Præsidēte R.P. Martino Luther, Artiū & S. Theologiæ Magistro, eiusdemꝗ ibidem lectore Ordinario. Quare petit ut qui non possunt uerbis præsentes nobiscum disceptare, agant id literis absentes. In nomine domini nostri Iesu Christi. Amen.

ſ   ᴅOminus & Magister noster Iesus Christus, dicendo pœnitentiā agite &c, omnem uitam fidelium, pœnitentiam esse uoluit.

ij   Quod uerbū pœnitentia de pœnitentia sacramentali(.i. confessionis & satisfactionis quæ sacerdotum ministerio celebratur) non potest intelligi.

iij   Non tamen sola intēdit interiorē: immo interior nulla est, nisi foris operetur uarias carnis mortificationes.

iiij   Manet itacꝗ pœna donec manet odium sui(.i. pœnitentia uera intus)scilicet usꝗ ad introitum regni cælorum.

v   Papa non uult nec potest, ullas pœnas remittere: præter eas, quas arbitrio uel suo uel canonum imposuit.

vj   Papa nō potest remittere ullam culpā, nisi declarādo & approbando remissam a deo. Aut certe remittēdo casus reseruatos sibi, quibus contēptis culpa prorsus remaneret.

vij   Nulli prorsus remittit deus culpam, quin simul eum subijciat humiliatum in omnibus sacerdoti suo uicario.

viij Canones pœnitentiales solū uiuentibus sunt impositi: nīhilꝗ morituris, secundū eosdem debet imponi.

ix   Inde bene nobis facit spiritussanctus in Papa: excipiēdo in suis decretis semper articulum mortis & necessitatis.

x   Indocte & male faciūt sacerdotes ij, qui morituris pœnitētias canonicas in purgatorium reseruant.

xj   Zizania illa de mutanda pœna Canonica in pœnā purgatorij, uidentur certe dormientibus Episcopis seminata.

xij   Olim pœnæ canonicæ nō post, sed ante absolutionem imponebantur, tanꝗ tentamenta ueræ contritionis.

A page from the first edition of Luther's The Ninety-Five Theses *(1517).*

This was demolishing heaven and consuming the earth with fire. I am accused by the pope, am cited to Rome, and the whole papacy rises up against me alone. All this happened in the year 1518. . . . (pp. 3-5)

In the year 1519, Leo X . . . sent the Rose with Karl von Miltitz, who urged me profusely to be reconciled with the pope. He had seventy apostolic briefs that if Prince Frederick would turn me over to him, as the pope requested by means of the Rose, he should tack one up in each city and so transfer me safely to Rome. But he betrayed the counsel of his heart toward me when he said, ''O Martin, I believed you were some aged theologian who, sitting behind the stove, disputed thus with himself; now I see you are still young and strong. If I had twenty-five thousand armed men, I do not believe I could take you to Rome, for I have sounded out the people's mind all along the way to learn what they thought of you. Behold, where I found one standing for the pope, three stood for you against the pope.'' But that was ridiculous! He had also asked simple little women and girls in the hostelries, what they thought of the Roman chair. Ignorant of this term and thinking of a domestic chair, they replied, ''How can we know what kind of chairs you have in Rome, wood or stone?''

Therefore he begged me to seek the things which made for peace. He would put forth every effort to have the pope do the same. I also promised everything abundantly. Whatever I could do with a good conscience with respect to the truth, I would do most promptly. I, too, desired and was eager for peace. Having been drawn into these disturbances by force and driven by necessity, I had done all I did: the guilt was not mine.

But he had summoned Johann Tetzel of the preaching order, the primary author of this tragedy, and had with verbose threats from the pope so broken the man, till then so terrible to all, a fearless crier, that from that time on he wasted away and was finally consumed by illness of mind. When I found this out before his death, I comforted him with a letter, written benignly, asking him to be of good cheer and not to fear my memory. But perhaps he succumbed a victim of his conscience and of the pope's indignation.

Karl von Miltitz was regarded as vain and his advice as vain. But, in my opinion, if the man at Mainz had from the start, when I admonished him, and, finally, if the pope, before he condemned me unheard and raged with his bulls, had taken this advice, which Karl took although too late, and had at once quenched Tetzel's fury, the matter would not have come to so great a tumult. The entire guilt belongs to the one at Mainz, whose smartness and cleverness fooled him, with which he wanted to suppress my doctrine and have his money, acquired by the indulgences, saved. Now counsels are sought in vain; in vain efforts are made. The Lord has awakened and stands to judge the people. Though they could kill us, they still do not have what they want, yes, have less than they have, while we live in safety. This some of them who are not entirely of a dull nose smell quite enough.

Meanwhile, I had already during that year returned to interpret the Psalter anew. I had confidence in the fact that I was more skilful, after I had lectured in the university on St. Paul's epistles to the Romans, to the Galatians, and the one to the Hebrews. I had indeed been captivated with an extraordinary ardor for understanding Paul in the Epistle to the Romans. But up till then it was not the cold blood about the heart, but a single word in Chapter 1 [:17], ''In it the righteousness of God is revealed,'' that had stood in my way. For I hated that word "righteousness of God," which, according to the use and custom of all the teachers, I had been taught to understand philosophically regarding the formal or active righteousness, as they called it, with which God is righteous and punishes the unrighteous sinner.

Though I lived as a monk without reproach, I felt that I was a sinner before God with an extremely disturbed conscience. I could not believe that he was placated by my satisfaction. I did not love, yes, I hated the righteous God who punishes sinners, and secretly, if not blasphemously, certainly murmuring greatly, I was angry with God, and said, "As if, indeed, it is not enough, that miserable sinners, eternally lost through original sin, are crushed by every kind of calamity by the law of the decalogue, without having God add pain to pain by the gospel threatening us with his righteousness and wrath!" Thus I raged with a fierce and troubled conscience. Nevertheless, I beat importunately upon Paul at that place, most ardently desiring to know what St. Paul wanted.

At last, by the mercy of God, meditating day and night, I gave heed to the context of the words, namely, "In it the righteousness of God is revealed, as it is written, 'He who through faith is righteous shall live.'" There I began to understand that the righteousness of God is that by which the righteous lives by a gift of God, namely by faith. And this is the meaning: the righteousness of God is revealed by the gospel, namely, the passive righteousness with which merciful God justifies us by faith, as it is written, "He who through faith is righteous shall live." Here I felt that I was altogether born again and had entered paradise itself through open gates. There a totally other face of the entire Scripture showed itself to me. Thereupon I ran through the Scriptures from memory. I also found in other terms an analogy, as, the work of God, that is, what God does in us, the power of God, with which he makes us strong, the wisdom of God, with which he makes us wise, the strength of God, the salvation of God, the glory of God.

And I extolled my sweetest word with a love as great as the hatred with which I had before hated the word "righteousness of God." Thus that place in Paul was for me truly the gate to paradise. Later I read Augustine's *The Spirit and the Letter,* where contrary to hope I found that he, too, interpreted God's righteousness in a similar way, as the righteousness with which God clothes us when he justifies us. Although this was heretofore said imperfectly and he did not explain all things concerning imputation clearly, it nevertheless was pleasing that God's righteousness with which we are justified was taught. Armed more fully with these thoughts, I began a second time to interpret the Psalter. And the work would have grown into a large commentary, if I had not again been compelled to leave the work begun, because Emperor Charles V in the following year convened the diet at Worms.

I relate these things, good reader, so that, if you are a reader of my puny works, you may keep in mind, that, as I said above, I was all alone and one of those who, as Augustine says of himself, have become proficient by writing and teaching. I was not one of those who from nothing suddenly become the topmost, though they are nothing, neither have labored, nor been tempted, nor become experienced, but have with one look at the Scriptures exhausted their entire spirit. (pp. 9-12)

Farewell in the Lord, reader, and pray for the growth of the Word against Satan. Strong and evil, now also very furious and savage, he knows his time is short and the kingdom of his pope is in danger. But may God confirm in us what he has accomplished and perfect his work which he began in us, to his glory, Amen. (p. 12)

Martin Luther, "Preface to the Complete Edition of Luther's Latin Writings," in Martin Luther: Selections from His Writings, *edited by John Dillenberger, Anchor Books, 1961, pp. 3-12.*

PHILIP MELANCHTHON   (eulogy date 1546)

[*In the following excerpt from his funeral oration for Luther, Melanchthon extols the man and his divinely inspired Reformation.*]

Though amid the public sorrow my voice is obstructed by grief and tears, yet in this vast assembly something ought to be said, not, as among the heathen, only in praise of the deceased. Much rather is this assembly to be reminded of the wonderful government of the Church, and of her perils, that in our distress we may consider what we are, most of all, to desire, and by what examples we are to regulate our lives. There are ungodly men, who, in the confused condition of human affairs, think that everything is the result of accident. But we who are illumined by the many explicit declarations of God, distinguish the Church from the profane multitude; and we know that it is in reality governed and preserved by God. We fix our eye on this Church. We acknowledge lawful rulers, and consider their manner of life. We also select suitable leaders and teachers, whom we may piously follow and reverence.

It is necessary to think on, and to speak of these things, so often as we name the name of the Reverend Doctor Martin Luther, our most dear Father and Preceptor, whom many wicked men have most bitterly hated; but whom we, who know that he was a minister of the Gospel raised up by God, love and applaud. We also have the evidence to show that his doctrine did not consist of seditious opinions scattered by blind impulse, as men of Epicurean tastes suppose; but that it is an exhibition of the will of God, and of true worship, an exposition of the Holy Scriptures, a preaching of the Word of God, that is, of the Gospel of Jesus Christ. (pp. 381-82)

It is both pleasant and profitable to contemplate the Church of all ages, and to consider the goodness of God, in sending useful teachers, one after another, that as some fall in the ranks, others may at once press into their places.

Behold the Patriarchs, Adam, Seth, Enoch, Methuselah, Noah, Shem. When in the time of the last named, who lived in the neighbourhood of the Sodomites, the nations forgot the teaching of Noah and Shem, and worshipped idols, Abraham was raised up to be Shem's companion and to assist him in his great work and in propagating sound doctrine. He was succeeded by Isaac, Jacob, and Joseph, which last lighted the torch of truth in all the land of Egypt, which at that time was the most flourishing kingdom in all the world. Then came Moses, Joshua, Samuel, David, Elijah, Elisha, Isaiah, Jeremiah, Daniel, Zechariah. Then Ezra, Onias, and the Maccabees. Then Simeon, Zacharias, the Baptist, Christ, and the Apostles. It is a delight to contemplate this unbroken succession, inasmuch as it is a manifest proof of the presence of God in the Church.

After the Apostles comes a long line, inferior, indeed, but distinguished by the divine attestations: Polycarp, Irenæus, Gregory of Neocæsarea, Basil, Augustin, Prosper, Maximus, Hugo, Bernard, Tauler, and others. And though these later times have been less fruitful, yet God has always preserved a remnant; and that a more splendid light of the Gospel has been kindled by the voice of Luther, cannot be denied.

To that splendid list of most illustrious men raised up by God to gather and establish the Church, and recognised as the chief glory of the human race, must be added the name of Martin Luther. Solon, Themistocles, Scipio, Augustus, and others, who established, or ruled over vast empires, were great men, indeed, but far inferior were they to our leaders, Isaiah, John the Baptist, Paul, Augustin, and Luther. It is proper that we of the Church should understand this manifest difference.

What, then, are the great and splendid things disclosed by Luther which render his life illustrious? Many are crying out that confusion has come upon the Church, and that inexplicable controversies have arisen. I reply that this belongs to the regulation of the Church. When the Holy Spirit reproves the world, disorders arise on account of the obstinacy of the wicked. The fault is with those who will not hear the Son of God, of whom the Heavenly Father says: "Hear ye him." Luther brought to light the true and necessary doctrine. That the densest darkness existed touching the doctrine of repentance, is evident. In his discussions he showed what true repentance is, and what is the refuge and the sure comfort of the soul which quails under the sense of the wrath of God. He expounded Paul's doctrine, which says that man is justified by faith. He showed the difference between the Law and the Gospel, between the righteousness of faith and civil righteousness. He also showed what the true worship of God is, and recalled the Church from heathenish superstition, which imagines that God is worshipped, even though the mind, agitated by some academic doubt, turns away from God. He bade us worship in faith and with a good conscience, and led us to the one Mediator, the Son of God, who sits at the right hand of the Eternal Father and makes intercession for us—not to images or to dead men, that by a shocking superstition impious men might worship images and dead men.

He also pointed out other services acceptable to God, and so adorned and guarded civil life, as it had never been adorned and guarded by any other man's writings. Then from necessary services he separated the puerilities of human ceremonies, the rites and institutions which hinder the true worship of God. And that the heavenly truth might be handed down to posterity he translated the Prophetical and Apostolic Scriptures into the German language with so much accuracy that his version is more easily understood by the reader than most commentaries.

He also published many expositions, which Erasmus was wont to say excelled all others. And as it is recorded respecting the rebuilding of Jerusalem that with one hand they builded and with the other they held the sword, so he fought with the enemies of the true doctrine, and at the same time composed annotations replete with heavenly truth, and by his pious counsel brought assistance to the consciences of many.

Inasmuch as a large part of the doctrine cannot be understood by human reason, as the doctrine of the remission of sins and of faith, it must be acknowledged that he was taught of God; and many of us witnessed the struggles through which he passed, in establishing the principle that by faith are we received and heard of God.

Hence throughout eternity pious souls will magnify the benefits which God has bestowed on the Church through Luther. First they will give thanks to God. Then they will own that they owe much to the labours of this man, even though atheists who

mock the Church declare that these splendid achievements are empty and superstitious nothings.

It is not true, as some falsely affirm, that intricate disputes have arisen, that the apple of discord has been thrown into the Church, that the riddles of the Sphynx have been proposed. It is an easy matter for discreet and pious persons, and for those who do not judge maliciously, to see, by a comparison of views, which accord with the heavenly doctrine, and which do not. Yea, without doubt these controversies have already been settled in the minds of all pious persons. For since God wills to reveal himself and his purposes in the language of Prophets and Apostles, it is not to be imagined that that language is as ambiguous as the leaves of the Sibyl, which, when disturbed, fly away, the sport of the winds.

Some, by no means evil-minded persons, have complained that Luther displayed too much severity. I will not deny this. But I answer in the language of Erasmus: "Because of the magnitude of the disorders God gave this age a violent physician." When God raised up this instrument against the proud and impudent enemies of the truth, he spoke as he did to Jeremiah: "Behold I place my words in thy mouth; destroy and build." Over against these enemies God set this mighty destroyer. In vain do they find fault with God. Moreover, God does not govern the Church by human counsels; nor does he choose instruments very like those of men. It is natural for mediocre and inferior minds to dislike those of more ardent character, whether good or bad. When Aristides saw Themistocles by the mighty impulse of genius undertake and successfully accomplish great achievements, though he congratulated the State, he sought to turn the zealous mind of Themistocles from its course.

I do not deny that the more ardent characters sometimes make mistakes, for amid the weakness of human nature no one is without fault. But we may say of such a one what the ancients said of Hercules, Cimon, and others: . . . "rough indeed, but worthy of all praise." And in the Church, if, as Paul says, he wars a good warfare, holding faith and a good conscience, he is to be held in the highest esteem by us.

That Luther was such we do know, for he constantly defended purity of doctrine and kept a good conscience. There is no one who knew him, who does not know that he was possessed of the greatest kindness, and of the greatest affability in the society of his friends, and that he was in no sense contentious or quarrelsome. He also exhibited, as such a man ought, the greatest dignity of demeanour. (pp. 382-86)

To his sixty-third year he spent his life in the most ardent study of religion and of all the liberal arts. No speech of mine can worthily set forth the praises of such a man. No lewd passions were ever detected in him, no seditious counsels. He was emphatically the advocate of peace. He never mingled the arts of politics with the affairs of the Church for the purpose of augmenting his own authority, or that of his friends. Such wisdom and virtue, I am persuaded, do not arise from mere human diligence. Brave, lofty, ardent souls, such as Luther had, must be divinely guided. (p. 387)

The removal of such a man from our midst, a man of the most transcendent genius, skilled in learning, trained by long experience, adorned with many superb and heroic virtues, chosen of God for the reformation of the Church, loving us all with a paternal affection—the removal of such a man from our midst calls for tears and lamentations. We are like orphans bereft of a distinguished and faithful father. (p. 388)

Contemporary engraving of the presentation of the Augsburg Confession of 1530.

Let us acknowledge that this man was a blessed instrument of God, and let us studiously learn his doctrine. Let us in our humble station imitate his virtues, so necessary for us: His fear of God, his faith, his devoutness in prayer, his uprightness in the ministry, his chastity, his diligence in avoiding seditious counsels, his eagerness for learning. And as we ought frequently to reflect on those other pious leaders of the Church, Jeremiah, John the Baptist, and Paul, so let us consider the doctrine and course of this man. Let us also join in thanksgiving and prayer, as is meet in this assembly. Follow me then with devout hearts:—We give thanks to thee, Almighty God, the Eternal Father of our Lord Jesus Christ, the Founder of thy Church, together with thy Coëternal Son, and the Holy Spirit, wise, good, merciful, just, true, powerful Sovereign, because thou dost gather a heritage for thy Son from among the human race, and dost maintain the ministry of the Gospel, and hast now reformed thy Church by means of Luther. We present our ardent supplications that thou wouldst henceforth preserve, fix, and impress upon our hearts the doctrines of truth, as Isaiah prayed for his disciples; and that by thy Holy Spirit thou wouldst inflame our minds with a pure devotion, and direct our feet into the paths of holy obedience. (pp. 390-91)

> *Philip Melanchthon, "Appendix: Funeral Oration over Luther," in* Philip Melanchthon: The Protestant Preceptor of Germany, 1497-1560, *by James William Richard, 1898. Reprint by Burt Franklin Reprints, 1974, pp. 381-92.*

JOHN BUNYAN   (essay date 1688)

[*An intensely devout Baptist minister, Bunyan is famous throughout the world as the author of* The Pilgrim's Progress (1678), *an allegory of man's journey to spiritual salvation. In the following excerpt from the 1688 edition of his spiritual autobiography,* Grace Abounding to the Chief of Sinners, *Bunyan describes the value of Luther's inspirational message in his* Commentarie upon Galathians.]

It would be too long here to stay, to tell you in particular how God did set me down in all the things of Christ, and how he did, that he might so do, lead me into his words; yea, and also how he did open them unto me, and make them shine before me, and cause them to dwell with me, talk with me, and comfort me over and over, both of his own Being, and the Being of his Son, and Spirit, and Word, and Gospel.

Only this, as I said before, I will say unto you again, that in general, he was pleased to take this course with me: first to suffer me to be afflicted with temptation concerning them, and then reveal them to me: As sometimes I should lie under great guilt for sin, even crushed to the ground therewith; and then the Lord would shew me the death of Christ; yea, and so sprinkle my Conscience with his Blood, that I should find, and that before I was aware, that in that Conscience, where but just now did reign and rage the Law, even there would rest and abide the peace and love of God, through Christ.

Now I had an evidence, as I thought, of my Salvation from Heaven, with many golden Seals thereon, all hanging in my sight: Now could I remember this manifestation, and the other discovery of Grace, with comfort; and should often long and desire that the last day were come, that I might be for ever inflamed with the sight, and joy, and communion of him, whose head was crowned with thorns, whose Face was spit on, and Body broken, and Soul made an Offering for my sins: For whereas before I lay continually trembling at the mouth of Hell, now me-thought I was got so far there-from, that I could not, when I looked back scarce discern it: And, Oh! thought I, that I were fourscore Years old now, that I might die quickly, that my Soul might be gone to rest.

But before I had got thus far out of these my Temptations, I did greatly long to see some ancient godly man's experience, who had writ some hundreds of years before I was born; for those who had writ in our days, I thought, (but I desire them now to pardon me,) that they had writ only that which others felt, or else had, through the strength of their Wits and Parts, studied to answer such Objections as they perceived others were perplexed with, without going down themselves into the deep. Well, after many such longings in my mind, the God in whose hands are all our days and ways, did cast into my hand (one day) a Book of *Martin Luther;* it was his [**Commentarie upon Galathians**]; it also was so old, that it was ready to fall piece from piece if I did but turn it over. Now I was pleased much that such an old Book had fallen into my hand; the which, when I had but a little way perused, I found my condition, in his experience, so largely and profoundly handled, as if his Book had been written out of my heart. This made me marvel; for thus thought I, *This Man could not know anything of the state of Christians now, but must needs write and speak the experience of former days.*

Besides he doth most gravely also in that Book, debate of the rise of these temptations, namely, Blasphemy, Desperation, and the like; showing that the Law of *Moses* as well as the Devil, Death, and Hell hath a very great hand therein: The which, at first, was very strange to me; but considering and watching, I found it so indeed. But of particulars here I intend nothing; only this methinks I must let fall before all men, I do prefer this book of *Martin Luther* upon the *Galatians,* (excepting the holy Bible,) before all the Books that ever I have seen, as most fit for a wounded Conscience. (pp. 40-1)

> *John Bunyan, in his* Grace Abounding *and* The Pilgrim's Progress, *edited by John Brown, Cambridge at the University Press, 1907, 432 p.*

HEINRICH HEINE   (essay date 1834)

[*One of the most prominent literary figures in nineteenth-century Europe and in the history of his native Germany, Heine is remembered for his poetry—characterized by passionate lyricism and wry irony—as well as for his distinctive commentaries on politics, art, literature, and society. Among his foremost writings are* Buch der Leider *(1827;* Heinrich Heine's Book of Songs, 1856) *and* Zur Geschicte der Religion und Philosophie in Deutschland *(1835;* Religion and Philosophy in Germany, *1882). In the following excerpt from a study originally published in 1834, Heine analyzes Luther's character and his contribution to German literature.*]

Luther is not only the greatest, but the *Germanest* man in our history; and as in his character all the virtues and weak points of Germans are united in the grandest manner, so he represented personally our strange Germany. For he had peculiar traits, such as we seldom find united, and which we generally regard as utterly contradictory. He was equally a dreamy mystic and yet a practical man. His thoughts had hands as well as wings; he spoke and acted; he was not only the tongue, but the sword of his time. And he was at once a cool scholastic picker and sifter of words and an inspired God-intoxicated prophet. When he had worked himself weary all day long with his dogmatic distinctions, he in the evening took his flute, and, while looking at the stars, melted away in melody and pious reverie. This man, who could scold like a fishwife, could also be as gentle as a tender maid. He was often wild as the storm which roots up oaks, and then soft as the zephyr playing with violets. He was filled with the most terrible fear of God and a sense of sacrifice to the Holy Ghost; he could lose himself in the depths of pure spirituality, and yet he knew full well the glories of this world and their worth, and from his mouth came the far-famed saying—

> Who loves not woman, wine, and song,
> Remains a fool his whole life long.

He was, I may say, a complete man, an absolute man, in whom spirit and matter were not divided. Therefore it would be as wrong to call him a Spiritualist as a Sensualist. How shall I express it?—there was in him something of an underived original, incomprehensible miraculous, such as we find in all prov-

Engraved title page of the first edition of the first German-language Bible, translated by Luther.

idential men; something terribly naïf, clumsily-clever, sub-limely narrow-minded, unconquerably dæmonic. (pp. 43-4)

Glory to Luther! glory to the valiant, valued man to whom we owe the rescue of our most precious possessions, and by whose benefits we now exist. It little becomes us to bewail his narrow views. The dwarf who stands upon the giant's shoulders can, of course, see farther than the giant himself, especially with spectacles; but to this elevated view is wanting elevation of feeling, or the giant heart which we cannot make our own. Still less does it become us to pass sentence on his failings; these faults have profited us more than the virtues of a thousand others. The refined subtlety of Erasmus and the mildness of Melanchthon would never have brought us so far as the godlike brutality of Brother Martin often did. Yes, his faults, which I have pointed out, have borne the most precious fruit—fruit by which all mankind has been refreshed. From that day of the Diet, when Luther denied the authority of the Pope, and openly declared "that his doctrines must be refuted by texts from the Bible itself or upon reasonable grounds," there began a new era in Germany. The chain with which St. Boniface had fettered the German Church to Rome was severed. This Church, which had been previously an integral part of the great hierarchy, crumbled away and divided into religious democracies. The religion itself changed its nature, the Indian-Gnostic element disappeared, and we see how the Judaic-deistic principle is rising in it. Evangelical Christianity is being developed. And as the most needed demands of matter are not only considered but made legitimate, religion becomes once more a truth. The priest becomes human and takes a wife and begets children as God ordained. On the other hand, God himself becomes a celestial old bachelor without family, the legitimacy of his son is contested, the saints are obliged to resign, the wings of the angels are clipped, the mother of God loses all claim to the heavenly crown, and she is forbidden to work miracles. And it may be observed that since that time, and especially since natural science has made such progress, miracles have ceased. Whether it be that the Lord does not like to have the doctors watch his fingering so closely, or that he will not enter into competition with Bosco, certain it is that in these later days, though religion is in such danger, he has disdained to help it by a brilliant miracle. Perhaps he intends in future to exclude all holy tricks from all the new religions which he may introduce here on earth, and prove the truths of the new doctrines, always by reason—which is indeed the most reasonable way. (pp. 45-7)

When Luther announced the proposition that his doctrine should only be refuted by the Bible itself or on reasonable grounds, he opened to human intelligence and reason the right to explain the Bible, and so reason was recognised as head-judge in all religious debates. Hence resulted in Germany the so-called spiritual liberty also known as freedom of thought. Thought became a right, and the decisions of reason were made legal. (p. 49)

Martin Luther gave us not only freedom of action, but the means to act—that is, he gave a body to the soul. He gave language to thought. He created the German language.

This he did by translating the Bible.

In fact, the Divine composer of this book seems to have known quite as well as we that it is not a matter of indifference by whom we are translated; therefore he chose his own translator, and gifted him with the wonderful power to translate from a language which was not only dead but buried into another which had not come to life.

Men had, it is true, the Vulgate, which was understood, and the Septuagint, which they might understand. But the knowledge of Hebrew was then utterly extinguished in all the Christian world. Only the Jews, who kept themselves hidden here and there in a corner of the world, preserved the traditions of this tongue. (pp. 54-5)

How Luther ever learned the language into which he translated the Bible is to me to this hour incomprehensible. The old Swabian dialect had utterly passed away with the knightly poetry of the imperial age of the Hohenstaufen. The old Saxon dialect—the so-called Platt-Deutsch—prevailed in only a part of North Germany, and, in spite of every effort, it never attained to a literary position. If Luther had used for his translation of the Bible the language which was spoken in the Saxony of the day, Adelung would have been right in declaring that the Saxon, especially the dialect of Meissen, is our real High German—that is, our written tongue. But this error has been long disproved. I must lay the more stress on it because it is still current in France. The present Saxon was never a dialect of the German people any more than Silesian, for both are born of Slavonic influence. I frankly confess I do not know how the language which we find in the Bible of Luther originated, but I know that it was through this Bible, of which the press—as yet in its youth—by its black art cast forth thousands of copies among the people, that in a few years the language of Luther spread all over Germany, and was raised to be that of our literature. This written language still prevails in Germany, and gives to our otherwise politically and religiously mangled and divided country a literary unity. Such an inestimable service may indemnify us for the fact that, in the present development of this language there is something wanting in the inward earnestness which we usually find in languages, developed from a single dialect. But the language in Luther's Bible does not need such genial expression, and this old book is an eternal fountain of youth for our tongue. All the expressions and turns of speech which are in the Lutheran Bible are German. The author may use them freely, and as the book is in the hands of the poorest people, they need no specially erudite preparation to express themselves in a literary form. This fact will, when the great political revolution breaks out, produce remarkable results. Freedom will speak everywhere, and its speech will be Biblical.

The original writings of Luther have not less contributed to fix the German language. By their polemic passion they drive deep in the heart of the time. Their tone is not always nice, but even religious revolutions are not made with rose-water. A tough log often needs a rough wedge. In the Bible, Luther's language is always kept within the bounds of a certain dignity out of reverence to the ever-present spirit of God. In his controversial writings, on the other hand, he often gives himself up to his plebeian coarseness, which is at times as grand as it is repulsive. His expressions and images then resemble those colossal stone figures which are found in Indian or Egyptian cave-temples, and whose harsh colouring and strange ugliness at once repel and attract us. In this *ba-rocky* style the bold monk often appears like a religious Danton, a preacher of the Mountain, who from its height hurls down varied blocks of words on the heads of his foes.

Far more remarkable and significant than his prose writings are Luther's poems, or the songs which sprung from his soul in battle and suffering. They often seem like a flower growing on a rock or a moon-ray quivering on a moving lake. Luther loved music; he even wrote a treatise on it [titled *Encomion Musices*]; hence his songs are remarkably melodious. And in this respect the name of the Swan of Eisleben was appropriate to him. But he was anything but a gentle swan in many songs, in which he fired the souls of his followers and inspired himself to the wildest joy of battle. That was a defiant war-song indeed with which he and his companions entered Worms. The old cathedral trembled at the new sounds, and the ravens were terrified in their obscure nests in the towers. That song, which was the Marseilles Hymn of the Reformation, has preserved its power of inspiration to this day, and we perhaps shall use the old mail-clad words ere long for other battles. . . . (pp. 56-9)

I have shown how much we owe to our dear Dr. Martin Luther for the freedom of thought which the new literature needed for its development. I have also shown how he shaped the Word in which this new literature could express itself. I have now only to add that he himself began this literature; that it, and in fact our pure literature begins with Luther; that his religious songs are the first appearances in it of any importance, and already announce the character which it was to assume. He who will speak of modern German literature must begin with Luther. . . . (p. 61)

Heinrich Heine, "Book I: Germany Till the Time of Luther," in his Germany, Vol. I, *translated by Charles Godfrey Leland, William Heinemann, 1892, pp. 1-67.*

RALPH WALDO EMERSON   (lecture date 1835)

[*Emerson was one of the most influential figures of the nineteenth century. An American essayist and poet, he founded the Transcendental movement, shaping a distinctly American philosophy which embraces optimism, individuality, and mysticism. His philosophy stresses the presence of ongoing creation and revelation by a god apparent in everything and everyone, as well as the essential unity of all thoughts, persons, and things in the divine whole. In the following excerpt from an 1835 lecture, Emerson pays tribute to Luther's strength and vision.*]

It sounds like a paradox but is a truth, that those talents and means which operate great results on society, are those which are common to all men. The greatest men are precisely those whose characters are easy to understand, and with whom we feel intimately acquainted. Whilst kings strive and armies are marshalled in vain; whilst great genius and incredible industry applied to bad ends produce no lasting consequence a simple honest man arises and accomplished wonders without effort and fills the world with his fame. This salutary truth breathes from every page of the life of Luther.

Martin Luther the Reformer is one of the most extraordinary persons in history and has left a deeper impression of his presence in the modern world than any other except Columbus. (p. 119)

The central fact in the history of Luther is the publication of his Thesis against Indulgences. This act is the crisis of his life, the cause out of which all his after actions flow. This involved him in the controversies, and nailed his attention to the ecclesiastical abuses which could not be seen by a sane eye without indignation.(pp. 119-20)

Luther's singular position in history is that of a scholar or spiritual man leading a great revolution, and from first to last faithful to his position. He achieved a spiritual revolution by spiritual arms alone. Let it be his eternal praise, and let it

stigmatize those who pretend the same cause with far different weapons, that Luther in the very spring and experiment of new Reformation, carrying with him the devotion of his countrymen, threatened though he was with prison and with fire by the papal power, and himself of that volcanic temper that his apologist Seckendorf says, "he will defend him against all charges but anger and jesting,"—that, Luther never appealed to force, and in every instance denounced those who did. (p. 127)

In his early youth he had discovered in a neglected corner of the convent library a copy of the Bible and with a presentiment of his Calling had given his days and nights to the study of it. The whole and every part of this book he esteemed omnipotent. He thought like Plato, "that the soul is unwillingly deprived of truth." He thought he saw the German nation—the European family—hungering after truth, and that it only needed to break down the barrier and let in the river of the Divine Word upon the impatient mind.

All his language and his actions are inspired with this thought. (p. 128)

He was not a philosopher; his speculations upon abstract questions are of no worth; Aristotle's logic had helped his dialectic, but not extended his views; he had no fitness to receive scientific truths, and he makes himself very merry with the recent astronomical discoveries, which he calls "starpeeping," and confounds ignorantly with astrology. Nay his theology is Jewish: His reform is directed at the corruptions of the Roman Church, not at its ancient creed, and if he can attain the Christianity of the first ages, he is quite content. (p. 131)

He was not more a general scholar and not more a philosopher than was Isaiah or Ezekiel among the ancient Hebrews. He was like them the Prophet, the Poet of his times and country. Out of a religious enthusiasm he acted on the minds of his contemporaries. He believed deepest what all believed. Reared up in the solemn traditions of the Christian Church and becoming at a later period under agitating events accurately acquainted with the Scriptures,—of a pious temper and in a believing age, he was himself wholly immersed in the Bible. This book gave a determination to his force. Giving heed to a divine impulse upon his mind or, feeling as all men of the first class, a reverence for the Unseen Source of their thoughts, he saw the impulse and the God through the medium of the Bible alone. There never has been since Luther a great man of the first class who believed as he did, unless Cromwell be deemed a sort of continuation of him. All others, if religious men as Milton, Newton, Leibnitz, Bacon, Montesquieu, Fenelon, Pascal, Locke, Cuvier, Goethe have joined Nature to Revelation to form their religion or like Spinoza, Rousseau, Laplace have worshipped like the Indian, Nature alone. Luther's religion is exclusively and literally from the Scriptures.

Luther was a Poet but not in the literary sense. He wrote no poems, but he walked in a charmed world. Everything to his eye assumed a symbolical aspect. All occurrences, all institutions, all persons seemed to him only occasions for the activity of supernatural agents. God in a personal form, angels, Satan, and his devils, are never out of his mind's eye. All objects, all events are transparent. He sees through them the love or malignity which is working behind them. "I shall go to Worms: I am determined to meet Satan, and to strike him with terror." The love and the hatred that are burning in his fervid mind, transform every object into similitudes and types of those things he loves and hates. His head is so full of Pope and friar and mass, that he sees nothing else look where he may,—at the walls, or the carpet, or the pictures in his apartment, or the herbs in the garden. ''That yellow flower,'' he says, ''which in the evening is like a bald friar,''—''The Pope is turned to a Poppy, and to a frothy mushroom.'' He exhausts his vocabulary of figurative terms in finding names for the Pope: ''Bear, Wolf, Huntsman, Ass, Sow, Ex-lex.'' ''Popedom is a slaughterhouse of consciences.'' Luther took in his hand a young sparrow and said, ''Thou barefoot friar with thy gray coat, thou art the most mischievous Bird.'' ''I am a bitter enemy to flies, *quia sunt imago Diaboli et Hereticorum* [''because they are the image of the devil and of heretics'']. . . . A pleasanter example of this poetic vision: ''One evening Luther saw cattle going in the fields into a pasture and said, Behold there go our preachers, our milkbearers, butter-bearers, cheese and wool bearers, which do daily preach unto us faith toward God, that we should trust in our loving father who will nourish us.'' (pp. 132-33)

It is true of him that his poetic vision mastered his own mind and whilst other poets describe their imaginations, he believed and acted his. He held all his opinions poetically, not philosophically; with poetic force but with poetic narrowness also. In his religious faith, there is no approach to the conception of God as the Pure Reason, which is the faith dear to philosophic minds, but he adhered to the lowest form of the popular theology,—I had almost said,—mythology. His view of the Deity is so extraordinary that no understanding of his character can be obtained without it. The expressions that have come down to us from the Dark Ages, from the Saxon Chronicles, from Gothic ballads and sermons, touching Divine agency are such as Luther uses. An old chronicle quoted by Mr. Hallam speaking of the desolation of England under the civil wars in Stephen's time says, ''Men said openly that Jesus and his saints were asleep.'' It was a proverb in the height of the prosperity of the Swiss Canton of Berne that ''God had been received a burgher of Berne.''

This gross and heathen theism is almost precisely that of Luther. Under this God he regarded himself a chosen instrument, and felt his commission with so much more intensity from the distinctness of which this idea of God was capable.

God is in Luther's mind a Genius or local and partial tutelary Daemon, the lover of his Church, the hater of its enemy, the chief of which are the Pope and the Turk.

He addresses the Deity therefore much as a subject who is conscious that his great services to his king and his known devotion to his service entitle to use great liberties of speech.

''We tell our Lord God plainly, If he will have his Church, he must look how to maintain and defend it; for we can neither uphold nor protect it. And well for us that it is so. For in case we could or were able to defend it, we should become the proudest asses under heaven. Who is the Church's Protector that hath promised to be with her to the end, and the gates of Hell shall not prevail against her? Kings, Diets, Parliaments, Lawyers? Marry, no such Cattle.''

''Dr. Justus Jonas asked me if the cogitations and words of Jeremy were Christian like where he curses the day of his birth? I answered him, We must now and then wake up our Lord God with such words. It was indeed a right murmuring in Jeremy.''

Treating of the selfish ambition of the Papal hierarchy he says, ''If I were as our Lord God and had committed the government to my son, as he hath done to his son and that these angry gentlemen were so disobedient as now they be, I would throw the world into a lump.''

''God could be rich soon and easily if he would be more provident, and would deny us the use of his creatures. If he would but keep back the sun that it should not shine or lock up the air or hold up the rain or quench out the fire, Ah! then would we willingly give all our money and wealth to have the use of his creatures.''

There are many expressions so indecorously familiar that I should shock you by their repetition.

It is unavoidable that there should in every mind be some correspondence between its conception of good and its conception of evil agents. Luther's man-like God required the same outstanding distinctness in the form of the Devil. His fidelity to this idea is as unflinching as his faith in the Confession of Augsburg. ''The Devil,'' he says, ''is God's Ape.'' He seems to have seen that great Enemy in bodily figure reaching along the path of his life from the cradle to the grave. ''We old people,'' he said, (at sixty-three years) ''must live thus long, to the end we should see the tail of the Devil, to be witnesses that he is such a wicked Spirit.'' ''The whole world is nothing else but a turned about Decalogue or the Ten Commandments backwards, a vizard and picture of the Devil.'' (pp. 133-35)

Brooding on such ideas, in the solitude of his convent or afterwards in his prison in the Castle of Warteburg, in hourly peril from the sword or the fagot, a man of tender conscience and seeing how far was the practice of the world, and (far worse) of the Church, from the plain letter of the Commandments, the movements of his heart took the form of visions, his thoughts became visible and audible, and he gave way to an irresistible conviction that he was summoned by God to set up a standard of Reform, and to do battle with the infernal hosts.

This persuasion betrays itself in all his writings and discourse. He esteemed himself a commissioned man, continuing the series of ancient prophets by whom the will of God was communicated to men. He called his prison, Patmos. His **Commentary on Galatians** is evidently writ under the impression that there was a strict parallelism between the historical position of St.Paul and his own, and he uses the Epistle to defend and explain his own acts.

He deemed himself the conspicuous object of hatred to Satan and his kingdom, and to be sustained against their malice by special interpositions of God. This is the secret of his indomitable Will. No man in history ever assumed a more commanding attitude or expressed a more perfect self-reliance. His words are more than brave, they threaten and thunder. They indicate a Will on which a nation might lean, not liable to sudden sallies or swoons, but progressive as the motion of the earth. (p. 136)

Luther was a fountain of strength, and resembled the torpedo which from the inexhaustible electricity within it affords an unceasing artillery of new shocks, each more violent than the last. This is the everlasting advantage which the simple sincere man possesses over the defective or half man. For as each animal and plant contains within itself all means for its defence and continuance so much and more has God made the soul of man entire and selfsufficing when Vice has not mutilated and distorted it. It can stand and it can go. It is elastic enough to recover from a blow. It can in its most violent actions regain the erect position. But to this end is it indispensable that its motions should be natural. None of its acts should be self-divided. There must be no crack, no schism between the man's act and his conviction. Whereas if a man's bravery does not arise out of love to the thing he defends but is assumed for appearance and pride, no wonder it has a limit. The sincere man's bravery is his struggle for being: for he fights for no other cause than that which involves all. But a man's bravery in a bad cause, is mere sauciness, and can easily faint. As there was nothing artificial in Luther's first opposition to Rome, but a result he could not help, because he was really angry with the brazen impudence of the Indulgence-mongers, so he did not feel it necessary to keep up the appearance of a boiling resentment as vulgar antagonists do, but when his first passion subsided, he continued the attack in good humor, occasionally with loud laughter, then waxing grave again, then merry, and sometimes in a towering passion, but always just as he felt, on the emergences of the controversy.

Society has now become so imitative and artificial that he stands in glaring contrast. Very hardly now could the great man be true. Appearances are always to be kept up. Parties are to be drilled and encouraged by this and that manoeuvre. Statesmen are to be made to say this and that nothing for effect, and half that a man does, is for example. And presently our real existence will be bowed out of the world by its own shadow.

But that was an earnest age and Luther the most earnest man. He believed and therefore spake, hit or miss, please or sting whom it might. If you tickled him, he would laugh,—if you pricked him, he would bleed. He loved, he hated, he feared God, he dared the world and the devils, he prayed, he sang, he desponded, he married, he served his prince, he abhorred dependence and became free, he erred, and repented, he worked unceasingly, he advanced unceasingly.

In the story of this singular person who was the instrument of the greatest of revolutions one moral appears, the superiority of immaterial to material power. His means being strictly spiritual called into life the deepest sentiments of men and the influence long outlived him who communicated it. A man mellowed by all the sweetness and tenderness of human nature, inspiring affection by the love in his own heart, astonishes and takes command of other men's minds by the energy of his own. Poor, loyal, abstemious, of irreproachable life, all men saw that it was not for earthly objects he contended, but taking his stand in the Invisible world as his basis, he operated on the sensible world. And so this enraged Poet, who did not write his visions in sonnets, but believed them, spoke them, and acted them, persuaded vast multitudes and many nations of their truth; and by the force of private thoughts, (with an impulse that is yet far from being exhausted), he shook to the centre, not only the Ecclesiastical empire, but, as all religious Revolutions must, the whole fabric of tyranny in the world. (pp. 141-43)

> *Ralph Waldo Emerson, "Biography: Martin Luther," in* The Early Lectures of Ralph Waldo Emerson: 1833-1836, Vol. I, *edited by Stephen E. Whicher and Robert E. Spiller, Cambridge, Mass.: Harvard University Press, 1959, pp. 118-43.*

N. F. S. GRUNDTVIG   (sermon date 1839)

[*Grundtvig was a preeminent nineteenth-century Danish historian, translator, and theologian. In the following excerpt from a sermon delivered in 1839 on All Saints' Day, he hails Luther's spiritual ascendancy and ecclesiastical legacy.*]

"The earth was without form and void, and darkness was upon the face of the deep; and the Spirit of God was moving over the face of the waters. And God said, 'Let there be light'; and there was light. And God saw that the light was good." (Gen. 1:2-4)

These well-known words from the book of Genesis may rightly be applied to the days of Martin Luther and to God's great deeds in and with him whom we are gathered to commemorate with joy and gratitude today!

Yes, my friends, the earth was in truth without form and void for the hearts who rejected this world and desired a commonwealth in heaven. For them the earth was more formless and empty than it had ever been since the Baptizer rose up and the Savior came down; since the host of angels proclaimed to God's people tidings of great joy, and the Word of eternal life on the lips of the Son of Man reached toward the ends of the earth. For a long time this true Word of God had been infiltrated by so much human learning, so many fables and dreams, that it was difficult to recognize it; but as long as there was life in the dreams about all God's saints who hovered about their enshrined bones and who proclaimed their saintliness with signs and wondrous deeds—life in the fabulous dream about the holy sepulcher where the Lord had lain, and angels descending and ascending with consolation for the penitent who knelt at the holy places, bringing their prayers to the throne of God—as long as there was life in these dreams, people were bewitched as by the evening glow of the day which had brought the glow of dawn from on high. But the hour of delusion had passed; darkness with all its horror had struck. The earth was without form and void, and darkness was upon the face of the deep.

For the earth is indeed without form and void in a spiritual sense when the Word about the earth's relationship to heaven—the word about the way to the land of the living—has been silenced or chilled to the point of petrification, rendering it dead and incapacitated. Thus it was at the time when Martin Luther appeared. The word of the Lord was scarce in those days, and the sun had set on the prophets who had said, "I have dreamed, I have dreamed!" (Jer. 23:25). There were no longer visions or songs, and all prophetic scriptures were like a book given to someone unable to read, or a sealed book no one could open.

Not only Christianity but also everything else which innately had exalted the spirit of the peoples and warmed their hearts had become dead and impotent. And the affliction was by no means caused by a scarcity of Bibles or other famous books, for through the invention of the printing press they were now easier to find and to possess. But when the living and powerful word, which the Creator has laid on the lips of man, is silenced, so that heartwarming and eloquent speech deals only with silver and gold and precious stones, eating and drinking, buffoonery and vanity, gambling and dancing and carnal pleasures, or with spears and swords, murder and manslaughter, raging revenge, and sly wiles—then all prophetic scriptures, both God's and man's, dealing with both heights and depths, have become like a closed book no one can open, or an open book no one can read.

Yes, in such spiritless and lifeless times Martin Luther was born and grew up. And there was darkness upon the face of the deep.... (pp. 88-89)

But the Spirit of God still moved over the face of the waters wherever the covenant had been kept by those who baptized in the name of the Father and the Son and the Holy Spirit.

Yes, precisely in areas where the papacy bore down on souls as a heavy yoke and made itself felt as darkness over the abyss, precisely there and there alone, the Spirit of God moved over the waters, in baptism. And therefore it was not an angel who descended from heaven and rolled back the stone from the tomb, nor a prophet from other parts of the world using his speech to dispel the darkness from the abyss. No, it was, as we know, a monk who as an infant in swaddling clothes had been brought to the Lord, who took him in his arms, blessing him and saying, "The Lord is with thee, go in peace!" Yes, to him in his monk's cage the Lord said, " 'Let there be light'; and there was light."

Yes my friends, Martin Luther felt the emptiness, found himself on the brink of the abyss over which the darkness brooded, and he detached himself from the world and fled to the monastery, which the serious-minded considered the only place one might escape the abyss and with repentance and penance save one's soul. There he sat sorrowing night and day; he read and prayed and tormented his soul, but found neither light nor peace; for it simply is not true that it was by reading he found peace. No, he believed in the Lord Jesus though he did not know him and was unaware of his goodness. And the Lord Jesus, who in baptism had made a covenant with him, fulfilled in him the words of the gospel for today, "Blessed are the poor in spirit, for theirs is the kingdom of heaven. Blessed are those who mourn, for they shall be comforted" (Matt. 5:3-4)

Yes, my friends, never has any mortal spoken in such a way on the strength of his own spirit, for who except a scoffer can declare that those who mourn are blessed, unless he is able to give them comfort and solace? But that the Lord Jesus both could and would do this—no less after fifteen hundred years following his ascension than when he declared to his disciples, " 'peace be with you!' and breathing upon them, 'Receive the Holy Spirit!' "—this Luther learned in the monastery from an old monk, whom the Lord had detained, like the ancient Simeon, in order to see his salvation and a light for revelation to the Gentiles. For when the old monk saw that Luther sorrowed for God and that it was his sins that overwhelmed and crushed him to the ground, he had compassion on him, searched his own heart for a buried treasure, and opened the sealed lips with the secret of the gospel, "Brother Martin, believe that the Lord Jesus has made full satisfaction for your sins, just as I believe he has done for me, and you will have peace." With these words a light was lit for Luther, a light over the abyss and glory to him who brings souls therefrom. And God saw that the light was good; for it was his own Word with life and light, it was the light which had shone in the darkness, though the darkness comprehended it not (John 1:5 King James Version).

Yes, my friends, "finished" was the last word the Savior uttered from the cross before he bowed his head and yielded up his spirit, and this "finished" is the word by which God creates light in the darkness of the soul from generation to generation. That light is good, because it is the true light of the world, Jesus Christ himself, the Lord, our light, our salvation, and our power of life!

Luther still sorrowed, sorrowed all his days, but not without hope and consolation, and less for himself than for the millions who sat in darkness and the shadow of death without seeing the great light which had dawned when the old sun darkened, the great light emanating from the God-given Word, "finished," and risen with him who died for us and shed his blood unto forgiveness of our sins! For those Luther now sorrowed, but only as one who finds the sorrow sweet in the consolation and solace which follows according to the Lord's word—in its fullness only when he rests in the bosom of Abraham, but also here, more often than mortal clay can figure and sweeter than our lips can tell.

Yes, my friends, God saw that the light was good, and Luther saw it; but our forefathers also saw it. Many people saw it and praised God who had given us such a man, had raised a great prophet among us, and had visited his people. And Martin Luther rejoiced as the woman who has sorrow because her hour has come, but who no longer remembers the anguish, for joy that a child is born into the world (John 16:21).

Yes, my friends, the light was so good that it spread abroad because it emanated from the Word of Life as the light for the living. Luther saw that only a living word in their own mother tongue could enlighten the peoples about God's great deeds; and the light placed such a living word on his lips for his people. God placed a new song in his mouth which gladdened the hearts and became a living word also on the lips of our forefathers in our mother tongue. This was not, as is usually alleged, because the Holy Scriptures were translated into Luther's and into our own native language, as well as others. The living word emanated not from the Book, but the word cast light upon the book so that the book was known by the Lord's light as a work by his Spirit and a masterly picture of him and his house, the house of living stones: his believing church.

Yes, my friends, let us join our forefathers in praise that the light, which dawned for Luther, was good and was communicated through words from his lips to those who heard him; for the light was Jesus Christ who accompanies his word from mouth to mouth and from heart to heart until the close of the age. Let us perceive and proclaim that through the dawning of that light a new creation began, a new day in Christendom, a creation through which not only the darkness upon the face of the deep was dispersed, but the earth which had been without form and void became bright and alive with the sun, moon, and stars above the firmament, with grass and flowers and all sorts of trees, with birds in the air and fish in the sea, with all kinds of animals, and finally man in God's image and after his likeness!

Let it not diminish our joy, but rather enhance it and our thanksgiving, that once again a period arrived when the earth was without form and void and with darkness upon the face of the deep. For it was evident that this was only a night between the days of creation, evening and morning before our eyes. Or it was as a winter's night superseded by a morn in spring in which we shall rejoice with the birds and look forward to behold the deeds of God toward which he graciously has called us to be co-workers.

Yes, let us thank God for Martin Luther who brought a dawn, this new Abraham, our father in Christ. Let those who now preach the gospel proclaim that word "finished," which creates light for our souls and peace with God in our hearts, so that they may join the Lord in saying that blessed are those who mourn in his house, for they shall be comforted with heavenly sweetness. May this father of our church, also of our children and grandchildren, become a father until the Lord comes in the glory of his Father, whom Martin Luther encouraged us to call upon freely in the name of him who healed our infirmities and bore our pains, in the blessed name of our Lord and Savior Jesus Christ! Amen! (pp. 90-3)

N. F. S. Grundtvig, "Sermons: All Saint's Day,"
translated by Enok Mortensen, in his Selected Writ-

ings, *edited by Johannes Knudsen, translated by Johannes Knudsen, Enok Mortensen, and Ernest D. Nielsen, Fortress Press, 1976, pp. 88-93.*

BLACKWOOD'S EDINBURGH MAGAZINE   (poem date 1844)

[*In the following poem, an anonymous critic exults in Luther's triumph over papal corruption.*]

Who sits upon the Pontiff's throne?
  On Peter's holy chair
Who sways the keys? At such a time
When dullest ears may hear the chime
Of coming thunders—when dark skies
Are writ with crimson prophecies,
  A wise man should be there;
A godly man, whose life might be
The living logic of the sea;
One quick to know, and keen to feel—
A fervid man, and full of zeal,
  Should sit in Peter's chair.

Alas! no fervid man is there,
  No earnest, honest heart;
One who, though dress'd in priestly guise,
Looks on the world with worldling's eyes;
One who can trim the courtier's smile,
Or weave the diplomatic wile,
  But knows no deeper art;
One who can daily with fair forms,
Whom a well-pointed period warms—
No man is he to hold the helm
Where rude winds blow, and wild waves whelm,
  And creaking timbers start.

In vain did Julius pile sublime
  The vast and various dome,
That makes the kingly pyramid's pride,
And the huge Flavian wonder, hide
Their heads in shame—these gilded stones
(O heaven!) were very blood and bones
  Of those whom Christ did come
To save—vile grin of slaves who sold
Celestial rights for earthy gold,
Marketing grace with merchant's measure,
To prank with Europe's pillaged treasure
  The pride of purple Rome.

The measure of her sins is full,
  The scarlet-vested whore!
Thy murderous and lecherous race
Have sat too long i' the holy place;
The knife shall lop what no drug cures,
Nor Heaven permits, nor earth endures,
  The monstrous mockery more.
Behold! I swear it, saith the Lord:
Mine elect warrior girds the sword—
A nameless man, a miner's son,
Shall tame thy pride, thou haughty one,
  And pale the painted whore!

Earth's mighty men are nought. I chose
  Poor fishermen before
To preach my gospel to the poor;
A pauper boy from door to door
That piped his hymn. By his strong word
The startled world shall now be stirr'd,
  As with a lion's roar!
A lonely monk that loved to dwell
With peaceful host in silent cell;
This man shall shake the Pontiff's throne:
Him kings and emperors shall own,
  And stout hearts wince before.

The eye profound and front sublime
  Where speculation reigns.
He to the learned seats shall climb,
On Science' watch-tower stand sublime;
The arid doctrine shall inspire
Of wiry teachers with swift fire;
  And, piled with cumbrous pains,
Proud palaces of sounding lies
Lay prostrate with a breath. The wise
Shall listen to his word; the youth
Shall eager seize the new-born truth
  Where prudent age refrains.

Lo! when the venal pomp proceeds
  From echoing town to town!
The clam'rous preacher and his train,
Organ and bell with sound inane,
The crimson cross, the book, the keys,
The flag that spreads before the breeze,
  The triple-belted crown!
It wends its way: and straw is sold—
Yea! deadly drugs for heavy gold,
To feeble hearts whose pulse is fear;
And though some smile, and many sneer,
  There's none will dare to frown.

None dares but one—the race is rare—
  One free and honest man:
Truth is a dangerous thing to say
Amid the lies that haunt the day;
But He hath lent it voice; and, lo!
From heart to heart the fire shall go,
  Instinctive without plan;
Proud bishops with a lordly train,
  Fierce cardinals with high disdain,
Sleek chamberlains with smooth discourse,
And wrangling doctors all shall force,
  In vain, one honest man.

In vain the foolish Pope shall fret,
  It is a sober thing.
Thou sounding trifler, cease to rave,
Loudly to damn, and loudly to save,
And sweep with mimic thunders' swell
Armies of honest souls to hell!
  The time on whirring wing
Hath fled when this prevail'd. O, Heaven!
One hour, one little hour, is given,
If thou could'st but repent. But no!
To ruin thou shalt headlong go,
  A doom'd and blasted thing.

Thy parchment ban comes forth; and lo!
  Men heed it not, thou fool!
Nay, from the learned city's gate,
In solemn show, in pomp of state,
The watchmen of the truth come forth,
The burghers old of sterling worth,
  And students of the school:
And he who should have felt thy ban
Walks like a prophet in the van;
He hath a calm indignant look,
Beneath his arm he bears a book,
  And in his hand the Bull.

He halts; and in the middle space
  Bids pile a blazing fire.
The flame ascends with crackling glee;
Then, with firm step advancing, He
Gives to the wild fire's wasting rule
The false Decretals, and the Bull,
  While thus he vents his ire:—
"Because the Holy One o' the Lord

Thou vexed hast with impious word,
Therefore the Lord shall thee consume,
And thou shalt share the Devil's doom
    In everlasting fire!''

He said; and rose the echo round
    ''In everlasting fire!''
The hearts of men were free; one word
Their inner depths of soul had stirr'd;
Erect before their God they stood
A truth-shod Christian brotherhood,
    And wing'd with high desire.
And ever with the circling flame
Uprose anew the blithe acclaim:—
''The righteous Lord shall thee consume,
And thou shalt share the Devil's doom
    In everlasting fire!''

Thus the brave German men; and we
    Shall echo back the cry;
The burning of that parchment scroll
Annull'd the bond that sold the soul
Of man to man; each brother now
Only to one great Lord will bow,
    One Father-God on high.
And though with fits of lingering life
The wounded foe prolong the strife,
On Luther's deed we build our hope,
Our steady faith—the fond old Pope
    Is dying, and shall die.

                                        (pp. 80-2)

> *''Martin Luther: An Ode,''* in Blackwood's Edin-
> burgh Magazine, *Vol. 56, No. 345, July, 1844, pp.
> 80-2.*

FRIEDRICH ENGELS   (essay date 1875)

[*A German social theorist, Engels collaborated with Karl Marx
to formulate the tenets of modern communism. In the following
excerpt from an essay first published in 1875, he views Luther's
actions and influences from a Marxist standpoint, declaring that
Luther became a ''flunky of the princes.''*]

When in 1517 Luther first opposed the dogmas and statutes of
the Catholic Church his opposition was by no means of a
definite character.... At that early stage all the opposition
elements had to be united, the most resolute revolutionary
energy displayed, and the sum of the existing heresies against
the Catholic orthodoxy had to find a protagonist. In much the
same way our liberal bourgeoisie of 1847 was still revolutionary, called itself socialist and communist, and clamored for
the emancipation of the working class, Luther's sturdy peasant
nature asserted itself in the stormiest fashion in that first period
of his activities.

> If the raging madness [of the Roman churchmen]
> were to continue, it seems to me no better counsel
> and remedy could be found against it than that kings
> and princes apply force, arm themselves, attack those
> evil people who have poisoned the entire world, and
> put an end to this game once and for all, *with arms,
> not with words.* Since we punish thieves with the
> halter, murderers with the sword, and heretics with
> fire, why do we not turn on all those evil teachers
> of perdition, those popes, cardinals, and bishops, and
> the entire swarm of the Roman Sodom *with arms in
> hand, and wash our hands in their blood?*

But this revolutionary ardor was short-lived. Luther's lightning
struck home. The entire German people was set in motion. On
the one hand, peasants and plebeians saw the signal to revolt

in his appeals against the clergy and in his sermon of Christian
freedom; on the other, he was joined by the moderate burghers
and a large section of the lesser nobility. Even princes were
drawn into the maelstrom. The former believed the day had
come to wreak vengeance upon all their oppressors, the latter
only wished to break the power of the clergy, the dependence
upon Rome, to abolish the Catholic hierarchy, and to enrich
themselves on the confiscation of church property. The parties
stood aloof of each other, and each had its spokesmen. Luther
had to choose between them. He, the protégé of the elector of
Saxony, the revered professor of Wittenberg who had become
powerful and famous overnight, the great man with his coterie
of servile creatures and flatterers, did not hesitate for a single
moment. He dropped the popular elements of the movement
and took the side of the burghers, the nobility, and the princes.
His appeals for a war of extermination against Rome resounded
no more. Luther now preached *peaceful progress* and *passive
resistance* (cf., for example, *Address to the Christian Nobility
of the German Nation,* 1520, etc.). Invited by Hutten to visit
him and Sickingen in the castle of Ebern, where the nobility
conspired against the clergy and the princes, Luther replied:
''I do not wish the gospel *defended by force and bloodshed.*
The world was conquered by the Word, the church is maintained by the Word, the Word will also put the church back
into its own, and Antichrist, who gained his own without violence, will fall without violence.''

From this tendency, or, to be more exact, from this more
definite delineation of Luther's policy, sprang that bartering
and haggling over institutions and dogmas to be retained or
reformed, that disgusting diplomatizing, conciliating, intrigu-
ing, and compromising, which resulted in the Augsburg
Confession, the finally imported articles of a reformed burgher
church. It was quite the same kind of petty bargaining as was
recently repeated in political form *ad nauseam* at the German
national assemblies, conciliatory gatherings, chambers of revision, and Erfurt parliaments. The Philistine nature of the
official Reformation was most distinctly evident at these
negotiations.

There were good reasons for Luther, henceforth the recognized
representative of the burgher reform, to preach lawful progress.
The bulk of the towns espoused the cause of moderate reform,
the petty nobility became more and more devoted to it, and a
section of the princes joined in, while another vacillated. Success was as good as won, at least in a large part of Germany.
The remaining regions could not in the long run withstand the
pressure of moderate opposition in the event of continued peaceful
development. Any violent upheaval, meanwhile, was bound
to bring the moderate party into conflict with the extremist
plebeian and peasant party, to alienate the princes, the nobility,
and many towns from the movement, leaving the alternative
of either the burgher party being overshadowed by the peasants
and plebeians or the entire movement being crushed by Catholic
restoration. There have been examples enough lately of how
bourgeois parties, after gaining the slightest victory, seek to
steer their way by means of lawful progress between the Scylla
of revolution and the Charybdis of restoration.

Under the general social and political conditions prevailing at
that time the results of every change were necessarily advan-
tageous to the princes and inevitably increased their power.
Thus it came about that the more completely the burgher reform
fell under the control of the reformed princes, the more sharply
it broke away from the plebeian and peasant elements. Luther
himself became more and more their vassal, and the people

knew perfectly well what they were doing when they accused him of having become, as the others, a flunky of the princes, and when they stoned him in Orlamünde.

When the Peasants' War broke out, Luther tried to strike a mediatory pose in regions where the nobility and the princes were mostly Catholic. He resolutely attacked the authorities. He said they were to blame for the rebellion in view of their oppression; it was not the peasants, but God himself, who rose against them. Yet, on the other hand, he said, the revolt was ungodly and contrary to the gospel. In conclusion, he called upon both parties to yield and reach a peaceful understanding.

But in spite of these well-meaning mediatory offers, the revolt spread swiftly and even involved Protestant regions dominated by Lutheran princes, lords, and towns, rapidly outgrowing the "circumspect" burgher reform. The most determined faction of the insurgents under Müntzer made its headquarters in Luther's immediate proximity at Thuringia. A few more successes and the whole of Germany would be in flames, Luther surrounded and perhaps piked as a traitor, and the burgher reform swept away by the tide of a peasant-plebeian revolution. There was no more time for circumspection. All the old animosities were forgotten in the face of the revolution. Compared with the hordes of peasants, the servants of the Roman Sodom were innocent lambs, sweet-tempered children of God. Burgher and prince, noble and clergyman, Luther and the pope, all joined hands "against the murderous and plundering peasant hordes." "They must be *knocked to pieces, strangled* and *stabbed, covertly* and *overtly,* by everyone who can, just as one must kill a *mad dog!*" Luther cried. "Therefore, dear sirs, help here, save there, stab, knock, strangle them everyone who can, and should you lose your life, bless you, no better death can you ever attain." There should be no false mercy for the peasant. Whoever hath pity on those whom God pities not, whom He wishes punished and destroyed, belongs among the rebels himself. Later the peasants would learn to thank God when they would have to give up one cow in order to enjoy the other in peace, and the princes would learn through the revolution the spirit of the mob that must be ruled by force only. "The wise man says: *cibus, onus et virga asino* ['food, pack, and lash to the ass']. The peasants must have nothing but chaff. They do not hearken to the Word, and are foolish, so they must hearken to the rod and the gun, and that serves them right. We must pray for them that they obey. Where they do not there should not be much mercy. *Let the guns roar among them,* or else they will do it a thousand times worse."

That was exactly what our late socialist and philanthropic bourgeoisie said when the proletariat claimed its share of the fruits of victory after the March events [the 1848 revolution in Germany and Austria].

Luther had put a powerful weapon into the hands of the plebeian movement by translating the Bible. Through the Bible he contrasted the feudalized Christianity of his day with the moderate Christianity of the first centuries, and the decaying feudal society with a picture of a society that knew nothing of the ramified and artificial feudal hierarchy. The peasants had made extensive use of this instrument against the princes, the nobility, and the clergy. Now Luther turned it against the peasants, extracting from the Bible such a veritable hymn to the God-ordained authorities as no bootlicker of absolute monarchy had ever been able to extract. Princedom by the grace of God, resigned obedience, even serfdom, were sanctioned with the aid of the Bible. Not the peasant revolt alone, but Luther's own mutiny against religious and lay authority was thereby disavowed; not only the popular movement, but the burgher movement as well, were betrayed to the princes. (pp. 102-05)

Friedrich Engels, "The Marxist Interpretation of Luther," translated by Vic Schneierson, in Luther: A Profile, *edited by H. G. Koenigsberger, Hill and Wang, 1973, pp. 97-105.*

FRIEDRICH NIETZSCHE   (essay date 1887)

[*Nietzsche is considered one of the most important figures in modern philosophy, and his thought has influenced nearly every aspect of modern culture. A forerunner of existentialism, he is credited with being the first philosopher to utilize it as a source for positive values. Nietzsche was also an important psychological theorist to whom Sigmund Freud was indebted for the psychoanalytic concepts of sublimation and repression. In general, he has had a crucial effect on the intellectual development of Western society: his thought signified the disintegration of the nineteenth century's social, religious, and scientific optimism and anticipated the nihilist sensibility of the modern world. In the following excerpt from an essay written in 1887, Nietzsche addresses the "unconscious" destructive and debilitating effects of Luther and the Reformation.*]

We Europeans find ourselves in view of an immense world of ruins, where some things still tower aloft, while other objects stand mouldering and dismal, where most things however already lie on the ground, picturesque enough——where were there ever finer ruins?——overgrown with weeds, large and small. It is the Church which is this city of decay: we see the religious organisation of Christianity shaken to its deepest foundations. The belief in God is overthrown, the belief in the Christian ascetic ideal is now fighting its last fight. Such a long and solidly built work as Christianity—it was the last construction of the Romans!—could not of course be demolished all at once; every sort of earthquake had to shake it, every sort of spirit which perforates, digs, gnaws and moulders had to assist in the work of destruction. But that which is strangest is that those who have exerted themselves most to retain and preserve Christianity, have been precisely those who did most to destroy it,— the Germans. It seems that the Germans do not understand the essence of a Church. Are they not spiritual enough, or not distrustful enough to do so? In any case the structure of the Church rests on a *southern* freedom and liberality of spirit, and similarly on a southern suspicion of nature, man, and spirit,— it rests on a knowledge of man an experience of man, entirely different from what the north has had. The Lutheran Reformation in all its length and breadth was the indignation of the simple against something "complicated." To speak cautiously, it was a coarse, honest misunderstanding, in which much is to be forgiven,—people did not understand the mode of expression of a *victorious* Church, and only saw corruption; they misunderstood the noble scepticism, the *luxury* of scepticism and toleration which every victorious, self-confident power permits. . . . One overlooks the fact readily enough at present that as regards all cardinal questions concerning power Luther was badly endowed; he was fatally short-sighted, superficial and imprudent—and above all, as a man sprung from the people, he lacked all the hereditary qualities of a ruling caste, and all the instincts for power; so that his work, his intention to restore the work of the Romans, merely became involuntarily and unconsciously the commencement of a work of destruction. He unravelled, he tore asunder with honest rage, where the old spider had woven longest and most carefully. He gave the sacred books into the hands of everyone,—they thereby got at last into the hands of the philologists, that is to say, the annihilators of every belief based upon books. He demolished the conception of ''the Church'' in that he repudiated the belief in the inspiration of the Councils: for only under the supposition that the inspiring spirit which had founded the Church still lives in it, still builds it, still goes on building its house, does the conception of ''the Church'' retain its power. He gave back to the priest sexual intercourse: but three-fourths of the reverence of which the people (and above all the women of the people) are capable, rests on the belief that an exceptional man in this respect will also be an exceptional man in other respects. It is precisely here that the popular belief in something superhuman in man, in a miracle, in the saving God in man, has its most subtle and insidious advocate. After Luther had given a wife to the priest, he had *to take from him* auricular confession; that was psychologically right: but thereby he practically did away with the Christian priest himself, whose profoundest utility has ever consisted in his being a sacred ear, a silent well, and a grave for secrets. ''Every man his own priest''— behind such formulæ and their bucolic slyness, there was concealed in Luther the profoundest hatred of ''higher men,'' and of the rule of ''higher men,'' as the Church had conceived them. Luther disowned an ideal which he did not know how to attain, while he seemed to combat and detest the degeneration thereof. As a matter of fact, he, the impossible monk, repudiated the *rule* of the *homines religiosi;* he consequently brought about precisely the same thing within the ecclesiastical social order that he combated so impatiently in the civic order,—namely a ''peasant insurrection.''—As to all that grew out of his Reformation afterwards, good and bad, which can at present be almost counted up,—who would be naïve enough to praise or blame Luther simply on account of these results? He is innocent of all; he knew not what he did. The art of making the European spirit shallower especially in the north, or more *good-natured*, if people would rather hear it designated by a moral expression, undoubtedly took a clever step in advance in the Lutheran Reformation; and similarly there grew out of it the mobility and disquietude of the spirit, its thirst for independence, its belief in the right to freedom, and its ''naturalness.'' If people wish to ascribe to the Reformation in the last instance the merit of having prepared and favoured that which we at present honour as ''modern science,'' they must of course add that it is also accessory to bringing about the degeneration of the modern scholar, with his lack of reverence, of shame and of profundity; and that it is also responsible for all naïve candour and plain-dealing in matters of knowledge, in short for the *plebeianism of the spirit* which is peculiar to the last two centuries, and from which even pessimism hitherto, has not in any way delivered us. ''Modern ideas'' also belong to this peasant insurrection of the north against the colder, more ambiguous, more suspicious spirit of the south, which has built itself its greatest monument in the Christian Church. Let us not forget in the end what a Church is, and especially in contrast to every ''State'': a Church is above all an authoritative organisation which secures to the *most spiritual* men the highest rank, and *believes* in the power of spirituality so far as to forbid all grosser appliances of authority. Through this alone the Church is under all circumstances a *nobler* institution than the State. (pp. 311-14)

> *Friedrich Nietzsche, ''Book Fifth: We Fearless Ones,''*
> *in his* The Joyful Wisdom, *translated by Thomas*
> *Common, 1910. Reprint by The Macmillan Company, 1924, pp. 273-354.*

ERNST TROELTSCH (essay date 1911)

[*A German Lutheran theologian, Troeltsch frequently examined the relationship between Christianity and political, intellectual,* *and economic history. In the following excerpt from an essay originally published in 1911, he discusses Luther's creation of the Protestant conception of the preeminence of personal faith in the attainment of grace.*]

[What Luther] laid all emphasis upon was the certainty of attaining the end for which he had always striven, assurance of salvation, complete assurance of deliverance from the condemnation entailed by original sin, by the grace which is revealed in Christ and made available by Him. That was his main interest, but that main interest was not something new, but only a vastly simplified and vividly realised form given to the old. The new thing that he introduced was a new means of reaching this goal, a means free from the uncertainties attaching to human contributory merit, to alien, uncomprehended authorities and purely material sacramental communication, a means which laid hold on the whole inner man to its very centre with absolute certainty and permanence, and could bring him directly into the closest touch with the Divine spiritual action. If to the Catholic it was precisely the external authority and the substantiality of grace which seemed to guarantee salvation, for Luther's feeling it was just that authority which was uncertain and alien, and that substantiality which was unintelligible and elusive. He needed for the personal life something purely personal. The means was therefore faith, *sola fides,* the affirmation, by the complete surrender of the soul to it, of that thought of God which has been made clear and intelligible to us in Christ. The assurance of salvation must be based on a miracle in order to be certain; but this miracle must be one occurring in the inmost centre of the personal life, and must be clearly intelligible in its whole intellectual significance if it is to be a miracle which guarantees complete assurance. Religion is completely transferred from the sphere of the substantial sacramental communication of grace, and of ecclesiastical, sacerdotal authority, to the psychologically intelligible sphere of the affirmation of a thought of God and of God's grace, and all the ethico-religious effects arise with psychological clearness and obviousness from this central thought. The sensuous sacramental miracle is done away with, and in its stead appears the miracle of thought, that man in his sin and weakness can grasp and confidently assent to such a thought. That is the end of priesthood and hierarchy, the sacramental communication of ethico-religious powers after the manner of a sensible substance, and the ascetic withdrawal from the world, with its special merits.

In all this Luther's sole object was the attainment of complete assurance of grace, which for him, while he followed the way of merit and the monastic life, of sacraments and sacerdotal authority, had threatened to become ever more alien and external, more human and conditional, and therefore more uncertain. The goal was the same as before, but the way to it was entirely new. But with this set of ideas it happened as it often does happen—that the new way to the old goal became more important than the goal itself; from that which was at first a new means there developed a new end and a new association of ideas. When, with the growth of Confessional wrangling, the tyranny of authoritative dogma became unbearable, and consequently dogma itself suspect, the centre of gravity was shifted from the doctrine of salvation and justification, which was closely bound up with the main Trinitarian and Christological doctrines, to personal subjective conviction, to the emotional experience of a sense of sin and of peace of heart. That, however, gave free scope for the establishment of the idea of faith on a purely subjective inward foundation, and consequently also for the possibility of its taking various forms not bound up with any official dogma. The Bible became, instead of the infallible rule of faith, a spiritual entity and power of a more fluid character, a witness to historical facts from which psychologically mediated religious energies streamed forth; in support of this view appeal was made to the living conception of the Bible, which Luther's religious instinct had always maintained alongside of the legalistic. Thus an approach was made to the Spiritualists, who from the first had drawn this inference, but who, repulsed on all sides and cleaving to the mystical tradition, had gradually withdrawn into an individualism which was without the power of creating social forms. Then follows that amalgamation of Protestantism with the subjective individualistic representatives of a religion of feeling and conviction, which now makes Protestantism as a whole appear as the religion of conscience and conviction, without compulsorily imposed dogma, and with a free Church-organisation independent of the State, and a certainty based on inner feeling independent of all rational proofs. (pp. 191-96)

For Luther, the being of God, the curse of sin, the existence of hell, were beyond question. What was problematical was only the application of grace and deliverance to one's own self, *fiducia specialis.* For the modern world, confronted with the new cosmology of the natural sciences, and the modern anti-anthropomorphic metaphysics, it was precisely the being of God which was the problematical point, while, on the other hand, it was beyond question that to be once certain of the being of God would be to have found the meaning and goal of life, salvation and grace. In these circumstances, the general principle of the "new way" discovered by Luther was infinitely more important than his special dogmatic goal. This "way" contained in itself the actual goal, assurance of the existence of God, escape from finitude into infinitude and the super-earthly in general—to have found the way was to have found the goal, the gaining of which brought with it necessarily everything else. All stress was now laid on the intuitive certainty of faith, on the inward movement and impulsion, on the inwardly necessary attainment of the idea of God in general, on the winning of a purely personal conviction of His real existence, for then everything further might be left to Him and His mysterious wisdom, if only this main decisive point was won. Thus Protestantism became the religion of the search for God in one's own feeling, experience, thought, and will, the seeking of an assurance of this supreme centre of all knowledge by the concentration of all personal convictions on this one point, while trustfully leaving open all the further obscure problems about which the Dogmatics of the earlier Protestantism had so much to say. (pp. 196-98)

Everywhere the idea of faith has triumphed over the content of faith, and only escapes weakness and sentimentality because, when all is said and done, the iron of the Protestant conception of faith rings through. (p. 199)

> *Ernst Troeltsch, "Protestantism and Modern Religious Feeling," in his* Protestantism and Progress: A Historical Study of the Relation of Protestantism to the Modern World, *translated by W. Montgomery, 1912. Reprint by Beacon Press, 1958, pp. 171-207.*

HARTMANN GRISAR, S.J.   (essay date 1911)

[*A German Jesuit scholar, Grisar was the author of an important Freudian analysis of Luther in which he assessed Luther's character in terms of his serious psychological disorders. In the following excerpt from this work (first published in German in 1911), he refutes the theology of three of Luther's Reformation Writings,* Address to the Nobility, On the Babylonian Captivity, *and* The Freedom of a Christian Man.]

It was at the time when the Bull of Excommunication was about to be promulgated by the Head of Christendom that Luther composed the Preface to the work entitled: *An den christlichen Adel deutscher Nation von des christlichen Standes Besserung.* The booklet appeared in the middle of August [of 1520]. . . . (p. 26)

This inflammatory pamphlet . . . was, with its complaints against Rome, in part based on the writings of the German Neo-Humanists.

Full of fury at the offences committed by the papacy against the German nation and Church, Luther here points out to the Emperor, the Princes and the whole German nobility, the manner in which Germany may break away from Rome, and undertake its own reformation, for the bettering of Christianity. His primary object is to show that the difference between the clerical and lay state is a mere hypocritical invention. All men are priests; under certain circumstances the hierarchy must be set aside, and the secular powers have authority to do so. "Most of the Popes," so Luther writes with incredible exaggeration, "have been without faith." "Ought not Christians, who are all priests, also to have the right [like them, i.e. the bishops and priests] to judge and decide what is true and what false in matters of faith?"

The work was, as Luther's comrade Johann Lang wrote to the author, a bugle-call which sounded throughout all Germany. Luther had to vindicate himself (even to his friends) against the charge of "blowing a blast of revolt." It is not enough to acquit him to point out in his defence that he had merely assigned to the Rulers the right of employing force, and that his intention was to "make the Word triumphant."

One of the most powerful arguments in Luther's work consisted in the full and detailed description of the Roman money traffic, Germany and other countries being exploited on the pretext that contributions were necessary for the administration of the Church. Luther had drawn his information on this subject from the writings of the German Neo-Humanists. . . . (pp. 26-7)

By the end of August another new book by Luther, which, like the former, is accounted by Luther's Protestant biographers as one of the "great Reformation-works," was in the press; such was the precipitancy with which his turbulent spirit drove him to deal with the vital questions of the day. The title of the new Latin publication which was at once translated into German was *Prelude to the Babylonish Captivity of the Church.*

He there attacks the Seven Sacraments of the Church, of which he retains only three, namely, Baptism, Penance, and the Supper, and declares that even these must first be set free from the bondage in which they are held in the Papacy, namely, from the general state of servitude in the Church; this condition had, so he opined, produced in the Church many other perverse doctrines and practices which ought to be set aside, among these being the whole matrimonial law as observed in the Papacy, and, likewise, the celibacy of the clergy.

The termination of this work shows that it was intended to incite the minds of its readers against Rome, in order to forestall the impending Ban.

This end was yet better served by the third "reforming" work *On the Freedom of a Christian Man,* a popular tract in Latin and German with its dangerously seductive explanation of his teaching on faith, justification and works.

In this work, as a matter of fact, Luther expresses with the utmost emphasis his theological standpoint which hitherto he had kept in the background, but which was really the source of all his errors. As before this in the pulpit, so here also he derives from faith only the whole work of justification and virtue which, according to him, God alone produces in us; this he describes in language forcible, insinuating and of a character to appeal to the people; it was only necessary to have inwardly experienced the power of faith in tribulations, temptations, anxieties and struggles to understand that in it lay the true freedom of a Christian man.

This booklet has in recent times been described by a Protestant as "perhaps the most beautiful work Luther ever wrote, and an outcome of religious contemplation rather than of theological study." It does, as a matter of fact, present its wrong ideas in many instances under a mystical garb, which appeals strongly to the heart, and which Luther had made his own by the study of older German models.

The new theory which, he alleged, was to free man from the burden of the Catholic doctrine of good works, he summed up in words, the effect of which upon the masses may readily be conceived: "By this faith all your sins are forgiven you, all the corruption within you is overcome, and you yourself are made righteous, true, devout and at peace; all the commandments are fulfilled, and you are set free from all things." "This is Christian liberty . . . that we stand in need of no works for the attainment of piety and salvation." "The Christian becomes by faith so exalted above all things that he is made spiritual lord of all; for there is nothing that can hinder his being saved." By faith in Christ, man, according to Luther, has become sure of salvation; he is "assured of life for evermore, may snap his fingers at the devil, and need no longer tremble before the wrath of God."

It was inevitable that the author should attempt to vindicate himself from the charge of encouraging a false freedom. "Here we reply to all those," he says in the same booklet, "who are offended at the above language, and who say: 'Well, if faith is everything and suffices to make us pious, why, then, are good works commanded? Let us be of good cheer and do nothing.' " What is Luther's answer? "No, my friend, not so. It might indeed be thus if you were altogether an interior man, and had become entirely spiritual and soulful, but this will not happen until the Day of Judgment."

But in so far as man is of the world and a servant of sin, he continues, he must rule over his body, and consort with other men; "here works make their appearance; idleness is bad; the body must be disciplined in moderation and exercised by fasting, watching and labour, that it may be obedient and conformable to faith and inwardness, and may not hinder and resist as its nature is when it is not controlled." "But," he immediately adds this limitation to his allusion to works, "such works must not be done in the belief that thereby a man becomes pious in God's sight"; for piety before God consists in faith alone, and it is only "because the soul is made pure by faith and loves God, that it desires all things to be pure, first of all its own body, and wishes every man likewise to love and praise God." (pp. 27-9)

As a matter of fact, experience soon showed that where the traditional Christian motives for good works (reparation for sin, the acquiring of merit with the assistance of God's grace, etc.) were given up, the practice of good works suffered.

There is, however, no doubt that there were some on whom the booklet, with its heartfelt and moving exhortation to communion with Christ, did not fail to make a deep impression, more particularly in view of the formalism which then prevailed.

"Where the heart thus hears the voice of Christ," says Luther with a simple, popular eloquence which recalls that of the best old German authors,

> it must needs become glad, receive the deepest comfort and be filled with sweetness towards Christ, loving Him and ever after troubling nothing about laws and works. For who can harm such a heart, or cause it alarm? Should sin or death befall, it merely recollects that Christ's righteousness is its own, and then, as we have said, sin disappears before faith in the Righteousness of Christ; with the Apostle it learns to defy death and sin, and to say: O death, where is thy victory? O death, where is thy sting? The sting of death is sin, but thanks be to God Who has given us the victory through our Lord Jesus Christ, so that death is swallowed up in victory (1 Cor. xv. 54 ff.).

Pious phrases, such as these, which are of frequent occurrence, demanded a stable theological foundation in order to produce any lasting effects. In Luther's case there was, however, no such foundation, and hence they are merely deceptive. The words quoted, as a matter of fact, detract somewhat from the grand thought of St. Paul, since the victory over sin and death of which he speaks refers, not to the present life of the Faithful, but to the glorious resurrection. The Apostle does, however, refer to our present life in the earnest exhortation with which he concludes (1 Cor. xv. 58): "Therefore, my beloved brethren, be ye steadfast and unmoveable, always abounding in the work of the Lord, knowing that your labour is not in vain in the Lord."

Protestants frequently consider it very much to Luther's credit that he insisted with so much force and feeling in his work *On the Freedom of a Christian Man* upon the dignity which faith and a state of grace impart to every calling, even to the most commonplace; his words, so they say, demonstrate that life in the world, and even the humblest vocation, when illumined by religion, has in it something of the infinite. This, however, had already been impressed upon the people, and far more correctly, in numerous instructions and sermons dating from mediæval times, though, agreeably with the teaching of the Gospel, the path of the Evangelical Counsels, and still more the Apostolic and priestly vocation, was accounted higher than the ordinary secular calling. A high Protestant authority, of many of whose utterances we can scarcely approve, remarks: "It is usual to consider this work of Luther's as the Magna Charta of Protestant liberty, and of the Protestant ideal of a worldly calling in contradistinction to Catholic asceticism and renunciation of the world. My opinion is that this view is a misapprehension of Luther's work." (pp. 29-30)

[It] may be worth our while to examine more closely two characteristics which [appear in the three works just mentioned] in singular juxtaposition. One is the deeply religious tone which . . . is so noteworthy in Luther's book *On the Freedom of a Christian Man.* The other is an unmistakable tendency to dissolve all religion based on authority.

Luther . . . positively refused to have anything to do with a religion of merely human character; yet, if we only draw the necessary conclusions from certain propositions which he sets up, we find that he is not very far removed from such a religion; he is, all unawares, on the high road to the destruction of all authority in matters of faith. This fact makes the depth of religious feeling evinced by the author appear all the more strange to the experienced reader.

Some examples will make our meaning clearer.

In the work addressed to the Christian nobility, Luther confers on every one of the Faithful the fullest right of private judgment as regards both doctrines and doctors, and limits it by no authority save the Word of God as explained by the Christian himself.

"If we all are priests"—a fact already proved, so he says—

> how then shall we not have the right to discriminate and judge what is right or wrong in faith? What otherwise becomes of the saying of Paul in 1 Corinthians ii. [15], "The spiritual man judgeth all things, and he himself is judged of no man," and again, "Having all the same spirit of faith," 2 Corinthians iv. [13]? How then should we not perceive, just as well as an unbelieving Pope, what is in agreement with faith and what not? These and many other passages are intended to give us courage and make us free, so that we may not be frightened away from the spirit of liberty, as Paul calls it (2 Cor. iii. [17]), by the fictions of the Popes, but rather judge freely, according to our understanding of the Scriptures, of all things that they do or leave undone, and force them to follow what is better and not their own reason.

"A little man," he had said already, "may have a right comprehension; why then should we not follow him?" and, with an unmistakable allusion to himself, he adds: surely more trust is to be placed in one "who has Scripture on his side."

Such assertions, as a matter of fact, destroy all the claims made by the visible Church to submission to her teaching. Further, they proclaim the principle of the fullest independence of the Christian in matters of faith; nothing but private judgment and personal inspiration can decide. Luther failed to see that, logically, every barrier must give way before this principle of liberty, and that Holy Scripture itself loses its power of resistance, subjectivism first invading its interpretation and then, in the hands of the extremer sort of critics, questioning its value and divine origin. The inner consequences of Luther's doctrine on freedom and autonomy have been clearly pointed out even by some of the more advanced Protestant theologians. Adolf Harnack, for instance, recently expressed the truth neatly when he said that "Kant and Fichte were both of them hidden behind Luther."

The second work *On the Babylonish Captivity,* with its sceptical tendency, of which, however, Luther was in great part unconscious, also vindicates this opinion.

The very arbitrariness with which the author questions facts of faith or usages dating from the earliest ages of the Church, must naturally have awakened in such of his readers as were already predisposed a spirit of criticism which bore a startling resemblance to the spirit of revolt. Here again, in one passage, Luther comes to the question of the right of placing private judgment in matters of religion above all authority. He here teaches that there exists in the assembly of the Faithful, and through the illumination of the Divine Spirit, a certain "interior sense for judging concerning doctrine, a sense, which, though it cannot be demonstrated, is nevertheless absolutely certain." He describes faith, as it comes into being in every individual

Christian soul, "as the result of a certitude directly inspired of God, a certitude of which he himself is conscious."

What this private judgment of each individual would lead to in Holy Scripture, Luther shows by his own example in this very work; he already makes a distinction based on the "interior sense" between the various books of the Bible, i.e. those stamped with the true Apostolic Spirit, and, for instance, the less trustworthy Epistle of St. James, of which the teaching contradicts his own. Köstlin, with a certain amount of reserve, admits: "This he gives us to understand, agreeably with his principles and experience; it is not our affair to prove that it is tenable or to vindicate it."

Luther says at the end of the passage in question: "Of this question more elsewhere." As a matter of fact, however, he never did treat of it fully and in detail, although it concerned the fundamentals of religion; for this omission he certainly had reasons of his own.

A certain radicalism is perceptible in the work *On the Babylonish Captivity,* even with regard to social matters. Luther lays it down: "I say that no Pope or Bishop or any other man has a right to impose even one syllable upon a Christian man, except with his consent; any other course is pure tyranny." It is true that ostensibly he is only assailing the tyranny of ecclesiastical laws, yet, even so, he exceeds all reasonable limits.

With regard to marriage, the foundation of society, so unguarded is he, that, besides destroying its sacramental character, he brushes aside the ecclesiastical impediments of marriage as mere man-made inventions, and, speaking of divorce based on these laws, he declares that to him bigamy is preferable. When a marriage is dissolved on account of adultery, he thinks remarriage allowable to the innocent party. He also expresses the fervent wish that the words of St. Paul in 1 Corinthians vii. 15, according to which the Christian man or woman deserted by an infidel spouse is thereby set free from the marriage tie, should also apply to the marriages of Christians where the one party has maliciously deserted the other; in such a case, the offending party is no better than an infidel. Regarding the impediment of impotence on the man's part, he conceives the idea that the wife might, without any decision of the court, "live secretly with her husband's brother, or with some other man." In the later editions of Luther's works this statement, as well as that concerning bigamy, has been suppressed.

Luther, so he says, is loath to decide anything. But neither are popes or bishops to give decisions! "If, however," says Luther, "two well-instructed and worthy men were to agree in Christ's name, and speak according to the spirit of Christ, then I would prefer their judgment before all the Councils, which are now only looked up to on account of the number and outward reputation of the people there assembled, no regard being paid to their learning and holiness." Apart from other objections, the stipulation concerning the "Spirit of Christ," here made by the mystic, renders his plan illusory, for who is to determine that the "Spirit of Christ" is present in the judgment of the two "well-instructed men"? Luther seems to assume that this determination is an easy matter. First and foremost, who is to decide whether these men are really well-instructed? There were many whose opinion differed from Luther's, and who thought that this and such-like demands, made in his tract *On the Babylonish Captivity,* opened the door to a real confusion of Babel.

Neither can the work *On the Freedom of a Christian Man* be absolved from a certain dangerous radicalism. A false spirit of liberty in the domain of faith breathes through it. The faith which is here extolled is not faith in the olden and true meaning of the word, namely the submission of reason to what God has revealed and proposes for belief through the authority He Himself instituted, but faith in the Lutheran sense, i.e. personal trust in Christ and in the salvation He offers. Faith in the whole supernatural body of Christian truth comes here so little into account that it is reduced to the mere assurance of salvation. All that we are told is that the Christian is "free and has power over all" by a simple appropriation of the merits of Christ; he is purified by the mere acceptance of the merciful love revealed in Christ; "this faith suffices him,"and through it he enjoys all the riches of God. And this so-called faith is mainly a matter of feeling; a man must learn to "taste the true spirit of interior trials," just as the author himself, so he says, "in his great temptations had been permitted to taste a few drops of faith." Faith is thus not only robbed of its true meaning and made into a mere personal assurance, but the assurance appears as something really not so easy of attainment, since it is only to be arrived at by treading the difficult path of spiritual suffering.

Luther thereby strikes a blow at one of the most vital points of positive religion, viz. the idea of faith.

The author, in this same work, again reminds us that by faith all are priests, and therefore have the right "to instruct Christians concerning the faith and the freedom of believers"; for the preservation of order, however, all cannot teach, and therefore some are chosen from amongst the rest for this purpose. It is plain how, by this means, a door was opened to the introduction of diversity of doctrine and the ruin of the treasure of revelation.

The religious tone which Luther assumed in the work *On the Freedom of a Christian Man,* and his earnestness and feeling, made his readers more ready to overlook the perils for real religion which it involved. This consideration brings us to the other characteristic, viz. the pietism which, as stated above, is so strangely combined in the three works with intense radicalism.

The religious feeling which pervades every page of the *Freedom of a Christian Man* is, if anything, overdone. In what Luther there says we see the outpourings of one whose religious views are quite peculiar, and who is bent on bringing the Christian people to see things in the same light as he does; deeply imbued as he is with his idea of salvation by faith alone, and full of bitterness against the alleged disfiguring of the Church's life by meritorious works, he depicts his own conception of religion in vivid and attractive colours, and in the finest language of the mystics. It is easy to understand how so many Protestant writers have been fascinated by these pages, indeed, the best ascetic writers might well envy him certain of the passages in which he speaks of the person of Christ and of communion with Him. Nevertheless, a fault which runs through the whole work is . . . his tendency to narrow the horizon of religious thought and feeling by making the end of everything to consist in the mere awakening of trust in Christ as our Saviour. Ultimately, religion to him means no more than this confidence; he is even anxious to exclude so well-founded and fruitful a spiritual exercise as compassion with the sufferings of our crucified Redeemer, actually calling it "childish and effeminate stupidity." How much more profound and fruitful was the religious sentiment of the genuine mystics of the Church, whom the contemplation of the sufferings of Christ furnished

with the most beautiful and touching subject of meditation, and who knew how to find a source of edification in all the truths of faith, and not only in that of the forgiveness of sins. Writers such as they, described to their pious readers in far greater detail the person of Christ, the honour given by Him to God and the virtues He had inculcated.

The booklet *To the Nobility,* likewise, particularly in the Preface, throws a strange sidelight on the pietism of the so-called great Reformation works.

Here, in his exordium to the three tracts, the author seeks to win over the minds of the piously disposed. The most earnest reformer of the Church could not set himself to the task with greater fear, greater diffidence and humility than he. Luther, as he assures his readers, is obliged "to cry and call aloud like a poor man that God may inspire someone to stretch out a helping hand to the unfortunate nation." He declares that such a task "must not be undertaken by one who trusts in his power and wisdom, for God will not allow a good work to be commenced in trust in our own might and ability." "The work must be undertaken in humble confidence in God, His help being sought in earnest prayer, and with nothing else in view but the misery and misfortune of unhappy Christendom, even though the people have brought it on themselves. . . . Therefore let us act wisely and in the fear of God. The greater the strength employed, the greater the misfortune, unless all is done in the fear of God and in humility."

Further on, even in his most violent attacks, the author is ever insisting that it is only a question of the honour of Christ: "it is the power of the devil and of End-Christ [Antichrist] that hinders what would be for the reform of Christendom; therefore let us beware, and resist it even at the cost of our life and all we have. . . . Let us hold fast to this: Christian strength can do nothing against Christ, as St Paul says (2 Cor. xiii. 8). We can do nothing against Christ, but only for Him."

In his concluding words, convinced of his higher mission, he declares that he was "compelled" to come forward. "God has forced me by them [my adversaries] to open my mouth still further, and, because they are cowards, to preach at them, bark at them, roar at them and write against them. . . . Though I know that my cause is good, yet it must needs be condemned on earth and be justified only by Christ in heaven." When a mission is Divine, then the world must oppose it.—One wonders whether everything that meets with disapproval must therefore be accounted Divine.

It is the persuasion of his higher mission that explains the religious touch so noticeable in these three writings. The power of faith there expressed refers, however, principally to his own doctrine and his own struggles. If we take the actual facts into account, it is impossible to look on these manifestations of religion as mere hypocrisy. The pietism we find in the tract *To the German Nobility* is indeed overdone, and of a very peculiar character, yet the writer meant it as seriously as he did the blame he metes out to the abuses of his age.

We still have to consider the religious side of the work *On the Babylonish Captivity.* Originally written in Latin, and intended not so much for the people as for the learned, this tract, even in the later German version, is not clad in the same popular religious dress as the other two. Like the others, nevertheless, it was designed as a weapon to serve in the struggle for a religious renewal, especially in the matter of the Sacraments. Among other of its statements, which are characteristic of the direction of Luther's mind, is the odd-sounding request at the very commencement: "If my adversaries are worthy of being led back by Christ to a more reasonable conception of things, then I beg that in His Mercy He may do so. Are they not worthy, then I pray that they may not cease to write their books against me, and that the enemies of truth may deserve to read no others." His conclusion is: He commits his book with joy to the hands of all the pious, i.e. of those who wish to understand aright the sense of Holy Scripture and the true use of the Sacraments. He further declares in an obstinate and mocking manner his intention of ever holding fast to his own opinion. His more enlightened contemporaries saw with anxiety how every page of his work teemed with signs of self-deception and blind prejudice, and of a violent determination to overthrow religious views which had held the field for ages. To those who cared to reflect, Luther's religiousness appeared in the light of a religious downfall, and as the chaotic manifestation of a desire to demolish all those venerable traditions which encumbered the way of the spirit of revolt. (pp. 31-7)

> *Hartmann Grisar, S.J., in his* Luther, Vol. II, *edited by Luigi Cappadelta, translated by E. M. Lamond, Kegan Paul, Trench, Trubner & Co., Ltd., 1916, 399 p.*

HAVELOCK ELLIS   (essay date 1917)

[*Ellis was a pioneering sexual psychologist and a respected English man of letters. His most famous work is his seven-volume* The Psychology of Sex *(1897-1928), a study containing frankly stated case histories of sex-related psychological abnormalities that was greatly responsible for changing British and American attitudes toward the hitherto forbidden subject of sexuality. In addition to his psychological writings, Ellis edited the Mermaid Series of sixteenth- to eighteenth-century English dramatists (1887-89) and retained an active interest in literature throughout his life. As a critic, according to Desmond MacCarthy, Ellis looked for the expression of the individuality of the author under discussion. "The first question he asked himself as a critic, was 'What does this writer affirm?' The next, 'How did he come to affirm precisely that?' His statement of a writer's 'message' was always trenchant and clear, his psychological analysis of the man extremely acute, and the estimate of the value of his contribution impartial. What moved him most in literature was the sincere expression of preferences and beliefs, and the energy which springs from sincerity." In the following excerpt, Ellis discusses Luther's fiery and contradictory character, basing his impressions "mainly on Luther's own highly instructive* Table-Talk."]

Four centuries have passed since, on All Saints' Eve, October 31st, 1517, the Reverend Father Martin Luther set up on the gate of the great church at Wittenberg those *Propositions* [*The Ninety-Five Theses*] by which was initiated the most revolutionary act ever performed by any German. This incident, it is true, was but part of an epoch-making series of deeds, and less important on the spiritual side than the moment, about a year later, when at last his rebellious indignation against the avenging "Justice" of God was finally settled by what Luther always believed to be the direct visitation of the Holy Spirit. That visitation came (there is no place closed to Divine revelation) to the privy in the tower of Wittenberg monastery, with the illumination: "The just shall live by faith"; and the gate of Paradise was opened *super cloacam* ["above the privy"]. It was the central event in Luther's inner life; but for the initiation of the mighty course of his external career the world has doubtless been right to select the publication of these *Propositions,* even though they were merely evoked by the extravagancies of a Dominican indulgence-monger who is disowned by his own Church, and even though Luther himself was at

times tempted to explain them away. That this centenary is being celebrated by Young Germany as joyously as it was in 1817, after the War of Liberation, under the inspiration of Father Jahn, "the new Luther," is improbable. But the occasion is still profitable for our own meditation. Luther has always been regardded as the central German. In the light of what we know to-day he may perhaps appear more typical than ever before. (pp. 108-09)

He was, above all, as he himself recognised, a rhetorician, not strong in logic. There is never any consistency in his opinions, even on the most vital subjects, as anyone who has ever sought to ascertain his precise standpoint on some important question (as, for instance, marriage) cannot fail to discover. He was quite unable to pursue an argument on measured and rational lines. He proved but a blustering child in controversy with the calm and lucid Erasmus. Luther realised his defeat, but he found consolation in the field of invective wherein he was easily a master, and henceforth "my dear Erasmus" became that scorpion, that bug, a mere hollow nut that fouls the mouth, yea, "the vilest miscreant that ever disgraced the earth." "Whenever I pray, I pray for a curse upon Erasmus." It is not surprising that Erasmus, who felt no need to retaliate in kind, again and again in his references to Luther uses the word "delirium." The turbulent flow of Luther's arrogant invective, obscure and vague as it may often be, yet with the vital warmth of the blood in it, is indeed almost delirious in its astonishing wealth and energy. The most incompatible elements are brought together in this stream, humility and egoism, exalted abstractions and a superb naturalism in the use of gross or familiar imagery scarcely before reached by the coarsest of mediæval preachers and doubtless the despair of all great preachers since. One cannot help being painfully affected, indeed, however remote one's sympathies from Rome, by the dogmatic contempt, the unmeasured vituperation, which, from the height of his personal infallibility as the special mouthpiece of God, Luther flung on the whole Church. It was magnificent in its daring and its horror, alike for friend and foe, but it had in it neither justice nor mercy, not even ordinary humanity. Luther had lived for years in a monastery, some of his best and wisest friends were monks, he had exercised authority in the Church, and even when he began to rebel the Pope had dealt with him considerately. But he had little but evil to say of the whole Church, while his letter to Leo X., in its reckless abuse under an air of condescending patronage, is the very perfection of insolence, the production, it seems, of a Teutonic Aretino.

Yet behind all this, and at times in the front of it, there is something homely, human, genial, almost lovable. If we ask how it should be so, we find the answer in the fact that this flow of passionate hatred and contempt is as little the outcome of disposition as of reason; it is a method, even a conscious method, of generating energy. "I never work better," he said, "than when I am inspired by anger; when I am angry, I can write well, pray well, preach well. My whole temperament is quickened and my understanding sharpened; the vexations of the world and the temptations of the Devil depart from me." Thus the great German's "Hymns of Hate," far from being the index of evil disposition, were simply a device comparable to that of the beast which instinctively lashes himself with his own tail in order to attain the degree of infuriation demanded by circumstances. It is a method which the German temperament, too phlegmatic to be easily moved to energetic action, especially requires; but, we must remember, the method is, in greater or less degree, universal. We see that in the present war, in the newspapers of the belligerent countries on both sides, not excluding our own. It is the distinction of Luther that, while he pushed this method to the extreme, he was entirely open with it. He was even prepared to admit what he called the "honest and pious lie." It is a point of view still recognised in Prussian statecraft.

Luther was a true German in his combination, alike in speech and act, of the abstract with the realistic, of the emotional with the material. To some people the German seems a creature of dreams and sentiment, of music and metaphysics. To others the German seems a creature of reckless materialism and crude fleshliness. Luther beautifully illustrates the fact that he is both. Here is all the sentiment, the simplicity, the enthusiasm for theological abstractions, and it is exhaled from a soil which for earthy coarseness can scarcely be matched in the history of genius. (p. 109)

One is constantly impressed by the expressive power of Luther's imagery, his plastic energy in moulding speech to emotional ends, the force with which even his casual sayings, pungent or poignant, cut to the core of experience. "When I am assailed by tribulation, I rush out among my pigs rather than remain alone," he said on one occasion at table. "The human heart is like a millstone in a mill; put wheat under it and it grinds the wheat to flour; put no wheat, and it still grinds on; but then 'tis itself it wears away." Such utterances of vital human truth, embodied in vivid or homely metaphors, occur again and again in the *Table-Talk*.

Luther's rhetoric, indeed, however turbulent, however turbid, is no mere voice. It springs hot from a human heart, itself as turbulent and as turbid. Luther's words and Luther's deeds are of a piece, alike human, violent, extravagant, the expression of a blindly impulsive force, the assertion of the most daring defiance the world had yet seen. Luther felt himself the child of God placed in a world under the direct rule of the Devil; what the exact relation of these two Cosmic Powers was he could never explain; but he felt himself the battlefield of their contest, and in the agony of this athletic struggle he has become one of the great spectacular figures of history. This Germanic temperament, we see, is made up of an incongruous mixture of gold and clay. But its great individualities moulded in the furnace of passion are devouring forces of Nature, and its ordinary common humanity, when hooped round in the lump by the iron bands of statecraft, becomes of an astonishing resistance.

The mighty effort of Luther changed the world. But that he had changed it into a better world was not so clear. It was not even clear, it is not clear to-day, what really the change was that he effected. The chief authorities are here hopelessly at variance. For some he is simply the superb expression in voice and deed of the obscurely seething movements beneath the surface of his time. For some he is the protagonist of modern Democracy, or even of "Kultur." For some he is a gigantic, belated figure thrust out from the Devil-haunted darkness of the Middle Ages and without any relation to his own world or ours. Even Harnack, the temperate theological representative of modern Germany, admits that Luther's Reformation delayed the political unity of Germany, brought on the Thirty Years' War, obscured the value of the Mediæval and even the Early Church, and permanently fostered all the evils of religious schism. It is doubtful whether Father Grisar, who has devoted so many years to the elucidation of his life and work, has formed any conclusion as to what precisely Luther stands for. Luther himself, in the end, seems to have been equally in the dark. As the close of his career drew nigh he was plunged into

ever deeper hours of gloom. In such moments of spiritual darkness he might obscurely have felt that he had become an involuntary, and more tragic, Samson Agonistes. The whole world seemed to him to grow swiftly and steadily worse; its end, he asserted, could not be far off. He lost his self-confident arrogance. He realised that he was unable to control the forces he had unchained. He saw himself struggling against great streams of tendency he had never set out to combat. The new stirrings of a social economic life he was unable to comprehend aroused his horror and hatred. On the one hand he would hang all rich farmers, such as nowadays would be termed "profiteers"; but, on the other hand, he was pitiless towards the struggling peasantry and heartily approved of serfdom. Shortly before his death a German princess, in fatuous compliment, wished him forty more years of life. "I would rather," he replied, "throw away my hopes of Paradise." He was mercifully spared that infliction. If he had lived forty years longer it would have been his fate to realise that the man who above all others had prepared the way for the purification and reinvigoration of the "Antichrist of Rome and his greasy crew," was that same Father Martin Luther who seemed to have dealt the Church so deadly a blow on All Saints' Eve, 1517. (p. 110)

> *Havelock Ellis, "Luther," in* New Statesman, *Vol. 10, No. 239, November 3, 1917, pp. 108-10.*

JACQUES MARITAIN   (essay date 1925)

> [*A French philosopher and educator, Maritain was the foremost spokesman for the Catholic Literary Revival in France as well as a vigorous proponent of the theology of Thomas Aquinas, which affirms the validity of Aristotelian philosophy and recognizes no conflict between reason and faith. His own philosophical system, which has been described as a modified form of Thomism, emphasizes the importance of rationality in theology, thereby opposing the intense mysticism of much nineteenth-century theology. Maritain wrote a large number of essays supporting his beliefs, and his works are universally applauded for their fluid and elegant prose and their logical coherence. In the following excerpt from a translation of* Trois Reformateurs: Luther—Descartes—Rousseau *(1925;* Three Reformers: Luther—Descartes—Rousseau, *1955), Maritain relates Luther's character traits to his doctrines, refuting Lutheran theology in the process.*]

Martin Luther, strong summoner of the great undefined powers which lie dormant in the heart of the creature of flesh, was gifted with a nature at once realistic and lyrical, powerful, impulsive, brave and sad, sentimental and morbidly sensitive. Vehement as he was, there yet was in him kindness, generosity, tenderness, and, with all, unbroken pride and peevish vanity. What was lacking in him was force of intellect. If by intelligence we mean capacity to grasp the universal, to discern the essential, to follow with docility the wanderings and refinements of reality, Luther was not intelligent, but limited,—stubborn, especially. But he had the understanding of the particular and practical to an amazing degree, and an astute and lively ingenuity, skill to detect even in others, the art of finding a thousand ways out of a difficulty and crushing his opponent—in short, all the resources of what philosophers call the "cogitative," the "particular reason." (pp. 4-5)

What first impresses us in Luther's character is *egocentrism*: something much subtler, much deeper, and much more serious, than egoism; a metaphysical egoism. Luther's self becomes practically the centre of gravity of everything, especially in the spiritual order. And Luther's self is not only his passing quarrels and passions, it has a representative value; it is the self of

the created being, the incommunicable stuff of the human individual. The Reformation unbridled the human self in the
spiritual and religious order, as the Renaissance (I mean the
hidden spirit of the Renaissance) unbridled the human self in
the order of natural and sensible activities.

After Luther decided to refuse obedience to the Pope and break
with the communion of the Church, his self is henceforth supreme, despite his interior agonies which increased until the
end. Every "external" rule, every "heteronomy", as Kant
said, becomes then an intolerable insult to his "Christian liberty".

"I do not admit," he writes in June 1522,"that my doctrine
can be judged by anyone, even by the angels. He who does
not receive my doctrine cannot be saved." "Luther's self,"
wrote Moehler, "was in his opinion the centre round which
all humanity should gravitate; he made himself the universal
man in whom all should find their model. Let us make no
bones about it, he put himself in the place of Jesus Christ."
(pp. 14-15)

Luther's doctrine is itself only a universalization of his self, a
projection of his self into the world of eternal truths. From this
point of view, what distinguishes the father of Protestantism
from the other great heresiarchs is that they started first from
a dogmatic error, from a false doctrinal view; whatever their
psychological origins may have been, the cause of their heresies
is a deviation of the intelligence, and their own fortunes only
count insofar as they conditioned that deviation. It is quite
different with Luther. What counts is his life, his history.
Doctrine comes as an extra. Lutheranism is not a system worked
out by Luther; it is the overflow of Luther's individuality. . . .
It is that which explains the "Reformer's" immense influence
on the German people. That is why a Lutheran like Seeberg
cannot contain his admiration of that truly *daimonic* man, as
he calls him, at that colossal figure of the superhuman which
it is blasphemous to presume to judge. The question is, whether
every flood is beautiful and good of itself, and whether a river
deserves our gratitude for simply spreading over the fields.

If you are looking for the translation of this egocentrism into
dogma, you will find it in some of the most noticeable characteristics of the Lutheran theology. What is the Lutheran dogma
of the certainty of salvation but the transference to the human
individual and his subjective state of that absolute assurance
in the divine promises which was formerly the privilege of the
Church and her mission? Because God was her centre, the
Catholic soul needed to know nothing with perfect certainty
except the mysteries of the faith, and that God is love and is
merciful. And if He sent her tokens of His love, she used these
experimental signs less to probe herself and judge of her state
before God than to live the imperfect certainties of hope with
greater strength, certainties all the dearer than the conscience
dare hardly receive the confession of them. But without perfect
certainty of her state of grace the heretical soul could not exist
without breaking for agony, because she has become the centre
and seeks her salvation in the justice with which she covers
herself, not in the abyss of the mercies of Another, Who made
her.

Why does the doctrine of salvation absorb all the Lutheran
theology, if it be not because the human self has become in
actual fact the chief preoccupation of that theology? For Luther,
one question towers above all the rest: to escape the judicial
wrath of the Almighty in spite of the invincible concupiscence
which poisons our nature. The truth is, that if it is essentially
important that we should save ourselves, it is less to escape

the devil than to see the face of God, and less to save our own
being from the fire than from love of Him Whom we love
more than ourselves. "Domine ostende nobis Patrem, et sufficit
nobis" ["Lord, reveal unto us yourself as God the Father, and
grant us strength"]. Catholic theology is ordered to God, and
it is, by that very fact, a science chiefly speculative. Lutheran
theology is for the creature; that is why it aims above all at
the practical end to be attained. Luther, who drives charity
away and keeps servile fear, so far as he has any, makes the
science of divine things revolve round human corruption.

Is not the salvation of man, however, the work of God and
His Christ? Beware: in the Lutheran theology grace is always
wholly extrinsic to ourselves, man is walled up in his nature
and can never receive in himself the seeds of true participation
in the divine life, nor (child of wrath as he is) can he produce
a substantially supernatural act. A flavour of the devil mingles
with everything he does. "I say that whether it be in man or
devil, the spiritual powers have been not only corrupted by
sin, but asbsolutely destroyed; so that there is now nothing in
them but a depraved reason and a will that is the enemy and
opponent of God, whose only thought is war against God."
"True piety, piety of value in God's eyes, is found in works
which are foreign to us (those of Christ), not in our own."
Can then the act of justifying faith, if it comes from us, come
also from God and from Christ acting in us? In fact it is ourselves, and we alone, who catch at Christ's cloak to "cover
all our shame with it," and use that "*skill* to leap from our
sin on to Christ's justice, and hence to be as certain of possessing Christ's piety as we are of having our own bodies."
The Pelagianism of despair! In fine, it is for man himself to
work his own redemption by driving himself to a desperate
truth in Christ. Human nature will only have to throw off as
an empty theological accessory the cloak of a meaningless grace
and turn its faith-trust on to itself, and it will become that
pleasant liberated beast whose continual and infallible progress
delights the universe to-day.

And thus in the person of Luther and in his doctrine, we are
present—and that on the level of the spirit and religious life—
at the Advent of the Self.

But then, surely Luther's case shows us precisely one of the
problems against which modern man beats in vain. It is the
problem of *individualism and personality*. (pp. 15-19)

What does Christian philosohy tell us? It tells us that the *person*
is "a complete individual substance, intellectual in nature and
master of its actions," *sui juris, autonomous,* in the authentic
sense of the word. And so the word *person* is reserved for
substances which possess that divine thing, the spirit, and are
in consequence, each by itself, a world above the whole bodily
order, a spiritual and moral world which, strictly speaking, is
not *a part* of this universe, and whose secret is hidden even
from the natural perception of the angels. The word *person* is
reserved for substances which, choosing their end, are capable
of themselves deciding on the means, and of introducing series
of new events into the universe by their liberty; for substances
which can say after their kind, *fiat,* and it is so. And what
makes their dignity, what makes their personality, is just exactly the subsistence of the spiritual and immortal soul and its
supreme independence in regard to all fleeting imagery and all
the machinery of sensible phenomena. And St. Thomas teaches
that the word person signifies the noblest and highest thing in
all nature: "Persona significat id quod est perfectissimum in
tota natura."

The word *individual,* on the contrary, is common to man and beast, to plant, microbe, and atom. And, whilst personality rests on the subsistence of the human soul (a subsistence independent of the body and communicated to the body which is sustained in being by the very subsistence of the soul), Thomist philosophy tells us that individuality as such is based on the peculiar needs of matter, *the principle of individuation* because it is the principle of division, because it requires to occupy a position and have a quantity, by which that which is *here* will differ from what is *there.* So that in so far as we are individuals we are only a fragment of matter, a part of this universe, distinct, no doubt, but a part, a point of that immense network of forces and influences, physical and cosmic, vegetative and animal, ethnic, atavistic, hereditary, economic and historic, to whose laws we are subject. As individuals, we are subject to the stars. As persons, we rule them. (pp. 19-21)

[We] gain our soul only if we lose it; a total death is needed before we can find ourselves. And when we are utterly stripped, lost, torn out of ourselves, then all is ours who are Christ's, and Christ Himself and God Himself is our good.

Luther's history . . . is a wonderful illustration of this doctrine. He did not free human personality, he led it astray. What he did free was the material individuality . . . , the animal man. Cannot we see it in his own life? As he gets older, his energy becomes less and less a soul's energy, and more and more the energy of a temperament. Driven by great desires and vehement longings which fed on instinct and feeling, not on intelligence; possessed by the passions, loosing the tempest around him, breaking every obstacle and all ''external'' discipline; but having within him a heart full of contradictions and discordant cries; seeing life, before Nietzsche, as essentially *tragic,* Luther is the very type of modern individualism (the prototype of modern times, Fichte calls him). But in reality his personality is disunited, ruined. There is much weakness of soul behind all his bluster.

It is significant that to free the human being he began by breaking the vows of religion; and the ''joyful tidings,'' as Harnack calls it, which he announced to Christendom, at once spread an epidemic of despair over Germany. German Protestants would have us recognize the *greatness* of Luther. Material greatness, quantitative greatness, animal greatness, yes, we will grant that, and, if you will, admire it; but truly human greatness, no. The confusion between these two kinds of greatness, or energy, between the individual and the person, is at the heart of Germanism, and it shows us why Germans conceive personality as a hurricane, a buffalo, or an elephant. It explains too why we see the old spring of the spirit of Luther gush out in all the great inspirers of Protestant Germany such as Lessing and Fichte. Fichte calls Luther the German *par excellence,* and that is true in so far as the Reformation succeeded in separating Germany from Catholicism. Happy the nation whose supreme incarnation of her own genius is not a mere individuality of flesh but a personality radiant with the Spirit of God! If we want to set against Luther's egocentrism an example of true personality, let us think of that miracle of simplicity and uprightness, of candour and wisdom, of humility and magnanimity, of loss of self in God,—Joan of Arc.

Luther has another striking characteristic. He is a man wholly and systematically ruled by his affective and appetitive faculties; he is a Man of Will only, characterized chiefly by power in action. All historians insist upon his stark energy; Carlyle calls him *a Christian Odin, a very Thor.* (pp. 26-8)

[He] was gifted by nature with a strong religious disposition: he prayed at length and liked to pray aloud, with a great flow of words which was the wonder of men; he was deeply moved at the sight of the harvest, the blue sky, a little bird which he watched in his garden. He wept over a violet found in the snow which he could not revive. Obsessed by a deep melancholy, no doubt the greatest and most human thing in him—by that melancholy of Saul which is so terrible to see because, if we did not know that Saul's eternal destiny, like Luther's, is reserved for the inscrutable judgement of God, we should be tempted to see in it the melancholy of those for whom it would have been better had they never been born,—that man who unloosed the Revolution on the world was soothed by music and took comfort in playing the flute. He tells us that the devils fled from his flute.

All that comes from the same cause: the absolute predominance of Feeling and Appetite. If the force of instinct and the power of feeling is still ruled by the spirit, then it provided the human being with incomparable material and emotional wealth, and these very things are used for the life of the spirit. On this score there is already a certain romanticism, if you like, in such as Suso, but in a conception of life which remains fundamentally rational, ordered, Catholic. With Luther it is otherwise; the will has the primacy, truly and absolutely; it is the very conception of life that is affected. We can say that he is the first great Romantic.

That attitude of soul would naturally go with a profound anti-intellectualism. . . . (pp. 29-30)

Has he a grudge against any particular system? No. He is attacking philosophy itself. ''Barking against philosophy is a homage he thinks to give to God. . . . One should learn philosophy only as one learns witchcraft, that is to destroy it; as one finds out about errors, in order to refute them.''

From him Carlstadt, as early as 1518, borrowed that fine thought, that ''logic is nowhere necessary in theology because Christ does not need human inventions.'' What? Dare to tie down a free Christian like Dr. Luther to the principle of contradiction? Argument was never anything for him but a boxing-match, in which he was past master, and where the thing was to knock out his opponent by any means. ''When I care to start writing,'' he said cynically to Philip of Hesse, ''I shall be able to get out of the difficulty easily and leave your Grace to stick in the mud.'' Finally, the Reformer declares war not only on philosophy, but essentially on reason. Reason has an exclusively pragmatic value, it is for use in earthly life. God has given it to us only ''to govern on earth, that is to say that it has power to legislate and order everything regarding this life, like drinking, eating, and clothes, as well as what concerns external discipline and a respectable life.'' But in spiritual things it is not only ''blind and dark,'' it is truly ''the whore of the devil. It can only blaspheme and dishonour everything God has said or done.'' (pp. 31-2)

Luther's contempt for reason is, moreover, in harmony with his general doctrine about human nature and original sin. According to Luther, sin has vitiated the very essence of our nature, and this evil is final; grace and baptism cover over, but do not efface, original sin. So that the most that reason could be granted would be a wholly practical part in life and human business. But it is incapable of knowing first truths; and all speculative knowledge, all metaphysics is a snare . . .— and the use of reason in matters of faith, the claim to establish a coherent science of dogma and of the revealed deposit by reasoning and the use of philosophy, in short, theology, as the scholastics understood it, is an abominable scandal. In a word, this corrupted Christian takes with gross liberalism and in absolutely opposite sense the passages in which spiritual writers speak of the annihilation of the natural faculties, debases the thoughts of Tauler and the German mystics as well as the texts of St. Paul and the Gospel, and declares that faith is *against* reason. "Reason is contrary to faith," he wrote in 1536. And a little later: "Reason is directly opposed to faith, and one ought to let it be; in believers it should be killed and buried."

I have quoted these passages because it is instructive to discern in the beginning, in its authentic tone and quality, the false anti-intellectualist mysticism which was to poison so may minds in more subtle and less candid guises in the nineteenth century. Luther in a word, brought a deliverance and an immense relief to humanity. . . . He delivered man from the intelligence, from that wearisome and besetting compulsion to think always and think logically. Yet this liberation has constantly to be begun again. For, as he wrote in his commentary on the Epistle to the Galatians, "Alas, in this life reason is never completely destroyed."

We know well the problem Luther sets before us here; it is classical, it is of to-day, we are soaked in it. It is the problem of intellectualism and voluntarism. Luther is at the source of modern voluntarism. To prove this in detail, we should have to stress the consequences of the anti-intellectualist pessimism of which I have just spoken. As reason is banished to the foulest place in the house, if not killed and buried, the other spiritual faculty, the will, must be correspondingly exalted in practice if not in theory, for the brute pure and simple will never be an ideal for man. And so in Luther the swollen consciousness of the self is essentially a consciousness of will, of *realisation of freedom*, as German philosophy said later on. We should have to stress too his egocentrism, and show how the self is the centre for him, not, certainly, as in Kant, from a claim of the human intelligence to be the measure of intelligible things, but from the claim of the individual will, cut off from the universal body of the Church, to stand solitary and naked before God and Christ in order to ensure its justification and salvation by its trust.

It will be enough for me to show how the mysticism of the self and of the will is brought in by Luther. His teaching of the nothingness of works does not proceed from a Quietist error. Far from exaggerating the primacy which Catholic theology grants to contemplation, he abhors the contemplative life, and in his doctrine, as union with God by charity is quite impossible, religion tends in fact to be reduced to the service of our neighbour. In short, actions and works are of no avail for salvation, and in this regard they are bad and corrupt. But they are good, devilish good (it is the right word here), for the present life. And as they can no longer be ordered to God, to what could they be ordered except to the realization of the human will? Rousseau dreams, but Luther acts. He does not say, like Jean-Jacques: I cannot resist my inclinations, but I am not wicked; I am good in Your sight, O my God, I am essentially good. He says: Adam's sin has corrupted me in my essence, I am unclean, I sin greatly, but I trust in You, O my God, and You take me and save me just as I am, covering me with your Son's cloak. (pp. 33-6)

Behind Luther's appeals to the redeeming Lamb, behind his outbursts of confidence and his faith in the forgiveness of sins, there is a human creature which raises its crest and manages very well in the mud in which it is plunged by Adam's sin.

This creature will get straight in the world, it will follow the will to acquire power, the imperialist instinct, the law of this world which is its own world, it will work *its will* in the world. God will only be an ally, a co-operator, a powerful partner. (p. 37)

If an error creeps into minds, it is always thanks to some truth which it twists. There must be some basic illusion at the heart of the Lutheran Reformation which we need to seek. For that, there is no method better than to question the reformed themselves.

What do they tell us? They tell us that the essence of the Reformation is to exalt the Spirit against Authority, the interior energy of man, master of his judgement, against dead ideas and lying conventions imposed from without. What Carlyle sees in Luther is "a man self-subsistent, true, original, *sincere*." "With spurious Popes," writes this naïve Hegelian,

> with spurious Popes, and Believers having no private judgement,—quacks pretending to command over dupes,—what can you do? Misery and mischief only. . . . In all this wild revolutionary work, from Protestantism downwards, I see the blessedest result preparing itself: not abolition of Hero-worship, but rather what I would call a whole world of Heroes. If Hero means *sincere man*, why may not every one of us be a Hero?

Why, indeed, why are not all sincere readers of Carlyle, Heroes? Why does not the *sincerity* of a scoundrel make him a martyr? The passage which I have just quoted is a good abridgement of anglo-modern stupidity, but I keep only the signs we are needing at the moment: the great ideas which the Lutheran error turned into illusions, the ideas of *liberty, inwardness, spirit*.

Here we touch the heart of the *immanentist* error. It consists in believing that liberty, inwardness, spirit, lie essentially in opposition to what is not the self, in a breach between what is *within* and what is *without*. Consequently truth and life must be sought only within the human subject; everything in us that comes from what is not ourselves (from what is "other,"), is a crime against the spirit and against sincerity. And thus everything *extrinsic* to us is the destruction and death of our interior. And every mean which common sense regards as uniting interior and exterior and bringing them into communication is in reality an "intermediary" which separates them. So, for modern Protestant individualism, the Church and the Sacraments separate us from God; so, for modern philosophic subjectivism, sensation and idea separate us from reality. I do not say that Luther formulated such a principle, far from it. On the contrary, he had personally an excessively dogmatic and authoritative conception of life and had nothing of the liberal about him. But I do say that it was he who in practice introduced this principle to modern thought in a very special and still wholly theological form, by setting up Faith against Works, the Gospel against the Law, and by actually falsifying that very faith to which alone he looked for salvation, an heretical pseudo-faith which could not but come down gradually to what it has become with many Protestants of our days, a transport of distress and trust towards the unknown from the deeps of the self.

What is remarkable here is, that this modern myth of Immanence with its exaltation of the dignity of the spirit is precisely based on a radical misunderstanding of the true nature of the spirit. To receive from others, from outside, is, indeed, in the world of bodies, in the world of transitive action, pure submission, and is most certainly contrary to living spontaneity, since there we are dealing precisely with lifeless things which, incapable of perfecting themselves, serve only for the passage and transformation of the energies of the universe. But to receive from others in the spiritual world, that is certainly submission in the first place, but only as a presupposed condition, and it is essentially action, to perfect oneself interiorly and manifest the autonomy of what is truly living. For the very quality of spiritual things is that they are not confined within their separate being and can increase intrinsically by the being of what is not themselves. If the law of the object, the law of being, imposes itself on the intelligence, it is in order that the intelligence may itself find vital completion in an action which is a pure immaterial quality, and in which the very thing which constitutes what is "*other*" becomes its own perfection. And if the law of the Last End, the law of the good, imposes itself on the will, it is that love may make us one with the Author of all good, and that we—by following His law, which has become ours,—may still follow our deepest and most intimate attraction. That is the mystery belonging to immanent activity, perfect *interiorization,* by knowledge and love, of what is "other", or of what comes from another than we.

In a still more transcendent order, before a yet deeper mystery,—that of the creating Spirit's action on created spirits,—Luther again isolates irremediably what is *ourselves* from what is "other", our spiritual vessel from the surrounding ocean. He turns our justice into a veneer under which we go on producing our bad works, bad because "men's works, even though they always seem beautiful and probably good, are mortal sins," whilst God's works, were they always ugly and apparently bad, are of eternal merit. "He does not even consider," says Bossuet, "that men's good works are at the same time God's works, since He produces them in us by His grace." This is the whole secret. For the immense God Who is in the very heart of all things because He creates them, and has dominion over Being itself, working in each creature as befits the nature He gave it, causes in spirits the action of spirits in the mode proper to spirits, with all the spontaneity, inwardness, and liberty which befit their nature. The absurd Lutheran externalism may well pretend to give all to grace; in reality, by regarding it as impossible that a work of man should be also a work of God, it lays down the principle of an unbridled naturalism which in a little more than two centuries ruined everything in Western thought before blossoming into contemporary immanentism. No longer is there any question of the indwelling of the Divine Persons in our soul. The soul is driven back into its solitude, it has become impenetrable to everything but self.

The Reformer, and with him the whole modern world, rises against two mysteries: the mystery of the divine operations, and the mystery of immanent activity and the capacity of spirits. Things perfectly clear until then because they were accepted become obscure because they are denied. They can no longer keep anything of the things of the spirit but what is accidental and accessory, conditioned by the material and human. Intellectual *magisterium,* human or divine, Church and revealed dogma, even more radically, authority of objective being and the moral law, are finally no longer conceivable except as external and mechanical restraints forced on a nature which suffers them under compulsion. Now the lists are open.

Immediately after Luther, there is, for reasons of public safety and to avoid perishing of anarchy, a reaction of authority in Protestant Germany under the most tyrannously social form.

What external compulsion is worse than to have princes legislating in spiritual matters and Churches separated from the Spirit of Christ? What discipline is more material and mechanical than Protestant scholasticism? What literalism is more oppressive than that of a dead theology and a "supernaturalism" based not on Primal Truth, but on the human reason of preachers paid by the State to interpret Scripture? What burden is heavier than their morality and that decalogue which terrified Luther and is terrible indeed, when the inward principle of grace no longer gives us strength and inclination to live in accordance with it?

But the spirit of Luther went on travelling underground, for new upheavals and new crises. And in such degree as the modern world and modern thought receive it, it gnaws them without respite and, because every spirit is stronger than matter, it swallows up, one after the other, all material prohibitions which restrain it for a time. The *essential* conflict of spirit and authority, of Gospel and Law, of subject and object, of intimate and transcendent, is a specifically Protestant conflict. It is meaningless in an order of things that takes account of spiritual realities, and modernism has tried in vain to carry it into the Catholic mind.

But see! By virtue of the principle of Immanence, since everything brought from outside is henceforth counted as oppression and force, it will, in the last analysis, be necessary to shut everything up in our spirit so that it may not have to receive anything from outside, and conclude all in man, including God Himself. Nature is itself dormant thought: in nature God is in process of becoming: and man will be the final stage of evolution at which that same nature will attain to self-consciousness.

The great "wild revolutionary work, from Protestantism downwards," thus prepares nonsense pure and simple as the "blessedest result."

It promises rest to the reason only in contradiction, it sets a universal war within us. It has inflamed everything, and healed nothing. It leaves us hopeless in face of the great problems, which Christ and His Doctors solved for redeemed humanity so long as it was faithful, problems which, nearly four centuries ago, once more began to rack the human heart like angelic instruments of torture. (pp. 45-50)

> *Jacques Maritain, "Luther," in his* Three Reformers: Luther—Descartes—Rousseau, *Charles Scribner's Sons, 1955, pp. 3-50.*

G. K. CHESTERTON (essay date 1933)

[*Regarded as one of England's premier men of letters during the first half of the twentieth century, Chesterton is best known today as a colorful bon vivant, a witty essayist, and as the creator of the Father Brown mysteries and the fantasy* The Man Who Was Thursday *(1908). Much of Chesterton's work reveals his childlike enjoyment of life and reflects his pronounced Anglican and, later, Roman Catholic beliefs. His essays are characterized by their humor, frequent use of paradox, and chatty, rambling style. In the following excerpt from an essay first published in 1933, Chesterton briefly compares Luther's character and intellect with Thomas Aquinas's.*]

We must be just to those huge human figures, who are in fact the hinges of history. However strong, and rightly strong, be our own controversial conviction, it must never mislead us into thinking that something trivial has transformed the world. So it is with that great Augustinian monk, who avenged all the ascetic Augustinians of the Middle Ages; and whose broad and burly figure has been big enough to block out for four centuries the distant human mountain of Aquinas. It is not, as the moderns delight to say, a question of theology. The Protestant theology of Martin Luther was a thing that no modern Protestant would be seen dead in a field with; or if the phrase be too flippant, would be specially anxious to touch with a bargepole. That Protestantism was pessimism; it was nothing but bare insistence on the hopelessness of all human virtue, as an attempt to escape hell. That Lutheranism is now quite unreal; more modern phases of Lutheranism are rather more unreal; but Luther was not unreal. He was one of those great elemental barbarians, to whom it is indeed given to change the world. To compare those two figures bulking so big in history, in any philosophical sense, would of course be futile and even unfair. On a great map like the mind of Aquinas, the mind of Luther would be almost invisible. But it is not altogether untrue to say, as so many journalists have said without caring whether it was true or untrue, that Luther opened an epoch; and began the modern world.

He was the first man who ever consciously used his consciousness; or what was later called his Personality. He had as a fact a rather strong personality. Aquinas had an even stronger personality; he had a massive and magnetic presence; he had an intellect that could act like a huge system of artillery spread over the whole world; he had that instantaneous presence of mind in debate, which alone really deserves the name of wit. But it never occurred to him to use anything except his wits, in defence of a truth distinct from himself. It never occurred to Aquinas to use Aquinas as a weapon. There is not a trace of his ever using his personal advantages, of birth or body or brain or breeding, in debate with anybody. In short, he belonged to an age of intellectual unconsciousness, to an age of intellectual innocence, which was very intellectual. Now Luther did begin the modern mood of depending on things not merely intellectual. It is not a question of praise or blame; it matters little whether we say that he was a strong personality, or that he was a bit of a big bully. When he quoted a Scripture text, inserting a word that is not in Scripture, he was content to shout back at all hecklers: ''Tell them that Dr. Martin Luther will have it so!'' That is what we now call Personality. A little later it was called Psychology. After that it was called Advertisement or Salesmanship. But we are not arguing about advantages or disadvantages. It is due to this great Augustinian pessimist to say, not only that he did triumph at last over the Angel of the Schools, but that he did in a very real sense make the modern world. He destroyed Reason; and substituted Suggestion. (pp. 194-95)

> G. K. Chesterton, ''The Sequel to St. Thomas,'' in his *Saint Thomas Aquinas, Image Books,* 1956, pp. 181-97.

REINHOLD NIEBUHR (essay date 1943)

[*Niebuhr is considered one of the most important and influential Protestant theologians in twentieth-century America. The author of such works as* The Children of Light and the Children of Darkness *(1944) and* Christian Realism and Political Problems *(1953), he consistently stressed the reality of original sin and emphasized the tragic condition of fallen humanity, opposing the secular and liberal Christian tendency to advance economic and political explanations of human misery. Nonetheless, Niebuhr believed it was the task of modern Christianity to minister to the worldly as well as the spiritual needs of humankind, and he attempted throughout his life to integrate Christian ethics with a practical political philosophy. In the following excerpt, Niebuhr*

examines some ethical and sociopolitical implications of the Lutheran doctrine of grace.]

Luther's approach to the ultimate problem of the Christian life was dominated by two considerations. The primary one was his conviction, established after bitter experience, that no final peace could be found by the effort to achieve righteousness. He had tried the method of monastic perfectionism and had failed; and the assurance of the Pauline word that ''the just shall live by faith,'' therefore came to him as a happy release from the bondage of ''the law,'' from the intolerable tension of an uneasy conscience which came the nearer to despair, the more imperious the demand for perfection appeared to it. The secondary consideration was the result of historical observation, rather than inner experience. He was convinced that the pretention of finality and perfection in the church was the root of spiritual pride and self-righteousness. His belief that the mystic-ascetic attempt at perfection was futile prompted his polemic against monasticism. His conviction that the pretension of finality was dangerous motivated his polemic against ecclesiasticism.

In elaborating his own theory of grace and the Christian life he was far from excluding that side of the paradox of grace according to which it is the source of a new life, of ''love, joy and peace.'' Luther has his own relation to the mystical tradition, and he followed the tendency of those who converted the classical mystical effort at union with God into a ''Christ-mysticism.'' The soul of the believer, he claimed, became so united with Christ that all his virtues flow into it: ''Since the promises of God are words of holiness, truth, righteousness, liberty and peace, and are full of universal goodness, the soul, which cleaves to them with a firm faith, is so united to them, nay thoroughly absorbed by them, that it not only partakes of, but is thoroughly saturated by all their virtues.''

Luther interprets the power of righteousness, psychologically, primarily as the motive of love and gratitude to God. This motive dispenses with the necessity of considering the gratitude or ingratitude, the praise or blame of fellowmen:

> Thus from faith now forth love and joy in the Lord, and from love a cheerful willing free spirit, disposed to serve our neighbour voluntarily, without taking into account any gratitude or ingratitude, praise or blame, gain or loss. Its object is not to lay men under obligation, nor does it distinguish between friends or enemies . . . but most freely spends its goods, whether it loses them through ingratitude or gains goodwill.

Here Luther comprehends the whole beauty and power of Christian *agape*, particularly its transcendent freedom over all the prudential considerations of natural ethical attitudes.

He does not deny, in other words, that the new life is capable of a new righteousness. He only insists that it is not justified by them: ''A Christian, being consecrated by his faith, does good works; but he is not by these works made a more sacred person or more a Christian. This is the effect of faith alone.''

Many of the emphases in Luther's thought combine the classical Christian doctrine shared by Catholicism and the Reformation, on the priority of grace, with a new emphasis on the place of forgiveness in grace. The soul is the ''poor little harlot'' who brings nothing to the spiritual marriage but a ''sackful of sins'' and her ''rich bridegroom Christ'' brings all the goodness. Or the soul is the ''parched earth'' which can bring forth no fruit unless grace as the ''rain from heaven'' water it. But with this rain the Christian will ''as a good tree bring forth good fruits.

For the believer has the Holy Spirit; and where He is He will not allow me to be idle but incites him to all exercises of piety, to the love of God, to patience in affliction, to prayer, thanksgiving and the showing of love towards all."

In picturing the possibilities of this love towards all Luther displays the most profound understanding of the meaning of Christian *agape*, particularly of its completely disinterested motives. He regards the ethic of the Sermon on the Mount as definitive for Christians, always so long as he is dealing with personal attitudes and relationships.

Despite these great merits of the Lutheran position there are quietistic tendencies in it, even when Luther is analysing the intricacies of personal religion, where he is on the whole most faithful to the Biblical paradox. Sometimes he lapses into mystic doctrines of passivity or combines quietism with a legalistic conception of the imputation of righteousness. "Without works" degenerates into "without action" in some of his strictures against the "righteousness of works." He writes: "This most excellent righteousness of faith . . . which God through Christ imputeth to us without works, is neither political nor ceremonial, nor the righteousness of God's law, nor consisteth in works, but is clean contrary: that is to say, a *mere passive* righteousness. . . . For in this we work nothing unto God, but only receive and suffer another to work in us, that is to say, God. Therefore it seemeth good to me to call this righteousness of faith, or Christian righteousness, the passive righteousness."

The mystic fear of action, because all action is tainted with sin, has its counterpart in the Lutheran fear of action, because it may tempt to a new pride. So Emil Brunner warns that "all energetic ethical activity carries with it a great danger. It may lead to the opinion that by such activity deliverance from evil is being accomplished." The danger cannot be denied. But if moral action is discouraged on that ground, the Reformation theologian is in no better position than the monastic perfectionist who disavows particular moral and social responsibilities because of the taint of sin which attaches to them. Ideally the doctrine of justification by faith is a release of the soul into action; but it may be wrongly interpreted to encourage indolence. The barren orthodoxy of seventeenth-century Lutheranism, in which the experience of "justification by faith" degenerated into a "righteousness of belief," was not an inevitable, but nevertheless a natural, destruction of the moral content of the Christian life, for which there was a certain warrant in Luther's own thought.

Possibly a greater weakness in the Lutheran analysis of grace is found in Luther's idea of the relation of grace to the law. His difficulty here is derived not so much from his theory of justification as from his idea of sanctification. Luther's vision of the "love, joy and peace" which the redeemed soul has in Christ, is of an ecstatic transcendence over all the contradictions of history, including the inner contradictions of the "ought," the sense of moral obligation. *Agape*, as the fulfillment of the law, results in a complete disappearance of the sense of obligation to the law, and in a consequent elimination of all the careful discriminations of justice which belong to "law" in the broadest sense. (pp. 185-89)

In [its] exposition of a highly personal and interior sanctification, the Reformation obscures the wisdom inhering in its doctrine of justification. For according to the doctrine of justification the inner contradiction of the soul is never completely healed. There are undoubtedly ecstatic moments when the conflict between self-love and the love of God, between conscience

Painting by Lucas Cranach the Younger depicting Luther among the other major Reformers, including Philipp Melanchthon, Johann Bugenhagen, Georg Spalatin, and (in honor of his scholarly achievements) Desiderius Erasmus, among several others.

and the anxious survival impulse of the ego are transcended. But these moments are merely "earnests" of the final fulfillment of life; and they do not describe the general condition of the life of the redeemed. In that condition the relation between law and grace is much more complex; for by the inspiration of grace the law is extended as well as overcome. Repentance and faith prompt a sense of obligation towards wider and wider circles of life. The need of this neighbour, the demands of that social situation, the claims of this life upon me, unrecognized today may be recognized and stir the conscience to uneasiness tomorrow. There is a constantly increasing sense of social obligation which is an integral part of the life of grace. To deny this is to be oblivious to one aspect of historic existence which the Renaissance understood so well: that life represents an indeterminate series of possibilities, and therefore of obligation to fulfill them. It is precisely because this is so that there can be no complete fulfillment; for "a man's reach should exceed his grasp" (Browning). The conception of the relation of grace to law in Luther need not lead to antinomianism, as is sometimes charged; but it is indifferent to relative moral discriminations. It does not relax moral tension at the ultimate point of moral experience; for there it demands the love which is the fulfillment, and not the negation of law. But it relaxes the tension at all intermediate points and does not deal seriously with all the possible extensions of justice to which men ought to be driven by an uneasy conscience.

The weakness of the Lutheran Reformation in dealing with the problem of law and grace in it becomes even more apparent when the issue is transferred from the inner life to the complexities of culture and civilization, and all expressions of the collective life of man. Here the "defeatism" of the Reformation becomes much more apparent. Its understanding of the ultimate problem of historical existence seems to preclude any understanding of all the proximate problems. The Reformation understands that every possible extension of knowledge and wisdom falls short of the wisdom which knows God. It realizes that the "world by its wisdom knew not God" and it rejoices in the grace, apprehended by faith, which overcomes the sinful ego-centricity of all human knowledge. But it has no interest in the infinite shades and varieties of the amalgam of truth and falsehood which constitutes the stuff of science and philosophy, and of all human striving after the truth. (pp. 189-91)

In confronting the problems of realizing justice in the collective life of man, the Lutheran Reformation was even more explicitly defeatist. Human society represents an infinite variety of structures and systems in which men seek to organize their common life in terms of some kind of justice. The possibilities of realizing a higher justice are indeterminate. There is no point in historical social achievement where one may rest with an easy conscience. All structures of justice do indeed presuppose the sinfulness of man, and are all partly systems of restraint which prevent the conflict of wills and interests from resulting in a consistent anarchy. But they are also all mechanisms by which men fulfill their obligations to their fellow men, beyond the possibilities offered in direct and personal relationships. The Kingdom of God and the demands of perfect love are therefore relevant to every political system and impinge upon every social situation in which the self seeks to come to terms with the claims of other life.

Luther denies this relevance explicitly. He declares:

> The way to discern the difference [between law and gospel] is to place the gospel in heaven and the law on the earth: to call the righteousness of the gospel heavenly, and the righteousness of the law earthly and to put as great a difference between [them] as God hath made between heaven and earth. . . . Wherefore if the question be concerning the matter of faith and conscience let us utterly exclude the law and leave it on earth. . . . Contrariwise in civil policy obedience to law must be severely required. There nothing *must be known* concerning the conscience, the Gospel, grace, remission of sins, heavenly righteousness or Christ himself; but Moses only with the law and the works thereof.

Here we have the complete severance between the final experience of grace and all the proximate possibilities of liberty and justice, which must be achieved in history. This principle of separation leads to a denial that liberty can have any other meaning for the Christian than liberty from "God's everlasting wrath. For Christ hath made us free not civilly nor carnally but divinely; that is to say our conscience is now made free and quiet, not fearing the wrath of God to come." Social antinomianism is guarded against by the injunction, "Let every man therefore endeavour to do his duty diligently in his calling and help his neighbour to the utmost of his power." But evidently no obligation rests upon the Christian to change social structures so that they might conform more perfectly to the requirements of brotherhood. In his attitude towards the peasant revolt Luther rigorously applied this separation between the "spiritual kingdom" and the "worldly" one; and met the demands of the peasants for a greater degree of social justice with the charge that they were confusing the two. He took a complacent attitude towards the social inequalities of feudalism and observed that on earth there will always be masters and slaves. Luther added an element of perversity to this social ethic by enlarging upon the distinction between an "inner" and an "outer" kingdom so that it became, in effect, a distinction between public and private morality. The rulers, as custodians of public morality, were advised to "hit, stab, kill" when dealing with rebels. For Luther had a morbid fear of anarchy and was willing to permit the *Obrigkeit* any instrument to suppress it. The peasants on the other hand, as private citizens, were admonished to live in accordance with the ethic of the Sermon on the Mount. They were told that their demand for justice violated the New Testament ethic of nonresistance.

By thus transposing an "inner" ethic into a private one, and making the "outer" or "earthly" ethic authoritative for government, Luther achieves a curiously perverse social morality. He places a perfectionist private ethic in juxtaposition to a realistic, not to say cynical, official ethic. He demands that the state maintain order without too scrupulous a regard for justice; yet he asks suffering and nonresistant love of the individual without allowing him to participate in the claims and counter-claims which constitute the stuff of social justice. The inevitable consequence of such an ethic is to encourage tyranny; for resistance to government is as important a principle of justice as maintenance of government. (pp. 192-95)

Even without this particular error, the Lutheran political ethic would have led to defeatism in the field of social politics. Its absolute distinction between the "heavenly" or "spiritual" kingdom and the "earthly" one, destroys the tension between the final demands of God upon the conscience, and all the relative possibilities of realizing the good in history. The spiritual and moral significance of various progressive realizations of justice is denied from two angles. On the side of its realism the Lutheran ethic finds all historical achievements equally tainted with sin and the distinctions between them therefore unimportant. On the side of its gospel perfectionism it finds them falling equally short of that perfect love of the Kingdom of God, which is alone the earnest of salvation.

The Lutheran Reformation is thus always in danger of heightening religious tension to the point where it breaks the moral tension, from which all decent action flows. The conscience is made uneasy about the taint of sin in all human enterprise; but the conviction that any alternative to a given course of action would be equally tainted, and that in any case the divine forgiveness will hallow and sanctify what is really unholy, eases the uneasy conscience prematurely. Thus the saints are tempted to continue to sin that grace may abound, while the sinners toil and sweat to make human relations a little more tolerable and slightly more just.

The weakness of the Lutheran position in the field of social ethics is accentuated to a further degree by its inability to define consistent criteria for the achievement of relative justice. Despite its conception of sanctification as an ecstatic love which transcends all law, and of its doctrine of justification which eases the conscience in its inability to realize the good perfectly, it is forced, nevertheless, to find some standards of relative good and evil. Since it rightly has less confidence than Catholicism in the untainted character of reason, it relegates the "natural law" that is, the rational analysis of social obligations, to the background, as an inadequate guide. But it has only odds and ends of systems of order to put in the place of "natural law." These consist primarily of two conceptions. The one is the order and justice which any state may happen to establish. This order is accepted uncritically precisely because a principle of justice, by which the justice of a given state could be criticized, is lacking. The other is the idea of a *Schoephungsordnung* an "order of creation," which is presumably, the directive given by God in the very structure of the created world. The difficulty with this concept is that human freedom alters and transmutes the "given" facts of creation so much that no human institutions can be judged purely by the criterion of fixed principles of "creation."

In the field of sex-relations for instance, bi-sexuality and those vocations of mother and father which are unalterably related to biological differentiation are the only factors which may rightfully be placed in the category of "order of creation."

Monogamy can certainly not be placed there, or for that matter any other form of marital union or standard of sex-relation. In political relations Luther sometimes regarded government as belonging to the "order of creation," and at other times seemed to think that its authority was derived from a special "divine ordinance," Scripturally validated, particularly in Romans 13. Government, however, can be regarded as belonging to "creation" only in the sense that both human freedom and the abuse of human freedom require that human society have a cement of cohesion transcending the natural sociality of animal existence. But no particular government can be derived from the "order of creation"; nor is the uncritical obedience to government, which Luther demanded, a part of the requirement of such an "order." (pp. 195-98)

> Reinhold Niebuhr, "The Debate on Human Destiny in Modern Culture: The Reformation," in his The Nature and Destiny of Man, a Christian Interpretation; Human Destiny, Vol. II, *Charles Scribner's Sons, 1943, pp. 184-212.*

UURAS SAARNIVAARA   (essay date 1947)

[*Saarnivaara is the author of* Luther Discovers the Gospel: New Light upon Luther's Way from Medieval Catholicism to Evangelical Faith *(first published in Finnish in 1947), a painstakingly detailed examination of Luther's progression from Catholic orthodoxy to his mature doctrinal views of grace and justification. In the following excerpt, drawn largely from the conclusion of this work, he recapitulates his arguments and judgments.*]

When Luther was seeking a way to peace with God and to an assurance of salvation, he had to find a solution to the greatest issue of life and death in man's personal relation to God: How can man, cut off from God by his sins and guilt, become acceptable to Him and enter into a living personal fellowship with Him? In Luther's life this quest for salvation was made up of two subissues: first, how could he find peace for his conscience through the forgiveness of sins?—second, how could he become justified or righteous in the sight of the Holy One?. . . Luther did not face these two sides, or aspects, at the same time. There was an interval of several years between the two crises of his life in which he found a solution to each of them. (p. xiii)

Though Luther possessed a saving faith already in 1512, his conception of justification was not that of his mature period. He understood justification as a gradual process of religious and moral renewal, or healing of the human nature from the corruption of sin. Non-imputation of sins, that is, non-reckoning of sins that remain, for the sake of Christ, was but a temporary supplement to this process of healing. True, Luther at times said, following Augustine, that this non-imputation formed the greater portion of justification, since the actual righteousness of the believer was a mere beginning in this earthly life.

This time, between the late fall of 1512 and the summer of 1518, may well be termed the twilight period of the Reformation. The first rays of the sun of grace and righteousness were already lighting the sky in Luther's spiritual life, but the actual daybreak had not yet taken place. The full light of the evangelical insight into justification had not yet reached his soul. The light which he did possess, however, was nearly sufficient to break the bonds of the Roman Church, as had been the case also with Wycliffe and Huss, who had about as much revealed to them as Luther at this particular time, but

who did not know the evangelical doctrine of justification. In his struggles against the abuses within the Church, Luther at this time directed his efforts toward removal of errors in the sphere of doctrines in which he had already or almost attained the evangelical insight, principally the doctrine of repentance.

The second great crisis, the actual day break, in Luther's development, was his tower experience toward the end of the year 1518. It resulted or consisted in his discovery of the evangelical or Reformation insight into justification. Two groups of historical documents give evidence of this great change: (1) Luther's *Preface* to his works, written in 1545, and scattered statements in his table talks of different dates; (2) Luther's lectures and writings. The first group of documents contains accounts of the nature and date of this discovery from the pen and mouth of Luther himself. The second group yields information concerning Luther's conception of justification in the early period of his life. Both in their own way testify irrefutably to the fact that Luther discovered his Reformation concept of justification toward the end of the year 1518. It is this year that marks the beginning of the Reformation movement in the deepest meaning of the word, with its watchword of justification by the gracious imputation of God appropriated through faith. This watchword was unknown prior to year 1519. Closely connected with the discovery of the true meaning of Rom. 1:17, as a kind of prerequisite, was the rejection of the fourfold meaning of Scripture and, as its inevitable consequence, the surrender of Mysticism.

The discovery in the tower, however, did not result in Luther's casting overboard his old views one and all. This was impossible since many of his pre-Reformation conceptions were perfectly Scriptural. To the very end he continued to teach that grace is bestowed only upon the humble and contrite in heart, that also the justified children of God are sinful in themselves, that therefore their struggle against sin and gradual mortification of the flesh must never cease in this present life. These beliefs, together with the conviction that man is dependent entirely upon the grace of God for salvation, belonged to the fundamental insights of Luther throughout his life. To the very end he agreed with Augustine in the interpretation of Romans 7, and of a similar passage in Gal. 5:16 ff., namely, that Paul speaks in them primarily as a believer. Consequently, many of the statements in the earlier and later writings of Luther are similar or almost so.

The basic difference between Luther's pre-Reformation and his Reformation doctrine of salvation is to be found in the conception of the nature and essence of justification. The tower experience opened his eyes to see that according to Scripture, and Paul in particular, justification by faith is not a gradual process of renewal or becoming righteous. It is rather the bestowal of the righteousness of Christ by imputation. God justifies the sinner by forgiving his sins and reckoning him innocent and blameless for the sake of the atoning work of Christ. This acquittal God pronounces through the Gospel promises proclaimed by the ministry of reconciliation. By faith the sinner receives this divine gift promised and offered to him. The foundation of justification and also the object of the believer's faith and trust is not what God has done and does *in* him, but what Christ has done *for* him. (pp. 121-23)

[Luther once said] that a volume containing his thoughts of the period prior to his discovery of the full Gospel was of little use in the new era of the noonday Gospel. These words may be applied to the entire literary heritage of the "young Luther." The writings of this period cannot be used alongside the works of the Reformation era. The Lutheran Church has followed the right instinct in owning as its true spiritual possessions only those writings of Luther which date from the year 1519 or later. Almost without exception the instruction in the Church has been based on these, while the writings produced prior to 1519 had been mostly forgotten until the Luther scholars of our own generation brought them to light. The church at large has had the feeling that the earlier works of Luther reflect a different and strange spirit and give expression to an unevangelical conception of the Christian faith and life. Truly ''Lutheran'' are only the writings after 1518.

Modern Luther research has reversed the stand at this point. Many of the studies of Luther's theology fail to distinguish between his earlier and later lectures and writings. On the basis of our study we must regard such a procedure as erring seriously as to method and causing much confusion. Since the literary production of Luther earlier than 1519 is of a pre-Reformation and sub-Reformation type, no sound Luther study can afford to make uncritical use of the writings before and after 1518-19, as though they were in every respect equal. However, a dangerously large part of modern Luther research has committed just this error and is, therefore, in need of thorough revision.

In 1938 Otto Wolff made the statement [in *Die Haupttypen der neueren Lutherdeutung*] that as far as the modern study of Luther is concerned the rediscovery of the full Reformation Gospel of the Reformer is still a thing of the future. The Luther research of our day is still living and groping largely in a ''pre-Reformation'' period. Is it too much to hope that as World War I was followed by a ''revival'' of the ''young Luther,'' World War II will be followed by a ''revival'' of the full Reformation Gospel of Luther—and of Scripture? (pp. 125-26)

> *Uuras Saarnivaara, in his* Luther Discovers the Gospel: New Light upon Luther's Way from Medieval Catholicism to Evangelical Faith, *Concordia Publishing House, 1951, 146 p.*

HEINZ BLUHM (essay date 1948)

[*Bluhm is a German-born American educator and scholar. In the following excerpt, he discusses the startling theological innovation of Luther's first publication,* Seven Penitential Psalms.]

Considerable interest attaches, or should attach, to Martin Luther's tract entitled *Die Sieben puszpsalm mit deutscher auszlegung nach dem schrifftlichen synne tzu Christi und gottis gnaden, neben seyns selben ware erkentniss grundlich gerichtet.* Appearing in the early spring of 1517, approximately half a year before the posting of the *Ninety-five Theses,* it is the first original publication that Luther himself saw through the press. Its success was instantaneous and widespread. As prominent a man as Johann von Staupitz lost no time in recommending it warmly. Luther's searching analysis of the human situation made a deep impression upon the many readers who, like the author's superior in the Augustinian order, gave the slender volume an enthusiastic reception. It is important to bear in mind that the book, besides stirring Luther's scholarly friends as well as the learned in general rather more than he himself had anticipated, found immediate favor also with the ''common man'' for whom it had primarily been written. There is no exaggeration in the claim that Luther's earliest publication straightway established him as one of the most widely read writers in the German tongue: his unparalleled success as an author can safely be said to have begun with the very first book he ever put out. (p. 103)

Die sieben Busspsalmen was, in a very real sense, the upshot of that comparatively peaceful quinquennium from 1512 to 1517, during which he was permitted, despite his many monastic duties and administrative functions, to devote himself largely to scholarly pursuits. These fairly quiet years of reflection, teaching, and study reached their acme in the preparation and publication of *Seven Penitential Psalms,* a work singularly free from strife and stress of an external kind.

[If] it was chiefly, even exclusively, the purely religious ideas set forth by Luther that caused the book to be devoured by so diverse a public practically before the ink was dry, the question arises quite naturally: what was it that caught the imagination of its impatient readers? exactly what was it that appealed to scholar and layman alike?

Two things impress the modern student eager to know the reasons for the striking success of Luther's first literary venture. It is an intensely personal record written in the white heat of passionate inquiry, and it presents within its relatively brief scope a whole philosophy or theology of life dealing as it does with fundamental problems of human existence. The reader senses instantly that he is under the spell of a searching mind individually concerned with what he is discussing: the book is, as Nietzsche wanted all books to be, written in blood. Moreover, the Christian view of life, supposedly long familiar, is seen in what must have seemed to contemporaries a new light. There is a splendor about the book and its bold reinterpretation of then prevalent ideas that cannot but have struck a responsive chord in the heart of every sensitive person. Still, after due credit has been given to the author, one should note the religious awareness of the man in the street who was ready to appreciate an admittedly difficult book proffering a challenging analysis of the meaning of Christian thought. An age not alive with religious questions could not have clamored for a treatise as exacting as *Die sieben Busspsalmen.* People were definitely interested in discussions of the nature of man, and they must have found some help in the answer that Luther provided. What was the picture of man that the youthful Wittenberg professor presented in his earliest essay?

Luther's ideas are at once original and traditional. Far removed from humanistic thought, whether of the twelfth and thirteenth or of the fourteenth and fifteenth centuries, he moves pretty much within the strictly theological realm suggested by the names of Paul and Augustine. Luther's tract is, in fact, a most severe attack on and indictment of the encroachment of philosophy upon theology. Relentlessly he drives home the point that the comparative humanism of the world in which he lives is the principal foe that needs to be battled. The extreme theocentricity of Pauline theology is to be enthroned again, completely, without the slightest trace of compromise with the contrary *Zeitgeist.*

The young scholar divides men into two main groups: the Old Man and the New. On both his thought is partly conventional and partly out of the beaten track. Beginning with his analysis of the Old Man we find that Luther is interested but very little in the common, ordinary sinner. The Old Man that he inveighs against is not primarily the thief, the murderer, the glutton, or the adulterer. It is hardly worth mentioning that Luther is of course as inflexibly opposed to such obvious sinners as the sternest moralist imaginable. But in his opinion, quite mature by 1517, this kind of Old Man, long recognized and universally fought against, is not the real or even the chief threat to a more profoundly interpreted Christian culture. All men with a modicum of interest in morality are patently against manifest vice.

Luther's implied argument is that you don't have to be a Christian to recognize and hate flagrant sin. He is convinced that a Christian, far transcending the bounds of mere Moral Man, is, or should be, concerned with incomparably deeper issues beyond the question of conspicuous misdemeanor. As a matter of fact, what Luther suggests in his first publication is that a Christian *qua* Christian is troubled by matters quite different from those of easily recognizable moral conduct. To be sure, the path of the Christian is also beset with difficulties of this sort, and Luther therefore points them out in passing. Naturally, he is painfully aware of the prevalence of gross sin, and he does pay heed to it in the course of his analysis of the condition of man. What is important for a proper understanding of this essay however is that a consideration of the crass sinner does not loom very large here: though it is clearly there it plays an altogether subordinate rôle when compared with Luther's presentation of an infinitely more insidious kind of sin infecting all people without exception, even the apparently upright and just. (pp. 104-06)

Inasmuch as Luther was above all troubled by the question of man's situation in the sight of God, he merely recorded as it were his profound displeasure with gross sin and sinners, particularly since such crimes lay pretty much within the jurisdiction of civil government. Perturbed by matters of infinitely greater weight in his view, he took up with vigor and insight the problem of man's existence before God. It is with this highest relationship then that Luther is almost exclusively concerned. The questions he tried to answer in this tract are those of the position of the Old Man and of the New Man before the seat of ultimate religious and ethical authority. We shall first examine the plight of the unredeemed sinner confronted with God.

The whole inwardness and amazing depth of Luther's thought dawn upon one when one remembers how markedly as moral a man as Sebastian Brant, the author of the most famous German book before Luther, differs from the latter in the approach toward and evaluation of human imperfection. What Brant attacks again and again, with pathos and bathos, in the *Ship of Fools* is what Luther all but passes over in **Seven Penitential Psalms**. While the humanist Brant attends almost exclusively to the outright vices and obvious sins of mankind, Luther endeavors to analyze the predicament of man in an infinitely more disturbing and upsetting manner. Though he is, naturally enough, as inveterate an enemy of open sin as Brant was or ever could be, Luther, the most kindred spirit Paul of Tarsus ever found, was not satisfied with showing up man's apparent foibles but went to what seemed to him to be the root of the trouble.

It goes without saying that this decision to see things whole took him far afield. Passionately concerned with ultimates, he emerged from his self-imposed task not so much the impatient detractor of indisputable vice as the sternest critic of the "good" men and women around him. Consciously disdaining to rail against the obvious and refusing to be just another voice in the chorus of the moralists of his generation, he proceeded to question the very "goodness" of those relatively few who strove to do justly and to love mercy. In a sense this was a shocking procedure on his part. With so much vice abroad in the land, with Rome practically burning, a Wittenberg professor, of some eminence to be sure but not yet of national or international prominence, undertook to arraign that distinguished minority which honestly tried to live the good life. What effrontery! What folly! How did this mad professor dare

to attack the salt of the earth, the people who really cared how they stood with God and who did express an active interest in the welfare of their fellows? Was it not, to say the least, impolitic and indiscreet to denounce the comparatively small number of those who were morally sensitive at all and to alienate men and women who made an honest effort to order their lives responsibly?

These are hard questions indeed. A satisfactory answer will not be found unless we are rather fully aware what manner of man this disquieting Augustinian really was. It is indispensable in this connection to recall some salient facts of his previous inner development. Whatever may have been the exact motives that drove the young master of arts and student of law into the monastery, once its doors had closed behind him he was a monk with all his heart and mind and soul. Not to be outdone by any of his fellow-monks, he resolutely strove to fulfill his every obligation, succeeding so well in his sincere endeavor that not even Heinrich Denifle, his modern archenemy, could detect any evidence to the contrary. He had been an upright man before he took the decisive step, and now he tried vigorously to increase in goodness and to hitch his wagon to the star of moral perfection. The outcome of these long and arduous labors was the painful discovery that the goal he had set for himself seemed ever out of reach, constantly receding while he pursued it hotly. It should perhaps be noted that in his ceaseless striving for irreproachable moral goodness his idea of what was morally good underwent progressive deepening and expansion. There is reason to think that he would probably have attained his goal if he had retained the concept of the good with which he had entered the monastery and which apparently rather satisfied him even in the earlier years of his monastic life. But the more he reflected on the nature of the good and the more earnestly he devoted himself to the study of the Scriptures, the more his uncertainty as to whether he was really advancing in his religious pursuits increased and weighed upon him.

We are fortunate enough to possess some remarkable literary records of his incessant struggle for more moral insight. Among the most precious documents clearly attesting to his spiritual growth are his university lectures on the Psalter, delivered from 1513 to 1516. Especially the lectures on the first psalm are a moving account of his unending wrestling with the problem and of his seeing the first glimmer of light on the new path on which he was, but few years later, boldly to lead much of Europe out of what might very fairly be called its moral complacency. By the time he began to lecture on Paul's Epistle to the Romans, in 1515, he was wholly in the clear, theoretically at least, and his characteristic view of the nature of the good had burst into full bloom. By 1515 at the very latest, his specific ideas on God and man and their mutual relationship had fully emerged. The work-laden years of the monk, priest, preacher, and professor had borne rich fruit. His heart and head were filed to overflowing with a "new" message or, to be more exact, with one that had long been forgotten. Luther, surveying the world in which he lived and moved, must have felt many a time, certainly since 1514 or 1515, that he had something important to say to his contemporaries. It is not at all improbable that in certain moments of heightened awareness and introspection he may have harbored the notion that the world was out of joint and that he was born to set it right. At any rate, the urge to penetrate beyond academic and monastic confines was partially gratified by ascending the pulpit and preaching to the people of Wittenberg. The great popularity and pronounced success he won as a preacher doubtless increased his ambition to give an even wider circulation to the religious ideas which were so enthusiastically and gratefully received by town and gown. A definite message, won in intense personal struggle, and the understandable desire to share the answer he had found inevitably put the pen in his eager hand. It cannot have taken him long to realize that, in addition to his proved mastery of the spoken word, he also had an extraordinary gift to express himself readily in the writing of the vernacular. His incredible powers as a writer cannot but have inspired him to go on to greater heights as a mover of men's minds. By the beginning of 1517, perhaps already before the end of 1516, he sat down and, for the first time in his life thus far, wrote a Goethean confession of faith in that language in which he was so soon to become a past master.

What the modern reader, weighing the intrepidness of the man's first attack upon generally prevailing ideas of the age, should ever bear in mind is that this severe book with all its harshness and even rashness was anything but the chance product of an irresponsible mind hungry to create a sensation. Instead, it is quite important to remember that *Die sieben Busspsalmen* was only the next further step that had to be taken after the preliminary work of the early university lectures and popular sermons: logically and psychologically, the evolution toward the German tract was both natural and inevitable. Responsibility rather than irresponsibility is the keynote of the new prophet. He could no longer withhold from the largest possible number the profoundly satisfying answer he had found after so many years of seeking. In an ever-expanding circle, from the lonely cell via the lecture hall and the pulpit, his course had taken him by 1517 to the forum where the whole nation could hear his voice: the German book. And the nation to which he addressed himself did listen. That it did listen so attentively to the difficult fare the famous professor placed before it surely redounds to its everlasting credit. Students of Luther have always marvelled that the common man read the challenging works as eagerly as he did. The author on whose lips he hung did not flatter him in the least. On the contrary, he mercilessly tore the mask of respectability off his face. It is little short of miraculous to behold that so tremendously serious a writer as Luther found a reading public of then unparalleled dimensions.

We had noticed that Luther refers only very briefly to the straightforward sinner, the ordinary idea of the Old Man. The preponderant majority of his utterances on the Old Man deal with a highly refined, inner conception of sin, a conception so inclusive that all men, even the best among them, are almost automatically classified as sinners. In no uncertain terms the Augustinian monk, disdaining to write at length on his basic hostility to the kind of open sin that everybody could easily detect, insisted vigorously that the way of life of what would commonly be called a good and just man is essentially evil and unjust and must therefore perish. The strangeness of this view of man does not keep Luther from believing it can be grasped by the average man, else he would not have spent a whole lifetime, beginning with *Die sieben Busspsalmen,* to expound it in detail over and over again.

Still, despite his hope—stronger to be sure in his youth than with the advancing years—that men would flock to his standards, there is discernible even in his earliest publication the uncomfortable realization that his is the voice of one crying in the wilderness. There is no doubt that Germany and Europe at large are overcrowded with theologians and priests. Yet all of them, with practically no exception of which Luther is aware, preach in an altogether different strain. Their preaching is of

course not immoral; far from it, it is very moral. In fact, the exhortation to live morally is at the very heart of their earnest preaching. Luther fully recognizes that they admonish their equally serious audiences to lead exemplary lives, and he freely admits that both clergy and laity exert themselves in many instances to their utmost in their concern for morality.

It is such preachers and such listeners, the very cream of Christian society, that Luther felt constrained to single out for his first major attack. These respectable men and women he identifies most closely, almost to the exclusion of ordinary sinners, with the Old Man. He spares no word in his assault upon their supposedly firm ramparts. Without the least perceptible hesitation he calls them "the most unrighteous" of all men, immeasurably worse than the most hardened sinners. In an impassioned passage he goes so far as to designate these pillars of church and state as the real as well as the only enemies Christendom has ever had in the past, has now in the present, and ever will have in the future. Nobody wars against the essence of the Christian religion more fiercely or more fundamentally than these apparently model people, looked up to by their less rigorous fellows and generally held in highest esteem.

In order to do a measure of justice to Luther's easily misunderstood pitiless onslaught it should always be borne in mind that he is here concerned with Christians, not with non-Christians no matter how high their ethical striving. Naturally Luther is far from denying that these valiant souls are sincerely working for, and sometimes even attaining, a considerable degree of justice and righteousness. Philosophically and humanly speaking, their eager search for the moral life is admirable and ever to be encouraged. If Aristotelian ethics were valid for Christians, all would be well, and Luther would either hold his peace or, what is more likely, join the throng of those devoted preachers untiringly urging their congregations to greater efforts in the quest for self-improvement. But for Martin Luther, primarily interested in re-establishing and preserving the uniqueness of the Christian message, the Aristotelian and even Thomistic conceptions of the righteousness required of men before God are basically wrong. While Aristotelian ethics, being a system of natural and philosophical ethics, will obviously do for pre-Christian and extra-Christian society, it is in Luther's opinion utterly inadequate within the Christian dispensation. At the heart of the Christian religion there is according to him a totally different idea of righteousness. The core of Luther's adamant opposition to the Christian church of his day resides in this very fact. It is not too much to say that the entire Lutheran Reformation springs from the early realization on the part of Luther that Christianity had largely forgotten its original genius and that it had consequently lost its mark of distinction.

Luther is therefore quite willing to concede that the earnest Christians of his generation possess all sorts of wisdom and justice except what he holds to be authentic *Christian* justice and wisdom. With all their resplendent goodness and their tireless pursuit of righteousness they lack the one thing needful, the only thing that makes one a Christian, namely, the righteousness that dwells in the cross of Christ. Insisting on this theology of the cross and its central significance for Christianity, Luther harshly charges that no one in the whole wide world fights more vehemently against Christ and the meaning of the cross than these would-be saints. Paradoxical as it may seem on the surface, the first are told that they are the last. Those who would rank highest in a human theory of justice are bluntly informed that they are lowest in the divine reckoning as revealed to Christians in the Scriptures. This judgment above all is the revolutionary note in the first book Luther published under his name.

The reasons for this Pauline-Augustinian view of man as held by Luther are not far to seek. So far as Luther himself is concerned, it is now agreed among informed Catholics and Protestants alike that he took God, God's relation to man, and man's relation to God exceedingly seriously, measuring all things by divine standards as set forth in the Bible. In the light of the moral requirements laid down there, Luther was compelled to admit that man's *seemingly* good works are not *really* good at all. Now those who strive after the moral life, i.e., actually the elite of men, have fallen prey to the idea that their noble deeds, often wrested from their resisting flesh, are worthy of being considered by God. In other words, their seemingly good works have made a fairly strong impression upon them. Subtly they have been led to take pleasure in their own piety, especially since it shines so brightly when compared with the obvious impiety of the multitude of men that do not care in the least. Their inner satisfaction with themselves, so easy to understand on the one hand, causes them on the other hand to love their own achievement in spiritual things even more than coarse sinners love fleshly things. It is their very eminence over their less spiritually concerned fellowmen which becomes their pitfall. They are pleased with what they have accomplished, and they think highly of themselves. Such an attitude Luther cannot but call the greatest blindness on earth.

Earnestly Luther recalls to them and to himself that all men are unrighteous in the sight of God. No matter how disagreeable or difficult the thought, the plain fact is that this situation before God applies not only to the ordinary sinner but also to those who exercise themselves in works of righteousness hoping thereby to get away from the unrighteousness of which they are so keenly aware. It is these morally sensitive people who have to be told over and over again that they cannot possibly work their way out of their fundamental unrighteousness. The highest act of which they are capable is thus condemned as the cause of their undoing before God. Although he fully realizes that he will shock the "just," Luther, bound by the word of God as he understood it, made bold to proclaim that those who strive to free themselves from sin are damned because of this very effort. Whoever regards himself as pious and takes consolation in his works, has not yet succeeded in knowing either himself or the God of the Bible. He has not yet come face to face with his real self as the word of God requires him to do. As long as a man thinks he can approach God by his own works, he belongs in Luther's judgment to the self-wise who teach the righteousness of men rather than the righteousness that avails before God. Thinking themselves wise they actually ascribe to themselves the honor solely due to God: instead of humbly permitting themselves to be justified, they proudly wish to achieve their own justification. Their ignorance of what constitutes the essence of sin in God's view is little short of catastrophic; they are charged by Luther not to penetrate beyond externals in that they fear God's judgment only in their manifestly evil deeds but not in their so-called good ones. Itching to be something by their own strength, they are thereby automatically excluded from becoming "material" with which God is willing to work. The almost insuperable difficulty resides in the fact that the "holy, all-too-holy" cannot be brought to a real experience of God's anger and of their own sin. Recklessly, they take themselves to be the most religious of all men. The root of the trouble is that they refuse to follow

God beyond what they can see with their own eyes; they insist, stubbornly, on understanding and comprehending God. After all has been said and done, they really throw in their lot with human reason, thereby declining to accept revelation as contained in the Bible. What they fail to see, because of their faith in human reason, is that good works not proceeding from divine grace are downright impious and unacceptable in God's sight. Thus all their moral striving must be adjudged to be in vain. Fighting the good fight in their opinion, they are nevertheless losing it. In their seeming justice they really war against true justice. The refusal to live steadfastly in the *via crucis* ["way of the cross"] and the failure to direct their attention away from themselves to God, mar all their well-intentioned acts. It makes no difference how their "good" works shine before men; they fool themselves if they hope to attain salvation in this human way. Following the light of reason with arrogance, they commit the grave error of shunning the only force that counts in these matters, faith. In their blindness they reach for Christ's own seat of judgment, allowing what seems rational to them to usurp the place of the revealed scheme of salvation, which has to be appropriated by faith and can never be apprehended and comprehended by reason.

Thus in a bold sweep Luther has led his readers to see that lack of faith is the essential and ultimate characteristic of the Old Man. (pp. 107-16)

It goes without saying that the religious thinker who had such a penetrating conception of the nature of the Old Man may be expected to have reflected just as keenly on the nature of the New Man. We shall now turn to a brief consideration of the ideal that Luther placed before the astonished eyes of his contemporaries.

Just as little as the Old Man was primarily, if indeed at all, an ordinary sinner or criminal, the New Man is not simply an upright individual in the usual meaning of that phrase. In fact, we have already found that this sort of respectable citizen is, for Luther at any rate, the veritable embodiment of the Old Man as he saw him. Since the New Man as commonly conceived is only the Old Man when thoroughly analyzed, Luther's idea of the New Man must be something radically and fundamentally different from the non-Lutheran picture. So it is.

The chief quality of the New Man is according to Luther first and foremost a profound conviction that he is every inch a sinner before God. He is of course aware that the life he is apt to lead is outwardly above reproach and that he is thus regarded as a valuable, even a model, member of society. He is just as sure of his good standing in civil estate as he is of his utter failing in the sight of God. It is this honest insight into his total sinfulness face to face with God which first starts him on the road to the New Man. However spotless and law-abiding he may be in the eyes of the world, and however much he may have to agree with his fellow-citizens that he is more than pulling his weight in communal and personal life, he nevertheless fully agrees with God's judgment of himself: he is in every aspect a lost sinner. Graciously he has been led to recognize more and more that his supposed piety, of which he himself may have boasted if ever so little, is in truth nothing but sin when God's standards are applied. Luther knows full well that the attainment of this knowledge of the self is no easy matter. Without a searching inquiry into one's ultimate motives it is impossible to begin to reach it. Since many refuse to examine themselves to this extent, they cannot understand why a model citizen and friend, whom they probably admire and may even try to emulate, should consider himself to be in reality an abject sinner. That is precisely the reason why Luther asserts time and again that nobody can become a New Creature without the deepest experience of his sinfulness. It is indispensable to have lain in the dust before God and to have cried out in contrition and terror. To have been alone with God and to have found oneself wanting are necessary prerequisites: without a trembling conscience in the encounter with God there is no path open into the realm of the New Man. (pp. 117-18)

The New Man then is the rare creature which, having come to the end of his own resources, is granted the vision that he must make a complete about-face. Though his inner resources are usually ampler than those of his more ordinary fellows, he has been led to believe that salvation does not lie in man's "active" striving but in his "passive" reception of the gift of that righteousness which God demands.

At the end of this brief presentation of Luther's early view of man we may perhaps be permitted to make some general statements about the work here analyzed. First of all, there is the matter of the amazing maturity of Luther's initial publication. In practically every essential aspect his theology appears to be fully developed or at least very near completion. This is of course not as surprising to us in the twentieth century as it would or should have been to earlier generations of scholars. The discovery and subsequent publication of the **Lectures on Romans,** delivered by Luther in 1515 and 1516, showed us in the first decade of our century how very far his theological thought had progressed by 1515. The significance of **Die sieben Busspsalmen**, in which similarly mature views are uttered, is partly to be found in the fact that this work was the first ever to be published by Luther himself. The Latin Lectures were intended for a restricted academic audience, and they were not made available to the public by Luther. Thus the first clear indication of what the celebrated professor, preacher, and prior meant was contained in the modest little book we have examined. It is, like its more famous brother **Von der Freiheit eines Christenmenschen,** small in size but of extraordinary importance embracing as it does the whole sum and substance of the Christian life. The German people as a whole received their first definite impression of what the Wittenberg friar was really after from this tract.

This fact of major historical interest does not, however, exhaust the significance of the work under review. It contains the gist of the ideas that Luther was prepared to lay before a larger public. The great early Latin Lectures on Psalms and Romans include much more than Luther actually communicated to even an intelligent student body. Only the notes taken by students give us, when compared with Luther's own manuscript, a rough idea of how little he saw fit to place even before an academic audience. In **Die sieben Busspsalmen** on the other hand we find what he was ready to submit, under his name, to the entire German reading public. This work was written for publication and presents thus the first formulation of the view of God and man that was to resound throughout Europe and to shake that continent to its foundations. From this point of view the significance of **Die sieben Busspsalmen** is almost incalculable. (pp. 121-22)

> *Heinz Bluhm, "Luther's View of Man in His First Published Work," in* Harvard Theological Review, *Vol. 41, No. 2, April, 1948, pp. 103-22.*

ROLAND H. BAINTON (essay date 1950)

[*Bainton was an American educator and scholar of religious history. In the following excerpt from his highly regarded biography*

of Luther, he discusses Luther's historical stature and wide-ranging influence on Germany, the church, and religious life, explicating four of his major works, Ninety-Five Theses, Babylonian Captivity, Address to the German Nobility, *and* Table Talk.]

On a sultry day in July of the year 1505 a lonely traveler was trudging over a parched road on the outskirts of the Saxon village of Stotternheim. He was a young man, short but sturdy, and wore the dress of a university student. As he approached the village, the sky became overcast. Suddenly there was a shower, then a crashing storm. A bolt of lightning rived the gloom and knocked the man to the ground. Struggling to rise, he cried in terror, "St. Anne help me! I will become a monk."

The man who thus called upon a saint was later to repudiate the cult of the saints. He who vowed to become a monk was later to renounce monasticism. A loyal son of the Catholic Church, he was later to shatter the structure of medieval Catholicism. A devoted servant of the pope, he was later to identify the popes with Antichrist. For this young man was Martin Luther.

His demolition was the more devastating because it reinforced disintegrations already in progress. Nationalism was in process of breaking the political unities when the Reformation destroyed the religious. Yet this paradoxical figure revived the Christian consciousness of Europe. In his day, as Catholic historians all agree, the popes of the Renaissance were secularized, flippant, frivolous, sensual, magnificent, and unscrupulous. The intelligentsia did not revolt against the Church because the Church was so much of their mind and mood as scarcely to warrant a revolt. Politics were emancipated from any concern for the faith to such a degree that the Most Christian King of France and His Holiness the Pope did not disdain a military alliance with the Sultan against the Holy Roman Emperor. Luther changed all this. Religion became again a dominant factor even in politics for another century and a half. Men cared enough for the faith to die for it and to kill for it. If there is any sense remaining of Christian civilization in the West, this man Luther in no small measure deserves the credit.

Very naturally he is a controversial figure. The multitudinous portrayals fall into certain broad types already delineated in his own generation. His followers hailed him as the prophet of the Lord and the deliverer of Germany. His opponents on the Catholic side called him the son of perdition and the demolisher of Christendom. The agrarian agitators branded him as the sycophant of the princes, and the radical sectaries compared him to Moses, who led the children of Israel out of Egypt and left them to perish in the wilderness. (pp. 21-2)

• • • • •

[**Ninety-Five Theses**] differed from the ordinary propositions for debate because they were forged in anger. The ninety-five affirmations are crisp, bold, unqualified. In the ensuing discussion he explained his meaning more fully. The following summary draws alike on the **Theses** and the subsequent explications. There were three main points: an objection to the avowed object of the expenditure [of the money raised from the sale of indulgences], a denial of the powers of the pope over purgatory, and a consideration of the welfare of the sinner.

The attack focused first on the ostensible intent to spend the money in order to shelter the bones of St. Peter beneath a universal shrine of Christendom. Luther retorted:

> The revenues of all Christendom are being sucked
> into this insatiable basilica. The Germans laugh at

calling this the common treasure of Christendom. Before long all the churches, palaces, walls, and bridges of Rome will be built out of our money. First of all we should rear living temples, next local churches, and only last of all St. Peter's, which is not necessary for us. We Germans cannot attend St. Peter's. Better that it should never be built than that our parochial churches should be despoiled. The pope would do better to appoint one good pastor to a church than to confer indulgences upon them all. Why doesn't the pope build the basilica of St. Peter out of his own money? He is richer than Croesus. He would do better to sell St. Peter's and give the money to the poor folk who are being fleeced by the hawkers of indulgences. If the pope knew the exactions of these vendors, he would rather that St. Peter's should lie in ashes than that it should be built out of the blood and hide of his sheep.

This polemic would evoke a deep *Ja wohl* among the Germans, who for some time had been suffering from a sense of grievance against the venality of the Italian *curia* and often quite overlooked the venality of the German confederates. Luther lent himself to this distortion by accepting Albert's picture of the money going all to Rome rather than to the coffers of the Fuggers. Yet in a sense Albert's picture was right. He was only being reimbursed for money which had already gone to Rome. In any case, however, the financial aspect was the least in Luther's eyes. He was ready to undercut the entire practice even though not a gulden left Wittenberg.

His second point denied the power of the pope over purgatory for the remission of either sin or penalty. The absolution of sin is given to the contrite in the sacrament of penance.

> Papal indulgences do not remove guilt. Beware of those who say that indulgences effect reconciliation with God. The power of the keys cannot make attrition into contrition. He who is contrite has plenary remission of guilt and penalty without indulgences. The pope can remove only those penalties which he himself has imposed on earth, for Christ did not say, "Whatsoever I have bound in heaven you may loose on earth."

The penalties of purgatory the pope cannot reduce because these have been imposed by God, and the pope does not have at his disposal a treasury of credits available for transfer.

> The saints have no extra credits. Every saint is bound to love God to the utmost. There is no such thing as supererogation. If there were any superfluous credits, they could not be stored up for subsequent use. The Holy Spirit would have used them fully long ago. Christ indeed had merits, but until I am better instructed I deny that they are indulgences. His merits are freely available without the keys of the pope.

> Therefore I claim that the pope has no jurisdiction over purgatory. I am willing to reverse this judgment if the Church so pronounces. If the pope does have the power to release anyone from purgatory, why in the name of love does he not abolish purgatory by letting everyone out? If for the sake of miserable money he released uncounted souls, why should he not for the sake of most holy love empty the place? To say that souls are liberated from purgatory is audacious. To say they are released as soon as the coin in the coffer rings is to incite avarice. The pope would do better to give away everything without charge. The only power which the pope has over purgatory is that of making intercession on behalf of souls, and

this power is exercised by any priest or curate in his parish.

Luther's attack thus far could in no sense be regarded as heretical or original. Even though Albert's instructions rested on papal bulls, there had as yet been no definite pronouncement, and many theologians would have endorsed Luther's claims.

But he had a more devastating word:

> Indulgences are positively harmful to the recipient because they impede salvation by diverting charity and inducing a false sense of security. Christians should be taught that he who gives to the poor is better than he who receives a pardon. He who spends his money for indulgences instead of relieving want receives not the indulgence of the pope but the indignation of God. We are told that money should be given by preference to the poor only in the case of extreme necessity. I suppose we are not to clothe the naked and visit the sick. What is extreme necessity? Why, I ask, does natural humanity have such goodness that it gives itself freely and does not calculate necessity but is rather solicitous that there should not be any necessity? And will the charity of God, which is incomparably kinder, do none of these things? Did Christ say, "Let him that has a cloak sell it and buy an indulgence"? Love covers a multitude of sins and is better than all the pardons of Jerusalem and Rome.

> Indulgences are most pernicious because they induce complacency and thereby imperil salvation. Those persons are damned who think that letters of indulgence make them certain of salvation. God works by contraries so that a man feels himself to be lost in the very moment when he is on the point of being saved. When God is about to justify a man, he damns him. Whom he would make alive he must first kill. God's favor is so communicated in the form of wrath that it seems farthest when it is at hand. Man must first cry out that there is no health in him. He must be consumed with horror. This is the pain of purgatory. I do not know where it is located, but I do not know that it can be experienced in this life. I know a man who has gone through such pains that had they lasted for one tenth of an hour he would have been reduced to ashes. In this disturbance salvation begins. When a man believes himself to be utterly lost, light breaks. Peace comes in the word of Christ through faith. He who does not have this is lost even though he be absolved a million times by the pope, and he who does have it may not wish to be released from purgatory, for true contrition seeks penalty. Christians should be encouraged to bear the cross. He who is baptized into Christ must be as a sheep for the slaughter. The merits of Christ are vastly more potent when they bring crosses than when they bring remissions.

Luther's *Ninety-Five Theses* ranged all the way from the complaints of aggrieved Germans to the cries of a wrestler in the night watches. One portion demanded financial relief, the other called for the crucifixion of the self. The masses could grasp the first. Only a few elect spirits would ever comprehend the full import of the second, and yet in the second lay all the power to create a popular revolution. Complaints of financial extortion had been voiced for over a century without visible effect. Men were stirred to deeds only by one who regarded indulgences not merely as venal but as blasphemy against the holiness and mercy of God.

Luther took no steps to spread his theses among the people. He was merely inviting scholars to dispute and dignitaries to define, but others surreptitiously translated the theses into German and gave them to the press. In short order they became the talk of Germany. What Karl Barth said of his own unexpected emergence as a reformer could be said equally of Luther, that he was like a man climbing in the darkness a winding staircase in the steeple of an ancient cathedral. In the blackness he reached out to steady himself, and his hand laid hold of a rope. He was startled to hear the clanging of a bell. (pp. 80-3)

• • • • •

During the summer of 1520 [Luther] delivered to the printer a sheaf of tracts which are still often referred to as his primary works: *The Sermon on Good Works* in May, *The Papacy at Rome* in June, and *The Address to the German Nobility* in August, *The Babylonian Captivity* in September, and *The Freedom of the Christian Man* in November. (p. 136)

The most radical of them all in the eyes of contemporaries was the one dealing with the sacraments, entitled *The Babylonian Captivity*, with reference to the enslavement of the sacraments by the Church. This assault on Catholic teaching was more devastating than anything that had preceded; and when Erasmus read the tract, he ejaculated, ''The breach is irreparable.'' The reason was that the pretensions of the Roman Catholic Church rest so completely upon the sacraments as the exclusive channels of grace and upon the prerogatives of the clergy, by whom the sacraments are exclusively administered. If sacramentalism is undercut, then sacerdotalism is bound to fall. Luther with one stroke reduced the number of the sacraments from seven to two. Confirmation, marriage, ordination, penance, and extreme unction were eliminated. The Lord's Supper and baptism alone remained. The principle which dictated this reduction was that a sacrament must have been directly instituted by Christ and must be distinctively Christian.

The removal of confirmation and extreme unction was not of tremendous import save that it diminished the control of the Church over youth and death. The elimination of penance was much more serious because this is the rite of the forgiveness of sins. Luther in this instance did not abolish it utterly. Of the three ingredients of penance he recognized of course the need for contrition and looked upon confession as useful, provided it was not institutionalized. The drastic point was with regard to absolution, which he said is only a declaration by man of what God has decreed in heaven and not a ratification by God of what man has ruled on earth.

The repudiation of ordination as a sacrament demolished the caste system of clericalism and provided a sound basis for the priesthood of all believers, since according to Luther ordination is simply a rite of the Church by which a minister is installed to discharge a particular office. He receives no indelible character, is not exempt from the jurisdiction of the civil courts, and is not empowered by ordination to perform the other sacraments. At this point what the priest does any Christian may do, if commissioned by the congregation, because all Christians are priests. (pp. 137-38)

But Luther's rejection of the five sacraments might even have been tolerated had it not been for the radical transformation which he effected in the two which he retained. From his view of baptism he was to infer a repudiation of monasticism on the ground that it is not a second baptism, and no vow should ever be taken beyond the baptismal vow.

Most serious of all was Luther's reduction of the mass to the Lord's Supper. The mass is central for the entire Roman Cath-

olic system because the mass is believed to be a repetition of the Incarnation and the Crucifixion. When the bread and wine are transubstantiated, God again becomes flesh and Christ again dies upon the altar. This wonder can be performed only by priests empowered through ordination. Inasmuch as this means of grace is administered exclusively by their hands, they occupy a unique place within the Church; and because the Church is the custodian of the body of Christ, she occupies a unique place in society.

Luther did not attack the mass in order to undermine the priests. His concerns were always primarily religious and only incidentally ecclesiastical or sociological. His first insistence was that the sacrament of the mass must be not magical but mystical, not the performance of a rite but the experience of a presence. . . . The teaching of the Church is that the sacraments cannot be impaired by any human weakness, be it the unworthiness of the performer or the indifference of the receiver. The sacrament operates by virtue of a power within itself *ex opere operato*. In Luther's eyes such a view made the sacrament mechanical and magical. He, too, had no mind to subject it to human frailty and would not concede that he had done so by positing the necessity of faith, since faith is itself a gift of God, but this faith is given by God when, where, and to whom he will and even without the sacrament is efficacious; whereas the reverse is not true, that the sacrament is of efficacy without faith. ''I may be wrong on indulgences,'' declared Luther, ''but as to the need for faith in the sacraments I will die before I will recant.'' This insistence upon faith diminished the role of the priest who may place a wafer in the mouth but cannot engender faith in the heart.

The second point made by Luther was that the priest is not in a position to do that which the Church claims in the celebration of the mass. He does not ''make God,'' and he does not ''sacrifice Christ.'' The simplest way of negating this view would have been to say that God is not present and Christ is not sacrificed, but Luther was ready to affirm only the latter. Christ is not sacrificed because his sacrifice was made once and for all upon the cross, but God is present in the elements because Christ, being God, declared, ''This is my body.'' The repetition of these words by the priest, however, does not transform the bread and wine into the body and blood of God, as the Catholic Church holds. The view called transubstantiation was that the elements retain their accidents of shape, taste, color, and so on, but lose their substance, for which is substituted the substance of God. Luther rejected this position less on rational than on biblical grounds. Both Erasmus and Melanchthon before him had pointed out that the concept of substance is not biblical but a scholastic sophistication. For that reason Luther was averse to its use at all, and his own view should not be called consubstantiation. The sacrament for him was not a chunk of God fallen like a meteorite from heaven. God does not need to fall from heaven because he is everywhere present throughout his creation as a sustaining and animating force, and Christ as God is likewise universal, but his presence is hid from human eyes. For that reason God has chosen to declare himself unto mankind at three loci of revelation. The first is Christ, in whom the Word was made flesh. The second is Scripture, where the Word uttered is recorded. The third is the sacrament, in which the Word is manifest in food and drink. The sacrament does not conjure up God as the witch of Endor but reveals him where he is.

To the degree that the powers of the priest were diminished, his prerogatives also were curtailed. In Catholic practice one of the distinctions between the clergy and the laity is that only the priest drinks the wine at the mass. The restriction arose out of the fear that the laity in clumsiness might spill some of the blood of God. Luther felt no less reverence for the sacrament, but he would not safeguard it at the expense of a caste system within the Church. Despite the risk, the cup should be given to all believers. This pronouncement in his day had an uncommon ring of radicalism because the chalice for the laity was the cry of the Bohemian Hussites. They justified their practice on the ground that Christ said, ''Drink ye all of it.'' Catholic interpreters explain these words as addressed only to the apostles, who were all priests. Luther agreed, but retorted that all believers are priests.

Such a view was fraught with far-reaching consequences for the theory of the Church, and Luther's own view of the Church was derivative from his theory of the sacraments. His deductions, however, were not clear-cut in this area, because his view of the Lord's Supper pointed in one direction and his view of baptism in another. That is why he could be at once to a degree the father of the congregationalism of the Anabaptists and of the territorial church of the later Lutherans.

His view of the Lord's Supper made for the gathered church of convinced believers only, because he declared that the sacrament depends for its efficacy upon the faith of the recipient. That must of necessity make it highly individual because faith is individual. Every soul, insisted Luther, stands in naked confrontation before its Maker. No one can die in the place of another; everyone must wrestle with the pangs of death for himself alone. ''Then I shall not be with you, nor you with me. Everyone must answer for himself.'' Similarly, ''The mass is a divine promise which can help no one, be applied for no one, intercede for no one, and be communicated to none save him only who believes with a faith of his own. Who can accept or apply for another the promise of God which requires faith of each individually?''

Here we are introduced to the very core of Luther's individualism. It is not the individualism of the Renaissance, seeking the fulfillment of the individual's capacities; it is not the individualism of the late scholastics, who on metaphysical grounds declared that reality consists only of individuals, and that aggregates like Church and state are not entities but simply the sum of their components. Luther was not concerned to philosophize about the structure of Church and state; his insistence was simply that every man must answer for himself to God. That was the extent of his individualism. The faith requisite for the sacrament must be one's own. From such a theory the obvious inference is that the Church should consist only of those possessed of a warm personal faith; and since the number of such persons is never large, the Church would have to be a comparatively small conventicle. Luther not infrequently spoke precisely as if this were his meaning. Especially in his earlier lectures he had delineated a view of the Church as a remnant because the elect are few. This must be so, he held, because the Word of God goes counter to all the desires of the natural man, abasing pride, crushing arrogance, and leaving all human pretensions in dust and ashes. Such a work is unpalatable, and few will receive it. Those who do will be stones rejected by the builders. Derision and persecution will be their lot. Every Abel is bound to have his Cain, and every Christ his Caiaphas. Therefore the true Church will be despised and rejected of men and will lie hidden in the midst of the world. These words of Luther might readily issue in the substitution for the Catholic monastery of the segregated Protestant community.

But Luther was not willing to take this road because the sacrament of baptism pointed for him in another direction. He could readily enough have accommodated baptism to the preceding view, had he been willing, like the Anabaptists, to regard baptism as the outward sign of an inner experience of regeneration appropriate only to adults and not to infants. But this he would not do. Luther stood with the Catholic Church on the score of infant baptism because children must be snatched at birth from the power of Satan. But what then becomes of his formula that the efficacy of the sacrament depends upon the faith of the recipient? He strove hard to retain it by the figment of an implicit faith in the baby comparable to the faith of a man in sleep. But again Luther would shift from the faith of the child to the faith of the sponsor by which the infant is undergirded. Birth for him was not so isolated as death. One cannot die for another, but one can in a sense be initiated for another into a Christian community. For that reason baptism rather than the Lord's Supper is the sacrament which links the Church to society. It is the sociological sacrament. For the medieval community every child outside the ghetto was by birth a citizen and by baptism a Christian. Regardless of personal conviction the same persons constituted the state and the Church. An alliance of the two institutions was thus natural. Here was a basis for a Christian society. The greatness and the tragedy of Luther was that he could never relinquish either the individualism of the eucharistic cup or the corporateness of the baptismal font. He would have been a troubled spirit in a tranquil age. (pp.138-42)

• • • • •

A mighty program of reformation was delineated by Luther in the *Address to the German Nobility.* The term ''nobility'' was broadly used to cover the ruling class in Germany, from the emperor down. But by what right, the modern reader may well inquire, might Luther call upon them to reform the Church? The question has more than an antiquarian interest, because some contend that in this tract Luther broke with his earlier view of the Church as a persecuted remnant and laid instead the basis for a church allied with and subservient to the state. Luther adduced three grounds for his appeal. The first was simply that the magistrate was the magistrate, ordained of God to punish evildoers. All that Luther demanded of the magistrate as magistrate was that he should hale the clergy before the civil courts, protect citizens against ecclesiastical extortion, and vindicate the state in the exercise of civil functions from clerical interference. This was the sense in which Luther often asserted that no one in a thousand years had so championed the civil state as he. The theocratic pretensions of the Church were to be repulsed.

The *Address to the German Nobility,* however, goes far beyond a mere circumscribing of the Church to her proper sphere. Luther was much less concerned for the emancipation of the state than for the purification of the Church. The stripping away of temporal power and inordinate wealth was designed to emancipate the Church from worldly cares that she might better perform her spiritual functions. The basis of the right of the magistrate to undertake this reform is stated in Luther's second reason, namely, ''The temporal authorities are baptized with the same baptism as we.'' This is the language of the Christian society, built upon the sociological sacrament administered to every babe born into the community. In such a society, Church and state are mutually responsible for the support and correction of each other.

Engraved title page of Luther's polemic Address to the Nobility of the German Nation *(1520).*

understand the mind of Christ. "Balaam's ass was wiser than
the prophet himself. If God then spoke by an ass against a
prophet, why should he not be able even now to speak by a
righteous man against the pope?" The third wall was that the
pope alone could call a council. Here again the priesthood of
all believers gave the right to anyone in an emergency, but
peculiarly to the civil power because of its strategic position.

Then follow all the proposals for the reforms to be instituted
by a council. The papacy should return to apostolic simplicity,
with no more triple crown and no toe kissing. The pope should
not receive the sacrament seated, proffered to him by a kneeling
cardinal through a golden reed, but should stand up like any
other "stinking sinner." The cardinals should be reduced in
number. The temporal possessions and claims of the Church
should be abandoned that the pope might devote himself only
to spiritual concerns. The income of the Church should be
curtailed—no more annates, fees, indulgences, golden years,
reservations, crusading taxes, and all the rest of the tricks by
which the "drunken Germans" were despoiled. Litigation in
Church courts involving Germans should be tried in Germany
under a German primate. This suggestion looked in the direction of a national church. For Bohemia it was definitely
recommended.

The proposals with regard to monasticism and clerical marriage
went beyond anything Luther had said previously. The mendicants should be relieved of hearing confession and preaching.
The number of orders should be reduced, and there should be
no irrevocable vows. The clergy should be permitted to marry
because they need housekeepers, and to place man and woman
together under such circumstances is like setting straw beside
fire and expecting it not to burn.

Miscellaneous recommendations called for the reduction of
Church festivals and a curb on pilgrimages. Saints should be
left to canonize themselves. The state should inaugurate legal
reform and undertake sumptuary legislation. This program was
comprehensive and for the most part would evoke hearty applause in Germany.

Underlying it all was a deep indignation against the corruption
of the Church. Again and again the pope was shamed by a
comparison with Christ. This theme went back through Hus to
Wyclif. An illustrated work in Bohemian on the disparity of
Christ and the pope was in the library of Frederick the Wise.
A similar work was later issued in Wittenberg with annotations
by Melanchthon and woodcuts by Cranach. The idea was already present in the *Address to the German Nobility,* where
reference was made to Christ on foot, the pope in a palanquin
with a retinue of three or four thousand mule drivers; Christ
washing the disciples' feet, the pope having his feet kissed;
Christ enjoining keeping faith even with an enemy, the pope
declaring that no faith is to be kept with him who has no faith,
and that promises to heretics are not binding. Still worse, constraint against them is employed. "But heretics should be vanquished with books, not with burnings. O Christ my Lord, look
down. Let the day of thy judgment break and destroy the devil's
nest at Rome!" (pp. 152-56)

• • • • •

Luther's *Table Talk* would deserve a notice if for no other
reason than its sheer volume. There are 6,596 entries, and it
is among the better known of his works because his students
after his death culled, classified, and produced a handy volume
adorned with a woodcut of Luther at the table with his family.
The classification obscures the lush profusion and unpredict-

In a third passage Luther gave the additional ground, that the
magistrates were fellow Christians sharing in the priesthood of
all believers, from which some modern historians have inferred
that Luther would concede to the magistrate the role of Church
reformer only if he were himself a convinced Christian, and
then only in an emergency. But no such qualification is stated
in this tract. The priesthood of all believers itself was made to
rest upon the lower grade of faith implicit in the baptized infant.
Luther's whole attitude to the reformatory role of the magistrate
is essentially medieval. What sets it off from so many other
attempts at the redress of grievances is its deeply religious
tone. The complaints of Germany were combined with the
reform of the Church, and the civil power itself was directed
to rely less on the arm of flesh than upon the hand of the Lord.

The program began with religious premises. Three walls of
Rome must tumble down like the walls of Jericho. The first
was that the spiritual power is above the temporal. This claim
Luther countered with the doctrine of the priesthood of all
believers. "We are all alike Christians and have baptism, faith,
the Spirit, and all things alike. If a priest is killed, a land is
laid under an interdict. Why not in the case of a peasant?
Whence comes this great distinction between those who are
called Christians?" The second wall was that the pope alone
might interpret Scripture. This assertion was met, not so much
by the vindication of the rights of Humanist scholarship against
papal incompetence, as by the claims of lay Christianity to

able variety of the original. Luther ranged from the ineffable majesty of God the Omnipotent to the frogs in the Elbe. Pigs, popes, pregnancies, politics, and proverbs jostle one another. Some random samples may convey a faint impression:

> The monks are the fleas on God Almighty's fur coat.
>
> When asked why he was so violent, Luther replied, "A twig can be cut with a bread knife, but an oak calls for an ax."
>
> God uses lust to impel men to marriage, ambition to office, avarice to earning, and fear to faith.
>
> The only portion of the human anatomy which the pope has had to leave uncontrolled is the hind end.
>
> Printing is God's latest and best work to spread the true religion throughout the world.
>
> I am a pillar of the pope. After I am gone he will fare worse.
>
> Birds lack faith. They fly away when I enter the orchard, though I mean them no ill. Even so do we lack faith in God.
>
> There are rumors that the world will end in 1532. I hope it won't be long. The last decade seems like a new century.
>
> A cartoon has appeared of me as a monster with seven heads. I must be invincible because they cannot overcome me when I have only one.
>
> A dog is a most faithful animal and would be more highly prized if less common.

(pp. 295-96)

The above selections speak well enough for themselves, but a word of comment is in order with regard to Luther's vulgarity, because he is often represented as inordinately coarse, and the *Table Talk* is cited by way of example. There is no denying that he was not fastidious, nor was his generation. Life itself stank. One could not walk around Wittenberg without encountering the odors of the pigsty, offal, and the slaughterhouse. And even the most genteel were not reticent about the facts of daily experience. Katie, when asked about the congregation on a day when Luther was unable to attend, replied, "The church was so full it stank." "Yes," said Luther, "they had manure on their boots." Erasmus did not hesitate to compose a colloquy in which the butcher and the fishmonger celebrated the offensiveness of each other's wares. Luther delighted less in muck than many of the literary men of his age; but if he did indulge, he excelled in this as in every other area of speech. The volume of coarseness, however, in his total output is slight. Detractors have sifted from the pitchblende of his ninety tomes a few pages of radioactive vulgarity. But there are whole volumes which contain nothing more offensive than a quotation from the apostle Paul, who "suffered the loss of all things," and counted them but dung, that he might win Christ. (pp. 296-98)

•　•　•　•　•

When one comes to take the measure of the man, there are three areas which naturally suggest themselves. The first is his own Germany. He called himself the German prophet, saying that against the papist asses he must assume so presumptuous a title, and he addressed himself to his beloved Germans. The claim is frequent that no man did so much to fashion the character of the German people. Their indifference to politics and their passion for music were already present in him. Their language was so far fashioned by his hand that the extent of

their indebtedness is difficult to recognize. If a German is asked whether a passage of Luther's Bible is not remarkable, he may answer that this is precisely the way in which any German would speak. But the reason is simply that every German has been reared on Luther's version. The influence of the man on his people was deepest in the home. In fact the home was the only sphere of life which the Reformation profoundly affected. Economics went the way of capitalism and politics the way of absolutism. But the home took on that quality of affectionate and godly patriarchalism which Luther had set as the pattern in his own household. The most profound impact of Luther on his people was in their religion. His sermons were read to the congregations, his liturgy was sung, his catechism was rehearsed by the father with the household, his Bible cheered the fainthearted and consoled the dying. If no Englishman occupies a similar place in the religious life of his people, it is because no Englishman had anything like Luther's range. The Bible translation in England was the work of Tyndale, the prayer book of Cranmer, the catechism of the Westminster divines. The sermonic style stemmed from Latimer; the hymnbook came from Watts. And not all of these lived in one century. Luther did the work of more than five men. And for sheer richness and exuberance of vocabulary and mastery of style he is to be compared only with Shakespeare.

The Germans naturally claim such a German for themselves. Yet when one begins to look over the centuries for those whom one would most naturally compare with this man, not a single one of his stature proves to be a German. In fact a German historian has said that in the course of three hundred years only one German ever really understood Luther, and that one was Johann Sebastian Bach. If one would discover parallels to Luther as the wrestler with the Lord, then one must turn to Paul the Jew, Augustine the Latin, Pascal the Frenchman, Kierkegaard the Dane, Unamuno the Spaniard, Dostoevski the Russian, Bunyan the Englishman, and Edwards the American.

And that is why in the second great area, that of the Church, Luther's influence extends so far beyond his own land. Lutheranism took possession of Scandinavia and has an extensive following in the United States, and apart from that his movement gave the impetus which sometimes launched and sometimes helped to establish the other varieties of Protestantism. They all stem in some measure from him. And what he did for his own people to a degree, he did also for others. His translation, for example, affected the English version. Tyndale's preface is taken from Luther. His liturgical reforms likewise had an influence on the *Book of Common Prayer*. And even the Catholic Church owes much to him. Often it is said that had Luther never appeared, an Erasmian reform would have triumphed, or at any rate a reform after the Spanish model. All of this is of course conjectural, but it is obvious that the Catholic Church received a tremendous shock from the Lutheran Reformation and a terrific urge to reform after its own pattern.

The third area is of all the most important and the only one which to Luther mattered much, and that is the area of religion. Here it is that he must be judged. In his religion he was a Hebrew, not a Greek fancying gods and goddesses disporting themselves about some limpid pool or banqueting upon Olympus. The God of Luther, as of Moses, was the God who inhabits the storm clouds and rides on the wings of the wind. At his nod the earth trembles, and the people before him are as a drop in the bucket. He is a God of majesty and power, inscrutable, terrifying, devastating, and consuming in his anger. Yet the

All Terrible is the All Merciful too. "Like as a father pitieth his children, so the Lord . . ." But how shall we know this? In Christ, only in Christ. In the Lord of life, born in the squalor of a cow stall and dying as a malefactor under the desertion and the derision of men, crying unto God and receiving for answer only the trembling of the earth and the blinding of the sun, even by God forsaken, and in that hour taking to himself and annihilating our iniquity, trampling down the hosts of hell and disclosing within the wrath of the All Terrible the love that will not let us go. No longer did Luther tremble at the rustling of a wind-blown leaf, and instead of calling upon St. Anne he declared himself able to laugh at thunder and jagged bolts from out the storm. This was what enabled him to utter such words as these: "Here I stand. I cannot do otherwise. God help me. Amen." (pp. 384-86)

Roland H. Bainton, in his Here I Stand: A Life of Martin Luther, *Abingdon-Cokesbury Press, 1950, 422 p.*

PAUL TILLICH   (lecture date 1953)

[*A Prussian-born American academic and Lutheran minister, Tillich is widely considered one of the most significant theologians of the twentieth century. In the following excerpt from a lecture given in 1953 and subsequently revised by Tillich's editor, he explicates several of Luther's essential doctrines.*]

The turning point of the Reformation and of church history in general is the experience of an Augustinian monk in his monastic cell—Martin Luther. Martin Luther did not merely teach different doctrines; others had done that also, such as Wyclif. But none of the others who protested against the Roman system were able to break through it. The only man who really made a breakthrough, and whose breakthrough has transformed the surface of the earth, was Martin Luther. This is his greatness. His greatness should not be measured by comparing him with Lutheranism; that is something quite different. Lutheranism is something which historically has been associated with Protestant Orthodoxy, political movements, Prussian conservatism, and what not. But Luther is different. He is one of the few great prophets of the Christian Church, and his greatness is overwhelming, even if it was limited by some of his personal traits and his later development. He is responsible for the fact that a purified Christianity, a Christianity of the Reformation, was able to establish itself on equal terms with the Roman tradition. From this point of view we must look at him. Therefore, when I speak of Luther, I am not speaking of the theologian who produced Lutheranism—many others contributed to this, and Melanchthon more than Luther—but of the man in whom the Roman system was broken through. . . . (p. 227)

Luther's breakthrough was externally occasioned by the sacrament of penance. There are two main sacraments in the Roman Church, the Mass, which is a part of the Lord's Supper, and the sacrament of penance, which is the subjective sacrament, dealing with the individual and having an immense educational function. This sacrament may be called the sacrament of subjectivity in contrast to the Mass as the pre-eminent sacrament of objectivity. The religious life in the Middle Ages moved between these two. Although Luther attacked the Mass, this was not the real point of criticism; the real issue had to do with the abuses connected with the sacrament of penance. The abuses stemmed from the fact that the sacrament of penance had different parts, contrition, confession, absolution,

and satisfaction. The first and last points were the most dangerous ones.

Contrition—the real repentance, the change of mind—was replaced by attrition, the fear of eternal punishment, which Luther called the repentance inspired by the imminent prospect of the gallows. So it had no religious value for him. The other dangerous point was satisfaction, which did not mean that you could earn your forgiveness of sins by works of satisfaction, but that you have to do them because the sin is still in you after it has been forgiven. The decisive thing is the humble subjection to the satisfactions demanded by the priest. The priest imposed on the *communicandus* all kinds of activities, sometimes so difficult that the people wanted to get rid of them. The church yielded to this desire in terms of indulgences, which are also sacrifices. One must sacrifice some money to buy the indulgences, and these indulgences remove the obligations to perform the works of satisfaction. The popular idea was that these satisfactions are effective in overcoming one's guilt consciousness. One can say that here a sort of marketing of eternal life was going on. A person could buy the indulgences and in this way get rid of the punishments, not only on earth but also in purgatory. The abuses brought Luther to think about the whole meaning of the sacrament of penance. This led him to conclusions absolutely opposed to the attitude of the Roman Church. Luther's criticisms were directed not only to the abuses but to the source of them in the doctrine itself. Thus Luther placed his famous ***Ninety-five Theses*** on the door of the Wittenberg church. The first of these is a classic formulation of Reformation Christianity: "Our Lord and Master, Jesus Christ, saying 'Repent ye,' wished that the whole life of the believers be penitence." This means that the sacramental act is only the form in which a much more universal attitude is expressed. What is important is the relationship to God. It is not a new doctrine but a new relationship to God which the Reformers brought about. The relationship is not an objective management between God and man, but a personal relationship of penitence first, and then faith.

Perhaps the most striking and paradoxical expression is given by Luther in the following words: "Penitence is something between injustice and justice.Therefore, whenever we are repenting, we are sinners, but nevertheless for this reason we are also righteous, and in the process of justification, partly sinners, partly righteous—that is nothing but repenting." This means that there is always something like repentance in the relationship to God. Luther did not at this time attack the sacrament of penance as such. He even thought that the indulgences could be tolerated. But he attacked the center out of which all abuses came, and this was the decisive event of the Reformation.

After Luther's attack had been made, the consequences were clear. The indulgence money can only help with respect to those works which are imposed by the pope, i.e., the canonical punishments. The dead in purgatory cannot be released by the pope; he can only pray for them; he has no power over the dead. The forgiveness of sins is an act of God alone, and the pope—or any priest—can only declare that God has already done it. There is no treasury of the church out of which the indulgences can come, except the one treasury of the work of Christ. No saint can do superfluous works because it is man's duty to do everything he can anyhow. The power of the keys, that is, the power of the forgiveness of sins, is given by God to every disciple who is with him. The only works of satisfaction are works of love; all other works are an arbitrary invention by the church. There is no time or space for them, because in our real life we must always be aware of the works of love demanded of us every moment. Confession, which is made by the priest in the sacrament of penance, is directed to God. One does not need to go to the priest for this. Every time we pray ''Our Father'', we confess our sins; this is what matters, not the sacramental confession. About satisfaction Luther said: This is a dangerous concept, because we cannot satisfy God at all. If there is satisfaction, it is done by Christ to God, not by us. Purgatory is a fiction and an imagination of man without biblical foundation. The other element in the sacrament of penance is absolution. Luther was psychologically alert enough to know that a solemn absolution may have psychological effects, but he denied its necessity. The message of the gospel, which is the message of forgiveness, is the absolution in every moment. This you can receive as the answer of God to your prayer for forgiveness. You do not need to go to church for this.

All of this means that the sacrament of penance is completely dissolved. Penitence is tranformed into a personal relationship to God and to the neighbor, against a system of means to obtain the release of objective punishments in hell, purgatory, and on earth. All of these concepts were in reality at least undercut by Luther, if not abolished. Everything is placed on the basis of a person-to-person relationship between God and man. You can have this relationship even in hell. This means that hell is simply a state and not a place. The Reformation understanding of man's relationship to God abolishes the medieval view. (pp. 231-33)

• • • • •

Whenever you see a monument of Luther, he is represented with the Bible in hand. This is somewhat misleading, and the Catholic Church is right in saying that there was biblicism throughout the Middle Ages. . . . [The] biblicistic attitude was especially strong in the late Middle Ages. . . . [In] Ockham, the nominalist, a radical criticism of the church was made on the basis of the Bible. Nevertheless, the biblical principle means something else in Luther. In nominalistic theology the Bible was the law of the church which could be turned against the actual church; but it was still law. In the Renaissance the Bible is the source-book of the true religion, to be edited by good philologists such as Erasmus. These were the two prevailing attitudes: the legal attitude in nominalism, the doctrinal attitude in humanism. Neither of these was able to break through the fundamentals of the Catholic system. Only a new principle of biblical interpretation could break through the nominalistic and humanistic docrines.

Luther had many of the nominalistic and humanistic elements within himself. He valued very highly Erasmus' edition of the New Testament, and he often fell back on a nominalistic legalism in his doctrine of inspiration whereby every word of the Bible has been inspired by the dictation of God. This happened in his defense of the doctrines of the Lord's Supper, when a literal interpretation of a biblical passage seemed to support his point of view. But beyond all this Luther had an interpretation of Scripture in unity with his new understanding of man's relationship to God. This can be made clear if we understand what he meant by the ''Word of God''. This term is used more often than any other in the Lutheran tradition and in the Neo-Reformation theology of Barth and others. Yet it is more misleading than we can perhaps realize. In Luther himself it has at least six different meanings.

Luther said—but he knew better—that the Bible is the Word of God. However, when he really wanted to express what he meant, he said that *in* the Bible there is the Word of God, the message of the Christ, his work of atonement, the forgiveness of sins, and the offer of salvation. He makes it very clear that it is the message of the gospel which is in the Bible, and thus the Bible contains the Word of God. He also said that the message existed before the Bible, namely, in the preaching of the apostles. As Calvin also later said, Luther stated that the writing which resulted in the books of the Bible was an emergency situation; it was necessary and it was an emergency. Therefore, only the religious content is important; the message is an object of experience. ''If I know what I believe, I know the content of the Scripture, since the Scripture does not contain anything except Christ.'' The criterion of apostolic truth is the Scripture, and the standard of what things are true in the Scripture is whether they deal with Christ and his work—*ob sie Christum treiben*, whether they deal with, concentrate on, or drive toward Christ. Only those books of the Bible which deal with Christ and his work contain powerfully and spiritually the Word of God.

From this point of view Luther was able to make some distinctions among the books of the Bible. The books which deal with Christ most centrally are the Fourth Gospel, the Epistles of Paul, and I Peter. Luther could say very courageous things. For instance, he said that Judas and Pilate would be apostolic if they gave the message of Christ, and Paul and John would not be if they did not give the message of Christ. He even said that anyone today who had the Spirit as powerfully as the prophets and apostles could create new Decalogues and another Testament. We must drink from their fountain only because we do not have the fullness of the Spirit. This is, of course, extremely anti-nominalistic and anti-humanistic. It emphasizes the spiritual character of the Bible. The Bible is a creation of the divine Spirit in those who have written it, but it is not a dictation. On this basis Luther was able to proceed with a half-religious, half-historical criticism of the biblical books. It does not mean anything whether the five books of Moses were written by Moses or not. He knew very well that the texts of the prophets are in great disorder. He also knew that the concrete prophecies of the prophets often proved to be in error. The Book of Esther and the Revelation of John do not really belong to the Scriptures. The Fourth Gospel excels the Synoptics in value and power, and the Epistle of James has no evangelical character at all.

Although Lutheran Orthodoxy was unable to preserve this great prophetic aspect of Luther, one thing was accomplished by Luther's freedom; it was possible for Protestantism to do something which no other religion in the whole world has been able to do, and that is to accept the historical treatment of the biblical literature. (pp. 242-44)

Luther was able to interpret the ordinary text of the Bible in his sermons and writings without taking refuge in a special pneumatic, spiritual, or allegorical interpretation alongside of the philological interpretation. The ideal of a theological seminary is to interpret the Bible in such a way that the exact philological method, including higher criticism, is combined with an existential application of the biblical texts to the questions we have to ask, and which are supposed to be answered in systematic theology. The division of the faculty into ''experts'' is a very unwholesome state of affairs, where the New Testament man tells me that I cannot discuss a certain problem because I am not an expert, or I say that I cannot discuss a matter because I am not an expert in Old or New Testament. Insofar as we all do this, we are sinning against the original meaning of Luther's attempt to remove the allegorical method of interpretation and to return to a philological approach which is at the same time spiritual. These are very real problems today, and students can do a great deal about them by refusing to let their professors be merely ''experts'' and no longer theologians. They should ask the biblical man about the existential meaning of what he finds, and the systematic theologian about the biblical foundation of his statements, in the actual biblical texts as they are philologically understood.

• • • • •

I want to emphasize Luther's doctrines of sin and faith very much because they are points in which the Reformation is far superior to what we find today in popular Christianity. For Luther sin is unbelief. ''Unbelief is the real sin.'' ''Nothing justifies except faith, and nothing makes sinful except unbelief.'' ''Unbelief is the sin altogether.'' ''The main justice is faith, and so the main evil is unbelief.'' ''Therefore the word 'sin' includes what we are living and doing besides the faith in God.'' These statements presuppose a concept of faith which has nothing whatsoever to do with the acceptance of doctrines. With respect to the concept of sin, they mean that differences of quantity (heavy and light sins) and of relativity (sins which can be forgiven in this or that way) do not matter at all. Everything which separates us from God has equal weight; there is no ''more or less'' about it.

For Luther, life as a whole, its nature and substance, is corrupted. Here we must comment on the term ''total depravity'' which we often hear. This does not mean that there is nothing good in man; no Reformer or Neo-Reformation theologian ever said that. It means that there are no special parts of man which are exempt from existential distortion. The concept of total depravity would be translated by a modern psychologist in the sense that man is distorted, or in conflict with himself, in the center of his personal life. Everything in man is included in this distortion, and this is what Luther meant. If ''total depravity'' is taken in the absurd way, it would be impossible for a man to say that he is totally depraved. A totally depraved man would not say that he is totally depraved. Even saying that we are sinful presupposes something beyond sin. What we can say is that there is no section in man which is not touched by self-contradiction; this includes the intellect and all other things. The evil are evil because they do not fulfill the one command to love God. It is the lack of love toward God which is the basis of sin. Or, it is the lack of faith. Luther said both things. But faith always precedes love because it is an act in which we receive God, and love is the act in which we are united with God. Everybody is in this situation of sin, and nobody knew more than Luther about the structural power of evil in individuals and in groups. He did not call it compulsion, as we do today in terms of modern psychology. But he knew that this is what it was, a demonic power, the power of Satan, which is greater than individual decisions. These structures of the demonic are realities; Luther knew that sin cannot be understood merely in terms of particular acts of freedom. Sin must be understood in terms of a structure, a demonic structure which has compulsory power over everyone, and which can be counterbalanced only by a structure of grace. We are all involved in the conflict between these two structures. Sometimes we are ridden, as Luther described it, by the divine compulsion, sometimes by the demonic. However, the divine structure of grace is not possession or compulsion, because it is at the same time liberating; it liberates what we essentially are.

Luther's strong emphasis on the demonic powers comes out in his doctrine of the devil, whom he understood as an organ of the divine wrath or as the divine wrath itself. There are statements in Luther which are not clear as to whether he is speaking of the wrath of God or of the devil. Actually, they are the same for him. As we see God, so he is for us. If we see him in the demonic mask, then he is that to us, and he destroys us. If we see him in the infant Jesus, where in his lowliness he makes his love visible to us, then he has this love to us. Luther was a depth psychologist in the profoundest way, without knowing the methodological research we know today. Luther saw these things in non-moralistic depths, which were lost not only in Calvinist Christianity but to a great extent in Lutheranism as well.

Faith for Luther is receiving God when he gives himself to us. He distinguished this type of faith from historical faith (*fides historica*), which acknowledges historical facts. Faith is the acceptance of the gift of God, the presence of the grace of God which grasps us. The emphasis is on the receptive character of faith—*nihil facere sed tantum recipere*, doing nothing but only receiving. These ideas are all concentrated in the acceptance of being accepted, in the forgiveness of sins, which brings about a quiet conscience and a spiritual vitality toward God and man. ''Faith is a living and restless thing. The right living faith can by no means be lazy.'' The element of knowledge in faith is an existential element, and everything else follows from it. ''Faith makes the person; the person makes the works, not works the person.'' This is confirmed by everything we know today in depth psychology. It is the ultimate meaning of life which makes a person. A split personality is not one which does not do good works. There are many people who do many good works, but who lack the ultimate center. This ultimate center is what Luther calls faith. And this makes a person. This faith is not an acceptance of doctrines, not even Christian doctrines, but the acceptance of the power itself out of which we come and to which we go, whatever the doctrines may be through which we accept it. In my book, *The Courage to Be*, I have called this ''absolute faith'', a faith which can lose every concrete content and still exist as an absolute affirmation of life as life and of being as being. Thus, the only negative thing is what Luther calls unbelief, a state of not being united with the power of being itself, with the divine reality over against the forces of separation and compulsion.

• • • • •

Luther's idea of God is one of the most powerful in the whole history of human and Christian thought. This is not a God who is a being beside others; it is a God whom we can have only through contrast. What is hidden before God is visible before the world, and what is hidden before the world is visible before God. ''Which are the virtues (i.e., powers of being) of God? Infirmity, passion, cross, persecution: these are the weapons of God.'' ''The power of man is emptied by the cross, but in the weakness of the cross the divine power is present.'' About the state of man Luther says: ''Being man means non-being, becoming, being. It means being in privation, in possibility, in action. It means always being in sin, in justification, in justice. It means always being a sinner, a penitent, a just one.'' This is a paradoxical way of speaking, but it makes clear what Luther means with respect to God. God can be seen only through the law of contrast.

Luther denies everything which can make God finite, or a being beside others. ''Nothing is so small, God is even smaller. Nothing is so large, God is even larger. He is an unspeakable being, above and outside everything we can name and think. Who knows what that is, which is called 'God'? It is beyond body, beyond spirit, beyond everything we can say, hear, and think.'' He makes the great statement that God is nearer to all creatures than they are to themselves.

> God has found the way that his own divine essence can be completely in all creatures, and in everyone especially, deeper, more internally, more present, than the creature is to itself and at the same time nowhere and cannot be comprehended by anyone, so that he embraces all things and is within them. God is at the same time in every piece of sand totally, and nevertheless in all, above all, and out of all creatures.

In these formulae the old conflict between the theistic and pantheistic tendencies in the doctrine of God is solved; they show the greatness of God, the inescapability of his presence, and at the same time, his absolute transcendence. And I would say very dogmatically that any doctrine of God which leaves out one of these elements does not really speak of God but of something less than God.

The same thing is expressed in Luther's doctrine of omnipotence. ''I call the omnipotence of God not that power by which he does not do many things he could do, but the actual power by which he potently does everything in everything.'' That is to say, God does not sit beside the world, looking at it from the outside, but he is acting in everything in every moment. This is what omnipotence means. The absurd idea of a God who calculates whether he should do what he could do is removed by this idea of God as creative power.

Luther speaks of creatures as the ''masks'' of God; God is hidden behind them. ''All creatures are God's masks and veils in order to make them work and help him to create many things.'' Thus, all natural orders and institutions are filled with divine presence, and so is the historical process. In this way he deals with all our problems of the interpretation of history. The great men in history, the Hannibals, Alexanders, Napoleons—and today he would add, the Hitlers—or, the Goths, the Vandals, the Turks—and today he would add, the Nazis and the Communists—are driven by God to attack and to destroy, and in this way God is speaking to us through them. They are God's Word to us, even to the church. The heroic persons in particular break through the ordinary rules of life. They are armed by God. God calls and forces them, and gives them their hour, and I would say, their *kairos*. Outside of this *kairos* they cannot do anything; nobody can apart from the right hour. And in the right hour no one can resist those who then act. However, in spite of the fact that God acts in everything in history, history is nonetheless the struggle between God and Satan and their different realms. The reason Luther could make these two statements is that God works creatively even in the demonic forces. They could not have being if they were not dependent on God as the gorund of being, as the creative power of being in them, in every moment. He makes it possible that Satan is the seducer; at the same time he makes it possible that Satan is conquered.

· · · · ·

What is interesting in Luther's christology is first of all his method, which is quite different from that of the ancient church. I would call it a real method of correlation; it correlates what Christ is for us with what we say about him. It is an approach from the point of view of the effects Christ has upon us. Melanchthon expressed the same idea in his *Loci*. He says that the object of christology is to deal with the benefits of Christ, not with his person and natures apart from his benefits. In decribing this method of correlation Luther says: ''As somebody is in himself, so is God to him, as object. If a man is righteous himself, God is righteous. If a man is pure, God is pure for him. If he is evil, God is evil for him. Therefore, he will appear to the damned as the evil in eternity, but to the righteous as the righteous, according to what he is in himself.'' This is a correlative way of speaking about God. For Luther, calling Christ God means having experienced divine effects which come from Christ, especially the forgiveness of sins. If you speak about God apart from his effects, this is a wrong objectifying method. You must speak of him in terms of the effects he can have. The One whose effects are divine must himself be divine—this is the criterion.

What we say about God always has the character of participation—suffering with him, being glorified with him; crucified with him, being resurrected with him. ''Preaching the Crucified means preaching our guilt and the crucifixion of our evils.'' ''So we go with him: first servant, therefore now King; first suffering, therefore now in glory; first judged, therefore now Judge. . . . So you must act: first humiliation, in order to get exaltation.'' ''Together condemned and blessed, living and dead, in pain and in joy.'' This is said of Christ and of us. The law of contradiction, the law of God always acting paradoxically, is fulfilled in Christ. He is the key to God's acting by contradicting the human system of valuation. This paradox is also valid in the church. In its visible form the church is miserable and humble, but in this humility, as in the humility of Christ, there is the glory of the church. Therefore, the glory of the church is especially visible in periods of persecution, suffering, and humility.

Christ is God for us, our God, God as he is in relationship to us. Luther also says that he is the Word of God. From this point of view Protestantism should think through its christology in existential terms, maintaining the immediate correlation of human faith and what is said about Christ. All the formulae concerning his divine and human natures, or his being the Son of God and Son of Man, make sense only if they are existentially understood.

Luther emphasizes very much the presence of God in Christ. In the incarnation the divine Word or Logos has become flesh. Luther's doctrine of the Word has different stages. First, there is the internal Word, which he also calls the heart of God, or the eternal Son. Only this internal Word, which is God's inner self-manifestation, is perfect. As the heart of man is hidden, so the heart of God is hidden. The internal Word of God, his inner self-manifestation, is hidden to man. But Luther says: ''We hope that in the future we shall look to this Word, when God has opened his heart . . . by introducing us into hs heart.'' The second meaning of the Word in Luther is Christ as the visible Word. In Christ the heart of God has become flesh, that is, historical reality. In this way we can have the hidden Word of the divine knowledge of himself, although only for faith, and never as an object among other objects. Thirdly, the Word of God is the spoken Word, by prophets, by Jesus, and the apostles. Thus, it becomes the biblical Word in which the internal Word is spoken forth. However, the revealing being of the eternal Word in Christ is more than all the spoken words of the Bible. They witness to him, but they are the Word of God only in an indirect way. Luther was never so bibliolatrous as so many Christians still are today. Word for Luther was the self-manifestation of God, and this was by no means limited to the words of the Bible, The Word of God is in, with, and under the words of the Bible, but not identical with them. The fourth meaning of the Word of God is the word of preaching, but this is only number four. If somebody speaks of the "church of the Word", whereby he is thinking of the predominance of preaching in the services, he is certainly not being a follower of Luther in this respect.

The special character of Luther's doctrine of the incarnation is the continual emphasis on the smallness of God in the incarnation. Man cannot stand the naked Absolute—God; he is driven to despair if he deals with the Absolute directly. For this reason God has given the Christ, in whom he has made himself small. "In the other works, God is recognized according to the greatness of his power, wisdom, and justice, and his works appear too terrible. But here (in Christ) appears his sweetness, mercy and charity." Without knowing Christ we are not able to stand God's majesty and are driven to insanity and hatred. This is the reason for Luther's great interest in Christmas; he wrote some of the most beautiful Christmas hymns and poems. He liked Christmas because he emphasized the small God in Christ, and Christ is the smallest in the cradle. This paradox was for Luther the real meaning of Christmas, that the One who is in the cradle is at the same time the Almighty God. The smallest and most helpless of all beings has withim himself the center of divinity. This is Luther's way of thinking of the paradoxical nature of God's self-revelation. Because God acts paradoxically the weakest is the strongest. (pp. 244-51)

Luther's handwritten translation of Psalm 43.

Paul Tillich, ''The Theology of the Protestant Reformers: Martin Luther,'' in his A History of Christian Thought, *edited by Carl E. Braaten, revised second edition, Harper & Row, Publishers, 1968, pp. 227-56.*

H. RICHARD NIEBUHR   (essay date 1955)

[*H. Richard Niebuhr, brother of Reinhold Niebuhr, was a major American Protestant theologian and the author of* Christ and Culture *(1951) and* Radical Monotheism and Western Culture *(1960). In the following excerpt, he evaluates Luther's moral, psychological, and theological thought.*]

[Martin Luther] is the key figure, the dominant leader in that profound movement of life and thought, the Reformation, which marked the end of the medieval and the beginning of the modern period in the history of Christianity. Though conjoined with the Renaissance, the rise of nationalities, the growth of capitalism, and the development of modern science, the Reformation was fundamentally a religious revolution. It resulted in a great popular revival of Christian faith and life, in an unprecedented influence of Biblical history and thought on the Western mind, in the adoption of new ethical ideas and ideals, in the organization of the Protestant churches and in the reconstruction—through the Counter Reformation and the constant rivalry with Protestantism—of the Roman Catholic church. The interrelations between the religious and the cultural, political, and economic movements of the periods are so complex, Luther's personality is so challenging, and his activities were so diversified that no consensus on the significance of his achievements is likely to be reached. But for a large part of the Christian church—far larger than that which calls itself by his name—he is a great prophetic figure and a theological genius from whose vital and penetrating utterances ever new insights are gained. In recent times even Roman Catholic theologians have paid tribute to his religious significance.

Luther's understanding of the Christian gospel and of Christian ethics is not so discontinuous with that of the thirteenth century as is often maintained by ardent disciples and ardent critics; it is particularly misleading to interpret him as standing in complete antithesis to Thomas Aquinas. Church, state, and society on the eve of the Reformation in the sixteenth century presented a radically different picture from the one that had obtained in the thirteenth; and Thomas' influence at the time was not great. Nevertheless Luther's ideas and the Reformation impulse were revolutionary in a large sense, for they sought to base Christian faith and practice directly on Biblical foundations without much concern for the conservation of the tradition and usages developed during fourteen centuries. The gospel—the central message of Scriptures—as Luther had discovered it in the course of desperate personal struggles supplied him with a new beginning and led him to call for a far more radical reform of the church and of Christian life than did his contemporaries. Hence the starting point of the Reformation is to be sought in that encounter with the gospel which marked Luther's personal conversion.

This conversion was in many respects similar to Paul's, for Luther, like the man who had been a zealous Pharisee, made his transition to a life of vital faith not from profligacy and moral carelessness but from intense ethical seriousness and religious devotion. The profound desire for a saintly life had come to appearance in the young Luther when he abandoned his plans for a career in law and, at the age of twenty-one, had entered an Augustinian monastery noted for the severity of its discipline. There he had distinguished himself by his asceticism as well as by his abilities that led to his appointment as a professor of Biblical studies in the university at Wittenberg. The combination of Bible study with intense personal concern for saintliness and salvation had led him into an enduring crisis. The Scriptural demand for holiness of life, for the complete fulfillment of the law to love God with heart, soul, mind and strength and to love the neighbor as one's self was irreducible. No less unavoidable was the Biblical picture of the divine wrath against sin. So the young monk had found himself involved in the dilemma of being required to love a fearsome God and of fulfilling for the sake of his own salvation commandments that could not be met by a self concerned for itself. He had found himself involved in what he later described as the ''curving in upon itself'' of human self-interestedness, that inversion which makes a man consider his own status and profit in everything that he does, be it in the pursuit of truth, in the practice of charity, in worship, or in the exercise of humility. The self curved in upon itself discovers that instead of loving God it is admiring or grieving over its own measure of love; instead of being concerned for the neighbor it is concerned about its acquisition of the virtue of neighbor-love; instead of being humble it seeks to excel in humility.

In consequence of his rigorous self-examination, but above all as a result of the illumination which came when at last the meaning of the Gospel struck home, Luther, more than any theologian since Paul, came to understand the difference between self-conscious moral aspiration after perfection or happiness and genuine goodness. He noted that there was as great an opposition between the self-centeredness of men who wanted to be saints and ''the grace of our Lord Jesus Christ'' as there was between the latter and the obvious immorality of passionate lovers of wealth or pleasure. In his later writings he often expressed the idea that there are two kinds of sinners, those who go off the road on the right-hand side and those who stray toward the left. The latter, like the publicans and ''sinners'' of the Gospels, succumb to their passions; the former, like Pharisees and scribes, fall prey to their egotism. Both fall short of the glory of God, and which sort does the greater harm to their companions is questionable. Where Bernard and Thomas had discerned stages of progress between perfectionist morality and the grace of Christ, Luther, with Paul, Augustine, Calvin and Edwards, saw only antithesis. There is no way, he believes, from self-love, though it be love even of one's best self, to love of God and neighbor, except through a radical change of direction—a change which may be easier in some respects for the profligate than for the self-righteous sinner.

This radical understanding of the sinfulness of the ''just and the unjust,'' which became a distinctive characteristic of the Christianity of the Reformation, had not, of course, been achieved by Luther so long as he wrestled only with his own inability to fulfill the commandments and achieve perfection. Insight into it came only in the double experience of despair and of faith. When it dawned upon Luther at last that ''the grace of our Lord Jesus Christ'' was less an example set for him than a deed done to him and for him, that he was loved and accepted by God prior to any achievement and in his perverseness, then all his ideas and values were subjected to a sharp change and transposition. What had been first became last and the last first. One may look for the secret of Luther's conversion, and so of the beginning of the Reformation, in the reversal of his understanding of the human situation before God. In the dialogue of self and God, present in religion, the self had forever been seeking to make itself heard by God, multiplying its

prayers, increasing its efforts so to change itself as to invite divine acknowledgment. It had never been silent long enough to listen to what God was saying; when it appeared to be listening it heard only what its stereotyped preconceptions allowed it to hear. When at last God's word and deed broke through this self-concentration, the whole situation between God and man was altered. The word of God and deed of God, focused in Jesus Christ, became the point of departure for a new relationship, a new self-knowledge, and a new response. Now the self recognized itself as both sinful and beloved, able to live before God in repentance and faith, in daily reliance on forgiveness, and in constant gratitude. The dialogue with God continued; outside it there was no possibility of existence, but in the dialogue God's word was always first, man's word or deed only response; and the word of God, harsh as it might sound at times, was always the word of the Saviour.

Luther's conversion, a relatively long drawn out process, led on his part to a manifold and intense activity. He was absorbed for thirty years and more in the tasks connected with the reformation of ecclesiastical abuses, the reorganization of the churches after the reformers had been rejected by the Roman authorities, the elimination of monasteries and the monastic life from reformed Christendom, the translation and explanation of the Bible, the development of popular religious education and of popular church services, the relations of churches and states. His work in these domains has well been called a ''reconstruction of morality.'' During these busy years he wrote, as occasion demanded, essays, sermons, treatises, and pamphlets without any thought of constructing a system of theology such as that of Thomas or of Calvin. The unity of his thought is, however, apparent in these manifold utterances; and the ethical interest is strong in all of them, for he was never a speculative thinker. Among these writings the following are especially important for the understanding of his view of the Christian life: *The Treatise on Good Works, The Treatise on Christian Liberty,* the [*Lectures on Romans,* the *Commentarie on Galathians*], and *The Large Catechism.* Special applications of his ideas to the field of political and economic ethics were made in such writings as the essays *Secular Authority, To What Extent It Should Be Obeyed; Whether Soldiers, Too, Can Be Saved; Address to the German Nobility; On Usury; Instructions for the Organization of a Community Chest.*

The insights and convictions that come to expression in Luther's writings are psychological as well as ethical and theological. On the psychological side two ideas in particular must be mentioned. The first of these is his voluntaristic, activist understanding of human nature. In distinction from the intellectualist view, which regards the human mind as fundamentally theoretical and for which the will translates the prior purposes of the intellect into action, Luther, with the voluntarists in general, notes that ''the being and nature of man cannot for an instant be without doing or not-doing something, enduring or running away from something, for life never rests.'' Man's moral problem, from this point of view, is less that of choosing the right means for the sake of attaining a chosen end than it is that of doing rightly the actions that issue from his nature. For voluntarism action, though always accompanied by understanding, does not begin with reflection. It is an expression of man's inner nature, of the set and disposition of his will. The voluntarist notes that man will eat, and that his moral problem in this realm is that of regulating his eating, not of choosing between fasting and eating, even though fasting seem to his mind a good means toward the attainment of a spiritual goal. So it is with his sexuality, his political existence, and his religion. The moral question is not about the *what* but about the *how* of our activity.

A second psychological insight of Luther's has been highly developed in modern times, though much ethical theory remains oblivious to it. It is the understanding that in all his actions man is subject to an inner bondage, a conflict and a self-contradiction which does not permit him to live at his full capacity. The internal bondage has many aspects. It appears in the sense of guilt, in anxiety, in self-centeredness and blindness to the values of others, in compulsive cravings for pleasure, and in abnormal scrupulosity. The fundamental moral problem of man is therefore the problem of freedom, not as the problem whether there is such a thing as liberty of choice, but as the problem of achieving liberation from these internal fetters so that man can serve his good causes without hindrance.

Closely connected with these psychological convictions are certain theological ideas which run through all of Luther's writings. Important among these is the principle that "good works do not make a good man but a good man produces good works." In common with a central tradition in Christian ethics Luther emphasizes the importance of good motives as compared with the consequences of action. While careful calculation of consequences is necessary in technical action when men deal with things, such calculation is misplaced when it is applied to persons and to personal relationships. There everything depends on the spirit, the source of the action. Luther illustrates the point in his ***Treatise on Good Works.***

> When a man and a woman love and are pleased with each other, and thoroughly believe in their love, who teaches them how they are to behave, what they are to do, leave undone, say, not say, think? Confidence alone teaches them all this and more. They make no difference in works: they do the great, the long, the much, as gladly as the small, the short, the little, and that too with joyful, peaceful, confident hearts. But where there is doubt search is made for what is best; then a distinction of works is imagined, whereby a man may win favor; and yet he goes about it with a heavy heart and great disrelish; he is, as it were, taken captive, more than half in despair, and often makes a fool of himself.

As the quotation indicates, Luther believed that the fundamental element in man's personal life, that which gives color and direction and meaning to every action, is man's trust or confidence—his real, not his official, religion. To have a god, says Luther, is to trust in something; whatever it is men trust in to give meaning to their lives, that is actually their god. Men are not either religious or irreligious, for none live without believing in something. They are either believers in the one true God or idolaters who trust in themselves, or in wealth, or reason, or civilization, or any one of the many actual and imagined beings to which they turn for a sense of security in their distrust and suspicion of the ultimate power on which they depend for being. When men distrust God and trust in themselves or in an idol, this becomes apparent in all their actions, no matter how much they profess to being religious or how ardently they try to conform to some ideal code of conduct. On the other hand, when the great gift of confidence in God, as Father and Saviour, is given, all their actions reflect this fundamental reorientation of their lives. In their assurance of being valued and sustained by the One who delivers from all evil they are set free from concern about themselves; their energies are released and integrated in the service of their neighbors. This is the theme of the ***Treatise On Christian Liberty.*** (pp. 235-41)

[For] Luther being a Christian is not primarily a matter of specifically religious actions. Indeed, in specifically religious matters man is to be receptive rather than active, *hearing* the word of God, *accepting* his forgiveness. On its active side this life is one of doing all the ordinary things demanded by the nature of life itself and the laws of society and conscience as well as those of the Scriptures. But the man of faith does all these things with a difference—in freedom from anxiety, without self-seeking, for the sake of the objective good, not for the sake of the agent. Christian vocation for Luther is, therefore, not religious vocation, though some men are required to preach and to organize churches. Any kind of constructive work in the world is a Christian vocation when it is carried on with confidence in God and with the repentance of a sinner in constant reliance on forgiveness. Although there are a few kinds of activities that evidently cannot be done in the right spirit— such as the activities of thieves and harlots on the one hand, or of seekers after saintliness on the other—there are none that carry the guarantee of the right spirit with them. Even the gospel may be preached in distrust of God and in pride. Every Christian in every vocation is involved in the constant problem of living as a sinner and yet by grace. There are even horrible things he may be required to do for the public good, such as going to war or acting as hangman. But if in a sinful world and as a sinfulman he acts in faith, he is justified as the seeker after personal virtue cannot be justified. Luther's conception of Christian vocation, especially as developed by Calvin, came to be of paramount significance in the later history of the Protestant countries. The heart of it is the understanding that a "good tree brings forth good fruit" and that the quarrels of men, including moralists, about the relative values of good pears, good cherries, and good persimmons exhibit human pride rather than knowledge of good and evil. (pp. 242-43)

> *H. Richard Niebuhr, "Martin Luther," in* Christian Ethics: Sources of the Living Tradition, *edited by Waldo Beach and H. Richard Niebuhr, The Ronald Press Company, 1955, pp. 235-43.*

JAROSLAV PELIKAN (essay date 1959)

[*An American educator and author, Pelikan is a Lutheran minister and a prominent Luther scholar. In the following excerpt, he analyzes Luther's biblical exegesis, concentrating on his understanding of the Eucharist, and indicates the continuing relevance of his principles and methods to modern biblical interpretation.*]

One of the most prominent motifs in medieval eucharistic exegesis was its idea that the Mass was a sacrifice. More than any other aspect of this exegesis, the notion that the Mass was a sacrifice which somehow repeated the sacrifice of Christ on Calvary provoked Luther's vigorous dissent. For this represented a denial of the New Testament teaching that Christ "has appeared once for all at the end of the age to put away sin by the sacrifice of Himself." At the same time Luther's repudiation of the sacrificial exegesis of "This do" in the Lord's Supper must not be permitted to obscure the sense in which the Lord's Supper still had sacrificial meaning according to Luther's exegesis. Here, as elsewhere, Luther brought care and precision to the task of Biblical exegesis. . . . (p. 237)

Luther's main work as a professor and theologian was the exegesis of the Old Testament. In this work he was aided not alone by his prodigious memory but especially by his capacity for ferreting out the basic meaning of Biblical words and phrases. He discerned the different terms which the Scriptures used to describe the same thing, as, for example, "justification" and "forgiveness." He was also sensitive to the tendency of the Bible to describe different things by the use of the same term; here he sought to distinguish the several meanings and to relate them to one another. Such distinguishing and relating was, according to Luther, one of the principal assignments of the expositor of the Scriptures.

As an expositor of the Scriptures, especially of the Old Testament, Luther had to give detailed attention to the sacrifices described and prescribed in the Scriptures. . . . This exegesis brought him to the observation that the word "sacrifice" had been used in the Scriptures to designate two distinct types of action. Luther sometimes distinguished these two types of action as "sacrifices of atonement" and "sacrifices of thanksgiving." A "sacrifice of atonement" was an action by which the favor of God was secured; its relation to the favor of God was that of cause to effect. A "sacrifice of thanksgiving," on the other hand, came from a person who already stood in a reconciled relation to God; its relation to the favor of God was that of effect to cause. The Scriptures used the word "sacrifice" for both types of action, and so did the early fathers of the church. It was, therefore, important that exegesis distinguish between the two meanings.

Failure to distinguish between the two meanings was, according to Luther, one of the sources of paganism in the ancient world. In his exegesis of the Old Testament, especially in his monumental [*Lectures on Genesis*], Luther pondered the question: How could the primitive revelation and promise given to Adam and again to Noah perish in the memory of so many nations and be replaced by pagan religion? The blurring of the distinction between "sacrifices of atonement" and "sacrifices of thanksgiving" was one of the basic reasons for this change. Since the basis of patriarchal religion was a covenant of grace with God, the patriarchs recognized that their sacrifices were not a means of appeasing God's wrath or of winning His favor but only a means of expressing gratitude to God and of bearing witness to God's grace given in the covenant. But when others saw the patriarchs offering up their sacrifices and then also discerned that the patriarchs stood in a special covenant with God, they concluded that the sacrifices were the basis of the covenant, and that God was gracious to the patriarchs because of sacrifices. Imitating the actions of the patriarchs rather than their faith, the Gentiles thus became pagans.

Here Luther's exegesis discerned a persistent tendency of man to turn his signs of gratitude toward God into devices for getting into God's good graces. So persistent was this tendency to confuse "sacrifices of thanksgiving" with "sacrifices of atonement" that Luther used it not only in his exegesis, as a way to explain the history of primitive religion in relation to the Old Testament, but also in his polemics, as a way to account for the fall of the church and the rise of notions like merit and satisfaction in the sacramental system of the church. (pp. 237-39)

Luther's exegesis of the Bible found one of its continuing themes in grace, and therefore it had to emphasize thanksgiving. In both Greek and Latin the words for "grace" and for "thanksgiving" are the same. . . . But it is interesting that many interpreters of Luther's theology and exegesis are unable to interpret his ideas about thanksgiving. For Luther thanksgiving was so basic in the Christian life precisely because the life of grace was a gift. Thanksgiving was always in response to a gift, as Luther pointed out in his exegesis of "O give thanks to the Lord" in the Psalms [**"Commentary on Psalm 118"**]. The giving of thanks thus included an acknowledgement of it as a gift rather than a reward. One did not need to give

thanks for that which he had earned, Luther pointed out in his exegesis. But when one had been the recipient of an unearned gift, then thanksgiving was the least (and the most) he could do.

Thanksgiving was also the outgrowth of a new relation between God and man. God's gift of grace in Christ was distinguished from human gifts by the basic change it brought about in the recipient. It was the grace of a new creation. Luther's favorite way of talking about this in his exegesis was to speak about the gift of the Holy Spirit. This was not a static gift to be clutched or saved. It was a dynamic gift, which effected a radical transformation in the recipient and made him a new being. Thanksgiving for the gift of grace was, therefore, not simply gratitude for favors received but the expression of that transformation which has been wrought by the Holy Spirit. Failure to recognize this meant the substitution of the Law for the Gospel. Despite its emphasis on thanksgiving, therefore, Luther's exegesis did not make gratitude the basis of Christian morality. The basis of Christian morality was the change which the Holy Spirit worked through the means of grace, and the dedication to God which that change made possible. Thanksgiving was the expression of such dedication.

The fundamental significance of the Lord's Supper in Luther's exegesis was, therefore, its function as an instrument of the grace to which thanksgiving responded. Through the grace communicated in the Sacrament the Holy Spirit accomplished the dedication out of which thanksgiving proceeded. The element of thanksgiving pervaded the entire Christian life, just as the grace given in the Word and the Sacraments affected the entire Christian life. Thanksgiving, therefore, was thanksgiving for the grace granted through the Word and the Sacraments, and it was the grace thus granted that made the thanksgiving possible. In this dynamic way Luther's exegesis joined thanksgiving and the Lord's Supper, because they were connected by the emphasis on grace. When thanksgiving was spoken of as duty in the legalistic sense of the word, its connection with the Lord's Supper was either destroyed or distorted. But when, on the other hand, the grace of the Lord's Supper was not related also to thanksgiving, its meaning shriveled up. This is why it is so important to realize that in Luther's exegesis both forgiveness of sins and thanksgiving had a role to play. (pp. 246-48)

What Luther managed to do by his careful exegesis was to eliminate from the motif of "sacrifice" all the connotations that contradicted the Biblical image of Christ's "sacrifice of Himself once for all." In the treatise *This Is My Body: These Words Still Stand* of 1527 Luther summarized his exegesis of "sacrifice" this way:

> It is certain that Christ cannot be sacrificed over and above the one single time when He sacrificed Himself. Thank God, even the papists now recognize that the daily sacrifice and the sale of this sacrifice to make up for our sins, as we have carried it on and maintained it heretofore, is the greatest blasphemy and abomination there has ever been on earth. None of the old theologians maintained, taught, or wrote this. For Irenaeus calls it a sacrifice in the sense that one sacrifices the bread and wine, out of which the Sacrament is made through the Word of God, only as an expression of thanksgiving, so that thereby one confesses that God nourishes us, as used to happen in the Old Testament. . . . Others call it a sacrifice because in it we remember the single sacrifice which Christ offered up on our behalf once and for all. Thus every year we call Easter "Resurrection" or the "Day

of Resurrection'' and say, ''Christ is risen today!''
This does not mean that Christ arises every year, but
that every year we recall the day of His resurrection.
It is in this sense that St. Augustine calls the Sacrament a sacrifice.

(pp. 253-54)

Luther the expositor was a virtuoso. No modern exegete can
fail to be moved by the depth of the Reformer's insights into
the meaning of the Biblical text. Next to his exegesis most
present-day commentaries seem either pedantic or shallow or
both. When one turns from such commentaries to Luther's
exegetical works . . . , one immediately recognizes the master's
touch. Where conservative commentators are often timid, Luther is bold and creative. Where critical commentators are often
irresponsible, Luther knows himself to be the servant of the
Word of God, not its master. Where scholarly commentators
sometimes seem interested in every detail of the text except
its theological meaning, Luther manages to find theological
meaning in the most unpromising parts of the Bible. Where
Roman Catholic allegorical commentators often practice an
exegetical alchemy that sets out to turn lead into gold but ends
up turning gold into lead, Luther labors to discover the literal
and historical sense of the text. Where Protestant commentators
often become so preoccupied with the literal sense that they
cannot tell prose from poetry, Luther's eye is always sensitive
to the spectrum of meanings in both the Old and the New
Testament. Surely the judgment of men like Ebeling and Bornkamm is correct: that Luther was one of the most important
figures in the history of Biblical exegesis. He was, in a sense
he could not have known when he took his degree in 1512, a
true *Doctor in Biblia* [''biblical theologian''].

Yet a virtuoso is often a failure as a composer—and worse
than a failure as a member of an orchestra. Many of the features
which we find most attractive and powerful in Luther's exegesis
are also the ones which we find most difficult to follow. It
would be an oversimplification to say that we are in a position
to imitate some of Luther's exegesis, while we are obliged to
depart from his pattern in other ways. Rather, what is impossible about Luther's exegesis is often his most telling and persuasive interpretation of the Scriptures. To put the problem in
a somewhat exaggerated form: A virtuoso certainly finds nu-
ances in the score which a less talented performer often misses.
But does this mean that the less talented performer should seek
to emulate the virtuoso? Now it is clear that the analogy between exegetical skill and musical virtuosity has decided limitations. No one is asked to stake his life and his hope on a
performer's reading of the score! The central message of the
Scriptures must be clear and unmistakable, whether the church
has a Luther to intepret that message or not. And it must be
possible for the church to discover the meaning of the Word
of God for problems and situations with which Lutehr never
dealt. What is at stake here is no merely aesthetic contrast, but
the very life of the church in the Gospel.

That is what makes the contemporary relevance of Luther's
exegesis so important, but also so problematical. . . . Some of
the problems in determining the relevance of Luther's exegesis
come from a consideration of his exegetical principles. . . .
Others arise from a study of Luther's exegetical practice. . . .
Still others emerge from the contrast between Luther's situation
and our own, with the inescapable realization that some of the
techniques and theories available to Luther have been closed
off to us. . . . [We], therefore, can do little more than review
for the present situation [Luther's exegetical principles] . . . as
these principles take embodiment in [his] exegetical prac-

tice. . . . Perhaps the most useful form for any such review,
following an effort at a reasonably objective account, is a series
of brief questions.

As a polemical theologian in his conflict with both Roman
Catholicism and Protestantism, Luther identified the Bible with
the Word of God. This identification made itself felt in his
exegesis of ''This is My body.'' By means of this identification
he tended to make the doctrine of the Word of God a matter
of knowledge. But as an exegetical theologian in his exposition
of the Biblical text, Luther noted the rarity of such an identification in the Scriptures themselves. This insight asserted
itself in his exegesis of ''You proclaim the Lord's death,'' in
which he made the Eucharist the visible Word of God, as well
as in his exegesis of ''For the forgiveness of sins.'' By means
of this insight he made the doctrine of the Word of God a
matter of grace and the means of grace rather than a matter of
mere knowledge. The question that emerges from this contrast
is: Is it possible to formulate the doctrine of the Word of God
today in such a way that the distinction between revelation and
Scripture, but also the connection between them, may be
safeguarded?

As the spokesman for a Biblically oriented Protestantism, Luther stressed the sovereignty of the Scriptures over all tradition
and dogma, however ancient. This stress enabled him to repudiate the sacrificial interpretation of the Eucharist, despite
its noble antiquity, on the basis of the Scriptural declaration
that Christ had ''appeared once for all at the end of the age to
put away sin by the sacrifice of Himself,'' and even to repudiate
the eucharistic exegesis of the sixth chapter of John. But as a
biblical interpreter, Luther made use of tradition and dogma
to find a meaning in the text that many other spokesmen for
a Biblically oriented Protestantism were unable or unwilling
to recognize as valid exegesis. This difference appeared in his
insistence on what he called ''the old meaning'' of passages
like ''This is My body,'' also in his traditional exegesis of
''participation in the body of Christ'' to mean the real presence
in the elements. The question raised by both his principle and
his practice is: Is it possible for exegesis today to assert the
sovereignty of Scripture over tradition (including the tradition
of Luther's exegesis of Scripture) and simultaneously to affirm
a continuity and affinity with the tradition and dogma of the
Christian centuries?

As a man of scholarship, Luther employed the best historical-
critical scholarship available to him and demanded that the
historical sense of the Scriptures receive the normative place
in exegesis. Therefore he took the phrase ''body of Christ'' in
''participation in the body of Christ'' in its ''historical'' rather
than in any ''spiritual'' sense. But as a man of faith, Luther
continually extracted something more than the simple and single historical sense from the Scriptures, and even found the
ministry of the Word in the narratives of Genesis. Thus he was
even willing, at least in his earlier exegesis, to give the ''spiritual'' sense of ''body of Christ'' a certain pre-eminence over
the ''historical'' or ''natural'' sense. This forces one to ask
the question: Is it possible to practice a spiritual or Christo-
centric exegesis of the Old Testament today without accepting
Luther's Christological exegesis or losing the ''historical'' sense
in the vagaries of unbridled allegorism?

As an obedient expositor of the whole Bible, Luther endeavored
to incorporate the full range of Biblical language into his theology. He therefore had room in his system for a pronounced
emphasis on the memorial aspects of the Eucharist, summarized
in the phrase ''in remembrance of Me,'' despite his primary

insistence on the real presence. But as a theological controversialist, Luther often gave the impression that he was concentrating on one strain of Biblical language to the exclusion, or at least the overshadowing, of others. This impression is conveyed by his almost exclusive emphasis on "the forgiveness of sins" as the benefit of the Eucharist. This circumstance compels the question: Is it possible to involve oneself in theological controversy (whether for Luther or against Luther or without Luther!) without being forced into an overemphasis that belies the work of the expositor?

These questions are obviously little more than examples, and they could be multiplied with ease. But they do serve to illustrate both the fascination and the embarrassment one feels in the study of Luther the expositor. As contemporary Protestant theology is re-examining the task of exegesis afresh, it is beginning to sense this fascination and to confess this embarrassment. Even some very dedicated defenders of Luther's eucharistic doctrine confess that they cannot follow Luther's eucharistic exegesis in all its aspects. Conversely, even some very vigorous critics of Luther's doctrine of justification must pay tribute to his method of exegesis. Here as elsewhere it is a distortion of the work of Luther to regard it as some sort of new revelation. For in his exegesis—as in his doctrine, piety, and ethic—the Reformer represented himself as a son of the church and as a witness to the Word of God revealed in Jesus Christ and documented in the Sacred Scriptures. To that church, to that Word, to that Christ, to those Scriptures Luther the expositor pointed.

He still does. (pp. 257-60)

> *Jaroslav Pelikan, in his* Luther the Expositor: Introduction to the Reformer's Exegetical Writings, *Concordia Publishing House, 1959, 286 p.*

PAUL ALTHAUS (essay date 1963)

[*Althaus was a German Lutheran theologian whose studies of Luther are highly respected. In the following excerpt from his* The Theology of Martin Luther (*first published in German in 1963*), *he outlines the basis and method of Luther's theological system.*]

Intensive study of Luther's theology is particularly rewarding because of his originality. The voice with which Luther speaks to us is unmistakably his own. Luther however did not intend to say anything particularly original. He felt he was commissioned only to explicate rightly the truth contained in the Holy Scriptures and the dogma of the orthodox church. All of his theological work presupposes the authority of Scripture and the derived authority of the genuine tradition of the church.

We shall begin at this point: All Luther's theological thinking presupposes the authority of Scripture. His theology is nothing more than an attempt to interpret the Scripture. Its form is basically exegesis. He is no "systematician" in the scholastic sense, and he is no dogmatician—either in the sense of the great medieval systems or in the sense of modern theology. He wrote neither a dogmatics, nor an ethics, nor a *Summa*: he never produced anything like Melanchthon's analyses of individual doctrines (*loci theologici*) or Calvin's *Institutes of the Christian Religion*.

Luther was professor of biblical exegesis at the University of Wittenberg. The major part of his literary work consists accordingly of exegetical lectures on the Old and New Testaments. Some he edited himself; some were edited by others.

Together with these lectures stand the sermons. Again, some were prepared for publication by Luther himself; others were taken down and published by his students. In these sermons we again hear Luther explicating biblical material. His larger and smaller topical writings too are saturated with quotations from Scripture and are largely exegetical in character. Luther also prepared theses for his students to defend in the open disputations that were part of the examinations for the theological degrees; and although he tried to cast these in the sharpest and briefest theological form possible, he constantly makes explicit as well as implicit references to biblical texts, using the language of his Latin Bible, the Vulgate.

A comparison of this aspect of Luther's work with the great theological works of scholasticism reveals the new and characteristic thrust which dominates Luther's theological method. There is no precedent for the way in which Luther, as an exegete and as a preacher, thinks in constant conversation with Scripture. Almost every single step in his theology receives its basis and direction from Scripture. To be sure, he also cites the church fathers and can occasionally—as in *The Bondage of the Will*—even call on philosophy or natural reason to provide secondary proof for theological theses. So far as his theology as a whole is concerned, however, that remains a secondary and peripheral addition to his method.

It is instructive to compare Thomas Aquinas and Luther on this point. Of course, Thomas also quotes Scripture; but in addition, we find references to the philosophical and ontological reflections of Aristotle and of Thomas himself. In contrast to this, Luther is always primarily oriented to Scripture, and often only to Scripture. In saying this, I do not mean to deny the influence which Occamistic philosophy actually had on Luther; what we are concerned with here however is the conscious intention of Luther's theological method. He distinguishes what he can say on the basis of Scripture from his own theological opinion. Since the latter cannot be proved from Scripture, Luther feels that no one is bound to accept it. For this reason he claims only that he has himself understood—and taught others to understand—the Holy Scripture somewhat better than the scholastic theologians had and sometimes better than the early fathers.

At this point, it is not a question of how far Luther may have gone in one-sided or forced interpretations of the Scripture. Neither would we speak about his criticism of the canon. These matters do not alter the fact that Luther—even when he criticized Scripture—never wanted to be anything else than an obedient hearer and student of the Scripture.

In this Luther was a perfect example of his own teachings concerning the authority of Holy Scripture in the church. The Scripture is the record of the apostolic witness to Christ and is as such the decisive authority in the church. Since the apostles are the foundation of the church, their authority is basic. No other authority can be equal to theirs. Every other authority in the church is derived from following the teaching of the apostles and is validated by its conformity to their teaching. This means that only the Scripture can establish and substantiate articles of faith. The Scripture offers all that is necessary to salvation. Christians need no other truth for their salvation beyond that proclaimed in Scripture. This applies to articles of faith as well as to ethical instruction. As the later dogmaticians put it, Scripture is "sufficient." No dogma or rule of the church not already contained in Scripture is necessary for salvation.

Neither the church therefore nor any of her representatives, not even the councils, have the authority to establish new articles of faith or new commandments. This does not mean that the teachers of the church and their theological work and teachings are to be despised and rejected. Their validity however depends on their conformity to Scripture. They must substantiate their statements from Scripture and may be judged and criticized on the basis of scripture. For it "alone is the true lord and master of all writings and doctrine on earth." Scripture alone is the authority capable of deciding in cases of doctrinal controversy. Furthermore, the statements of the teachers and fathers of the church are never placed on a level with articles of faith. For they do not provide the unconditional certainty which the conscience needs and which Scripture, the word of God, gives. We may trust unconditionally only in the word of God and not in the teaching of the fathers; for the teachers of the church can err and have erred. Scripture never errs. Therefore it alone has unconditional authority. The authority of the theologians of the church is relative and conditional. Without the authority of words of Scripture, no one can establish hard and fast statements of dogma in the church.

Those parts of the tradition of the church however which prove to be based on Scripture also have authority, even though it is only a derived authority. This was Luther's attitude toward the three so-called ecumenical creeds of the ancient church. Luther accepted them, not because they had been adopted by councils (that does not guarantee their orthodoxy), but because he was convinced that they conform to Scripture. He therefore explicitly accepted them for himself and emphasized them, especially against the anti-Trinitarians. Beginning in 1533, the oath required of students receiving the doctor's degree at Wittenberg included the subscription to these three creeds. Luther published them with his own commentary in 1538. In 1528, he had expressly confessed his agreement with the content. Now, ten years later, he wishes "once again to bear witness that I hold to the true Christian church, which up until now has preserved these creeds or confessions." He praises the Apostles' Creed as "the finest of all, a brief and true summary of the articles of faith." He values the Athanasian Creed as "a creed that protects" the Apostles' Creed.

With these creeds, Luther accepted the basic dogmas of the early church on the Trinity and the person of Christ. He also agreed with the church in its rejection of the heretics. On individual points, however, Luther frequently criticized the terminology of the dogmas; he maintained for himself and granted to others freedom not to use the terminology, provided that the substance of the dogmas was preserved.

The authority of the word of God which confronts us in Scripture and in the creeds establishes itself in our spirit and heart through experience. Of course, Luther also knows that there are elements of Christian truth which are beyond experience and must simply be "believed." But when it comes to the heart and center of the gospel, the message of sin and grace, Luther appeals not only to Scripture and the consensus of the church, but also to his own experience in spiritual matters. There can be no doubt that experience is one of the principles of his theology. It is, of course, not a source of knowledge in and by itself, but it definitely is a medium through which knowledge is received. Theological knowledge is won by experiencing it.

This is the ground on which Luther's theology stands. He intends to bring the old truth of Scripture and of dogma out of obscurity into the light, and to let its real meaning shine forth. His theology is intended as a commentary, an exposition of the received texts of Scripture and of the creeds. In this process

of exposition, the old truth admittedly becomes new truth because it is received in a new situation by men whose theological concerns and frame of reference are determined by medieval theology. And Luther knew that situation at first hand. He knew from experience the agony of asking its deepest questions—and also the freedom of the man who has found the answer. (pp. 3-8)

Paul Althaus, in his The Theology of Martin Luther, *translated by Robert C. Schultz, Fortress Press, 1966, 464 p.*

JAMES ATKINSON   (essay date 1968)

[*Atkinson is an educator and clergyman of the Church of England. He has written extensively on Luther. In the following excerpt, he discusses Luther's 1520* Reformation Writings.]

Luther was not only a prodigious writer, but wrote with a readiness, effectiveness and colour that has perhaps never been excelled. He is responsible for nearly a hundred massive volumes, each containing several major works.... Whether in Latin or German, he wrote in a style facile and fluent, full of humour and homely truth, of poetry and simplicity. He wrote to the point every time. His power rested in that he felt he had something from God to say and felt called by God to say it. There was nothing mealy-mouthed about him. The tragedy within the Reformation was the failure of Rome to give any proper answer to Luther. They condemned him, yet never answered his arguments. As Israel in that dark hour turned a deaf ear to Jeremiah and thereby forfeited her destiny, so did Catholicism, in rejecting her noblest son, choose for herself a disinherited and disunited existence. Nevertheless, Luther left more than a message; he conserved a remnant of the true people of God. (pp. 182-83)

Of special interest is his book *On Good Works,* a subject on which Luther, then as now, was misunderstood. His principles are clear. Good works are good only in that God commands them, and are never those which we opt to do as good, for example fasting. As Christ taught, the first and only work is faith, from which stem all the good works God requires of us. This is in no sense a contribution we put into the bargain, something we do or offer, something we struggle to attain, for then faith would be a human work or striving. Faith is confidence in God, an assurance, almost a reassurance, of His favour towards us, which takes root in the soul when the news of the Gospel has been given or preached to us. It is something that was not there before; it is something wholly new; it is something that God created, that man cannot create; it is a gift of God (Ephesians ii, 8). Anything that is done in response to this faith is a good work, anything that is done by this faith is transformed into a good work. Good works are not specifically 'religious'. The work may simply be mother washing the baby, the little miller's girl putting the corn on to the ass's back, the farmer tending his beasts or ploughing his ground, the cobbler at his last, the scholar reading his book and teaching his students, the prince governing his people, and so on. These are the good works. These are the works God wants His people to do for one another, and He calls them to do these in His sight so that His world may continue in peace and harmony. Going on pilgrimages, reciting paternosters, paying for masses as holy merchandise, counting beads and all the rest are not good works at all. Moreover, once faith has taken root in the heart, a man never needs any telling as to what work is good and what is not. He knows it instinctively and intuitively, as a husband who is loved by his wife does all things large or small for her (and the home) in utter faith and without distinction. Only where there is doubt does he seek to please her and curry favour and approval by devised deeds rather than the ordinary good works of daily life. For those who are young and for those who have not grown to the stature of knowing this truth, God gave the Ten Commandments, and these Luther then proceeded to elucidate for his readers.

This writing has rarely been accorded its due weight, possibly because it was never classed with the *Reformation Writings* of 1520. Yet in showing the ethical meaning of life it wrought a transformation. It utterly turned upside down (or better, the right way up) the dualism, the intellectualism and the absurd arbitrariness of medieval ethics. The distinction between the so-called sacred and secular, characteristic alike of ancient and classical religion as of medieval religion, was removed by Luther. In his view, all that the man of faith did within the framework of his relationship of faith towards God, was holy: all that a man did who had not this relationship of faith to God, was unholy, even the accepted religious activities such as fastings, pilgrimages, etc. Consequently, monkish morality was not higher than secular morality.

He also wrote a book on the mass, entitled *Treatise on the New Testament.* The title is significant. The essence of the mass to Luther was the new covenant, the forgiveness of sins, which Christ confirmed under the signs of bread and wine. 'This is my body, this is the cup of the new testament in my blood which is shed for you for the forgiveness of sins.' In the first instance, this was God's gift, but now it had been made into a gift from man to God, a sacrifice, a meritorious work, though the only sacrifice a Christian man can make is of himself and his prayers. Of the souls in purgatory, Luther argued that it was neither scriptural nor reasonable to believe that a celebration of a mass could release a departed soul from his misery. Where a mass did not serve to underline the new covenant, that is, the forgiveness of sins, it was otiose. Endowed masses should be reduced, the institution made audible and in German. If the sacrifice of the mass was that of oneself and one's prayers, all believers might make such a sacrifice, not only priests. Faith made everybody a priest. (Luther, of course, unlike the sectaries and enthusiasts, allowed the place of ordained clergy, commissioned and called by lawful authority, to preach and teach and minister.)

Not the least important, Luther had clarified his attitude towards Rome by 1520. In May he wrote a book entitled *The Papacy at Rome,* in which he showed that the Church was not to be identified with the institution Rome had made of it, but was to be thought of as that congregation of men of faith who are called of God and listen to His Word. . . . By now Luther, who had earlier suspected the authenticity of the papal decretals (notably, if uncertainly at Leipzig), had received certain proof, arising from the publication by von Hutten (1517) of the researches of Valla, who had demonstrated in 1440 that the Isidorian decretals were a forgery, as was the alleged Donation of Constantine. It was shown to the world that the authority of the papacy based on these ancient decretals and the alleged gift of the Western Empire to the papacy by Constantine were based on common fraud and plain deceit. Luther was like a young man returning home from abroad to find the fiancée he loved fallen to the level of a street woman. He was filled with dismay. To him the Antichrist was now in command at Rome.

But it is as important to see how Luther understood this term as it is to know how he combated the reality it represented.

His grasp of the situation was far more profound than John Wyclif's or that of any of his predecessors. He did not think of the Antichrist as some person or being who would appear at the end of time. Nor did he identify the papacy with the Antichrist. The Antichrist was to him some sort of demoniacal power which had gradually infected the court of Rome, and in the course of centuries thoroughly corrupted it. He saw its worst manifestation not in its striving after earthly power and riches, nor in its moral depravity, intensely aware as he was of these vices. It lay essentially in the papal claim to infallibility. In Luther's eyes the worst feature of this claim was that it meant that the papacy set itself above scripture, thereby claiming an authority over God and His Word and holding the faithful in spiritual bondage and tutelage. Luther also found great offence in the way in which the papacy arrogated to itself the right to release men from oaths and vows. Still worse, the closer knowledge of ecclesiastics which recent events had given him had convinced him that few of these agents of the papacy seemed to believe what they were professing. He was forced to the conclusion that the papal curia consisted of religious nihilists, even atheists. History has shown that Luther was largely right in this belief.

This state of affairs at Rome convinced Luther that he was living 'in the last days', understood in the real New Testament apocalyptic sense. He fought the Roman Sodom as a devilish institution, as an enemy of the Gospel, as a city set against God. It was to responsible laymen he wrote his book, *An Open Letter to the Christian Nobility of the German Nation Concerning the Reform of the Christian Estate,* as a call to resist the papacy. Clearly Rome would not reform herself, so Luther appealed to lay Christians. He began writing his book in June and it went to the press in August. It was an enormous success. Even his staunch enemy Duke George was fascinated by it. This was the first of those works, all written in 1520, which subsequently earned the title *The Reformation Writings (Die Reformationsschriften).*

Luther appealed to the leaders of Germany, to the young Emperor, the princes and knights and cities, though warning them that they must never imagine that they could heal Christendom by force of arms. They were dealing not with flesh and blood but with the princes of hell, who could fill the world with war and bloodshed but never themselves be overcome by them. It was faith in God that they must have. He struck at once at the quasi-divine power supposed to be inherent in the Church and priesthood, a power which had cowed Europe for centuries. Rome had entrenched herself behind three walls: (1) the claim that her spiritual power was superior to the temporal power of kings and princes, (2) the claim that no one could interpret scripture but the Pope, (3) the claim that only the Pope could summon a general council. Luther set about demolishing these three walls.

The Romanists asserted that there were two estates of man, the spiritual and the secular. The Pope, bishops, priests and monks constituted the spiritual estate while the princes, lords, artisans and peasants constituted the secular. But the whole idea that there was a higher spiritual estate and a lower secular estate was a disastrous delusion. The real 'spiritual estate' as such was constituted not by the clerics but by the whole body of believers in Jesus Christ, clerical and lay alike, for God had called all such, and all such were alike kings and priests by the calling. There was only one body under Christ the Head. All Christians belonged to the same spiritual estate. Baptism, the Gospel, faith, these alone made a Christian and spiritual people. We were all kings, all priests (I Peter ii, 9; Revelation V, 10). A farmer belonged to the spiritual estate as much as a bishop. The clergy were not distinguished by some indelible character given them at ordination, but simply because they had been set apart to do the particular work of a priest by and on behalf of the community. What all could do, not all might do; only the men properly called and duly set apart might perform the office and work of a priest in the Church of God. The spiritual priesthood of all believers blasted to pieces the first wall of the Romanists.

The second wall tumbled just as readily. To allege that scripture needed interpreting before it could be understood and that only the interpretation of the Pope was valid was absurd. If this were true, then there was no need of Holy Scripture at all. 'Let us burn the scriptures and be content with the unlearned boys at Rome!' Holy Scripture was plain to all, and could be interpreted by all 'who have the true faith, spirit, understanding, word and mind of Christ'.

The third wall collapsed with the other two. There was no historical foundation to the pretension that only the Pope had the power to call a council. The Church itself might call a council, as it did in Jerusalem in Acts XV; even the Emperor might call a council, as happened at Nicaea in 325. Certainly the calling of an ecumenical council had never been the prerogative of a Pope.

In the second part Luther chastised the worldly pomp of the Pope and cardinals, their greed, their exactions. It was a very telling indictment. He referred to the three thousand papal secretaries at Rome, and called the whole lot a swarm of vermin misappropriating the wealth of Germany and other countries. The details of the annates, the buying and selling of benefices, plurality, simony, make very dismal reading to Christian men, but doubtless quickened the interest of the self-interested masses in the consequences of a religious reformation. The latter is an important point. Luther's only concern was religious: to declare God and brings souls to Him in Christ. When he re-furbished the house of God, there were too many influential people interested in what would happen to Church endowments, lands, properties and resources, rather than in the establishment he sought to rebuild. One of the tragedies of the Reformation is what worldly men made of it. Much of Luther's wild anger in later life was aroused by the men who refused to accept the spiritual and theological nature of the Reformation, and whose self-interest made of his mission a kind of socialism, a new kind of libertinism, the end of which he saw as disastrous for society as well as for Christianity.

In the third part Luther gave a long, practical list of reforms which needed to be carried out. A few are listed here: the abolition of annates; of the buying and selling of benefices; of the extravagant papal court and all the customs that gave adulation to the Pope, such as kissing his feet and carrying him on men's shoulders; of saints' days and wakes; of interdict and ban; of masses for the dead with the concomitant carnivals and processions. He further advocated that the Pope should renounce temporal power and re-dedicate himself to prayer and the Word; the restriction of mendicants; that every town should have its own parish parson elected by the congregation and that he should be free to marry or not as he chose; that schools and universities should be reformed; that common life should be simplified and luxury and prostitution abolished; that drinking should be controlled; that care should be taken of young people.

What Luther sought in the main was the complete abolition of papal power over the state, the creation of a German Church with its own court of final appeal, together with a religious and ethical reform of the whole of Christendom. He wrote to Spalatin at this time, 'I am beyond injury. Whatever I have done and do, I do under constraint, ever ready to keep quiet if only they do not demand that the truth of the Gospel be quiet'. The effect of the book was instantaneous.

At the end of the Appeal Luther promised another book, and this was to be the *Prelude on the Babylonian Captivity of the Church,* a book written for the clergy and the humanists which appeared in October 1520 within a matter of weeks. It had far-reaching consequences, for it severed the tap root of Romanism, namely, the sacramental system by which Rome controlled the life of every member from birth to death under the power of the priest. It should not be assumed that Luther had no sacramental theology. There was nothing of the radical or liberal about him; he was intensely sacramental in his theology as well as in his religion. When he severed this tap root he was cutting not sacramentalism but clericalism in the guise of sacramentalism.

Luther first discussed the sacrament of the Holy Communion and exposed three errors of Roman practice as a three-fold bondage: the exclusion of the laity from the cup, the doctrine of transubstantiation, and the sacrifice of the mass.

With regard to the withholding of the cup, Luther proved from the Gospels of Matthew, Mark and Luke, as well as from Paul, that early Christians not only partook of the cup but were intended to partake. 'Drink ye all of this.' It was the Romanists who were the heretics and schismatics in excluding the laity.

The doctrine of transubstantiation he regarded as a product of scholasticism. He disbelieved in any miraculous change of the substance of bread, but maintained the coexistence of the body and blood in, with and under the elements. He was a total believer in the real presence, but thought that the Body of Christ could be included within the substance without the substance having to be transubstantiated, rather in the manner of the Incarnation when Christ dwelt in a human body without any transubstantiation of human flesh and blood. Luther's views are generally described as 'consubstantiation' as distinct from transubstantiation, but this is misleading. He never used the word, which implies 'inclusion' or 'circumscription.' This view he never held. He thought of Christ in terms of an illocal presence. In other words, Christ was present, but that presence was not to be thought of in terms of a place or a thing.

The sacrifice of the mass meant the offering to God of the very body and blood of Christ by the hands of the priest after consecration. It was a repetition of the atoning sacrifice of the cross in an unbloody manner. This institution is central both to Roman Catholic and Greek Catholic worship and theology. Luther argued that the original Lord's Supper was instituted by Christ to serve as a perpetual and thankful memory of the atoning death of Christ: to it a blessing was attached, namely the forgiveness of sins, a blessing to be appropriated by faith. The burden of the sacrament was the promise of forgiveness and its appropriation by faith. But of course this promise was larger than the sacrament proper, and was not restricted to the sacrament. It was established and proved in Christ's total ministry, and was true even without the confirmation of the sacrament. This promise is the Gospel, and the sacrament its acted Word. It is something God is offering, not man. We have nothing whatever to offer. It is exactly like baptism, to be received not given. The Romanists had changed all this into a good work of man, an *opus operatum,* by which they imagined they please God. They had surrounded it with vestments and incense, gestures and ceremonies, so that its original evangelical meaning was beclouded. According to Luther it is God who is doing all the offering, and who gives the free gift of undeserved forgiveness. All man can do is respond with thanks, with all that he has and is. Luther never sought to abolish the mass but rather to reinstate the true mass. He also quite sensibly wanted the service in the vernacular.

Luther then turns to the sacrament of baptism. Here is a clear example of how he was more of a sacramentalist than the Romanists themselves. He was thankful that this sacrament at any rate had largely remained untouched by avarice and unspoilt by bad theology. The only serious theological difference was that Rome diminished baptism by relying much more on 'the second plank' of penance, the plank that saved a man from drowning. Luther objected to this. Instead of placing his confidence in priestly absolution, a man should rely on the remission of sins offered in baptism. A penitent man should return to faith in his baptism, where he received and receives the promise of remission of sins. Luther preferred immersion as a better significance of death and resurrection of the old man. He also accepted the baptism of children as an ancient and justifiable practice of the Church. There is no satisfactory way of reconciling Luther's clear teaching on justification by faith alone with his views on baptismal regeneration. His contemporaries saw this chink in his armour, and so have many radicals who succeeded them. Perhaps the least unsatisfactory way of resolving the problem is to recall Luther's simple defence of the example of Jesus in blessing the children and the long practice of the Church in bringing up the young. Further, it emphasizes that in a sacrament what comes first and matters most is God's work not ours.

Finally, Luther attacked the number of the sacraments as then held. He believed that there should be baptism and bread, in that both of the were instituted by Christ, and both promised remission of sins. Penance he used as a means to return to the grace of baptism. The rest of the seven sacraments he rejected on the grounds that they were common to the heathen world, or were not taught by Christ, or could not by proved from scripture.

Although Rome had finally condemned Luther, Milititz persuaded him to write once more to the Pope. This was Luther's third and last letter. With the letter he sent a book entitled ***The Freedom of a Christian Man.*** Written in some twelve days, it is in effect a popular summing up of the Christian life. The leading idea is a kind of dual paradox, namely that the Christian man is the lord of all and subject to none, by virtue of faith; and that he is also the servant of all and subject to everyone, by virtue of love. A Christian's life is made up of faith and love: faith expresses his relationship to God, love his relationship to man. Man is made free by faith which alone justifies, but faith manifests itself in love to one's fellows and in good works. The person must first be good before he can do good works; good works proceed from a good man. Faith, as it makes man a believer, by the same process makes his works good; but works in themselves do not make a man into a believing man nor a justified man. The error of good works is in seeking justification in doing them. Faith unites the soul to Christ in perfect union, therefore whatever is Christ's is the soul's also. This is more than communion as such; it is victory and redemption and freedom. By faith we are all kings and priests.

It is not sufficient to preach the words and works of Christ in a historic manner, but rather (as St John did) to promote faith in Him, so that Christ is Christ for us. We must preach why Christ came; He has given us liberty and made us kings and priests—kings in what we are lords of all things, priests in that we stand continually in His presence.

Luther then turns to his second principle, that a Christian man is the servant of all. Faith issues in works, for a Christian enjoys that most free of all servitudes in which he serves others of his own will and for nought. He should empty himself and serve his neighbour, in the same way as he sees that God has acted and is acting towards him through Christ. A Christian lives in Christ and in his neighbour, in Christ by faith and in his neighbour by love. What Luther criticized in the Romish doctrine was that Christian men were there taught to seek merits and rewards, so that Rome turned the Gospel into Law.

What the Pope thought of the book we do not know. He was much too worldly to like it, or even to read it. The letter accompanying it destroyed all prospects of reconciliation. In his first letter to the Pope (1518) Luther threw himself at his feet, in his second letter (1519) he addressed him as his humble servant but would not recant, in his third letter (1520) he addressed him as an equal and pitied him as a poor Daniel in a den of lions. He made the devastating remark that the Pope was called the vicar of Christ for a vicar was there because someone else was absent, and it was Christ who was absent from Rome. (pp. 184-93)

James Atkinson, in his Martin Luther and the Birth of Protestantism, *Penguin Books, 1968, 352 p.*

H. G. HAILE   (essay date 1977)

[*Haile is an American educator and author of a biography of Luther. In the following excerpt from an earlier work, he approaches Luther from a literary rather than a theological standpoint, examining his songs and his treatment of the Bible as a work of literature.*]

Luther formulated a theory of literature that for the first time enabled the people to understand the great works from ancient Hebrew as relevant to their own personal lives. This is the aspect of Luther's work that our own era, languishing in a new scholasticism, can most admire. Let us think of Luther as the consummate popular artist who democratized South European humanism. While the aristocratic Italian Renaissance tends to evoke visions of clear and balanced form, Northern Europe learned to take delight in the profusions of the poet and satirist Johann Fischart, and of Rabelais and Shakespeare with their endless combinations and bold juxtapositions. In this more boisterous sense, Luther is also a man of the Renaissance, who from long experience as professor and debater consciously played to the gallery.

As a lyricist, Luther is kin to Scottish poet Robert Burns, our own Woody Guthrie, and others whose songs arose from the native strength of popular language, words and music coming as a coherent inspiration. Learned arguments, long and bravely fought, concerning the originality of Luther's melodies, quite miss the point that such artists as these scorn originality. When school children patriotically sing "This Land Is Your Land," when resolute Lutherans sing **"Ein feste Burg,"** or when "Auld Lang Syne" unites Anglo-Saxons, they are not singing national hymns but modes that hark back to a common Indo-European background. He who places great store by originality must seek

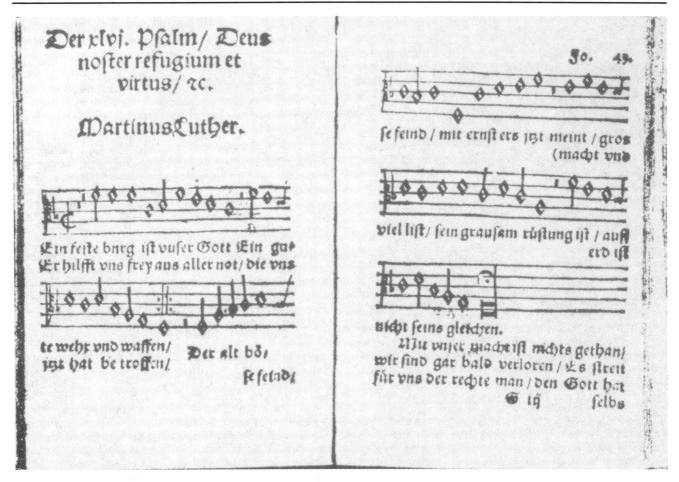

Words and music of "Ein' feste Burg ist unser Gott" ("A Mighty Fortress Is Our God"), Luther's best-known hymn.

it in the craftsmanship with which these artists match lyric and melodic line. Any of Luther's songs might serve us as examples, but the very first one that has come down to us seems most naïve and appealing: **"Ein neues Lied wir heben an"** **("We raise a new song").**

The occasion was the public burning of two Antwerp Augustinians (July 1, 1523) at the beginning of the inquisition set up by Charles V in the Netherlands—the first martyrdom of the emerging sect. The song is a tendentious narrative which makes claim to art by its masterful recall of topoi.... (pp. 144-45)

The narrative is strongly partisan, and the melody emphasizes conflict of good with wicked in melodramatic fashion, as is appropriate for the historical folk song. (p. 145)

Singing or playing this song immediately conveys its propagandistic effectiveness. Luther has hewed faithfully to the form of the historical folk song, widely cultivated from earliest times. In his day this genre was an important and accepted vehicle for recording and disseminating news, just as in our own era it can still be used to inform or shape public opinion. "Jesse James" and "John Henry" of the last century, as well as union workers' songs of this century are modern examples. Especially in the latter we hear the traditional techniques of sarcasm and vitriolic attack, which Luther applied so well.

The craftsmanship that went into Luther's polemical pamphlets is equally naïve. The most famous (and effective) example is

his *Address to the Christian Nobility of the German Nation.* The body of the work takes its simple organization from twenty-seven complaints familiar from their presentation at numerous Imperial diets. Luther lets us know at the outset that his will be an especially entertaining presentation of them, delivered by the universal favorite of the Renaissance, the fool. Who could be better suited to play the fool, he asks, than a monk? "No one need buy a cap or trim the coxcomb for me. We shall see, however, who is to be belled." It is one of the most familiar conceits of an age that delighted in puns and double entendre. Equally familiar in popular culture with the fool was siege imagery. Somewhat earlier Luther had complained that the papacy "laid a bar across the door to guard its rascality." Now he develops his celebrated conceit of the three walls that, like the walls of Jericho, shield the impious papists (Canon Law, ultimate authority in interpreting the Bible, and exclusive right to call a council). The twenty-seven articles constituting Luther's treatise become in this frame a mere vessel for the many tricks of popular debate known to a practiced debater. Let us examine some of them in detail, as representative of Luther's numerous polemics.

At the lowest level, techniques may be simply invective and appeal to chauvinism and prejudice in harsh epithet of the sort which the sixteenth century loved. Luther likes crude neologisms. Among his many debater's tricks is the direct appeal to his audience, to his enemy the pope, or to Jesus Christ himself. He maintains a jovial tone by making fun of himself and ridiculing the pretensions of his opponents (''Why, it's just the same as if I called the keeper of the whorehouse: Madam Mayor.'') From Luther's style we infer an audience that loved puns and had an endless tolerance of repetition. They obviously took delight in sheer prolixity. While Luther does shape his flood of words—most frequently with crescendo—we often feel that he is just venting his spleen in a tradition later to be taken up by Fischart and Abraham a Sancta Clara. He knows how to use the proverb in an argumentative, very convincing way: *O wie ein schlechter Schatz ist der Zoll am Rhein gegen dieses heilige Haus* (what a poor source of revenue a customs house on the Rhine is, compared with the church).

Proverbs are convincing because they distill the wisdom of the ages, with which one just does not quibble—but their use also certifies the native son, who can make a special claim on credence. In this connection, note that Luther imprints his slogans on our mind not with end rhyme (of Latin provenience) so often as with stave rhyme, a Germanic device. In *To the Christian Nobility* we have *Gewurm und Geschwurm* (vermin), *lügen und trügen* (deceive), *die Schrift zwingen und dringen* (distort Scripture), etc.; but uses of alliteration (stave rhyme) are much more numerous and inventive: *prachten und prangen* (extravagance), *Schätzerei und Schinderei* (gouging), *nur frisch mit füssen treten* (go ahead and kick it down), *irre laufen auf dem Land* (get lost in the wilds), of Hus's tormentors: *es hat sie der Teufel toll und töricht gemacht* (the devil drove them mad). Stave rhyme linkages reinforce the logic of an argument, as when Luther says that we (not only) put up with (but even) praise God's shame: *solche Unehre Gottes leiden und loben.* He ties together greed and Canon Law: *der Geiz und das geistliche Recht.* It is fascinating to follow this highly associative mind as it seeks poetic release, now in fairy tale motif *(zehn Brüder, Königskinder, in eine Wüste gesetzt)*, now into metaphor: to give a celibate monk a housekeeper is to put fire and straw together, and forbid them to burn. Luther knows how to turn his poetic gift to great harshness (''The pope gives you lead for gold, hide for meat, cord for purse, comb for honey, words for wares, letter for spirit, and if you ride toward heaven on his parchment and wax, your coach will soon break down and plunge you into hell''), or gently, especially when guided by his beloved Bible: *So doch allein die Schrift unser Weingarten ist* (For Scripture alone is our vineyard).

The untiring delight of medieval man in discovering his everyday life exemplified in the Bible puts forth its most stunning flower in Martin Luther. . . . The Bible becomes for Luther an immense storehouse in which the tiniest jewels are immediately accessible. On the subject of universities, he confesses his concern for young people that the professors are so unlearned: ''Mine eyes do fail with tears and my bowels spill upon the ground . . .'' Thus begins a lengthy recitation of Lamentations II—from memory no doubt—ten years before he translated it! Heinz Bluhm, who has compiled an index of Luther's Bible translations outside his Bible, comes to the conclusion that some of Luther's greatest successes occur in just such extempore quotations. Luther seems to have been a true artist in the sense that substance and beauty seemed one to him.

Not only did involvement in doctrinal dispute make Germans literate in the modern, democratic sense of the word, and soon other north Europeans as well. The Scriptures as doctrinal court of fine appeal became the all-time literary classic of the West. Above all others, it seems to have been Luther who taught us

to read these ancient songs and tales of the Near East in terms of immediate relevance to our own daily lives and thought.

In this, he became a shining example to all literature teachers. With the literary riches of an ancient, noble herdsman civilization of the south, he was able to transform superstitious tribesmen of the dark north European forest into an enlightened, even scholarly race—for a time. (pp. 146-49)

There seems to be no question that we do have with Luther some first beginnings of a view of the Bible as a literary document, i.e., a work that bears testimony to the limited time and place of its origins and undergoes its own history. This is especially apparent in his appreciation of specifically Hebrew devices—''barbarisms of the Holy Ghost.'' Fragmentary features of the prophetic books seem explicable to him now in terms of the passions of the prophets themselves, or now because of faulty transmission: ''These sayings were not arranged by the prophet, but excerpted by scribes.'' Bornkamm conjectures that one reason motivating later publishers of Luther's Bible to drop his excellent prefaces may have been Luther's freely expressed doubts as to authorship of books in the Bible. He repeatedly questions Moses' authorship of the Pentateuch, and his outright rejection of certain books of the New Testament is notorious (James, Revelation).

In calling attention to these things I am trying to map out a broad common ground where Luther's approach to the Bible resembles our own approach to great literature. The most striking difference between Luther and a reader such as myself may be in Luther's confident assurance that the written word holds high *practical* value for men of his day. As a professor, that was the chief ax he had to grind. He was sure that interpretation as practiced by his own contemporaries, whom he contemptuously called ''the Sophists,'' although it boasted a highly refined method for extracting and expanding upon the so-called spiritual senses of the text, was oblivious to the real spiritual needs of the congregation. It is probably true that scholastic interpreters had become more wrapped up in the fine art of distilling various abstract meanings from the text than concerned with its practical value. Luther seems to have felt that once this happens, once the process loses sight of the ends it serves, then interpretation itself degenerates. We have to concede that he was stunningly successful in his own interpretation while at the same time effecting unprecedented popularity of the text itself.

Is not a Renaissance in Luther's sense precisely what every literature teacher longs for—a return to the sources as they are reborn in a new immediacy? ''Renaissance'' probably takes on its full meaning only in this religiously colored sense, which suffuses the sources in new affect and lends them relevance for and in the individual life.

With this in mind I offer this summing up of Luther's principles of interpretation from a literary point of view, as distinct from the more usual theological approach.

1. Surely the most striking feature of Luther's exegesis is that it does not aim at finality. On the contrary, the typical interpretation begins and ends with a statement that it is tentative, that it may be replaced tomorrow by a better one based on increased experience and understanding. As we grow, so does our appreciation—and the text helps us grow.

2. Luther insisted that the text was generally comprehensible, an elaborate interpretive technique unnecessary. ''The Holy Ghost is the simplest of all scribes and counsellors in heaven

and earth so that his words could not have more than one simplest sense, which we call the scriptural or literal sense.'' He readily allows for allegory . . .'' as if I said: Emser is a crude ass, and a simpleton took me at my word and understood that Emser were a real ass with long ears and four legs—he would be deceived by the literal sense.'' But aside from allegory clearly intended by the author, Luther flatly refused to accept the time-hallowed manifold sense of Scripture. The humanists approved of allegorical interpretation and often could come to terms with the text in no other way. Luther, in lashing out at the *ludicri et lusores* who thus made a game of Scripture, enhanced respect for the Bible as a document that must be accepted on its own terms.

3. Luther's confidence in the simplicity of Biblical expression corresponds with his sure assumption of one simple, i.e., *uniform* sense or—as he put it with the Aristotelian term—*skopos* for the entire Bible: ''All of Scripture would make us acquainted with Christ. This is the *skopos* of all Scripture.'' Rabbinical interpretation, for example, could never be correct, because it missed this simple, literal sense of the Old Testament. An interpreter must know the entire Bible intimately. The meaning of the Old Testament will normally arise from the New Testament. Luther's own detailed acquaintance with the Bible was fantastic—he scorned users of concordances.

4. The text is its own best interpreter—in Luther's words: ''Scripture itself is in itself most certain, simple, and apparent. It is its own interpreter, testing, judging, and illuminating all things.'' There are, to be sure, obscure and difficult passages aplenty. They must be illuminated by the clearer ones. This principle presupposes, of course, the simple, uniform sense of Scripture just discussed. Furthermore, both notions operate under the ''analogy of faith'' that the entire Bible is concerned with Christ and with His meaning for man and that hence no passage, when it is rightly construed, can contradict this fundamental article of belief.

5. So far, I have only listed principles that in one way or another are treated by theologically oriented Luther scholarship. I as student and teacher of literature find one more important principle arising almost everywhere Luther interprets a text. I will call it the *analogia experientiae:* analogy to shared experience. . . . My emphasis, however, recognizes that Luther never interprets except that he is consciously interpreting for someone, be it in lectures to his students, introductions to books of his Bible translation, sermons and other kerygmatic writings, or in his tough polemics. He is always trying to communicate to others his special interpretation of the text. In doing so, his constant appeal is to the experience of his audience.

Of course this was not new with Luther, and it continues to be a most popular preacher's and teacher's device. It even embodies a whole philosophy of textual understanding. But Luther was highly adept at it, and I believe that his use of the analogy to experience must be regarded as a major characteristic of his entire attitude toward Scripture. Especially do I think that Luther's example here is likely to be useful to teachers of all texts in all societies. ''No one,'' he declares, ''can understand a text unless he experiences it.''

Let me just conclude with a few examples. Luther's explanation as to how Christians should regard Mosaic Law is deservedly famous. He concedes that it is excellent, ''Not that it should be imposed by force, but let the emperor take an example of a fine government from Moses, just as the Romans had fine laws, and just as the Germanic peoples had fine laws in the

Sachssenspiegel [an early corpus of Germanic law], by which our land was governed. Gentiles don't have to obey Moses. Moses is the Jewish *Sachssenspiegel*''—by means of analogy, a brilliant demythologization of the Ten Commandments.

Rather than continue with numerous examples, I will conclude with what turned out to be Luther's last written words:

''Nobody can understand Vergil in his *Bucolics* and *Georgics* unless he has first been a shepherd or a farmer for five years.

''Nobody understands Cicero in his letters unless he has twenty years experience in important public office.

''Let no one think that he sufficiently savors Holy Scripture unless he has governed the churches with the prophets for a hundred years. Because the wonders are great, first of John Baptist, then of Christ, and third of the Apostles. Touch not this divine *Aeneid*, but bow down and adore his footsteps. *Wir sein pettler. Hoc est verum.*''

In short, Luther assumes—and often says explicitly—that the true medium of communication from soul to soul is shared passion and experience. Letters cannot be separated from life. The spirit must first bring meaning to the letter. A typical comment from his *scholia* on Psalms is: ''Only passion and experience will reveal the meaning.'' (pp. 150-54)

> H. G. Haile, *''Luther as Renaissance Writer,''* in The Renaissance and Reformation in Germany: An Introduction, *edited by Gerhart Hoffmeister, Frederick Ungar Publishing Co., 1977, pp. 141-56.*

WALTHER VON LOEWENICH (essay date 1982)

[*In the following excerpt from his biographical and critical study of Luther (originally published in German in 1982), von Loewenich explicates five of Luther's most famous and influential works:* Ninety-Five Theses, Treatyse on Good Works, On the Papacy in Rome, Address to the Nobility, *and his German Bible.*]

Around noon on October 31, 1517, the day before All Saints' Day, Luther, accompanied by his teaching assistant Johann Schneider of Eisleben, called Agricola, walked the short way from the Black Cloister to the castle church and posted on the north door a sheet of paper with 95 theses opposing indulgences. (p. 109)

The first thesis established in a concise way what penance was. ''When our Lord and Master Jesus Christ said, 'Repent,' he willed the entire life of believers to be one of repentance.'' Penance, in other words, cannot be limited to a sacramental act. It is a basic orientation of the Christian life. The pope cannot remit sin, he can only affirm that it has been remitted by God (thesis 6). The only punishments he can remit are those prescribed by the church; this does not include purgatory (thesis 5). God has made priests responsible for our absolution (thesis 7). Canonical punishments are valid only for the living; one cannot postpone them for purgatory (theses 8-19). Therefore the pope cannot release anyone from the punishments of purgatory (theses 20-29). The pope can only achieve an amelioration of punishment for those in purgatory through intercessory prayer *(per modum suffragii).* It is a human teaching (not divine) to assert that as soon as the money rings in the coffer, the soul is freed from purgatory (theses 26-27). How are indulgence and true confession related (theses 30-40)? Those who believe that their salvation is assured by indulgence certificates are eternally damned (thesis 32). Thesis 33 was directed specifically against [*Instructio summaria,* an instruction manual for indulgence preachers]: Persons cannot be reconciled to God through indulgences. So is thesis 35: It is unchristian to teach that contrition is not required to obtain certificates of indulgence. Quite the opposite is true: true contrition receives both the forgiveness of sin and the remission of punishment; it makes indulgences unnecessary (thesis 36). This also makes it impossible for the most learned theologian to commend both indulgences and true contrition to the people (thesis 39). True faith cherishes punishment; indulgences attempt to avoid it (thesis 40). Contrition and indulgences are therefore opposites. Moreover, indulgences also conflict with good works (theses 41-52). Love of one's neighbor and the giving of alms are better than indulgences (thesis 43). "Because love grows by works of love, man thereby becomes better. Man does not, however, become better by means of indulgences but is merely freed from penalties" (thesis 44). Those who have little to spare should not spend their money on indulgences, but ought rather to care for their own (thesis 46). Indulgences are useful only if one does not rely on them (thesis 49). The pope would rather have our intercession than our money (thesis 48); he would rather see St. Peter's lie in ashes than allow it to be built with the skin of his sheep (thesis 50). The preaching of the gospel is more important than the preaching of indulgences (theses 52-55). The "treasure of the church" is neither its earthly wealth, nor the merits of Christ and the saints, nor the poor, as Laurentius maintained, but rather, "The true treasure of the church is the most holy gospel of the glory and grace of God" (thesis 62). The current preaching of indulgences contradicts the gospel (theses 69-80). Theses 81-91, in order to preserve the honor of the pope from the disturbance brought about by the unrestrained preaching of indulgences, address several "shrewd questions of the laity." Why does the pope not decrease purgatory apart from money—purely out of love (thesis 82)? Why are the rules of penance, which have already been abolished, still considered valid for indulgences (thesis 85)? Why doesn't the pope, who is richer by far than wealthy Crassus, build St. Peter's with his own money (thesis 86)? Luther concluded with four powerful theses stated in the spirit of his theology of the cross: "Away then with all those prophets who say to the people of Christ, 'Peace, peace,' and there is no peace! (thesis 92). "Blessed be all those prophets who say to the people of Christ, 'Cross, cross,' and there is no cross! (thesis 93). Christians should be exhorted to be diligent in following Christ, their head, through penalties, death, and hell (thesis 94). And thus be confident of entering into heaven through many tribulations rather than through the false security of peace (thesis 95)."

Luther obviously intended to absolve the pope of responsibility for these abuses (see theses 20, 26, 38, 42, 50, 53, 70, 91). He was thoroughly convinced that he was teaching in the tradition of the church (see also thesis 7). He did not expound the entire riches of his newly acquired Pauline theology in these theses. Nevertheless, one cannot read them without detecting a new theological direction: Luther's ideal church was a church characterized by contrition, the Word, and love. (pp. 114-15)

Luther was not pleased with the widespread circulation of his theses among the laity. In order to place something more suitable into their hands he published the German *Sermon on Indulgences and Grace* in March 1518. It was written with far more clarity than the theses: God asks nothing more of sinners than sincere repentance; there is nothing in the Bible about works of satisfaction. Indulgences are only for lazy Christians who do not wish to do good works. One ought not speak for

Luther's room in the Wartburg.

or against indulgences. Yet it was Luther's desire and counsel that no one obtain indulgences. He was not certain whether souls could be freed from purgatory by purchasing indulgences on their behalf, but he did not believe it. Moreover, he didn't place much importance on the fact that those whose business he had destroyed called him a heretic.

Luther had become conscious of the things that needed to be said in this little pamphlet for the laity during his preparration of his *Explanations of the 95 Theses (Resolutiones disputationum de indulgentiarum virtute)*. . . .

The *Explanations* was more than just a commentary; it also expanded the theses and developed them. Luther had studied hard to prepare it. He did not want his statements to be taken as definitive assertions, but as propositions for discussion. He repeatedly declared his willingness to respect ecclesiastical authority. But this did not hinder him from expressing revolutionary thoughts. (p. 118)

In the *Explanations* many of the thoughts in the original *95 Theses* are restated and dealt with in greater detail. He reaffirmed his statements on penance in thesis 1: The absolution of the priest assures us of the forgiveness that we have already received. Where there is no faith in the promise of Christ, there can be no forgiveness. Without faith the sacraments cannot effect salvation. The surplus merits of the saints, which are said to be the treasure of the church, do not exist, since no human being has ever satisfactorily fulfilled the commandments of God. Papal authority must be respected and obeyed, but the conscience is not bound by the judicial pronouncements of the pope, including excommunication, if they are injust. The primacy of the papacy over the whole church did not exist from the beginning. Luther rejected the medieval doctrine of the two swords—the spiritual and the secular—in the hands of the pope. The church is not permitted to use the secular sword, even against heretics. Errors must be disposed of with spiritual weapons. In view of the circumstances within the church, Luther declared near the end of the *Explanations*, ''The church needs a reformation which is not the work of one man, namely, the pope, or of many men, namely the cardinals, both of which the most recent council has demonstrated, but it is the work of the whole world, indeed it is the work of God alone. However, only God who has created time knows the time for this reformation.'' The *95 Theses* did in fact introduce the Reformation of the church. (p. 119)

Among Luther's many publications during [the opening years of the Reformation] the *Sermon on Good Works* is one of the most important. It is often rightly included as being among the most significant Reformation writings. . . . In fact it did become one of the finest presentations of evangelical ethics, as superb in practical matters as it was in theory.

Luther used the Ten Commandments as a framework for expressing his views, expanding them evangelically. In the preface he assured his readers that he was not ashamed of preaching to the ''uneducated laity.''. . . . Luther chose the theme of ''good works'' because it brought to the surface many common misconceptions; accusations were being made already at that time that he held good works to be unimportant.

Luther introduced the sermon with two theses: (1) Only those works that God has commanded are good; only those works that God has forbidden are sinful. Therefore one must hold fast to the Ten Commandments, and not seek out those works that human beings have determined to be good. (2) The first and greatest good work is faith in Christ. ''For in this work all good works exist, and from faith these works receive a borrowed goodness.'' There are many who pray, fast, provide endowments for the church, and lead good lives before others; but when one asks whether these deeds are pleasing to God, they do not know. Then the theologians come along and say that such certainty is not really necessary; but without this certainty the works are dead. Without faith, ''their works are pointless and their life and goodness all amount to nothing.''

When Luther exalted faith in this way and rejected works done without faith, his opponents accused him of forbidding good works; but it was really his intention to teach nothing more than the truly good works of faith. When we rely confidently on God there is no distinction between pious and profane works; every deed is good even if it is as insignificant as picking up a single straw. However, where confidence in God fails, no deed is good, even if we should raise the dead or allow ourselves to be burned at the stake. Since the works please God because of faith and not because of their own nature, they are all equal; there is no distinction between great and small.

Whoever lives by faith, that is, out of the confidence God himself creates, does not need to be instructed in doing good works; he or she already does ''whatever the occasion calls for,'' whatever is at hand. ''For faith does not permit itself to be bound to any work or to refuse any work.'' It is like the love between those who are truly partners in marriage: they do everything out of joyful hearts and without the need of ethical teaching. ''Thus a Christian man who lives in this confidence toward God knows all things, can do all things, ventures everything that needs to be done, and does everything gladly and willingly, not that he may gather merits and good works, but because it is a pleasure for him to please God in

doing these things. He simply serves God with no thought of reward, content that his service pleases God.'' Where this trust fails, people turn to St. James, to Rome, to Jerusalem, do penance in this place and in that, yet never find peace.

Yet faith remains small in works; it receives its testing through suffering. There faith is not simply a matter of trusting in God and looking forward to receiving something better from him, as we are prone to think. There God is hidden, and yet he wants to help us. There God stands as though he were behind a wall, but through ''the window of dim faith'' God lets himself be seen. But the highest degree of faith is to hold fast to God when he appears as if he wants to condemn us forever. ''To believe at such times that God is gracious and well-disposed toward us is the greatest work that may ever happen to and in a man.'' Luther had already spoken of this *''resignatio ad infernum''* in the lectures on Romans.

This then is the work required by the First Commandment, to place our entire trust alone in God. ''For you do not have a god if you [just] call him God outwardly with your lips, or worship him with the knees or bodily gestures; but [only] if you trust him with your heart and look to him for all good, grace, and favor, whether in works or suffering, in life or death, in joy or sorrow.'' The words are reminiscent of Luther's famous explanation of the First Commandment in the *Large Catechism*. Faith is trust in God; this is the heart of Luther's piety. Over against all external churchliness, true Christianity consists of this inner attitude that Luther called faith. Since life never stands still, faith never finds itself without opportunities for doing good works. Indeed, even idleness finds its rightful place only within the activities and practice of faith.

Admittedly not everyone is sufficiently mature to practice the ethics of faith. Many people must still be forced by the law to do that which is good and refrain from doing evil. They must be supported by those who are truly Christian and gently led to faith. And those who stand in faith are not therefore morally perfect. Faith is not an ordinary work like other works; it lives entirely from God's mercy, and it knows that we are God's children and sinners as well. So faith takes refuge in the love of God in Christ. The First Commandment then leads us to Christ.

The Second and Third Commandments flow directly out of the First. We are to praise God's name, practice worship, and hear God's Word. This includes opposing all injustice and combating every misuse of spiritual power. Even trials lead us to call on God's name, and who is not without trials, even for an hour? But the most dangerous trial of all is when there is no trial, and therefore we forget God.

In his exposition of the Third Commandment Luther denounced the excesses of church life. There were far too many festivals that only contributed to idleness and loose living. Absurd fables ought to be banished from sermons. Prayer ought not be mere prattle. One must pray believing that one will be heard, but not ''prescribe to him the measure or the manner, the limits or the place'' in which God must respond. The disciplines of fasting and self-denial are also among the works called for by the Third Commandment, but they ought not be carried to the extreme of harming one's body. The Old Testament command to keep the Sabbath is no longer binding, but a day must be set aside on which people can go to church to hear God's Word. The Sabbath commandment can also be understood spiritually (allegorically): God wants us to rest from our works and allow his work to occur among us, even God's "alien work." The first three commandments are interlocked like a golden ring.

In his treatment of the Fourth Commandment Luther focused on the duties of parents and children. He discussed evils in ecclesiastical and temporal government and denounced extravagance, prostitution, and exorbitant interest rates. The remaining commandments were expounded much more briefly, though their relationshp to faith was constantly emphasized. Good works are the natural outcome of faith. Faith is not one work among others, but the foundation of works. There is no faith without works; nor are there isolated "good works" in the casuistic sense. In this sermon Luther overcame the medieval dualism that distinguished between holy and profane actions and between the ethics of monks and the ethics of the laity.

No less consequential for the existing social order was Luther's work of 1520, *On the Papacy at Rome, Against the Most Celebrated Romanist in Leipzig* [Augustine of Alfeld]. (pp. 152-56)

Luther began by insisting that the papacy was not concerned about divine order, but rather with money above all else. How much longer should the "drunken Germans" continue to put up with this? Alfeld had argued that every community on earth must have a physical head; Christianity is such a community, therefore it too must have a head, and this is the pope. Luther contradicted this. First, reason was not the judge of this question. Second, Alfeld's notion did not even follow reason; there were also republics without a monarchial head, such as ancient Rome or Switzerland. Christendom was not a civic community, but far more "an assembly of hearts in one faith." External unity made persons neither Christians nor heretics.

Christendom was a "spiritual community," whose life, according to Col. 3:3, was hidden with Christ in God. The Holy Scriptures did not say that the external church, where it is by itself, is ordained by God. The true head of Christendom is Christ alone, who resides in the heavens, and not the pope. Nor was the pope Christ's representative, for he did not carry on the work of Christ in the church, namely faith, hope, and love. St. Paul knew nothing of the primacy of Peter. Peter was a messenger [*Bote*] of Christ, like all the other apostles, for the word *apostle* should be translated into German as *Bote*. "Not Rome or this or that place, but baptism, the sacrament, and the gospel are the signs by which the existence of the church in the world can be noticed externally." Where Baptism and the gospel are, there is the church, even if it rests only on children in their cradles.

The opponents supported papal primacy by quoting Christ's words to Peter in Matt. 16:18-19. Luther did not consider this "proof text" to be valid. According to Matt. 18:18 and John 20:20, the office of the keys was not conferred solely upon Peter, but upon all of the apostles. Moreover, the authority of the keys was something quite different from the authority to govern. The promise, "the powers of death shall not prevail against it," was meant for true faith and not for an external institution. Furthermore the history of the papacy had been marked by numerous instances of subjugation to secular power.

Christ's command to Peter was "feed my sheep." That did not mean "tyrannize them," but "preach to them"; the pope did not do that. Luther had been accused of being excessively "biting"; he was concerned that he had not been biting enough. "I should have pulled even more [at the sheep's] clothing of these raving wolves." Nevertheless the papacy had to be supported, for it did not come into being without God's provi-

dence—though it was an angry providence. Yet in spite of this forbearance, two things needed to be held firmly: (1) No one should dare establish new articles of faith such as that of papal primacy; (2) the pope should remain subject to Christ and allow himself to be judged by Holy Scripture. If, however, the pope refused to acknowledge these two points (God forbid), then one needed to say "openly" that he was the Antichrist. Luther concluded with an appeal to the civil authorities to put an end to the robbery of the pope. (pp. 156-58)

By early June he had devised a plan that called on the emperor and the German nobility to engage in open warfare against the Roman tyranny. Out of this plan came the work, *To the Christian Nobility of the German Nation Concerning the Reform of the Christian Estate.* (p. 158)

The serious struggles for reform of the late Middle Ages and the burdens of the German nation here found expression in the shimmering language and clear tone of the gospel. (p. 159)

Luther opened his treatise *To the Christian Nobility of the German Nation Concerning the Reform of the Christian Estate* by addressing his most illustrious, all-powerful, imperial majesty, and the Christian nobility of the German nation. Since the councils had not accomplished anything, he set his hope on the secular authorities, particularly the emperor, the "young man of noble birth." He warned against self-confident activism when beginning the work of reform: "For God cannot and will not suffer that a good work begin by relying upon one's own power and reason," even if all the power in the world were theirs. This was the very reasons the "precious princes," Emperor Frederick I, Frederick II, and so many other German emperors were so "wretchedly" treated by the popes, put down, and trodden under foot. "It may be that they relied on their own might more than on God. . . . We must tackle this job by renouncing trust in physical force and trusting humbly in God. . . . Otherwise . . . [there will be] such confusion that the whole world will swim in blood." This was not a cause that could be helped by war and bloodshed. (p. 160)

The Romanists (Luther's term for the papal court) had built three walls with which they had protected themselves against every attempt at reformation. The first wall was the thesis that spiritual power is superior to secular power. The second wall was the thesis that the pope alone had the right to interpret Holy Scripture. The third wall was the thesis that only the pope could convene a council. "May God help us, and give us just one of those trumpets with which the walls of Jericho were overthrown to blast down these walls of straw and paper in the same way."

Against the first wall Luther pitted the priesthood of all believers: "all Christians are truly of the spiritual estate, and there is no difference among them except that of office." The external rite of ordination and priestly garb might indeed make one a hypocrite and a puppet, but never a Christian or a spiritual person. All who had come "out of the water of baptism" had the same spiritual authority, but they assigned it to someone from their midst, who exercised the office in the congregation on their behalf. Priests did not have a *character indelebilis* (indelible character) that was presumably conferred on them through their ordination. When they no longer fulfilled the duties of their office they became farmers or citizens like everyone else. The only distinction was in the office, not in the estate. Civil authorities also held an office, namely that of exercising secular power. When those who exercised this office now saw that spiritual authority was breaking down, they had to come to its aid, even as each member of a physical body supports the others. In such situations the secular authorities were exercising their emergency authority in the church. Occam had already expressed these thoughts in the late Middle Ages; they became a reality with the establishment of the evangelical territorial churches. Church and state together formed the *Corpus Christianum,* therefore the church could not claim special rights or privileges. Crimes of the clergy had to be punished just as those of the laity were. In its existing form Christendom reflected the image of "the Antichrist, or at any rate that [of his] forerunner. . . ."

The second wall was no more than a "fancied fable" for which one could not point to a single letter of Scripture. Had not the pope erred many times? If it were true that the pope was always right, they would have to have confessed, "I believe in the pope at Rome." "It is the duty of every Christian to espouse the cause of the faith, to understand and defend it, and to denounce every error."

The third wall collapsed on its own along with the other two. Neither the Apostolic Council nor the Council of Nicaea were convened or authorized by the pope; the latter was convened by Emperor Constantine. When there is a fire, everyone has the duty of putting it out, even though they may not have been commissioned to do so by the mayor. Since the pope was now an offense to Christendom, it was the duty of the secular powers to convene a just and free council. "There is no authority in the church except to promote good." If a pope used this power to oppose the good and to prohibit the convening of a council, one should not be swayed. Such a council would surely not fail to find plenty of work to do.

In the second part of his treatise Luther outlined a comprehensive program of reform. In the first 25 segments he concentrated on religious problems, and he dealt with the deplorable state of secular affairs in the 26th. The "drunken Germans" paid the bills for the worldly splendor and arrogance of the pope and the curia. But the Germans were now waking up and seeing through the Roman practices. The never-ending payments to Rome had to cease: the *annates,* that is, the taxes paid to Rome by newly-appointed bishops; the palliums, or special payments required of archbishops; the monies paid to the Datarius, the Roman court of justice; the *compositiones,* such as Albert of Mainz had to pay; the indulgence monies; the dispensations; and a host of others. This robbery ruined both the body and soul of Christendom. What could one do against it?

"If we want to fight against the Turks, let us begin here where they are worst of all. If we are right in hanging thieves and beheading robbers, why should we let Roman Avarice go free? He is the worst thief and robber that has ever been or could ever come into the world, and all in the holy name of Christ and St. Peter!" One should "henceforth forbid" the payment of *annates.* The bishops should no longer remain the "ciphers and dummies" of the pope. When the next Roman lackey came with potential appointments for the office of bishop, he should be told "to keep out, to jump into the Rhine or the nearest river, and give the Romish ban with all its seals and letters a nice, cool dip."

Luther would like to have seen the practices of the early church reintroduced. The appointment of a bishop should be made with the approval of the neighboring bishops, and at the head of the bishops there should be a German primate. The pope should have nothing to do with the exercise of secular power;

instead he ought to be "the most learned in the Scriptures" and concern himself with the things that pertain to faith and the holy life of Christians. The pope was not the successor of the Roman emperor; the "Donation of Constantine" was an "impossible lie.". . . The papal states had been stolen by the papacy by means of this document.

The kissing of feet was to be abolished; pilgrimages to Rome should cease. There was nothing good to learn there; "'The nearer Rome, the worse Christians.'" "They say the first time a man goes to Rome he seeks a rascal; the second time he finds one; the third time he brings him back home with him." Pilgrimages were costly affairs; it would be better and more God-pleasing to use the money for one's own family. Not only the papacy, but the entire life of the church was in need of reform. The number of begging monks had to be reduced; they had become a plague on the countryside. The cloisters ought once again to become Christian schools in which one learned Holy Scripture and Christian discipline, rather than continuing to make "an eternal prison" out of them through the monastic vow. Celibacy should be abolished, at least for parish priests; it was not observed anyway, and it led to a guilty conscience. It was neither biblical nor founded on the traditions of the ancient church.

Luther severely judged the rules and regulations of the church: the interdict, the laws of marriage, the regulations concerning fasting, dispensations, the granting of privileges, and others. Festivals should be abolished and limited to Sundays. Begging was an evil; every city ought to look after its own poor and expel other beggars. It was high time that the schism with the Bohemians be set aside; it needed to be admitted that the burning of Hus was an injustice. Safe conduct was a divine decree. "We should overcome heretics with books, not with fire, as the ancient Fathers did. If it were wisdom to vanquish heretics with fire, then the public hangmen would be the most learned scholars on earth." Reconciliation with the Pickards, the community of Bohemian brethren, was important. The doctrine of transubstantiation was not an article of faith; it was sufficient to believe that the body and blood of Christ are in the bread and wine. One ought to give the cup to the laity.

The universities also needed to be reformed. To begin with, Aristotle needed to be done away with—that "conceited, rascally heathen" who denied the immortality of the soul and knew nothing of the grace of God. Luther knew what he was talking about; he claimed to have studied Aristotle in greater depth than had either Thomas or Scotus. Only his *Logic, Poetics,* and *Rhetoric* were worthy of being kept. Instead of Aristotle, languages, mathematics, and history should be taught. The jurists ought to concentrate on practical reason and forget canon law. The "dear theologians" should, above all, study Holy Scripture and not the *Sentences.*

One became a proper theologian through the Holy Spirit; the study of books alone wouldn't do it. "The number of books on theology must be reduced and only the best ones published. It is not many books that make men learned, nor even reading. But it is a good book frequently read, no matter how small it is, that makes a man learned in the Scriptures and godly." The church Fathers should lead one into the Scriptures, not out of them, as was then the case. For the Scripures alone are "our vineyard in which we must all labor and toil." In the elementary schools, too, the reading of the gospel ought to be given a primary place. "And would to God that every town had a girls' school as well, where the girls would be taught the gospel for an hour every day either in German or in Latin." Those who withheld the gospel from their youth would be severly judged.

Luther considered secular evils and injustices more briefly, since he had already dealt with them in his *Treatise on Good Works*. He spoke out against luxurious clothing, against the importation of exotic articles, and against excessive interest rates, a subject on which he was very critical of the Fuggers. He did not understand how one could earn 20 gulden on 100 gulden in a year. "I leave this to men who understand the ways of the world. As a theologian I have no further reproof to make on this subject except that it has an evil and offending appearance." Luther declared his support for agriculture: "I know full well that it would be a far more godly thing to increase agriculture and decrease commerce." There was still much uncultivated land in Germany. A dreadful vice of the Germans was excessive "gorging and boozing," which resulted in murder, adultery, robbery, and other crimes. Public brothels were a disgrace. Secular authorities had their work cut out for them in curbing all the deplorable conditions. (pp. 160-64)

Luther concluded his courageous appeal with these high-spirited, yet confident words:

> I know full well that I have been very outspoken. I have made many suggestions that will be considered impractical. I have attacked many things too severely. But how else ought I to do it? I am duty-bound to speak. If I had the power, these are the things I would do. I would rather have the wrath of the world upon me than the wrath of God. The world can do no more to me than take my life.

He had previously proposed peace, but his adversaries had given him no rest. "Well, I know another little song about Rome and the Romanists. If their ears are itching to hear it, I will sing that one to them, too—and pitch it in the highest key! You understand what I mean, dear Rome." "God give us all a Christian mind, and grant to the Christian nobility of the German nation in particular true spiritual courage to do the best they can for the poor church."

Luther had indeed "sung high." The book was written in so captivating a style that one would like to quote much more from it. It is packed full of fruitful ideas and practical insights. The proposed program of reform was as comprehensive as it was biblically grounded. In Ranke's opinion, "These few pages both prepare the way for and predict the content of further developments in world history." Johann Lang was disturbed by its "terribly wild" tone, and many agreed with him. Luther himself admitted that he may have "attacked many things too severely," but the situation did not call for a detached academic discussion. It was no unholy passion, but rather a holy zeal for reform of the muddled state of affairs and indignation over outrageous corruption that determined Luther's tone. Without this zeal he might have been a professor, but he would never have become a reformer. . . . (pp. 165-66)

The greatest service [Luther] contributed to "his Germans" was the translation of the Bible. Luther had the Bible to thank for everything. He could not keep it to himself; he had to pass it on to the laity so they could draw from it and so realize the priesthood of all believers.

It is understandable that Luther did not immediately attempt the whole Bible, but rather began with the New Testament. The completion of the translation took him a mere 11 weeks—an incredible achievement. His translation differed from pre-

vious German versions in two ways: it was based on the original Greek text rather than on the inaccurate Latin Vulgate, and it made use of a style of German the people could understand. (pp. 209-10)

Luther's preface to the entire volume and his introductions to the individual books are gems. The gospel was "a good story and report, sounded forth into all the world by the apostles." Romans was truly the chief part of the New Testament. Luther explained that book's most important concepts. Faith is "a divine work in us which changes us and makes us to be born anew of God. . . . O it is a living, busy, active, mighty thing, this faith. It is impossible for it not to be doing good works incessantly." Luther did not hesitate in assigning each of the individual books a different rank. The gospel of John was rightly "the one, fine, true, and chief gospel."

Compared with John and the most important of Paul's letters, James was "an epistle of straw . . . for it has nothing of the nature of the gospel about it." In his preface to James, Luther especially criticized that book for teaching justification through works and saying nothing about Christ. The "true test" for all books was whether or not they "inculcate Christ." "Whatever does not teach Christ is not yet apostolic, even though St. Peter or St. Paul does the teaching. Again, whatever preaches Christ would be apostolic, even if Judas, Annas, Pilate, and Herod were doing it." Even though Luther did not consider James one of the major books of the Bible, he admitted that there were many good sayings in it.

Luther also looked critically at Hebrews; although the author could not have been Paul, he was nevertheless a learned man. Yet the book's rejection of the possibility of a second repentance after Baptism was a "hard knot" to unravel and contrary to all of the Gospels and to Paul. Concerning the Revelation of John, "My spirit cannot accommodate itself," because the book dealt with pictures and visions, and he found it difficult to learn rightly about Christ from it. In a later preface to the Apocalypse Luther expressed himself more positively, having in the meanwhile accepted the church-historical interpretation.

In his day Luther stood alone in his completely free and varied judgment of the biblical canon; only since the Enlightenment have we been able to recapture his spirit. (pp. 210-11)

Luther defended his translation in *On Translating: An Open Letter*, published in 1530. He took issue with various criticisms that had been leveled by persons such as Hieronymus Emser. When translating it was no use asking the letters of the Latin language how to speak German. "Rather we must inquire about this of the mother in the home, the children on the street, the common man in the marketplace. We must be guided by their language, the way they speak, and do our translating accordingly. That way they will understand it and recognize that we are speaking German to them." Where Matt. 12:34 literally says, "Out of the abundance of the heart the mouth speaks," Luther had translated, "What fills the heart overflows the mouth." The angelic greeting, "Hail Mary, full of grace" was best translated, "Dear Mary." To Rom. 3:38 he had added the word *alone* after *faith* because only then did the correct sense of the passage become clear. His opponents had accused him of distorting the Bible with this addition; a modern catholic exegete of our own day maintains that Luther was correct. Luther had good reason to remark that his enemies were "stealing" his language. In fact the grim Duke George himself had said, "if only the monk would translate the whole Bible into German, and then go to the place he ought to go."

The Old Testament gave Luther the most trouble. ''It has often happened that for two or three or four weeks we have searched and inquired for a single word.'' At times in translating Job they took four days to complete only three sentences. ''Now that it is translated and finished, everybody can read and criticize it . . . without realizing what boulders and clods had once lain there where he now goes along as over a smoothly-planed board. . . . The plowing goes well when the field is cleared. But rooting out the woods and stumps, and getting the field ready—this is a job nobody wants.''

In order to visualize the 12 pearls of the new Jerusalem Luther visited a jeweler. Before describing the sacrifices of Leviticus he visited the butcher. ''Translating is not every man's skill as the mad saints imagine. It requires a right, devout, honest, sincere, God-fearing, Christian, trained, informed, and experienced heart.'' Luther was guided not only by what was being spoken by the common people, but also by what was in the heart of the saints. He translated the Bible into German, but his translation was not a distortion.

Luther was not only an unparalleled master of words who possessed a finely tuned musical ear for the rhythm of a sentence, he was also a person who was immersed in the spirit of the Bible in a way that has seldom been equalled. He lived in the Scriptures. He himself once said, ''The Scriptures are a vast forest, but there's no tree in it that I haven't shaken with my hand.'' His translation was not a slave to the letter but rather served the spirit. Luther had the gift of discerning the divine heart of Scripture and of couching it so totally and completely in human forms that the words came to light and life. For that we cannot sufficiently thank him. (pp. 212-13)

> *Walther von Loewenich, in his* Martin Luther: The Man and His Work, *translated by Lawrence W. Denef, Augsburg Publishing House, 1986, 446 p.*

HENRY ZECHER (essay date 1983)

[*In the following excerpt, Zecher summarizes Luther's achievements as a writer.*]

Martin Luther was many things to the sixteenth-century Christian church: reformer, teacher, orator, translator, theologian, composer, and family man. He came to symbolize everything the Protestant Reformation stood for.

Yet, had it not been for his powerful influence as a writer, all the changes he brought about and all he taught on the interpretation and practice of the Christian faith would have never had such a universal and long-lasting impact.

The man whose five-hundredth birthday is being celebrated all around the world this year published some 420 works on a wide range of topics, from *The Babylonian Captivity of the Church* to *A Marriage Booklet for Simple Pastors.* He wrote prefaces to, and brilliant sermons and commentaries on, every book of the Bible, his translation of which into German changed forever his country's language, literature, and dramatic arts. He also composed several hymns, most notably **''Ein' feste Burg ist unser Gott''** (**''A Mighty Fortress Is Our God''**). With all of that, he still found time to be a tender and witty correspondent of such enormous output that over 3,000 letters have survived.

In a time of intense restlessness, revolt, and violence, Luther's pen took the place of the sword he refused to wield, and its influence reached far into the future. (pp. 10-11)

Luther's greatest and most popular commentary was the one on Galatians, his favorite Pauline epistle. Wrote John Bunyan, ''I do prefer this book of Martin Luther upon the Galatians, excepting the Holy Bible, before all books that I have ever seen'' [see excerpt dated 1688].

The fact that Luther could say so clearly and succinctly what few others could even express, and with an impact that erased international boundaries, had more to do with the early spread of the Protestant Reformation than any other factor. In this once-obscure German monk, the people of Europe found a true champion of the faith who would not be beaten or silenced, for Luther's teachings not only expressed sound doctrines, but they touched sentiments that had been brewing in the hearts of oppressed people for centuries. Nearly everything Luther wrote was rushed into print and circulated as quickly as possible, with an immediate and widespread effect.

Secular Authority: To What Extent It Should Be Obeyed was the first and most definitive statement on the separation of church and state. Using the Book of Romans as his scriptural base for the Christian's obedience to the temporal government, he taught that ''whatever powers exist and flourish, they exist and flourish because God has ordained them.''

He noted the apostle Paul's instructions regarding the church in chapter 12 and the government in chapter 13, explaining that ''the former serves the guidance and peace of the inner (*spiritual*) man and his concerns; the latter serves that of the outward (*earthly*) man and his concerns. (*That is, the Church directs people as Christians; the state, as citizens.*)''

Luther concluded, ''These two kingdoms must be sharply distinguished, and both be permitted to remain; the one to produce piety, the other to bring about external peace and prevent evil deeds; neither is sufficient without the other.''

Luther's writing went hand in hand with his restructuring of the church liturgy. To teach the basics of the Christian faith to the people, particularly the children, Luther wrote his two Catechisms in 1529; one for adults [the *Large Catechism*] containing training for pastors, teachers, married couples, and parents; and the *Small Catechism* for children. These two books form the shortest, simplest, and clearest explanation of Christianity ever written. They are still used by Lutheran churches today.

He composed numerous hymns based, not on the old Gregorian chants, but on the popular music of his day. He included his own with those composed by others in the hymnals used during the service by the entire congregation, including the women, who were allowed to sing for the first time in more than a thousand years.

But, far and away, Luther's greatest achievement was the German Bible. No other work has had nearly the direct impact on a nation's development and heritage as did this book. (p. 11)

One reason for its lasting influence and popularity was its credibility. While previous translations had been based on the errant Latin Vulgate Bible, Luther relied on the work of humanists John Reuchlin, Gerson Ben Mosheh, and Desyderius Erasmus, who had compiled the best original Hebrew and Greek manuscripts then available. When his territorial ruler had him hidden away for safekeeping in the castle at Wartburg following the Diet of Worms, Luther settled down and translated Erasmus's Greek New Testament in only 11 weeks—a phenomenal feat considering the darkened days, the poor lighting, and his own generally poor health.

Das Newe Testament Deutzsch was published in September 1522. A typographical masterpiece containing woodcuts from Lucas Cranach's workshop and selections from Albrecht Dürer's famous Apocalypse series, the *September Bibel* sold an estimated 5,000 copies in the first two months alone.

Luther then turned his attention to the Old Testament, but as brilliant a scholar as he was (largely self-taught in both Greek and Hebrew), he would not attempt it alone. "Translators must never work by themselves," he wrote. "When one is alone, the best and most suitable words do not always occur to him." Luther thus anticipated C. S. Lewis by four centuries with his own version of the Oxford don's Inklings, which Luther called his "Sanhedrin." If the notion of a translation committee seems obvious today, it is because such scholars as Philipp Melanchthon, Justus Jonas, John Bugenhagen, and Gasper Cruciger joined Luther in setting the precedent. Never before, and not for many years after, was the scholarship of this body equaled.

Luther remained the principal translator, and his was the spirit that motivated and guided the Sanhedrin in producing a translation that was not literal in the truest sense of the word. He wanted this Bible to be in *spoken* rather than bookish or *written* German. Before any word or phrase could be put on paper, it had to pass the test of Luther's ear, not his eye. It had to *sound* right. This, of course, was the German Bible's greatest asset, but it meant that Luther had to straddle the fence between the free and the literal. (pp. 11-12)

It was Luther's desire to express the original Hebrew in the best possible German, but the task was not without its difficulties. "We are now sweating over a German translation of the Prophets," he wrote.

> O God, what a hard and difficult task it is to force these writers, quite against their wills, to speak German. They have no desire to give up their native Hebrew in order to imitate our barbaric German. It is as though one were to force a nightingale to imitate a cuckoo, to give up his own glorious melody for a monotonous song he must certainly hate. The translation of Job gives us immense trouble on account of its exalted language, which seems to suffer even more, under our attempts to translate it, than Job did under the consolations of his friends, and seems to prefer to lie among the ashes.

In spite of this, the Sanhedrin worked rapidly but accurately, translating in a tone more apologetic than scientific. The result was a German Bible of such incomparable literary quality that those competent to say so consider it superior even to the King James Version that followed it. And because it sounded natural when spoken as well as read, its cadence and readability have made it the most popular Bible in Germany to this day.

Germans everywhere bought it, not only for the salvation of their souls (if such was their concern), but also for the new middle-class prestige it conferred. It was the *must* book to have in their homes, and many Germans had no choice but to read it because it was likely to be one of the few books they could afford to buy.

It was the first time that a mass medium, in the form of the printed word, had ever penetrated everyday life. Everyone read it or listened to it being read. Its phrasing became the people's phrasing, its speech patterns their speech patterns. So universal was its appeal, and so thoroughly did it embrace the entire range of the German tongue, that it formed a linguistic rallying point for the formation of the modern German language and a more formal restructuring of German literature and the German

performing arts. Its impact, and Luther's in general were so awesome that Frederick the Great later called Luther the personification of the German national spirit, and scholars today consider him the most influential German who ever lived. . . .

Luther was exceptionally gifted in most everything he did, but that aspect of his genius most responsible for the impact he had is the one least heralded through the centuries—his skill and power as a writer. Had it not been for that, the Protestant Reformation and the growth of a united German nation would have taken an entirely different course. (p. 13)

> *Henry Zecher, "How One Man's Pen Changed the World," in* Christianity Today, *Vol. XXVII, No. 16, October 21, 1983, pp. 10-13.*

ADDITIONAL BIBLIOGRAPHY

Atkinson, James. *The Great Light: Luther and Reformation*. Grand Rapids, Mich.: Wm. B. Eerdmans Publishing Co., 1968, 287 p.
Narration of Luther and the German Reformation, Ulrich Zwingli and the Swiss Reformation, John Calvin, and the Reformation in Britain.

Bacon, Thomas I. *Martin Luther and the Drama*. Amsterdam: Editions Rodopi N.V., 1976, 86 p.
Analyzes Luther's conception of and influence on the religious drama of his time.

Beard, Charles. *Martin Luther and the Reformation in Germany until the Close of the Diet of Worms*. 1889. Reprint. Ann Arbor, Mich.: University Microfilms International, 1977, 468 p.
Respected study of the political, intellectual, and religious milieu of sixteenth-century Germany including an account of Luther's life up to the Diet of Worms in 1521.

Bluhm, Heinz. *Martin Luther: Creative Translator*. St. Louis, Mo.: Concordia Publishing House, 1965, 236 p.
Pioneering comparative textual analysis of selected portions of Luther's German Bible, which Bluhm considers a "literary and a religious achievement of the first order."

———. "The Literary Quality of Luther's *Septembertestament*." *PMLA*, LXXXI, No. 5 (October 1966): 327-33.
Compares Luther's New Testament translation with Latin, Greek, and High German versions. Bluhm praises Luther's work as "the most important work of German literature in the sixteenth century."

Boehmer, Heinrich. *Luther & the Reformation in the Light of Modern Research*. Translated by E. S. G. Potter. New York: Dial Press, 1930, 380 p.
Comprehensive, frequently cited study of Luther and Luther scholarship.

Carlyle, Thomas. "Lecture VIII." In his *Lectures on the History of Literature*, edited by J. Reay Greene, pp. 124-45. New York: Charles Scribner's Sons, 1892.
Contains a brief biography of Luther (written in 1838), concentrating on his bravery before the council at the Diet of Worms. Carlyle says of Luther that "he is the image of a large, substantial, deep man, that stands upon truth, justice, fairness, that fears nothing, considers the right, and calculates on nothing else."

Cranz, F. Edward. *An Essay on the Development of Luther's Thought on Justice, Law, and Society*. Cambridge: Harvard University Press, 1959, 197 p.
Examines the relationship Luther's social, political, and religious thought.

Davies, Rupert E. *The Problem of Authority in the Continental Reformers: A Study in Luther, Zwingli, and Calvin.* 1946. Reprint. Westport, Conn.: Greenwood Press, Publishers, 1978, 158 p.
Historical approach to the three reformers and their individual challenges of ecclesiastical authority.

Dickens, A. G. *Martin Luther and the Reformation.* London: English Universities Press, 1967, 184 p.
Analysis of Luther and Lutheranism in historical context.

Dünnhaupt, Gerhard, ed. *The Martin Luther Quincentennial.* Detroit: Wayne State University Press, 1985, 315 p.
Collection of studies presented at a 1983 Michigan conference on Luther. The essays included cover Luther and his contemporaries, his literary legacy, and his rhetorical techniques.

Ebeling, Gerhard. *Luther: An Introduction to His Thought.* Translated by R. A. Wilson. London: Wm. Collins Sons & Co., 1970, 287 p.
Examination of Luther's personality and theology, focusing on such topics as "The Kingdom of Christ and the Kingdom of the World," "Freedom and Bondage," and "The Way Luther Speaks of God."

Eck, John. *Enchiridion of Commonplaces against Luther and Other Enemies of the Church.* Translated by Ford Lewis Battles. Grand Rapids, Mich.: Baker Book House, 1979, 312 p.
1541 defense of the sovereign authority of the Church and denunciation of the heresy of Luther and his followers.

Edward, Mark U., Jr. *Luther and the False Brethren.* Stanford: Stanford University Press, 1975, 242 p.
Examines the nature and targets of Luther's theological disputes from 1522 until his death.

Erikson, Erik H. *Young Man Luther: A Study in Psychoanalysis and History.* New York: W. W. Norton & Co., 1962, 280 p.
Psychoanalytic study of Luther's early development emphasizing his major neuroses and emotional crises.

Fife, Robert Herndon. *Young Luther: The Intellectual and Religious Development of Martin Luther to 1518.* New York: Macmillan Co., 1928, 232 p.
Study of Luther's early intellectual and theological development based on the premise that the Reformation "must be approached from the standpoint of Luther's break with the scholastic traditions."

————. *The Revolt of Martin Luther.* New York: Columbia University Press, 1957, 726 p.
Biographical treatment of Luther from his early years to the Diet of Worms in 1521.

Forell, George Wolfgang. *Faith Active in Love: An Investigation of the Principles Underlying Luther's Social Ethics.* Minneapolis: Augsburg Publishing House, 1954, 198 p.
Discusses Luther's existential approach to ethical problems and central belief that the Gospel may serve as a guide to virtually all earthly matters.

Froude, James Anthony. "Luther: Parts I and II." *Contemporary Review* 44 (July, August 1883): 1-18, 183-202.
Anecdotal biography attesting to Luther's singular greatness.

Gritsch, Eric W. *Martin—God's Court Jester: Luther in Retrospect.* Philadelphia: Fortress Press, 1983, 289 p.
Study that "tries to distill . . . the historical Luther as well as the most significant research findings into a condensed retrospective which aims to be both an introduction to and an appraisal of Martin Luther." The book is divided into three parts: a historical/biographical background, a discussion of Luther's "neuralgic heritage" (described by Gritsch as those controversial and disturbing aspects of his thought that have caused "considerable pain . . . along the curves of many Christian nerves"), and a consideration of Luther's ecumenical legacy. The final chapter of the work is particularly helpful to those interested in a clear, concise history of Luther scholarship.

Hagen, Kenneth. *A Theology of Testament in the Young Luther: The Lectures on Hebrews.* Leiden, The Netherlands: E. J. Brill, 1974, 129 p.
Examination of Luther's exegetical writings on Hebrews, with comparative reference to classical and medieval exegetical texts.

Haile, H. G. *Luther: An Experiment in Biography.* Princeton: Princeton University Press, 1980, 422 p.
Biography of Luther's later life by a noted Luther scholar. Haile describes his engaging yet scholarly work as an attempt at pure biography, unadulterated by explications of theological and intellectual history, and designed with the sole purpose of rendering an "authentic impression" of Luther's character.

Hillerbrand, Hans J. *The Reformation: A Narrative History Related By Contemporary Observers and Participants.* New York: Harper & Row, Publishers, 1964, 495 p.
Overviews the Reformation through a selection of original source material by Luther and other principal figures of the era.

Hoffman, Bengt R. *Luther and the Mystics: A Re-examination of Luther's Spiritual Experience and His Relationship to the Mystics.* Minneapolis: Augsburg Publishing House, 1976, 285 p.
Detailed view of Luther's mystical theology, including his concepts of salvation, supernatural beings, occultism, and the afterlife.

Hoffmann, Manfred, ed. *Martin Luther and the Modern Mind: Freedom, Conscience, Toleration, Rights.* New York and Toronto: Edwin Mellen Press, 1985, 278 p.
Collection of 1983 essays on Luther. Among the lectures included are "Divine Right and Human Rights in Luther," by Martin Brecht and "Free by Faith: Luther's Contribution to a Theological Anthropology," by Otto Hermann Pesch.

Janz, Denis R. *Luther and Late Medieval Thomism: A Study in Theological Anthropology.* Waterloo, Ontario: Wilfred Laurier University Press, 1983, 186 p.
Comparative study of Luther, Thomas Aquinas, and Thomist scholars including John Capreolus, Conrad Koellin, and Cajetan.

Kaufman, Peter Iver. "Luther's 'Scholastic Phase' Revisited: Grace, Works, and Merit in the Earliest Extant Sermons." *Church History* 51, No. 3 (September 1982): 280-89.
Documents Luther's predisposition toward the concept of divine grace in his earliest sermons.

Kierkegaard, Søren. "For Self-Examination." In his *For Self-Examination and Judge for Yourselves! and Three Discourses,* translated by Walter Lowrie, pp. 27-106. Princeton: Princeton University Press, 1944.
Reveals, in an essay first published in 1851, Kierkegaard's encounter with Luther's doctrine of justification by faith, wherein he imagines himself undergoing—and failing—Luther's acid test of faith.

Koenigsberger, H. G., ed. *Luther: A Profile.* New York: Hill and Wang, 1973, 233 p.
Collection of historical and critical essays on Luther's career, theology, and work.

Leo X. "The Bull 'Decet Romanum': The Condemnation and Excommunication of Martin Luther, the Heretic, and His Followers." In *Martin Luther,* edited by E. G. Rupp and Benjamin Drewery, pp. 63-7. New York: St. Martin's Press, 1970.
Excommunicates "the slave of a depraved mind," Luther.

Lienhard, Marc. *Luther: Witness to Jesus Christ.* Translated by Edwin H. Robertson. Minneapolis: Augsburg Publishing House, 1982, 412 p.
Comprehensive analysis of Luther's Christology.

Lindberg, Carter. "Mask of God and Prince of Lies: Luther's Theology of the Demonic." In *Disguises of the Demonic: Contemporary Perspectives on the Power of Evil,* edited by Alan M. Olson, pp. 87-103. New York: Association Press, 1975.
Discusses Luther's conception of the demonic linked to his understanding of divine wrath.

Lindhardt, Jan. *Martin Luther: Knowledge and Mediation in the Renaissance.* Lewiston, N.Y.: Edwin Mellen Press, 1986, 259 p.
Evaluation of Luther and his doctrines in the light of Renaissance humanist philosophy.

MacLaurin, C. "Luther's Devil." In his *Mere Mortals: Medico-Historical Essays,* pp. 117-27. New York: George H. Doran Co., 1925.
Posits that Luther's personal encounters with the devil throughout his life were actually caused by the symptoms of Meniere's disease, an inner ear disorder.

Marty, Martin E. "A Man of Grand Contradictions." *Christianity Today* XXVII, No. 16 (21 October 1983): 8-9.
Explores Luther's contradictory stances on a variety of subjects, including language, women, civil disobedience, and God's attitude—of wrath or of mercy?—toward humanity.

Mee, Charles, L., Jr. *White Robe, Black Robe.* New York: G. P. Putnam's Sons, 1972, 316 p.
Dual biography of Pope Leo X and Luther centering on the ideological clash between the two.

Mullet, Michael. "Luther: Conservative or Revolutionary?" *History Today* 33 (December 1983): 39-44.
Denies that Luther was a radical reformist, concluding that he "was the author of one Reformation, the 'moderate' Reformation of the centre."

Oberman, Heiko A., ed. *Luther and the Dawn of the Modern Era: Papers for the Fourth International Congress for Luther Research,* Leiden, The Netherlands: E. J. Brill, 1974, 219 p.
Essay collection. Topics include "Conscience and Authority in Luther," "Luther and the Beginning of the Modern Age," and "Renaissance and Reformation: An Essay in Their Affinities and Connections."

Pelikan, Jaroslav, ed. *Interpreters of Luthers: Essays in Honor of Wilhelm Pauck,* Philadelphia: Fortress Press, 1968, 374 p.
Collection of essays wherein modern scholars explicate selected earlier critics' views of Luther. Subjects include John Calvin, Joseph Priestley, Søren Kierkegaard, and Paul Tillich.

Priestley, Joseph. "The Progress of the Reformation, from the Accession of Charles V. to the Empire, to the Citation of Luther to Appear at the Diet at Worms." In his *The Theological and Miscellaneous Works, &c., of Joseph Priestley,* Vol. X, edited by J. T. Rutt, pp. 112-27. New York: Kraus Reprint Co., 1972.
History (written in 1800) of Luther's actions and writings in the progress of the Reformation. Priestley describes Luther as an "extraordinary man, who had been raised up by God to be a principal instrument in promoting the great and necessary work of reformation."

Ritter, Gerhard. *Luther: His Life and Work.* Translated by John Riches. Westport, Conn.: Greenwood Press, Publishers, 1963, 256 p.
Biographical and critical account of Luther based on the premise that "Luther is a religious prophet: his public acts, his militancy, his efforts as organiser of church life—all stem from this."

Rupp, [E.] Gordon. *The Righteousness of God: Luther Studies.* London: Hodder and Stoughton, 1953, 375 p.

Collection of lectures on a wide variety of Luther topics.

Rupp, E. G[ordon], and Drewery, Benjamin, eds. *Martin Luther.* New York: St. Martin's Press, 1970, 180 p.
Excerpts from Luther's works and correspondence and from documents written by his contemporary supporters and opponents, chronologically arranged to present an evolving picture of Luther's life and the progress of the Reformation.

Spelman, Leslie P. "Luther and the Arts." *The Journal of Aesthetics and Art Criticism* 10, No. 2 (December 1951): 166-75.
Discusses Luther's understanding of and influence on German art, poetry, music, and architecture.

Steinmetz, David C. *Luther and Staupitz: An Essay in the Intellectual Origins of the Protestant Reformation.* Durham, N.C.: Duke University Press, 1980, 149 p.
Provides comparative research into the theological thought of Luther and his mentor, Johann von Staupitz, whose influence on Luther's Reformation thought has been the subject of considerable speculation. Steinmetz believes that "Luther perceived Staupitz as a crucial influence in his development as a theologian and reformer.

———. *Luther in Context.* Bloomington: Indiania University Press, 1986, 146 p.
Examines several aspects of Luther's thought by placing his views in historical context while comparing them with those of his antecedents and contemporaries. Chapter topics include: "Luther and Calvin on Church and Tradition" and "Luther and Augustine on Romans 9."

Todd, John M. *Luther: A LIfe.* London: Hamish Hamilton, 1982, 396 p.
Biography written for nonspecialists delineating Luther's personal life through liberal use of his letters.

Waring, Luther Hess. *The Political Theories of Martin Luther.* 1910. Reprint. Port Washington, N.Y.: Kennikat Press, 1968, 293 p.
Analysis of Luther's views on the powers, limitations, and fundamental sovereignty of the state.

Wicks, Jared, ed. *Catholic Scholars Dialogue with Luther.* Chicago: Loyola University Press, 1970, 228 p.
Collection of essays on Luther written by prominent Catholic scholars. Wicks explains in the book's introduction that "each essay offers in its own way an evaluation of Luther's theology from a Catholic standpoint."

Will, George F. "Martin Luther, Founding Father." In his *The Morning After: American Successes and Excesses, 1981-1986,* pp. 222-24. New York: Free Press, 1986.
Reprints a 1983 essay in which Will pays tribute to Luther on the quincentenary of his birth.

Zeeden, Ernst Walter. *The Legacy of Luther: Martin Luther and the Reformation in the Estimation of the German Lutherans from Luther's Death to the Beginning of the Age of Goethe.* Translated by Ruth Mary Bethell. Westminster, Md.: Newman Press, 1954, 221 p.
Useful history of Luther critical scholarship by German Lutherans from the sixteenth century to the end of the eighteenth.

John Milton

1608-1674

English poet, essayist, dramatist, and historian.

Milton is recognized as one of the greatest writers in the English language and as a thinker of world importance. He is best known for two poems: *Paradise Lost,* an epic of humanity's fall from grace, and *Paradise Regained,* a sequel in which grace is restored. Both of these works are celebrated for their consummate artistry and searching consideration of God's relationship with the human race. Milton also wrote copious prose, some of which is considered among the finest in English. In such essays as *Areopagitica, The Doctrine and Discipline of Divorce,* and *The Tenure of Kings and Magistrates* he questioned prevailing beliefs about human liberty, helping to promote intellectual and social freedom as natural rights. Controversial in his day, during which he was principal propagandist of the Cromwellian Protectorate and frequently characterized as a seditious upstart and self-promoter, Milton also became known as the supreme champion in England of the then-embryonic concept of political self-determination. Today he is simply considered a master of his art and a literary craftsman of the highest order.

Milton's life was an intellectual and literary one. He was born in Cheapside, London in 1608, the son of a prosperous scrivener and notary. His father, who was exceptionally devoted to the boy, early provided his son with a private tutor, retaining him even after Milton had entered St. Paul's School sometime between 1615 and 1620. Milton was a model student: he excelled in Latin, Greek, and Hebrew; wrote poetry in Latin and English; and studied the classics voraciously. (Milton acknowledged that in his youth he rarely quit his books before midnight, and he attributed his later blindness to excessive reading by lamp- and candlelight.) Under the guidance of both his tutor and his father, he also learned several modern languages and the niceties of music. These subjects—especially music and the classics—remained lifelong interests for Milton and colored much of his literary work. Milton entered Christ's College, Cambridge in 1625. There, his handsome face, delicate appearance, and lofty but unpretentious bearing earned him the sobriquet "the Lady of Christ's"—an appellation he was apparently never wont to put down, distinguishing him as it did from some of the coarser students. At first unpopular, Milton eventually made a name for himself as a rhetorician and public speaker. While at Cambridge he probably wrote "L'Allegro," "Il Penseroso," and "On the Morning of Christ's Nativity," three of his earliest great poems in English. Upon leaving the university in 1632 with an M. A. degree, Milton retired to Hammersmith for three years and later to Horton, Buckinghamshire, where he devoted himself to intense study and writing. To this period scholars assign the composition of some of Milton's finest so-called "minor" poems (critics agree that this is a label of convenience only, for there is nothing minor about most of these works), including "Lycidas," "Arcades," and the sonnet "How Soon Hath Time." While still in Hammersmith, he also wrote his first extended work, *Comus,* on commission for the Bridgewater family. In May 1638, Milton embarked on an Italian journey which was to last nearly fifteen months. The experience, which he described in *Defensio se-*

cunda pro populo anglicano (Second Defence of the People of England), brought him into contact with the leading men of letters in Florence, Rome, and Naples, including Giovanni Battista Manso, Marquis of Villa, who had been an intimate of the epic poet Torquato Tasso. Because until now Milton had published almost nothing under his name—*Comus* was issued anonymously, and "Lycidas," which was signed only "J. M.," was buried in an otherwise undistinguished anthology—and therefore had no notable personal connections with English writers, scholars view the Italian tour as seminal in Milton's literary development. For a new self-confidence emerged in the letters he wrote during his travels, and it was in Italy that Milton first proposed to write a great epic. Upon his return to England, Milton took lodgings in St. Bride's Churchyard, London, where he took in boys for tuition. Around this time he also wrote the Italian-inspired *Epitaphium Damonis (Damon),* a Latin elegy on his longtime friend Charles Diodati. Critics have seen this work as Milton's first heralding of his ambition to be a great poet in the Renaissance vein, the author of classically inspired works on elevated themes.

But with the coming of the English Civil War and Commonwealth, Milton's life changed utterly as he moved from private to public concerns. Abruptly he left off writing poetry for prose, pouring out pamphlets during the early 1640s in which he opposed what he considered rampant episcopal tyranny. Having, as he related, embarked from a sense of duty upon "a troubled sea of noises and hoarse disputes," he declared his Puritan allegiance in such antiprelatical tracts as *Of Reformation Touching Church-Discipline in England* and *The Reason of Church-Governement*. The theme of these works was always the same: the need to purge the Church of England of all vestiges of Roman Catholicism and restore the simplicity of the apostolic church. Around this time Milton also published *The Doctrine and Discipline of Divorce*, in which he maintained that incompatibility is a valid reason for divorce. This work was presumably inspired by his precipitate marriage in 1642 to his first wife, Mary Powell, who left her husband shortly after the wedding (but returned to him three years later; ironically, though Milton was to marry two more times, he was never divorced). In 1644 Milton published *Areopagitica,* a now-classic plea for unlicensed printing in England. During the next few years Milton worked on his *History of Britain* and *De doctrina christiana (A Treatise of Christian Doctrine).* With the execution of Charles I in 1649, however, Milton entered the political fray with *The Tenure of Kings and Magistrates,* an assertion of the right of a people to depose or execute a ruling tyrant. This view constituted a complete about-face for Milton, who had written as a good monarchist in his early antiprelatical works. Henceforth Milton was permanently of the left. He accepted an invitation to become Cromwell's Latin secretary for foreign affairs and soon issued a number of tracts on church and state issues, including *Pro populo anglicano defensio (A Defence of the People of England)* and *Second Defence of the People of England,* two highly laudatory reviews of the achievements of the Commonwealth. The Restoration of Charles II in 1660 left Milton disillusioned and hastened his departure from public life. As a noted defender of the regicides, he lived for a time in peril of his life, but for reasons not entirely clear he was spared harsh punishment.

The remaining fourteen years of Milton's life were spent in relatively peaceful retirement in a succession of houses and lodgings in and around London. Now completely blind—he had been since 1652—Milton increasingly devoted his time to poetry. Amanuenses, assisted sometimes by Milton's two nephews and his daughter Deborah, were employed to take dictation, correct copy, and read aloud, and Milton made rapid progress on projects he had put off many years before. According to early biographers and to Milton's own account of the making of *Paradise Lost,* Milton spent mornings dictating passages he had composed in his head at night. *Paradise Lost* was published in 1667, followed in 1671 by *Paradise Regained. Samson Agonistes,* a metrical tragedy, appeared in the same volume as *Paradise Regained.* In 1673 Milton embraced controversy once again with *Of True Religion,* a short defense of Protestantism. Milton died in November 1674, apparently of heart failure. (An early biographer, John Aubrey, claimed simply: "the gout struck in.") His funeral, wrote John Toland in 1698, was attended by "All his learned and great Friends in *London,* not without a friendly concourse of the Vulgar. . . ."

Milton's works fall neatly into two categories, poetry and prose, and there is very little crossover of theme or purpose from one category to the other. This is because poetry was chiefly an artistic medium for Milton, prose being reserved for exposition only. Milton believed that the great poet had first to be a great man. His early poems, consisting chiefly of Psalm paraphrases, Latin elegies, a few sonnets in Italian, and ruminations on the Gunpowder Plot, show him working hard toward greatness, attempting, as had many classical writers, to civilize himself

and society through literature. His success at this manifested itself boldly in the twin lyrics "L'Allegro" and "Il Penseroso," in which are contrasted the active and contemplative lives. Critics agree that the poet's voice in these lyrics is a mature and studied one. The imagery, drawn from classical mythology and English folkore, is cultivated and stylized, and both works are tightly argued. Milton's next major poem, *Comus,* is in the Elizabethan court mask tradition. Here, in exchanges between two young brothers, a lady, and the tempter Comus, Milton explored the merits of "moral discipline" and the dangers of sexual license, emphasizing Christian-Platonic idealism as it mirrors divine grace. Milton drew on the works of Homer, Ovid, Edmund Spenser, Shakespeare, and others for his theme, plot, and imagery in *Comus.* Critics agree that with "Lycidas," his next major work, Milton came into his own as a poet. In editing his poems in 1645, he called this pastoral a "Monody" in which "the Author bewails a learned Friend, unfortunately drown'd . . . on the *Irish* Seas, 1637. And by occasion foretells the ruin of our corrupted Clergy then in their height." The purpose of the poem was twofold: to honor the late Edward King, who had been at Christ's College in Milton's time, and to denounce hireling, incompetent clergy—a perennial concern of Milton's. Incidentally, the poem reveals Milton's own ambitions as a poet while foreshadowing the mission of *Paradise Lost:* to justify God's ways to men. Many critics consider "Lycidas" the finest short poem in the English language.

Milton's best-known poems are also his longest ones: *Paradise Lost, Paradise Regained,* and *Samson Agonistes.* Of these, *Paradise Lost* is deemed the supreme achievement by far. As early as the Italian tour, Milton had planned an epic which was to be to England what Homer's works were to Greece and the *Aeneid* was to Rome. Originally, he contemplated an Arthurian subject for his national poem. Only later, around 1657 or 1658, did he abandon this idea for the biblical subject he considered the most fitting: the Fall of Man as described in the Book of Genesis. The work was finished by 1665. The first edition of 1667 was in ten books; in one of the issues of 1668, Milton added summary arguments and a note on his use of blank verse. In the second edition (1674), Books VII and X were each split into two, a few passages were revised, and the arguments, which were initially prefixed to the poem as a whole, were placed at the head of the respective books. This is the final form of the poem as Milton conceived it. The Fall of Man as a literary subject was not original to Milton—it had received imaginative treatment from Guillaume du Bartas and Hugo Grotius, among others—but Milton infused it with a strikingly fresh aspect. As a classicist, he was powerfully aware of his antique antecedents; he therefore began the poem in medias res, invoking his muse and plunging into the action with a description of Satan in Hell—actually the poem's third crisis, which chronologically follows Satan's revolt in Heaven and descent with his followers through Chaos to Hell. The remainder of the poem treats Satan's deception of Eve in Eden, her deception of Adam, their fall from perfect fellowship with God and with each other, and their banishment from Paradise. Along the way, Milton established the Son of God's right to reign in heaven, described the creation of the universe, and unfolded the reconciliation of Adam and Eve. Everywhere the poem is strong in its appeal to the ear, the intellect, and the visual imagination. While the iambic pentameter line is the norm, Milton played with the model, contriving syllables and stresses to complement the sense. (Commentators attribute many of Milton's superb metrical effects to his deep knowledge of music and his acutely sensitive ear.) Descriptive passages evoke images at once vague and minute, exposing in precise detail the character (but usually not the exact composition) of Heaven, Pandemonium, Chaos, and the universe. Eden is revealed as a sensuous feast. Milton's high purpose in the poem, to "justify the ways of God to men," is ever in the forefront of the action. Critics agree that this challenging objective, made all the more difficult by the complicated issue of divine foreknowledge of the Fall, is effected chiefly by imbuing Adam with a will as well as a mind of his own, enabling him to disobey God and thus mar an omnipotent Creator's perfect creation. The whole of the poem is bound together both by imagination and organization, with form and matter closely knit through analogue and juxtaposition. *Paradise Regained*—less of an epic poem than a dramatic one—completes the action of *Paradise Lost.* Shorter and conceptually much simpler than the earlier work, it shows Christ in the wilderness overcoming Satan the tempter. By this action, Christ proves his fitness as the Son of God, thereby preparing himself for his human, substitutionary role in the Crucifixion and thus, above all, making the Redemption possible. *Samson Agonistes* departs from the form and theme of *Paradise Lost* and *Paradise Regained,* but it is clear that Milton recognized affinities among the three works. A retelling of the story of Samson in the Book of Judges, *Samson* is in the tradition of Greek tragedy and is highly ironic, evocative, and ambiguous. Like Christ in *Paradise Regained,* Samson is terribly isolated, "Eyeless in Gaza at the mill with slaves," and undergoes a severe testing of his spiritual strength. He triumphs, gaining renewed faith in God and an improved understanding of his soul. Critics have seen this as Milton's final testament. If it is this, it is an essentially optimistic one.

Milton's prose is less known than his poetry, but commentators agree that it is compelling in several respects. The themes of the major works have been discussed above: *Areopagitica,* a plea for unlicensed printing; *The Tenure of Kings and Magistrates,* an assertion of a people's right to rid itself of a tyrant; *A Defence of the People of England* and *Second Defence of the People of England,* Commonwealth propaganda; and antiprelatical tracts urging the completion of the English Reformation. These works are recognized as excellent examples of English polemic. They are liberally infused with rhetorical devices drawn from classical models; make their points forcefully but with dignity; evidence a marked sensitivity to syntax and sentence length; do not refrain from autobiography when personal notes are thought useful for strengthening the argument; and are resoundingly clear, ordered, and measured—in thought, degree, and execution. All the while, much of the prose reveals Milton's first love, poetry, in its suggestive diction, vigorous movement, and overall impassionedness. (It will be remembered that Milton the poet turned pamphleteer not by preference but from a compelling sense of duty.) In addition to antiprelatical tracts and other topical treatises on religion, Milton wrote on more general theological issues. His most important work in this field is *A Treatise of Christian Doctrine,* in which he surveyed at length the emergence of institutionalized Christianity and commented on major tenets of Christian belief. Milton also wrote studies not prompted by strictly political or religious concerns. The short works *A Brief History of Moscovia* and *Accedence Commenc't Grammar* treat Russian history and Latin grammar respectively. In *The Doctrine and Discipline of Divorce* he argued that wedded couples should be allowed release from their marriage commitment if perfect companionship proved impossible. His views here were not popular and were opposed in print, leading him to write three further pamphlets on the subject: *The Judgment of Martin Bucer concerning Divorce, Colasterion,* and *Tetrachordon. Of Ed-*

ucation, written in the form of a letter, is the most frequently quoted example of Milton's minor prose. Here, drawing no doubt on his own experience as a student and teacher, Milton petitioned for the creation of an elite class through the careful instruction of boys in small regional academies. Milton's objective for the students, "to repair the ruins of our first parents by regaining to know God aright," had a practical end: "I call therefore a complete and generous education that which fits a man to perform justly, skilfully, and magnanimously all the offices, both private and public, of peace and war." Milton was especially proud of this work, and its reputation as a major contribution to educational theory endures to this day.

More scholarship and criticism is devoted to Milton than to any other English author save Shakespeare and possibly Chaucer. In life Milton was both praised and scorned: praised for his achievements in poetry, scorned for his writings on church and state. Political opponents lashed out at him mercilessly in print, damning him as a rebel and traitor. But he was not without advocates. Andrew Marvell, for example, allied himself closely with Milton, defending him against detractors at the Restoration and, later, praising him in print in an encomium on *Paradise Lost.* The first few decades after Milton's death saw the writing or publication of a number of biographies—strong testimony to Milton's growing eminence. According to one estimate, more than 1,750 critical statements and allusions concerning Milton's life and works had appeared in print and manuscript by 1700, and writings by him were included in over one hundred discrete publications. *Paradise Lost,* which initially was only moderately successful, attracted keen minds soon after Milton's death and has remained the work on which the poet's reputation largely rests. In an epigram first printed in the 1688 edition of the poem, John Dryden linked Milton with Homer and Vergil, and in 1695 Patrick Hume issued an annotated text of the poem—the first scholarly edition of any English poet. Serious criticism of the poem began in 1712 with Joseph Addison's series of essays in the *Spectator.* Addison, whose judgments were carefully argued and mostly laudatory, approached *Paradise Lost* as a neoclassicist; like Dryden, he considered Milton an epic poet of world importance. Eighteenth-century English poets immersed themselves in *Paradise Lost, Paradise Regained,* and *Samson Agonistes.* The impact was tremendous: immensely impressed by Milton's use of blank verse (which hitherto had been practically confined to the drama) and his treatment of the sublime, imitators and would-be Miltons adapted, mimicked, and emulated the Miltonic style in their works. The result was a mass of Milton-inspired poems by major and minor writers alike. But Samuel Johnson, for one, was not so positively inclined toward Milton. In a lengthy study of the poet, he attacked "Lycidas" as "harsh," anachronistic, unfeeling, and pretentious; maintained that Milton's poetic idiom was in general a foreign one; and belittled the language and, to a degree, the argument—the thematic structure—of *Paradise Lost.* While commentators agree that Johnson's views are not without merit and are clearly the product of honest, careful deliberation, most believe that his opinions were colored as much by political and religious prejudice as by understanding and critical sensitivity. The Romantic vision of Milton, which insists that he made Satan the hero of *Paradise Lost,* was heralded in 1790 by William Blake, who wrote in *The Marriage of Heaven and Hell* that Milton was "a true Poet, and of the Devil's party without knowing it." (Blake, however, appears to have been only a catalyst here and not, as is sometimes claimed, an originator, for Dryden also pointed to Satan as the hero of *Paradise Lost.*) Percy Bysshe Shelley exalted Satan as a Promethean rebel, Samuel Taylor Coleridge extolled Milton the artist, and William Wordsworth, taking a different tack, saw Milton as a liberator and champion of independent thinking. "Milton! thou shouldst be living at this hour," he wrote. Shelley represents one of two dominant strains in nineteenth-century Milton criticism: Milton the Romantic, projecting himself into Satan. This view, which insists that Milton conceived God in *Paradise Lost* as wicked or, in any case, did not portray God as compellingly as he might have, was strongly challenged by later critics, notably the twentieth-century commentators C. S. Lewis and E. M. W. Tillyard. The other approach, exemplified by Wordsworth, William Hazlitt, and Ralph Waldo Emerson, centered on the epic qualities of *Paradise Lost*. Advocates promoted the sensual aspects of Milton's verse—its sublime utterances—to the near-total exclusion of all else, including the poet's ideas and beliefs.

Milton's reputation remained high until the 1920s or so, when his poetical works suffered their fiercest denunciation ever. Aspects of the poem once praised now came under fire. T. S. Eliot, for one, attacked the Milton canon, ranking Milton the poet far below John Donne. Eliot modified his views somewhat later on, but F. R. Leavis and others subscribed to them wholeheartedly. These critics faulted the perceived rigid syntax, rhythm, and argument of *Paradise Lost;* lamented Milton's apparent inability to infuse the poem with Spenserian richness and sensuality; and, perhaps most of all, regretted Milton's influence on later poets, which they saw as stifling and pernicious. In a word, they viewed Milton as a mechanical poet—a poetry machine, of sorts, without feeling or human sentiment—whose poetic legacy was worse than nil. By the 1940s, however, thanks to a new and systematic revaluation, such approaches had been dismissed almost entirely, freeing critics to explore Milton from an astonishing variety of viewpoints. Hitherto practically buried, the prose works were examined rigorously and with fervor. Commentators soon came to consider Milton a shaping influence during the Commonwealth period in matters concerning religious appointment, education, and the limits of government. Most significant of all, critics recognized Milton as a major figure in the history of ideas, one whose thoughts on self-determination and unlicensed printing, though not initially embraced or especially influential, touched later generations and helped form opinion in Britain and abroad. At the same time, *Paradise Lost* attained a new eminence. Once considered by Leavis and his school to be overly logical and argumentative, the poem is now celebrated for its breadth and complexity. So, too, are *Paradise Regained* and *Samson Agonistes*—both now appreciated as outstanding works of literature. In demonstrating the greatness of the poetry, commentators have examined imagery, argument, motive, characterization, and form. All these features have been deemed superlative in almost every case, inviting critics to quarrel over precisely what makes them so. As aesthetic achievements, then, Milton's poems are now recognized as among the finest in the language. And as the work of a man who sought to justify the ways of God to men, they—and much of the prose, too—are considered uniquely penetrating and successful.

It would be difficult to overestimate Milton's importance in English letters. In *Paradise Lost* he gave his country its greatest epic, surpassing, most commentators believe, even Spenser in the magnitude of his achievement in this form. And as the author of "Lycidas," "L'Allegro," and "Il Penseroso" he established himself as a master of the shorter poem, too. He also helped fuel Commonwealth reform and argued eloquently for major social amendment. Perhaps most telling of all, he

wrote, unlike his nearest English rivals for literary eminence, Chaucer and Shakespeare, in numerous forms on a tremendous range of issues. Of Milton it may therefore be truly said that his scope was wide, his sweep broad, and his capacity for thought deep—the touchstone of intellectual achievement. For, in the words of James Russell Lowell, "If [Milton] is blind, it is with the excess of light, it is a divine partiality, an overshadowing with angels' wings."

PRINCIPAL WORKS

A Maske Presented at Ludlow Castle, 1634, on Michaelmas Night, before the Right Honorable John Earle of Bridgewater, Viscount Brackly (drama) 1637

"Lycidas" (poetry) 1638; published in *Obsequies to the Memorie of Mr. Edward King, Anno. Dom. 1638*

Epitaphium Damonis (poetry) 1640
[*Damon*, 1900]

"On Hobson the Carrier" (poetry) 1640; published in *Witts Recreatons, Selected from the Finest Fancies of Moderne Muses*

Animadversions upon the Remonstrants Defence, against Smectymnuus (essay) 1641

An Answer to a Book Entituled "An Humble Remonstrance," in Which the Originall of Liturgy Episcopacy Is Discussed (essay) 1641

Of Prelatical Episcopacy, and Whether It May Be Deduc'd from the Apostolical Times by Vertue of Those Testimonies Which Are Alledg'd to That Purpose in Some Late Treatises (essay) 1641

Of Reformation Touching Church-Discipline in England and the Causes That Hitherto Have Hindred It (essay) 1641

An Apology against a Pamphlet Call'd "A Modest Confutation of the Animadversions upon the Remonstrant against Smectymnuus" (essay) 1642

The Reason of Church-Governement Urg'd against Prelaty (essay) 1642

The Doctrine and Discipline of Divorce, Restor'd to the Good of Both Sexes from the Bondage of Canon Law (essay) 1643

Areopagitica: A Speech of Mr. John Milton for the Liberty of Unlicenc'd Printing, to the Parlament of England (essay) 1644

The Judgement of Martin Bucer concerning Divorce, Written to Edward the Sixt, in His Second Book of the Kingdom of Christ, and Now Englisht, Wherin a Late Book Restoring the Doctrine and Discipline of Divorce Is Heer Confirm'd and Justify'd By the Authoritie of Martin Bucer (essay) 1644

Of Education: To Master Samuel Hartlib (essay) 1644

Colasterion: A Reply to a Nameless Answer against "The Doctrine and Discipline of Divorce" (essay) 1645

†*Poems of Mr. John Milton, Both English and Latin, Compos'd at Several Times* (poetry) 1645

Tetrachordon: Expositions upon the Foure Chief Places in Scripture Which Treat of Mariage, or Nullities in Mariage (essay) 1645

‡*ΕΙΚΟΝΟΚΛΑ΄ΣΤΗΣ in Answer to a Book Intitl'd Ε΄ΙΚΩ΄Ν ΒΑΣΙΛΙΚῊ, the Portrature of His Sacred Majesty in His Solitudes and Sufferings* (essay) 1649

"Observations upon the Articles of Peace with the Irish Rebels" (essay) 1649; published in *Articles of Peace Made and Concluded with the Irish Rebels, and Papists, by James Earle of Ormond*

*This work is commonly known as *Comus: A Maske*.

†This work was revised as *Poems upon Several Occasions* in 1673 and 1695.

‡This work is commonly known by its transliterated title, *Eikonok-lastes*.

§Milton's role in the writing of this work is disputed.

‖This work was written chiefly between 1625 and 1632.

SIR ROBERT FILMER   (essay date 1652)

[*Filmer was an ardent English royalist who, having been knighted by Charles I and suffered hardships under Cromwell, viewed the Civil War as repugnant. He is known to be the author of several short political essays, including* The Anarchy of a Limited or Mixed Monarchy *(1648) and* The Necessity of the Absolute Power of All Kings *(1648). In the following excerpt from his "Obser-vations on Master Milton against Salmasius," which was origi-nally published as part of a pamphlet entitled* Observations con-cerning the Originall of Government *in 1652, he replies to Milton's* Defence of the People of England *and comments briefly on his views concerning kingship in* The Tenure of Kings and Magistrates.]

Among the many Printed Books, and severall Discourses touch-ing the Right of *Kings*, and the Liberty of the *People*, I cannot finde that as yet the first and chief point is agreed upon, or indeed so much as once Disputed. The word *King* and the word *People* are familiar, one would think every simple man could tell what they signified; but upon examination it will be found, that the learnedst cannot agree of their meaning.

Ask *Salmasius* what a King is, and he will teach us that *a King is he who hath the Supreme power of the Kingdome, and is accountable to none but God, and may do what he please, and is free from the Laws.* This definition *J. M.* abominates as being the definition of a Tyrant: And I should be of his minde, if he would have vouchsafed us a better, or any other definition at all, that would tell us how any King can have a Supreme Power, without being freed from humane Laws: To finde fault with it, without producing any other, is to leave us in the dark: But though Mr. *M.* brings us neither Definition nor Description of a King, yet we may pick out of several passages of him, something like a definition, if we lay them together. He teaches us [in *A Defence of the People of England*] that *power was therefore given to a King by the people, that he might see by the authority to him committed, that nothing be done against Law: and that he keeps our Laws and not impose upon his own: Therefore there is no regal power but in the Courts of the Kingdome, and by them.*

And again he affirmeth, *the King cannot Imprison, Fine or punish any man, except he be first cited into some Court; where not the King, but the usual Judges give Sentence,* and before we are told, *not the King, but the Authority of Parliament doth set up and take away all Courts.*

Lo here the description of a King, He is *one to whom the People give power, to see that nothing be done against Law:* and yet he saith there is *no regal power but in the Courts of*

Justice and by them, where not the King, but the usual Judges give Sentence. This description not only strips the King of all power whatsoever, but puts him in a condition below the meanest of his Subjects.

Thus much may shew, that all men are not agreed what a King is. Next, what the word *People* means is not agreed upon: ask *Aristotle* what the People is, & he will not allow any power to be in any but in free Citizens. If we demand who be free Citizens? that he cannot resolve us, for he confesseth that *he that is a free Citizen in one city, is not so in another City.* And he is of opinion that *no artificer should be a free Citizen, or have voice in a well ordered Commonwealth;* he accounts a *Democratic* (which word signifies the Government of the people) *to be a Corrupted sort of Government;* he thinks *many men by nature born to be Servants, and not fit to govern as any part of the people.* Thus doth *Aristotle* curtal the people, and can give us no certain rule to know who be the people: Come to our Modern Politicians, and ask them who the people is, though they talk big of the people, yet they take up, and are content with a *few Representors* (as they call them) *of the whole people;* a point *Aristotle* was to seek in, neither are these Representors stood upon to be the whole people, but the *major part of these Representors must be reckoned for the whole people;* nay *J. M.* will not allow the major part of the Representors to be the people, but the *sounder and better part only* of them, & in right down terms he tells us *to determine who is a Tyrant, he leaves to Magistrates, at least to the uprighter sort of them and of the people, though in number less by many, to judge as they finde cause.* If the *sounder, the better, and the uprighter* part have the power of the people, how shall we know, or who shall judge who they be?

Our Text is urged by Mr. *Milton,* for the peoples power: Deut. 17.14. *When thou art come into the Land which thy Lord thy God giveth thee, and shalt say, I will set a King over me, like as all the Nations about me.* It is said, by the tenure of Kings *these words confirm us that the right of choosing, yea of changing their own Government, is by the Grant of God himself in the people:* But can the foretelling or forewarning of the *Israelites* of a wanton and wicked desire of theirs, which God Himself condemned, be made an argument that God gave or granted them a right to do such a wicked thing? or can the narration and reproving of a future fact be a donation and approving of a present right, or the permission of a sin be made a commission for the doing of it? the Author in his Book against *Salmasius,* falls from making God the Donor or Grantor, that he cites him onely for a *Witness, Teste ipso Deo penes populos arbitrium semper fuisse, vel ea, que placeret formareipub, utendi, vel hanc in aliam mutandi; de Hebrais hoc diserte dicit Deus: de religuis non abnuit.*

That here in this Text *God himself being witness, there was alwayes a power in the people, either to use what form of Government they pleased, or of changing it into another: God saith this expressly of the* Hebrews, *and denies it not of others.* Can any man finde that God in this Text expressly saith, that there was always a right in the People, to use what form of Government they please? The Text not warranting this right of the People, the foundation of the defence of the People is quite taken away; there being no other grant or proof of it pretended. (pp. 12-14)

Jus Regni is much stumbled at, and the definition of a King, which saith *His power is supreme in the Kingdome, and he is accountable to none but to God, and that he may do what he please, and is not bound by Laws:* it is said if this definition

be good, no man is or ever was, who may be said to be a Tyrant, for *when he hath violated all divine and humane Laws, nevertheless he is a King, and guiltless jure Regio.* To this may be answered, That the definition confesseth he is accountable to God, and therefore not guiltless if he violate Divine Laws: Humane Laws must not be shuffled in with Divine, they are not of the same authority: if humane Laws binde a King, it is impossible for him to have supreme power amongst men. If any man can finde us out such a kinde of Government, wherein the supreme power can be, without being freed from humane Laws, they should first teach us that; but if all sorts of popular Government that can be invented, cannot be one minute, without an Arbitrary power, freed from all humane Laws: what reason can be given why a royal Government should not have the like freedom? if it be tyranny for one man to govern arbitrarily, why should it not be farre greater tyranny for a multitude of men to govern without being accountable or bound by Laws? It would be further enquired how it is possible for any Government at all to be in the World without an arbitrary power; it is not power except it be arbitrary: a legislative power cannot be without being absolved from humane Laws, it cannot be shewed how a King can have any power at all but an arbitrary power. We are taught, that *power was therefore given to a King by the People, that he might see by the authority to him committed, that nothing be done against Law, and that he keep our Laws, and not impose upon us his own: therefore there is no royal Power, but in the Courts of the Kingdome, and by them* and again it is said, *the King cannot imprison, fine or punish any man except he be first cited into some Court, where not the King but the usual Judges give sentence,* and before we are told *not the King, but the Authority of* Parliament *doth set up and take away all Courts.*

Lo here we have Mr. *Miltons* perfect definition of a King. He is one to whom the People gave *power to see that nothing be done against Law, and that he keep our Laws, and not impose his own.* Whereas all other men have the faculty of seeing by nature, the King only hath it by the gift of the People, other power he hath none; he may see the Judges keep the Laws if they will; he cannot compel them, for he may not imprison, fine, nor punish any man, the Courts of Justice may, and they are set up and put down by the Parliament: yet in this very definition of a King, we may spy an arbitrary power in the King, for he may wink if he will: and no other power doth this description of a King give, but onely a power to see: whereas it is said *Aristotle doth mention an absolute Kingdome, for no other cause, but to show how absurd, unjust and most tyrannical it is:* There is no such thing said by *Aristotle,* but the contrary, where he saith, that *a King according to Law makes no sort of Government;* and after he had reckoned up five sorts of Kings, he concludes that there were in a manner but two sorts, the *Lacedemonian* King, and the absolute King; whereof the first was but as a General in an Army, and therefore no King at all, and then fixes and rests upon the *absolute King, who ruleth according to his own will.* (pp. 16-17)

To the Text, *Where the word of a King is, there is power, and who may say to him, What dost thou?* J. M. gives this answer, *It is apparent enough that the Preacher in this place gives precepts to every private man, not to the great Sanedrin, nor to the Senate:—shall not the Nobles, shall not all the other Magistrates, shall not the whole People dare to mutter, so oft as the King pleaseth to dote?* We must here note, that the great Councel, and all other Magistrates or Nobles, or the whole People compared to the King, are all but private men, if they derive their power from him: they are Magistrates under him and out of his presence, for when he is in place, they are but so many private men. *J. M.* asks, *Who swears to a King, unless the King on the other side be sworn to keep Gods Laws, and the Laws of the Country?* We finde that the Rulers of *Israel* took an Oath at the Coronation of *Jehoash.* But we finde no Oath taken by that King, no not so much as to God's Laws, much less to the Laws of the Countrey. (p. 20)

Kings have been and may be vitious men, and the Government of one, not so good as the Government of another; yet it doth not follow that the form of Government is or can be in its own nature ill, because the Governour is so: it is Anarchy or want of Government, that can totally destroy a Nation. We cannot finde any such Government as Tyranny mentioned or named in Scripture, or any word in the Hebreiw Tongue to express it. After such time as the Cities of *Greece* practised to shake off Monarchy, then and not till then (which was after *Homers* time) the name of Tyrant was taken up for a word of disgrace, for such men as by craft or force wrested the power of a City from a multitude, to one man onely; and not for the *exercising,* but for the ill *obtaining* of the Government: but now every man that is but thought to govern ill, or to be an ill man, is presently termed a Tyrant, and so judged by his Subjects. Few remember the prohibition, *Exod. 22.28. Thou shalt not revile the Gods, nor curse the Ruler of thy people:* and fewer understand the reason of it. Though we may not one judge another, yet we may speak evil or revile one another, in that which hath been lawfully judged, and upon a Tryal wherein they have been heard and condemned: this is not to judge, but onely to relate the judgement of the Ruler. To speak evil or to revile a Supreme Judge, cannot be without judging him who hath no Superior on earth to judge him, and in that regard must alwayes be presumed innocent, though never so ill, if he cannot lawfully be heard.

J.M. That will have it Tyranny in a King not to regard the Laws, doth himself give as little regard to them as any man, where [in **The Tenure of Kings and Magistrates**] he reckons that *contesting for Priviledges, Customs, Forms, and that old entanglement of Iniquity, their gibrish Laws, are the badges of ancient Slavery....* (pp. 21-2)

J.M. is also of opinion, that *If at any time our Fore-fathers out of baseness have lost any thing of their right, that ought not hurt us, they might if they would promise Slavery for themselves, for us certainly they could not, who have alwayes the same right to free our selves, that they had to give themselves to any man in slavery.* This Doctrine well practised, layeth all open to constant Anarchy.

Lastly, if any desire to know what the liberty of the People is which *J.M.* pleads for, he resolves us, saying, that *he that takes away from the people, the right of choosing what form of Government they please, takes away truly that in which all liberty doth almost consist.* It is well said by *J.M.* that all liberty doth almost consist in choosing their form of Government, for there is another liberty exercised by the people, which he mentions not, which is the liberty of the peoples choosing their Religion; every man may be of any Religion, or of no Religion; *Greece* and *Rome* have been as famous for *Polytheisme,* or multitudes of gods, as of Governors, and imagining Aristocraty and Democraty in Heaven, as on Earth. (p. 22)

> *Sir Robert Filmer, "Observations on Master Milton against Salmasius," in* Milton's Contemporary Reputation: An Essay *by William Riley Parker, The Ohio State University Press, 1940, pp. 12-22.*

SIR ROGER L'ESTRANGE   (essay date 1660)

[*L'Estrange was a prominent Tory journalist and pamphleteer who wrote prolifically for the royalist cause. Described by Sir Sidney Lee as "no friend to the Revolution," he bitterly opposed Milton's political views. Nevertheless, his name figures among the subscribers to the fourth edition of* Paradise Lost *in 1688. In the following excerpt from an essay originally published in 1660, he rebuts Milton's* Brief Notes upon a Late Sermon, Titl'd, "The Fear of God and the King."]

Mr. Milton,

Although in your *Life,* and *Doctrine,* you have *Resolved one* great *Question;* by *evidencing* that *Devils may indue Humane shapes;* and proving your *self,* even to your own *Wife,* an *Incubus:* you have yet *Started Another;* and that is, whether *you* are not of *That* Regiment, *which carried the Herd of Swine headlong into the Sea: and moved the People to beseech Jesus to depart out of their coasts. (This* may be very well imagined, from your suitable practises *Here)* Is it possible to read your *Proposals of the benefits of a Free-State,* without Reflecting upon your Tutours—*All this will I give thee, if thou wilt fall down, and worship me?* Come, come Sir, lay the Devil aside; do not proceed with so much *malice,* and against *Knowledge:*— Act like a *Man;*—that a good Christian may not be afraid to pray for you.

Was it not *You,* that scribled a Justification of the *Murther* of the *King,* against *Salmasius:* and made it *good* too, Thus? *That murther was an Action meritorious, compared with your superiour wickedness.* 'Tis *There,* (as I remember) that you *Common place* your *self* into *Set forms of Rayling,* two Pages thick: and left, your *Infamy* should not extend it self enough, within the Course and Usage of your *Mother tongue,* the *Thing* is Dress'd up in a *Travailing Garb,* and *Language;* to blast the English Nation to the Universe; and to give every man a Horrour for *Mankind,* when he Considers, *You are of the Race.* In This, you are above all *Others;* but in your *Iconoclastes,* you exceed your *self.*

There, not content to see that Sacred Head divided from the *Body;* your piercing Malice enters into the private Agonies of his struggling *Soul;* with a Blasphemous Insolence, invading the Prerogative of God himself: (Omniscience) and by Deductions most *Unchristian,* and *Illogical,* aspersing his *Last Pieties,* (the almost certain *Inspirations* of the *Holy Spirit*) with *Juggle,* and *Prevarication.* Nor are the *Words* ill fitted to the *Matter.* The Bold *Design* being suited with a conform *Irreverence of Language.* (but I do not love to Rake long in a Puddle.)

To take a view in particular of all your Factious Labours, would cost more time, than I am willing to afford them. Wherefore I shall stride over all the *rest,* and pass directly to your **Brief Notes upon a Late SERMON, Titl'd, "The Fear of God and the King." Preach'd, and since Publish'd by MATTHEW GRIFFITH D. D. and Chaplain to the late KING, &c.**

Any man that can but *Read* your *Title,* may *understand* your *Drift* & that you Charge the *Royal Interest, & Party* thorough the *Doctour's* sides. I am not *bold* enough to be his *Champion,* in all particulars; nor yet so *Rude,* as to take an Office most properly to him Belonging, out of his Hand: Let him acquit *himself,* in what concerns the *Divine;* and I'll adventure upon the most material parts of the *Rest.* (but with this Profession, that I have no design in exposing *your* Mistakes, saving to hinder them from becoming the *Peoples.)*

Your *Entrance* is a little *Peremptory,* and *Magisterial,* me-thinks (but that shall be allowed you)' please you, wee'll see how *Pertinent* it is, and *Rational.*

> I Affirmed in the Preface of a late discourse, Entitl'd, **The Ready Way to Establish a Free Commonwealth, and the Dangers of Readmitting Kingship in This Nation,** that *the humor of returning to our old bondage, was instilld of late by some deceivers;* and to make good, that what I then affirmd, was not without just ground, one of those deceivers I present here to the people; and if I prove him not such, I refuse not to be so accounted in his stead.

To the *First:* give me leave to mind you, that you make an *Observation* of things *Past,* amount to a *foretelling* of what's to *come.* This *Sermon* was not *Preach'd,* when *that Humor* you mention, was *Instill'd.* Next; You'll as hardly satisfie the *people,* that you your self, are *no Deceiver,* as prove the *Doctor* one of those you *meant.* And thus I'll Instance; KINGSHIP, is *your old bondage;* RUMPSHIP, ours: (Forgive the Term) *You* were *Then,* Past the *One:* we are now (God be thanked) past the *Other:* and should be as loth to Return, as *You.* Yet you are Tampering to *delude the People,* and to withdraw them from a *Peaceable,* and *Rational expectancy* of *good,* into a *mutinous,* and *hopless attempt* of *mischief.*

By your own Rule now, who are the Deceivers: We, that will *not Return to our old Bondage;* or *you,* that would *perswade* us to't?

Your next Paragraph talks of *Purgatives, Myrrhe, Aloes, &c.*— It may be an Apothecaries Bill, for ought I know, and I have no skill in Physique. (pp. 1-3)

Your 4th Page, runs away in some mistakes concerning *Gideon;*—(a Person, *Call'd* and set apart by God himself; guided by Divine *Inspirations;* and Acting without Partnership, the work he was employ'd upon)

A little further, you deny the King, *the Power of life and death,* urging [*Page 4.*] *that tis against the declared Judgements of our Parliaments, nay of our Laws; which reserve to themselves only the power of life and death, &c.*

I'll not deny, but a Parliament is above the King: (That is: The King is greater in Conjunction with his two *Houses,* than by *Himself*) but still this weakens not the force of my assertion; which is; that Kings must necessarily have that power: *without* it, they're no Kings (and 'tis the same thing in all Governments whatsoever, 'tis one of the Prerogatives Inseparable from Supreme Authority) But since you urge *the Declar'd Judgements of our Parliaments,* in favour of your opinion, I should be glad to see them.

Now for the Laws; 'tis true; they Pronounce Life, or Death; but the King's left at Liberty to Take, or to Remit the forfeiture, at pleasure. Enough is said of this.

If I were bent to *Cavil;* your 5th. Page would afford matter abundantly, where you extravagate upon the word *Anointed:* but That is more Peculiarly the *Doctor's* Businesse, and I refer you to him. So are your slips, [*Page 6.*] but *Those,* I cannot passe without a marque: For *There,* you shew your *Teeth.* (I might have said, your *Eares* to boot)

> But how will you confirm one wrested Scripture with another: *I Sam.* 8,7. *They have not rejected thee, but me:* grossly misapplying these words, which were not spoken to any who had *resisted or rejected* a King, but to them who much against the will of God

had sought a King, and rejected a Commonwealth, wherein they might have liv'd happily under the Reign of God only, their King. Let the words interpret themselves: *v.6,7. But the thing displeased Samuel, when they said, give us a King to judge us. And Samuel prayed unto the Lord. And the Lord said unto Samuel, harken unto the voice of the people in all that they say unto thee; for they have not rejected thee, but they have rejected me, that I should not reign over them* Hence you conclude, *so indissoluble is the Conjunction of God and the King.* O notorious abuse of Scripture! when as you should have concluded, So unwilling was God to give them a King, So wide was the disjunction of God from a King.

Mr. *Milton,* when your hand was *In,* another verse methinks should not have over-charg'd you: and 'tis the very next too. *As they have ever done* (sayes God to Samuel) since I *brought them out of Egypt, even unto this Day,* (and *have forsaken me, and served other Gods) even so doe they unto thee. This,* would have given you light to read the *Rest* by; and (possible) have done *you* the *same* service, which you pretend to doe the *Doctour.* (But none so Blind as they that will not see) especially, had you but taken in likewise the verse next Antecedent to your Quotation, which speaks the *motive* to their such *Desires;* as the other does fairly imply the *Reason* of Gods *Disapproval* of them, 'twas a hard misse, and an industrious one (I fear) to scape the 5, and 8, verses, without the which, the 6 and 7, (which you make use of) have no intelligible Coherence. *Make us a King,* (say they) *to Judge us like the* NATIONS *v.* 5. and after That, *v.* 8. God charges them with inclinations to *Idolatry;* so that the inference is open; They had a hankering after the *Gods* of the Nations, as well as the *Kingship;* and *That* moved the All-seeing wisdome, (that knew their hearts) to tell *Samuel,* saying, *they have not Rejected Thee, bùt Mee:* a Speech applyable to their *Disobedience,* rather, than to their *Proposition: God* is rejected, in the rejection of his *Ministers.*—This is a stubborn Text Sir, and will not mould as you would have it.

Had not they against the will of God, sought a KING, *and rejected a Common-wealth,* you tell us, *that they might have liv'd* HAPPILY *under the reign of God onely their King.* (Indeed you have the best intelligence)—I beseech you how doe you know this: whom God *loves,* he *chastens:* and *persecution,* in *this* world, is the Portion of the Saints. It's true; their obedience to God *here,* would certainly have rendered them Happy *hereafter;* but *this* is not the Happinesse you drive at. Look back now upon the *3. verse* of the same Chapter; and there you'll find some Reason to apprehend the contrary. For *Samuel* being Old, and having made his sonnes *Judges* over *Israel;* the Text sayes, that *his sonnes walked not in his wayes, but turn'd aside after Lucre, and took Rewards, and perverted Judgement, &c.* now, if from *hence,* you can perswade your self into a good opinion of a *Popular Government;* I cannot blame your stickling for the *Rump;* But that this *mis-rule* should please *God,* your modesty I hope will not pretend to offer. You'll say however, that the *Popular form* did; I'll not contend about it; Did not the *Regall* too, as much in *David;* a *King* of God's particular *choice,* and a *man* after his Own *Heart?* So that you gain little by the odds of a *Free-State* in ballance against *Monarchy.* In one word: The *Saviour* of the *world* was a KING, and a *King* of *Jewes.*

Grant, or *Denie* at pleasure, I have you in a Net. Why would you meddle with a Chapter, that you were sure would burn your fingers? There's no Relief you see, against Authority. 'Tis well you stopp'd short of that *Lex Regni* which *Samuel* opens to the People; (beginning at the II. *verse* of the same

Chapter;) from whence, lyes *no* Appeal. Truly, your insincerity in this Section, is more exposed, than I could with it.

Under the Reign of God onely their King you say. This expression, doubtfully implies you a Millenary. Doe you then, really expect to *see* Christ, Reigning upon Earth, even with *those very eyes* you *Left* (as 'tis reported) *with staring too long, and too sawcily upon the Portraiture of his Vicegerent, to breake the* Image, as your Impudence Phrases it? (It is generally indeed believed, you never wept them out for this *Losse.*) (pp. 5-8)

> Sir Roger L'Estrange, "No Blinde Guides," in Milton's Contemporary Reputation: An Essay *by William Riley Parker, The Ohio State University Press, 1940, pp. 1-13.*

THE CENSURE OF THE ROTA   (essay date 1660)

[*The following excerpt is from the anonymous* Censure of the Rota upon Mr. Milton's Book, Entituled, "The Ready and Easie Way to Establish a Free Common-wealth," *published in 1660. Although this work has sometimes been attributed to James Harrington, most critics agree that it cannot be by him or by any other member of the London debating club known as the Rota, for both the club and Harrington himself are satirized in the essay.* The Censure of the Rota *is widely acknowledged to be one of the best attacks on Milton's political opinions. Of it, William Riley Parker wrote in 1940: "The authorship of the pamphlet remains a secret, which is a pity, for of all the contemporary attacks on Milton it is probably the cleverest and most penetrating. The writer avoids abuse and name-calling; he uses the rapier of satire against the learned bludgeon of Milton, and with telling effect. . . . The anonymous* Censure *is a fine piece of prose satire in the best Restoration tradition." Here, the anonymous critic purports to record the Rota's unfavorable opinion concerning Milton's promotion of commonwealth government.*]

SIR,

I am commanded by this ingenious Convention of the *Rota*, to give you an account of some Reflections that they have lately made upon a Treatise of yours, which you call, **The ready and easie way to establish a Free Commonwealth**; in which I must first bespeak your pardon, for being forced to say something, not onely against mine own sense, but the Interesse which both you and I carry on; for it is enjoyn'd me to acquaint you with all that was said, although I take as little pleasure to repeat it, as you will do to hear it. For whereas it is our usuall custom to dispute every thing, how plain or obscure soever, by knocking Argument against Argument, and tilting at one another with our heads (as Rams fight) untill we are out of breath, and then refer it to our wooden Oracle the *Box;* and seldom any thing, how slight soever, hath appear'd, without some Patron or other to defend it. I must confesse, I never saw Bowling-stones run so unluckily against any Boy, when his hand has been out, as the Ballots did against you, when anything was put to the question, from the beginning of your Book to the end. For it was no sooner read over, but a Gentleman of your acquaintance said, he wish'd for your own sake, as well as the Cause you contend for, that you had given your Book no name (like an Anabaptist's child) untill it had come to years of discretion, or else that you had got some friend to be Gossip, that has a luckier hand at giving Titles to Books than you have: For it is observ'd, you have always been very unfortunate that way, as if it were fatall to you to prefix Bulls and Nonsense to the very fronts of your learned Works, as when you call *Salmasius, Claudius Anonymus,* in the very Title

of that admired piece [**Pro populo anglicano defensio, contra Claudii Anonymi**], which you writ to confute his Wife and his Maid. As also in that other learned Labor of yours, which you style **Tetrachordon,** that is to say, a Fiddle with four strings; but, as you render it, a Four-fold Cord, with which you undertake (worse then Captain *Ottor,* and *Cuibbert* the Barber) not to bind, but (most ridiculously) to unty Matrimony. But in this Book, he said, you were more insufferable; for you do not onely style your Declamation, *The ready and easie way,* as if it were the best or onely way, to the disparagement of this most ingenuous Assembly, who are confident, they have propos'd others much more considerable; but do very indiscreetly profess in the same place, to compare the Excellencies of a Common-wealth with the inconveniences and dangers of Kingship; this, he said, was foul play, and worse Logick: For, as all conveniences in this world carry their inconveniences with them, to compare the Best of one thing with that Worst of another, is a very unequall way of comparison. He had observ'd, that Comparisons were commonly made on the wrong side, and so was this of yours, by your owne confession. To this, another added, He wondred you did not give over writing, since you have always done it to little or no purpose; for though you have scribled your eyes out, your works have never been printed but for the Company of Chandlers and Tobacco-men, who are your Stationers, and the onely men that vend your Labors. He said, that he himself reprieved the **Whole Defence of the People of England** for a groat, that was sentenced to vile *Mundungus,* and had suffer'd inevitably (but for him) though it cost you much Oyle and Labor, and the *Rump* 300 l. a year, to whose service it was more properly intended; although in the close, you pronounce them to be very Rascalls as *Salmasius,* and all the Christian world calls them, if ever they suffered any of their fellow-Members to invade the Government (as O. *Cromwell* and others have since done) and confesse your self fool'd and mistaken, and all you have written to be false, howsoever you give your self the second lye in writing for them again. After this, a grave Gentleman of the long Roab, said, You had broken the heads of all the Sages of the Law, and plaid false in the very first word of your Treatise. For the Parliament of *England* (as you call the *Rump*) never consisted of a pack'd Party of one House, that by fraud and covin had disseaz'd the major part of their Fellows, and forfeited their own right, by abetting the ejectment of the whole House of Peers, and the greater part of their own (which was always understood to be the whole House) with whom they had but a joynt Right. That they had been severall times justly dissolv'd by the Army, from whom they really deriv'd their Authority; and the generall Voices of the People, in whom they had declar'd the supream Power to reside; and their own confession upon Record in their Journall-Book. But this, he said, you stole from Patriot *Whitlock,* who began his Declaration for a Free State with the same words; and he wondred you would filch and pilfer Nonsense and Fallasies, that have such plentifull store of your own grouth. Yet this was as true as that which follows, *That a great number of the faithfullest of the People assisted them in throwing off Kingship;* for they were a very sleight number in respect of the whole, and none of the faithfullest that forswore themselves, to maintain and defend that which they judg'd dangerous, and resolv'd to abolish. And therefore they turn'd Regall Bondage (as you word it) into a Free Common-wealth, no more justly and magnanimously, than other Knights of the Post do their feats, by plain downright perjury. And the Nation had little reason to trust such men with their Liberty or Propriety, that had no right to their own ears, but, among the rest of their Cheats, had defrauded the very Pillory of its due. This being put to the Ballot was immediately carried on in the Affirmative, without a dissenting Pellet. When presently a Gentleman, that hath been some years beyond-Seas, said, He wonder'd you would say anything so false and ridiculous, as that this Common-wealth was the terrour and admiration of *France* it self; for if that were true, the Cardinall and Councell were very imprudent to become the chief Promoters of it, and strive by all means to uphold that, which they judg'd to be dangerous to themselves, and for the Interesse of a Nation, which they hate and fear so much as they do us; for if this Free State be so terrible to them, they have been very unwise in assisting it to keep out the King all this while; especially if they saw the people of *Paris* and *Burdeaux* disposed (as you say) to imitate us, which appears very strange; for by their history, any man would judge we had catch'd the disease of them. As for our actions abroad, (which you brag of) he said, he never heard of any where he was, untill *O. Cromwel* reduc'd us to an absolute Monarchy under the name of a Free state; and then we beat the Potent and flourishing Republique of the *United Provinces*. But for our actions at home, he had heard abroad, that they favoured much of *Goth* and *Vandal* barbarism, if pulling down of Churches, and demolishing the noblest Monuments in the Land, both Publick and Privat, (beside Religion and all Laws, Human and Divine) may amount to so much. And yet, he said, he granted what you affirm, That they were not unbecomming the rising of a glorious Common-wealth, for such are usually founded in Fiction, Sedition, Rebellion, Rapine, and Murther. And how much soever you admire the Romans . . . , they were at first but a Refuge for Thieves and Murtherers. In all *Asia, Africa,* and the New World, there is no such thing as Republick, nor ever was; but onely that of *Carthage,* and some paltry Greek Colonies upon the skirts of *Asiaminor;* and for one Common-wealth there have been a hundred Kingdoms in the world, which argues, they should be the more agreeable to Mankind. He added, Commonly Republicks arise from unworthy causes, not fit to be mention'd in History; and that he had heard many Persons of Honor in *Flanders* affirm, That it was not the Tyranny of *Spain,* nor the cruelty of Duke *D'Alva,* nor the blood of their Nobility, nor Religion, nor Liberty, that made the Dutch cast off their obedience to their Prince; but one penny Excise laid upon a pound of Butter, that made them implacably declare for a Common-wealth. That the *Venetians* were banish'd into a Free State by *Atila,* and their glorious Liberty was at first no other, then he may be said to have that is turn'd out of his house. That the *Romans* were Cookolded into their Freedom, and the *Pisans* Trepand into theirs by *Charls* the eighth. That as Common-wealths sprung from base Originalls, so they have ruin'd upon as slight occasions. That the same *Pisans,* after they had spent all they had upon a Freak of Liberty, were sold (like Cattle) by *Lewis* the 12th. The *Venetians* Hector'd, and almost ruin'd by *Maximilian* the first, a poor Prince, for refusing to lend him mony, as they were not long before by *Francesco Sforza* about a Bastard. The *Florentines* utterly enslav'd for spoyling an Embossador's Speech, and disparaging *Petrode' Medici's* fine Livereys. The *Genoeses*——— But as he was going on, he was interrupted by a Gentleman that came in and told us, that Sir *Arthur Hazlerig,* the *Brutus* of our Republique, was in danger to be torn in pieces (like a *Shrovetuesday* Bawd) by the Boys in *Westminster-Hall;* and if he had not shewn himself as able a Foot-man as he that cudgell'd him, he had gone the way of Doctor *Lamb* infallibly. This set all the company a laughing, and made the Traveller forget what he was saying. After a little pause, a learned Gentleman of this Society stood up, and said, He could not but take notice of one absurdity in your Discourse, and that is, where you speak of Liberty gloriously fough for, and Kingly Thraldome abjur'd by the people, &c. for if by liberty, you mean Common-wealth, (as you do) There was never any such thing, as either the one, or the other; unlesse yon will state the Quarrell at the end of the Warre, which is very senselesse, and directly contrary to all Oaths and Engagements: or can prove that Hanging, Drawing, and Quartering of some of the People, and selling others as Slaves, for taking up Arms in all parts of the Nation for the *King,* are abjurations of his Authority; and he wonder'd, you could be so weak, or impudent to play foul in matters of Fact, of which there are so many thousands witnesses to disprove you. But he was of opinioin, that you did not believe your selfe, nor those reasons you give in defence of Commonwealth, but that you are sway'd by something else, as either by a Stork-like Fate, (as a modern Protector-Poet calls it, because that Foul is observ'd to live no where but in Commonwealths) or because, you have unadvisedly scribled your selfe obnoxious, or else you fear such admirable eloquence as yours, would be thrown away under a Monarchy, (as it would be) though of admirable use in a Popular Government, where Orators carry all the Rabble before them: For who knows to how Cheap a rate this goodly Eloquence of yours, (if well manadg'd) might bring the price of Sprats, as no wiser Orators then your selfe have done heretofore, in the petty factions, Greek Republiques, whom you chiefly imitate; for all your Politiques are derived from the works of Declamers, with which sort of Writers, the Ancient Common-wealths had the fortune to abound, who left many things behind them in favour, or flattery of the Governments they liv'd under, and disparagement of others, to whom they were in opposition, of whom we can affirm nothing certain, but that they were partiall, and never meant to give a true account of things, but to make them finer or worse then they really are; Of which men, one of their owne Common-wealth Poets, gives a just Character, by sorting them among the worst of men. (pp. 3-8)

> *"The Censure of the Rota upon Milton's Book,"* in Milton's Contemporary Reputation: An Essay *by William Riley Parker, The Ohio State University Press, 1940, pp. 3-8.*

JOHN MILTON   (poem date 1667)

[*In the following excerpts from Books I and IX of* Paradise Lost, *Milton proposes the subject of the poem and comments on its method of composition.*]

Of Man's First Disobedience, and the Fruit
Of that Forbidden Tree, whose mortal taste
Brought Death into the World, and all our woe,
With loss of *Eden,* till one greater Man
Restore us, and regain the blissful Seat,
Sing Heav'nly Muse, that on the secret top
Of *Oreb,* or of *Sinai,* didst inspire
That Shepherd, who first taught the chosen Seed,
In the Beginning how the Heav'ns and Earth
Rose out of *Chaos:* Or if *Sion* Hill
Delight thee more, and *Siloa's* Brook that flow'd
Fast by the Oracle of God; I thence
Invoke thy aid to my advent'rous Song,
That with no middle flight intends to soar
Above th' *Aonion* Mount, while it pursues
Things unattempted yet in Prose or Rhyme.
And chiefly Thou O Spirit, that dost prefer
Before all Temples th' upright heart and pure,
Instruct me, for Thou know'st; Thou from the first

Wast present, and with mighty wings outspread
Dove-like satst brooding on the vast Abyss
And mad'st it pregnant: What in me is dark
Illumine, what is low raise and support;
That to the highth of this great Argument
I may assert Eternal Providence,
And justify the ways of God to men.

(pp. 211-12)

No more of talk where God or Angel Guest
With Man, as with his Friend, familiar us'd
To sit indulgent, and with him partake
Rural repast, permitting him the while
Venial discourse unblam'd: I now must change
Those Notes to Tragic; foul distrust, and breach
Disloyal on the part of Man, revolt,
And disobedience: On the part of Heav'n
Now alienated, distance and distaste,
Anger and just rebuke, and judgment giv'n,
That brought into this World a world of woe,
Sin and her shadow Death, and Misery
Death's Harbinger: Sad task, yet argument
Not less but more Heroic than the wrath
Of stern *Achilles* on his Foe pursu'd
Thrice Fugitive about *Troy* Wall; or rage
Of *Turnus* for *Lavinia* disespous'd,
Or *Neptune's* ire or *Juno's*, that so long
Perplex'd the *Greek* and *Cytherea's* Son;
If answerable style I can obtain

Of my Celestial Patroness, who deigns
Her nightly visitation unimplor'd,
And dictates to me slumb'ring, or inspires
Easy my unpremeditated Verse:
Since first this Subject for Heroic Song
Pleas'd me long choosing, and beginning late;
Not sedulous by Nature to indite
Wars, hitherto the only Argument
Heroic deem'd, chief maistry to dissect
With long and tedious havoc fabl'd Knights
In Battles feign'd; the better fortitude
Of Patience and Heroic Martyrdom
Unsung; or to describe Races and Games,
Or tilting Furniture, emblazon'd Shields,
Impreses quaint, Caparisons and Steeds;
Bases and tinsel Trappings, gorgeous Knights
At Joust and Tournament; then marshall'd Feast
Serv'd up in Hall with Sewers, and Seneschals;
The skill of Artifice or Office mean,
Not that which justly gives Heroic name
To Person or to Poem. Mee of these
Nor skill'd nor studious, higher Argument
Remains, sufficient of itself to raise
That name, unless an age too late, or cold
Climate, or Years damp my intended wing
Deprest; and much they may, if all be mine,
Not Hers who brings it nightly to my Ear.

(pp. 378-79)

John Milton, "Paradise Lost, Book I and Book IX" in his Complete Poems and Major Prose, *edited by Merritt Y. Hughes, The Odyssey Press, 1957, pp. 211-31, 378-405.*

JOHN MILTON   (essay date 1668)

[*In the following statement, which was inserted in editions of* Paradise Lost *in 1668 "for the satisfaction of many that have desired it," Milton describes the verse form of the poem and supplies "a reason of that which stumbled many . . .* [readers], *why the Poem Rimes not."*]

The measure [of *Paradise Lost*] is *English* Heroic Verse without Rime, as that of *Homer* in *Greek,* and of *Virgil* in *Latin;* Rime being no necessary Adjunct or true Ornament of Poem or good Verse, in longer Works especially, but the Invention of a barbarous Age, to set off wretched matter and lame Meter; grac't indeed since by the use of some famous modern Poets, carried away by Custom, but much to thir own vexation, hindrance, and constraint to express many things otherwise, and for the most part worse than else they would have exprest them. Not without cause therefore some both *Italian* and *Spanish* Poets of prime note have rejected Rime both in longer and shorter Works, as have also long since out best *English* Tragedies, as a thing of itself, to all judicious ears, trivial and of no true musical delight; which consists only in apt Numbers, fit quantity of Syllables, and the sense variously drawn out from one Verse into another, not in the jingling sound of like endings, a fault avoided by the learned Ancients both in Poetry and all good Oratory. This neglect then of Rime so little is to be taken for a defect, though it may seem so perhaps to vulgar Readers, that it rather is to be esteem'd an example set, the first in *English,* of ancient liberty recover'd to Heroic Poem from the troublesome and modern bondage of Riming.

John Milton, "The Verse," in his Complete Poems and Major Prose, *edited by Merritt Y. Hughes, The Odyssey Press, 1957, p. 210.*

Paradiſe loſt.

A

P O E M

Written in

TEN BOOKS

By ɟOHN MILTON.

Licenſed and Entred according to Order.

L O N D O N

Printed, and are to be ſold by *Peter Parker* under *Creed* Church neer *Aldgate* ; And by *Robert Boulter* at the *Turks Head* in *Biſhopſgate-ſtreet* ; And *Matthias Walker*, under St. *Dunſtons* Church in *Fleet-ſtreet*, 1 6 6 7.

Title page of the first edition of Paradise Lost *(1667).*

ANDREW MARVELL   (poem date 1674)

[One of the last of the seventeenth-century English metaphysical poets, Marvell is noted for his intellectual and allusive poetry. His work incorporates many of the elements associated with the metaphysical school: tension of opposing values, metaphorical complexities, logical and linguistic subtleties, and unexpected twists of thought and argument. Although in the past his work has been considered of minor stature next to that of John Donne, the most renowned of the metaphysical poets, Marvell is now recognized as an important poet in his own right. He was also a sometime political writer, but his shifting positions on the issues of the day have obscured his intentions for later readers. Wherever his sympathies lay, it is clear that for a time he, like Milton, supported Cromwell's assumption of the Protectorate, and this fact may have helped cement the close friendship that existed between the two men. In the following encomium, originally published in a 1674 edition of Paradise Lost, *Marvell describes how he came to recognize the greatness of the poem.]*

When I beheld the Poet blind, yet bold,
In slender Book his vast Design unfold,
Messiah Crown'd, God's Reconcil'd Decree,
Rebelling Angels, the Forbidden Tree,
Heav'n, Hell, Earth, Chaos, All; the Argument
Held me a while misdoubting his Intent,
That he would ruin (for I saw him strong)
The sacred Truths to Fable and old Song
(So *Sampson* grop'd the Temple's Posts in spite)
The World o'erwhelming to revenge his sight.
   Yet as I read, soon growing less severe,
I lik'd his Project, the success did fear;
Through that wide Field how he his way should find
O'er which lame Faith leads Understanding blind;
Lest he perplex'd the things he would explain,
And what was easy he should render vain.
   Or if a Work so infinite he spann'd,
Jealous I was that some less skilful hand
(Such as disquiet always what is well,
And by ill imitating would excel)
Might hence presume the whole Creation's day
To change in Scenes, and show it in a Play.
   Pardon me, Mighty Poet, nor despise
My causeless, yet not impious, surmise
But I am now convinc'd, and none will dare
Within thy Labours to pretend a share.
Thou hast not miss'd one thought that could be fit,
And all that was improper dost omit:
So that no room is here for Writers left,
But to detect their Ignorance or Theft.
   That Majesty which through thy Work doth Reign
Draws the Devout, deterring the Profane.
And things divine thou treat'st of in such state
As them preserves, and thee, inviolate.
At once delight and horror on us seize,
Thou sing'st with so much gravity and ease;
And above human flight dost soar aloft
With Plume so strong, so equal, and so soft.
The Bird nam'd from that Paradise you sing
So never flags, but always keeps on Wing.
   Where couldst thou words of such a compass find?
Whence furnish such a vast expense of mind?
Just Heav'n thee like *Tiresias* to requite
Rewards with Prophecy thy loss of sight.
   Well mightst thou scorn thy Readers to allure
With tinkling Rime, of thy own sense secure;
While the *Town-Bayes* writes all the while and spells,
And like a Pack-horse tires without his Bells:
Their Fancies like our Bushy-points appear,
The Poets tag them, we for fashion wear.
I too transported by the Mode offend,

And while I meant to Praise thee must Commend.
Thy Verse created like thy Theme sublime,
In Number, Weight, and Measure, needs not Rime.

                         (pp. 209-10)

Andrew Marvell, "On Paradise Lost," in Complete Poems and Major Prose *by John Milton, edited by Merritt Y. Hughes, The Odyssey Press, 1957, pp. 209-10.*

JOHN DRYDEN   (essay date 1688)

[Regarded by many scholars as the father of modern English poetry and criticism, Dryden dominated literary life in England during the last four decades of the seventeenth century. In the following epigram, which was originally published beneath the frontispiece portrait of Milton in the 1688 folio edition of Paradise Lost, *he praises Milton as the sum of the best of Antique literary practice.]*

Three poets, in three distant ages born,
Greece, Italy, and England did adorn.
The first in loftiness of thought surpass'd,
The next in majesty, in both the last:
The force of Nature could no farther go;
To make a third, she join'd the former two.

John Dryden, "Epigram on Milton," in his The Poetical Works of John Dryden, *Houghton Mifflin Company, 1909, p. 253.*

JOHN DENNIS   (essay date 1692)

[Dennis was an eighteenth-century English man of letters who is esteemed for his astute, wide-ranging literary criticism. His several abusive attacks on the character and writings of Alexander Pope, however, served to diminish his posthumous status as a critic. In the following excerpt from the preface to his 1692 translation of Ovid's Passion of Byblis, *he praises the verse form of* Paradise Lost.]*

I must beg Pardon for the Liberty which I have taken in the numbers which is so great that it may well be entitled License. But then the Reader will have the greater Variety, and if those Numbers are not harmonious, it is not for want of care about them: I have particularly taken care to be exact in the Rhimes, in which the former Translators of this passage have been very defective. I am not so miserably mistaken, as to think rhiming essential to our *English* Poetry. I am far better acquainted with *Milton*, than that comes to. Who without the assistance of Rhime, is one of the most sublime of our *English* Poets. Nay, there is something so transcendently sublime in his first, second, and sixth Books [of *Paradise Lost*], that were the Language as pure as the Images are vast and daring, I do not believe it could be equall'd, no, not in all Antiquity. But tho' I know that Rhiming is not absolutely necessary to our Versification, yet I am for having a Man do throughly what he has once pretended to do. Writing in blank Verse looks like a contempt of Rhime, and a generous disdain of a barbarous Custom; but Writing in such Rhimes as a Boy may laugh at, at *Crambo*, looks at the best like a fruitless Attempt, and an impotent Affectation.

John Dennis, "Preface to 'The Passion of Byblis'," in his The Critical Works of John Dennis, 1692-1711, *Vol. I, edited by Edward Niles Hooker, The Johns Hopkins Press, 1939, pp. 1-5.*

JOHN DRYDEN   (essay date 1693)

[*In the following excerpt from* A Discourse concerning the Original and Progress of Satire *(1693), Dryden outlines what he considers the merits and faults of the verse of* Paradise Lost.]

As for Mr. Milton, whom we all admire with so much justice, his subject [in *Paradise Lost*] is not that of an Heroic Poem, properly so called. His design is the losing of our happiness; his event is not prosperous, like that of all other epic works; his heavenly machines are many, and his human persons are but two. But I will not take Mr. Rymer's work out of his hands. He has promised the world a critique on that author; wherein, though he will not allow his poem for heroic, I hope he will grant us, that his thoughts are elevated, his words sounding, and that no man has so happily copied the manner of Homer, or so copiously translated his Grecisms, and the Latin elegancies of Virgil. 'Tis true, he runs into a flat of thought, sometimes for a hundred lines together, but it is when he is got into a track of Scripture. His antiquated words were his choice, not his necessity; for therein he imitated Spenser, as Spenser did Chaucer. And though, perhaps, the love of their masters may have transported both too far, in the frequent use of them, yet, in my opinion, obsolete words may then be laudably revived, when either they are more sounding, or more significant, than those in practice; and when their obscurity is taken away, by joining other words to them, which clear the sense; according to the rule of Horace, for the admission of new words. But in both cases a moderation is to be observed in the use of them: for unnecessary coinage, as well as unnecessary revival, runs into affectation; a fault to be avoided on either hand. Neither will I justify Milton for his blank verse, though I may excuse him, by the example of Hannibal Caro, and other Italians, who have used it; for whatever causes he alleges for the abolishing of rhyme, (which I have not now the leisure to examine,) his own particular reason is plainly this, that rhyme was not his talent; he had neither the ease of doing it, nor the graces of it; which is manifest in his *Juvenilia*, or verses written in his youth, where his rhyme is always constrained and forced, and comes hardly from him, at an age when the soul is most pliant, and the passion of love makes almost every man a rhymer, though not a poet. (pp. 29-30)

> John Dryden, *"A Discourse Concerning the Original and Progress of Satire,"* in his Essays of John Dryden, Vol. II, *edited by W. P. Ker, Oxford at the Clarendon Press, 1926, pp. 15-114.*

JOHN DRYDEN   (essay date 1697)

[*In the following excerpt from the dedication to his 1697 translation of Vergil's* Aeneid, *Dryden faults Milton for making Satan the hero of* Paradise Lost.]

There have been but one great *Ilias* and one *Æneis* in so many ages. The next, but the next with a long interval betwixt, was the *Jerusalem:* I mean not so much in distance of time, as in excellency. After these three are entered, some Lord Chamberlain should be appointed, some critic of authority should be set before the door, to keep out a crowd of little poets, who press for admission, and are not of quality. Mævius would be deafening your Lordship's ears with his

Fortunam Priami cantabo, et nobile bellum;

mere fustian, as Horace would tell you from behind, without pressing forward, and more smoke than fire. Pulci, Boiardo, and Ariosto, would cry out, 'make room for the Italian poets,

the descendants of Virgil in a right line:' Father Le Moine, with his *Saint Louis*, and Scudery with his *Alaric*, for a godly king and a Gothic conqueror; and Chapelain would take it ill that his *Maid* should be refused a place with Helen and Lavinia. Spenser has a better plea for his *Fairy Queen*, had his action been finished, or had been one. And Milton, if the Devil had not been his hero, instead of Adam; if the giant had not foiled the knight, and driven him out of his stronghold, to wander through the world with his lady errant; and if there had not been more machining persons than human in his poem. (pp. 164-65)

> John Dryden, *"Dedication of the Aeneis,"* in his Essays of John Dryden, Vol. II, *edited by W. P. Ker, Oxford at the Clarendon Press, 1926, pp. 154-240.*

JOSEPH ADDISON   (essay date 1712)

[*An English statesman and man of letters, Addison is considered one of the most important essayists of the early eighteenth century. With Richard Steele he founded the influential daily the* Spectator, *which aimed at improving the morals and manners of the day. Addison's best essays are those in which he adopted the persona of the fictitious country squire Sir Roger de Coverley. These works are trenchant, pointed observations of life, literature, and society. Didactic and moralizing, yet witty and ironic, Addison's style epitomizes neoclassical lucidity and moderation. As Samuel Johnson remarked, Addison's work is characterized by "an English style familiar but not coarse, elegant but not ostentatious." In the following excerpt from a series of essays originally published in the* Spectator *in 1712, Addison applies Aristotle's conception of epic formula to* Paradise Lost.]

There is Nothing in Nature so irksome as general Discourses, especially when they turn chiefly upon Words. For this Reason I shall wave the Discussion of that Point which was started some Years since, Whether *Milton's* **Paradise Lost** may be called an Heroick Poem? Those who will not give it that Title, may call it (if they please) a *Divine Poem*. It will be sufficient to its Perfection, if it has in it all the Beauties of the highest Kind of Poetry; and as for those who alledge it is not an Heroick Poem, they advance no more to the Diminution of it, than if they should say *Adam* is not *Aeneas*, nor *Eve Helen*.

I shall therefore examine it by the Rules of Epic Poetry, and see whether it falls short of the *Iliad* or *Aeneid*, in the Beauties which are essential to that Kind of Writing. The first Thing to be consider'd in an Epic Poem, is the Fable, which is perfect or imperfect, according as the Action which it relates is more or less so. This Action should have three Qualifications in it. First, It should be but one Action. Secondly, It should be an entire Action; and Thirdly, it should be a great Action. To consider the Action of the *Iliad, Aeneid,* and **Paradise Lost,** in these three several Lights. *Homer* to preserve the Unity of his Action hastens into the Midst of Things, as *Horace* has observed: Had he gone up to *Leda's* Egg, or begun much later, even at the Rape of *Helen*, or the Investing of *Troy*, it is manifest that the Story of the Poem would have been a Series of several Actions. He therefore opens his Poem with the Discord of his Princes, and with great Art interweaves in the several succeeding Parts of it, an Account of every Thing material which relates to them, and had passed before that fatal Dissension. After the same Manner *Aeneas* makes his first Appearance in the *Tyrrhene* Seas, and within Sight of *Italy*, because the Action proposed to be celebrated was that of his settling himself in *Latium*. But because it was necessary for the Reader to know what had happened to him in the taking of *Troy,* and in the preceding Parts of his Voyage, *Virgil* makes his Heroe relate it by Way of Episode in the second and third Books of the *Aeneid.* The Contents of both which Books come before those of the first Book in the Thread of the Story, tho' for preserving of this Unity of Action, they follow them in the Disposition of the Poem. *Milton,* in Imitation of these two great Poets, opens his *Paradise Lost,* with an infernal Council plotting the Fall of Man, which is the Action he proposed to celebrate; and as for those great Actions which preceded, in Point of Time, the Battle of the Angels, and the Creation of the World, (which would have entirely destroyed the Unity of his principal Action, had he related them in the same Order that they happened) he cast them into the fifth, sixth, and seventh Books, by way of Episode to this noble Poem.

Aristotle himself allows, that *Homer* has nothing to boast of as to the Unity of his Fable, tho' at the same Time that great Critick and Philosopher endeavours to palliate this Imperfection in the *Greek* Poet, by imputing it in some Measure to the very Nature of an Epic Poem. Some have been of Opinion, that the *Aeneid* labours also in this Particular, and has Episodes which may be looked upon as Excrescencies rather than as Parts of the Action. On the contrary, the Poem which we have now under our Consideration, hath no other Episodes than such as naturally arise from the Subject, and yet is filled with such a Multitude of astonishing Incidents, that it gives us at the same Time a Pleasure of the greatest Variety, and of the greatest Simplicity.

I must observe also, that as *Virgil* in the Poem which was designed to celebrate the Original of the *Roman* Empire, has described the Birth of its great Rival, the *Carthaginian* Commonwealth: *Milton* with the like Art in his Poem on the Fall of Man, has related the Fall of those Angels who are his professed Enemies. Besides the many other Beauties in such an Episode, it's running parallel with the great Action of the Poem, hinders it from breaking the Unity so much as another Episode would have done, that had not so great an Affinity with the principal Subject. In short, this is the same Kind of Beauty which the Criticks admire in the *Spanish Fryar,* or the *Double Discovery,* where the two different Plots look like Counterparts and Copies of one another.

The second Qualification required in the Action of an Epic Poem is, that it should be an *entire* Action: An Action is entire when it is compleat in all its Parts; or as *Aristotle* describes it, when it consists of a Beginning, a Middle, and an End. Nothing should go before it, be intermix'd with it, or follow after it, that is not related to it. As on the contrary, no single Step should be omitted in that just and regular Process which it must be supposed to take from its Original to its Consummation. Thus we see the Anger of *Achilles* in its Birth, its Continuance and Effects; and *Aeneas*'s Settlement in *Italy,* carried on through all the Oppositions in his Way to it both by Sea and Land. The Action in *Milton* excels (I think) both the former in this Particular; we see it contrived in Hell, executed upon Earth, and punished by Heaven. The Parts of it are told in the most distinct Manner, and grow out of one another in the most natural Method.

The third Qualification of an Epic Poem is its *Greatness.* The Anger of *Achilles* was of such Consequence, that it embroiled the Kings of *Greece,* destroy'd the Heroes of *Troy,* and engaged all the Gods in Factions. *Aeneas*'s Settlement in *Italy* produced the *Caesars,* and gave Birth to the *Roman* Empire. *Milton*'s Subject was still greater than either of the former; it does not determine the Fate of single Persons or Nations, but of a whole Species. The united Powers of Hell are joined together for the Destruction of Mankind, which they effected in Part, and would have completed, had not Omnipotence it self interposed. The principal Actors are Man in his greatest Perfection, and Woman in her highest Beauty. Their Enemies are the fallen Angels: The Messiah their Friend, and the Almighty their Protector. In short, every Thing that is great in the whole Circle of Being, whether within the Verge of Nature, or out of it, has a proper Part assigned it in this noble Poem.

In Poetry, as in Architecture, not only the Whole, but the principal Members, and every Part of them, should be Great. I will not presume to say, that the Book of Games in the *Aeneid,* or that in the *Iliad,* are not of this Nature, nor to reprehend *Virgil*'s Simile of the Top, and many other of the same Nature in the *Iliad,* as liable to any Censure in this Particular; but I think we may say, without derogating from those wonderful Performances, that there is an unquestionable Magnificence in every Part of *Paradise Lost,* and indeed a much greater than could have been formed upon any Pagan System.

But *Aristotle,* by the Greatness of the Action, does not only mean that it should be great in its Nature, but also in its Duration, or in other Words, that it should have a due Length in it, as well as what we properly call Greatness. The just Measure of the Kind of Magnitude he explains by the following Similitude. An Animal, no bigger than a Mite, cannot appear perfect to the Eye, because the Sight takes it in at once, and has only a confused Idea of the Whole, and not a distinct Idea of all its Parts; If on the contrary you should suppose an Animal of ten thousand Furlongs in Length, the Eye would be so filled with a single Part of it, that it could not give the Mind an Idea of the Whole. What these Animals are to the Eye, a very short or a very long Action would be to the Memory. The first would be, as it were, lost and swallowed up by it, and the other difficult to be contained in it. *Homer* and *Virgil* have shewn their principal Art in this Particular; the Action of the *Iliad,* and that of the *Aeneid,* were in themselves exceeding short, but are so beautifully extended and diversified by the Invention of *Episodes,* and the Machinery of Gods, with the like poetical Ornaments, that they make up an agreeable Story sufficient to employ the Memory without overcharging it. *Milton*'s Action is enriched with such a Variety of Circumstances, that I have taken as much Pleasure in reading the Contents of his Books, as in the best invented Story I ever met with. It is possible, that the Traditions on which the *Iliad* and *Aeneid* were built, had more Circumstances in them than the History of *The Fall of Man,* as it is related in Scripture. Besides it was easier for *Homer* and *Virgil* to dash the Truth with Fiction, as they were in no danger of offending the Religion of their Country by it. But as for *Milton,* he had not only a very few Circumstances upon which to raise his Poem, but was also obliged to proceed with the greatest Caution in every Thing that he added out of his own Invention. And, indeed, notwithstanding all the Restraints he was under, he has filled his Story with so many surprising Incidents, which bear so close an Analogy with what is delivered in Holy Writ, that it is capable of pleasing the most delicate Reader, without giving Offence to the most scrupulous. (pp. 294-98)

. . . . .

Having examined the Action of *Paradise Lost,* let us in the next Place consider the Actors. This is *Aristotle*'s Method of considering; first the Fable, and secondly the Manners, or as we generally call them in *English,* the Fable and the Characters. (p. 312)

If we look into the Characters of *Milton,* we shall find that he has introduced all the Variety his Poem was capable of receiving. The whole Species of Mankind was in two Persons at the Time to which the Subject of his Poem is confined. We have, however, four distinct Characters in these two Persons. We see Man and Woman in the highest Innocence and Perfection, and in the most abject State of Guilt and Infirmity. The two last Characters are, indeed, very common and obvious, but the two first are not only more magnificent, but more new than any Characters either in *Virgil* or *Homer,* or indeed in the whole Circle of Nature.

Milton was so sensible of this Defect in the Subject of his Poem, and of the few Characters it would afford him, that he has brought into it two Actors of a shadowy and fictitious Nature, in the Persons of Sin and Death, by which Means he has interwoven in the Body of his Fable a very beautiful and well invented Allegory. But notwithstanding the Fineness of this Allegory may atone for it in some Measure; I cannot think that Persons of such a chymerical Existence are proper Actors in an Epic Poem; because there is not that Measure of Probability annexed to them, which is requisite in Writings of this Kind. . . . (p. 313)

Another principal Actor in this Poem is the great Enemy of Mankind. The Part of *Ulysses* in Homer's *Odyssey* is very much admired by *Aristotle,* as perplexing that Fable with very agreeable Plots and Intricacies, not only by the many Adventures in his Voyage, and the Subtilty of his Behaviour, but by the various Concealments and Discoveries of his Person in several Parts of that Poem. But the crafty Being I have now mentioned, makes a much longer Voyage than *Ulysses,* puts in Practice many more Wiles and Stratagems, and hides himself under a greater Variety of Shapes and Appearances, all of which are severally detected, to the great Delight and Surprise of the Reader.

We may likewise observe with how much Art the Poet has varied several Characters of the Persons that speak in his infernal Assembly. On the contrary, how has he represented the whole Godhead exerting it self towards Man in its full Benevolence under the Three-fold Distinction of a Creator, a Redeemer and a Comforter!

Nor must we omit the Person of *Raphael,* who amidst his Tenderness and Friendship for Man, shews such a Dignity and Condescention in all his Speech and Behaviour, as are suitable to a Superior Nature. The Angels are indeed as much diversified in *Milton,* and distinguished by their proper Parts, as the Gods are in *Homer* or *Virgil.* The Reader will find nothing ascribed to *Uriel, Gabriel, Michael* or *Raphael,* which is not in a particular manner suitable to their respective Characters.

There is another Circumstance in the principal Actors of the *Iliad* and *Aeneid,* which gives a peculiar Beauty to those two Poems, and was therefore contrived with Very great Judgment. I mean the Authors having chosen for their Heroes Persons who were so nearly related to the People for whom they wrote. *Achilles* was a *Greek,* and *Aeneas* the remote Founder of *Rome.* By this means their Countrymen (whom they principally proposed to themselves for their Readers) were particularly attentive to all the Parts of their Story, and sympathized with their Heroes in all their Adventures. A *Roman* could not but rejoice in the Escapes, Successes and Victories of *Aeneas,* and be grieved at any Defeats, Misfortunes or Disappointments that befel him; as a *Greek* must have had the same Regard for *Achilles.* And it is plain, that each of those Poems have lost this great Advantage, among those Readers to whom their Heroes are as Strangers, or indifferent Persons.

Milton's Poem is admirable in this respect, since it is impossible for any of its Readers, whatever Nation, Country or People he may belong to, not to be related to the Persons who are the principal Actors in it; but what is still infinitely more to its Advantage, the principal Actors in this Poem are not only our Progenitors, but our Representatives. We have an actual Interest in every Thing they do, and no less than our utmost Happiness is concerned, and lies at Stake in all their Behaviour. (pp. 313-15)

· · · · ·

We have already taken a general survey of the Fable and Characters in *Milton's* **Paradise Lost**: The Parts which remain to be considered, according to *Aristotle's* Method, are the *Sentiments* and the *Language.* (p. 330)

Milton's chief Talent, and indeed his distinguishing Excellence, lies in the Sublimity of his Thoughts. There are others of the Moderns who rival him in every other Part of Poetry; but in the Greatness of his Sentiments he triumphs over all the Poets both Modern and Ancient, *Homer* only excepted. It is impossible for the Imagination of Man, to distend it self with greater Ideas, than those which he has laid together in his first, second, and tenth Books. The Seventh, which describes the Creation of the World, is likewise wonderfully sublime, tho' not so apt to stir up Emotion in the Mind of the Reader, nor consequently so perfect in the Epic Way of Writing, because it is filled with less Action. Let the Reader compare what *Longinus* has observed on several Passages in *Homer,* and he will find Parallels for most of them in the **Paradise Lost.** (pp. 331-32)

Having already treated of the Fable, the Characters, and Sentiments in the **Paradise Lost,** we are in the last Place to consider the *Language;* and as the learned World is very much divided upon *Milton,* as to this Point, I hope they will excuse me if I appear particular in any of my Opinions, and encline to those who judge the most advantagiously of the Author.

It is requisite that the Language of an heroick Poem should be both perspicuous and sublime. In proportion as either of these two Qualities are wanting, the Language is imperfect. Perspicuity is the first and most necessary Qualification; insomuch, that a good-natured Reader sometimes overlooks a little Slip even in the Grammar or Syntax, where it is impossible for him to mistake the Poet's Sense. Of this Kind is that Passage in *Milton,* wherein he speaks of *Satan.*

> . . . *God and his Son except,*
> *Created Thing Nought valued he nor shunn'd.*

And that in which he describes *Adam* and *Eve.*

> *Adam the goodliest Man of Men since born*
> *His Sons, the fairest of her Daughters* Eve.

It is plain, that in the former of these Passages, according to the natural Syntax, the Divine Persons mentioned in the first Line are represented as created Beings; and that in the other, *Adam* and *Eve* are confounded with their Sons and Daughters. Such little Blemishes as these, when the Thought is great and natural, we should, with *Horace,* impute to a pardonable Inadvertency, or to the Weakness of humane Nature, which cannot attend to each minute Particular, and give the last finishing to every Circumstance in so long a Work. The ancient Criticks therefore, who were acted by a Spirit of Candour, rather than that of Cavilling, invented certain Figures of Speech, on purpose to palliate little Errors of this Nature in the Writings of those Authors, who had so many greater Beauties to atone for them.

If Clearness and Perspicuity were only to be consulted, the Poet would have Nothing else to do but to cloath his Thoughts in the most plain and natural Expressions. But, since it often happens that the most obvious Phrases, and those which are used in ordinary Conversation, become too familiar to the Ear, and contract a Kind of Meanness by passing through the Mouths of the Vulgar, a Poet should take particular Care to guard himself against idiomatick Ways of Speaking. *Ovid* and *Lucan* have many Poornesses of Expression upon this Account, as taking up with the first Phrases that offered, without putting themselves to the Trouble of looking after such as would not only have been natural, but also elevated and sublime. *Milton* has but few Failings in this Kind, of which, however, you may meet with some Instances, as in the following Passages.

> *Embrio's and Idiots, Eremites and Fryars*
> White, Black, and Grey, *with all their* Trumpery.
> *Here Pilgrims roam . . .*
> *. . . A while Discourse they hold,*
> No fear lest Dinner cool; *when thus began*
> *Our Author . . .*
> *Who of all Ages to succeed, but feeling*
> *The Evil on him brought by me, will curse*
> *My Head, ill fare our Ancestor impure.*
> *For this we may thank Adam . . .*
>
> (pp. 348-50)

Aristotle has observed, that the Idiomatick Stile may be avoided, and the Sublime formed, by the following Methods. First, by the Use of Metaphors, like those in *Milton*.

> *Imparadised in one another's Arms,*
> *. . . And in his Hand a Reed*
> *Stood waving* tipt *with Fire; . . .*
> *The grassie Clods now* calv'd. . . .

In these and innumerable other Instances, the Metaphors are very bold, but beautiful: I must however observe, that the Metaphors are not thick sown in *Milton,* which always savours too much of Wit, that they never clash with one another, which as *Aristotle* observes, turns a Sentence into a Kind of an Enigma or Riddle; and that he seldom makes Use of them where the proper and natural Words will do as well.

Another Way of raising the Language, and giving it a poetical Turn, is to make Use of the Idioms of other Tongues. *Virgil* is full of the *Greek* Forms of Speech, which the Criticks call *Hellenisms,* as *Horace* in his Odes abounds with them much more than *Virgil*. I need not mention the several Dialects which *Homer* has made Use of for this End. *Milton* in conformity with the Practice of the ancient Poets, and with *Aristotle's* Rule, has infused a great many *Latinisms,* as well as *Graecisms,* and sometimes *Hebraisms,* into the Language of his Poem, as towards the Beginning of it.

> Nor *did they not perceive the evil Plight*
> *In which they were, or the fierce Pains not feel.*
> *Yet to their Gen'ral's Voice they soon obey'd.*
> *. . . Who shall tempt with wandring Feet*
> *.The dark unbottom'd infinite Abyss,*
> *And through the* palpable Obscure *find out his Way,*
> *His uncouth Way, or spread his airy Flight*
> *Upborn with indefatigable Wings*
> *Over the* vast Abrupt! *. . .*
> *. . . So both ascend*
> *In the Visions of God. . . .*

Under this Head may be reckoned the placing the Adjective after the Substantive, the Transposition of Words, the turning the Adjective into a Substantive, with several other foreign Modes of Speech, which this Poet has naturalized to give his Verse the greater Sound, and throw it out of Prose.

The third Method mentioned by *Aristotle,* is what agrees with the Genius of the *Greek* Language more than with that of any other Tongue, and is therefore more used by *Homer* than by any other Poet. I mean the length'ning of a Phrase by the Addition of Words, which may either be inserted or omitted, as also by the extending or contracting of particular Words by the Insertion or Omission of certain Syllables. *Milton* has put in Practice this Method of raising his Language, as far as the Nature of our Tongue will permit, as in the Passage abovementioned, *Eremite,* for what is Hermite in common Discourse. If you observe the Measure of his Verse, he has with great Judgment suppressed a Syllable in several Words, and shorted those of two Syllables into one, by which Method, besides the abovementioned Advantage, he has given a greater Variety to his Numbers. But this Practice is more particularly remarkable in the Names of Persons and of Countries, as *Beelzebub, Hessebon,* and in many other Particulars, wherein he has either changed the Name, or made Use of that which is not the most commonly known, that he might the better deviate from the Language of the Vulgar.

The same Reason recommended to him several old Words, which also makes his Poem appear the more venerable, and gives it a greater Air of Antiquity.

I must likewise take Notice, that there are in *Milton* several Words of his own Coining, as *Cerberean, miscreated, Helldoom'd, Embryon* Atoms, and many Others. If the Reader is offended at this Liberty in our *English* Poet, I would recommend him to a Discourse in *Plutarch,* which shews us how frequently *Homer* has made Use of the same Liberty.

Milton, by the abovementioned Helps, and by the Choice of the noblest Words and Phrases which our Tongue would afford him, has carried our Language to a greater Height than any of the *English* Poets have ever done before or after him, and made the Sublimity of his Stile equal to that of his Sentiments. (pp. 350-52)

[Next I shall] remark the several Defects which appear in the Fable, the Characters, the Sentiments, and the Language of *Milton's* **Paradise Lost;** not doubting but the Reader will pardon me, if I alledge at the same Time whatever may be said for the Extenuation of such Defects. The first Imperfection which I shall observe in the Fable is, that the Event of it is unhappy.

The Fable of every Poem is according to *Aristotle's* Division either *Simple* or *Implex*. It is called Simple when there is no Change of Fortune in it, Implex when the Fortune of the chief Actor changes from Bad to Good, or from Good to Bad. The Implex Fable is thought the most perfect; I suppose, because it is more proper to stir up the Passions of the Reader, and to surprize him with a greater Variety of Accidents.

The Implex Fable is therefore of two Kinds: In the first the chief Actor makes his Way through a long Series of Dangers and Difficulties, 'till he arrives at Honour and Prosperity, as we see in the Story of *Ulysses*. In the second, the chief Actor in the Poem falls from some eminent Pitch of Honour and Prosperity, into Misery and Disgrace. Thus we see *Adam* and *Eve* sinking from a State of Innocence and Happiness, into the most abject Condition of Sin and Sorrow.

The most taking Tragedies among the Antients were built on this last Sort of Implex Fable, particularly the Tragedy of *Oedipus,* which proceeds upon a Story, if we may believe *Aristotle,* the most proper for Tragedy that could be invented by the Wit of Man. . . . [This] Kind of Implex Fable, wherein the Event is unhappy, is more apt to affect an Audience than that of the first Kind; notwithstanding many excellent Pieces among the Antients, as well as most of those which have been written of late Years in our own Country, are raised upon contrary Plans. I must however own, that I think this Kind of Fable, which is the most perfect in Tragedy, is not so proper for an Heroick Poem.

Milton seems to have been sensible of this Imperfection in his Fable, and has therefore endeavoured to cure it by several Expedients; particularly by the Mortification which the great adversary of Mankind meets with upon his Return to the Assembly of Infernal Spirits, as it is described in a beautiful Passage of the tenth Book; and likewise by the Vision, wherein *Adam* at the Close of the Poem sees his Off-spring triumphing over his great Enemy, and himself restored to a happier *Paradise* than that from which he fell.

There is another Objection against *Milton*'s Fable, which is indeed almost the same with the former, tho' placed in a different Light, namely, That the Hero in the **Paradise Lost** is unsuccessful, and by no means a Match for his Enemies. This gave Occasion to Mr. *Dryden*'s Reflection, that the Devil was in reality *Milton*'s Hero [see excerpt dated 1697]. I think I have obviated this Objection in my first Paper. The **Paradise Lost** is an Epic, or a Narrative Poem; he that looks for an Hero in it, searches for that which *Milton* never intended; but if he will needs fix the Name of an Hero upon any Person in it, 'tis certainly the *Messiah* who is the Hero, both in the Principal Action, and in the chief Episodes. Paganism could not furnish out a real Action for a Fable greater than that of the *Iliad* or *Aeneid,* and therefore an heathen could not form a higher Notion of a Poem than one of that Kind, which they call an Heroick. Whether *Milton*'s is not of a sublimer Nature I will not presume to determine: It is sufficient that I shew there is in the **Paradise Lost** all the Greatness of Plan, Regularity of Design, and masterly Beauties which we discover in *Homer* and *Virgil.*

I must in the next Place observe, that *Milton* has interwoven in the Texture of his Fable some particulars which do not seem to have Probability enough for an Epic Poem, particularly in the Actions which he ascribes to *Sin* and *Death,* and the Picture which he draws of the *Lymbo of Vanity,* with other Passages in the second Book. Such Allegories rather savour of the Spirit of *Spencer* and *Ariosto,* than of *Homer* and *Virgil.*

In the Structure of his Poem he has likewise admitted too many Digressions. It is finely observed by *Aristotle,* that the Author of an Heroick Poem should seldom speak himself, but throw as much of his Work as he can into the Mouths of those who are his principal Actors. *Aristotle* has given no Reason for this Precept; but I presume it is because the Mind of the Reader is more awed and elevated when he hears *Aeneas* or *Achilles* speak, than when *Virgil* or *Homer* talk in their own Persons. Besides that assuming the Character of an eminent Man is apt to fire the Imagination, and raise the Ideas of the Author. *Tully* tells us, mentioning his Dialogue of Old Age, in which *Cato* is the chief Speaker, that upon a Review of it he was agreeably imposed upon, and fancied that it was *Cato,* and not he himself, who uttered his Thoughts on that Subject.

If the Reader would be at the pains to see how the Story of the *Iliad* and the *Aeneid* is delivered by those Persons who act in it, he will be surprized to find how little in either of these Poems proceeds from the Authors. *Milton* has, in the general Disposition of his Fable, very finely observed this great Rule; insomuch, that there is scarce a third Part of it which comes from the Poet; the rest is spoken either by *Adam* and *Eve,* or by some Good or Evil Spirit who is engaged either in their Destruction or Defence.

From what has been here observed it appears, that Digressions are by no means to be allowed of in an Epic Poem. If the Poet, even in the ordinary Course of his Narration, should speak as little as possible, he should certainly never let his Narration sleep for the sake of any Reflections of his own. I have often observed, with a secret Admiration, that the longest Reflection in the *Aeneid* is in that Passage of the Tenth Book, where *Turnus* is represented as dressing himself in the Spoils of *Pallas,* whom he had slain. *Virgil* here lets his Fable stand still for the sake of the following Remark. *How is the Mind of Man ignorant of Futurity, and unable to bear prosperous Fortune with Moderation? The Time will come when* Turnus *shall wish that he had left the Body of* Pallas *untouched, and curse the Day on which he dressed himself in these Spoils.* As the great Event of the *Aeneid,* and the Death of *Turnus,* whom *Aeneas* slew because he saw him adorned with the Spoils of *Pallas,* turns upon this Incident, *Virgil* went out of his way to make this Reflection upon it, without which so small a Circumstance might possibly have slipped out of his Reader's Memory. *Lucan,* who has an Injudicious Poet, lets drop his Story very frequently for the sake of his unnecessary Digressions, or his *Diverticula,* as *Scaliger* calls them. If he gives us an Account of the Prodigies which preceded the Civil War, he declaims upon the Occasion, and shews how much happier it would be for Man, if he did not feel his Evil Fortune before it comes to pass, and suffer not only by its real Weight, but by the Apprehension of it. *Milton*'s Complaint for his Blindness, his Panegyrick on Marriage, his Reflections on *Adam* and *Eve*'s going naked, of the Angels eating, and several other Passages in his Poem, are liable to the same Exception, tho' I must confess there is so great a Beauty in these very Digressions, that I would not wish them out of his Poem.

I have, in a former Paper, spoken of the *Characters* of *Milton*'s **Paradise Lost,** and declared my Opinion, as to the Allegorical Persons who are introduced in it.

If we look into the *Sentiments,* I think they are sometimes defective under the following Heads; First, as there are several of them too much pointed, and some that degenerate even into Punns. Of this last Kind I am afraid is that in the First Book, where, speaking of the Pigmies, he calls them.

> . . .*The small* Infantry
> *Warr'd on by Cranes.* . .

Another Blemish that appears in some of his Thoughts, is his frequent Allusion to Heathen Fables, which are not certainly of a Piece with the Divine Subject, of which he treats. I do not find fault with these Allusions, where the Poet himself represents them as fabulous, as he does in some Places, but where he mentions them as Truths and Matters of Fact. The Limits of my Paper will not give me leave to be particular in Instances of this Kind: The Reader will easily remark them in his Perusal of the Poem.

A third Fault in his Sentiments, is an unnecessary Ostentation of Learning, which likewise occurs very frequently. It is certain that both *Homer* and *Virgil* were Masters of all the Learning of their Times, but it shews it self in their Works after an indirect and concealed Manner. *Milton* seems ambitious of letting us know, by his Excursions on Free-Will and Predestination, and his many Glances upon History, Astronomy, Geography and the like, as well as by the Terms and Phrases he sometimes makes use of, that he was acquainted with the whole Circle of Arts and Sciences.

If, in the last Place, we consider the *Language* of this great Poet, we must allow what I have hinted in a former Paper, that it is often too much laboured, and sometimes obscured by old Words, Transpositions, and Foreign Idioms. *Seneca*'s Objection to the Stile of a great Author, *Riget ejus oratio, nihil in ea placidum, nihil lene,* is what many Criticks make to *Milton*; As I cannot wholly refute it, so I have already apologized for it in another Paper; to which I may further add, that *Milton*'s Sentiments and Ideas were so wonderfully sublime, that it would have been impossible for him to have represented them in their full Strength and Beauty, without having Recourse to these Foreign Assistances. Our Language sunk under him, and was unequal to the Greatness of Soul, which furnished him with such glorious Conceptions.

A second Fault in his Language is, that he often affects a Kind of Jingle in his Words as in the following Passages, and many others:

> *And brought into the* World *a* World *of woe.*
> *. . . Begirt th' Almighty throne*
> *Beseeching or besieging. . .*
> *This tempted our Attempt. . .*
> *At one slight Bound high overleapt all Bound.*

I know there are Figures for this Kind of Speech, that some of the greatest Antients have been guilty of it, and that *Aristotle* himself has given it a place in his Rhetorick among the Beauties of that Art. But as it is in itself poor and trifling, it is I think at present universally exploded by all the Masters of polite Writing.

The last Fault which I shall take notice of in *Milton*'s Stile, is the frequent Use of what the Learned call *Technical Words,* or Terms of Art. It is one of the greatest Beauties of Poetry, to make hard Things intelligible, and to deliver what is abstruse of it self in such easy Language as may be understood by ordinary Readers: Besides that the Knowledge of a Poet should rather seem born with him, or inspired, than drawn from Books and Systems. I have often wondered how Mr. *Dryden* could translate a Passage out of *Virgil* after the following manner.

> *Tack to the Larboard, and stand off to Sea.*
> *Veer Star-board Sea and Land. . . .*

Milton makes use of *Larboard* in the same manner. When he is upon Building he mentions *Doric Pillars, Pilasters, Cornice, Freeze, Architrave.* When he talks of Heavenly Bodies, you meet with *Ecliptic* and *Eccentric, the Trepidation, Stars dropping from the Zenith, Rays culminating from the Equator.* To which might be added many Instances of the like Kind in several other Arts and Sciences. (pp. 385-89)

> *Joseph Addison, in a review of "Paradise Lost," in*
> The Spectator, *Vol. II, edited by Gregory Smith,*
> *1906. Reprint by Dutton, 1950, pp. 294-389.*

ALEXANDER POPE (essay date 1726)

[*Pope has been called the greatest English poet of his time and one of the most important poets in world literature. As a critic*

and satirical commentator, he wrote works that epitomize eighteenth-century neoclassicism. His famous remark, "The proper study of mankind is man," perfectly illustrates the temperament of his age, a time when influential thinkers severely narrowed the limits of human speculation. All of Pope's works demonstrate a love of restraint, clarity, order, and decorum. His greatness lies in his cultivation of style and wit rather than sublimity and pathos—an inclination that shaped his criticism of other writers. In the following excerpt from the postscript to his translation of Homer's* Odyssey, *he briefly considers the poetic style of* Paradise Lost *and assesses the value of the speeches in the poem as exemplars.*]

The imitators of *Milton*, like most other imitators, are not *Copies* but *Caricatura's* of their original; they are a hundred times more obsolete and cramp than he, and equally so in all places: Whereas it should have been observed of *Milton*, that he is not lavish of his exotick words and phrases every where alike, but employs them much more where the subject is marvellous vast and strange, as in the scenes of Heaven, Hell, Chaos, &c. than where it is turn'd to the natural and agreeable, as in the pictures of Paradise, the loves of our first parents, the entertainments of Angels, and the like. In general, this unusual style better serves to awaken our ideas in the descriptions and in the imaging and picturesque parts, than it agrees with the lower sort of narrations, the character of which is simplicity and purity. *Milton* has several of the latter, where we find not an antiquated affected or uncouth word, for some hundred lines together; as in his fifth book [of *Paradise Lost*], the latter part of the eighth, the former of the tenth and eleventh books, and in the narration of *Michael* in the twelfth. I wonder indeed that he, who ventur'd (contrary to the practice of all other Epic Poets) to imitate *Homer*'s Lownesses in the *Narrative*, should not also have copied his plainness and perspicuity in the *Dramatic* parts: Since in his speeches (where clearness above all is necessary) there is frequently such transposition and forced construction, that the very sense is not to be discover'd without a second or third reading: And in this certainly he ought to be no example. (pp. 390-91)

> *Alexander Pope, "Postscript," in* The Odyssey of
> Homer: Books XIII-XXIV, *edited by Maynard Mack,*
> *translated by Alexander Pope, Methuen & Co. Ltd.,*
> *1967, pp. 382-97.*

VOLTAIRE (essay date 1727)

[*A prolific French philosopher and man of letters, Voltaire was a major figure of the eighteenth-century European Enlightenment, a movement in which reason and empiricism superseded reliance on prescription, faith, and authority. As a man of diverse and intense interests, he wrote on many subjects and in a variety of genres, always asserting the absolute primacy of personal liberty—be it intellectual, social, religious, or political. Consequently, he opposed religious traditions and political organizations that he believed thwarted or curtailed individual freedom. Voltaire's most valuable contribution to literature is usually considered his invention of the philosophical* conte, *or tale, in which the story is a vehicle for an ethical or philosophical message. The most famous of these* contes *is the highly regarded* Candide *(1759). In the following excerpt from another work originally published in 1727, he enumerates what he considers the principal merits and faults of* Paradise Lost.]

Milton is the last in *Europe* who wrote an *Epick* Poem, for I wave all those whose Attempts have been unsuccessful, my Intention being not to descant on the many who have contended for the Prize, but to speak only of the very few who have gain'd it in their respective Countries. (pp. 102-03)

If the Difference of Genius between Nation and Nation, ever appear'd in its full Light, 'tis in *Milton's* **Paradise Lost.**

The *French* answer with a scornful Smile, when they are told there is in *England* an *Epick* Poem, the Subject whereof is the Devil fighting against God, and *Adam* and *Eve* eating an Apple at the Persuasion of a Snake. As that Topick hath afforded nothing among them, but some lively Lampoons, for which that Nation is so famous; they cannot imagine it possible to build an *Epick* Poem upon the Subject of their Ballads. And indeed such an Error ought to be excused; for if we consider with what Freedom the politest Part of Mankind throughout all *Europe,* both Catholicks and Protestants, are wont to ridicule in Conversation those consecrated Histories; nay if those who have the highest Respect for the Mysteries of the Christian Religion, and who are struck with Awe at some Parts of it, yet cannot forbear now and then making free with the *Devil,* the *Serpent,* the Frailty of our first Parents, the Rib which *Adam* was robb'd of, and the like; it seems a very hard Task for a profane Poet to endeavour to remove those Shadows of Ridicule, to reconcile together what is Divine and what looks absurd, and to command a Respect that the sacred Writers could hardly obtain from our frivolous Minds.

What *Milton* so boldly undertook, he perform'd with a superior Strength of Judgment, and with an Imagination productive of Beauties not dream'd of before him. The Meanness (if there is any) of some Parts of the Subject is lost in the Immensity of the Poetical Invention. There is something above the reach of human Forces to have attempted the Creation without Bombast, to have describ'd the Gluttony and Curisoity of a Woman without Flatness, to have brought Probability and Reason amidst the Hurry of imaginary Things belonging to another World, and as far remote from the Limits of our Notions as they are from our Earth; in short to force the Reader to say, ''If God, if the Angels, if Satan would speak, I believe they would speak as they do in *Milton.*''

I have often admir'd how barren the Subject appears, and how fruitful it grows under his Hands.

The **Paradise Lost** is the only Poem wherein are to be found in a perfect Degree that Uniformity which satisfies the Mind and that Variety which pleases the Imagination. All its Episodes being necessary Lines which aim at the Centre of a perfect circle. Where is the Nation who would not be pleas'd with the Interview of *Adam* and the *Angel?* With the Mountain of Vision, with the bold Strokes which make up the Relentless, undaunted and sly Character of Satan? But above all with that sublime Wisdom which *Milton* exerts, whenever he dares to describe God, and to make him speak? He seems indeed to draw the Picture of the Almighty, as like as human Nature can reach to, through the mortal Dust in which we are clouded.

The *Heathens* always, the *Jews* often, and our Christian Priests sometimes, represent God as a Tyrant infinitely powerful. But the God of *Milton* is always a Creator, a Father, and a Judge, nor is his Vengeance jarring with his Mercy, nor his Predeterminations repugnant to the Liberty of Man. These are the Pictures which lift up indeed the Soul of the Reader. *Milton* in that Point as well as in many others is as far above the ancient Poets as the Christian Religion is above the *Heathen* Fables.

But he hath especially an undisputable Claim to the unanimous Admiration of Mankind, when he descends from those high Flights to the natural Description of human Things. It is observable that in all other Poems Love is represented as a Vice,

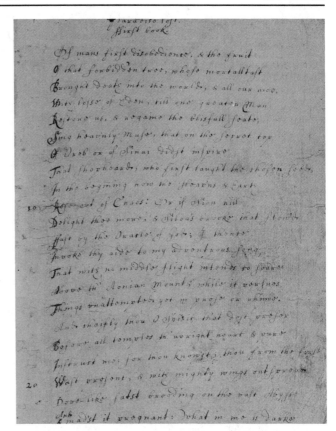

Manuscript page of Paradise Lost, *Book I.*

in *Milton* only 'tis a Virtue. The Pictures he draws of it, are naked as the Persons he speaks of, and as venerable. He removes with a chaste Hand the Veil which covers every where else the enjoyments of that Passion. There is Softness, Tenderness and Warmth without Lasciviousness; the Poet transports himself and us, into that State of innocent Happiness in which *Adam* and *Eve* continued for a short Time: He soars not above human, but above corrupt Nature, and as there is no Instance of such Love, there is none of such Poetry. (pp. 104-07)

It is an easy and pleasant Task to take Notice of the many Beauties of *Milton* which I call universal: But 'tis a ticklish Undertaking to point out what would be reputed a Fault in any other Country.

I am very far from thinking that one Nation ought to judge of its Productions by the Standard of another, nor do I presume that the *French* (for Example) who have no *Epick* Poets, have any Right to give Laws on *Epick* Poetry.

But I fancy many *English* Readers, who are acquainted with the *French* Language, will not be displeas'd to have some Notion of the Taste of that Country: And I hope they are too just either to submit to it, or despise it barely upon the Score of its being foreign to them. (p. 109)

I'll venture to say that none of the *French* Criticks could like the Excursions which *Milton* makes sometimes beyond the strict Limits of his Subject. They lay down for a Rule that an Author himself ought never to appear in his Poem; and his own Thoughts, his own Sentiments must be spoken by the Actors he introduces. Many judicious Men in *England* comply with that Opinion, and Mr. *Addison* favours it. I beg Leave in this

Place to hazard a Reflexion of my own, which I submit to the Reader's Judgment.

Milton breaks the Thread of his Narration in two Manners. The first consists of two or three kinds of Prologues, which he premises at the Beginning of some Books. In one Place he expatiates upon his own Blindness; in another he compares his Subject and prefers it to that of the *Iliad,* and to the common Topicks of War, which were thought before him the only Subject fit for *Epick* Poetry; and he adds that he hopes to soar as high as all his Predecessors, unless the cold Climate of *England damps his Wings.*

His other Way of interrupting his Narration, is by some Observations which he intersperses now and then upon some great Incident, or some interesting Circumstance. Of that Kind is his Digression on Love in the fourth Book;

> Whatever *Hippocrites* austerely talk
> Defaming as impure, what God declares
> Pure, and commands to some, leaves free to all.
> Our Maker bids increase, who bids abstain
> But our Destroyer foe to God and Men?
> Hail wedded Love, &c.

As to the first of these two Heads, I cannot but own that an Author is generally guilty of an impardonable Self-love, when he lays aside his Subject to descant on his own Person; but that human Frailty is to be forgiven in *Milton;* nay I am pleas'd with it. He gratifies the Curiosity, it raises in me about his Person, when I admire the Author, I desire to know something of the Man, and he whom all Readers would be glad to know, is allow'd to speak of himself. But this however is a very dangerous Example for a Genius of an inferior Order, and is only to be justified by Success.

As to the second Point I am so far from looking on that Liberty as a Fault, that I think it to be a great Beauty. For if Morality is the aim of Poetry, I do not apprehend why the Poet should be forbidden to intersperse his Descriptions with moral Sentences and useful Reflexions, provided he scatters them with a sparing Hand, and in proper Places either when he wants Personages to utter those Thoughts, or when their Character does not permit them to speak in the Behalf of Virtue.

'Tis strange that *Homer* is commended by the Criticks for his comparing *Ajax* to an Ass pelted away with Stones by some Children, *Ulysses* to a Pudding, the Council-board of *Priam* to Grashoppers: 'Tis strange, I say, that they defend so clamourously those Similes tho' never so foreign to the Purpose, and will not allow the natural Reflexions, the noble Digressions of *Milton* tho' never so closely link'd to the Subject.

I will not dwell upon some small Errors of *Milton,* which are obvious to every Reader, I mean some few Contradictions, and those frequent Glances at the *Heathen* Mythology, which Fault by the by is so much the more unexcusable in him, by his having premis'd in his first Book that those Divinities were but Devils worshipp'd under different Names, which ought to have been a sufficient Caution to him not to speak of the Rape of *Proserpine,* of the Wedding of *Juno* and *Jupiter,* &c. as Matters of Fact.

I lay aside likewise his preposterous and aukward Jests, his Puns, his too familiar Expressions so inconsistent with the Elevation of his Genius, and of his Subject.

To come to more essential Points and more *liable* to be debated. I dare affirm that the Contrivance of the *Pandæmonium* would have been entirely disapprov'd of by Criticks like *Boyleau, Racine,* &c.

That Seat built for the Parliament of the Devils, seems very preposterous: Since Satan hath summon'd them altogether, and harangu'd them just before in an ample Field. The Council was necessary; but where it was to be held, 'twas very indifferent. The Poet seems to delight in building his *Pandæmonium* in *Doric* Order with Freeze and Cornice, and a Roof of Gold. Such a Contrivance favours more of the wild Fancy of our Father *le Moine* then of the serious Spirit of *Milton.* But when afterwards the Devils turn dwarfs to fill their Places in the House, as if it was impracticable to build a Room large enough to contain them in their natural Size; it is an idle Story which would match the most extravagant Tales. And to crown all, Satan and the chief Lords preserving their own monstrous Forms, while the Rabble of the Devils shrink into Pigmees, heightens the Ridicule of the whole Contrivance to an unexpressible Degree. Methinks the true Criterion for discerning what is really ridiculous in an *Epick* Poem, is to examine if the same Thing would not fit exactly the Mock heroick. Then I dare say that nothing is so adapted to that ludicrous way of Writing, as the Metamorphosis of the Devils into Dwarfs.

The Fiction of *Death* and *Sin* seems to have in it some great Beauties and many gross Defects. In order to canvass this Matter with Order. We must first lay down that such shadowy Beings, as *Death, Sin, Chaos,* are intolerable when they are not allegorical. For Fiction is nothing but Truth in Disguise. It must be granted too, that an Allegory must be short, decent, and noble. For an Allegory carried too far or too low, is like a beautiful Woman who wears always a Mask. An Allegory is a long Metaphor; and to speak too long in Metaphor's must be tiresom, because unnatural. This being premis'd, I must say that in general those Fictions, those imaginary Beings, are more agreable to the Nature of *Milton*'s Poem, than to any other; because he hath but two natural Persons for his Actors, I mean *Adam* and *Eve.* A great Part of the Action lies in imaginary Worlds, and must *of course* admit of imaginary Beings.

Then *Sin* springing out of the Head of Satan, seems a beautiful Allegory of Pride, which is look'd upon as the first Offence commited against God. But I question if *Satan,* getting his Daughter with Child, is an Invention to be approv'd off. I am afraid that Fiction is but a meer Quibble; for if Sin was of a masculine Gender in *English, as it is in all the other Languages,* that whole Affair Drops, and the Fiction vanishes away. But suppose we are not so nice, and we allow Satan to be in Love with *Sin, because this Word is made feminine in* English (as Death passes also for masculine) what a horrid and loathsome Idea does *Milton* present to the Mind, in this Fiction? *Sin* brings forth Death, this Monster inflam'd with Lust and Rage, lies with his Mother, as she had done with her Father. From that new Commerce, springs a Swarm of Serpents, which creep in and out of their Mother's Womb, and gnaw and tear the Bowels they are born from.

Let such a Picture be never so beautifully drawn, let the Allegory be never so obvious, and so clear, still it will be intolerable, on the Account of its Foulness. That Complication of Horrors, that Mixture of Incest, that Heap of Monsters, that Loathsomeness so far fetch'd, cannot but shock a Reader of delicate Taste.

But what is more intolerable, there are Parts in that Fiction, which bearing no Allegory at all, have no Manner of Excuse. There is no meaning in the Communication between Death and

Sin, 'tis distasteful without any Purpose; or if any Allegory lies under it, the filthy Abomination of the Thing is certainly more obvious than the Allegory.

I see with Admiration, *Sin,* the *Portress* of Hell, opening the Gates of the Abiss, but unable to shut them again. That is really beautiful, because 'tis true. But what signifies Satan and Death quarrelling together, grinning at one another, and ready to fight?

The Fiction of *Chaos, Night,* and *Discord,* is rather a Picture, than an Allegory; and for ought I know, deserves to be approv'd, because it strikes the Reader with Awe, not with Horror.

I know the Bridge built by Death and Sin, would be dislik'd in *France.* The nice Criticks of that Country would urge against that Fiction, that it seems too common, and that it is useless; for Men's Souls want no paved Way, to be thrown into Hell, after their Separation from the Body.

They would laugh justly at the Paradise of Fools, at the Hermits, Fryars, Cowles, Beads, Indulgences, Bulls, Reliques, toss'd by the Winds, at *St. Peter*'s waiting with his Keys at the Wicket of Heaven. And surely the most passionate Admirers of *Milton,* could not vindicate those low comical Imaginations, which belong by Right to *Ariosto.*

Now the sublimest of all the Fictions calls me to examine it. I mean the War in Heaven. The Earl of *Roscommon,* and Mr. *Addison* (whose Judgment seems either to guide, or to justify the Opinion of his Countrymen) admire chiefly that Part of the Poem. They bestow all the Skill of their Criticism, and the Strength of their Eloquence, to set off that favourite Part. I may affirm, that the very Things they admire, would not be tolerated by the *French* Criticks. The Reader will perhaps see with Pleasure, *in what consists so strange a Difference,* and what may be the Ground of it.

First, they would assert, that a War in Heaven being an imaginary Thing, which lies out of the Reach of our Nature, should be contracted in two or three Pages, rather than lengthen'd out into two Books; because we are naturally impatient of removing from us the Objects which are not adapted to our Senses.

According to that Rule, they would maintain, that 'tis an idle Task to give the Reader the full Character of the Leaders of that War, and to describe *Raphael, Michael, Abdiel, Moloch,* and *Nisroth,* as *Homer* paints *Ajax, Diomede* and *Hector.*

For what avails it to draw at length the Picture of these Beings, so utterly Strangers to the Reader, that he cannot be affected any Way towards them; by the same Reason, the long Speeches of these imaginary Warriors, either before the Battle, or in the Middle of the Action, their mutual Insults, seem an injudicious Imitation of *Homer.*

The aforesaid Criticks would not bear with the Angels plucking up the Mountains, with their Woods, their Waters, and their Rocks, and flinging them on the Heads of their Enemies. Such a Contrivance (they would say) is the more puerile, the more it aims at Greatness. Angels arm'd with Mountains in Heaven, resemble too much the Dipsodes in *Rabelais,* who wore an Armour of *Portland* Stone six Foot thick.

The Artillery seems of the same Kind, yet more trifling, because more useless.

To what Purpose are these Engines brought in? Since they cannot wound the Enemies, but only remove them from their Places, and make them tumble down: Indeed (if the Expression

may be forgiven) 'tis to play at Nine-Pins. And the very Thing which is so dreadfully great on Earth, becomes very low and ridiculous in Heaven.

I cannot omit here, the visible Contradiction which reigns in that Episode. God sends his faithful Angels to fight, to conquer and to punish the Rebels. Go (says he, to *Michael* and *Gabriel*)

> ———And to the Brow of Heaven
> Pursuing, drive them out from God and Bliss,
> Into their Place of Punishment, the Gulph
> Of *Tartarus,* which ready opens wide
> His fiery Chaos to receive their Fall.

How does it come to pass, after such a positive Order, that the Battle hangs doubtful? And why did God the Father command *Gabriel* and *Raphael,* to do what he executes afterwards by his Son only.

I leave it to the Readers, to pronounce, if these Observations are right, or ill-grounded, and if they are carried to far. But in case these Exceptions are just, the severest Critick must however confess there are Perfections enough in *Milton,* to attone for all his Defects.

I must beg leave to conclude this Article on *Milton,* with two Observations.

His Hero (I mean *Adam,* his first Personage) is unhappy. That demonstrates against all the Criticks, that a very good Poem may end unfortunately, in Spight of all their pretended Rules. Secondly, The **Paradise Lost** ends compleatly. The Thread of the Fable is spun out to the last. *Milton* and *Tasso* have been careful of not stopping short and abruptly. The one does not abandon *Adam* and *Eve,* till they are driven out of *Eden.* The other does not conclude, before *Jerusalem* is taken. *Homer* and *Virgil* took a contrary Way, the *Iliad* ends with the Death of Hector, the *Æneid* with that of *Turnus:* The Tribe of Commentators have upon that enacted a Law, that a House ought never to be finish'd, because *Homer* and *Virgil* did not compleat their own; but if *Homer* had taken *Troy,* and *Virgil* married *Lavinia* to *Æneas,* the Criticks would have laid down a Rule just the contrary. (pp. 110-21)

Voltaire, ''An Essay on Epick Poetry,'' in Le Bossu and Voltaire on the Epic, *Scholars' Facsimiles & Reprints, 1970, pp. 102-30.*

JONATHAN RICHARDSON   (essay date 1734)

[*The following excerpt is from* Explanatory Notes and Remarks on Milton's ''Paradise Lost'' *(1734), which was written jointly by Jonathan Richardson and his son, Jonathan junior. Richardson senior, sole author of the section excerpted below, is best known today as a portrait painter, but, according to Samuel Johnson, during his life he was celebrated chiefly for his writings on aesthetics, including* Essay on the Theory of Painting *(1715) and* An Argument in Behalf of the Science of a Connoisseur *(1719). He was careful to point out his debt to his son in the following passage from* Explanatory Notes: *''My Son is my Learning, as I am That to Him which He has Not; We make One Man; and Such a Compound Man (what Sort of One Soever He is whom We make) May Probably, produce what no Single Man Can. When therefore I, in my Own Person talk of Things which in my Separate Capacity I am known to be a Stranger to, let Me be Understood as the Complicated* Richardson.'' *In printing the excerpt, the typographical peculiarities of the original have been preserved. Of these, the Richardsons remarked: ''We have Us'd Great Letters, wherever any particular Weight is to be laid on the Word; and not Else, though at the beginning of a Paragraph in Prose, or of a Line in Verse, where there is no Other Pretence for One than*

Custom, and an Imagin'd Beauty in it; for 'tis Imagination Only; or if it Really was Handsomer to the Eye; or if So many Great Letters as We put into the Page Look'd not So well as None at all, or very Few, as in the Old Italian Books by Giolito or the Giunti and Some Others, is That Sufficient to stand in Ballance with what is so much more Important?'' Here, Richardson senior praises Milton's character, literary motivation, and the ''Musick of His Verse.'']

Milton appears to have had a Natural Greatness, Warmth and Vigour of Mind, together with an Openness and Generosity, all which is True Magnanimity. This Blazes wherever he goes from One End of his Life to the Other. Such Minds are apt to take Strong and Deep Impressions; and as He was Fully persuaded he was engag'd in the Cause of God, and of Liberty, he exerted every Nerve. (p. 215)

Milton had Always a Firm Belief of the Being of a God, and a Mind which could not fail from his Existence to Infer his Government of the Universe, and all This in such a One must Produce True Piety, Veneration, Submission, Dependance, Love mix'd with Filial Awe, Joy, &c. This Appears Perpetually to every Observing Reader of his Works, Verse or Prose. His Other Speculative Religious Opinions whereby he is Distinguish'd, are rather Political than Religious, Such as relate to the Circumstantials rather than to the Essentials or Substance of Religion; Church-Government, Church-Communion, Ceremonies, the Millenium, &c. on which 'tis not necessary to Enlarge, and I am Glad it is not. (p. 240)

Verse and Prose have Each their Peculiar Musick, and whether One, or the Other 'tis Different according to the Subject. All kinds of Verses have Sounds of their Own; Blank Verse comes nearest to Prose, and as the Prose of Some Writers Approaches Verse, *Milton's* Blank Verse, That of *Paradise Lost,* has the Beauty of Both; it has the Sweetness of Measure, without stopping the Voice at the end of the Line, or Any where else but as the Sense requires; One Verse runs into Another, and the Period concludes in any part of a Line Indifferently, and as if 'twas his Choice 'tis very often Not at the End of One or of a Couplet, as is too Frequent with Those who write in Rime. He has frequently Eleven Syllables in a Verse, but 'tis rarely So unless Those are no more in Quantity than the Ten of Another.

> Fall'n Cherube, to be Weak is Miserable
> Doing or Suffering: but of This be Sure,

the *e* in the Middle of the Word *Suff'ring* must be Melted in the Pronunciation, as if written Without it as here; and the two Syllables made by that Vowel, and the *a* that follows in *Miserable* are so Short as to be Equal to but One in any part of the Line. So

> Assur'd me and still Assure. though what thou tell'st

here *Me* and *and* are both so Short as to be no more in Quantity than if they were but One Syllable. to read right requires Some Judgment, and some Experience in *Milton's* Manner who Abounds More with These Instances than most English Poets; but, well Read, the Musick of His Verse is Exceeding Delicate and Noble, though Somwhat Peculiar to Himself; for He, (as in his Language) has Profited Himself of the Greeks and Latins; His *Ictus,* or *Cadence,* or Musick bears towards Them, as he has form'd himself Upon Their Examples into Somthing of his Own, by his Own Ear, and which was a very Musical, Experienc'd and Judicious One. See further concerning his Versification in his Short Discourse before the Poem [see excerpt dated 1668]. (pp. 311-12)

Milton's Language is English, but 'tis *Milton's* English; 'tis Latin, 'tis Greek English; not only the Words, the Phraseology, the Transpositions, but the Ancient Idiom is seen in All he Writes, So that a Learned Foreigner will think *Milton* the Easiest to be Understood of All the English Writers. This Peculiar English is most Conspicuously seen in *Paradise Lost,* for This is the Work which he Long before Intended should Enrich and Adorn his Native Tongue. . . . (p. 313)

Milton's true Character as a Writer is that he is an Ancient, but born two Thousand Years after his Time. his Language indeed is Modern, but the Best, next to Greek, and Latin, to Convey those Images Himself Conceiv'd; and That moreover Greek'd and Latiniz'd and made as Uncommon and Expressive as our Tongue could be, and yet Intelligible to us for whom he Wrote. But All his Images are Pure Antique. So that We read *Homer* and *Virgil* in reading Him. We hear Them in our Own Tongue, as we See What They Conceiv'd when *Milton* Speaks; Yes, and We find Our Selves amongst Persons and Things of a more Exalted Character. *Connoisseurs* in Painting and Sculpture can Best tell what is the Difference of Taste in Ancient and Modern Work, and can therefore Best Understand what I am now Saying; it must Suffice that I tell Others that there is a Certain Grace, Majesty and Simplicity in the Antique which is its Distinguishing Character. the Same Kind of Taste is Seen in Writing; and *Milton* has it, I think, to a Degree beyond what We have ever found in Any Modern Painter or Sculptor, not Excepting *Rafaelle* Himself. (p. 318)

[If] Ever any Book was Truly Poetical, if Ever Any Abounded with Poetry, 'tis *Paradise Lost.* What an Expansion of Facts from a Small Seed of History! What Worlds are Invented, What Embellishments of Nature upon what our Senses Present Us with? Divine things are More Nobly, more Divinely Represented to the Imagination than by Any Other Poem, a More Beautiful Idea is given of Nature than any Poet has Pretended to; Nature as just come out of the Hand of God, in its Virgin Loveliness, Glory, and Purity; and the Human Race is Shown, not as *Homer's,* More Gigantick, more Robust, more Valiant, but without Comparison more Truly Amiable, more So than by the Pictures and Statues of the Greatest Masters. and all These Sublime Ideas are Convey'd to Us in the most Effectual and Engaging Manner. the Mind of the Reader is Tempered, and Prepar'd, by Pleasure, 'tis Drawn, and Allured, 'tis Awaken'd and Invigorated to receive Such Impressions as the Poet intended to give it: it Opens the Fountains of Knowledge, Piety and Virtue, and pours Along Full Streams of Peace, Comfort and Joy to Such as can Penetrate the true Sense of the Writer, and Obediently Listen to his Song.

In reading the *Iliad* or *Æneis* we Treasure up a Collection of Fine Imaginative Pictures as when we read *Paradise Lost*; Only that form Thence we have (to speak like a *Connoisseur*) More *Rafaelles, Correggios, Guidos,* &c. *Milton's* Pictures are more Sublimely Great, Divine and Lovely than *Homer's,* or *Virgil's* or those of Any Other Poet, or of All the Poets, Ancient, or Modern. (pp. 327-28)

O *Milton* thou hast employ'd all thy Vast Treasure of Wit, Learning, and Ability, all the Beauty, Energy, and Propriety of Words Our Language was Capable of, all the Sweetness and Harmony of Numbers thy Musical and Judicious Ear furnish'd thee with, All the Fire and Beauty and Sublimity of Imagination Peculiar to thy Self, Added to what could be Supply'd by Those who have most Excell'd in That Angelical Faculty, in whatever Ages or Languages, All the Firmness, Force and Dignity of Mind thy Vertue and Piety Excited in thee, or Rewarded thee with; and together with All These a Genius Perfectly Poetical, if Ever Any Man's was, and That Regulated by a most Solid Judgment. All These thou hast Consecrated to Produce a Poem, more Instrumental than any Other Human Composition, to Calm and Purify the Mind, and through the Delightful Regions of Poetry, to Exalt and Fix it to the Mysteries, Sublimities and Practice of Religion; to a State of Tranquility and Happiness, the Utmost Mortality is Capable of. (pp. 329-30)

> *Jonathan Richardson, "The Life of Milton, and a Discourse on 'Paradise Lost',"* in The Early Lives of Milton, *edited by Helen Darbishire, Constable & Co. Ltd., 1932, pp. 199-330.*

SAMUEL JOHNSON (essay date 1779)

[Johnson is one of the outstanding figures in English literature and a leader in the history of textual and aesthetic criticism. Popularly known in his day as the "Great Cham of Literature," he was a prolific lexicographer, essayist, poet, and critic whose Dictionary of the English Language *(1775) and* Prefaces, Biographical and Critical, to the Works of the English Poets *(10 vols., 1779-81; reissued in 1783 as* The Lives of the Most Eminent English Poets) *were new departures in lexicography and biographical criticism, respectively. Johnson the critic was neither a rigid theorist nor a strict follower of neoclassical rules, tending instead to rely on common sense and empirical knowledge. He had in his criticism one criterion in mind: the power of a work to please and instruct. At his best a direct and pungent prosodist, Johnson was a perceptive and acute judge of a work's defects as well as merits, but because of his forceful style his listings of defects are often more memorable than his extensive general praise. In the following excerpt from an essay originally published in 1779, he surveys Milton's major poetry.]*

In the examination of Milton's poetical works, I shall pay so much regard to time as to begin with his juvenile productions. For his early pieces he seems to have had a degree of fondness not very laudable; what he has once written he resolves to preserve, and gives to the publick an unfinished poem, which he broke off because he was *nothing satisfied with what he had done,* supposing his readers less nice than himself. These preludes to his future labours are in Italian, Latin, and English. Of the Italian I cannot pretend to speak as a critick; but I have heard them commended by a man well qualified to decide their merit. The Latin pieces are lusciously elegant; but the delight which they afford is rather by the exquisite imitation of the ancient writers, by the purity of the diction, and the harmony of the numbers, than by any power of invention, or vigour of sentiment. They are not all of equal value; the elegies excell the odes; and some of the exercises on Gunpowder Treason might have been spared.

The English poems, though they make no promises of *Paradise Lost,* have this evidence of genius, that they have a cast original and unborrowed. But their peculiarity is not excellence; if they differ from verses of others, they differ for the worse; for they are too often distinguished by repulsive harshness; the combination of words are new, but they are not pleasing; the rhymes and epithets seem to be laboriously sought, and violently applied.

That in the early parts of his life he wrote with much care appears from his manuscripts, happily preserved at Cambridge, in which many of his smaller works are found as they were first written, with the subsequent corrections. Such reliques shew how excellence is required; what we hope ever to do with ease, we may learn first to do with diligence.

Those who admire the beauties of this great poet, sometimes force their own judgement into false approbation of his little pieces, and prevail upon themselves to think that admirable which is only singular. All that short compositions can commonly attain is neatness and elegance. Milton never learned the art of doing little things with grace; he overlooked the milder excellence of suavity and softness; he was a *Lion* that had no skill *in dandling the Kid.* One of the poems on which much praise has been bestowed is **"Lycidas"**; of which the diction is harsh, the rhymes uncertain, and the numbers unpleasing. What beauty there is, we must therefore seek in the sentiments and images. It is not to be considered as the effusion of real passion; for passion runs not after remote allusions and obscure opinions. Passion plucks no berries from the myrtle and ivy, nor calls upon Arethuse and Mincius, nor tells of rough *satyrs* and *fawns with cloven heel.* Where there is leisure for fiction there is little grief.

In this poem there is no nature, for there is no truth; there is no art, for there is nothing new. Its form is that of a pastoral, easy, vulgar, and therefore disgusting: whatever images it can supply, are long ago exhausted; and its inherent improbability always forces dissatisfaction on the mind. When Cowley tells of Hervey that they studied together, it is easy to suppose how much he must miss the companion of his labours, and the partner of his discoveries; but what image of tenderness can be excited by these lines!

> We drove a field, and both together heard
> What time the grey fly winds her sultry horn,
> Battening our flocks with the fresh dews of night.

We know that they never drove a field, and that they had no flocks to batten; and though it be allowed that the representation may be allegorical, the true meaning is so uncertain and remote, that it is never sought because it cannot be known when it is found.

Among the flocks, and copses, and flowers, appear the heathen deities; Jove and Phoebus, Neptune and Aeolus, with a long train of mythological imagery, such as a College easily supplies. Nothing can less display knowledge, or less exercise invention, than to tell how a shepherd has lost his companion, and must now feed his flocks alone, without any judge of his skill in piping; and how one god asks another god what is become of Lycidas, and how neither god can tell. He who thus grieves will excite no sympathy; he who thus praises will confer no honour.

This poem has yet a grosser fault. With these trifling fictions are mingled the most awful and sacred truths, such as ought never to be polluted with such irreverent combinations. The shepherd likewise is now a feeder of sheep, and afterwards an ecclesiastical pastor, a superintendent of a Christian flock. Such equivocations are always unskilful; but here they are indecent, and at least approach to impiety, of which, however, I believe the writer not to have been conscious.

Such is the power of reputation justly acquired, that its blaze drives away the eye from nice examination. Surely no man could have fancied that he read **"Lycidas"** with pleasure, had he not known its author.

Of the two pieces, **"L'Allegro"** and **"Il Penseroso,"** I believe opinion is uniform; every man that reads them, reads them with pleasure. The author's design is not, what Theobald has remarked, merely to shew how objects derived their colours from the mind, by representing the operation of the same things upon the gay and the melancholy temper, or upon the same man as he is differently disposed; but rather how, among the successive variety of appearances, every disposition of mind takes hold on those by which it may be gratified.

The *chearful* man hears the lark in the morning; the *pensive* man hears the nightingale in the evening. The *chearful* man sees the cock strut, and hears the horn and hounds echo in the wood; then walks *not unseen* to observe the glory of the rising sun, or listen to the singing milkmaid, and view the labours of the plowman and the mower; then casts his eyes about him over scenes of smiling plenty, and looks up to the distant tower, the residence of some fair inhabitant; thus he pursues rural gaiety through a day of labour or of play, and delights himself at night with the fanciful narratives of superstitious ignorance.

The *pensive* man, at one time, walks *unseen* to muse at midnight; and at another hears the sullen curfew. If the weather drives him home, he sits in a room lighted only by *glowing embers;* or by a lonely lamp outwatches the North Star, to discover the habitation of separate souls, and varies the shades of meditation, by contemplating the magnificent or pathetick scenes of tragick and epick poetry. When the morning comes, a morning gloomy with rain and wind, he walks into the dark trackless woods, falls asleep by some murmuring water, and with melancholy enthusiasm expects some dream of prognostication, or some musick played by aerial performers.

Both Mirth and Melancholy are solitary, silent inhabitants of the breast that neither receive nor transmit communication; no mention is therefore made of a philosophical friend, or a pleasant companion. The seriousness does not arise from any participation of calamity, nor the gaiety from the pleasures of the bottle.

The man of *chearfulness*, having exhausted the country, tries what *towered cities* will afford, and mingles with scenes of splendor, gay assemblies, and nuptial festivities; but he mingles a mere spectator, as, when the learned counsels of Jonson, or the wild dramas of Shakespeare, are exhibited, he attends the theatre.

The *pensive* man never loses himself in crowds, but walks the cloister, or frequents the cathedral. Milton probably had not yet forsaken the Church.

Both his Characters delight in musick; but he seems to think that chearful notes would have obtained from Pluto a compleat dismission of Eurydice, of whom solemn sounds only procured a conditional release.

For the old age of Chearfulness he makes no provision; but Melancholy he conducts with great dignity to the close of life. His Chearfulness is without levity, and his Pensiveness without asperity.

Through these two poems the images are properly selected, and nicely distinguished; but the colours of the diction seem not sufficiently discriminated. I know not whether the characters are kept sufficiently apart. No mirth can, indeed, be found in his melancholy; but I am afraid that I always meet some melancholy in his mirth. They are two noble efforts of imagination.

The greatest of his juvenile performances is the *Mask of Comus;* in which may very plainly be discovered the dawn or twilight of *Paradise Lost*. Milton appears to have formed very early that system of diction, and mode of verse, which his maturer judgment approved, and from which he never endeavoured nor desired to deviate.

Nor does *Comus* afford only a specimen of his language; it exhibits likewise his power of description and his vigour of sentiment, employed in the praise and defence of virtue. A work more truly poetical is rarely found; allusions, images, and descriptive epithets, embellish almost every period with lavish decoration. As a series of lines, therefore, it may be considered as worthy of all the admiration with which the votaries have received it.

As a drama it is deficient. The action is not probable. A Masque, in those parts where supernatural intervention is admitted, must indeed be given up to all the freaks of imagination; but, so far as the action is merely human, it ought to be reasonable, which can hardly be said of the conduct of the two brothers; who, when their sister sinks with fatigue in a pathless wilderness, wander both away together in search of berries too far to find their way back, and leave a helpless Lady to all the sadness and danger of solitude. This however is a defect overbalanced by its convenience.

What deserves more reprehension is, that the prologue spoken in the wild wood by the attendant Spirit is addressed to the audience; a mode of communication so contrary to the nature of dramatick representation, that no precedents can support it.

The discourse of the Spirit is too long: an objection that may be made to almost all the following speeches: they have not the spriteliness of a dialogue animated by reciprocal contention, but seem rather declamations deliberately composed, and formally repeated, on a moral question. The auditor therefore listens as to a lecture, without passion, without anxiety.

The song of Comus has airiness and jollity; but, what may recommend Milton's morals as well as his poetry, the invitations to pleasure are so general, that they excite no distinct images of corrupt enjoyment, and take no dangerous hold on the fancy.

The following soliloquies of Comus and the Lady are elegant, but tedious. The song must owe much to the voice, if it ever can delight. At last the Brothers enter, with too much tranquillity; and when they have feared lest their sister should be in danger, and hoped that she is not in danger, the Elder makes a speech in praise of chastity, and the Younger finds how fine it is to be a philosopher.

Then descends the Spirit in form of a shepherd; and the Brother, instead of being in haste to ask his help, praises his singing, and enquires his business in that place. It is remarkable, that at this interview the Brother is taken with a short fit of rhyming. The Spirit relates that the Lady is in the power of Comus; the Brother moralises again; and the Spirit makes a long narration, of no use because it is false, and therefore unsuitable to a good Being.

In all these parts the language is poetical, and the sentiments are generous; but there is something wanting to allure attention.

The dispute between the Lady and Comus is the most animated and affecting scene of the drama, and wants nothing but a brisker reciprocation of objections and replies, to invite attention, and detain it.

The songs are vigorous, and full of imagery; but they are harsh in their diction, and not very musical in their numbers.

Throughout the whole, the figures are too bold, and the langauge too luxuriant for dialogue. It is a drama in the epick style, inelegantly splendid, and tediously instructive.

A MASKE

PRESENTED

At Ludlow Castle,

1 6 3 4 :

On Michaelmasse night*, before the*

RIGHT HONORABLE,

IOHN *Earle of Bridgewater*, Vicount BRACKLY,
Lord President *of* WALES, And one of
His MAIESTIES moft honorable
Privie Counfell.

Eheu quid volui mifero mihi ! floribus auftrum
Perditus ————

LONDON,
Printed for HVMPHREY ROBINSON,
at the figne of the *Three Pidgeons* in
Pauls Church-yard. 1 6 3 7.

Title page of the first edition of the work more commonly known as Comus: A Maske *(1637).*

The *Sonnets* were written in different parts of Milton's life, upon different occasions. They deserve not any particular criticism; for of the best it can only be said, that they are not bad; and perhaps only the eighth and the twenty-first are truly entitled to this slender commendation. The fabrick of a sonnet, however adapted to the Italian language, has never succeeded in ours, which, having greater variety of termination, requires the rhymes to be often changed.

Those little pieces may be dispatched without much anxiety; a greater work calls for greater care. I am now to examine *Paradise Lost;* a poem, which, considered with respect to design, may claim the first place, and with respect to performance the second, among the productions of the human mind.

By the general consent of criticks, the first praise of genius is due to the writer of an epick poem, as it requires an assemblage of all the powers which are singly sufficient for other compositions. Poetry is the art of uniting pleasure with truth, by calling imagination to the help of reason. Epick poetry undertakes to teach the most important truths by the most pleasing precepts, and therefore relates some great event in the most affecting manner. History must supply the writer with the rudiments of narration, which he must improve and exalt by a nobler art, must animate by dramatick energy, and diversify by retrospection and anticipation; morality must teach him the exact bounds, and different shades, of vice and virtue; from policy, and the practice of life, he has to learn the discrimi-

nations of character, and the tendency of the passions, either single or combined; and physiology must supply him with illustrations and images. To put these materials to poetical use, is required an imagination capable of painting nature, and realizing fiction. Nor is he yet a poet till he has attained the whole extension of his language, distinguished all the delicacies of phrase, and all the colours of words, and learned to adjust their different sounds to all the varieties of metrical modulation.

Bossu is of opinion that the poet's first work is to find a *moral,* which his fable is afterwards to illustrate and establish. This seems to have been the process only of Milton; the moral of other poems is incidental and consequent; in Milton's only it is essential and intrinsick. His purpose was the most useful and the most arduous; *to vindicate the ways of God to man;* to shew the reasonableness of religion, and the necessity of obedience to the Divine Law.

To convey this moral, there must be a *fable,* a narration artfully constructed, so as to excite curiosity, and surprise expectation. In this part of his work, Milton must be confessed to have equalled every other poet. He has involved in his account of the Fall of Man the events which preceded, and those that were to follow it: he has interwoven the whole system of theology with such propriety, that every part appears to be necessary; and scarcely any recital is wished shorter for the sake of quickening the progress of the main action.

The subject of an epick poem is naturally an event of great importance. That of Milton is not the destruction of a city, the conduct of a colony, or the foundation of an empire. His subject is the fate of worlds, the revolutions of heaven and of earth; rebellion against the Supreme King, raised by the highest order of created beings; the overthrow of their host, and the punishment of their crime; the creation of a new race of reasonable creatures; their original happiness and innocence, their forfeiture of immortality, and their restoration to hope and peace.

Great events can be hastened or retarded only by persons of elevated dignity. Before the greatness displayed in Milton's poem, all other greatness shrinks away. The weakest of his agents are the highest and noblest of human beings, the original parents of mankind; with whose actions the elements consented; on whose rectitude, or deviation of will, depended the state of terrestrial nature, and the condition of all the future inhabitants of the globe.

Of the other agents in the poem, the chief are such as it is irreverence to name on slight occasions. The rest are lower powers;

> ————of which the least could wield
> Those elements, and arm him with the force
> Of all their regions;

powers, which only the controul of Omnipotence restrains from laying creation waste, and filling the vast expanse of space with ruin and confusion. To display the motives and actions of being thus superiour, so far as human reason can examine them, or human imagination represent them, is the task which this mighty poet has undertaken and performed.

In the examination of epick poems much speculation is commonly employed upon the *characters.* The characters in the *Paradise Lost,* which admit of examination, are those of angels and of man; of angels good and evil; of man in his innocent and sinful state.

Among the angels, the virtue of Raphael is mild and placid, of easy condescension and free communication; that of Michael is regal and lofty, and, as may seem, attentive to the dignity of his own nature. Abdiel and Gabriel appear occasionally, and act as every incident requires; the solitary fidelity of Abdiel is very amiably painted.

Of the evil angels the characters are more diversified. To Satan, as Addison observes, such sentiments are given as suit *the most exalted and most depraved being*. Milton has been censured, by Clarke, for the impiety which sometimes breaks from Satan's mouth. For there are thoughts, as he justly remarks, which no observation of character can justify, because no good man would willingly permit them to pass, however transiently, through his own mind. To make Satan speak as a rebel, without any such expressions as might taint the reader's imagination, was indeed one of the great difficulties in Milton's undertaking, and I cannot but think that he has extricated himself with great happiness. There is in Satan's speeches little that can give pain to a pious ear. The language of rebellion cannot be the same with that of obedience. The malignity of Satan foams in haughtiness and obstinacy; but his expressions are commonly general, and no otherwise offensive than as they are wicked.

The other chiefs of the celestial rebellion are very judiciously discriminated in the first and second books; and the ferocious character of Moloch appears, both in the battle and the council, with exact consistency.

To Adam and to Eve are given, during their innocence, such sentiments as innocence can generate and utter. Their love is pure benevolence and mutual veneration; their repasts are without luxury, and their diligence without toil. Their addresses to their Maker have little more than the voice of admiration and gratitude. Fruition left them nothing to ask, and Innocence left them nothing to fear.

But with guilt enter distrust and discord, mutual accusation, and stubborn self-defence; they regard each other with alienated minds, and dread their Creator as the avenger of their transgression. At last they seek shelter in his mercy, soften to repentance, and melt in supplication. Both before and after the Fall, the superiority of Adam is diligently sustained.

Of the *probable* and the *marvellous*, two parts of a vulgar epick poem, which immerge the critick in deep consideration, the ***Paradise Lost*** requires little to be said. It contains the history of a miracle, of Creation and Redemption; it displays the power and the mercy of the Supreme Being; the probable therefore is marvellous, and the marvellous is probable. The substance of the narrative is truth; and as truth allows no choice, it is, like necessity, superior to rule. To the accidental or adventitious parts, as to every thing human, some slight exceptions may be made. But the main fabrick is immovably supported.

It is justly remarked by Addison [see excerpt dated 1712] that this poem has, by the nature of its subject, the advantage above all others, that it is universally and perpetually interesting. All mankind will, through all ages, bear the same relation to Adam and to Eve, and must partake of that good and evil which extend to themselves.

Of the *machinery*, so called from Θεὸς ἀπὸ μηχανῆς, by which is meant the occasional interposition of supernatural power, another fertile topic of critical remarks, here is no room to speak, because every thing is done under the immediate and visible direction of Heaven; but the rule is so far observed, that no part of the action could have been accomplished by any other means.

Of *episodes*, I think there are only two, contained in Raphael's relation of the war in heaven, and Michael's prophetick account of the changes to happen in this world. Both are closely connected with the great action; one was necessary to Adam as a warning, the other as a consolation.

To the compleatness or *integrity* of the design nothing can be objected; it has distinctly and clearly what Aristotle requires, a beginning, a middle, and an end. There is perhaps no poem, of the same length, from which so little can be taken without apparent mutilation. Here are no funeral games, nor is there any long description of a shield. The short digressions at the beginning of the third, seventh, and ninth books, might doubtless be spared; but superfluities so beautiful, who would take away? or who does not wish that the author of the *Iliad* had gratified succeeding ages with a little knowledge of himself? Perhaps no passages are more frequently or more attentively read than those extrinsick paragraphs; and, since the end of poetry is pleasure, that cannot be unpoetical with which all are pleased.

The questions, whether the action of the poem be strictly *one,* whether the poem can be properly termed *heroick,* and who is the hero, are raised by such readers as draw their principles of judgement rather from books than from reason. Milton, though he intituled ***Paradise Lost*** only a *poem,* yet calls it himself *heroick song.* Dryden, petulantly and indecently, denies the heroism of Adam [see excerpt dated 1697], because he was overcome; but there is no reason why the hero should not be unfortunate, except established practice, since success and virtue do not go necessarily together. Cato is the hero of Lucan; but Lucan's authority will not be suffered by Quintilian to decide. However, if success be necessary, Adam's deceiver was at last crushed; Adam was restored to his Maker's favour, and therefore may securely resume his human rank.

After the scheme and fabrick of the poem, must be considered its component parts, the sentiments and the diction.

The *sentiments,* as expressive of manners, or appropriated to characters, are, for the greater part unexceptionably just.

Splendid passages, containing lessons of morality, or precepts of prudence, occur seldom. Such is the original formation of this poem, that as it admits no human manners till the Fall, it can give little assistance to human conduct. Its end is to raise the thoughts above sublunary cares or pleasures. Yet the praise of that fortitude, with which Abdiel maintained his singularity of virtue against the scorn of multitudes, may be accommodated to all times; and Raphael's reproof of Adam's curiosity after the planetary motions, with the answer returned by Adam, may be confidently opposed to any rule of life which any poet has delivered.

The thoughts which are occasionally called forth in the progress, are such as could only be produced by an imagination in the highest degree fervid and active, to which materials were supplied by incessant study and unlimited curiosity. The heat of Milton's mind might be said to sublimate his learning, to throw off into his work the spirit of science, unmingled with its grosser parts.

He had considered creation in its whole extent, and his descriptions are therefore learned. He had accustomed his imagination to unrestrained indulgence, and his conceptions therefore were extensive. The characteristick quality of his poem is sublimity. He sometimes descends to the elegant, but his element is the great. He can occasionally invest himself with grace; but his natural port is gigantick loftiness. He can please when pleasure is required; but it is his peculiar power to astonish.

He seems to have been well acquainted with his own genius, and to know what it was that Nature had bestowed upon him more bountifully than upon others; the power of displaying the vast, illuminating the splendid, enforcing the awful, darkening the gloomy, and aggravating the dreadful: he therefore chose a subject on which too much could not be said, on which he might tire his fancy without the censure of extravagance.

The appearances of nature, and the occurrences of life, did not satiate his appetite of greatness. To paint things as they are, requires a minute attention, and employs the memory rather than the fancy. Milton's delight was to sport in the wide regions of possibility; reality was a scene too narrow for his mind. He sent his faculties out upon discovery, into worlds where only imagination can travel, and delighted to form new modes of existence, and furnish sentiment and action to superior beings, to trace the counsels of hell, or accompany the choirs of heaven.

But he could not be always in other worlds: he must sometimes revisit earth, and tell of things visible and known. When he cannot raise wonder by the sublimity of his mind, he gives delight by its fertility.

Whatever be his subject, he never fails to fill the imagination. But his images and descriptions of the scenes or operations of Nature do not seem to be always copied from original form, nor to have the freshness, raciness, and energy of immediate observation. He saw Nature, as Dryden expresses it, *through the spectacles of books;* and on most occasions calls learning to his assistance. The garden of Eden brings to his mind the vale of *Enna,* where Proserpine was gathering flowers. Satan makes his way though fighting elements, like *Argo* between the *Cyanean* rocks, or *Ulysses* between the two *Sicilian* whirlpools, when he shunned *Charybdis* on the *larboard.* The mythological allusions have been justly censured, as not being always used with notice of their vanity; but they contribute variety to the narration, and produce an alternate exercise of the memory and the fancy.

His similes are less numerous, and more various, than those of his predecessors. But he does not confine himself within the limits of rigorous comparison: his great excellence is amplitude, and he expands the adventitious image beyond the dimensions which the occasion required. Thus, comparing the shield of Satan to the orb of the Moon, he crowds the imagination with the discovery of the telescope, and all the wonders which the telescope discovers.

Of his moral sentiments it is hardly praise to affirm that they excel those of all the other poets; for this superiority he was indebted to his acquaintance with the sacred writings. The ancient epick poets, wanting the light of Revelation, were very unskilful teachers of virtue: their principal characters may be great, but they are not amiable. The reader may rise from their works with a greater degree of active or passive fortitude, and sometimes of prudence; but he will be able to carry away few precepts of justice, and none of mercy.

From the Italian writers it appears, that the advantages of even Christian knowledge may be possessed in vain. Ariosto's pravity is generally known; and though the *Deliverance of Jerusalem* may be considered as a sacred subject, the poet has been very sparing of moral instruction.

In Milton every line breathes sanctity of thought, and purity of manners, except when the train of the narration requires the introduction of the rebellious spirits; and even they are compelled to acknowledge their subjection to God, in such a manner as excites reverence, and confirms piety.

Of human beings there are but two; but those two are the parents of mankind, venerable before their fall for dignity and innocence, and amiable after it for repentance and submission. In their first state their affection is tender without weakness, and their piety sublime without presumption. When they have sinned, they shew how discord begins in mutual frailty, and how it ought to cease in mutual forbearance; how confidence of the divine favour is forfeited by sin, and how hope of pardon may be obtained by penitence and prayer. A state of innocence we can only conceive, if indeed, in our present misery, it be possible to conceive it; but the sentiments and worship proper to a fallen and offending being, we have all to learn, as we have all to practise.

The poet, whatever be done, is always great. Our progenitors, in their first state, conversed with angels, even when folly and sin had degraded them, they had not in their humiliation *the port of mean suitors;* and they rise again to reverential regard, when we find that their prayers were heard.

As human passions did not enter the world before the Fall, there is in the *Paradise Lost* little opportunity for the pathetick; but what little there is has not been lost. That passion which is peculiar to rational nature, the anguish arising from the consciousness of transgression, and the horrours attending the sense of the Divine Displeasure, are very justly described and forcibly impressed. But the passions are moved only on one occasion; sublimity is the general and prevailing quality in this poem; sublimity variously modified, sometimes descriptive, sometimes argumentative.

The defects and faults of *Paradise Lost,* for faults and defects every work of man must have, it is the business of impartial criticism to discover. As, in displaying the excellence of Milton, I have not made long quotations, because of selecting beauties there had been no end, I shall in the same general manner mention that which seems to deserve censure; for what Englishman can take delight in transcribing passages, which, if they lessen the reputation of Milton, diminish in some degree the honour of our country?

The generality of my scheme does not admit the frequent notice of verbal inaccuracies; which Bentley, perhaps better skilled in grammar than poetry, has often found, though he sometimes made them, and which he imputed to the obtrusions of a reviser whom the author's blindness obliged him to employ. A supposition rash and groundless, if he thought it true; and vile and pernicious, if, as is said, he in private allowed it to be false.

The plan of *Paradise Lost* has this inconvenience, that it comprises neither human actions nor human manners. The man and woman who act and suffer, are in a state which no other man or woman can ever know. The reader finds no transaction in which he can be engaged; beholds no condition in which he can by any effort of imagination place himself; he has, therefore, little natural curiosity or sympathy.

We all, indeed, feel the effects of Adam's disobedience; we all sin like Adam, and like him must all bewail our offences; we have restless and insidious enemies in the fallen angels, and in the blessed spirits we have guardians and friends; in the Redemption of mankind we hope to be included; in the description of heaven and hell we are surely interested, as we are all to reside hereafter either in the regions of horrour or of bliss.

But these truths are too important to be new; they have been taught to our infancy; they have mingled with our solitary thoughts and familiar conversation, and are habitually interwoven with the whole texture of life. Being therefore not new, they raise no unaccustomed emotion in the mind; what we knew before, we cannot learn; what is not unexpected, cannot surprise.

Of the ideas suggested by these awful scenes, from some we recede with reverence, except when stated hours require their association; and from others we shrink with horrour, or admit them only as salutary inflictions, as counterpoises to our interests and passions. Such images rather obstruct the career of fancy than incite it.

Pleasure and terrour are indeed the genuine sources of poetry; but poetical pleasure must be such as human imagination can at least conceive, and poetical terrour such as human strength and fortitude may combat. The good and evil of Eternity are too ponderous for the wings of wit; the mind sinks under them in passive helplessness, content with calm belief and humble adoration.

Known truths, however, may take a different appearance, and be conveyed to the mind by a new train of intermediate images. This Milton has undertaken, and performed with pregnancy and vigour of mind peculiar to himself. Whoever considers the few radical positions which the Scriptures afforded him, will wonder by what energetick operation he expanded them to such extent, and ramified them to so much variety, restrained as he was by religious reverence from licentiousness of fiction.

Here is a full display of the united force of study and genius; of a great accumulation of materials, with judgement to digest, and fancy to combine them: Milton was able to select from nature, or from story, from ancient fable, or from modern science, whatever could illustrate or adorn his thoughts. An accumulation of knowledge impregnated his mind, fermented by study, and exalted by imagination.

It has been therefore said, without an indecent hyperbole, by one of his encomiasts, that in reading **Paradise Lost** we read a book of universal knowledge.

But original deficience cannot be supplied. The want of human interest is always felt. **Paradise Lost** is one of the books which the reader admires and lays down, and forgets to take up again. None ever wished it longer than it is. Its perusal is a duty rather than a pleasure. We read Milton for instruction, retire harassed and overburdened, and look elsewhere for recreation; we desert our master, and seek for companions.

Another inconvenience of Milton's design is, that it requires the description of what cannot be described, the agency of spirits. He saw that immateriality supplied no images, and that he could not show angels acting but by instruments of action; he therefore invested them with form and matter. This, being necessary, was therefore defensible; and he should have secured the consistency of his system, by keeping immateriality out of sight, and enticing his reader to drop it from his thoughts. But he has unhappily perplexed his poetry with his philosophy. His infernal and celestial powers are sometimes pure spirit, and sometimes animated body. When Satan walks with his lance upon the *burning marle,* he has a body; when, in his passage between hell and the new world, he is in danger of sinking in the vacuity, and is supported by a gust of rising

vapours, he has a body; when he animates the toad, he seems to be mere spirit, that can penetrate matter at pleasure; when he *starts up in his own shape,* he has at least a determined form; and when he is brought before Gabriel, he has a *spear and a shield,* which he had the power of hiding in the toad, though the arms of the contending angels are evidently material.

The vulgar inhabitants of Pandaemonium, being *incorporeal spirits,* are *at large, though without number,* in a limited space; yet in the battle, when they were overwhelmed by mountains, their armour hurt them, *crushed in upon their substance, now grown gross by sinning.* This likewise happened to the uncorrupted angels, who were overthrown the *sooner for their arms, for unarmed they might easily as spirits have evaded by contraction or remove.* Even as spirits they are hardly spiritual; for *contraction* and *remove* are images of matter; but if they could have escaped without their armour, they might have escaped from it, and left only the empty cover to be battered. Uriel, when he rides on a sun-beam, is material; Satan is material when he is afraid of the prowess of Adam.

The confusion of spirit and matter which pervades the whole narration of the war of heaven fills it with incongruity; and the book, in which it is related, is, I believe, the favourite of children, and gradually neglected as knowledge is increased.

After the operation of immaterial agents, which cannot be explained, may be considered that of allegorical persons, which have no real existence. To exalt causes into agents, to invest abstract ideas with form, and animate them with activity, has always been the right of poetry. But such airy beings are, for the most part, suffered only to do their natural office, and retire. Thus Fame tells a tale, and Victory hovers over a general, or perches on a standard; but Fame and Victory can do no more. To give them any real employment, or ascribe to them any material agency, is to make them allegorical no longer, but to shock the mind by ascribing effects to nonentity. In the *Prometheus* of Aeschylus, we see *Violence* and *Strength,* and in the *Alcestis* of Euripides, we see *Death,* brought upon the stage, all as active persons of the drama; but no precedents can justify absurdity.

Milton's allegory of Sin and Death is undoubtedly faulty. Sin is indeed the mother of Death, and may be allowed to be the portress of hell; but when they stop the journey of Satan, a journey described as real, and when Death offers him battle, the allegory is broken. That Sin and Death should have shewn the way to hell, might have been allowed; but they cannot facilitate the passage by building a bridge, because the difficulty of Satan's passage is described as real and sensible, and the bridge ought to be only figurative. The hell assigned to the rebellious spirits is described as not less local than the residence of man. It is placed in some distant part of space, separated from the regions of harmony and order by a chaotick waste and an unoccupied vacuity; but *Sin* and *Death* worked up a *mole of aggravated soil,* cemented with *asphaltus;* a work too bulky for ideal architects.

This unskilful allegory appears to me one of the greatest faults of the poem; and to this there was no temptation, but the author's opinion of its beauty.

To the conduct of the narrative some objections may be made. Satan is with great expectation brought before Gabriel in Paradise, and is suffered to go away unmolested. The creation of man is represented as the consequence of the vacuity left in heaven by the expulsion of the rebels; yet Satan mentions it as a report *rife in heaven* before his departure.

To find sentiments for the state of innocence, was very difficult; and something of anticipation perhaps is now and then discovered. Adam's discourse of dreams seems not to be speculation of a new-created being. I know not whether his answer to the angel's reproof for curiosity does not want something of propriety: it is the speech of a man acquainted with many other men. Some philosophical notions, especially when the philosophy is false, might have been better omitted. The angel, in a comparison, speaks of *timorous deer,* before deer were yet timorous, and before Adam could understand the comparison.

Dryden remarks, that Milton has some flats among his elevations. This is only to say, that all the parts are not equal. In every work, one part must be for the sake of others; a palace must have passages; a poem must have transitions. It is no more to be required that wit should always be blazing, than the sun should always stand at noon. In a great work there is a vicissitude of luminous and opaque parts, as there is in the world a succession of day and night. Milton, when he has expatiated in the sky, may be allowed sometimes to revisit earth; for what other author ever soared so high, or sustained his flight so long?

Milton, being well versed in the Italian poets, appears to have borrowed often from them; and, as every man catches something from his companions, his desire of imitating Ariosto's levity has disgraced his work with the *Paradise of Fools;* a fiction not in itself ill-imagined, but too ludicrous for its place.

His play on words, in which he delights too often; his equivocations, which Bentley endeavours to defend by the example of the ancients; his unnecessary and ungraceful use of terms of art; it is not necessary to mention, because they are easily remarked, and generally censured, and at last bear so little proportion to the whole, that they scarcely deserve the attention of a critick.

Such are the faults of that wonderful performance *Paradise Lost*; which he who can put in balance with its beauties must be considered not as nice but as dull, as less to be censured for want of candour, than pitied for want of sensibility.

Of *Paradise Regained,* the general judgement seems now to be right, that it is in many parts elegant, and everywhere instructive. It was not to be supposed that the writer of *Paradise Lost* could ever write without great effusions of fancy, and exalted precepts of wisdom. The basis of *Paradise Regained* is narrow; a dialogue without action can never please like an union of the narrative and dramatick powers. Had this poem been written not by Milton, but by some imitator, it would have claimed and received universal praise.

If *Paradise Regained* has been too much depreciated, *Sampson Agonistes* has in requital been too much admired. It could only be by long prejudice, and the bigotry of learning, that Milton could prefer the ancient tragedies, with their encumbrance of a chorus, to the exhibitions of the French and English stages; and it is only by a blind confidence in the reputation of Milton, that a drama can be praised in which the intermediate parts have neither cause nor consequence, neither hasten nor retard the catastrophe.

In this tragedy are however many particular beauties, many just sentiments and striking lines; but it wants that power of attracting the attention which a well-connected plan produces.

Milton would not have excelled in dramatick writing; he knew human nature only in the gross, and had never studied the shades of character, nor the combinations of concurring, or the perplexity of contending passions. He had read much, and knew what books could teach; but had mingled little in the world, and was deficient in the knowledge which experience must confer.

Through all his greater works there prevails an uniform peculiarity of *Diction,* a mode and cast of expression which bears little resemblance to that of any former writer, and which is so far removed from common use, that an unlearned reader, when he first opens his book, finds himself surprised by a new language.

This novelty has been, by those who can find nothing wrong in Milton, imputed to his laborious endeavours after words suitable to the grandeur of his ideas. *Our language,* says Addison, *sunk under him.* But the truth is, that, both in prose and verse, he had formed his style by a perverse and pedantick principle. He was desirous to use English words with a foreign idiom. This in all his prose is discovered and condemned; for there judgement operates freely, neither softened by the beauty, nor awed by the dignity of his thoughts; but such is the power of his poetry, that his call is obeyed without resistance, the reader feels himself in captivity to a higher and a nobler mind, and criticism sinks in admiration.

Milton's style was not modified by his subject: what is shown with greater extent in *Paradise Lost,* may be found in *Comus.* One source of his peculiarity was his familiarity with the Tuscan poets: the disposition of his words is, I think, frequently Italian; perhaps sometimes combined with other tongues. Of him, at last, may be said what Jonson says of Spenser, that *he wrote no language,* but has formed what Butler calls a *Babylonish Dialect,* in itself harsh and barbarous, but made by exalted genius and extensive learning, the vehicle of so much instruction and so much pleasure, that, like other lovers, we find grace in its deformity.

Whatever be the faults of his diction, he cannot want the praise of copiousness and variety: he was master of his language in its full extent; and has selected the melodious words with such diligence, that from his book alone the Art of English Poetry might be learned.

After his diction, something must be said of his *versification. The measure,* he says, *is the English heroick verse without rhyme* [see excerpt dated 1668]. Of this mode he had many examples among the Italians, and some in his own country. The Earl of Surrey is said to have translated one of Virgil's books without rhyme; and, besides our tragedies, a few short poems had appeared in blank verse; particularly one tending to reconcile the nation to Raleigh's wild attempt upon Guiana, and probably written by Raleigh himself. These petty performances cannot be supposed to have much influenced Milton, who more probably took his hint from Trisino's *Italia Liberata;* and, finding blank verse easier than rhyme, was desirous of persuading himself that it is better.

Rhyme, he says, and says truly, *is no necessary adjunct of true poetry.* But perhaps, of poetry as a mental operation, metre or musick is no necessary adjunct: it is however by the musick of metre that poetry has been discriminated in all languages; and in languages melodiously constructed with a due proportion of long and short syllables, metre is sufficient. But one language cannot communicate its rules to another: where metre is scanty and imperfect, some help is necessary. The musick of the English heroick line strikes the ear so faintly that it is easily lost, unless all the syllables of every line co-operate together: this co-operation can be only obtained by the preservation of every verse unmingled with another, as a distinct system of sounds; and this distinctness is obtained and preserved by the artifice of rhyme. The variety of pauses, so much boasted by the lovers of blank verse, changes the measures of an English poet to the periods of a declaimer; and there are only a few skilful and happy readers of Milton, who enable their audience to perceive where the lines end or begin. *Blank verse,* said an ingenious critick, *seems to be verse only to the eye.*

Poetry may subsist without rhyme, but English poetry will not often please; nor can rhyme ever be safely spared but where the subject is able to support itself. Blank verse makes some approach to that which is called the *lapidary style;* has neither the easiness of prose, nor the melody of numbers, and therefore tires by long continuance. Of the Italian writers without rhyme, whom Milton alleges as precedents, not one is popular; what reason could urge in its defence, has been confuted by the ear.

But, whatever be the advantage of rhyme, I cannot prevail on myself to wish that Milton had been a rhymer; for I cannot wish his work to be other than it is; yet, like other heroes, he is to be admired rather than imitated. He that thinks himself capable of astonishing, may write blank verse; but those that hope only to please, must condescend to rhyme.

The highest praise of genius is original invention. Milton cannot be said to have contrived the structure of an epick poem, and therefore owes reverence to that vigour and amplitude of mind to which all generations must be indebted for the art of poetical narration, for the texture of the fable, the variation of incidents, the interposition of dialogue, and all the stratagems that surprise and enchain attention. But, of all the borrowers from Homer, Milton is perhaps the least indebted. He was naturally a thinker for himself, confident of his own abilities, and disdainful of help or hindrance: he did not refuse admission to the thought or images of his predecessors, but he did not seek them. From his contemporaries he neither courted nor received support; there is in his writings nothing by which the pride of other authors might be gratified, or favour gained; no exchange of praise, nor solicitation of support. His great works were performed under discountenance, and in blindness, but difficulties vanished at his touch; he was born for whatever is arduous; and his work is not the greatest of heroick poems, only because it is not the first. (pp. 111-34)

> *Samuel Johnson, ''Milton,'' in his* Lives of the English Poets, Vol. I, *1779. Reprint by Oxford University Press, 1955, pp. 63-134.*

JOHN ADAMS   (essay date 1787)

[*Adams was a prominent American statesman who served a single term (1797-1801) as second president of the United States. He helped draft the Declaration of Independence and, according to Thomas Jefferson, was "the pillar of its support on the floor of congress." In 1785 he was made envoy to the court of St. James's. While in England, he wrote his three-volume* Defence of the Constitutions of Government of the United States of America against the Attack of Mr. Turgot *(1787). In the following excerpt from this work, he hypothesizes what would have become of England if Milton's plan for a commonwealth had been implemented there.*]

A man may be a greater poet than Homer, and one of the most learned men in the world; he may spend his life in defence of liberty, and be at the same time one of the most irreproachable moral characters; and yet, when called upon to frame a consititution of government, he may demonstrate to the world that

he has reflected very little on the subject. There is a great hazard in saying all this of John Milton; but truth and the rights of mankind demand it. In his *Ready and Easy Way to Establish a Free Commonwealth,* this great author says,

> I doubt not but all ingenuous and knowing men will easily agree with me, that a free commonwealth, without single person or house of lords, is by far the best government, if it can be had; . . .

> For the ground and basis of every just and free government, is a general council of ablest men chosen by the people to consult of public affairs, from time to time, for the common good. In this grand council must the sovereignty, not transferred, but delegated only, and, as it were, deposited, reside; with this caution, they must have the forces by sea and land committed to them for preservation of the common peace and liberty; must raise and manage the public revenue, at least with some inspectors deputed for satisfaction of the people how it is employed; must make or propose civil laws, treat of commerce, peace, or war with foreign nations; and, for the carrying on some particular affairs with more secrecy and expedition, must elect, as they have already, out of their own number and others, a council of state.

> And although it may seem strange at first hearing, by reason that men's minds are prepossessed with the notion of successive parliaments, I affirm that the grand or general council, being well chosen, should be perpetual; for so thier business is, or may be, and ofttimes urgent; the opportunity of affairs gained or lost in a moment. The day of council cannot be set as the day of a festival; but must be ready always to prevent or answer all occasions. By this continuance they will become every way skilfullest, best provided of intelligence from abroad, best acqaunted with the people at home and the people with them. The ship of the commonwealth is always under sail; they sit at the stern, and if they steer well, what need is there to change them, it being rather dangerous? Add to this, that the grand council is both foundation and main pillar of the whole state; and to move pillars and foundations, not faulty, cannot be safe for the building. I see not, therefore, how we can be advantaged by successive and transitory parliaments; but that they are much likelier continually to unsettle, rather than to settle a free government; to breed commotions, changes, novelities, and uncertainties; to bring neglect upon present affairs and opportunities, while all minds are in suspense with expectation of a new assembly, and the assembly, for a good space, taken up with the new settling of itself. . . . But if the ambition of such as think themselves injured, that they also partake not of the government, and are impatient till they be chosen, cannot brook the perpetuity of others chosen before them; or if it be feared that long continuance of power may corrupt sincerest men, the known expedient is, that annually, (or if the space be longer, so much perhaps the better,) the third part of senators may go out, &c.

Can one read, without shuddering, this wild reverie of the divine, immortal Milton? If no better systems of government had been proposed, it would have been no wonder that the people of England recalled the royal family, with all their errors, follies, and crimes about them. Had Milton's scheme been adopted, England would have been a scene of revolutions, carnage, and horror, from that time to this, or its liberties would have been at this hour the liberties of Poland, or the island would have been a province of France. What! a single assembly to govern England? an assembly of senators for life too? What! did Milton's ideas of liberty and free government extend no further than exchanging one house of lords for another, and making it supreme and perpetual? What! Cromwell, Ireton, Lambert, Ludlow, Waller, and five hundred others of all sects and parties, one quarter of them mad with enthusiasm, another with ambition, a third with avarice, and a fourth of them honest men, a perpetual council to govern such a country! It would have been an oligarchy of decemvirs on the first day of its sitting; it would have instantly been torn with all the agitations of Venice, between the aristocracy and oligarchy, in the assembly itself. If, by ballots and rotations and a thousand other contrivances, it could have been combined together, it would have stripped the people of England of every shadow of liberty, and grown in the next generation a lazy, haughty, ostentatious group of palatines; but if they had fallen into divisions, they would have deluged the nation in blood, till one despot would have ruled the whole. John Milton was as honest a man as his nation ever bred, and as great a friend of liberty; but his greatness most certainly did not consist in the knowledge of the nature of man and of government, if we are to judge from this performance, or from **The Present Means and Brief Delineation of a Free Commonwealth,** in his letter to General Monk. (pp. 464-66)

> *John Adams, "Opinions of Historians," in his* The Works of John Adams, Vol. IV, *Charles C. Little and James Brown, 1851, 435-468.*

WILLIAM WORDSWORTH   (poem date 1802)

[*An English poet and critic, Wordsworth is recognized as one of the principal exponents of English Romanticism. His literary criticism reflects his belief that neither the language nor the content of poetry should be stylized or elaborate and that poets should feel and express the relation between man and nature. In the following sonnet, originally written in 1802, he praises Milton's intellectual and literary achievements.*]

> MILTON, thou shouldst be living at this hour:
> England hath need of thee: she is a fen
> Of stagnant waters: altar, sword, and pen,
> Fireside, the heroic wealth of hall and bower,
> Have forfeited their ancient English dower
> Of inward happiness. We are selfish men;
> Oh! raise us up, return to us again;
> And give us manners, virtue, freedom, power.
> Thy soul was like a Star, and dwelt apart;
> Thou hadst a voice whose sound was like the sea:
> Pure as the naked heavens, majestic, free,
> So didst thou travel on life's common way,
> In cheerful godliness; and yet thy heart
> The lowliest duties on herself did lay.

(p. 183)

> *William Wordsworth, "Milton! Thou Shouldst be Living at This Hour," in* The Prelude, *edited by Carlos Baker, Holt, Rinehart and Winston, 1954, p. 183.*

S. T. COLERIDGE   (lecture date 1818)

[*An English poet and critic, Samuel Taylor Coleridge was at the center of the English Romantic movement and is considered one of the greatest literary critics in the English language. In addition to his poetry, which is itself often pioneering in form and subject, his most important intellectual contributions include his formulation of Romantic theory and introduction of German Romantic thought to England. He also produced much Shakespearean crit-*icism, *helping to overthrow the neoclassical approach to Shakespeare's works by focusing on the dramatist as a masterful portrayer of human character. In the following excerpt from a lecture originally delivered in 1818, he probes the purpose and method of* Paradise Lost.]

[In Milton's mind] there were purity and piety absolute; an imagination to which neither the past nor the present were interesting, except as far as they called forth and enlivened the great ideal, in which and for which he lived; a keen love of truth, which, after many weary pursuits, found a harbor in the sublime listening to the still voice in his own spirit, and as keen a love of his country, which, after a disappointment still more depressive, expanded and soared into a love of man as a probationer of immortality. These were, these alone could be, the conditions under which such a work as the **Paradise Lost** could be conceived and accomplished. By a life-long study Milton had known—

> What was of use to know,
> What best to say could say, to do had done.
> His actions to his words agreed, his words
> To his large heart gave utterance due, his heart
> Contain'd of good, wise, fair, the perfect shape;

And he left the imperishable total, as a bequest to the ages coming, in the **Paradise Lost.**

Difficult as I shall find it to turn over these leaves without catching some passage, which would tempt me to stop, I propose to consider, 1st, the general plan and arrangement of the work, 2dly, the subject with its difficulties and advantages;—3rdly, the poet's object, the spirit in the letter, the ενθύμιου εν μύθω, the true school-divinity; and lastly, the characteristic excellencies of the poem, in what they consist, and by what means they were produced.

1. As to the plan and ordonnance of the Poem.

Compare it with the Iliad, many of the books of which might change places without any injury to the thread of the story. Indeed, I doubt the original existence of the Iliad as one poem; it seems more probable that it was put together about the time of the Pisistratidæ. The Iliad—and, more or less, all epic poems, the subjects of which are taken from history—have no rounded conclusion; they remain, after all, but single chapters from the volume of history, although they are ornamental chapters. Consider the exquisite simplicity of the **Paradise Lost.** It and it alone really possesses a beginning, a middle, and an end; it has the totality of the poem as distinguished from the *ab ovo* birth and parentage, or straight line, of history.

2. As to the subject.

In Homer, the supposed importance of the subject, as the first effort of confederated Greece, is an after-thought of the critics; and the interest, such as it is, derived from the events themselves, as distinguished from the manner of representing them, is very languid to all but Greeks. It is a Greek poem. The superiority of the Paradise Lost is obvious in this respect, that the interest transcends the limits of a nation. But we do not generally dwell on this excellence of the Paradise Lost, because it seems attributable to Christianity itself;—yet in fact the interest is wider than Christendom, and comprehends the Jewish and Mohammedan worlds;—nay, still further, inasmuch as it represents the origin of evil, and the combat of evil and good, it contains matter of deep interest to all mankind, as forming the basis of all religion, and the true occasion of all philosophy whatsoever.

The FALL of man is the subject; Satan is the cause; man's blissful state the immediate object of his enmity and attack; man is warned by an angel who gives him an account of all that was requisite to be known, to make the warning at once intelligible and awful, then the temptation ensues, and the Fall; then the immediate sensible consequence; then the consolation, wherein an angel presents a vision of the history of man with the ultimate triumph of the Redeemer. Nothing is touched in this vision but what is of general interest in religion; any thing else would have been improper.

The inferiority of Klopstock's Messiah is inexpressible. I admit the prerogative of poetic feeling, and poetic faith; but I can not suspend the judgment even for a moment. A poem may in one sense be a dream, but it must be a waking dream. In Milton you have a religious faith combined with the moral nature; it is an efflux; you go along with it. In Klopstock there is a wilfulness; he makes things so and so. The feigned speeches and events in the Messiah shock us like falsehoods; but nothing of that sort is felt in the *Paradise Lost,* in which no particulars, at least very few indeed, are touched which can come into collision or juxtaposition with recorded matter.

But notwithstanding the advantages in Milton's subject, there were concomitant insuperable difficulties, and Milton has exhibited marvellous skill in keeping most of them out of sight. High poetry is the translation of reality into the ideal under the predicament of succession of time only. The poet is an historian, upon condition of moral power being the only force in the universe. The very grandeur of his subject ministered a difficulty to Milton. The statement of a being of high intellect, warring against the supreme Being, seems to contradict the idea of a supreme Being. Milton precludes our feeling this, as much as possible, by keeping the peculiar attributes of divinity less in sight, making them to a certain extent allegorical only. Again poetry implies the language of excitement; yet how to reconcile such language with God! Hence Milton confines the poetic passion in God's speeches to the language in Scripture; and once only allows the *passio vera,* or *quasi humana* to appear, in the passage, where the Father contemplates his own likeness in the Son before the battle:—

> Go then, thou Mightiest, in thy Father's might,
> Ascend my chariot, guide the rapid wheels
> That shake Heaven's basis, bring forth all my war,
> My bow and thunder; my almighty arms
> Gird on, and sword upon thy puissant thigh;
> Pursue these sons of darkness, drive them out
> From all Heaven's bounds into the utter deep:
> There let them learn, as likes them, to despise
> God and Messiah his anointed king.

3. As to Milton's object:

It was to justify the ways of God to man! The controversial spirit observable in many parts of the poem, especially in God's speeches, is immediately attributable to the great controversy of that age, the origination of evil. The Arminians considered it a mere calamity. The Calvinists took away all human will. Milton asserted the will, but declared for the enslavement of the will out of an act of the will itself. There are three powers in us, which distinguish us from the beasts that perish:—1, reason; 2, the power of viewing universal truth; and 3, the power of contracting universal truth into particulars. Religion is the will in the reason, and love in the will.

The character of Satan is pride and sensual indulgence, finding in self the sole motive of action. It is the character so often seen *in little* on the political stage. It exhibits all the restless-ness, temerity, and cunning which have marked the mighty hunters of mankind from Nimrod to Napoleon. The common fascination of men is, that these great men, as they are called, must act from some great motive. Milton has carefully marked in his Satan the intense selfishness, the alcohol of egotism, which would rather reign in hell than serve in heaven. To place this lust of self in opposition to denial of self or duty, and to show what exertions it would make, and what pains endure to accomplish its end, is Milton's particular object in the character of Satan. But around this character he has thrown a singularity of daring, a grandeur of sufferance, and a ruined splendor, which constitute the very height of poetic sublimity.

Lastly, as to the execution:—

The language and versification of the *Paradise Lost* are peculiar in being so much more necessarily correspondent to each than those in any other poem or poet. The connection of the sentences and the position of the words are exquisitely artificial; but the position is rather according to the logic of passion or universal logic, than to the logic of grammar. Milton attempted to make the English language obey the logic of passion, as perfectly as the Greek and Latin. Hence the occasional harshness in the construction.

Sublimity is the pre-eminent characteristic of the *Paradise Lost.* It is not an arithmetical sublime like Klopstock's, whose rule always is to treat what we might think large as contemptibly small. Klopstock mistakes bigness for greatness. There is a greatness arising from images of effort and daring, and also from those of moral endurance; in Milton both are united. The fallen angels are human passions, invested with a dramatic reality.

The apostrophe to light at the commencement of the third book is particularly beautiful as an intermediate link between Hell and Heaven; and observe, how the second and third book support the subjective character of the poem. In all modern poetry in Christendom there is an under consciousness of a sinful nature, a fleeting away of external things, the mind or subject greater than the object, the reflective character predominant. In the *Paradise Lost* the sublimest parts are the revelations of Milton's own mind, producing itself and evolving its own greatness; and this is so truly so, that when that which is merely entertaining for its objective beauty is introduced, it at first seems a discord.

In the description of Paradise itself, you have Milton's sunny side as a man; here his descriptive powers are exercised to the utmost, and he draws deep upon his Italian resources. In the description of Eve, and throughout this part of the poem, the poet is predominant over the theologian. Dress is the symbol of the Fall, but the mark of intellect; and the metaphysics of dress are, the hiding what is not symbolic and displaying by discrimination what is. The love of Adam and Eve in Paradise is of the highest merit—not phantomatic, and yet removed from every thing degrading. It is the sentiment of one rational being towards another made tender by a specific difference in that which is essentially the same in both; it is a union of opposites, a giving and receiving mutually of the permanent in either, a completion of each in the other.

Milton is not a picturesque, but a musical, poet; although he has this merit, that the object chosen by him for any particular foreground always remains prominent to the end, enriched, but not encumbered, by the opulence of descriptive details furnished by an exhaustless imagination. I wish the *Paradise Lost* were more carefully read and studied than I can see any ground for believing it is, especially those parts which, from the habit of always looking for a story in poetry, are scarcely read at all,—as for example, Adam's vision of future events in the 11th and 12th books. No one can rise from the perusal of this immortal poem without a deep sense of the grandeur and the purity of Milton's soul, or without feeling how susceptible of domestic enjoyments he really was, notwithstanding the discomforts which actually resulted from an apparently unhappy choice in marriage. He was, as every truly great poet has ever been, a good man; but finding it impossible to realize his own aspirations, either in religion or politics, or society, he gave up his heart to the living spirit and light within him, and avenged himself on the world by enriching it with this record of his own transcendent ideal. (pp. 477-81)

> *S. T. Coleridge, "Literary Criticism: Milton," in his* Selected Poetry and Prose, *edited by Donald A. Stauffer, The Modern Library, 1951, pp. 475-81.*

JOHN KEATS   (poem date 1818)

[*Keats is considered a key figure in the English Romantic movement and a major poet in the English language. He achieved remarkable intellectual and artistic development in a creative career that spanned only four years. His poems are valued not only for their sensuous imagery, simplicity, and passionate tone, but also for their insight into aesthetic and human concerns, particularly the conflict between art and life. The artistic philosophy delineated in Keats's poetry—a philosophy perhaps best mirrored in the words "beauty is truth, truth beauty" in "Ode on a Grecian Urn" (1820)—is illuminated by his correspondence, which critics place among the most sensitive ever written. In the letters, Keats set down poetic theories that have become standards of literary criticism, including his theory of "Negative Capability, that is when man is capable of being in uncertainties, mysteries, doubts, without any irritable reaching after fact and reason." The following poem, entitled "On Seeing a Lock of Milton's Hair," grew directly from an event in early 1818. "I was at [Leigh] Hunt's the other day," Keats wrote to Benjamin Bailey on 23 January 1818, "and he surprised me with a real authenticated lock of Milton's Hair. I know you would like what I wrote thereon, so here it is—as they say of a sheep in a Nursery Book." After copying the poem, he added, "This I did at Hunt's at his request—perhaps I should have done something better alone and at home." Here, he praises Milton extravagantly for his multifarious achievements.*]

> CHIEF of organic numbers!
>   Old Scholar of the Spheres!
>   Thy spirit never slumbers,
>   But rolls about our ears,
>   For ever and for ever!
>   O what a mad endeavour
>   Worketh he,
> Who to thy sacred and ennobled hearse
> Would offer a burnt sacrifice of verse
>   And melody.
>
> How heavenward thou soundest,
>   Live Temple of sweet noise,
> And Discord unconfoundest,
>   Giving Delight new joys,
> And Pleasure nobler pinions!
>   O, where are thy dominions?
>   Lend thine ear
> To a young Delian oath,—ay, by thy soul,
> By all that from thy mortal lips did roll,
> And by the kernel of thine earthly love,
> Beauty, in things on earth, and things above,

>   I swear!
> When every childish fashion
>   Has vanish'd from my rhyme,
> Will I, grey-gone in passion,
>   Leave to an after-time,
>   Hymning and harmony
> Of thee, and of thy works, and of thy
>   life;
> But vain is now the burning and the strife,
> Pangs are in vain, until I grow high-rife
>   With old Philosophy,
> And mad with glimpses of futurity!
> For many years my offering must be hush'd;
>   When I do speak, I'll think upon this
>   hour,
> Because I feel my forehead hot and flush'd.
>   Even at the simplest vassal of thy
>   power,—
>   A lock of thy bright hair—
>   Sudden it came,
> And I was startled, when I caught thy name
>   Coupled so unaware;
> Yet, at the moment, temperate was my
>   blood.
> I thought I had beheld it from the flood.
>
>   (pp. 39-40)

> *John Keats, "On Seeing a Lock of Milton's Hair," in his* The Complete Poetical Works and Letters of John Keats, *edited by H. E. Scudder, Houghton Mifflin Company, 1899, pp. 39-40.*

PERCY BYSSHE SHELLEY   (essay date 1819)

[*Shelley was a leading figure in the English Romantic movement. His* Defence of Poetry *(written in 1821 but not published until 1840), in which he investigated the relation of poetry to the history of civilization, is considered an important contribution to nineteenth-century aesthetics. Influenced by the French philosopher Jean-Jacques Rousseau and the German poet and pre-Romanticist Johann Gottfried von Herder, Shelley viewed poetry, as he did human society, as a continuing evolution of ideas, a "fountain forever overflowing with the waters of wisdom and delight," which, when exhausted by one age, will be succeeded by "another and yet another . . . and new relations are ever developed." Accordingly, he labeled all poets "legislators and prophets" who, even unconsciously or when in least prominence, contribute to the spiritual and political evolution of humankind. In the following excerpt from his "Essay on the Devil and Devils," a work believed to have been written in 1819 or 1820, he discusses Milton's conception of Satan.*]

[In his account of the origin of Hell] Milton supposes that, on a particular day, God chose to adopt as his son and *heir*, (the reversion of an estate with an immortal incumbent would be worth little) a being unlike the other Spirits, who seems to have been supposed to be a detached portion of himself, and afterwards figured upon the earth in the well-known character of Jesus Christ. The Devil is represented as conceiving high indignation at this preference, and as disputing the affair with arms. I cannot discover Milton's authority for this circumstance; but all agree in the fact of the insurrection, and the defeat, and the casting out into Hell. Nothing can exceed the grandeur and the energy of the character of the Devil, as expressed in *Paradise Lost*. He is a Devil, very different from the popular personification of evil, and it is a mistake to suppose that he was intended for an idealism of evil. Malignity, implacable hate, cunning, and refinement of device to inflict the utmost anguish on an enemy, these, which are venial in a slave, are not to be forgiven in a tyrant; these, which are redeemed by much that ennobles in one subdued, are marked by all that dishonours his conquest in the victor. Milton's Devil, as a moral being, is as far superior to his God, as one who perseveres in a purpose which he has conceived to be excellent, in spite of adversity and torture, is to one who in the cold security of undoubted triumph inflicts the most horrible revenge upon his enemy—not from any mistaken notion of bringing him to repent of a perseverance in enmity, but with the open and alleged design of exasperating him to deserve new torments.

Milton so far violated all that part of the popular creed which is susceptible of being preached and defended in argument, as to the allege no superiority in moral virtue to his God over his Devil. He mingled as it were the elements of human nature as colours upon a single palett, and arranged them into the composition of his great picture, according to the laws of epic truth; that is, according to the laws of that principle by which a series of actions of intelligent and ethical beings, developed in rhythmical tale, are calculated to excite the sympathy and antipathy of succeeding generations of mankind. The writer who would have attributed majesty and beauty to the character of victorious and vindictive omnipotence, must have been contented with the character of a good Christian; he never could have been a great epic poet. It is difficult to determine, in a country where the most enormous sanctions of opinion and law are attached to a direct avowal of certain speculative notions, whether Milton was a Christian or not, at the period of the composition of *Paradise Lost*. Is it possible that Socrates seriously believed that Æsculapius would be propitiated by the offering of a cock? Thus much is certain, that Milton gives the Devil all imaginable advantage; and the arguments with which he exposes the injustice and impotent weakness of his adversary, are such as, had they been printed, distinct from the shelter of any dramatic order, would have been answered by the most conclusive of syllogisms—persecution. As it is, *Paradise Lost* has conferred on the modern mythology a systematic form; and when the immeasurable and unceasing mutability of time shall have added one more superstition to those which have already arisen and decayed upon the earth, commentators and critics will be learnedly employed in elucidating the religion of ancestral Europe, only not utterly forgotten because it will have participated in the eternity of genius. The Devil owes everything to Milton. Dante and Tasso present us with a very gross idea of him. Milton divested him of a sting, hoof, and horns, and clothed him with the sublime grandeur of a graceful but tremendous spirit. (pp. 387-90)

> *Percy Bysshe Shelley, "On the Devil, and Devils,"*
> *in his* The Prose Works of Percy Bysshe Shelley,
> *edited by Harry Buxton Forman, 1876? Reprint by*
> *Reeves and Turner, 1880, pp. 382-406.*

JOHN KEATS   (essay date 1821?)

[*In the following undated remarks from the flyleaf of his personal copy of* Paradise Lost, *Keats comments on a variety of Miltonic issues, noting especially the poet's genius as it is revealed in* Paradise Lost.]

The Genius of Milton, more particularly in respect to its span in immensity, calculated him, by a sort of birthright, for such an 'argument' as the *Paradise Lost*: he had an exquisite passion for what is properly, in the sense of ease and pleasure, poetical Luxury; and with that it appears to me he would fain have been content, if he could, so doing, have preserved his self-respect and feel of duty performed; but there was working in him as

it were that same sort of thing as operates in the great world to the end of a Prophecy's being accomplish'd: therefore he devoted himself rather to the ardours than the pleasures of Song, solacing himself at intervals with cups of old wine; and those are with some exceptions the finest parts of the poem. With some exceptions—for the spirit of mounting and adventure can never be unfruitful or unrewarded; had he not broken through the clouds which envelope so deliciously the Elysian field of verse, and committed himself to the Extreme, we should never have seen Satan as described—

> But his face
> Deep scars of thunder had entrench'd, &c.
>
> (pp. 256-57)

There is a greatness which the *Paradise Lost* possesses over every other Poem—*the Magnitude of Contrast*, and that is softened by the contrast being ungrotesque to a degree. Heaven moves on like music throughout. Hell is also peopled with angels; it also moves on like music, not grating and harsh, but like a grand accompaniment in the Base of Heaven. (p. 257)

Milton is godlike in the sublime pathetic. In Demons, fallen Angels, and Monsters the delicacies of passion, living in and from their immortality, is of the most softening and dissolving nature. It is carried to the utmost here—"Others more mild"— nothing can express the sensation one feels at "Their song was partial" &c. Examples of this nature are divine to the utmost in other poets—in Caliban "*Sometimes a thousand twangling instruments*" &c. In Theocritus, Polyphemus—and Homer's Hymn to Pan where Mercury is represented as taking his "*homely fac'd*" to Heaven. There are numerous other instances in Milton—where Satan's progeny is called his "*daughter dear*," and where this same Sin, a female, and with a feminine instinct for the showy and martial, is in pain lest death should sully his bright arms, "*nor vainly hope to be invulnerable in those bright arms.*" Another instance is "*Pensive I sat alone.*" We need not mention "Tears such as Angels weep." (pp. 261-62)

The management of [Book III lines 1 and 15-19 of *Paradise Lost*] is Apollonian. Satan first "*throws round his baleful eyes*", the[n] awakes his legions, he consults, he sets forward on his voyage—and just as he is getting to the end of it we see the Great God and our first parent, and that same Satan all brought in one's vision—we have the invocation to light before we mount to heaven—we breathe more freely—we feel the great author's consolations coming thick upon him at a time when he complains most—we are getting ripe for diversity—the immediate topic of the Poem opens with a grand Perspective of all concerned. (p. 262)

There are two specimens of a very extraordinary beauty in the *Paradise Lost*; they are of a nature as far as I have read, unexampled elsewhere—they are entirely distinct from the brief pathos of Dante—and they are not to be found even in Shakespeare—these are according to the great prerogative of poetry better described in themselves than by a volume. The one is in the fol[lowing]—"which cost Ceres all that pain"—the other is that ending "Nor could the Muse defend her son"—they appear exclusively Miltonic without the shadow of another mind ancient or Modern. (p. 264)

Milton in every instance pursues his imagination to the utmost—he is "sagacious of his Quarry," he sees Beauty on the wing, pounces upon it and gorges it to the producing his essential verse. "So from the root springs lighter the green stalk" &c. But in no instance is this sort of perseverance more exemplified, than in what may be called his *stationing or statuary*.

He is not content with the simple description, he must station,—thus here we not only see how the Birds *"with clang despised the ground,"* but we see them *"under a cloud in prospect."* So we see Adam *"Fair indeed, and tall—under a plantane"*—and so we see Satan *"disfigured—on the Assyrian Mount."* This last with all its accompaniments, and keeping in mind the Theory of Spirits' eyes and the simile of Galileo, has a dramatic vastness and solemnity fit and worthy to hold one amazed in the midst of this Paradise Lost. (pp. 264-65)

> John Keats, *"Notes on Milton's 'Paradise Lost',"* in his The Complete Works of John Keats, Vol. III, edited by H. Buxton Forman, Gowans & Gray, 1901, pp. 256-65.

LORD MACAULAY (essay date 1825)

[*Thomas Babington, Lord Macaulay was a distinguished English historian, essayist, and politician. For many years he was a major contributor of erudite, highly opinionated articles to the* Edinburgh Review. *Besides these essays, which were collected in 1843 in* Critical and Historical Essays, *his most enduring work is his five-volume* History of England from the Accession of James II *(1849-61), which, despite criticism of its strong Whig bias, is revered for its rhetorical and narrative prose. According to Richard Tobias, Macaulay was a writer who "feared sentiment and preferred distance, objectivity, dispassionate vision. Yet withal, he was a brilliant writer who . . . is still capable of moving a reader by sheer verbal excitement." In the following excerpt from an essay originally published in the* Edinburgh Review *in 1825, Macaulay surveys Milton's major poems, commenting on the poet's character and comparing* Paradise Lost *with Dante's* Divine Comedy.]

Milton, it is well known, admired Euripides highly, much more highly than, in our opinion, Euripides deserved. Indeed the caresses which this partiality leads our countryman to bestow on "sad Electra's poet," sometimes remind us of the beautiful Queen of Fairy-land kissing the long ears of Bottom. At all events, there can be no doubt that this veneration for the Athenian, whether just or not, was injurious to the *Samson Agonistes.* Had Milton taken Æschylus for his model, he would have given himself up to the lyric inspiration, and poured out profusely all the treasures of his mind, without bestowing a thought on those dramatic proprieties which the nature of the work rendered it impossible to preserve. In the attempt to reconcile things in their own nature inconsistent, he has failed, as every one else must have failed. We cannot identify ourselves with the characters, as in a good play. We cannot identify ourselves with the poet, as in a good ode. The conflicting ingredients, like an acid and an alkali mixed, neutralise each other. We are by no means insensible to the merits of this celebrated piece, to the severe dignity of the style, the graceful and pathetic solemnity of the opening speech, or the wild and barbaric melody which gives so striking an effect to the choral passages. But we think it, we confess, the least successful effort of the genius of Milton.

The *Comus* is framed on the model of the Italian Masque, as the *Samson* is framed on the model of the Greek Tragedy. It is certainly the noblest performance of the kind which exists in any language. It is as far superior to the Faithful Shepherdess, as the Faithful Shepherdess is to the Aminta, or the Aminta to the Pastor Fido. It was well for Milton that he had here no Euripides to mislead him. He understood and loved the literature of modern Italy. But he did not feel for it the same veneration which he entertained for the remains of Athenian and Roman poetry, consecrated by so many lofty and endearing recollections. The faults, moreover, of his Italian predecessors were of a kind to which his mind had a deadly antipathy. He could stoop to a plain style, sometimes even to a bald style; but false brilliancy was his utter aversion. His muse had no objection to a russet attire; but she turned with disgust from the finery of Guarini, as tawdry and as paltry as the rags of a chimney-sweeper on May-day. Whatever ornaments she wears are of massive gold, not only dazzling to the sight, but capable of standing the severest test of the crucible.

Milton attended in the *Comus* to the distinction which he afterwards neglected in the *Samson.* He made his Masque what it ought to be, essentially lyrical, and dramatic only in semblance. He has not attempted a fruitless struggle against a defect inherent in the nature of that species of composition; and he has therefore succeeded, wherever success was not impossible. The speeches must be read as majestic soliloquies; and he who so reads them will be enraptured with their eloquence, their sublimity, and their music. The interruptions of the dialogue, however, impose a constraint upon the writer, and break the illusion of the reader. The finest passages are those which are lyric in form as well as in spirit. "I should much commend," says the excellent Sir Henry Wotton in a letter to Milton, "the tragical part if the lyrical did not ravish me with a certain Dorique delicacy in your songs and odes, whereunto, I must plainly confess to you, I have seen yet nothing parallel in our language." The criticism was just. It is when Milton escapes from the shackles of the dialogue, when he is discharged from the labour of uniting two incongruous styles, when he is at liberty to indulge his choral raptures without reserve, that he rises even above himself. Then, like his own good Genius bursting from the earthly form and weeds of Thyrsis, he stands forth in celestial freedom and beauty; he seems to cry exultingly,

> Now my task is smoothly done,
> I can fly or I can run,

to skim the earth, to soar above the clouds, to bathe in the Elysian dew of the rainbow, and to inhale the balmy smells of nard and cassia, which the musky winds of the zephyr scatter through the cedared alleys of the Hesperides.

There are several of the minor poems of Milton on which we should willingly make a few remarks. Still more willingly would we enter into a detailed examination of that admirable poem, the *Paradise Regained,* which, strangely enough, is scarcely ever mentioned except as an instance of the blindness of the parental affection which men of letters bear towards the offspring of their intellects. That Milton was mistaken in preferring this work, excellent as it is, to the *Paradise Lost,* we readily admit. But we are sure that the superiority of the *Paradise Lost* to the *Paradise Regained* is not more decided, than the superiority of the *Paradise Regained* to every poem which has since made its appearance. Our limits, however, prevent us from discussing the point at length. We hasten on to that extraordinary production which the general suffrage of critics has placed in the highest class of human compositions.

The only poem of modern times which can be compared with the *Paradise Lost* is the *Divine Comedy.* The subject of Milton, in some points, resembled that of Dante; but he has treated it in a widely different manner. We cannot, we think, better illustrate our opinion respecting our own great poet, than by contrasting him with the father of Tuscan literature.

The poetry of Milton differs from that of Dante, as the hieroglyphics of Egypt differed from the picture-writing of Mexico. The images which Dante employs speak for themselves; they stand simply for what they are. Those of Milton have a sig-nification which is often discernible only to the initiated. Their value depends less on what they directly represent than on what they remotely suggest. However strange, however grotesque, may be the appearance which Dante undertakes to describe, he never shrinks from describing it. He gives us the shape, the colour, the sound, the smell, the taste; he counts the numbers; he measures the size. His similes are the illustrations of a traveller. Unlike those of other poets, and especially of Milton, they are introduced in a plain, business-like manner; not for the sake of any beauty in the objects from which they are drawn; not for the sake of any ornament which they may impart to the poem; but simply in order to make the meaning of the writer as clear to the reader as it is to himself. The ruins of the precipice which led from the sixth to the seventh circle of hell were like those of the rock which fell into the Adige on the south of Trent. The cataract of Phlegethon was like that of Aqua Cheta at the monastery of St. Benedict. The place where the heretics were confined in burning tombs resembled the vast cemetery of Arles.

Now let us compare with the exact details of Dante the dim intimations of Milton. We will cite a few examples. The En-glish poet has never thought of taking the measure of Satan. He gives us merely a vague idea of vast bulk. In one passage the fiend lies stretched out huge in length, floating many a rood, equal in size to the earth-born enemies of Jove, or to the sea-monster which the mariner mistakes for an island. When he addresses himself to battle against the guardian angels, he stands like Teneriffe or Atlas: his stature reaches the sky. Con-trast with these descriptions the lines in which Dante has de-scribed the gigantic spectre of Nimrod. "His face seemed to me as long and as broad as the ball of St. Peter's at Rome; and his other limbs were in proportion; so that the bank, which concealed him from the waist downwards, nevertheless showed so much of him, that three tall Germans would in vain have attempted to reach to his hair." We are sensible that we do no justice to the admirable style of the Florentine poet. But Mr. Cary's translation is not at hand; and our version, however rude, is sufficient to illustrate our meaning.

Once more, compare the lazar-house in the eleventh book of the **Paradise Lost** with the last ward of Malebolge in Dante. Milton avoids the loathsome details, and takes refuge in in-distinct but solemn and tremendous imagery, Despair hurrying from couch to couch to mock the wretches with his attendance, Death shaking his dart over them, but, in spite of supplications, delaying to strike. What says Dante? "There was such a moan there as there would be if all the sick who, between July and September, are in the hospitals of Valdichiana, and of the Tuscan swamps, and of Sardinia, were in one pit together; and such a stench was issuing forth as is wont to issue from decayed limbs."

We will not take upon ourselves the invidious office of settling precedency between two such writers. Each in his own de-partment is incomparable; and each, we may remark, has wisely, or fortunately, taken a subject adapted to exhibit his peculiar talent to the greatest advantage. The Divine Comedy is a per-sonal narrative. Dante is the eye-witness and ear-witness of that which he relates. He is the very man who has heard the tormented spirits crying out for the second death, who has read the dusky characters on the portal within which there is no hope, who has hidden his face from the terrors of the Gorgon, who has fled from the hooks and the seething pitch of Bar-bariccia and Draghignazzo. His own hands have grasped the

shaggy sides of Lucifer. His own feet have climbed the moun-tain of expiation. His own brow has been marked by the pu-rifying angel. The reader would throw aside such a tale in incredulous disgust, unless it were told with the strongest air of veracity, with a sobriety even in its horrors, with the greatest precision and multiplicity in its details. The narrative of Milton in this respect differs from that of Dante, as the adventures of Amadis differ from those of Gulliver. The author of Amadis would have made his book ridiculous if he had introduced those minute particulars which give such a charm to the work of Swift, the nautical observations, the affected delicacy about names, the official documents transcribed at full length, and all the unmeaning gossip and scandal of the court, springing out of nothing, and tending to nothing. We are not shocked at being told that a man who lived, nobody knows when, saw many very strange sights, and we can easily abandon ourselves to the illusion of the romance. But when Lemuel Gulliver, surgeon, resident at Rotherhithe, tells us of pygmies and giants, flying islands, and philosophising horses, nothing but such circumstantial touches could produce for a single moment a deception on the imagination. (pp. 217-23)

[The poetry of Milton and Dante] has in a considerable degree taken its character from their moral qualities. They are not egotists. They rarely obtrude their idiosyncrasies on their read-ers. They have nothing in common with those modern beggars for fame, who extort a pittance from the compassion of the inexperienced by exposing the nakedness and sores of their minds. Yet it would be difficult to name two writers whose works have been more completely, though undesignedly, col-oured by their personal feelings.

The character of Milton was peculiarly distinguished by lof-tiness of spirit; that of Dante by intensity of feeling. In every line of the Divine Comedy we discern the asperity which is produced by pride struggling with misery. There is perhaps no work in the world so deeply and uniformly sorrowful. The melancholy of Dante was no fantastic caprice. It was not, as far as at this distance of time can be judged, the effect of external circumstances. It was from within. Neither love nor glory, neither the conflicts of earth nor the hope of heaven could dispel it. It turned every consolation and every pleasure into its own nature. It resembled that noxious Sardinian soil of which the intense bitterness is said to have been perceptible even in its honey. His mind was, in the noble langauge of the Hebrew poet, "a land of darkness, as darkness itself, and where the light was as darkness." The gloom of his character dis-colours all the passions of men, and all the face of nature, and tinges with its own livid hue the flowers of Paradise and the glories of the eternal throne. All the portraits of him are sin-gularly characteristic. No person can look on the features, noble even to ruggedness, the dark furrows of the cheek, the haggard and woful stare of the eye, the sullen and contemptuous curve of the lip, and doubt that they belong to a man too proud and too sensitive to be happy.

Milton was, like Dante, a statesman and a lover; and, like Dante, he had been unfortunate in ambition and in love. He had survived his health and his sight, the comforts of his home, and the prosperity of his party. Of the great men by whom he had been distinguished at his entrance into life, some had been taken away from the evil to come; some had carried into foreign climates their unconquerable hatred of oppression; some were pining in dungeons; and some had poured forth their blood on scaffolds. Venal and licentious scribblers, with just sufficient talent to clothe the thoughts of a pandar in the style of a bellman, were now the favourite writers of the Sovereign and of the public. It was a loathsome herd, which could be compared to nothing so fitly as to the rabble of *Comus,* grotesque monsters, half bestial half human, dropping with wine, bloated with gluttony, and reeling in obscene dances. Amidst these that fair Muse was placed, like the chaste lady of the Masque, lofty, spotless, and serene, to be chattered at, and pointed at, and grinned at, by the whole rout of Satyrs and Goblins. If ever despondency and asperity could be excused in any man, they might have been excused in Milton. But the strength of his mind overcame every calamity. Neither blindness, nor gout, nor age, nor penury, nor domestic afflictions, nor political disappointments, nor abuse, nor proscription, nor neglect, had power to disturb his sedate and majestic patience. His spirits do not seem to have been high, but they were singularly equable. His temper was serious, perhaps stern; but it was a temper which no sufferings could render sullen or fretful. Such as it was when, on the eve of great events, he returned from his travels, in the prime of health and manly beauty, loaded with literary distinctions, and glowing with patriotic hopes, such it continued to be when, after having experienced every calamity which is incident to our nature, old, poor, sightless and disgraced, he retired to his hovel to die.

Hence it was that, though he wrote the *Paradise Lost* at a time of life when images of beauty and tenderness are in general beginning to fade, even from those minds in which they have not been effaced by anxiety and disappointment, he adorned it with all that is most lovely and delightful in the physical and in the moral world. Neither Theocritus nor Ariosto had a finer or a more healthful sense of the pleasantness of external objects, or loved better to luxuriate amidst sunbeams and flowers, the songs of nightingales, the juice of summer fruits, and the coolness of shady fountains. His conception of love unites all the voluptuousness of the Oriental harem, and all the gallantry of the chivlaric tournament, with all the pure and quiet affection of an English fireside. His poetry reminds us of the miracles of Alpine scenery. Nooks and dells, beautiful as fairy land, are embosomed in its most rugged and gigantic elevations. The roses and myrtles bloom unchilled on the verge of the avalanche.

Traces, indeed, of the peculiar character of Milton may be found in all his works; but it is most strongly displayed in the Sonnets. Those remarkable poems have been undervalued by critics who have not understood their nature. They have no epigrammatic point. There is none of the ingenuity of Filicaja in the thought, none of the hard and brilliant enamel of Petrarch in the style. They are simple but majestic records of the feelings of the poet; as little tricked out for the public eye as his diary would have been. A victory, an expected attack upon the city, a momentary fit of depression or exultation, a jest thrown out against one of his books, a dream which for a short time restored to him that beautiful face over which the grave had closed for ever, led him to musings, which, without effort, shaped themselves into verse. The unity of sentiment and severity of style which characterise these little pieces remind us of the Greek Anthology, or perhaps still more of the Collects of the English Liturgy. The noble poem on the Massacres of Piedmont [**"On the Late Massacre in Piemont"**] is strictly a Collect in verse.

The Sonnets are more or less striking, according as the occasions which gave birth to them are more or less interesting. But they are, almost without exception, dignified by a sobriety and greatness of mind to which we know not where to look for a parallel. It would, indeed, be scarcely safe to draw any

decided inferences as to the character of a writer from passages directly egotistical. But the qualities which we have ascribed to Milton, though perhaps most strongly marked in those parts of his works which treat of his personal feelings, are distinguishable in every page, and impart to all his writings, prose and poetry, English, Latin, and Italian, a strong family likeness. (pp. 229-33)

> *Lord Macaulay, "Milton," in his* Critical, Historical and Miscellaneous Essays, *Vol. I,* Sheldon and Company, 1860, pp. 202-66.

JOHN GREENLEAF WHITTIER   (essay date 1828)

[*Whittier was an American poet, abolitionist, journalist, and critic. His works are noted for their moral content, simple sentiment, and humanitarianism. As a critic, Whittier often praised the moralistic efforts of obscure writers over the sensational, "immoral" attempts of such well-known writers as Lord Byron. Most importantly, Whittier encouraged the idea of American literary nationalism. In the following excerpt from an essay originally published in the* Essex Gazette *in 1828, he favorably reviews Milton's prose works.*]

There is strength and boldness in [the prose works of Milton], which cannot fail to please, even those, who are attached to the smooth and graceful periods of modern authors. They are distinguished by that sublimity of sentiment and loftiness of diction, to which none but Milton has ever attained.—The elements of poetry are scattered in every page, and need but the melody of numbers to fix them indelibly on our memories.

There is much of beauty and sublimity in the following, from the speech for the liberty of the Press *Areopagitica*].

> Methinks I see in my mind, a noble and puissant nation, rousing herself like a strong man after sleep, and shaking her invincible locks. Methinks I see her as an eagle muing her mighty young, and kindling her undazzled eyes at the full mid-day beam, purging and unscaling her long abused sight at the fountain itself of heavenly radiance.

The reader, who has become familiar with the austere antiquity of Milton's style, who is able to follow his vigorous flights of imagination, and fathom the depth of his reasonings, will not fail to acknowledge in those writings, the presence of the same unrivalled power, which has stamped its undying seal of remembrance on the readers of *Paradise Lost.*

It is to be regretted that those truly valuable writings have been so long neglected. They need only to be known to be extensively admired.

> Their power is of the brighter clime,
>   Which in our birth has part;
> Their tones are of the world, which time
>   Sears not within the heart.

(pp. 18-19)

> *John Greenleaf Whittier, "The Prose Works of Milton," in* Whittier on Writers and Writing: The Uncollected Critical Writings of John Greenleaf Whittier *by Edwin Harrison Cady and Harry Hayden Clark, Syracuse University Press, 1950, pp. 18-19.*

RALPH WALDO EMERSON   (lecture date 1835)

[*Emerson was an American essayist and poet who is recognized today as one of the most influential figures of the nineteenth century. A chief proponent of Transcendentalism in America, he shaped a distinctly American philosophy based on optimism, individuality, and mysticism, stressing all the while the essential unity of thoughts, persons, and things in the divine whole. In the following excerpt from a lecture delivered in Boston in 1835, he briefly considers Milton's major works and comments on his motivation as a writer.]*

[The perception we attribute] to Milton, of a purer ideal of humanity, modifies his poetic genius. The man is paramount to the poet. His fancy is never transcendant, extravagant; but, as Bacon's imagination was said to be "the noblest that ever contented itself to minister to the understanding," so Milton's ministers to character. Milton's sublimest song, bursting into heaven with its peal of melodious thunder, is the voice of Milton still. Indeed, throughout his poems, one may see under a thin veil, the opinions, the feelings, even the incidents of the poet's life, still reappearing. The sonnets are all occasional poems. **"L'Allegro"** and **"Il Penseroso"** are but a finer autobiography of his youthful fancies at Harefield. The **Comus** is but a transcript, in charming numbers, of that philosophy of chastity, which, in the **Apology for Smectymnuus,** and in the **Reason of Church Government,** he declares to be his defence and religion. The **Samson Agonistes** is too broad an expression of his private griefs, to be mistaken, and is a version of the **Doctrine and Discipline of Divorce.** The most affecting passages in **Paradise Lost,** are personal allusions; and, when we are fairly in Eden, Adam and Milton are often difficult to be separated. Again, in **Paradise Regained,** we have the most distinct marks of the progress of the poet's mind, in the revision and enlargement of his religious opinions. This may be thought to abridge his praise as a poet. It is true of Homer and Shakspeare, that they do not appear in their poems; that those prodigious geniuses did cast themselves so totally in to their song, that their individuality vanishes, and the poet towers to the sky, whilst the man quite disappears. The fact is memorable. Shall we say, that, in our admiration and joy in these wonderful poems, we have even a feeling of regret, that the men knew not what they did; that they were too passive in their great service; were channels through which streams of thought flowed from a higher source, which they did not appropriate, did not blend with their own being? Like prophets, they seem but imperfectly aware of the import of their own utterances. We hesitate to say such things, and say them only to the unpleasing dualism, when the man and the poet show like a double consciousness. Perhaps we speak to no fact, but to mere fables of an idle mendicant, Homer; and of a Shakspeare, content with a mean and jocular way of life. Be it how it may, the genius and office of Milton were different, namely, to ascend by the aids of his learning and his religion,—by an equal perception, that is, of the past and the future,—to a higher insight and more lively delineation of the heroic life of man. This was his poem; whereof all his indignant pamphlets, and all his soaring verses, are only single cantos or detached stanzas. It was plainly needful that his poetry should be a version of his own life, in order to give weight and solemnity to his thoughts; by which they might penetrate and possess the imagination and the will of mankind. The creations of Shakspeare are cast into the world of thought, to no farther end than to delight. Their intrinsic beauty is their excuse for being. Milton, fired "with dearest charity to infuse the knowledge of good things into others," tasked his giant imagination, and exhausted the stores of his intellect, for an end beyond, namely, to teach. His own conviction it is, which gives such authority to his strain. Its reality is its force. If out of the heart it came, to the heart it must go. What schools and

epochs of common rhymers would it need to make a counterbalance to the severe oracles of his muse.

> In them is plainest taught and easiest learnt,
> What makes a nation happy, and keeps it so.

The lover of Milton reads one sense in his prose and in his metrical compositions; and sometimes the muse soars highest in the former, because the thought is more sincere. Of his prose in general, not the style alone, but the argument also, is poetic; according to Lord Bacon's definition of poetry, following that of Aristotle, "Poetry, not finding the actual world exactly conformed to its idea of good and fair, seeks to accomodate the shows of things to the desires of the mind, and to create an ideal world better than the world of experience." Such certainly is the explanation of Milton's tracts. Such is the apology to be entered for the plea for freedom of divorce; an essay, which, from the first until now, has brought a degree of obloquy on his name. It was a sally of the extravagant spirit of the time, overjoyed, as in the Frnech revolution, with the sudden victories it had gained, and eager to carry on the standard of truth to new heights. It is to be regarded as a poem on one of the griefs of man's condition, namely, unfit marriage. And as many poems have been written upon unfit society, commending solitude, yet have not been proceeded against, though their end was hostile to the state; so should this receive that charity, which an angelic soul, suffering more keenly than others from the unavoidable evils of human life, is entitled to. (pp. 160-63)

> *Ralph Waldo Emerson, "John Milton," in his* The Early Lectures of Ralph Waldo Emerson: 1833-1836, *Vol. I, edited by Stephen E. Whicher and Robert E. Spiller, Cambridge, Mass.: Harvard University Press, 1959, pp. 144-63.*

JAMES RUSSELL LOWELL   (essay date 1872)

[A celebrated American poet and essayist, Lowell edited two of the literary journals of his day, the Atlantic Monthly *and the* North American Review. *He is best known for his satirical and critical writings, including* A Fable for Critics *(1848), a book-length poem featuring witty portraits of his contemporaries. Although often awkwardly phrased and occasionally vicious, A Fable is distinguished by the enduring value of its literary assessments. Commentators generally agree that Lowell displayed a judicious critical sense, even though he sometimes relied upon impressions rather than precepts in his writings. In the following excerpt from an essay originally published in the* North American Review *in 1872, he isolates the distinctive qualities of Milton's poetry and considers the impact of the poet's personality on his literary works.]*

Milton cannot certainly be taxed with any partiality for low words. He rather loved them tall, as the Prussian King loved men to be six feet high in their stockings, and fit to go into the grenadiers. He loved them as much for their music as for their meaning,—perhaps more. His style, therefore, when it has to deal with commoner things, is apt to grow a little cumbrous and unwieldy. A Persian poet says that when the owl would boast, he boasts of catching mice at the edge of a hole. Shakespeare would have understood this. Milton would have made him talk like an eagle. His influence is not to be left out of account as partially contributing to that decline toward poetic diction which was already beginning ere he died. If it would not be fair to say that he is the most artistic, he may be called in the highest sense the most scientific of our poets. If to Spenser younger poets have gone to be sung-to, they have sat at the feet of Milton to be taught. Our language has no finer poem than **Samson Agonistes,** if any so fine in the quality of austere dignity or in the skill with which the poet's personal experience is generalized into a classic tragedy.

Gentle as Milton's earlier portraits would seem to show him, he had in him by nature, or bred into him by fate, something of the haughty and defiant self-assertion of Dante and Michael Angelo. In no other English author is the man so large a part of his works. Milton's haughty conception of himself enters into all he says and does. Always the necessity of this one man became that of the whole human race for the moment. There were no walls so sacred but must go to the ground when *he* wanted elbow-room; and he wanted a great deal. Did Mary Powell, the cavalier's daughter, find the abode of a roundhead schoolmaster *incompatible* and leave it, forthwith the cry of the universe was for an easier dissolution of the marriage covenant. If *he* is blind, it is with excess of light, it is a divine partiality, an over-shadowing with angels' wings. Phineus and Teiresias are admitted among the prophets because they, too, had lost their sight, and the blindness of Homer is of more account than his *Iliad*. After writing in rhyme till he was past fifty, he finds it unsuitable for his epic, and it at once becomes "the invention of a barbarous age to set off wretched matter and lame metre" [see excerpt dated 1674]. If the structure of *his* mind be undramatic, why, then, the English drama is naught, learned Jonson, sweetest Shakespeare, and the rest notwithstanding, and he will compose a tragedy on a Greek model with the blinded Samson for its hero, and he will compose it partly in rhyme. Plainly he belongs to the intenser kind of men whose yesterdays are in no way responsible for their to-morrows. And this makes him perenially interesting even to those who hate his politics, despise his Socinianism, and find his greatest poem a bore. (pp. 113-15)

It results from the almost scornful withdrawal of Milton into the fortress of his absolute personality that no great poet is so uniformly self-conscious as he. We should say of Shakespeare that he had the power of transforming himself into everything; of Milton, that he had that of transforming everything into himself. Dante is individual rather than self-conscious, and he, the cast-iron man, grows pliable as a field of grain at the breath of Beatrice, and flows away in waves of sunshine. But Milton never let himself go for a moment. As other poets are possessed by their theme, so is he *self*-possessed, his great theme being John Milton, and his great duty that of interpreter between him and the world. I say it with all respect, for he was well worthy translation, and it is out of Hebrew that the version is made. Pope says he makes God the Father reason "like a school-divine." The criticism is witty, but inaccurate. He makes Deity a mouthpiece for his present theology, and had the poem been written a few years later, the Almighty would have become more heterodox. Since Dante, no one had stood on these visiting terms with heaven.

Now it is precisely this audacity of self-reliance, I suspect, which goes far toward making the sublime, and which, falling by a hair's-breadth short thereof, makes the ridiculous. Puritanism showed both the strength and weakness of its prophetic nurture; enough of the latter to be scoffed out of England by the very men it had conquered in the field, enough of the former to intrench itself in three or four immortal memories. It has left an abiding mark in politics and religion, but its great monuments are the prose of Bunyan and the verse of Milton. It is a high inspiration to be the neighbor of great events; to have been a partaker in them and to have seen noble purposes by their own self-confidence become the very means of ignoble

ends, if it do not wholly depress, may kindle a passion of regret deepening the song which dares not tell the reason of its sorrow. The grand loneliness of Milton in his latter years, while it makes him the most impressive figure in our literary history, is reflected also in his maturer poems by a sublime independence of human sympathy like that with which mountains fascinate and rebuff us. But it is idle to talk of the loneliness of one the habitual companions of whose mind were the Past and Future. I always seem to see him leaning in his blindness a hand on the shoulder of each, sure that the one will guard the song which the other had inspired. (pp. 115-17)

> *James Russell Lowell, "Milton," in his* The Writings of James Russell Lowell: Literary Essays, Vol. IV, *1890. Reprint by Houghton, Mifflin and Company, 1897, pp. 58-117.*

MATTHEW ARNOLD   (lecture date 1888)

[*Arnold is considered one of the most important authors of the later Victorian period in England. While he is well known today as a poet, in his own time he asserted his greatest influence through his prose writings. His forceful literary criticism, which is colored by a humanistic belief in the value of balance and clarity in literature, significantly shaped modern theory. In the following excerpt from an address delivered in 1888 at St. Margaret's Church, Westminster upon the unveiling of a window honoring Milton's second wife, Arnold praises Milton as the supreme English epic poet.*]

[In] calling up Milton's memory we call up, let me say, a memory upon which, in prospect of the Anglo-Saxon contagion and of its dangers supposed and real, it may be well to lay stress even more than upon Shakespeare's. If to our English race an inadequate sense for perfection of work is a real danger, if the discipline of respect for a high and flawless excellence is peculiarly needed by us, Milton is of all our gifted men the best lesson, the most salutary influence. In the sure and flawless perfection of his rhythm and diction he is as admirable as Virgil or Dante, and in this respect he is unique amongst us. No one else in English literature and art possesses the like distinction.

Thomson, Cowper, Wordsworth, all of them good poets who have studied Milton, followed Milton, adopted his form, fail in their diction and rhythm if we try them by that standard of excellence maintained by Milton constantly. From style really high and pure Milton never departs; their departures from it are frequent.

Shakespeare is divinely strong, rich, and attractive. But sureness of perfect style Shakespeare himself does not possess. I have heard a politician express wonder at the treasures of political wisdom in a certain celebrated scene of *Troilus and Cressida*; for my part I am at least equally moved to wonder at the fantastic and false diction in which Shakespeare has in that scene clothed them. Milton, from one end of **Paradise Lost** to the other, is in his diction and rhythm constantly a great artist in the great style. Whatever may be said as to the subject of his poem, as to the conditions under which he received his subject and treated it, that praise, at any rate, is assured to him.

For the rest, justice is not at present done, in my opinion, to Milton's management of the inevitable matter of a Puritan epic, a matter full of difficulties, for a poet. Justice is not done to the *architectonics,* as Goethe would have called them, of **Paradise Lost**; in these, too, the power of Milton's art is remarkable. But this may be a proposition which requires discussion and development for establishing it, and they are impossible on an occasion like the present.

That Milton, of all our English race, is by his diction and rhythm the one artist of the highest rank in the great style whom we have; this I take as requiring no discussion, this I take as certain.

The mighty power of poetry and art is generally admitted. But where the soul of this power, of this power at its best, chiefly resides, very many of us fail to see. It resides chiefly in the refining and elevation wrought in us by the high and rare excellence of the great style. We may feel the effect without being able to give ourselves clear account of its cause, but the thing is so. Now, no race needs the influences mentioned, the influences of refining and elevation, more than ours; and in poetry and art our grand source for them is Milton.

To what does he owe this supreme distinction? To nature first and foremost, to that bent of nature for inequality which to the worshippers of the average man is so unacceptable; to a gift, a divine favour. 'The older one grows,' says Goethe, 'the more one prizes natural gifts, because by no possibility can they be procured and stuck on.' Nature formed Milton to be a great poet. But what other poet has shown so sincere a sense of the grandeur of his vocation, and a moral effort so constant and sublime to make and keep himself worthy of it? The Milton of religious and political controversy, and perhaps of domestic life also, is not seldom disfigured by want of amenity, by acerbity. The Milton of poetry, on the other hand, is one of those great men 'who are modest'—to quote a fine remark of Leopardi, that gifted and stricken young Italian, who in his sense for poetic style is worthy to be named with Dante and Milton—'who are modest, because they continually compare themselves, not with other men, but with that idea of the perfect which they have before their mind.' The Milton of poetry is the man, in his own magnificent phrase, of 'devout prayer to that Eternal Spirit that can enrich with all utterance and knowledge, and sends out his Seraphim with the hallowed fire of his altar, to touch and purify the lips of whom he pleases.' And finally, the Milton of poetry is, in his own words again, the man of 'industrious and select reading.' Continually he lived in companionship with high and rare excellence, with the great Hebrew poets and prophets, with the great poets of Greece and Rome. The Hebrew compositions were not in verse, and can be not inadequately represented by the grand, measured prose of our English Bible. The verse of the poets of Greece and Rome no translation can adequately reproduce. Prose cannot have the power of verse; verse-translation may give whatever of charm is in the soul and talent of the translator himself, but never the specific charm of the verse and poet translated. In our race are thousands of readers, presently there will be millions, who know not a word of Greek and Latin, and will never learn those languages. If this host of readers are ever to gain any sense of the power and charm of the great poets of antiquity, their way to gain it is not through translations of the ancients, but through the original poetry of Milton, who has the like power and charm, because he has the like great style.

Through Milton they may gain it, for, in conclusion Milton is English; this master in the great style of the ancients is English. Virgil, whom Milton loved and honoured, has at the end of the *Æneid* a noble passage where Juno, seeing the defeat of Turnus and the Italians imminent, the victory of the Trojan invaders assured, entreats Jupiter that Italy may nevertheless survive and be herself still, may retain her own mind, manners, and language, and not adopt those of the conqueror.

Sit Latium, sint Albani per secula reges!

Jupiter grants the prayer; he promises perpetuity and the future to Italy—Italy reinforced by whatever virtue the Trojan race has, but Italy, not Troy. This we may take as a sort of parable suiting ourselves. All the Anglo-Saxon contagion, all the flood of Anglo-Saxon commonness, beats vainly against the great style but cannot shake it, and has to accept its triumph. But it triumphs in Milton, in one of our own race, tongue, faith, and morals. Milton has made the great style no longer an exotic here; he has made it an inmate amongst us, a leaven, and a power. Nevertheless he, and his hearers on both sides of the Atlantic, are English, and will remain English—

Sermonem Ausonii patrium moresque tenebunt.

The English race overspreads the world, and at the same time the ideal of an excellence the most high and the most rare abides a possession with it for ever. (pp. 61-8)

> *Matthew Arnold, "Milton," in his* Essays in Criticism, *second series, 1889. Reprint by The Macmillan Company, 1924, pp. 56-68.*

FRANCIS THOMPSON   (essay date 1900)

[*Thompson was one of the most important poets of the Catholic Revival in nineteenth-century English literature. Often compared to the seventeenth-century metaphysical poets, especially Richard Crashaw, he is best known for his poem "The Hound of Heaven" (1893), which displays his characteristic themes of spiritual struggle, redemption, and transcendent love. Like other writers of the English fin de siècle period, Thompson wrote poetry and prose noted for rich verbal effects and a devotion to the values of aestheticism. In the following excerpt from an essay originally published in the* Academy *in 1900, he examines Milton's prose style.*]

"This manner of writing," said John Milton regarding his prose, "wherein knowing myself inferior to myself, led by the genial power of nature to another task, I have the use, as I may account, but of my left hand." It is a sentence strange to encounter, in the strong and copious prose-work of the great Puritan—copious in style and diction, if not in quantity. Most poets, nevertheless, must have been ready to echo it; must have felt the new-born hesitancy of their accustomed ready handmaid, Expression, when she was called to walk with them in the dusty and frequented ways of prose. Yet not a beaten way was that when Milton adventured on it—wittingly we say *adventured*. It had for the poet an attraction which has fallen from it to-day, in that—no less than poetry—if offered him the privileges of the conqueror and explorer; a new empire to be founded, a new region to be reduced under obedience and law. And this, to some its difficulty, to the poet must have been its allurement. In poetry the great traditions had been set; in prose they remained to be set. In this medium, the language lay plastic under his hands; the whole question of its style expected his formative touch; its whole structural laws hearkened for his creative *fiat*. Such an unsullied and virgin opportunity comes not twice in a language.

Milton, whose authoritative sanction lies large over English poetry, made, it must be confessed, no equivalent use of his vast chance in prose. He did fine things with it, but he estated no tradition on his successors, he laid no mandate on the language: not to him have our fathers gone for a precedent, nor can we go for a resurrecting voice in prose. It has passed as an axiom that poets' prose (when poets do write prose) is peculiarly clean, pure, forthright, and workmanly; that, in fact (contrary to probable anticipation) it has no tincture of "poetic prose,'' but is as distinctively prose as their verse is distinctively poetry. It would be interesting to inquire whether this be so. It is so with Byron, Cowper, and Southey, who were not imaginative poets; it is so with Wordsworth when he treats philosophically of poetic principle. But when he writes on the Cintra Convention he adopts the raised manner of Hooker and his fellows; nor does the law hold exactly good with Coleridge, still less with Rossetti or Swinburne. Dryden and Matthew Arnold can be cited for it, and the prose of Shakespeare's plays; but against it again is Sidney, and against it again is Milton. Under his large motions, the garment of prose intermittently falls aside, revealing the immortal limbs of poetry.

But this alone will not explain why he is a splendidly impossible model. Browne is full of rhetoric that hovers on the confines of poetry, yet from the grand physician of Norwich it is possible to learn, as Johnson learned, and Stevenson. Browne's sentences are admirable in structure, and (apart from diction) need little, if anything, to be quite modern—we do not say fashionably modern. Therein is the difference. Milton was Milton to the last. As he went to Virgil for the structural art of his blank verse, he went to Cicero for the structure of his prose. But the Latinisation which his genius triumphantly imposed on poetry failed against the stubborn native grain of English prose. It is true (as Professor Vaughan remarks, in this ''Temple Classics'' edition of the *Areopagitica*) that he is looser in structure than Hooker; his long sentences are in the main ''not a synthesis of clauses, but an agglomeration.'' Clearly he discerned that rigid Latinisation would not work, and sought for such a successful compromise as he had carried out in verse. But the two elements of the compromise are only reined in equal yoke by his powerful hand; they must needs break loose

Milton at age 10.

from any other. Even in his hand the combination is often less than masterly, sometimes downright cumbersome and awkward. The *accretions* of sentence are tagged on in almost slovenly fashion. Such are the changes brought about by the fixing of a language that a child can now smile at the difficulties of the great Milton. We (so to speak) have but to touch a spring, where he had all to do with his own hand. That we may not appear to censure without giving testimony of the infelicity, consider this passage:

> What if I had written as your friend the author of the aforesaid mime, *Mundus alter et idem*, to have been ravished like some young Cephalus or Hylas, by a troop of camping housewives in Viraginea, and that he was there forced to swear himself an uxorious varlet: then after a long servitude to have come into Aphrodisia, that pleasant country that gave such a sweet smell to his nostrils among the shameless courtezans of Desvergonia?

Here clause is inartificially hooked on to clause; with an unpleasant effect intensified by the changes of construction; not absolutely ungrammatical, but perplexing and inelegant.

Yet again examine another sentence, where the like faulty looseness of structure is pushed to a final obscurity of expression:

> So if my name and outward demeanour be not evident enough to defend me, I must make trial if the discovery of my inmost thoughts can: wherein of two purposes, both honest and sincere, the one perhaps I shall not miss; although I fail to gain belief with others, of being such as my perpetual thoughts shall here disclose me, I may yet not fail of success in persuading some to be such really themselves, as they cannot believe me to be more than what I feign.

This, despite its intended openness of structure, is truly involved, not *evolved* after the manner of a long sentence justly builded. And such is the fault which may rightly be charged against Milton. Of occasional Latinisms we make less account. As thus:

> But these frequent songs throughout the law and the prophets . . . may be easily made appear over all the kinds of lyric poetry to be incomparable.

Or, again: ''The chief of learned men reputed in this land.'' The like may be found, much more frequently, in Hooker; and Milton is rather to be praised that they appear so seldom, than censured that they appear sometimes. The former, indeed, exemplifies a construction which we could wish Milton had succeeded in recommending, the inversion not being violent, while there is force and propriety in bringing down the close upon the emphatic word. Next to the genius of the language, the great power which fought against the splendid host of Latinising writers was doubtless the English Bible. The Bible had decided before Dryden that the language should not set in their mould.

But if not as an imitable model, yet as a magnificent study and recreation, like the hearing of grave and lofty music, the prose-work of Milton deserves to pass from the exclusive hands of scholars into those of all who care for exalted English. Though critics have dwelt on his Latinised diction, the substance is fine and virile Saxon, on which the Latin is a stately broidery, harmonised with rare art. He can pass from it at will to the most energetic simplicity, as one might conjecture in the author of *Comus.*

> They thought themselves gallant men, and I thought them fools; they made sport, and I laughed; they

mispronounced, and I misliked; and, to make up the
atticism, they were out, and I hissed.

Were ever unlucky actors assailed with more vernacular scorn?
That it can exceed, at times, in too rough abuse, we might
surmise from passages in the poems. But the cudgel, if too
knotty, is sound English wood; and one has a laughing relish
in hearing its hearty ring—the savagery of the blows deadened
by a distance of two centuries. And when Milton's matter gives
him scope, how those long sentences drop like a cloak all
suspicion of stiffness or pedantry, and advance in sweet and
noble measure! Listen to this, if you will to hear music:

> Next . . . that I may tell ye whither my younger feet
> wandered, I betook me among those lofty fables and
> romances, which recount in solemn cantos the deeds
> of knighthood founded by our victorious kings, and
> from hence had in renown over all Christendom.
> There I read it in the oath of every knight, that he
> should defend to the expense of his best blood, or of
> his life, if so befell him, the honour and chastity of
> virgin or matron; from whence even then I learned
> what a noble virtue chastity sure must be, to the
> defence of which so many worthies, by such a dear
> adventure of themselves, had sworn. And if I found
> in the story afterward, any of them, by word or deed,
> breaking that oath, I judged it the same fault of the
> poet as that which is attributed to Homer, to have
> written indecent things of the gods. Only this my
> mind gave me, that every free and gentle spirit, with-
> out that oath, ought to be borne a knight, nor needed
> to expect the gilt spur, or the laying of a sword upon
> his shoulder, to stir him up both by his counsel and
> his arms to secure and protect the weakness of any
> attempted chastity. So that even those books, which
> to many others have been the fuel of wantonness and
> loose living, I cannot think how, unless by divine
> indulgence, proved to me so many incitements, as
> you have heard, to the love and steadfast observation
> of that virtue which abhors the society of bordelloes.

The language of this is as pure and austerely beautiful as the
thought, which is (so to speak) the finest blend of chivalry and
Puritanism.

There is in the above passage a certain strain of exalted declamation, which appears yet more notable in Milton's most
splendid outbursts. *Outbursts* they are, so that one continually
considers what an orator might have been in him. Always he
seems perorating to some august assembly, like his own Satan
in Pandemonium: the very rhythm seems designed to swell
through resounding distances and reverberate above the multitudinous murmur of frequent congregations. This suits, also,
the essential spaciousness of the man's mind, its love of large
grandeurs, of massed and massive sound, of all imperial am-
plitudes, alike in conception, expression, and ambitions. It is
in such mood and at such opportunities, therefore, that his
great and entirely personal style is most completely under his
control, can deploy its full resources and rejoice unafraid in
its own power. At such moments his style is the prose counterpart of the supreme numbers which awe us in *Paradise Lost,*
so far as the occasion and the lesser range of prose will admit.
Sometimes it comes and passes in a single gust, as when he
speaks of the "poet, soaring in the high region of his fancies,
with his garland and singing robes about him." Or, yet more
magnificent:

> The Apocalypse of St. John is the majestic image of
> a high and stately tragedy, shutting up and intermin-
> gling her solemn scenes and acts with a sevenfold
> chorus of hallelujahs and harping symphonies.

To keep on such a level would be to make his prose purely
lyrical; and, therefore, in the sustained passages, Milton starts
from a lower stage. Take that fine passage in the *Areopagitica:*

> Books are not absolutely dead things, but do contain
> a potency of life in them to be as active as that soul
> was whose progeny they are; nay, they do preserve
> as in a vial the purest efficacy and extraction of that
> living intellect that bred them. I know they are as
> lively, and as vigorously productive, as those fabu-
> lous dragon's teeth; and being sown up and down
> may chance to spring up armed men. And yet, on
> the other hand, unless wariness be used, as good,
> almost, kill a man as kill a good book. Who kills a
> man kills a reasonable creature, God's image; but he
> who destroys a good book, kills reason itself, kills
> the image of God, as it were, in the eye. Many a
> man lives a burthen to the earth; but a good book is
> the precious lifeblood of a master spirit, embalmed
> and treasured up on purpose to a life beyond life.
> 'Tis true, no age can restore life, . . . and revolutions
> of ages do not oft recover the loss of rejected truth,
> for the want of which whole nations fare the worse.

This weighty piece of reflection is almost modern in form.
From it Milton rises or descends at will, until he reaches his
majestic and characteristic level, shown in the following passage:

> Good and evil we know in the field of this world
> grow up together almost inseparably; and the knowl-
> edge of good is so involved and interwoven with the
> knowledge of evil, and in so many cunning resem-
> blances hardly to be discerned, that those confused
> seeds which were imposed upon Psyche as an in-
> cessant labour to cull out, and sort asunder, were not
> more intermixed. It was from out the rind of one
> apple tasted, that the knowledge of good and evil,
> as two twins cleaving together, leaped forth into the
> world. . . . He that can apprehend and consider vice
> with all her baits and seeming pleasures, and yet
> abstain, and yet distinguish, and yet prefer that which
> is truly better, he is the true wayfaring Christian. I
> cannot praise a fugitive and cloistered virtue, unex-
> ercised and unbreathed, that never sallies out and
> sees her adversary, but slinks out of the race, where
> that immortal garland is to be run for, not without
> dust and heat. Assuredly we bring not innocence into
> the world, we bring impurity much rather; that which
> purifies us is trial, and trial is by what is contrary.
> That virtue therefore which is but a younging in the
> contemplation of evil, and knows not the utmost which
> vice promises to her followers, and rejects it, is but
> a blank virtue, not a pure; her whiteness is but an
> excremental whiteness.

Praise is impotent before such prose as this, which only Milton
could transcend. Often quoted, we must yet quote again the
words in which he achieves that feat:

> Methinks I see in my mind a noble and puissant nation
> rousing herself like a strong man after sleep, and
> shaking her invincible locks. Methinks I see her as
> an eagle mewing her mighty youth, and kindling her
> undazzled eyes at the full midday beam: purging and
> unscaling her long-abused sight at the fountain itself
> of heavenly radiance; while the whole noise of ti-
> morous and flocking birds, with those also that love
> the twilight, flutter about, amazed at what she means,
> and in their envious gabble would prognosticate a
> year of sects and schisms.

So puissant a passage (to use Milton's own word) is not to be
found elsewhere, and could hardly be written again. We could
no more build like the builders of Egypt than we could write

in this colossal manner. The Miltonic prose overtops our praise, and seems framed for a larger generation. It stands with the columns of Memphis and Babylonian gardens, and all primeval survivals which have testified, or still testify, to the living little, of the spacious dead. Let us not overlay it with the parasitical growth of vain words. (pp. 83-9)

> Francis Thompson, "Milton," in his Literary Crit-
> icisms, edited by Rev. Terence L. Connolly, S.J.,
> E. P. Dutton and Company, Inc., 1948, pp. 83-9.

LYTTON STRACHEY   (essay date 1908)

[Strachey was an early twentieth-century English biographer, critic, essayist, and short story writer. He is best known for his biographies Eminent Victorians *(1918),* Queen Victoria *(1921), and* Elizabeth and Essex: A Tragic History *(1928). Critics agree that these iconoclastic reexaminations of historical figures revolutionized the course of modern biographical writing. Strachey's literary criticism is also considered incisive. In the following excerpt from an essay originally published in 1908 in honor of the tercentenary of Milton's birth, he discusses Milton's love of art and comments on his character as it is revealed in his works.]*

The tercentenary of the year of Milton's birth, which is being celebrated at Cambridge by an Exhibition of portraits and manuscripts, to be followed later by a performance of *Comus*, suggests, after the manner of anniversaries, some questionings as to the value of Milton's achievement and his place in the history of letters. That his place is a very high one no lover of poetry today would wish to dispute, for never has Milton's fame been more assured or more widely recognized than at the present moment. But if the quantity of his merit can admit of no doubt whatever, its quality is not quite so easy to decide upon. In more ways than one Milton's genius presents difficulties and contradictions to the critic who attempts to sum up in a single judgment the nature of his work as a whole. To the world at large he stands out as before all things the poet of sublimity, of austere and awful grandeur, walking in a noble severity among the highest places of art. But if we open his pages, we are struck by a very different impression; we are overwhelmed by a flowing river of enchanting sound, by a mass of words which seem to be there for no other reason than because they are beautiful, and we begin to feel that the real fascination of poetry such as this is simply the fascination of rhetoric. Traditionally, Milton is the greatest of religious poets, and that fundamentally the temper of his mind was profoundly religious it is impossible to doubt. Yet the part of his work which has least withstood the assaults of time—which is most obviously and certainly out of date at the present day—is his theology, while his highest claim to immortality rests upon the amazing splendour and the imperishable glamour with which he has invested the ministers of vice. It is, however, easy to perceive one common element in all these conflicting qualities—one characteristic which, from the beginning to the end of his poetic career, never deserted Milton—his noble and passionate love of art. He is the supreme artist of our race; that, surely, must be the first and last word in any appreciation of the author of *Paradise Lost*. And it is precisely from this point of view that Milton may be most clearly contrasted with the only figure in English literature which, without a shadow of a doubt, towers above his own. Shakespeare was not primarily an artist, in the sense in which the word may be applied to Milton—the sense which connotes a method no less than a result. He worked as no conscientious artist would work, hastily and unevenly; he produced a *King Lear* one day, a *Timon*

of Athens the next; he was 'fancy's child'. No doubt his method was that best adapted to his temperament, and it would be rash indeed to affirm that any other method could have produced a greater body of achievement; but it was not the method of the artist. Who can imagine Milton even dreaming of writing the kind of stuff that it pleased Shakespeare to throw off in some of his careless hours? But the comparison becomes still more clearly marked if for Shakespeare we substitute one of the average poets of Milton's youth. What a difference there is between the exquisite unforced lyrics of the Elizabethans and the consummate songs of *Comus*! It is the difference between a wild rose and a rose in a garden bed. Sir Henry Wotton, who was an acute critic, noticed the change at once. He was 'ravished', he wrote to Milton, by 'a certain Dorique delicacy in your Songs and Odes, wherunto I must plainly confess to have seen yet nothing parallel in our Language.' The publication of *Comus* did indeed mark an epoch in English literature; henceforward our poetry could never be the half-unconscious thing it had been before. In Milton's hands it became an elaborate product, the outcome of patient care and infinite craft. The ideal poem was 'not to be raised from the heat of youth, or the vapours of wine, like that which flows at waste from the pen of some vulgar amorist, or the trencher fury of a rhyming parasite, nor to be obtained by the invocation of Dame Memory and her Siren daughters, but by devout prayer to that eternal Spirit who can enrich with all utterance and knowledge, and sends out his Seraphim with the hallowed fire of his altar to touch and purify the lips of whom he pleases; to this must be added industrious and select reading, steady observation, insight into all seemly and generous arts and affairs.' Such was the spirit which went to the making of *Paradise Lost*.

It is the artist that appears most distinctly in what is perhaps the most sympathetic of the many portraits now gathered together at the Memorial Exhibition at Christ's College—the charming presentment of Milton as a young man, which usually hangs in the College Hall. . . . The authenticity of the picture is merely traditional; but it is impossible to believe that the beautiful oval face with the great eyes and the arched nose and the long hair could have belonged to any save a poet, or to any poet save John Milton. There is a curious delicacy, an aristocratic refinement, about these fascinating features which inevitably put one in mind of Milton's own account of that 'certain niceness of nature, an honest haughtiness and self-esteem either of what I was or what I might be,' which, he says, kept him above the 'low descents of mind' when he was a young man. The expression of the countenance is full of the exclusiveness and of the preciosity of a youthful artist who has just begun to recognize his own high worth; but there is more in it than that. There is a dreamy sensuousness in the eyes and in the full lips which betrays the author of the lovely and delicious cadences of "L'Allegro" and the "Arcades" and "Lycidas". That, in spite of his Puritanism, there was a strain in Milton of what might almost be called paganism, no reader of his works can doubt. His well-known observation upon the chief attributes of poetry—that it is simple, sensuous, and passionate—is in itself an indication of this, and his poems show clearly enough that the definition was by no means a random one. The truth is, it would be difficult to name a poet who was more completely occupied with the 'sensuous' side of things—the side, that is to say, which appeals directly to the senses. He has none of the intellectual subtlety of Donne, none of the psychological intensity of Pope, none of the spiritual tenderness of Wordsworth; his merits depend almost entirely upon a faculty of lofty and grandiose vision coupled with a complete mastery of the resources of verbal sound. His imagination, within its own province, was supreme; but it was, so to speak, a material imagination, perpetually concerned with objects which, however vast and however splendid, still remained objects of sense. Between his imagination and that of Shakespeare, with its lightning flashes into the heart of man and the mystery of the universe, what a gulf is fixed! Perhaps the most remarkable fact about Milton's genius is that he never allowed his 'sensuousness' to get the better of his art. It is certain that he realized the danger, for, alike in his earliest work and in his latest, in *Comus* as in *Samson,* there are traces of an inward struggle, of an effort to shake off the thraldom of physical beauty, of a determination to worship only the highest and best. 'Yet beauty, though injurious, hath strange power,' exclaim the Chorus in *Samson* after the departure of Dalila, and the phrase might be taken as a summary of the curious conflict of ideals which finds its synthesis in Milton's art.

Underlying and supporting his artistic consciousness there was, of course, that force of character which makes Milton so striking and eminent a figure in the history, not only of literature, but of the world. The high determination with which at the beginning of his career he set out to accomplish a task of superhuman difficulty, and the triumphant success which crowned the guiding resolution of his life—these are things for which it is difficult to find a parallel, and which, when one reflects upon them, seem more thrilling than the strangest romance. Yet the moral qualities that enabled him to achieve so much brought with them another characteristic of a less pleasant nature—a characteristic which is the chief cause of the often-expressed dislike of Milton as a man—his lack of humour. If he had taken himself less seriously, perhaps he would never have written *Paradise Lost;* and the author of *Paradise Lost* no doubt had a right to take himself seriously; but who can help regretting that he took himself as seriously as he did? One wonders what Shakespeare would have said to some of the autobiographical references in Milton's prose works. But it is uncharitable to raise comparisons. We must, after all, take great men as we find them. If Milton was a confirmed egotist, he was none the less the creator of Satan; and even his egotism, if we are to believe Coleridge, was not without its value. 'It is a sense of his intense egotism,' says that fine critic, 'that gives me the greatest pleasure in reading Milton's works. The egotism of such a man is a revelation of spirit.' (pp. 104-08)

> *Lytton Strachey, "Milton," in his* Spectatorial Essays, *Harcourt Brace Jovanovich, Inc., 1964, pp. 104-08.*

ANDREW LANG   (essay date 1912)

[One of England's most powerful men of letters during the closing decades of the nineteenth century, Lang is remembered today as the editor of the "color fairy books," a twelve-volume series of fairy tales which began with The Blue Fairy Book *in 1889 and ended with* The Lilac Fairy Book *in 1910. The stories in these volumes were drawn from various cultures and grew out of Lang's extensive research into early languages, literatures, folktales, myths, and legends. As one of the chief proponents of Romanticism in a critical battle that pitted revivalist Romanticists against defenders of Naturalism and Realism, Lang espoused a strong preference for romantic adventure novels. His critical works therefore show little sympathy for the works of Realists or Naturalists. In the following excerpt from a literary history originally published in 1912, he favorably surveys a selection of Milton's poetry.]*

A man's best poems are usually written before he is 30. Milton was 21 when (1629) he produced the ode **"On the Morning of Christ's Nativity"**. In this splendid and immortal piece he invokes, as always, "the heavenly Muse," and, in addition to the beautiful measure of the Hymn, in harmony rivalling Spenser's, he already strikes his own sonorous note, as in "The trumpet spoke not to the armed throng," a glorious combination and harmony of sounds. Here advance

> The helmed cherubim
> And sworded seraphim,

who are, in *Paradise Lost,* to make the floor of heaven

> Ring to the roar of an angel onset.

The stanzas on the flight of the ancient classic deities, even the genius of "haunted spring and dale," and the nymphs, are of a high and melancholy imagination. But Milton "found the subject to be above the years he had when he wrote it," and "was nothing satisfied with what he had done". After deliberately selecting and weighing many themes, for example that of Arthur, he returned when old, blind, and fallen on what he deemed "evil days," to the topic of wars in heaven, and man's Fall and Redemption.

"L'Allegro" and **"Il Penseroso"** are impeccable early poems. Milton is not yet so Puritan as to denounce Merry England, "the jocund rebecks," the dancing youths and maids, the tales of fairy Mab and the Brownie, and the stage: if Jonson and sweetest Shakespeare be the playwrights. Milton was deeply learned in the classics, but there is none of the pedantry of his age in his allusions to Prince Memnon, or "that starr'd Aethiop Queen," though now many readers must turn to notes for information about them. Octosyllabic lines had never before been written with such variety of grave and gay as by Milton, who in verse is a supreme master and "inventor of harmonies". Spenser had not his variety: in Milton's poems, as in his lines **"On a Solemn Music"**

> The bright Seraphim, in burning row
> Their loud uplifted angel-trumpets blow.

Yet Milton's party in the State set its face like a flint against the "solemn music" of the churches as against the "joyous rebecks" of the lads and lasses.

In 1634 Milton produced a masque, the one great and enduring masque of the many that were played in the halls of princes and peers. *Comus* was presented at Ludlow Castle, the house of Lord Bridgewater, President of Wales, and the actors were his family. The Muse is heavenly, the theme is divine Chastity: there is no such awful contrast to the purity of the Lady as that which Fletcher, in "The Faithful Shepherdess," presents in the person of the deplorable Cloe. As in the plays of Euripides, an explanatory prologue is spoken by a Spirit, who later appears as the shepherd Thyrsis. We learn that Comus (Revelry) the son of Dionysus the Wine God and Circe the enchantress of the "Odyssey," has settled in "this ominous wood" in Britain; tempts travellers with the crystal cup of his sorceries, and changes them into beast-headed adventurers. Then Comus enters with his torch-bearing company, swine, bulls, goats, bears, and in beautiful lines, recommends his unholy ethics.

> Come, let us our rites begin,
> 'Tis only daylight that makes sin.

But something warns him that a chaste being draws near; he dismisses his troop; the Lady enters, she has lost her way in the dark wood, her brothers have strayed apart, she hopes to meet merry peasants who will guide her; she calls them by a song, and Comus appears, summoned by the notes

> How sweetly did they float upon the wings
> Of silence, through the empty-vaulted night
> At every fall smoothing the raven down
> Of darkness, till it smiled.

Thinking Comus an honest shepherd, the Lady follows him: her brothers enter in search of her, the Spirit warns them of her danger, and gives them such virtuous herbs as Hermes gives to Odysseus in Circe's isle. Armed with these they scatter the satyrs of Comus, but only Sabrina, nymph of the Severn, called and replying in lyrics of ineffable beauty, can release the Lady from the enchanted chair of Comus. The majesty, delicacy, and beauty of the ideas are matched by the exquisite music of the blank verse and lyric passages, for at the age of 26 and in his poetic prime of youth, Milton was already a master of every technical resource of poetry; of everything, except humour and the power of creating human characters. He might compose poetry more august and sustained than *Comus* but he never could be a better poet than he was in 1634. Sanity, order, form, absence of vain conceit and ingenious antithesis were as natural to Milton as they were unknown to Donne and the Fletchers.

Milton's next great poem, **"Lycidas,"** was composed shortly before he left Horton, early in 1638, on a visit to Italy. The occasion, which other Cambridge poets celebrated, was the death of a friend, Edward King, drowned in crossing the Irish Channel. We do not know from external evidence that Milton was more attached to King, personally, than Shelley was to Keats. **"Lycidas"** is not a cry from an almost broken heart, as are parts of the "In Memoriam" of Tennyson. It has been said that admiration of **"Lycidas"** is a test of a man's capacity for appreciating poetry,—a hard saying for Dr. Johnson. That Milton had a true affection for King the classic allusions and the pastoral guise of his ode may cause some to doubt. But there is deep natural feeling in the plangent words,

> But oh! the heavy change now thou art gone,
> Now thou art gone and never must return!

The story disguised as a friendship between Theocritean shepherds is really that of a college friendship between two boyish poets, and no later friendships can be so tender, close, dear; the lost voice ever echoing in the memory. The verse is a solemn music: the mingling of the figures of classical mythology with St. Peter, and with Camus, "reverend sire," vexed Dr. Johnson [see excerpt dated 1779], but he would have been equally vexed by the only Oxford pendant to this Cambridge lament, the "Thyrsis"of Matthew Arnold.

Indeed what really annoyed the good Doctor was the certainly regrettable introduction of an attack on his beloved Church of England, and the ominous mention of "that two-handed engine at the door," which did not strike once, but often, nor only at the neck of an Archbishop, but slew Strafford, Hamilton, and the King.

"The dread voice" comes across the shepherd's dirge; the Sicilian Muse, the Muse of Theocritus, is bidden to return, but to Milton she will not come again. We think of him, at this time, as "young but intolerably severe," like Apollo in Matthew Arnold's "Empedocles on Etna". Like Wordsworth and Shelley he was devoid of humour,—and thus fails—as Shelley did not fail, thanks to his geniality, and kindness and charms— to win universal sympathy. Think of Shakespeare,—who does not love the man, and who does dare to love Milton! He was

not vain with the childlike vanity of some poets, but he was as proud as his own Satan. He not only had genius next to the highest, but he knew it, tended it, cared for it, and could scarcely find a task that was great enough for his powers. We respect his self-knowledge, applaud his resolution, and are much happier with Shakespeare and Scott, who never gave a thought to their genius.

On returning from Italy to his country, the country of "the Bishops' Wars," Milton, in Aldersgate Street, devoted himself to the education of his nephews, to sonnets, and then to prose works . . . , all written in the cause of sacred Liberty. He, like the old Scots Earl, did not love "the new liberty" as offered by the Presbyterian, whose name was "old priest writ large". His marriage, in 1643, to a lady of a loyal family, Mary Powell, was unhappy: she went back, in a short time, to her own people. In 1645 she returned, had three daughters, and died in 1652. His private unhappiness made Milton plead vainly for freedom of divorce, a remedy which has its own unsatisfactory aspect. In 1652 Milton lost his eyesight, like his

> Blind Thamyris and blind Maeonides,
> And Teiresisas and Phineus, prophets old.

His sonnets are his only poems of this period; when he argued for divorce, and for liberty of printing, defended the slaying of his King, wrangled with political opponents in English and Latin, and was Latin Secretary to the Commonwealth. An accomplished sonneteer in Italian, Milton in English observed, usually, the strict Petrarchian rules; and had the wisdom and self-restraint to write not too many sonnets, most of them choicely good. Even that in which he commemorates the noble Aboyne, and the son of Col of the left hand, and Gilespie Grumach is a good sonnet. He mourned for the late Massacre in Piedmont, but not for those of Drogheda and Dundee. His nobility of soul never declares itself more gloriously than in the sonnets on his blindness, of these eyes.

> Overplied,
> In Liberty's defence, my glorious task.

But there was no liberty left for Anglicans, Catholics, or Presbyterians in Scotland, who were turned out of their court of General Assembly.

After rejecting many topics which had occurred to him as possible subjects for his life-long purpose to write a great Epic, Milton returned to the inspiration of the Heavenly Muse, and settled (1655-1667) on *Paradise Lost*. He did wisely, for a human epic like the others, the "Iliad," the "Odyssey," and all the Greek, Roman, Italian, and French imitations of these, demands a pell-mell of human characters, noble, treacherous, and humorous. In creating human characters Milton had little skill, and, in *Paradise Lost* there are but two, Adam and Eve. In Genesis they are extremely human, but Milton had to make them at first perfect, and place them in a situation where no other human beings ever were. For the rest, he had the magnificent Satan, fallen through a pride and independence of character with which the poet was in sympathy; while Belial and Abdiel are also, each in his own way, heroic. The heavenly angels are less clearly marked and discriminated.

In Athens, Milton would have rivalled Æschylus; with Euripides he does not pair. He has the greatest of stages, the universe, chaos, heaven and hell. His theme is the mystery of human fortunes; man, what he might be, what he is. He uses a non-Biblical poetic legend, the war in heaven, which had been treated. . .by an Anglo-Saxon poet, and has a parallel in the mythology of the Kaitish, a savage tribe of Central Australia. There too the great self-created Atnatu of the highest heaven hurls his disobedient children down to earth. It was inevitable that Satan, not Adam, should become the Hero, as Mephistopheles, not Faust, is the hero of Goethe's play—is the interesting character. Milton in his Puritan way describes himself as "Not sedulous by nature to indite wars," hitherto "alone heroic deemed," while modest domestic patience and heroic martyrdom are unsung, or as in the case of Jeanne d'Arc, have proved too lofty a theme for any poet. But Milton being a poet is subject to inevitable poetic limitations. The patience which Eve displayed in everyday domestic life, after her expulsion from Paradise, would not be a theme for the epic; and Milton "never stoops his wing" when he sings of the Raising of the Banner of Satan, and "the banner cry of Hell".

In the true spirit of epics, his poem ends with no clash of arms, no blare of trumpets, but with "a dying fall";

> They, hand in hand, with wandering steps and slow,
> Through Eden took their solitary way;

in such manner, too, ceases the "Iliad,"

> Thus held they funeral for knightly Hector.

Milton's blank verse is the stateliest, most variously tuneful, and most relieved by varieties of pause, most sonorous with the mysterious music of ancient names. All in this is perfect. The verse-paragraphs—the opening paragraphs is of thirty lines— could only be arrayed by Milton. We do not often meet what seems to us a bathos, as when Satan, fallen from heaven, "views the dismal situation". After viewing the dismal situation Satan is himself again:—

> All is not lost; the unconquerable will,
> And study of revenge, immortal hate,
> And courage never to submit or yield,
> And what is else not to be overcome,
> That glory never shall His wrath or might
> Extort from me.

Milton is not pedantic, but as Homer has his catalogue of ships and heroes, Milton outdoes him with *his* catalogue of fallen angels, gods of the nations, Moloch, Chemosh, Ashtoreth, Dagon, Osiris, Isis, Horus, "the Ionian gods of Javan's issue," and they

> who with Saturn old
> Fled over Adria to the Hersperian fields,
> And o'er the Celtic roam'd the utmost isles.

Milton's knowledge was equal to every demand, and his were

> the unconquerable will
> And courage never to submit or yield.

But, magnificent as he is, Milton has always his eye on that Achæan "father of the rest," and he copies Homer's bridal-bed of Zeus and Hera

> under foot the violet,
> Crocus and hyacinth with rich inlay
> Broidered the ground.

"And beneath them the divine earth sent forth fresh new grass, and dewy lotus, crocus, and hyacinth." But Milton gives twenty lines where Homer gives four.

In comparing the two greatest of epic poets—the first, Homer, with the last, Milton,—we observe that each sums up in himself the whole thought and experience, and the poetic expression of a world that lies behind him. Each "takes his own where he finds it," "makes all men's wit his own," as Ben Jonson said, in an invidious sense, of Shakespeare. Homer has his

debts to old nameless poets; Milton displays his debts to Homer, and to Greek, Roman, and Celtic poets and historians, to Anglo-Saxons, Dutch, Italians, to all song and all learning, and all that he takes he transfigures, and rounds into a harmonious whole, the immortal Epic. (pp. 347-54)

In *Paradise Regained,* a sequel which Mr. Ellwood, a Quaker, reports himself to have suggested to Milton, the great qualities of the poet are unimpaired. His verse is that which he alone could wield. His sonorous catalogues, the music of names, the eagle glance over all the kingdoms of earth and the glory of them, the triumph of the pure spirit over carnal joys; nay the haunting memories of old romance,

> Of fairy damsels, met in forest wide,
> By knights of Logres, or of Lyones,
> Lancelot, or Pelleas, or Pellenore,

these are all present, all are captivating.

It is natural to wish that, while young, Milton had followed his dominant motive into Arthur's fairy land, and told the story of Galahad and the Holy Grail: the purity that wins the Beatific Vision.

His *Samson Agonistes,* in the severest style of Greek tragedy, sets forth his own strength foiled by blindness, mocked by the dull triumphs of the wanton crowd, and triumphant in death. The occasional unrhymed verse of the chorus, not in decasyllabic lines, stands for Milton's curious antipathy for rhyme, in which, when he chose, he excelled. The subtleties and sophistries of Delilah express his idea of one type of womanhood, the other type shines in the steadfast love of the repentant Eve. The poem, with all the strength, has less of the charm of Milton than his other great works.

Milton died in 1674; a poet who in one sense might be styled "self-taught," for while he was so deeply read, his verse was no echo, nor ever can be re-echoed. It is foolish but natural to appraise the relative greatness of great poets, but, Shakespeare apart, it is to the lonely Milton that the world has always awarded the crown of England's greatest. (pp. 354-55)

> *Andrew Lang, "Caroline Poets: Milton," in his* History of English Literature: From "Beowulf" to Swinburne, *1912. Reprint by Longmans, Green and Co., 1928, pp. 347-55.*

GILBERT K. CHESTERTON (essay date 1917)

[*Regarded as one of England's premier men of letters during the first half of the twentieth century, Chesterton is best known today as a colorful bon vivant, a witty essayist, and as the creator of the Father Brown mysteries and the fantasy* The Man Who Was Thursday (1908). *Much of his work reveals his childlike enjoyment of life and reflects his pronounced Anglican and, later, Roman Catholic beliefs. His essays are characterized by their humor, frequent use of paradox, and chatty, rambling style. In the following excerpt, he studies the apparent contrast between Milton the man and Milton the poet and considers Milton's place among his contemporaries.*]

All the mass of acute and valuable matter written or compiled about Milton leaves eternally an unanswered question; a difficulty felt by all, if expressed by few, of his readers. That difficulty is a contrast between the man and his poems. There exists in the world a group of persons who perpetually try to prove that Shakespeare was a clown and could not have written about princes, or that he was a drunkard and could not have written about virtue. I think there is a slight fallacy in the argument. But I wonder that they have not tried the much more tempting sport of separating the author of "L'Allegro" from the author of the *Defensus Populi Anglicani*. For the contrast between the man Milton and the poet Milton is very much greater than is commonly realized. I fear that the shortest and clearest way of stating it is that when all is said and done, he is a poet whom we cannot help liking, and a man whom we cannot like. I find it far easier to believe that an intoxicated Shakespeare wrote the marble parts of Shakespeare than that a marble Milton wrote the intoxicated, or, rather, intoxicating, parts of Milton. Milton's character was cold; he was one of those men who had every virtue except the one virtue needful. While other poets may have been polygamists from passion, he was polygamous on principle. While other artists were merely selfish, he was egoistic.

The public has a quick eye for portraits, a very keen nose for personality; and across two centuries the traditional picture of Milton dictating to his daughters till they were nearly dead has kept the truth about Milton; it has not taken the chill off. But though the mass of men feel the fact Milton after two hundred years, they seldom read the poetry of Milton at all. And so, because Milton the man was cold, they have got over the difficulty by saying that the poet Milton is cold too; cold, classical, marmoreal. But the poetry of Milton is not cold. He did in his later years, and in a fit of bad temper, write a classical drama, which is the only one of his works which is really difficult to read. But taken as a whole he is a particularly poetical poet, as fond of symbols and witchery as Coleridge, as fond of colored pleasures as Keats. He is sometimes sufficiently amorous to be called tender; he is frequently sufficiently amorous to be called sensual. Even his religion is not always heathen in his poetry. If you heard for the first time the line,

> By the dear might of Him that walked the waves,

you would only fancy that some heart of true religious heat and humility, like Crashaw or George Herbert, had for a moment achieved a technical triumph and found a faultless line. If you read for the first time,

> But come, thou Goddess fair and free,
> In heaven yclept Euphrosyne,

you would think that the most irresponsible of the Elizabethans had uttered it as he went dancing down the street, believing himself in Arcady. If you read

> Blossoms and fruits at once of golden hue
> Appeared, with gay enamelled colors mixed,

or

> Silence was pleased. Now glowed the firmament
> With living sapphires,

you would think that all the rich dyes of the Orient and the Middle Ages had met, as they do in some quite modern poet, such as Keats or even Swinburne. If you read the account of the ale and the elf and the Christmas sports in "L'Allegro," you might think them written by the most rollicking of rustic poets; if you read some lines about Eve in *Paradise Lost,* you might think them written at once by the most passionate and the most chivalrous of lovers. *Paradise Lost* is not dull; it is not even frigid. Anyone who can remember reading the first few books as a boy will know what I mean; it is a romance, and even a fantastic romance. There is something in it of *Thalabe the Destroyer;* something wild and magical about the image of the empire in the abyss scaling the turrets of the

magician who is king of the cosmos. There is something Oriental in its design and its strange colors. One cannot imagine Flaxman illustrating Milton as he illustrated Homer. Nor is it even true that the rich glimpse of tropical terrors are conveyed in a clear outline of language. No one took more liberties with English, with metre, and even with common sense than Milton; an instance, of course, is the well-known superlative about Adam and his children.

Milton was not a simple epic poet like Homer, nor was he even a specially clear epic poet like Virgil. If these two gentlemen had studied his verse, they would have certainly acknowledged its power; but they would have shrunk from its inversions, its abrupt ellipses, its sentences that sometimes come tail foremost. I might even say that Homer reading Milton might have much the same feelings as Milton reading Browning. He would have found

> Or of the eternal coeternal beam

a trifle obscure, and

> nor sometimes forget,
> Those other two, equalled with me in fate, etc., etc.,

almost entirely unintelligible. In this sense it is absurd to set up Milton as a superlatively clear and classic poet. In the art of turning his sentences inside out he never had an equal; and the only answer is to say that the result is perfect; though it is inside out, yet somehow it is right side out.

Nevertheless, the tradition which puts Milton with Virgil and the large and lucid poets, must possess and does possess some poetic significance. It lies, I think, in this: the startling contrast between Milton and the century in which he lived. He was not supremely classical; but he was classical in a time when classicism was almost forgotten. He was not specially lucid; but he was moderately intelligible in an age when nearly all poets were proud of being unintelligible; an age of one hundred Brownings gone mad. The seventeenth century was a most extraordinary time, which still awaits its adequate explanation. It was something coming after the Renaissance which developed and yet darkened and confused it, just as a tree might be more tangled for growing. The puns that had been in Shakespeare few and bad became numberless and ingenious. The schisms of thought which under Wickliffe and Luther had at least the virtue of heartiness, and were yet full of a human hesitation, became harsh, incessant, exclusive; every morning one heard that a new mad sect had excommunicated humanity. The grammars of Greek and Latin, which the young princes of the Renaissance had read as if they were romances, were now being complicated by bald-headed pedants until no one on earth could read them. Theology, which could always in light moments be given the zest of an amusement, became a disease with the Puritans. War, which had been the sport of gentlemen, was now rapidly becoming the ill-smelling science for engineers it still remains. The air was full of anger; and not a young sort of anger; exasperation on points of detail perpetually renewed. If the Renaissance was like a splendid wine, the sevententh century might be compared to the second fermentation into vinegar. But whatever metaphor we use the main fact is certain; the age was horribly complex; it was learned, it was crabbed, and in nearly all its art and utterance, it was crooked.

Remember the wonderfully witty poets of Charles I.; those wonderfully witty poets who were incomprehensible at the first reading and dull even when one could comprehend them. Think of the scurrilous war of pamphlets, in which Milton himself engaged; pages full of elaborate logic which no one can follow, and elaborate scandals which everyone has forgotten. Think of the tortured legalities of Crown and Parliament, quoting against each other precedents of an utterly different age; think of the thick darkness of diplomacy that covers the meaning (if it had any) of the Thirty Years' War. The seventeenth century was a labyrinth; it was full of corners and crotchets. And against this sort of background Milton stands up as simple and splendid as Apollo. His style, which must always have been splendid, appeared more pure and translucent than it really was in contrast with all the mad mystification and darkness. (pp. 463-66)

Gilbert K. Chesterton, "Milton: Man and Poet," in
The Catholic World, *Vol. CIV, No. 622, January,*
1917. pp. 463-70.

E. M. W. TILLYARD (essay date 1930)

[*Tillyard was an English scholar of Renaissance literature whose studies of John Milton, William Shakespeare, and the epic form are widely respected. In the following excerpt from his study* Milton, *he considers the meaning and unity of* Comus *and comments on the work's place in the Milton canon.*]

Readers of **Comus** have usually failed to see that it is an experiment, not entirely unsuccessful, in drama. Johnson wrote as follows:

> As a drama it is deficient. The action is not probable. A Masque, in those parts where supernatural intervention is admitted, must indeed be given up to all the freaks of imagination; but, so far as the action is merely human, it ought to be reasonable, which can hardly be said of the conduct of the two Brothers; who, when their Sister sinks with fatigue in a pathless wilderness, wander both away together in search of berries too far to find their way back, and leave a helpless Lady to all the sadness and danger of solitude . . . The discourse of the Spirit is too long; an objection that may be made to almost all the following speeches; they have not the sprightliness of a dialogue animated by reciprocal contention, but seem rather declamations deliberately composed, and formally repeated, on a moral question [see excerpt dated 1779].

The usual answer to this charge is that Johnson was looking for what is not there, that Milton does not intend to be dramatic. 'We must not read **Comus** with an eye to the stage,' wrote Warton, 'or with the expectation of dramatic propriety. . . . **Comus** is a suite of speeches, not interesting by discrimination of character; not conveying a variety of incidents, nor gradually exciting curiosity: but perpetually attracting attention by sublime sentiment, by fanciful imagery of the richest vein, by no exuberance of picturesque description, poetical allusion, and ornamental expression.' And the general opinion would be that such blemishes as the improbability of the plot and the singular dramatic ineptitude of the Elder Brother's discourse on chastity can easily be forgiven for the sheer splendour of the poetry.

All such criticism rests on a fallacy, because not a little of **Comus** is deliberately and successfully dramatic. Johnson and Warton overlook the really dramatic portions altogether; and those elements that are usually regarded as blemishes would not be blemishes at all, had not Milton, by writing dramatically in parts, forced us to exact in the other parts a kind of probability new in his writing. The fact is that Milton is not always certain whether or not he is in Arcadia. The Elder Brother's speech on chastity, beautiful in itself, would be perfectly in

place in the unalloyed Miltonic Arcadia; but a few lines later (480) Milton begins writing in the vein of the Elizabethan dramatists and arouses a new set of expectations.

> *Eld. Bro.* List, list I hear
> Som far off hallow break the silent Air.
>   *2 Bro.* Me thought so too; what should it be?
>   *Eld. Bro.* For certain
> Either som one like us night-founder'd here,
> Or els som neighbour Wood-man, or at worst,
> Som roaving Robber calling to his fellows.
>   *2 Bro.* Heav'n keep my sister, agen agen and neer,
> Best draw, and stand upon our guard.
>   *Eld. Bro.* Ile hallow,
> If he be friendly he comes well, if not,
> Defence is a good cause, and Heav'n be for us.

> *The attendant Spirit habited like a Shepherd*

>   That hallow I should know, what are you? speak;
> Com not too neer, you fall on iron stakes else.
>   *Spir.* What voice is that, my young Lord? speak agen.
>   *2 Bro.* O brother, 'tis my father Shepherd sure.

Whereupon, with a sudden relapse into Arcadianism, the Elder Brother says

> *Thrysis?* Whose artful strains have oft delaid
> The huddling brook to hear his madrigal,
> And sweeten'd every muskrose of the dale.

Indeed, the mixture of styles in **Comus** has never been sufficiently recognised. But until it is, one cannot put **Comus** in its right place among the early poems of Milton. Let us examine the fluctuations of style at the beginning.

The opening speech of the Attendant Spirit is a Euripidean prologue in which drama is not looked for, and the opening, rhymed, section of Comus's first speech leaves the sequel in doubt; but as soon as he begins speaking blank verse with

> Break off, break off, I feel the different pace
> Of som chast footing neer about this ground,

we see that Milton has definitely ventured beyond the undramatic couplet-writing he had used for "**Arcades.**" The rest of the speech is vigorous and, though not particularly reminiscent in style of any of the Elizabethan dramatists, yet dramatic enough to interest one in the action as well as in the poetry. And the Lady in the opening lines of her speech,

> This way the noise was, if mine ear be true,
> My best guide now,

fulfils the interest Comus's words has raised. But not for long. In spite of her plight, she exchanges the language of feeling for the exquisite circumlocutions of the pastoral. She cannot say plainly that her brothers left her when it was growing dark, but

> They left me then, when the gray-hooded Eev'n
> Like a sad Votarist in Palmers weed
> Rose from the hindmost wheels of *Phoebus* wain;

and from this she falls into a delightful conceit (betokening an ordered and leisurely exercise of the wits):

>   els O theevish Night
> Why shouldst thou, but for som fellonious end,
> In thy dark lantern thus close up the Stars,
> That nature hung in Heav'n, and fill'd their Lamps
> With everlasting oil;

from which she rises into lines which in their self-contained beauty can be detached with no loss of value from their histrionic setting:

> What might this be? A thousand fantasies
> Begin to throng into my memory
> Of calling shapes, and beckoning shadows dire,
> And airy tongues, that syllable mens names
> On Sands, and Shoars, and desert Wildernesses.

When the Lady speaks such poetry, we heed only the poetry and forget her desperate plight. Then follows a strain of rapturous meditation, and only the last few lines of the speech have a cadence faintly dramatic:

> I cannot hallow to my Brothers, but
> Such noise as I can make to be heard farthest
> Ile venter, for my new enliv'nd spirits
> Prompt me; and they perhaps are not far off.

Then follows the Echo Song, and with Comus's enthusiastic appreciation of it the dramatic interest rises again, for by now he is much more anxious than before to capture the Lady. In passing it may be noted that Comus is easily the livest character in the masque. There is a fullness and an opulence in his speeches not found in any of the others. Warburton and Newton object to Comus's hyperbolic description of what would happen to the world if strict temperance reigned:

> Th' earth cumber'd, and the wing'd air dark't with plumes,
> The herds would over-multitude their Lords,
> The Sea o'refraught would swell, and th' unsought diamonds
> Would so emblaze the forehead of the Deep,
> And so bestudd with Stars, that they below
> Would grow inur'd to light, and com at last
> To gaze upon the Sun with shameless brows.

Here the case is very different from what it was in the Lady's first speech: we need the dramatic context to justify the sentiments. Comus has worked himself up (he has been drinking too) and the hyperboles match the excited flashing of his eyes. To return from the digression, after describing with rapture the beauty of the Lady's song Comus hails her as if she were the Miranda of the desert; the Lady replies, and the two fall into a most curious stichomythia, that sounds like a very indifferent translation from Greek tragedy, ending

> *Co.* Imports their loss, beside the present need?
> *La.* No less then if I should my brothers loose.
> *Co.* Were they of manly prime, or youthful bloom?
> *La.* As smooth as *Hebe's* their unrazor'd lips.

In strange contrast to this classicising interlude there follows Comus's description of when he saw the two brothers, a description whose Elizabethan character Raleigh has already noted. And after a few lines the Lady, wondering whether the spot can now be found, slips back for a moment into the manner of the stichomythia;

> To find out that, good Shepherd, I suppose,
> In such a scant allowance of Star-light,
> Would overtask the best Land-Pilots art
> Without the sure guess of well-practiz'd feet.

Comus replies in the vein of *A Midsummer Night's Dream:*

> I know each lane, and every alley green.

In the next speech the Lady thinks good to be more dramatic and ends in the style of the post-Elizabethan drama:

> In a place
> Less warranted then this, or less secure
> I cannot be, that I should fear to change it.
> Eie me blest Providence, and square my triall
> To my proportion'd strength. Shepherd lead on.

An examination of the rest of the play before the lyrical close reveals much the same mixture of styles.

It is all the more noteworthy that Milton should have tried to be really dramatic in parts, because there was no apparent need for the attempt. He had written a very good masque in "**Arcades**" and he did not need to alter his style to write another. In fact, had he stuck to the earlier style, the masque, as a masque, would have been very much better. The inference is that Milton, in writing *Comus* as he did, had motives other than those of supplying a suitable entertainment for the Bridgewater family; and it would seem that he used *Comus* as a private experiment in dramatic style, in preparition for the great tragedy or Morality he at that time intended should be the end or one of the ends of his years of preparation. Although in *The Reason of Church Government* he states that it was in Italy he decided to use his life for writing a great poem, there can be no doubt that such had been his *hope* from much earlier years. In his poem to Manso ["**Mansus**"], written in 1639, he is meditating an epic; in his schemes preserved in the Trinity College Manuscript and dating in the next year he is planning a tragedy. In his earlier years, too, he probably had not made up his mind between the claims of these two great forms, if indeed he did not intend to use both; and it was inevitable that at some time he should have considered writing in the dramatic form that was the inheritance of the Elizabethan age. In *Comus* his dramatic aspirations are reflected.

That Milton was peculiarly conscious of the imperfections of *Comus* is made likely by the motto he prefixed to the first edition, published in 1637, and perhaps by the first lines of "**Lycidas**." The motto, which runs

> Eheu, quid volui misero mihi! floribus austrum
> Perditus,

is part of a sentence from Virgil's second Eclogue completed by the words

> et liquidis immisi fontibus apros.

'Alas, what was I thinking of; unhappy man, I have let the wind blow on my flowers.' Milton would hardly have expressed his fear of public opinion had he felt satisfied with what he had written. If the opening lines of "**Lycidas**" refer to *Comus,* as in all probability they do, there is additional proof that Milton was not satisfied with his dramatic experiment.

One of the passages, found in the Egerton and Trinity Manuscripts but omitted in the printed editions, shows how tentatively Milton could write in *Comus*. The Elder Brother's speech beginning at line 407 runs

> I do not, brother,
> Inferr, as if I thought my sisters state
> Secure without all doubt,

and in the manuscripts it continues thus,

> or question, no;
> I could be willing though now I' th' darke to trie
> A tough encounter with the shaggiest villain
> That lurks by hedge or lane of this dead circuit
> To have her by my side, though I were sure
> She might be free from perill where she is.

Moreover for 'I could be willing' Milton first wrote 'Beshrew me but I would,' and for 'encounter' 'passado.' Clearly he felt he had pushed his experiment too far towards realism and the language of men, and backed out before publication.

To bring a fresh unprejudiced judgment to bear on a poem so familiar as *Comus* is exceedingly difficult. During the years one has known it all sorts of extraneous and personal prejudices, whose origin is altogether forgotten, must have crept in. But the attempt is worth making. The final impression I get from *Comus* viewed as a whole is that when Milton wrote it he was not inspired by any compelling mood to give it unity. But this impression is not shared by all readers. Saurat writes: 'The theme of *Comus* is no artificial choice; it corresponds to one of the deepest needs in the poet: the need to triumph over sensuality which in itself implies sensuality.' Hanford seems to agree when he writes: 'The intensity with which Milton seized upon this virtue [chastity] as the center and test of his ethical idealism is explained by the strength of his own romantic passion, a passion which is still the chief force of his imaginative life.' Both statements seem to me greatly exaggerated. Of course Milton was concerned personally in the doctrine of chastity, but I cannot see that it had this great, almost exclusive, hold on his imagination. There were several other topics that held his mind at this time: such as ambition, the craving for knowledge, the desire for personal perfection (which would include other things than chastity), and absorption in poetic experiment. Milton may have been sufficiently interested in the question of chastity to choose it (in accordance with the example of Spenser and Fletcher) as the subject of his poem; but he did not feel strongly enough about it, he was not enough in earnest, to make it the instrument of a true poetic unity, the instrument for evoking and fusing a considerable portion of what most occupied his mind. *Comus* remains a by-product of his total activity. And as an artistic unity it cannot compare with the "**Nativity Ode**," "**L'Allegro**" and "**Il Penseroso**," and "**Lycidas**."

This does not mean that the parts are not superlatively good. There is in *Comus* finer poetry than anything Milton wrote earlier. Sir Henry Wotton was perfectly justified in writing, 'Wherein I should much commend the Tragical part, if the Lyrical did not ravish me with a certain Dorique delicacy in your Songs and Odes, whereunto I must plainly confess to have seen yet nothing parallel in our Language.' We do not know what Sir Henry Wotton really thought of the tragic part—the compliment he pays it is doubtful enough—but he certainly chooses to praise the parts of the poem rather than the whole.

By reason of the experiments it contains *Comus* corresponds to "**In Quintum Novembris**" and the fragment of "**The Passion**," but by the nature of those experiments it is far more interesting and important. Though the more dramatic passages may be stitched onto the smooth Arcadian texture of the rest, they go, some of them, to prove that Milton, had he persisted, could have compassed a style lively enough for a certain kind of tragedy. The meeting of the two Brothers and the Attendant Spirit, already quoted, is tense and exciting. Of a striking and dramatic opening to a speech Milton is already master: indeed several of the least dramatic speeches give good examples; like the Lady's first speech, the Elder Brother's which opens so splendidly with

> Unmuffle ye faint stars,

and Comus's

> Why are you vext Lady? why do you frown?

And once or twice a character will detach itself from its author and create for a moment the genuine dramatic illusion. When

the Lady, imprisoned in Comus's magic chair, begins her final speech with

> I had not thought to have unlockt my lips
> In this unhallow'd air,

the reader is transported in imagination to the enchanter's bower and watches the drama rather than listens to the melody of the speech. Such examples suffice to prove my contention. Milton was not a man to let slip what he had acquired. In *Comus* he had mastered the elements of drama, and had he thought good he might later have combined them to make a great tragedy. But he put off his attempt till too late in life. By the time he wrote *Samson Agonistes* his style had hardened: it could never be suppled to the degree of flexibility necessary for the writing of authentic drama.

More remains to be said of the manner in which Milton was concerned with the doctrine of chastity as set forth in *Comus*. Did he choose the subject because it happened to be sanctioned by Spenser and John Fletcher, or because self-expression was a relief or a necessity? Although the subject was far from occupying the whole of his attention, I think it had some relation to his recent experience. In his letter to an unknown friend he had admitted his inclination to marriage but had chosen celibacy for the time being, in order to devote his whole attention to self-discipline. But in his studious retirement this curbing of inclination would tend to irk him more than in the fuller social life of Cambridge. His thoughts would run on questions of chastity and marriage. Having in the first instance chosen celibacy purely as a matter of expediency, he is gradually impelled by the force of his feelings to seek a stronger justification for his abstention. By a process of compensating fiction he would invest chastity with some unusual power, turning a negation into an active principle. There are signs of this mystical notion of chastity in *Comus*. Chastity is a 'sublime notion and high mystery,' it is a hidden strength and a protection against all perils.

> So dear to Heav'n is Saintly chastity
> That when a soul is found sincerely so,
> A thousand liveried Angels lacky her,
> Driving far off each thing of sin and guilt,
> And in cleer dream, and solemn vision,
> Tell her of things that no gross ear can hear.

In Milton, who believed in, or came later to believe in, the natural goodness of the flesh, the notion was unhealthy. It lasted perhaps in his mind till his journey to Italy; anyhow all traces of it have vanished in *Paradise Lost*, where not merely is human love exalted, but the angels enjoy some higher physical mingling. Milton was no mystic, and his dallying in *Comus* with a magical view of chastity was no more than an interlude. (pp. 66-75)

> *E. M. W. Tillyard, in his* Milton, *1930. Reprint by Chatto & Windus, 1949, 396 p.*

ALLEN TATE   (essay date 1931)

[*Tate's criticism is closely associated with two American critical movements, Agrarianism and New Criticism. The Agrarians were concerned with political and social issues as well as with literature and were dedicated to preserving traditional Southern values. In particular, they attacked Northern industrialism as they sought to preserve the Southern farming economy. The New Critics, among whom are counted Cleanth Brooks and Robert Penn Warren, did not subscribe to a single set of principles. Yet all believed that a work of literature should be examined as an object in itself, not as a manifestation of ethics, sociology, or psychology. Accordingly, examinations were accomplished by a close analysis of symbol, image, and metaphor. Tate, however, adhered to a different vision of the purpose of literature than did other New Critics. A conservative thinker and convert to Catholicism, he attacked the tradition of Western philosophy, believing that it alienated persons from themselves, from each other, and from nature by divorcing intellectual functions from natural human ones. Tate considered literature to be the principal form of human knowledge and revelation and saw it as restoring human beings to a proper relationship with nature and the spiritual realm. Although this vision informs much of his work, Tate is like T. S. Eliot insofar as an appreciation of his criticism is not wholly dependent upon an acceptance of his spiritual convictions. In the following excerpt, he describes ways in which Milton's works may be read profitably and examines Milton's use of mythology.]*

From the time of Addison's praise of Milton in 1694, the stream of criticism has carried the poet to our own day, the most referred to, but, in the last half-century, the least read of all the great poets. The scholars know him but the poets do not, and on the whole it must be said that we flatter him with neglect. We must not be misled by the dubious fact that every year sees the publication of enough critical routine about Milton to bemuse the whole of any man's time. In the most important sense the poet is without influence. His style, his "philosophy," his methods of composition, above all his attitude toward his material, have had no effect on the best poets since Tennyson. There is enough exegesis left to be done on Milton to entertain the profession of letters forever: **"Lycidas"** alone is one of those jokers that will always beguile the historical critic who cannot understand what is meant when one says that it is a great poem meaning nothing. Textual interpretation and biography have their own value; one hopes that all the problems may some time be solved. There is one new and great problem for the historical critic, who, however, had also better be a philosopher: we now hear that the Massonized Milton was fiction, that Milton's Puritanism was the most convenient set of terms in that age into which he might throw the whole energy of an insight that exceeded all brands of nonconformity. This new Milton will probably win a large new following among those men who do not know they are living in the backwash of the Renaissance and can thus enjoy it. The new Milton is a Renaissance hero. It is to be hoped that neither Masson nor the Renaissance can keep him from being a poet, or us from seeing that no historical controversy is so important as the task of making him available to the living poets. . . .

[One] may suggest two ways in which the moderns might read Milton with profit. The first is as craftsman; the second, closely connected with the first, goes deeper, and raises the question that Mr. I. A. Richards has discouraged us about: this is the place of poetic fiction in the modern mind.

Modern critical practice explicitly demands of poetry a great many features that were taken for granted in Milton's time, or called by different names. The early eighteenth century said perspicuity; we say psychological sincerity—that is, does the poetry come out of an actual core of experience? (The corollary to this demand, one of our most typical dogmas, that the experience must be *personal*, or even almost purely sensory, I pass by as irrelevant to the main issue.) Another demand that we habitually make is this: Is the poetry peculiarly the poet's own? He must speak in his own character; his rhythms and images must bear his personal stamp, and in every case it must be said, for him to win our praise, that he has created a style. This personal or psychic kind of sincerity means that the poet must be careful to distinguish his sensations from those of other poets, for this alone will make the poetry his and suffuse over his imagery a certain emotional tone that gives to the verse its specific esthetic quality. To demand these qualities is only just; Milton had them—from the point of view of his own age. Does Milton, in these respects, survive our judgment? We believe that an elaborate mythology lies beyond the possibility of experience, and we denounce the continued use of mythological personages in poetry as unreal and insincere. No poet has ever experienced the physicist's ether, or the mathematician's *quantum;* nevertheless, such fictions compete gloriously amongst us against Chaos or the Spirit of the Wood.

At what moment in Milton's poetry does this relative insincerity first appear? I call it relative because it is only a matter of taste in fiction. In the early poems—for example, the **"Nativity Ode,"** which before **"Lycidas"** has the most elaborate machinery—there is not, even as we see it, any pretense of "belief" in the physical existence of the Christian and pagan gods who amplify the theme. They are there as allusion, as metaphor; and a metaphor, at that stage of the mental process which the term implies, has never been a mythology. It is so with **"Arcades,"** and with the twin poems; so barefaced is the make-believe in *Comus,* it is so with that poem—although the full-bodied and subtly contrived anthropomorphisms of Comus seem to promise an even more elaborate performance of that kind. In Milton's poetry from first to last there is a steady growth of the personifying power, a sheer love of sensible fictions for their own sake, beginning with the casual figures in the early work and mounting to the systematized mythology of the epic. Was Milton less sincere at the end than at the beginning?

There is no need of discussing the quality of the early style; if we like it we can surely accept the kind of experience that it sets forth, and we nearly all do; which means that we are perfectly capable of accepting an incipient myth, a small fiction but not a large fiction. It is not that Milton was increasingly irresponsible about reality, and insincere, but rather that the character of our imaginations has changed and taken on a defect. On principle, the **"Epitaph on the Marchioness of Winchester"** requires as much willing suspension of disbelief as Raphael's story of the war in Heaven: we can make a little suspension but not a big one.

For we fail to see any great portions of our experience as wholes: I use the verb *see* to mean actual vision, which as Milton employed it reduced the chief human passions to a perceptible scale, for the sake of truth, certainly, but mostly for our richest kind of delight. To represent as action, and as a whole, any human experience, one must make a fable, and when the fable is typical of one kind of action it becomes a myth, which conveys its meaning dramatically. When we read poetry we bring to it the pseudo-scientific habit of mind; we are not used to joining things up in vague disconnected processes in terms that are abstract and thin, and so our sensuous enjoyment is confined to the immediate field of sensation. We are bewildered, helpless, confronted with one of those immensely remote, highly sensuous and perfectly make-believe worlds of poetry that rise above our scattered notions of process. The dramatic character of the myth offends us with its pretentiousness; it is hateful to *l'homme moyen et sensuel,* who is modern man; for it implies that the action is undertaken by superior beings (who are not allowed to exist), reaching beyond our personal experience. Our great myths make their appeal to those people, at last remarkably few, who have a sense of destiny, of poise above life, and who look at the vast distraction of the world, its shift and disintegration, with a controlling detachment.

Mythology as Milton understood it was no mere pictorial exercise. We must remember that the greatest Anglo-Saxon master of the myth is the most perfectly self-conscious technician in English poetry: without the sense of myth, of fable, of ordered wholes in experience, he would have had no protection against our modern disease—miscellaneous sensation. He never wrote the same poem twice; there is no repetition. He was not overwhelmed by personal emotion; his personal emotion was caught up and purified by a succession of objective themes. Not even any two sonnets are technically the same; and what one expects is actually true—the emotion of every sonnet is distinctive. The moment he touched his medium, the feeling began to be transformed. There is, in the background of all the poems, an exalted presence, but there are no special Miltonic emotions comparable to the Byronic melancholy or the Leopardian despair. He is capable of every effect, but of no two effects twice. His great secret, as Saintsbury said, is his infallible sense of form: a violent, passionate man, he did not let passion betray him into incomplete expression. He is the supreme English craftsman because he never violated the exact relation between his chosen subject and its demands upon his technique. His one unfinished poem, "**The Passion,**" is evidence of a great artistic integrity; his instinct for form told him he had better drop it (it was "beyond his years"), although the last stanza is his high point in the minor poems before "**Lycidas**":

> Or should I thence hurried on viewles wing,
> Take up a weeping on the Mountains wilde,
> The gentle neighborhood of grove and spring
> Would soon unbosom all their Echoes milde,
> And I (for grief is easily beguild)
>   Might think th' infection of my sorrows loud
> Had got a race of mourners on som pregnant cloud.

Unless we are convinced Spenglerians, it is time for the Miltonic sense of form to reappear in Anglo-American poetry. It is high time that the modern poets, who feel strongly other seventeenth-century influences, came to a better view of Milton's significance for style. This does not mean that we must repeat "**Lycidas,**" or try to write Miltonic blank verse; I have no specifications for modern style. In his time (as in ours) there was a good deal to be said for the Spenserian school against the technical breakdown to which the Jacobean dramatists had ridden English verse. Webster is a great moment in English style, but the drama was falling off, and blank verse had to survive in a non-dramatic form, which required a more rigid treatment than the stage could offer it. In substance, it needed stiffer and less sensitive perceptions, a more artificial grasp of sensation to offset the supersensitive awareness of the school of Shakespeare, a verification less imitative of the flow of sensation and more architectural. What poetry needed Milton was able to give. It was Arnold who, in the 1853 preface to his own poems, remarked that the sensational imagery of the Shakespearean tradition had not been without its baleful effect on poetry down to Keats: one may imitate a passage in Shakespeare without penetrating to the mind that wrote it, but to imitate Milton one must be Milton; one must have all of Milton's resources in myth behind the impulse: it is the myth, ingrained in his very being, that makes the style. From Milton we learn only the meaning of craftsmanship—without a prescription for reproducing it; but it is a great lesson. There is no discouragement in the fact that Milton has never been successfully imitated (even Keats failed), and never will be.

It is still easy for us to oppose Spenser and Milton, and follow Donne. The school of T. S. Eliot is the modern school of

POEMS
OF
Mr. *John* ℳ*ilton* ,
BOTH
ENGLISH and LATIN,
Compos'd at several times.

Printed by his true Copies.

The **S**o**n**g**s** were set in Musick by
Mr. **Henry Lawes** Gentleman of
the **Kings** Chappel, and one
of His **Maiesties**
Private Musick.

—————*Baccare frontem*
Cingite, ne vati noceat mala lingua futuro,
Virgil, Eclog. 7

Printed and publish'd according to
ORDER.

Jan: 2   LONDON,
Printed by *Ruth Raworth* for *Humphrey Moseley;*
and are to be sold at the signe of the Princes
Arms in S.*Pauls* Church-yard. 1645.

Title page of the first edition of Poems of Mr. John Milton
(1645).

Donne; it most probably would have appeared (such is the atmosphere of the age) without Donne's direct influence. In this generation we have had little use for Milton's lack of sensation, for his abstract orotundity. The enormous complexity of the sensibility in "**Lycidas**" contains no surprises, no shocks, and we do not like it. We like the oxymoron of feeling in the school of Donne. Milton asks us to attend not to his experience as such, but to his mythology; and this is the source of our belief in his psychological insincerity. He asks us to consider his fictions. Does he ask us to believe them? He asks us to contemplate them, and then to think what we please. We cannot see that *Paradise Lost* no more than "**Lycidas**" was written to enhance the idea of God; God and the death of Edward King—whom Milton had known slightly and probably disliked—were seized upon to satisfy a deep sense for form: Milton was devout, and the glorification of God was close to his personal impulse, but the finished work shows his motive to have been something else. The cabinetmaker takes the need of his patron for a table as the occasion to exercise his gift for form; Milton's poetry is just as mysterious, and just as simple, as that.

There is still work to be done on Milton's mythology. Possibly the critic ought to assume that it was qualitatively present at the outset of his career, and then grew from the acorn. He demands that we accept it, for that is all he is. If we cannot do this, the inference is in no one's favor in the matter of metaphysical knowledge. But it is against us in another respect; it means that we have lost the imagination. Milton does not ask us to believe his heavenly fictions in any sense that he did not believe them; Lucifer needs the same quality of belief as ''old Damœtas.'' He does ask us to exercise as much philosophical insight, passively, as he actively puts into his poetry. His philosophy is neither right nor wrong; it is comprehensive. It covers and puts in its philosophical place the modern short-sightedness that we short-sightedly call the revolution of the human mind, which is said to have made Milton's poetry obsolete. There has never been a revolution of the mind: there are only styles in fiction. Milton's fiction is not in our style, and it seems inadequate to the solution of our problems. It is not diverting; it has no personality. We do not like it because it lacks these modern features; because it is creative in the purest sense. I think it was Warton who said that **''Lycidas''** was the absolute test of the sense of poetry; it still is. It is well to have one fixed criterion, for there is no abstract formula under the glassy cool translucent wave. (pp. 266-68)

> *Allen Tate, ''A Note on Milton,'' in* The New Republic, *Vol. LXVIII, No. 881, October 21, 1931, pp. 266-68.*

PAUL ELMER MORE   (essay date 1936)

[*More was an American critic who, along with Irving Babbitt, formulated the doctrines of New Humanism. The New Humanists were strict moralists: in an age of scientific and artistic self-expression, they adhered to traditional conservative values, believing that a work's implicit support for classic ethical norms is as important as its aesthetic qualities. More was particularly opposed to Naturalism, which he viewed as accentuating the animal nature of humans, and to any literature that broke with established tradition. His importance as a critic derives from his rigidly coherent ideology, which polarized American critics into hostile opponents (Van Wyck Brooks, Edmund Wilson, H. L. Mencken) or devoted supporters (Norman Foerster, Stuart Sherman, and, to a lesser degree, T. S. Eliot). He is especially esteemed for the philosophical and literary erudition of his multi-volume* Shelburne Essays *(1904-21). In the following excerpt from the third volume of* New Shelburne Essays, *he assesses Milton's literary achievement in ''Lycidas'' and suggests why the poet chose the form and theme he did.*]

After passing, as I might say, through the valley of the shadow of death, after months of physical prostration when reading of any sort was beyond the strength of a depleted brain, the poet to whom I turned instinctively with the first renewal of health was Milton. And so I have been reading Milton again and books about him, with the old zest I had as a boy, and with an added joy of almost tremulous excitement such as a miser might feel at the rediscovery of a treasure of gold stolen from him and long buried out of sight. But with this delight have been mingled certain scruples which vexed me a little more than they did in the old days. Again, as many times before, on laying down one of the poems the familiar words of Tennyson would come unbidden to my mind:

> O mighty-mouth'd inventor of harmonies,
> O skill'd to sing of Time or Eternity,
>   God-gifted organ-voice of England,
>   Milton, a name to resound for ages.

Of the mighty harmonies there would be no doubt; God-gifted voice certainly, organ-voice certainly, for those who have ears to hear. If any one in English, Milton had the divine craft of words, the mastery of sonorous speech. His is not Shake-

speare's incalculable gift; it lacks the element of magic that captures us in Shakespeare; it is, or soon after his earliest experiments it was, an art that came by reflection, and as we read him we imagine that we might by equal deliberation attain the same perfection—only we never do attain it. And something of this distinction Milton himself seems to have felt when he wrote of Shakespeare:

> For whil'st to th' shame of slow-endeavoring Art
> Thy easie numbers flow.

The same distinction, I think, was present to Irving Babbitt when he spoke, as I have heard him do more than once, of his experience in quoting. It was Babbitt's custom in the first draught of his essays to cite from memory, and then, before printing, to verify the quotation by reference to the text. He would find occasionally that even his retentive memory had slipped and that he had substituted a word of his own for the poet's. And sometimes, he would say, he could not see that the substitution was inferior to the original—except in the case of Shakespeare. He never made a change in Shakespeare's language but some force or charm was lost. That was not so even with Milton.—Such a difference exists between the seemingly careless spontaneity and the elaborated art of our two supreme masters of poetical diction; and he would be a rash judge who should say that the advantage was all on one side or the other.

But to return to the question that vexed my mood of acquiescent joy. God-gifted organ-voice Milton possessed in full measure—but ''voice of England''? Does he speak for the whole of England, or, that being scarcely possible, does he speak from the heart of England, giving articulate expression to that central quality which has made England what we know and love? And by his influence did he maintain that balance and moderation, that sense of law enveloping the individual, which made of Falkland a true type of the Englishman that was to be? Here the question begins with style, but extends beyond mere style to psychology and to principles of government and life.

Now, if there be any hesitation with me to accept Milton's style as the norm of good English, it is certainly not on the ground of that ''dissociation of sensibility'' which draws a school of modern critics and poets to repudiate what may be called the Miltonic line of development and to seek their parentage in Shakespeare and Donne and the ''Metaphysicals.'' If I understand what the leader of that Choir means by this rather obscure phrase, it is that Milton by conscious choice and judgement dissociated his mind from one whole range of perceptions, refusing to respond to them emotionally as foreign to his fixed theory of values, and by the same deliberate act of selection created a more or less artificial language; whereas the poets proceeding from Donne held their sensibility open to any and every perception and employed words to convey the sharp immediate impression of each fact of sense and experience without discrimination. The distinction is valid, and it is interesting; for the ''modernist'' in poetry it is of vital significance. But I am not sure that the ''dissociation of sensibility,'' so taken, has been the source of dead monotony and of verbal unreality in our literature; and I am sure that if Milton failed in national leadership it was not for this reason. Rather I should say that his influence in this respect has made for sanity and form and for limitations which are characteristically English. Rather I should maintain that Milton's failure, so far as he failed, was owing to something essentially un-English, or only partially English, to something belonging to his individual temperament, which passed into his philosophy of life and diverted a noble love of liberty into a morbid and isolating passion. Here too Milton was clear-headed in his application of the law to others, but curiously perverse when his own interests were affected. In the second of the sonnets on the book called **Tetrachordon,** he berates his fellow countrymen as "Owles and Cuckoos, Asses, Apes and Doggs" for the very reason that they have lost the true meaning of liberty, while they

> bawle for freedom in this senceless mood,
> And still revolt when truth would set them free.
> Licence they mean when they cry libertie;
> For who loves that, must first be wise and good;
> But from that mark, how far they roave we see
> For all this wast of wealth, and loss of blood.

That is sound doctrine, but—alas to say it!—Milton did not see how apt would be the retort, *de te fabula;* how easy the reply: License he meant when he cried liberty.

This book called **Tetrachordon,** written by Milton himself, was the second of his treatises on divorce, and is a bitter invective against those who, by opposing the facile freedom of marital separation, enslave the soul under man-made laws, forgetting that which "makes us holiest and likest to God's immortal image," and who, for the law of liberty, set up "that which makes us most conformable and captive to civil and subordinate precepts: . . . although indeed no ordinance, human or from heaven, can bind against the good of man." By "the good of man," as Mr. Tillyard observes in his comment on the passage, Milton means what elsewhere he calls "nature"—damnable word, I add, into which have been distilled all the fallacies of human wit through thousands of years. If you track the word down through its many ambiguities, you will discover that in the end it signifies that which a man temperamentally and personally desires as distinguished from that which is prescribed for him by human rule or divine precept. So it was that Milton, fretted and humiliated because his wife, finding existence with him intolerable, left him and ran away home,— so it was that incontinently he rebelled against the human and divine laws of marriage, and wrote his pleas for freedom of divorce as complying with natural law and the good of man. If ever there was a case of liberty becoming license, it was here. However they may have differed in other respects, in this quality Milton resembled Shelley: they both identified what they desired at any moment with the natural good of man; they both made self-righteousness the law of right.

That was the beginning of Milton's public career and of his prose writings, and it was typical of what ensued. If the bishops in any way interfered with his personal idea of worship, then down with episcopacy and away with the Church; if the monarchical form of government hampered his political independence, then down with monarchy and away with the Constitution. There is no more painful reading in English literature than these apologies for free divorce and regicide which occupied the greatest genius of the age between **"Lycidas"** and **Paradise Lost,** and the style in which they are written is as heavy and un-English as their spirit is perverse. There are purple patches scattered through these treatises, which are all that most readers know of Milton's prose and which would give the impression that he is as magnificent here as in his verse; but if these passages are examined it will be found that, taken apart from their context, they are expressions of personal ambition, legitimate in itself and magnificent in its devotion to the aim of a poet, while all about them floats and rages a sea of rebellious discontent. I will not endorse Hilaire Belloc's

sweeping condemnation of the prose works, but in the mass they do certainly form a repellent body of reading. Following the ideas of the tractates through the surging verbiage, one is reminded of the monsters in the account of creation, "wallowing unweildie" in

> the vast immeasurable Abyss
> Outrageous as a Sea, dark, wasteful, wilde,
> Up from the bottom turn'd by furious windes.

There is something disconcerting in the spectacle of a supreme artist, as Milton was in his verse, so losing his craftsmanship in another medium; what I would insist on is that the very style of his prose has a close relation to the fact that when he passes from imagination to theory his voice is not that of his people but of an exasperated individual. The seventeenth century, with all its greatness, is an age of frustration, filled with fine promises that, except in the field of science, came to no fruition, replete with noble utterance that somehow failed to convince. In the Church, in the State, in society, the one thing needed and not found was a commanding genius that should have been indeed the voice of England. It is the tragedy of the time that he who had the genius so to speak should have wasted his energies in querulous complaints against what was, and in the future was to show itself, the true spirit of the land. In a word that spirit may be described precisely as liberty, not license, as centrality, not dissent.

But I am not concerned to pass judgement on Milton's character and its effect upon his work as a whole; that is a longer theme than I care now to discuss. What I started out to do was to consider one small piece of his output, the **"Lycidas,"** and to ask myself how it should be read. To this question, at least in its acuter form, I was moved by chancing to take up at the same time Mr. Tillyard's estimation of the poem and Dr. Johnson's. As a whole I should regard Mr. Tillyard's *Milton* as about the best book we have on the man and the poet, a study admirable for its scholarship and discrimination, and particularly notable for its treatment of the philosophical problems raised by **Paradise Lost,** such as Milton's conception of the nature of evil and the cause of man's fall. Now to Mr. Tillyard "**'Lycidas'** is the last and greatest English poem of Milton's youth; though shorter, it is greater than **Comus,** written with newly won but complete mastery and expressing a mental experience both valuable and profound." That is a sentiment with which my own judgement is in perfect accord; indeed, I should go further and hold it to be the greatest short poem of any author in English, the very criterion and touchstone of poetical taste. Yet with that opinion I have felt bound to remember the sweeping condemnation of Johnson, to whom "the diction" of the poem "is harsh, the rhymes uncertain, and the numbers unpleasing" [see excerpt dated 1779]. It is without passion and without art. In part no doubt Johnson's lack of appreciation can be set down to his known deficiency in the higher faculty of imagination. His comment on the diction and rhythm does nothing more than indicate a certain insensitiveness to the finer and more delicate effects of poetry in general. But one cannot read the whole essay without perceiving that his hostile criticism of the art of **"Lycidas"** sprang not so much from his miscomprehension and aesthetic obtuseness as from hostility to the poet and to all that Milton as a man stood for. Touching Milton's plea for looser laws of divorce, the neglect of which by the ruling Presbyterians turned him against that sect, Johnson observes, and justly: "He that changes his party by his humour is not more virtuous than he that changes it by his interest; he loves himself rather than truth." As for the political tirades, Johnson in his attack ran true to form: "Milton's republicanism was . . . founded in an envious hatred of greatness, and a sullen desire of independence. . . . He hated monarchs in the State, and prelates in the Church; for he hated all whom he was required to obey. . . . He felt not so much the love of liberty as repugnance to authority.'' Now for myself I do not like Belloc's summary and contemptuous dismissal of Milton as ''a man rotten with the two worst vices: falsehood and pride''; for somehow one shrinks from using such language of a very great poet. To Johnson's charge, on the contrary, I can subscribe without reservation (indeed I have already said much the same thing in weaker language), and I do not see how the charge, in substance, can be countered by any impartial student of Milton's life. But to Johnson the faults of the man were ruinous to the earlier work of the poet, and he denounced **"Lycidas"** because he read into it the author's ecclesiastical and political heresies; whereas I must reject the maker whilst admiring what he has made. And there the difficulty lies—or has lain for me: how can one so combine detestation and love? how can one make so complete a separation between Milton the destroyer of Church and State, and Milton the artist? how is one to read **"Lycidas"**?

That particular difficulty, it will be observed, opens up into one of the major problems of criticism in general: the relation between the content of a poem and the art of a poem independent of its content. In the beginning, when that distinction first presented itself to the Greek mind, it took a very simple form and indeed was scarcely a question at all: the *Iliad* and the *Odyssey* were valued primarily, not for their charm and interest, but because in them the statesman, the soldier, the athlete, the man who desired to live honourably, could find the wisest precepts and the best models. For later times, and for us of the West, the principle involved was formulated by Horace in his famous saying that the most successful poet was he who knew how to mix the *utile* and the *dulce*. What Horace meant by the *dulce* is clear enough; it is just that in a poem which gives pleasure to the reader. And what he meant by the *utile* is equally clear; it is that in a poem from which we draw instruction. So in one of the *Epistles* he tells a friend, held in Rome by the practice of declaiming, no doubt about the schools of philosophy, that he is the country reading Homer, who is a better teacher than all the philosophers. . . . (pp. 184-93)

But a change came with the advent of the romantic movement. The *utile* and the *dulce* took on new significance, and the old division was sharpened to something like an absolute contrast between two irreconcilable criteria of excellence. The *utile* was broadened so as to embrace the whole substance of a poem whether instructive or not, its sense or meaning. The *dulce* on the other side was refined to a conception of pure poetry, the quintessence of art, as a sort of abstract entity which could be felt and judged somehow apart from any articulate thought or story conveyed; indeed the ideal poem would be a succession of beautiful words with no meaning at all. Such a thesis, baldly stated, is manifestly bare nonsense; but practically the early romantics applied it to criticism by taking *Kubla Khan* as the ideal poem, because, while the content was no more than the shimmering matter of a dream, it reeked of that mysterious entity called pure poetry. And it was not so long ago that the theory flared up again in France under the impulse of the Abbé Bremond's monograph on *La Poésie pure*. The discussion that ensued was confused by the Abbé's association of aesthetic rapture with a mystical view of the function of prayer. More illuminating, to me at least, is T. S. Eliot's pursuit and final rejection of the same ideal of absolute poetry. In his earlier essays, particularly those on Seneca, Shakespeare, and Dante,

you will see him eagerly pursuing this *ignis fatuus* as the ultimate standard of value. In the first of those studies he ranks Shakespeare and Dante together as the supreme poets of the world, and the two are equally great though the Italian has taken up into the *Commedia* the profoundest wisdom of human experience as expounded in the Thomistic theology, whereas the Englishman has no interpretation of life's riddle beyond the stale platitudes of Seneca. ''Perhaps it was Shakespeare's special rôle in history to have effected this peculiar union—perhaps it is a part of his special eminence to have expressed an inferior philosophy in the greatest poetry.'' It is true that Mr. Eliot has his reservations in supporting this romantic dream of pure poetry which came to him from certain early and, as I think, unfortunate associations. It is more important to note that in his latest enunciation he has worked himself quite clear of the disturbing inheritance. There lies before me now his recently published volume of *Essays Ancient and Modern,* and in the opening paragraph of one of the ''modern'' (that is, hitherto unprinted) essays I am held by this sentence: ''The 'greatness' of literature cannot be determined solely by literary standards; though we must remember that whether it is literature or not can be determined only by literary standards.'' That I take to be a complete truth perfectly expressed; and the whole essay on ''Religion and Literature'' is a masterly application of this sentence to modern currents in verse and fiction. It is the critic come to full maturity after years of probation.

And so, to apply this canon of taste to **"Lycidas,"** it may be possible for a young man, enamoured of the sheer beauty of words and untroubled as yet by the graver issues of life, to enjoy the marvellous art of the poem with no thought of what the poem means if connected with the poet's place in the world of ideas and action. But such a rupture between the form and the substance of literature cannot long be maintained with the ripening of experience. Sooner or later we are bound to make up our account with that law of taste so ably formulated: ''The 'greatness' of literature cannot be determined solely by literary standards; though one must remember that whether it is literature or not can be determined only by literary standards.'' That **"Lycidas"** is literature, poetry and not mere verse, depends on the language, the images, the form, on that mysterious working of the imagination which we can feel but cannot ultimately analyse or adequately describe; that it is great literature must depend on the junction of such qualities with nobility of content. And such nobility is there, in full measure.

The poem is an elegy prompted by the drowning of a college friend of the author. It has been the complaint of more than one critic that the expression of grief has little of that warmth which might be expected from such a subject. Dr. Johnson can find no ''effusion of real passion, for passion runs not after remote allusions and obscure opinions.'' Against this charge of frigidity Mr. Tillyard contends with great acumen that the true theme of the poem is not the death of Edward King at all, but the possible death of the poet himself. Milton was writing just before he set out on his voyage to Italy, when such an adventure was more or less perilous and the chance of shipwreck and drowning might very well have occupied his mind. So taken, the charge of coldness towards a friend might be changed to one of cowardice or egotism. But Milton was no coward and, however he may have shown himself elsewhere, the note of egotism is relieved by the artful, though doubtless unconscious transference of anxiety for himself to sorrow for another. And it was not the mere termination of life that made him anxious, but the fear that his one all-absorbing passion might so be left unfulfilled. To understand his state of mind and the emotion that was impelling him to write, the elegy should be read in the light of those passages of self-dedication scattered through his prose works. These purple patches laid upon the coarse cloth of controversy are too well known to need repeating here. The keynote is given by the words inserted in the gross *Apology for Smectymnuus:*

> He who would not be frustrate of his hope to write
> well hereafter in laudable things, ought himself to be
> a true poem; that is, a composition and pattern of the
> best and honourablest things; not presuming to sing
> high praises of heroic men, or famous cities, unless
> he have in himself the experience and the practice of
> all that which is praiseworthy.

And joined with this personal ambition was the conviction that no loftier or purer service could be rendered to one's country and to the world than such a work as he was preparing himself to produce. Under the spell of a great heroic poem the mind of the people would respond in efforts towards great and heroic living. That was Milton's faith. It was the spirit of the reformer engrafted upon the temperament of the artist. In such a profession, wherein personal glory is identified with public welfare, pride with humility, there lurks, let us admit, a subtle danger; to fall short of brilliant success must leave the professor a monument of ridicule, like the mountains in labour that brought forth only a mouse. But, on the other hand, such a purpose, if carried through valiantly to a successful issue, makes the ordinary ambition of the artist and poet to appear in comparison no more than a cheap display of vanity. And Milton had the courage of conviction and the genius to succeed. In the history of English letters there is nothing like this determination carried through from youth to age, except the solemn dedication of Wordsworth to a similar purpose. All this must be read into **"Lycidas."** Under the pretext of grief for the loss of a comrade in hope the poem is in reality as it were the quintessence of those prose passages through which there speaks a self-confidence as sublime as it was justified.

It is in the light of this life-long ambition that we should read the savage attack on the abuses in Church and State which raises the note of elegy to the "higher mood" of righteous indignation:

> Last came and last did go,
> The Pilot of the *Galilean* lake. . . .
> He shook his Miter'd locks, and stern bespake,
> How well could I have spar'd for thee, young swain,
> Anow of such as for their bellies sake,
> Creep and intrude, and climb into the fold? . . .
> But that two-handed engine at the door,
> Stands ready to smite once, and smite no more.

And apart from any theory of episcopacy and royalty the abuses were there and cried out for remedy. Laud knew them as well as did Baxter, Charles as well as Cromwell; but none but Milton possessed the "dread voice" which—alas, but for defects of temper!—might have done so much to set them right.

In this light also we should interpret the allegorical symbolism of the poem:

> The hungry Sheep look up, and are not fed.

To Dr. Johnson all this masquerade of sheep and shepherds is "easy, vulgar, and therefore disgusting," a cheap device of images without passion and without art. Johnson had good reason to be suspicious of a *genre* that has invited so many weak poets to indulge in flim-flam. But he should not have forgotten how all through the Old Testament, from the call that

came to Amos, "who was among the herdmen of Tekoa," and all through the New Testament, from the angelic vision that broke upon the shepherds who were "abiding in the field" about Bethlehem to the parable that Jesus spake to his disciples, "I am the good shepherd and know my sheep,"—how all through the Bible this pastoral allegory of the Church runs like the very music of religion.

These were the thoughts that haunted the memory of the poet when he linked himself with his friend as shepherds:

> Together both, ere the high Lawns appear'd
> Under the opening eye-lids of the morn,
> We drove a field.

Together they were practising their "rural ditties" in preparation for the louder chant that was to stir the nation from its ignoble lethargy, when one of the twain was washed away by the sounding sea, and his voice forever silenced. And what if a like fate awaited the other, who also was about to start on a voyage? "What boots it with incessant care . . . to meditate the thankless Muse," of what avail to "Live laborious dayes," when, just as we

> think to burst out into sudden blaze,
> Comes the blind *Fury* with th' abhorred shears,
> And slits the thin spun life?

"But not the praise," he exclaims; the reward and the outcome are not confined to this world nor are they measured by success "on mortal soil," but in heaven before the "witness of all judging *Jove.*" I do not know how others are affected, but I can never peruse the climax of the poem without a thrill such as scarcely any other verses of the language excite.

> Weep no more, woful Shepherds weep no more,
> For *Lycidas* your sorrow is not dead,
> Sunk though he be beneath the watry floar,
> So sinks the day-star in the Ocean bed,
> And yet anon repairs his drooping head,
> And tricks his beams, and with new spangled Ore,
> Flames in the forehead of the morning sky:
> So *Lycidas* sunk low, but mounted high,
> Through the dear might of him that walk'd the waves
> Where other groves, and other streams along,
> With *Nectar* pure his oozy Lock's he laves,
> And hears the unexpressive nuptiall Song,
> In the blest Kingdoms meek of joy and love.
> There entertain him all the Saints above,
> In solemn troops, and sweet Societies
> That sing, and singing in their glory move,
> And wipe the tears for ever from his eyes.

Milton always rang true when he wrote of the world to come, but never before nor after did he attain quite this elevation, or achieve so realistic an expression of the invisible mysteries wrapt in the future. A few of his contemporaries possessed this power of giving substance to the hopes of eternity—notably Vaughan—but none of them approaches the master. And in later times the art was simply lost. Choose the best of the moderns, Newman for instance in *The Dream of Gerontius,* and they will appear cold and unconvincing beside Milton. Nor did any of the great poets of the earlier ages of faith quite equal him in this field. I would not compare the few lines of an elegy with the mighty structure of Dante's *Paradiso*, but for myself at least there is no single incident in Dante's voyage through the celestial spheres that touches me with the shock of actuality like that which I feel when I read **"Lycidas."** I am not competent to explain by what devices, by what choice of words, Milton obtains his sublime effect. It would be easy of course, if it seemed worth while, to point to the rich manipulation of vowel sounds in this or that verse, to note the startling ob-viousness of the allusion to the might of him that walked the waves, but the final alchemy of art escapes such an analysis; indeed I question whether any skill of criticism can penetrate to the heart of that mystery of the word which we call inspi-ration, and leave at that. But one phase of Milton's method impresses me: the fact that his images are borrowed from the simplest commonplaces of faith,—the return of dawn after the sinking of the sun in the ocean-stream, the tears wiped away, the heavenly choiring of the blest. A comparison of Newman's attempt to translate the subtler speculations of theology into a poetic account of the soul's awakening after death shows how inevitably right was Milton's choice. There are regions of spir-itual experience where the untutored imagination of the people goes deeper into reality than all the groping wisdom of philosophy.

One thing in the end is certain, the "greatness" of **"Lycidas"** is determined by an intimate marriage of form and matter, expression and substance. He who would read the poem wor-thily must see this, and must be equally sensitive to the delicacy of its art and to the sublimity of its ideas. This does not mean that he will forget or slur over the disagreeable traits of the poet's character or the repulsiveness of his ecclesiastical and political theories. But for our good fortune what repels us in the man and roused Johnson to a fury of protest is reserved for his prose and is excluded from his poetry—not completely indeed, for, not to mention the more outrageous sonnets, oc-casionally the bitterness of his disappointed soul breaks out in his later works, yet to such an extent that it is not impossible to keep the poet and the controversialist apart as two almost separate powers. That divorce has its unhappy aspect; for one thing it debars Milton, in his total effect, from being accepted as the voice of England. But it leaves to him the high credit of having raised in *Paradise Lost,* to the honour of his native land, the one monumentally successful product of that hu-manistic culture of the Renaissance in which originality of genius and faithfulness to the classical tradition are combined in perfect union. And for **"Lycidas"** there is this further apol-ogy, that the elegy was composed before Milton's splendid spirit of liberty was exacerbated by opposition into petulant license, when his personal pride flamed with a yet undiverted zeal to make of his own life a true poem and so to train himself for creating such a work of art as would lift his people from the ugly slough of faction and greed, where they were grov-elling, into the finer atmosphere where pure religion and the love of beauty might flourish together. (pp. 193-202)

Paul Elmer More, "How to Read 'Lycidas'," in his On Being Human: New Shelburne Essays, Vol. III, *Princeton University Press, 1936, pp. 184-202.*

T. S. ELIOT (essay date 1936)

[*Perhaps the most influential poet and critic to write in the English language during the first half of the twentieth century, Eliot is closely identified with many of the qualities denoted by the term Modernism: experimentation, formal complexity, artistic and in-tellectual eclecticism, and a classicist's view of the artist working at an emotional distance from his or her creation. He introduced a number of terms and concepts that strongly affected critical thought in his lifetime, among them the idea that poets must be conscious of the living tradition of literature if their work is to have artistic and spiritual validity. In general, Eliot upheld values of traditionalism and discipline, and in 1928 he annexed Christian theology to his overall conservative worldview. Of his criticism, he stated: "It is a by-product of my private poetry-workshop: or*

a prolongation of the thinking that went into the formation of my verse." In the following essay, which was originally published in Essays and Studies *in 1936, he offers a mixed assessment of Milton's poetic legacy.*]

While it must be admitted that Milton is a very great poet indeed, it is something of a puzzle to decide in what his great-ness consists. On analysis, the marks against him appear both more numerous and more significant than the marks to his credit. As a man, he is antipathetic. Either from the moralist's point of view, or from the theologian's point of view, or from the psychologist's point of view, or from that of the political philosopher, or judging by the ordinary standards of likeable-ness in human beings, Milton is unsatisfactory. The doubts which I have to express about him are more serious than these. His greatness as a poet has been sufficiently celebrated, though I think largely for the wrong reasons, and without the proper reservations. His misdeeds as a poet have been called attention to, as by Mr. Ezra Pound, but usually in passing. What seems to me necessary is to assert at the same time his greatness—in that what he could do well he did better than anyone else has ever done—and the serious charges to be made against him, in respect of the deterioration—the peculiar kind of de-terioration—to which he subjected the language.

Many people will agree that a man may be a great artist, and yet have a bad influence. There is more of Milton's influence in the badness of the bad verse of the eighteenth century than of anybody's else: he certainly did more harm than Dryden and Pope, and perhaps a good deal of the obloquy which has fallen on these two poets, especially the latter, because of their influence, ought to be transferred to Milton. But to put the matter simply in terms of 'bad influence' is not necessarily to bring a serious charge: because a good deal of the responsi-bility, when we state the problem in these terms, may devolve on the eighteenth-century poets themselves for being such bad poets that they were incapable of being influenced except for ill. There is a good deal more to the charge against Milton than this; and it appears a good deal more serious if we affirm that Milton's poetry could *only* be an influence for the worse, upon any poet whatever. It is more serious, also, if we affirm that Milton's bad influence may be traced much farther than the eighteenth century, and much farther than upon bad poets: if we say that it was an influence against which we still have to struggle.

There is a large class of persons, including some who appear in print as critics, who regard any censure upon a 'great' poet as a breach of the peace, as an act of wanton iconoclasm, or even hoodlumism. The kind of derogatory criticism that I have to make upon Milton is not intended for such persons, who cannot understand that it is more important, in some vital re-spects, to be a *good* poet than to be a *great* poet; and of what I have to say I consider that the only jury of judgment is that of the ablest poetical practitioners of my own time.

The most important fact about Milton, for my purpose, is his blindness. I do not mean that to go blind in middle life is itself enough to determine the whole nature of a man's poetry. Blind-ness must be considered in conjunction with Milton's person-ality and character, and the peculiar education which he re-ceived. It must also be considered in connexion with his devotion to, and expertness in, the art of music. Had Milton been a man of very keen senses—I mean of *all* the five senses—his blind-ness would not have mattered so much. But for a man whose sensuousness, such as it was, had been withered early by book-learning, and whose gifts were naturally aural, it mattered a great deal. It would seem, indeed, to have helped him to concentrate on what he could do best.

At no period is the visual imagination conspicuous in Milton's poetry. It would be as well to have a few illustrations of what I mean by visual imagination. From Macbeth:

> This guest of summer,
> The temple-haunting martlet, does approve
> By his loved mansionry that the heaven's breath
> Smells wooingly here: no jutty, frieze,
> Buttress, nor coign of vantage, but this bird
> Hath made his pendent bed and procreant cradle:
> Where they most breed and haunt, I have observed
> The air is delicate.

It may be observed that such an image, as well as another familiar quotation from a little later in the same play,

> Light thickens, and the crow
> Makes wing to the rooky wood

not only offer something to the eye, but, so to speak, to the common sense. I mean that they convey the feeling of being in a particular place at a particular time. The comparison with Shakespeare offers another indication of the peculiarity of Milton. With Shakespeare, far more than with any other poet in English, the combinations of words offer perpetual novelty; they enlarge the meaning of the individual words joined: thus 'procreant cradle', 'rooky wood.' In comparison, Milton's images do not give this sense of particularity, nor are the separate words developed in significance. His language is, if one may use the term without disparagement, *artificial* and *conventional*.

> O'er the smooth enamel'd green . . .
> . . . paths of this drear wood
> The nodding horror of whose shady brows
> Threats the forlorn and wandering passenger.

['Shady brow' here is a diminution of the value of the two words from their use in the line from *Dr. Faustus*

> Shadowing more beauty in their airy brows.]

The imagery in **"L'Allegro"** and **"Il Penseroso"** is all general:

> While the ploughman near at hand,
> Whistles o'er the furrowed land,
> And the milkmaid singeth blithe,
> And the mower whets his scythe,
> And every shepherd tells his tale,
> Under the hawthorn in the dale.

It is not a particular ploughman, milkmaid, and shepherd that Milton sees [as Wordsworth might see them]; the sensuous effect of these verses is entirely on the ear, and is joined to the concepts of ploughman, milkmaid, and shepherd. Even in his most mature work, Milton does not infuse new life into the word, as Shakespeare does.

> The sun to me is dark
> And silent as the moon,
> When she deserts the night
> Hid in her vacant interlunar cave.

Here *interlunar* is certainly a stroke of genius, but is merely combined with 'vacant' and 'cave', rather than giving and receiving life from them. Thus it is not so unfair, as it might at first appear, to say that Milton writes English like a dead language. The criticism has been made with regard to his involved syntax. But a tortuous style, when its peculiarity is aimed at precision [as with Henry James], is not necessarily a

dead one; only when the complication is dictated by a demand of verbal music, instead of by any demand of sense.

> Thrones, dominations, princedoms, virtues, powers,
> If these magnific titles yet remain
> Not merely titular, since by decree
> Another now hath to himself engrossed
> All power, and us eclipsed under the name
> Of King anointed, for whom all this haste
> Of midnight march, and hurried meeting here,
> This only to consult how we may best
> With what may be devised of honours new
> Receive him coming to receive from us
> Knee-tribute yet unpaid, prostration vile,
> Too much to one, but double how endured,
> To one and to his image now proclaimed?

With which compare:

'However, he didn't mind thinking that if Cissy should prove all that was likely enough their having a subject in common couldn't but practically conduce; though the moral of it all amounted rather to a portent, the one that Haughty, by the same token, had done least to reassure him against, of the extent to which the native jungle harboured the female specimen and to which its ostensible cover, the vast level of mixed growths stirred wavingly in whatever breeze, was apt to be identifiable but as an agitation of the latest redundant thing in ladies' hats.'

This quotation, taken almost at random from *The Ivory Tower*, is not intended to represent Henry James at any hypothetical 'best', any more than the noble passage from **Paradise Lost** is meant to be Milton's hypothetical worst. The question is the difference of intention, in the elaboration of styles both of which depart so far from lucid simplicity. The sound, of course, is never irrelevant, and the style of James certainly depends for its effect a good deal on the sound of a voice, James's own, painfully explaining. But the complication, with James, is due to a determination not to simplify, and in that simplification lose any of the real intricacies and by-paths of mental movement; whereas the complication of a Miltonic sentence is an active complication, a complication deliberately introduced into what was a previously simplified and abstract thought. The dark angel here is not *thinking* or conversing, but making a speech carefully prepared for him; and the arrangement is for the sake of musical value, not for significance. A straightforward utterance, as of a Homeric or Dantesque character, would make the speaker very much more real to us; but reality is no part of the intention. We have in fact to read such a passage not analytically, to get the poetic impression. I am not suggesting that Milton has no idea to convey which he regards as important: only that the syntax is determined by the musical significance, by the auditory imagination, rather than by the attempt to follow actual speech or thought. It is at least more nearly possible to distinguish the pleasure which arises from the *noise*, from the pleasure due to other elements, than with the verse of Shakespeare, in which the auditory imagination and the imagination of the other senses are more nearly fused, and fused together with the thought. The result with Milton is, in one sense of the word, *rhetoric*. That term is not intended to be derogatory. This kind of 'rhetoric' is not necessarily bad in its influence; but it may be considered bad in relation to the historical life of a language as a whole. I have said elsewhere that the living English which was Shakespeare's became split up into two components one of which was exploited by Milton and the other by Dryden. Of the two, I still think Dryden's development the healthier, because it was Dryden who preserved, so far as it was preserved at all, the tradition of conversational language in poetry: and I might add that it seems to me easier to get back to healthy language from Dryden than it is to get back to it from Milton. For what such a generalization is worth, Milton's influence on the eighteenth century was much more deplorable than Dryden's.

If several very important reservations and exceptions are made, I think that it is not unprofitable to compare Milton's development with that of James Joyce. The initial similarities are musical taste and abilities, followed by musical training, wide and curious knowledge, gift for acquiring languages, and remarkable powers of memory perhaps fortified by defective vision. The important difference is that Joyce's imagination is not naturally of so purely auditory a type as Milton's. In his early work, and at least in part of *Ulysses,* there is visual and other imagination of the highest kind; and I may be mistaken in thinking that the later part of *Ulysses* shows a turning from the visible world to draw rather on the resources of phantasmagoria. In any case, one may suppose that the replenishment of visual imagery during later years has been insufficient; so that what I find in *Work in Progress* is an auditory imagination abnormally sharpened at the expense of the visual. There is still a little to be seen, and what there is to see is worth looking at. And I would repeat that with Joyce this development seems to me largely due to circumstances: whereas Milton may be said never to have seen anything. For Milton, therefore, the concentration on sound was wholly a benefit. Indeed, I find, in reading *Paradise Lost,* that I am happiest where there is least to visualize. The eye is not shocked in his twilit Hell as it is in the Garden of Eden, where I for one can get pleasure from the verse only by the deliberate effort not to visualize Adam and Eve and their surroundings.

I am not suggesting any close parallel between the 'rhetoric' of Milton and the later style of Joyce. It is a different music; and Joyce always maintains some contact with the conversational tone. But it may prove to be equally a blind alley for the future development of the language.

A disadvantge of the rhetorical style appears to be, that a dislocation takes place, through the hypertrophy of the auditory imagination at the expense of the visual and tactile, so that the inner meaning is separated from the surface, and tends to become something occult, or at least without effect upon the reader until fully understood. To extract everything possible from *Paradise Lost,* it would seem necessary to read it in two different ways, first solely for the sound, and second for the sense. The full beauty of his long periods can hardly be enjoyed while we are wrestling with the meaning as well; and for the pleasure of the ear the meaning is hardly necessary, except in so far as certain key-words indicate the emotional tone of the passage. Now Shakespeare, or Dante, will bear innumerable readings, but at each reading all the elements of appreciation can be present. There is no interruption between the surface that these poets present to you and the core. While therefore, I cannot pretend to have penetrated to any 'secret' of these poets, I feel that such appreciation of their work as I am capable of points in the right direction; whereas I cannot feel that my appreciation of Milton leads anywhere outside of the mazes of sound. That, I feel, would be the matter for a separate study, like that of Blake's prophetic books; it might be well worth the trouble, but would have little to do with my interest in the poetry. So far as I perceive anything, it is a glimpse of a theology that I find in large part repellent, expressed through a mythology which would have better been left in the Book of

Genesis, upon which Milton has not improved. There seems to me to be a division, in Milton, between the philosopher or theologian and the poet; and, for the latter, I suspect also that this concentration upon the auditory imagination leads to at least an occasional levity. I can enjoy the roll of

> . . . Cambula, seat of Cathaian Can
> And Samarchand by Oxus, Temir's throne,
> To Paquin of Sindean kings, and thence
> To Agra and Lahor of great Mogul
> Down to the golden Chersonese, or where
> The Persian in Ecbatan sate, or since
> In Hispahan, or where the Russian Ksar
> On Mosco, or the Sultan in Bizance,
> Turchestan-born. . .,

and the rest of it, but I feel that this is not serious poetry, not poetry fully occupied about its business, but rather a solemn game. More often, admittedly, Milton uses proper names in moderation, to obtain the same effect of magnificence with them as does Marlowe—nowhere perhaps better than in the passage from **"Lycidas"**:

> Whether beyond the stormy Hebrides,
> Where thou perhaps under the whelming tide
> Visit'st the bottom of the monstrous world;
> Or whether thou to our moist vows deny'd
> Sleep'st by the fable of Bellerus old,
> Where the great vision of the guarded Mount
> Looks toward Namancos and Bayona's hold . . .

than which for the single effect of grandeur of sound, there is nothing finer in poetry.

I make no attempt to appraise the 'greatness' of Milton in relation to poets who seem to me more comprehensive and better balanced; it has seemed to me more fruitful for the present to press the parallel between *Paradise Lost* and *Work in Progress:* and both Milton and Joyce are so exalted in their own kinds, in the whole of literature, that the only writers with whom to compare them are writers who have attempted something very different. Our views about Joyce, in any case, must remain at the present time tentative. But there are two attitudes both of which are necessary and right to adopt in considering the work of any poet. One is when we isolate him, when we try to understand the rules of his own game, adopt his own point of view: the other, perhaps less usual, is when we measure him by outside standards, most pertinently by the standards of language and of something called Poetry, in our own language and in the whole history of European literature. It is from the second point of view that my objections to Milton are made: it is from this point of view that we can go so far as to say that, although his work realizes superbly one important element in poetry, he may still be considered as having done damage to the English language from which it has not wholly recovered. (pp. 156-64)

> *T. S. Eliot, "Milton I," in his* On Poetry and Poets, *Farrar, Straus and Cudahy, 1957, pp. 156-64.*

CHARLES WILLIAMS (essay date 1940)

[Williams was a writer of supernatural fiction, a poet whose best works treat the legends of Logres (Arthurian Britain), and one of the central figures in the literary group known as the Oxford Christians, or "Inklings." The religious, the magical, and the mythical are recurrent concerns in his works, reflecting his devout Anglicanism and lifelong interest in the preternatural. Although his writings are not as well known today as those of his fellow-Inklings C. S. Lewis and J. R. R. Tolkien, Williams was an im-

portant source of encouragement and influence in the group. In the following excerpt from an essay originally published in 1940, he reviews criticism of Milton's poetry and cites evidence of Milton's fundamental humanity in his works.]

We have been fortunate enough to live at a time when the reputation of John Milton has been seriously attacked. The result of this attack, which has come from various sources otherwise not noticeably sympathetic with each other, has been to distract the orthodox defenders of Milton, and to compel the reconsideration everywhere of his power as a poet. This reconsideration of poetic glory has now reached everyone but Shakespeare—and, it seems, the metaphysicals and W. B. Yeats. All these, it is true, are united by one general tendency—the tendency to suggest, by one means or another, 'the feeling intellect' of which Wordsworth spoke. It has been because of his supposed lack of that intellect that Milton has been chiefly repudiated. He has been supposed to be a heavy and, if resounding, yet, one might say, a comatose poet. He has been called, personally, a bad man. Mr. Middleton Murry has said so in so many words: 'On the moral and spiritual side I find it easy enough to place him; he is, simply, a bad man of a very particular kind.' But Mr. Murry went on to profess himself puzzled: 'The difficulty is . . . that a poet so evidently great in some valid sense of the word, should have so little intimate meaning for us. We cannot make him real. He does not, either in his great effects or his little ones, trouble our depths.'

The success of such an attack—I do not suggest that that particular demonstration was confined to Mr. Murry; I quote him because those sentences form a convenient and compact epigram of the Opposition—lay chiefly in two things: (i) the lack of power in the orthodox party; (ii) the chance that Mr. Eliot had, about the same time, defined certain weaknesses in Milton. The orthodox Chairs of Literature, it must be admitted, had for long professed the traditional view of an august, solemn, proud, and (on the whole) unintelligent and uninteresting Milton. Professor Oliver Elton had already committed himself to the hint that Milton's subject could not concern us. 'What is made of the central myth? Does it in Milton's hands embody some enduring truth that speaks to the imagination? I doubt it.' The great academic teachers confined themselves to analyses of his diction and his rhythm. Remote from us (they, in fact, declared) was his pre-empted Eden; the pride of his Satan was his own pride, and he approved it. They argued over his Arianism or his Calvinism. They confined his instrument to the organ. They denied him cheerfulness and laughter (he who, it is said, used to sing while he had the gout!). They gloomed over him, as (they supposed) he, in his arrogant self-respect, gloomed over the world.

In the midst of this monotonous and uncritical praise, there emerged the calm voice of Mr. Eliot commenting on their subject—already admitted by them to be, to all intents and purposes, poetically alien from us. The present writer, disagreeing firmly with the effect of Mr. Eliot and indeed with some of Mr. Eliot, may admit his gratitude to Mr. Eliot for one or two critical statements. But 'the corrupt following' of Mr. Eliot went to lengths which Mr. Eliot (so far as I know) never suggested. Some writer—I have forgotten whom and I certainly will not look him up—said that Mr. Eliot had 'destroyed Milton in a parenthesis'. In fact, it might be permissible to say that no critic of Milton ought to be uninformed of Mr. Eliot's article, 'A Note on the Verse of John Milton' [see excerpt dated 1936]. I shall not discuss it here, because, frankly, I wish to discuss Milton; it is why other distinguished critics must also be ignored.

The general opposition resolved itself into four statements: (i) that Milton was a bad man; (ii) that Milton was, especially, a proud man and was continually writing approvingly about his own pride (Blake's incorrect epigram—that Milton 'was of the devil's party without knowing it'—was generally used here); (iii) that Milton's verse is hard, sonorous, and insensitive; (iv) that Milton's subject was remote and uninteresting. This being almost exactly what the orthodox party had been, for centuries, saying with admiration, they were quite helpless when they found it said with contempt. The solemn rituals in praise of Milton were suddenly profaned by a change of accent, but the choruses had not altered; what then were the pious worshippers to do?

There had been, of course, another possibility all along; it may be put very briefly by saying that Milton was not a fool. The peculiar ignorance of Christian doctrine which distinguished most of the academic Chairs and of the unacademic journalists who had been hymning Milton had not prevented them from arguing about the subtle theological point of the Nature of the Divine Son in *Paradise Lost*. The peculiar opposition to high speculations on the nature of chastity felt in both academic and unacademic circles had prevented any serious appreciation of that great miracle of the transmutation of the flesh proposed in *Comus*. And the peculiar ignorance of morals also felt everywhere had enabled both circles to assume that Milton might be proud and that yet he might not at the same time believe that pride was wrong and foolish. It was never thought that, if he sinned, he might repent, and that his repentance might be written as high in his poetry as, after another manner, Dante's is in his. Finally, it was not supposed, in either of those circles, that Satan could be supposed to be Satan, and therefore a tempter; that Christ (in *Paradise Regained*) could be supposed to hold human culture a poor thing in comparison with the salvation of the soul; or that Samson, in the last great poem, could in fact reach a point of humility at which he could bring himself occasionally to protest like Job against the apparent dealings of God with the soul.

I have said nothing here against the explicit denial to Milton of any drama or of any humanity. Those denials, as well as the others, had been consecrated by custom and a false *pietas*. Yet there was no need for them. The great and sensitive poetry of that august genius had escaped his admirers. 'Milton', said Landor, 'wrote English like a learned language'; no one had thought it worth while to learn it as a living language. All *Paradise Lost* was supposed to be an image of pride; and yet much of *Paradise Lost* can be felt to revolve, laughingly and harmoniously, round the solemn and helpless image of pride. To discuss this in full would need a volume. All that can be done here is to dwell on a few chief points in the discussion of *Paradise Lost*, with one or two comments on the other poems. And we may begin with *Comus*.

Comus is a kind of philosophical ballet. Comus himself is, no doubt, a black enchanter, but he talks the most beautiful poetry, and he does not seriously interrupt the dance of the three young creatures opposed to him, with their heavenly attendant: there is a particular evasion of violence (when Comus is 'driven in'). But what is this ritual ballet about? It is about an attempted outrage on a Mystery. The mystery which Comus desires to profane is the Mystery of Chastity. It is no use trying to deal with *Comus* and omitting chastity; *Hamlet* without the Prince would be an exciting melodrama compared to the result of that other eviction. Chastity (not only, though perhaps chiefly, that particular form of it which is Virginity; it will be observed that

Sabrina, the chaste goddess, is particularly favourable to herds and shepherd life) is the means, in *Comus,* by which all evils are defeated, the flesh is transmuted, and a very high and particular Joy ensured. It may be true that we ourselves do not believe that to be so, but our disbelief is largely as habitual as our admiration of *Comus.* That is why it has been possible to admire *Comus* without any serious realization of the mystery of chastity, in spite of John Milton.

> To him that dares
> Arm his profane tongue with contemptuous words
> Against the Sun-clad power of Chastity,
> Fain would I something say, yet to what end? . . .

And that, as one may say, is that. Comus is a fool in these matters, and

> worthy that thou should'st not know
> More happiness than is thy present lot.

But the Lady and her brothers and the Attendant Spirit and Sabrina do know. They know that Chastity is the guardian and protector of fruitfulness, that Temperance is the means of intense Joy. In their eyes Comus, by refusing to admit the general principle of things and to be obedient to it, is foolishly and sinfully limiting the nature of Joy. He prefers drunkenness to the taste of wine and promiscuousness to sensitiveness. He knows nothing about that other power which can make the flesh itself immortal; he prefers to sit about in sepulchres. Let him, cries the whole lovely dance.

Obedience then and Joy are the knowledge, in their degree, of those three Youths of *Comus.* And *Paradise Lost,* following long after, did not forget its prelude. It dealt with the same subject, but differently. Obedience, in the longer poem, is no longer that of a particular devotion to a particular law; it is the proper order of the universe in relation to a universal law, the law of self-abnegation in love. This, like chastity, is a mystery, but a mystery so simple that only the two sublimely innocent figures of Adam and Eve—beautiful, august, pure, and lucid— are able to express it; they, and the glowing fires of the celestial hierarchy; they, and beyond them the passionate deity of the Divine Son. It is not only a law—something that ought to be obeyed—but a fact—something that obeys and is obeyed. There remains, nevertheless, the possibility of disobedience to the law, of revolt against the fact. That disobedience depends on choice; and it is that choice on which the poem concentrates.

Comus had not gone so far. There is challenge there but no analysis of choice. Indeed, that is a problem which has been very rarely attacked in English verse. Generally the poets have confined themselves, sooner or later, to showing the decision; and certainly the actual motion of the will in its pure essence is inconceivable by the human imagination. Even Shakespeare, in *Macbeth,* when he reached that point, disguised it; Macbeth is half-determined; he asks if he will be safe; and when he is assured of safety he finds that he is wholly determined. But the actual decision is not there. Twice in *Paradise Lost* Milton attempted that problem: the first effort is contracted into Satan's speech on Niphates (iv. 32-113); the second is expanded into Eve's temptation, which begins with her dream (v. 8-135) and ends with the sensual degradation of her and Adam, so that the two of them, in another sense than *Comus* had foreseen, are 'lingering and sitting by a new-made grave'. Her temptation certainly is greater than that of her younger sister, the Lady, though it depends on the same method of flattery. To be praised and lured aside by such lines as 'love-darting eyes or tresses

like the morn' is well enough; but Eve needs a lordlier and more subtle, even a more metaphysical, attraction:

> Wonder not, sovran Mistress, if perchance
> Thou canst, who art sole Wonder.

This flattery is, however, of the same kind as Satan has previously, one may say, offered to himself; and, in a lesser degree, to the angels whom he persuades to follow him, in that speech (v. 796-802) which is the nearest thing in English poetry to Antony's speech in *Julius Caesar,* though Milton's lines are perhaps even more highly wrought, as they had to be, the speech being shorter. Every word echoes another; each accent is calculated—'magnific titles . . . merely titular', and so on. The aim in all three instances is the same; it is the awakening, in Satan, in Eve, in the angels, of a sense of proper dignity, of self-admiration, of rights withheld, of injured merit. This, it is asserted, Milton himself felt about himself. Perhaps; but if he did, then he certainly also thought it foolish and wrong. We need not fall back on any exterior evidence for that nor on any exposition of Christian morals; the evidence is in the poem itself. Satan thinks himself impaired, and what is the result? 'deep malice thence conceiving and disdain'. He is full of injured merit; what is the result? 'high disdain'. He is the full example of the self-loving spirit, and his effort throughout the poem is to lure everyone, Eve, Adam, the angels, into that same state of self-love. His description of himself in the first two books is truthful enough—

> that fixt mind
> And high disdain from sense of injured merit
> That with the mightiest raised me to contend. . . .

But it is also ironical. Certainly Satan has this sense; only this sense has landed him in hell—and in inaccuracy. Hell is always inaccurate. He goes on to say of the Omnipotence that he and his followers 'shook his throne': it is only afterwards that we discover that this is entirely untrue. Milton knew as well as we do that Omnipotence cannot be shaken; therefore the drama lies not in that foolish effort but in the terror of the obstinacy that provoked it, and in the result; not in the flight but in the fall. The irrepressible laughter of heaven at the solemn antics of 'injured merit', of the 'self impair'd', breaks out. Love laughs at anti-love.

> 'Nearly it now concerns us to be sure
> Of our Omnipotence' . . .
> To whom the Son, with calm aspect and clear
> Lightning divine, ineffable, serene,
> Made answer: 'Mighty Father, thou thy foes
> Justly hast in derision.'

In fact, the rebel angels only get as far through heaven as they do because God precisely suspends their real impairment—

> What sin hath impaired, which yet hath wrought
> Insensibly, for I suspend their doom.

So much for Milton's approval of the self-loving spirit. He thought pride, egotism, and a proper sense of one's own rights the greatest of all temptations; he was, no doubt, like most people, subject to it. And he thought it led straight to inaccuracy and malice, and finally to idiocy and hell. Milton may sometimes have liked to think of himself as proud, but it is extraordinarily unlikely that he liked to think of himself as malicious and idiotic. Yet it is those two qualities he attributes to Satan as a result of his energy of self-love. When Satan sees Eve:

> Her graceful Innocence, her every air
> Of gesture or least action overawed
> His malice . . .
> That space the Evil one abstracted stood
> From his own evil, and for the time remained
> Stupidly good.

It is not, however, Eve alone who is the image of some state of being opposite to Satan's. It is all the rest of the poem, but especially it is the Divine Son. Precisely as the mark of Satan and the rebel angels is that they will not consent to be derived from anyone else; he will have it that he was like Topsy and grew by himself; so the mark of the Son, of the angels, of Adam, of Eve, is that they derive, and take delight in deriving, from someone else. Their joy is in that derivation-in-love. The Divine Son carries it into the highest state—

> this I my glory account,
> My exaltation and my whole delight,
> That thou in me well pleased declar'st thy will
> Fulfilled, which to fulfil is all my bliss.

So Eve, in a state of passionate and pure love, to Adam:

> My author and disposer, what thou bid'st
> Unargued I obey.

Milton had his own views on the relation between the sexes, which (like almost any other views of the relation between the sexes) were probably wrong. But this last quotation does not spring from that only; it springs from the essential fact of things; which is everywhere this derivation-in-love. The Son is the Image of that, as Satan is the Image of personal clamour for personal independence. The casting-out of the rebel angels from heaven is the result of the conflict between the two Images—in so far as there can be any conflict between the state which is in utter union with Omnipotence and the state which is only in union with itself—if that, and the Niphates speech suggests that it is not even that. The obstinate figure of Satan does but throw up the intertwined beauty and lightness of the universe beyond him, the universe (and more than the universe) which understands, enjoys, and maintains, its continuous derivation, lordship, and obedience.

In this sense, therefore, the poem is concerned with a contrast and a conflict between two states of being. But those states are not only mythological; they are human and contemporary, and thus the poem has a great deal of interest for us. The overthrow of the rebel angels is the overthrow, spiritually, of all in whom that deriving and nourishing Love is dead. The very blaze of eyes from the chariot which the Divine Son rides is the spectacle of a living and stupendous universe rolling on the 'exhausted' rebels. There needs no battle; the exposition of the Divine Nature is enough.

> Sole Victor, from the expulsion of his foes,
> Messias his triumphal chariot turned.

It is we who are involved, one way or the other: it is not only to Adam that the Archangel's word is addressed—'Remember, and fear to transgress'.

Paradise Lost then is chiefly concerned with the choice between these two states of being, with the temptations which provoke men and women to that sense of 'injured merit', as Eve and Satan are provoked, and with the terrible result of indulging that sense. It is true that John Milton was not a man for compromise. When Adam, in the fullness of his passion for Eve, really does abandon heaven and his knowledge of God for her, Milton denounced his act. But it was, after all, Milton who imagined his passion so intensely as to make us almost wish that it could be approved. There and elsewhere *Paradise Lost* is full of the senses—even Shakespeare hardly made the human hand more moving. This would perhaps be more obvious if we were more attentive to the tenderness of some of the verse. It is no doubt as a result of the long tradition of the organ-music of Milton that the shyness of some of his verse passes unnoticed. The famous prayer to 'justify the ways of God to man' is a prayer of humility. This is seen by considering the lines that lead up to it. Milton, invoking the Holy Spirit, says:

> Thou from the first
> Was present, and with mighty wings outspread
> Dove-like sat'st brooding on the vast Abyss
> And mad'st it pregnant: what in me is dark
> Illumine. . . .

And so on. Now the point is that 'Dove-like' and 'pregnant' are words which cannot be sonorous and tremendous; it would make nonsense of them emotionally. The passage is daring in its hope, but shyly and modestly daring, palpitating with its own wonder at its own audacity. Milton may have been proud on earth (and repented of it), but he was not proud in his approach to heaven.

There is another word, at the other end of the poem, which is another example of a certain misreading. The renewed and repentant passion of Eve for Adam expresses itself.

> In me is no delay; with thee to go
> Is to stay here, without thee here to stay
> Is to go hence unwilling; thou to me
> Art all things under heaven, all places thou,
> Who for my wilful crime art banished hence.

This again is derivation (she from him and he from her), and the knowledge of derivation. After which outbreak of human love, the lines sink again into a shy softness of hope.

> This further consolation yet secure
> I carry hence; though all by me is lost,
> Such favour I unworthy am vouchsafed,
> By me the promised Seed shall all restore.

'The promised Seed' is, of course, Christ. But Milton did not choose to use any such august title. He preferred, there, the word Seed, and the literal meaning is not to be forgotten in the metaphorical. The metaphorical refers back to the glorious, devoted, self-abandoned figure—glorious because self-abandoned—which has again and again been deliberately contrasted with Satan throughout the poem; I need name only the pause in heaven and the pause in hell (ii. 417-29; iii. 217-26), the two progresses through Chaos (ii. 871-1033; vii. 192-221; and the Chaos is not only exterior; it is also the interior chaos of the human soul); and, of course, the conflict in heaven. But the literal meaning of 'Seed' is of the new, tiny, important thing, the actuality of the promise, the almost invisible activity upon which all depends. So small, so intimate, so definite, is the word that the line becomes breathless with it and with the hope of it. That breathless audacity of purpose towards the beginning of the poem is answered by a breathless audacity of expectation towards the end. And at the very end humanity has its turn in the hand again, the hand which has meant so much at certain crises of the poem: at the separation, as if symbolically, of a derived love from its source—

> So saying, from her husband's hand her hand
> Soft she withdrew;

and in the sin (the derived love working against its human and Divine sources):

> So saying, her rash hand in evil hour
> Forth reaching to the fruit, she plucked, she ate;

and so now in the rejoined union of that penitence and humility which Milton knew so well:

> They hand in hand with wandering steps and slow
> Through Eden took their solitary way.

There are no linked lovers in our streets who are not more beautiful and more fortunate because of those last lines; no reunion, of such a kind, which is not more sad and more full of hope. And then it is said that Milton is inhuman. The whole of our visibility, metaphysical, psychological, actual, has been increased by him.

It is the word 'solitary', however, which looks forward to the last two poems—to *Paradise Regained* and to *Samson*. The first is completely different from *Paradise Lost*. The verse is, on the whole, less infinitely sensitive than that of the earlier poem; it is already changing to something else. There are few personages; in the earlier there had been many. They are brooding rather than active. And whereas in *Paradise Lost* everything had been exposed from the beginning, now the chief thing is hidden. The centre had previously been a spectacle; now it is a secret. The Blessed Virgin is in a state of expectation:

> his absence now
> Thus long to some great purpose he observes.

Christ himself waits:

> to what intent
> I learn not yet, perhaps I need not know.
> For what concerns my knowledge God reveals.

The urgency is in Satan, but even he is here haunted by the unknown: 'who this is we must learn.'

It is the discovery of this nature, which Satan does not know, and which Christ only half-knows, that is the theme of the poem. Christ's answers to Satan's efforts to find out are, in a sense, riddles, for they are given half in his own terms and half in Satan's. Food; glory; kingdoms; earthly wisdom—these are the temptations; through all of them, in Milton's phrase,

> the Son of God
> Went on and stayed not.

He goes on—or in ('into himself descended'). It is precisely into his Nature that the argument plunges to seek its discovery, but the moral trials are hardly enough; at the end Milton used something else. He came to the mysterious 'standing'; moral temptation is lost in what lies behind it. 'Stand or cast thyself down': be whatever you are. But the answer is still a riddle; it has precisely the lightness, almost the happiness, certainly the heavenly mockery which is always the answer to the hellish sneer. Satan is as hopelessly foolish as ever, and Jesus speaks to him, in the technique of this poem, as the Divine Son had spoken of him to the Father in the *Paradise Lost*:

> To whom the Son with calm aspect and clear
> Lightning divine, ineffable, serene,
> Made answer.

> To whom thus Jesus: Also it is written
> Tempt not the Lord thy God; he said and stood.
> But Satan, smitten with amazement, fell.

He and his had been in the same case before—

> They astonished all resistance lost,
> All courage; down their idle weapons dropped . . .
> Exhausted, spiritless, afflicted, fallen.

'So, strook with dread and anguish, fell the Fiend.' Heaven is always unexpected to the self-loving spirit; he can never understand whence it derives, for he has himself renounced all derivation, as do those who follow him. It was this great and fundamental fact of human existence which Milton very well understood; it was this which his genius exerted all its tenderness and all its sublimity to express; it was this which is the cause of the continual laughter of *Paradise Lost,* and it was because of this that Milton invoked that Spirit which Itself derives from the co-equal Two.

It is not possible in the remaining space to discuss *Samson*. The verse again has changed, and I doubt if we have yet properly learnt its style. 'A little onward lend thy guiding hand'—to what? To the 'acquist Of true experience from this great event'. What then is our true experience from the poem? Much every way; perhaps not the least is the sense of the union of Necessity and Freewill. That had been discussed in *Paradise Lost,* as an accompaniment to the spectacle and analysis of man choosing. But there the actual stress had been a little on the choice; here it is a little on 'dire Necessity'. Here 'the cherub contemplation' is allowed even fuller view. The persons, if they do not exactly accuse God, at least indicate to God the unanswered questions. There is no humility in refraining from asking the questions; the humility consists in believing that there may be an answer. Both asking and believing are desirable, and both are here. In the earlier poems the sense of a full comprehension had been chiefly felt in the Figure of the Divine Son—and therefore either in heaven or (if among men) then prophesied for the future. But in *Samson* there is more than a hint that the great satisfaction of all distresses is already there. It is perhaps not by a poetic accident that here and there in the poem Milton wrote like Shakespeare; in other places, like himself with a new song. The modest and appealing courage of the opening of *Paradise Lost*—'and justify the ways of God to man' [see excerpt dated 1667]—becomes an angelic beauty of victory—

> Just are the ways of God,
> And justifiable to men,
> Unless there be who think not God at all.
> If any be, they walk obscure,
> For of such doctrine never was there school
> But the heart of the fool,
> And no man therein doctor but himself.

That is precisely Satan—and men and women. But 'Nothing is here for tears' is here no Stoic maxim, but something beyond—something 'comely and reviving'.

The phrase would cover most of Milton. So far from being granite, his verse is a continual spring of beauty, of goodness, of tenderness, of humility. The one thing he always denounced as sin and (equally) as folly was the self-closed 'independent' spirit, the spirit that thinks itself of 'merit', especially 'of injured merit'. It does not seem a moral entirely without relevance to us. All things derive in love—and beyond all things, in the only self-adequate Existence, there is the root of that fact, as of all. It is known in God; the Father speaks—

> and on his Son with rays direct
> Shone full; he all his Father manifest
> Ineffably into his face received,
> And thus the Filial Godhead answering spake.

'Filial . . . answering.' Milton has been too long deprived of half his genius. He did his best to make clear what he was saying. But then, as his admirer John Dryden wrote:

> Dim as the borrowed beams of moon and stars
> To lonely, weary, wandering travellers
> Is Reason to the soul.

(pp. 26-36)

Charles Williams, ''John Milton,'' in his The Image of the City and Other Essays, *edited by Anne Ridler, Oxford University Press, London, 1958, pp. 26-36.*

HUNTINGTON CAIRNS, ALLEN TATE, AND MARK VAN DOREN (conversation date 1941)

[*An American lawyer and literary critic, Cairns is the author of* Law and the Social Sciences *(1935) and* Legal Philosophy from Plato to Hegel *(1949). Tate, a prominent American man of letters, is associated with two critical movements: Agrarianism and New Criticism. Van Doren, perhaps best known as a poet, was also a respected critic. His criticism is aimed at the general reader, rather than the scholar or specialist, and is noted for its lively perception and wide interest. In the following excerpt from the transcript of a radio broadcast aired in 1941, the critics discuss* Paradise Lost, *emphasizing the importance of understanding the poem rather than simply reading it for what Matthew Arnold called "the great style."*]

Cairns: John Dryden, who was Milton's friend and first critic, observed that Milton combined the "loftiness of mind" exhibited by Homer with the "majesty" of expression exhibited by Virgil [see excerpt dated 1688]. It has always seemed to me that subsequent criticism has not improved upon that judgment. (p. 309)

[*Van Doren*:] Dryden's epithets—loftiness and majesty—do fit Milton. These epithets seem to refer chiefly, however, to the manner of Milton and to the quality of his mind. I am not at all convinced that the poem we have before us this evening is—well, let me put it this way—more than lofty and majestic.

Cairns: Mr. Tate, would you say that he had any rival in those two characteristics except Dante?

Tate: He is almost wholly unlike Dante in that respect. The loftiness that Dryden attributed to Milton is what Matthew Arnold meant by "high seriousness." It is all on one level. There is no letdown; the tone is the same throughout.

Cairns: It is what Matthew Arnold called the "grand style."

Van Doren: The great style [see excerpt dated 1888]. And that great style in Milton is something which he must write or else fall from poetry altogether. We agree in an earlier discussion that the difference between him and a poet like Shakespeare, if there is a poet like Shakespeare—or one like Dante, or one like Homer—is that those men have no style which they must pursue at peril of complete failure otherwise.

Cairns: Shakespeare's style was absolutely free; he used all the forms of blank verse and employed other metres as well. Milton as an extremely self-conscious artist—something Shakespeare was not—was much more on the side of strictness, although, of course, both his verse and his style vary.

Tate: In Books X and XI of **Paradise Lost,** in which there is so much description of the physical universe, in which there are prophecies of the future after the Fall of Man—in those passages we get Milton thinking, and his language loses its elevation. In fact, it seems to me to become dull. Milton has not been able to think and to imagine at the same time.

Van Doren: The old epigram to the effect that Milton wrote English as if it were a dead language applies there. You cannot think in a dead language. When Milton needs to think, his style shows the strain.

Cairns: He apparently thought in Latin just as easily as he thought in English; but I believe we ought to recognize what he attempted to do. He attempted the greatest undertaking in poetry ever ventured by an English poet. In doing that he teaches us that poetry is no trivial matter. He shows us also how important a thing form is.

Tate: Now, Mr. Cairns, don't you think we ought to get that undertaking clearly in mind? The fundamental subject in **Paradise Lost** is the dramatization of the origin of evil.

Van Doren: Let me interrupt you just a minute, Mr. Tate; please go on with the point later. I should like to quarrel with Mr. Cairns' use of the word "great." I do not see that this is the "greatest" undertaking, judging at any rate by the success achieved. If you judge by success rather than ambition in a poet, any one of a dozen plays by Shakespeare was a greater undertaking. *King Lear* is a greater undertaking.

Cairns: Let me explain what I meant. I expressly used the word "attempted" in referring to Milton's undertaking so as to negate the notion that the enterprise was necessarily successful. I meant a number of things by the phrase "greatest undertaking": first, that, at the time Milton wrote, the epic was generally regarded as the highest form of poetry; Milton therefore resolved he would write an epic.

Van Doren: Or, as they said in those days, heroic.

Cairns: Sometimes called the heroic poem. Since we are still without a satisfactory epic, it might be possible to draw the conclusion that an epic is the most difficult of all verse to write successfully and that Milton therefore undertook the poet's most difficult task. Second, the language in which Milton wrote is the most dangerous language that a poet can employ, I believe.

Tate: What do you mean by that?

Cairns: Because he must maintain at its full intensity the poetic note, or the language becomes absolutely flat. A poet could not possibly utilize a language more full of pitfalls than that in which Milton wrote.

Tate: What you say may be very true, but I do not see exactly what you mean by it. Dante's purpose in the *Divine Comedy* was certainly just as lofty, but Dante varies his language; he does not need to maintain the grand style.

Cairns: But Milton, in writing his kind of blank verse, had to maintain the grand style. He undertook that risk. He said: "I will write an heroic poem in twelve books in blank verse of the most difficult kind. I am certain I will be successful. At least I will undertake that risk." I can think of no other poem to put beside **Paradise Lost** in its kind of greatness.

Tate: There is another kind of blank verse altogether which Shakespeare used. Shakespeare's blank verse varies. It is not the same from play to play, but it shows that blank verse is a very flexible instrument. There is no reason why it cannot be varied.

Van Doren: You did not mean blank verse alone, did you, Mr. Cairns, when you referred to his style?

Cairns: I was thinking specifically of blank verse. It was created by Marlowe and the other dramatists. Of course, Milton's verse is quite varied. By dropping or doubling stresses he can achieve effects of grace or solidity and emphasis.

Van Doren: But the blank verse of Shakespeare comes between Marlowe and Milton. The style we are talking about in Milton's case is not necessarily wedded to the measure that he uses. Style, I should say, is his way of thinking about his material. If we can interpret a man's style as meaning something about his whole mind and his whole intention, as I am sure we can, then we discover that Milton's style, since it is as artificial as it is (of course, only at its worst is it stilted; at its best it is magnificent), means that his subject was in his own mind somehow above him, somehow out of reach. There is always the effort to reach up, to put himself on a level with subject matter which he assumes to be almost beyond human grasp.

Cairns: I was not speaking of the importance of the subject. That is a different matter. I was emphasizing the risk Milton ran in using his kind of blank verse which did not possess the freedom of Shakespeare's. His subject, like all subjects, was dictated to him by the age he lived in.

Tate: It seems to me that he never embodies the subject in the language. Now doesn't that bring us back to the theme of the poem?

Cairns: Tell us what you think the theme is.

Tate: The theme is the dramatization of the origin of evil in the world. If you look at the story of the Fall of Man, it is a very limited thing within this poem. The simple narrative running through the poem is concerned with that story, and Milton is at his best while he is telling that story, or leading up to it. Satan's escape from Hell, the temptation and the fall—all that is beautifully done.

Cairns: He is at his best, in my opinion, when he is most similar to Dante. That is to say, when he is concrete, as in his description of Pandemonium, the capital of Hell, or in his description of Satan's conversation with Sin and Death at the gates of Hell. When he is misty and unsubstantial, when he deals in images that are difficult or impossible to visualize, then he is least satisfactory.

Tate: But isn't he weakest in the description of this universe in which these events take place? Then his language becomes stilted, as Mr. Van Doren says; it becomes inflated and vague. Don't you think that is due to the fact that Milton never successfully imagined his universe? You might even call it a jerry-built universe. It is arbitrary and magical. For example, the bridge built from the gates of Hell to the Earth after the fall of man is an arbitrary trick incomprehensible in any real mathematical universe. It was arbitrary and almost perverse on Milton's part.

Van Doren: That bridge is something you cannot believe in. It does not seem any more substantial than a rainbow. Now your use of the word "imagination" interested me. Might it not be true that the trouble with Milton's universe—if there is any trouble with it, and there must be for us from the way we are talking—is that it is not as solid and convincing as Dante's. The trouble with it is that for Milton himself it was something that had to be imagined. It was not something that he believed, that he knew. Dante can be understood as making his universe out of all that he knew, out of all that he could think in any capacity at all—as a scientist, as a theologian, as a poet—whereas Milton, who was a Puritan, had a special view of the spirit. It is something much less substantial than it was for Dante; so he has to make his poetry out of something unsubstantial too, and imagined. Perhaps when we have to imagine a world, we are bound to fail. No man can imagine a world.

Tate: But don't you think that the structure of Dante's world was recognizable to men at that time and is still recognizable to us?

Cairns: I think so. The features of Dante's world are recognizable because Dante visualized them precisely and was artist enough to put that visualization on paper. There is a technical term applicable to the point you are making, the so-called

"Miltonic vague." It describes those vast but indeterminate pictures that Milton drew. I don't think anyone, even of Milton's own time, saw concretely the whole of what Milton had in mind, as they saw concretely what was in Dante's imagination.

Tate: Now, in the first place, Mr. Cairns, I agree with you when you say that he is at his best when he is most concrete, most Dantesque, let us say. But at the same time, there are certain passages in Milton—for example, the description of Satan that you get in Book I which he develops through elaborate Homeric similes. He always begins with *As* and he goes on for eight or ten, sometimes twenty, lines. They are like great Renaissance frescoes. It is word-painting. It is what Lessing would call descriptive poetry, and it is magnificent in its kind, but those fine passages tend to be just thrown into the poem. Then the narrative is resumed. The texture of the poem is not all of a piece.

Van Doren: He surely is a descriptive poet. The architecture of this poem is something like a veneer, something applied, the structure being invisible behind it and perhaps not so certain. I find myself more and more uncertain as I read *Paradise Lost* as to what its structure is, and I can doubt that this structure is sound, in view of the fact that Milton must borrow so many things for it. For instance, his God is not like the God of Dante, whom Dante is satisfied to speak of briefly from time to time

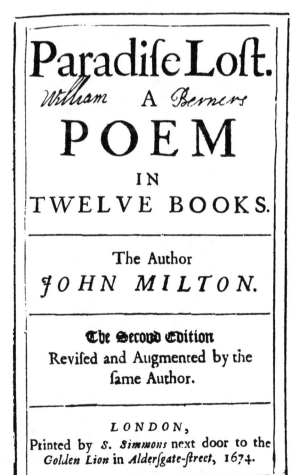

Title page of the second edition (1674) of Paradise Lost, *"revised and augmented by the . . . author."*

as king of the universe or Him whose will cannot be withstood. Milton does not believe in God in that simple and complete way. He must give us a Charlemagne, a military leader, a stuffed shirt.

Cairns: He also gives you the colonel of a British regiment.

Van Doren: This God, incidentally, is a synthetic God. He hangs out scales in the sky, the way the Zeus of Homer does, or he nods and thunder shakes the world.

Tate: He laughs too, occasionally, but there is no humor in the laughter.

Cairns: Milton is absolutely humorless. At least, I do not find any humor in him.

Tate: None whatever.

Van Doren: The very synthetic nature of his God and of his Christ, and of his whole universe, for that matter, leads me to suspect that somehow his conception of what he wanted to do, his conception of his subject, has not that clarity and that substantiality which we find in Homer, Dante and Shakespeare.

Cairns: We must not forget that Milton has survived for a long time and many fine judges have praised him. We have dwelt upon his defects, which is proper. But I should like to consider his good qualities also. To begin with, he has an exactness of expression which is admirable; also the associations he employs when he wishes to suggest images leave him few rivals in English. I have two stanzas here which may illustrate my point; one describing the gates of Heaven and the other the gates of Hell. You will notice how the character of the words changes when he switches from Heaven to Hell. His words are sweet and harmonious in describing the gates of Heaven; for the gates of Hell they are rasping and rough. This is the description of the gates of Heaven:

> Heaven opened wide
> Her ever-during gates, harmonious sound
> On golden hinges moving.

He describes the other gates:

> On a sudden open fly,
> With impetuous recoil and jarring sound,
> The infernal doors, and on their hinges grate
> Harsh thunder that the lowest bottom shook
> Of Erebus.

The point can be illustrated another way. Here is a line of Wordsworth, in which Wordsworth is perhaps attempting to say the same thing that Milton had said before him. Wordsworth says, "Negro ladies in white muslim gowns." Milton says, "Dusk faces with white silken turbans wreathed."

Tate: I prefer Wordsworth.

Cairns: I was afraid of that. Why do you prefer Wordsworth?

Tate: Because it is sharp and direct, and Wordsworth's words denote objects which are brought before you.

Cairns: I prefer Milton because his line is more poetic and because of his suggestion of mystery.

Van Doren: Well, here is another passage from Milton which magnificently explores in words—note the sheer weight of the words it uses, and their quality—the mysterious realm, the no-

man's realm, between Hell and what is above it. Satan is asking who shall be sent on that first exploratory flight toward Earth.

> Who shall tempt with wandering feet
> The dark, unbottomed, infinite abyss,
> And through the palpable obscure find out
> His uncouth way, or spread his aery flight
> Upborne with indefatigable wings
> Over the vast abrupt ere he arrive
> The happy isle?

Now that suggests to me Milton's greatest quality as poet, and anyone who knows the capacities of the English language for verse knows that Milton has no competitor. He explores these capacities, however, chiefly in musical terms. Milton is the greatest of all our versifiers on the musical side, not merely for the sonorousness that you so often hear about, not merely for the organ tones, but also for the really very precise fitting of the movement of a line, as here where the movement suggests effort, suggests titanic effort, to its subject. We all, I am sure, recognize his mastery of these verbal arts. Our only point—and it is one that should be made—is that the English-speaking people still have no first-rate epic poem. This poem does not compare for a moment with the *Iliad*.

Tate: I agree. Bearing that in mind, I think we can say it is a great poem. It seems to me that the musical quality that you …

Van Doren: I beg your pardon, Mr. Tate. I should say it was a great piece of writing. I should not call it a great poem; its structure and its conception are not first rate.

Cairns: May I add one thing to that? I should like to suggest that the chief interest that the modern reader has in Milton today is in his craftsmanship as a poet and, secondly, in the moral personality that is reflected in this poem.

Tate: I should like to say something about those two points if you are finished.

Cairns: Let me explain what I mean by the second point. The *Divine Comedy* has a human interest in the story itself. There is also a human interest in **Paradise Lost,** but of an entirely different kind. Its human interest is to be found in Milton's moral personality, which comes out in nearly every line.

Tate: In the personal passages about himself, and, of course, in the domestic relations of Adam and Eve which are in their way very charming. I must confess that if Milton had faced the humorous possibilities of that situation, it would be still more charming. The humor is largely unconscious.

Cairns: Of course, I am criticizing Milton when I say that we read him just for his craftsmanship, because the poem is too long to read for its craftsmanship alone; and Milton's personality can be found as easily, even more attractively sometimes, in his prose.

Tate: I don't know about that, Mr. Cairns. A point Mr. Van Doren made just a minute ago about the musical qualities of Milton's verse ought to be elaborated a little. Nobody can read Milton very long without realizing the masterly way in which he organizes what has been called by the critics the "verse paragraph." Now another poet, using the same material and having Milton's ability line by line, could write a magnificent line the way Milton does, but might cease to interest us because he lacks Milton's power of organization. The poem is actually broken up into units—the books—and the books are broken up into small units of attention which are managed very cunningly. Our attention is not exhausted over too long a stretch.

And that is all a part of this musical quality. The units of thought are expressed in units of rhythm.

Van Doren: Would you agree that here Milton has no competitor?

Tate: None whatever.

Van Doren: In English verse, or possibly anywhere at all?

Tate: None whatever. For example, Tennyson's blank verse, which, of course, is inferior to Milton's on many counts. But just on that count alone it is inferior. Tennyson does not know how to make the verse paragraph in the blank verse structure a unit of attention. It tends to be diffuse. In other words, Tennyson merely holds our attention line by line. Milton is far too cunning for that.

Cairns: I take it that you agree that we read him for his craftsmanship, but, at the same time, you do not want the poem any shorter. I cannot help thinking of Samuel Johnson's remark: ''No one ever wished it longer than it is.'' It is only fair to say that he also said: ''I cannot wish Milton's work other than it is.'' That is to say, I assume, he did not want it any shorter either.

Van Doren: We continue to read **Paradise Lost,** and I hope we shall do so for a long time. But the English-speaking peoples read **Paradise Lost** chiefly for its style. Here is our epic, if you will, but an epic which we can praise most for its language. We have said in the past that the greatest poets can be translated. That is to say, there is more in them than their language, important as language is. And one sign of this is that Homer and Dante and Shakespeare translate easily, translate well. They seem to keep their important qualities in whatever language they adopt. It is difficult to imagine Milton succeeding in Hungarian.

Cairns: It is their substance that is translated, not their craftsmanship. Take away Milton's craftsmanship and there is little left to interest the modern reader. Altogether apart from his style, his theme would baffle most people. I recall that Voltaire said that the French laugh when they are told that in the great English epic Satan struggles against God and a serpent persuades a woman to eat an apple. He said that is a subject that should be treated in a farce. The French just cannot get interested in it.

Tate: That brings us back to Milton's myth, and I have a great deal of respect for it, I must say.

Van Doren: But let me ask you whether that myth is not something which almost necessarily is to be treated briefly—treated as most myths are, in a few sentences, a few lines.

Cairns: The myth cannot support the burden it is designed to carry. No matter what the apple signifies, it is not convincing to have Adam and Eve behave the way they do after Eve eats the apple. Why should their love be less innocent? The modern reader merely smiles and flips the pages.

Tate: But what about the myth of Prometheus? Now, of course, the *Prometheus Bound,* which we have discussed, is relatively short.

Cairns: Prometheus is in this poem in the person of Satan.

Tate: That is what I am getting around to. He is Lucifer.

Cairns: In the Greek tradition he is Prometheus, and like Prometheus, Lucifer is rebelling against Omnipotence.

Tate: It seems to me that the symbolism of the Tree of Knowledge brings us very close to the Promethean myth. But I grant you that Milton's way of doing it is much longer than it should be.

Van Doren: We might put it this way: The myth is perfectly handled in a few verses of the Book of Genesis. It is also, if you like, treated at length by two poets, Aeschylus and Milton. Aeschylus chose the wiser way, as a poet, and this is where we can test his true greatness. He did not attempt the impossible. He made his drama into nothing more than a series of conversations. Prometheus is stationary, and to him come certain significant persons whose conversation with him reveals the depth and the sources of the myth. Milton makes the mistake, the technical error, of trying to set the whole universe in motion in order to elucidate his myth, and the universe he constructs for the purpose, of course, does not move simply and quietly enough to do the job. His universe, rather, gets in our way.

Cairns: That is an important point that can be extended: Milton in taking in the whole universe for his field of operation leaves out too much that is familiar and therefore necessary for the modern mind, if it is to feel at home in the poem. There is no love in the poem; there is no child in the poem; his description of the Garden of Eden is a place that we just do not recognize if we have ever been in the country.

Tate: That is a revival of Saturn's reign, the myth of the Golden Age again. I should put that same notion in slightly different terms. There is too great a discrepancy between this enormous universe and this central event which occurs in it. There is only one sin. There is not enough moral discrimination. In Dante you get a wonderful gradation of sins in which they are all related, in which all human experience is comprehended. The whole human experience in Milton is merely implied. You are given this one thing, the Fall of Man, and you are asked to arrange the rest for yourself.

Van Doren: Adam and Eve in the Garden of Eden have nothing to do except prune a few vines.

Cairns: There are no ice ponds or hay stacks; no barns or smoke from chimneys. They just ate nuts. They did not even drink wine, although Milton himself loved it.

Van Doren: And of course, this question is never really answered by the poem: Why should they not have plucked the fruit of the Tree of Knowledge? Why was knowledge so dreadful a thing for them to have? We never learn.

Tate: If we consider what he meant by knowledge, though, we have to concede the point. Isn't the state of Adam and Eve in the Garden a unity of being? This rational knowledge of the forbidden tree brings disunity of being.

Cairns: Not only does his argument fail there, but I think his whole theme fails when he attempts to justify the ways of God to man. If he had reversed his theme and tried to justify the ways of man to God, he would have been more interesting. He lacks the modernity of Shakespeare and Dante. (pp. 309-20)

Huntington Cairns, Allen Tate, and Mark Van Doren, from a conversation in their Invitation to Learning, *Random House, 1941, pp. 307-24.*

C. S. LEWIS (lecture date 1941)

[*Lewis is considered one of the foremost mythopoeic authors of the twentieth century. Indebted principally to George MacDonald, G. K. Chesterton, Charles Williams, and the writers of ancient Norse sagas, he is regarded as a formidable logician and Christian polemicist, a perceptive literary critic, and—perhaps most highly—as a writer of fantasy literature. Also a noted academic and scholar, Lewis held posts at Oxford and Cambridge, where he was an acknowledged authority on medieval and Renaissance literature. Lewis was a traditionalist in his approach to life and art: he opposed the modern critical movement toward biographical and psychological interpretation, preferring instead a theory of criticism that stresses the author's intent rather than the reader's presuppositions and prejudices. In the following excerpt from a lecture originally delivered in 1941, he studies the nature of Eve's and Adam's falls in* Paradise Lost.]

Eve fell through Pride. The serpent tells her first that she is very beautiful, and then that all living things are gazing at her and adoring her (IX, 532-541). Next he begins to make her "feel herself impair'd." Her beauty lacks spectators. What is one man? She ought to be ador'd and served by angels: she would be queen of heaven if all had their rights (IX, 542-548). God is trying to keep the human race down: Godhead is their true destiny (703, 711), and Godhead is what she thinks of when she eats (790). The results of her fall begin at once. She thinks that earth is a long way from Heaven and God may not have seen her (811-816); the doom of Nonsense is already at work. Next she decides that she will not tell Adam about the fruit. She will exploit her secret to become his equal—or no, better still, his superior (817-825). The rebel is already aiming at tyranny. But presently she remembers that the fruit may, after all, be deadly. She decides that if she is to die, Adam must die with her; it is intolerable that he should be happy, and happy (who knows?) with another woman when she is gone. I am not sure that critics always notice the precise sin which Eve is now committing, yet there is no mystery about it. Its name in English is Murder. If the fruit is to produce deity Adam shall have none of it: she means to do a corner in divinity. But if it means death, then he must be made to eat it, in order that he may die—for that reason and no other, as her words make perfectly plain (826-830). And hardly has she made this resolve before she is congratulating herself upon it as a singular proof of the tenderness and magnanimity of her love (830-833).

If the precise movement of Eve's mind at this point is not always noticed, that is because Milton's truth to nature is here almost too great, and the reader [of *Paradise Lost*] is involved in the same illusion as Eve herself. The whole thing is so quick, each new element of folly, malice, and corruption enters so unobtrusively, so naturally, that it is hard to realize we have been watching the genesis of murder. We expect something more like Lady Macbeth's "unsex me here." But Lady Macbeth speaks thus after the intention of murder has already been fully formed in her mind. Milton is going closer to the actual moment of decision. Thus, and not otherwise, does the mind turn to embrace evil. No man, perhaps, ever at first described to himself the act he was about to do as Murder, or Adultery, or Fraud, or Treachery, or Perversion; and when he hears it so described by other men he is (in a way) sincerely shocked and surprised. Those others "don't understand." If they knew what it had really been like for him, they would not use those crude 'stock' names. With a wink or a titter, or in a cloud of muddy emotion, the thing has slipped into his will as something not very extraordinary, something of which, rightly understood and in all his highly peculiar circumstances, he may even feel

proud. If you or I, reader, ever commit a great crime, be sure we shall feel very much more like Eve than like Iago.

She has still a further descent to make. Before leaving the Tree she does "low Reverence" before it "as to the power that dwelt within," and thus completes the parallel between her fall and Satan's. She who thought it beneath her dignity to bow to Adam or to God, now worships a vegetable. She has at last become 'primitive' in the popular sense.

Adam fell by uxoriousness. We are not shown the formation of his decision as we are shown the formation of Eve's. Before he speaks to her, half-way through his inward monologue (896-916) we find the decision already made—"with thee Certain my resolution is to Die." His sin is, of course, intended to be a less ignoble sin than hers. Its half-nobility is, perhaps, emphasized by the fact that he does not argue about it. He is at that moment when a man's only answer to all that would restrain him is: "I don't care"; that moment when we resolve to treat some lower or partial value as an absolute—loyalty to a party or a family, faith to a lover, the customs of good fellowship, the honour of our profession, or the claims of science. If the reader finds it hard to look upon Adam's action as a sin at all, that is because he is not really granting Milton's premises. If conjugal love were the highest value in Adam's world, then of course his resolve would have been the correct one. But if there are things that have an even higher claim on a man, if the universe is imagined to be such that, when the pinch comes, a man ought to reject wife and mother and his own life also, then the case is altered, and then Adam can do no good to Eve (as, in fact, he does no good) by becoming her accomplice. What would have happened if instead of his "compliance bad" Adam had scolded or even chastised Eve and then interceded with God on her behalf, we are not told. The reason we are not told is that Milton does not know. And I think he knows he does not know: he says cautiously that the situation "*seemd* remediless" (919). This ignorance is not without significance. We see the results of our actions, but we do not know what would have happened if we had abstained. For all Adam knew, God might have had other cards in His hand; but Adam never raised the question, and now nobody will ever know. Rejected goods are invisible. Perhaps God would have killed Eve and left Adam "in those wilde Woods forlorn": perhaps, if the man had preferred honesty to party loyalty or established morals to adultery, a friend would have been ruined or two hearts broken. But then again, perhaps not. You can find out only by trying it. The only thing Adam knows is that he must hold the fort, and he does not hold it. The effects of the Fall on him are quite unlike its effects on the woman. She had rushed at once into false sentiment which made murder itself appear a proof of fine sensibility. Adam, after eating the fruit, goes in the opposite direction. He becomes a man of the world, a punster, an aspirant to fine raillery. He compliments Eve on her palate and says the real weakness of Paradise is that there were too few forbidden trees. The father of all the bright epigrammatic wasters and the mother of all the corrupting female novelists are now both before us. As critics have pointed out, Adam and Eve "become human" at this point. Unfortunately what follows is one of Milton's failures. Of course, they must now lust after each other. And of course this lusting must be something quite different from the innocent desires which Milton attributes to their unfallen intercourse. Wholly new, and perversely delicious, a tang of evil in sex is now to enter their experience. What will reveal itself on waking as the misery of shame now comes to them (they are growing "sapient," "exact of taste") as the delighted discovery that obscenity is possible. But could poetry suffice to draw such a distinction? Certainly not Milton's. His Homeric catalogue of flowers is wide of the mark. Yet something he does. Adam's hedonistic calculus—his cool statement that he has never (except perhaps once) been so ripe for "play" as now—strikes the right note. He would not have said that before he fell. Perhaps he would not have said "to enjoy thee." Eve is becoming to him a *thing*. And she does not mind: all her dreams of godhead have come to that. (pp. 121-24)

> *C. S. Lewis, in his* A Preface to Paradise Lost, *revised edition, Oxford University Press, London, 1942, 139 p.*

E. M. FORSTER (broadcast date 1944)

[*Forster was a prominent English novelist, essayist, and critic whose works are marked by a strong strain of liberal humanism. His most celebrated novel,* A Passage to India *(1924), is a complex examination of personal relationships amid the conflicts of the modern world. Although some of Forster's critical essays are considered naive, his discussion of the techniques of fiction in* Aspects of the Novel *(1927) is regarded as a minor classic in literary criticism. In the following essay, which was written in 1944 in honor of the tercentenary of the publication of* Areopagitica, *he analyzes the argument of the work and applies Milton's message to contemporary events.*]

Milton's *Areopagitica* was published exactly three hundred years ago. The Parliament was fighting the King. Milton upheld Parliament, but it had just given him a very unpleasant shock. It had passed a defence regulation for the control of literature, and had placed all printed matter under a censorship. "No book etc. shall from henceforward be printed or exposed for sale unless the same be first approved of and licensed by such persons" as Parliament shall appoint.

There are usually two motives behind any censorship—good, and bad. The good motive is the desire of the authorities to safeguard and strengthen the community, particularly in times of stress. The bad motive is the desire of the authorities to suppress criticism, particularly of themselves. Both these motives existed in 1644, as they do in 1944, and, in Milton's judgment, the bad then predominated over the good. He was profoundly shocked that Parliament, which fought for liberty, should be suppressing it, and he issued his *Areopagitica* as a protest. It is the most famous of his prose works—partly because it is well written, but mainly because it strikes a blow for British freedom. It has been much praised, and sometimes by people who do not realise what they are praising and what they are letting themselves in for. In celebrating its tercentenary let us do so with open eyes.

To begin with one of Milton's smaller points: the inconvenience of a censorship to a creative or scholarly writer. All that he says here is true, though not of prime importance. It is intolerable, he exclaims, that "serious and elaborate writings, as if they were the theme of a grammar lad, must not be uttered without the eyes of a temporising and extemporising licenser." It is being treated like a schoolboy after one is grown up. The censor is probably some overworked and dim little official who knows nothing about literature and is scared of anything new. Yet the writer has to "trudge" to him to get his script passed, and if he makes any alteration afterwards, he must make application again. "I hate a pupil teacher, I endure not an instructor," proud Milton cries, and when he is reminded that the censor does after all represent the State, he hits back fiercely with "The State shall be my governors but not my critics."

All this is very much what a scholar or a creative artist might charge against a censor today: the big mind having to apply for permission to the fidgety small mind, and the small mind being supported by the authority of the State. It is all quite true; though why should not distinguished writers be put to trouble if it is to the general good? Why should they not submit to censorship if the national welfare requires it?

But there is much more to the problem, and the bulk of the *Areopagitica* is occupied with larger questions. Censorship means—uniformity and monotony: and they mean spiritual death. "Where there is much desire to learn, there of necessity will be much arguing, much writing, and many opinions: for opinion in good men is but knowledge in the making." And he apostrophises London at war in words we might gladly use today:

> Behold now this vast City: a city of refuge, the mansion house of liberty; encompassed and surrounded with God's protection; the shop of war hath not there more anvils and hammers working . . . than there be pens and heads there, sitting by their studious lamps, musing, searching, revolving new notions and ideas . . . others at fast reading, trying all things, assenting to the forces of reason and convincement.

All this free writing and reading will pass with the institution of the censorship, and its disappearance means the spiritual impoverishment of us all, whether we write and study or not. Intellectuals, in Milton's opinion, are not and cannot be apart from the community, and are essential to its health.

And then he tackles the problem of bad or harmful books. Might it not be well to prohibit them? The answer, No. It is preferable that bad books should be published rather than that all books should be submitted before publication to a government official. What is bad will be forgotten, and free choice in reading is as important as in action. "Truth is a perpetual progression." Also who is to settle what is bad? Who indeed? I recall in this connection an argument I had with an acquaintance during the first war. He was for prohibiting bad books, and when I asked him which books he answered "Conrad's novels." He did not care for them. He was an able public-spirited fellow, and later on he became an M.P.

If there is no censorship, is the writer or the newspaper editor to be above the law? Not at all. That is not Milton's position. If a book or pamphlet or newspaper is illegal it can, after publication, be prosecuted. The grounds of prosecution in his day were two—blasphemy and libel—and they hold good in our day, prosecutions for blasphemy now being very rare and prosecutions for libel very frequent. Milton did not set writers above the law. He did insist on punishment afterwards rather than censorship beforehand. Let a man say what he likes and then suffer if it is illegal. This seems to me the only course appropriate to a democracy. It is for the courts, and for no one else, to decide whether a book shall be suppressed.

Milton, would'st thou be living at this hour? "Yes and No," Milton would answer. He would certainly be heart and soul with us in our fight against Germany and Japan, for they stand for all that he most detested. And he would note with approval that there is no direct censorship of books. But he would disapprove of the indirect censorship operating on them through the paper control. At the present moment, most of the paper available goes to government departments, the publication of new books gets cut down, and most of our great English classics have gone out of print. Nor would he have approved of any attempt of publishers to combine and decide what books should be published. Would he have liked the wireless? Yes and No. He would have been enthusiastic over the possibilities of broadcasting, and have endorsed much it does, but he would not approve of the "agreed script" from which broadcasters are obliged to read for security reasons. He believed in free expression and in punishment afterwards if the expression turned out to be illegal: but never, never supervision beforehand, and whether the supervision was called censorship or licensing or "agreed script" would have made no difference to him. You can argue that the present supervision of broadcasters is necessary and reasonable, and that a silly or cranky speaker might do endless harm on the air. But if you feel like that, you must modify your approval of the *Areopagitica.* You cannot have it both ways. And do not say "Oh, it's different today—there's a war on." There was equally a war on in 1644. The fact is we are willing enough to praise freedom when she is safely tucked away in the past and cannot be a nuisance. In the present, amidst dangers whose outcome we cannot foresee, we get nervous about her, and admit censorship. Yet the past was once the present, the seventeenth century was once "now," with an unknown future, and Milton, who lived in his "now" as we do in ours, believed in taking risks.

In places, then, the *Areopagitica* is a disturbance to our self-complacency. But in other places it is an encouragement, for Milton exalts our national character in splendid words. He was intensely patriotic—on the grounds that when France was a tyranny and Germany a muddle, we were insisting on freedom of speech and being admired for it by European scholars. He had travelled on the Continent before the civil war, and sat among her learned men, "and," he goes on,

> I bin counted happy to be born in such a place of philosophic freedom as they supposed England was, while they themselves did nothing but bemoan the servile conditions with which learning amongst them was brought. . . . I tooke it as a pledge of future happiness that other nations were so persuaded of her liberty.

And he is proud—and how justly—of the variety of opinion incidental to our democracy of "this flowering crop of knowledge and new light" as opposed to "that dark conjealment of wood and hay and stubble" engendered by the pressure of totalitarianism. Our enemies, he notes, mistake our variety for weakness—exactly the mistakes the Germans were to make about us both in 1914 and in 1939.

> The adversary applauds and waits the hour: "When they have branched themselves out," saith he, "small enough into parties and partitions, then will be our time."Fool! he sees not the firm root of which we all grow, though into branches, nor will beware until he sees our small divided maniples cutting through at every angle of his ill-united and unwieldy brigade.

"Ill-united and unwieldy brigade"—could there be a phrase more prophetic of the Axis? But we must not dwell on the phrase too much, for the subject of the *Areopagitica* is not tyranny abroad but the need, even in wartime, of liberty at home. Not the beam in Dr. Goebbels' eye, but the mote in our own eye. Can we take it out? Is there as much freedom of expression and publication in this country as there might be? That is the question which, on its tercentenary, this explosive little pamphlet propounds. (pp. 51-5)

> *E. M. Forster, "The Tercentenary of the 'Areopagitica'," in his* Two Cheers for Democracy, *Harcourt Brace Jovanovich, Inc., 1951, pp. 51-5.*

CLEANTH BROOKS   (essay date 1947)

[*Brooks is the most prominent representative of the New Critics, a group of American literary critics that included Allen Tate, John Crowe Ransom, and Robert Penn Warren. Although the New Critics did not subscribe to a single set of principles, all believed that a work of literature should be examined as an object in itself, not as a manifestation of ethics, sociology, or psychology. Accordingly, examinations were accomplished by a close analysis of symbol, image, and metaphor. The third of these elements, metaphor, was the primary element of literary art for Brooks, and the effect of metaphor was of primary importance to him. His most characterisic essays are therefore detailed studies of metaphoric structure, particularly in poetry. According to René Wellek, Brooks "analyzes poems as structures of opposites, tensions, paradoxes, and ironies with unparalleled skill." Moreover, irony "indicates the recognition of incongruities, the ambiguity, the reconciliation of opposites which Brooks finds in all good, that is, complex poetry." Brooks's criticism strongly influenced critical writing and the teaching of literature in the United States during the 1940s and '50s. In the following excerpt, he studies light symbolism in "L'Allegro" and "Il Penseroso."*]

The most amusing and at the same time probably the most penetrating comment on **"L'Allegro-Il Penseroso"** has to be credited to Dr. Samuel Johnson. True, Johnson sometimes seems brutally obvious as when he points out that "the gaiety [of **"L'Allegro"** does not spring] from the pleasures of the bottle" [see excerpt dated 1779]. We scarcely need to be warned against attempting to visualize Milton's demure and academic Platonist tippling his way through the morning landscape. Some of Johnson's other comments seem quite as pointless without having the merit of seeming amusing. For example, Johnson tells us that "the *pensive* man never loses himself in crowds." To be sure, he does not; and if he does not, what of it? Yet it has remained for Dr. Johnson to point out the essential character of the speaker in the two poems, and several of the pertinent passages are worth quoting:

> Both Mirth and Melancholy are solitary, silent inhabitants of the breast, that neither receive nor transmit communication; no mention is therefore made of a philosophical friend, or a pleasant companion. The seriousness does not arise from any participation of calamity, nor the gaiety from the pleasures of the bottle . . . but [the cheerful man] mingles [as] a mere spectator. . . .

The *pensive* man never loses himself in crowds. . . .

> His Cheerfulness is without levity, and his Pensiveness without asperity. . . .
>
> No mirth can, indeed, be found in his melancholy; but I am afraid that I always meet some melancholy in his mirth. They are two noble efforts of imagination.

The passage ends with what is apparently one of the most astonishing *non sequiturs* in criticism. What have the facts given above to do with the fact that the two poems are "noble efforts of imagination"?

Actually they have a great deal to do with it, but Dr. Johnson did not see fit to point out why, and with the critical tools at his disposal, he may very well have had difficulty in doing so. It is characteristic of his honesty and his bluntness that he penetrated so far into the secret, and then rather clumsily appended his concluding judgment.

But Johnson is definitely about the critic's proper job. He inspects the poems—he does not emote over them. And for his failure to connect his observations on the poems with his judgment of their nobility, I hazard the following explanation: Milton is using in these poems something which looks curiously like symbolism, and a symbolism too delicate and indeterminate to be treated in terms of the coarser modes of it such as allegory, for example, with which Dr. Johnson was acquainted.

The typical critic since Johnson has done little more than express his appreciation of the delicious quality of the double poem, feeling perhaps that the beauty of the poem was so obvious as to require no further comment, and the effect given so simple as to render any consideration of architectonics a mere intrusion. This view is based upon a sound consideration of the effectiveness of the poem; but great art is never so simple that it will not repay careful reading, and the result has been that except for communication between admirers of the poem, the "criticism" has been quite useless. Confronted with the skeptic or the honest ignoramus, the admirer has frequently found himself embarrassed in attempting to demonstrate that the poem is so fine, or in explaining its difference from the numerous eighteenth-century imitations of it, which, though filled with the same details of landscape, are so wooden and dull.

Professor Tillyard has got much nearer the point in those of his comments which emphasize the element of tone: the poems, he says, are characterized by a "subtle friendliness of tone," and further, Milton displays in them "a perfect social tone." Tillyard has even gone so far as to suggest that the opening passage in **"L'Allegro"** represents conscious burlesque on Milton's part: "what possessed him," Tillyard asks, "that he should write such bombast? By what strange anticipation did he fall into the manner of the worst kind of eighteenth-century ode? If Milton meant to be noble, he failed dreadfully. If, however, he knew what he was doing, he can only have meant to be funny. And if he meant to be funny, to what end? There is nothing in the rest of the poem that suggests humour—at least of the burlesque sort."

This is all very shrewd. But Professor Tillyard, in his preoccupation with the problem of dating the poems—a matter that has its own importance, certainly—has hardly followed up the implications of his surmise. The alleged burlesque is justified by Tillyard on what are really extrapoetic grounds: the poems were written for an academic audience and the parody on the high-flown style, meant for their amusement, "can perhaps be justified" as the "high spirits of a young man." Tillyard does not relate the justification to the tone of the rest of the double poem, nor to its total effect.

With regard to the symbolism of the poem also, Tillyward has come close to the main matter. In pointing out the close connections between **"L'Allegro-Il Penseroso"** and Milton's First Prolusion (**"Whether Day or Night is the more excellent"**), he has indicated how important the day-night contrasts are in determining the general architecture of the poem. But he has not seen that the light-shade imagery amounts to a symbolism and that this symbolism is related ultimately to the "meaning" of the poem, including its tone.

Precisely how these symbols work—how Milton gives the illusion of full day, dawn, noon, and night, and yet manages to keep both poems bathed in their special quality of coolness, is a matter to be discussed in detail a little later on. For the moment, it is sufficient to prepare for such a discussion by examining a little further Dr. Johnson's observation that the protagonist of both poems is a mere spectator who avoids crowds and who has no companion, and the further observation

that mirth and melancholy in this poem "are solitary, silent inhabitants of the breast."

Mirth and melancholy need not be solitary—mirth in particular need not be. Dr. Johnson's reference to the pleasures of the bottle is definitely *not* beside the point; for, if Milton had intended to exploit mere contrast, **"L'Allegro"** would have been sociable; **"Il Penseroso,"** solitary; **"L'Allegro,"** boisterous; **"Il Penseroso,"** prim and sober. A little consideration, however, will show that Milton could not afford to exploit mere contrast. If he had, the two halves would have been driven poles apart. They would have ceased to be twin halves of *one* poem, for the sense of unity in variety would have been lost. We are almost justified in putting the matter in this way: by choosing the obvious contrast between mirth and melancholy, Milton obligated himself to bring them as close together as possible in their effect on the mind. For the tension between the two choices depends upon their presentation as choices which can appeal to the same mind; and the element of choice is worth emphasizing. Such pleasures and such sorrows as are intruded upon the character—"public," convivial mirth, or "public" melancholy, a funeral in the family—deprive the protagonist of conscious choice and render him chosen rather than choosing. Milton, one feels, is quite as emphatic in his belief that the aesthetic requires a deliberate act of will as was Immanuel Kant in insisting that the ethical involves deliberate choice.

It is not for nothing that the "Mountain Nymph, sweet Liberty" presides over **"L'Allegro"** and that the "Cherub Contemplation" dominates **"Il Penseroso."** Yet, as a matter of fact, the "Mountain Nymph" and the "Cherub," as we shall see, tend to merge into the same figure.

If, under the influence of Milton's later political career, we tend to give Liberty any political significance, we find her in **"L'Allegro"** in very strange company, consorting with

> Jest and youthful Jollity,
> Quips and Cranks, and wanton Wiles,
> Nods, and Becks, and Wreathed Smiles . . .
> Sport that wrincled Care derides,
> And Laughter holding both his sides.

The petition to Mirth

> To live with her, and live with thee,
> In unreproved pleasures free . . .

indicates, of course, plainly enough why Liberty walks at the right hand of Mirth: the pleasures are those which are unreproved. They are, moreover, the pleasures which can be had for the asking—the pleasure of drifting through the landscape or through the city, and watching the varying beauties of the landscape or the pageantry of men. But such pleasures pertain to liberty in another sense also: they depend upon one's freedom from business appointments and dinner engagements. One must be able to move along, unhurried and undetained, or the spell is broken. The necessity for being at a particular place at a particular time would wreck the cheerful man's day as described in the poem quite as completely as it would the day of the pensive man.

Dr. Johnson, always on the alert to ruffle up at the presence of Milton's somewhat aggressively republican goddess, does not betray any irritation at the presence of Liberty here. Perhaps he recognized in her, in spite of the mountain-nymph disguise, the same deity who presided over some of his own most delightful rambles. And if we find it difficult to associate Dr. Johnson, whose pleasures were uncompromisingly eighteenth-century, with either of Milton's cool and leisurely observers, we might recall such a passage as the following, in which Boswell describes a typical Johnsonian jaunt: "We landed at the Old Swan, and walked to Billingsgate, where we took oars, and moved smoothly along the silver Thames. It was a very fine day. We were entertained with the immense number and variety of ships that were lying at anchor, and with the beautiful country on each side of the river." The parallelism is at once destroyed when talkative Boswell, "the philosophical friend, or . . . pleasant companion," begins again to draw the great man out. But the delight in moving through a busy and fascinating world, leisurely and aimlessly, himself unbusied, was one which Johnson found most attractive. If the indulgence in such pleasures sometimes caused the rigid moralist to reprove himself for idleness, still, idle with such an idleness, he remained to the end. For all their differences over "liberty," the great republican and the great tory find themselves in close agreement here.

I have remarked that the mountain nymph and the cherub tend to merge into the same figure. One can easily see why. The more serious pleasures of Il Penseroso are so obviously "unreproved pleasures free" that the poet does not even need to point out that they are unreproved; yet, on the other hand, they are hardly more "contemplative" than those which delight L'Allegro. The happy man, too, is the detached observer, gliding through his world, a spectator of it, and preserving a certain aesthetic distance between it and himself. It is true that the spectator as the happy man emphasizes the spontaneity, the effortless freedom of his pleasures; and that the more austere observer is more consciously the man dedicated to the contemplative life. But here, as elsewhere in these poems, Milton's oppositons tend to come together.

The cheerful man's day is balanced by the pensive man's day at every point: a cheery dawn scene played off against a somber evening scene; Elizabethan comedy balanced against Greek tragedy; Lydian airs in antithesis to

> Such notes as warbled to the string,
> Drew Iron tears down *Pluto's* cheek. . . .

There is no need to detail them here; they are charming, and everyone knows them. What may be more to the point is to note that the tendency for these opposites to merge comes out even here. Both music passages, for example, refer to Orpheus; in **"L'Allegro,"** to an Orphean strain which might have won Eurydice completely; in **"Il Penseroso,"** to the Orphean strain played when Orpheus won her only to lose her. Or, to take another instance, the reference to supernatural lore in the one case involves *Faery Mab,* the most charming and harmless of folklores; in the other, the "unsphering" of

> The spirit of *Plato* to unfold
> What Worlds, or what vast Regions hold
> The immortal mind that hath forsook
> Her mansion in this fleshly nook:
> And of those *Dæmons* that are found
> In fire, air, flood, or under ground. . . .

But in neither case are we dealing with vulgar superstition— with the person in terror of spooks. In **"L'Allegro"** the superstition is reduced to a charming and poetic fancy; in **'Il Penseroso,"** it has been elevated to the level of the philosophical imagination.

Even more striking is the tendency for the opposed items to cross over from their usual antitheses in a fashion which associates the same object with both mirth and melancholy. Here,

the network of patternings is less obvious, and the instances given here may well be thought to be merely trivial. Perhaps they are; and yet in poetry so rich and cunningly contrived as this, we shall probably err less in putting down apparent relationships as meant and meaningful than in assuming that Milton threw materials into the double poem "every which way," and that the relations among them have no part in the total effect because we do not consciously associate them with the effect.

In **"Il Penseroso,"** one of the finest passages is that in which Milton describes his Platonist toiling on at his studies:

> Or let my Lamp at midnight hour,
> Be seen in som high lonely Tower,
> Where I may oft out-watch the *Bear* . . .

Yet if "high" and "lonely" seem inevitably associated with the tower, and the tower itself, the inevitable symbol of the meditative, ascetic life, one remembers that towers are to be found all through **"L'Allegro"**—yet they're associated with anything but lonely solitude. The lark scares away the dull night by singing "From his watch-towre in the skies." And again, the next tower that appears is one which is "Boosom'd high in tufted Trees." "Boosom'd" is almost shockingly unascetic. (One is tempted to pursue the parallel with the **"Il Penseroso"** passage further. There, in the tower he outwatches the stars of the Bear; here the tower contains the "star" which all watch, for "Cynosure" is the constellation of the Lesser Bear.)

Lastly, "Towred" is the adjective which Milton chooses to apply to the cities to which the cheerful man will turn at nightfall after his day in the country—

> Towred Cities please us then,
> And the busie humm of men. . . .

Or, take another example. The most sociable and crowded scene that occurs in **"L'Allegro"** is perhaps that in which

> . . . throngs of Knights and Barons bold,
> In weeds of Peace high triumphs hold,
> With store of Ladies, whose bright eies
> Rain influence, and judge the prise. . . .

It is a court scene of some pomp and circumstance. But the only parallel to it in **"Il Penseroso"**—and Milton has of course provided a parallel—is one of the most poignant of the melancholy delights. The knights have been shifted out of reality into Spenser's Faeryland:

> And if ought els, great *Bards* beside,
> In sage and solemn tunes have sung,
> Of Turneys and of Trophies hung;
> Of Forests, and inchantments drear,
> Where more is meant than meets the ear.

But the most important device used to bring the patterns of opposites together—to build up an effect of unity in variety— is the use of a basic symbolism involving light. The symbolism never becomes quite explicit, but it is most important, nevertheless, and in the use of it Milton brings all the oppositions of the poem together, and orders and unifies them. I have said that Milton never declares his symbolism explicitly, but he comes very close to it in the preamble of each poem: Melancholy is born "of . . . blackest midnight"; the fancies of Mirth are like the "gay motes that people the Sun Beams." This is more than a broad hint; and to have **"L'Allegro"** begin with a dawn scene and **"Il Penseroso,"** with an evening scene, emphasizes it.

But "L'Allegro," as we know, is not consistently a daylight poem, just as "Il Penseroso" is not consistently a night poem. The day, for both the cheerful man and the pensive man, embraces the whole round of the twenty-four hours. If both poems are characterized by a leisurely flowing movement as the spectator in each case drifts from pleasure to pleasure, and if in both poems he *is* the detached spectator—not the participant in the world he wanders through—in neither of the poems do we get the flaring sunbeam in which the dust motes swim or the unrelieved blackness of midnight. In both poems the spectator moves through what are predominantly cool half-lights. It is as if the half-light were being used in both poems as a sort of symbol of the aesthetic distance which the cheerful man, no less than the pensive man, consistently maintains. The full glare of the sun would then symbolize the actual workaday world over which neither the "Mountain Nymph, sweet Liberty" nor the "Cherub Contemplation" presides.

I have said that in this symbolism all the problems of the double poem head up. Let me mention a specific one: the landscape through which the spectator (as cheerful or pensive) moves must seem—even in its variety—cool, inviting, delightful. It must seem subdued to a mood; but more than that, it must present, when seen from every varying vantage-point, an aesthetic object. Yet even in a poem which skirts the *tour de force* as narrowly as this one does, it must seem *real*. It must be a world in which a real sun glares and real people sweat at their work; otherwise, it will seem a reduced world, or even an unreal, paper-thin world. The point is highly important. Milton must not merely, through his selection of materials, rule out the unpleasant or ugly. That is easy enough to do on the mechanical level. His selectivity must operate on a much higher plane: Milton must give the illusion of a real world, and of a full life—the whole round of the day—while at the same time presenting a world which meets at every point L'Allegro's cheer or Il Penseroso's melancholy.

To see how important this is, it is only necessary to recall the "Miltonic" landscapes of Akenside or the Wartons, poets who tend to heap up mechanically the characteristic details of Milton's poem, and yet fail of the characteristic atmosphere.

Since the progression of both "L'Allegro" and "Il Penseroso" is based upon the chronology of the day, Milton's light symbolism comes in naturally (and apparently inevitably), for the clock of the day is the sun; and the allusions to morning, noon, twilight, and moonlight provide Milton all the opportunities which he could wish to develop his symbolism of light and shade.

After the somewhat rhetorical exorcism of Melancholy, "Of *Cerberus,* and blackest midnight born," Mirth comes in with the morning. The first scene is a dawn scene—sunrise and people going to work: the plowman, the milkmaid, the mower, and the shepherd. But though we see people going to work, we never see them *at* their work, just as we do not ever feel the full glare of the sun. Even after the cottage dinner, when we are told of Phillis that

> . . . then in haste her Bowre she leaves,
> With *Thestylis* to bind the Sheaves;
> Or if the earlier season lead
> To the tann'd Haycock in the Mead. . . .

we do not accompany them to the haycock, nor do we feel the sun which "tans" it. Instead, with "secure delight" we slip

with the observer over to one of the "up-land Hamlets" where we watch

> . . . many a youth, and many a maid,
> Dancing in the Chequer's shade;
> And young and old com forth to play
> On a Sunshine Holyday,
> Till the live-long day-light fail. . . .

There is the illusion of a real world and of a daylight world; but the basic scenes of the daylight sequence in "L'Allegro" are dominated by the whistling plowman, the rustics at their noon meal, and the dancing in the "Chequer'd shade." The sunshine is that of a "Sunshine Holyday." Nobody sweats in the world of "L'Allegro"·—except the goblin:

> Tells how the drudging *Goblin* swet,
> To ern his Cream-bowle duly set,
> When in one night, ere glimps of morn,
> His shadowy Flale hath thresh'd the Corn. . . .

(Perhaps it is overingenious to suggest that in this scene—the only depiction of strenuous activity in the poem—Milton has "cooled" it off by making the flail "shadowy," by presenting it as part of a night scene, and by making the laborer, not a flesh-and-blood man, but a goblin. And yet the scene has been carefully patterned: it is balanced by the passage in "Il Penseroso," where the spectator having taken refuge from the sun, listens

> While the Bee with Honied thie,
> . . . at her flowry work doth sing. . . .

Goblins and bees are the only creatures presented "at work" in the two poems.)

If we get merely holiday sunshine in the country-scene sequence of "L'Allegro," we get, of course, no sunshine at all in the city sequence. But Milton has attended very carefully to the lighting of the scene displayed. The "high triumphs" of the knights and barons are presided over by the "bright eies" of the ladies, eyes which "Rain influence." "Rain influence" suggests a star metaphor: the stars were supposed to rain influence and determine events. The court ceremonial is succeeded by a wedding ceremony presided over by Hymen with his "Taper clear." The light in these scenes, then, is starlight or candlelight, not, to be sure, presented as the actual physical lighting of the scenes, but certainly insinuated into the mood of the scenes. The "thronged" scenes of "L'Allegro" are thus softened—the aesthetic distance from which they are viewed is thus indicated—just as the scenes of physical work have been softened and pushed back from the immediate presence of the observer.

The common-sense reader who distrusts the ingenious and wants his poetry to be explicit, declared, and forthright, may well ask why, if all this elaborate handling of the lighting is going on, Milton has to handle it so indirectly. Why doesn't Milton declare himself? But Milton does—at least with regard to the central element of the symbol, the association of the raw glare of the sun with the workaday world. In "Il Penseroso," when the showery morning has passed and the sun has broken forth, the speaker says:

> And when the Sun begins to fling
> His flaring beams, me Goddes bring
> To arched walks of twilight groves,
> And shadows brown that *Sylvan* loves
> Of Pine, or monumental Oake,
> Where the rude Ax with heaved stroke,

> Was never heard the Nymphs to daunt,
> Or fright them from their hallow'd haunt.
> There in close covert by som Brook,
> Where no profaner eye may look,
> Hide me from Day's garish eie. . . .

We are not told in so many words that the sun ("Day's . . . eie") is one of the "profaner" eyes; but it is "garish"; and it is associated definitely with the "heaved stroke." The pensive man withdraws from both—to the "twilight groves" where he may hear only the "work" of the bee—"flowry work," at which the bee sings—labor which is a part of nature itself. But the cheerful man too, as we have seen, has been kept out of "Day's garish eie" almost as completely as has Il Penseroso himself.

On the other hand, **"Il Penseroso"** avoids "blackest midnight" too. And at this point we are prepared to take up Tillyard's point about the burlesque style of the passage in which Melancholy is dismissed. The reprehension of Melancholy as loathsome, and the identification of her with the blackness of midnight are associated with a consciously stilted rhetoric which forms an ironical contrast with the freer and more casual rhythms in which the pensive man's actual experience of melancholy is expressed. It is the most delicate kind of qualification that a poet can give. For those who feel with Tillyard that the opening *is* bombastic, the presence of the bombast thus becomes meaningful. Melancholy as actually experienced by the pensive man is not a monstrosity at all. In contrast to her "literary" and abstract caricature, the actual goddess moves in a solid and "real" world, a beautiful world, and not a world of midnight black.

The poem has her come in with evening into a scene dominated by the moon. But even when the pensive man goes within doors and the moonlight is shut out, there are the "glowing Embers" which "Teach light to counterfeit a gloom." Midnight itself, when it is mentioned, is relieved by the speaker's studious lamp, and above the tower the stars are shining:

> Or let my Lamp at midnight hour,
> Be seen in som high lonely Towr,
> Where I may oft out-watch the *Bear*. . . .

The night scene here balances the starlight and candlelight of its companion scene in **"L'Allegro,"** with starlight and lamplight—though the stars here are not the eyes of brilliant women which "Rain influence, and judge the prise" but the cold, watchful stars of Ursa Major.

More important still, the sequence which follows, with its references to Plato, "Gorgeous Tragedy," Chaucer, and the other "great *Bards*," emphasizes the light accorded to the "inward eye," and thus provides a concrete realization of the paradox hinted at earlier in the poem: that the black of night, "staid Wisdoms hue," is merely a necessary veil to conceal a brightness which is in reality too intense for human sight.

This, of course, is the point which Milton was to make years later when he wrote his *Paradise Lost,* where, addressing the celestial light, he says:

> Shine inward, and the mind through all her powers
> Irradiate, there plant eyes, all mist from thence
> Purge and disperse, that I may see and tell
> Of things invisible to mortal sight.

When **"Il Penseroso"** was being written, that day was far in the future, and it is not my purpose to suggest that the poem gives a calculated foresight of that sterner time to come. What one may fairly say, however, is that the light symbolism, used so powerfully, though unobtrusively, in these earlier poems, was perfectly consonant with Milton's thinking, and was to emerge later in the great poem quite explicitly.

Actually, the connection of the life of contemplation with the higher life, and of the shades associated with melancholy with the brightest visions (though unearthly visions) is made quite explicitly at the end of **"Il Penseroso."** This concluding passage, by the way, has no parallel in the twin poem: **"Il Penseroso"** is twenty-four lines longer than its companion piece.

Here the secular life is made to pass over into the religious—the semipaganism of the "Genius of the Wood" frankly gives way to Christianity, and the measure of aesthetic distance with which the world has been consistently viewed is extended into the hermit's avowed withdrawal from the secular world altogether. The light symbolism accommodates itself to the change:

> . . . storied Windows richly dight,
> Casting a dimm religious light.

The pensive man is now bathed neither in midnight nor in the moted sunbeam. The daylight of the senses, dimmed and enriched by the storied windows, has been brought nearer to darkness, and yet at the same time prepared for the vision of the inward eye:

> Dissolve me into extasies,
> And bring all Heav'n before mine eyes.

Is the light "dimm" because religious, or religious because "dimm"? Or is it paradoxically dim, though religious—dim to the physical eye, though actually the proper light for one who would have the vision too insupportably bright for human sight to receive? To unravel these question is to recapitulate the entire symbolism of the two poems. Suffice it to say that the collocation, if it seems inevitable, seems so because of Milton's cunning development of the light passages throughout the poems. (pp. 50-66)

> *Cleanth Brooks, "The Light Symbolism in 'L'Allegro- Il Penseroso'," in his* The Well Wrought Urn: Studies in the Structure of Poetry, *1947. Reprint by Harcourt, Brace & World, Inc., 1956, pp. 50-66.*

NORTHROP FRYE   (essay date 1950)

[*A Canadian critic and editor, Frye is the author of the highly influential and controversial* Anatomy of Criticism: Four Essays *(1957), a study of four kinds of literary criticism: historical, ethical, archetypal, and rhetorical. In this work Frye argued that the methods and results of criticism can be scientific and that judgments are not inherent in the critical process. Believing that literature is wholly structured by myth and symbol, Frye considers the critic's task to be the exploration of the archetypal characteristics of a work. In the following excerpt from the 1950 preface to his edition of* Paradise Lost *and other poems, he discusses the versification, vocabulary, and imagery of Milton's major poetry.*]

Some poets—Spenser is a good example—start with experiment and end with conventional forms. Milton, like Shakespeare, begins in convention and becomes increasingly radical as he develops. The **"Nativity Ode"** is written in a tight, intricate stanza: the rhythm is not thereby prevented from bringing out every ripple and curve of the meaning—

> She, crowned with olive green, came softly sliding
> Down through the turning air

—but it is still exactly confined to the pattern of the stanza. It is a miraculous feat of technical skill, but even Milton could not always be performing miracles. He began a complementary poem on the Passion, but abandoned it after eight stanzas, and the stanzaic poem along with it. In the lovely tripping octosyllabics of **"L'Allegro"** and **"Il Penseroso"** he escaped into a more freely moving and continuous rhythm, and one that he uses for a good part of **Comus.** From that time on he sought mainly for long-range rhythmical units, and consequently moved away from rhyme, with its emphatic recurrence of sound, to the more austere but freer patterns of blank verse. He had a keen appreciation of music, and perhaps the continuity of rhythm in music influenced his poetry: it is noteworthy that in the Preface to **Paradise Lost** he speaks of "musical delight" [see excerpt dated 1668] as consisting among other things in "the sense variously drawn out from one verse [that is, line] into another."

The epic in any case makes heavy demands on the more sustained and cumulative rhythms, and Milton may have found his twenty years of practice in writing prrose also of some help. Prose gives the fullest scope for long-range rhythmical construction, and Milton, though he complains about having only the use of his "left hand" in prose, took every advantage of what prose had to give him. His vast periodic sentences that almost never end, his dizzy flights of prayer and peroration, and his labyrinths of subordinate clauses, qualifying epithets, and parenthetical allusions do not always make for what we should now consider ideal prose. But they may well have played some part in developing the motor power that makes **Paradise Lost,** apart from all its other qualities, the most readable epic in English. Milton's long postponement of his epic had its reward in the almost effortless mastery of the final performance. His reference to "Easy my unpremeditated verse" is no idle boast,and from beginning to end it is clear that **Paradise Lost** was not so much written as written out.

As Milton moves from the stanza into the more linear and continuous pentameter forms, a much bigger type of stanza develops, containing a number of pentameter lines in a rhythmic unit for which the most convenient name is "verse paragraph." The opening lines of **"Lycidas,"** down to "without the meed of some melodious tear," constitute an intricately organized verse paragraph, held together by the rhymes to "sere" in the second line and by a varied but consistent pattern of alliteration. The real secret of the unity behind its irregularity, however (the first line, for instance, is unrhymed and the fourth line is not a pentameter), defies all critical analysis. Many of the sonnets, too, are much more verse paragraphs than they are conventional sonnets. This paragraph forms a larger rhythmical unit in **Paradise Lost** too, and its presence enables Milton to handle the pentameter line with such a large number of run-on lines and medial pauses. In **Samson Agonistes** the paragraph achieves a much greater independence from the line and forms the basis for those amazing passages of recitativo which are perhaps the "freest" and most radically experimental verse that English poetry has yet reached.

The elements of versification are sound, vocabulary, rhythm, and imagery, and all four demand the closest attention from the reader of major poetry. Let us take a passage from **"L'Allegro"** and compare it with one from **"Il Penseroso"**;

> While the cock with lively din,
> Scatters the rear of darkness thin,
> And to the stack, or the barn-door,
> Stoutly struts his dames before.
> To behold the wandering moon,
> Riding near her highest noon,
> Like one that had been led astray
> Through the heaven's wide pathless way.

We can see how each of these four elements helps to make the contrast between the two poems. The **"L'Allegro"** passage has sharp, light vowels and abrupt, explosive consonants; the **"Il Penseroso"** one has resonant vowels and soft liquids. **"L'Allegro"** has vigorous words like "scatters," "struts," and "din"; **"Il Penseroso,"** quiet and pensive words like "wandering" and "behold." The **"L'Allegro"** rhythm flutters away in the almost unscannable third line and swaggers in the fourth; the **"Il Penseroso"** rhythm, especially in the fourth line, is full of slow and sonorous heavy accents. The first passage describes the clucks and crows of a poultry yard at dawn; the second dwells on the silence of a moonlit night. These points are simple enough, though it takes the highest kind of genius to produce the simplicity, and the principles involved are applicable everywhere in Milton.

Every language has its own body of descriptive sounds, and every poet accepts what his language affords him as a matter of course. *S* is always a hissing letter, suitable for serpents:

> And Dipsas (not so thick swarmed once the soil . . .)

R (which Milton is said to have pronounced very hard) is a martial one:

> Innumerable force of spirits armed;

W is for loneliness and terror:

> Through the world's wilderness long wandered man

and the long *a* and *o* sounds (even more resonant in seventeenth-century pronunciation) herald the approach of the prince of darkness:

> Meanwhile upon the firm opacous globe
> Of this round world, whose first convex divides
> The luminous inferior orbs, enclosed
> From Chaos and th' inroad of darkness old,
> Satan alighted walks.

Milton's poetry is proverbial for its resonance: the sonnet on the massacre in Piedmont, for instance, is a deeply felt and powerfully indignant poem, but this does not prevent it from being also a kind of étude, a technical exercise in sombre vowels. It is natural that we should find what makes most noise easiest to hear. This is one reason why Satan makes the strongest initial impact on the reader of **Paradise Lost,** for in the great variety of Milton's orchestration Satan gets most of the heavy brass. It is true also that the gloom and terror of hell is not less impressive for being obviously impressive. But it would be a pity to neglect the woodwinds and strings, and fail to hear how the brothers in **Comus** murmur to each other what they have read in praise of chastity; how the flowers are dropped one by one on Lycidas' grave; how the Christ child lies asleep with his legions of angels sitting quietly around him; how the fragrance of Eden is diffused over the earth by lazy breezes. The great hymn of creation in the seventh book of **Paradise Lost,** in which everything seems to dance in the joy of its deliverance from chaos and the release of its form, is a particularly wonderful example of Milton's skill in the subtler and softer harmonies:

> Forth flourished thick the clustering vine, forth crept
> The smelling gourd, up stood the corny reed
> Embattled in her field; and th' humble shrub
> And bush with frizzled hair implicit: last
> Rose, as in dance, the stately trees.

Passing from the sounds to the words, we notice that Milton uses an unusually large proportion of long words of Latin origin. Also that he often uses such words in an original Latin sense different from ours: "frequent" means crowded, "horrid" means bristling, "explode" means to hiss off or drive away, and so on. Many of these Latin words have become dead robot words in our speech, with nothing left in them of the vivid concrete metaphors they once were. But Milton uses them with the whole weight of their etymology behind them, and in reading him we have to wake up this part of our vocabulary. It comes as something of a shock to read in *Paradise Regained* of "elephants endorsed with towers," because we no longer think of *dorsum,* back, in connection with the word. But in Milton "astonished" means not mildly surprised but struck with thunder; "aspect" and "influence" are still partly technical terms in astrology, and "insinuating" has its visual meaning of wriggling as well as its abstract meaning. This principle of traditional weight applies not only to words, but to phrases as well, and the reader should be warned that it is precisely in such lines as "He for God only, she for God in him," where Milton seems to be most typically Miltonic, that he is most likely to be quoting verbatim from the Bible.

Another feature of Milton's vocabulary, the catalogues of proper names, also needs a word of warning. There are two reasons for which these catalogues are never used. They are never used to show off Milton's learning, and they are never used as an easy way of increasing the resonance. When they are lists of strange gods, they suggest the incantation or muttered spell of the magician who commands them, as in the summoning of Sabrina in *Comus,* and, less obviously, in the roll call of baffled demons in the **"Nativity Ode."** In *Paradise Lost* the rumble and crash of Satan's armies is echoed in the place names of epic and romance; the garden of Eden calls up the luxuriant and fruitful spots of earth, and the storms of advancing chaos sweep from point to point over the wastes of Asia and America. In each case the reader who has to look up several dozen references at once may miss the fact that the vagueness and strangeness of the names is exactly the poet's reason for using them. There are exceptions to this, of course: one should not miss the irony of "Vallombrosa," with its echo of "valley of shadows" in reference to hell, nor of the fateful epithet of Eden, "this Assyrian garden," which links it prophetically with the ferocious children of Nimrod who annihilated the Ten Tribes.

Some of the peculiar features of Milton's rhythm have been mentioned. The prosody of *Paradise Lost* has been exhaustively studied, but the general principle is that Milton can do anything he likes with the pentameter line. One may notice particularly the use of trochaic rhythms to describe falling movement:

> Hurled headlong flaming from th' ethereal sky,
> Exhausted, spiritless, afflicted, fallen;

the placing of two strong accents together in the middle of a line to describe something ominous or foreboding:

> Which tasted works knowledge of good and evil,
> Deep malice to conceal, couched with revenge;

the use of extra syllables to suggest relaxation or lateral movement:

> Luxuriant; meanwhile murmuring waters fall;

and the use of a weak or enjambed ending that pushes the rhythm into the next line to describe the completing of a movement:

> Intelligent of seasons, and set forth
> Their airy caravan high over seas
> Flying.

The long Latin words in Milton's vocabulary also have the rhythmical function of relaxing or increasing the speed. A monosyllable always means a separate accent, however slight, and a series of them produces a slow, emphatic sonority that would soon become intolerable unless relieved:

> Scarce half I seem to live, dead more than half.
> O dark, dark, dark, amid the blaze of noon,
> Irrecoverably dark!

The same principles of variation apply to the other verse forms as well as to the pentameter, and usually the sense will warn us when a change of pace is coming:

> I can fly, or I can run
> Quickly to the green earth's end,
> Where the bowed welkin slow doth bend.

Milton's imagery is more difficult to appreciate than any other aspect of his work. Except perhaps in **"L'Allegro"** and **"Il Penseroso,"** he is not one of the intensely visualizing poets: we are more conscious of degrees of light and shade than of sharply outlined objects. In this Milton is more characteristic of his age than elsewhere: in such painters as Rembrandt and Claude Lorrain, who were Milton's contemporaries, we find the same mysterious shadows and diffused brilliance that we find in Milton's hell and heaven. The relative vagueness of vision in *Paradise Lost* can hardly be due primarily to Milton's blindness, for we find it also in the early poems: in the formless shadows of the old gods retreating from the tiny point of light at the center of the **"Nativity Ode"**; in the dark wood of *Comus* and in the stylized pastoral world of **"Lycidas."** In *Samson Agonistes,* where the hero is blind, the vision is outside the poem: it is focused with unbearable intensity on the hero himself, whose inability to stare back is his greatest torment, an agony of humiliation that makes him, in one of the most dreadful passages in all drama, scream at Delilah that he will tear her to pieces if she touches him. The precision of Milton's poetry is aural rather than visual, musical rather than pictorial. When we read, for instance:

> Immediately the mountains huge appear
> Emergent, and their broad bare backs upheave

the mountains cannot be *seen:* it is the ear that must hear in "emergent" the splash of the water falling from them, and in the long and level monosyllables the clear blue line of the horizon. In every major poem of Milton's there is some reason why the ear predominates over the eye. In the **"Nativity Ode,"** it is because of the pattern of light and shade already mentioned; in *Comus,* it is because of the dark "leafy labyrinth" where one listens intently for rustles and whispers; in **"Lycidas,"** it is because the ritual lament generalizes the imagery; in *Paradise Lost* it is because the three states of existence, heaven, hell, and Paradise, all transcend visualization; in *Samson Agonistes* it is because the Classical form of the tragedy makes it a discussion or reporting of offstage events. The prominence of temptation among Milton's themes is significant too, as temptation is an attempt to persuade one through aural suggestion to seize something that is illusory.

In *Paradise Lost* Milton uses the same Ptolemaic onion-shaped universe that Dante does, with the earth at the center and the *primum mobile* at the circumference. But Dante puts heaven and hell inside this universe; Milton puts them outside, and the impersonal remoteness of the Copernican universe, with its unthinkable stretches of empty space, thus forms part of his poetic vision. Dante relies on symmetry; Milton on disproportion. Satan is a colossal angel and a toad; Christ is to become a despised son of the Adam he creates; Raphael is a hero of a war that rocks heaven, yet he drops in on Adam and Eve for a cold lunch; all the armies of heaven and hell and the fate of the created universe hang on one apple, and on whether or not a hungry girl will reach for it. What holds this farrago together is nothing that the eye or mind can accept, but the steady flow of the powerful working words that, exactly like the temptations in the poems, persuade us to seize the illusion. Milton, the agent of the Word of God, is trying to awaken with his words a vision in us which is, in his own language, the Word of God in the heart, and in the possession of which we may say with Job, "I have heard thee with the hearing of the ear, but now mine eye seeth thee." If we surrender to his charming and magical spell, and seize his fables of hell and Paradise, they will become realities of earth, and the stories of Adam and Samson our own story. And then, perhaps, we may consider a further question:

> what if Earth
> Be but the shadow of Heaven, and things therein
> Each to other like, more than on Earth is thought?
>
> (pp. xxi-xxx)

Northrop Frye, in an introduction to "Paradise Lost" and Selected Poetry and Prose by John Milton, edited by Northrop Frye, Holt, Rinehart and Winston, 1951, pp. v-xxx.

ROBERT GRAVES (essay date 1957)

[*Graves was a versatile English poet, novelist, translator, and critic. First associated with the Georgian poets of World War 1, he later followed a nontraditional yet highly ordered line, being influenced during the 1920s and 1930s by the American poet Laura Riding. Graves's reputation rests largely on his verbal precision and strong individuality as a poet. He is also considered a great prose stylist and is well known for such historical novels as* I, Claudius *(1934) and* Wife to Mr Milton *(1943). Witty, imaginative, and seldom concerned with the ordinary, Graves's novels are at once eccentric and scholarly, and his characters are considered larger than life. In the following excerpt, he suggests how Milton may have gone about composing "L'Allegro" and "Il Penseroso" and judges the overall success of the two poems.*]

Poetry (need I say?) is more than words musically arranged. It is sense; good sense; penetrating, often heart-rending sense. Children who enjoy verse-jingles are not reliable critics of poetry, and though a few nursery-rhymes happen to be poems, most have nothing but their engaging rhythms to recommend them. Yet how few readers ever get beyond the jingle-loving or, at best, the music-loving, stage of poetic appreciation! How few give any thought to the sense of a poem, though it often has layer after layer of meaning concealed in it!

I don't enjoy generalizing, unless I can support my argument by practical examples. I assume that almost everyone has read Milton's **"L'Allegro,"** but I, for one, hadn't read it carefully until the other day, when my thirteen-year-old daughter Lucia, finding herself obliged to learn it by heart (as I had done at the same age) asked me: "Isn't this rather a muddle, Father?"

How could I deceive an innocent and intelligent girl? I admitted, after a closer scrutiny of the text, that **"L'Allegro"** was indeed a dreadful muddle, and that most of it could be "appreciated" only in the Burkian sense, as one appreciates deformed gorgons and hydras.

Lucia's anthology version began straight away with:

> Haste thee, Nymph, and bring with thee
> Jest, and youthful Jollity . . .

(There was something awkward about '*youthful* Jollity,' I felt at once—it must have been put there for some dishonest reason.) Then the same Nymph was asked to bring along two other allegorical figures:

> . . . Sport that wrinkled Care derides,
> And Laughter holding both his sides.

Jest, Jollity, Sport, Laughter—four figures not easily distinguished, as one distinguishes the plaster saints in a Catholic repository by the emblems they bear: Peter's keys, Isidore's spade, Lawrence's gridiron, and so on. I found this conjunction rather fuzzy.

One way of appreciating a poem is first to write it out in longhand; then to imagine oneself composing the lines, and so creep inside the poet's skin. The process of getting a rough verse draft into presentable form will be familiar to most of you. And with practice one can often deduce, from some slight awkwardness surviving in the final version, what the grosser faults of the original were.

Well, when I tried the longhand test, my little finger told me (and I never argue with my little finger) that Milton had written:

> Hasten, Mirth, and bring with thee
> Jest and Youth and Jollity,
> Sport that wrinkled Care derides
> And Laughter holding both his sides . . .

Afterwards he had wondered whether the difference betwen Mirth and Jollity could be justified or, alternatively, the difference between Mirth and Laughter. He shook his head, changed "Mirth" to "Nymph," and kept her anonymous. Then, disliking the two *n's* of "Haste thee, Nymph"—not noticing another "thee" at the end of the line—and went on:

> And in the right hand lead with thee
> The mountain nymph sweet Liberty . . .

But it was clear that some lines were needed to separate this couplet from the first one, in which he had not only used the same rhyme—*with thee* and *Jollity*—but also the word *Nymph*. So between the figures of Mirth, Jest, Youth, Jollity, and their companions, Sport, Care and Laughter, he introduced a crowd of impersonalized nouns:

> Quips and Cranks and Wanton Wiles,
> Nods and Becks and gleeful Smiles . . .

And, to prove that he was a Cambridge graduate, Milton added a mythological reference to Hebe, Goddess of Youth. Having decided on Hebe, he prudently removed the figure of Youth from the second line by changing *Youth and Jollity* to *youthful Jollity*. I suspect that the first draft ran:

> Wreathed about sweet Hebe's cheek
> Which is dimpled, fair and sleek . . .

but Milton realized that "*Wreathed about sweet Hebe's cheek*" was far too heavy for a tripping measure, and that *wreathed* made an ugly assonance with *sweet* and *cheek*. So he substituted *wreathed smiles* for *gleeful smiles* and let the next line read:

> Such as hang on Hebe's cheek . . .

Clearly smiles don't hang on cheeks, and wreaths don't either, and Milton knew it; but the revised line was much more musical, with its alliteration of *hang* and *Hebe:* and in these minor poems Milton always put music before sense, if he ever got stuck. Besides, all nouns were capitalized in his day (whether common or proper); so Quips, Cranks, Wiles, Nods, Becks and Smiles could be read as allegorical imps or animalcules. Smiles, for example, might be tinsy, whimsical little atomies, wearing wreaths around their heads, and hanging merrily from Hebe's cheeks. He hoped to get by with that.

On re-reading:

> Which is dimpled, fair and sleek . . .

Milton disliked the three adjectives in a row, immediately after all those nouns in a row—Quips, Cranks, Wiles, Smiles, etc. So he considered:

> And love to live on skin so sleek . . .

But the double alliteration—*love, live; skin, sleek*—was excessive; so he decided to retain the dimples and let the tinsy whimsical little Smiles keep house in them. He wrote:

> And love to live in dimple sleek . . .

Cheek, not *cheeks*, for the sake of the rhyme; and *dimple*, not *dimples*—because of dimple*s s*leek. Though it was only natural to suppose that Hebe had two cheeks, there's a hoary Latin verse-convention that allows the use of singular for plural, and Milton took advantage of it. And he knew, of course, that dimples aren't sleek; however, another hoary Latin verse-convention, called "transference of epithet," allowed him to call the *dimple* "sleek," instead of the cheek. But this is not honest English.

That it was a "tripping measure" suggested the next line:

> Come and trip it as you go . . .

The rhyme would be *toe*, meaning *toes*. So he used another transferred epithet, making *fantastic* govern *toe*. But this is not honest English either. In English, toes are not "fantastic," unless one is a Charles Addams monster, or has been forced to wear tight shoes as a child.

So Milton was now back at:

> And in the right hand lead with thee
> The Mountain Nymph, sweet
> Liberty . . .

and rattled on:

> I'll live with her, and live with thee
> In unrestrained pleasures free . . .

He then thought of his Puritanical father, who was paying him a modest allowance to write poems in a cottage at Chalfont St. Giles, rather than enter the family scrivener's office. What would Father say about "*unrestrained*"? He changed it to "*unreproved*," which made the line sound less orgiastic. Yet condonation of wanton wiles, including a derision of serious, careworn men, still seemed a bit dangerous, so he dissociated himself from the poem by making it describe the ideal, mirthful man—and not himself, John Milton.

The next trouble was that he had carelessly repeated the '*with thee-ee*' rhyme. He corrected this by inserting two more lines of padding:

> And if I give thee honour due,
> Nymph, admit me of thy crew . . .

'*Nymph*,' again! Very well, he'd call her by her real name and risk it:

> Mirth, admit me of thy crew,
> To live with her, and live with thee,
> etc., etc.

Then the poem got underway at last:

> To hear the lark begin his flight
> And singing startle the dull night . . .

Milton now asks Mirth's permission (unnecessarily, I think) to hear the lark begin his flight and sing, etc., until the dappled dawn doth rise; and then to come and bid her good-morrow at his window, peering out through the sweet brier, vine, or twisted eglantine, at the cock in the barnyard crowing and stoutly strutting before his dames. So far, not so bad. But while distractedly bidding good-morrow, at the window, to Mirth, with one ear cocked for the hounds and horn, he sometimes, we are told, goes "*walking, not unseen, by hedgerow elms, on hillocks green.*" Either Milton had forgotten that he was still supposedly standing naked at the open window—(the Jacobeans always slept raw)—or else the subject of "walking" is the cock who escapes from the barnyard, deserts his dames, ceases to strut and, anxiously aware of the distant hunt, trudges far afield among ploughmen and shepherds in the dale. But why should Milton give twenty lines to the adventures of the neighbour's wandering cock? And why "*Walking, not unseen*"? Not unseen by whom?

Please, do not think that I am joking when I suggest that a chunk of the poem formed the sixth page of Milton's manuscript and got accidentally misplaced as the third page. (Always number your pages, girls!) Milton laid the poem aside for a few days, perhaps, while he visited London to see whether Jonson's learned socks were on and, when he returned, did not notice the mistake.

Well, when Milton had finished **"Il Penseroso,"** he took **"L'Allegro"** up again and found it far too countrified. In **"Il Penseroso"** he had sown Classical allusions with the sack; but apart from Hebe's cheek and a reference at the end to Orpheus and Eurydice, **"L'Allegro"** might have been written by any poetic bumpkin (Shakespeare, poor fellow, for example—"father lost his money in the meat trade and couldn't send young Will to college.") So, Milton tacked on that ponderous "*Hence, loathed Melancholy*" piece to "*Haste thee, Nymph*," and there introduced the Nymph in due Classical form as Euphrosyne; giving her, for good measure, two variant mythical parentages.

He also, I believe, inserted that most un-English passage about Corydon's meeting with his boy-friend Thyrsis at the cottage between the oaks. Phillis prepares their luncheon and scurries discreetly off in pretended haste, saying that she has to bind the August sheaves, or perhaps cart the June hay, she isn't sure which. Milton, incidentally, not having access to an Apollodorus in Chalfont St. Giles, misreported Euphrosyne's birth. Her mother was neither Venus nor Aurora, but the Moongoddess Eurynome; her father neither Zephyr nor ivy-crowned Bacchus, but jolly old Father Zeus himself, with a thunderbolt in his fist and a grog-blossom on his nose.

If you think that I'm exaggerating Milton's pride in his Cambridge education, you will have to account for these lines:

> Thou goddess fair and free
> In Heav'n ycleped Euphrosyne,
> And by men heart-easing Mirth . . .

—which made Milton an immortal and mortalized all the uneducated Chalfont clods who could talk only English, who called Thyrsis "Maister Jack Melton" and who called Corydon "that young furriner, Maister Charley Deodati, or somesuch."

The legitimacy of this sort of chiseling ''appreciation'' is tested when one applies it to other, similar songs of mirthful invocation such as Shakespeare's:

> Come unto these yellow sands,
> And then take hands . . .

or the nursery-rhyme:

> Girls and boys, come out to play:
> The moon doth shine as bright
> as day . . .

There the probing cold-chisel of criticism rings against the true rock of poetry. With **"L'Allegro,"** the plaster flakes away and the rubble tumbles out.

I grant that **"L'Allegro"** is cunning verbal music—''linked sweetness long drawn out'' as he called it—and that Milton is a cunning musician who can cheat you of your inheritance of common sense as easily as he once cheated his Royalist mother-in-law, Mrs. Powel, of her ''widow's third.'' Shakespeare, on the other hand, was an English poet, and always played fair, except sometimes when he knocked off verses too hurriedly for patching up some old play. He burlesqued the ''University wits'' who wrote English as if it were Latin, and never did so himself, though his grammar school education seems to have been a sound one.

The genius of the English language, whether transplanted to Wales, Scotland, Ireland or America remains literal, logical, and anti-hypothetical. No sensitive poet or critic can accept without a blush Milton's pastoral affectations:

> Ye daffodillies fill your cups with tears
> And strew them on the hearse where
> Lycid lies . . .

in what is supposed to be an elegy for his dead college friend. Especially after Shakespeare had written in *The Winter's Tale* the wholly unpastoral lines:

> Yellow daffodils
> That come before the swallow dares,
> and take
> The winds of March with beauty . . .

which no true poet who has lived through an English winter can read without a catch at the heart.

A poem is legitimately judged by the standards of craftsmanship implied in the form used. One expects little from a fo'csle ballad where even false rhymes do not matter so long as the tune is brisk. But Milton was not writing a fo'csle ballad. Why pretend that English poetry is held in a Latin straitjacket, from which one has to wriggle out with the artful aid of grammatical and syntactical license? (pp. 17-19)

> *Robert Graves, "John Milton Muddles Through,"
> in* The New Republic, *Vol. 136, No. 21, May 27,
> 1957, pp. 17-19.*

A. E. DYSON   (essay date 1961)

[*Dyson is an English literary critic who is recognized as an exponent of two schools of critical thought. Once an adherant of ''liberal humanism,'' he has for some time considered himself a Christian ''traditionalist.'' ''Literature is a celebration,'' he has stated. ''Almost everything that makes life rich was said or written or created by people who are no longer living; almost all the color and joy came from religious men.'' In the following excerpt from an essay written during the earlier stage of his critical*

outlook, he examines the nature of Milton's Christ in Paradise Regained.]

The regaining of Paradise [in ***Paradise Regained***] is directly associated with Christ's temptation in the wilderness. All the emphasis falls on Christ's power to endure testing; when this is proved, he is already established as a superior to Adam and Eve—a conquerer where they fell. The problem haunting the background of ***Paradise Lost*** is here inescapably to the fore. To all apparent purposes Christ and Satan face one another as equals: or at least on a basis which makes Christ's fall possible, and therefore his victory real. Yet from the start, we know Christ is not going to fall; and we know that his victory will in essence be that of Truth over Error, not of superior prowess in deeds of arms. The challenge Milton faced was to make of this a real drama instead of a puppet-show; and . . . had he stressed Christ's compassion, his forgiveness, his sufferings, success might have been fully possible. Instead, the Christ we see is no humbled God, but magnanimous man. His victory is a stoic one, and marked by the type of pride—even insolence— to which the tradition of magnanimity lends itself. All that the theological placing does is to confer on him invulnerability: a gift which turns his tone and manner from a justified human reaction to a totally insufferable pretense. If he were really equally matched with Satan, his insolence would be at least understandable. If he were really the Christ of the gospels, his victory would ring true, though his manner, of course, would be different. As it is, the theology sabotages the heroism, and the heroism the theology. And . . . we find Milton's imaginative engagement is with the heroic values, though his intelligence is busied with the blackening of Satan in ways demanded by the myth.

Not that the blackening of Satan is at all difficult under the circumstances—for consider the unenviable nature of the Archfiend's task. In ***Paradise Lost*** he had a fair chance of success. Even with Job, to whom frequent reference is made, he was matched on very fair terms. In ***Paradise Regained,*** he has no hope at all, as both he and his opponent very well know from the start.

His tribulations begin with the disguise, which is seen through at a glance, and does nothing but make him look absurd. It is seen through, moreover, not because any depravity is apparent either in his mien or in his opening remarks, but because Christ has a magic insight (''For I discern thee other than thou seem'st'') against which it would be useless to argue. Satan's first words, indeed, are an offer of help which is the least that any human being could have made in the circumstances, and Christ's crushingly ungracious reply is an immediate assertion of superiority not only over Satan, but over anyone who might try to give help.

This is only the start of Satan's trials. More seriously embarrassing is the fact that he has nothing to offer. How can you tempt someone who already possesses all he desires, and enjoys total immunity from the rest? Comus had the Lady's natural sexuality to work upon; Satan in ***Paradise Lost*** had Eve's vanity (illegitimately smuggled in to a prelapsarian nature as Dr. Tillyard has shown it to be [in *Studies in Milton* (1951); see Additional Bibliography]). Here, Satan has nothing. When he conjures up a splendid banquet, Christ waves it aside—not on the scriptural ground that man cannot live by bread alone, but with the discouraging reply that anything Satan can do, he can do better:

> To whom thus Jesus temperately reply'd.
> Said'st thou not that to all things I had right?
> And who withholds my pow'r that right to use?

Shall I receive by gift what of my own,
When and where likes me best, I can command?
I can at will, doubt not, as soon as thou,
Command a Table in this Wilderness,
And call swift flights of Angels ministrant
Arrayd in Glory on my cup to attend:
Why shouldst thou then obtrude this diligence,
In vain, where no acceptance it can find,
And with my hunger what hast thou to do?

The tone, though described as temperate, is surely nearer to aristocratic hauteur. It is Christ's magical power, not his moral, that is invoked; what he asserts is not greater humility, but greater power.

And throughout the poem, Christ's triumphs bring him closer and closer to a tested and unbreakable self-sufficiency. He can exist without help from Satan—without help from anyone—and the knowledge turns, in his tone, to arrogance.

When Satan offers knowledge, he stands less hope of success than he does with his offers of food. Christ already knows all that there is to be known, and is well aware that views other than his own are dangerous errors:

To whom our Savior sagely thus repli'd.
Think not but that I know these things, or think
I know them not; not therefore am I short
Of knowing what I ought: he who receives
Light from above, from the fountain of light,
No other doctrin needs, though granted true;
But these are false, or little else but dreams,
Conjectures, fancies, built on nothing firm.

Here, it is true, Christ claims a knowledge which might be presumed not peculiar to his magical status, but available to all who use Reason: at this point we are nearer to *Comus,* where the Lady's wisdom is, at least, part of a human tradition. Nevertheless, Christ at once goes on to *reject* the wisdom of the Greeks as being exactly the "conjectures, fancies, built on nothing firm" he has warned against, and to assert, instead, the absolute supremacy of Hebrew revelation. Might it be, one wonders, that Milton is here recognizing human reason as his own last temptation and greatest treason? He certainly makes Christ speak against the Greeks with a bitterness new in his works, and talk of knowledge almost as a personal possession.

If Satan cannot tempt successfully, neither can he harm. When he sends a storm sufficient to put a normal man in his grave, Christ sleeps "patiently" through it, and greets his tormentor the following day with the words,

Me worse than wet thou find'st not; other harm
Those terrors which thou speak'st of, did me none;
I never feard they could.

No wonder Milton has difficulty in making the battle seem real, and Satan in any meaningful sense dangerous. He solves the problem, as he did to a lesser extent in *Paradise Lost,* by applying to Satan heavily charged words and epithets of disapproval, and by constantly asserting that Satan's weak arguments have been defeated by superior virtue. The truth is, however, as any impartial reader is likely to see, that a few of Satan's arguments are sound—one or two of them to the verge of being unanswerable—just as some of his offers of help are the least that any occupant of the wilderness could have made without active discourtesy. And Christ's answers are characterized by the arrogance of superior strength rather than by a truly moral insight and compassion.

The nature of Milton's Christ is naturally the central crux. Clearly he is nothing like the figure in the gospels. If anything, he resembles more closely a strong human hero from the Old Testament—Job, perhaps, or King David, though with the divine status safeguarding him from their human doubts and fears. But who, in literature, is he really like? I suggest Shakespeare's Coriolanus; and for one or two moments at least, Marlowe's Tamburlaine.

In Book I we find God the Father thinking of his Son in terms of glory, much as Priam might have thought of Hector. Smiling with characteristic aloofness, he ponders the humiliations which Satan is to receive at the Savior's hands:

He now shall know I can produce a man
Of femal Seed, far abler to resist
All his sollicitations, and at length
All his vast force, and drive him back to Hell,
Winning by Conquest what the first man lost
By fallacy surpriz'd. But first I mean
To exercise him in the Wilderness,
There he shall first lay down the rudiments
Of his great warfare, ere I send him forth
To conquer Sin and Death the two grand foes,
By humiliation and strong Sufferance.

In Christ's first long meditation (a speech which many commentators have felt to reflect Milton's own early sense of election to greatness) there is reference to heroic and warlike dreams of youth, which his mother encourages in a tone and mood that might remind us of Volumnia. It very soon becomes clear that Christ regards temptation solely as a trial of his strength, and the task of "saving" as a demonstration of his superiority to those he has come to save. Two of the truly remarkable passages in the poem, both spoken by Christ, will have to be quoted:

For what is glory but the blaze of fame,
The peoples praise, if always praise unmixt?
And what the people but a herd confus'd,
A miscellaneous rabble, who extoll
Things vulgar, and well weighd, scarce worth the praise;
They praise and they admire they know not what,
And know not whom, but as one leads the other;
And what delight to be by such extolld,
To live upon their tongues and be their talk,
Of whom to be disprais'd were no small praise?

We are undoubtedly reminded, I think, of Coriolanus' reluctance to submit to the judgment, or the approval, of the people. In the tone, there is contempt for the vulgar—for those he has supposedly come to save. And as later passages make clear, what Christ renounces is not true fame, but a fame unworthy of his deeds. The praises of men are by and large worthless; it is the applause of angels and of God that he desires.

The second passage is similar. Christ is speaking, at first, of the corrupt Emperor, whom Satan has tempted him to subdue by political power:

Let his tormentor Conscience find him out,
For him I was not sent, nor yet to free
That people victor once, now vile and base,
Deservedly made vassal, who once just
Frugal, and mild, and temperat, conquerd well,
But govern ill the Nations under yoke,
Peeling thir Provinces, exhausted all
By lust and rapine; first ambitious grown
Of triumph that insulting vanity;
Then cruel, by thir sports to blood enur'd
Of fighting beasts, and men to beasts expos'd,
Luxurious by thir wealth, and greedier still,

> And from the daily Scene effeminate.
> What wise and valiant man would seek to free
> These thus degenerat, by themselves enslav'd,
> Or could of inward slaves make outward free?

What Christ says here is that most men are not worth saving, and that his mission is something other than to these. At the end of the passage he caps these surprising reflections with the hint that true salvation is from within; that it comes, in fact, from what the goddess Athene in Tennyson's *Oenone* was to call "self-reverence, self-knowledge, self-control"—the three that alone lead on to sovereign power. Christ sees himself as an example of salvation, rather than a bringer of it: and despite the explicit rejection of stoicism, there is difficulty in finding how his own wisdom differs very greatly from the Greek. In another passage, at the end of Book II, the similarity is plainer to see. Rejecting the temptation to "riches and realms," Christ goes on to talk about true kingship, which is achieved from within:

> Yet he who reigns within himself, and rules
> Passions, Desires, and Fears, is more a King;
> Which every wise and vertuous man attains:
> And who attains not, ill aspires to rule
> Cities of men, or head-strong Multitudes,
> Subject himself to Anarchy within,
> Or lawless passions in him which he serves.

He adds that "to give a Kingdom" has been thought "greater and nobler done" than to win one, "to lay down Far more magnanimous than to assume."

This will remind us, no doubt, of Christ's first appearance, when he accepts isolation as the lot of an exceptional man. And isolation he thinks of not as deprivation, or loneliness, but as the natural state of one whose visions outsoar those of normal humanity, and whose thoughts are infinitely to be preferred to any discourse:

> And he still on was led, but with such thoughts
> Accompanied of things past and to come
> Lodg'd in his brest, as well might recommend
> Such Solitude before choicest Society.

Willed isolation is the fruit of "obedience"; its tone is one of superiority, even contempt. Perhaps, looking back at the earlier Milton, this might be the inner logic of much that went before—even amid the idealism, and the enchantments of *Comus*. The Lady in *Comus* is *right,* of course: and her rightness relates, as I have argued [in the 1955 *Essays and Studies* article, "The Interpretation of Comus"], to a moral scheme more clearly realized than anything in *Paradise Regained.* But how strategically placed she is to despise Comus!—in his power physically, yet spiritually free, and above him:

> I had not thought to have unlockt my lips
> In this unhallow'd air, but that his Jugler
> Would think to charm my judgment, as mine eyes,
> Obtruding false rules prankt in reasons garb.

With this, one can compare the words of Christ to Satan in *Paradise Regained:*

> Whom thus our Saviour answered with disdain.
> I never lik't thy talk, thy offers less,
> Now both abhorr, since thou hast dar'd to utter
> Th' abominable terms, impious condition;
> But I endure the time, till which expir'd,
> Thou hast permission on me.

Christ not only takes no pains to conceal his contempt, but he threatens Satan also with violence. In Book I his attitude reminds one not only of Coriolanus, but even of Tamburlaine:

> thou com'st indeed,
> As a poor miserable captive thrall
> Comes to the place where he before had sat
> Among the Prime in Splendour, now depos'd,
> Ejected, emptied, gaz'd, unpitied, shunnd,
> A spectacle of ruin or of scorn
> To all the Host of Heaven.

For Milton this harshness was the other side of truth. He was always temperamentally ready to persecute error, and it is at this level that one can often feel him identified with his own Christ. Yet he believed passionately that truth must be openly vindicated after the battle, and Satan led captive and degraded in the end through the mocking ranks of the unfallen. For Fame was always the spur: the last infirmity of noble minds like Satan's; the crowning glory of noble minds like Christ's.

And so one returns, again, to Satan. I have pointed out how he has been deliberately played down; his reasonable arguments said to be unreasonable, his disguises made to seem ridiculous, his whole temptation doomed from the start. And one sees that the main force of the poem, as Milton planned it, depends on the reader's knowing of Christ's triumph in advance and enjoying a vicarious pleasure in its inevitability. Yet if one ignores this explicit framework, it is not hard to see how little there is to choose between Satan and Christ in the end. Each understands well enough the aspiration, the will, the arrogance of the other. Satan even recognizes in Christ a worthy foe, using much the same standards by which Christ himself dismisses the vulgar: he scorns to tempt with weaknesses of the flesh, which would be beneath the dignity of them both, choosing only the noble temptations to glory and power which he himself has followed.

Theologically, of course, the difference is that Christ has every right to glory and power, since he was born to them, whilst Satan has none, and cannot aspire to them without sin. But the corollary of this is that Christ has no need to rebel to fulfill his nature; if you reversed their positions, would not both be still basically the same? For beneath the theological, the technical difference, the motives of both are heroic. And it is no real surprise that if one of the noblest, the most Miltonic speeches in the poem should go to Christ, another should come from the mouth, and the predicament, of Satan:

> To whom the Tempter inly rackt reply'd.
> Let that come when it comes; all hope is lost
> Of my reception into grace; what worse?
> For where no hope is left, is left no fear;
> If there be worse, the expectations more
> Of worse torments me than the feeling can.
> I would be at my worst; worst is my Port,
> My harbour and my ultimate repose,
> The end I would attain, my final good.
> My error was my error, and my crime
> My crime; whatever for it self condemnd,
> And will alike be punisht; whether thou
> Raign or raign not.

This is the Satan of the first two books of *Paradise Lost,* noble in ruin, strong and uncowed in defeat. It is also uncommonly like the Samson Milton is shortly to create, in whom a similar acceptance of his own sin and destiny, almost fanatical in intensity, becomes virtue, and a similar force of heroic will the very secret of his becoming acceptable to God again. It is not unlike the voice of Milton himself in his *Second Defence*

PARADISE

REGAIN'D.

A

POEM.

In IV *BOOKS*.

To which is added

SAMSON AGONISTES.

The Author

JOHN MILTON.

LONDON,

Printed by *J. M.* for *John Starkey* at the
Mitre in *Fleetstreet*, near *Temple-Bar.*
MDCLXXI.

Title page of the first edition of Paradise Regain'd *and* Samson Agonistes *(1671).*

Of The English People, where a noble acceptance of his own pain and suffering, even in unhappiness, is at the heart of one of the most moving personal documents in our literature. One knows, as I have acknowledged, that Samson and Milton himself are on God's side, Satan against God, and that here the gulf is in theory fixed. One knows, too, that one of Milton's great emotional needs was to think of truth and error as two opposite poles, with himself as a crusader for truth—and that this also was a dynamic that influenced everything he wrote. At the heroic level, however, of courage, endurance, vigor, "plain heroic magnitude of mind," there is little to choose between them: Christ, Satan, Samson, Milton himself. And the purpose of this paper has been to suggest that the force of the poetry, and the realized values, serve to underline the similarity, not the difference.

Only by accepting this, I think, can one finally see why Milton is one of the greatest, the most indispensable of our poets. Those who point to discrepancies in his ideas as a reason for thinking him overrated are almost as mistaken, to my mind, as those who adversely criticize his poetry against alien standards. Yet one can readily see how the mistake comes about. If you go on trying to see him as a great Christian poet, you are likely to become increasingly bewildered by theological splits and dislocations: by endless riddles concerning his exact doctrines of the Godhead, or the angels, or the fall, and the

difficulty both of elucidating these and of reconciling them with the impact of the poem as a whole. You are likely, indeed, to plunge into an intellectual maze in an attempt to see how Milton is a good Christian, and to emerge with a dazed sense that he is not even a good poet.

If one looks, instead, at the heroic level—the one for which the style was forged—most of the problems fall into place and dwindle. There is no longer any need to worry if love, mercy, humility, forgiveness are hard to discern: they are not virtues one expects to find in Homer or Virgil, nor the epic tradition in general. It is no longer even unduly worrying to discover that the last thing either Milton himself or his Savior really believes in is salvation. What we find, instead, is one of the noblest monuments of humanism ever erected: an assertion of the greatness of the human spirit to aspire, to conquer new worlds, above all perhaps to endure even the ultimate insults and misfortunes without loss of will, and dignity, and individual identity. In Christ, as in Samson when he destroys the Philistines at the end, Milton dramatizes his sense that one man can hold a world's destiny in his hands, if he is big enough. In Satan, and in Samson during his captivity, there is an assertion that even in tragedy man need not surrender his will, or curse the day of his nativity. In all of these figures, Milton recognizes a worth which he can identify as part of his experience, and also as part of his hope of mankind. One can be sorry, perhaps, tht he did not choose Job or Prometheus for his themes, since both of these might have been nearer to providing a myth he could use without discrepancies. Yet when all is said, the magnificence of **Paradise Lost, Paradise Regained,** and **Samson Agonistes** is the first impression one gains; it is also the impression that remains longest, confirming itself as the true center of the Miltonic experience.

In an age of conflict like our own we shall value Milton not as a Christian poet, and not, one hopes, for his own political beliefs or methods, but as one who affirms that man is great in suffering as well as in success: proud in victory, and resilient in defeat. We shall also value him, maybe, as one who offers inner discipline and integrity as the secret of greatness.

Milton cannot help us to love, or to be gentle. He certainly cannot teach us tolerance, or poise, or what Keats called negative capability. But he can reassure us about the greatness that men *have* known: the majesty of the dreams that have been dreamed, the vastness of possible destiny. (pp. 202-11)

> *A. E. Dyson, "The Meaning of 'Paradise Regained'," in* Texas Studies in Literature and Language, *Vol. III, No. 2, Summer, 1961, pp. 197-211.*

DOUGLAS BUSH   (essay date 1964)

[Bush was a Canadian-born American educator, literary historian, and critic whose works include Mythology and the Renaissance Tradition in English Poetry *(1932) and* Science and English Poetry *(1950). He is recognized as one of the leading twentieth-century authorities on Milton and his works. In the following excerpt, he relates* Samson Agonistes *to its Greek antecedents.]*

Samson Agonistes may have been composed at any time during 1660-1670, but, since **Paradise Lost** was apparently not finished until 1663-1665, it seems unlikely that Milton would have interrupted the epic to write the drama, and unlikely also that he would not have followed up the epic with its sequel. We may then—if we are quite unmoved by recent arguments for a date before 1660—think of **Samson** as his last poetic utterance. For some readers it is the most completely satisfying of the later works. While it has not the vast scope, complexity, variety, and splendor of *Paradise Lost,* it presents no theological barriers; and, in contrast with *Paradise Regained,* its hero (though in theological tradition one of the prototypes of Christ) is a wholly human sinner who attains spiritual regeneration only after touching the depths of misery and despair.

Milton was experimental to the last, and *Samson* was a bold novelty in form and style. The blank verse, obviously remote from the sweeping periods of *Paradise Lost,* has a colloquial irregularity more massive, rugged, and sinewy than the "prosaic" plainness of *Paradise Regained.* The texture, it has been truly said, gives the Greekless reader a more authentic sense of the style of Greek tragedy than any translation of an actual play. This general character and tone are heightened by Milton's use, in choric odes and some speeches, of more or less short lines which have a special expressive value in following closely the movement of thought and feeling. These short lines are not free verse of the modern kind; they can be scanned as irregular combinations of regular metrical feet, although Milton doubtless composed them in accordance with the free syllabic principles that governed his verse, and they are commonly parts of larger rhythmical and syntactic units. Some effects are illustrated in lines 80-82 of Samson's first speech:

> Ó dárk, / dárk, dárk, // ămíd / thĕ bláze / ŏf nóon,
> Ĭrrĕcóv / ĕráb / lў dárk, // tótăl / ĕclípse,
> Wĭthóut / áll hópe / ŏf dáy.

The first four syllables, all long, depict Samson's condition, in contrast with the three following iambs that depict the bright world about him. In the second line the rising—one might say struggling—rhythm of the first half (an anapest and two iambs) shifts to a trochee in "total"; and the juxtaposition of two stressed syllables at the caesura explosively shatters the rhythm and intensifies the emotion. The third line links itself in sense and rhythm to the second half of the first, but with the negation that belongs to Samson's darkness. Other effects appear in 631-635:

> Thĕnce fáint / ĭngs, // swóon / ĭngs ŏf / dĕspáir,
> Ănd sénse / ŏf Héav'n's / dĕsér / tĭon.
> Í wás / hĭs núrs / lĭng ónce // ănd chóice / dĕlíght,
> Hĭs dés / tĭned frŏm / thĕ wómb,
> Prómĭsed/bў héaven/lў més/săge//twíce/dĕscénd/ĭng.

Here the smooth flow and strong endings of the third and fourth lines sustain the idea of Samson's former glory and assurance; in the other lines feminine caesuras and feminine line-endings suggest failure and loss.

Whatever Milton's early admiration for Shakespeare, he himself was not writing for the stage, and we should expect such a scholarly poet to follow the Greeks (and, as he notes in his preface, the Italians). The drama reminds us in various ways of all three of the Greek tragic poets. The epic simplicity of form, the predominance of the protagonist, and the author's passionate concern with righteousness may be called Aeschylean. The repeated testing of the protagonist's will and integrity, the pervasive irony, and the function of the chorus recall Sophocles. The strain of intellectualism and the self-defensive prominence given to a "bad" woman suggest Euripides. But of course Milton did not deliberately aim at such a combination of qualities; he had not only a life-long saturation in Greek tragedy but temperamental and artistic affinities with its authors, so that, as usual, he could work with entire ease and freedom within a convention. *Samson* is the one tragedy in English that can stand beside the ancient originals. Two plays

which are relatively close to it—though not very close—are *Prometheus Bound* and *Oedipus at Colonus.*

Beginning, like the Greeks, on the eve of the catastrophe, Milton brings in other events of Samson's career by way of retrospective allusion. The brawny warrior of the book of Judges, the Heracles of Hebrew story, is endowed with a heroic character and a Hebraic conscience. As the drama opens, on the festival of Dagon, the Philistine god, the blind captive is led out of prison for a breath of fresh air. His long speech describes the pains of blindness and captivity, his utter debasement, his bitter sense of God's desertion:

> Ask for this great deliverer now, and find him
> Eyeless in Gaza at the mill with slaves. . . .

But although the bulk of Samson's speech is self-centered, a few lines near the middle of it contain the seed of ultimate recovery, an acknowledgement of his own responsiblity for his lot. As the drama develops, self-pity and wounded pride and reproaches of God give way by degrees to clear-eyed and humble recognition of his sins and deserved sufferings.

In the large ironic pattern, each of the first four "acts" brings about a result contrary to that expected by the interlocutor. The chorus, though sympathetic, are "Job's comforters" and they turn the knife in Samson's wound by questioning his marriages with Philistine women. He is roused to the defense "That what I motioned was of God"; moreover, if the Israelites are still in subjection, it is because they failed to follow up his successes. (We meet here that recurrent Miltonic conviction, which usually seems to be topical as well as historical, that nations grown corrupt fall readily into bondage.) Samson's well-meaning but unimaginative father likewise rouses Samson to opposition, but on a higher level: Manoa's blaming of God elicits Samson's full confession of his own guilt and a declaration that his present servitude is much less base than his former servitude to Dalila. Manoa also turns the knife in his son's wound by reminding him that he has brought contempt upon the God of Israel and glory to Dagon, a reproach that draws from his son a still more contrite confession, and with it the belief that God will yet assert himself and make Dagon stoop. Manoa's happy report of his negotiations with the Philistines for ransom further deepens Samson's misery. Indeed the upward movement—which, if wholly steady, might have come to seem contrived—now undergoes a prolonged reversal. Samson sinks into abject despair and longs only for death. And the choric ode is an arraignment of God's ways which goes far beyond Adam's and which, though it will be answered in the end, is unmitigated here.

An extravagant nautical image heralds the approach of Dalila, who has all the finery and perfume and attendants she has gained with the proceeds of betrayal. Samson is stirred at once to vehement anger. Dalila's apologies and defenses are spiced with sensual invitation, but her "fair enchanted cup, and warbling charms" have no more power over him (this last of Milton's allusions to Circe takes us back to his first Latin Elegy). Her allurements failing, Dalila turns on Samson to rejoice in the enduring fame she has won as a heroine of her nation. His renewed strength and confidence are carried further in his colloquy with the Philistine giant Harapha, who comes to inspect the fallen champion. When Samson's contempt for Harapha's armor brings the charge of black art in his own martial feats, Samson replies: "My trust is in the living God . . . ," and he challenges Harapha to decide by combat between Israel's God and Dagon. A still stronger testimony of his state of mind is his next speech, a humble admission, to his scornful enemy, of his sins and just punishment, joined with the hope of God's pardon and a repeated challenge. Harapha goes off "in a sultry chafe," and Samson shows a quietly lucid understanding of Harapha's embarrassment and of the limits of affliction he can himself endure; if death is to be his fate,

> it may with mine
> Draw their own ruin who attempt the deed.

The chorus recall his former prowess, when he was

> With plain heroic magnitude of mind
> And celestial vigor armed,

but they assume that he can now be only a hero of patient suffering.

The cause of Samson's new confidence is made clearer when he refuses to go to the feast and entertain the Philistines. To the officer's warning, "Regard thyself, this will offend them highly," he answers "Myself? my conscience and internal peace"; he has come far from "Myself my sepulchre, a moving grave." Even the chorus urge him to obey, pointing out that he works daily for his captors. He replies:

> Not in their idol-worship, but by labor
> Honest and lawful to deserve my food
> Of those who have me in their civil power.

The reply is of the same kind as that of Socrates to the friends who wished to arrange his escape from prison and death. One of the impressive and Miltonic things in the latter part of the drama is that Samson's humble repentance and faith in God's restored favor bring, not emotionalism, but a quiet Socratic rationality, fortitude, and fearlessness. When he changes his mind and goes, because of "Some rousing motions in me," a recognition of God's directing providence, he can assure the chorus that he will incur no dishonor: "The last of me or no I cannot warrant." In pronouncing a benediction the chorus recall the angel who attended his birth, the divine blessing Samson had recalled in his first despairing speech.

The last act is the last irony. Manoa's good hopes of a ransom, of nursing his son at home, give place to the messenger's account of the feast and Samson's feats of strength ("performed, as reason was, obeying") and his prayerful approach to the final one. The choric lament contrasts the *hubris* of the Philistines, upon whom God sent "a spirit of frenzy" (akin to the Greek Ate or Furies), with the inward illumination of the blind Samson, who in a climactic image is likened to the phoenix, the age-old Christian symbol of death and rebirth (though here expressly used of earthly fame). Manoa sadly glorifies his son in lines which may represent the last phase of Milton's "classical" art:

> Nothing is here for tears, nothing to wail
> Or knock the breast, no weakness, no contempt,
> Dispraise, or blame, nothing but well and fair,
> And what may quiet us in a death so noble.

Manoa will raise a monument to be kept as a shrine—a contrast with the one that Dalila anticipates. But Manoa, and the chorus, see only the external fact, that God has unexpectedly returned

> And to his faithful champion hath in place
> Bore witness gloriously:

they have not comprehended the nature of Samson's inward struggle and victory.

The briefest outline indicates the larger ironies of the drama, and the texture is full of ironic ambiguities. "Agonistes" means

more than an ordinary participant in public games; and Samson's opening line, "A little onward lend thy guiding hand," is more than an injunction to his attendant. If Greek decorum is violated by the sense, especially in Samson, of an immediate relationship with God, the violation is hardly felt as such, in the main because Milton keeps ideas and beliefs strictly within the Hebraic frame. A few classical allusions—to Atlas, Stoic consolations against calamity, Circe—are more or less veiled. What is much more important, no specifically Christian doctrines are admitted, no clear statement of the working of grace, not even faith in Samson's immortality (unless that is contained in Manoa's literal "Home to his father's house"); no flights of angels sing him to his rest. It has been said that a Christian with an assured belief in Providence cannot write a tragedy. But Milton was a Christian, and *Samson* is a tragedy; belief in Providence does not preclude what, in a limited human view, is tragic catastrophe. But one does not need any religious beliefs to be greatly moved by Milton's picture of pride, guilt, suffering, despair, and recovery; and the final vindication of God's providential order does not, any more than in some Greek plays, nullify the tragic sense of the mystery of pain and evil.

It seems clear that in Samson Milton saw a partial parallel to his own experience. One passage in the chorus's indictment of God's justice (692 f.) must allude to the Restoration government's treatment of the regicides, dead and living; and the lines go on to the "Painful diseases and deformed" of premature old age, which remind us of Milton's severe pangs of gout. In general, of course, we think of the blind and defeated revolutionist in Restoration London as "Eyeless in Gaza at the mill with slaves"; but parallels need not be stretched to include Mary Powell and Milton's father ("I cannot praise thy marriage choices, son"). Though the early biographers do not suggest dormant fires under the quiet routine of Milton's later life, the subject itself and the excitement of composition could hardly fail to stir thoughts of the revolution and its failure; and if we remember his tracts of 1660, we may think that his chief temptation, like Samson's, was despair. Such personal involvement helps to explain the energy and intensity of the drama. Yet it is not less significant that even in such a work Milton preserved complete impersonality; there is not a detail or sentiment that does not belong to the story of Samson, and the poet's emotions, whatever they may have been, were wholly sublimated. If Samson is in some sense Milton, or an England which may rouse herself after sleep, that is an overtone; Milton's theme is the grand theme of all his last works (as, in less dark days, it had been of *Comus* and "**Lycidas**"), God's providence sustaining and guiding individual righteousness or regeneration. (pp. 194-201)

> *Douglas Bush, in his* John Milton: A Sketch of His Life and Writings, *The Macmillan Company, 1964, 224 p.*

LIONEL TRILLING   (essay date 1967)

[*An American critic and literary historian, Trilling was also an essayist, editor, novelist, and short story writer. His exploration of the application of liberal arts theory to the conduct of life led him to become a social commentator as well. A liberal and a humanist, Trilling judged the value of a text by the contribution it makes to culture. In turn, he regarded culture as indispensable for human survival. In his literary criticism Trilling focused on the conflict between the individual and culture, maintaining that art has the power to "liberate the individual from the tyranny of his culture in the environmental sense and to permit him to stand beyond it in an autonomy of perception and judgement." In the following excerpt from a work originally published in 1967, he considers why Milton chose the pastoral mode for "Lycidas."*]

It is often said by critics and teachers of literature that **"Lycidas"** is the greatest lyric poem in the English language, and very likely it is. But the word "greatest" applied to a work of art is not always serviceable; the superlative judgment can immobilize a reader's response to a work, or arouse his skeptical resistance. It may be that we are given a more enlightening introduction to the poem by a critic who held it in low esteem—so far from thinking that **"Lycidas"** was superlatively great, Samuel Johnson thought it a very bad poem [see excerpt dated 1779]. Without doubt Dr. Johnson was wrong in this judgment and the grounds on which he bases it are quite mistaken. But his erroneous views, stated in his characteristically bold and unequivocal fashion, make plain how the poem ought to be regarded.

The sum of Dr. Johnson's objections is that **"Lycidas"** is insincere. It purports to be a poem of mourning; the poet is expressing grief over the death of a friend. But can we possibly believe in the truth of his emotion? Grief, Dr. Johnson says in effect, inclines to be silent or at least to be simple in its utterance. It does not express itself so elaborately, with as much artifice as Milton uses or with such a refinement of fancy and such a proliferation of reference to ancient legend and lore. "Passion plucks no berries from myrtle or ivy," Dr. Johnson said, "nor calls upon Arethuse and Mincius, nor tells of rough *satyrs* or *fauns with cloven heels*. Where there is leisure for fiction, there is little grief."

Of the poem's elaborateness of artifice, even of artificiality, there can be no question. The poet does not speak in his own person but in the guise of a "shepherd" or "swain." That is to say, he expresses his grief, such as it is, through the literary convention known as the pastoral, so called because all the persons represented in it are shepherds (the Latin word for shepherd is *pastor*). This convention of poetry has a long history. It goes back to the Greek poet Theocritus (c. 310-250 B.C.), who, in certain of his poems, pretended that he and his poet-friends were shepherds of his native Sicily. Far removed from the sophistication and corruption of cities, the fancied shepherds of Theocritus devoted themselves to the care of their flocks and to two innocent pursuits—song and the cultivation of love and friendship. Their only ambition was to be accomplished in song; their only source of unhappiness was a lost love or the death of a friend, the latter being rather more grievous than the former and making the occasion for an *elegy*, a poem of lament. Virgil brought the pastoral convention into Roman literature with his *Eclogues*, and it was largely through his influence that it became enormously popular in the Renaissance. This popularity continued through the eighteenth century, but the mechanical way in which it came to be used in much of the verse of that period justifies Dr. Johnson in speaking of the pastoral mode as "easy, vulgar, and therefore disgusting." In the nineteenth century the convention lost its vogue, but even then it was used for two great elegies, Shelley's "Adonais" and Matthew Arnold's "Thyrsis." For the poets of our time it seems to have no interest.

The fictional nature of the pastoral was never in doubt. Nobody was supposed to believe and nobody did believe that the high-minded poetic herdsmen were real, in charge of actual flocks. Yet the fiction engaged men's imaginations for so long a time because it fulfilled so real a desire of mankind—it speaks of simplicity and innocence, youth and beauty, love and art. And although the poets were far from claiming actuality for their pastoral fancies, they often used the convention to criticize actual conditions of life, either explicitly as Milton does in the passage on the English clergy (lines 108-131) or by implication.

The traditional and avowedly artificial nature of the pastoral was exactly suited to the occasion which produced **"Lycidas."** Milton could scarcely have felt at Edward King's death the "passion" that Dr. Johnson blames him for not expressing, for King, although a college mate, had not been a close friend. He composed **"Lycidas"** not on spontaneous impulse but at the invitation of a group of Cambridge men who were bringing out a volume of poems to commemorate King. For Milton to have pretended to an acute sense of personal loss would have been truly an insincerity. Yet he could not fail to respond to what we might call the general pathos of a former comrade's dying "ere his prime," and by means of the pastoral elegy he was able to do what was beautifully appropriate to the situation—he associated King's death with a long tradition in which the deaths of young men had been lamented. Ever since the dawn of literature the death of a young man has been felt to have an especial pathos—how often it is evoked in the *Iliad*; and few things in the Bible are more affecting than David's mourning for his young friend Jonathan and his young son Absalom. It is this traditional pathos that Milton evokes from the death of Edward King. Had he tried to achieve a more personal expression of feeling, we should have responded not more but less. What engages us is exactly the universality of the emotion.

The pastoral convention is also appropriate to King's commemoration in two other respects. One is the extent to which the pastoral elegy was known and cultivated by young men in the English universities of Milton's time, if only because in their study of the ancient languages they were assigned the task of composing verses in this genre. Milton's own earliest-known poems are such college exercises, and all the poets who are mentioned or referred to in **"Lycidas"**—Theocritus, Virgil, Ovid—were subjects of university study. And in Milton's age as in ours, the college days of a young man were thought to have something like a pastoral quality—from mature life men look back to that time as being more carefree, and to their relationships then as having been more generous, disinterested, and comradely than now: why else do college alumni return each spring to their old campuses? Our very word *alumnus* expresses what Milton means when he says that he and King were "nurs'd upon the self-same hill," for an *alumnus* is a foster child, a nursling of *alma mater*, the fostering mother.

Dr. Johnson did not make it an item in his charge of insincerity that Milton, mourning a young man dead, is so preoccupied with a young man alive—himself. But we cannot fail to see that this is the case. Milton begins his poem with an unabashed self-reference, to his feeling about himself as a young poet who has not yet reached the point in his development when he is ready to appear before the public. One reason he gives for overcoming his reluctance and undertaking the poem in memory of King is his hope that this will make it the more likely that someone will write to commemorate him when he dies. When he speaks about the poetic career and about poetic fame in relation to death, it is manifestly his own career and fame and his own death that he has in mind—the thought arouses him to a proud avowal of his sense of his high calling. And as the poem concludes, it is again to himself that he refers. Having discharged his duty of mourning, he turns from death and sorrow back to life and his own purposes:

> At last he rose, and twitch'd his mantle blue:
> To-morrow to fresh woods, and pastures new.

These passages have led many readers to conclude that **"Lycidas"** is not about Edward King at all but about John Milton. They are quite content that this should be so. They take the view that though the poem may fail in its avowed intention, it succeeds in an intention that it does not avow—they point to the fact that the most memorable and affecting parts of the poem are those in which Milton is his own subject. But in weighing this opinion we might ask whether it is ever possible to grieve for a person to whom we feel akin without grieving for ourselves, and, too, whether the intensity with which we are led to imagine our own inevitable death is not a measure of the kinship we feel with the person who has already died. Certainly nothing in **"Lycidas"** more strongly enforces upon us the pathos of untimely death than that it puts the poet in mind of his own death—for what he says of himself we are bound to feel of ourselves. And how better represent the sadness of death than to put it beside the poet's imagination of the fulness of life?

It must also be observed that Milton speaks of the death of Edward King and of his own imagined death and actual life in a context that does not permit our mere ordinary sense of the personal to prevail. He brings them into conjunction not only with the traditional pathos of young men dead ere their prime but also with the traditional evocations of the death of young gods, and their resurrection. No religious ceremonies of the ancient peoples were more fervently performed than those in which the death of a young male deity—Osiris, Adonis, Atys, Thammuz—was mourned and his resurrection rejoiced in. The myths of these gods and the celebration of their death and rebirth represented the cycles of the vital forces; the dying and reborn god symbolized the sun in its annual course, the processes of vegetation, the sexual and procreative energy, and sometimes, as in the case of Orpheus, poetic genius. Once we are aware of this, Milton's concern with himself takes on a larger significance. It is not himself-the-person that Milton is meditating upon but himself-the-poet: that is, he is thinking about himself in the service not of his own interests but of the interests of the "divine" power that he bears within him.

In this service Milton is properly associated with Edward King, who was also a poet—it does not matter that King was not distinguished in his art. But there was yet another aspect of the service of divine power in the fact that King was a clergyman, a priest of the Church of England, which licenses the inclusion in the elegy of St. Peter's explosion of wrath against the negligent and corrupt clergy of the time. This famous passage constitutes only a small part of the poem, but the importance that Milton gave it is made plain by his extended reference to it in the "argument." Some readers will find a bitter condemnation of clerical corruption inappropriate to an elegy, and will be jarred and dismayed by the sudden introduction of Christian personages and considerations into a poem that has been, up to this point, consistently pagan. That Milton is himself quite aware that the passage will seem incongruous to the pastoral form is indicated in the lines in which he invokes the "return" of the "Sicilian Muse," who has been scared away by St. Peter's "dread voice." But in Milton's thought ancient pagan literature and mythology and the Judaeo-Christian religion were never really at odds with each other. It is a salient characteristic of his great and enormously learned mind that Milton gave allegiance to both, and used for Christian ideas the literary forms of paganism. In the pastoral convention he found a natural conjunction of the two: we can readily see that the poetic convention has affinity with the feelings attached to the pastoral life by Biblical Judaism and, more elaborately, by

Christianity. The peaceable Abel was a shepherd and so was Abraham. So was David, and a poet-shepherd at that, one of whose psalms begins, "The Lord is my Shepherd, I shall not want." It was shepherds who saw the Star of Bethlehem rise; Jesus is both the Lamb of God and the Good Shepherd. *Pastor* is the name for the priest of a parish, the congregation being his flock, and the form of a bishop's crozier is the shepherd's crook.

As the poem moves toward its conclusion the mingling of pagan and Christian elements is taken wholly for granted. This conjunction of the two traditions exemplifies yet another characteristic of the poem, its inclusiveness. **"Lycidas"** gathers up all the world, things the most disparate in space and time and kind, and concentrates them in one place and moment, brings them to bear upon one event, the death of the poet-priest. The poem's action is, as it were, summarized in the lines about "the great Vision" of St. Michael the Angel who, from Land's End, the southernmost tip of England, looks afar to Spain but is adjured to "look homeward."So the poem looks afar to the ancient world and also turns its gaze upon contemporary England. From "the bottom of the monstrous world" it turns to heaven, and from all the waters of the world to all the flowers of all the seasons of the Earth, and from the isolation of Lycidas in death to the "sweet societies" of his resurrection and everlasting life through the agency of Christ. It plays literary games with the most solemn subjects, and juxtaposes the gravest ideas with the smallest blossoms, using their most delicate or homely names (culminating in the daffadillies, which sound like the very essence of irresponsible frivolity). And then, when it has brought all the world together, and life out of death and faith out of despair, it has its "uncouth swain," the shepherd-poet, with the jauntiness of a task fully discharged, announce that the mourning is now at an end. Life calls the poet to other work and he must answer the call. (pp. 194-200)

> *Lionel Trilling, "John Milton: 'Lycidas'," in his* Prefaces to The Experience of Literature, *Harcourt Brace Jovanovich, 1979, pp. 194-200.*

JOHN T. SHAWCROSS (essay date 1969)

[Shawcross is an American authority on seventeenth-century English literature. In the following excerpt, he analyzes the genre of Paradise Lost, *focusing on claims that the poem is an epic.]*

The difficulties inherent in discussing style grow out of individual preferences, knowledge, and point of view. No definition is quite acceptable, for the components of style, its techniques, and its effects do not seem determinable as a formula to satisfy all tastes. Yet the codifications Aristotle and other rhetoricians devised have proved useful, and have accordingly been "applied" to classify the style of such works as *Paradise Lost*. This technique of definition continues to underlie recent investigations of both the style and the genre of the poem. Since literary style is discussed primarily through an author's language and uses of language, Milton's style has been termed "grand" and "sublime." Christopher Ricks, devoting a full book to the subject [see Additional Bibliography], states the basic concept that places the poem in these categories: "Decorum (in the sense both of epic tradition and of aptness to Milton's subject) demanded that he should elevate his style by deviating greatly from common usage." Elevation of style and wide deviation from common usage have confirmed the grandness and sublimity of Milton's verse for generations of readers; but I must demur not only because of the rather facile acceptance of this concept by so many students of *Paradise Lost* but because I am convinced that Milton's intentions and achievements are in opposition to the statement. Ricks implies a limitation upon Milton by "epic tradition" and by "aptness to subject." And, of course, he also begs the question of what that subject is.

The present paper has not been written to take anyone to task for not recognizing in the poem that which I do. Indeed others have in recent years offered readings that are closely akin to some of my thoughts, but incidentally and in different frameworks. Rather it is my hope to show that the poem's genre, though epic, is a modification of tradition not previously noted, while abiding by the "rules"; to illustrate that its generic classification depends upon point of view; to establish the style as complex in range; and to argue that the style is calculated to drive home Milton's "message." This last point fits the demands of decorum but in a different way from that advanced by critics in the past with a different view of the poem's subject, intention, and achievement. Because the principles postulated by Aristotle and others are useful, even from my perspective, though I believe a reexamination of them when in the hands of Milton will counter usual interpretations, and because this technique of definition continues to be employed in one form or another, I choose to pursue my ideas of the style and genre of *Paradise Lost* within this framework. A summary of previous scholarship on style and genre seems hardly necessary: the views presented here owe inspiration to many other people and their ideas, but despite remarks that hint at conclusions I shall present, my thoughts have a heretical cast that does not color such remarks.

Milton's modification of tradition, while working within it, can be observed in such poems as "Lycidas," the "Ode to John Rouse," and the translations of Psalms 1-8. Therefore, to assume that *Paradise Lost* necessarily was conditioned by what is "standard" for epic tradition and what is "apt" for its alleged subject is not justified. A more logical expectation would be that Milton created his own decorum, for he boasts that the poem "pursues things unattempted yet in Prose or Rime" [see excerpt dated 1667]. First, however, the tradition must be investigated, and the full subject examined. Of significance in determining the tradition of the poem are its mode and its effect; of significance in determining the subject in the sense that Ricks uses the word are its thesis, its theme, and its intention. Recently I have argued [in "The Balanced Structure of *Paradise Lost*" (1965) and "The Son in his Ascending: a Reading of *Paradise Lost*" (1966)] that the mode and the effect of *Paradise Lost* are comic rather than tragic. My conclusion arises from what I see as Milton's thesis, "message," structural orgainzation, and central vision. With an emphasis upon the good that comes out of the evil within the poem, including the Fall, and upon the victory of the Son over Satan in time past, present, and future (at Judgment), with its accompanying return to the Godhead, the poem cannot be considered tragic of effect but hopeful, inspirational, and glorious. There has been no wastage of good in the poem by driving out of evil. Only Satan and the fallen angels illustrate a wastage of good but by no means in the process of driving out evil, and the good that Man loses is not wasted. The stated subject is Man's disobedience, but the thesis is that eternal providence will justify to Man God's ways toward him, and the theme is God's love. God's love for Man best illustrates His providence and best justifies His ways. The intention of the poem is thus the didactic aim of inculcating virtue in Man by showing God's truth, justice, and mercy, leading to peace, and Satan's deceit,

injustice, and hate, leading to war. Fundamentally the poem is concerned with the opposition of Eros and Thanatos, that is, the opposition of love and hate, life and death, creation and uncreation. Thus if the "tradition" within which Milton wrote is different from what it has been considered and if the full subject is also different, then the decorum must likewise differ and the style demanded will need reexamination. Whether this style is to be considered "grand" or "sublime," "elevated," and "deviating greatly from common usage" follows as a necessary concern.

Part of the tradition of the poem is its genre. The classification of *Paradise Lost* as an epic has led to a number of predications: it is in the "high" style, it has a hero of noble status or virtue, it is concerned with heroic achievement. Consideration of the first must wait for a few pages, but it is obvious to twentieth-century readers of Milton that the last two are the basis for the so-called Satanic interpretation of the poem and its alleged failure. This censure of Milton's artistry thus implied has been laid to rest for scholars (although not for the general reader), for Satan is not a hero to the poem and by the same reasoning neither is the Son, who throughout is a contrast to Satan. Should we therefore search out a hero in Adam (or Adam and Eve, that is, Mankind)? This view held by E.M.W. Tillyard (and others) is not borne out by Adam's action or character. He cannot be thought of as "epic hero" despite the likenesses of the poem to such as the *Aeneid* and despite Adam's likeness to Aeneas as a progenitor. The worriment over the hero which has gone on seems to me to be pointless: to me there is no hero in the poem although Adam and Eve constitute a protagonist as representatives of Mankind in the drama of life. This is that kind of protagonist one finds in a morality play, a central character about whom the action revolves. He is not truly a "doer," an exemplar of achievement; he is one who plays out a part against great life forces, an example of what life encompasses. The poem was first outlined as a morality drama, and thus seen, it offers the Son and his attributes of love and faith as antagonist against Satan and his attributes of hate and unbelief as opposing antagonist (his name means "Adversary"). I do not wish to overstress the morality relationship of the poem, although appropriately its major structural and imagistic pattern is balance through contrast; yet an awareness of this relationship moves us far from requiring a hero (in the usual sense) for the poem and thus from requiring the presence of certain traditional epic qualities.

Placing the poem in the epic tradition has also sent readers in search of heroic achievement within it; but Adam neither achieves nor shows heroic action, and Satan corrupts, whether other angels or man, and intends uncreation. In no way can this be construed as fighting bravely for a cause against incalculable odds ("hitherto the onely Argument / Heroic deem'd," IX, 28-29). It is positive Promethean action that is the heroic action of the poem: such action sacrifices self for the love of others. It is the action of the Son or of Man when he follows the Son's example that predicates high achievement. But the Son is greater than Prometheus since he obeys the Father and shows faith. Full heroic action is magnanimous, in Aristotle's definition of the word. Milton calls *Paradise Lost* a Heroic Poem in the forenote on the verse, and this he justifies in the proem to Book IX. He does not mention any "hero." This passage alone, it seems to me, should direct readers to the differences from "epic tradition" that Milton was developing. His task is to tell of distrust, disloyalty, revolt, and disobedience—a sad task. In balance are the trust, loyalty, acceptance, and obedience of the Son throughout the poem and the admonitions (like Raphael's, "first of all / Him whom to love is to obey, and keep / His great command," just before in Book VIII, lines 633-635) which loom with ironic persistence. Here is an argument not less, but more heroic than those of the Greek and Roman epics. The word "argument" means subject as Milton indicates in line 24, but it also retains the meaning "proof" in a persuasive discourse. Quintilian (V. 8-11) called an argument the plot of a play or the theme of a speech, but added that proof and credibility are not the result of reason only but of *signa* (i.e., "indications"). Book IX, with its recounting of the Fall and the immediate aftermath, gives best proof of how Satan works, how Man is deceived, and what disobedience can bring.

Both as subject and as proof, this "argument" ranges throughout the poem. Book IX with the fall of Eve to Satan's blandishments and Adam's fall through his love for Eve becomes the hinge of Man's action in life. With this climax Satan has seemingly triumphed and Man must hew a path upward to God through repentance and faith, or through obedience and love. It is interesting to note that whereas Death is introduced in Book II in line 666, the number of the Great Beast of Revelation, Adam perversely falls (and completes the entry of death into the world) at line 999 in Book IX. On the other hand the climax of Book III indicates the Son's future victory on earth as Man; and in this way the "argument" of Book IX will be totally reversed. It is part of the "great argument" of the full poem, for the Son's action will furnish the means by which Man will be saved. Those who will have preceded the Son as Man will receive salvation through the harrowing of Hell; those who will come after will have learned the way to fly from woe. The climax of Book III is the hinge of Man's salvation. But it is the climax of Book VI that is the keystone of the poem. With the rebellion and defeat of Satan and his cohorts,the need to create Man has arisen. Without the falsely "heroic" action of the War in Heaven, there would have been no Man, no Fall, no Redemption, and no poem with its "great argument."

Certainly Man'a action in life, whether Adam and Eve's in Book IX or most of their progeny's as related in Books XI and XII, is not heroic. The only heroic achievement is such as Noah's: faith in God, and love, implying obedience to Him. It is the example of the Son. But this does not constitute the narrative; it is rather the intended result of the narrative. Quintilian (V. 12) explicitly tells us that in each argument there is something requiring no proof, by means of which we can prove something else. What justly gives heroic name to person or to poem, Milton implies, is striving valiantly for good against opposing forces, and when those forces are basic, the term "heroic" is most suitable. What he will now present in Book IX gives higher argument (proof) to yield that name "heroic" for his poem. Though Adam and Eve fall, we see paradoxically the heroic action by which Man may prove heroic. Milton is concerned only with the name for his poem, not for a person. The meaningfulness of the definition I am posing can be appreciated when we remember Dryden's remarks. He rejected *Paradise Lost* as a heroic poem in "Original and Progress of Satire" because "His design is the losing of our happiness; his event is not prosperous, like that of all other epic works. . . ." [see excerpt dated 1693]. It is thus understandable that Dryden was the first to cast Satan as hero, for he centers on the Fall rather than on the greater happiness that now may ensue, according to Michael in Book XII.

On the basis of the preceding, we can define the genre of the poem by looking at the properties of the epic-heroic poem found

therein. First, there are the poem's sweep and length, its catalogues and war, and its organization of events. These are the elements that have so frequently categorized the poem for readers, but they are only narrative and structural motifs whose differences from epic form or use (in *Paradise Lost*) are more significant than their superficial likenesses. These elements we may label the "plot," which, according to Aristotle, is the arrangement of the incidents. In *Paradise Lost* motifs are arranged in a contrasting form (for example, the creation of Pandaemonium in Book I and the creation of the Universe in Book VII) and in comparative (or repetitious) form (for example, the assault on Eve in Book IV and the actual Fall in Book IX). Contrast shows disorder (the world of Satan); comparison shows order (the world of God). (pp. 15-21)

[The] structure works in two ways, one emphasizing contrast, disorder, and cause and effect, the other emphasizing comparison, order, and the way to God. Books I and II contrast with VII and VIII; III with IX; IV with X; and V and VI with XI and XII. For example, Satan's soliloquy in IV, his means of entry into Eden, and his routing by Gabriel contrast with Adam's soliloquy in X, the ease of entry of Sin and Death into the world, and Satan's reception by the devils; IV has paved the way for the disorder of X. But seen the other way, Books I and II compare with XI and XII; III with X; IV with IX; and V and VI with VII and VIII. For example, the Judgment of God the Father in III compares with the Judgment pronounced by the Son in X, for both are merciful; the stairs to Heaven which Satan sees shining forth between the Universe and Heaven compare with the repentance that ends X, for both lead by steps to God. This comparison suggests order in things and the ultimate order that these specific acts will bring. Both views are necessary to make one aware of Good by knowing Evil and because all of life is made up of such opposites. The Spirit of God may be a dove and the meek may inherit the Earth, but to defeat Satan one must be eagle-winged. A human being is the fusion of Man and Woman, and though he needs the power of the Father to achieve by great deeds, he also needs the compassion of the Mother to achieve by small.

The two-part poem of contrasting halves which is achieved by this first structuring principle shows cause (the devils' decision of revenge, the begetting of Sin and Death, the nature of Satan's evil, the problems of innocence, the pride and envy of Satan, the rebellion and defeat of a third of the angels) and effect (the creation of the Universe, the creation of Man and Woman, the Fall, lust, anger, the seasons, etc., repentance, the Judgment, Man's history, and the First Coming). The movement upward and downward of the second structuring principle creates a mountain hieroglyphic, the mythic (or magic) mountain of Truth and Virtue. To scale the mountain to reach the Plains of Heaven one need only follow the example of the Son (difficult though some may find this path) and conclude with Adam

> that to obey is best,
> And love with fear the onely God, to walk
> As in his presence, ever to observe
> His providence, and on him sole depend . . .
> (XII, 561-564)

Through following the Son's example, one metaphorically takes on the Father's three-bolted thunder with which the Son defeated Satan in Book VI, lines 760-766.

The chronological disruption of narrative—the beginning *in medias res*—was a staple of the epic, but Milton's use of it illustrates the thesis of the poem and becomes analogous to a major narrative element and motif. We have a disordered poem out of which comes order once we take perspective of the whole. But it is not just the poem that is disordered; it is Man too who can be made an ordered person through Milton's leading him to acknowledge the poem's theme and its theses. Those who will not be led are disordered eternally, in Milton's philosophy.

Paradise Lost is itself a creation, a type of God's creation. All parts have importance in the full scheme; all parts look forward to the period after that creation has ceased to be: for God's creation, life after the Final Judgment; for Milton's creation, the life his readers are leading which will subtend their ultimate life after the Final Judgment. Of course the poem can remain disordered for those who do not see its integrity, just as God's providence and ways, Milton would have surely felt, will not be acceptable to those who see from Satan's perspective only.

The structural motifs derive from epic example, but they are used more hieroglyphically, more metaphorically, more extensively and fully than in previous epics. *Paradise Lost* is epical but far from traditional.

Secondly, further properties of the epic-heroic poem can be discerned through consideration of other dicta for the epic. To Aristotle (*Poetics*, XIII. 11-13) the epic should be embraced in one view; it should unify beginning, middle, and end. Only a perspective view, therefore, of the complete, received *Paradise Lost* will allow understanding of the poem as epic. The emphasis on one aspect of "plot" (the Fall) or the classification of certain sections as unnecessary (the vision of Books XI and XII) or the dismissal of other elements as poorly articulated (the War in Heaven) do not permit perspective. When, however, we see it whole, the poem becomes unified and possible of embracement in one view. The theme that I have urged before is the view that thus arises, not the theme of the Fall, not the elements of plot which are rather Quintilian's *signa*. Awareness of the preceding is necessary to progress to a discussion of two further epic qualities of this heroic poem.

First, epic affords greater scope for the inexplicable, Aristotle observed (*Poetics*, XXIV. 15), because we do not actually see the persons of the story. The differences between *Samson Agonistes*, for example, where we are presented with definite persons speaking in character and performing specific actions (static as this dramatic poem is), and the *Aeneid*, where the epic voice comments and leads and unifies, illustrate what Aristotle was noting. In *Samson* we are limited by the dramatis personae, although the chorus at times—but certainly not always—seems to present part of Milton's "message," and although close reading of the speeches of the main characters will lead us to understand the inexplicable that Milton is trying to enunciate. The epic allows the author to insert his view and to lead the reader to awareness of what is happening, what the characters are like, how what they say is to be interpreted, and how the work itself should be read. The difference in point of view perhaps can be realized in this way: contrast what **"Lycidas"** says to us when we read the poem (the first ten verse paragraphs) as the author's direct and contemporary musing, and when we read it as the reflective musing of the uncouth swain of the last stanza observed by some superior voice (though swain and superior voice both be Milton).

In this regard *Paradise Lost* falls between *Samson* and the *Aeneid*. The fact that it was first planned as a play surely was influential in creating this dramatic-epic classification. Allan H. Gilbert in *On the Composition of Paradise Lost* has shown evidence that earlier brief tragedies were incorporated into the final epic.

If we minimize the narrator's position and stress the dramatic speeches of certain characters—of the fallen angels in Books I and II; of Satan, Eve, and Adam in Books IX and X—we read drama and tend to interpret the speeches as "truth" and the characters a "real" people. If we recognize the role of the narrator—and it is noteworthy that Anne Davidson Ferry's extensive discussion of *Milton's Epic Voice* has caused many critics of the poem to reread it with surprising results—and realize that the characters are presented "in character," we read epic and, through perspective, see the range of "truth" from disobedience to obedience, and the characters as representative of ways of thinking and exercisers of will.

As drama *Paradise Lost* allows us to go wrong in Milton's view (even if some may think we are broaching the intentional fallacy); as epic it allows us to choose right in Milton's view. The form of the heroic poem thus becomes the very embodiment of Milton's full message. This is another example of the break with tradition; it is neither drama nor epic in an unrelenting classic definition. As Roy Daniells has argued in *Milton, Mannerist and Baroque*, it is an example of the baroque by virtue, here, of its placement between the manneristic and the neoclassic (or late baroque), despite some tendency toward the latter. By casting his work in epic form, while deriving it from drama and retaining dramatic sections, Milton acquired greater scope for the inexplicable and obtained answerable style.

Second, what is convincing though impossible, Aristotle wrote concerning epic (*Poetics*, XXIV. 19), should be preferred to what is possible and unconvincing. The application to a heroic poem like *Paradise Lost* as opposed to a drama like Jack Gelber's *The Connection* (I do not say *all* dramas) is obvious. Of course God cannot be depicted and quoted, nor how angels eat or make love, but these achieve conviction for Milton's theme through anthropomorphism and accommodation or symbolic meaning. We are convinced that we ourselves are involved in the cosmic scene before us. Gelber's narcotic addicts are all too real—they even sit next to the audience during the play and approach them at intermission for money for a fix. Actuality is before and around the audience, but they are unconvinced that they may become addicts or that the "scene" is a basic philosophic problem. The drama has the defensible and most necessary effect of making us aware of a *real* problem, but it has reservations in scope and depth. Or we may look at *Samson* where the scope and depth of what Milton is saying arises from our interpretation of such phrases as "inward eyes." Proof that *Samson* remains "unconvincing" in the sense that Aristotle meant can be seen in the denial by a number of present-day critics that Samson is regenerated or that he is intended as a type of Christ. The difficulty for them lies in not being able to accept Samson as more than a folk hero of biblical writing, who is employed to delineate the conquering of self and despair in himself and only by vicarious projection in us. *Paradise Lost* employs epic elements by moving into the impossible, which in the full view convinces that Eternal Providence exists and that God's ways are justified. It presents that which is possible only symbolically, but those who see Adam and Eve and Satan as true people doing real things have not been convinced of Milton's epical achievement.

A final point classifying the poem as epic is that it is a kind of praise: a praise of God rather than of hero and nation. We can call it epideictic because the example of the Son is seen and alluded to in Books III, VI, XII (or one like him—Abdiel, V, or Noah, XI) and because evil is shown so unfavorably in Books II, V, VI, IX, X, XI (the admonitory epic seen through blame). But besides this, the poem is an apostrophe to God's greatness and love for Man, to the need and wisdom of obeying Him. Milton's admonishment is to join in the forces of life (Eros) and renounce the forces of death (Thanatos). Looked at thus, the epic is a full-scale argument leading to the Song of Moses and the Song of the Lamb, sung by those who have achieved victory over the beast and his image and his mark: "Great and marvelous *are* thy works, Lord God Almighty; just and true *are* thy ways, thou King of saints" (Rev. 15: 3). Milton, in his divine inspiration, becomes the voice of the multitude, singing, "Alleluia: for the Lord God omnipotent reigneth" (Rev. 19: 6). The angelic praise of God figures prominently, of course, in the poem itself: III, 344-415; VI, 742-745, 882-888; VII, 180-192, 557-632; X, 641-648. The last is drawn from Revelation 15: 3. This structure of praise in terms of the earlier ten-book version is balanced and paralleled.

Thus labeling **Paradise Lost** as epic, but an epic with a difference, we can examine what sense of decorum Milton would employ. The prior discussion suggests that Milton's decorum should be based on classical definitions of epic decorum but that it should also be altered within that framework in the direction of its more heroic argument. "This great Argument" involves the bringing of dovelike creatures out of the vast abyss. Decorum cannot therefore be defined in the simpler terms of hero or "standard" heroic action; rather it calls for a seeming disorder out of which will arise order, a new form representing the action considered heroic, and a code that implies praise of God and his works.

Literary decorum is defined as the fitting of the various parts of a poem together, the sound agreeing with the sense, the style with the thought. "Propriety of style will be obtained," wrote Aristotle (*Rhetoric*, III. vii. 1-2), "by the expression of emotion and character, and by proportion to the subject matter. Style is proportionate to the subject matter when neither weighty matters are treated offhand nor trifling matters with dignity. . . ." Order, characterization, tone, vocabulary, style, and meter should all accord.

Classically, the epic (based on praise) should be in a high style and its subject matter should concern gods, heroes, members of the nobility, great men, great occasions, or noble abstractions. Comedy (based on blame) should be in a middle style and its subject matter should concern the middle class, the person of the poet, or middle-class occasions (such as birth, marriage, and death). High style in **Paradise Lost** adheres to the subject matter concerned with God and the Son; middle style to the narratives concerned with Adam and Eve and their progeny, which includes Milton, the narrative voice. The scenes involving Satan pretend to the high style as Satan and his crew envision themselves noble and as they undertake their great action; but he is instead an *eiron*, a staple of a comic mode (satire), when viewed from Man's reality, and an *alazon*, also a staple of comic mode (romance), when viewed with God's omniscience.

The speech of God the Father (III, 274-343) is illustrative of the high style of the epic. The Father's joy at the Son's offer to become Man to redeem Mankind pervades the passage: by this act heavenly love will overcome hellish hate; the Son will be more glorified thereby, and He will reign on God's throne as both God and Man. The joy of Judgment will peal forth when the sign of the Son appears in the sky: the world will dissolve in a great conflagration and from its ashes will spring a new Heaven and Earth for the Just, who will dwell with Joy and Love and Truth. Then the Son's scepter put by, all will

have been reduced (led back) to God who will once again be All in All.

The language is most appropriate. Note the reduplication: for example, line 292, "Thir own both *righteous* and un*righteous* deeds": line 301, "So easily *destroy'd,* and still *destroyes*"; line 316, "*Both God and Man,* Son *both* of *God and Man*"; line 337, "*See Golden d*ays, fruitful of *golden dee*ds" lines 339-340, "*Then* thou thy *regal Scepter shalt* lay by, / For *regal Scepter then* no more *shall* need"; line 341, "*God* shall be *All* in *All.* But *all* ye *Gods*." Note the lack of resting places within the periods of this passage: there are grammatical pauses (such as lines 280, 286, 289, 294, etc.) but there is no resting, as such a transition word as "So" in line 294 or line 298 makes clear. Note the specific words: "complacent," "transplanted," "ransomd," "fruition," "Humiliation," "incarnate," "dread," "tribulations," "compass"; the accents: line 279, "Thée frõm my bósom añd right hañd tõ sáve"; line 320, "Throñes, Prińcedoms, Pówers, Domiñioñs I rēdúce"; line 338, "Wīth Jóy añd Lóve trïúmphiñg, añd fáir Trúth"; and the sound: lines 313-314, "Therefore thy Humiliation shall exalt / With thee thy Manhood also to this Throne"; line 329, "Shall hast'n, such a peal shall rouse thir sleep." The diction is elevated as in "all Power / I give thee" (lines 317-318); "All knees to thee shall bow" (line 321); or "Then all thy Saints assembl'd" (line 330). The symbol of the sign of the Son (to figure so importantly in Milton's account of the Son's previous defeat of Satan at the beginning of time [VI, 776] and drawn from Matt. 24: 30) and of the Phoenix along with allusions to Isaiah 65: 17-25, II Peter 3: 12-13, and I Corinthians 15: 28 manifest the high style of the passage.

Adam's denunciation of Eve in Book X, lines 867-908, may not be typical of the human sections, but it does indicate the mean style to be found in the poem. The wallowing blame with which Adam assails Eve pervades the passage: she is called a serpent and likened to Satan; except for her, Adam now laments, he would have continued happy. "O why did God create this noveltie on Earth?" God (who now receives Adam's censure) should have filled the world with men as angels or have found some other way to achieve generation. (Adam has forgotten the omnipotence and omniscience of God.) To Adam, Woman (not Man like himself) will be the cause of infinite calamity to human life.

The language again is appropriate. Note such puns as calling Eve Serpent, her name supposedly being an aspirated form of *Heva*, "serpent"; or the line "To trust thee from my side" soon followed by reference to his rib "More to the part sinister from me drawn," the adjective meaning both from the "left" and "evil"; or the sexually graphic "straight conjunction with this Sex"; or the word "fell" referring to Satan, who is both "dangerous" and "fallen." Note the way duplication is made trivial and comic: "supernumerarie," "number," "innumerable"; "Serpent," "Serpentine"; "snare," line 873, and "Femal snares," line 897. Hyperbole, employed by comic poets for comic effect and yielding a "frigid" style, occurs throughout: "Out of my sight, thou Serpent," "proof against all assaults," "Crooked by nature, bent," "innumerable Disturbances," "infinite calamitie," "and houshold peace confound." There is a feeling of choppiness in the passage, for phrases are interrupted and the flow of thought tends toward an arid style: "nothing wants // but that thy shape // Like his // and colour . . ."; "Fool'd and beguil'd // by him thou // I by thee // To trust thee from my side // imagin'd wise // Constant, / mature / proof against all assaults // And understood . . ."; "By a farr worse // or if she love // withheld By Parents // or his. . . .'' Symbols and allusions that are integral to God's passage do not appear; the sounds are more plosive and sibilant, and the words themselves are not generally unusual or unusually employed. The middle-class concern is especially emphasized by the domestic strife lamented in the final lines of the passage.

Any one of his ''glorious'' speeches will suffice to show the false high style of Satan, dissembler and buffoon. Look at Book I, lines 622-662. Satan recounts his high exploit against God in the past and looks forward to further heroism in the future. Heroic war (''open or understood'') has shown the rebellious angels to be ''matchless'' (except against the Almighty) and ''puissant''; they have ''emptied Heav'n''; they have shown God that ''who overcomes / By force, hath overcome but half his foe.'' They will now resolve by new war to ''repossess thir native seat.'' We need not cite the high-sounding rhetoric and language, or ringing accents, for those who have advanced Satan as hero have done so frequently. Dissembling—and thus the irony underlying all that Satan says—is always evident. The fallen angels are not ''matchless'' against God or his presence in others. The power of mind that could presage that they would be repulsed by God is in everyone who admits God's omnipotence. The War in Heaven has removed only a third of the angels (as Death and Raphael both report in II, 692, and V, 710). None of the fallen angels should illogically believe that they will reascend. In this speech Satan implies that they have lost hope (1. 637) and that they must come to a resolution because ''Peace is despair'd'' (note the etymological pun), although in line 190 he had been hopeful and denied that resolution could come from despair. God's concealment of His strength wrought their fall, according to Satan. They had hoped to gain by force although now, defeated, Satan says, as if he aways knew, that force overcomes only half one's foe (note, too, his implied denial of God's omniscience). A comic element is seen thus in his self-deception; Milton is really so unsubtle that Satan becomes a caricature of the pompous braggart.

This effect is underlined by the contrasts that the poet builds. When we hear Satan say that the Abyss cannot long cover celestial spirits under darkness, we remember shortly before the dovelike creature that sits on the vast Abyss and makes it pregnant. The falseness of Satan's images is impressed upon us by contrast, and calling the fallen angels ''Sons of Heav'n''—true though it may be—sharply reminds us of their unfilial love; the Son's filial love later will undercut this epithet more patently.

But over all lies the hint of Satan's soliloquies that all this heroic, high-flown language is but trivia: for, Milton makes clear throughout the poem, God is omnipotent, omniscient, and omnipresent. The important text from Psalms 2, that the Lord will have the kings of the earth in derision, alluded to by Belial in Book II, line 191, hangs over these sections, and shows the self-aggrandized devils to be but the swarm of bees or pygmies they become about one hundred lines after this particular passage. They are giants only to themselves. Their pettiness is here seen in their ''prying'' (1. 655); their pride in their desired and heretical ''self-raising'' of themselves to Heaven; their envy appears everywhere. As vacuous orator, Satan becomes a buffoon; viewed from God's position, the fancifulness of Satan's speech is sheer romance and laughable besides. The rhetorical devices become obvious and ''contrived'': the opening apostrophes, the rhetorical questions (II. 626-630, 631-643, 661), the deliberate repetitions (''Warr then,

Warr''). These caricature when read fully. It is Milton's genius that has led so many astray, not Satan.

What then is the style? It is high, and it is middle, and it is falsely high but really low. Its style depends on how we read the poem, but if we read it with Milton's thesis and theme firmly in mind, we see that the middle style predominates, the high offset by the low, though that is superficially high. (The style is a part of the total dialectic of the poem: it represents thesis, antithesis, and synthesis as much as the contrasts of good and evil, and the like. The point, of course, is that Man partakes of both the thesis which is God and the antithesis which is Satan.) Yet we realize a striving upward and we have a feeling that as we accept the ''message'' we soar with Milton with no middle flight. As a heroic poem, *Paradise Lost* partakes of epical style, but it is not limited by what is epic style any more than its author is by other elements of epic tradition. Milton's style is appropriate to his subject, Man's disobedience, but it also shifts aptly as the subject matter and characters shift. Milton has kept ''propriety of style'' if we recognize the shifts in expression of emotion and character and subject matter. Triviality does enter—when it should; and dignity is maintained—when it should be. The more heroic argument, encompassing *all* the basics of life, requires the full gamut of styles. It is not limited and it is a product of modified tradition.

Nonetheless we can apply the terms ''grand'' and ''sublime'' to the whole rather than just to certain parts; but these terms will not mean quite what they summarized for the eighteenth century, under the influence of Longinus and John Dennis. Rather than a mere equation of ''sublime'' with ''high'' or ''epic'' style, we have the sublimity of being upraised when the full effect and message of the poem is allowed to work upon us. It does not derive merely from language used and literary devices employed; it arises largely from the joy that pervades the whole poem when we recognize God's presence and the paradise within, happier far. It uplifts us when we see what is above the false grandeur of Satan and the mean existence of mankind. And we have this concept impressed upon us by the dignity (or grandness) of God's creations and ultimate plan. Justification of God's ways lies in recognition of true Good, impossible before the Fall, and in recognition of the need for joint endeavor of Man and God to reach high goals.

The poem is sublime in its elevation of the spirit and its tremendous joy: the elevation of the spirit is achieved through the style that moves from low to mean to high, and the joy is achieved by realizing that what has befallen Man is not tragic but ultimately blissful, once the seat has been regained. Rhetorically the style is grand in part, but not all parts are stylistically grand. The total effect may reach grandness, but that is not the same thing as classifying Milton's style in one traditional category.

Milton's style is answerable to the Renaissance concept of epic, and it satisfies the expectations of decorum. And though the impersonal and universal strain toward the individual and personal (see Arnold Stein's essay in *Answerable Style*, pp. 136-137), this is all carefully calculated to bring God's message down from high to the common man, thereby to raise man up. In fact it is the individual and personal in the poem that are raised and supported. Man's habitat is the middle ground; the poet *intends* to soar with no middle flight above the Aonian mount. That he was successful is evident from the three centuries of readers who have soared with the poet. But the total view of the style of the poem and thus its answerability is not that simple.

The narrator inspired by God's spirit well exhibits the point being made in the poem: God works through Man to reach Man; He purges and disperses the mists, and, as it were, with inward eyes illuminated, the poet's intended wing is in no way depressed. Man's normal style is mean, his audience receives the mean best; but the spirit moves upward and the goal is upward, and fit audience will be led upward with the poet as he moves into the high and ultimately answerable style. The fusion of genres and the fusion of styles created a "new" genre and a "new" style, and thereby was wrought the only possible answer to argument above heroic. (pp. 21-33)

> *John T. Shawcross, "The Style and Genre of 'Paradise Lost'," in* New Essays on "Paradise Lost," *edited by Thomas Kranidas, 1969. Reprint by University of California Press, 1971, pp. 15-33.*

EARL MINER (essay date 1974)

[*Miner is the author of numerous scholarly works on Japanese fiction and English Renaissance literature. In the following excerpt, he discusses the genre of* Paradise Regained *and describes its narrative structure.*]

Paradise Regained strikes every reader as something quite distinct in experience from **Paradise Lost,** and although the admirers of the brief epic have been distinguished, not many have troubled themselves to present with "reason and convincement," as Milton says, the virtues of that poem. Any other writer would have achieved fame with Milton's brief epic, but since he had already written a longer and richer one, he fails to get the credit he might have for **Paradise Regained.** The first thing that strikes a reader moving from the longer to the shorter epic is a spareness of style that at first seems deficient in interest but that, on better acquaintance, becomes as hard and clear as one would wish for in a debate between two formidable antagonists. The complete lucidity of the style answers perfectly to the minds of the narrator and of Jesus in challenging the falsehoods of Satan. **Paradise Regained** is a poem of related (sometimes joined, sometimes conflicting) perspectives, those of Satan, of the Son, of the narrator, and of the reader. Certain lesser perspectives also contribute to the first and part of the second books of the poem: the proto-Christians, Mary, and the fallen angels. In my view, these other perspectives help establish the situation and the scene but otherwise exist only to be subtracted in that gradual process of taking away that reduces the four other perspectives to two clear and crucially focused choices.

In writing his brief epic Milton seems less interested than he had been in writing **Paradise Lost** to observe and renovate the pagan epic conventions, or even their modern counterparts. He does begin, however, in very characteristic fashion: "I who e're while the happy Garden sung . . ." **Paradise Lost** was a pastoral? We shake our heads. Of course Milton knows what he is doing. The four prefatory lines to the *Aeneid* (beginning, "Ille ego, qui quondam gracili modulatus avena / carmen," whose first four words Milton closely follows) spoke of Virgil's changing from the pastoral and georgic worlds to that of war for his epic. Before Milton, Spenser had begun *The Faerie Queene* with an echo of the same Virgilian preface:

> Lo I the man, whose Muse whilome did maske,
> As time her taught in lowly Shepheards weeds,
> Am now enforst a far unfitter taske,
> For trumpets sterne to chaunge mine Oaten reeds,
> And sing of Knights and Ladies gentle deeds;
> Whose prayses having slept in silence long,
> Me, all too meane, the sacred Muse areeds
> To blazon broad emongst her learned throng:
> Fierce warres and faithfull loves shall moralize my song.

Numerous matters emerge from this. Milton's strength and lucidity are apparent at once in the contrast with Spenser's leisurely style. We observe once again the hold that the *Aeneid* has on Milton's imagination. More important, we do *not* infer from what is said that Milton will now essay a larger form hitherto, or one more martial. No, what Milton is saying is that **Paradise Lost** ought to have been a pastoral, and in some sense was in Books IV to VIII. With the pastoral as it were totally lost as a world-genre, a new genre (again in a universal, typological sense a pastoral) is necessary.

> I who e're while the happy Garden sung,
> By one man's disobedience lost, now sing
> Recover'd Paradise to all mankind
> By one man's firm obedience fully tri'd
> Through all temptation, and the Tempter foil'd
> In all his wiles, defeated and repuls't,
> And *Eden* rais'd in the wast Wilderness.

Five of the first seven lines of the poem end with verbs, a highly unusual procedure for any seventeenth-century poet, especially since the first two lines thereby suggest a couplet, and the fourth, fifth, and sixth a Drydenian triplet. The activity of most of the verbs also heightens the sense of action or movement. When Blake declared that we would not cease from *mental* fight (I take it that the sword in his hand was his pen) until Jerusalem had been rebuilt in England, he caught something of the temper of Milton's beginning. Milton himself stresses contrast and transformation. As "one man's disobedience" had turned a pastoral into a tragic epic, so now "one man's firm obedience" will make out of that the new pastoral ("*Eden* rais'd in the wast Wilderness"). "For as by one man's disobedience many were made sinners, so by the obedience of one shall many be made righteous." The opening lines of **Paradise Lost** have been recalled and transformed.

"By one man's firm obedience": experienced readers of Milton know that the problem-word of the phrase is "man's." Setting aside the christological considerations, and deferring other problems, we must ask why, having chosen Jesus as his hero, Milton takes that "man's" heroism to be exemplified in the temptations in the desert? The question has often been raised in one way or another, and perhaps the best answer is another question: what alternatives were there? Two, really: the Passion and Resurrection or the Second Coming. Apart from the difficulties involved in narrating both of those subjects (the one too familiar and the other, as Milton had learned, not familiar enough), only the temptation in the wilderness answered symbolically and logically to that in Eden. "By one man's firm obedience": we can now see the kind of elaborate interlingual and typological pun that had existed, or that is now brought into existence, in the opening lines of **Paradise Lost.** "Mans First Disobedience" and "one greater Man" obviously refer to the two Adams in a kind of reverse typology, because after all in Hebrew "Adam" means "man."

In the epic trying the obedience of the new Adam, Milton once again isolates the scene of temptation and again presents one-to-one confrontation. We have very simple and momentous confrontation and choice. And yet the surprise **Paradise Regained** reimposes on one in each reading is the extraordinary degree of uncertainty in most of the poem. The fallen angels meeting twice in the "gloomy consistory" of the air have not the faintest notion of their problem or what to do about it (except Satan, to whose problems we shall return). The newly baptized have a chorus of anxiety at the absence of Jesus, and Mary's brief appearance conveys her fearful trust in her mysterious son. Even the brief scene in Heaven makes us long for the School Divine of *Paradise Lost* whose plain-speaking now seems a most valuable virtue, especially in a diety. God addresses Gabriel (traditionally the angel of the Annunciation) about the fulfillment of the promise to Mary ''that she should bear a Son . . . call'd the Son of God.'' Particularly in the context of *Paradise Regained* that simple ''call'd'' carries something of the dubiety of a Spenserian ''seem'd'': ''Men call'd him Mulciber . . . Thus they relate erring.'' Why, in an account so familiar and, one would have thought, so well established, is Jesus merely ''call'd the Son of God''? We learn indeed about Mary's conception: ''on her should come / The Holy Ghost,'' engendering a son, ''This man . . . of birth divine.''

In the *Christian Doctrine* Milton denies trinitarian orthodoxy. He accepts of course the existence of the Son of God as Messiah, and also the existence of the Holy Spirit, but as we have seen he treats them both as ''posterior'' creatures rather than as beings coeternal and coessential with God. As for the Holy Spirit, who acts for God (''the power of the highest,'') in visiting Mary, he was ''created . . . later than the Son, and far inferior to him'' (*Christian Doctrine*). Now no one can pretend that orthodox trinitarianism proves any clearer that Milton's idea, or that the mystery of the Incarnation is less difficult. But by giving us an Incarnation without trinitarianism, Milton presents the Son of God created after the angels but superior to all other creatures, and one ''call'd the Son of God'' who was conceived by Mary when visited by that Holy Spirit (acting God's mission) who was created after the Son of God and far inferior to him. A ''man'' of ''birth divine'' is indeed a man of mystery, and the working-out of that mystery constitutes the action of *Paradise Regained.*

After Satan's second consistory (i.e., after II, 234) we find the scene reduced in effect to only two characters, the Son and Satan. With such simplification the air of uncertainty thickens. Jesus tells of God's voice at his baptism, calling him ''his beloved Son.'' That baptismal appellation is rehearsed three times, growing less certain with repetition. Indeed the whole central point of Jesus's being in the wilderness is in one sense his ignorance:

> And now by some strong motion I am led
> Into this Wilderness, to what intent
> I learn not yet, perhaps I need not know;
> For what concerns my knowledge God reveals.

Again we observe the extraordinarily verbal character of the style at a crucial moment, with three of the four lines ending with verbs, with the sequence from ''led'' to ''learn,'' and from ''not know'' *via* ''knowledge'' to ''God reveals.'' Jesus trusts divine revelation, and whatever ''Son of God'' may mean, Jesus plays the role that Christians must emulate, trusting God's revelation. Jesus has made the central Protestant and Miltonic point about the supreme importance of faith: ''Now faith is the substance of things hoped for, the evidence of things not seen'' (Hebrews 11:1). In *Paradise Regained,* faith is also acquiescence in the divine will although unknown; it is patience; it is obedience. Like reason, faith is heroic choice. The faithful Jesus, *deo profugus,* does not know why he is in the wilderness, and he does not speculate on *who* he is.

That speculation which I found difficult to sort through is the chief business of Satan in the poem, and he too speaks about the baptismal pronouncement:

> Who this is we must learn, for man he seems
> In all his lineaments, though in his face
> The glimpses of his Fathers glory shine.

The metrical agitation of the first line quoted well expresses Satan's concern. Satan seems to possess the answer to his implied question, since he says that although Jesus looks like a man his Father's—surely only ''God's'' can be meant?—glory shines in his face. But as we have been seeing all along, knowing is virtually impossible in this poem. More than that, knowing is not the *essential* thing. Faith is essential, *sola fides,* as the Reformers insisted. Satan lacks faith and declares: ''we must learn.'' He lacks knowledge of just what ''Son of God'' means in reference to Jesus (all angelic creatures as well as human creatures deserve the phrase, as with the ''sons of God'' in Job and elsewhere). He has something more than suspicion from the outset that this is *the* Son of God who will spell the end of his reign over the sinful world. To the extent that the poem is, like *Paradise Lost,* something of a Sataniad, the irony directed toward Satan is enormous and grows with each action he takes. Increasingly frustrated by the ease with which Jesus rejects his temptations and by Jesus's calm refusal to say who he is, Satan employs ''All his wiles'' for an essential but profoundly ironic reason. He cannot afford not to know what will undo him. To accept not knowing would be faith in God, and Satan just will not believe, He would rather *know*, which, as this poem points out again and yet again, and more clearly than anything else written by Milton, without faith is perverse. To Satan knowing means defeat, destruction, the fulfillment of the prophecy made to Eve that her seed would avenge her on the serpent. And yet he must know.

Amid uncertainty at least as great as that in our own lives, and meant by Milton to answer to our own lives, the two antagonists meet. Satan, deceiver that he is, appears as a hungry old man, he the ''great Dictator'' as he is now styled, the magician. [According to Arnold Stein in *Heroic Knowledge* (1957),] Jesus, the hero, is the man of pure faith, one of ''the rarest and most hopeful of images, wisdom without bodily decrepitude, early, with the hero young, at the flower, unbruised.'' As the two interact, Satan becomes more and more desperate, the Son more and more in control. We can regard the course of the action in the poem in an easy way. Following Milton's invitation, we can compare this with the earlier epic. Let us consider part of the first book of *Paradise Regained.*

1-7: Epic proposition and forecast.

8-17: Epic invocation; talk of style.

18-32: John the Baptist, line 20, ''Heavens Kingdom nigh at hand'' (the kingdom and time motifs); first version of the baptism.

33-125: Satan's gloomy consistory (*Par. Lost,* I-II); second version of baptism (''A perfect Dove,'' rather than the Holy Spirit); question of sonhood; play on time and timelessness; the kingdom motif in Satan's view of dictatorship; his thoughts on the Son's nature.

126-81: God's conversation with Gabriel; angelic hymns (*Par. Lost,* III).

182-293: Jesus in meditation (actual soliloquy is employed) on events precedent (like Raphael and Adam, *Par. Lost,* IV-VIII); the Son's knowledge that he is the Messiah; his lack of assurance of how to act, except that his faith and will are unshaken.

Following the invited parallel, we see that Milton has used up as it were the first eight books of *Paradise Lost* in as few as 293 lines of the first book of *Paradise Regained.*

Most of what follows is concerned with direct encounter between Satan and the Son. All of us refer to those encounters as temptations, as choices between good and evil, but it proves no easy thing to say what in Jesus is being tested or how many temptations he endures. One view that is particularly appropriate to the central question of Jesus's identity as one "call'd Son of God," is that in each approach Satan seeks out a different one of the "natures of the Son of God." The initial temptation, to turn stones into bread, tests the manhood of Jesus insofar as he hungers at last after forty days of fasting. But to perform that miracle, Jesus would have to enter on his role as Messiah before God's will had been revealed to him. As is well known, the three traditional roles of Christ are those of prophet, priest, and king. The long temptation (or temptations) of the kingdoms obviously plays on the Son's nature as king. His rejection of the kingdoms offered by Satan points to his role as "*Israels* true King," as also king of the (typologically) true Israel, his Christian Church. But more than anything else, the temptations show Jesus in his role of prophet. In writing "Of the Office of the Mediator" in the *Christian Doctrine,* Milton says that as prophet the Son has an internal "manner of administering," the "illumination of the understanding"; and an external manner, "the promulgation of divine truth." The internal clearly predominates in the Son himself until his last utterance to Satan on the pinnacle of the temple. Satan fears that he has not only a man but also a king to deal with, and his temptations drive at those two natures of the Son. He is defeated by those two natures in that they rebuff him constantly. But the defeat is made whole by Jesus's taking on the role of prophet at the moment he accepts his ministry as priest.

It is possible to consider the poem under one or three aspects, then—or four, or two, or six. A major function of the lucidity of *Paradise Regained* is the clarification less of our ignorance than that we *are* ignorant and will continue to be until in faith we accept our ignorance. Milton does not help us to number the temptations, nor does he aid us in distinguishing whether there is one or more temptations of the kingdoms. The real point is that one choice is like another, that no matter what Satan does he does and fails at the same thing, and that as long as the Son maintains faith until God reveals some new larger matter, his every reply is essentially the same. Some simplification of Milton's clarity, and some ordering of his constants, can assist us in understanding what happens as it were in the poem after it reaches its equivalent of Book IX of *Paradise Lost.* The distinctions are based on episodes involving either a different time or locale or a different object of view:

I, 294-502: Tempted action: to turn stones into bread
II, 1-235: Interlude: the "new baptiz'd"; Mary; Satan in consistory
II, 235-406: The Banquet
III, I-IV, 194: The Kingdoms (power)
IV, 195-393: The Kingdoms (wisdom)
IV, 394-450: The Storm
IV, 451-580: The Pinnacle
IV, 581-631: Denouement

It should be stressed that these divisions are offered only as convenience. Fewer or further divisions make perfect sense: perhaps one should distinguish in the section I have termed the temptation of the Kingdoms (power) a further temptation. After suffering various rebuffs over Rome and Parthia (each of which is worth being termed a separate temptation), Satan suddenly utters his price: Jesus must bow down and serve him. How very crude that seems. But the complete shift of front and its very crudity are well calculated to arouse the unguided anger

and self-betrayal that Satan has all along been looking for. As a master psychological stroke, the sub-episode deserves to be set apart. But once again we see that, far from being crucial, the difference in Satan's approach makes no difference whatsoever as long as the Son's faith and choice remain unshaken. The Son has but one way of defeating his opponent, faith, but Satan has numerous ways of losing. The opposition between those two facts sustains the tension of the poem.

The opposition of those two perspectives on common experience leaves the narrator and the reader somewhere between. We think that we can distinguish various temptations, but it turns out that they may be very many or very few and that they all seem in succession to repeat their predecessors. In creating such perspectives of choice, Milton in general gives us another version of that discriminating whole, *Paradise Lost.* But his brief epic is more original than the earlier (not that that means better), more independent of earlier epics. The recapitulative *Aeneid*-form is ignored; there is none of the descent to the underworld, the epic shield, the epic catalogue, or of those things so carefully renovated for *Paradise Lost.* Instead we discover a series of episodes basically all one, as if *Paradise Lost* in its central ten books dealt with the temptation of Adam and Eve. Another related characteristic is the amount of talk in the poem. *Paradise Lost* had obviously included more talk than any previous epic, because of its exaggeration of the *Aeneid*-form. But that unusual structure also makes most of the talk seem to be the action that the talk relates. In *Paradise Regained,* speech follows speech so persistently that one might wish to follow an interpretation of the poem as a drama. What is acceptable in such speech-making in narrative, however, would be precisely the thing that would be thought non-dramatic, because tediously extended, on the stage. Allowing that, however, we must also allow that Milton's climax shares a great deal with drama in that it involves a reversal and recognition of enormous impact. The placing of that climax so near the end of the poem, and the nature of the climax, both make the poem a novelty in the epic tradition. At that moment, all perspectives become one. And it happens so quickly. When Satan suddenly sweeps the Son to the pinnacle of the Temple in Jerusalem, he leaves him on the perilous footing, scoffing that he stand or fall:

> To whom thus Jesus: also it is written,
> Tempt not the Lord thy God, he said and stood.
> But Satan smitten with amazement fell
> As when Earths Son *Antaeus* (to compare
> Small things with greatest) in *Irassa* strove
> With *Joves Alcides,* and oft foil'd still rose,
> Receiving from his mother Earth new strength,
> Fresh from his fall, and fiercer grapple joyn'd,
> Throttl'd at length in the Air, expir'd and fell;
> So after many a foil the Tempter proud,
> Renewing fresh assaults, amidst his pride
> Fell whence he stood to see his Victor fall.
> And as that *Theban* Monster that propos'd
> Her riddle, and him, who solv'd it not, devour'd;
> That once found out and solv'd, for grief and spight
> Cast her self headlong from th' *Ismenian* steep,
> So strook with dread and anguish fell the Fiend,
> And to his crew, that sat consulting, brought
> Joyless triumphals of his hop't success,
> Ruin, and desperation, and dismay,
> Who durst so proudly tempt the Son of God.

Having made so much of falling and its Latinate variants, "ruined," etc. in *Paradise Lost,* Milton dwells on the opposite here, standing when standing is difficult. The metaphorical play about the image of those two figures on the perilous pinnacle, one of them standing, one falling, unfolds suddenly in our minds. The éclaircissement contradicts itself in some sense by being that manifestly paradoxical thing, a religious epiphany without an apotheosis. What, after all, is the Son of God? He is, as the poem started by saying, that man who can overcome all temptation, who can obey in faith. At the end of the poem, we are at one with Milton. We have discovered what each episode of the poem has taught us again and again, and which we have simply not learned and so had to be taught again and again. The answer to our quest or disposition to know is that we need not know. We need only believe and understand.

The coming of the grandest climactic episode at the very end of *Paradise Regained* resembles no other work of Milton's so much as *Samson Agonistes*. Likewise the "strong motion" leading Jesus to the wilderness is reminiscent of Samson's "rousing motions" once Dalila leaves. It also resembles in that the detective story. As in that genre, so here we also have the investigator, the search for clues in a series of episodes, and the revelations of the last few pages. Of course Milton "renovates" a genre as yet unborn by reversing the guilt and putting it in the investigator, as also by making something profound out of such a form of plot. *Paradise Lost* also anticipates a later genre, science fiction, by combining two human creatures at the center and supernatural ones from places other than the earth converging on the human pair. We also find battles in space, strange weapons, magic, and a controller of the universe. The interest of the detective story and of science fiction in themselves is as legitimate as such other conventions as the blazon or the epic itself. Our minds are well exercised in reaching out into space, in rattling through chaos, and above all in our concern for threatened humanity. Similarly, the mystery-story atmosphere of *Paradise Regained* creates a genuine compulsion and suspense. Satan's irresistible and fatal curiosity arouses both a similar response and a counter-response in us. The divergence of perspectives sometimes puts our own in peril. There are those who criticize Milton for having run a risk that he failed. But after all, he does not write detective stories or science fiction, and we can trust what happens as we read his brief epic. (pp. 268-82)

> *Earl Miner, "Milton's Laws Divine and Human,"*
> *in his* The Restoration Mode from Milton to Dryden,
> *Princeton University Press, 1974, pp. 198-287.*

CHRISTOPHER HILL　　(essay date 1977)

[*Hill is a distinguished English essayist and historian. In the following excerpt from a work originally published in 1977, he discusses the origin and intent of* Areopagitica *and comments on Milton's understanding of toleration.*]

Areopagitica was published on 28 November 1644, selling at 4d a copy. It was Milton's reply to Herbert Palmer's attack on him in a sermon before the House of Commons. Many of its ideas were commonplaces among the radicals. We may quote Servetus, for instance. 'It would be easy to judge if it were permitted to all to speak in peace in the church, that all might vie in prophesying.' So far from his *Restitutio Christianismi* disturbing Christendom, Servetus argued at his trial, Christendom would profit by it and the truth would be worked out little by little: things are often at first repressed which are afterwords received. In England radical sectaries had worked out a theory of toleration long before Milton wrote. John Stoughton had said in a sermon preached at Paul's Cross 'take heed thou strike

not a schismatic, and a saint be found to lie a-bleeding and thou to answer it.' But Stoughton quoted Pico della Mirandola for the sentiment, so Milton may have got it direct. Compare 'If I . . . should meet a poor soul wandering from parish to parish, from sermon to sermon, to find her well-beloved, I durst not wound her.' But some shepherds, Stoughton added, are wolves. Stoughton was a friend of Dury and Hartlib. The latter published his millenarian *Felicitas ultimi saeculi* after Stoughton's death—a work in which he linked Bacon, Comenius and Dury.

Many passages in Milton's *Of Prelatical Episcopacy* echo or are echoed by (scholars are not quite sure) passages on toleration in Lord Brooke's *Discourse on Episcopacie*. In the year or so before *Areopagitica* appeared, its arguments had been anticipated by William Walwyn, later the Leveller, by Henry Robinson and by Henry Burton. Walwyn in June or July 1644 recognized the necessity of restricting Royalist propaganda in wartime, but pointed out that 'by reason of the qualifications of the licensers' this had 'wrought a wrong way, and stopped the mouths of good men'.

Areopagitica starts from the assumption that, given freedom of debate, the reason which is common to all men is likely to lead them to recognize the same truths. Such a view would appeal to those whose economic life demanded freedom of trade from monopoly: it did not seem self-evident to the big

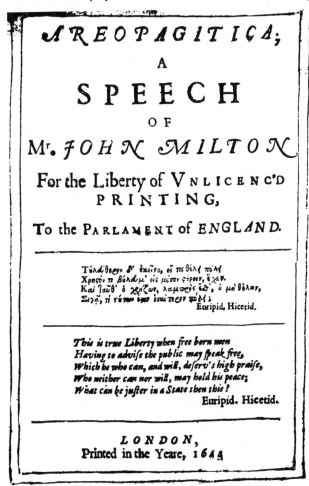

Title page of the first edition of Milton's famous call for the liberty of unlicensed printing.

City merchants who read *Gangraena*. We can see *Areopagitica* as Milton's attempt to focus the tolerationist case on one point, liberty of printing, using arguments from the attack on monopolies; or we can see him trying to unite the Protestant nation against priests, the Westminster Assembly and the censorship, as he had earlier tried to unite the nation against bishops. His immediate object was to appeal to Parliament against the Assembly of Divines, and especially to Erastians in and out of Parliament, who came nearest to sharing his views at this time. Thomas Coleman, one of the few Erastian ministers to preach before Parliament, cited Milton with approval in August 1643. Coleman's most famous Erastian sermon was preached eight months after *Areopagitica* appeared.

The leading figure among the Erastians was John Selden, whose books Milton had been reading and annotating since at least 1638. In 1642-5 he studied Selden's *De Jure Naturali* in connection with his divorce pamphlets, quoting it and praising its author in *The Doctrine and Discipline of Divorce*. In *Areopagitica* he again cited 'the chief of learned men reputed in this land', this time in support of the view that 'all opinions, yea errors, can help us to attain truth.' Selden's *Uxor Hebraica* of 1646 seemed to confirm some of Milton's positions on divorce, and was quoted triumphantly in *The Second Defence* and in the *De Doctrina*. In *The Likeliest Means* Milton again quoted Selden against the necessity for marriage to be administered by a priest. Selden was a favourite of the Spenserian poets, a friend of William Browne. It was to Selden that in 1636 George Wither dedicated his translation of Nemesius's *The Nature of Man*, used by R. O. in *Mans Mortalitie*. Selden was said by some to have been Oliver Cromwell's first choice when a reply to *Eikon Basilike* was needed. There are many convergences between Selden's ideas and Milton's. Selden, for instance, thought that 'there's no such thing as spiritual jurisdiction', and that ''tis a vain thing to talk of a heretic'.

So long as Milton retained confidence in the ability and willingness of the Erastians in Parliament to curb Presbyterian intolerance, he did not insist on the necessity for separating church and state, notwithstanding his attack on Constantine. Anxious to enlist the support of 'anyone' who would 'bring his helpful hand to the slow-moving Reformation which we labour under', he felt that 'those neighbouring differences, or rather indifferences, ... in some point of doctrine or discipline, ... need not interrupt the unity of spirit, if we could but find among us the bond of peace.' We shall often find Milton exhibiting this sort of tactical moderation in the interests of strategic extremism.

What must also be emphasized, however, is the apocalyptic atmosphere of the early sixteen-forties, in which men could believe in progressive revelation, in the evolution of truth, and could hope for a state of permanent reformation. Here writers as diverse as the Smectymnuans, the Five Dissenting Brethren of the Westminster Assembly, Lord Brooke, Thomas and John Goodwin, Henry Robinson, Roger Williams, Walter Cradock and John Saltmarsh can be linked. Hence the necessity of toleration, said the anonymous author of *The Ancient Bounds* (1645), without which truth 'cannot be so easily brought forth'. 'Better many errors of some kind suffered than one useful truth be obstructed or destroyed.' Similarly Cromwell would rather tolerate Mohammedanism than persecute one of the elect. Truth, said Milton, 'may have more shapes than one'. Fifteen years later, in a phrase that suggests a reference to Hobbes, he argued that 'no man or body of men in these times can be the infallible judges or determiners in matters of religion to any other men's consciences but their own.'

We may recall some long-standing radical Protestant traditions: Foxe's paean in praise of the printing press, Peter Wentworth's demand for liberty of speech, John Penry's for liberty of printing, the contempt for expurgatory indexes shown by Thomas James, Bodley's first librarian, who used the Papal Index to help him to decide what books to order for his Library. Or we may compare the *Homily on Reading of Holy Scripture:* ''If you will not know the truth of God . . . lest you fall into error; by the same reason you may then lie still and never go [i.e. walk] lest, if you go, you fall into the mire.' Even more important in the history of toleration was the stand of radical sectaries—Baptists like Leonard Busher and John Murton, Socinians like Crell—who said that truth would always prevail in fair argument.

Milton himself had argued in *Animadversions* for the right of 'the freeborn people of England' at long last to speak their minds, and in *The Reason of Church Government* against using the existence of sects and errors as an excuse for delaying reform. There was tactical wiliness in Milton's determination to prove that censorship should be rejected because it was popish. Protestantism—and here Milton echoes Walwyn and Robinson—is opposed to implicit faith, because all believers are priests. If he takes it at second hand, 'a man may be a heretic in the truth.' Toleration, Milton argued, followed necessarily from that reliance on the Bible which was common to all Protestants, and only to them. This made persecution of Protestants by Protestants even more inexcusable than by papists. In 1659, echoing Hobbes, Milton was to argue that popery was 'but a Roman principality . . ., endeavouring to keep up her old universal dominion under a new name and mere shadow of a catholic religion'. The only heretic is he who maintains opinions which cannot be proved by Scripture—the papist. Nearly thirty years after *Areopagitica* Milton was still saying that 'no true protestant can persecute, or not tolerate, his fellow-protestant' without rejecting the principles on which his own religion was founded. 'What is freedom but choice?' he had asked; but the literal meaning of the word heresy *is* choice.

Censorship, Milton argued, favours a dull conformity; the censor's 'commission enjoins him to let pass nothing but what is vulgarly received already'. In a revolutionary age, when ideas were developing as rapidly as they were in the England of 1644, this was intolerable. It was also unsuccessful: suppressing sects only helped them to spread. Unanimity was neither possible nor desirable. Here Milton abandoned age-old assumptions, expressed by Hooker and more recently by Hobbes, that anarchy was the only possible consequence of religious diversity, liberty of expression and publication, were permitted. Milton consequently abandons the attempt at (or pretence of) a one-minded community. It is a very big step towards the modern world, though Milton is only one of many who took it in the sixteen-forties.

One of the earliest entries in Milton's Commonplace Book, made before his Italian journey, noted that 'in moral evil much good can be mixed': evil exists to exercise the good. 'If there were no opposition', he asked in *The Reason of Church Government,* 'where were the trial of an unfeigned goodness? . . . Virtue that wavers is not virtue, but vice revolted from itself.' The line of thought runs from *Comus* to *Areopagitica.* It runs through *Paradise Lost,* where the evil angels and Adam fall of their own free will, and the Son freely offers to die in order to redeem man's sin. Christian liberty is triumphantly asserted in the *De Doctrina*, whose Preface proclaims 'how much it is in the interests of the Christian religion that men should be free not only to sift and winnow any doctrine, but also openly to give their opinions of it, and even to write about it, according to what each believes. Without this freedom . . . there is no religion and no gospel. Violence alone prevails, and it is disgraceful and disgusting that the Christian religion should be supported by violence.' Here the idea that truth evolves, that revelation is progressive, seems to link up with the Protestant stance of which Oliver Cromwell is a prominent exemplar, of waiting on God, of watching for providences, signs, before acting: truth may appear in unexpected places, but it is none the less divine for that. And truth once known must lead to action, as Michael told Adam to 'add/Deeds to thy knowledge answerable'.

Although in *Areopagitica* Milton says that Arminius was 'perverted', he describes him as 'acute and distinct'; Milton's definition of freedom as choice is already leading him on the road from Calvin to Arminius in theory, at the same time as his revulsion from 'new Presbyter' is leading him further away from Presbyterianism in practice. The argument of *Areopagitica*—'that which purifies us is trial, and trial is by things contrary'—assumes that men are free to choose good or evil. So the cultural crisis which became a political crisis becomes a theological crisis as well. Milton had to rethink his position not only on discipline but also on doctrine. It is not so much a change in fundamental outlook—for virtue was purified by trial in *Comus*—as a realization of the full significance, in political, social and theological terms, of a conception of Christian liberty which started from the absolute integrity of the individual conscience.

The idea of being a heretic in the truth can be found in Giordano Bruno, in Paolo Sarpi and among the Socinians, as well as in Bishop Carleton, William Chillingworth, John Fry, John Knowles, Robert Boyle, James Nayler, Thomas Hobbes and Robert Barclay. It too is a logical conclusion of the radical Protestant doctrine that revelation may be progressive. When Agricola Carpenter, a mortalist, called in 1652 for 'some wiser Columbus' to reveal 'an America of knowledge yet unfound out', he may have been echoing Milton, but more probably he was repeating ideas that were current in radical circles. John Bunyan in 1657 thought that truth profited from heresy.

We recall the importance in sixteenth- and seventeenth-century Protestant thinking of the linked themes of spiritual struggle and spiritual pilgrimage, warfaring and wayfaring. Lemot in Chapman's *An Humerous Dayes Mirth* (1599) asked 'how can you conquer that against which you never strive, or strive against that which never encounters you?' This is 'to make virtue an idle huswife, and to hide herself [in] slothful cobwebs that still should be adorned with actions of victory'. The intention here is ironical, but the sentiment recurs. John Warr, like William Sedgwick, Milton (and Bruno) recognized that liberty in its full appearance would darken the eye newly recovered from blindness, and therefore approved of gradual methods of reform.

It is difficult to be patient with those critics, innocent of historical knowledge, who tut-tut at Milton's refusal of toleration for Roman Catholics, suggesting that he failed to understand the logic of his own *Areopagitica*. Milton knew very well what he was doing, and it is evidence of the complete change in the politico-religious atmosphere since his day that this still has to be explained. Milton, like Marvell, regarded popery not primarily as a religion—that might have been tolerated—but as 'a priestly despotism under the cloak of religion', which 'extirpates all religious and civil supremacies'. He saw it as 'a

Roman principality', the outward arm of the Italian potentate whom he regarded as Antichrist, leader of a potential Spanish or French fifth column in England. Milton early wrote Latin poems to celebrate England's escape on Guy Fawkes Day; and what he saw in Italy did not change his belief in the existence of an international Catholic plot aiming at total suppression of free discussion. Milton swallowed whole the stories of Irish massacres of English Protestants, and himself subscribed to the suppression of the Irish revolt. He would not be at all surprised when a papal nuncio headed the Irish rebels. The Irish were 'an accursed race', Royalist support for whom was 'criminal madness'.

Milton further regarded Roman Catholic worship as idolatry, and therefore as one of the most grievous sins described in the Bible, the main offence of the chosen people, against which they had to be warned again and again. Popish (and Laudian) idolatry subordinated the dignity of man to the sanctity of material things, whether they were the bread and wine of the sacrament or consecrated churches. 'When all our fathers worshipped stocks and stones' was his summary dismissal of the Catholic Middle Ages. Milton knew that idolatry was a sin to which too many of the common people were addicted. He also believed that popery, even more than prelacy, encouraged laxness and corruption, since through 'easy confession, easy absolution, pardons, indulgences, masses' a man could 'buy out his peace with money which he cannot with repentance'. It was the negation of that strenuous self-discipline which Milton thought fundamental to Christian liberty. In view of popish idolatry, freedom of worship for papists, if allowed, would pander to all that was worst, least rational, most backward-looking, most lax, in the natural man. Popery, because of its refusal to accept the fundamental status of the Bible and conscience, could not be met on equal terms. By insistence on implicit faith, Rome 'forfeits her Christian liberty'. For these reasons, political and cultural as well as religious, Milton in common with many other Englishmen felt that although Roman Catholics might be allowed liberty of conscience in secret, 'for just reason of state' they must not be permitted 'the public and scandalous use' of worship.

Here Milton represented the normal English Protestant attitude, shared by liberals from Hooker through Selden to Locke. More in need of explanation than Milton's position is that of those eccentric tolerationists who would have been prepared to extend liberty of worship to Catholics—Roger Williams, Richard Overton, William Walwyn, Colonel John Jubbes. None of them was a practical politician in the sense that Milton was, nor was ever associated with any government. Their views would have made this impossible. Sir Henry Vane, who may privately have favoured toleration for Catholics, did nothing in his public capacity to achieve this end. We may admire the consistency in charity of Williams, Walwyn, Overton and Jubbes; to contemporaries they must have seemed, in this respect, totally unrealistic. (I speak only of tolerationists on the radical wing of the Parliamentarians: no explanation is needed for those Laudians who favoured liberty of conscience for papists for exactly the same political reasons as led Milton and his like to oppose it.) Nor did Milton urge the extension of toleration to Jews, as Roger Williams and Oliver Cromwell were prepared to do. A radical like William Erbery was prepared for toleration to Jews and Turks, but not to papists.

In *Areopagitica* Milton advocated limitations on publishing: the Commonwealth should 'have a vigilant eye how books demean themselves as well as men; and thereafter to confine, imprison and do sharpest justice on them as malefactors'. He recommended abolition of licensing in advance of publication, not the abolition of laws preventing publication of that 'which is impious or evil absolutely, either against faith or manners'. It is possible—though I could not prove this—that Milton is here making tactical concessions to those whose views were more conservative than his own. This seems to me more plausible than the suggestion that *Areopagitica* is a party-line document, 'a rationale of revolutionary censorship', 'a militant and exclusivist revolutionary pamphlet', which scholars have misinterpreted. We should be grateful to John Illo for reminding us that Milton was indeed a revolutionary, not a nineteenth-century liberal. He did not 'misunderstand' the logic of his own argument, as liberal scholars have plaintively suggested. On the contrary: Milton was facing not only the tactical problem of how to preserve the greatest possible unity among the opponents of intolerance, but also the difficulties resulting from the shock of new light breaking on 'eyes bleared and dimmed with prejudice and custom': the problem of how to establish liberty before all men were educated up to it. His tolerance, like Cromwell's, was limited to those with 'the root of the matter' in them. Milton and Cromwell would have thought it was necessarily so limited, since to extend toleration to the intolerant would have defeated its fundamental object—the establishment of a better society.

The proponents of unfreedom—Rome, Charles I, the Presbyterians—were prepared to use violence to prevent the establishment of what Milton, and posterity, regarded as necessary freedoms. Milton's policy of toleration to the left, toleration of nearly all Protestants, could have been a very wide toleration; if it excluded the advocates of intolerance ('to suppress the suppressors'), it would have excluded only those whose views had in the past been widely propagated. New ideas came from the radical Protestant left, and could do so only given the liberty of printing which Milton advocated so warmly. Milton's tolerance had its limits, but it is not quite fair to sneer at him as if he were a twentieth-century fellow traveller who had learnt nothing from the career of Joseph Stalin.

Milton had been drawn towards Baconianism at Cambridge. In his anti-episcopal tracts he made especially good use of Bacon's *Certain Considerations touching the Church* and *Advertisement concerning the Controversies of the Church of England*, which the liberation of the press had allowed to be printed in 1640 and 1641 respectively. Even earlier Milton had noted Bacon's remarks on the unwisdom of prohibiting books. The extent of Bacon's influence over Milton at this period has perhaps not been sufficiently noted. The remark in *Of Education* that 'the end . . . of learning' was 'to repair the ruins of our first parents' is pure Baconianism. The denunciation in *Areopagitica* of the rich man who resolves 'to find himself out some factor, to whose care and credit he may commit the whole managing of his religious affairs' and resign 'the whole warehouse of his religion' also echoes Bacon's 'when men have once made over their judgment to others' keeping'. Milton had in fact quoted Bacon a page or two earlier. 'It is reserved only for God and angels to be lookers-on', Bacon had written, refusing to praise a fugitive and cloistered virtue; and he attacked 'men of a devout policy' who discourage 'stirring in philosophy, lest it may lead to an innovation in divinity'. I am not necessarily suggesting direct Baconian influence here. More relevant perhaps is the common Puritan background. 'Not to try is a greater risk than to fail', wrote Bacon in the true vein of *Areopagitica*. If we look forward to *Paradise Lost,* there too we can trace echoes of Bacon's view that the Fall was caused

not by curiosity about the secrets of nature but by a desire for moral omniscience which would make man self-sufficient. In the *Defence of the People of England* Milton declared in Baconian style that things were more important than the names given to them. Towards the end of his life Milton still insisted that 'the habit of learned vapouring should rather be ejected from the schools than retained.'

So Milton, who in the pamphlets on episcopacy had gone out of his way to defend Anabaptists and Familists, by 1644 was sought after by the Hartlib group of reformers. His divorce pamphlets had outraged conservative Parliamentarians, who savagely attacked him as a subverter of morals; this brought him perhaps embarrassing allies on the libertine wrong of the supporters of Parliament. In the *Apology* he had defended the right of smiths, carpenters, weavers, to a voice in the election of ministers, and attacked those who condemned 'the Christian congregation' as 'rabble'. In *Areopagitica* he summed up with superb eloquence the radical demand for freedom of speech, and especially of printing. Experience taught him that new Presbyter was but old priest writ large. As divisions grew between radical and conservative Parliamentarians, Milton moved naturally and inevitably towards the radicals—to those like Oliver Cromwell who demanded religious toleration and a career open to the talents; to those like Walwyn who called for wider religious and political liberty.

The important transformation was in Milton's conception of the poet's role. In the sixteen-thirties, church-outed, he had seen himself as the dedicated poet, isolated in his purity from a corrupt society. The long preparatory period of study and travel was related to the fact that the world of affairs was closed to him. But now, in the Utopian enthusiasm of the early forties, Milton began to envisage the possibility of a reconstructed society in which the true poet could step forward as the acknowledged legislator of mankind. That is the point of the prayer at the end of *Of Reformation,* and of the autobiographical passage in *The Reason of Church Government.*

Poetry and politics thus got inextricably mingled. The 'impertinent yoke of prelaty' first cast off, the press must next be set free from the attempts of new presbyters to re-establish the old control, if the life of the spirit is to flourish. Then a mighty and puissant nation can emerge, a nation chosen by and dedicated to God, a nation of creative searchers for truth, among whom the poet will have an honoured and supremely important function. At this stage Milton's romantic belief in the chosen English nation was explicit. Censorship is 'an undervaluing and vilifying of the whole nation', a reproach to the common people. 'Now the time has come, wherein . . . all the Lord's people are become prophets.' This last sentence no doubt refers to the elect members of the nation; but other passages appear to think of the nation itself as elect. Such distinctions were forced on Milton only later, when he began to doubt whether the English people was in fact chosen. (pp. 149-60)

Christopher Hill, in his Milton and the English Revolution, *1977. Reprint by The Viking Press, 1978, 541 p.*

THOMAS KRANIDAS   (essay date 1984)

[*Kranidas is a distinguished American academic and scholar who is noted for his many contributions to Milton studies. In the following excerpt, he offers a close reading of* Areopagitica, *isolating elements in the work that add strength to the argument.*]

Milton chose the title for his greatest prose piece [*Areopagitica*] for two reasons. One was public and historical: from the Hill of Mars radiated the aura of Mars himself, of Athena, Apollo, Aeschylus, Socrates, and St. Paul. The rule of humane law under divine aegis had been founded at the *Areopagus*, at least for the Christian humanist. St. Paul had confirmed that dignity and linked it with the Christian dispensation in his shrewd, courteous speech (Acts 17. 18-31). The hill was an emblem for Justice confirmed and Word proclaimed.

The second reason was less grand. Milton had engaged in a small rant with Bishop Joseph Hall over the grammatical use of the word *Areopagi* by Smectymnuus. In the *Animadversions,* Milton had accused Hall of the "capricious *Paedantie* of hot-liver'd Grammarians." Hall's defender, The Modest Confuter, had gone on about the issue for several pages and in fact had accused Milton of a cover-up: "Yes, yes, anything, rather than acknowledge the least errour." In his response to the Confuter, Milton did not mention the word again. I suspect he was ashamed of the pettiness of the issue, something fit only for "grammarians," whom he despised. It would have been a pleasure for Milton to rescue the term, and his use of it, from petty personalism. By analogy, and more urgently, the immediate reason for this defense of unlicensed printing would be subordinated to larger issues. The great *Doctrine and Discipline of Divorce* had been censured publicly and the public licenser had apologized for its printing. The urge to defend himself was immediate for Milton; his movement to objectivity was one of the major achievements of the tract. One can assume he worked hard for this success.

Milton displays then subsumes the personal issues in the *Areopagitica,* just as he displays then subsumes the classical pedigree of the Areopagus. It is part of his technique of emphasizing contrasts, of pushing images and definitions to poleimically useful extremes, then synthesizing them in visionary images. The structure of the oration arises out of a series of polarities; that structure is as real as "the model of a regular speech," which is Milton's own description. (pp. 175-76)

The contrasts and assertions begin on the title page. Milton did not set the type, but surely the author's eye approved, or at least allowed as not inconsistent, the blazoned title, the emphasized SPEECH, the prominence of his name. Surely it was Milton who chose the epigraph from Euripides, first in Greek, then in his own English. Also he himself arranged the remarkable blend of the personal and conceptual: the personal delivery by Mr. John Milton to the Parliament of a speech on liberty derived from the Greek, translated into the English, at London in 1644. The typography enacts the message of the epigraph which pleads for the speaker's liberty to advise the public as true liberty, the height of justice, worthy of praise, since time remembered.

This blend of private assertion and public images to support those assertions is also used to begin the oration with a traditional presentation of the speaker's truthfulness, his lack of flattery, the confirmed appropriateness of his praise of parliament. There is an immediate invidious comparison between a present-day England, which has been delivered by God and Parliament, and the England of Laud's day: "wee are already in good part arriv'd, and yet from such a steepe disadvantage of tyranny and superstition grounded into our principles as was beyond the manhood of a *Roman* recovery." By the end of the first full page of text the speaker has suggested a connection between English and Greek, and a contrast between England and Rome.

The language of truth is opposed to flattery; the language in which "complaints are freely heard, deeply consider'd, and speedily reform'd" is opposed to the language which did not provide a vehicle for a Roman recovery. The language of that "old and elegant humanity of Greece" is opposed to "the barbarick pride of a *Hunnish* and *Norwegian* stateliness." The language of truth and reason and political vision is Greek-English. The language of repression and falsehood is un-Greek un-English; for the chief purposes of this tract, as will shortly be seen, it is monkish Latin. There is of course good, Republican, Latin which opposes the barbarian stateliness; there is bad Greek, but it is the Greek co-opted by Scholastic philosophy or "Papistical" ceremony. Nevertheless, in the first sections especially, the language of repression and deceit is Latin; the language of truth and liberty is Greek-English.

As an English heir to the truth-telling tradition of the Greeks, Milton presents his proposition that the licensing order be judged over again. He links the licensing order with "his brother *quadragesimal* and *matrimonial*," contemptuously italicized and thus identified as Latinisms. Then he turns to his outline: "first the inventors of it to bee those whom ye will be loath to own; next what is to be thought in generall of reading, what ever sort the Books be; and that this Order avails nothing to the suppressing of scandalous, seditions, and libellous Books, which were mainly intended to be supprest. Last, that it will be primely to the discouragement of all learning, and the stop of Truth." The speaker is at pains to state his outline, to emphasize his transitions, and to establish clear guideposts for our convenience in following the argument. But even as stated above, the argument is loose, and the parallelisms irregular. Even an ardent admirer of Milton's "architectonics" will recognize that much of the power of the piece comes from imagistic and thematic interplay and polarization.

The pattern of Greek-English versus Latin is not consistent in the *Areopagitica*. Yet, it is a real pattern and Milton derives considerable effect from it, especially in the first section, where the history of censorship ends in the Inquisition. It is, surely, designed to end in the Inquisition. Villainous, popish, Spanish and Italian repression usurps and absorbs the entire survey and lays its Latin curse upon the English present: "I refuse not the paines to be so much Historicall, as will serve to shew what hath been done by ancient and famous Commonwealths, against this disorder, [libel and blasphemy], till the very time that this project of licencing crept out of the *Inquisition*, was catcht up by our Prelates, and hath caught some of our Presbyters." The ancient and famous commonwealths are Athens, Sparta, Republican Rome; and the "objective" survey leaves the reader with a clear sense of the relative limits of censorship in Athens, or of its uselessness in enforcing or raising public morality. Here in fact Athens, Plato, Dionysius, Chrysostom form a net of approval of freedom of the press. The "*Spartan* surlinesse" is put in its place by Lycurgus and Euripides' *Andromache*. And the episode of Republican Roman severity ends in Cato's recantation. If Milton is actually sympathetic to the uses of censorship against blasphemy and libel, his sympathy is qualified. When speaking of Augustus' punishment of libelers, he adds drily, "the like severity no doubt was us'd if ought were impiously writt'n against their esteemed gods." The practical comment, a strong strain amongst the gorgeous images of this tract, remains: many sharp, satirical, troublesome writings were never suppressed. The survey of ancient times produces very few examples of censorship.

The early Church, too, is presented as relatively free of censorship. The books of "grand Hereticks were examin'd, refuted, and condemn'd in the generall Councels; and not till then were prohibited, or burnt by autority of the Emperor." Heathen authors were not prohibited until 400. Only after 800, the Popes "extended their dominion over mens eyes." The rhythm of repression is expressed in the list of Councils, popes, and "popish" words: *burning, prohibiting, censures, Martin the 5, excommunicated, hereticall, Papall court, Leo the 10, Councell of Trent.* The lovely image of the vital, truth-telling book has lingered from the first pages: "a good Booke is the pretious life-blood of a master spirit, imbalm'd and treasur'd up on purpose to a life beyond life." Now that image is violated by the Censor-Killer of the Catholic Inquisition: "the Councell of Trent, and the Spanish Inquisition engendring together brought forth, or perfeted those Catalogues, and expurging Indexes that rake through the entralls of many an old good Author, with a ·violation wors then any could be offer'd to his tomb." It is a fine confluence of the images to this point and a shrewd anticipation of the argument to come. In a characteristic transference of images, the homely "many a old good Author" is set upon by the perverse offspring of Trent and the Inquisition.

Although the hand of the Inquisition is not a dead hand, it is a very heavy one. Milton invests the censorial motion throughout with as many associations as possible which are repugnant to the Protestant Englishman of the 1640s. The censors condemn what is "not to their palat" or "had it strait into the new Purgatory of an Index." They "ordain that no Book, pamphlet, or paper should be Printed . . . unlesse it were approv'd and licenc't under the hands of 2 or 3 glutton Friers." There follows a series of examples, Italian names and Catholic titles paraded in ironic disparagement. The series ends with witty contempt: "It may be Printed, *July* 15. Friar *Simon Mompei* d'*Amelia* Chancellor of the holy office in *Florence.*" Milton did not write shaped verse; nevertheless, in prose he is a master of typographical effects. In these effects the printed word often assumes its own physical life. And the most impressive example is now presented. First, the word is raised: "Sure they have a conceit, if he of the bottomlesse pit had not long since broke prison, that this quadruple exorcism would barre him down." Then it is "exercised" in the repressed (and eye-exercising) marginal note. It would be as easy to license Satan as to license the passage of wind. Now the real, virulent display on the page:

> Voutsafe to see another of their forms the Roman stamp:
> *Imprimatur,* If it seem good
> to the reverend Master
> of the holy Palace,
>
> *Belcastro* Vicegerent
> *Imprimatur*
> Friar *Nicolo Rodolphi*
> Master of the holy Palace.

The intimacy of Milton's invitation "Voutsafe to see," the easy shared contempt of "the Roman stamp," the genuinely funny parade of bureaucratic deference and pomposity—all these contribute to the further devaluation of the already corrupt Latin and Latin-dependent word. We are reminded too that the *Areopagitica* is a speech designed to be read. Our visual imagination is now directed to enfranchise silly words as live actors:

> Sometimes 5 *Imprimaturs* are seen together dialoguewise in the Piatza of one Title page, complementing and ducking each to other with their shav'n reverences, whether the Author, who stands by in perplexity at the foot of his Epistle, shall to the Presse or to the spunge. These are the prety responsories, these are the deare Antiphonies that so bewitcht of

late our Prelats, and their Chaplaines with the goodly Eccho they made; and besotted us to the gay imitation of a lordly *Imprimatur,* one from Lambeth house, another from the West end of *Pauls;* so apishly Romanizing, that the word of command still was set down in Latine.

The contempt gathers, and anyone familiar with the antiprelatical tracts will recognize the vocabulary which depicts trivial ceremony: dialoguewise, ducking, shaven reverences, prety responsories, dear Antiphonies, bewitched, Prelates, Echo, besotted, gay, imitation, lordly, apishly, and of course, Romanizing. The words are common in Milton's early prose, and a number of them are common in the literature of Puritan vituperation against the Laudian church and its Roman predecessors. Literally before our eyes, the *Imprimatur* of a distant censor has been invested with the venality and venom of contemporary and just-defeated political repression, then transformed into two silly Anglican censors singing antiphonally from opposite ends of London. The word can jump off the page; it can live magnificently and freely as "the precious life blood of a master spirit"; it can also live foolishly and repressively like an "envious Juno" sitting "cros-leg'd over the nativity of any man's intellectuall off spring."

Milton's first confirmation ends in a rousing and brilliantly cohered argument; censorship has been exposed as the plot of the worst elements of the Roman-Laudian corruption which the readers of this piece have just fought to shake off. The anti-Catholic history ends with the proud sense of English virtue and English courage:

> —so apishly Romanizing, that the word of command still was set downe in Latine; as if the learned Grammaticall pen that wrote it, would cast no ink without Latine: or perhaps, as they thought, because no vulgar tongue was worthy to expresse the pure conceit of an *Imprimatur;* but rather, as I hope, for that our English, the language of men over famous, and formost in the atchievements of liberty, will not easily finde servile letters anow to spell such a dictatorie presumption English.

Milton's brisk, efficient survey has shown two strains of censorship. One is very restricted, cautiously applied, and rational. This strain is Greek, Republican Roman, and English, associated with strong, free commonwealths. The second is heavy-handed, fearful, and irrational. This strain is Imperial Roman, medieval, popish, Spanish, associated with corrupt, irrational, and fearful tyrannies. In Milton's eyes the Laudian Church adopted this second strain. Having fought against and defeated the other aspects of that "apish Romanizing," the English choice ought to be clear. England has no word for censorship; the concept is foreign.

Milton is not denying the classical legacy, he is carefully distinguishing its parts. Through argument, through much rhetorical affect in the title and the epigraph, and through the treatment of foreign words on the page, he has suggested that England's intellectual parent is Greece, not Rome—certainly not Imperial Rome. The first part of the speech has provided a strong argument against censorship: not merely guilt by association but a real analysis of its origins. It has also prepared the audience, thematically and imagistically, for the soaring eloquence of national pride that illuminates the ending of Milton's piece.

But the first section is not yet complete. The speaker does to the censor what the censor does to the book: "And thus ye have the Inventors and the originall of Book-licencing ript up, and drawn as lineally as any pedigree.'' The source of licensing tradition is not ''any ancient State, or politie, or Church, nor by any Statute left us by our Ancestors elder or later; nor from the moderne custom of any reformed Citty, or Church abroad; but from the most Antichristian Councel, and the most tyrranous Inquisition that ever inquir'd''. Rich images are again used to separate the two traditions and to keep the polarities of intellectual vitality and repression in mind:

> But that a Book in wors condition than a peccant soul, should be to stand before a Jury ere it be borne to the World, and undergo yet in darknesse the judgement of *Radamanth* and his Collegues, ere it can passe the ferry backward into light, was never heard before, till that mysterious iniquity provokt and troubl'd at the first entrance of Reformation, sought out new limbo's and new hells wherein they might include our Books also within the number of their damned. And this was the rare morsell so officiously snatcht up, and so ilfavourdly imitated by our inquisiturient Bishops.

Milton cleverly decorates his censorship scene with words and concepts repugnant to the Puritan imagination, words like *limbo* and concepts like excommunication. And he ends with coinage worthy of Marprelate, a coinage both contemptuous and damningly linking the Inquisition with the Bishops: *inquisiturient* is sinister and perverse, yet pompously silly in sound and in meaning. Milton has skilfully attached it to the prelacy and their presbyterial imitators.

These fearful and tyrannous images are the sources of the prelatical policy towards censorship. The Parliament and people of England are heirs to the other tradition; they are the party of reason, of liberty, of nature, of assurance, of the future—of England, the visionary commonwealth that will enact the climax of the painful and glorious Reformation. How can that Parliament and that people align themselves with the ''mysterious iniquity''? Milton's eclectic history of censorship lacks the memorable texts of the other two sections of this argument, but it prepares with cunning economy for the vision of English national destiny in the last confirmatio.

The *Areopagitica* is an internationalist document, drawing for its evidence and ornament from myths and histories as varied and contrasting as Isis and Osiris, Pythagoras, ''the *Persian* wisdom,'' Zwingli, Calvin. But it also deliberately distances the abstract intellectualism of ''*Atlantick* and *Eutopian* polities, which never can be drawn into use, will not mend our condition.'' The final confirmatio, ''the manifest hurt'' which licensing does to leaning, is the most personal, the most timely, and the most English. There is for example the theme of the release from tutelage, a topic of personal concern for Milton during these years. A learned man ought to be allowed the academic freedom to teach without a tutor. It is wrong ''not to count him fit to print his mind without a tutor and examiner . . . how can a man teach with autority, which is the life of teaching . . . whenas all he teaches, all he delivers, is but under the tuition, under the correction of his patriarchal licencer. . . . I hate a pupil teacher.''

Although the culminating vision absorbs the major strands of argument and image, the oration does not proceed regularly from specific to general. For example, there is a movement from images of states and nations to images of the city. In one sense the *Areopagitica* now becomes a London City document. Similarly, Truth moves from strength to vulnerability. At first, Truth is a grand and living thing, the ''pretious life-blood of a master spirit, imbalm'd and treasur'd up on purpose to a life beyond life''; Truth ''came once into the world with her divine Master, and was a perfect shape most glorious to look on.'' Now fragmented, her ''body'' is still ''*homogeneal,* and proportionall''; Truth is a wrestler, ''give her but room, & do not bind her when she sleeps''; ''a streaming fountain; if her waters flow not in a perpetuall progression, they sick'n into a muddy pool of conformity and tradition.'' Truth is neither containable nor marketable; ''Truth and understanding are not such wares as to be monopoliz'd and traded in by tickets and statutes, and standards. We must not think to make a staple commodity of all the knowledge in the Land, to mark and license it like our broad cloath, and our wooll packs.'' Sardonically Milton gives us a brisk parable of the merchant who finds religion too complicated: ''he cannot skill to keep a stock going upon that trade. . . . [He finds] himself out som factor, to whose care and credit he may commit the whole managing of his religious affairs. . . . So that a man may say his religion is now no more within himself, but is becom a dividuall movable.'' The parable is courageous as well as charming. This particular focus on mercantile vocation could offend a substantial and influential portion of the Parliamentary supporters.

Nonetheless Milton's sympathies are as broad as his antagonisms are sharp. At this point the *Areopagitica* becomes a London merchant piece in a positive sense, and commercial vitality becomes one of the most important aspects of the imagery. England's ''richest Marchandize'' is Truth. Images of husbandry are closely linked to images of merchandising: ''should ye suppresse all this flowry crop of knowledge and new light sprung up and yet springing daily in this City?'' English leadership of the Reformation is presented in images of the City's commercial energy:

> Now once again by all concurrence of signs, and by the generall instinct of holy and devout men, as they daily and solemnly express their thoughts, God is decreeing to begin some new and great period in his Church, ev'n to the reforming of Reformation it self: what does he then but reveal Himself to his servants, and as his manner is, first to his English-men; I say as his manner is, first to us, though we mark not the method of his counsels, and are unworthy. Behold now this vast City; a City of refuge, the mansion house of liberty, encompast and surrounded with his protection; the shop of warre hath not there more anvils and hammers waking, to fashion out the plates and instruments of armed Justice in defence of beleaguer'd Truth, then there be pens and heads there, sitting by their studious lamps, musing, searching, revolving new notions and idea's wherewith to present, as with their homage and their fealty the approaching Reformation: others as fast reading, trying all things, assenting to the force of reason and convincement.

Milton has taken the vituperative Anglican commonplace of pugnacious, sectarian, busybody scribblers and made it the ''mansion house of liberty'' (the echo of scripture is clear). This is an English commerce, sober but vigorous and successful. It is an answer to Anglican, and now Presbyterian, attacks on the proliferation of arguments in print and from the pulpit. The Anglican attack could range from stately to sardonic:

> Never did any age produce more fasting, more
> preaching, more praying. Never did those holy
> exercises produce less fruit.
> the irrational licentious practice of our times,
> wherein either sex and any profession
> crowds in a finger to the moulding of the design'd

               Reformation.
they would have *peace* with *truth.* But who can
believe them? when they *make lies their refuge,*
and daily unrest and pervert the *word* of truth to
                encourage to warre.
And now the books, and now the bells,
And now our arts the Preacher tells
              to edifie the people;
All our Divinity is news,
And we have made of equall use
   the pulpit and the steeple
And shall we kindle all this flame
Only to put it out againe,
           and must we now give ore,
And only end where we begun,
In vaine this mischiefe we have done
           if we can do no more.

It is unnecessary to cite Thomas Edwards' *Gangraena,* the classic Presbyterian way of viewing Independent and independent debate. Milton himself was to be attacked in that loathsome, popular compendium. In the *Areopagitica* what is death for Edwards is clearly life for Milton.

The imagery of the great, busy city, really about its father's business, is powerful and central. The activity depicted is brisk, forward, even irritating: "Where there is much desire to learn, there is of necessity will be much arguing, much writing, many opinions; for opinion in good men is but knowledge in the making. Under these fantastic terrors of sect and schism, we wrong the earnest and zealous thirst after knowledge and understanding which God hath stirr'd up in this City." "This pious forwardness" is set against "this Prelaticall tradition of crowding free consciences and Christian liberties into canons and precepts of men." The house of God is not a finished structure; its very grace rests on oppositions: "it cannot be united into a continuity, it can but be contiguous in this world; . . . nay rather the perfection consists in this, that out of many moderat varieties and brotherly dissimilitudes that are not vastly disproportionall arises the goodly and the graceful symmetry that commends the whole pile and structure." This image of righteous, energetic search for truth is the practical face of the lovely parable of Truth and the wicked deceivers who "hewd her lovely form into a thousand peeces":

> We have not yet found them all, Lords and Commons, nor ever shall doe, till her Masters second comming. . . . The light which we have gain'd, was giv'n us, not to be ever staring on, but by it to discover onward things more remote from our knowledge. . . . To be still searching what we know not, by what we know, still closing up truth to truth as we find it (for all her body is *homogeneal,* and proportionall) this is the golden rule in *Theology* as well as in Arithmetick, and makes up the best harmony in a Church; not the forc't and outward union of cold, and neutrall, and inwardly divided minds.

The "mansion house of liberty" fuses political, historical, and visionary energies: the immediate praise of those whom Milton is petitioning; the sense of present and recent threat; the transformation of an image contemptible to Anglican and Presbyterian polemic into an image of *thriving* in matters spiritual; the fusion of it all under the mythic and parasacramental search for Truth; and the placing of this brilliant, complexly resonating present in the anteroom of Apocalypse. It is an appropriate proem to one of Milton's greatest images:

> Methinks I see in my mind a noble and puissant Nation rousing herself like a strong man after sleep, and shaking her invincible locks: Methinks I see her

as an Eagle muing her mighty youth, and kindling her undazl'd eyes at the full midday beam; purging and unscaling her long abused sight at the fountain it self of heav'nly radiance; while the whole noise of timorous and flocking birds, with those also that love the twilight, flutter about, amaz'd at what she means, and in their envious gabble would prognosticat a year of sects and schisms

This is the most powerful single emblem in Milton's prose. Comprehensive, dynamic, intense, it is an appropriate climax to the argument. The *Areopagitica* celebrates the energies of truth-seeking and contemns the weaknesses of truth-hiding. The vehicle for that vigorous search for truth is an England at the height of her "masculine" intellectual powers, full of movement—rousing, shaking, ascending. England as Samson. She as He. The vigor actually fuses the sexes. On the other hand, the powerful androgyny increases the sense of awe. We are made to look up, and the repetitions increase the sense of ascension: "Methinks I see in my mind. . . . Methinks I see her as an Eagle muing her mighty youth." Grace and energy abound. In freedom England renews herself at "the fountain it self of heav'nly radiance." Yet that renewal must include purging and unscaling the eyes of the whole corrupt tradition of knowledge, the encrusted theological tradition of Scripture itself. (We feel a special intensity here, as Milton generalizes the poignant wish for clear sight.) The Eagle is Eagle with a dash of Phoenix—soaring, muing, kindling; the Eagle is Samson, championing his cause and rejecting the first three temptations of Delilah; the Eagle is England, leading the Reformation, marching on to total knowledge at the last day; the Eagle is Parliament, bursting the secondhand manacles of prelatical tradition and pursuing Truth to its very source in Scripture; the Eagle is John Milton soaring in language, unscaling his now blurring eyes at the Fountain of light. And all about this composite figure of ascending, energetic majesty flutter the detractors, the modest confuters, the humble remonstrators, the censors. They are ridiculous, like small flocking birds, and they are sinister, bat-like: "while the whole noise of timorous and flocking birds, with those also that love the twilight, flutter about, amaz'd at what she means, and in their envious gabble would prognosticate a year of sects and schisms." The Eagle's language—free, lofty, purified—is Truth. The language of the small birds is gabble, prognostication—a good Greek word for Latin priests. . . . What would these augurbats prognosticate but a year of fluttering and gabbling motions? Milton has again commandeered the adversaries' image for Puritan controversy and used it against them. *They* are the flutterers and gabblers, the sects and schisms, reacting impotently against England's potent ascent to the true light of Scripture, Heavenly Revelation itself. From the many of free inquiry England arrives at the radiant one of Truth.

The tract is not over. The proposition is restated in quite practical terms, including the infamous qualification on "tolerated popery." But the climax has been reached and we are in denouement. The "flowry crop of knowledge and new light sprung up" is set against "an *Oligarchy* of twenty ingrossers" who would measure to us "by their bushel." Parliament's "mild, and free, and human government" is directly the cause of this "liberty which is the nurse of all great wits." Only if Parliament denies its true nature and becomes oppressive will England become "ignorant again, brutish, formall, and slavish, as ye found us." Parliament has "propagated in us," and "our hearts are now more capacious, our thoughts more erected to the search and expectation of greatest and exactest things."

The section ends with the clearest of statements: "Give me the liberty to know, to utter, and to argue freely according to conscience, above all liberties." It is generally agreed that the peroration starts here, "according to the model of a regular speech." The peroration reinforces and tidies up the argument. It reinforces with the testimony of Lord Brooke (one of the extremely rare references by Milton to a contemporary) who had emphasized the need for "patience and humility"; his dying words, "so full of meekness and breathing charity," are now invoked to suggest the dual nature of Truth. On the one hand, Truth is strong: "Let her and Falshood grapple; who ever knew Truth put to the wors, in a free an open encounter. Her confuting is the best and surest suppressing." On the other hand, building on Brooke's plea for tolerance, Milton emphasizes the difficulties, even the fragility, of Truth. She is "*hidd'n treasures*" "if it come to prohibiting, there is not ought more likely to be prohibited then truth it self." We need the "charity of patient instruction to supple the least bruise of conscience . . . gentle meetings and gentle dismissions." This is the immediate context of the decision against "tolerated popery." It does not arise out of a context of aggressive images and statements. It is defensive, not offensive.

The strength of Truth has been celebrated: "Truth is strong next to the Almighty; she needs no policies, nor stratagems, nor licencings to make her victorious . . . give her but room & do not bind her when she sleeps." But at this time she is vulnerable; for all the energy of Eagle-Truth, there is a need for gentleness, encouragement, and attention. And part of that attention is the defense against popery: "I mean not tolerated Popery, and open superstition, which as it expirpats all religions and civill supremacies, so it self should be extirpat, provided first that all charitable and compassionat means be us'd to win and regain the weak and the misled." The modern reader experiences a lurch of disappointment. And yet in this context the proscriptive elements must not be overemphasized. Specifically the reader must keep clearly in mind the "charitable and compassionat means"—"gentle meetings, gentle dismissions." Most of our contemporaries have their own prohibitions: the drug pusher on the school grounds, the child pornographer, the terrorist of one passion or another. Milton's compromise with repression does dim his vision with what is after all a practical political position for his time. But in his vision those shadows of danger were always present: the night birds, the yoke, the "stark and dead congealment of *wood and hay and stubble* forc't and frozen together."

The peroration raises the image of a vulnerable Truth and, once more, of a virulent threat to that Truth from Roman tyranny: "Priests," "Pharisees," "*Imprimatur*," "*Dominican*," "Inquisition," "*authentic* Spanish," "Star-chamber decree," "*Lucifer*," "*patentees* and *monopolizers*," "*Sophisms* and *Elenchs*." Truth is supple, gentle, shy in these last pages; for all her shining she needs to be protected. The character of the polarized terms has changed sharply. Surely there is no clear Greek-Latin opposition, although the bad Greek words are those (like "*Sophisms* and *Elenchs*" or *prognosticate*) within the priestly and scholastic traditions. Nevertheless, polarities still function. Righteous, ultimately triumphant but presently vulnerable Truth opposes the corrupt, ultimately vanquished but still virulent Falsehood.

The prohibition of popery is relegated to the peroration. It is in no way the climax, and in my reading it cannot be the ironic pivot of the piece. On the contrary, the prohibition is consistent with the pattern of polarities that have at once suffused and

girded up the structure of the *Areopagitica*. The extirpation of popery does not bring the main argument to climax; it reflects it. That argument has steadily contrasted true and false language, politics, religion, most forcefully in images of Greek and Latin, English and foreign; ascending unity and fluttering disunity; clear sight and blurring; brilliant, impregnating light and twilight; energetic competition and bureaucracy; the firm poetic voice which is true sight—Prophecy—against gabble. Milton sustains the polarities to the end, aware of evil and its persistence, aware "that errors in a good government and in a bad are equally almost incident." The process of closing up truth to truth is dialogic, as that other great emblem, near the beginning of the tract, suggests: "I cannot praise a fugitive and cloister'd vertue, unexercis'd & unbreath'd, that never sallies out and sees her adversary, but slinks out of the race, where that immortall garland is to be run for, not without dust and heat." The epic *Paradise Lost* and the tragedy *Samson Agonistes* are implicit in the strenuous grandeur, the nourishing polarities of Milton's greatest prose work. (pp. 177-90)

Thomas Kranidas, "Polarity and Structure in Milton's 'Areopagitica'," in English Literary Renaissance, *Vol. 14, No. 2, Spring, 1984, pp. 175-90.*

ANN BAYNES COIRO (essay date 1988)

[*Coiro is an American scholar and academic. In the follow excerpt, she compares the educational program described in* Of Education *with Adam's education in* Paradise Lost.]

In *Of Education* Milton proposed a radical change in traditional educational strategies. Subjects normally taught to young children—rhetoric, logic, and original composition—were to be left until the very end of the process of education; instead, the concrete, pragmatic phases of education were to come first, preparing the student intellectually and emotionally for his leap into metaphysics and controversy. Milton's educational tractate has been compared before to the education of Adam in *Paradise Lost* but the similarities critics have noted have been general, drawn mainly from the first few paragraphs of the tractate where Milton enunciates the purposes of education. Furthermore, previous discussions of *Of Education* and *Paradise Lost* have found their parallels in Raphael's education of the unfallen Adam in Books V and VI. It is, however, striking and significant that in Books XI and XII of *Paradise Lost* Michael leads Adam through an education that exactly parallels, down to the smallest detail, the "methodical course" that Milton had delineated with such precision in his educational tractate. Even the sharp and disturbing shift from vision to narration between Books XI and XII can be seen as a reflection of the bipartite structure of Milton's ideal education between the practical education of the senses and the more difficult education of the intellect and the conscience.

Books XI and XII demonstrate a clear shift in Milton's handling of his material, a shift which has been variously attributed to a loss of poetic power or of interest in the poem, on the one hand, or, on the other, to an intentional strategy to alter both Adam's perception of reality and our own. The most striking difficulties which the conclusion of *Paradise Lost* presents are its shift from the evocative complexity of the body of the poem to a bare lean style; the compression of all human history into so brief a space after the poem dwells expansively upon the initial creation and fall; and the further difficulty of the shift in Book XII from visions of history to a long narrative of events to come. The similarity of procedures between the education outlined in the tractate and the angelic education of Adam can, I believe, serve to illuminate some of these persistent difficulties and serve as well to illuminate Milton's stance as poet and teacher at the conclusion of *Paradise Lost.*

Indeed, the explicit statement of intent with which Milton begins the body of *Of Education* almost insists, in retrospect, upon a comparison with the epic:

> The end . . . of learning is to repair the ruins of our first parents by regaining to know God aright. . . . But because our understanding cannot in this body found itself but on sensible things, nor arrive so clearly to the knowledge of God and things invisible as by orderly conning over the visible and inferior creature, the same method is necessarily to be followed in all discreet teaching.

In every detail, the clear, optimistic "method" of the tractate can be traced in Michael's education of Adam. But this recall of Milton's early work on education adds a dark resonance to the conclusion of *Paradise Lost,* especially because the procedures are so close as to seem at times almost an intentional self-parody of "that voluntary idea which hath long in silence presented itself to me, of a better education, in extent and comprehension far more large, and yet of time far shorter, and of attainment far more certain, than hath been yet in practice."

Of Education divides the process of teaching into two distinct halves: these two stages correspond to the division of Adam's education between Book XI and Book XII. Before placing tractate and poem together, let me give a summary list of the

Milton at age 21.

precisely arranged series of lessons Milton proposes for younger pupils before they reach the age capable of moral reasoning. They are to learn first the basic rules of grammar. Then they are to learn arithmetic and the practical sciences—agriculture, geography, geometry and trigonometry, fortification, architecture, engineering, navigation, geology, botany, biology, human anatomy, and medicine. The students are to consolidate this practical learning by observing demonstrations performed by visiting craftsmen. Finally, this phase of their education is to be capped by reading pastoral and georgic poetry. Even such a skeletal overview suggests the lessons of Book XI; retracing in more detail the early lessons of Milton's academy while at the same time moving through the lessons of Book XI demonstrates, I believe, close similarities of educational procedure—and profound differences of purpose.

The very youngest pupils at Milton's ideal academy were to learn the proper use of language by a simple grounding in the rules of grammar and pronunciation. This very early stage of learning is, of course, unnecessary for the unfallen Adam who, untaught, can speak perfectly the names of all created things. But in *Of Education* Milton further recommends that in order to make young students adept at grammar "and withal to season them and win them early to the love of virtue and true labor, ere any flattering seducement or vain principle seize them wandering, some easy and delightful book of education would be read to them" for "here the main skill and groundwork will be to temper them such lectures and explanations upon every opportunity as may lead and draw them in willing obedience." This passage from early in *Of Education* may be read as a synopsis of Raphael's education of Adam before the Fall. But the passage is also charged with the tensions, even the very words that fill Books IX and X of *Paradise Lost* when, in spite of their "easy and delightful" education, Eve is by "flattering seducement" and Adam by "vain principle" seized wandering and drawn away from "willing obedience."

In the pamphlet on education Milton placed his faith in the power of a great teacher, "he who hath the art and proper eloquence to catch them with, what with mild and effectual persuasions and what with the intimation of some fear, if need be, but chiefly by his own example" who could thereby "in a short space gain them to an incredible diligence and courage, infusing into their young breasts such an ingenuous and noble ardor, as would not fail to make many of them renowned and matchless men." The bitter lesson of *Paradise Lost,* however, is that not even mild Raphael, the perfect teacher of uncorrupted man, could prevent the fall into the knowledge of evil. Adam and Eve disobey; and all the rest of education must attempt to salvage something from that destruction.

Significantly, the early lessons outlined by Milton in *Of Education* were to be from "some easy and delightful book of education [which] would *be read to them*" (italics added). As the boys grew older, however, they were to become increasingly engaged in the process of their own education, first watching, then doing; first being read to, then reading, and finally writing themselves. It is the cornerstone of Milton's educational theory that a young student be *shown* first and experience directly what he is to learn, rather than be confined immediately to the dry theories of books. Clearly, Michael uses this "same method . . . to be followed in all discreet teaching" when he teaches Adam, first by showing him visions which gradually sharpen his responses, and the by withdrawing visions and lecturing the more sophisticated Adam on the history of Man after the Fall.

The close parallels between the tractate and Books XI and XII begin when the children in Milton's academy move beyond passive reception of knowledge and themselves begin to read. The first books that the young students should attempt are practical works of agriculture, "for the matter is most easy" and will be "an occasion of inciting and enabling them hereafter to improve the tillage of their country, to recover the bad soil and to remedy the waste that is made of good."

The first lesson that Michael teaches Adam is the simple knowledge of his fate:

> to remove thee I am come,
> And send thee from the Garden forth to till
> The ground whence thou wast tak'n, fitter Soil.

Michael here repeats exactly the message that God the Father charged him to deliver and every lesson Michael teaches Adam will be a version of this one. It is not an "easy" lesson: expulsion from paradise, limited knowledge, limited ambition, the inevitable linking of birth with death. Adam's lesson in "agriculture" is his first, but not his easiest; it is not a stepping stone to more difficult lessons, but the first strand in an interwoven web of self-knowledge.

For Milton's hypothetical students it will next be "seasonable . . . to learn . . . the use of the globes and all the maps, first with the old names and then with the new." So also, at the very beginning of his lessons, Michael gives Adam a vantage point from which to "command wherever stood / City of old or modern Fame, the Seat / Of mightiest Empire," described in a catalogue of twenty-five lines (XI, 385-411). This gorgeous series of places beginning—

> Of *Cambalu*, seat of *Cathaian Can*,
> And *Samarchand* by *Oxus, Temir's* Throne,
> To *Paquin* of *Sinaean* Kings, and thence
> To *Agra* and *Lahor* of great *Mogul*
> Down to the golden *Chersonese,* or where
> The *Persian* in *Ecbatan* sat, or since
> In *Hispahan*, or where the *Russian Ksar*
> In *Mosco*, or the Sultan in *Bizance*,
> *Turchestan*-born

—Michael spreads before Adam in a dazzling display of both temporal power and the power of magnificent words. Suddenly, however, Michael undercuts the hypnotic vision (and litany) with one concluding half-line—"but to nobler sights." Adam's vision must be cleared so that he can see again without the cloud cast over his eyes by the forbidden fruit. What he will see will not be the panoply of human magnificence, but the sordid details of death; what he will hear will not be sonorous, magical place names, but stark statements of reality. The maps and globes that in *Of Education* will be a means of opening children's eyes to the world around them, in Adam's more somber education is his first lesson "that God attributes to place / No sanctity."

Since the primary thesis of *Of Education* is that before a student advances to abstract concepts he must have an education thoroughly grounded in sensible, physical knowledge, Milton recommends that the preliminary study of agriculture and geography be followed by practical sciences, culminating in anatomy and medicine so that the student "may at some time or other save an army by this frugal and expenseless means only, and not let the healthy and stout bodies of young men rot away under him for want of this discipline—which is a great pity, and no less a shame to the commander." At the parallel moment in Adam's much more brutal and pessimistic education, Michael introduces him to the grotesque aspects of anatomy—

deliberate murder in the vision of Cain and Abel and disfiguring disease in the vision of the Lazar-house of Death. Adam is shown personified diseases, not to make him a more efficient military leader, but in order to demonstrate to him the need for temperance, a lesson vividly and ruthlessly impressed since it was through intemperance that Eve and he fell. He must learn to negotiate between his instinctive desire for pleasure and life and, after the fall, Eve's brave and horrifying suggestion: "Let us seek death" (X, 1001). Adam's lessons in the human body thus go far beyond the jaunty utility proposed in *Of Education.*

The younger boys at the academy Milton outlined in 1644 were at this stage to have mastered "the principles of arithmetic, geometry, astronomy, and geography, with a general compact of physics" and were now to "descend in mathematics to the instrumental science of trigonometry, and from thence to fortification, architecture, enginery, or navigation." As they learn the principles of these subjects they will be allowed to share "the helpful experiences of hunters, fowlers, fishermen, shepherds, gardeners, apothecaries; and in the other sciences, architects, engineers, mariners, anatomists" which should "give them such a real tincture of natural knowledge as they shall never forget, but daily augment with delight."

These practical arts Adam also sees and delights in as Michael allows him the analogous visions of the sons of God and the sons of Lamech. But Adam's delight is a sad deception and Michael must warn him:

> studious they appear
> Of Arts that polish Life, Inventors rare,
> Unmindful of thir Maker, though his Spirit
> Taught them, but they his gifts acknowledg'd none.

The *purpose* of the practical lessons in *Of Education* is to inspire a lasting delight in the pupils; the delight that these same lessons give Adam is not the purpose of the lessons, but the means to a very different end. His delight is another fall into sin. He must learn to recognize the temptation of delight and temper it with moral judgment. Indeed, what Michael teaches him is that all of these worldly arts tend toward one end—and that is war. *Of Education* enunciates as one of its explicit goals the training of its students for military excellence. Milton concluded the introduction to his tractate by calling "a complete and generous education that which fits a man to perform justly, skilfully, and magnanimously all the offices, both private and public, of peace and war." But war and military heroism run like a sinister thread throughout Adam's education: Cain kills Abel, pastures are soaked with human blood (XI, 646-54), the spokesman for "Justice," "Religion," "Truth and Peace" (XI, 667) is threatened by violent hands. The students of 1644 were at this point to have enjoyed the pastoral and georgic poets; by the end of Book XI, Adam also sees pastoral and georgic visions, but, in every case, violence has intruded to destroy the idyll.

In *Of Education* the culmination of the practical phase of learning is the moment when Milton judged his pupils had by "years and good general precepts" been furnished with "that act of reason which in ethics is called Proairesis; that they may with some judgment contemplate upon moral good and evil. Then will be required a special reinforcement of constant and sound indoctrinating to set them right and firm, instructing them more amply in the knowledge of virtue and the hatred of vice; while their young and pliant affections are led through all the moral works of Plato, Xenophon, Cicero, Plutarch, Laertius, and those Locrian remnants." This process of reinforcement that

Milton touches on briefly in the tractate is the cornerstone of Michael's pedagogy. He teaches Adam his lessons over and over again, allowing him to contemplate moral good and evil that he may judge correctly for himself. Over and over again, Adam judges incorrectly and learns from his mistake. The tractate, perhaps because it is so brief, never considers the possibility that students will *not* learn all the lessons spread so carefully before them. But Michael seems to expect that possibility and to use it in order to teach Adam.

Most delightful of all to Adam, for example, is the vision of the ''Bevy of fair Women''—the vision which must be his most humiliating lesson. For Adam falls again and entirely into his original sin and cries:

> True opener of mine eyes, prime Angel blest,
> Much better seems this Vision, and more hope
> Of peaceful days portends, than those two past;
> Those were of hate and death, or pain much worse,
> Here Nature seems fulfill'd in all her ends.

Tellingly, it is on this one crucial point that the students of the 1644 tractate were to receive a very tentative and insufficient lesson. When they reached the age of moral judgment, they were to be allowed ''but with wariness and good antidote . . . [to] taste some choice comedies, Greek, Latin, or Italian; those tragedies also that treat of household matters, as *Trachiniae, Alcestis,* and the like.'' In this ''complete and generous education which [should fit] a man to perform justly, skilfully, and magnanimously all the offices, both private and public, of peace and war,'' a few plays are to be his only introduction to women and marriage. The two plays Milton specifically recommends would demonstrate a wife whose jealousy inadvertently caused her husband's painful death and a wife so perfect that she gave her own life to save her husband's. What lesson is to be drawn from these instances of fallible and perfect woman is not clear except that it should be circled warily and with ''good antidote.'' Characteristic of the tractate, the hero of both plays is the warrior Hercules, the kind of hero who is cast in a very problematic light in *Paradise Lost.* At this parallel point in Book XI, Michael specifically warns Adam against the heroic ideal that Hercules embodies:

> styl'd great Conquerors,
> Patrons of Mankind, Gods, and Sons of Gods,
> Destroyers rightlier call'd and Plagues of
> men.

The first lesson Milton's students were to learn once they had advanced to the second, contemplative stage of education was ''the study of politics; to know the beginning, end, and reasons of political societies, that they may not in a dangerous fit of the commonwealth be such poor, shaken, uncertain reeds, of such a tottering conscience, as many of our great counsellors have lately shown themselves, but steadfast pillars of the state.'' Milton wrote these contemptuous words during the first steps of the commonwealth. Underneath his sarcasm seems to lie a belief that it will be possible to educate English youth truly to be ''steadfast pillars of the state.'' In bitter contrast, the political lesson that Adam receives from Michael seems to reflect Milton's actual experience of the state he had endowed with so much hope. The lesson of politics becomes in *Paradise Lost* the central pivot of Adam's education—the same lesson taught over and over again—first by a vision of Enoch, ''daring single to be just,'' speaking out in his nation's counsels, then in a vision of Noah reprimanding the assemblies of his decadent nation and a vision of the destruction of the Flood, then again, once Adam's visions are withdrawn, in Michael reiteration and

interpretation of the story of Noah, ''One Man expect, the only Son of light / In a dark Age'' (XI, 808-809).

The lesson of Noah is of crucial significance both to the education of Adam and to the problematic structure of *Paradise Lost*'s conclusion. It is the cruelest vision that Michael shows to Adam and he subjects him to it twice—once in a vision and then again as a narration. This double lesson is a replication of the larger shift from vision to narration between Books XI and XII. It is Adam's lesson in proairesis, moral education, the moment when he must finally abandon his false optimism about man's happiness on earth and recognize the ''only Son of light / In a dark Age.'' It is finally here, at the end of Book XI, that Adam must face the stunning humiliation of seeing men who do not give in to temptation as he has done, men whom he must recognize as morally superior to himself.

Finally, Adam's lesson in politics closes with the story of Nimrod, the rebel and tyrant who

> shall rise
> Of proud ambitious heart, who not content
> With fair equality, fraternal state,
> Will arrogate Dominion undeserv'd
> Over his brethren, and quite dispossess
> Concord and law of Nature from the Earth.

Adam, indignant, once again misunderstands his lesson here at the beginning of the second phase of his education, but there is added poignance to his protestation against Nimrod since he could so easily be voicing Milton's own ideals before the realities of the commonwealth were borne in upon him:

> but Man over men
> He made not Lord; such title to himself
> Reserving, human left from human free.

Michael must explain that ''Since thy original lapse, true Liberty / Is lost, which always with right Reason dwells'' (XII. 82-83). Instead,

> Tyranny must be,
> Though to the Tyrant thereby no excuse.
> Yet sometimes Nations will decline so low
> From virtue, which is reason, that no wrong,
> But Justice, and some fatal curse annext
> Deprives them of thir outward liberty,
> Thir inward lost.

Adam receives a lesson in politics that goes far beyond what Milton had envisioned in 1644, a darker, sadder lesson than Milton would ever have intended for the students of his academy.

Following their readings in politics, the students in Milton's early academy were to cover ''the grounds of law and legal justice; delivered first and with best warrant by Moses.'' At this point, Adam must go much further and come to understand the bitter underlying necessity of law. When Michael tells him the story of Moses, Adam, whose responses have become increasingly sophisticated as his education advances, asks why God should wish to live with men so sinful that they must be fenced in with innumerable laws. Michael replies:

> Law appear imperfet, and but giv'n
> With purpose to resign them in full time
> Up to a better Cov'nant, disciplin'd
> From shadowy Types to Truth, from Flesh to Spirit,
> From imposition of strict Laws, to free
> Acceptance of large Grace, from servile fear
> To filial, works of Law to works of Faith.

Michael crowns his lesson with the story of Christ and the ''Law of Faith'' which his sacrifice to his Father shall institute.

The penultimate stage outlined in the pamphlet on education is the study of "the highest matters of theology and church history ancient and modern." The whole fabric of Michael's teaching, especially in the latter part of Book XI and in Book XII, has been theological and, at the end of Book XII, Adam listens to the history of the degeneration of the Church to the point where the Church would interfere in the laws that should spring from the heart of man. Readers of *Paradise Lost* have been disappointed and critics have been severe because Michael passes so quickly over the triumphant, climactic moment of Christ's act of salvation and then moves directly to the story of the Church's decay. It would indeed be comforting if Michael's lessons ended in a splendid burst of glory and optimism as Christ saved us all from ourselves. But it would not be the truth. Such a soft and happy ending would have been suitable for a young boy at the early stage of Milton's educational process when the teacher tells him "the easy grounds of religion and the story of scripture" as a relaxing bedtime story, carefully protecting his students from harsh truth, nurturing instead their curiosity and idealism. By the time Milton wrote *Paradise Lost,* however, his ideal teacher regarded it as unsuitable, even dangerous, to send a young man into the world without a forewarning that:

> Wolves shall succeed for teachers, grievous Wolves,
> Who all the sacred mysteries of Heav'n
> To thir own vile advantages shall turn
> Of lucre and ambition.

The most striking difference between *Of Education* and Michael's education of Adam is that in *Paradise Lost* each lesson is weighted down by a darker, more complex vision of man's capability for corruption and failure and weighted by the admission that knowledge can lead not only to good, but to evil. It is understandable that Adam and the reader would want *Paradise Lost* to end on a great swelling note of triumph. The most important lesson of *Paradise Lost,* however, is that man has fallen, that dangers lurk around us and within us, and that we must both suffer because of our first parents' fall and learn from it.

The crowning movement of the education outlined in the tractate is the study of logic, rhetoric, and poetry so that the students may realize "what religious, what glorious and magnificent use might be made of poetry, both in divine and human things." Then, Milton concludes triumphantly, his students will be "fraught with an universal insight into things." Adam's final lesson, however, is very different; he acknowledges the rightful limitations of his knowledge and Michael approves: "thou hast attain'd the sum / Of wisdom; hope no higher" (XII, 575-76). In the disparity between these concluding lessons, the profound difference between Milton's early sketch of an ideal education and his later dramatization is most apparent.

Paradise Lost does not end with Michael's voice, however. There is one final lesson for us, if not for Adam. Michael's stern, rather unsympathetic voice ceases, and once again at the close of the poem the narrator's voice resumes and we do learn *Of Education*'s final lesson: "what religious, what glorious and magnificent use might be made of poetry, both in divine and human things."

In recent years impressive scholarly work has focused our attention upon the narrator of *Paradise Lost,* the central intelligence of the work whose mediating, meditative, and inspired presence adds rich dimensions to the first ten books. At the same time, some of Milton's most sympathetic critics have rejected Books XI and XII as a relative failure or have devised elaborate explanations for the aridity of the final books. Certainly a crucial factor in our response to Books XI and XII is the virtual disappearance of the narrator. The Cambridge Manuscript preserves four different stages of Milton's early plan for a drama, *Adam Unparadis'd.* The drama was to have had a narrator, and for this role Milton considered, in turn, Michael, Moses, and Gabriel. Books XI and XII, then, are a curious return to Milton's earliest conception of a drama of the fall, in which the responsibility for shaping and narrating the story of man falls upon Michael.

[In *The War in Heaven: "Paradise Lost" and the Tradition of Satan's Rebellion* (1980)] Stella Revard has delineated a composite portrait of the archangel Michael as he was traditionally portrayed in the Renaissance. The militant angel of judgment and expulsion, his strength lies in his sword and in his almost Roman figure of military charisma. In *Paradise Lost,* however, Milton subverts Michael's traditional stature as the supreme angel of undefeatable physical prowess, giving his traditional role of defeater of Satan to the Son and radically changing the means of that defeat from physical force to moral strength. Having limited Michael's traditional military power, Milton instead portrays him, still in his military garb, as teacher of fallen man.

There is no precedent for Milton as teacher; it is a curious and significant innovation on Milton's part. Yet Michael's soldierly demeanor perfectly embodies the military project of the early tractate on education:

> In which methodical course it is so supposed they
> must proceed by the steady pace of learning onward,
> as at convenient times for memory's sake to retire
> back into the middle ward, and sometimes into the
> rear of what they have been taught, until they have
> confirmed and solidly united the whole body of their
> perfected knowledge, like the last embattling of a
> Roman legion.

The final military metaphor is appropriate to a work that has advocated the training of civic and military leaders. It is also prophetic of Milton's soldier-teacher Michael who, having been superceded by the Son on the field of battle, his physical prowess superceded by spiritual strength, is sent by God to teach fallen man. He is to teach man reality and give him hope, but, finally, it will be Christ who will complete man's education. *Of Education* is shot through with confidence that the military skills Milton proposes for his students will be a powerful good for the state. That confidence is deeply shaken in the conclusion of *Paradise Lost,* spoken by Michael, who has been an actor in God's comedy of warfare. Adam's horror at the vision of Homeric heroes—

> Death's Ministers, not Men, who thus deal Death
> Inhumanly to men, and multiply
> Ten thousandfold the sin of him who slew
> His Brother

—is a lesson learned by both pupil and teacher.

Milton framed *Of Education* with a telling image of his own stance as educational reformer: "I shall . . . straight conduct ye to a hillside, where I will point ye out the right path of a virtuous and noble education; laborious indeed at the first ascent, but else so smooth, so green, so full of goodly prospect and melodious sounds on every side, that the harp of Orpheus was not more charming." When Michael leads Adam to the top of the Hill of Paradise, he begins an education much more difficult than the lesson Milton had envisioned years before. A central theme of *Paradise Lost* and indeed, it may be argued, the central *action* of *Paradise Lost* is education, the pursuit of knowledge. Education was Milton's conscious concern throughout his life: from his own extended self-education, from his years as a teacher, from the publication of the tractate in 1644 for "the reforming of education . . . for want whereof this nation perishes," to Milton's republication of *Of Education* with the *Poems* of 1673 as part of his self-conscious presentation of his youthful work. But the traces of the tractate's "discreet method" which structure the education of Adam serve to dramatize how Milton's thinking evolved. For Michael's lessons complicate the agenda and the imagery of *Of Education* and play its optimism against the tragic story of human history. Michael must lead Adam and the reader down from "this top of Speculation," out of the sympathetic clarity of the epic narrator's primeval world, out of the ideal academy, and into the dark, cold confusion of our contemporary world. (pp. 133-45)

Ann Baynes Coiro, " 'To Repair the Ruins of Our First Parents': Of 'Education' and Fallen Adam," in Studies in English Literature, 1500-1900, Vol. 28, No. 1, Winter, 1988, pp. 133-47.

ADDITIONAL BIBLIOGRAPHY

Adams, Richard P. "The Archetypal Pattern of Death and Rebirth in Milton's *Lycidas.*" *PMLA* LXIV (1949): 183-88.
  Explores the theme of immortality in "Lycidas."

Aldington, Richard. "Milton's Shorter Poems." *The Nation and the Athenaeum* XXXVII, No. 10 (6 June 1925): 297.
  Briefly surveys Milton's major poems, noting that "parts of *Paradise Lost* seem. . .dull and laboured."

[Arnold, Matthew]. "A French Critic on Milton." *The Quarterly Review* 143, No. 285 (January 1877): 186-204.
  A review of Edmond Sherer's discussion of Milton in his *Etudes critiques de littérature* (1876), focusing on Scherer's evaluation of Milton criticism written by Joseph Addison, Samuel Johnson, and Lord Macaulay.

Baumlin, James S. "Epic and Allegory in *Paradise Lost,* Book II." *College English* XIV, No. 2 (Spring 1987): 167-77.
  Studies Book II of *Paradise Lost* as one component of "a typically Renaissance poem of mixed genre."

Belloc, Hilaire. "On Milton." In his *On Anything,* pp. 142-48. 1910. Reprint. Freeport, N.Y.: Books for Libraries Press, 1969.
  Briefly considers Milton's importance in English letters.

———. "The Sonnets of Milton." In his *Selected Essays by Hilaire Belloc,* edited by John Edward Dineen, pp. 133-64. Philadelphia: J. B. Lippincott Co., 1936.
  Considers Milton's sonnets "*as verse* by themselves, disconnected from the rest of his writing."

Birrell, Augustine. "John Milton." In his *The Collected Essays & Addresses of the Rt. Hon. Augustine Birrell, 1880-1920,* Vol. I, pp. 1-34. New York: Charles Scribner's Sons, 1923.
  A biographical sketch of Milton, with commentary on his development as an author.

Bowra, C. M. "Milton and the Destiny of Man." In his *From Virgil to Milton,* pp. 194-247. London: Macmillan, 1967.
  Discusses Milton as "the last great practitioner of literary epic."

Brooks, Cleanth. "Milton and Critical Re-estimates." *PMLA* LXVI, No. 6 (December 1951): 1045-54.
  Reviews recent criticism of *Paradise Lost,* noting the need for a study of myth, metaphor, and symbolic structure in the poem.

———. "Eve's Awakening." In *Essays in Honor of Walter Clyde Curry,* edited by the Editorial Committee of the Vanderbilt University Department of English, pp. 281-98. Vanderbilt Studies in the Humanities, Vol. II. Nashville: Vanderbilt University Press, 1954.
  Studies Milton's theological and philosophical consistency as it is revealed by the portrayal of Eve in *Paradise Lost.*

———. "Milton and the New Criticism." In his *A Shaping Joy: Studies in the Writer's Craft,* pp. 330-48. New York: Harcourt Brace Jovanovich, 1971.
  A close examination of Milton's use of metaphor in *Paradise Lost,* noting similarities in the poetry of John Donne.

Bush, Douglas. Introduction to *The Portable Milton,* by John Milton, pp. 1-28. New York: Viking Press, 1949.
  Surveys Milton's life and literary career, emphasizing his choice of subject matter for his works.

Canavan, Francis. "The True Wayfaring Christian: John Milton." In his *Freedom of Expression: Purpose as Limit,* pp. 41-53. Durham, N.C.: Carolina Academic Press, 1984.
  A careful examination of *Areopagitica,* focusing on the work's relationship to the American right to freedom of speech and the press.

Chambers, R. W. *Poets and Their Critics: Langland and Milton.* London: Humphrey Milford for The British Academy, 1941, 48 p.
  Cites parallels between *Paradise Lost* and William Langland's *Piers Plowman,* chiefly those involving characterization and allegory.

Chesterton, G. K. "Milton and His Age." *The Oxford and Cambridge Review,* No. 7 (1909): 3-13.
  Attempts to explain the apparent contrast between Milton the man and Milton the poet: a poet "whom we cannot help liking, and a man whom we cannot like."

———. "Milton and Merry England." In his *Fancies versus Fads,* pp. 252-74. New York: Dodd, Mead & Co., 1923.
  Discusses Milton's moral earnestness and places him among the religious poets of his day.

———. "The Taste for Milton." In his *A Handful of Authors: Essays on Books & Writers,* edited by Dorothy Collins, pp. 75-7. New York: Sheed and Ward, 1953.
  Argues that far from being for everyone, Milton's poetry "is really a matured taste, a taste that grows."

Clark, Donald Leman. *John Milton at St. Paul's School: A Study of Ancient Rhetoric in English Renaissance Education.* New York: Columbia University Press, 1948, 269 p.
  A rigorous study of primary and secondary education in Milton's day, suggesting of what Milton's formal training consisted and positing how it influenced his literary career.

Coleridge, Samuel Taylor. "Poetry: John Milton." In his *Coleridge on the Seventeenth Century,* edited by Roberta Florence Brinkley, pp. 541-612. Durham: Duke University Press, 1955.
  Collects the author's lectures, notes, and scattered marginalia on Milton and his works.

Cottle, Basil. "The Seventeenth Century: Milton." In his *The Language of Literature: English Grammar in Action,* pp. 57-64. London: Macmillan, 1985.
  Scrutinizes the phrasings, locutions, and diction of *Paradise Lost.*

Daiches, David. *Milton.* Rev. ed. London: Hutchinson University Library, 1959, 254 p.
  A general survey of Milton's life and major writings.

Darbishire, Helen, ed. *The Early Lives of Milton.* London: Constable & Co., 1932, 353 p.
  Introduces and edits early biographies of Milton by six authors: John Aubrey (1681); John Phillips (after 1681); Anthony à Wood (1691); Edward Phillips (1694); John Toland (1698); and Jonathan Richardson (1734).

Dobrée, Bonamy. "Milton and Dryden: A Comparison in Poetic Ideas and Poetic Method." In his *Milton to Ouida: A Collection of Essays,* pp. 1-21. New York: Barnes & Noble, 1970.
> Cites likenesses and differences in the works of John Dryden and Milton.

Donoghue, Denis. "God with Thunder." In his *Thieves of Fire,* pp. 33-58. New York: Oxford University Press, 1974.
> Approaches *Paradise Lost* as an expression of the Aeschylean impression that "men are the creation only of a minor god, and have only a minor status in the universe and a minor place in the attention of the gods."

Dos Passos, John. "Liberty to Speak to Print." In his *The Ground We Stand On: Some Examples from the History of a Political Creed,* pp. 85-100. New York: Harcourt, Brace and Co., 1941.
> Describes Milton's role in the development of the English idea of freedom of the press.

Duncan, Joseph. *Milton's Earthly Paradise: A Historical Study of Eden.* Minnesota Monographs in the Humanities, Vol. 5. Minneapolis: University of Minnesota Press, 1972, 329 p.
> Uses *Paradise Lost* as a touchstone for explaining the meaning and character of Edenic paradises in the Renaissance.

Du Rocher, Richard J. *Milton and Ovid.* Ithaca: Cornell University Press, 1985, 241 p.
> Traces Milton's historical and philosophical debt to Ovid in *Paradise Lost* and other poems.

Dyson, A. E. "Virtue Unwavering: Milton's *Comus.*" In his *Between Worlds: Aspects of Literary Form,* pp. 15-40. London: Macmillan, 1972.
> Suggests how *Comus* might have impressed an educated seventeenth-century audience.

————, and Lovelock, Julian. "Event Perverse: Milton's Epic of Exile." In their *Masterful Images: English Poetry from Metaphysics to Romantics,* pp. 47-70. New York: Barnes & Noble, 1976.
> Cites evidence of Milton's faith in freedom in *Paradise Lost* and comments on the nature of the Fall in the poem.

————, eds. *Milton: "Paradise Lost": A Casebook.* London: Macmillan, 1973, 253 p.
> Collects and introduces 28 previously published critical views of *Paradise Lost,* ranging from the earliest appraisals to the most recent ones.

Eliot, T. S. "Milton." *Sewanee Review* LVI, No. 2 (Spring 1948): 185-209.
> Retracts, in part, the critic's earlier claim that Milton's influence on later writers was a bad one.

————. "Milton II." In his *On Poetry and Poets,* pp. 165-83. New York: Farrar, Straus and Cudahy, 1957.
> A close analysis of Milton's versification, emphasizing the unwholesomeness of the poet's influence on later writers and the English language in general.

Empson, William. *Milton's God.* Rev. ed. London: Chatto & Windus, 1965, 320 p.
> Probes Milton's major works for evidence of his beliefs about the nature of God.

Fallon, Stephen M. "Milton's Sin and Death: The Ontology of Allegory in *Paradise Lost.*" *English Literary Renaissance* 17, No. 3 (Autumn 1987): 329-50.
> Rebuts Samuel Johnson's contention (see excerpt dated 1779) that "Milton's allegory of Sin and Death [in *Paradise Lost*] is undoubtedly faulty."

Fiske, John. "John Milton." In his *Essays Historical and Literary,* Vol. I: *Scenes and Characters in American History,* pp. 35-68. New York: Macmillan, 1902.
> A brief biography, focusing on Milton's "precocious boyhood" and early poems.

Flannagan, Roy. "Milton Criticism, Present and Future." *Études Anglaises* XXVII, No. 4 (October-December 1974): 399-403.
> A commentary on the present state of Milton scholarship, by the editor of *Milton Quarterly.*

Fletcher, Harris Francis. *The Intellectual Development of John Milton.* 2 vols. Urbana: University of Illinois Press, 1956.
> A searching study of Milton's boyhood education.

Fowler, Alastair. "'To Shepherd's ear': The Form of Milton's *Lycidas.*" In *Silent Poetry: Essays in Numerological Analysis,* edited by Alastair Fowler, pp. 170-84. New York: Barnes & Noble, 1970.
> Explores the external form of "Lycidas," chiefly in terms of meter and stanza length.

————. Introduction to *Paradise Lost,* by John Milton, pp. 3-39. London: Longman, 1971.
> Treats some of the major issues concerning *Paradise Lost:* composition, characterization, printing history, language and style, prosody, chronology, and Milton's conception of the universe.

French, J. Milton. "Lamb and Milton." *Studies in Philology* XXXI, No. 1 (January 1931): 92-103.
> Discusses Lamb as one who "mentions Milton more often and with greater admiration than any other writer before 1660 except Shakspere."

Frye, Northrop. "The Typology of *Paradise Regained.*" *Modern Philology* LIII, No. 4 (May 1956): 227-38.
> Approaches *Paradise Regained* in the light of theological views expressed in Milton's other works.

————. *God, Man, and Satan: Patterns of Christian Thought and Life in "Paradise Lost," "Pilgrim's Progress," and the Great Theologians.* Princeton: Princeton University Press, 1960, 184 p.
> Examines the character of evil, denial of humanity, and God's plan of salvation in *Paradise Lost,* with commentary on related theology in John Bunyan's *Pilgrim's Progress.*

————. "The Revelation to Eve." In his *The Stubborn Structure: Essays on Criticism and Society,* pp. 135-59. Ithaca: Cornell University Press, 1970.
> Examines Adam's dream of Eve in *Paradise Lost* as a complement of Eve's own dreams in the poem.

————. "Agon and Logos." In his *Spiritus Mundi: Essays on Literature, Myth, and Society,* pp. 201-27. Bloomington: Indiana University Press, 1976.
> An investigation of the meaning and purpose of Milton's use of classical genres in his major poetry.

Graves, Robert. *Wife to Mr. Milton: The Story of Marie Powell.* New York: Creative Age Press, 1944, 380 p.
> A book-length biography of Milton's first wife, offering commentary on how she may have influenced her husband's political and literary career.

Grierson, H. J. C. "John Milton I and II." *The Criterion* VII, Nos. 30, 31 (September 1928; December 1928): 7-26, 240-57.
> Attributes the perceived egotistical and idealistic character of *Paradise Lost* to parental coddling during Milton's boyhood and youth.

Hamilton, G. Rostrevor. *Hero or Fool? A Study of Milton's Satan.* London: George Allen & Unwin, 1944, 41 p.
> Synthesizes critical opinion concerning the nature of Satan in *Paradise Lost,* concluding: "The pride of the ruined Archangel is itself the ruin of a virtue, the sense of glory which is eminently found in a great spirit."

Hannay, Margaret P. "A Preface to *Perelandra.*" In *The Longing for a Form: Essays on the Fiction of C. S. Lewis,* edited by Peter J. Schakel, pp. 73-90. Kent, Ohio: Kent State University Press, 1977.
> Considers C. S. Lewis's contention that Milton made mistakes in his portrayal of the Edenic myth.

Hart, Jeffrey. "*Paradise Lost* and Order: 'I Know Each Lane and Every Valley Green'." *College English* 25, No. 8 (May 1964): 576-82.

An anagogical and autobiographical reading of *Paradise Lost*, focusing on the poem as "a paradigm of every soul's journey to salvation."

Hazlitt, William. "On Milton's 'Lycidas'"; "On Milton's Versification"; "On the Character of Milton's Eve." In his *The Round Table; Characters of Shakespear's Plays*, edited by Catherine MacDonald MacLean, pp. 31-36, 36-41, 105-11. London: J. M. Dent & Sons, 1936.
    Three essays. The first challenges Samuel Johnson's claim (see excerpt dated 1779) that "Lycidas" suffers from pedantry and want of feeling; the second considers the verse form of *Paradise Lost*; the third contrasts the Miltonic Eve with Shakespeare's female characters.

Henley, W. E. "In Milton's Hand." *The Pall Mall Magazine* XXI, No. 85 (May 1900): 135-39.
    Describes Milton's writing processes as evidenced in the Trinity Manuscript of his poems.

Hill, Christopher. "Milton the Radical." *The Times Literary Supplement*, No. 3795 (29 November 1974): 1330-32.
    Examines Milton's political partisanship, arguing that during the 1640s the author was as closely related to an underworld culture of heretical ideas as he was to official Puritanism.

Howison, Patricia M. "Memory and Will: Selective Amnesia in *Paradise Lost*." *The University of Toronto Quarterly* 56, No. 4 (Summer 1987): 523-39.
    Studies Milton's apparent belief that "the proper co-operation of memory and will makes it possible to know and understand truths which cannot be apprehended merely through the evident facts."

Hughes, Merritt Y., ed. *John Milton: Complete Poems and Major Prose*, by John Milton. Indianapolis: The Odyssey Press, 1957, 1059 p.
    An outstanding one-volume edition of Milton's principal works, with succinct, balanced introductions by the editor and copious notes and annotations.

Hunt, Leigh. "On the Latin Poems of Milton." In his *Leigh Hunt's Literary Criticism*, edited by Lawrence Huston Houtchens and Carolyn Washburn Houtchens, pp. 177-207. New York: Columbia University Press, 1956.
    A comparison, originally published in the *Literary Examiner* in 1823, of Milton's Latin poetry with that of his contemporaries.

Huttar, Charles A. "The Passion of Christ in *Paradise Regained*." *English Language Notes* XIX, No. 3 (March 1982): 236-60.
    Summarizes criticism of *Paradise Regained* and analyzes images of the Cross and Christ's crucifixion in the work.

Johnson, William C. *Milton Criticism: A Subject Index*. Folkestone, England: Dawson, 1978, 450 p.
    Indexes 150 selected works of Milton criticism, principally of the twentieth century.

Kermode, Frank. "*Samson Agonistes* and Hebrew Prosody." *The Durham University Journal* XLV, No. 2 (March 1953): 59-63.
    Maintains that Milton imitated Hebrew lyric rhymes and measures in certain passages of *Paradise Regained*.

————. "Milton's Hero." *Review of English Studies* n. s. 4, No. 16 (October 1953): 317-30.
    Examines Milton's portrayal of heroic virtue in *Paradise Regained*.

————, ed. *The Living Milton: Essays by Various Hands*. New York: Barnes & Noble, 1968, 180 p.
    Contains ten specifically commissioned essays on Milton and his works. Contributors include J. B. Broadbent, "The Nativity Ode"; Bernard Bergonzi, "Criticism and the Milton Controversy"; and Frank Kermode, "Adam Unparadised."

Kirkconnell, Watson. *The Celestial Cycle: The Theme of "Paradise Lost" in World Literature, with Translations of the Major Analogues*. Toronto: University of Toronto Press, 1952, 701 p.
    Examines the major analogues of *Paradise Lost*, stressing the overall orginality of the poem.

Knight, G. Wilson. "Milton." In his *The Golden Labyrinth: A Study of British Drama*, pp. 124-29. New York: W. W. Norton & Co., 1962.
    Approaches Milton as a dramatist, focusing on the artistry of *Comus*.

————. "Chariot of Wrath: On Milton's Prose and Poetry." In his *Poets of Action*, pp. 70-162. London: Methuen & Co., 1967.
    A wide-ranging survey of Milton's literary career, emphasizing the relationship between the author's prose and poetry.

Kranidas, Thomas. "Adam and Eve in the Garden: A Study of *Paradise Lost*, Book V." *Studies in English Literature, 1500-1900* IV (1964): 71-83.
    Examines Milton's idea of decorum as evidenced by the portrayal of Raphael in *Paradise Lost*, Book V.

————. "'Decorum' and the Style of Milton's Antiprelatical Tracts." *Studies in Philology* LXII, No. 2 (April 1965): 176-87.
    Considers the prose style of Milton's antiprelatical tracts.

————. *The Fierce Equation: A Study of Milton's Decorum*. Studies in English Literature, Vol. X. The Hague: Mouton & Co., 1965, 165 p.
    Explores Milton's conception of literary decorum, noting its application in selected verse and prose.

————. "Dalila's Role in *Samson Agonistes*." *Studies in English Literature, 1500-1900* VI, No. 1 (Winter 1966): 125-37.
    Maintains that Milton's portrayal of Dalila in *Samson Agonistes* evidences his dramatic skill.

————. "Style and Rectitude in Seventeenth-Century Prose: Hall, Smectymnuus, and Milton." *The Huntington Library Quarterly* 46, No. 3 (Summer 1983): 237-69.
    A close study of *Animadversions upon the Remonstrants Defence*, focusing on the origin and purpose of the discourse.

————, ed. *New Essays on "Paradise Lost."* Berkeley and Los Angeles: University of California Press, 1971, 180 p.
    Contains seven essays by leading Milton scholars. Contributors include Stanley Eugene Fish on "Discovery as Form in *Paradise Lost*" and Michael Fixler on "The Apocalypse within *Paradise Lost*."

Lamb, Charles. Letter to Charles Lloyd. In his *The Letter of Charles Lamb, to Which Are Added Those of His Sister Mary Lamb*, Vol. I, edited by E. V. Lucas, pp. 81-3. New Haven: Yale University Press, 1935.
    An 1809 letter in which Lamb states: "Nothing can be more unlike to my fancy than Homer and Milton. Homer is perfect prattle. . . compared to the deep oracular voice of Milton."

Leavis, F. R. "Milton's Verse." *Scrutiny* II, No. 2 (September 1933): 123-36.
    Studies the verse forms used by Milton in *Paradise Lost* and comments briefly on the versification of Milton's Latin poetry.

————. "Mr. Eliot and Milton." *Sewanee Review* LVII, No. 1 (January-March 1949): 1-30.
    An overview of T. S. Eliot's vacillating opinions about Milton and his literary works.

————. "In Defence of Milton." In his *The Common Pursuit*, pp. 33-43. Harmondsworth, England: Penguin Books, 1976.
    Defends Milton against critics who maintain that his works are confusing, poorly planned, or dreadful failures.

Leishman, J. B. *Milton's Minor Poems*. Edited by Geoffrey Tillotson. London: Hutchinson & Co., 1969, 360 p.
    A full-length study of the themes and forms of Milton's minor poetry.

Lewalski, Barbara Kiefer. "Milton: Political Beliefs and Polemical Methods, 1659-60." *PMLA* LXXIV, No. 3 (June 1959): 191-202.
    Studies the political tracts Milton wrote during the Puritan Revolution.

————. "Milton on Women—Yet Once More." *Milton Studies* VI (1975): 3-20.

Asserts the limitations of feminist studies of *Paradise Lost.*

————. "On Looking into Pope's Milton." *Milton Studies* XI (1978): 29-50.
    Considers the impact of Milton's poetry upon Alexander Pope.

————. "The Genres of *Paradise Lost:* Literary Genre As a Means of Accommodation." *Milton Studies* XVII (1983): 75-103.
    Isolates the generic elements of *Paradise Lost,* arguing that genre permutations provide multiple viewpoints and thereby exercise the reader's moral sense.

Lewis, C. S. "A Note on *Comus.*" *Review of English Studies* VIII, No. 30 (April 1932): 170-76.
    Examines Milton's revisions in the manuscript of *Comus.*

————. "Variation in Shakespeare and Others." In his *Rehabilitations and Other Essays,* pp. 159-80. London: Oxford University Press, 1939.
    Contains a brief comparison of Milton's method of developing a literary theme with that of William Shakespeare.

MacKail, J. W. "Milton." In his *The Springs of Helicon: A Study in the Progress of English Poetry from Chaucer to Milton,* pp. 135-204. New York: Longmans, Green, and Co., 1909.
    Surveys Milton's literary career, emphasizing the poet's choice of verse forms and interest in the epic.

Martz, Louis L., ed. *Milton: A Collection of Critical Essays.* Englewood Cliffs, N. J.: Prentice-Hall, 1966, 212 p.
    Reprints selected twentieth-century Milton criticism. Essayists include William Empson, Geoffrey Hartman, and Arnold Stein.

Merton, Thomas. "Satan, Milton, and Camus: Can We Survive Nihilism?" *Saturday Review* L, No. 15 (15 April 1967): 16-19.
    Studies the character of Satan in *Paradise Lost* and isolates "modern" elements in the poem.

Miles Josephine. *Poetry and Change: Donne, Milton, Wordsworth, and the Equilibrium of the Present.* Berkeley and Los Angeles: University of California Press, 1974.
    Contains a discussion of how Milton's poetry mirrors its age as a time of change and transition.

Milton Quarterly (formerly *Milton Newsletter*) I— (1967—).
    A quarterly publication, currently edited by Roy Flannagan, that includes scholarly articles on Milton's life, works, and the Miltonic milieu.

Milton Society of America Bulletin (formerly *Proceedings of the Milton Society of America*) I— (1953—).
    An annual review of Milton studies.

Milton Studies I— (1969—).
    An annual forum for Milton scholarship and criticism.

Miner, Earl. "*Felix Culpa* in the Redemptive Order of *Paradise Lost.*" *Philological Quarterly* XLVII, No. 1 (January 1968): 43-54.
    Explores the paradox of the Fortunate Fall in *Paradise Lost.*

Mirsky, D. S. Introduction to *A Brief History of Moscovia,* by John Milton, pp. 9-26. London: Blackamore Press, 1929.
    A general appreciation of *A Brief History of Moscovia,* with a commentary on Milton's sources for the work.

Mueller, Janel. "The Mastery of Decorum: Politics as Poetry in Milton's Sonnets." *Critical Inquiry* 13, No. 3 (Spring 1987): 475-508.
    Surveys Milton's major political works, emphasizing the political content of selected sonnets.

Murry, John Middleton. "John Milton: 'I Am That Satan'"; "John Milton: Lear without Cordelia"; "John Milton: 'Tendering the Whole'." In his *Heroes of Thought,* pp. 142-52, 153-62, 163-77. New York: Julian Messner, 1938.
    Three essays. The first examines Satan's function in *Paradise Lost*; the second attempts to isolate the elements that make Milton's poetry peculiarly English; the third explores the origin of *Areopagitica.*

Nott, Kathleen. "Old Puritan Writ Large." In her *The Emperor's Clothes,* pp. 159-93. Bloomington: Indiana University Press, 1958.
    Reviews criticism of Milton's major works and considers the author's theological point of view.

Parker, William Riley. *Milton's Contemporary Reputation.* Columbus: Ohio State University Press, 1940, 299 p.
    An overview of Milton's literary reputation during his lifetime. The work also contains a tentative list of printed allusions to Milton through 1674 and facsimile reproductions of early printed responses to several of Milton's works.

Patrides, C. A. *Milton and the Christian Tradition.* Oxford: Oxford University Press, Clarendon Press, 1966, 302 p.
    Focuses on Milton's "conception and presentation of the principal themes of the Christian faith."

————. *An Annotated Critical Bibliography of John Milton.* New York: St. Martin's Press, 1987, 200 p.
    Lists selected works on Milton and his art.

————, ed. *Milton's "Lycidas": The Tradition and the Poem.* New York: Holt, Rinehart and Winston, 1961, 246 p.
    A collection of important "Lycidas" criticism dating from 1779 to the middle of the twentieth century. The work also contains a discussion of the poem's textual problems and an annotated reading list.

Poggioli, Renato. "Milton's *Lycidas.*" In his *The Oaten Flute: Essays on Pastoral Poetry and the Pastoral Ideal,* pp. 83-104. Cambridge, Mass.: Harvard University Press, 1975.
    Examines the pastoral character of "Lycidas" and comments on the poem's apparent indebtedness to Jacopo Sannazaro's *Arcadia.*

Pointon, Marcia R. *Milton & English Art.* Toronto: University of Toronto Press, 1970, 276 p.
    An illustrated overview of responses in the visual arts to Milton's works, especially *Paradise Lost.*

Ransom, John Crowe. "The Idea of Literary Anthropologist and What He Might Say of the *Paradise Lost* of Milton: A Speech with a Prologue." *The Kenyon Review* XXI, No. 1 (Winter 1959): 121-40.
    Approaches *Paradise Lost* as a reflection of the culture of its age.

————. "A Poem Nearly Anonymous." In his *The World's Body,* pp. 1-28. Baton Rouge: Louisiana State University Press, 1968.
    Suggests that Milton deliberately sought to be "anonymous as a poet" in "Lycidas."

Ricks, Christopher. *Milton's Grand Style.* Oxford: Oxford University Press, Clarendon Press, 1963, 154 p.
    Describes the major elements of Milton's versification.

Romanticism Past and Present (formerly *Milton and the Romantics*) I— (1975—).
    A semiannual periodical that publishes articles on Milton's relation to the English Romantics.

Rowse, A. L. "The Milton Country." In his *The English Past: Evocations of Persons and Places,* pp. 85-112. London: Macmillan, 1951.
    Describes the countryside, chiefly around Oxford, that may have inspired passages in Milton's poetry.

————. *Milton the Puritan.* London: Macmillan, 1977, 297 p.
    A wide-ranging study of Milton's mind, focusing on his ideas, prejudices, and the line he took about issues that led to the Civil War.

Saurat, Denis. *Milton Man and Thinker.* New York: The Dial Press, 1925, 363 p.
    Maintains that Milton was a highly original thinker and not just a derivative one.

————. *Blake and Milton.* 1935. Reprint. New York: Russell & Russell, 1965, 159 p.
    Examines the relationship between William Blake and Milton, describing Blake as Milton's "wild brother . . . a Milton gone mad."

Sayers, Dorothy L. ''Dante and Milton.'' In her *Further Papers on Dante*, pp. 148-82. New York: Harper, 1957.

> Notices parallels between the careers of Milton and Dante Alighieri.

————. ''The Faust Legend and the Idea of the Devil.'' In her *The Poetry of Search and the Poetry of Statement and Other Posthumous Essays on Literature, Religion and Language*, pp. 227-41. London: Victor Gollancz, 1963.

> Comments briefly on the devil in *Paradise Lost,* maintaining that Milton did not consider Satan to be the hero of the poem.

Sensabaugh, George F. *Milton in Early America*. Princeton: Princeton University Press, 1964, 320 p.

> Argues that Milton influenced poetry in early America as much as he affected poetry in eighteenth-century England.

Shawcross, John T. *Milton: A Bibliography for the Years 1624-1700*. Binghamton, N.Y.: Medieval & Renaissance Texts & Studies, 1984, 452 p.

> A useful bibliography of Milton through 1700, citing 416 primary works and 1,753 secondary ones.

Stein, Arnold. *The Art of Presence: The Poet and ''Paradise Lost.''* Berkeley and Los Angeles: University of California Press, 1977, 190 p.

> Attempts to show how the ''presence'' of Milton himself in *Paradise Lost* works upon the reader.

Tillyard, E. M. W. *Studies in Milton*. London: Chatto & Windus, 1951, 176 p.

> Collects and revises the critic's principal essays on Milton. The subjects include Milton's humor, the portrayal of Christ in *Paradise Regained,* and the author's private correspondence and academic exercises.

————. ''Milton.'' In his *The Metaphysicals and Milton*, pp. 61-74. London: Chatto & Windus, 1956.

> Places Milton among the English poets of his day, concluding: ''Milton was a great figure looking back to the Middle Ages and forward to the spirit and the achievements of eighteenth-century puritanism.''

Trevor-Roper, Hugh. ''The Elitist Politics of Milton.'' *The Times Literary Supplement,* No. 3717 (1 June 1973): 601-3.

> Maintains that by 1660 Milton's political philosophy was ''in ruins'' and his role as a pamphleteer was over.

Tuve, Rosemond. ''New Approaches to Milton'' and ''Baroque and Mannerist Milton?'' In her *Essays by Rosemond Tuve: Spenser, Herbert, Milton,* edited by Thomas P. Roche, Jr., pp. 255-61, 262-80. Princeton: Princeton University Press, 1970.

> Two essays. The first, originally published in 1958, reviews recent criticism of Milton. The second, originally published in 1961, warns against applying the label ''baroque'' to Milton too freely.

Visiak, E. H. *Milton Agonistes: A Metaphysical Criticism*. London: A. M. Philpot, n. d., 104 p.

> Approaches *Paradise Lost* as a tragedy in the Greek sense.

————. *The Portent of Milton: Some Aspects of His Genius*. London: Werner Laurie, 1958, 148 p.

> Collects and revises a selection of the author's essays on Milton. The subjects include Milton's marriages, his prose, and the public perception of Milton in his own day.

Wagenknecht, Edward. *The Personality of Milton*. Norman: University of Oklahoma Press, 1970, 170 p.

> Probes instances of self-revelation in Milton's works.

Wain, John. ''Reflections on the First Night of *Comus*.'' In his *Professing Poetry*, pp. 134-56. New York: Viking Press, 1978.

> Explores the origin and purpose of *Comus* and considers the merits of the work as poetry.

Webber, Joan Malory. *Milton and His Epic Tradition*. Seattle: University of Washington Press, 1979, 244 p.

> Attempts to ''chart more fully the extent to which Milton's central concerns are compatible with those of earlier epic writers.''

Williams, Charles. ''Milton.'' In his *The English Poetic Mind*, pp. 110-52. New York: Russell & Russell, 1963.

> Examines Milton's technical achievement as a poet in *Paradise Lost, Paradise Regained,* and *Samson Agonistes*.

Wordsworth, William. Letter to Isabella Fenwick. In his *The Letters of William and Dorothy Wordsworth: The Later Years*, Vol. III: *1841-50,* edited by Ernest de Selincourt, pp. 1229-31. Oxford: Oxford University Press, Clarendon Press, 1939.

> Laments Milton's having abandoned poetry for a time to ''take an active part in the troubles of his country.''

(Lady) Mary (Pierrepont) Wortley Montagu

1689-1762

(Also Montague) English epistler, poet, essayist, translator, and dramatist.

Known to her contemporaries and to posterity alike simply as Lady Mary, Montagu is celebrated as a consummate writer of intelligent, witty, candid—and frequently scandalous—letters. She was a controversial figure in her own day and has intrigued readers ever since with the self-portrait she left in her letters. Spanning the years 1708 to 1762, Montagu's correspondence is addressed to a wide variety of recipients and is considered remarkable for its versatility and range. By turns gossipy, philosophical, descriptive, eccentric, affectionate, worldly, thoughtful, and sarcastic, the letters share one common attribute: the forceful imprint of their author's personality.

Born in London to an aristocratic family, Mary Pierrepont (Lady Mary after her father became the earl of Kingston in 1690) supplemented the scanty education then commonly afforded young noblewomen with a rigorous academic program of her own devising. From a young age, she read and studied tirelessly, even teaching herself Latin. While she was yet in her teens, her unusual erudition and beauty captured the attention of Edward Wortley Montagu (usually referred to simply as Wortley), a politician eleven years her senior. Lady Mary's first extant letters were written ostensibly to Wortley's sister Anne, but were very likely read, and in part answered, by Wortley himself. After Anne Wortley's death in 1709, Lady Mary and Wortley began their own curious correspondence, passionate and reticent by turns, alternately loving and querulous. At length Wortley applied to Lady Mary's father for her hand, but the two men were unable to agree on financial settlements. Thus the courtship seemed over until, in 1712, after much bickering and indecision, the couple eloped. Montagu spent the first few years of her marriage alone in the country while Wortley attended to business in London; biographers note that her letters to him there indicate her dissatisfaction with the arrangement and her growing concern over his seeming indifference to her.

In 1715 Montagu joined her husband in the capital, where his political career was flourishing. She moved with ease in prominent social and literary circles, counting among her many friends and admirers Alexander Pope. It was probably in collaboration with him and with poet John Gay that she wrote *Town Eclogues*, six clever and defamatory satires of well-known society personalities. Montagu had no intention of publishing the work, but in 1716 three of the eclogues were pirated, with coy hints of their authorship, as *Court Poems*. Later that year, having been appointed ambassador to Turkey, Wortley took his wife and young son with him to Constantinople. There, displaying her customary curiosity and enthusiasm, Montagu studied Turkish life and language and wrote several letters detailing her observations and experiences to friends and acquaintances back in England. One of her principal correspondents was Pope, who regularly sent elaborately stylized and effusive love letters to which Montagu returned friendly but comparatively distant replies. (To what extent Pope's amorous sentiments were sincere and not mere social and literary convention is still a matter of speculation.) Montagu later revised

her letters from Turkey to form her famous "Turkish Embassy Letters." But her sojourn in Turkey is important from a medical as well as a literary standpoint: noting the success of the Turkish practice of smallpox inoculation, Montagu (who had herself suffered from the disease in 1715) had the procedure performed on her son and, later, on her daughter. Through her example and her anonymously published essay "A Plain Account of the Inoculating of the Small Pox by a Turkey Merchant," she was instrumental in convincing her countrymen of the practical merits of the procedure.

Returning to England in 1718, Montagu resumed her social and literary friendships and diversions, accepting Pope's invitation to take a cottage in Twickenham, with her husband, so as to be neighbors. The cause of their famous quarrel, which began sometime around 1728, is unknown; one apocryphal explanation has it that Pope became her enemy after she laughed derisively at his declaration of love. Another story holds that Pope became outraged after loaning the Montagus some bed linens which were later returned unwashed. Whatever the cause, their estrangement was bitter and public. Pope, who had once written that joy "only dwells where W——— casts her eyes," now lampooned Montagu ("Sappho") in *The Dunciad* and elsewhere in his poetry, recklessly indicting her for offenses ranging from exhibiting solvenliness and malice to having loose morals and veneral disease. Disagreement exists as to whether an anonymous retaliatory attack, *Verses Address'd to the Imitator of the First Satire of the Second Book of Horace*, was actually written by Montagu, but this satirical invective against Pope and his work was attributed to Montagu by her contemporaries, and Pope continued to castigate her in his own satires.

In 1736 Montagu met and fell in love with Francesco Algarotti, an Italian count several years younger than she. (As biographers observe, the early doubts she and Wortley had expressed in their courtship letters were prophetic; though their relationship was amicable, it had become distant and unfulfilling.) Montagu declared her love for Algarotti in passionate, giddy letters quite unlike those she had written to Wortley in their early days. Though the Italian's response was apparently less ardent than she wished, she resolved in 1739 to leave her country, husband, and grown children to live with him in Italy. But Algarotti, by all accounts an opportunist, albeit a charming one, changed his mind and failed to meet her in Venice. Montagu's decision to remain on the Continent regardless has never been fully accounted for, but remain she did, mainly in Italy, for the next twenty years. She and Wortley exchanged polite and affectionate letters but made no effort to meet. She wrote many other letters during these years, most to her married daughter, Mary, Lady Bute. Critics call these letters her most gentle, reflective, and philosophical. After Wortley died in 1761, Montagu set out for England. En route, she encountered an English clergyman to whom she entrusted the manuscript of her reworked letters from Turkey, apparently with the understanding that they would be published after her death. Within mere months of her return to London, Montagu died of cancer.

The "Turkish Embassy Letters," apparently the only ones Montagu intended for publication, were printed (surreptitiously and over the objections of Montagu's family) two years after her death under the title *Letters of the Right Honourable Lady M—y W——y M——e*. The fifty-two letters in the collection are thought to be based in part on Montagu's real letters and in part on a journal she kept during her travel to Turkey and her stay in that country. So great was their popularity that successive editions were augmented with Montagu's other, private correspondence as it became available. Among the series of correspondence unearthed and published by nineteenth-century editors were her letters to Wortley, to her sister Frances, Lady Mar, and to Lady Bute. However, the complete array of Montagu's correspondence was not available until Robert Halsband's definitive edition of 1965-67.

Montagu jestingly predicted her own fame in a 1726 letter to her sister: "The last pleasure that fell in my way was Madam Sevigny's Letters; very pretty they are, but I assert without the least vanity that mine will be full as entertaining 40 years hence. I advise you therefore to put none of 'em to the use of Wast paper." Indeed, despite the letters' history of piecemeal publication, their critical reception has remained surprisingly stable and consistently approving throughout the years. Due to the personal nature of her epistolary work, critics have traditionally focused as much on Montagu's character as on her writing, describing the woman as well as the letters as intelligent, articulate, high-spirited, and somewhat hard-hearted. The "Turkish Embassy Letters" are generally considered Montagu's most accomplished. Since their first publication, the letters have been highly praised for both style and substance: witty, polished, and entertaining, they are also valued for Montagu's informative, accurate observations of Turkish life as well as her penetrating and remarkably unprejudiced insights into Middle Eastern culture. Nineteenth-century commentators echoed

eighteenth-century appreciation of the "Turkish Embassy Letters" and were generally approving of the new correspondence as it came to light. They frequently described Montagu's letters as "masculine," referring to her character traits of common sense, confidence, and candor. Many critics were disturbed, however, by the "unsavoury strain of impropriety" running through the letters, considering her cynicism and "coarseness" of language particularly noxious in a woman writer. Nevertheless, as Walter Bagehot wrote, while the letters might not be suitable for "the youngest of young ladies," they would repay the attention of "maturer" readers.

Twentieth-century critics are less concerned with indecency than were their counterparts of the preceding century, but share their tendency to evaluate Montagu's character as much as her letters. She has been found wanting in kindness, particularly in her witty social-gossip letters to Lady Mar, which have on occasion come under fire for their sarcasm and evident (many say malicious) delight in scandal and slander. Still, this does not detract from the letters' entertainment value; indeed, it may enhance it. Critics have observed that while Montagu's letters are always unaffected and candid, they rarely exhibit deeply felt personal emotion—the notable exception being the series of emotionally abandoned letters to Algarotti. "Brilliant as her letters are," according to Lewis Gibbs, "they have very little humanity, and give more light than warmth. They appeal to the mind but not to the heart, and arouse admiration rather than affection." Montagu's letters are noted for conveying poise and self-possession, being clearly written to interest and amuse, but retaining nonetheless naturalness and spontaneity. Above all, Montagu and her letters are celebrated for intelligence and wit, qualities that provide unity to her diverse epistolary subjects and styles.

Montagu's work in other genres is considered minor compared to her letters. Halsband, modern editor of the essay collection *The Nonsense of Common-Sense*, has written that the essays therein "played a minor but distinguished part in [the] pageant of eighteenth-century manners, morals, and politics," while several critics have described her poetry as competent if not brilliant. However, the minor works have received little critical consideration, and prevailing opinion might be best summed up in Gamaliel Bradford's words: "Lady Mary Wortley Montagu. . .wrote poems, essays, and translations of some note in her own day, of none in ours."

Montagu's letters, however, are "perenially readable," as George Saintsbury has said. The penetration and polish of the "Turkish Embassy Letters," the tortuous indecision of the early letters to Wortley, the hard brilliance and casual malice of the letters to Lady Mar, the impassioned and high-flown love letters to Algarotti, the thoughtful and philosophical correspondence to her daughter from Italy: these series and Montagu's others have charmed critics and general readers alike in their evocation of a multifaceted and fascinating woman.

PRINCIPAL WORKS

Court Poems [with others] (poetry) 1716
"A Plain Account of the Inoculating of the Small Pox by a Turkey Merchant" (essay) 1722; published in newspaper *The Flying-Post; or, Post-Master*
Verses Address'd to the Imitator of the First Satire of the Second Book of Horace (poetry) 1733
Six Town Eclogues with Some Other Poems [with others] (poetry) 1747

Letters of the Right Honourable Lady M—y W———y M———e: Written, during Her Travels in Europe, Asia and Africa, to Persons of Distinction, Men of Letters, &c. in Different Parts of Europe. Which Contain, among Other Curious Relations, Accounts of the Policy and Manners of the Turks; Drawn from Sources That Have Been Inaccessible to Other Travellers. 3 vols. (letters) 1763

The Poetical Works of the Right Honourable Lady M—y W———y M———e (poetry) 1768

†*The Nonsense of Common-Sense* (essays) 1947

The Complete Letters of Lady Mary Wortley Montagu. 3 vols. (letters) 1965-67

‡*Essays and Poems and Simplicity, a Comedy* (essays, poetry, and drama) 1977

*This work includes the earlier *Court Poems*.

†This work was published as a periodical from December 16, 1737 to March 14, 1738.

‡This work contains the drama *Simplicity*, a free translation/adaptation of Pierre Carlet de Chamblain de Marivaux's *Le jeu de l'amour et du hasard* (1730).

M[ARY] A[STELL]   (essay date 1724)

[*Astell was an English writer of controversial feminist and theological essays. When her friend Montagu loaned her the manuscript of the "Turkish Embassy Letters" in 1724, Astell wrote a preface to the work on the blank pages of the manuscript. In the following excerpt from this preface, she enthusiastically recommends the letters.*]

> Let the *Male-Authors* with an envious eye
> Praise coldly, that they may the more decry:
> *Women* (at least I speak the Sense of some)
> This little Spirit of Rivalship o'recome.
> I read with transport, and with Joy I greet
> A Genius so Sublime and so Complete,
> And gladly lay my Laurels at her Feet. . . .

To the Reader.

I was going, like common Editors, to advertise the Reader of the Beautys and Excellencys of the Work laid before him; to tell him that the Illustrious Author had oppertunitys that other Travellers, whatever their Quality or Curiosity may be, cannot obtain, and a Genius capable of making the best Improvement of every oppertunity. But if the Reader, after perusing *one Letter* only, has not discernment to distinguish that natural Elegance, that delicacy of Sentiment and Observation, that easy gracefulness and lovely Simplicity (which is the Perfection of Writing) in which these **Letters** exceed all that has appear'd in this kind, or almost in any other, let him lay the Book down and leave it to those who have.

The noble Author had the goodness to lend me her M.S. to satisfy my Curiosity in some enquirys I made concerning her Travels. And when I had it in my hands, how was it possible to part with it! I once had the Vanity to hope I might acquaint the Public that it ow'd this invaluable Treasure to my Importunitys. But alas! The most Ingenious Author has condemn'd it to obscurity during her Life, and Conviction, as well as Deference, obliges me to yeild to her Reasons. However, if these **Letters** appear hereafter, when I am in my Grave, let *this*

attend them in testimony to Posterity, that among her Contemporarys *one Woman*, at least, was just to her Merit. (pp. 466-67)

I confess I am malicious enough to desire that the World shou'd see to how much better purpose the LADYS Travel than their LORDS, and that whilst it is surfeited with Male Travels, all in the same Tone and stuft with the same Trifles, a *Lady* has the skill to strike out a New Path and to embellish a worn-out Subject with variety of fresh and elegant Entertainment. For besides that Vivacity and Spirit which enliven every part and that inimitable Beauty which spreds thro the whole, besides that Purity of Style for which it may justly be accounted the Standard of the *English* Tongue, the Reader will find a more true and accurate Account of the Customs and Manners of the several Nations with whom the Lady Convers'd than he can in any other Author. But as her Ladyship's penetration discovers the inmost follys of the heart, so the candor of her Temper passes over them with an air of pity rather than reproach, treating with the politeness of a Court and gentleness of a Lady what the severity of her Judgment cannot but Condemn.

In short, let her own Sex at least do her Justice; Lay aside diabolical Envy and its Brother Malice with all their accursed Company, Sly Whispering, cruel backbiting, spiteful detraction, and the rest of that hideous crew, which I hope are very falsely said to attend the *Tea Table*, being more apt to think they haunt those Public Places where Virtuous Women never come. Let the Men malign one another, if they think fit, and strive to pul down Merit when they cannot equal it. Let us be better natur'd than to give way to any unkind or disrespectful thought of so bright an Ornament of our Sex, merely because she has better Sense. For I doubt not but our hearts will tell us that this is the Real and unpardonable Offence, whatever may be pretended. Let us be better Christians than to look upon her with an evil eye, only because the Giver of all good Gifts has entrusted and adorn'd her with the most excellent Talents. Rather let us freely own the Superiority of this Sublime Genius as I do in the sincerity of my Soul, pleas'd that a *Woman* Triumphs, and proud to follow in her Train. Let us offer her the *Palm* which is justly her due, and if we pretend to any Laurels, lay them willingly at her Feet. (p. 467)

M[ary] A[stell], "Mary Astell's Preface to the Embassy Letters," in The Complete Letters of Lady Mary Wortley Montagu: 1708-1720, Vol. I, *edited by Robert Halsband, Oxford at the Clarendon Press, 1965, pp. 466-67.*

ALEXANDER POPE   (poem date 1732-34)

[*Pope has been called the greatest English poet of his time and one of the most important in the history of world literature. As a critic and satirical commentator on eighteenth-century England, he was the author of work that represents the epitome of neoclassical thought. His famous remark, "The proper study of mankind is man," perfectly illustrates the temperament of his age, a time when influential thinkers severely narrowed the limits of human speculation. All of Pope's work demonstrates his love of restraint, clarity, order, and decorum. His greatness lies in his cultivation of style and wit, rather than sublimity and pathos, and this inclination shaped his criticism of other writers. Although he had once extravagantly praised Montagu, Pope frequently attacked her in his poetry after they quarreled sometime around 1728. The following excerpt (from a poem written sometime between 1732 and 1734) is just one example of his many scattered and scurrilous allusions to his former friend. Here, he slights Montagu ("Sappho") for slovenly habits. ("Rufa" is thought to*]

"The Rejected Poet," an 1854 painting by William Powell Frith, depicts Montagu laughing airily at an obviously smoldering Alexander Pope after hearing his declaration of love for her.

be Catharine Trotter, a dramatist and outspoken defender of John Locke's philosophy.)]

> Rufa, whose eye quick-glancing o'er the Park,
> Attracts each light gay meteor of a Spark,
> Agrees as ill with Rufa studying Locke,
> As Sappho's diamonds with her dirty smock,
> Or Sappho at her toilet's greasy task,
> With Sappho fragrant at an ev'ning Mask:
> So morning Insects that in muck begun,
> Shine, buzz, and fly-blow in the setting-sun.

                                        (p. 561)

> Alexander Pope, "Epistle II. To a Lady," in The Poems of Alexander Pope, *edited by John Butt, Yale University Press, 1963, pp. 559-69.*

[FRANCIS JEFFREY] (essay date 1803)

[*Jeffrey was a founder and editor of the* Edinburgh Review, *an influential magazine that helped raise the standards of periodical reviewing in early nineteenth-century Britain. Jeffrey's literary criticism is a characteristic example of the sentimental, or "impressionistic," critical thought common at the time. Jeffrey promoted a personal approach to literature that was sympathetic to the general principles of Romanticism. He believed that literature should be judged by a criterion of beauty, a beautiful work being one that inspired sensations of tenderness or pity in the reader. However, to inspire these emotions the artist must "employ only such objects as are the natural signs, or the inseparable concomitants of emotions, of which the greater part of mankind are susceptible." Thus it can be said that Jeffrey wanted literature* to be realistic, to avoid mysticism and metaphysics, and to observe standards of propriety. He also repudiated the influence of French aesthetics and stressed the dependence of literature on society. Jeffrey roundly attacked writers, such as William Wordsworth, who did not meet his standards, while exalting Shakespeare and the Elizabethan writers. He had little good to say about the Augustans, believing that they displayed wit but lacked imagination, lyricism, or an understanding of the elements of true poetry: of his own generation he praised the work of John Keats, Lord Byron, and Walter Scott. Jeffrey was also active politically, and his political beliefs often color his criticism. A liberal Whig, he supported the inclusion of the middle class in government and believed in principles of moderate social progress. In the following excerpt from a review of *The Works of the Right Honourable Lady Mary Wortley Montagu *(1803), Jeffrey appraises each series of Montagu's correspondence, treating as well her other works.*]

These volumes [of **The Works of the Right Honourable Lady Mary Wortley Montague**] are so very entertaining, that we ran them all through immediately upon their coming into our possession; and at the same time contain so little that is either difficult or profound, that we may venture to give some account of them to our readers without farther deliberation....

[The] very first series of letters with which we are presented, indicates a great deal of that talent for ridicule, and power of observation, by which [Lady Mary] afterwards became so famous and so formidable. These letters (about a dozen in number) are addressed to Mrs Wortley, the [sister] of her future husband; and, along with a good deal of girlish flattery and affectation, display such a degree of easy humour and sound penetration, as is not often to be met with in a damsel of nineteen, even in this age of precocity. (p. 507)

In the course of this correspondence with the [sister], Lady Mary appears to have conceived a very favourable opinion of the [brother]; and the next series of letters contains her antenuptial correspondence with that gentleman from 1710 to 1712. Though this correspondence has interested and entertained us as much at least as anything in the whole book, we are afraid that it will afford but little gratification to the common admirers of love letters. Her Ladyship, though endowed with a very lively imagination, seems not to have been very susceptible of violent or tender emotions, and to have imbibed a very decided contempt for sentimental and romantic nonsense, at an age which is commonly more indulgent. There are no raptures nor ecstacies, therefore, in these letters; no flights of fondness, nor vows of constancy, nor upbraidings of capricious affection. To say the truth, her Ladyship acts a part in this correspondence that is not often allotted to a female performer. Mr Wortley, though captivated by her beauty and her vivacity, seems evidently to have been a little alarmed at her love of distinction, her propensity to satire, and the apparent inconstancy of her attachments. Such a woman, he was afraid, would make rather an uneasy and extravagent companion to a man of plain understanding and moderate fortune; and he had sense enough to foresee, and generosity enough to explain to her, the risk to which their mutual happiness would be subjected by a rash and indissoluble union. Lady Mary, who probably saw her own character in a different light, and was at any rate biassed by her inclinations, appears to have addressed a great number of letters to him upon this occasion, and to have been at considerable pains to relieve him of his scruples, and restore his confidence in the substantial excellencies of her character. These letters, which are written with a great deal of female spirit and masculine sense, impress us with a very favourable notion of the talents and disposition of the writer (pp. 508-09)

[The letters] are certainly very uncommon productions for a young lady of twenty; and indicate a strength and elevation of character, that does not always appear in her gayer and more ostentatious performances. Mr Wortley was convinced and re-assured by them; and they were married in 1712. The con-cluding part of the first volume contains her letters to him for the two following years. There is not much tenderness in these letters, nor very much interest indeed of any kind. Mr Wortley appears to have been rather indolent and unambitious; and Lady Mary takes it upon her, with all delicacy and judicious man-agement, however, to stir him up to some degree of activity and exertion. There is a good deal of election news and small politics in these epistles. (p. 511)

To the end of [the first volume] is annexed a translation of the Enchiridion of Epictetus, executed by Lady Mary, when she was under twenty years of age. We have only read the first paragraph of it, in which we see, that 'opinion, appetite, aver-sion, desire, &c. are said to be altogether *in our power*;' which is evidently a false translation: Epictetus says only, that these things are our proper business and concern.

The second volume, and a part of the third, are occupied with those charming letters, written during Mr Wortley's embassy to Constantinople, upon which the literary reputation of Lady Mary has hitherto been exclusively founded. It would not be-come us to say any thing of productions which have so long engaged the admiration of the public. The grace and vivacity, the ease and conciseness, of the narrative, and the description which they contain, still remain unrivalled, we think, by any epistolary compositions in our language, and are but slightly shaded by a sprinkling of obsolete tittle-tattle, or womanish vanity and affectation. (p. 512)

[Another] series of letters consists of those written to her sister the Countess of Mar, from 1723 to 1727. These Letters have at least as much vivacity, wit, and sarcasm, as any that have been already published; and though they contain little but the anecdotes and scandal of the time, will long continue to be read and admired for the brilliancy and facility of the com-position. Though Lady Mary is excessively entertaining in this correspondence, we cannot say, however, that she is either very amiable, or very interesting; there is rather a negation of good affection, we think, throughout, and a certain cold-hearted levity that borders sometimes upon misanthropy, and some-times on indecency. (pp. 513-14)

In spite of all this gaiety, Lady Mary does not appear to have been happy. Her discreet biographer is silent upon the subjects of her connubial felicity; and we have no desire to revive forgotten scandal: but it is a fact, which cannot be omitted, that her Ladyship went abroad without her husband, on account of bad health, in 1739, and did not return to England till she heard of his death in 1761. Whatever was the cause of their separation, however, it did not produce any open rupture be-tween them; and she seems to have corresponded with him very regularly for the first ten years of her absence. These letters, which occupy the latter part of the third volume, and the beginning of the fourth, are by no means so captivating as any of the preceding series. They contain but little wit, and no confidential or striking reflections: They are filled up with accounts of her health and her journies, with short and general notices of any extraordinary customs she meets with, and little scraps of stale politics picked up in the petty courts of Italy. They are cold, in short, without being formal; and are gloomy and constrained, when compared with those which were spon-taneously written to show her wit, or her affection to her cor-

respondents. She seems extremely anxious to impress her hus-band with an exalted idea of the honours and distinction with which she was every where received; and really seems more elated and surprised than we should have expected the daughter of an English Duke to be, with the attentions that were shewn her by the noblesse of Venice, in particular. (pp. 516-17)

The last series of letters, which extends to the middle of the fifth volume, and comes down to the year 1761, consists of those that were addressed by Lady Mary, during her residence abroad, to her daughter the Countess of Bute. These letters, though somewhat less brilliant than those to the Countess of Mar, have more heat and affection in them than any other of her Ladyship's productions; and abound in lively and judicious reflections. They indicate at the same time a very great share of vanity, and that kind of contempt and indifference for the world, into which the veterans of fashion are most apt to sink. With the exception of her daughter and children, Lady Mary appears to have cared nothing for any human being; and rather to have beguiled the days of her declining life with every sort of amusement than to have soothed them with affection or friendship. (p. 517)

[Our] readers will easily be enabled to judge of the character and genius of this extraordinary woman. A little spoiled by flattery, and not altogether, 'undebauched by the world,' she seems to have possessed a masculine solidity of understanding, great liveliness of fancy, and such powers of observation and discrimination of character, as to give her opinions great au-thority on all the ordinary subjects of practical manners and conduct. After her marriage, she seems to have abandoned all idea of laborious or regular study, and to have been raised to the station of a literary character merely by her vivacity, and her love of amusement and anecdote. The great charm of her letters is certainly the extreme ease and facility with which every thing is expressed, the brevity and rapidity of her rep-resentations, and the elegant simplicity of her diction. While they unite almost all the qualities of a good style, there is nothing of the professed author in them: nothing that seems to have been composed, or to have engaged the admiration of the writer. She appears to be quite unconscious either of merit or of exertion in what she is doing; and never stops to bring out a thought, or to turn an expression, with the cunning of a practised rhetorician. The letters from Turkey will probably be more universally read than any of those that are now given for the first time to the public; because the subject commands a wider and more permanent interest, than the personalities and unconnected remarks with which the rest of the correspondence is filled. At the same time, the love of scandal and of private history is so great, that these letters will be highly relished, as long as the names they contain are remembered; and then they will become curious and interesting, as exhibiting a truer pic-ture of the manners and fashions of the time, than is to be found in any other publication.

The Fifth Volume contains also her Ladyship's poems, and two or three trifling papers that are entitled her ***Essays***. Poetry, at least the polite and witty sort of poetry, which Lady Mary has attempted, is much more of an art than prose-writing. We are trained to the latter, by the conversation of good society; but the former seems always to require a good deal of patient labour and application. This her Ladyship appears to have disdained; and accordingly, her poetry, through abounding in lively conceptions, is already consigned to that oblivion in which mediocrity is destined, by an irrevocable sentence, to slumber till the end of the world. The ***Essays*** are extremely insignificant, and have no other merit, that we can discover, but that they are very few and very short. (pp. 520-21)

[*Francis Jeffrey*], *"Lady Mary Wortley Montagu's Works,"* in The Edinburgh Review, *Vol. II, No. IV, July, 1803, pp. 507-21.*

THOMAS CARLYLE (essay date 1830)

[*A noted nineteenth-century essayist, historian, critic, and social commentator, Carlyle was a central figure of the Victorian Age in England. In his writings, Carlyle advocated a work ethic and stressed the importance of order, piety, and spiritual fulfillment. Known to his contemporaries as the "Sage of Chelsea," Carlyle exerted a powerful moral influence in an era of rapidly shifting values. In the following excerpt from an essay originally published in* The Edinburgh Encyclopaedia *in 1830, Carlyle comments approvingly on Montagu's letters.*]

Concerning the merits of Lady Montagu's poems, it is not necessary to say much. Suggested chiefly by ephemeral topics, they seem to have been written without great care. They are not polished, but across their frequent harshness and infelicity of expression, we can easily discern considerable vivacity of conception, accompanied with some acuteness in discriminating character and delineating manners. It is to be regretted that they are not always free from indelicacy.

But Lady Mary's principal merit is to be sought for in her letters. Those written during the embassy were loudly applauded at first, and they have since maintained a conspicuous place in this still scanty department of English literature. The official character of Mr. Wortley procured her admittance to whatever was splendid or attractive in every country which they visited. She seems to have been contented with herself, and therefore willing to be pleased with others; and her cheerful sprightly imagination, the elegance, the ease, and airiness of her style, are deservedly admired. Succeeding and more minute observers have confirmed the accuracy of her graphic descriptions. Her other letters are of a similar stamp. The continual gaiety, the pungent wit, with which she details the passing follies of a court, but too successfully imitating that of Louis xv., render her letters extremely amusing. In those written from her retirement at Lover, we discern the same shrewdness of observation, with a little more carelessness of expression. The pensive, calm regret, which they breathe, and, above all, the tender affection for her daughter, the Countess of Bute, to whom they are generally addressed, perhaps more than compensate for the absence of that flow of spirits and exuberance of incident, which distinguished the correspondence of her youth. In a literary point of view, Lady Mary's writings certainly do not belong to a very elevated class, but they occupy the first rank in their class. Considering the times and the circumstances of the writer, they may safely be called extraordinary. And, though the general diffusion of knowledge within the last century has rendered it common for females to write with elegance and skill upon far higher subjects, Lady Mary deserves to be remembered as the first Englishwoman, who combined the knowledge of classical and modern literature with a penetrating judgment and correct taste. (pp. 76-7)

Thomas Carlyle, "Lady Mary Wortley Montagu," in his Critical and Miscellaneous Essays, *Vol. V, Charles Scribner's Sons, 1901, pp. 70-7.*

[J. W. CROKER] (essay date 1837)

[*A noteworthy critic of literature and historical writings, Croker was instrumental in establishing the* Quarterly Review *as the preeminent conservative periodical of early-nineteenth-century Britain. In the following excerpt from a review of the 1837 edition of Montagu's works edited by her great-grandson Lord Wharncliffe, Croker evaluates the newly published letters, drawing on their evidence to judge also Montagu's character.*]

[*The Letters and Works of Lady Mary Wortley Montagu*] will, we fear, disappoint in some degree the public expectation; indeed it could hardly be otherwise. When a work is known to have been published with certain prudential restrictions, there is always a strong curiosity excited about the suppressed parts; and it is supposed that what has been concealed must be much more *piquant* than what has been published. This feeling exists especially with regard to private letters and memoirs, and in no case was it more likely to be pushed to its extreme than with regard to the gay, witty, and superabundantly frank correspondence of Lady Mary Wortley. 'When such things have been printed, what,' it is naturally asked, 'must that be which is kept back?' Now, in truth, in this as in most cases, it turns out that the suppressions have been much less important than was fancied; they bear but a small proportion to the whole work, and generally apply to matters—delicate perhaps at the moment of the first publication, but—of very little interest to the general reader of after-times. We cannot but suspect, also, that every reperusal of Lady Mary's *Letters* will tend to a doubt whether her merit has not been somewhat exaggerated. When they first appeared, a traveller and an author of Lady Mary's rank and sex was a double wonder—which was much increased by Lady Mary's personal circumstances, and by the vivacity, spirit, and boldness of her pen. But now that the extraneous sources of admiration have run dry, we confess that the intrinsic value of the letters seems less striking; and that if we were to deduct from Lady Mary's pleasantry and wit, those passages which a respectable woman ought not, perhaps, to have written, we should very considerably reduce her claims to literary eminence. The additional letters now produced will add little to Lady Mary's fame, and take little from her reputation. They exhibit her neither wittier nor looser than she was already known to be—on the contrary, the pleasantry and the coarseness being diluted, as it were, by a large addition of very commonplace matter, the *peculiarities* of Lady Mary appear on the whole, we think, less pungent than in the earlier editions. (pp. 147-48)

Besides the additions to the former correspondence, and Lady Louisa's anecdotes [see excerpt dated 1837], the editor states—

> The most considerable novelties to which this edition pretends, consist in the letters to Lady Pomfret, those to Sir James Steuart of Coltness, and Lady Frances;

but he does not here notice a more important class than either of those which he mentions, which is equally new to us, namely, twenty-four letters written between 1744 and 1750, to the Countess of Oxford. These letters are of a more sober cast than any of the others—the character of the amiable and respectable lady to whom they were addressed, seems to have sobered Lady Mary's fancy and formalized her style. The letters to Lady Pomfret are in a tone rather more lively; but the notes and letters to Sir James and Lady Frances Steuart—twenty-seven in number—seem to us as destitute of any talent or interest, as any batch of familiar letters in our language; and neither they nor even the letters to Ladies Oxford and Pomfret will, we are satisfied, add anything to Lady Mary's epistolary fame—but we do not, therefore, blame the noble editor for inserting them. His edition being intended *'to give a complete view of the character of Lady Mary,'* he has inserted much that a less honest editor might have suppressed, and he, therefore, does quite right in giving us the less lively but more respectable portion of her correspondence.

Indeed, we have been struck with the kind of instinctive skill which guided Lady Mary in suiting—we suspect unconsciously—her style to the characters of her correspondents. To her late and transient acquaintance, Sir James and Lady Frances Steuart, her letters are verbose and empty—to Lady Oxford, a high-bred lady of the old school, she talks the language of a grave and somewhat formal friendship—to Lady Pomfret, a kind of *Blue*, she intersperses her chit-chat with scraps of learning and antiquarianism—with her sister and Mrs. Hewet, the companions and confidants of her youth, she is giddy, sarcastic, and even coarse—towards her husband she always employs a sober, respectful, and business-like style—to her daughter, she mingles maternal tenderness with a decent pleasantry and much good sense—and finally (to end almost where she began), in the celebrated *Letters during the Embassy,*—which she obviously intended for the world at large, and which she therefore addressed to a variety of correspondents—there is a combination of the easy grace—the polished wit—the light humour—the worldly shrewdness of the clever and not over scrupulous woman of fashion. (pp. 151-52)

It is not without some hesitation that we venture to give any specimen of her ante-nuptial correspondence with Mrs. Hewet, which is replete with wit and shrewdness, but superabundantly sprinkled with something more than levity; but that which the Reverend Mr. Dallaway thought not unfit to be printed, and which Lord Wharncliffe has republished, we hope we may be forgiven for quoting, not merely as a sample of Lady Mary herself, but as a fact in the history of female manners, if not morals, in England. (p. 153)

> My poor head is distracted with such a variety of *gallimatias,* that I cannot tell you one bit of news. The fire I suppose you have had a long and true account of, though not perhaps that we were raised at three o'clock, and kept waking till five, by the most dreadful sight I ever saw in my life. It was near enough to fright all our servants half out of their senses: however, we escaped better than some of our neighbours. Mrs. Braithwayte, a Yorkshire beauty, who had been but two days married to a Mr. Coleman, ran out of bed *en chemise,* and her husband followed her in his, in which pleasant dress they ran as far as St. James's-street, where they met with a chair, and prudently crammed themselves both into it, observing the rule of dividing the good and bad fortune of this life, resolved to run all hazards together, and ordered the chairman to carry them both away, perfectly representing—both in love and nakedness, and want of eyes to see that they were naked—our first happy parents. Sunday last I had the pleasure of hearing the whole history from the lady's own mouth.

We do not pretend to know whether there is more female *virtue* now-a-days than 'in the reign of good Queen Anne,'—but we are confident that there is more both of *decency* and *delicacy,* and that there is not now an unmarried *Lady Mary* in England who would or *could* sully her paper with that species of wit which constitutes the chief merit of these letters to Mrs. Hewet.

To Lady Mary's strange argumentative love-letters to Mr. Wortley before marriage, already published, there is an addition

of half-a-dozen, exhibiting the same combination of sober calculation and headlong giddiness. (p. 154)

So odd a mixture of prudence and temerity,—so keen an eye to her own personal objects, and such blindness to all other considerations,—are very indicative of that wayward head and selfish heart which continued to misguide all her subsequent life. (p. 155)

Next to [the] *Letters during the Embassy,* the most important class for wit and cleverness at least, are those addressed to her sister Lady Mar, between 1720 and 1726. To about thirty letters of this class, thirteen or fourteen are now added. They are like their predecessors, light and gay, seasoned with a good deal of scandal and some rather coarse wit. (pp. 156-57)

We next arrive at the letters to Lady Pomfret, which commence in July, 1738, and end in 1742; they are of two classes; the first ten are written from London to Lady Pomfret in Italy, and are full of the tittle-tattle of the town—the other twenty-five were written abroad, and contain chiefly the anecdotes that she picks up of the travelling English, who then, as now, swarmed in Italy. (p. 161)

The next series of letters (which is divided, we know not why, into two, one ending in March, and the other beginning in May, 1744,) extends from her going abroad in 1739 to her return about 1760, and comprises her letters to her husband and her daughter Lady Bute, during that period, and are the most respectable, though not the most entertaining portion of the volumes. (p. 163)

To conclude. We are strongly persuaded, that Lady Mary Wortley's fame, both as an author and a woman, stood highest when it rested on the *Letters* during the embassy, in which her literary talent shines brightest and purest; and her maternal and moral courage in the introduction of innoculation by trying the experiment on her own son, gives her an honourable immortality as one of the benefactors of the human race. We regret to be obliged to express our opinion that every subsequent publication has impaired her character for good nature and good conduct—and, judging by the last of all which has appeared—this Appendix—we are warranted in suspecting that the more her life is examined, and the more her history is sifted, the less personally creditable they will be found. (p. 196)

> [*J. W. Croker*], *in a review of "Lady Mary Wortley Montagu's Letters &c.," in* The Quarterly Review, *Vol. LVIII, No. CXV, February, 1837, pp. 147-96.*

[LEIGH HUNT]   (essay date 1837)

[*An English poet, essayist, and cofounder of the liberal weekly the* Examiner, *Hunt is remembered as a literary critic who encouraged and influenced several fledgling Romantic poets, especially John Keats and Percy Bysshe Shelley. In his criticism, Hunt articulated the principles of Romanticism, emphasizing imaginative freedom and the expression of a personal emotional or spiritual state. Although his critical works were overshadowed by those of more prominent Romantic critics, such as his friends Samuel Taylor Coleridge, William Hazlitt, and Charles Lamb, his essays are considered both insightful and generous. In the following excerpt taken from the conclusion of an essay on Montagu's life and character, Hunt bids his subject farewell, defining and appraising her as he does so.*]

And so farewell, poor, flourishing, disappointed, reconciled, wise, foolish, enchanting Lady Mary! fair English vision in Turk-land; Turkish vision in ours; the female wit of the days of Pope; benefactress of thy species, irritating satirist of the circles. Thou didst err for want of a little more heart, perhaps for want of finding heart enough in others, or for loss of thy mother in infancy; but thy loss was our gain, for it gained us thy books and thy inoculation. Thy poems are little, being but a little wit in rhyme—*vers de société;* but thy prose is much; admirable, better than accurate, idiomatical, off-hand, conversational without inelegance, fresh as the laugh on thy young cheek, and full of brain. The conventional shows of things could not deceive thee: pity was it that thou didst not see a little farther into the sweets of things unconventional—of faith in the heart, as well as in the blood and good sense. Loveable indeed thou wert not, whatever thou mightst have been rendered; but admirable thou wert, and ever wilt thou be thought so, as long as pen writeth straight-forward, and sense or Sultana hath a charm. (pp. 163-64)

> [Leigh Hunt], *"Lady Mary Wortley Montagu," in*
> The London and Westminster Review, *Vol. XXVII,*
> *No. 1, April, 1837, pp. 130-64.*

LADY LOUISA STUART   (essay date 1837)

[*The first edition of Montagu's works to be sanctioned by her family appeared in 1837, edited by her great-grandson Lord Wharncliffe. The following excerpt is taken from a memoir, first published in this edition, written by Montagu's granddaughter (Lady Bute's daughter) Lady Louisa Stuart. Here, she compares her grandmother's letters with those of a well-known French predecessor, Marie de Rabutin-Chantal, Marquise de Sévigné.*]

Lady Mary Wortley's insensibility to the excellence, or, let us say, the charm of Madame de Sévigné's *Letters*, is the thing most surprising in her observations on liberary subjects; and it can only be accounted for by a marked opposition of character between the two women. The head was the governing power with the one, the heart with the other. If they had lived at the same time, and in the same country and society, they would not have accorded well together. Madame de Sévigné would have respected Lady Mary's talents, but rather dreaded than coveted her acquaintance. Lady Mary, in lieu of prizing that simplicity of mind which Madame de Sévigné so wonderfully preserved in the midst of such a world as surrounded her, might have been apt to confound it with weakness; and to hold in contempt not only her foible for court favour, but her passionate devotion to her daughter.

As writers also they were dissimilar: Lady Mary wrote admirable letters; *letters*—not dissertations, nor sentimental *effusions,* nor strings of witticisms, but real letters; such as any person of plain sense would be glad to receive. Her style, though correct and perspicuous, was unstudied, natural, flowing, spirited; she never used an unnecessary word, nor a phrase savouring of affectation; but still she meant to write well, and was conscious of having succeeded. Madame de Sévigné had no such consciousness; she did not so much *write,* as talk and think upon paper, with no other aim than to make Madame de Grignan present at every incident, and partaker of every feeling, throughout the twenty-four hours of her day. By this means she makes us present likewise; as we read, we see her, hear her, feel with her, enter into all her concerns. Not that she ever dreamt of pleasing us. "If the post knew what it carried," says she, "it would leave these packets by the wayside." "Keep my letters," said Lady Mary, on the contrary; "they will be as good as Madame de Sévigné's forty years hence." And in some measure she said true. What she terms the tittle-tattle of a fine lady would have lost nothing in her hands. She

could relate passing events, and satarise fashionable follies with as much vivacity and more wit than Madame de Sévigné herself; and there was more depth in her reflections, for she had the superiority in strength of understanding. But all that she sought to degrade by the epithet "tittle-tattle of an old nurse," including, as it does, so many touches of truth and nature; all the little traits that bring before our eyes the persons spoken of; all the details which render Les Rochers and Livry as interesting to us as Versailles; all this part, it must be confessed, lay out of Lady Mary's province; and she proved it did so by viewing it with disdain. (pp. cxxv-cxxvii)

> *Lady Louisa Stuart, "Introductory Anecdotes," in*
> The Letters and Works of Lady Mary Wortley Montagu, *Vol. I, edited by Lord Wharncliffe, revised edition, George Bell and Sons, 1887, pp. lxxi-cxxxviii.*

WALTER BAGEHOT   (essay date 1862)

[*Bagehot is regarded as one of the most versatile and influential authors of mid-Victorian England. In addition to literary criticism, he wrote several pioneering works in the fields of politics, sociology, and economics. As editor of the London* Economist, *he was instrumental in shaping the financial policy of his generation. Despite their diverse subject matter, Bagehot's works are unified by his emphasis on factual information and his interest in the personalities of literary figures, politiciams, and economists. Many modern commentators contend that it is partially because of the readable quality of his prose that Bagehot's writings, which were primarily composed as journalistic pieces, are still enjoyed today. In the following excerpt from an essay originally published in the* National Review *in 1862, Bagehot assesses the interest and worth of Montagu's letters to a nineteenth-century audience.*]

Nothing is so transitory as second-class fame. The name of Lady Mary Wortley Montagu is hardly now known to the great mass of ordinary English readers. A generation has arisen which has had time to forget her. Yet only a few years since, an allusion to the 'Lady Mary' would have been easily understood by every well-informed person; young ladies were enjoined to form their style upon hers; and no one could have anticipated that her letters would seem in 1862 as different from what a lady of rank would then write or publish as if they had been written in the times of paganism. The very change however, of popular taste and popular morality gives these letters now a kind of interest. The farther and the more rapidly we have drifted from where we once lay, the more do we wish to learn what kind of port it was. We venture, therefore, to recommend the letters of Lady Mary Wortley Montagu as an instructive and profitable study, not indeed to the youngest of young ladies, but to those maturer persons of either sex 'who have taken all knowledge to be their province,' and who have commenced their readings in 'universality' by an assiduous perusal of Parisian fiction.

It is, we admit, true that these letters are not at the present day very agreeable reading. What our grandfathers and grandmothers thought of them it is not so easy to say. But it now seems clear that Lady Mary was that most miserable of human beings, an ambitious and wasted woman; that she brought a very cultivated intellect into a very cultivated society; that she gave to that society what it was most anxious to receive, and received from it all which it had to bestow;—and yet that this all was to her as nothing. The high intellectual world of England has never been so compact, so visible in a certain sense, so enjoyable, as it was in her time. She had a mind to understand it, beauty to adorn it, and wit to amuse it; but she chose to pass a great part of her life in exile, and returned at last to die at home among a new generation, whose name she hardly knew, and to whom she herself was but a spectacle and a wonder. (pp. 221-22)

She lived abroad for more than twenty years, at Avignon and Venice and elsewhere; and, during that absence, she wrote the letters which compose the greater part of her works. And there is no denying that they are good letters. The art of note-writing may become classical—it is for the present age to provide models of that sort of composition—but letters have perished. Nobody but a bore now takes pains enough to make them pleasant; and the only result of a bore's pains is to make them unpleasant. The correspondence of the present day is a continual labour without any visible achievement. The dying penny-a-liner said with emphasis, 'That which I have written has perished.' We might all say so of the mass of petty letters we write. They are a heap of small atoms, each with some interest individually, but with no interest as a whole; all the items concern us, but they all add up to nothing. In the last century, cultivated people who sat down to write a letter took pains to have something to say, and took pains to say it. The postage was perhaps ninepence; and it would be impudent to make a correspondent pay ninepence for nothing. Still more impudent was it, *after* having made him pay ninepence, to give him the additional pain of making out what was half expressed. People, too, wrote to one another then, not unfrequently, who had long been separated, and who required much explanation and many details to make the life of each intelligible to the other. The correspondence of the nineteenth century is like a series of telegrams with amplified headings. There is not more than one idea; and that idea comes soon, and is soon over. The best correspondence of the last age is rather like a good light article,—in which the points are studiously made,—in which the effort to make them is studiously concealed,—in which a series of selected circumstances is set forth,—in which you feel, but are not told, that the principle of the writer's selection was to make his composition pleasant.

In letter-writing of this kind Lady Mary was very skilful. She has the highest merit of letter-writing—she is concise without being affected. Fluency, which a great orator pronounced to be the curse of orators, is at least equally the curse of writers. There are many people, many ladies especially, who can write letters at any length, in any number, and at any time. We may be quite sure that the letters so written are not good letters. Composition of any sort implies consideration; you must see where you are going before you can go straight, or can pick your steps as you go. On the other hand, too much consideration is unfavourable to the ease of letter-writing, and perhaps of all writing. A letter too much studied wants flow; it is a museum of hoarded sentences. Each sentence sounds effective; but the whole composition wants vitality. It was written with the memory instead of the mind; and every reader feels the effect, though only the critical reader can detect the cause. Lady Mary understood all this. She said what she had to say in words that were always graphic and always sufficiently good, but she avoided curious felicity. Her expressions seem choice, but not chosen. (pp. 251-53)

Lady Mary did not live long after her return to England. . . . *Requiescat in pace;* for she quarrelled all her life. (p. 254)

Walter Bagehot, "Lady Mary Wortley Montagu," in his Literary Studies, Vol. 1, *edited by Richard Holt Hutton, 1878. Reprint by Longmans, Green, and Co., 1884, pp. 221-54.*

LYTTON STRACHEY   (essay date 1905)

[*Strachey was an English literary critic and biographer whose iconoclastic reexaminations of historical figures helped fix the course of modern biography. Conceiving of biography as an integration of established facts, speculative psychological interpretations, and imaginative recreations of his subjects' thoughts and actions, Strachey wrote biographies considered lively, perceptive, and above all "human" portraits. Like his biographies, Strachey's literary criticism is deemed incisive and interestingly written. In the following excerpt from an essay written in 1905, Strachey describes Montagu's personality and character of thought as revealed in her letters.*]

It is curious that the two ladies who have won the greatest reputation as letter writers should present so complete a contrast. Lady Mary Wortley Montagu certainly bears out Professor Raleigh's dictum that in the eighteenth century man lived up to his definition and was a rational animal; and "a rational animal" is precisely the last designation which anyone would dream of applying to Madame de Sévigné. "How many readers and admirers," exclaims Lady Mary, "has Madame de Sévigné, who only gives us, in a lively manner and fashionable phrases, mean sentiments, vulgar prejudices, and endless repetitions! Sometimes the tittle-tattle of a fine lady, sometimes that of an old nurse, always tittle-tattle." Nothing could be more unjust; and the injustice obviously springs from an utter lack of sympathy. Lady Mary was the least feminine of women, and Madame de Sévigné was the most. The delicacy, the charm, the tenderness, of the French lady's letters were lost upon the virile mind of the English one. Lady Mary's flashing wit tossed aside the elegance of Madame de Sévigné's with the disdain of a steel rapier tossing aside a piece of silver filigree-work. What could be the value of such a bauble? It was only meant for show!

"Few women would have spoken so plainly as I have done," Lady Mary wrote in the first of her letters to Edward Wortley; "but to dissemble is among the things I never do." And a certain outspoken clarity is perhaps the most conspicuous characteristic of all her letters. She is always absolutely frank and absolutely sensible; yet she manages never to be heavy. Her wit has that quality which is the best of all preservatives against dullness—it goes straight to the point. If she had been a little less sensible, she would have been an eccentric; if she had been a little less witty she would have been a prig. "To say truth," she wrote, at the age of sixty-six, "I think myself an uncommon kind of creature, being an old woman without superstition, peevishness, or censoriousness." The account was true of all the periods of her life.

Her freedom from prejudice, which was so strikingly demonstrated by her introduction into England of the practice of inoculation, adds a peculiar interest to her letters. Her views on the education of women were especially in advance of her age. (pp. 22-3)

Lady Mary is not always . . . serious. Her letters abound in pointed remarks and spicy anecdotes; and her comments on the persons of her acquaintance are usually most amusing when they are most vitriolic. She is at her best when she is telling her correspondent of the history of some "beauteous virgin of forty," and how "after having refused all the peers in England, because the nicety of her conscience would not permit her to give her hand when her heart was untouched, she remained without a husband till the charms of that fine gentleman, Mr. Smith, who is only eight-two, determined her to change her condition." (p. 24)

Every reader of Lady Mary must observe, without subscribing to Pope's scurrilities about "Sappho," that a sense of propriety seems rarely to stand in the way of her sense of humour. She was the last person to beat about the bush, when there was a point to be made by plain speaking; and such were precisely the points which presented themselves most frequently to her mind. Thus, when she is coarse, she is always coarse directly; she does not wrap up her meaning in a veil of innuendoes; so that her indecencies have at least this merit: they are nothing if not healthy. Nor can they be denied the saving grace of wit. (p. 25)

Lady Mary's straightforwardness was not without its drawbacks. It is only by striking very hard that one can hit the nail on the head; and Lady Mary, solely occupied with that operation, wasted none of her energies in delicate touches. Her letters are all in one key—the C major of this life. They express no subtleties, no discriminations, no changes of mood. They flash; but with a metallic light. Their writer, one feels, was far too sensible either to sink or to soar; and it is an open question whether she was ever much excited. Describing her discussions with the Jesuits, she wrote: "I have always the advantage of being quite calm on a subject which they cannot talk of without heat." And that was her attitude in every relation of her life. Her very love-letters were made up of arguments upon the ethics of marriage. Her philosophy of life, though it was too witty to be dull, was too dispassionate to be true. The real nature of things was hidden from her, because she could never throw herself into its midst. (p. 26)

Lytton Strachey, "Lady Mary Wortley Montagu and Lord Chesterfield," in his Characters and Commentaries, *Harcourt Brace Jovanovich, 1933, pp. 22-30.*

GEORGE PASTON [PSEUDONYM OF EMILY MORSE SYMONDS] (essay date 1907)

[*An English author, Symonds wrote novels and plays of a feminist cast, including* A Modern Amazon *(1894) and* Nobody's Daughter *(1910). In the following excerpt from a biography of Montagu, Symonds renders her impression of the letters and personality of her enigmatic subject.*]

Although the *dossier* of Lady Mary Wortley is voluminous enough in all conscience, the problem of her complex "personality" still remains unsolved. Her character has stood its trial now for a century and a half, but when the evidence for the prosecution and the defence is impartially examined, an open verdict must be pronounced. Was she a woman of gallantry, heartless and shameless, as described by Pope and Horace Walpole, or was she a brilliant specimen of the eighteenth-century great lady, witty, charming, and beautiful, as she appeared to her numerous admirers? Or yet again, was she the intelligent, thoughtful woman, of exceptional culture and blameless conduct, who won the friendship of such irreproachable dames as Mary Astell, Lady Oxford, and the Duchess of Portland? Contemporary witnesses contradict each other so flatly that the answer to each of these questions must be "not proven."

Lady Mary's personal correspondence only confuses the points at issue, for she was mistress of a bewildering variety of styles. As one of her critics has pointed out, when writing to her sister and her early friend, Mrs. Hewet, she is giddy, sarcastic, and sometimes coarse; to Lady Oxford she talks the language of a grave and formal friendship; to Lady Pomfret she intersperses her chit-chat with scraps of learning; to her late and transient acquaintances, the Steuarts, her letters are verbose and empty;

towards her husband she employs a sober, business-like style; to her daughter she mingles maternal tenderness with a decent complacency and much good sense; and, finally, in the *Letters during the Embassy,* which she intended for the world at large, there is a combination of the easy grace, the polished wit, the light humour, the worldly shrewdness of the clever and not over-scrupulous woman of fashion. (pp. 539-40)

It will hardly be contended nowadays, even by her most ardent admirers, that Lady Mary was a "poet," for her mind was the reverse of poetical. Her verses are always fluent, often lively, and sometimes forcible. She is at her best when she paints the manners of her times, as in the *Town Eclogues,* for her serious satires, even at their highest level, are but a far-away imitation of Pope. The prose *Essays* that are published with her other Remains, are trite enough, and show that her talent did not work easily in that form. It is to the *Letters,* and the *Letters* alone, that she owes her little niche in the Temple of Fame. And yet Lady Mary was lacking in many of the qualities that are generally found in famous letter-writers. She had little sympathy or imagination, and no sentiment. She was not even strikingly witty in the modern sense of the word, for her writings contain no fireworks, and few bons-mots or set epigrams. But then the "wit" of the eighteenth century was nothing so trivial as the cracking of jokes; it might better be defined as the felicitous expression of a glorified common sense. Lady Mary, in her youth, wrote in a dashing, high-spirited, vigorous

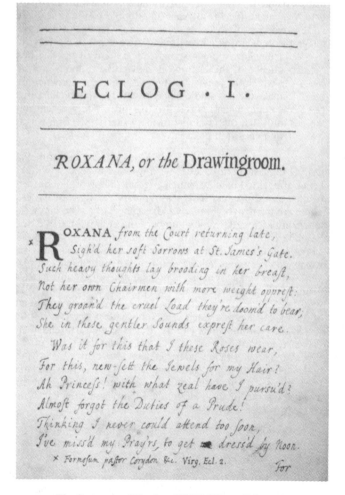

The first page of the first (1716) "Town Eclogue."

style; she was not always accurate, consistent, or impartial, but she dealt freely and fearlessly with the people she knew, and with the social topics of the day. It was, of course, her good fortune to live in exciting times and among famous people, but it is her own keen interest in the life about her that compels the interest of her readers. In her later letters, when her high spirits had sobered down, and the philosophy that she fondly believed to be founded on the purest Stoicism, was tinctured by the natural bitterness of the disappointed elderly woman, she makes less effort to entertain. She gives out the fruits of her long experience of the narrow clique that to her represented "the world," and of her eager though not impartial study of the fashionable folk that to her represented "human nature." She does not attempt to shine, but there is something curiously impressive in her downright, matter-of-fact, forcible style, as she records her opinions and recollections, or chronicles some dramatic incident from the life in her Italian village. (pp. 542-43)

> *George Paston [pseudonym of Emily Morse Symonds], in her* Lady Mary Wortley Montagu and Her Times, *G. P. Putnam's Sons, 1907, 559 p.*

PAUL ELMER MORE   (essay date 1908)

[*More was an American critic who, along with Irving Babbitt, formulated the doctrines of New Humanism in early twentieth-century American thought. The New Humanists were strict moralists who adhered to traditional conservative values in reaction to what they deemed an age of scientific and artistic self-expression. In regard to literature, they considered a work's implicit reflection of support for the classic ethical norms to be as important as its aesthetic qualities. More is especially esteemed for the philosophical and literary erudition of his multi-volume* Shelburne Essays *(1904-21). In the following excerpt from an essay originally published in the* Atlantic Monthly *in 1908, he favorably appraises Montagu's skill as a writer of travel letters.*]

In 1716 Mr. Wortley was appointed Ambassador to the Porte, and on August 1, he, with his wife, three-year-old son, and suite set out for Constantinople. I shall not follow them on their journey across the Continent, nor try to give an account of what Lady Mary saw, and so vividly described, in Paris and Vienna, in the wild regions of Hungary, and then in the home of the Turk. She was an ideal traveller, adapting herself facilely to the customs of the place, and feeling no prudish alarm at the different moral codes that met her. In particular she writes with curious complacency of the Austrian "sub-marriages," and remarks of the Italian ladies that "the custom of cicisbeos has very much improved their airs." It is only fair to add her amusing apology from Vienna: "I'll assure you, a lady, who is very much my friend here, told me but yesterday, how much I was obliged to her for justifying my conduct in a conversation on my subject, where it was publicly asserted that I could not possibly have common-sense, that I had been about town above a fortnight, and had made no steps toward commencing an amour." And at Constantinople she found the ways of life peculiarly to her taste; the Turkish women she declared to be "the only free people in the empire."

All these things she described in letters of which, after the manner of the age, she kept faithful, or unfaithful, copies, or which she afterwards wrote up for the half-public from her diaries. On them her fame as a writer depends almost exclusively to-day, and it must be admitted that they fully deserve their reputation. Letters of travel somehow have generally less staying power than those from home; what they give can be better given in a formal treatise, while they miss the little

touches of satire and friendship, the pleasant familiarities, the display of character at ease in its proper environment, which make the charm or the humour of the best correspondence. These homelier qualities for the most part Lady Mary's epistles, as they may be called, do not possess. But they have other traits, rarer, if less engaging. She shows a kind of familiarity with things strange, which carries the reader with her. Her language is clear and firm, but less formal than that of Pope and Bolingbroke and the other professed epistolary authors of the day. She puts a curb on their incurable trick of dealing in moral platitudes. In a word, she strikes the happy and difficult balance between the general and the particular, the descriptive and the personal. She stands to the front among the second grade of letter-writers. (pp. 165-67)

> *Paul Elmer More, "Lady Mary Wortley Montagu,"*
> in his With the Wits: Shelburne Essays, tenth series,
> Houghton Mifflin Company, 1919, pp. 153-85.

GEORGE SAINTSBURY   (essay date 1916)

[*The author of numerous studies of European literature, Saintsbury has been called the most influential English literary historian and critic of the late nineteenth and early twentieth centuries. René Wellek has praised Saintsbury's critical qualities: his "enormous reading, the almost universal scope of his subject matter, the zest and zeal of his exposition," and "the audacity with which he handles the most ambitious and unattempted arguments." In the following excerpt, Saintsbury observes general characteristics of Montagu's "perennially readable" letters.*]

[Lady Mary Wortley Montagu's] verse flashes with the very best paste in Dodsley; and, for its purposes and in its place, we do not care to test it for pure diamond quality. In prose the famous letters have found few detractors, though somehow it seems to me that of late years she has found fewer eulogists than formerly, and than she deserves. If this means that she has fewer readers it is a pity, because it would be an additional proof of that apparently *incapacitating* effect of modernity . . . which seems to be making it more and more impossible for people to take an interest in anything but the "cackle of their bourg" and their day. The brilliant and varied pictures of scenes and manners, both in her earlier and in her later time; the occasional shrewd literary criticisms (she was, it must be remembered, Fielding's cousin, and had other literary blood in her); the unfailing acuteness (sometimes no doubt passing into "cuttingness") of her remarks on men and things; the easy, fluent style, neither slipshod nor stilted; the interest in all manner of things which brought about her famous introduction of inoculation, and lasted through her life—all these merits and others make her perennially readable. There may be . . . too much "light without love;" a somewhat hard intellectualism, which, if there were nothing else on the earth, would make rather arid pasture. . . . Lady Mary is not "adorable" like her French predecessor [Mme. de Sévigné] but she is very frequently admirable and always enjoyable. She never "wrote herself out"; the later letters (sometimes idly doubted as questionably genuine) are as good as the earlier, and even show a certain progress. (pp. 215-16)

> *George Saintsbury, "Letters, Diaries, and the Like,"*
> in his The Peace of the Augustans: A Survey of
> Eighteenth Century Literature as a Place of Rest and
> Refreshment, *G. Bell and Sons, Ltd., 1916, pp.
> 213-57.*

LEWIS MELVILLE [PSEUDONYM OF LEWIS SAUL BENJAMIN] (essay date 1925)

[*"Lewis Melville" was the pen name of Lewis Saul Benjamin, an early-twentieth-century English biographer. He wrote lives of William Makepeace Thackeray, Tobias Smollett, John Gay, and Montagu, among others. In the following excerpt from his biography of Montagu, Benjamin offers a general assessment of her status as a writer of letters, emphasizing her relations with her contemporaries.*]

Lady Mary Wortley Montagu has her niche in the history of medicine as having introduced inoculation from the Near East into England; but her principal fame is as a letter-writer.

Of her gifts as a correspondent she was proud, and with reason. It was in all sincerity that in June, 1726, she wrote to her sister, Lady Mar: "The last pleasures that fell in my way was Madame Sévigné's letters: very pretty they are, but I assert, without the least vanity, that mine will be full as entertaining forty years hence. I advise you, therefore, to put none of them to the use of waste paper." And again, later in the year, she said half-humorously to the same correspondent: "I writ to you some time ago a long letter, which I perceive never came to your hands: very provoking; it was certainly a *chef d'œuvre* of a letter, and worthy any of the Sévigné's or Grignan's, crammed with news." That Lady Mary's belief in herself was well founded no one has disputed. Even Horace Walpole, who detested her and made attacks on her whenever possible, said that "in most of her letters the wit and style are superior to any letters I have ever read but Madame de Sévigné's" [see Additional Bibliography]. A very pleasant tribute from one who had a goodly conceit of himself as a letter-writer.

Walpole, as a correspondent, was perhaps more sarcastic and more witty; Cowper undoubtedly more tender and more gentle; but Lady Mary had qualities all her own. She had powers of observation and the gift of description, which qualities are especially to be remarked in the letters she wrote when abroad with her husband on his Mission to the Porte. She had an ironic wit which gave point to the many society scandals she narrated, a happy knack of gossip, and a style so easy as to make reading a pleasure.

Some of the incidents which Lady Mary retails with so much humour may be accepted as not outraging the conventions of the early eighteenth century when it was customary to call a spade a spade; when gallantry was gallantry indeed, and the pursuit of it openly conducted. What is not mentioned by those who have written about her is that she was possessed of a particularly unsavoury strain of impropriety which outraged even the canons of her age. Some twenty years after her death, it was mentioned in the *Gentleman's Magazine* that Dr. Young, the author of *Night Thoughts,* had a little before his death destroyed a great number of her letters, assigning as a reason of his doing so that they were too indecent for public inspection. (pp. vii-viii)

Lady Mary's most redoubtable assailants were Pope and Horace Walpole, and both were biassed. . . . Walpole, it has been suggested, disliked her much because she had championed her father's mistress, Molly Skerritt, against the mother to whom he was devoted. Pope, of course, knew her well; but Walpole, who was twenty-eight years her junior, only met her in her late middle age. Walpole's prejudice was so great that when Lady Mary said, "People wish their enemies dead—but I do not, I say, give them the gout, give them the stone," he reported it solemnly.

Of course, it is not to be assumed that Lady Mary had not her full share of malice—she was undoubtedly well equipped with that useful quality—and she did not turn the other cheek when she was assailed. She could even stand up to the vitriolic Sarah, Duchess of Marlborough, and stand up so effectively that they tacitly agreed to an armed neutrality that verged perilously upon friendship. The young Duke of Wharton sometimes beat her in open fight, but she harboured no very angry feelings towards him. As regards Pope, if it was not tit-for-tat with him, at least she gave him hard knocks. Pope, great poet as he was, never played fair in war.

"Lady Mary, quite contrary," she might have been dubbed, for she was frequently in trouble. . . . [Her] witty tongue made her many enemies and cost her many friends. Had the contents of her letters about London society become known at the time, nearly every man's and all women's hands would have been against her. She had, in fact, little that was kind to say about people; when she had, she usually refrained from mentioning it. (pp. xi-xii)

Lewis Melville [*pseudonym of Lewis Saul Benjamin*], *in his* Lady Mary Wortley Montagu: Her Life and Letters (1689-1762), *Houghton Mifflin Company, 1925, 320 p.*

LEWIS GIBBS [PSEUDONYM OF JOSEPH WALTER COVE] (essay date 1949)

[*In the following excerpt from his biography of Montagu, Gibbs favorably appraises her letters—for which, he claims, "she belongs to the classics"—and other writings.*]

It is chiefly for the sake of her letters that [Lady Mary] is remembered. Letters are personal and even intimate things, but hers, though written with perfect ease, were never careless. The public could have looked in on them at any moment and found them dressed and fit to be seen. No doubt the thought often occurred to her that they might one day make their appearance in all the dignity of print, but it was not for this reason that she wrote them so excellently. Her artistic instinct forbade her to do otherwise. This is the only sense in which they can be called artificial, for affectation was no failing of hers.

'Nothing,' observes Walter Bagehot, 'is so transitory as second-class fame. The name of Lady Mary Wortley Montagu is hardly now known to the great mass of ordinary English readers. A generation has arisen which has had time to forget her. Yet only a few years since, an allusion to "Lady Mary" would have been easily understood by every well-informed person; young ladies were enjoined to form their style upon hers; and no one could have anticipated that her letters would seem in 1862 as different from what a lady of rank would then write or publish as if they had been written in the times of paganism' [see excerpt dated 1862]. *Popular taste and poular morality* had changed by 1862—but then, they have since changed again. And there is more than one kind of second-class fame, and one kind, at least, is not transitory; namely, that which depends on real, though limited, excellence. Now this is Lady Mary's case: her quality is that of the artist, and it is for this reason that her letters have endured. In other words, she belongs to the classics, and though her place among them is a comparatively humble one, she shares their peculiar power to defy time and change.

Letters may be interesting because they deal with great events and important persons; because they are written by someone about whom people want to know as much as possible; or because they lay before the reader, with unexpected and fascinating clearness, the character of the writer. Lady Mary's letters depend hardly at all upon any of these things. It is true that she went to Constantinople, and lived a long while in Italy; and that her relations and friends belonged to the world of fashion and distinction. But these were only accidents and she owes none of her excellence to them. When Horace Walpole read the Embassy letters in 1763, he found them entertaining, but, on the whole, was disappointed: they had very little *personal interest*. The same remark might be made of nearly all Lady Mary's letters. She tells us what she sees and hears, and something of what she does. She makes reflections and passes judgments. But all this does not reveal, and is not intended to reveal, herself. She had no turn for self-revelation, and would certainly have considered it indecent. Now and then she lets fall something which surprises us—something not at all in keeping with the idea we had formed of her. Who would have thought she had any skill in making custards, French rolls, and so forth? And who would have expected the quaint touch of prudery which appears in her being shocked because Richardson's Mr. Lovelace kissed his cousins? 'I should have been much astonished,' she told her daughter primly, 'if Lord Denbigh should have offered to kiss me; and I dare swear Lord Trentham never attempted such an impertinence to you.'

She was not at all unwilling that her own letters should be compared with those of Madame de Sévigné, whom she surpassed in strength of intellect, keenness of wit, and vigorous grace of style. These were the qualities by which she herself set most store: the Frenchwoman had others which the world rightly thinks more valuable, and which were notably wanting in Lady Mary. For her part she did not care about such qualities, and thought them suitable for nothing better than *tittle-tattle*. It was inevitable that her own subject-matter should often have a feminine air, but there was something decidedly masculine in her style, and likewise in her way of looking at things. Brilliant as her letters are, they have very little humanity, and give more light than warmth. They appeal to the mind but not to the heart, and arouse admiration rather than affection. Still, when these limitations have been admitted, she has virtues enough left and will not lack readers until wit, elegance, independent thought, and a complete freedom from cant are no longer valued.

As for her other writings, Jeffrey, dealing in the *Edinburgh Review* with the 1803 edition, dismissed her essays as having no other merit 'but that they are very few and very short' [see excerpt dated 1803]. They are, in fact, far too few and too short for much to be said about them: still, they are well written and sensible. 'Her poetry,' observed the same critic (whose opinions were quite as positive as those of Lady Mary herself), 'though abounding in lively conceptions, is already consigned to that oblivion in which mediocrity is destined, by an irrevocable sentence, to slumber till the end of the world.'

The eighteenth century was over and the day of the romantics had dawned. Pope himself had to suffer the same kind of treatment as Lady Mary: the question was not what rank he should hold among the poets, but whether he was a poet at all. Her reputation does not depend on her verses, but Jeffrey was too hasty in consigning them so lightly to oblivion. They have real merit, though not of a very high kind. The truth is, they do not aspire very high, for it was a virtue of Lady Mary's that she generally confined her attempts to what she knew she was fitted to do well. The best of her pieces would make a

Letter, dated 15 August 1712, from Montagu to her husband.

creditable figure in any extensive collection of verse, and there are few which fail to provide the discerning reader with entertainment—praise to which many a far greater poet cannot justly lay claim. (pp. 239-42)

> *Lewis Gibbs [pseudonym of Joseph Walter Cove], in his* The Admirable Lady Mary: The Life and Times of Lady Mary Wortley Montagu (1689-1762), *William Morrow and Company, 1949, 255 p.*

ROBERT HALSBAND (essay date 1978)

[*In the following excerpt, Halsband investigates Montagu's feminism as it is displayed throughout her writings.*]

[Lady Mary Wortley Montagu's] ideas and writings on feminism and her career as a miscellaneous writer deserve re-examination now because they are clarified and amplified in the recenty published edition of her wide-ranging prose and verse [*Essays and Poems and Simplicity,* edited by Halsband and Isobel Grundy]. It may seem anachronistic to call an eighteenth-century woman a feminist, a word applied to that movement a century later, yet Lady Mary, because of her life-long preoccupation with women as women, their privileges and disabilities, rights and wrongs, deserves an honorable place in that movement.

Lady Mary was an aristocratic, stubborn, and self-educated woman. Her dates, 1689 to 1762, span the lifetimes of the two most conspicuous feminist women of the century—Mary Astell (whom she knew) and Mary Wollstonecraft. She is thus one of a trinity of Marys. Unlike the other two she did not enunciate feminist principles in boldly signed pamphlets and books advocating that cause with revolutionary fervor. Yet she states or clearly implies this doctrine in her private correspondence with friends and family, and in her essays and poems, whether published or not. As a feminist she earns her credentials also by her vigorous activity in the profession of writing, which in her time was dominated by men. What better proof of women's equality with the other sex than competing on this intellectual battlefield!

Lady Mary's feminist ideas were not static, but became emancipated as she grew older. Whether or not women are inferior to men was a frequently debated question, and often decided on a theological basis. When Lady Mary, at the age of twenty-one, translated the *Enchiridion* of Epictetus (from a Latin version) and sent it to Bishop Burnet for correction she says this of women: "I am not now arguing for an Equality for the 2 Sexes; I do not doubt God and Nature has thrown us into an Inferior Rank. We are a lower part of the Creation; we owe Obedience and Submission to the Superior Sex; and any Woman who suffers her Vanity and folly to deny this, Rebells against the Law of the Creator and indisputable Order of Nature." No doubt her conventional posture was stiffened by her awareness that the good Bishop was not guilty of holding advanced notions of creatures whose genealogy begins with Adam's rib. (It was he who probably dissuaded the future Queen Anne from endowing the college for women as envisioned by Mary Astell.) Like any sensitive letter-writer Lady Mary tailored her ideas to her correspondents' interests and expectations.

Forty years later, as an expatriate in Italy—when she boasted of being "old without peevishness, superstition, or slander"—she writes that in her opinion "Nature has not plac'd us in an inferior Rank to Men, no more than the Females of other Animals, where we see no distinction of capacity, thô I am persuaded if there was a Common-wealth of rational Horses (as Doctor Swift has suppos'd) it would be an establish'd maxim amongst them that a mare could not be taught to pace." Whether or not women were intrinsically inferior to men was a moot question since they were undoubtedly treated as though they were, especially in their education.

Certainly Lady Mary believed that women were worthy of a more thorough and advanced education than they were allowed; and she proved it by her own strenuous self-education as well as by her general prescription. While living in Avignon (in the 1740's) she composed a brief essay in French on the subject of women's education. Apparently written only for her own amusement, it is in the form of an imaginary letter to an unnamed literary lady of a past age who now resides in the Elysian Fields. At the present time, writes Lady Mary, everything is decided from a political point of view, "and it is by this that I should aspire to prove that learning is very necessary for women." Most women, she continued,

> are brought up in such gross ignorance that it is enough for them to mumble some paternosters, in order to believe themselves inspired by Heaven, and consequently worthy of managing everything at home, scorning their husbands and maltreating their servants. I dare boldly say that the behaviour of most women does more harm than good. . . . I attribute this corruption to the bad education which stifles the nat-

ural wit of some, and increases the foolishness of others. If men would only see us as an element in the state (for I submit to inferiority although I could name a thousand who have written, as you know, to prove the equality of the sexes) they ought to strive to use all talents profitably. Our frailty prevents us from serving in war, but this same frailty gives us great leisure for study. Those who succeed will be able to contribute to the Republic of Letters, and those who do not succeed will at least avoid idleness with all its consequences.

A few years later, from her Italian retirement, she returned to the subject in letters to her daughter. In England, she insists, women are treated with contempt; they "are educated in the grossest ignorance, and no art [is] omitted to stiffle [their] natural reason"—as though, she adds—"the same Studies which raise the character of a Man should hurt that of a Woman." The paradox of this injustice, she points out, is men's fear that improving the understanding of women would only "furnish [them] with more art to deceive them, which is directly contrary to the Truth."

At the same time Lady Mary admitted that excessive show of learning in a woman could be as undesirable as ignorance; she had always "thought the reputation of learning a misfortune to a woman." Indeed, while surreptitiously studying Latin as a young woman she sent Bishop Burnet her translation and acknowledged that the world despised and ridiculed "a Learned Woman. Them words imply. . .a tatling, impertinent, vain, and Conceited Creature." But, she continued, only superficial learning has this effect. Many years later she still believed that a woman of genuine learning should conceal it "with as much solicitude as she would hide crookedness or lameness," for it would draw the envy and hatred of most people. In her own letters she tactfully adjusted her intellectual exhibitionism to her correspondents: when writing to learned friends like the Abbé Conti and Sir James Steuart, the political economist, she flaunted her erudition, whereas to her daughter and the dull Countess of Oxford she presented herself merely as a sharp-witted, opinionated woman, rich in common sense and common reading.

These then are Lady Mary's opinions of women's intellect and capacity for education; and they affected her own career and her status as a writer. For, as her French essay on women's education implies, she regarded herself as one who had succeeded in her studies and could contribute to what she calls the Republic of Letters. Certainly she was not a professional writer in the sense of one who earns a living by her writing; her wealth and rank made that both unnecessary and indecorous. (pp. 35-7)

But whether she is classified as professional or amateur, there can be no doubt that as a writer she was engaged by feminist topics—that, in other words, she combines both roles of my title, feminist and writer. Her very first publication, in fact, was an essay in the *Spectator* that satirically treated marriage from a wife's point of view. (She was the only woman, incidentally, who contributed to that periodical.) In June 1714 the *Spectator* had printed a letter written by Addison in the role of "a tall, broad-shouldered, impudent, black Fellow . . . every way qualified for a rich Widow." He complains that he has been unable to capture a rich widow in marriage because his courtships have been obstructed by the Widow-Club, made up of "nine experienced Dames" who meet to pool their information about widow-hunters, and are thus able to resist suitors like himself. "Their Conversation," he continues, "often turns upon their former Husbands, and it is very diverting to hear them relate their several Arts and Strategems, with which they amused the Jealous, pacified the Cholerick, or wheedled the Good-natured Man, 'till at last, to use the Club-phrase, *They sent him out of the House with his Heels foremost.*'' In its gentle raillery and condescension Addison's fictitious letter is typical of his attitude toward women in most of his essays.

A month later, *Spectator* No. 573 printed a reply from Mrs. President, head of the Widow-Club, and it was Lady Mary who had held her pen. ''You are pleased to be very Merry, as you imagine, with us Widows,'' she begins; and then in her counter-attack as well as defence of the club she relates the history of her own extensive marital career: having disposed of six husbands, she intends to take a seventh. (She thus outranks Chaucer's Wife of Bath, who could boast of only five husbands.) Her constant suitor, the seventh husband-to-be, is called the Hon. Edward Waitfort, evidently Lady Mary's private little joke about her husband Edward Wortley's long and querulous courtship. At the end of her account she sums up her marriages: ''I do not believe all the unreasonable Malice of Mankind can give a Pretence why I should have been constant to the Memory of any of the deceased, or have spent much time in grieving for an insolent, insignificant, negligent, extravagant, splenatick, or covetous Husband; my first insulted me, my second was nothing to me, my third disgusted me, the fourth would have ruined me, the fifth tormented me, and the sixth would have starved me. If the other Ladies you name would thus give in their Husbands Pictures, at length, you would see, they have had as little Reason as my self to lose their Hours in weeping and wailing.'' At the head of the essay Lady Mary put a Latin motto from Juvenal that sums up her reply: ''Being reproved they bite back.'' This needs to be kept in mind, for the portrait of the widow is far from idealized; she displays some characteristics that are less than admirable. Mrs. President shows herself to be both frivolous and mercenary, but her various husbands easily surpass her in their faults. Lady Mary as a feminist regarded women as human creatures of mixed qualities and not as idealized saints.

She had more opportunity to ''bite back'' in a periodical that she herself conducted in 1737-38. The chief mission of her paper, which she called *The Nonsense of Common-Sense,* was political, as its title implied, for it supported Robert Walpole's administration against the Opposition paper *Common Sense.* Of the nine essays that Lady Mary wrote for her paper during its brief run she devoted two to women—in contrasting ways. Other essays simply glanced at them, like the first paper (in December 1737), where they are urged to wear wool instead of silk in order to support the domestic woolen trade, and the third paper, where they are teased for adoring the reigning *castrato* singers.

In Number II of *The Nonsense of Common-Sense,* which deals with women directly, the anonymous Author begins, ''I have allways been an Humble Admirer of the Fair Sex, nay, I beleive I think of them with more tenderness than any Man in the World. [Readers could not have seen the irony here.] I do not only look upon them as Objects of pleasure, but I compassionate the many Hardships both Nature and Custom has subjected them to. I never expose the Foibles to which Education has enclin'd them; and (contrary to all other Authors) I see with a favourable Eye the little vanitys with which they amuse themselves, and am glad they can find in the imaginary Empire of Beauty, a consolation for being excluded every part of Government in the State.'' But the Author is shocked, the essay

continues, to see that the influence of women—specifically ''Brittish Mothers, sisters, and mistresses (for Wives are out of the Question)''—has caused the defeat in Parliament of a bill to reduce interest on government bonds from four to three per cent. Women are urged to forego luxury and self-indulgence in favor of patriotic support of the lower interest rate. Two elements of this essay are puzzling: the Author presents no evidence that women opposed the bill; and the scolding could have no effect since it had been defeated in Parliament eight months earlier. Perhaps Lady Mary, thinking it might be brought forward again, was campaigning early. Still, the essay assures women that although they may be excluded from a direct voice in government their duty is to use their personal power beneficently when they can.

In Number VI of *The Nonsense of Common-Sense,* Lady Mary devotes the entire paper to an impassioned and enlightened defence of womankind. After starting as a ''Freind . . . of the Fair sex,'' the Author attacks *Common Sense* for its pernicious advice to avoid plays because they teach immorality and to attend operas instead. Declaring himself opposed to such a dangerous pastime for women, the Author writes: ''I am for treating them with more dignity, and as I profess my selfe a protector of all the oppressed I shall look upon them as my peculiar care.'' As a moralist the Author intends to defeat vulgar prejudices, the most universal of which is ''that of treating the weaker sex with a contempt, which has a very bad Influence on their conduct''; they are treated as though their reason is weaker than men's—a prejudice that men cling to in order to rationalize their own selfish desires. For that reason, a paper that ridicules or declaims against women is very welcome in the coffee-houses, ''where there is hardly one Man in ten but fancys he has one reason or other, to curse some of the Sex most heartily.''

When using a theological argument Lady Mary does not stoop this time to the humility of her statement to Bishop Burnet many years earlier. ''If I was a divine,'' she writes (as Author), ''I would remember that in their first Creation [the beautiful halfe of Mankind] were design'd a Help for the other Sex, and nothing was ever made incapable of the end of its Creation.'' If men cannot find proof to justify their claim to superiority, they simply invoke the traditional prejudice that only they have been endowed with reason. ''I am seriously of another Opinion,'' continues the Author: ''as much greatness of Mind may be shewn in submission as in command.'' Women's virtue entitles them to the greatest respect because they are cut off from the kind of glory that only men can win; a woman ''who has performe'd her Duty as a Daughter, a Wife, and a Mother, appears to my Eyes with as much veneration as I should look on Socrates or Xenophon, and much more than I should pay either to Julius Caesar or Cardinal Mazarine. . . .'' Women are advised to value themselves not merely for beauty but for ''rational, sensible'' minds that will enable them to make the most estimable figures in life. ''Begin then Ladies,'' the Author concludes, ''by paying those Authors with Scorn and contempt who with the sneer of affected Admiration would throw you below the Dignity of the Human Species.''

In the entire canon of Lady Mary's letters, essays, and poems this is her most extended, articulate, and reasoned defence of women. Compared to the feminist doctrine in the *Tatler* and *Spectator* it is more advanced in its tenets, more forthright in its advocacy, and more vigorous in its expression. It was reprinted almost immediately by the *London Magazine* for January 1738, which gave it the ambiguous title: **''An Apology for the Ladies.''**

Besides essays in a weekly journal, an earnest propagandist could utilize pamphlets, especially if the argument could be spun out in elegant verse couplets. (The recently issued bibliography by David Foxon lists the enormous number of verse pamphlets that were published between 1700 and 1750). Lady Mary used this means at least twice for feminist propaganda: once to defend women in general against a satirist's scorn, and once to set forth her thoughts on courtship and marriage.

Jonathan Swift's *The Lady's Dressing Room,* published in 1732, vividly depicts how a naif Strephon explores his Celia's dressing room, with its evidence of slatternly filth (including an unemptied chamber-pot), and steals away disgusted,

> Repeating in his amorous Fits,
> Oh! *Celia, Celia, Celia* shits!

Among the various responses to the poem—it caused Mrs. Pilkington's mother to vomit—four writers issued anonymous pamphlets; one of them has only recently been identified as being by Lady Mary. Swift's poem, like others of his "excremental vision," is sometimes cited as proof of misogyny; one may wonder how a woman writer would treat it. She might scold him for his lack of charity, reprove him for his obscenity, accuse him of undue bias in choosing such a nymph as heroine. Lady Mary does none of these; the title of her poem indicates her strategy: ***The Dean's Provocation for Writing the Lady's Dressing Room*** (1734). She spins out a fiction of how he had gone to a prostitute, who demanded payment before her services; how when he proved impotent and demanded the return of his payment, the prostitute refused; whereupon he vowed that in revenge he would ruin her trade by describing her dressing room.

In her *jeu d'esprit* Lady Mary very cleverly parodies Swift's own verse style—his octosyllabic couplets, his blunt, unpoetic diction, his digressions, animal parallels, sententiae, and even his use of scatological words—as in her concluding lines. The prostitute, refusing to return the money, says:

> Perhaps you have no better Luck in
> The Knack of Rhyming than of ——.

When the Dean replies with the threat that he will describe her dressing-room:

> She answer'd short, I'm glad you'll write,
> You'll furnish Paper when I Sh—e.

In this poem Lady Mary is not at all lady-like, but why should she be? Although "condemned to petticoats" (as she phrased it) she neither demanded nor expected consideration for being a woman. Is that not the frame of mind fitted for sexual equality, the "equal opportunity" that feminists strive for today?

Her other feminist poem, published as a pamphlet (in 1733), is about courtship and marriage. It is ***The Answer*** to a love elegy (printed along with it) by James Hammond, an impecunious young man who had fallen in love with a young woman at court. In her reply to the man's love-poem Lady Mary, answering for the woman, realistically points out that a marriage without financial safeguards would cause bitter regret for both: the woman would be "a poor *Virtuous* Wretch for Life"; and as for both: "*Love* soon would cease to smile, when *Fortune* frown'd." And so at the conclusion the woman makes a firm resolve not to encourage him:

> Whilst other Maids a shameless Path pursue,
> Neither to Honour, nor to Int'rest true;
> And proud to swell the Triumphs of their Eyes,

> Exult in Love from Lovers they despise;
> Their Maxims all revers'd, I mean to prove,
> And tho' I like the Lover quit the Love.

In her view of marriage Lady Mary recognizes the stringencies of her social class, where in a successful match financial settlements had to accompany love as a protection for the wife (as well as the husband). At the same time she sharply condemns a purely mercenary marriage, a "Nuptial Sale," and characterizes women who marry for that reason "legal Prostitutes." The phrase had already been used, in slightly different forms, by Steele in the *Tatler* and by Defoe; it was made famous by Mary Wollstonecraft in *A Vindication of the Rights of Woman.* With or without Lady Mary's consent, her printer revealed her authorship by putting on the pamphlet's title page "By a Lady, Author of the Verses to the Imitator of Horace." The printer no doubt hoped to profit by the notoriety of her feud with Alexander Pope.

Lady Mary had already devoted a long poem to women's disabilities after marriage, to the cruel punishment suffered by wives because of the double moral standard imposed by society. In the **"Epistle from Mrs. Y[onge] to her Husband,"** purportedly written by a cast-off wife, Lady Mary criticizes the moral code that permits a husband to commit adultery with impunity yet punishes his wife for the same crime:

> Too, too severely Laws of Honour bind
> The Weak Submissive Sex of Woman-kind.

She then asks:

> From whence is this unjust Distinction grown?
> Are we not form'd with Passions like your own?
> Nature with equal Fire our Souls endu'd,
> Our Minds as Haughty, and as warm our blood,
> O're the wide World your pleasures persue,
> The Change is justify'd by something new;
> But we must sigh in Silence—and be true.

The eloquence of this poem seems to reflect Lady Mary's urgent convictions; and whether or not she intended it to be printed, it remained unpublished among her manuscripts.

Adultery and divorce were so common among those she knew that she once suggested (in a letter to her sister) "a genneral Act of Divorceing all the people of England. You know, those that pleas'd might marry over again, and it would save the Reputations of several Ladys that are now in peril of being expos'd every day." Often in verse as well as in prose she scornfully attacked men's "gallantry," whether in or out of marriage, and particularly condemned the injustice of punishing or ostracizing women when their seducers were really the guilty ones.

She developed this notion in a long French essay refuting the maxim of La Rochefoucauld that there are some convenient marriages but not delightful (*délicieux*) ones. On the contrary, argues Lady Mary: the marriage of a man and woman who are in love and who are intelligent and sensible will bring far greater happiness than any alternative to such a union. "It appears to me a life infinitely more delightful, more elegant, and more pleasurable," she writes, "than the most conducted and most happy gallantry. A woman capable of reflection cannot but look upon her lover as her seducer, who would take advantage of her weakness to give himself a momentary pleasure, at the expence of her repose, of her glory, and of her life." In a true marriage, by contrast, the wife "must strive to heighten the charms of a mistress by the good sense and solidity of a friend. When two persons, prepossessed with sentiments so reasonable, are united by eternal ties, all nature smiles upon them. . . .'' But she concludes, realistically, that since two such persons are very extraordinary, it is not surprising that such unions are very rare.

Lady Mary's scattered comments elsewhere on marriage may sound cynical, for although she believed that it could lead to happiness, as a realist she observed that it rarely did. Her own failed marriage was a persuasive example. Her cynicism was thus the obverse of her idealism. By refuting La Rochefoucauld's genuinely cynical maxim she was reaffirming the idealism that she had so fervently set forth in her courtship letters. Her essay on marriage was never published in her lifetime; instead she allowed friends to read it and to make copies. In this modest private circulation she showed her desire to propagandize in a cause that would benefit women.

How do her ideas on marriage contribute to her advocacy of feminism? The faults of conventional marriage of the time are to the woman's disadvantage—the mercenary principle that treats her as a financial commodity, and the double standard of morality that permits a husband's infidelity but harshly punishes a wife's. Woman's lot would be improved, Lady Mary implies, if the institution of marriage were accepted honestly and seriously as a union between equals.

All of her writings that I have so far discussed illustrate both parts of my title simultaneously: her ideas on feminism and her activity as a writer concerned with those ideas. But in most of her writings she did not confine herself to that subject; she stands out as a woman whose literary energy and passion drove her to compete in an activity ruled by men. She is thus a feminist in practice. (pp. 38-44)

With all [her] . . . varied writings, in prose and in verse, published and in manuscript, Lady Mary would seem to deserve a place in the Republic of Letters. Yet I have not mentioned the *Turkish Embassy Letters,* her most ambitious work, and one which—surrounded as it is with ironies, puzzles, and paradoxes—won her a substantial European reputation as a woman of letters. She composed these letters during her journey to Turkey and residence there, an experience unique for a woman writer. As a young wife, she had accompanied her husband, British Ambassador to Turkey in 1716, remaining only sixteen months because Wortley bungled his diplomatic mission so disastrously that he was recalled. But Lady Mary succeeded brilliantly in her unannounced, self-appointed mission of interpreting Moslem culture for Western Europe.

The status of Turkish women could not fail to pique her curiosity, for Western Europe had always been intrigued by a society in which polygamy was practiced and women were confined to the harem, unseen by any men except their husbands and attendant eunuchs. As the first woman traveller in Turkey to record what she saw of her own sex Lady Mary set down particularly trustworthy and vivid observations. After visiting a women's bagnio in Adrianople and joining them in their bathing, she reported that at this social gathering women behaved with modesty, grace, and good manners. She also found that women of the upper class, whom she visited in their palaces, were as charming and sophisticated (and of course beautiful) as any court-ladies in London or Paris.

Implicitly, as well as explicitly, she opposes the idea current in Europe that Turkish women were abject slaves, deprived of all rights and privileges. Aaron Hill's popular book on the Ottoman empire (in 1709) emphasized women's inferior position and the complete subjection of wives, who—he states—

Lady M-y W-r-t-l-y M-nt-g-e
The Female Traveller
In the Turkish Dress.

Let Men who glory in their better sense,
Read, hear, and learn Humility from hence;
No more let them Superior Wisdom boast,
They can but equal M-nt-g-e at most.

Eighteenth-century engraving of Montagu as ''The Female Traveller.''

had no liberty at all; and the travel-writer Dumont bluntly states that 'There is no Slavery equal to that of the *Turkish* Women.'' Such opinions seem based not on open-minded observation but rather on the misconception that women confined to the harem were bereft of all rights. Instead, Lady Mary develops the paradoxical notion that Turkish women enjoy more liberty than western women, for when they go out in public they cannot be recognized, even by their own husbands, because their shapeless garments hide their features from head to toe. ''This perpetual Masquerade,'' she writes, ''gives them entire Liberty of following their Inclinations without danger of Discovery.'' In addition to this personal liberty—for which, she adds, their religion does not threaten them with punishment in afterlife— Turkish women have the privilege of owning property and money; and if divorced they receive additional support from their husbands. ''Upon the Whole,'' she concludes, ''I look upon the Turkish Women as the only free people in the Empire.'' (pp. 48-9)

[The] progress of the *Turkish Embassy Letters* from their origin to their publication charts the evolution of Lady Mary's career as a feminist and writer. In their earlier form they were private correspondence with friends and family; she then arranged them to make a collection to be read and admired by her private circle of friends, including . . . Mary Astell; and finally, she arranged for their publication so that although decorum forbade her practising the trade of authorship, their posthumous appearance would establish her status as a liberated woman not inferior to men in the Republic of Letters. (p. 50)

> *Robert Halsband, "'Condemned to Petticoats': Lady Mary Wortley Montagu as Feminist and Writer," in* The Dress of Words: Essays on Restoration and Eighteenth Century Literature in Honor of Richmond P. Bond, *edited by Robert B. White, Jr., University of Kansas Libraries, 1978, pp. 35-52.*

ELIZABETH WARNOCK FERNEA (essay date 1981)

[*An American educator and specialist in Middle Eastern studies, Fernea is the author of* Guests of the Sheik *(1965; also published as* Guests of the Sheik: An Ethnography of an Iraqi Village, *1969) and* A Street in Marrakech *(1975). In the following excerpt from a later work, she discusses Montagu's role as an ethnographer of Middle Eastern life—and in particular of the status of women—in her letters from Turkey.*]

"I am now got into a new world, where every thing I see appears to me a change of scene," wrote Lady Mary Wortley Montague to her friend Lady Rich in London. (p. 329)

Robert Halsband, her most recent biographer, has pointed out that Lady Mary's [*Turkish Embassy Letters*] are used by scholars in many disciplines for their comments on politics, diplomacy, music, health, art, medical history (she campaigned for smallpox inoculation in England), and social history ("for her analysis of religion, customs and morality in Ottoman Turkey"). But her work has another important dimension; she can be justly called one of the earliest ethnographers of Middle Eastern women. Lady Mary, in 1717, was among the first to suggest that Muslim women were not benighted "others" bound by a cruel code of restriction and oppression, but might have values and customs that were worthy, if not of emulation, at least of study and respect.

"I went to the (Turkish) bagnio," Lady Mary continued in her letter to Lady Rich, "about ten o'clock. It was already full of women. . . ." She goes on to describes in detail the design and construction of the bath, the system of heating and cooling water, and the furniture, including sofas covered with cushions and carpets on which the ladies and their slaves could recline. The ladies were, she noted:

> without any distinction of rank by their dress, all being in the state of nature, that is, in plain English, stark naked, without any beauty or defect concealed. Yet there was not the least wanton smile or immodest gesture amongst them. They walked and moved with the same majestic grace, which Milton describes our general mother with. . . .

To make the scene and the people in the scene especially sympathetic and human to her English reader, Lady Mary here employs one of the basic techniques of a conscientious ethnographer trying to communicate the humanity of the peoples of another culture. She likens their appearance or behavior to a figure, an institution, or an object with which the audience is familiar. Using Milton's name and work in relation to a Turkish bath full of naked women immediately lends an air of virtue and artistry to what could otherwise be perceived rather differently. And, adding another familiar comparison to her account, she goes on. "In short, (the bath) is the women's coffee-house, where all the news of the town is told, scandal invented, etc. . . ." Finally, she involves herself in the en-

counter, which brings her audience even closer to the scene. And she is not afraid of the reactions.

> The lady that seemed the most considerable among them, entreated me to sit by her, and would fain have undressed me for the bath. I excused myself with some difficulty. They being however all so earnest in persuading me, I was at last forced to open my shirt, and show them my stays; which satisfied them very well; for, I saw, they believed I was so locked up in that machine, that it was not in my own power to open it, which contrivance they attributed to my husband. . . .

(pp. 329-30)

It is not only Lady Mary's considerable wit and descriptive powers that concern us here, but also her interest in her surroundings and her remarkable openness to the values and ideas of another culture, an openness rare in any century, including our own. In short, Lady Mary seems remarkably free of ethnocentrism. Her comment about the beautiful Fatima, wife of the Kahya, or Second Officer after the Grand Vizier of the Sultan, might well apply to herself. "She is very curious after the manners of countrys [*sic*] and has not that partiality for her own, so common to little minds." (p. 330)

Lady Mary's ethnographic contributions are limited in time and space, but they are important in three areas: religious belief and ritual, the recording of material culture and "vie quotidienne" ["daily life"] of early eighteenth century Turkish court life, and the status of women. Another contribution is her sense of the relationship between cultures, the common elements in Islamic Turkey and the Christian West, which she welcomes. She also is careful to identify areas of difference and does not let her "enlightenment" views lead her to overlook problems in the two societies.

Lady Mary did not collect data in the sense that the modern ethnographer is instructed to do. But she listened and looked carefully, and she offers pointed observations and uses specific incidents to illustrate general trends she sees in Turkish society. Her comparisons, as in the Turkish bath description above, lead the reader into the strange culture by offering familiar signposts. She tries to correct stereotypes currently in existence. Her anecdotes are chosen with care to both entertain and subtly instruct the reader. (pp. 331-32)

Not content with set and formal glimpses of social life in Constantinople she pushed further, donning native dress to travel about the city, sometimes with friends, sometimes alone. "The asmak, or Turkish veil, is become not only very easy but agreeable to me, and if it was not, I would be content to endure some inconveniency to content a passion so powerful with me as curiosity," she wrote Lady Bristol in April 1718. In May 1718 she wrote the Countess of —, "I ramble every day, wrap'd up in my *ferige* and *asmak*, about Constantinople, and amuse my selfe with seeing all that is curious in it." Garbed in her veils, she visited the Bosphorus, the Seraglio and its gardens, the mosques, the Church of Santa Sophia, and also made some forays into the markets. These she described by again using an English analogy, as holding "365 shops furnish'd with all sort of rich goods expos'd to sale in the same Manner as the New Exchange in London." She also goes out to view the camps of the Ottoman army, preparing for a move to the frontiers, and describes the tents of the Sultan and his court.

The complicated social schedule of a diplomatic wife and the organization of a household of servants seemed able to accommodate these anonymous wanderings as well as the care of her young son, the beginning of her second pregnancy, her journal-keeping and letter-writing, and her study of Turkish. She wrote Alexander Pope that she spends Wednesdays ''studying the Turkish language (in which, by the way, I am already very learned).'' She sent Pope samples of her translations of Turkish poetry and described to him and other readers some of the particular technical problems of Turkish verse.

From translating and learning the language; from describing the sights, sounds, and scenes around the Golden Horn, the mosques, the fountains, the markets, cloisters, and monasteries, ''the fine painted meadows by the side of the sea of Marmora''; she turns next to subjects which she knows will interest not only her intellectual and literary friends, but every lady (and gentleman) of the English court. The furniture, houses, music, dance, the clothes, jewels, food, the customs of hospitality of the Turkish upper-class household—the material culture of a vanished class and epoch—are lovingly delineated here for future generations to enjoy and to learn from. (pp. 332-33)

Conversations with the Sultana are employed by Lady Mary to dispose of various questions concerning the harem and the seraglio.

> The Emperor precedes his visit by a Royal present and then comes into her (the chosen lady's) apartment. Neither is there any such thing as her creeping in at the bed's feet. Sometimes the Sultan diverts him selfe in the Company of all his Ladies, who stand in a circle round him, and she confess'd they were ready to dye with Jealousie and envy of the happy She that he distinguish'd by any appearance of preference. But this seem'd to me neither better nor worse than the Circles in most Courts where the Glance of the Monarch watch'd and every Smile waited for with impatience and envy'd by those that cannot obtain it.

Again the comparison with a known, familiar cultural pattern.

Lady Mary was clever enough to forestall criticisms of her detailed descriptions. After all, many of her correspondents had read the tales of the *Arabian Nights* by this time. She wrote her sister, Lady Mar:

> Now do I fancy that you imagine I have entertain'd you all this while with a relation that has (at least) receiv'd many Embellishments from my hand. . . . This is but too like (says you) the Arabian Night tales; these embrodier'd Napkins, and a jewel as large as a Turkey's egg!—You forget, dear Sister, those very tales were writ by an Author of this Country and (excepting the Enchantments) are a real representation of the manners here.
>
> (p. 333)

Lady Mary was impressed with what she observed of the status of Turkish women in contrast to the observations made by others. Her analysis was of course confined to the upper class, and she found the fact that women owned property in their own right particularly striking, given the situation of English women in the eighteenth century. She confided to her sister in April 1717:

> Neither have they much to apprehend from the resentment of their Husbands, those Ladys that are rich having all their money in their own hands, which they take with 'em upon a divorce with an addition which he is oblig'd to give 'em. Upon the whole, I look upon the Turkish women as the only free people

in the Empire. . . .' 'Tis true their Law permits (the men) four (4) wives, but there is no Instance of a Man of Quality that makes use of this Liberty, or a woman of Rank that would suffer it. . . .

The all-enveloping ferigee and veil, seen as a disadvantage by most observers, was viewed in quite a different light by Lady Mary. After her own freedom of wandering in veiled garb, she wrote her sister,

> 'Tis very easy to see that they have more liberty than we have, no Woman of what rank so ever being permitted to go in the streets (without the veil and the ferigee) . . . you may guess how effectively this disguises them, that there is no distinguishing the great Lady from the slave, and 'tis impossible for the most jealous Husband to know his wife when he meets her, and no Man dare either touch or follow a Woman in the Street. . . . This perpetual Masquerade gives them entire Liberty of following their Inclinations without danger of Discovery.
>
> (p. 334)

The key importance of motherhood as giving role and status is mentioned several times in the letters, and the Turkish woman's fear of being barren is seen as so great that

> they do not content themselves with using the natural means, but fly to all sort of Quackerys to avoid the Scandal of being past Child bearing and often kill themselves by 'em . . . when I have ask'd them sometimes how they expected to provide for such a Flock as they desire, They answer that the Plague will certainly kill half of 'em; which, indeed generally happens. . . .
>
> (p. 335)

And although she admires the ''liberty'' of the Turkish ladies, she is not so blinded by romanticism that she is not aware of the many problems. The news of the death of a young woman by an unknown hand prompts a discussion of crimes of ''honor.''

> 'Tis true the same customs that give them so many opportunitys of gratifying their evil Inclinations (if they have any) also puts it very fully in the power of their Husbands to revenge them if they are discover'd and I don't doubt but that they suffer sometimes for their Indiscretions in a very severe manner.

Lady Mary provides descriptions of pre-nuptial baths, of marriage processions and gift giving, of childbirth, of slavery, of enchantments, sorceries, and the so-called balm of Mecca. Accounts of the performances of the Whirling Dervishes had already reached Europe, so Lady Mary took it upon herself to witness a session of their devotions. She described it carefully, concluding ''The whole is perform'd with the most solemn gravity. Nothing can be more austere than the form of these people.''

She also takes up the subject of comparative religion. While in Belgrade, en route to Constantinople, she and her husband had been housed with a religious judge, the Cadi Effendi Achmet-Beg. To Abbé Conti, she related the substance of some of their conversations:

> Mahometism is divided into as many Sects as Christianity, and the first institution as much neglected and obscur'd by the interpretations. I cannot here forebear reflecting on the natural Inclination of Mankind to make Mysterys and Noveltys. The Zeidi, Kadara, Jabari, etc., put me in mind of the Catholic, Lutheran, Calvinist, etc., and are equally zealous against one another. But the most prevailing Opinion,

if you search into the Secret of the Effendis, is plain Deism. . . . (The Cadi) assur'd me that if I understood Arabic I should be very well pleas'd with reading the Alcoran, which is far from the nonsense we charge it with, tis the purest morality deliver'd in the very best language. I have since heard impartial Christians speak of it in the same manner, and I don't doubt but all our translations are from Copys got from the Greek Preists, who would not fail to falsify it with the extremity of Malice.

She ended the letter by adding:

> I don't ask your pardon for the Liberty I have taken in speaking of the Roman. I know you equally condemn the Quackery of all Churches as much as you revere the sacred Truths in which we both agree.

Her belief in Deism is enunciated in many letters, a Deism which she saw as a bridge between East and West, between Islam and Christianity, between rational beings in both worlds. (pp. 335-36)

Lady Mary would no doubt be surprised at being termed an ethnographer, since the word hardly existed at the time, and anthropology as the study of other cultures was not to appear as a serious discipline for another hundred years. We might speculate, however, that she would have been pleased to be praised for the qualities of the ethnographer: the openness to new ideas, the non-judgmental attitude; the eye for the important details that illuminate the broader picture; the ability to see oneself and one's culture from another point of view; the talent to convey these perceptions so vividly that an ordinary audience not only learns, but is cheered and entertained. For these are literary as well as ethnographic accomplishments. . . .

After two hundred and fifty years, the freshness of the *Turkish Embassy Letters* reminds us what ethnography could and should be. Middle Eastern women and we who admire, write, and study about Middle Eastern women are indebted to Lady Mary Wortley Montagu for the warm-hearted, clever, and faithful portrait of Turkish court life she left behind for later generations. (p. 338)

> *Elizabeth Warnock Fernea, "An Early Ethnographer of Middle Eastern Women: Lady Mary Wortley Montagu (1682-1762)," in* Journal of Near Eastern Studies, *Vol. 40, No. 4, October, 1981, pp. 329-38.*

PATRICIA MEYER SPACKS (essay date 1984)

[*An American essayist, biographer, and educator, Spacks has written extensively on eighteenth-century literature. In the following excerpt, she analyzes the correspondence between Montagu and Alexander Pope, discerning a subtext of struggle beneath Pope's stylized, amorous letters and Montagu's airy and determinedly intellectual responses.*]

In Alexander Pope's "Epistle to Miss Blount, with the Works of Voiture" (1712), reflection on the French master of the romantic epistle leads the speaker to imagine his own life as "an innocent gay Farce . . . more Diverting still than Regular." Four years later, Pope inaugurated a correspondence with Lady Mary Wortley Montagu, then beginning her travels to Turkey. He adopted for his letters Voiture's elegant tone, enacting half of an epistolary romance—apparently undeterred by Lady Mary's attempted self-representation in quite another mode. Lady Mary's letters to Pope do not survive in their original form; we have only the redactions which she subsequently published in the *Embassy Letters*. Pope's responses, however, as well as

Lady Mary's extant summaries of her own letters, suggest that in substance the published letters bear a close relation to texts actually sent. The twelve letters from Pope to Lady Mary, with eight letters and two summaries of letters from her to him, sketch a farce of incomprehension—a farce not devoid of pathos or serious implications, and one hardly "innocent," although sufficiently "diverting." Its participants appear to possess utterly opposed private agendas, suggested by their differing relations to literary convention. The letters delineate a full and vivid male-female transaction and call attention to its implications.

The specific male and female involved in the interchange resemble one another in their intense literary self-consciousness. Both see themselves, in this correspondence, always as *writers*. The impression of minds at cross purposes that the letters convey is doubtless heightened by Lady Mary's revisions for publication, which presumably excised personal material. Yet the letters to Pope differ from others of the *Embassy Letters* in the kind of personal references they include as well as the kind conspicuously lacking. To Lady Rich, Lady Mary writes, confidently, "I expect from you that you should love me and think of me when you don't see me." To Pope, on the other hand, she sounds suspicious: "Perhaps you'll laugh at me for thanking you very gravely for all the obliging concern you express for me. 'Tis certain that I may, if I please, take the fine things you say to me for wit and railery, and it may be it would be taking them right." She may have been reacting to Pope's July letter, which begins, "So natural as I find it is to me, to neglect every body else in your company, I am sensible I ought to do any thing that might please you." Lady Mary obviously is wary about letting herself be pleased.

Her wariness, perhaps, responds to an emotion which she might feel beneath Pope's compliments: his delight in his mastery of the epistolary situation. He points out that his correspondent lives in his memory and imagination; the warmth and tenderness of his fancy preserves her reality. "If to live in the memory of others have any thing desirable in it, 'tis what you possess with regard to me, in the highest sense of the words. There is not a day in which your Figure does not appear before me, your Conversations return to my thought, and every Scene, place, or occasion where I have enjoyed them are as livelily painted, as an Imagination equally warm & tender can be capable to represent them" ([June 1717]). Lady Mary chooses not to comment or, at any rate, not to preserve her comment. If Pope (as he claims) believes himself to inhabit and generate a romance, Lady Mary locates herself in a more realistic fiction. The story of these correspondents in conjunction hardly promises a happy ending. (pp. 207-08)

From Pope's point of view, she would have seemed an ideal partner for literary flirtation: intelligent, verbal, more or less at loose ends, apparently interested in him and in matters that concerned him. But she perceived herself, of course, as a *self*, not a partner.

Lady Mary's early letters to Wortley obsessively proclaim their writer's self-definition as an unusual young woman. She wishes her lover to understand whom he's dealing with; she begs him not to commit himself further unless he really wants her in all her specialness, with all her difficulties of personality. In the letters to Pope, she takes herself more for granted. Pope, on the contrary, offers frequent protestations about his own nature, proclaiming his romanticism, his "artlessness," and, above all, his sincerity. His letters, he maintains, in the first of the series written to Lady Mary on her travels, "will be the most

Lady Mary's husband, Edward Wortley Montagu.

impartial Representations of a free heart, and the truest Copies you ever saw, tho' of a very mean Original'' (18 Aug. [1716]). Whatever he writes ''will be the real Thought of that hour.'' ''If I don't take care,'' he complains, ''I shall write myself all out to you'' ([1716-17]). ''This is really true,'' he insists, after telling her of his wishes for her happiness ([1718]). Although his self-presentation—including the insistence on his spontaneity and authenticity—depends heavily on literary convention, he implicitly and explicitly denies the fact.

Best exemplified in the romantic epistles of Vincent de Voiture, the conventions Pope followed involved elaborate protestations of feeling and of sincerity. . . . Sensibility supplies the main counter in the game the correspondents play.

The appropriate female response to such letters as Voiture's involved equivalent protestations of feeling. Lady Mary, however, chose to resist the convention, although alternative literary models did not readily present themselves. Not until 1726 did she read Madame de Sevigné's letters, and although she found them entertaining, she also thought them trivial. In the form in which she offered her own letters for publication, they reject triviality, although not the aim of entertainment. They implicitly declare her stand of resistance—resistance to her own feelings, which might make her vulnerable, and to the epistolary conventions which reduce women to romantic adjuncts or to retailers of tittle-tattle. Her first letter of response to Pope, the one that begins with her suggestion that he may laugh at her for believing him sincere, continues, ''but I never in my Life was halfe so well dispos'd to believe you in earnest, and that distance which makes the continuation of your Friendship improbable has very much encreas'd my Faith for it, and I find that I have (as well as the rest of my sex), whatever face I set on't, a strong disposition to believe in miracles'' (14 Sept.

[1716]). Revealing her human need—distant from her friends, she must keep faith in their constancy, she needs their reality—leads her promptly to self-deprecation. By ironically attributing her belief in Pope to a weakness of her sex, she suggests a covert theme of the entire correspondence: the problem of what a women can do and be. Made ever more conscious of the status of women by her experience of a country where women go veiled and live in harems, she wants to understand herself as a woman without understanding herself also as deficient. Although she offers increasingly emphatic intellectual claims for herself, she would never receive much affirmation from her correspondent.

Nor would her correspondent receive much affirmation from her. After this first letter, she hardly acknowledges Pope's persistent announcements of intense feeling. He develops, over several letters, an elaborate conceit about a Circassian slave: he wishes Lady Mary to bring him back a girl who looks like her; he proposes to be at once master and slave of this girl; he will thus gratify vicariously—he says it almost directly—his desire for Lady Mary. The extravagant, transparent disguise declares the pain of Pope's sexual situation. Lady Mary never mentions this proposal in the published letters; one cannot imagine that she offered a very satisfactory response in the private ones. Indeed, what satisfactory response *could* she offer? Occasionally she throws out a compliment. She has not written for a long time, she explains, because she wants to modify Pope's exaggerated good opinion of her; once she mentions how highly she values his friendship and Congreve's. On the whole, though, she eschews the language of feeling characteristic of women's letters even in print, and she ignores her correspondent's indulgence in the male equivalent. She refuses to accept the role of his romantic counterpart.

''Nothing that regards the Countries you pass thro' engages so much of my Concern.'' Pope writes, ''as what relates purely to yourself. You can make no Discoveries that will be half so valuable to me as those of your own mind, temper, and thoughts'' (20 Aug. [1716]). Rosemary Cowler comments about these sentences, ''It is characteristic of his preoccupation with his own moral nature that Pope's concern for his friends also goes to the core of their beings, not to their activities.'' Lady Mary's response, however, raises the possibility of another interpretation. She may have felt the intrusiveness of such implicit demands; she may have seen them as part of Pope's effort to subsume her into his fantasies. Less than two months later, she begins a letter from Vienna by apologizing for herself as correspondent [Spacks explains in a footnote that it is not known for certain that Pope was the recipient of this particular letter, but adds: ''Whoever the recipient, the letter makes explicit what other letters to Pope imply in their resolute concentration on scene and event.''] First she says that she will show Pope his mistake in esteeming her so highly. Then she adds, ''if you are sincere when you say you expect to be extremely entertain'd by my Letters, I ought to be mortify'd at the disappointment that I am sure you will receive when you hear from me, tho' I have done my best endeavors to find out something worth writeing to you. I have seen every thing that is to be seen with a very diligent Curiosity.'' She thus introduces an account of villas and jewels. This denial of her correspondent's professed desire for knowledge of her mind, temper, and thoughts dominates the succeeding letters as well. She will write regularly, wittily, informatively, and fluently, but she will not write of herself (or, for that matter, of her husband, about whom Pope inquires; or her children, although her self-published letters to other correspondents mention children and husband alike). She will not declare herself romantic or sincere or impassioned. "For Gods sake, Madam, when you write to me, talk of your self," Pope begs in his next letter, "there is nothing I so much desire to hear of" (10 Nov. [1716]). He hears instead of the weather in Hungary, with a promise that Lady Mary will report her next adventure to him if it ends comically, or of the Turkish soldiery and the mob-murder of a great official. Lady Mary explains that she has written "in the discharge of my own Conscience"—a phrase which, Halsband points out, evidently appeared in a letter actually sent, since Pope repeats it (12 Feb. [1717]). She is telling her correspondent that she writes not from feeling but from duty. One begins to feel sorry for Pope.

But one may feel sorry also for Lady Mary, in her effort of self-preservation. Pope's powerfully articulated version of their respective positions leaves her little space. Such extravagant virtue as hers, he observes (with reference to her insistence on following her husband to Constantinople), belongs only "in a Romance" ([Oct. 1716]). He makes her into a fictional character: the countess who turned nun after arranging for her lover's extravagant tomb, the poet's enslaver, the object of his own and others' devotion. These images flatter their subject, but only by placing her in roles not chosen by her. Pope, on the other hand, selects for himself the fantasy of the man who will follow a woman anywhere, and gladly die for love. As he writes Lady Mary in expectation of her homecoming, he remarks that he looks upon her three years' residence in the East as making her "so many years Younger than you was, so much nearer Innocence (that is, Truth) & Infancy (that is Openness)" (1 Sept. [1718]). He would not value the truth of innocence or the openness of infancy for himself; to attribute them to Lady Mary covertly insists on his superiority, his adulthood as opposed to her infancy, or his knowledge in contrast with her "Innocence." Later in the same letter, Pope praises Lady Mary's body: "For in the very twinkle of one eye of it, there is more Wit; and in the very dimple of one cheek of it, there is more Meaning, than in all the Souls that ever were casually put into Women since Men had the making of them."

Here is Pope at his epistolary best—that is, his most charming, witty, imaginative, controling the rhythms of his prose as he does those of his verse. Lady Mary, however, may have glimpsed dark undertones, whether or not she recognized a possible allusion to the theological controversy over whether women have souls at all. Pope acknowledges that men imagine women and call their imaginings real, and he demonstrates the process as he assures Lady Mary that he values her dimple and the twinkle of her eye, but he locates wit and meaning there rather than in her mind. Lady Mary's half of the correspondence has revealed a pathetic effort to assert her powers of interpretation and commentary—an effort pathetic not in its inadequacy, since the writer both sees and articulates brilliantly, but in the lack of response it elicits. She ignores Pope's romantic gambits; he ignores her intellectual ones. Her boat almost overturns in the Hebrus; she imagines how she might be celebrated if she had swum down the river where Orpheus's head floated. "I dispair of ever having so many fine things said of me as so extraordinary a Death would have given Occasion for," she concludes, the ironic tone not altogether concealing her wistfulness over the idea of fame (1 Apr. [1717]). She speculates about the relation of poetry to truth, about the situation of women, about Turkish politics. She studies Arabic poetry, sending Pope her own adaptation of a love lyric. The letter containing it ends, "You see I am pritty far gone in Oriental Learning, and to say

truth I study very hard. I wish my studys may give me occasion of entertaining your curiosity, which will be the utmost advantage hop'd from it by etc." (1 Apr. [1717]). (Evidence exists that this letter too was actually sent.) Her learning, in fact, must be its own reward; she knows that she can attain public recognition only by entertaining the curiosity of a male arbiter. (pp. 209-14)

The subtext of this correspondence, on both sides, concerns power. Pope's putative sexual insecurity helps to explain the will to control expressed by his insistence on incorporating Lady Mary into his fantasies. Literary convention and tradition made the exercise easy. He could express gracefully and unostentatiously his dominance over a female partner—even while attributing to her the power to make him her slave. For Lady Mary, no accessible convention supplied a ready means to express her countervailing will. She could evade and ignore, she could dwell resolutely in the external, she could deprecate her own accomplishment, but she could not soon discover an attractive mode of self-presentation which would unite her to a viable tradition yet preserve her sense of herself as woman. Women had long asserted control in private relationships by withholding and refusal. In the Turkish correspondence with Pope, one can see Lady Mary adapting and enlarging this private convention for her own literary purposes, willing to make herself forceful. The seeds of the future rupture may lie buried here, as well as those of the feminism which Robert Halsband has documented [see excerpt dated 1978]. In the later letters to her daughter, Lady Mary would express a generous, reflective, and open personality, aware of the difficulties of the female situation but rarely combative about them. Those letters communicate a more private sense of self. Pope, by his reliance on literary convention, had urged her too to find a voice publicly as well as privately viable; her own desire for literary reputation encouraged her to use the letters as a means of developing such a voice. Her search for a personal rhetoric of power led her to the antiromantic, antitender, self-presentation of refusal. (pp. 214-15)

> *Patricia Meyer Spacks, "Imaginations Warm and Tender: Pope and Lady Mary," in* South Atlantic Quarterly, *Vol. 83, No. 2 Spring, 1984, pp. 207-15.*

ADDITIONAL BIBLIOGRAPHY

Barry, Iris. *Portrait of Lady Mary Wortley Montagu.* London: Ernest Benn, 1928, 294 p.
> Fictionalized biography. Barry stresses that her story ("in almost every detail based on fact") is an attempt to portray Montagu "not as a museum piece, but as a real person."

Byron, George Gordon. Letter to John Murray. In his *"The Flesh is Frail": Byron's Letters and Journals, Vol. 6: 1818-1819,* edited by Leslie A. Marchand, pp. 30-1. Cambridge: Harvard University Press, Belknap Press, 1976.
> Letter dated 12 April 1818 from Venice, where Byron had discovered specimens of Montagu's private correspondence to Algarotti. He writes that "the *Short* French love letters *certainly* are Lady M. W. Montague's—the *French* not good but the Sentimentals beautiful . . .'"

Bradford, Gamaliel. "Lady Mary Wortley Montagu." In his *Portraits of Women,* pp. 1-22. Boston: Houghton Mifflin Co., Riverside Press, 1916.
> Assessment of Montagu's character in many aspects of her life, including love, domestic affairs, financial concerns, social life,

and attitude toward education and religion. Bradford finds the tenor of Montagu's mind predominantly "masculine."

Drew, Elizabeth. "Lady Mary Wortley Montagu: 1689-1762." In her *The Literature of Gossip: Nine English Letterwriters*, pp. 67-90. New York: W. W. Norton & Co., 1964.
Concise yet comprehensive biography.

Gibbon, Edward. Letter to Dorothea Gibbon. In his *The Letters of Edward Gibbon, Vol. 1: 1750-1773*, edited by J. E. Norton, pp. 168-69. New York: Macmillan Co., 1956.
Letter of 17 February 1763, in which Gibbon says of Montagu's "Turkish Embassy Letters": "They have entertained me very much. What fire, what ease, what knowledge of Europe and of Asia."

Halsband, Robert. Introduction to *The Nonsense of Common-Sense: 1737-1738*, by Lady Mary Wortley Montagu, edited by Robert Halsband, pp. ix-xxx. Evanston: Northwestern University, 1947.
Describes and critiques Montagu's periodical essays, providing political and social background information.

———. "Pope, Lady Mary, and the *Court Poems* (1716)." *PMLA* LXVIII, No. 1 (March 1953): 237-50.
Argues that, of the three eclogues published as *Court Poems*, "The Toilet" was written by John Gay and "The Basset-Table" and "The Drawing-Room" by Montagu.

[Oliphant, Margaret]. "Historical Sketches of the Reign of George II: No. IV—Lady Mary Wortley Montagu." *Blackwood's Edinburgh Magazine* CIV, No. DCXXXIII (July 1868): 1-25.
Biography including many extracts from Montagu's letters. Oliphant concludes that "there is little to be said about Lady Mary Wortley's writings," as "she . . . is in herself more interesting, more curious, a thousand times closer to us, than any of her works."

Perry, Ruth. "Two Forgotten Wits." *The Antioch Review* 39, No. 4 (Fall 1981): 431-38.
Illuminates both the personal and intellectual relationship between Montagu and feminist Mary Astell. Perry surmises that Astell "probably saw Lady Mary as a sort of spiritual daughter, an inheritor."

Spacks, Patricia Meyer. "Borderlands: Letters and Gossip." *The Georgia Review* XXXVII, No. 4 (Winter 1983): 791-813.
Interesting analysis of the analogous relationship between gossip as a form of verbal communication and published letters as literature. Spacks concentrates on the letters of Montagu, Horace Walpole, and E. B. White to elucidate her discussion.

Spence, Joseph. Letter to his mother. In his *Letters from the Grand Tour*, edited by Slava Klima, pp. 356-57. Toronto: McGill-Queen's University Press, 1975.
Letter dated 25 February 1741 in which Spence discusses Montagu, whom he describes in superlatives.

Strachey, Lytton. "Lady Mary Wortley Montagu." In his *Characters and Commentaries*, pp. 115-24. New York: Harcourt, Brace and Co., 1933.
Discusses, in an essay written in 1907, the poignancy of Montagu's courtship letters to Wortley.

Tillotson, Geoffrey. "Lady Mary Wortley Montague and Pope's 'Elegy to the Memory of an Unfortunate Lady'." *The Review of English Studies* XII, No. 48 (October 1936): 401-12.
Speculates that Montagu was the inspiration for Pope's elegy in that her absence from England during her sojourn in Turkey constituted a "death" of sorts to the lovelorn poet.

Waddell, Helen. "Lady Mary Wortley Montagu." *The Fortnightly Review* n.s. CVIII, No. DCXLV (1 September 1920): 503-14.
Account of Montagu's relationship with her husband—as shown in her letters—from their first communication through the early days of their marriage.

Walpole, Horace. *Horace Walpole's Correspondence*. 48 vols. Edited by W. S. Lewis and others. New Haven: Yale University Press, 1937-83.
Prints several letters containing Walpole's remarks on his acquaintance with Montagu. In one of the few critical comments, contained in a letter to Horace Mann dated 14 October 1751, Walpole notes that in Montagu's letters "the art and style are superior to any letters I ever read but Madame Sévigné's." Elsewhere, however, he exhibits a marked animosity toward Montagu, reviling her appearance and character.

Henry More

1614-1687

(Also wrote under pseudonyms of Alazonomastix Philalethes, Franciscus Palaeopolitanus, and Philophilus Parresiastes) English philosopher, poet, and essayist.

A prominent seventeenth-century English religious and philosophical figure, More is one of the foremost representatives of the Cambridge Platonists, a group of English philosophers united against both materialism and Puritan dogmatism. Interested mainly in theology and essentially latitudinarian in spirit, More spent his life contemplating questions concerning the existence and eternalness of the soul. In his quest to understand the interrelatedness of man, the universe, and divine will, he voiced some of the major philosophical and intellectual ideas of his age, a time when Europe stood poised between the eras commonly designated the Age of Faith and the Age of Reason. His work therefore reflects the difficulty of reconciling religious faith with both the growing skepticism of the time and the emerging materialism expounded by such contemporaries as Thomas Hobbes.

The youngest of eleven children, More was born in 1614 in Grantham, Lincolnshire. His father was a strict Calvinist who believed in predestination and led an austere life of religion. Yet the elder More also had a penchant for reading aloud from Edmund Spenser's *The Faerie Queene* (1590-96), a chivalric romance in which basic Calvinist principles are indirectly contradicted. More later attributed his poetical taste to Spenser's work; indeed, he began his literary career with a poem in the Spenserian vein: *Psychodia platonica; or, A Platonicall Song of the Soul*, a reflection of More's deep admiration of Spenser's work in its careful imitation of the structure and diction of *The Faerie Queene*. Further, Spenser's humane vision of God may have initially led More to question Calvinism. Attending a local school until 1627, he then went to Eton College, where he studied Greek and Latin. At Eton, he became obsessed with theological questions, and by age fourteen he had disproven to himself the validity of the doctrine of predestination.

In 1631 More entered Christ's College, Cambridge, where he studied philosophical works by such authors as Aristotle, Geronimo Cardano, and Julius Scaliger. More worked chiefly toward one end: gaining "the knowledge of natural and divine things." Four years later, however, he reached a point of spiritual crisis, questioning seriously his conviction that the highest spiritual truths, those regarding immortality and the purpose of life, would be revealed to him if he gained knowledge of all things. More's crisis lasted until he took his M.A. and holy orders in 1639, at which time he discovered two important philosophical sources. The first was the Platonic writers—Plato, Plotinus, Philo of Alexandria, Justin Martyr, Mercurius Trismegistus, and Marsilio Ficino—in whose writings he found support for his emerging belief that attaining spiritual purity, rather than supreme knowledge, would lead to divine inspiration and understanding. From Neoplatonic thought More also adopted his belief in the transcendence of spirit over matter, his philosophical idealism, his principle of the immortality of the soul, and his view of the harmonious relationship between beauty and virtue. From Plotinus he drew his concept of God: the maker and controller of the universe, God is the uncreated

creator of all things. More's second philosophical source was the medieval mystical text cherished by Martin Luther, *Theologia germanica*, which emphasizes the understanding of God's will through the extinction of self-will. Upon reading *Theologia germanica*, More later claimed, he was instantly converted, his spiritual crisis and skepticism ending. Soon after his conversion, he became a tutor and fellow at Christ's College, settling permanently in Cambridge where he continued his intense philosophical study and quiet reflection.

At mid-seventeenth-century Cambridge, the predominant philosophical school was Aristotelian and the dominant strain of religion, Calvinism. Having rejected both, More established ties with three Cambridge scholars, Ralph Cudworth, Benjamin Whichcote, and John Smith, who preferred Plato's thought to that of Aristotle and had, like More, rejected the Calvinist beliefs that man is inherently corrupt, that salvation or damnation is preordained, and that formal rituals and dogma are necessary to true religion. Instead, More and the other scholars emphasized reason and morality, believing the two to be intimately linked. Later known as the Cambridge Platonists, these men and their disciples, though differing on many points of religion and philosophy, all believed in a rational, "enlightened" approach to Christianity based on Neoplatonic thought.

In the late 1640s, More began reading the works of René Descartes, who shared the Cambridge Platonists' interest in discovering truth through reason. In More's opinion, Descartes had successfully integrated Plotinus's philosophy with modern science and religion. For almost twenty years More was one of Descartes's strongest advocates, citing Cartesian philosophy in several essays and arguments. (The most notable of his ethical writings, *Enchiridion ethicum*, shows the marked influence of Descartes, particularly his *Les passions de l'âme* [1649; *The Passions of the Soul*, 1650]). Eventually, however, More came to believe that Descartes had reduced God to a mere abstraction, one with only a perfunctory role in the universe, and that Descartes's intent was to discredit the principles of religious belief. More's perception of Descartes's failure to interpret God as omnipotent and omniscient ultimately led him to reject all Cartesian arguments and to label Descartes a Nullibist, or materialist.

More was a vehement opponent of the rising philosophical materialism and atheism he perceived in England. Considering the materialist Hobbes his chief philosophical opponent, More directed many of his works against him. More believed that divine will and the immortality of the soul were "demonstrable from the knowledge of nature and the light of Reason." Hobbes, though, extended the concept of empirical reason to the point of mechanistic determinism, denying the existence of a transcendent order from which humanity derives its laws and standards of conduct. All events, in Hobbes's system, even in the realms of memory and thought, are reduced to solely physical and physiological phenomena. Individual will is declared nonexistent and the intellect is demoted to a passive role in determining human actions. To discredit Hobbes, More attempted in two critical works, *Enchiridion ethicum* and *The Immortality of the Soul*, to demonstrate the necessary role of will and intellect in shaping human destiny. In the former, More presented his practical moral philosophy on leading a holy life and discussed the psychological ramifications of free will. Further, More credited the human ability to reason to a communication from God and, in an idea far in advance of his contemporaries, deemed the passions both good and vital to spiritual existence. In the latter belief he relied heavily upon mystical and supernatural occurrences to counteract Hobbes's doctrine of egoism, claiming that Hobbes's disbelief in the supernatural proved he was an atheist.

To More, belief in spiritualistic phenomena was essential to understanding the human soul and its relation to the universe. Implicit in his Christian faith was a belief in the existence and immortality of the soul. Many of his major essays, including *An Antidote Against Atheisme, The Immortality of the Soul, Divine Dialogues,* and *Enchiridion metaphysicum,* are concerned with this subject. Through his lifelong correspondent, Lady Anne Conway, More was introduced to two important men of occult medicine, Baron Jean VanHelmont and Valentine Greatrakes. From them and other mystics, More heard stories of witchcraft and apparitions as well as testimony concerning human disembodiment. Convinced that a knowledge of mystic phenomena presupposes an understanding of the nature of the human soul, More collected these stories in *An Antidote Against Atheisme* and *The Immortality of the Soul.*

A believer in the supernatural, More was deeply concerned that false claims of illumination and mystical experience might sometimes be made at the expense of reason. Thus, in his first prose work, *An Antidote Against Atheisme,* he argued against belief in the "inner light" by which some claimed to receive divine inspiration, theorizing that both it and atheism stem from the same problematic source: a deluded, excessive imagination. More's opposition to "enthusiasts"—ardent believers in special, personal revelations from the Holy Spirit—culminated in a literary quarrel with the hermetic alchemist Thomas Vaughan, brother of the poet Henry Vaughan. Upon reading three of Vaughan's works, *Anthroposophia theomagica* (1650), *Anima magica abscondita* (1650), and *Magia adamica* (1650), which state that ancient magicians are the only true source of philosophy, More attacked Vaughan in *Observations upon "Anthroposophia theomagica" and "Anima magica abscondita"* for ignorantly deeming flights of fancy illumination from God. Vaughan responded to More's criticism in *The Man-Mouse Taken in a Trap and Tortured to Death* (1650), labeling More "a scurril, senseless piece, and—as he well styles himself— a chip of a block-head." More replied in *The Second Lash of Alazonomastix,* criticizing Vaughan as "driven by heedlesse intoxicating imaginations under pretense of higher strains of Religion and supernaturall light." After several similarly insulting written exchanges, More ended the quarrel in 1652, though many of his later treatises, especially *Enthusiasmus triumphatus,* indirectly continued his argument. Concurring with him, such later writers as John Locke, Jonathan Swift, and Joseph Addison supported More's definition of "enthusiasm" as an undisciplined melancholic imagination.

Although he continued to study philosophy, even after denouncing Descartes, More became predominantly interested in the Bible. Increasingly he emphasized the lessons of Scripture, becoming highly suspicious of extrabiblical philosophy and regretting his earlier passion for it. More continued to write until his death in 1687 at age seventy-three, never losing sight of his goal to discover and teach the highest spiritual truths. Throughout his career he had declined numerous offers of pres-

tigious preferments, believing he could "do the church of God better service in private than in public station." Having inherited a substantial fortune, More had suffered few financial burdens and apparently had entertained little interest in current affairs outside Cambridge. Although a loyal royalist and life-long defender of the Church of England, he appears to have been personally untouched by the political and religious upheavals which occurred during the English Civil War, the Protectorate, the Commonwealth, and the Restoration.

During his lifetime, More was a well-known religious figure. His numerous tracts were said to have "ruled all the booksellers in London for twenty years after the Restoration," according to one Mr. Chishull, a prominent seventeenth-century London bookseller. Many of More's works went through several printings, and numerous extracts and abridgements published after his death attest to an abiding public interest in his ideas. Even Hobbes, despite More's adamant opposition to him, stated that were he obliged to relinquish his own philosophy, his next choice would be More's. One of More's pupils, John Norris, extolled his mentor's virtues in a poem, writing, "His Worth *now shines* through Envy's base Alloy; / 'Twill *fill* her [the Muse's] widest Trump, and *all* her Breath employ." Yet another pupil (and More's biographer), Richard Ward, while personally affording More unconditional praise, also noted as early as 1710, "'Tis very certain that his writings are not generally (I will not say read, but) as much known, and many scholars themselves are in a great measure strangers to them." This confusion as to whether More's works were actually read or simply admired by reputation remains unresolved. The influence of the Cambridge Platonists in general was neither pervasive nor long-lasting. Only their latitudinarian approach to religion carried over into the eighteenth century, paving the way, ironically, for the philosophy that eclipsed their own: the Deistic rationalism of such men as Hobbes, Locke, and Descartes.

Nineteenth-century criticism mirrored that of the eighteenth century in its mixed appraisal, with the majority of commentators praising More's religious ideals and latitudinarian spirit while negatively criticizing both his writing ability (as frequently stilted and archaic) and his philosophy (as unoriginal and unenduring). An admirer, novelist J. H. Shorthouse, extracted several pages of More's work almost verbatim for his historical novel *John Inglesant* (1880). But in a caustic essay written earlier in the century, Robert Southey deemed More antiquated and found no literary value in his poetry whatsoever: "More could express [a strain of feeling] in no better language than an inharmonious imitation of Spenser's, barbarized by the extremes of carelessness the most licentious, and erudition the most pedantic." Samuel Taylor Coleridge's critique aptly reflects this dual reaction: "More's theological writings . . . contain more original, enlarged, and elevating views of the Christian dispensation than I have met with in any other single volume. For More had both the philosophic and the poetic genius, supported by immense erudition. But unfortunately the two did not amalgamate. . . . [He lacked] that critique of the human intellect, which, previously to the weighing and measuring of this or that, begins by assaying the weights, measures, and scales themselves." Many scholars agree with this statement, theorizing that More would probably have written more insightfully had he actively participated in the world outside Cambridge instead of choosing to seclude himself among his books.

Today More is generally considered a laborious writer whose works would have profited from greater objective critical attention on the part of their author—attention that might have helped develop the brilliance that occasionally appears therein. More's texts are rarely read except by students of Cambridge Platonism or seventeenth-century religious philosophy in general. None of these readers praises him in such glorifying terms as did Ward, nor do they condemn him as unforgivingly as did Southey. Most concur that he is more notable for his religious views and passion for mysticism than for his philosophy. Surprisingly modern, he is credited with accommodating the beliefs of others at a time when numerous religious and political groups were embattled in a fierce struggle. Striving to defend Christianity during a time of growing materialism and atheism, More attempted to combine the positive aspects of all religions in order to form one "church of God." Unable to separate the fideistic and emotional aspects of the past from the rational emphasis of the new materialists, he wrote philosophical poetry which is considered neither enduring philosophy nor especially good poetry. Geoffrey Bullough has summed up More's legacy in his comment that More's writing is "interesting, less for its artistic value, and its influence, than for its psychological significance and its embodiment of the religious ideals of an epoch."

PRINCIPAL WORKS

Psychodia platonica; or A Platonicall Song of the Soul, Consisting of Foure Several Poems, viz, Psychozoia, Psychathanasia, Antipsychapannychia, Antimonopsychia (poetry) 1642

Democritus platonissans; or, An Essay Upon the Infinity of Worlds Out of Platonick Principles (verse) 1646

Philosophical Poems (poetry) 1647

Observations upon "Anthroposophia Theomagica" and "Anima Magica Abscondita" (prose) 1650

The Second Lash of Alazonomastix; Conteining a Solid and Serious Reply to a Very Uncivil Answer to Certain Observations Upon Anthroposophia Theomagica, and Anima Magica Abscondita (prose) 1651

An Antidote Against Atheisme, or an Appeal to the Natural Faculties of the Minde of Man, Whether There Be Not a God (prose) 1652

Enthusiasmus triumphatus; or, A Discourse of the Nature, Causes, Kinds and Cures of Enthusiasme [as Philophilus Parresiastes] (prose) 1656

The Immortality of the Soul, So Farre Forth as it is Demonstrable from the Knowledge of Nature and the Light of Reason (poetry) 1659

Enchiridion ethicum, praecipua moralis philosophiae rudimenta complectens [as Franciscus Paleopolitanus] (essay) 1667

[*An Account of Virtue: or, Dr. Henry More's Abridgment of Morals,* 1690]

Divine Dialogues, Containing Sundry Disquisitions & Instructions Concerning the Attributes of God and His Providence in the World (prose) 1668

Enchiridion metaphysicum: sive, De rebus incorporeis succincta & luculenta dissertatio (prose) 1671

A Brief Discourse of the Real Presence of the Body and Blood of Christ in the Celebration of the Holy Eucharest (prose) 1686

JOHN NORRIS   (poem date 1687)

[*Norris was an English poet, mystical writer, and philosopher whose chief philosophical work,* An Essay Towards the Theory of an Ideal and Intelligible World *(1701-04), reflects the theories of Nicolas Malebranche and strongly opposes the philosophy of John Locke. In the following excerpt from his poem "To Dr. More, an Ode" (1687), he extols More as a man of knowledge and truth.*]

> Go *Muse,* go hasten to the *Cell of Fame,*
>   (Thous know'st her reverend aweful Seat:
>   It stands hard by your Blest Retreat)
> Go with a risk Alarm, assault her Ear;
>   Bid her her loudest Trump prepare,
>   To sound a *more* than *Humane* Name,
>   A *Name* more *Excellent* and *Great*
>   Than She could ever publish yet:
> Tell her; She need not stay till *Fate* shall give
> A *License* to his *Works,* and bid them *live;*
> His Worth *now shines* through Envy's base Alloy;
> 'Twill *fill* her widest Trump, and *all* her Breath employ.
>
> *Learning,* which long, like an *Enchanted Land,*
>   Did *Human Force* and *Art* defie,
> And stood the *Virtuoso's* best Artillery,
>   Which nothing *mortal* could subdue,
> Has yielded to *this Heer's Fatal* hand;
>   Like Seas that border on the Shore,
> The *Muses Suburbs* some *Possession* knew;
> But like the deep Abyss their *inner* Store
> Lay *unpossess'd,* till seiz'd and own'd by *You:*
>   Truth's *Outer Courts* were trod before:
> Sacred was her *Recess:* that Fate reserv'd for MORE.
>
> *Others* in *Learning's Chorus* bear their part;
>   And the great Work *distinctly* share:
> *Thou* our great *Catholick Professor* art;
> *All Science* is annexed to thy *unerring Chair.*
>   Some lesser *Synods* of the *Wise*
> The *Muses* kept in *Universities;*
>   But never yet, till in *thy Soul,*
> Had they *a Council Oecumenical.*
>   An *Abstract* they'd a mind to see
> Of all their *scatter'd Gifts,* and *summ'd* them up in *Thee.*
>   *Thou* hast the *Arts* whole *Zodiack* run;
>   And fathom'st all that *here* is known.
>   Strange restless *Curiosity!*
>   *Adam* himself came short of *Thee.*
> He *tasted* of the *Fruit,* Thou *bear'st* away the *Tree.*
>
>   Whilst to be *Great* the *most* aspire,
> Or with *low Souls* to raise their *Fortunes higher;*
> *Knowledge* the *chiefest Treasure* of the *Blest,*
>   *Knowledge,* the *Wise* Man's *best Request,*
> Was made *thy Choice:* For *this* thou hast declin'd
> A Life of *Noise, Impertinence* and *State:*
>   And whate're else the *Muses* hate;
> And mad'st it thy own *Business* to *Enrich* thy *Mind,*
> How *Calm* thy *Life,* how *Easie,* how *Secure,*
>   Thou *Intellectual Epicure!*
> *Thou,* as another *Solomon,* hast try'd
> *All Nature* through; and nothing thy Soul *deny'd.*
>   Who can two *such* Examples shew?
> *He* All things try'd *t'enjoy,* and *you* All things *to know.*
>
> By *Babel's* Curse, and our *Contracted Span,*
> *Heaven* thought to check the swift Career of Man:
>   And so it prov'd till *now;* Our Age
> Is much too *short* to run so *long* a Stage:
> And to learn Words is such a vast *Delay,*
> That we're *benighted* e're we come half way.

Thou with *unusual Hast* driv'st on;
And dost even *Time* it self *out-run.*
No Hindrance can retard *thy* Course,
Thou rid'st *the Muses winged Horse;*
Thy Stage of *Learning* ends e're that of *Life* be done.
There is now no Work left for *thy* Accomplish'd Mind,
But *to survey* thy *Conquests,* and *inform Mankind.*

(pp. xlvi-xlvii)

John Norris, "To Dr. More; an Ode" in The Complete Poems of Dr. Henry More (1614-1687), *edited by Rev. Alexander B. Grosart, 1878. Reprint by Georg Olms Verlagsbuchhandlung, 1969, pp. xlvi-xlvii.*

RICHARD WARD   (essay date 1710)

[*Ward was an English clergyman. In the following excerpt from a work originally published in 1710, he extols More as a champion of virtue and piety.*]

It is not only Customary, but seems to be the Right of illustrious Persons to have the most considerable Passages of their Lives transmitted to Posterity. Nor is the Design any other of the Divine Providence, in raising up great and extraordinary Men, than that the World should take particular Notice of their Virtues; and of such Performances of theirs as, both for the Illustration of its own Glory and the Good of others, have proceeded from them.

But in attempting so great an Enterprise as the present, I am sensible of the Peculiarity and Difficulty of the Province I undertake. I know the Expectation there will soon be of finding something that is Extraordinary in this Performance; something, I mean, suitable to the Character of this excellent Person [Henry More]; to the Singularity of his Learning and Genius; to that Esteem he hath so justly gained in the World; that Sense of him, in short, and that especial Reverence for him, which many have; from whence they will be prone to conceive Hopes of seeing it all answered by these Papers; and of a full Life to be offer'd in them to publick view. (pp. 55-6)

My design in brief is, to offer to the Publick, the best Account that I can of this great both Divine and Philosopher: and because he was a Person really extraordinary, and yet not so universally taken notice of in the World, or as I shall otherwise be able, to set him in a fair, or at least tolerable Light; and to collect together such Things concerning him as may best recommend his Wisdom and Writings and Piety unto all. (p. 56)

[What] an anxious and thoughtful Genius he was from his very Childhood; as he hath expresly in a certain Place [***Divine Dialogues***] told us, so is it abundantly to be collected from his Works in General; and from that which we have heard already concerning him. And assuredly, that Wit, Learning, and Piety, which shone so bright afterwards in the Highest Orb of Reason, Wisdom, and Virtue, could not fail of giving early very Signal Discoveries of it self, and even Hercules-like perform Wonders in its Cradle.

And here it is highly Remarkable, How, from the Beginning of his Time, all things in a Manner came flowing to him; and, as the Beams of the Sun in the cool early Day, rose and shone in upon him with their Golden and unexpressible Light. And having thus "his Mind (to use his own elegant Expression) enlightened with a Sense of the Noblest Theories in this Morning of his Days," he proceeded (as it is said concerning Wisdom) "to shine more and more unto the Perfect Day:" And thus vigorously residing in his Sphere of Light, he continued

his Course to the very Evening of his Age: Though then (as the Sun is often after the clearest Days) overtaken and Enveloped with Vapours and Clouds; in which this bright Lamp set; yet to rise with so much the greater Lustre in a New and more Glorious Region.

But here, I say, is that which is greatly Observable; How in his Youthful Years, at the Writing of his Poems, he is found to be endow'd with all that rich Sense of Mind in Relation to God, His Works and Providence which He afterwards so excellently cultivated and improv'd. For there we find him singing the Infinity of Worlds; the Prae-existency of the Soul; the Immensity, nay Infinity both of Time and Space; (though the latter of these, viz. the Infinity, he afterwards on his cooler thoughts retracted; not from any Deficiency in the Goodness of God, but from the Nature, as he speaks, and Incompossibility of the thing); the Soul's Immortality; the Soul's highest Life, Virtue, and Divine Joy; the Dreams and Fondnesses of many both in Philosophy and Religion; the eternal First Good; with the whole both Platonick and Christian Triad; the Unexceptionableness of Providence over all Men and Creatures, from their first Production to this very Day; the adorning of the Earth with Universal Righteousness in due time; the Earth's both Original and Conflagration; With such other lofty and glorious Theorems as make up the Strength and Beauty of that incomparable Work; and of which he writes in a Strain greatly to be admir'd but not easily imitated. (pp. 73-5)

[More] had a wonderful Sense of God, Sacred and Ineffable, and of his unconceivable Attributes; So he soon found All things, to his high Satisfaction, not unsuitable to them. And partly from a free Exercise of his own Reason and Faculties, and, what is much more, the Advantages of a Holy and Purified Nature; partly from the Sense of such ancient Sages as have ever been in greatest Honour and Esteem for their Wisdom and Virtue; partly from the Discoveries of the New Philosophy, and the known State and Phaenomena of the World; and lastly from either the open Expressions, or else more secret Intimations of Holy Scripture. . . . (pp. 76-7)

[He] took a very special Care to guard his Philosophy and free Principles with the duties of Virtue and Piety; and to make them all subservient to nothing but the purposes of Wisdom and Goodness; that so all Men might attain unto the highest Truth and Righteousness at once. And if all that pretend to Freedom of Knowledge, would make this their design, and accordingly to the utmost of their Power prosecute it; we should soon see a New, and much other Scene of things amongst us: Neither would the Church be disturb'd, nor Religion be prejudic'd; but God of all persons most exceedingly Honour'd: And, I will be bold to say, the Memory and the Writings of this his Servant esteem'd; Vice confounded; and the Christian Institution look'd upon, as it is, the most Adorable Mystery that could ever be communicated unto Men.

This then is the upshot of the Doctor's Free Way, whether in Matters of Nature or of Revelation. And he seems therefore to have been rais'd up by a Special Providence in these Days of Freedom, as a Light to those that may be fitted or inclin'd to High Speculations; and a General Guide to all that want it, how they are to mix the Christian and the Philosophic Genius together; and make them rightly to accord in one common End, *viz.* the Glory of God, with the highest both Felicity and Perfection of Man. (pp. 78-9)

Richard Ward, in his The Life of the Learned and Pious Dr. Henry More, *edited by M. F. Howard, The Theosophical Publishing Society, 1911, 310 p.*

ROBERT SOUTHEY (essay date 1812)

[A late-eighteenth and early-nineteenth-century English man of letters, Southey was a key member of the Lake School of poetry, a group which included the celebrated authors William Wordsworth and Samuel Taylor Coleridge. Southey's poetry consists mainly of short verse, ballads, and epics, many of which are notable for their novel versification and meter. His prose writings—which are generally more highly praised than his poetry—include ambitious histories, biographies, and conservative social commentaries. Today Southey is primarily remembered as a conservative theorist and as the biographer of such figures as Horatio Nelson, Thomas More, and John Wesley. In the following excerpt from Omniana—*a work originally published in 1812 and interlarded with commentary by his friend Coleridge in later editions—Southey unfavorably critiques More's attempts to combine poetry and philosophy in such works as* A Platonicall Song of the Soul.]*

Henry More whose philosophical works contain the most extraordinary instances of credulity, is not less curious as a poet than a philosopher. (p. 244)

[Mr. Henry John] Todd enumerates the **Song of the Soul,** among the poems which have been written in Spenser's metre, and praises it for "often presenting as just an allegory and as sweet a stanza as the original, which it professes to follow." It is my good fortune to be gifted with some perseverance; and in some of those remnants and fractions of time which are so often left to waste, and which if summed up and carried to account, amounts to so much in the course of an ordinary life, I have read this work through. Few persons perhaps have done this before, and still fewer will do it after me. "Lend me your *eyes*," reader, and in a very few minutes you shall know as much about it, as can be known without a thorough perusal . . . and in fact, almost as much as is worth knowing.

There is perhaps no other poem in existence, which has so little that is good in it, if it has any thing good. [In the margin of his copy of Southey's *Omniana,* Coleridge at this point wrote: "Mr. (J. H.) Frere . . . observed this very day to me how very grossly Southey had wronged this poem. I cannot understand in what mood S. could have been: it is so unlike him."] Henry More possessed the feelings of a poet; but the subject which he chose is of all others least fitted for poetry, and in fact there is no species of poetry so absurd as the didactic. The memory, when mere memory is concerned, may best be addressed in metre; old Lilly knew this, and the Memoria Technia is good proof of it. In these instances it is necessary to impress words, and nothing but words upon the recollection; which is facilitated by their chiming in. But philosophy set to tune only serves to puzzle the composer, without assisting the student. There is only one way of adapting it to the nature of poetry, which is, by allegorizing it: Henry More attempted this in a small part of his song, and the success of this attempt is not such as to induce a wish that he had extended it. Mr. Todd's praise is ill founded. The allegory in Spenser is the worst part of his poem, but the worst allegory in Spenser is far better than the best in Henry More. This the following specimen will convince. (pp. 244-45)

> A lecture strange he seem'd to read to me,
> And though I did not rightly understand
> His meaning, yet I deemed it to be
> Some goodly thing.

Henry More's readers seem to have agreed with old Mnemon [the character through which More tells of the pilgrimage of life], in thinking it strange and in not understanding it. Yet this is the best part of the whole allegory, and of the whole poem. He soon begins to imitate John Bunyan in his nomen-

clature . . . but oh! what an imitation of that old King of the Tinkers . . . ! [In a second margin note, Coleridge exclaims: "False, cruelly false! Again and again I puzzle myself to guess in what most un-southeyan mood Southey could have been, when he thought and wrote the above!—And the phrase, old king of the Tinkers! applied to the Author of the inimitable *Pilgrim's Progress,* that model of beautiful, pure, and harmonious English, no less than of still higher merits, outrages my moral Taste"]—The passage is curious in another respect . . . it may have suggested the name of Pandaemonium to Milton, who was a friend of Henry More's.

> On Ida hill there stands a Castle strong,
> They that it built call it *Pantheothen;*
> Hither resort a rascal rabble throng
> Of miscreant wights; but if that wiser men
> May name that fort, *Pandemoniothen*
> They would it cleep. It is the strongest delusion
> That ever Dæmon wrought, the safest pen
> That ere held silly sheep for their confusion.
> Ill life and want of love, hence springs each false conclusion.
>
> That rabble rout that in this Castle won
> Is *Irefull-Ignorance, Unseemly-Zeal,*
> *Strong-self-conceit, Rotten Religion,*
> *Contentious-reproach-gainst-Michael-*
> *If-he-of-Moses'-body-aught-reveal-*
> *Which-their-dull-skonses-cannot-easily-reach.*
> *Love-of-the-carkass, an-inept-appeal-*
> *T'-uncertain-papers, a-false-formal-fetch-*
> *Of-feigned-sighs. Contempt-of-poor-and-sinful-wretch.*

Two more stanzas follow full of these Praise-God-Barebones names. The next contains one of those rare gleams of poetry which redeem the author . . . not indeed from neglect . . . but certainly from contempt.

> These and such like be that rude regiment
> That from the glittering sword of Michael fly;
> They fly his outstretched arm, else were they shent,
> If they unto this Castle did not hie,
> Strongly within its walls to fortifie
> Themselves. Great Dæmon hath no stronger hold
> Than this high Tower. *When the good Majesty*
> *Shines forth in love and light,* a vapour cold
> And a black hellish smoke from hence doth all infold.

Here too are lines which none but a true poet could have written, and here the reader will again be reminded of Milton.

> Fresh varnished groves, tall hills, and *gilded clouds*
> *Arching an eyelid for the gloring morn,*
> Fair clustred buildings which our sight so crouds
> At distance, with high spires to heaven yborn,
> *Vast plains with lowly cottages forlorn*
> *Rounded about with the low-wavering sky.*

But in general the language of this poem is the most barbarous that can be conceived. (pp. 248-49)

Henry More could express [a strain of feeling] in no better language than an inharmonious imitation of Spenser's, barbarized by the extremes of carelessness the most licentious, and erutition the most pedantic. (p. 251)

In looking over this account of Henry More's strange poems, I do not perceive that any thing too harsh has been said of their defects, and yet it leaves a more unfavourable opinion of the author's talents, than I feel myself, or by any means wish to communicate. It is generally acknowledged that a man may write good verses, and yet be not poet; it is not so generally acknowledged that he may be a poet and yet write bad ones. Three fourths of the English poets have had less genius than

Henry More, but not one of them who possessed any has contrived so completely to smother it, and render it useless. (p. 257)

Robert Southey, "Henry More's Song of the Soul," in Omniana, or Horae Otiosiores *by Robert Southey and S. T. Coleridge, edited by Robert Gittings, Southern Illinois University Press, 1969, pp. 244-57.*

SAMUEL TAYLOR COLERIDGE   (essay date 1834?)

[*An English poet and critic, Coleridge was central to the English Romantic movement and is considered one of the greatest literary critics in the English language. Besides his poetry, his most important contributions to literature include his formulation of Romantic theory and his introduction of the ideas of the German Romantics to England. His Shakespearean criticism overthrew the neoclassical approach to William Shakespeare by focusing on the dramatist as a masterful portrayer of human character. In the following excerpt from fragments of his various writings on More, Coleridge condemns More's philosophy and adversely criticizes his literary style.*]

In Henry More who blended the doctrine of Des Cartes (viz. that matter is mere extension and that Body and Soul or Spirit are especially heterogeneous) with the Notions of Plotinus, which are built, on the assumption of their being differences in degree, Body being the dying away of Spirit, and it's last vibrations & echoes, this incongruity is especially prominent and revolting. Matter is mere Potentiality, Potentiality mere non-entity, & yet this non-entity plays the part of a most energetic Figurante in all possible forms, attracts and is attracted, exerts magic influences, bird-limes Spirits &c. In short, the πρῶτον ψεῦδος of all these Schemes is that they commence with an Abstraction, that is, an *Object.* Hence whatever is in it's nature incapable of being contemplated objectively, as the I, We, with all the Affections and Passions, are not explained at all, or with more than Stoical Bravado called Nothings, that require and permit no explanation—tho' in every Object these Subjects are supposed, in order to it's being an Object.—And yet from the same cause Explanations are endlessly sought for, in lieu of that insight which Ideas alone can afford—for an Abstraction quoad Abstraction is necessarily incomplete, and supposes a something from which it is abstracted; but this again is an Abstraction, and so on ad infinitum. This, however, is an evil common to the Pseudo-Platonists with the Epicurean-Naturalists; but it is peculiar to the former, that their Objects being either properly Subjective, as the Soul, or Transcendent, as Deity, their Explanations are all not so much Suppositions or hypotheses, as *Suffixions* or hypopoieses ex. gr. the Eight orbs, orbs Monadical, Intellectual, Psychical, Imaginative, Sensitive, Spermatical, Quantitative, and Hyle or Coactive. And yet the Attention of the Soul being throughout intentionally and professedly directed to her highest interests, these Writers have and cannot but have a charm for minds, that feel and struggle up against the insight and witchery of Custom and yearn for an evidence and a reality beyond what the flux of the Senses can afford: and after all, if there be not some third better than either, it is nobler and perhaps wiser to dream about realities than to be grave-awake about dreams!

More, ***Poems,*** *written on the flyleaf at the beginning of the volume.*

Ah! what strength might *I* gather, what comfort might *we* derive, from these Proclo-plotinian Platonists' doctrine of the Soul, if only they or their Spinozistic imitators, the Natur-philosophers of present Germany, had told or could tell us what

they meant by *I* and *we,* by Pain and Remorse. Poor *we* are nothing in *act* but everything in suffering.

(*A manuscript note in a different hand, with Coleridge's added remark*)

Dr. More uses many words that are obsolete, many that are provincial, and many that are entirely his own coinage, which the novelty of the subject may in some degree have rendered necessary. His elisions appear to be more licentious than have either been adopted before or since.

Spenser he acknowledges in his Dedication was a favourite author with him from childhood, and his partiality is sufficiently obvious from following his antiquated diction, and from writing in the same octave stanza, which Spenser borrowed from the Italian poets.

Which is not an octave but an ennead (*i.e.* a stanza of nine lines) and which Spenser did *not* borrow from the Italians, but after many and various experiments invented for himself, as a perfect ✳ whole, as it is indeed, and it only.

✳ That I mean, to which nothing can be added and from which nothing can be removed. (pp. 621-22)

H. More was a poetical philosophist who amused himself in calling Aristotelian abstractions by the names of Platonic Ideas; but by no means a philosophic poet, framing in the life-light of a guiding Idea. (p. 623)

The 5 main faults characteristic of our elder poets not of the first class, and of none more than of H. More, are:

1. That in the pursuit of strength and vigour they fall into, may eagerly rush upon, the hateful and loathsome, and particularly the offensive to the sense of smell, aggravated by moral disgust and associations of disease, "fed with stinking gore suck'd from corrupted corse"(**"Psychathanasia"**).

2. That from a predilection for the lively and exact in similitudes and descriptions, they recur to the mean, the ludicrous, and the odd.

3. That generally they are regardless of the influence of associations, not merely such as are the accidental growth of a particular age and fashion, but of those that are grounded on the nature of man and his circumstances.

4. That they sacrifice the grand keeping and total impression to particular effects, and if it only be *bene* sonans per se, care not though it should be dissonant in the concert.

5. That they construct their metre in correspondence to their own passionate humouring and often peculiar and mannered mode of reading or reciting their verses—a mode always more influenced by what they intended the words to mean than by the necessary or obvious sense of the words themselves. (p. 625)

Samuel Taylor Coleridge, "Poetry: Henry More," in his Coleridge on the Seventeenth Century, *edited by Roberta Florence Brinkley, Duke University Press, 1955, pp. 617-26.*

REV. GEORGE GILFILLAN   (essay date 1860)

[*Gilfillan was a Scottish clergyman and poet as well as a prolific critic and biographer. In the following excerpt, he comments on More's occasional brilliance as well as the philosophic short-comings of More and the Cambridge Platonists.*]

More's prose writings give us, on the whole, a higher idea of his powers than his poem. This is not exactly, as a recent critic calls it, 'dull and tedious,' but it is in some parts prosaic, and in others obscure. The gleams of fancy in it are genuine, but few and far between. But his prose works constitute, like those of Cudworth, Charnock, Jeremy Taylor, and John Scott, a vast old quarry, abounding both in blocks and in gems—blocks of granite solidity, and gems of starry lustre. The peculiarity of More is in that poetico-philosophic mist which, like the autumnal gossamer, hangs in light and beautiful festoons over his thoughts, and which suggests pleasing memories of Plato and the Alexandrian school. Like all the followers of the Grecian sage, he dwells in a region of 'ideas,' which are to him the only realities, and are not cold, but warm; he sees all things in Divine solution; the visible is lost in the invisible, and nature retires before her God. Surely they are splendid reveries those of the Platonic school; but it is sad to reflect that they have not cast the slightest gleam of light on the dark, frightful, faith-shattering mysteries which perplex all inquirers. The old shadows of sin, death, damnation, evil, and hell, are found to darken the 'ideas' of Plato's world quite as deeply as they do the actualities of this weary, work-day earth, into which men have, for some inscrutable purpose, been sent to be, on the whole, miserable,—so often to toil without compensation, to suffer without benefit, and to hope without fulfilment. (pp. 221-22)

> *Rev. George Gilfillan, "Dr. Henry More," in his* Specimens with Memoirs of the Less-Known British Poets, Vol. II, *James Nichol, 1860, pp. 219-22.*

GEORGE MacDONALD   (essay date 1868)

[*A Scottish man of letters, MacDonald was a key figure in shaping the fantastic and mythopoeic literature of the nineteenth and twentieth centuries. Such novels as* Phantastes *(1858) and* The Princess and the Goblin *(1872) are considered classics of fantasy literature. These works have influenced C. S. Lewis, Charles Williams, J. R. R. Tolkien, and other seekers of divine truth, adventure, and escape from mortal limitations. During his long, prolific career, MacDonald also wrote in several other genres, achieving particular success with his novels of British country life. These, like his work in all genres but fantasy, are nearly forgotten today. In the following excerpt, MacDonald praises the spiritual ideals and philosophy in More's poetry.*]

Chiefly known for his mystical philosophy, which he cultivated in retirement at Cambridge, and taught not only in prose, but in an elaborate, occasionally poetic poem, of somewhere about a thousand Spenserian stanzas, called *A Platonicall Song of the Soul,* [Dr. Henry More] has left some smaller poems [as well]. . . . Whatever may be thought of his theories, they belong at least to the highest order of philosophy; and . . . they must have borne their part in lifting the soul of the man towards a lofty spiritual condition of faith and fearlessness. The mystical philosophy seems to me safe enough in the hands of a poet: with others it may degenerate into dank and dusty materialism. (p. 223)

> Yea, though the soul should mortal prove,
> So be God's life but in me move
> To my last breath—I'm satisfied
> A lonesome mortal God to have died.

This last paragraph [from his poem **"Resolution"**] is magnificent as any single passage I know in literature.

Is it lawful, after reading [the entire poem], to wonder whether Henry More, the retired, and so far untried, student of Cambridge, would have been able thus to meet the alternations of

suffering which he imagines? It is one thing to see reasonableness, another to be reasonable when objects have become circumstances. Would he, then, by spiritual might, have risen indeed above bodily torture? It is *possible* for a man to arrive at this pefection; it is absolutely *necessary* that a man should some day or other reach it; and I think the wise doctor would have proved the truth of his principles. But there are many who would gladly part with their whole bodies rather than offend, and could not yet so rise above the invasions of the senses. Here, as in less important things, our business is not to speculate what we would do in other circumstances, but to perform the duty of the moment, the one true preparation for the duty to come. (pp. 226-27)

There are strange things and worth pondering in [the poems **"Resolution," "Devotion," "The Philosopher's Devotion,"** and **"Charity and Humility"**]. An occasional classical allusion seems to us quite out of place, but such things we must pass. The poems are quite different from any we have had before [in the history of English poetry]. There has been only a few of such writers in our nation, but I suspect those have had a good deal more influence upon the religious life of it than many thinkers suppose. They are in closest sympathy with the deeper forms of truth employed by St. Paul and St. John. [**"Charity and Humility"**], concerning humility as the house in which charity dwells, is very truth. A repentant sinner feels that he is making himself little when he prays to be made humble: the Christian philosopher sees such a glory and spiritual wealth in humility that it appears to him almost too much to pray for. (pp. 231-32)

> *George MacDonald, "Henry More and Richard Baxter," in his* England's Antiphon, *Macmillan & Co., 1868, pp. 223-37.*

JOHN TULLOCH   (essay date 1874)

[*Tulloch was a Scottish theological writer and historian. His principal work,* Rational Theology and Christian Philosophy in the Seventeenth Century *(1874), has been a standard authority. In the following excerpt, Tulloch considers why More's writings have failed to remain popular.*]

As the Cambridge movement reached its highest, or at least its most elaborate, intellectual elevation in Cudworth, so it ripened into its finest personal and religious development in Henry More. Cudworth is much less interesting than his writings; More is far more interesting than any of his. He was a voluminous author. His writings fill several folio volumes; they are in verse as well as prose; they were much read and admired in their day; but they are now wellnigh forgotten. Some of them are hardly any longer readable. Yet More himself is at once the most typical and the most vital and interesting of all the Cambridge school. He is the most Platonical of the Platonic sect, and at the same time the most genial, natural, and perfect man of them all. We get nearer to him than any of them, and can read more intimately his temper, character, and manners—the lofty and serene beauty of his personality—one of the most exquisite and charming portraits which the whole history of religion and philosophy presents. (p. 303)

More's poems are now hardly known; they have fallen out of the rank which even the poems of Donne and Davies maintain, and are not found in any collection. In some respects they form the most singular attempt in literature to turn metaphysics into poetry. Apart from the "notes" and "interpretation general," which he has himself happily furnished, they are barely intelligible. Even with such assistance they are a most intricate and perplexing study. Not only the strain of thought and complexities of Neo-Platonic allusion, but the involutions and phantasies of the verse itself, contribute to this. Yet there are here and there not a few genuine gleams both of poetic and spiritual insight; and the mental picture which the poems present is altogether so curious as to reward the patience of a congenial student. No one unless such a student, animated in some degree by the "Platonic rage," from which they "powerfully flow forth," need attempt them. The eye must be profound as well as "clear," which would penetrate their "deep searching thoughts often renewed." (pp. 313-14)

If More's life as a student kept him retired from the world, it greatly stimulated his productivity as an author. Probably, also, it contributed in some degree to the endless prolixity and repetitions of his writings. We feel especially with him—as more or less with all the Cambridge school, except Whichcote—that we are conversing with a mind too little braced by active discipline, and the prompt, systematic, compact habits which come from large intercourse with men, and the affairs which stir men to powerful movement or great ambitions. The air of a school, which was after all confined to a narrow if influential sphere, is more pervading in his writings than in any of the others. Christ College, with its books, is never far out of sight; and all the sweetness and seclusion of Ragley, "the solemness of the place, its shady walks and hills and woods, where he lost sight of the world and the world of him," did not help to let the light of day or the breath of the common air into his "choice theories," however they may have assisted him in "finding them out" and elaborating them. . . . It may be pleasant to keep away from the "bustles and affairs of the world without," as it is pleasant to contemplate the peculiar beauty and serenity of character which ripen amidst such retirements; but, after all, no man can escape from his fellow-men, and the rough facts of ordinary human life, without spiritual and intellectual injury. The product may be finer that is grown in solitude, but it will neither be so useful, nor, in many respects, so true and good.

And so More's writings, largely as they bulk in his life, and deeply interesting as some of them are to the religious and philosophical student, have long ceased to exert any influence. They never became literature. (pp. 339-40)

[Of all More's] writings, the only one which can be said to have retained any literary popularity, or to be commendable to the modern reader, is his *Divine Dialogues,* . . . illustrative of his mental and spiritual growth. It is of this volume that Dr. Blair speaks in his Lectures on Rhetoric, as "one of the most remarkable in the English language." "Though the style," he adds, "be now in some measure obsolete, and the speakers be marked with the academic stiffness of those times, yet the dialogue is animated by a variety of character and a sprightliness of conversation beyond what are commonly met with in writings of this kind." The *Divine Dialogues* are certainly, upon the whole, the most interesting and readable of all More's works. The current of thought runs along smoothly, with less tendency than in any of his other writings to digressive absurdity and wearisome subdivisions; the style is here and there fresh and powerful, and there is not only some liveliness of movement in the successive conversations, but an attempt is made, as Blair implies, to impart a definite portraiture to the several speakers, and to preserve throughout their individuality and consistency. This attempt is not very successful, but it is one in which scarcely any modern writer of dialogues has succeeded, and More may in this respect compare happily even

with Berkeley, in an age of far more literary brilliancy. The *Divine Dialogues,* moreover, possess for the common reader the advantage of condensing his general views in philosophy and religion. In fact, most of his characteristic principles may be gathered from them.

The year 1668, in which he composed the *Dialogues,* may be said to mark the apex of More's intellectual activity. It is true that after this he composed his *Manual of Metaphysics,* and attacked both Jacob Böhme and Spinoza in elaborate treatises. But the elasticity and temper of his philosophical genius are less buoyant in these efforts. His *Metaphysics,* elaborate though they be, are in the main only a systematic and somewhat desultory expansion of views regarding the nature and proof of incorporeal substances, which he had already more than once expressed; while his cabbalistical and prophetical studies have acquired a stronger hold of his mind. (pp. 343-45)

The character of More's genius and thought has been sufficiently set before our readers. As a thinker he is much less systematic, but more fertile and genial, than Cudworth. He is poet, moralist, and mystic, rather than thinker. It is difficult to bring his varied speculations to a unity, or to fix his opinions into a definite system. His attitude is sufficiently determinate; but his sympathies and views are apt to vary with his temporary enthusiasms and the altered pressure of the moral and theological atmosphere around him. He is never inconsistent with himself—whether commending Descartes or abusing him— whether warning Lady Conway against the Quakers, and exposing their fanaticism, or transported by the wonder-working vagaries of Van Helmont or the ghost-stories of Glanvill. But his genius is rich, complex, and enthusiastic—swayed by passionate and lofty emotion—rather than clear, penetrating, and illumined by a definitely rational purpose. He is less philosopher or theologian than prophet and gnostic—with his mind brimful of divine ideas, in the delighted contemplation of which he lives, and moves, and writes. All his works are inspired by a desire to make known something that he himself has felt of the Divine. The invisible or celestial, so far from being hard for him to apprehend, is his familiar haunt. He has difficulty in letting himself down from the higher region of supernal realities to the things of earth. This celestial elevation is the most marked feature at once of his character and his mind. It is the key to his beautiful serenity and singular spiritual complacency—a complacency never offensive, yet raising him somewhat above common sympathy. It is the source of the dreamy imaginings and vague aerial conjectures which fill his books. These may seem to us now poor and unreal, and some of them absurd, but they were to him living and substantial. Nay, they were the life and substance of all his thought. He felt himself at home moving in the heavenly places, and discoursing of things which it hath not entered into the ordinary mind to conceive or utter. He was a spiritual realist. It was his passion and study so to feel and describe divine facts, that others might see and know them as he himself did. Thus it was that he delighted to dwell on such subjects as the existence of God and the immortality of the soul; and felt that when he was drawn aside from these, even to ethical questions and rules, he was drawn from a pleasant and congenial atmosphere to a dry and uninviting one.

The substantive value of More's thought cannot be judged high. It is impossible indeed to overestimate the tone, character, and spiritual ideal after which he aimed in all his life and work. But so far as the progress of truth is concerned—the removal of prejudice—the simplification of belief—the conciliation of natural and spiritual knowledge—he accomplished little. With all his enthusiasm of reason, he is an imperfect representative of the rational movement. The Cambridge philosophy, while it showed in him some of its finest fruit, yet also brought forth in him all its weakness. The Neo-Platonic extravagances which lay hidden in it from the first, came in his writings into luxuriant blossom. Originally a protest against spiritual fanaticism, no less than dogmatic bigotry, it remained free in all its course from any taint of the latter; but it certainly reached in More a new species of fanaticism. He is not merely inspired, but possessed by his favourite ideas. They not only guide but dominate him, and sometimes in the most traditionary and outworn forms. They are never kept calmly before him in an attitude of inquiry. His aim is not to purify, enlarge, and harmonise them, but to teach them even in exaggerated and fantastic forms. All this bespeaks the decadence rather than the growth of reason.

Withal, More is true to the two great springs of the movement. He loves inquiry, although he is himself an imperfect inquirer. He never shrinks from reason, if he fails to give it free play and scope, and to draw it into the full light of day. Again, he believes profoundly in the harmony of natural and spiritual truth. He has lost the threads of this harmony, and some of his own speculations have rather tended to obscure than to illuminate it. But if he must be pronounced in many things a spiritual dreamer rather than a Christian Rationalist, his dreams are not merely of a higher world, fashioned by his own imaginings, but of a cosmos of nature and spirit—of life here and life hereafter, united by continuity of effort in the beneficient designs of divine love. (pp. 406-09)

> John Tulloch, "Henry More-Christian Theosophy and Mysticism," in his Rational Theology and Christian Philosophy in England in the Seventeenth Century, Vol. II, *second edition, William Blackwood and Sons, 1874, pp. 303-409.*

REV. ALEXANDER B. GROSART (essay date 1878)

[*A Scottish clergyman, editor, and essayist, Grosart is best known for editing and reprinting rare Elizabethan and Jacobean literature. In the following excerpt, he praises More's poetry, philosophy, and character.*]

I limit myself here to the Poetry of our Worthy [Henry More]. The preceding portion of our Memorial-Introduction has made it clear that it was to 'sing' his Philosophy that he became a Poet, and that his Poetry was designed as the vehicle of his highest reach of attainment as a Philosopher. Nevertheless it is not for its philosophy *per se,* but for its imaginative qualities and vividness of fancy and exquisite nicety of expression of the most gossamery thinking and feeling, and its pre-Raphael-like studies of nature, and now and again—alas! at long intervals, and mainly in the minor Poems—wonderfulness of rapture and aspiration, that we hold the Poetry of Henry More to be worthy of prolonged study. (p. xxix)

[In] one of the most memorable of the minor poems ["**Cupid's Conflict**"] he admits his unskilfulness and obscurity and 'barbarous words,' as against mellifluous love-lays that he might have sung. (p. xxxii)

[This] and other admissions will win for More forgiveness—such as Spenser had to ask in his 'Shepherd's Calendar,' because of his Chaucerian and older words—for inevitable obscurantism and irritating neologies. Many of the new words and new 'ideas' were as hierogylphs rather than expressions

of his thoughts, intelligible or semi-intelligible to himself, but hidden to the multitude.

Notwithstanding all this, when you compare the little volume of 1642 with the larger of 1647, you find that he did more than merely enlarge. In our quotation from the *Epistle to the Reader,* it is to be observed that he professes—'I have taken the pains to peruse these Poems of the soul, and to lick them into some more tolerable form and smoothnesse;' and the reader who will emulate the Author's 'pains' to peruse and re-peruse, and compare, will be interested with the marks of revision and nicety of labour in the most unlooked-for places. But so far as I have discovered, the more 'tolerable form and smoothnesse' belong rather to the additional stanzas inserted throughout, so as to give a firmer *nexus,* and a less abrupt succession to the philosophising and fancies. I have been struck with the untouched perfection of all that arrests you in reading, when the portions are common to both the editions. Not verbal but structural and constructural were his endeavours 'to lick them' into shape. . . . That More had an ear for the melody of versification, and an eye for the colouring of choice words, many and many a stanza in his *Philosophical Poems,*—as finely wrought in workmanship as gem from Holland,—goes to demonstrate. I can only cull a few flowers from the rich Garden, and like Alexander Wilson's little friend say, 'The woods are full of them,' the book will yield well-nigh innumerable such. (pp. xxxiii-xxxiv)

Others of his minor Poems ["**The Son of God,**" "**The Eagle,**" "**Dawn of Day and Sunset,**" "**The Sunbeams,**" "**Mnemon,**" "**The Shrew-Wife,**" "**Spring,**" "**Horses,**" "**A Nymph,**" "**Body and Soul,**" and "**The Visible and Invisible: Soul and Sense**"], are equally exquisite in adaptation of word to 'idea.' His 'Hymns'—strong, severely simple, hearty—I place far above the effusive sentimentalisms of our popular Hymnology. It is a scandal and a sorrow that some of them have not long since been used in the Churches. . . .

I have already stated and illustrated More's Wordsworthian self-scrutiny and lofty self-estimate. The most cursory reader will be struck with his ingenuity in working into his arguments his own experiences and likings. . . .

Of his personal opinions and characteristics revealed in his Poetry, I value inestimably his catholicity. He was a clergyman of the Anglican Church, and he 'defended' her with courage and force when she was on the losing side. He is full of tart and even sarcastic rebuke of the infinite factions and fractions of Nonconformity who broke off from the National Church. But he rose far above mere Churchism, and estimated a man's religion by what the man was and did, not by the Church-name he bore. Thus common-sensely does he put the matter in his *Epistle to the Reader:*— . . .

> I would be very loth to be so farre mistaken as to be thought a Censurer or Contemner of other mens Religions or Opinions, if they serve God in them in the simplicity and sincerity of their hearts, and have some more precious *substratum* within, then inveterate custome or naturall complexion. All that I mean is this: That neither eager promoting of Opinion or Ceremony, nor the earnest opposing of the same, no not the acuteness of Reason, nor yet a strong, if naked conceit, that we have the Spirit of God, can excuse a man from being in any better condition then in the Land of Brutes or in the mere animal nature. . . . [It] would prevent a great deal of bloud and bitternesse in the Christian world, if we reserved the flower and strength of our zeal for the undoubted Truth of God and His immutable Righteousnesse, and were more

mildly and moderately affected concerning the Traditions and determinations of the Elders.

(pp. xxxiv-xxxvii)

Of his own devoutness and 'walking with God,'—as walked the two of Emmaus,—there are everywhere heart-stirring evidences. . . .

As the corollary of all this, the student-Reader will be half-awed half-touched by the pervading sanctity of the man and of the Poet. With beaming eye and tremble in his voice he thus greets 'virgin youth as yet immaculate:'—

> Dear lads! How do I love your harmlesse years
> And melt in heart while I the Morning-shine
> Do view of rising virtue which appears
> In your sweet faces, and mild modest eyne.
> Adore that God that doth himself enshrine
> In your untainted breasts; and give no eare
> To wicked voice that may your souls encline
> Unto false peace, or unto fruitlesse fear,
> Least loosened from your selves Harpyes away you bear.

(p. xxxviii)

It is questionable if any man is complete, or of kin to the highest, who has no humour. The finest Humourists of all literatures have had the largest and strongest intellect. Shakespeare is so utterly supreme and exceptional all round, that it needeth not to adduce him. But apart from him, I know none of the mighties who lacked this element. JOHN MILTON and WILLIAM WORDSWORTH are vulgarly supposed to have been without it. It is a 'Vulgar Error.' I was glad in studying More to discern, amid all his restraint and gravity, sufficient indications that he had humour and pleasantry of wit. None but a genuine Humourist could have drawn these portraits:—

> All the nice questions of the School-men old
> And subtilties as thin as cobwebs bet,
> Which he wore thinner in his thoughts yrold.
> And his warm brains, they say, were closer set
> With sharp distinctions than a cushionet
> With pins and needles; which he can shoot out
> Like angry Porcupine, where e're they hit.
> Certes a doughty Clerk and Champion stout
> He seem'd and well appointed against every doubt.

> 'The other rod on a fat resty jade
> That neighed loud. His rider was not lean.
> His black plump belly fairly outward swai'd
> And pressed somewhat hard on th'horses mane.
> Most like methought to a Cathedrall Dean.
> A man of prudence and great courtesie
> And wisely in the world he knew to glean.
> His sweaty neck did shine right greasily
> Top heavy was his head with earthily policy.

(p. xxxix)

Has your materialist ever been more keenly ridiculed than here?—

> For then our soul can nothing be but bloud
> Or nerves or brains, or body modifide.
> Whence it will follow that cold stopping crud,
> Hard moldy cheese, dry nuts, when they have rid
> Due circuits through the heart, at last shall speed
> Of life and sense, look thorough our thin eyes
> And view the Close wherein the Cow did feed
> Whence they were milk'd; grosse Pie-crust will grow wise,
> And pickled Cucumbers sans doubt Philosophize.

(p. xl)

No grim ascetic, no misanthropic recluse, but a whole-hearted, clean-conscienced man was Henry More. I like him all the better that he manfully avowed his love of the nutbrown ale

of his College, and that he did not believe in 'Fasting'—for everybody. (pp. xl-xli)

[His love of nature] comes out very much as in the great ancient Painters, whose backgrounds of portraits or sacred personalities rather than land-scape, or sea-scape, or sky-scape proper, assure us that they had eyes to look into, and not merely on, this so radiant and beautiful earth of ours. That is to say, you have nothing of the later Wordsworthian clarity and intuition of seeing, that *humanizing* of 'the meanest flower that blows,' which is part of Wordworth's measureless gift to our English-speaking race. But you have snatches of description, elect *traits* of the visible and audible, dainty epithet and interblended perception and emotion. And so you have him crying out with a great joy:—

> How sweet it is to live! what joy to see the Sunne.

(p. xli)

I am thankful to have More's avowal of a 'purpose' and disavowal of purpose-less-ness. His manly words come across our mephitic atmosphere with the freshness of a salt wind blown across the sea. That he should win such Readers as he coveted, and not be forgotten, he was tranquilly assured. . . . While he had this calm confidence in and for himself, his was no absurd magnifying of his poetic gift. He had sung because he must sing. (p. xlv)

There is nothing of the spasmodic or ambitious in all this. He knows that he sang 'true' alike to himself and the truth; and in his lowly sphere, he recognises his Verse as having the stuff of imperishableness in it; and so as with the Meteor—according to the old belief—'whose materiall is low unwieldy earth, base unctuous slime,' but having 'its inward spright' fired of 'great Phoebus lamp:'—

> . . . then even of it self doth climb;
> That earst was dark becomes all eye, all sight.

he sees his Poetry as a—

> Bright starre, that to the wise, of future things gives light.

And now I ask for the Poetry of Henry More new and sympathetic Readers and Students. I have no hesitation in affirming substantive additions to philosophic thought and opinion in his Prose. Were it for no more than his strenuous assertion of the ethical, as well as intellectual, side of all truth, and his wise scorn of any attempt to 'intermeddle' with either ethical or divine things without a clear and purified spiritual vision, and his co-equal rejection of any religion that rested on mere dogma and creed and untouched of aspiration as of action, and above all, his self-introspection as an exemplar of a human soul—as lovingly and lingeringly as anything in 'The Prelude' itself—I should so regard his Prose. Because of this, your Historians of Ethical-metaphysical Philosophy must imitate WHEWELL'S and COLERIDGE'S and MAURICE'S appreciation, not MACKINTOSH'S and LEWES' and BAIN'S, and others' neglect. But as furnishing his complete Poems, I am naturally most of all concerned to win readers for them. Granted that there is much barbarous and uncouth wording, recondite and obscurant speculation, hard and barren controversy, and all too often absence of finished art and consequent discords—granted every abatement, there nevertheless remains in these Poems—in nearly all the minor, and in well-nigh every page of the larger—ample to vindicate their revival, and to reinscribe the venerable name of Henry More among our real Makers and Singers to the full extent of his own modest claim. (pp. xlv-xlvi)

Rev. Alexander B. Grosart, "Memorial-Introduction: Critical," in The Complete Poems of Dr. Henry
More (1614-1687), edited by Alexander B. Grosart,
1878. Reprint by Georg Olms Verlagsbuchhandlung, 1969, pp. ix-xlvii.

ARTHUR CHRISTOPHER BENSON   (essay date 1888)

[*Benson was an English educator and author. Although he was
a prolific poet, novelist, and biographer, it is as an essayist that
he is best known; his three volumes of essays,* The Upton Letters
(1905), From a College Window *(1906), and* Beside Still Waters
*(1907) remain his most commended works. In the following ex-
cerpt from an essay originally published in 1888 in the* Contemporary Review, *Benson illuminates the reflection of the author's
personality in More's style and subject matter.*]

[More] was a very laborious writer; his works fill folio volumes, and are full of curious learning, with a strange streak
of humour, descending at times to a coarseness of expression
which would not be tolerated now. (p. 55)

The *Divine Dialogues* are the **"Mystery of Godliness"** and the
"Mystery of Iniquity"; the first of these being an exhuastive
inquiry, in many books, into the nature and spirit of heathen
religions. It may be said at once that his method of treating
the subject is unjust; he is far too anxious, in his zeal for the
Truth, to attribute to them a licentious or contemptible origin
and obscene or meaningless ceremonies. The "Mysteries of
Eleusis," which, according to Socrates, had much symbolism
of a strangely exalted type, are treated by More as both superstitious and dissolute—even Apollonius of Tyana, who,
whether he existed actually or not, at least exhibits a high type
of the Stoic ideal, is a solemn puppet in his eyes. When he
has, then, to his satisfaction demonstrated the worthless and
debasing character of these rites—which is surely to shut the
eyes to the inextinguishable hunger for the holy expression of
life, in worship, that has never really deserted the human race—
he proceeds to bring the Christian faith upon the stage, and to
show how it satisfies the deepest and highest instincts of
humanity.

But More cannot be said to have been a Christian in the sense
that Thomas-à-Kempis or Francis of Assisi were Christians;
he did not hunger for the personal relation with Christ which
is so profoundly essential to the true conception of the Christian
ideal. He was a devout, a passionate Deist; he realised the indwelling of God's spirit in the heart, and the divine excellence
of the Son of Man. But it was as a pattern, and not as a friend,
that he gazed upon Him; the light that he followed was the
uncovenanted radiance. For it is necessary to bear in mind that
More and the Cambridge Platonists taught that the Jewish
knowledge of the mysteries of God had passed through some
undiscovered channel into the hands of Pythagoras and Plato;
and that the divinity of their teaching was directly traceable to
their connection with Revelation. They looked upon Plato and
Pythagoras as predestined vehicles of God's spirit, appointed
to prepare the heathen world for the reception of the true mysteries, though not admitted themselves to full participation in
the same.

Besides these books, which are profound and logical, and composed in a style which is admirable by comparison to the ordinary writing of the times, More drifted away into some rather
grotesque speculations on the subject of Apocalyptical interpretation; of this, he says, humorously, himself, that while he

was writing it "his nag was over free, and went even faster
than he desired, but he thought it was the right way." (pp. 55-7)

Besides these there are published letters of Henry More's,
prolix for the general reader, but interesting enough if the man's
own personality appeals to you: some very disappointing hymns
and didactic poems, stiff and unlovely to a strange degree for
so deep and graceful a writer; and many other scattered works,
such as the **Enchiridion Ethicum,** which it is impossible to
analyse here. (p. 58)

Though he produced very voluminous writings, yet he sometimes manifested a strong and healthy repugnance to the task
of expressing himself: he had none of the gloomy laboriousness
that is never satisfied with its performance, and yet never takes
a lively pleasure in it. When he had finished one of his more
lengthy works, he said pleasantly to a friend, as he threw down
his pen: "Now for three months I will neither think a wise
thought, nor speak a wise word, nor do a wise thing." (p. 59)

He had no turn for dry and laborious criticism: he studied things
more than words: of his own skill in dead languages, though
it was in reality very considerable, he spoke jestingly, in that
deprecating ironical way that he always used of himself—that
he was like the man that passed by a garrison with a horseshoe
hanging at his belt, when a bullet being shot at him struck right
upon it, upon which he remarked, "that a little armour was
sufficient, if well placed;"—and he often said, in writing his
books, that when he came to criticism and quotation, it was
"like going over ploughed lands." (p. 60)

[More] dwelt much on the next world. "I am glad to think
when I am gone," he said, "that I shall still converse with
this world in my writings. But it is a greater satisfaction to me
that I am going to those with whom I shall be as well acquainted
in a quarter of an hour as if I had known them many years."
(p. 64)

The great and singular charm of such a life is its union of
mystical tendencies with such perfect sanity. For nearly half
a century Henry More lived in a light which he did not invent,
but found. He cannot be suspected of fanaticism or weakness;
from the day that he found peace in life to the day that he
entered into rest, he lived in the strength of a magnificent ideal.
(p. 65)

> Arthur Christopher Benson, "Henry More, the Pla-
> tonist," in his Essays, Macmillan and Co., 1896,
> pp. 35-67.

EDWARD AUGUSTUS GEORGE   (essay date 1908)

[*George was an American clergyman and essayist. In the following excerpt, he praises More's latitudinarian attempts to modern-
ize Christian doctrine and practice.*]

More's writings are voluminous, but are less interesting than
his personality, and in large part are so foreign to the modern
mind as to be almost unreadable. His autobiography . . . is far
more interesting than the philosophical works to which it is
the preface. **An Antidote against Atheism** presents a noble Transcendentalism, and carries one along with its argument, until
it flies off on a tangent into discussions of witchcraft, apparitions, and extravagant manifestations of the occult. Mystic
that he was, More was far from despising matter, and displays
a surprising interest in physical phenomena, to which he applies
an observation almost scientific. He makes laudable attempts
at physiological psychology in his discussions of the spinal

marrow, conarium and ventricles of the brain as possible seats of the reasoning faculty. Interesting as are these essays in primitive science from an historical point of view, they could hardly be expected to speak in modern phrase. Worthless as are the results, the spirit of these investigations is altogether admirable. The principle by which More explains physical phenomena is the ''spirit of nature.'' (p. 119)

Newton's principle was soon to dissipate More's ''spirit of-nature'' and Descartes' ''vortices,'' but such speculations have value as showing men's interest in natural science in the seventeenth century, and more particularly in the case of More as showing the attitude of certain Christians of that much -abused century toward science in its beginnings and the startling ideas which it was introducing. These times of ours are not the first in which Christianity has adapted itself to new ideas with sympathy and grace. Not all heralds of new truth have been burned at bigotry's stake. It is good to behold Henry More, than whom his century produced few more profound and devoted Christians, in his attitude toward the new truths of his day.

> The times we are in, and are coming on are times wherein Divine Providence is more universally loosening the minds of men from the awe and tyranny of mere accustomary superstition, and permitting a freer perusal of matters of religion than in former ages.

It sounds like a voice from the present. ''Blind obedience to the authority of the church'' is being swept away. Scepticism and atheism are resulting: and these should be met not by stemming the tide of the times, but by adapting Christianity to the new conditions. A new Christian phraseology and point of view are demanded, which shall appeal to the naturalist.

> The atheist will boggle at whatever is fetched from established religion, and fly away from it, like a wild colt in a pasture at the sight of a bridle. But that he might not be shy of me, I have conformed myself as near his own garb as I might, without partaking of his folly or wickedness: and have appeared in the plain shape of a mere naturalist myself, that I might, if it were possible, win him off from downright atheism. For he that will lend his hand to another fallen into a ditch, must himself, though not fall, yet stoop and incline his body: and he that converses with a barbarian must discourse to him in his own language; so he that would gain upon the more weak and sunken minds of sensual mortals, is to accommodate himself to their capacity.

Here is a Henry Drummond of the seventeenth century! (pp. 120-21)

More realized that it would be ''hugely disadvantageous to religion and theology to seem to be left so far behind, or to appear to be opposite to that, which I foresaw might probably become the common philosophy of the learned.'' Therefore to prevent all contempt and cavil against the sacredness of Christianity, as holding anything against the solid truths of approved reason and philosophy, by fantastic and allegorical interpretation he discovers Cartesianism and Platonism in the books of Moses. The method was bad, but the object good. Cabalistic exegesis is absurd, but the demand that science, philosophy and religion speak one language is beyond all praise.

Responsiveness to new views and on the other hand downright opposition to them are not uncommon: but to be responsive to new views and at the same time to sympathize with the feelings of those who oppose them, to pass to the new without making a rupture with the old, this is the rare spirit. Such a truly

mediating position was More's. He endeavored to write ''without any offence or scruple to the good and pious, or any real exception or probable cavil from those whose pretensions are greater to reason than religion.'' He refuses to be destructive. He will not tear down what others reverence, but is content to build up what he reverences himself, and for the final result trust to the survival of the fittest. Arguments for the existence of God, which he considers illogical, he will still not confute, for the reason that they help some, and he would not cause any to stumble by the removal even of an unsteady prop. (pp. 122-23)

With rare magnanimity More, believing himself in the new truth, respects its opposers, and understands their opposition. He realizes that ''that which is strange has something of the face of that which is hostile.''

> It is a piece of rudeness and unskilfulness in the nature of things and in the perfection of Divine Providence (who has generally implanted a tenacious adhesion to what has accustomarily been received, that the mind of man might be a safer receptacle when it lights upon what is best) to conceit that because a truth is demonstratively evident in itself, that therefore its opposite shall immediately surrender the castle.
>
> (p. 123)

In a remarkable passage More explains how authority should be respected, and how disregarded. Only where authority demands belief contrary to the teaching of the Scriptures is it to be rebelled against. It may well be compromised with, especially in terms of expression, in matters of speculation and science. (p. 124)

> [The] conscience of every holy and sincere Christian is as strictly bound up in matters of religion plainly and expressly determined by the infallible oracles of God, as it is free in philosophical speculations: and though out of love to his own ease, or in a reverential regard to the authority of the church, which undoubtedly every ingenuous spirit is sensible of, he may have a great desire to say, profess and do as they would have him; yet in cases of this kind, where anything is expected contrary to the plain and express sense of those divine writings, he will use that short but weighty apology of the apostle, that God is to be obeyed rather than men.
>
> (p. 125)

For a thorough mystic, More's interest in physical science was remarkable, but it was a spiritual interest. He is always in antagonism to Hobbes, ''that confident exploder of immaterial substances,'' and to the materialism of the *Leviathan*. It was the ''spirit of nature'' that he saw behind all material forms and phenomena. He looked in, in order to understand what he saw as he looked out.

In theology More is a transcendentalist. He argues the reality of God from the existence in us of the idea of a perfect and necessary being. The object must exist as the correlate of the idea. The soul is furnished with innate ideas and the natural emanations of the mind are to be trusted as faithful guides. The principles of the circle and triangle are appreciated by the mind, though they are nowhere exhibited in visible form. The geometrical propositions we feel are true of all triangles and circles, the mind confidently leaping to universal conceptions. As a musician sings the whole song at the suggestion from another of a few notes, so the soul leaps to universals and sings out the whole song upon the first hint, ''as knowing very well before.'' ''It is plain that we have some ideas that we are not beholding to our senses for.'' There is more of reality than matter offers through the senses. Man dwells in the borders of two worlds, the spiritual and the material, responding to influences from each, ''tugging upward and downward.'' Man is supernatural. Matter is utterly incapable of such operations as we find in ourselves, therefore there is in us something immaterial or incorporeal. As our spirit understands and moves corporeal matter, so behind the phenomena of nature is there reason and spirit. The soul of man is a ''little medal of God.'' ''As cattle are branded with their owner's name, so God's character sealed upon our souls marks us as his people and the sheep of his pasture.'' ''No bishop, no king''; and ''No spirit, no God.''

But reason does not yield the great certainties. The comprehension of spiritual truth requires ''a certain principle more noble and inward than reason itself and without which reason will falter, or at least reach but to mean and frivolous things. I have a sense of something in me while I thus speak, which I must confess is of so retruse a nature that I want a name for it, unless I should endeavor to term it divine sagacity.'' (pp. 126-27)

This mystic was not obliged to soar to worlds unknown for the beatific vision. Within and without he saw God, whenever his heart was pure. To him there were ''two temples of God, the one the universe in which the divine Logos is high priest: the other, the rational soul whose priest is the true man'': and in both temples he worshipped. (pp. 127-28)

> Edward Augustus George, ''Henry More, 1614-1687,'' in his Seventeenth Century Men of Latitude: Forerunners of the New Theology, Charles Scribner's Sons, 1908, pp. 109-28.

M. F. HOWARD (essay date 1911)

[*In the following excerpt, Howard uses* A Platonicall Song of the Soul *to illustrate both the virtues and faults of More, the Cambridge Platonists, and their followers.*]

The first-fruits of the new thought [of the Cambridge school] appeared in 1642—''Psychozoia,'' a curious and fantastic metaphysical poem by Henry More, then a young Fellow of Christ's College, and a contributor to the ''Lycidas'' volume of elegies. He was already fascinated by Neoplatonism, and described the first part of his poem as the allegorical story of his own conversion from self-will to a union with the Divine Will, and from doubt and conflict to peace and joy. He explained that owing to its autobiographical character it was intended to be obscure, and was only published in response to the eager desire of his friends. Its form and style were suggested by the *Faerie Queene*—which, More writes in the dedication, his father had read to him as a boy, in the long winter evenings,—but the ideas have more affinity with Spenser's Platonic hymns and the didactic poems of Sir John Davies.

The ''Psychozoia'' contains many beautiful lines, and some whole stanzas are almost excellent, but the allegory is so difficult and pedantic (in spite of a key and ample notes) that the poem has come to be considered amongst the curiosities of literature. This is much to be regretted, for, apart from its actual merits, Henry More's *Song of the Soul* is the representative poem of the Cambridge Platonists, and one of the most comprehensive statements of their theories and speculations. It shows their great weakness—that aloofness from the every-

day world and its affairs (not uncharacteristic of severe scholarship) which kept them in comparative tranquillity all through political strife and civil war. But the inwardness and self-knowledge of the first part of the poem, and the breadth of thought and strength of faith which could deal with such subjects as those of the later sections—the questions of the Pre-existence and Unity of Souls, and the Infinity of Worlds—are typical of the scope of their speculations. (pp. 4-5)

[More's] *Song of the Soul* was too difficult and involved, even for the subtle minds of his contemporaries, and at length in 1652 a new sympathy with the pressing needs of his time induced him to write a more lucid prose treatise on an equally vast scale. He had been in London, probably staying with his pupil, Sir John Finch, and was shocked and alarmed by the atheistical tendencies of young men of the world outside the universities. He had also been aroused and stimulated by that platonic friendship with his pupil's sister, Lady Anne Conway, which became one of the strongest factors in his life. To her he dedicated this first essay in prose apologetics, the *Antidote against Atheism,* which was probably the most curious tribute of respect and affection received by a lady even in that ingenious century. It consists of three parts: the first section proving the existence of God from metaphysical arguments; the second, from the revelation of mind and purpose in the visible world; the third, from the probabilities of the supernatural or spirit-world discovered in well-attested ghost-stories of every age.

From this time onward Henry More expounded his theories in volume after volume—enlarging or condensing them, and approaching them from the theological, philosophical, or scientific standpoint, but always with a singular consistency. He wrote little more poetry, and it is clear from his **''Cupid's Conflict''**—the record of a temptation to live and write with lower ideals to court success and popularity—that he had realised the incongruity of metaphysics and poetry, and the fact that the mere form of verse was not a sufficient disguise for philosophy.

> But now thy riddles all men do neglect,
> Thy rugged lines of all do ly forlorn.
> Unwelcome rhymes that rudely do detect
> The Reader's ignorance. Men holden scorn,
>   To be so often non-plus'd or to spell,
>   And on one stanza a whole age to dwell.

Probably his work both in prose and poetry would have had more lasting value if he had encouraged such moods of self-criticism. (pp. 8-9)

[His] aloofness from the everyday world accounts for many of his failures in authorship. His abundant leisure led him to write too much (his many apologies and pseudonyms show that he himself realised this), too widely, and sometimes enigmatically and carelessly. Moreover, although he had many friends and disciples, he did not succeed in influencing and developing men of sufficient power to carry on his work effectively. They were usually kindred spirits—gentle, devout souls and lovers of mysticism; but none of them had enough strength of intellect or personality to impress their master's teaching upon the materialistic eighteenth century. (pp. 9-10)

The real value of [More's] work, which cannot deteriorate although his metaphysical speculations are obsolete and worthless, lies in his moral philosophy, his mysticism, and the poetry which is even more apparent in the short poems and some passages of his prose than in the monumental *Song of the Soul.* It is unlikely that his writings will ever regain much attention, but, just as in his own day his disciples were won by his character even more than by his theories—the personality of Henry More becomes increasingly interesting and significant in the light of newer knowledge of psychology. (pp. 34-5)

> *M. F. Howard, in an introduction to* The Life of the Learned and Pious Dr. Henry More *by Richard Ward, edited by M. F. Howard, The Theosophical Publishing Society, 1911, pp. 1-53.*

MARJORIE H. NICOLSON   (essay date 1922)

[*An American essayist, editor, and educator, Nicolson was the first woman president of the Modern Language Association, an editor of the* American Scholar, *and Dean of Smith College. Fascinated with the influence science and philosophy had on literary minds of the seventeenth and eighteenth centuries, she wrote prolifically on the subject, examining the ideas of such authors as John Milton, Alexander Pope, and Samuel Pepys. In the following excerpt, Nicolson argues that More borrowed from classical and medieval authors when composing "Psychozoia."*]

It is interesting . . . to find a poem which combines, together with undoubted references to contemporary science, at least seven of the most popular allegorical devices of the Middle Ages. Henry More's "Psychozoia," first published in 1648, was the first of the *Philosophical Poems* which may be said to be the earliest publication of the great school of Cambridge Platonism. Written when More was about twenty-five years of age, the poem is a combination of frequently undigested learning based on the scholastic training of Cambridge, and a youthful enthusiasm for the newly discovered Plotinian philosophy in which More at that time believed that all contradictions were to be finally resolved. In the midst of what is admittedly a metaphysical study, sometimes nothing but a versification of portions of the *Enneads,* one comes across the pilgrimage theme; the device of the marriage of abstractions; the figure of Alain de Lille's Nature; the contest of the Vices and Virtues; the assault of the castle of the soul; the debate; even the birds' matins. (pp. 141-42)

[While there are] many Spenserian reminiscences—even direct imitations and borrowings—which we find throughout **"Psychozoia"**; yet there are many themes in the poem which came rather from the medieval originals.

In the first canto More is dealing with one of the most difficult of all problems: the doctrine of the unity of the Trinity; and attempting, in addition, to reconcile the Christian and neo-Platonic doctrines of the Trinity; to prove, in other words, not only that the three are one, but that the Christian Father, Son, and Holy Ghost are paralleled by the Plotinian Good, Mind, and Spirit, or even that the one conception is included in the other. The allegorical form which he uses to express this complex idea is the marriage of abstractions. Ahad, or Hattove, variously spoken of as the Father and the Good, is represented as joining in marriage his children: Aeon, the Son, or the Mind, and Psyche, or the Holy Spirit. Ahad, the Father, being in his own nature infinite and incomprehensible, is represented as hidden in his own light:

> . . . deeply cover'd o're
> With unseen light. No might imaginall
> May reach that vast profunditie.

Neither Ahad nor Aeon is, in himself, visible to mortal eye; they may be known only through the third person of the Trinity, Psyche; and Psyche herself is visible only through the robe of Nature which she wears. In his prolonged description of this figure, More is using that great medieval conception of Nature,

suggested probably by Claudian in his *Rape of Proserpina,* but fully worked out for the first time, in Alain de Lille's *Complaint of Nature.* Upon the flowing robes of More's Psyche there are pictures which remind one of the pictures on the robe of the earlier Nature; but More has added to his figure a "number of goodly balls" which "pendant was at the low hem of this large garment gay"—most of which danced about, though one stood among them "steady"; "a glance," as he expresses it, "at Copernicus his system." Besides this More has added to the medieval description the fourfold robe, combined of Aristotelian elements: Physis, the outer robe, sprinkled with dark little spots which increase continuously, each developing to the full its own potentiality, yet never allowing the robe to lose that shape which is its nature; the second fold, Arachnea, a web "so thin as to deceive the spider's curious touch," in the midst of which sits the third element, Haphe, the sense of touch, these two together forming the life of sensation; the fourth fold, largest and loosest of all, spreading over and transforming all things, Semele, universal imagination.

It is through this four-fold robe that man can know Psyche, and it is through Psyche that he can comprehend the Trinity. Then the poet shows the union of the Trinity under the symbol of the marriage of abstractions, a device which in medieval allegory had its inception in the *De Nuptiis Philologiae et Mercurii* of Martianus Capella, which we find used again and again throughout the Middle Ages. In addition to the marriage of Aeon and Psyche, More shows us the Father also placing his hand eternally upon the clasped hands of the Son and Spirit, with which action the union of the Trinity is accomplished.

From this macroscosmic allegory, More passes on, in the next canto, to a microcosmic one—the pilgrimage of the life of man. At first this tale, which is by far the most readable part of the *Philosophical Poems,* seems to have no connection with the first canto, but as the reader proceeds he finds that all souls are the children of Psyche, the great original scource, each life on earth being a ray from the vast central sphere; the spirit, however, appears in as many guises as there are persons on the earth. The character through which More tells of the pilgrimage of life is Mnemon, who was a young man when the pilgrimage began, but whose years now number ten times ten—the Pythagorean symbol of the perfect life. . . . Throughout the pilgrimage of Mnemon, the influence of Spenser upon More is evident to the most casual reader.

The scene of the pilgrimage is Psychania, the Land of Souls, which More describes as divided into two parts: the good, or the dwelling place of these souls which are most like God, is called therefrom Theoprepia; while the other part is Autaesthesia, the land of brute sensation. . . . It is in the province of Beiron, the country of mere sensation, that the wandering of Mnemon begins. The first district in which he finds himself is Psittacusa-Land, the dwelling place of the parrot people, who speak significant words, the meaning of which they do not comprehend. On his way, Mnemon meets with other travellers, and for awhile they journey on together, in true allegorical style. The first of these, Don Psittaco himself, discourses glibly of all the problems of the universe and says the last word in regard to each. Pithecus joins them for a short time, but rapidly proceeds to his own country, the land of the apes. It is while Don Psittaco is discoursing of religious forms and observances that there occurs that episode which is, from the point of view of allegory, one of the most interesting things in the entire poem, the birds' mass, an extraordinary device for this particular period. This carries us back historically to *La Messe des*

Oisaus of Jean de Conde of the early fourteenth century, in which occurs an elaborate parody of the church service, when Venus bids the nightingale to sing mass. . . . The two principal treatments of the theme in English are to be found in Lydgate's *Devotions of the Fowles* and *A Proper New Boke of the Armonye of Byrdes,* sometimes attributed to Skelton. In **"Psychozoia"** More goes into details in regard to the setting of the matins, and then comments on the service as the birds perform it. . . . The travellers do not remain for the entire service, but they do remark that each bird, as it enters the enclosure, bows to the east, that at various periods throughout the service, all the other birds do the same. (pp. 142-45)

At this the travellers leave the birds' church and take up their journey again. A short distance further on, they meet two friends of Psittaco, well named Corvino and Graculo—the description of whom is strongly reminiscent of Chaucer. There follows one of those 'debates' so common in medieval allegory and romance, in which the question is not however love, either earthly or heavenly, but is the conflict between the believers in rational and revealed religion. Eventually the discussion is ended, so far as Mnemon is concerned, by the fact that the travellers reach the crossroads; the others, still disputing, keep on in the kingdom of the brutish life, but Mnemon goes straight forward and comes at last to a high wall which completely bars his progress. This and what follows is definitely reminiscent of the *Roman de la Rose,* with its high wall and low wicket gate. Mnemon calls, and in answer there appears a youth, "in decent russet clad," who is Simon, or, as he explains it "obidentall Nature." He points out to the traveller that he has looked too high for the gate, "for that same doore where you must passe in deep descent doth lie." The wall, the traveller learns, is Self-Conceit; the low door, overgrown with stinging nettles, is Humility. Simon from this time becomes the guide usual to medieval allegory, explaining what else were dark to the traveller. Simon is accompanied by two strangely complex characters; his father, an old man, is represented as holding continually at his heart a bloody knife; his mother's back is bent beneath burdens, and her face distorted with pain. All three, we find later, are phases of the human soul, one being Patience, the other Self Denial, and Simon the complete soul which is in the end to include the other two.

The strange band passes through the gate of Humility and finds the valley of Dizoia, where all life is dual because man opposes his will to the will of God. All is darkness, the air filled with chill fog and mist; the travellers wander about fearfully, the only sounds at first the barking of dogs. There follows an episode evidently taken directly from the *Faerie Queene* where Sir Scudamour visits the cottage of the blacksmith Care. In all this valley there are no dwellings save great forges where giants work unceasingly at the anvils. There is no rest, for when the night bird of sleep swoops down to the weary, it is driven away by the clanging of the great hammers. Thus there begins a long season of penance for the sinful man.

After many days, the light begins to appear, and the fog and mist to disperse. Above the hill, the weary man can see the first light of the sun, but something else must happen before the valley can behold the pure light, for on that hill, its shadow obscuring the sun, stands a great castle, the stronghold of Daemon. Here the author combines two of the most popular themes in medieval allegory: the siege of the castle, and the war between the Vices and Virtues, both of which had their first form in Prudentius, the one in *Hamartigenia,* the other in *Psychomachia.* This particular castle has been called Pan-

theothen, but the wanderer understands at last that it should have been Pandaemoniothen. In it is the rabble rout of the Vices—many of them bearing the names of medieval Vices, but some of the others reminding the reader that the poem is a product of seventeenth-century England, as do also the names of the walls which surround the castle: Inevitable-Destiny-of-God's-Decree and Invincible-Fleshlie-Infirmitie. Both of these, the poet reminds his readers, are invincible only because man has thought them so. Here, moreover, are all those pagan torments of Hades, which the medievalists delighted in introducing. . . . (pp. 146-47)

But the pilgrimage is not over yet for the wanderer. Accompanied by Simon and his strange parents, Mnemon goes on through flowery fields until he comes to a hill, the ascent of which he insists upon beginning. Here he meets three sisters, Justice, Philosophy, and Apathy, with whom he wishes to linger, thinking that now at last he has reached truth. But he finds, contrary to custom, that it is not on the hill that truth dwells, and he is forced to descend to a dark valley—the valley of the vapors which arise as long as man chooses to remain in the land of beasts. In passing through the fumes which are of self, he loses himself, for this is the valley of Nothingness. There too, the aged parents, Patience and Self-Denial—which are of self—give up their lives to their son, who becomes thereby the complete soul; vitality being lost, reality and spirit remain. Casting off the last vapors of self, Mnemon finds in the newly understood Simon his own soul; he pushes through the last of the black vapors and comes out upon that country of God where

> there's no fear of Death's dart-holding hand;
> Fast love, fix'd life, firm peace in Theoprepia land.

With that comes the end of the seventeenth-century pilgrimage of the soul, and Mnemon, now an old man, sinks back upon his seat beneath the trees, lost in memory of youth. (pp. 147-48)

Marjorie H. Nicolson, "More's 'Psychozoia'," in Modern Language Notes, *Vol. XXXVII, No. 3, March, 1922, pp. 141-48.*

BASIL WILLEY (essay date 1934)

[*An English author and educator, Willey has written several highly praised works of literary criticism including* The Seventeenth Century Background *(1934),* The Eighteenth Century Background *(1940), and* Nineteenth Century Studies *(1949). In the following excerpt, he traces More's initial acceptance and subsequent rejection of Descartes's philosophy.*]

With Henry More, as with Cudworth, the existence of the spiritual world was the first of certainties, and most of his works are designed to prove its reality. More was the most mystical of the Cambridge Platonists; with him the reality of 'spirit' was more than an intellectual conviction, it was an experience. (p. 160)

Beginning life . . . with his interpretation of existence unalterably fixed by his emotional experience, More was at once confronted with the two main philosophical systems of his own time, those of Hobbes and Descartes. His repugnance for Hobbism may be guessed, and indeed he clearly regarded himself as the champion of all vital truth against Hobbes's materialism and its dire consequences. Nothing, he felt, was of more urgent importance than 'to root out this sullen conceit' of Hobbes, 'that the very Notion of a Spirit or Substance Immaterial is a perfect Incompossibility and pure Non-sense'. For the implications of this view, as he clearly saw, were

> That it is impossible that there should be any God, or Soul, or Angel, Good or Bad; or any Immortality or Life to come. That there is no religion, no Piety nor Impiety, no Vertue nor Vice, Justice nor Injustice, but what it pleases him that has the longest Sword to call so. That there is no Freedome of Will, nor consequently any Rational remorse of Conscience in any Being whatsoever, but that all that is, is nothing but *Matter* and *Corporeal Motion;* and that therefore every trace of man's life is as *necessary* as the tracts of Lightning and the fallings of Thunder; the blind *impetus* of the *Matter* breaking through or being stopt every where, with as certain and determinate *necessity* as the course of a Torrent after mighty storms and showers of Rain.

In his *Immortality of the Soul* he places Hobbes, 'that confident exploder of *Immaterial Substances* out of the world', as it were in the witness-box by quoting eight of his clearest statements for the sole reality of body, and then proceeds to refute him point by point. We shall understand his position best, perhaps, by considering what he took to be the *True Notion of a Spirit.* In this treatise, which belongs to his last period, we find him in opposition to Descartes as well as to Hobbes. More had formerly been one of the earliest transmitters of Cartesian ideas to England. . . . What had especially attracted him in Descartes, apart from the precision and charm of all his work, was his clear affirmation of the existence of the soul and of God as the fundamental certainties. Here, he felt, was the great, the incomparable philosopher of the modern age, who could not only explain the hidden workings of nature but who could do it without falling, like Hobbes, into materialism. A theory of the world which accepted the last results of science, but which yet confirmed the metaphysics of Platonism and Christianity: what more could be desired? Gradually, however, More's youthful enthusiasm for Descartes, like Coleridge's for Hartley, gave way to a misgiving that there was a fundamental cleavage between them; and Descartes, to whom he had written in 1648 that 'All the great leaders of philosophy who have ever existed, or who may exist, are pygmies in comparison with your transcendent genius,' at length became for him 'that pleasant Wit *Renatus des Cartes,* who by his jocular *Metaphysical Meditations* has so luxated and distorted the rational faculties of some otherwise sober and quick-witted persons'. This remarkable change was brought about by the realisation that Descartes did not teach the 'True Notion of a Spirit'; that his conception of 'soul', that is, was not 'true' to More's own experience. More's technique for expressing his divergence from Descartes was strictly confined by the contemporary modes of thought, but he seems nevertheless to be feeling after and endeavouring to expose, that very quality in Cartesianism which . . . made it ultimately a force hostile to poetry and to religion. He singles out for attack Descartes's definition of the soul as a *res cogitans,* a thinking substance, having no extension in space. For one who, though affirming the reality of spirit, yet denies it 'extension' or location in space, More coins the term 'Nullibist'. To say that a thing is, and yet is nowhere, seems to him dangerous nonsense. He agrees with the Nullibists that 'whatever real Being there is that is somewhere, is also extended', but differs in believing that the soul, which his adversaries agree to be real, not only is, but is *somewhere,* that is, occupies space. To strip spirit of all attributes save that of thought is, he fears, to reduce it to a mere abstraction. The Cartesians have wrongly assumed that because we can conceive the soul merely as cogitation, therefore it has no other con-

ceivable attributes, such as location. He points out that the mind can conceive many things in abstraction from many of their attributes, and urges that

> from the precision of our thoughts to infer the real precision or separation of the things themselves is a very putid and puerile sophism.

The view that the Mind is not 'in space' seems to More to imply that 'the Mind, in so far as it is conceived to be an *Incorporeal Substance,* is to be exterminated out of the Universe, as a useless figment and Chimaera.'

Such authority had the notion of 'Extension', in the seventeenth century, as the essential attribute of the admittedly 'real' (matter), that unless one could attribute extension to a substance, that substance was in danger of evaporating into nothingness. This was More's fear for 'spirit'; Descartes by affirming spirit as a mere abstraction was really, in spite of all appearances to the contrary, beginning upon the slippery slope towards materialism and atheism. It was safer, in More's opinion, to admit frankly that extension is a necessary attribute of all that exists, and to demonstrate, further, that spirit, as a real being, must be extended also. He was anxious to claim extension for spirit,

> that it may be conceived to be some real Being and true Substance, and not a vain Figment, such as is everything that has no Amplitude and is in no sort extended.

It is a queer situation: More, the champion of 'spirit', appears, at least at first sight, to be paying unconscious tribute to the sovereignty of 'matter', for he can only defend the reality of spirit by endowing it with extension, which was supposed to be the peculiar and essential attribute of matter. He attempts to avoid the implications of this in two ways. First he denies that extension is the formal principle of matter, and substitutes for it 'impenetrability'; spirit, on the other hand, is penetrable. Secondly, the property of 'divisibility', which was agreed to be inseparable from extended matter, does not belong to extended spirit. The extension of spirit is true extension, and yet it is different from material extension; it is what he calls 'metaphysical extension', a notion which becomes little clearer when he describes it as a 'fourth dimension' or 'essential spissitude'. Spirit, it seems, is to have extension so that it may be deemed as real as matter, but it must have it without any of the awkward conditions which attend upon material extension; it must be penetrable and 'indiscerpible'. More retorts the charge of 'corpority' upon his opponents; they cannot conceive of extension apart from matter because they wrongly hold that whatever is extended is the object of imagination, not of intellect. The fact is, he continues, in a characteristic manner of philosophic invective, that they are suffering from that very 'materious disease' of which I was accusing More himself a moment ago:

> their Imagination is not sufficiently defecated and depurated from the filth and unclean tinctures of corpority; their mind is so illaqueated and lime-twigged, as it were, with the Ideas and Properties of corporeal things,

that they mix up metaphysical with physical extension. Metaphysical extension, then, is the idea of extension contemplated by the intellect in abstraction from 'corporeal affections'. In trying to substantiate this conception More frequently appeals for proof to the idea of 'infinite extension' which, he says, is imprinted on our intellects (not our *imaginations*) so that we cannot think it away. He asks his readers to refer to the 'internal sense' of their minds, and see whether they can fail to conceive of a certain infinite, immovable extension having necessary, actual existence—the equivalent, I take it, of infinite space—and of themselves as in this. The conception of infinite space seems to him to be an example of extension conceived without the attributes of matter, and hence to be a proof of his proposition. As is well known, this infinite extension or space became with More, by a very natural analogy, an attribute of God, the Infinite Spirit. In thus making space the divine ground of the universe he was followed by Locke and Newton.

More's arguments can perhaps best be viewed, from our present point of view, as an endeavour to reunite matter and spirit, which the rigid logic of Descartes had left in unbridgeable opposition, and to give greater 'body,' or actuality, to both conceptions, which in Cartesianism were too nakedly abstract. More wants his 'spirit' to be more than abstract 'cogitation'; he will have it to be activity, and the activity must be *there where* it is at work, penetrating and moving matter.

More had thus demonstrated to his own satisfaction that the notion of a spirit contained no inherent contradiction or absurdity. His further proofs, from reason, of the actual existence of spirit, as a substance distinct from matter—proofs from the necessary existence of God, from the incapacity of matter to think, move, or organise itself, and so forth—follow the usual lines, and need not be recapitulated here. But there was a further class of proofs on which he placed increasing reliance in his later years, the 'proofs' from testimonies of apparitions and witchcraft. In his treatise on the *Immortality of the Soul* he had spoken of the 'pre-eminence of the arguments drawn from reason above those from story.' But later he appears to have felt that the increase of infidelity made well-attested stories of witches and apparitions especially requisite, since the sceptics and worldlings who denied 'spirit' were still afraid of 'ghosts', and their 'dull souls', unable to rise to rational conviction, might thereby be 'rubbed and awakened with a suspicion, at least, if not assurance, that there are other intelligent beings besides these that are clad in heavy earth and clay'. More includes evidence of this kind in several of his works, devoting to it, for instance, the whole of Book III. even of his early *Antidote against Atheism.* For More

> Millions of spiritual creatures walk the earth,

and ascend upwards, in unbroken hierarchical degrees, through the air to heaven. It was typical of the seventeenth century situation that this pilgrim of the skies should welcome blasts from Hell as 'evidence' for the reality of the heavenly spirit-world in which he was so entirely at his ease; that this Cambridge rationalist, after proving his faith in the language of loftiest metaphysics, should proceed to buttress it by stories of 'Coskinomancy', of 'Margaret Warine discharged upon an Oake at a Thunder-clap', or of the 'vomiting of Cloth stuck with Pins, Nails and Needles, as also Glass, Iron and Haire, by Wierus his Patients'. The fact is that in appealing to demonology More, like Browne and Glanvill, was tapping a reservoir of traditional supernatural belief which lay deeper in the national consciousness than Christianity itself, and deeper, certainly, than the new ice-crust of rationalism which now covered it. Christianity, as is well known, had not abolished the older divinities, it had merely deposed and demonised them; and Protestantism, aiming at the purification of Christianity from the 'pagan' accretions of the middle ages, had produced at first not a diminished but a greatly heightened Satan-consciousness, so that the later sixteenth and earlier seventeenth centuries, when witch-burnings reached their maximum, were Satan's palmiest time in England. By the time of More, it is true, this Puritan horror of the powers of darkness, which had persecuted

without pity much that had been tolerated in the less self-conscious pre-Reformation days, had greatly weakened, under 'philosophic' influences. But primitive picture-thinking is not destroyed at a blow, and the persistent if furtive acknowledgment of things undreamed of in the 'new philosophy' was now unexpectedly available as a reinforcement to the philosophic defence of the faith. It may be, one may now conjecture, that in making the most of this crude material the defenders of religion were guided by a sound instinct. They may have obscurely felt, though they could not have realised or admitted it, that the ancient springs of popular demonology were also those of religion itself, and that in the emotion of the supernatural, however evoked, they had a surer foundation for faith than all the 'proofs' of philosophic theism. (pp. 162-69)

> *Basil Willey, "Rational Theology—The Cambridge Platonists," in his* The Seventeenth Century Background: Studies in the Thought of the Age in Relation to Poetry and Religion, *1934. Reprint by Columbia University Press, 1950, pp. 133-69.*

MARJORIE HOPE NICOLSON   (essay date 1959)

[In the following excerpt, Nicolson analyzes More's conception of the relation of space and infinity to God.]

Only the scholar now reads More's tortuous *Philosophical Poems,* his cabbalistical interpretations of Daniel and the Apocalypse, his verbose theological works. Unfortunately More lacked the gift of true poetry, yet in spite of the ineptitude of his meter and rhyme, the harshness of his style, the abstruseness of his allegory, his "Platonic Poems" were contagious. The verbosity and superabundance of his prose did not disturb his contemporaries. His philosophical and theological works were widely read. Even more important was the fact that More was one of the most persuasive and compelling teachers of his generation. The charm of his personality, his native enthusiasm, his gentle mysticism laid its spell upon students who went out from Cambridge to teach his philosophy to another generation of pupils.

More's influence lived on in his pupil's pupil, Isaac Newton, in Leibniz, who found him one of the most congenial of English philosophers, in Barrow and Berkeley, in Shaftesbury, who acknowledged his debt, yet still owed him more than he knew. It was revived again in Coleridge, whose philosophy was even more influenced by the Christian Platonists than by the German idealists, and it powerfully affected the "Vermont Transcendentalists," who gave new direction to American idealism in the nineteenth century. Today we have been discovering More again and beginning to realize the extent to which he anticipated modern movements of thought. However, it is not primarily because of More's influence that I select him as a guide to the seemingly confused issues of the mid-century in which he lived but because he affords a better index to tendencies of his generation than would a more systematic thinker, such as Hobbes or Descartes. Henry More was immensely susceptible to ideas and often uncritical of those he accepted. His response was frequently emotional rather than logical. He was touched by the "enthusiasm" against which he warned his generation. (pp. 114-15)

"INFINITIE OF WORLDS!" More had written when he first faced the ultimate implications of the new astronomy, "A thing monstrous if assented to, and to be startled at." But his recoil was momentary, for, granted the God of Plenitude in whom More believed, the idea of an infinity of worlds was not monstrous but inevitable, not appalling but enthralling.

Henry More was the first English poet to express and the first English philosopher to teach the idea of infinite space and an infinity of worlds. "Roused up," as he said, "by a new Philosophick furie," he denied "the Hypothesis of either the world or time being infinite; defending the infinitude of both." He forgot the Reason he had so carefully cultivated and gave free rein to his own native enthusiasm. He broke the bonds of finite time and space and shattered the Circle of Perfection from which he had formerly deduced an ethics and aesthetics of limitation, restraint, and proportion.

As a philosopher Henry More's greatest contribution to the history of thought lies in his development of the concept of absolute space and, to a lesser degree, absolute time. More's ideas on the subject first appeared in his poem, *Democritus Platonissans; or, An Essay upon the Infinity of Worlds Out of Platonick Principles,* published in 1646. They were further developed through his correspondence with Descartes and most fully discussed in the *Enchiridion Metaphysicum* and *Divine Dialogues,* though many of his later works treat the ideas of space that lay behind Barrow, Newton, Locke, and Berkeley. Space was the vehicle of Deity, by means of which finite man might come closer to comprehension of the true Infinite, God. We do not know it with our intellects, as we do not know God, yet we feel and sense it. And think as we will, we cannot think away space, as we cannot think away God. In his *Enchiridion Metaphysicum* More transferred to space some twenty attributes formerly associated with God. . . . Space is One, Incorruptible, Eternal, Complete, Independent, Immense, Uncreated, Omnipresent, Incorporeal. Yet though More seemed to be approaching the identification of Space with God, he refused to go the whole way and declare, with some later philosophers, that Space *is* God. Space is divine, as the dwelling place of Deity. More might indeed have used the phrase of Newton, whose conception of space was so largely drawn from him, and said that Space is "the sensorium of Deity." But though Space was a way to God, it was not God. "The spiritual object that we call space," he wrote, "is only a passing shadow, which represents for us, in the weak light of our intellect, the true and universal nature of the continuous divine presence, till we are able to perceive it directly with open eyes and at a nearer distance."

In spite of his place in the history of metaphysics, More would not be so significant for our purposes if his feeling for the new space had not been basically that of a poet. As Wordsworth said,

> Oh! many are the Poets that are sown
> By Nature; men endowed with highest gifts,
> The vision and the faculty divine;
> Yet wanting the accomplishment of verse.

The *Infinity of Worlds* was a song of praise to an infinite universe, created by an Infinite God, His nature such that He could never be satisfied with less than all. In contemplating Space as in contemplating God, the soul of man was elated; released from finite limitations, it stretched its wings and took off into a vast universe of which there was no end, to seek the inexhaustible Good, and experienced triumph rather than despair because its quest must always remain unfinished:

> Unseen, incomprehensible He moves
> About himself each seeking entity
> That never yet shall find that which it loves.
> No finite thing shall reach infinity,
> No thing dispers'd comprehend that Unity. . . .
> Still falling short they never fail to seek,
> Nor find they nothing by their diligence;
> They find repast, their lively longing eek
> Rekindled still.

Into the new universe of stars and suns and space, More sent his ecstatic soul to rove and range and be filled with the "astonishment," "amazement," "rapture" that are reiterated strains in his poetry and prose whenever he approaches the theme of the vastness of the universe. Attempting to grasp the whole, imagination and spirit grow vast as they feed on vastness. "Then all the works of God with close embrace," More wrote in a minor poem, "I dearly hug in my enlargéd arms"—arms of the spirit, arms of the imagination, growing with the universe. In the new philosophy More felt the "psychology of infinity," the insatiability of man, striving for what he can never reach, yet feeling not failure but delight in the effort.

In the new philosophy More discovered, too, arguments for variety and diversity more significant than those he had used before. "If these globes be regions of life, And severall kinds of plants therein do grow," what difference varieties of "Grasse, flowers, hearbs, trees"—perhaps men—must exist even in this one cosmic universe? How much more elsewhere, in worlds and universes of the past and future, for "Long ago there Earths have been, Peopled with men and beasts before this Earth . . . and after this shall others be again, And still another in endless repedation." The cosmos created to infinity and eternity by a God of Plenitude must be infinitely filled with every sort of variety and diversity. One world, one universe was not enough. More felt as Thomas Traherne wrote in "Insatiableness":

> 'Tis mean Ambition to desire
>   A single World.
>   To many I aspire,
>   The one upon another hurl'd,
> Nor will they all, if they be all confin'd
>   Delight my mind.
>
> This busy, vast, enquiring Soul
>   Brooks no Controul;
>   'Tis very curious too,
> Each one of all these Worlds must be
> Enricht with infinite Variety
> And Worth; or 'twill not do.

The *Divine Dialogues,* More's wisest and most charming work, was written in full maturity, yet the reader feels much of the youthful exuberance and enthusiasm of the earlier poems. This was More's most complete reply to Hobbes and other "atheists;" it was also the finest expression of Cambridge Platonism. In the *Divine Dialogues* More not only "accepted the universe" but rejoiced in every aspect of its richness, fullness, diversity, variety. There was room in his universe for all possible things, even for those which narrow-minded men called "evils." The waste places of the world, the uninhabitability of torrid and frigid zones, the "morbidness" of extremes of climate, the occurrence of untimely death seem evils to man merely because of his limited point of view. Without the scenery of the world would be languid and flat, unworthy of the dramatist who contrived it. Henry More's Great Dramatist—the figure is a favorite of his—was no classicist, following the rules and the unities, but a Shakespeare or a Marlowe, an Author who crowded into his "Tragick Comedy" beauty and ugliness, laughter and tears, birth and death, with overflowing bounty seeming to say, "Here is God's plenty!" Even such supposed distortions of Nature as mountains have become ornaments. More's Nature-vocabulary changed with the development of his ethics and aesthetics. (pp. 134-38)

As Henry More's theater of the world seems to look back to the superabundance of the Elizabethans, so it looked forward to Shaftesbury's diverse and varied universe, to Leibniz' "best of all possible worlds." In an age when the shades of French classicism were closing around English literature, More was carrying on the native English romantic temperament. If he did not travel all the way, nevertheless in his mature works, most of all in the ***Divine Dialogues,*** he had cast aside his earlier belief in restraint and limitation and allowed full play to his natural enthusiasm, his love of variety, diversity, irregularity as principles of Nature. (pp. 139-40)

> *Marjorie Hope Nicolson, "New Philosophy," in her* Mountain Gloom and Mountain Glory: The Development of the Aesthetics of the Infinite, *Cornell University Press, 1959, pp. 113-40.*

AHARON LICHTENSTEIN (essay date 1962)

[*In the following excerpt, Lichtenstein examines More's theory of the relationships of "right reason" to divine will, self-will, morality, and knowledge.*]

Not in vain has More's name found its way into the histories of rational theology. The attempt to approach religious problems philosophically, often scientifically, is evident throughout his works. This attitude, furthermore, is often made explicit. Up and down in his writings are strewn passages underscoring the validity of human reason and the importance of rational guidance in all spheres of life, particularly the religious. "For what greater satisfaction can there be to a rational Spirit," More asks, "than to find himself able to appeal to the strictest Rules of Reason and Philosophy?".... Writing against the "enthusiasts'" reliance upon the "inner light" of subjective inspiration, More argues that those who "would, by their wild Rhetorick, disswade men from the use of their Rational faculties, under pretence of expectation of an higher and more glorious Light, do as madly" as "some furious Orator" who should persuade a group of nocturnal travelers to beat out their torches and lanterns by convincing them that, in the glory of their present condition, they could proceed in the dark, unaided by auxiliary artificial light. Against his other theological bugbear, the Roman Catholic Church, More presents a similar charge. By its "pretended infallibility," it has, in taking away the rights of the individual's reason, reduced him to the level of the brute: "Nay what Conspiracy against humane Nature can be more tragical or direful, or what so palpable a Plot to make Mankind mere Slaves and Vassals, and to take away from them that Privilege by which alone they are distinguishable from brute beasts?" More sees "enthusiasm" regarding reason as unnecessary, and Catholicism dismissing it as untrustworthy. His own *via media* is firmly based upon the belief that it is both indispensable and reliable. It represents, indeed, one aspect of man's deiformity:

> But for mine own part, Reason seems to me to be so far from being any contemptible Principle in man, that it must be acknowledged in some sort to be in God himself. For what is the Divine Wisdom but that steady comprehension of the Ideas of all things, with their mutual respects one to another, congruities and incongruities, dependencies and independencies?... And what is this but *Ratio stabilis,* a kind of steady and immoveable Reason, discovering the connexion of all things at once? But that in us is *Ratio mobilis* or Reason in evolution, we being able to apprehend things only in a successive manner one after another.

While the mode differs, in its essence, More concludes, human reason resembles the divine: "But so many as we can comprehend at a time, while we plainly perceive and carefully view

their Ideas, we know how well they fit, or how much they disagree one with another, and so prove or disprove one thing by another: which is really a participation of that Divine Reason in God, and is a true and faithful Principle in man, when it is perfected and polished by the Holy Spirit."

The validity of this "true and faithful Principle" derives from the nature and source of the human soul. For deiformity, to the Platonists, is not only a religious ideal; it is likewise a metaphysical fact. To quote Whichcote: "We are made in the image of God; not only upon a moral consideration, but upon a natural account: as we are invested with intellectual natures, and so stand in another relation to God, than the creatures below us." Indeed, that reason is connatural to the soul because God is reason and the soul is of God, is one of his most persistent themes. More discusses this conception somewhat less frequently, but clearly accepts it no less firmly. "The soul of man," he declares, "is as it were *agalma theou,* a compendious Statue of the Deity; her substance is a solid Effigies of God." And he is fully explicit in making this metaphysical deiformity the basis for assuming the validity of human intellect—"the Deiform intellect," More had called it in the *Poems*. "The Intellect of man is as it were a small compendious Transcript of the Divine Intellect, and we feel in a manner in our own Intellects the firmness and immutability of the Divine, and of the eternal and immutable Truths exhibited there."

We are here touching upon the familiar concept of "right reason," which asserts the universal correspondence of the human soul with a set of fundamental absolute truths.... In More, "right reason" ... was bound up with the theory of innate ideas.... [It] served as a bond linking man with God—as an ideal and as a fact.

In itself, however, reason is a neutral factor. It is not only insufficient but indeterminate, equally capable of being directed to good or to evil, towards God or the devil. More sees it as "the general Principle or common Root" of a "Middle Life," intermediate between the animal and the divine, and inclinable to either:

> This is a short Description of the Middle Life which is neither Animal nor Divine, but is really (what the Astrologians phansy Mercury to be) such as that with which it is conjoined, whether Good or Bad, Divine or Animal. For if Reason be swallowed down into the Animal Life, it ceases not to operate there, but all her Operations then are tinctured with that Life into which she is immers'd.

The light of reason may become a captive organ of rationalization, to the point that, as More pointed out in a letter, it becomes "scarce in the Power of any Man to undeceive one thus impos'd upon by his own Wit, Fancy, and Subtilty of Reason." It is the will, as the innermost spring of the soul, that determines the character of human life. For it is, first, in itself, the deepest, the most essential element in the psyche: "And deep desire (the desire of which More speaks is of course for 'near Union with God')," More declares,

> And deep desire is the deepest act,
> The most profound and centrall energie,
> The very selfnesse of the soul.

Secondly, as a motive force, it gives purpose and direction to all other facets of the personality, the intellect included. It is consequently in terms of the will that More's conception of the divine life is molded. As the source of human conduct, the will, above all, must be properly channeled. Else, even a small turn may divert all subsequent actions from their true object, God, and toward man's selfish interests.

We verge here upon one of More's loftiest and most persistent themes. It is that which he had learned from the *Theologia Germanica*—the eradication, root-and-branch, of self-will, the negation of I-hood. If Plotinus had taught More to find God in himself—*reverere teipsum*—the Taulerians had taught him to find—or rather, to place—himself in God. Deiformity in the simplest sense, assimilating ourselves *to* God, is insufficient; one must assimilate *into* Him. Both in his formal works and in his correspondence, More returns to this theme again and again, ringing all the changes upon it. . . . In allegorizing his early spiritual experience in **"Psychozoia,"** More makes "Anautaesthesie" the road to "Fast love, fix'd life, firm peace in Theoprepia land" and the same note is struck in the concluding paragraph of his *Theological Works:*

> This therefore is the Supreme Law and Will of God touching the Purity of his Worship, That we have no Will nor End of our own. For as we are to have but one God, 'Hear, O Israel, the Lord thy God is one God,' Deut. 6.4. so we are to have but one Will, even the Will of the God whom we worship. Which we have not, if we have any Self-will or Self-ends unsubordinate to the Will of God.

The theme runs like a refrain through More's letters to Lady Conway, letters in which the inveterate sufferer is repeatedly urged to find comfort in resignation to the Divine Will. "We must," he writes, "submitt our selves to the will of God and possess our selves in patience, extinguish in our selves the desire of all things but of being of one will with him who has a complete power over us to deal with us as he pleases.". . . Self-will, whether or not it directly contravenes the expressed Divine Will, is, in its very essence, sin. "We are only forbidden," Adam tells Satan, "to feed on our own Will, and to seek pleasures apart, and without the approbation of the Will of God." It is with the abandonment of "our own will" that regeneration must begin.

In thus becoming—as far as humanly possible—of one will with God, man approaches the state of deiformity; and this in two ways. First, and most obviously, the "vital Center" of his soul henceforth acts in accordance with its great Archetype. Implanted within him is the "Tree of Life" which More interprets as referring to "the Essential Will of God," by which

> is understood the Will of God becoming Life and Essence to the Soul of Man; whereby is signified a more thorough union betwixt the Divine and humane nature, such as is in them that are firmly regenerated and radicated in what is good. Philo makes the Tree of Life to be *eusebeia*, that is, Piety or Religion; but the best Religion and Piety is to be of one will with God.

Secondly, its very act of abnegation is an *imitatio Dei*. For in renouncing its own selfish pursuits in favor of the highest objective Good, it acts just as "God himself, who is that pure, free, and perfectly unselfed Love" acts—in a spirit of disinterestedness. Man thus attains the Kingdom of God within him, whose essence More summarizes in a single sentence:

> To be brief, It is the Rule of the Spirit of God in the Soul, who takes the Reins of all our Powers, Faculties, and Affections into his own hand, and curbs them and excites them according to his own most holy Will, that is carried to no particular Self-interest, but ever directs to that which is simply and absolutely the best.

As the source and matrix of the soul's faculties, then, the will directs all human activity. With respect to intellection, however, the will does not merely guide; it affects—and enters into—the very operation. The conception that true knowledge can be achieved only in conjunction with moral virtue is a familiar aspect of the idealism of the Platonic tradition. . . . [More's view of the dependence of knowledge upon morality is] indeed present throughout his works, and has been emphasized by all student of More. It should be noted, however, that the conception is variously expressed. At times, More is content simply to make a purely negative claim; immorality may obscure the mind, making real knowledge impossible. If "the eye of the understanding be shut through Pride, Prejudice, or Sensuality, the mysteries of Philosophy are thereby vailed from it; but if by true vertue and unfeigned sanctity of mind that eye be opened, the Mysteries of Philosophy are thereby the more clearly discovered to it." "Sanctity of mind" is here apparently a prelude to knowledge; it seems to precede intellection rather than enter into it. (pp. 55-62)

Elsewhere, however, the relation between knowledge and morality is expressed in positive terms. The purified heart is not merely a prerequisite to knowledge. Nor does it only serve as an impetus, stirring the mind to exertion in the search for truth. Rather, it is itself an aspect of that search. More does not envision simply "the sweet counsels *between* head and heart" of which Wordsworth was to speak. The moral will not only facilitates the quest for knowledge—in the sense, say, that sheer determined will power helped Ben Hogan become a great golfer—but participates in it. For it is only through the united endeavor of the heart and mind that the soul can attain true knowledge. . . . The heart is here not merely a prerequisite to wisdom, but its very seat.

Equally positive is More's fullest description of the purified intellect, presented in the preface to *A Collection of Several Philosophical Writings*. More envisions a principle which, while intellectual in nature and therefore *of* reason, he nevertheless prefers to treat as a separate endowment, thus distinguishing it from "reason" as usually conceived. This "principle" More calls "Divine Sagacity":

> I should commend to them that would successfully philosophize, the belief and endeavor after a certain Principle more noble and inward then Reason it self, and without which Reason will faulter, or at least reach but to mean and frivolous things. I have a sense of something in me while I thus speak, which I must confess is of so retruse a nature that I want a name for it, unless I should adventure to term it Divine Sagacity, which is the first Rise of successful Reason, especially in matters of great comprehension and moment, and without which a man is as it were in a thick wood, and may make infinite promising attempts, but can find no Out let into the open Champain, where one may freely look about him every way (the *pedion te aletheias*) without the safe conduct of this good Genius. . . .

Subjectively, "Divine Sagacity" is the reflection of the objective Divine Presence. . . . Reason in the highest sense is by no means to be equated with the intellect and its logical faculty. More would have agreed fully with the recent remarks of the very differently oriented Karl Jaspers: "In common parlance Reason is identical with intellect. It can, in fact, take no step without the intellect, but it goes beyond it." And, More would have added, it goes beyond it precesely because it starts above and beyond it, because it is "the Gift of God" to a soul seeking assimilation to Him. More is careful to distinguish between ordinary ''Reason'' and ''souls Deiform intellective.'' Where the ''dispred exility / Of slyer reason fails, some greater power / Found in a lively vigorous Unity / With God'' must be invoked, and only then does man find his true rational nature. Suffused with this ''Divine Sagacity,'' the human mind is transmuted; and, transported to higher levels, gains a direct insight into truth. Moral virtue informs the purified intellect, and in the process of catharsis the ethical will is itself integrated as a facet of the regenerate mind.

Of course, this is not to say that the will is henceforth directly involved in any and every ratiocinative step. More is not quite so naïve. For one thing, he apparently sees morality as having a bearing only upon religious and philosophical thought. Here he speaks of its being relevant ''especially in matters of great comprehension and moment,'' and elsewhere he makes it clear that he does not include scientific problems. ''The Heart,'' he writes, ''is the seat of Conscience; i.e. of Desire, or bent of Will and Knowledge; Knowledge of things Moral or Divine. So in Scripture, we have oft mention of a wise and understanding Heart. And surely if a man observe; in Moral and Pious matters, a man communeth with his Heart, and discovereth deceit and hypocrisie there; as he doth incongruities and falsities in his Brain, where imagination is placed, in Natural and Mathematical Theories.'' Secondly, More recognizes that the processes of discursive thought, the ''Reason'' to which he refers as following upon ''Divine Sagacity,'' are not identical with it. The actual development of a logical proof may, for instance, be a purely ''intellectual'' endeavor, even taking the term in its usual sense. But More does mean—and this should be emphasized—that the purified will is indissolubly linked with the intellect, actively engaged in the quest for truth. It is very definitely a facet of reason itself—''Aaron's Rationale, his *Logion* or Oracle of Reason, did it not include in it the Urim and Thummim, Purity and Integrity of the Will and Affections, as well as the Light of the Understanding?'' ''Divine Sagacity'' is not manifested in all intellection; but it always remains an aspect of intellect. (pp. 63-6)

> *Aharon Lichtenstein, in his* Henry More: The Rational Theology of a Cambridge Platonist, *Cambridge, Mass.: Harvard University Press, 1962, 250 p.*

M. V. DePORTE (essay date 1966)

[*DePorte is an American critic and educator and the editor of* Discourse on Madness *by the seventeenth-century writer Thomas Tryon. In the following excerpt, DePorte examines More's opposition to religious enthusiasm as exemplified in* Enthusiasmus triumphatus.]

At first sight Henry More might seem an unlikely man to have written what is perhaps the best of the many seventeenth-century attacks on enthusiasm. More was not only, as Basil Willey has said, ''the most mystical of the Cambridge Platonists'' [see excerpt dated 1934], he was also a believer in ghosts, witches, and pacts with the devil, and an admirer of Valentine Greatraks, the faith healer who made so great a name for himself in the 1660s with his stroking cures. But whatever there was of the enthusiast in More never encouraged him to belittle reason. On the contrary, he was a vigorous rationalist who conceived reason to be no less than a ''participation of that Divine Reason in God,'' and who devoted his life to providing an intellectual defense of religion sound enough to withstand the attacks of Hobbes and other materialists. His mysticism and interest in supernatural phenomena do not stem from any distrust of in-

tellect; they are simply an expression of his continuing need to find proofs for the existence of spiritual forces in personal experience and in recorded events as well as through rational demonstration. Since he had only contempt for those dissenting sects that would abandon reason for the easy certitude of ''inner light,'' he was understandably anxious to dissociate his position from theirs. Like many liberal Anglicans of his day, More cherished the hope that the great majority of Christians would eventually come together once more in a broad church affirming the basic truths of Christianity. Such a reunion would never be achieved, however, unless men agreed to discuss their differences rationally. One of the most obvious liabilities of founding religious belief on ''inner light'' was, as Truman Steffan has pointed out, that there was ''no way of convincing a second person that one was inspired.'' Enthusiasm by its very nature emphasized what was private and divisive in men and, carried to its logical extreme, might end in a cry for ''one man, one religion.'' In writing *Enthusiasmus Triumphatus,* therefore, More had two objectives: first, to call attention to the danger of relying on ''inner light'' rather than reason, and second, to distinguish clearly between true and false inspiration, lest the excesses of the enthusiasts cast a shadow on the possibility of genuine illumination.

Enthusiasmus Triumphatus grew out of a pamphlet war with Thomas Vaughan, twin brother of the poet. Vaughan, an ardent student of chemistry, a dabbler in magic, and a Rosicrucian, published in 1650 two theosophical tracts, *Anthroposophia Theomagica* and *Anima Magica Abscondita* under the pseudonym ''Eugenius Philalethes.'' The tracts contained, amid farfetched speculations on the nature of man and the universe, some acrimonious jibes at Aristotle (Vaughan calls him an ''ape,'' his writings ''vomit'') and Descartes which irritated More. He was particularly irked by the criticism of Descartes, of whom he was then an extravagant admirer, and the same year brought out his *Observations upon Anthroposophia Theomagica and Anima Magica Abscondita,* signing himself ''Alazonomastix Philalethes,'' and calling Vaughan a presumptuous upstart, a magician, and a deluded enthusiast. . . . As he said at the beginning of the *Observations* he wrote against Vaughan primarily because he saw in him a symptom of the disease ''growne even Epidemicall in our Nation, *viz.* to desire to be filled with high-swolne words of Vanity, rather then to feen on sober Truth, and to heate and warme our selves rather by preposterous and fortuitous imaginations, then to move cautiously in light of a purified minde and improved Reason.'' (pp. i-ii)

[More republished] his two pamphlets in 1656 . . . ''for the discountenancing and quelling of vain *Fantastry* and *Enthusiasme,*'' which are most easily kept down by ridicule since ''*Fantasticks* and *Enthusiasts* seek nothing more than the admiration of men, wherefore there is no such soveraign Remedy as scorn and neglect, to make them sober.'' He evidently felt, however, that the attacks on Vaughan were too occasional to accomplish this purpose by themselves, for he decided to write a preliminary treatise under the new pseudonym ''philophilus Parresiastes'' which, as a kind of anatomy of enthusiasm, would establish the broader context in which the earlier works were to be read. This treatise he called *Enthusiasmus Triumphatus, or a Discourse of the Nature, Causes, Kinds, and Cure of Enthusiasme,* and in it he gave a thorough analysis of enthusiasm as the cause of absurdities in both religion and philosophy.

Enthusiasts were usually treated by seventeenth-century writers either as conniving hypocrites or as collaboraters with the Devil.

But More was not one to stir up hatred. He had no desire "to incense the mindes of any against *Enthusiasts* as to persecute them"; he wished only to dissuade others from following their teachings and so preferred to view them as victims of mental disorder, as madmen suffering from a "misconceit of being inspired." More assigned the cause of their delusions to melancholy, which he knew from his reading of Burton was a disease particularly apt to set some "absurd imagination upon the Mind so fast that all the evidence of Reason to the contrary cannot remove it." More noted that melancholy was also a disease which generated strong passions, and since men were by nature "very prone to suspect some special presence of God in any thing that is *great* or *vehement*"—the early pagans, for example, commonly deified awesome natural objects—they would likely respond to the passions stirred up in them by melancholy as if they were impulses sent from heaven. (pp. iii-iv)

Enthusiasmus Triumphatus was clearly superior to the tracts it was written to introduce, and when More issued a collection of his philosophical writings in 1662, he included it to reinforce the unifying theme of the volume: "*The knowledge of God, and therein of true Happiness*, so far as *Reason* can cut her way through those darknesses and difficulties she is incumbred with in this life." The 1662 text . . . contains several significant additions. More changed the opening section from an explanation of his plan to preface the attacks on Vaughan with a general consideration of enthusiasm, to one which provides a link with the preceding treatise, **An Antidote against Atheism,** by showing the similarity between enthusiasm and atheism. He also added three new sections: one accounting for the willingness of enthusiasts to suffer martyrdom, another aimed at preventing this account from being used as an argument against all religion, in which he says that the misguided zeal of enthusiasts no more implies "there is no Religion, than *Madness* that there is no *Reason*," and a third insisting that though the immediate cause of enthusiasm is physiological, a man is still to blame for allowing himself to become melancholy.

In 1679 More published a Latin translation of *Enthusiasmus Triumphatus* in his **Scriptorum Philosophicum,** to which he added a number of scholia. . . . The most important of the scholia are those which further qualify his ridicule of enthusiasm. He renews the assurances given in the last pages of the attack that he by no means opposes "*true* and *warrantable Enthusiasm*," where man experience divine rapture, but profess no unique insight into scripture nor special authority given them by God; he says, in fact, that "they very ill deserve the name of Christians, who so indulge a sort of dry and hungry Reason, as wholly to exclude all manner of Enthusiasm." He elaborates too upon the notion . . . that melancholy, in its milder forms, can be of great aid to religious sensibility by imbuing one with a "salutary sadness" which excites concern for the state of his soul and disposes him to shun worldly pleasures and seek mercy through prayer and meditation. (p. iv-v)

The central point of **Enthusiasmus Triumphatus** is that true religious experience, however emotionally satisfying or disturbing it may be, is never irrational. Those dissenters who talk of giving over reason to rely on a "higher and more glorious light" More compares to fools that would put out their torches on a dark night because they were not so bright as the sun. He is at pains throughout to contrast genuine illumination, "a Principle of the *purest Reason* that is communicable to humane Nature," with the illumination of the enthusiasts, a delusion of divine favor. There is nothing, he tells us, that "*the holy Spirit* did ever suggest to any man but it was agree-

able to, if not demonstrable from, what we call *Reason*." It is worth noting that More defines reason as a faculty specifically opposed to imagination: "By *Reason* I understand so settled and cautious a Composure of Mind as will suspect every high-flown & forward Fancy . . ."; it is swayed neither by the attractiveness nor by the force of her illusions but tests them "by the known Faculties of the Soul, which are either the *Common notions* that all men in their wits agree upon, or the *Evidence of outward Sense*, or else a *clear and distinct Deduction from these*." If a man lay claim to an inspiration which cannot survive this test, it is a sure sign that the inspirtion comes not from God but from his own imagination; he is like one asleep who, insensible to reason or the report of his senses, mistakes his dreams for reality. Phillip Harth has seen in this pitting of reason against fancy as rival faculties of knowledge, the one trustworthy, the other deceptive, an "epistemological dualism" which sets More apart from earlier Anglican apologists, and especially from Hooker, to whom he was otherwise greatly indebted. Hooker, whose view derived from Aquinas, and ultimately from Aristotle, saw imagination as the vital mediary between reason and the senses which, by transforming sensory impressions into images, and communicating them to the intellect, enables it to form ideas. More's suspicion of imagination is no doubt connected with his admiration of Platonism, in which he discovered a congenial expression of his belief in the supreme reality of immaterial substances. He would have found in the earlier dialogues of Plato and in the writings of the Neoplatonists ample disparagement of imagination as a delusive agency capable only of reflecting or distorting the world of appearances. He consistently represents the imagination as a faculty of dangerous "strength and vigour," and in his warning that its unruliness is such that "though it be in some sort in our power, as *Respiration* is, yet it will also work without our leave," we have an early instance of the kind of misgivings which led to the insistence by some in the late seventeenth and early eighteenth century on the need to keep a tight rein on fancy.

By associating enthusiasm with unrestrained imagination, and depicting the enthusiast as mad, More helped set the pattern for attacks on Dissenters for the next one hundred years. (pp. v-vi)

> *M. V. DePorte, in an introduction to* Enthusiasmus Triumphatus (1662) *by Henry More, William Andrews Clark Memorial Library, 1966, pp. i-x.*

C. A. STAUDENBAUR (essay date 1968)

[*Staudenbaur is an American philosopher, essayist, and educator. In the following excerpt, he compares the structure of "Psychathanasia" to that of Marsilio Ficino's* Theologia Platonica, *maintaining that More used Ficino's text as his principal authority. For a response to Staudenbaur's argument, see the excerpt by Alexander Jacob dated 1985.*]

A connection between Marsilio Ficino and the Cambridge Platonists has been often asserted, commonly assumed, and never proved. In this paper I shall present evidence for such a connection, evidence conclusive enough to warrant the hypothesis that Henry More composed his **"Psychathanasia Platonica: or a Platonicall Poem of the Immortality of Souls"** with a quill in one hand and a copy of Ficino's *Theologia Platonica de Immortalitate Animorum* in the other.

More's **"Psychathanasia"** . . . rehearses the stock arguments for the immortality of the soul, and with her sister poems provided the English reader of the seventeenth century with a rhapsodic repository of Neoplatonic lore. For this reason it has interested intellectual historians and especially literary historians, but both seventeenth- and twentieth-century critics have found much in it that is perplexing, for the *Psychodia Platonica* presents an exotic blend of Neoplatonism and Christianity dressed out in archaic English and ornamented with Greek and Hebrew terms. For "the better understanding," not only of his poetry, "but of the Principles of Plato's Philosophy," More added a set of notes and a glossary of terms to the second edition, but at least one perplexity is only increased by this kind gesture. Since 30 of the 33 pages of notes to the "**Psychathanasia**" are devoted to astronomical theory, complete with diagrams of the Copernican system of the world copied out of Galileo's *Dialogue on the Great World Systems*, the reader cannot help being reminded that the longest canto of the "**Psychathanasia**" expounds and defends in considerable detail the heliocentric theory of Copernicus. What has Copernicanism to do with "the Principles of Plato's Philosophy"? And how does an exposition of Copernican theory contribute to the argument for the immortality of the soul in the "**Psychathanasia**"? (pp. 565-66)

The Canto on Copernican astronomy has received considerable attention in a critical edition of the "**Psychathanasia**" by Lee Haring, who has explored in some detail the relation of the Canto to Galileo's *Dialogue on the Great World Systems*. While he finds this relationship reasonably definite and clear he finds the relation of the Canto to the "**Psychathanasia**" both tenuous and obscure.

> The logical connection between Canto 3 and the rest of the poem may seem weak to modern readers, who may forget that the Cartesian division between the worlds of mind and matter did not exist for Henry More. They should remember too that More, "a seventeenth-century weather vane," was exceedingly responsive to currents of contemporary thought, of which astronomy was one of the most influential. "Henry More was immensely susceptible to ideas, and often uncritical of those he accepted. His response was frequently emotional rather than logical" [see excerpt by Marjorie Hope Nicolson dated 1959]. No clearer support for this characterization need be sought than the seemingly unplanned sequence of thought in Book III of "**Psychathanasia**."

Certainly More does function as a weather vane for the intellectual historian; his work provides evidence that the winds of Copernicanism were blowing in seventeenth-century England. But the metaphor is not a wholly innocent one if it leads us to be content with the implication that More's changes of direction were passive and mechanical, or if active, emotional rather than intellectual. That they were emotional as well as intellectual we would not deny, but we assume that More had some reason for his emotion. He was not passively and mindlessly carried before the wind; for some reason near the end of "**Psychathanasia**" he spread his canvas and his Platonic bark sailed off in a new direction.

But perhaps we are creating a perplexity where there is none by our suggestion that the Canto on Copernican theory represents "a new direction" either for More or for the argument of the "**Psychathanasia**." For it is the case that astronomical speculation has enjoyed a long and hallowed history in the Platonic tradition; beginning with Book X of the *Republic,* the *Timaeus,* the *Laws* and the *Epinomis,* it continues through the Hellenistic commentators and is carried into the Middle Ages by the Latin treatises of Chalcidius and Macrobius. But Book III, Canto 3, of the "**Psychathanasia**" makes no reference to

this tradition; it directs all of its attention to post-Copernican developments. Moreover, there are many strands in the Platonic tradition. A theme more prominent than astronomical theorizing is that of contempt for the realm of "becoming," and for the futile attempts which are made to explain the images which make their appearance in this realm. This attitude is dramatized by Plato in the allegory of the cave in Book VII of the *Republic,* and it is endemic in Neopythagorean and Neoplatonic writers, both Christian and pagan. (pp. 566-67)

[Two] themes—the emphasis on the ethical use of knowledge, and the suspicion that knowledge of appearances is impossible to attain—are combined by Henry More with another theme prominent in Plato's *Phaedo* and in Plotinus, namely, the need for purification. The mind must be purified—set free from the body—liberated from bondage to the senses and the passions they arouse. The first Canto of the "**Psychathanasia**" is devoted to this theme. Preoccupation with the world of appearance strengthens the passions and darkens the intellect; it blinds the mind's eye to the reality which lies behind appearance, namely the hidden life of the soul. More develops his theme by plunging the "naturalist" into the Platonic cave. "Like men new made contriv'd into a cave / That ne're saw Light . . ." they philosophize,

> Busying their brains in the mysterious toyes
> Of flittie motion, warie well advize
> On 'ts inward principles and hid Entelechies:
>
> This is that awful cell where Naturalists
> Brood deep opinion, as they themselves conceit;
> This errors den where in a Magick mist
> Men hatch their own delusion and deceit,
> And grasp vain shows. . . .

More's poetic rage against "the stupid state of drooping soul, / That loves the body and false forms admires; / Slave to base sense, . . ." draws him to a threefold condemnation of natural knowledge as vain, false, and useless. The very violence of his condemnation suggests that he is not merely posing in traditional garments for literary effect; even More himself in later years seemed to feel that the extreme emphasis on purification in his early poems demanded some further explanation, and he sought to provide it in an autobiographical preface to his *Opera Omnia.*

In this preface More recounts the experiences which led him to compose the several poems of the *Psychodia Platonica.* As an undergraduate he had immersed himself in the study of natural science as it was understood in the Renaissance. After four years of reading Aristotle, Cardan, Scaliger, and other eminent men in the field of natural philosophy, and the Thomists and Scotists on metaphysics, he recounts how he found himself in a state of scepticism and despair; the studies which he had undertaken with the expectation of deriving from them "knowledge of things natural and divine" had precipitated a crisis both intellectual and emotional. At this point he discovered the "Platonic Writers Marsilius Ficinus, Plotinus himself, Mercurius Trismegistus; and the Mystical Divines; among whom there was frequent mention made of the Purification of the Soul, and the Purgative Course that is previous to the illuminative; . . . ." More embarked on a course of study and purification which led him to a new intellectual and religious orientation, to a conversion so profound and complete that he felt the need to express it in poetry. The first major poem he completed was the "**Psychozoia, or a Christiano-Platonicall display of Life,**" which he finished in 1640. In the first Canto of this work More sketched the Plotinian metaphysical world, and against this background presented in the following two Cantos a lengthy account of an allegorical journey from doubt and despair to religious peace through purification, an account inspired by Spenser's *Faerie Queene*. To complete the exposition of Neoplatonism he composed the ''Psychathanasia.'' . . . (pp. 568-70)

As a result of his experiences More returns constantly to the theme of purification. Purification is accomplished by setting the mind free from the senses and redirecting intellectual inquiry and interest from the physical world of appearances to the spiritual world, to reality. He develops his theme by contrasting spirit and matter, inward life and outward appearance, vital principle and dead form, illumination and darkness, reason and sense. In the first poem of the volume entitled ''To the Reader,'' More warns the unpurified reader against expecting too much.

> But whom lust, wrath and fear controule,
> Scare know their body from their soul.
> If any such chance hear my verse,
> Dark numberous Nothings I rehearse
> To them; measure out an idle sound
> In which no inward sense is found.

The unpurified reader may also be hard-put to understand Henry More's doctrine of purification. I suspect that this is partly the fault of More himself, since he has conflated two distinct theories of purification, the Christian and the Platonic. The Christian theory, which More found in the *Theologia Germanica*, stresses moral purification—purging the self of pride, self-will, *etc.*; to such as are morally prepared illumination comes as a divine gift, for there is no natural or causal connection between the moral victory of the self and the supernatural illumination which follows. In Plato and Plotinus purification is primarily intellectual and is described as separating the soul from the body so that it may attain truth by its own natural powers unimpeded by the senses and physical appetites. In the allegorical journey of the soul in his ''Psychozoia'' Henry More presents an essentially Christian account of purification. The soul escapes the land of Beirah (the ''brutish'' life) over the wall of self-conceit and through the door of humility, to be accompanied further by Self-denial and Patience. In the ''Psychathanasia'' we have the Platonic theory. The concern is not with purging the self of spiritual sins but with freeing the mind from the senses. Something of a Christian attitude remains in More's posture toward the unpurified—they are regarded as not simply unenlightened but also in a state of sin, and this accounts for the violence of his condemnation of the ''naturalist.'' (pp. 570-71)

Originally we were concerned with explaining what positive contribution to the argument for the soul's immortality was made by the Canto on Copernican astronomy. Now it appears that the very presence of this Canto is in violation of the opening stanzas of the poem, in which explanations of natural phenomena are condemned as vain, useless, and spiritually dangerous. In the ''Psychozoia'' More had addressed to the ''blundring Naturalist'' the demand: ''Therefore thy God seek out, and leave Nature behind.'' How is the Canto in question consistent with this demand? We may now pose two distinct questions: (1) How can one explain the organization of the ''Psychathanasia'' so as to account for the ''seemingly unplanned sequence of thought in Book III'' which results from including a long Canto on astronomy? (2) How is this Canto consistent with the dominant theme of this poem and the rest of the volume, namely the need for purification? The answer to both questions will be forthcoming when we have described the

relation of More's poem to Ficino's *Theologia Platonica*. (pp. 571-72)

It will not be necessary, nor even useful to our purpose to show by content analysis the influence of Ficino's work on More. Our task is much simpler. Since our primary interest is in the structure of **Pyschathanasia,** it will be sufficient to show how this structure is derived from Ficino's work. Kristeller has described the plan of the *Theologia Platonica* as follows:

> In his principal work, the *Theologia Platonica*, Ficino sets forth the philosophical doctrine of Platonism as a whole. The subject matter is not divided systematically, as might be expected, but proceeds with a succession of formal arguments, applying, so to speak, on a large scale the medieval form of disputation which seeks to establish a proposed thesis by a series of independent proofs. The thesis of the whole work is the immortality of the Soul, as the subtitle indicates.
>
> (p. 573)

More's *Psychathanasia* is divided in the same manner. After the introductory Canto condemning ''naturalism'' it proceeds to reproduce the structure of the *Theologia Platonica*, as the following table illustrates.

	THEOLOGIA PLATONICA	''PSYCH-ATHANASIA''
Degrees of Being	Libri I-IV	Book I, Canto 2
Rationes Communes for the immortality of the soul,	Liber V	Book I, Cantos 3, 4
Rationes propriae for the immortality of the soul drawn from the vegetative powers of the soul,	Liber VI	Book II, Canto 1
sensitive powers of the soul,	Liber VII	Book II, Canto 2
intellectual powers of the soul,	Liber VIII	Book II, Canto 3
soul's independence of the body,	Liber IX	Book III, Cantos 1, 2
general order of things,	Liber X	
soul's unity with eternal objects, and the fact of its	Liber XI	
formation by the divine mind.	Liber XII	
Signa for the immortality of the human soul.	Libri XIII, XIV	Book III, Canto 3
Solutiones quaestionum raised by Averroists,	Liber XV	''Antimonopsychia''
Epicureans, and	Liber XVI	''Antipsychopannychia''
Platonists.	Libri XVII, XVIII	''The Preexistence of the Soul'' (added to the 1647 edition)

The parallelism of structure is easily confirmed if one compares the book headings of the 1559 edition with the Canto headings of More's poem. Moreover, there is the matter of titles, in which More has rather pedantically both revealed and concealed his indebtedness. The complete title of Ficino's work is *Theologia Platonica de Immortalitate Animorum.* We have noted that the subtitle translates as "the immortality of souls," not as "the immortality of the soul." The plural form "souls" sounds strange to the ear since the phrase "the immortality of the soul" is a habit of speech dating back to the *Phaedo* in the Platonic tradition and consecrated as the title of *Ennead* IV, vii, the *locus classicus* of neoplatonic arguments for the soul's immortality. . . . The editor of the 1559 edition of Ficino reverts to the singular in the book headings he has supplied, and the page headings of More's poem read "The Immortality of the Soul." A later prose work of Henry More is also entitled ***The Immortality of the Soul,*** but the subtitle of the "**Psychathanasia Platonica**" is faithful to Ficino's treatise.

Why did Ficino and More use the plural form in spite of tradition and linguistic habit? Undoubtedly to proclaim their oppostition to the Averroist interpretation of Aristotle which held that only the active intellect shared by all men is immortal; there is no individual immortality. Ficino devoted Liber XV of his work to an explicit attack on this doctrine, and More added a sister poem to the "**Psychathanasia**" for the same purpose, which he entitled "**Antimonopsychia, or That all Souls are not one.**"

Averroism was hardly a living issue in seventeenth-century Cambridge, and More was conscious of this to the point of being self-conscious. "Onely let me excuse myself," he remarks in the preface to the poem, "if any chance to blame me for my "**Antimonopsychia,**" as confuting that which no man will assert. For it hath been asserted by some; . . . " namely, "That learned Arab . . . Aven-Roe." And it has loomed as one of the major intellectual heresies to some, especially to Ficino, and so More felt his argument for the soul's immortality incomplete without some mention of it.

In the table exhibiting the parallelism of "**Psychathanasia**" and her sister poems with the *Theologia Platonica* we have indicated that in Canto 3 of Book III More is presenting the Copernican theory as a *signum* of the soul's immortality. The parallelism with Ficino's work is less exact just prior to this point. More skips over Libri X, XI, and XII to XIII, the book presenting *signa* for the soul's immortality. In Cantos 1 and 2 of Book III, corresponding to Liber IX in Ficino. More explores the relation of body and soul, and asserts the soul's independence of the body with various arguments; then in Canto 3 he presents the Copernican theory as a *signum* confirming this theory. His argument that Copernicanism is a sign that the soul is independent of and superior to the body will be better understood if we look briefly at the argument of Liber XIII in Ficino's work.

In the opening sentence of Liber XIII Ficino distinquishes between demonstrating a thesis by arguments and confirming it by signs; he claims to have demonstrated the divinity of the soul in the previous books and now seeks to confirm his thesis by citing facts, events, theories, *etc.*, which the thesis he is maintaining explains, but which would presumably be inexplicable on any other thesis. In the first chapter of Liber XIII, Ficino argues that the power of imagination to affect the body is a sign of the soul's domination of the body. The imagination (*phantasia*) is the faculty which by means of its power to produce images can also produce passions such as desire, de-

light, fear, and sadness. These passions in turn affect the body; for example, the greed of a pregnant mother leaves a mark on the embryo, a sign of the object desired; the passion of some gluttons for certain foods imbues their saliva with the flavor of the desired viand; and Sophocles reportedly dropped dead from delight at the news of the success of one of his tragedies. All of these "phenomena" are cited by Ficino as *signa* that the soul dominates the body by its power of imagination, and indeed it might seem difficult to account for some of them in any other way. One might argue, however, that these passions and their effects are simply physical responses to physical stimuli. But this theory will not explain certain other facts. If it were true then all men would experience similar passions in the presence of similar stimuli, yet cold weather bothered most Greeks but not Socrates; Diogenes the Cynic marched barefoot over ice and through cold rivers. These occurrences are signs that the soul is independent of the body; that while sense experience may be the occasion of judgment and imagination, it does not determine it.

> To perceive and to judge are acts of the soul. Thus the soul is disturbed by its own proper act and not through the power of the body; it moves itself and is not moved by the body.

This doctrine is an ancient and honorable one in the Platonic tradition. While Ficino sought to confirm it by numerous and curious signs collected from various ancient authors, More illustrates it in a more contemporary and to some readers an even more curious way by developing at some length a single sign—the Copernican theory. His argument may be stated briefly. To the senses the sun appears to move across the sky and the earth to remain at rest. But sense experience does not compel the soul to judge that this is the case, for in triumphal opposition to the senses the soul judges that the sun is at rest and the earth is moving. Copernicanism is a *signum* of the independence of the soul's own proper act of judgment from effects of sense perception considered as an act of the body. The data of the senses are no more than evidence which the soul considers in coming to a decision, and if the soul is a wise judge she heeds reason more than sense.

> The busie soul it is that hither hent
> By strength of reason, the true distancies
> Of the erring Planets, and the vast extent
> Of their round bodies without outward eyes
> Hath view'd, told their proportionalities,
> Confounded sense by reason's strange report
> (But wiser he that on reason relies
> Then stupid sense low-sunken into dirt)
> This weapon I have got none from me may extort.

Since in More's opinion Copernicanism has "confounded sense by reason's strange report," it is apparent that he regards his exposition of it as perfectly consistent with his sense-purified posture, since it is a sign of the essential correctness of that posture. The geocentric theory is the natural one for the man who "dotes on sense," for "sense pleads for Ptolemee." The rational arguments for Copernicanism are so strong, More believes, that we must accept it even though it "utterly oppugne our outward sense." (pp. 573-77)

[More] started to compose the "**Psychathanasia,**" to present in a more systematic way the Platonic theory of immortality, and in this poem he was guided by the *Theologia Platonica.* In 1641 he acquired a Latin translation of Galileo's dialogue very probably while he was in the process of writing the "**Psychathanasia,**" perhaps even while he was considering what to include as *signa* of the soul's immortality, and the result was a "Copernican revolution" in his thinking. The Copernican theory, as it was defended and interpreted in a rationalistic spirit by Galileo, seemed to fit in perfectly with the aims and theme of **"Psychathanasia."** Here was a physical theory which in its central doctrine proclaimed that things were not what they seemed, that "confounded sense by reason's strange report." More's reaction was enthusiastic; the new cosmology reinforced rather than threatened his purified Platonic point of view. Before the second edition of his poems appeared More discovered the same attitude in Descartes—that the senses are deceptive, that things are not really what they appear—and he embraced Cartesian physics with equal enthusiasm. (pp. 577-78)

> *C. A. Staudenbaur, "Galileo, Ficino, and Henry More's 'Psychathanasia',"* in Journal of the History of Ideas, *Vol. XXIX, No. 4, October-December, 1968, pp. 565-78.*

JOHN HOYLES (essay date 1971)

[*In the following excerpt, Hoyles evaluates the critical history of More's poetry as literature and compares it to that of Thomas Vaughan, John Keats, and William Blake.*]

Southey wrote of **"Psychozoia"**: "There is perhaps no other poem in existence which has so little that is good in it, if it has anything good" [see excerpt dated 1812]. Coleridge commented: "Southey must have wearied himself out with the poem, till the mists from its swamps and stagnants had spread over its flowery plots and bowers." Southey on reflection agreed: "I have not done full justice to him as a poet. Strange and sometimes uncouth as he is, there are lines and passages of the highest poetry and most exquisite beauty." And so began Henry More's literary reputation.

The Victorians added little to Coleridge's judgment, though some seemed to enjoy wallowing in the swamps and stagnants. Thus Campbell likened More's poetry to "a curious grotto, whose gloomy labyrinths we might be curious to explore for the strange and mystic associations they create." Gilfillan referred to "that poetico-philosophic mist, which like the autumnal gossamer, hangs in light and beautiful festoons over his thoughts, and which suggests pleasing memories of Plato and the Alexandrian school" [see excerpt dated 1860]. And Grosart took up the refrain, valuing More's poetry "for its imaginative qualities and wildness of fancy and exquisite niceness of expression of the most gossamery thinking and feeling, and its pre-Raphaelitelike studies of nature, and now and again—alas! at long intervals, and mainly in the minor poems—wonderfulness of rapture and aspiration" [see excerpt dated 1878]. No doubt they found what they were looking for—mystic associations and pre-Raphaelite gossamer; but even if such Romantic empathy can be justified on the grounds that otherwise More would have no literary reputation, it is hardly fair to isolate elements of his poetry which are susceptible to such empathy, and construct a critical evaluation thereon. More's contribution to literature cannot be evaluated outside the context of his life and work, and without understanding it as an outcome of his philosophical, religious and aesthetic insights. (pp. 65-6)

In More's prose and poetry there are passages which are detachable from the backcloth of polemical speculation, and indicate an emerging modern consciousness. Usually the patches of literary value are moments when More uses the anachronistic or disintegrating material of Renaissance imagination, notably Spenserian diction and Metaphysical wit, but manages to ap-

propriate such material to his introspective expressionism. A key passage which will help to show how he does this is the following:

> He hath made me full lord of the four elements; and hath constituted me emperor of the world. I am in the fire of choler and am not burned; in the airy sanguine, and yet not blown away with every blast of transient pleasure, or vain doctrines of men; I descend also into the sad earthly melancholy, and yet am not buried from the sight of God. I am, Philalethes (though I dare say thou takest me for no bird of paradise) Incola Coeli in Terra, and inhabitant of paradise and heaven upon earth—I sport with the beasts of the earth; the lion licks my hand like a spaniel; and the serpent sleeps upon my lap and stings me not. I play with the fowls of heaven; and the birds of the air sit singing on my fist.

At first sight it is difficult to see in what sense this Biblical rhapsody points to an emergence of the modern consciousness; it represents the style and content of pre-Augustan prose. Just so; this is what it is meant to be, almost a pastiche of the style and content of Thomas Vaughan, to whom More is writing. More is arguing with Vaughan in Vaughan's own idiom; and, as the passage goes on to show, he is appropriating, to consolidate the reality of his divine life and free imagination, all the manifestations of magic and the old cosmology, which Vaughan has hurled at him. More pursues his rhapsody at the same high pitch:

> All these things are true in a sober sense. And the dispensation I live in, is more happiness above all measure, than if thou could'st call me down the moon so near thee by thy magic charms that thou may'st kiss her, as she is said to have kissed Endymion; or could'st stop the course of the sun; or, which is all one, with one stamp of thy foot stay the motion of the earth.

As Ward pointed out, "it is hard to represent the wit, reason, zeal, fancy, sportfulness and seriousness, divine boast, and rapture of mind there is contained in this writing."

It is instructive to compare those qualities in More's prose, which Ward pinpoints with such enthusiasm, with Vaughan's particularly spicy brand of personal abuse. One senses that Vaughan's most telling blows come, when he descends from the realm of speculative polemic, into the arena of libellous vituperation. In the preface to his *The Man Mouse Taken in a Trap and Tortured to Death for Gnawing the Margins of Eugenius Philalethes,* he draws More's character in that combination of Baconian and Rabelaisian style, so beloved of English satirists from Hall and Marston to Oldham and Cleveland:

> It is supposed he is in love with his Faerie Queen, and this hath made him a very elf in philosophy. He is indeed a scurvy, flabby, snotty-snouted thing. He is troubled with a certain splenetic looseness, and hath such squirts of the mouth, his readers cannot distinguish his breath from his breech. . . . But I have studied a cure answerable to his disease, I have been somewhat corrosive, and in defiance to the old phrase, I have washed a Moore clean. I have put his hog-noddle in pickle, and here I present him to the world, a dish of soused nonsense.

A purple passage in identical vein occurs in Vaughan's preface to *Magia Adamica* (1650), with which *The Man Mouse* was published. More is once again subjected to a flourish of excremental wit:

His observations are one continued ass's skin and the oysterwhores read the same philosophy every day. 'Tis a scurril, senseless piece, and—as he well styles himself—a chip of a block-head. His qualities indead are trancendent abroad but they are peers at home. His malice is equal to his ignorance. I laughed to see the fool's disease—a flux of gale which made him still at the chops whiles another held the press for him, like Porphyry's basin to Aristotle's well. There is something in him prodigious. His excrements run the wrong way, for his mouth stools, and he is so far from man that he is the aggravation to a beast. These are his parts, and for his person I turn him over to the dog-whippers, that he may be well-lashed and bear the errata of his front imprinted in his rear.

Vaughan has his place in English prose, half way between the gusto of Nashe and the conciseness of Swift; and on this ground More could hardly hope to compete with his opponent. But for More, polemic as well as abuse was distasteful; in an even battle Vaughan had slightly the better of the argument. The distinction between the two lies elsewhere. While Vaughan excels in his forte of Rabelaisian vituperation, More excels in giving rein to a rhapsodic expressionism. In Ward's words, More "was not for a mere notional apprehension of these high matters." More's refusal to be limited to notional controversy results in a negative capability which creates its own gusto out of his imaginative vision.

More's gusto embraces relics of Renaissance wit as well as intimations of Romantic imagination. Vaughan's own language was clearly infectious; and More enjoys a fair share of pun and paradox in his polemic with Eugenius Philalethes. We have seen his Bird of Paradise witticism; and very similar is this retort:

> If I be a Precisian,. . . it must be from hence, that I precisely keep myself to the naked truth of Christianity. If this be to be a Puritan, Eugenius, I am a Puritan: But I must tell thee that by how much more a man precisely takes this way, the more Independent he will prove.

More's double pun, first on "Precisian" and "precisely," then on "Independent," was part of the game of Renaissance polemic, and fair ripost to a man who had written, "in defiance to the old phrase, I have washed a Moore clean." The gothic elements in More's prose are very often part and parcel of a Metaphysical wit that has not completely lost its old habits of gratuitous speculation. . . . [Usually] More makes use of Metaphysical wit in the service of truth. . . . At other times, what seems to us gratuitous speculation, is in fact a seriously held piece of scientific theory, which the Metaphysical wit serves to demonstrate; as when More writes:

> The low spirit of the universe, though it go quite through the world, yet it is not totally in every part of the world; also we should hear our antipodes if they did but whisper: Because our lower man is a part of the inferior spirit of the universe.

Grosart's facetious comment—"Is this an anticipation of the telephone?"—illustrates the dangerous path More was following in using wit to support truth.

More may use Metaphysical wit to sharpen the edge of notional controversy; it nevertheless remains true that, as literature, such passages interest us for the impression they give of More's imaginative consciousness, whether it be grappling with speculative truths on the basis of the fourth ground of certainty, or whether it be flexing its muscles and rejoicing in its scope and energy. It is at this level of literary appreciation, that isolated passages, purple or otherwise, take on a meaning above that of style or content, and form an image of More's real literary achievement. This image does not distinguish between the motions of ordinary life, the search for speculative truth, and the sense of creative imagination. As such it approximates to Keats's "poetical character." More's poetical character is by no means a purely literary one; but with the reservation that its aesthetic implications are secondary to its philosophical and religious dimensions, it does relate the various facets of More's work to their organising and unitive source, and provide the only satisfactory criterion by which to measure his contribution to literature.

More's poetical character is best seen, as is Keats's, in his letters. This autobiographical articulation is in itself a no mean contribution to literature. The tone of the following passage is that of frank and casual introspection, with no hint of exhibitionism or self-pity. The gusto is Keatsian because it betrays a confidence in the solidity and validity of its intuitions, without claiming to be more than a means of self-expression:

> I scarce find myself here at all, saving in the trouble of my body, which has been as sad as lead, which I conceive is from the flaccidity of the mouth of my stomach, which Helmont makes the seat of the soul. . . . Either this or my incessant tumbling down too much small beer and fruit to mitigate that troublesome and wasting heat in my body caused by those fierce elements and materials of green choler, is the reason of this flaccidness of the mouth of my stomach, as that of my extreme proneness to heaviness and sorrow. . . . But I never deal with any passion that troublesomely invades me with sleights and diversions but bid them battle on the open field, and by a serious ramble for a whole afternoon . . . I got some considerable ground against my enemy, after which I was better in both body and mind. . . . Madame, what you speak in compliment I acknowledge if rightly understood, to be a real truth, viz. that in what place so ever I enjoy most of myself that I am sure to have the best company there. For I profess, if I know myself aright, I am nothing else but an aggregate of my friends.

The Metaphysical arguments in this passage are identical to those out of which Lord Herbert of Cherbury wove his subtle lyrics and elegies. More appropriates the machinery of the Metaphysical conceit to the expression of personality. His method of dealing with troublesome passions reminds one of Keats putting on his best clothes to gain ground against melancholy. In this way the motions of ordinary life reveal More's poetical character.

Keats expressed his sense of the creative imagination in his theory of the "chamber of maiden thought," and the various passages which issued from it. More had a similar sense of the imagination's autonomy. Describing the strange sights and lively forms which people his mind, he compares them to

> men ybrought
> Into some spacious room, who when they've had
> A turn or two, go out, although unbad.
> All these I see and know, but entertain
> None to my friend but who's most sober sad;
> Although, the time my roof doth them contain
> Their presence doth possess me till they out again.

More's sense of creative imagination, although he is not wholly happy with it, constitutes a second aspect of his poetical character.

The third ingredient of More's poetical character, his commitment to the search for truth, was of course geared to his fourth ground of certainty. Speculative truth might often be misleading, but it had to square with imaginative insight if it was to have any meaning. Keats, with equal foresight, saw that one had to be a philosopher, even if all the philosophical minds one knew were never content with a half-truth. False philosophy had to be castigated, and the life of the imagination upheld. With such a poetical character, More could hardly not write just a little bit like Blake and Keats. The following passages are eloquently exemplary:

> Such is thy putid muse, Lucretius,
> That fain would teach that souls all mortal be:
> The dusty atoms of Democritus
> Certes have fall'n into thy feeble eye,
> And thee bereft of perspicacity.
> Others through the strong steam of their dull blood
> Without the help of that philosophy,
> Have with more ease the truth not understood,
> And the same thing conclude in some sad drooping mood.

> What doth move
> The nightingale to sing so sweet and clear,
> The thrush, or lark that mounting high above
> Chants her shrill notes to heedless ears of corn
> Heavily hanging in the dewy morn?

The striking affinities to poems by Blake and Keats are no mere accidents of style or content; they are the visible tip of the iceberg of More's total enterprise, as it emerges out of Renaissance culture into the modern mind. (pp. 66-72)

> *John Hoyles, "More's Work as Literature," in his*
> The Waning of the Renaissance, 1640-1740: Studies
> in the Thought and Poetry of Henry More, John Nor-
> ris and Isaac Watts, *Martinus Nijhoff, 1971, pp. 65-72.*

THOMAS L. CANAVAN   (essay date 1973)

[Canavan is an American educator and essayist. In the following excerpt, he explores the anti-Puritan sentiments prevalent in the works of More, Jonathan Swift, Robert Burton, and Meric Casaubon.]

During the seventeenth century, attacks on the excesses of Puritan "enthusiasm" came from many sources: from Anglican divines who feared that the social and political implications of Puritan religious zeal would destroy their church, from rationalists who saw in religious fervor the antithesis of reason, from reformers who believed that the true Christian Commonwealth would never emerge from the Puritan community. Robert Burton's *Anatomy of Melancholy* (1621) and Jonathan Swift's *Tale of a Tub* (1704) express the Anglican clergyman's rejection of Puritan enthusiasm, while in other works Meric Casaubon and Henry More, writing with less obvious partisan intentions, warn of the threat of enthusiasm to both liberty and rationality.

In Meric Casaubon's *Treatise Concerning Enthusiasm* and Henry More's *Enthusiasmus Triumphatus,* it is quite clear that both authors, like Burton, Swift, and others, are concerned with the Puritan belief in the "inner light" of divine inspiration and are writing against that form of enthusiasm which was popularly accepted in the Puritan assemblies as a manifestation of one's prophetic role. Essentially, Casaubon and More demand a rather sophisticated attitude toward the preaching of those who affirm their own "inner light" and expect, indeed sometimes require, respect as inspired speakers of God's word. Although neither of these men rejects the possibility of individual inspiration,

both do insist upon a cynicism which would ask the prophet to "manifest" himself and to "prove," insofar as proof is possible, that he is in fact a "vessel" of the Holy Spirit endowed with the preternatural gift of prophecy. They propose that a distinction be drawn between the inspired sermon of the true prophet and the preaching of the deluded enthusiast whose sense of his own self-importance has led him to believe in himself as a "messenger" of the diety.

Since Casaubon and More present themselves as men who require rationality and free assent in all human activity, especially religious activity, they introduce their discussions of enthusiasm with the assumption that "true religious experience, however emotionally satisfying or disturbing it may be, is never irrational." It is not surprising, then, that their ideas are developed in a somewhat syllogistic fashion, despite the seemingly loose and arbitrary structure of their works. They proceed from a belief in the essential goodness of man's faculties and assume that the exercise of free will and rationality is a necessary part of man's worship of God. Seeing no virtue in self-induced emotional excitement, they criticize the behavior of those "Saints" who demean their own humanity by deliberately generating in themselves a nonrational response to religious worship. In Casaubon's and More's opinion, to deny reason in one area of human activity is to deny the efficacy of reason altogether. It is their contention that "there is nothing . . . that *the holy Spirit* did ever suggest to any man but it was agreeable to, if not demonstrable from, what we call *Reason.*" And if the prophet cannot make an appeal to reason, if his so-called inspired words cannot stand the test of reason, then he is to be abjured and his preaching is to be rejected. But such a man is not to be ostracized unless it can be shown that he remains adamant in his delusion and continues to preach his delusion to others. In that case, he is to be condemned, his preaching is to be publicly exposed, and his delusion, or his madness, is to be regarded as the result of his sin or his demonic possession.

Given these general principles, it is impossible to ignore the intellectual tradition which supplied the framework for much of the anti-Puritan literature of the seventeenth century. To be sure, many operated within the tradition, and some of their works influenced those writers now being discussed, but Casaubon and More provide detailed examples of the development of the tradition in the seventeenth century. Moreover, the ideas presented in their works suggest an intellectual relationship between Burton and Swift and a continuity in the approach of anti-Puritan writers. As the first of these four writers to consider the validity of Puritan enthusiasm, Burton offered that criticism which was to be elaborated in the religious treatises of Casaubon and More and which was to find unique expression in the satire of Swift's *Tale.* It was not, however, a criticism that was contained solely in the works of these major figures; instead, it was a criticism that extended through all modes of literary expression, finding its most complete elaboration in the works of these four authors.

In their books, Burton, Casaubon, More, and Swift explicitly acknowledge the actuality of divine inspiration in particular cases, most notably in the prophetic books of the Bible. They also admit the presence of the Holy Spirit, through grace, in the souls of men, but they reveal their opposition to the self-determined "Saints" who use zeal as the measure of morality and religious sincerity. Casaubon, for example, while accepting the virtuous zeal of the prophet whose gift is manifested through reason, cautions that among those who are "true, sanctified, orthodox Christians, some may be found, that have more zeal then they have discretion; to discern between time and time, persons and persons, and other circumstances, by which they that intend to do good, ought, as by word of God they are directed, to guide their zeal." But in the seventeenth century, few Saints were interested in "guiding" their zeal, with a resulting series of anti-Puritan attacks on unwarranted enthusiasm. Although all four writers treat the possible physical causes of misdirected zeal, they emphasize the religious importance of false prophecy. One can sympathize with the man who becomes mad or irrational because of an excess of vapor in his brain, but one must expose the man who, maddened himself, attempts to lead others to accept his delusion as truth. Such a man must be revealed as a false prophet; the irrational must be overcome by the rational. Unfortunately, it is not always possible to distinguish between the enthusiasm which proceeds from true inspiration and the enthusiasm which results from an excess of wind in the body. (pp. 227-29)

It has been suggested that only Burton, Casaubon, More, and some anonymous pamphleteers "pictured the Puritans as sincere victims of delusion." However, these writers are linked not only by their attitude toward enthusiastic Puritans, but also by their determination of the nature of enthusiasm. Although Burton had found no adequate discussion of melancholy by a physician, still he was able to satisfy himself that enthusiasm was a form of melancholy, and in this he was followed by Casaubon, More, and Swift. Indeed, there is a developmental pattern in the writings of these authors when their comments on enthusiasm and melancholy are considered in relation to the tradition of anti-Puritan attack. Burton was uncertain of the connection between the melancholic humor and the enthusiasm of the Saints. Yet despite his uncertainty, Burton insisted that a connection existed. Casaubon, writing approximately thirty years after Burton, agreed with Burton in the assumption that enthusiasm is a species of melancholy. Then More, following Burton and Casaubon, made specific the relationship between melancholy and enthusiasm by approaching the subject "scientifically": that is, he used medical terms to explain the relationship. And finally, Swift applied More's reduction directly to his fictional presentation of the Puritan enthusiasts in the *Tale.*

Burton and Casaubon, acknowledging, in general, two possible causes of melancholic enthusiasm, endeavored to show that those causes are related. For example, they declare in their books that enthusiasm may result from physiologial imbalance of the humors or from demonic possession. Then each assumes that these two causes are related, that the physiological imbalance serves only to make the mind and soul of man more readily subject to demonic possession. Early in the century, Burton wrote:

> Many think [the Devil] can work upon the body, but not upon the mind. But experience pronounceth otherwise, that he can work upon both body and mind. . . .
>
> [The Devil] *begins first with the phantasy, & moves that so strongly, that no reason is able to resist.* Now he moves the *phantasy* by mediation of humours; although many Physicians are of opinion, that the Devil can alter the mind, and produce this disease himself.

Casaubon, placing himself in the same tradition as Burton, later affirmed that medical history supports the opinion of those "Physicans [who] acknowledge [that] a preparation and disposition of the body, through distemper of humours,. . . giveth

great advantage to the Devil to work upon." And this advantage, when it leads to genuine demonic possession, often produces the enthusiast who is known to the general community by his ability to "prophesy, speak several languages, talk of Astronomy, & other unknown sciences" (Burton). But it must be noted that these abilities are demonically generated and that the "disease" of the soul is a reflection of the disease of the body. Indeed, in the works of Burton and Casaubon, it is only one small step from melancholic enthusiasm to melancholic madness. (pp. 231-32)

While Burton merely allows for the existence of mechanical enthusiasm, Casaubon and those who wrote after him more explicitly acknowledge the place of mechanical enthusiasm in Puritan worship. Casaubon, strangely, includes such enthusiasm in his listing of types, but fails to discuss it. However, in his attribution of zeal to physiological causes, with Burton he admits that the mind and soul of man may be so possessed that the individual is forced to act as the devil dictates. In this sense, and only this sense, is enthusiasm mechanical. Printed just one year after Casaubon's work, More's *Enthusiasmus Triumphatus* continues this approach to the mechanical aspects of enthusiasm. More states that

> the Originall of such preemptory delusion as mankind are obnoxious to, is the enormous strength and vigour of the *Imagination;* which Faculty though it be in some sort of power, as *Respiration* is, yet it will also work without our leave, as I have already demonstrated: and hence men become mad and fanaticall whether they will or no.

Here More has in fact affirmed the existence of demonically inspired enthusiasm which does not necessarily result from sin and which does not reflect the sure damnation of an individual's soul. As in the *Treatise Concerning Enthusiasm,* it is suggested that some Puritan enthusiasts are simply victims of their own humoral imbalances. Because they have been deluded by the vapors which rise to the brain, they have not wilfully involved themselves in heresy and false prophecy.

> The *Spirit* then that wings the *Enthusiast* in such a wonderful manner is nothing else but that *Flatulency* which is in the *Melancholy* complexion, and rises out of the *Hypochondriacal* humour.

But that some Puritan "Saints" were guilty of heresy and false prophecy was recognized by More, for if all "Saints" were merely deluded and were not guilty of generating their delusions, then part of the purpose of Casaubon's and More's treatises would be obviated. Their books do not simply warn Englishmen of the existence of false prophets; they also provide the bases for the public condemnation of false prophets. However, the writer who was to involve himself more overtly than Casaubon or More in direct condemnation was Jonathan Swift. In his *Tale of a Tub* and his *Mechanical Operation of the Spirit,* he is clearly less generous than his predecessors, for he does not "[picture] the Puritans as sincere victims of delusion." (pp. 235-36)

Endeavoring to give his work a pseudo-philosophical tone, Swift asks his readers, perhaps in the style of a scholastic philosopher, "to distinguish, First between an Effect grown from *Art* into *Nature,* and one that is natural from its Beginning; Secondly, between an Effect wholly natural, and one which has only a natural Foundation, but where the Superstructure is entirely Artificial." After making this distinction, the reader is prepared for Swift's recounting of the physiological causes of inspiration—the rising of vapor from the lower part of the body—and for his contention that the ''Saints'' wilfully subject themselves to the force of these vapors in their effort to provoke an ''inspired'' frenzy.

> I am apt to imagine, that the Seed or Principle, which has ever put Men upon *Visions* in Things *Invisible,* is of a Corporeal Nature.

Mechanical enthusiasm is, then, the wilful submission of the spirit to the bodily sickness, and since Swift's Puritans are wilfully submissive, they are, in contrast to the enthusiasts described by Burton, Casaubon, and More, always condemnable as false prophets. In their works, ''the *Thorn in the Flesh* serves for a *Spur* to the *Spirit*'' (Swift), for ''it is agreed among Physicians, that nothing affects the Head so much, as a tentiginous Humor, repelled and elated to the upper Region, found by daily practice, to run frequently up into Madness'' (Swift). This final assertion differentiates Swift from his seventeenth-century predecessors who accepted the view that the enthusiast, although deluded and possibly mad, could be cured of his zeal. Swift's enthusiasts, on the contrary, cannot be cured, because they are knowing contributors to their own madness and, ultimately, to their own perversion of true religion.

But More, to a greater extent than Casaubon, is the author who provides, in relation to the tradition of anti-Puritan invective, the link between Burton and Swift. That More was familiar with Burton's *Anatomy* cannot be questioned, for he refers directly to ''Democritus Junior'' in the **Enthusiasmus Triumphatus.** And to disregard More's influence on *A Tale of a Tub* is to ignore Swift's own notes to the work.

In *Swift and Anglican Rationalism,* Phillip Harth, stressing the development of anti-Puritan literature from Burton to Swift, has studied Henry More's **Enthusiasmus Triumphatus** as the work which provided Swift with the background for his attack on enthusiasts in the *Tale.* Moreover, Harth contends that an important source for Swift's satiric approach can be found in Burton's *Anatomy,* although there is, in his opinion, nothing that specifically links Burton and Swift directly. More, then, becomes the intermediary between Burton and Swift, and in More's explanation for the physiological causes of enthusiasm, Harth believes that he ''did not have to go beyond the analysis of melancholy already mapped out by Burton.''

> All More had to do was to turn for the details of his discussion, not to the vague account of religious melancholy which appears toward the end of Burton's book, but to the clinical discussion of the causes and kinds of melancholy which Burton provides early in *The Anatomy of Melancholy.*
>
> According to Burton, the immediate physiological cause of melancholy depends upon the prevalence and condition of the victim's humors.

More accepted, as did Casaubon and many other authors, this diagnosis of the physiological cause not only of melancholy, but of enthusiasm as well. But More followed Burton more closely than Casaubon and used in his study of enthusiasm Burton's analysis of the source of vapors. Burton had said that a pathological melancholic condition results from ''*vapours which arise from the other parts, and fume up into the head, altering the animal faculties.*'' More adapted to his own use the statement that the vapors arise from the lower organs of the body and abuses Puritan enthusiasts by suggesting that enthusiasm proceeds from an excess of vapor. In this approach, More was followed by Swift, who wrote that ''Human Understanding, seated in the Brain, must be troubled and over-

spread by Vapours, ascending from the lower Faculties, to water the Invention, and render it fruitful'' (*Tale*).

Burton, More, and Swift are united not merely by a somewhat conservatively religious attitude toward Puritanism, but by a very real suspicion that enthusiasm is likely to result in the wrongful exercise of individual liberty. The enthusiast in the seventeenth century did not live privately; he demanded that his ''light'' be communicated to others. In short, he saw himself as a leader whose duty provoked him to require of others respect as a prophet. Thus, in dealing with the religious aspects of enthusiasm, anti-Puritan writers arrived at conclusions which related immediately to the Dissenters in their societal roles. The three authors being discussed share several common convictions, and beyond their religious feeling and their attribution of enthusiasm to a physiological imbalance, they convey in their anti-Puritan works a genuine fear of enthusiasm as a socially destructive force which must, because of its very nature, grow out of a mistaken religious belief or a misdirected prophetic impulse.

Because it never occurred to Burton, More, and Swift to treat religion separately from social problems, their works contain the assumption that whatever is religiously wrong is socially evil. They admit that the factionalism existing among religious sects produces only greater factionalism in essentially non-religious areas of social activity. In the *Anatomy* Burton condemns the preacher who is a servant of the devil, whether knowingly or unknowingly, because he ''[omits] no opportunities, according to men's several inclinations, abilities, to circumvent and humour them, to maintain his superstitions; sometimes to stupify, besot them; sometimes again by oppositions, factions, to set all at odds, and in an uproar; sometimes he infects one man, and makes him a principal agent; sometimes whole Cities, Countries.'' Such a man cannot be criticized merely as a false prophet, for his prophecy almost always results in political action. (pp. 237-39)

Although More is not merely as thorough as Burton in his recounting of examples that reflect the relationship between religion and politics, he does nevertheless comment on the relationship and imply that religious enthusiasts are to be quieted because they instigate in their preaching a dangerous tendency toward social radicalism. He asserts that enthusiasm naturally leads to a desire to reform the world, a desire which may be religious in origin but which is clearly political in its social import. The enthusiast so affected is dangerous not only because he is a threat to existing religion, but because he is also a threat to the social *status quo.*

> . . . A *Melancholist* . . . must be very highly puffed up, and not only fancy himself *inspired,* but believe himself such a special piece of *Light* and *Holiness* that God has sent into the world, that he will take upon him to *reform,* or rather *annull,* the very *Law* and *Religion* he is born under, and make himself not at all inferiour to either *Moses* or *Christ,* though he have neither any sound *Reason* nor visible *Miracle* to extort belief.

And to More, Moses and Christ were politically important, for no religious leader of stature is socially neutral. More, accepting this position as inevitable and true, indicates that the physiology of the religious enthusiast is also the physiology of the political radical, for both are subject to hypochondriacal melancholy and the deleterious vapor which, ''mounting into the Head, being first actuated and spirited and somewhat refined by the warmth of the Heart, fills the Mind with variety of *Imaginations.''* Such imaginations can direct the enthusiast into actions and statements which disrupt the order of society and, perhaps, endanger the peace. Indeed, the same impulse which allows the religious enthusiast to believe in himself as a Messias permits him, when his activity has taken on some political importance, to assume a very aristocratic posture. More says:

> Wherefore those whose Temper carries them most to *Political* affairs,who love rule and honour, and have a strong sense of Civil Rights, *Melancholy* heating makes them sometimes fancy themselves great Princes (at least by divine assignment) and Deliverers of the people sent from God.

The religious purpose of the enthusiast, then, becomes inextricably united to his political and social role, and the self-styled Messias presents himself to his countrymen as their political savior. Such an enthusiast, no doubt unwillingly, was fulfilling the role that proved so frightening to the theologian-philosophers of seventeenth-century Cambridge: such a falsely motivated man was following the Calvinistic dictate to become to his people a "religious politician." To the Cambridge Platonists, to men like Henry More, the Calvinistic precedent at Geneva, in its restriction of human freedom, was as anathema as the Catholic insistence on the unquestioned authority of the Roman pontiff. (pp. 240-41)

[Politics] and religion, are never utterly separable, as is indicated directly by More's *Enthusiasmus Triumphatus* and satirically, by indirection, in Swift's *Tale*.

Attention to religion and politics as areas of Puritan influence was not restricted to Burton, More, and Swift. But their interest in both the internal piety and public politics of the enthusiasts affirms the complex nature of the anti-Puritan literary tradition, a tradition concerned equally with private religious motivation and the social consequences of zeal. Attacking the Puritan community for its religious excesses as well as its presumed social ambitions, writers like Burton and Swift, Casaubon and More, believed that they were at once defending the bases of true Christianity and apprising their readers of a serious threat to the health of their souls and the peace of their country. These authors believed themselves justified in their exposure of, and objections to, the Puritans on both moral and political grounds; their self-appraisals revealed only the best intention, a desire to emulate the Messiah by becoming physicians of the soul and the body-politic. For Burton and Swift, Casaubon and More, the correspondence between the purity of the soul and the security of the state was unquestionable. It is this correspondence which is central to their anti-Puritan writings. (pp. 241-42)

> *Thomas L. Canavan, "Robert Burton, Jonathan Swift, and the Tradition of Anti-Puritan Invective," in Journal of the History of Ideas, Vol. XXXIV, No. 2, April-June, 1973, pp. 227-42.*

EARL MINER   (essay date 1974)

[*An American educator, editor, literary critic, and translator, Miner has been the general editor of the Augustan Reprint Society and* The Works of John Dryden *(15 vols., 1965-72). In the following excerpt, he evaluates More's narrative poetry, focusing specifically upon* Psychodia Platonica.]

The revival of narrative poetry coincided with deep political strains and the outbreak of civil war [in England]. Such coincidence was not necessary, but it was a factor that affected poets differently, making some concerned with glancing at the troubles of the day and others looking inward to the consolations of philosophy. Above all, however, there was a struggle to achieve something great, something commensurate with the scale of contemporary events. The most useful of predecessors at first were Spenser and the Fletchers, who soon yielded to a tradition of romance going back as far as Chaucer but more and more wrought with aspirations for the heroic. A constant problem facing these narrative poets was that facing all writers of narrative: creation of a story that seemed at once interesting and important. From our beginnings in Henry More and Sir Francis Kynaston we can see this problem. At one extreme, a writer may invest his narrative with all the philosophical or other significance in his mind, and so lose hold of simple plot. Or at the other extreme, he may write a plot that moves so jauntily and quickly that when it is over one doubts that it has meant a blessed thing. (p. 57)

The Christian, or Cambridge, Neoplatonist Henry More first produced a narrative entitled *Psychodia Platonica: or A Platonicall Song of the Soul* at Cambridge in 1642. More's scientific interests emerge more clearly in a collection supplementary to the former poem in 1646: *Democritus Platonissans, or an Essay upon the Infinity of Worlds out of Platonic Principles.* Epicurus, Ficino, Descartes, and Christianity mingle in an allegory. In 1647 *Democritus Platonissans* was printed with Psyche's **"Song"** under the general title of *Philosophical Poems.* By now, however, More had woven the two together in a way requiring, for full explanation, the reader to have a copy in his hand. Suffice it to say that the working title of the whole is *A Platonicall Song of the Soul* and that More himself usually refers to his work as the *Song of the Soul.* The 1647 *Philosophical Poems* is of capital importance to understanding More, because he added to it an index of characters and ideas, "The Interpretation Generall."

Among most students of Renaissance literature, the possibility of Neoplatonism increases at once the value of a literary work. If ever there was a Neoplatonic English poet, Henry More was the one. Of course his Neoplatonism has very little connection with Plato, who was not fully extracted from Ficino and other interpreters until the last century. But Psyche's **"Song"** is unquestionably "platonick." In "To the Reader," More sets out an analogy between Neoplatonism and Christianity.

> —*Ahad, Aeon,* and *Psyche* [his heroes and heroine] are all omnipresent in the World, after the most perfect way that humane reason can conceive of. For they are in the world all totally and at once every where.

> This is the famous Platonicall Triad: which though they that slight the Christian Trinity do take for a figment; yet I think it is no contemptible argument, that the Platonists, the best and divinest of Philosophers, and the Christians, the best of all that do professe religion, do both concur that there is a Trinity. In what they differ, I leave to be found out according to the safe direction of that infallible Rule of Faith, the holy Word.

The first part of the poem has the separate title, **"Psychozoia, or The Life of the Soul"**; and this part "has," we are told, "the first spontaneous glow of the satisfying revelation the author's passionately hungry soul had sought and found"; it is further reassuring that "The most Spenserian and most attractive of these poems" is **"Psychozoia,"** because I confess it difficult to get much beyond it. (pp. 58-9)

It seems improbable to me that any reader of **"The Life of the Soul"** will single out its plot for praise. But that the poem has had readers can be demonstrated by the echoes of More's Hyle in Milton's chaos, and of More's Pandaemoniothen in Milton's Pandemonium. The difference between the two poems is more radical than these connections. If proof of that be necessary, we need only compare More's evil characters with Milton's fallen angels in the first two books of *Paradise Lost*.

> That rabble rout that in this Castle won [dwells],
> Is Irefull-ignorance, Unseemly-zeal,
> Strong-self-conceit, Rotten-religion,
> Contentious-reproch-'gainst-Michael-
> If-he-of-*Moses*-body-ought-reveal-
> Which-their-dull-skonses[-]cannot-eas'ly-reach,
> Love-of-the-carkas, An[-]Inept-appeal-
> T'uncertain[-]papyrs, a-False-formall-fetch-
> Of[-]feigned-sighs, Contempt-of-poore-and-sinfull-wretch.

The charms of Neoplatonism hardly extend to a character named Contentious-reproch-'gainst-Michael-If-he-of-*Moses*-body-ought-reveal-Which-their-dull-skonses[-]cannot-eas'ly-reach. (How much finer are Bunyan's conjugate names.) More is not done, for he has more—two stanzas of this nonsense in which I find it particularly difficult to detect "the first spontaneous glow of the satisfying revelation" of anything poetic. These evil ones are later defeated by "the mighty warlick Michaels host," and in one stanza (except for its bathetic last line) we hear true poetry.

> In perfect silver glistring panoply
> They ride, the army of the highest God.
> Ten thousands of his Saints approachen nie,
> To judge the world, and rule it with his rod.
> They leave all plain whereever they have trod.
> Each Rider on his shield doth bear the Sun
> With golden shining beams dispread abroad,
> The Sun of righteousness at high day noon,
> By this same strength, I ween, this Fort is easily wonne.

All Henry More need do is turn from religious action (the Angels Militant under Michael) to platonick allegory and the art of sinking is mastered. In spite of Aristotle, Sidney, and Dryden, we believe that when the "language" of the poem is so palpably incompetent, any discussion of further issues seems superfluous. Anyone who can marry brother to sister and both to father, bedding them at once under the world (Psyche's robe), leads us to ask why he wrote a poem when he might have written a prose treatise. I fear that the answer is that writers of the Neoplatonic persuasion fancy themselves poetic *ipso facto*, as do many of their admirers, but that the kind of poet wholly attracted to such beliefs usually lacks the requisite talents. More's poem (of which we have considered the first, best part) shows the extraordinary difficulties that lie in the way of anyone seeking to be a narrative poet, even if he knows full well what he designs his poem to mean. There is something, in the end, altogether pathetic about More's attempt to write a fully philosophical poem. (pp. 61-2)

> *Earl Miner, "The Search for New Language and Form: Narrative Poetry from More to Chamberlayne," in his* The Restoration Mode from Milton to Dryden, *Princeton University Press, 1974, pp. 53-128.*

GEORGE A. PANICHAS (essay date 1974)

[*Panichas is an American educator, literary scholar, and editor. He has written extensively on the works of D. H. Lawrence, Fedor Dostoevski, and Simone Weil, and on the literature written be-* *tween the two world wars. A self-described Christian Humanist, Panichas characterizes himself as a "dissident critic" whose work is often concerned with the "spiritual bankruptcy"—lack of a moral imperative—he perceives in much of modern literature. Since 1984 he has edited the conservative quarterly* Modern Age. *In the following excerpt, Panichas explicates More's philosophy, comparing aspects of it to the thought systems of Plotinus, Hobbes, and Descartes.*]

Platonic philosophy has often been identified as the "old loving nurse" of the Church. The Cambridge Platonists appealed to Plato, condemned by some in the course of the centuries as the "mad theologian" and "bombastic poet," as a confederate against the empiricism, sensualism, and materialism which negated access to religious experience. More and the other Cambridge men, embodying the Greek spirit, venerated both Plato and Plotinus, in contradistinction to the Calvinists and Puritans who took careful precautions to give Christianity unquestioned precedence over antiquity. The goal of More and the other English Platonists was the discovery of being. In order to achieve this discovery, as Cassirer points out [in his *The Platonic Renaissance in England* (1953)], they did not hesitate "to say that the good will of a heathen is godlier than the angry zeal of a Christian." The fact is that More and the others did not openly distinguish between Plato and Plotinus, Platonism and Plotinianism. But both of these, especially to More, were philosophies of values, not form; and both supplemented Christianity in relation to certain eternal values and a common indifference to worldly preoccupations. More and his colleagues at Cambridge did not seek to superimpose Platonism upon Christianity. They simply wished to find philosophical support in a system which was essentially religious, which taught the sole reality of the spiritual world, and which proclaimed the immortality of the soul and the upward ascent of the soul in the quest for divine union.

Religious mysticism owes a great deal to Plotinus, to whom the phenomenal world was not evil nor burdened with the defilement of original sin, but was simply the "image" or reflection of the highest perfection of the world above, a realm sought beyond all images, from the image to the prototype. Henry More was strongly influenced by Plotinus, and his poems of 1642 and 1647 show this throughout. More's conception of the Trinity was comparable to Plotinus' trinity of the One or the Good, above existence, or God as the Absolute; the Intelligence, the sphere of real existence, or the organic unity; and the Soul, the sphere of appearance, of imperfect reality, or God as action. More's Plotinianism is clearly brought out in a stanza from his poem **"Psychathanasia"** showing the flowing, emanating, goodness of God:

> When nothing can to Gods own self accrew,
> Who's infinitely happy; sure the end
> Of this creation simply was to shew
> His flowing goodness, which he doth out-send
> Not for himself; for naught can him amend;
> But to his creature doth his good impart,
> This infinite Good through all the world doth wend
> To fill with heavenly blisse each willing heart:
> So the free Sunne doth 'light and 'liven every part.

In the thinking of More and the other Platonists the soul was looked upon as the Plotinian principle of motion. . . . More further argued, always drawing on Plotinus, that the soul was immaterial and immortal because it was independent of the body. First of all, More believed that the body, which was dependent on the soul, was in the soul; second, that the soul could be occupied with its own thoughts without affecting the body, thus centering its attention upon the contemplative quest of its own well-being; third, that since the soul does not emanate from sensual things, it could resist the desires of the body, sublimating material lusts and devoting itself to the intellectual love of divine qualities; and fourth, that the soul was a continuum of existence, growing in force and strength, whereas sense, fancy, and memory faded away with the gradual disintegration of the body. More refers to the soul's independence of the body in the following:

> What disadvantage then can the decay
> Of this poore carcase do, when it doth fade?
> The soul no more depends on this frail clay
> Then on our eye depends bright Phoebus glist'ring ray.

More also believed in the preexistence of the soul. He contended that God was good; and if the soul was also good, as he believed, God would naturally have created the soul early in the divine scheme. For More the pilgrimage of the soul through earthly life was primarily a "return to the source from which all being emerged and . . . [a] unification with the realm of divine entities above the world of material Things." The end of this pilgrimage was marked by spiritual catharsis and mystical union with God. More realized that this ecstatic vision would not be granted without one's fulfilling certain conditions which Plotinus best describes: "The very soul, once it has conceived the straining love towards this, lays aside all shape it has taken, even to the intellectual shape that has informed it. There is no vision, no union, for those handling or acting by any thing other; the soul must see before it neither evil nor any thing else, that alone it may receive the Alone." Also, in true Plotinian fashion, More argued in favor of three realms of the soul: the *terrestrial*, the combination of soul and body; the *aereal*, the separation of the soul and body and the former's attachment to the particles in the air; and the *ethereal*, the union with the highest category of Being, above reason and intelligence. (pp. 316-18)

Essentially More's concept of God was Plotinian: God was the force producing all things but produced by none, the source of all beauty, the end of all things, the highest good and wisdom, the transcendence of all existence itself, the highest abstraction, superior even to the Platonic Idea. To More, as to Plotinus, the human mind would return to and unite with the absolute only after passage between vulgar opinion and philosophical knowledge. More believed that the innate idea of God existed in man. "It remains therefore undeniable," he wrote, "that there is an inseparable Idea of a Being absolutely Perfect ever residing, though not always acting, in the Soul of Man." More, closely adhering to Plotinian emanatistic theory, looked upon the world as an *overflow* of the divine life, and believed in the return of the being to its divine source, made possible through contemplation. He believed that the mind of man is as the image of God, drawn and descending from Him. More's faith in the Holiness and greatness of God is seen in his lines:

> From thy Works my Joy proceeds:
> How I triumphed in thy Deeds!
> Who thy Wonders can express?
> All thy Thoughts are fathomless,
> Hid from Men in Knowledge blind,
> Hid from Fools to Vice inclin'd.

With Philo, More agreed that man's rational faculty was a temple of God, and with Plotinus that the human intellect was an image of the divine rationality which was the emanation of God. Indeed, More believed in the excellence and necessity of reason for the maintaining of the truth of Christian religion.

He enthusiastically quoted Cicero's saying "*Rationem, quo ea me cunque ducet, sequar*" in his attempts to bolster the "two grand pillars" of religion, the existence of God and the immortality of the soul. But he was convinced that piety was the key to knowledge, that keenness of insight proceeded from purity of life, that the life of contemplation was superior to that of pleasure and statesmanship. Being religious was to More of supreme importance in a life that was really a struggle between the lofty and the low, between the sacred and the profane. More's emphasis on reason, however, did not become an arrogant and impossible demand for a foolproof system of theology free from mystery. More felt that reason should "construct a philosophy round these two pivots, God and Man." And even when More sought to establish a free intercourse between religion and the natural sciences and philosophies, he kept uppermost in his mind that scientific discoveries were nothing more than the revelations of the immanence, beneficence, and wisdom of God.

The Greek concept of man's life as a continual effort to achieve the beautiful and good was central to More's ethical point of view. Ethical living was part of divine living, and the harmonious unity of both brought man to a point of perfection. Goodness and happiness were identical to More. Along with Cudworth he felt that human nature was inherently divine: "I come from Heaven; am an immortal Ray / of God; O Joy! and back to God shall goe." Both stressed that all appetites and passions "yet fall into proper subordination to the higher divine faculty or reason, which distinguishes man, and stamps him a moral being." More observed in his *Enchiridion Ethicum* ("a middle ground of ethical doctrine"), which was really an answer to Hobbesianism, that "Passions therefore are not only good, but singularly needful to the perfecting of human life." He emphasized that proper guidance and regulation were necessary at all times, in order to avoid sensualism of an extreme sort. He did not fail to introduce an element of mysticism and religious faith into his ethics, pointing out that the end of human life was purification and assimilation with divinity. The existence of a divine moral faculty in man was always a primary belief in More's thinking. He called this the "Boniform Faculty of the Soul," which represented the moral sense of the soul, and which was the image of God in man's soul, containing right reason.

Henry More steadfastly believed in absolutes: absolute good, absolute evil, absolute values, absolute justice. The publication of Thomas Hobbes's *Leviathan* in 1651 contributed a great deal to the maturity of More and the Cambridge Platonists, since they had not only to answer Hobbes's materialism, which denied the existence of the soul and the freedom of the will, but also to combat his belief that the source of all moral obligation lay in power and civil authority. Hobbes's materialistic theory of perception affirmed the reality of the "body," but More affirmed the reality of the spirit. (pp. 319-20)

The Cambridge Platonists wished to look on nature as plastic, not mechanical; More, wishing to reunite matter and spirit, looked on spirit as an active force, penetrating and moving matter. In the work of his contemporary René Descartes, More sought an ally, one whose science might augment the metaphysical beliefs of the English Platonists. At first More admired the rational clearness of the Cartesian speculations which had departed from the scholastic tradition and which unified and reconciled philosophical truths through reason. Descartes' ideas especially fascinated More because they affirmed the existence of the soul and of God as fundamental certainties. "By the name of God," said Descartes, "I understand a substance infinite [eternal, immutable], independent, all-knowing, all-powerful, and by which I myself, and every other thing exists, if any such there be, were created. . . . And thus . . . God exists: for though the idea of substance be in my mind owing to this, that I myself am a substance, I should not, however, have the idea of an infinite substance, seeing I am a finite being, unless it were given me by some substance in reality infinite."

However, when More began to reflect upon Descartes' findings, it became clear that the work of the latter was rooted in logic and epistemology, not in metaphysics and theology. More strongly believed that all existence, spiritual or material substance, was extended, *res extensa*; for if God were unextended, He was necessarily nowhere. More's early admiration of Cartesianism was dampened when Descartes' dualistic system was understood; for how could More ever separate, as did Descartes, *res cognitans*, the realm of thought and knowledge of God and soul, from *res extensa*, the realm of physical phenomena? More and the other English Platonists felt that Cartesianism condemned nature to a standstill, since in Descartes' mechanistic system spiritual substance was put in a realm of its own with no unifying and spiritual bond with the phenomenal world. "There would be no purposive deity. There would be no causative spiritual power. There would be no organizing force." More felt that Descartes was guilty of the unpardonable sin of denuding the spirit of all attributes, and placing God in a spiritual realm that was not attached to the natural world of phenomena. Thus Descartes was affirming God as a mere abstraction. The Cartesians, to More, were "Nullubists" who affirmed that a spirit is "nullubi," *nowhere*. He had no choice but to oppose Cartesianism because it excluded the influence of every nonmaterial cause of natural phenomena.

Henry More was throughout his life a contemplative mystic, a "divinely intoxicated genius." His love of God was made fuller and truer by his reverence for the Greek spirit of interpretation and for the ancient and divinely inspired philosophers. He fought atheism, skepticism, and materialism in every possible way, and he upheld absolutes without fear or hesitation. Culture of itself was not enough for More, since his was the life of theological mysticism. In true Platonic fashion, he cried out:

> O thou eternall Spright, cleave ope the skie,
> And take thy flight into my feeble breast,
> Enlarge my thoughts, enlight my dimmer eye,
> That wisely of that burthen closely prest
> In my straight mind, I may be dispossest:
> My Muse must sing of things of mickle weight;
> The souls eternity is my quest:
> Do thou me guide, that art the souls sure light,
> Grant that I never erre, but ever wend aright!

Henry More was the embodiment of the Christian spirit in his sincerity and devotion, and his life exemplified and realized the excellence of Christian virtue in its pristine beauty. His life was of "an inwardness too deep for words." (pp. 321-22)

> *George A. Panichas, "Henry More: Cambridge Platonist," in his* The Reverent Discipline: Essays in Literary Criticism and Culture, *The University of Tennessee Press, Knoxville, 1974, pp. 309-22.*

MICHAEL BOYLAN (essay date 1980)

[*Boylan is an American educator and essayist. In the following excerpt, he relates More's theory on God and space to his attempt*

to prove the existence of a link between divine will and the material world.]

How should the relation of the corporeal and the incorporeal, of bodies and spirits, be conceived? If a dualistic account such as Descartes's were to be accepted, there would be numerous difficulties for a man wishing to affirm the existence of an immanent God. If one accepted that all physical phenomena could be explained by mechanical means alone, there then seemed no need for God's presence (except perhaps to have started the machine). Such acceptance seemed to exclude God from the daily affairs and operations of the world, or at least to remove him from active maintenance of the physical order. Was the new science excluding God? In the face of mechanical explanation, what role remained for God to play? More saw Hobbes as attempting to exclude God by reducing all motion to mechanical laws. Against this, More favored Descartes's effort to maintain an efficacy of spiritual substance within his system, but contended that Descartes's division between the corporeal and the incorporeal was too radical. Unless, More argued, one admits a physical tie between God and the physical world, God will remain excluded from that world.

More accepted the classical distinction between "soul" and "matter" (ψυχή and ὑλη). This distinction, according with scholastic precedent, was not seen to be problematic. Even though the "new science" made a similar distinction (for example, in Descartes), it was the mutually exclusive way in which the division was asserted that More rejected. He couches his definitions of spirit and body as follows:

> I will define therefore a Spirit in generall thus: A substance penetrable and Indiscerpible. The fitness of which definition will be better understood if we divide Substance in generall into these first Kindes, viz., Body and Spirit and then define Body A Substance impenetrable and discerpible. Whence the contrary Kind to this is fitly defined, A Substance penetrable and indiscerpible.

The significant difference between the two is that the corporeal is impenetrable and the incorporeal is penetrable. Also, the incorporeal can expand and contract at will, whereas the corporeal cannot (this latter point being an area of agreement with Descartes against earlier theories which cited such examples as sponges to claim that physical bodies could also expand).

> But for mine own part I think that the nature of anything else. . . . [It] consists of these severall powers or properties, viz., Self-Penetration, Self-Motion, Self-Contraction and Dilatation, and Indivisibility. . . . These are those that I reckon . . . is plainly distinguished from a Body.

Now these spirits could be divided into three classes. In the first class are spirits which are "regular": "four kinds of spirits viz. the λόγοι σπέομαλιχοι or Seminal forms, the Souls of Brutes, the Humane Soul and the Soul or Spirit which activates informs the vehicles of Angels" [*The Immortality of the Soul*]. These regular spirits reinforce the world order as mechanical. Thus, these spirits regulate the world, making it possible that the phenomena we observe as mechanical necessity actually continue. An important contrast can be seen here with Aristotle. For Aristotle, *psuchē* marked the difference between the animate and the inanimate. The various grades of nutritive, sensitive, and rational soul acted as a principle along with matter. They were one, just as form was one with matter. The soul was the *archē* of the thing, being prior in being but posterior in its development (*genesis*). More adopts similar categories, but he makes his spirits control matter. They act *in* matter (through the physical medium of space). Thus, while at first glance it might appear that More was simply adopting Aristotelian categories via St. Thomas, it is now seen that a strong neo-Platonic motif concerning the priority of soul both in formula (*logos*) and in function (*ergon*) as well as in activity makes More's theory of regular souls different from those of his predecessors. On this point alone More would be unique. But he also introduces matter to the domain of spirit. For this he has to invent another kind of spirit: the spirit of nature. This spirit is:

> A Substance incorporeal but without sense or animadversion, pervading the whole matter of the Universe, and exercising a plastic power therein, according to the sundry predispositions and occasions of the parts it works upon, raising such Phenomena in the world, by directing the parts of the matter and their motion, as cannot be resolved into mere mechanical power.

From this quotation it is evident that the spirit of nature deals with matter only when the event cannot be explained mechanically. It is used to demonstrate the extraordinary. In the *Immortality of the Soul,* it is suggested that these extraordinary events demonstrate the existence of God. The rationale for this is roughly the same as that for miracles: if a natural law is broken, then the law is not ultimate. That which broke the law is of greater power and stands as the ground for the law itself. The types of events that this spirit of nature could affect are of two sorts: intermittent or regular. An example of the first would be monstrous births such in a story More relates of a woman giving birth to an ape. There are many such exotic examples. Physical examples include, as violations of gravity, a wooden disc rising to the surface in a pail of water and the piston in Boyle's air pump experiment rising in a vacuum.

Even though More was willing to accept mechanical explanations constructed in the work of Galileo, Boyle, and Kepler, he eagerly cited whatever told, in his judgment, against mechanical accounts taken as complete or conclusive. Even if the orbits predicted by Kepler were true according to all the present data, More believed that exceptions could occur—exceptions which had no physical explanation. A contrast to Aristotle is useful to illustrate this point. Aristotle's chance (*tuchē*) and fortune (*automaton*) both conform to the laws of necessity. They are considered aberrations only with reference to some particular end or purpose. More's chance is really contrary to nature, not just to some specific purpose.

Sometimes these violations of mechanical laws were regular events and not statistical freaks. These illustrate the spirit of nature as regular. Gravity is an illustration of this function of the spirit of nature. More does not consider gravity to be an essential property of corporeal substance. He rejects both Hobbes's and Descartes's accounts as inadequate on the grounds that the universe would disintegrate if none but physical forces were at work. That it does not is proof that there is something in nature which is "more than mechanical," that is, a spiritual force.

The two functions of the spirit of nature require it to play disparate roles, but More never rejects one in favor of the other. He embraces both in attempting to show that mechanical explanations fall short either because they do not cover irregular events or because they do not make a place for regulative spirit. In doing so, he invokes hidden mysterious powers as though

these not only saved miracles but came to the rescue of otherwise deficient mechanical explanation.

More's *anima mundi* ["spirit of nature"] incorporates a paraphysical force which is generalized into a world picture that Hobbes had filled with only bodies. This paraphysical force is "mechanical" in the sense that it offers an account for why everything happens (using the new science when it worked and the *anima mundi* when it did not). More is, in fact, radically antimechanical with his invocation of spirits to explain natural events. But he had a reason for this which is based upon his fear that God was being excluded from the universe. If God were to be radically separated from the material world, then there would be no way for God to interact with it. If God were separated from matter, then without a third medium for interaction, God would be unable to control the world. . . . [More] believed that all entities must physically exist somewhere or at least have direct physical contact with the empirical world. He agreed with the tenets of the new science which said that physical effects have physical causes. At the same time he sought to posit a scheme of regular spirits, a spirit of nature, and a God in which they do not act in their traditional roles. This is the central problem which faced More: how to combine God and the physical world.

To make matters more complicated, there are several theological issues that also had to be met. More believed that God created the universe. Therefore, God had to be in some way placed above his creation. Secondly, God must have sovereignty over the world so that he would not be just one of the elements *in* nature. Thirdly, God is immanent in the world and must have power over physical objects (for the purposes of miracles, and so on, which are found throughout the Bible). Therefore, God must have some instrument by which he can act in the world. This instrument must consist in some shared characteristic which is common to both God and the world. The Cartesians could not admit such a conception. More claimed that Descartes's God had no place in the world; God was nowhere, *nullibi*. This nickname, nullibists, was to stick to Cartesians during the period as testimony to More's claim that the Cartesian depiction must lead to atheism. It was thus necessary to create a system whereby God and the world could interact. This was accomplished by defining existence as extension,

> the very essence of whatsoever is, to have parts or extension in some measure or other. For, to take away all extension, is to reduce a thing only to a mathematical point, which is nothing else but pure negation or nonentity, and there being no medium betwixt extended and nonextended, no more than there is betwixt entity and nonentity, it is plain that if a thing be at all it must be extended.

This quotation seems primarily directed at material substances; that is, if some corporeal object had no extension, then it would be no more than a point. But More wants to make extension define the existence of incorporeal spirits as well. In his first letter to Descartes, More declares:

> Your first definition of matter or body is too broad. For it is to be seen that not only God, but also the angels and everything that exists by itself, is a being which is extended—from this extension possesses no narrower limits than the absolute essence of things. . . . The reason why I believe God is extended in his fashion is that he is omnipresent and fills all of the mechanical universe with his spirit (filling all of the parts) for how could he impart motion to matter, as

> he has done, and is doing, according to you, if he
> did not have immediate contact with matter. . . . God
> is therefore extended and expanded in his own mode,
> and so God is an extended being.

God has extension in his own mode. But what is this mode? If it is immaterial, how does More avoid the problems he attributes to Descartes? One is tempted to think that More might reply that the common link was extension. But what could the nature of such a common extension be? The difference between the corporeal and incorporeal is principally penetrability, though as has been mentioned earlier, spirits can also expand and contract as well as pass through bodies. What More had in mind in this description were various phenomena which were nonmaterial and visibly influenced material, such as gravity and magnetism. Both of these regular spirits could move bodies. Light also seems to More to be a tangible, yet incorporeal medium which could help explain the kind of link that he needed to show. What is left (once the existence of possible links has been established) is to show how God fits into all of this. That God exists More proved through a form of the ontological argument. Once God's existence has been established the ''mode'' of this existence must be described. It is at this point that More is vague. It is not clear *how* God exists beyond the fact that he is extended. Now this could mean several things. First, God could be space itself. In this case God would have corporeal contact with the objects of the world. God would *be* space. But this seems odd when compared to other things that More says. For instance, More attacks the Cartesian conception of space (it is remembered that Descartes wanted to assert a plenum of matter). There was no empty space. Space and place were identified with matter. By doing this, More claimed that Descartes left room for nothing else. To make room for God, More proclaimed that space and place (or locus) were different so that bodies had loci within space. This seems to make space a kind of receptacle in which bodies can move. Indeed, More saw this as the only possible explanation for movement. For if everything were filled with matter, then how could one thing move? Everything would be packed together and therefore static. But if God were space itself, then all things would be *in* God. God would be the receptacle. There would be something everywhere (where ''something'' is defined as that which has extension). (pp. 395-99)

The interpretation that God is space *simpliciter* seems to contradict other aspects of More's cosmology. It makes his attacks against the Cartesian plenum weaker and contradicts his idea of space as an area in which other substances can be found. If this analysis is correct, then either More has to make a sharp distinction between God and space or he has to make it clear just what he means by God's ''mode'' (that is, what is the special nature of God's extension).

More is not willing to take the first step and make a clear distinction between God and space. In fact, More goes to great lengths to show how closely they are related. The two most important points in his argument concern demonstrating that like God, space is one, simple, and immovable, and that it is necessary and uncircumscribed. These categories come from the list More gives in his **Enchiridium Metaphysicum:**

> One, simple, immobile, eternal, complete, independent, existing in itself, incorruptible, necessary, immense, uncreated, uncircumscribed, incomprehensible, omnipresent, incorporeal, all-penetrating, all-embracing, essential being, actual being, and pure actuality. . . .

To make his first point that space is one, simple, and immovable requires the acceptance of the difference between space and matter. Once this distinction has been made, then space's indepenence is demonstrated. That it is one and simple is clear because space has no parts. It is homogeneous. That it is immobile can be derived from its simplicity. Remember, movement has to occur within some medium for More. If space as a unit could move, it would be necessary for it to move *in* something, but since there is no medium ''outside'' space, because space is infinite, it follows that space as a whole entity cannot move. But even within itself, space cannot move. For in order to move internally it would require moving parts, but since space is simple this cannot occur.

The implication of this first point is that space is absolute. By ''absolute'' More meant that, given that something is absolutely at rest in space, a body can act as a real point of reference for motion. More's arguments on absolute space may seem comparatively simple next to Isaac Barrow's. But they were not without their influence. There are two varieties of arguments given by More for this position: empirical and a priori. On the empirical side, More displays several arguments. These arguments are not *for* absolute space as much as they are refutations of Descartes's relativism. More saw the problem of space as reduced to only two positions so that if he could discredit the one, he could indirectly prove his own. He could not see the possibility of a third position such as Mach's principle, which incorporates aspects of each position. The target was Descartes's theory of philosophical motion as stated in the *Prinicipia* and not the ordinary or vulgar theory of motion. (pp. 399-400)

The rational reasons that More has for positing absolute space revolve around whether motion in space is relative or can be judged in terms of a body absolutely at rest in an unmoving, fixed space. If More allowed motion to be relative, then space would not be the proper abode for God. Space would be seen merely as a relational medium dependent upon objects to give it definition. An absolute space, on the other hand, is prior to its objects. The corporeal would be defined in terms of the incorporeal and thus would be more basic. Naturally, the God of More's ontological argument must have all perfections, among which is omnipotence. This power cannot be dependent upon anything, and so space (if it is to be identified with God in some way) must be absolute.

This leads to the arguments concerning space as necessary. In the rational argument for the absolute nature of space it was shown that space had to be absolute, for if it was not, then it would not be a fitting abode for God. In this argument (which More presents only in a rational or a priori manner without any empirical arguments), More wants to demonstrate that among the types of beings (corporeal and incorporeal), space, or the incorporeal, is necessary and is a precondition for matter. There are three arguments for this position that are very similar. First, More says, in elaborating ''existing by itself'' (one of the list of space's attributes), that space is the precondition for our experiencing anything. We cannot imagine an object except as it is in space. That is, we cannot imagine a body just as a body, for its very extension requires the extension of space to contain it. On the other hand, space is easily imagined without anything in it. Since we can think of space and not objects, but cannot imagine (i.e., actually picture or form a schema of) the converse, space must be a necessary precondition for the existence of objects.

The second argument concerns the limits of the material world. Is the corporeal infinite or finite? Obviously, More wants to argue that space is infinite and the world is finite. He sees as his foes the Aristotelians and the Cartesians. The Aristotelian conception of a finite world with no space outside it is obviously unacceptable, for More cannot allow the universe (whose basic component is absolute space) to have boundaries, spherical or otherwise. (pp. 401-02)

What More wants to do is to claim that space and place are separate and that any limitation on space is illegitimate. Sometimes More is a little confusing because he becomes careless with his use of language. For example, even though he wishes to distinguish space and place, he refers to space in his list of its attributes as "an infinite internal place (locus)." Now More was very careful to refute the equation of place (locus) with space in his letters with Descartes. Yet here he is in an important passage employing a confusing phrase. An "internal place" *is* the locus of some *x* in space. But to call space itself an "internal place" implies that it (space) is *in* something else, which is impossible through the categories of independence and self-existence. One must attribute such careless use of language to an attempt at metaphor or some such figure of speech, which, if one reads More's poetry, is frequently uncontrollable in his hands.

More wants seriously to assert that the universe has no limit. What he has in mind is a nonmathematical infinite: a universe which is conceptually without end. Unlike Barrow and Newton, More has no infinite sets or geometrical compositions in his mind. He wanted to assert positively that the universe, space, stretched out forever. Since this is an often repeated point, the reader must interpret his occasional epithet "uncircumscribed" as being equivalent to "infinite" and not to "indefinite," which was a term he was to attack in Descartes. With this view in mind, More takes any argument on the limitation of the universe as directly implying that absolute space (a part of his universe) is also limited. He rejects the implication of the claim that the universe is finite because the universe consists of space and matter and that while matter *is* finite, space is infinite.

It is in this manner that More attacks Descartes's claim that the world is indefinite. More takes this to mean that with respect to our knowledge there is no limit to the universe, for regardless of where we might put a boundary in our mind, the universe extends beyond that. But this, More claims, is the same thing as saying it is finite, for the universe's indefiniteness is stated only with respect to us. It is not indefinite in itself and so must have boundaries. This logical argument resembles the argument about absolute space versus relative motion. More assumes that a thing is infinite or it is not. Since Descartes views the world as not infinite, it must be finite. Indeed, the very claim of indefiniteness rests upon the universe being a function of a finite imagination (that of men), and so the parameters of such an assertion are only as wide as that finite imagination; hence, the universe is finite to exactly that degree. . . .

Descartes could not make the world infinite, because then it would be necessary, a position that only God can hold. He therefore opted for a middle course between these two positions. More found this middle course untenable because it depended upon the human mind's limitations and because he basically saw the position as a choice between two mutually exclusive positions (the infinite vs. the finite universe). By showing again through indirect proof that the universe could not be finite, he showed that it was infinite. Being infinite

meant that it was necessary, a position More could accept since space was identified with God and therefore had to be necessary.

The third argument hangs on the subject-attribute distinction. The first two arguments set forth space as necessary and infinite. That space also contains matter cannot be disimagined (we cannot imagine a world with no space). These three features are real attributes, and since real attributes imply real substances, space is a real substance. "It is therefore necessary that, because it is a real attribute, some real subject support this extension" [*Enchiridion Metaphysicum*]. In showing that space is a substance More believes that the necessary nature of space is obvious, given that it is the only abode for God. (p. 403)

These three arguments have all been directed toward showing how absolute space is necessary. The arguments on the most part work indirectly by saying that (1) God is necessary and must exist somewhere (from the ontological argument); (2) existence requires extension; (3) the only modes having extension are matter and space; (4) matter is not necessary; (5) therefore, space is necessary and must be the abode of God. Compare this argument with those given for there being a spirit of nature: (1) All phenomena must have some explanation (a mechanical assumption of the time). (2) There are two types of phenomena which cannot be mechanically explained—sporadic events such as monstrous births and regular events such as gravity. These violate existing natural laws. (3) Therefore, these events have no mechanical explanation, and their explanation must be found elsewhere. If the mechanical explanation is inadequate (i.e., the realm of the corporeal is insufficient as an explanation), then the explanation must be found in the spiritual realm. These explanations fall under the spirit of nature.

Both of these arguments hinge upon the inadequateness of the material realm. In the case of absolute space, this leads to an affirmation of necessity and in the case of the spirit of nature to one of sufficiency. What is the relationship between these two spirits? Though several commentators, such as Burtt and Baker, comment upon both parts of More's philosophy, these two elements, to my knowledge, have not been connected. The main reason for this is that the spirit of nature, unlike space (God), is described in terms of a force which acts without intelligence. This appears to make the *anima mundi* into a paramechanical force. But as was mentioned earlier, the spirit of nature is really antimechanical in that it offers exceptions to the mechanical rules and overtly breaks others. It is both capricious and regular. In this way it points to God's existence in much the same way miracles do. Thus, the spirit of nature appears to support and not to support the mechanical view of the world. But beyond this, as the earlier discussion on spiritual explanations illustrated, even the regular invocations of the spirit are not mechanical in the true sense of there being a proper analogy between nature and a machine. More's spirit of nature acts to obscure any possible *mechanical* explanation for the phenomena described by *anima mundi*. In this way, More's scheme is profoundly antimechanical.

But again, one is led to the interesting questions of how the *anima mundi* points to God. Would this somehow mean that the spirit of nature is a power invoked by God? And since it represents the Divine directly in a way that reason cannot, perhaps the spirit of nature is God working directly in nature. This view is never directly argued by More, but it does fit nicely with the times and with More's own theological views. For example, the commonly held belief that God created an orderly world which he set in motion and then forgot about would be attacked since the spirit of nature affirms that God created an orderly world, one in which he holds things together through gravity, magnetism, and the like, but also one in which he produces miracles. Without God actively in the world, composite bodies would disintegrate. The purely mechanical explanation becomes insufficient to explain the world. God must be invoked as working through an *anima mundi*.

This aspect of God emphasized is the Divine as immanent in the corporeal world. It is therefore appropriate that most of the arguments for the presence of the spirit of nature are made through appeals to empirical data read off as evidence of regulation or of intervention. The rational arguments fall principally under the question of why space is necessary and, ineluctably, the abode of God. (More's epistemology specifies three ways to knowledge: the senses, reason, and common opinion, with the last deriving from the first two and acting as a check against "bad sense or sensibility.") The material world, the spirit of nature, and God extend within space, but only the first is a kind of extension divisible into parts.

How does More fit together his conceptions of God, the spirit of nature, and space? God is not space itself. Though there are many descriptions which mutually apply to space and God, to make space the actual godhead would demote God in relation to the things of his creation. The material world created by God is ontologically lower than God. Space as the container of the world is not asserted to be also its creative source. Nonetheless, it is through or by an extension common to God and the world that the spirit of nature is efficacious in physical events. But could not an all-powerful God interact with the world directly via his own spirit? More believed that God could, but that a declaration of such a belief would not of itself suffice to show a disbelieving deist *where* and *how* intervention and regulation could be effectuated. By positing the spirit of nature extending throughout the world and serving as a tool of God for the governance of physical events, More thought he had supplied a convincing description. (As extending throughout the universe, the spirit of nature is not localized like other spirits, i.e.; as seminal, and as the souls of brutes, men, and angels.)

In the soul of man, God's own spirit may be immanent for his salvation; but in the material world, the spirit of nature is operative as the instrument of the Divine will. The spirit of nature acts according to the will of God both as a regular and as a miraculous force in absolute space. Space, in attributes applicable both to it and to God, is not an instrument. It is, for More, an ontological condition *sine qua non* of existence predicable of any thing, God not excepted. More fundamentally is seeking to defend powers and governance traditionally attributed to God in Christian thought against dangers he perceived in Hobbes and Descartes and in the rise of mechanistic explanations in the new science. The glorification of space and the ambidextrous functions assigned to the spirit of nature constitute two principle weapons contrived for the defense. (pp. 404-05)

> *Michael Boylan, "Henry More's Space and the Spirit of Nature," in* Journal of the History of Philosophy, *Vol. XVIII, No. 4, October, 1980, pp. 395-405.*

ALEXANDER JACOB (essay date 1985)

[*In the following excerpt, Jacob refutes C. A. Staudenbaur's theory, set out above in an excerpt from the critic's 1968 essay, that*

More imitated the structure of Marsilio Ficino's Theologia Platonica *in "Psychathanasia."*]

Let us examine the precise relationship between More's poems and Ficino's treatise a little more closely than Staudenbaur chooses to do [see excerpt dated 1968], for I do not think that literary structure is wholly independent of content, especially in rhapsodic verse such as More's. "Psychathanasia" was composed after his first poem "Psychozoia," during the anxious days of the Civil War, when it was especially appropriate to clarify the question of the soul's immortality. Although it lacks the allegorical representations of "Psychozoia, "Psychathanasia" continues the discussions of the world-soul, the spirit of nature, and the individual soul that are to be found in the 1st canto of "Psychozoia" and the first twenty-three stanzas of its 2nd canto. More's cosmogony in "Psychozoia" is based on a "Christiano-Platonicall" trinity constituted of Ahad, or Atove, the "first Principle of all beings, the Father of all existence"; Aeon, or the "universall Intellect," traditionally identified with Christ as Logos; and Psyche, or Love, the equivalent of the Holy Ghost. Early in the poem, More acknowledges as his philosophical authority Plotinus, whom he venerates even above Plato (who is called just "Plato" while Plotinus is "deep Plotin") as the restorer of "th'antique roll/Of Chaldee wisdome." In fact, the names of the cosmic entities in "Psychozoia" are a mixture of Neoplatonist, Chaldean, and Hebrew terminology, and his notes to the poem are replete with quotations from the works of Plotinus and Trismegistus.

The phenomena of the world arise from the marriage of Aeon to Psyche when Psyche is decked with an "outward vest" which is the azure expanse of the universe itself. Essentially invisible, it is "thickened" for sensuous human enjoyment by the sons of "Love." Already at this early stage in the unfolding of his song of the soul, More emphasizes the difference between sensual awareness and intellectual:

> But well I wot that nothings bare to sense
> For sense cannot arrive to th' inwardnesse
> Of things, nor penetrate the crusty fence
> Of constipated matter close compresse

—a fact which belies Staudenbaur's neat distinction between "Psychozoia" and "Psychathanasia" as representing the Christian account of purification and the Platonic, respectively. As we shall see, "Psychathanasia" and the other poems are not without their Christian aspects too. The eight folds of Psyche's vest include Physis (vegetative nature, later reified as the Spirit of Nature), Arachnea (the web of sense perception) with her chief Haphe (touch), Semele (intellectual imagination), Proteus and Idothea (the changeability of forms),Tasis (extension) and, finally, Hyle (matter). This "universall Ogdoas" is both the ground of phenomenal individuation and the basis of the unity of the universe "as one ample uniform being from Ahad to Hyle." At the "low hem" of Psyche's garment hang the planets that constitute the solar system. Interestingly, More glosses this section of the poem as being "A glance at *Copernicus* opinion, as at theirs also that make the first starres so many Sunnes, and all the planets to be inhabited," a comment which reveals his interest in the Copernican system even at the time of composing "Psychozoia" in 1640. Staudenbaur, following Haring, believes that since the diagrams More used to illustrate his astronomical examples in "Psychathanasia" refer to the 1641 Latin edition of Galileo's *Dialogue on the Great World Systems*, this was the date at which More read the Galilean interpretation of Coperican astronomy. But More's note to I,30 of "Psychozoia" suggests that he had read an earlier version of Copernicanism—whether Galileo's or some other—already in 1640 when he first wrote the poem. Whatever the case may have been, More's representation of the planetary system as a sign of the materialization of the world soul for the purpose of human admiration,

> O gladsome life of sense that doth adore
> The outward shape of the worlds curious frame!

should make us less certain that the longer Copernican canto in "Psychathanasia" was exclusively designed to serve as a Ficinian *signum* for the soul's domination of the senses. (pp. 505-07)

"Psychathanasia" aims at proving the immortality of the soul in a more elaborate manner through Platonic arguments. The first canto, as Staudenbaur indicates, is a condemnation of all philosophies that are preoccupied with naturalism, especially those of Epicurus, Democritus, and Aristotle, who in different ways delved into "Hyle's hell" to find "the root of life." This abjuration of naturalism does not include astronomy, as Staudenbaur claims: "it appears that the very presence of this Canto (III,3) is in violation of the opening stanzas of the poem, in which explanations of natural phenomena are condemned as vain, useless, and spiritually dangerous." More was never against the explanation of natural phenomena, only against their explanation in materialistic terms. In fact, as we shall shortly see, astronomical study is one way of allowing the mind to expand beyond the confines of this terrestrial realm and move towards, first, the physical sun and, then, its Ideal archetype, God. This outward movement of the soul is facilitated by Platonic philosophy and then by the "purer flame of Love" which, as we have seen in "Psychozoia," is the grace of God that draws pure souls back to their source. (pp. 507-08)

More's structural imitation of Ficino is supposed by Staudenbaur to begin with the second canto. Following Kristeller's classification in *The Philosophy of Marsilio Ficino* (1943), Staudenbaur groups Libri I-IV as dealing with Degrees of Being. A careful study of Ficino will reveal that these books deal, respectively, with the five characteristic levels of the Ficinian system of the universe—God, angels, soul, quality, and body (Liber I); the several virtues of God (Liber II); the exact nature of the connection between the different levels of Ficino's hierarchy (Liber III); and the subdivision of the central level, soul, into the world-soul, the souls of the spheres, and the souls of the living beings contained in each of these spheres (Liber IV). Canto ii of "Psychathanasia," on the other hand, is exclusively concerned with the human soul, even though More too, as we have seen, believed in various sorts of soul, such as Psyche or the world-soul, Physis or the spirit of nature, and individual souls. More distinguishes within the human soul three parts, vegetative, sensitive, and rational, the last being the sole prerogative of man, especially evident in his "full grasp of vast *Eternitie*." Though the common feature of all these parts of the soul is self-motion, More carefully studies the different operations of the soul in its three aspects. Once again, in his discussion of the rational virtue of the soul, we find him emphasizing astronomical study:

> Or when quite heedlesse of this earthie world
> She lifts herself unto the azure skie
> And with those wheeling gyres around is hurl'd
> Turns in herself in a due distance
> The erring Seven, or a stretch'd line doth tie
> O'th' silver-bowèd moon from horn to horn;
> Or finds out Phoebus vast soliditie
> By his diametre, measures the Moon,
> Girds the swoln earth with linear list, though earth she scorn.

> All this is done, though bodie never move;
> The soul about it self circumgyrates
> Her various forms

Having established that all of the operations of the body derive from the motion of the soul, More concludes the canto with a brief discussion of the nature of spiritual extension constituted as it is of points that defy the laws of physical measurement;

> But if't consist of points, then a Scalene
> Ill prove all one with an Isosceles.
>
> (pp. 508-09)

Liber V of the *Theologia Platonica* offers *rationes communes* for the soul's immortality—fifteen in all: 1. The rational soul moves by itself in a circular movement; 2. it remains stable in its own substance; 3. it adheres to the divine; 4. it controls matter; 5. it is independent of matter; 6. it is indivisible; 7. it has an essential existence; 8. it is never separated from its form; 9. it exists by itself; 10. it naturally refers to God; 11. it cannot be decomposed into parts; 12. it cannot not be; 13. it receives its being directly from God; 14. it is life itself; and 15. its life is superior to that of the body. If anything, this book is a source for the final section of the second canto of Book I of "Psychathanasia," which we have just considered, for it has nothing whatsoever in common with the third canto, as Staudenbaur's table would indicate. The third canto recounts a vision that More had of a nymph who shows him a lunar rainbow with the help of which she explains to him the true constitution of the universe. . . . Canto iv continues the vitalistic explanation of the soul's immortality by pointing to the passive, potential nature of Hyle, so that only that which borders on Hyle is subject to death while all the other higher orders are "unfading lives from fount of livelihood." In both these cantos we observe that More never loses sight of his larger cosmic framework, and his efforts to prove the soul's immortality at this point are both more visionary and comprehensive than Ficino's concentration on the rational soul in the fifth book of the *Theologia Platonica*.

Libri VI-VIII of the *Theologia Platonica* present *rationes propriae* for the soul's immortality. These are based on the soul's virtue as the principle of nutrition and growth, as the principle of sense-perception, and as the principle of intellection. The three cantos of Book II of "Psychathanasia" do bear a general resemblance to the Ficinian ordering of arguments, since the first canto deals with vegetative life, the second with sense-perception, and the third with intellection. But, again, the contents of the two works are not always the same. While Ficino emphasizes the incorporeality of the soul by elaborating the differences between the inert body and its vivifying form, More explains the vegetative power of the soul as being derived from

> that vitality,
> That doth extend this great Universall,
> And move th'inert materiality
> Of great and little worlds.

In his vitalistic philosophy, the lower plastic part of the soul is continuous with the spirit of nature which molds all things in their proper forms:

> The lower man is nought but a fair plant,
> Whose grosser matter is from the base ground;
> The Plastick might thus finely did him paint
> And fill'd him with the life that doth abound
> In all places of the world around.

Although More, like Ficino, focusses on the spiritual nature of the common sense (stanzas 26ff), he does not stop to refute the other notions of the soul as the quality, temperament or harmony of the body as Ficino does through half of Liber VII (Chs. 7-15). Besides, More's characteristic notion of spirit as being present in every part of the body "not by extension but by a totall self-reduplication" is original. Though Ficino, too, attempts to explain this Platonic mystery by quoting Augustine, Augustine's notion of "vital intensity" is not as carefully worked out as More's unique conception of spirit as a substance capable of self-reduplication on account of what he was later, in *The Immortality of the Soul,* to call its "essential spissitude."

Canto iii of the second book of "Psychathanasia" is the only one which depends to a great extent on Ficino's work. In Liber VIII Ficino describes the intellectual aspect of the soul by 1. its ascent from the body to the spirit through the four degrees of sense, imagination, phantasy and intelligence; 2. its nourishment by truth; 3. its indivisibility; 4. its ability to receive species and ideas; 5. its independence of physical touch and motion in the act of intellection; 6. its comprehension of things in their totality; 7. its retention of its own form at the same time as it receives the forms of objects; 8. its ability to conceive universals; 9. its ability to contain other intelligence within itself in mutual comprehension; 10. its ability to conceive a multitude of corporeal forms as well as incorporeal ones; 11. its improvement in rest whereas the body improves by motion; 12. its ability to receive contrary impressions simultaneously; 13. its retention of its original form even while receiving external ones; 14. its characteristic operation of simplification, whereas the body is always composite; 15. the fulfillment of action within itself whereas the body's always extends to matter; and 16. its possession of an infinite power. Book II, canto iii of "Psychathanasia" also discusses the soul's ascent to God when it rises above the senses, its nourishment by "verity," its power of abstraction, its indivisibility, its incorporeal mode of comprehension, its aspiration to higher incorporeal forms, its ability to receive contraries, its retention of the original form while receiving others, its simplifying operation, its ability to contain a multitude of forms, its self-contained action, and its apprehension of infinity and eternity. This is the only canto that More may be said to have borrowed almost entirely from Ficino, a fact which reveals that More's originality was restricted to his mathematical conception of spirit as a substance and to his development of the soul's vital relation to the rest of the universe. His almost complete dependence on Ficino in his analysis of the soul's purely intellectual faculty highlights his inadequacy as a theoretical philosopher. Rather, More's special importance as a vitalist was his ingenious attempt to reconcile his vivid view of the sympathetic union between different parts of the macrocosm and the microcosm to the stricter quantitative science of the seventeenth century.

Cantos i and ii of Book III of "Psychathanasia" resemble Liber IX of *Theologia Platonica* in that they deal with the "soul's free independency" of the body. But whereas Ficino offers six proofs of the soul's independent action (1. it reflects in itself 2. the more removed it is from body the better it works 3. it despises the body 4. it operates with free-will 5. it operates independently of the body in volition and intellection 6. it participates in a divine nature as well as in an animal one), More elaborates his notion of the soul as a vitalistic entity comprised of three essences (or vehicles as they are otherwise called), a vegetative essence, a central essence, and deiform. (pp. 510-12)

He reaffirms his theory of the centrality of the soul as being linked to God's own "outgone Centre," which fact is most evident in "the conversion/Into herself" and in its exercise of the Intellect and the Will. Further proof of the soul's independent action removed from corporeal commerce is provided by *signa,* such as those Ficino offers in Chap. 2 of Liber IX. . . . (p. 513)

The following stanzas describe the joy of the soul as it detaches itself from its bodily chains, and in stanzas, More, like Ficino, proves the soul's free power in commanding the body and its desires in order to follow the laws of reason. But having followed Ficino's arguments so far, More then turns back to his own conception of the soul's link to the spirit of the world. Since imagination, memory, and ideas are produced by the interaction between the soul and the mundane spright:

> Of old Gods hand did all forms write
> In Humane souls, which waken at the knock
> Of Mundane shapes

it is not surprising that, with the course of time, "The common life sucks back the common spright", and disease or injury can hurt the lower spright so as to impair sense, wit, imagination, and memory. Fortunately, the soul's upper part is directly linked to "The ever-live-Idees, the lamping fire/Of lasting Intellect" as well as to the lower Mundane spright, and it is from this higher link that the soul shows, in animadaversion, its superiority to the lower life of the common world-soul: "She knows that spright, that spright our soul can never know."

The soul's independent action when it is free of the mundane spright and joined to the eternal ideas is illustrated in the third canto by the example of Copernican astronomy. This is *not* More's equivalent of the whole of Libri XIII and XIV of the *Theologia Platonica,* as Staudenbaur suggests. The *signa* that Ficino offers in Liber XIII of the soul's control of the body include supernatural phenomena, effects of the imagination, effects of intellectual intuition such as poetic, religious, and philosophical inspiration, the artistic and political achievements of men, and miracles. The *signa* in Liber XIV focus on different ways in which the human soul strives to attain a God-like knowledge and power. None of this, except the third *signum* of Liber XIII, has anything to do with Book III, canto iii of "Psychathanasia. In the third *signum* of the soul's independence of the body, namely, from the accomplishments of government and the arts, we note the inclusion of astronomical observation as a sign of pure intellectual effort:

> Subtilis computatio numerorum figurarum curiosa descriptio, linearum obscurissimi motus, superstitiosa musicae consonanta, astrorum observatio diuturna, naturalium inquisitio causarum, diuturnorum investigatio, oratorum facundia poetarumque furores. In ijs omnibus animus hominis corporis despicit ministerium, utpote qui quandoque possit, et iam nunc incipiat sine corporis auxilio vivere

> [The precise calculation of numbers, the minute descriptions of figures, the obscure movements of lines, the careful harmony of music, the daily observation of the stars, the inquiry into natural causes, the examination of lasting things, the eloquence of orators and the frenzy of poets. In all these things, the human spirit despises the authority of the body seeing that it can live eventually without the body and even begins to do so now.]

What makes it especially certain that this is the section that inspired More is that Ficino here attributes the natural aptitude for astronomical study to the celestial element in the soul: "Merito coelesti elemento solum coeleste animal delectatur. Coelesti virtute ascendit coelum, atque metitur" (*Ibid*). So, too, More exclaims at the beginning of canto iii, "*What comes from heaven onely can there ascend.*" Then follows a denunciation of Ptolemy and a praise of, significantly, not Copernicus but, first, Plato. Staudenbaur tries to dissociate More from the traditional Platonic emphasis on astronomical speculation as a spiritual discipline by pointing to the practical and ethical use that was made of it in Hellenistic times and that was favored by Renaissance Humanists. He gives, as a proof of this bias, More's concentration on post-Copernican astronomy to the exclusion of the classical and medieval contributions to the subject. This observation ignores the repeated references to "Plato's school" in the first part of the canto. The reason More gives for his invocation to the "the Theologie of heavenly Plato" is that the sun in Plato's philosophy is the physical counterpart of the archetypal "Idee/of Steddie Good, that doth his beames dilate/Through all the worlds, all lives and beings propagate." He elaborates this correspondence with a definition of Good:

> One steddy Crood, centre of essencies
> Unmoved Monad that Apollo hight
> The *Intellectual* sunne whose energies
> Are all things that appear in vitall light

which maintains a link with the vitalistic accounts of the universe in earlier parts of this poem and "**Psychozoia.**" All things move round this unity "in distinct *circumference*," as the planets "wheel round the fixed sunne, that is the shade/Of steddy good" (III, iii, 15).

After this prelude about the Ideal Sun, More begins his account of the visible sun, and, again, we notice a marked reliance on his theory of the plastic spirit of the world to explain, simultaneously, the planetary arrangements and the phenomenon of gravity. The more particular scientific proofs of the Copernican system that More proceeds to give are from Galileo. However, one of his final reasons for the motion of the earth is that

> The Eternall Son of God, who Logos hight
> Made all things in a fit proportion,

—a proportion that would be upset by the rival theory of epicycles which present

> A heap of Orbs disorderly perplext
> Thrust in on every hint of motion
>
>   (pp. 514-16)

[Unlike] Ficino in Liber XIV, More emphasizes not the soul's God-like power but rather God's infinite goodness and justice which guarantee the immortality of "good mens souls." The concluding stanzas answer objections that may be raised against his spectacular view of God's Providence as represented in an infinite universe. He particularly addresses the problem of the world's duration, and in the first edition of the poem denies that it is *ab aeterno:*

>   . . . Certain deficiency
> Doth alwayes follow evolution
> Nought's infinite but tight eternity,
> Close thrust into itself: extension
> That's infinite implies a contradiction

This opinion, however, he was to reverse in 1646 with the publication of **Democritus Platonissans,** which—if it corresponds to any of the books of the *Theologia Platonica*—is the counterpart of Liber XVIII, Ch. 1 . . . where Ficino discusses teleological cosmology. This correspondence, incidentally, does

not seem to have been noted by Staudenbaur, who asigns the whole of Liber XVIII to "**The Preexistency of the Soul.**" (pp. 516-17)

[Both] in the last two cantos of "**Psychathanasia**" and in its later appendix, **Democritus Platonissans,** More is motivated primarily by his admiration of the infinity of the universe as a physical proof of the immense goodness of God. An explanation of these parts of the **Psychodia Platonica** by reference to the structure of the *Theologia Platonica* fails to consider why More chose one brief example among the various *signa* that Ficino offers of the soul's independence of the body and why he elaborated it so enthusiastically both in 1641 and, later, in 1646.

What about the remaining poems? "**Antipsychopannychia**" originally followed "**Psychathanasia.**" Having established the soul's immortality, More describes in "**Antipsychopannychia**" the activity of the soul after its release from the body. This activity is based on the higher ideas that the mind contains within itself in direct sympathy with the Eternal Ideas. Those who develop this intellectual memory, which is distinct from the 'Mundane memory' produced by the soul's interaction with the lower spirit of the world, will be drawn up to God, while those whose activities have been diverted to the 'outworld' will sink down again to the infernal realm of matter. (p. 518)

It is difficult to see how any of this material could be accommodated, either structurally or contextually, to Liber XVI of the *Theologia Platonica* which answers three Epicurean questions: 1. Why are souls enclosed in terrestrial bodies? 2. If souls are divine, why are they subject to bodily distress? 3. Why do souls leave the body with regret? Rather than deal with the condition of the soul after its departure from the body, Ficino here is wholly concerned with its imprisonment in it.

The "**Preexistency of the Soul**" was added to "**Antipsychopannychia**" in the 1647 edition since it completes the discussion of the soul's extracorporeal life begun in that poem, with special reference to the Neoplatonic theory of the soul's three vehicles, terrestrial, airy, and ethereal. This theory is found in Ficino too (Libri XVII, XVIII), but More's concentration on the aerial spirits is different from Ficino's representation in his final chapters of a traditional, that is, Roman Catholic, eschatology constituted of blessed ethereal angels (Liber XVIII, Ch. 8), the damned (Ch. 9), and the inhabitants of Purgatory (Ch. 10). Rather, More's account of the different sorts of aerial spirits is derived from Michael Psellus' *De Operatione Daemonum.* The reason for this shift of emphasis is clearly his lack of interest in Roman Catholic eschatological doctrines and, more importantly, his desire to combat "Sadducisme and Atheisme," as he himself admits in his general preface to the second edition of the poems:

> I have also added another [poem] of the Praeexistency of the Soul, where I have set out the nature of *Spirits* and given an account of *Apparitions* and *Witchcraft* very answerable I conceive to experience and story, invited to that task by the frequent discoveries of this very age. Which if they were publicly recorded, and that course continued in every Parish, it would prove one of the best antidotes against that earthy and cold disease of Sadducisme and Atheisme, which may easily grow upon us; if not prevented, to the hazard of all Religion, and the best kinds of Philosophy.

The final section of this poem discusses the way in which the soul insinuates itself into the body, the topic of Ch. 2-7 of Liber XVIII of the *Theologia Platonica.* More repudiates the rival theories of Traducianism and Creationism and offers, instead, his own theory of the emanation of individual souls from the "immense Orb of wast vitality," which with all its Lives and Souls is everywhere."

This theory, however, contains an inherent problem:

> But sooth to say though his opinion
> May seem right fair and plausible to be
> Yet toils it under an hard difficulty
> Each where this Orb of life's with every soul;
> Which doth imply the souls ubiquity.

The last poem of the *Psychodia Platonica*, "**Antimonopsychia**," is precisely a denial of the idea of monopsychism that is implied in More's account of the origin of souls in the "eternall store of lives and souls ycleep'd the world of life." We see from this sequence of ideas that More was not sedulously following the order of Ficino's books in the *Theologia Platonica*, but rather evolving a pattern with its own internal logic which, at least in the case of the last three poems, is superior to Ficino's. While Ficino's adds Liber XV as a separate academic problem—that of Averroe's unified Intellect—after having proved the soul's immortality by its God-like aspirations in Liber XIV, More moves more naturally from the individual soul to the world soul "**Antipsychopannychia**," III and "**The Preexistency of the Soul**" and from there to the universal Intellect ("**Antimonopsychia**").

Staudenbaur suggests that More felt obliged to add a poem on this Averroistic question since he was following Ficino's model throughout the last five poems of the *Psychodia Platonica*. More himself admits, in the Preface, to the strangeness of the topic "as confuting that which no man will assert." But he justifies the inclusion of this poem by quoting Ficino's example of the "Mauri" who held this opinion and, more significantly, Plotinus' efforts to refute the unity of the soul in his *Enneads*, IV, 9: "This is that which both Plotinus and I endeavour to destroy, which is of great moment." . . . More's poem does draw upon Ficino's arguments of the operations of the individual intellect as well as on his *signa* and *rationes*. In stanza 7 he appeals to the common experience of individuality in all men and to the fact of independent will in stanza 10. And like Ficino, he reasons from the absurdity of positing a single apprehension of intellectual forms, from the impossibility of contradicitons being contained simultaneously in the same subject, and from the preposterous unity of knowledge amongst all mankind that would result from the Averroistic theory.

But More does not stop here, as Ficino does. Rather, he goes on to explain the plurality of souls from his own theory of the soul's "self-centrall essence" which issues from God "with proper raies embew'd." The main reason for More's displeasure with the Averroistic doctrine is that it comes too close to pantheism:

> Wherefore if creatures intellectual
> (And in that order humane souls will fall)
> Were God himself, they would be alike wise,
> Know one anothers thoughts imaginall

—a danger that he seeks to avoid with his insistence on the soul's "proper raies." After adducing the authority of the Scriptural account of creation, More reaffirms his conviction of the *Deiformity* of the individual soul which will reunite it, once it is purified, to the goodness of God. Another proof of the soul's individuality that More offers is the vital link of memory after death, which ensures "Coherence." . . . In this discussion of the soul's memory, More follows Plotinus, *En-*

neads: "The loftier, on the contrary, must desire to come to a happy forgetfulness of all that has reached it through the lower." But the lower soul, says Plotinus, "must always be striving to attain to memory of the activities of the higher." So, too, More asks, "But can she here forget our radiant sunne/ Of which its maker is the bright Idee?" The desire of the deiform soul for the Deity is so strong that it will ever seek to return to its source:

> And deep desire is the deepest act
> The most profound and centrall energie
> The very selfnesse of the soul, which backt
> With piercing might, she breaks out, forth doth flie
> From dark contracting death, and doth descry
> Herself unto herself

Here, again, we note an echo of Plotinus' final passage in the *Enneads*: 'When the soul begins to mount, it comes out not to something alien but to its very self: thus detached, it is in nothing but itself." As an illustration of this final apotheosis of the soul, More appropriately concludes his vast Neo-platonic song of the soul with a "Paraphrasticall Interpretaton" of Porphyry's description of the beautitudinous soul of Plotinus in his *Life of Plotinus*.

We see that in the last poem of the *Psychodia Platonica* and its epilogue, More moves from Ficino's scholastic arguments against monopsychism to his own vitalistic conception of the individuation of souls from the matrix of Psyche and, finally, to a vision of the soul's highest bliss derived from his spiritual idol "deep Plotin". Throughout the *Psychodia Platonica*, More's reliance on Ficino is almost exclusively for theoretical reasons to substantiate various points about the soul's operation in the body. This is confirmed by his statement in his Preface to "**Psychathanasia**" regarding his choice of arguments: "I must confess I intended to spin it out to a greater length; but things of greater importance then curious *Theory* take me off," which is, clearly, a reference to the scope of his reliance on Ficino's treatise. More is not bound to Ficino's order of books in the *Theologia Platonica* except when, in the second book of "**Psychathanasia**" and the first two cantos of the third book, he discusses the different operations of the individual soul that reveal its independence of the body. Not only do the other parts of his song of the soul develop their own organic structure based on the dynamic relation between the microcosm and the macrocosm, but they are also independent of Ficino's metaphysical categories. Far from being a neat structural imitation of the *Theologia Platonica*, More's debt to Ficino in the *Psychodia Platonica* is, indeed, restricted to incidental borrowings of scholastic arguments for the independent activities of the soul within the body (especially in "**Psychathanasia**" and "**Antimonopsychia**," while his larger vision of the cosmos— the various spirits that inhabit it, the Mundane spright, Psyche, and the grand Providence of Divine Goodness—is informed by the various Platonist philosophies of the Chaldaic oracles, Plotinus, Psellus, and Galileo. Given such a rich store of information, what wonder is it that More himself acknowledges the wide-ranging course of his philosophical speculations in the opening verse of his last poem thus:

> Who yields himself to learning and the Muse
> Is like a man that leaves the steddy shore
> And skims the Sea. He nought then can refuse
> Whatever is designed by Neptunes power,
> Is fiercely drove in every stormy stoure
> Slave to the water and the whistling wind:
> Even so am I, that whylom meant recover
> The wished land, but now against my mind
> Am driven fiercely back, and so new work do find.

(pp. 518-22)

Alexander Jacob, "Henry More's 'Psychodia Platonica' and Its Relationship to Marsilio Ficino's 'Theologia Platonica'," in *Journal of the History of Ideas*, *Vol. XLVI, No. 4, October-December, 1985, pp. 503-22.*

ADDITIONAL BIBLIOGRAPHY

Baker, John Tull. "Henry More and Kant: A Note to the Second Argument on Space in the *Transcendental Aesthetic*." *The Philosophical Review* XLVI, No. 3 (May 1937): 298-306.
    Analyzes the arguments of Kant and More on the existence of space and its relationship to matter.

Brann, Noel L. "The Conflict between Reason and Magic in Seventeenth-Century England: A Case Study of the Vaughan-More Debate." *The Huntington Library Quarterly* XLIII, No. 2 (Spring 1980): 103-26.
    Studies the events and arguments of More's theological debate with Thomas Vaughan regarding the role philosophy should play in servicing religion.

Bullough, Geoffrey. Introduction to *The Philosophical Poems of Henry More Comprising "Psychozoia" and Minor Poems,* by Henry More, edited by Geoffrey Bullough, pp. xi-lxxxi. Manchester: Manchester University Press, 1931.
    Critically explicates "Psychozoia" and assesses the impact of such writers as Marsilio Ficino, Plotinus, Benjamin Whichcote, and John Tauler upon More's philosophical development.

Cole, Rosalie L. "Henry More and Spinoza" and "Henry More and the Spinozan Opposition in Holland." In her *Light and Enlightenment: A Study of the Cambridge Platonists and the Dutch Arminians,* pp. 66-93, 94-116. London and New York: Cambridge University Press, 1957.

Considers More's condemnation of Spinozan doctrines as heresies.

Coleridge, Samuel Taylor. "Henry More's Theological Works." In *Selected Poetry and Prose of Coleridge,* by Samuel Taylor Coleridge, edited by Donald A. Stauffer, pp. 554-56. New York: Random House, 1951.
    Posits three principal causes for the failure of the theological schemes of More and the Cambridge Platonists.

Dolson, Grace Neal. "The Ethical System of Henry More." *The Philosophical Review* VI, No. 6 (November 1897): 593-607.
    Explicates More's philosophical concept of human nature.

Harrison, A. W. "Henry More, The Cambridge Platonist." *The London Quarterly and Holborn Review* CLVIII, 6th ser., No. 2 (October 1933): 485-92.
    Provides a brief overview of More's life and work.

Hunter, William B., Jr. "Henry More." In his *The English Spenserians: The Poetry of Giles Fletcher, George Wither, Michael Drayton, Phineas Fletcher and Henry More,* pp. 395-450. Salt Lake City: University of Utah Press, 1977.
    Examines More's attempts to prove that the soul is a separate substance distinct from and preexistent to the body.

Nicolson, Marjorie Hope. "The Spirit World of Milton and More." *Studies in Philology* XXII, No. 4 (October 1925): 433-52.
    Compares More's concept of angels to that of John Milton.

Powicke, Frederick J. "Henry More." In his *The Cambridge Platonists: A Study,* pp. 150-73. London and Toronto: J. M. Dent and Sons, 1926.
    Traces the stages of More's development as a philosopher and his opinions of mysticism and Quakers.

Thompson, Elbert N. S. "A Forerunner of Milton." *Modern Language Notes* XXXII, No. 8 (December 1917): 479-82.
    Likens the astronomical theories discussed by More in "Psychathanasia" to those put forth by John Milton in *Paradise Lost.*

Jean-Baptiste Rousseau

1671-1741

French poet, dramatist, and librettist.

Celebrated by his contemporaries as "le grand Rousseau," Rousseau was the chief French lyric poet of his age. He was primarily noted for his odes, both sacred and secular, and his *cantates,* or *odes en musique*: short, lyrical pieces set to music. He also wrote epigrams, poetical epistles, and allegories, infusing his whole canon with the dignified, harmonious, neoclassical spirit of his era.

Few details are known of Rousseau's early life. He was born into a lower-class Parisian family and obtained a sound education in classical literature during his youth. As a young man of twenty or twenty-one, he began frequenting the city's cafés, particularly the Laurent, a haunt of intellectuals and litterateurs. There Rousseau quickly gained both admirers and enemies by circulating a number of witty epigrams: some satirically lampooning fellow poets and others written to divert through scatological humor (describing, for example, the sexual escapades of monks and nuns.) He tried his hand at drama with *Le café,* a one-act farce, and *Le flatteur,* an attempt at comedy of character on the order of Molière's *Tartuffe* (1669), but met with little success. A few opera librettos and a third play, *Le capricieux,* were also unsuccessful. Rousseau continued to circulate his verses but, popular though they were among many readers throughout Paris, these highly critical satires of his fellow poets roused a deep animosity in the targets themselves. This enmity surfaced in 1701 with the advent of the so-called Affair of the Couplets. A series of anonymous, particularly scurrilous verses began to circulate among the café clientele and were immediately attributed to Rousseau, who indignantly denied authorship. Although the furor appeared to die down before the year's end, Rousseau had by then acquired several open, avowed enemies, including philosopher and geometrician Joseph Saurin. Nine years later, Saurin and other offended parties would take up their quarrel with Rousseau again. Nonetheless, Rousseau's literary achievement and potential were officially recognized late in 1701 with his admission to the Académie royale des inscriptions et belles-lettres.

During the next ten years, Rousseau wrote prolifically and his fame grew in Paris—this though only a few of his poems were yet published. Early in 1710, soon after he was denied an expected election to the prestigious Académie française, the Affair of the Couplets revived. Following a volley of satirical verses exchanged between Rousseau and his adversaries, an anonymous manuscript of defamatory couplets began circulating and was attributed to Rousseau. A group of prominent Parisians, among them Saurin, took legal action, filing charges of libel against Rousseau. The charges were eventually dropped, but Rousseau, angry and unwilling to let the matter rest there, instituted a case against Saurin, accusing *him* of writing the libel. The ensuing court trial resulted in Saurin's acquittal and Rousseau's subjection to public stricture and a heavy fine. Rousseau appealed the verdict at once. Then, apparently in an effort to discredit Saurin, he traveled to Switzerland to obtain evidence of Saurin's alleged swindlings there years earlier. Meanwhile, Rousseau's detractors succeeded in re-opening the case against him, broadening it to include defamatory verses

The Bettmann Archive

as well as his acknowledged obscene epigrams. In his absence, Rousseau was convicted and sentenced to perpetual banishment from France.

For the remainder of his life, Rousseau drew upon the protection and aid of continental acquaintances; he lived in Solothurn, Switzerland, then Vienna, and, finally, Brussels. Soon after his departure from France, the Parisian journal *Mercure galant* published a number of poems said to be Rousseau's, though some were corrupt versions and others not Rousseau's work at all. This prompted the poet to supervise an edition of his odes, *cantates,* epistles, allegories, epigrams, and miscellaneous pieces in 1712. Although he was never able to return to France for more than a brief, surreptitious visit, Rousseau's works were well known there, for new editions of his collected work appeared frequently throughout his lifetime. In addition, Rousseau corresponded with a number of French literary figures, including Voltaire. The younger poet initially wrote to Rousseau requesting literary advice but in time a quarrel arose between the two (possibly due to the patronizing tone Rousseau adopted in critiquing Voltaire's work) and Voltaire became one of Rousseau's most influential and implacable enemies. Among Rousseau's later literary works are adaptations of such dramas as Ben Jonson's *Epicœne; or, The Silent Woman* (1609) and Pierre Corneille's *Le cid* (1637). Having lived a life filled with controversy and animosity, then suffering two damaging strokes and a lingering sickness, Rousseau died in Brussels in 1741.

Rousseau is perhaps best known as an odist. His nineteen *odes sacrées,* or sacred odes, are theological meditations based on the Psalms. They ''sing the trials and triumphs of the heart,'' according to Robert Finch, and reflect the spiritual passion of their originals. Rousseau's thirty-five secular odes, most of them Horatian, address a variety of topics and encompass personal, social, moral, political, and artistic concerns. Among his best-known odes are ''Ode à la fortune'' and ''Ode au comte du Luc.'' The former (translated by John Quincy Adams for his own diversion) is a didactic reminder of the power of fortune in human affairs, while the latter—extravagantly furnished with the mythological metaphors often favored by Rousseau—is an expression of gratitude to a patron. Common to all the odes is evidence of Rousseau's adherence to the French neoclassical ideals of formal harmony and balance. Concurrently, the poet strove to achieve two other ideals of the early-eighteenth-century French odist: ''beau désordre'' (''controlled, attractive disorder'') and ''enthousiasme'' (''enthusiasm''). Believing that beyond the prescribed rules of poetry which the poet is charged to follow there exists a superior poetic impulse—the ''divine afflatus'' of Plato—Rousseau sought to integrate strict technical control with imaginative freedom. Drawn to the popular Italian cantata, a musical composition with lyrics, Rousseau developed the French *cantate,* placing greater emphasis on the lyrics and standardizing the form for this type of poetry. Henry A. Grubbs has described such typical Rousseau *cantates* as ''Circé'' and ''Le triomphe de l'amour'' as stories, ''dealing usually with love, picked from classical mythology, and capable of a simple allegorical application.'' Another of Rousseau's poetic innovations is the French allegorical poem: while he did not invent the form, his was one of the first sustained attempts to employ it. Didactic and frequently satirical, his thirteen poems of this type ''constitute a school of ethics,'' in the opinion of Finch. Grubbs, however, has remarked that while ''they are correct enough in technique,'' they are ''insufferably long, heavy and dull.'' Rousseau's poetical epistles, including ''Epître aux muses'' and ''A Louis Racine,'' are also didactic but more successful; they have been described by Grubbs as ''smoothly versified, well expressed,'' and containing ''a judicious blend of autobiography, criticism and satire.'' The epigrams fall into several categories: satirical pieces of literary criticism and fulmination against inept writers; those dealing, like the *cantates,* with love; those that tell a brief, usually amusing, story; the *epigrammes libres,* or comic and risqué pieces; and poems addressing general moral and human concerns.

As criticism of Rousseau's work has evolved almost entirely within the boundaries of France, scholarship available in English is an inadequate barometer of the author's critical history. Rousseau's rise to fame was extraordinarily rapid, outpacing the actual publication of his poetry. Moreover, his exile detracted not at all from his stature, for throughout his lifetime he garnered critical superlatives: he was ''le grand lyrique français,'' the best of lyric poets, the French Horace or Pindar. His literary enemies abounded, however, and were powerful. Voltaire was among those who attacked his character and work, maintaining that his talent declined after his departure from France, that his poetry suffered badly from poor reasoning, and that his satirical attacks were wicked and malicious. Nevertheless, as Grubbs has asserted, Rousseau became ''a classic during his own lifetime.'' The frequent reprinting of his poetry attests to his popularity after his death and into the nineteenth

century. During these years, selections from his works formed a regular part of secondary school curricula in France.

Rousseau's reputation suffered an abrupt reversal in 1829, when eminent French critic Charles Augustin Sainte-Beuve published a wholesale condemnation of the poet's life and work. Lambasting Rousseau as the least lyrical of poets in the least lyrical of literary eras, Sainte-Beuve denounced the poet as deficient in imagination, sense, and even the technical skill for which he was renowned. This assessment (or ''polemic,'' as Grubbs would have it) apparently went unopposed and seems to have had a strong effect, for subsequent critics rarely mentioned Rousseau at all, and, when they did, summarily dismissed him. The chief modern critic of Rousseau, Grubbs has attempted to restore Rousseau's lost prestige, particularly in his 1941 study *Jean-Baptiste Rousseau: His Life and Works.* Describing Rousseau as a technical virtuoso of the neoclassical era, Grubbs praised the poet's harmony, rhythmic musicality, and complete mastery of the various forms he employed. More recently, Robert Finch has examined the themes and tones of Rousseau's poetry, emphasizing the poet's ''heart'': his central interest in expressing emotional and spiritual profundities.

Today, in one of the more dramatic of critical reversals, the works of ''le grand Rousseau'' are rarely read or studied and his literary reputation has declined to the point where he is a virtual unknown. Grubbs has attributed this largely to changing poetic tastes: Rousseau's work, with its emphasis on formal order and convention, lacks appeal to an audience preferring spontaneity and individual expression. But whatever Rousseau's intrinsic merit for the reader of today, Grubbs has emphasized that he played an important role in the development of the French lyric ode, the *cantate,* the epigram, and the allegory. As Grubbs has summed up: ''Rousseau is, historically, a poet of considerable importance, since he is the best representative of a significant, though little-known, phase in the evolution of French poetry. From the absolute point of view, he is a poet who followed an ideal which no longer seems adequate to us, and who was a great master in the use of a technique which is now almost completely forgotten.''

PRINCIPAL WORKS

Le café (drama) 1694
Le flatteur (drama) 1696
Le capricieux (drama) 1700
La ceinture magique (drama) 1702
　　[*The Magic Girdle,* 1770]
''A une veuve'' (poetry) 1703; published in journal *Mercure galant*
*''Ode à la fortune'' (poetry) 1712; published in *Oeuvres diverses du sieur R**
　　[*John Quincy Adams's Verse Translation of Jean-Baptiste Rousseau's ''Ode à la fortune,''* 1970]
*Oeuvres diverses du sieur R** (poetry) 1712
Oeuvres diverses de mr. Rousseau. 2 vols. (poetry and dramas) 1723
Pièces dramatiques choisies et restituées [adaptor] (dramas) 1734
Lettres de Jean-Baptiste Rousseau sur différents sujets de littérature. 5 vols. (letters) 1749-50
†*Portefeuille de J.-B. Rousseau.* 2 vols. (poetry and dramas) 1751
Oeuvres de Jean-Baptiste Rousseau. 5 vols. (poetry and dramas) 1820

Correspondance de Jean-Baptiste Rousseau et de Brossette. 2 vols. (letters) 1910-11.

*The English translation of this work was written in 1803.

†This work contains *L'hypocondre; ou, La femme qui ne parle point,* adapted from Ben Jonson's *Epicœne; or, The Silent Woman* (1609) in 1733 but not performed at the time.

FRANÇOIS MARIE AROUET DE VOLTAIRE   (poem date 1733)

[*A French philosopher and man of letters, Voltaire was a major figure of the eighteenth-century European Enlightenment, a movement in which reason and empiricism markedly superseded reliance on prescription, faith, and authority. As a man of diverse and intense interests, Voltaire wrote prolifically on many subjects and in a variety of genres, always asserting the absolute primacy of personal liberty—be it intellectual, social, religious, or political. Consequently, he opposed religious traditions and political organizations that he believed thwarted or curtailed individual freedom. Voltaire's most valuable contribution to literature is usually considered his invention of the philosophical* conte, *or tale, in which the story is a vehicle for an ethical or philosophical message; the most famous of these* contes *is the highly regarded* Candide (1759). *The following excerpt is taken from Voltaire's 1733 poem* Le temple du goût, *which describes the poet's fanciful, satirical journey to the literary "temple of taste." Here, he imagines Rousseau's encounter with the guard of the temple, Criticism.*]

[There arrived a] versifier supported by two little satires, and crowned with laurels and thistles.

> "I come hither to laugh, to sport, and to play,
> And make merry," said he, "till the dawn of the day."

"What's this I hear?" said Criticism. "'Tis I," answered the rhymer; I am just come from Germany to visit you, and I have chosen the spring of the year to travel in.

> Spring, the season in which the young Zephyrs dissolve
> The bark of the floods, and to fluid resolve."

The more he spoke in this style, the less was Criticism disposed to open the door to him. "What," said he, "am I then taken for

> A frog, who from his narrow throat
> Still utters, in discordant note.
> Boekekex, roax, roax?"

"Heavens," cried Criticism, "what horrible jargon is this!" She could not immediately guess who the person was that expressed himself in this manner. She was told it was Rousseau, and that the Muses had altered his voice as a punishment for his misdeeds. She could not believe it, and refused to open the door. He blushed and cried out,

> "A rigor so extreme abate,
> I come to seek Marot, my mate;
> Like him, ill luck I had awhile,
> But Phœbus now does on me smile;
> I'm Rousseau, and to you well known;
> Here's verses against the famed Bignon.
> O thou, who always didst inspire
> My bosom with sacred fire,
> Kind Criticism a welcome give
> To one who elsewhere cannot live."

Criticism, upon hearing these words, opened the door and spoke thus:

> "Rousseau, my temper better know,
> I'm just, and ne'er with gall o'erflow;
> Unlike that fury, whose fell rage
> Suggested thy malicious page;
> Who poured her poison in your heart,
> And armed you with the deadly dart.
> The calumnies you strove to spread,
> Drew Themis' vengeance on your head;
> Your muse was into banishment
> For certain wicked couplets sent.
> And for a wretched, ill-writ case,
> Which added to your dire disgrace;
> But Phœbus quickly did pursue
> Your malice with the vengeance due;
> Your soul of genius he deprived,
> Genius which you from him derived,
> Of harmony he robbed your lays,
> Which by that only merit praise;
> Yet you the scribbling itch retain,
> Whilst Phœbus disavows each strain."

Criticism, after having given this advice, adjudged that Rousseau should take place of La Motte as a versifier; but that La Motte should have the precedence whenever genius or understanding were the subjects of dispute. (pp. 50-2)

> *François Marie Arouet de Voltaire, "The Temple of Taste," in his* The Works of Voltaire: A Contemporary Version, *edited by Tobias Smollett, translated by William F. Fleming, revised edition, E. R. DuMont, 1901, pp. 40-69.*

HENRY A. GRUBBS   (essay date 1940)

[*An American scholar, Grubbs was the twentieth century's foremost English-speaking authority on Rousseau. In the following excerpt, he compares Rousseau's* L'hypocondre *with its source, Ben Jonson's* Epicœne; or, The Silent Woman (1609).]

Jean-Baptiste Rousseau, that almost forgotten eighteenth-century poet, who was known as "le grand Rousseau" in the days before his reputation began to slip, owed his vogue mainly to his lyric poetry. Even in the time of his greatest renown he was considered a failure as a dramatist. That is probably the main reason why his posthumous play **L'Hypocondre, ou la femme qui ne parle point** has attracted little attention. . . . One of the poet's friends, the abbé Séguy, when he published a posthumous edition of his works, apparently judged **L'Hypocondre** unworthy of being printed. It did not appear until 1751, when the so-called **Portefeuille de J.-B. Rousseau** was issued. It attracted no attention whatever and has not since. And yet this forgotten play is of considerable interest to us today: it is one of the first French imitations of an Elizabethan dramatist; the first French adaptation of a play by Ben Jonson [*Epicœne, or the Silent Woman*]. (p. 170)

The Silent Woman, produced in 1609 or 1610, is the gayest of Jonson's comedies and has remained the most popular, if not the best-known and the most admired. (p. 171)

This play, because of the conception of comedy upon which it is based (that is, a central figure who is ridiculous because he represents some trait of character carried to an extreme), is closest to Molière of all of Jonson's plays. Rousseau was violently opposed to the tendencies of French comedy about 1730, when Destouches, La Chaussée and Marivaux were reigning favorites; he was anxious to guide the French comic muse back to what he felt was the true comic tradition: that represented by Molière. As we examine the manner in which he adapted Jonson's comedy we must keep that fact in mind.

The French poet kept the name Morose for the main character, called the nephew Léandre, suppressed Clerimont, and called Truewit Eutrapel. Epicœne was changed to Androgyne, which may have seemed to the French poet to have a more easily grasped significance. The minor characters were cut down in numbers and were linked more closely to the main characters.

In general, as the changes made with regard to the characters suggest, the plot of the French play is simpler than the source, Rousseau obviously having decided to eliminate everything that seemed to him to violate the unities. Although the first acts of both plays contain the same amount of exposition, Rousseau did not keep Jonson's opening scene, in which Clerimont, Truewit and Dauphine converse wittily and entertainingly and bring in Morose and the situation involving him only incidentally and gradually. This may have seemed to the French poet to violate Boileau's rule:

> Que des les premiers vers l'action préparée
> Sans peine du sujet aplanisse l'entrée

[From the very start the prepared action ought effortlessly to smoothen the introduction of the subject.]

(*Art poétique*, III).

He substituted for this opening scene a monologue by the barber, followed by a scene between the barber and the nephew, both of which stick pretty much to exposition. There is a significant difference at the end of the first act. In Jonson's play, Truewit and the others coöperate with Dauphine mainly out of pure love of mischief, and, along with the audience, are kept in the dark with regard to the most important detail of Dauphine's plot (that is, the real nature of Epicœne). In Rousseau's version the first act ends with Léandre promising, as he leaves the stage with Eutrapel, to give the details of the plot, which he does between the acts. These are not revealed to the audience, although the name Androgyne might serve as a fairly good clue.

In the second acts of both plays, the three most important scenes are similar: that is, the scenes between Morose and his servant, between Morose and his nephew's friend and the scene where the barber introduces the silent woman to Morose. It goes almost without saying that Rousseau maintains the unity of place, and thus is obliged to omit one of Jonson's scenes, that which takes place in Sir John Daw's house.

In the third and fourth acts the two plays are similar as far as the general lines of the plot go, but there are considerable differences in the details of the action. Rousseau has simplified a great deal. He certainly found a lack of unity of action, as he understood it, in Jonson's play. He would have decided that many details based upon conditions of London life in the Elizabethan period would have been unintelligible and probably repugnant to any French audience. He therefore suppressed such details, but he endeavored to keep the most important comic devices found in the third and fourth acts of his source: the sudden change in the silent woman, the ludicrous distress and frenzy of Morose, the hubbub caused by the invasion of uninvited guests. He kept whatever comic details of Jonson's he judged suitable and added others of his own of far from negligible quality to replace those he suppressed.

The highly effective and comic fifth act of Jonson was adapted by Rousseau with little change. The French poet shortened it—especially by cutting down greatly the amount of Latin used by the supposed authorities on divorce whom Morose consults. It is interesting to note that he also gave his Morose a little more dignity: his Morose protests more violently against being obliged to confess impotence and refuses to admit it in words; instead he signs reluctantly a confession of impotence dictated to him.

From this comparison, it is seen that, in all essential portions of the action, Rousseau followed Jonson as closely as he thought the French rules would allow, with the exception of the detail mentioned above concerning the revelation of Dauphine's plot to the other characters. Rousseau possibly decided that the behavior of Eutrapel and the women would not be sufficiently motivated, hence not *vraisemblable*, [''verisimilitudinous''], if it were not made clear that they were consciously coöperating in Léandre's plot. The parts suppressed by the French poet were parts which, amusing in themselves, were not essential to the development of the plot and hence violated the unity of action.

As far as the character of Morose goes—in Rousseau's mind certainly the most important feature of the play—the original was reproduced carefully, with the exception of one curious point. At the end, when Epicœne's identity is revealed, Jonson's Morose exits without a word, whereas Rousseau's delivers a final tirade in which he reviles the characters who have made a game of him, but declares himself satisfied anyway, as he is certain now that he can have rest and quiet. This seems in line with the French author's apparent desire to keep the character of Morose unchanged and intact (as Molière would have done), but to allow him maintain a certain amount of dignity.

When we consider the matter of similarities of detail in the two plays, we must remark at once that Rousseau's play, even in scenes that correspond exactly, is in no way a translation of Jonson's. It should be remembered that the English play is in prose, and the French in verse, in regular Alexandrines. Furthermore, although, as far as language went, considerably greater freedom was permitted in French comedy than in French tragedy, there is a great and fundamental difference between rich, vigorous, earthy Elizabethan prose and classical French verse, even when the latter is taken in its familiar and realistic moments. Hence, the closest Rousseau came to his English source is in making use of specific ideas or themes within scenes that correspond in function. (pp. 172-74)

In short, *L'Hypocondre* is a respectable adaptation of a very good English comedy. At the time it was written, however, and for long afterwards, Rousseau's effort was, if noticed at all, treated as beneath contempt, a thing that had better not be mentioned and that should be forgotten as quickly as possible. Hence it passed into oblivion, an oblivion so complete that though recent English editors of Jonson's works mention the fact that a ''bad French translation'' of *the Silent Woman* was said to have been made in the eighteenth century, they are unable to give further precisions. (pp. 175-76)

> *Henry A. Grubbs, ''An Early French Adaptation of an Elizabethan Comedy: J. B. Rousseau as an Imitator of Ben Jonson,''* in Modern Language Notes, *Vol. LV, No. 3, March, 1940, pp. 170-76.*

HENRY CARRINGTON LANCASTER (essay date 1940)

[*An American scholar and educator, Lancaster was the author of* A History of French Dramatic Literature in the Seventeenth Cen-

tury. In the following excerpt from this work, he assesses Le café, Le flatteur, *and* Le capricieux.]

[Rousseau's] first comedy was *le Caffé,* a farce in one act and in prose. . . . The scene is laid in a café, where, at the beginning of the play, a poet meditates, an abbé slumbers, a game of draughts is being played, and two coffee-drinkers argue. The manners of those who frequent the house, brought out by means of a slight intrigue that shows resemblance to earlier plays, constitute the principal subject of the play. Mme Jérome is a thrifty woman who has laid up enough to make a handsome dowry for her daughter, complains of patrons who do not pay their debts, and is very much afraid of scandal. Her daughter is an ingénue, fresh from a convent, who stands in awe of her mother and loves Dorante, an impecunious officer chiefly interested in her on account of her 20,000 écus. His clever valet disguises himself first as an officer in search of a recruit, then as a police official. He pretends to be drunk, deceives Jobelin into thinking that he will be easy to defeat, and brings the intrigue to a successful termination.

Rousseau's introduction of an abbé follows an example recently set by Dancourt in *l'Eté des coquettes,* but here there is less doubt about the permanency of his profession. Though he is on the hero's side, he is hardly an honor to his cloth. He claims to have spent the day with three companions and to have consumed with their assistance twenty-five bottles of wine. He seems to be asleep at the beginning of the play, but this may be partly pretense, as he has been able to gather information for Dorante, who is also aided by Coronis, a talkative Gascon, and by a lively Chevalier. The rival, Jobelin, makes love in the language of a notary, fails to attract the girl, and is easily deceived by La Flèche. He is a knave himself, concealing from Mme Jérome the fact that he is in debt and has not paid for his position as a notary, and hoping to take advantage at cards of a man he believes to be drunk. His friend, La Sourdière, seems to be a hanger-on of the café, interested in news of the war, but so ignorant of geography that he supposes Belgrade to be a seaport. Rousseau adds three characters that have nothing to do with the plot, but help complete the picture of the café: two players of draughts, one of whom ''blows'' one of the other's pieces and asks for a cup of coffee when he wins the game, and a poet who is trying desperately to complete an epithalamium for Jobelin in the confusion of the establishment.

The conversation is concerned not only with the love intrigue, with drinking wine and coffee, with playing draughts and piquet, but with war, *mésalliances,* tapestries, and operas. . . . The vivacious dialogue and rapid movement must have made this seem a promising play, even if the unity of action is not preserved. It had, however, little success. First given on Aug. 2, 1694, it was acted only 14 times in this year and the next. (pp. 848-50)

Rousseau determined to bring out a comedy of character and wrote **le Flatteur** in five acts and in prose, subsequently turning it into verse. He selected Molière as his model, choosing for his flatterer the name of Philinte, who had been made famous in *le Misanthrope,* getting suggestions from the characters of Maître Jacques in *l'Avare* and Toinette in *le Malade imaginaire,* but following especially *Tartuffe.* As in the latter play, the head of a family becomes infatuated with an intriguer and offers him his daughter, his plans are opposed by the girl, her lover, and a *suivante* [''lady's maid''], he is in danger of losing a considerable sum of money to the villain, is finally convinced that the latter is an evil person, keeps his money, and allows

his daughter to marry the man to whom she had been originally engaged. (p. 850)

Philinte is not merely a flatterer, but an intriguer and . . . many of the methods he uses have nothing to do with flattery. As this is true, the study is not that of a typical flatterer, but of a villain who uses flattery along with slander, misrepresentation, and forgery to gain his ends. While Philinte begins his intrigue with flattery, he makes no extensive use of it when he sees it progressing. Flattery is not, moreover, the unique possession of Philinte, for Justine employs it in order to get from Francisque the essential document. The play is intended to be a comedy of character and may be entitled to this designation as the study of character makes a greater impression in the play than intrigue or manners, but Rousseau does not display the skill in the conception of the leading figure that is shown by Molière when he created corresponding characters. There is, moreover, weakness in the dénouement, for Philinte entrusts the *dédit* too readily to Francisque and Chrysante is too easily convinced. There is also too much chance in Justine's discovery that Francisque has the document in his possession.

On the other hand, the play has several interesting characters and a number of striking scenes. (pp. 850-51)

The exposition is skillfully made in the first act, where the characters of Chrysante and Philinte are explained to us before they are shown in their dialogue. The action begins there, too, with Philinte's insinuations, calculated to separate the lovers and prepare the way for his own triumph. In Act II we learn of the danger he is in and see the first result of his flattery and slander. By letting Angélique know that her father would marry her to another man than Damon, but not to whom, the author is able to create a scene in which the lamb appeals to the wolf and to keep for Act III the situation resulting from the knowledge that Philinte is the man her father has selected. The latter act contains also the scene of the *dédit* and the scene in which Philinte outwits Damon. Act IV is largely concerned with the lovers' quarrel and with the beginning of Justine's counterattack, while in Act V she cleverly secures the *dédit* from Francisque and exposes Philinte's villainy. With this structure, several interesting characters, and various dramatic situations, the play deserved greater success than it received. Perhaps its resemblance to *Tartuffe* made it less acceptable to the public than a more original play would have been. It was not a failure, but it was far less successful than a number of other plays of the decade in which it was written. Acted first on Nov. 24, 1696, it was played sixteen times in that and the two following years and was revived in 1717, 1721, 1730, and 1732. The total number of performances was forty-five. (pp. 852-53)

Le Capricieux is distinctly inferior. It was the first play that Rousseau wrote in verse, for, as we have seen, *le Flatteur* was originally in prose. Perhaps the recent success of Regnard's *Joueur* was what induced him to prefer poetry to prose. Dufresny's more recent *Esprit de contradiction* may well have suggested the principal kind of caprice in which his protagonist was to indulge. Rousseau may have been guided, too, by Boileau, whom he greatly admired and whose description of an ''inconstant'' in the eighth satire has some resemblance to a passage in *le Capricieux,* I, 2. . . . The idea of a father who exalts his own method of instructing his child over his friend's and discovers that he has nothing to be proud of resembles *Scapin* II, 1; Albert's saying to Pamphile, ''touchez-là'' [''let's shake on it''], and then telling him that he will not have his daughter, *le Bourgeois Gentilhomme,* V. 4; while the two fathers recall those of *le Dépit amoureux,* one of whom, as in this play, is named Albert, while two characters in both comedies are called Valère and Lucile. Most of the intrigue, however, appears to be original.

Rousseau apparently meant to write a comedy of character, but he succeeded in producing a play of intrigue in which the title-rôle does not satisfactorily live up to the title. In the preface he tries to answer the criticism that Albert acts not so much by caprice as by a desire to contradict, by arguing that contradiction is due to caprice. He considers the matter of little importance as, at worst, it is only a question of the title. . . . [Albert] is moved at times by fear of being unhappily married and he may change his mind without intending to thwart the plans of anyone else. A good deal of the play is dependent, moreover, on a misunderstanding with which Albert has nothing to do. A more serious fault is that the character is entirely unconvincing and uninteresting in the monotonous series of changes. Pamphile is a somewhat grotesque gentleman of fifty, ten years younger than Albert and equally indifferent to his daughter's happiness. The two girls resemble each other closely, as do the young lovers. Jacinte alone has any real cleverness, but she is little more than an imitation of the maid in *le Flatteur.* The characters are constantly running about in order to create new surprises. There is little more logic in their actions than there is charm in their conversation. Acted first on Dec. 17, 1700, it was given only seven times in that year and three in the following. Rousseau claimed in a letter to Duché that it could have been acted twenty times if the troupe had been willing to produce it with a "petite pièce." The actors were, however, probably quite right in refusing to play it more often.

It is by these three plays that J.-B. Rousseau must be judged, for they alone were acted in public. He had begun by a farce of manners, in a way that recalls Dancourt. As he made his greatest reputation in odes and epigrams, it would seem that his talents were at their best in short works and that he should have continued writing farce. But the high opinion that he had of his own powers made him seek to be the successor of Molière and to compose comedies of character. In *le Flatteur* he was fairly successful, though his leading character was only partially a flatterer and his play suffered by the comparison it invited with *Tartuffe*, but *le Capricieux* showed his inability to improve upon his earlier full-length play, or even to equal it. In this last comedy he abandoned the study of manners in his effort to create character, but succeeded in producing only a play with a complicated plot and mechanical personages. He tacitly admitted his defeat by turning to other *genres* while he was in Paris and his exile kept him from recovering the reputation he had lost by the failure of *le Capricieux.* (pp. 853-55)

> *Henry Carrington Lancaster, "Comedy from April, 1689, to the End of 1700," in his* A History of French Dramatic Literature in the Seventeenth Century, Part IV: The Period of Racine, 1673-1700, Vol. II, *The Johns Hopkins University Press, 1940, pp. 818-907.*

HENRY A. GRUBBS (essay date 1941)

[*In the following excerpt from the most comprehensive examination of Rousseau available in English, Grubbs surveys Rousseau's lyric odes and* cantates, *concluding with a summary of the poet's ultimate literary importance.*]

It was above all as a lyric poet that Jean-Baptiste Rousseau was known and admired in the eighteenth century. "Le grand lyrique français," ["the great French lyric poet"], "le Pindare de nos jours" ["the Pindar of our time"] are terms that were frequently applied to him. Up to the end of the classical period the ode was considered to be the principal type of lyric poem, and it is because of this that the larger part of Rousseau's lyric production was classed under the heading "Odes," the paraphrases from the Psalms being called "odes sacrées" and the cantatas being given the subtitle of "odes allégoriques" or "odes en musique." Actually, the sacred odes, the odes proper and the cantatas are distinct and separate types of lyric poems, differing in inspiration, in form and in intent, and they will be considered in separate sections. (p. 226)

• • • • •

A large number of French writers before Rousseau had written poems imitated from the Bible. The most important of these are Marot, Malherbe, Racan and Racine. Strange as it may seem, in view of the obvious and certain influence that Marot exerted upon Jean-Baptiste's lighter verse, there is no evidence that he was even acquainted with Marot's psalms. . . . As for Malherbe, whose paraphrases of the Psalms are few in number, but distinguished in quality, his example may have served as a stimulus, but there is no indication of influence in detail. (pp. 227-28)

[Rousseau] was familiar with the sacred odes of Racan, and, though we must admit that the common source might be the explanation for some similarity in expression and idea, it seems certain that Rousseau imitated Racan to a definite if limited extent. In several of the odes there is no resemblance whatsoever, either in form, content or details, but there is more or less vague resemblance in others, and in at least two, specific evidence of imitation. Rousseau's eighth sacred ode: **"Béni soit le Dieu des armées"** is similar in form and in certain details to the corresponding psalm of Racan (CXLIII). Furthermore, the theme of the last two or three stanzas, in the two poems, shows exactly the same curious twist away from the theme of the Biblical original. The mere fact that Rousseau followed Racan in going outside of the Psalms to make a paraphrase of the Song of Hezekiah (*Isaiah 38*) shows influence, but there are also striking resemblances of detail, especially in the first stanza.

The influence of the Biblical poetry of Racine upon the sacred odes of Jean-Baptiste Rousseau is mainly a matter of general inspiration, though commentators have also pointed out vague similarities of detail, quite possibly the result of the unconscious influence of poetry so thoroughly studied as to have been completely assimilated into the poet's nature. Racine wrote one psalm paraphrase (it was not published until 1808 and was probably unknown to Rousseau) and four *cantiques*, but it was probably the lyric portions of the Biblical tragedies, *Esther* and *Athalie*, that had the most effect upon Rousseau and that served as an important source of inspiration to him. The idea that Jean-Baptiste had of the grandeur and simplicity of the poetry of the Bible must have come to him from those two plays, for the terms that he uses in his preface to characterize that poetry apply much better to them than they do to the prose of the Vulgate, admirable as it may be.

Rousseau was stating the case mildly when he explained that his imitations of the Psalms were free. They are not translations by any manner of means, and although the author seemed to think that they were not free enough to be called paraphrases, the modern reader would call them paraphrases in the broadest sense of the term. They take as point of departure a theme found in a Psalm, and then proceed to amplify and develop it, making use of many details from the source, but being continually guided by the exigencies of the rhythm, the harmony, the stanza form used, and being also constantly restrained and restricted by the narrow classical rules of *bienséance* in language and imagery. There is another point that explains the great differences that may be found between the Psalms and the sacred odes of Rousseau. Like all Catholic French poets of his period, in paraphrasing Psalms, Jean-Baptiste tended, consciously or unconsciously, to introduce Catholic and Christian elements that did not exist in the Hebrew original. Thus, to the simple, dry, earthy—if also eloquent and occasionally grandiose—morality of the Jewish Psalms, are added abstractions such as immortality, the eternal felicity of the blessed, the everlasting misery of the damned. This, along with the general tendency towards abstraction in the language and imagery in the noble style of that period, produced a tone, an aura, often very different from that of the source.

The psalm paraphrase was a popular form in the eighteenth century. Many of Rousseau's contemporaries and successors emulated him, with more or less success. To name only a few of the better known, we can mention Lamotte, Desfontaines, Louis Racine, Lefranc de Pompignan, Piron, Lebrun, Gilbert, Laharpe and Delille. Jean-Baptiste was considered the master of all, and his sacred odes were the most generally admired of all of his works. Even Voltaire praised them. The necessary simplicity, the necessary absence of classical mythology, pleased one current in the taste of the time. And the grandiloquence, the enthusiasm, could not, as in the case of some of Rousseau's profane odes, be called factitious or artificial. They were taken from the source and were appropriate to the theme. Even the *philosophes,* the deists, would find nothing to reproach in these poems, for, in the picture they give so vividly of a "Dieu rémunérateur et vengeur" ["rewarding and avenging God"], they harmonize quite well with the tenets of natural religion.

The first to suggest that Rousseau did not deserve too much credit for these sacred odes, beautiful as they were, because in them he was an imitator rather than a creator, was Vauvenargues. For Vauvenargues Rousseau's psalm paraphrases contained passion that his other odes . . . did not have, but that passion did not come from him, it came from great masters. This reproach was renewed during the Romantic period by Sainte-Beuve [see Additional Bibliography], and, inconsistently and unjustly, it was combined with the accusation that in imitating the Bible, Rousseau had failed to make use of the most poetic details in his source. He was thus, at the same moment, being accused of lack of originality and too much originality!

Though the Romantic poets rebelled against J.-B. Rousseau as an authority in poetry, they probably knew well, and were influenced by, the sacred odes. This is most likely in the cases of Lamartine and Hugo. (pp. 228-31)

· · · · ·

The "profane" ode, that is, the ode proper, was considered, in the classical period, to be the principal form of lyric poetry. . . .

Rousseau seems to have been stimulated to serious effort in the field of the ode by rivalry with Lamotte. (p. 231)

The crux of the controversies with regard to the ode consisted in the question: what is this *beau désordre* or *enthousiasme* which is said to be the principal beauty of the ode? (p. 232)

Not having found in the odes of Lamotte that *beau désordre,* that enthusiasm, which should reign in the ode, and having stated so publicly, Rousseau felt it incumbent upon himself to endeavor to show what a real ode was. With that in view, he wrote his **"Ode sur la naissance du Duc de Bretagne."** He tried to explain to his friend De Machy the difficulties that he faced, and how he was trying to present a *beau désordre* to the public. The question was still confused, involved. In 1707 he was not ready to go farther than Boileau or even Lamotte. The prestige of rationalism still weighed upon him, and he endeavored, just like Boileau and Lamotte, to justify enthusiasm by reason. . . . (p. 233)

Later, his ideas became bolder, and he put forth the theory that poetic enthusiasm should rise above reason, dominate it, be independent of it. (p. 234)

[Rousseau said of Lamotte's odes that] they resembled letters rather than odes "commençant toutes, pour ainsi dire, par le *Monsieur,* et finissant par le *très humble serviteur*" ["all beginning, so to speak, with the 'Sir', and ending with the 'very humble servant"]. In other words, instead of being the inspired product of the poet's enthusiasm for some heroic subject, they were cold amplifications constructed according to the rules of geometric logic, and addressed to some individual whom they were designed to flatter. When we examine, as we shall now, the practice of Rousseau as opposed to his theory, the reader will have the opportunity of determining for himself whether the odes approach the poet's rather vague ideal more than they do the condemned practice of his enemy.

Jean-Baptiste wrote some thirty-five odes. He distributed thirty of these into three books of ten each, placing the rest, for various reasons, among his "poésies diverses." The ten odes of the second book (the first book was devoted to the sacred odes) were written before 1710, most of them probably being written 1707-1710. The odes of the third book and the first five of the fourth were written 1713-1724. The last five were written 1734-1738. Thus we have three main divisions: the odes written in full maturity (between the ages of thirty-five and forty), the odes of middle age, and the odes of old age.

As to the first group of odes, Rousseau tells us in his preface that he made them varied:

> . . . à l'exemple d'Horace, sur lequel j'ai tâché de me former, comme lui-même s'était formé sur les anciens lyriques. . . .
>
> [. . . according to the example of Horace, on whom I tried to model myself, as he modeled himself on the ancient lyric poets. . . .]

And in fact they possess a wide variety in stanza form, in subject matter and in tone. Two are of the heroic type, one dealing with the birth, one with the death, of a prince. These two differ greatly, however. The **"Ode sur la naissance du Duc de Bretagne"** is an attempt to provide an example of Pindar's *beau désordre,* whereas the **"Ode sur la mort du Prince de Conti"** is far more restrained, and contains a long moral digression on the dangers of flattery. Two others, the famous **"Ode à la Fortune** and the **"Ode à La Fare,"** on Reason, are didactic odes, elaborate amplifications of moral commonplaces, illustrated with examples drawn mainly from history. They make little attempt to be anything but eloquent rhetoric, though there are occasional lyrical touches in the figures used by way of illustration. Three other odes addressed to friends (the **"Ode à Caumartin,"** formerly dedicated to Rouillé du Coudrai, the **"Ode au Marquis d'Ussé,"** and the **"Ode à Duché"**), while remaining grave, are lighter in tone. A certain characteristic eighteenth-century grace (which, since Sainte-Beuve, Jean-Baptiste has been accused of lacking totally) is conspicuous in a few stanzas of these odes. Finally, the three remaining odes in the second book (the odes to Courtin and to Chaulieu, and the "**Ode à une Veuve**") are successful enough attempts to express in light, easy-going verses [an] amiable Epicurean philosophy. . . . (pp. 235-36)

The predominant inspiration of the odes that we have just been discussing was Horatian. If Pindaric and Anacreontic traits appear in them, it is because similar traits are to be found also in the odes of Horace. The "**Ode sur la naissance du Duc de Bretagne,**" at least in its primitive version, owed something also to Boileau's "Ode sur la prise de Namur." It cannot have been a mere coincidence that, in both poems, each dealing with a heroic subject, the poet returns to himself at the end, and exalts his own ability at the expense of that of a despised rival. . . .

In this, the only group of profane odes published in the first edition of Rousseau's works, the *beau désordre* that was considered the main beauty of the ode, was not very well represented. The "**Ode sur la naissance du Duc de Bretagne**" was the only one which made a serious attempt to express this *beau désordre,* and it contains imperfections which betray the poet's inexperience in that type of ode. The most successful of these odes was the "**Ode à la Fortune.**" It is really in no way different, except in greater perfection of form and in greater richness of imagery, from the didactic odes of Lamotte. This type of ode seems to have appealed to the taste of the time, and the theme of the "**Ode à la Fortune**" was well calculated to please the France of 1712. Its teaching is that it is fortune, rather than greatness of character, that creates most so-called heroes, that most of the great conquerors have merely been fortunate brutes. (p. 237)

If one examines carefully the odes in the third book, the inaccuracy of Voltaire's judgment, that Rousseau's poetry written after his exile was worthless, becomes apparent. These odes were written between 1713 and 1718, while Rousseau was in Solothurn and in Vienna. As a body of poems they are equal if not superior to the preceding group, and one of them is generally considered the best of Rousseau's odes. He himself said that in the majority of these odes he had tried to give an idea of the poetry of Pindar, and, in fact, eight out of the ten are heroic odes of the type in which *beau désordre* is highly desirable. The first (the "**Ode au Comte du Luc**") is a powerful expression of tribute and gratitude to a protector; two (the second, "**Au Prince Eugène,**" and the tenth, "**Sur la bataille de Peterwardein**") deal with the greatness and the heroic deeds of Prince Eugene; three deal with wars and warlike expeditions (the odes "**Aux Princes chrétiens, Au Prince de Vendôme**" and "**A M. de Grimani**"); one (the "**Palinodie**") is a diatribe against those disrespectful to the memory of Louis XIV; and one (the "**Ode à Malherbe**") attacks the detractors of Homer. The two other odes resemble the lighter types to be found among those written earlier. The "**Ode au Comte de Sinzendorff**" resembles, in theme, in tone and in rhythm, the ode to Caumartin. The "**Ode à Bonneval**" is like the light, Epicurean odes of the second book.

To give an example of what Rousseau meant by a Pindaric ode, we shall analyze in some detail the "**Ode au Comte du Luc.**" He probably would have been willing to have this ode taken as an example of the desired *beau désordre* or *enthousiasme.* It was considered his great masterpiece, as long as he was thought to have written masterpieces. . . . [The casual reader today] would fine *désordre* in it, but the *désordre* would hardly seem *beau* to him. His principal reaction would probably be:

if the poet wants to express gratitude to his protector, why doesn't he do just that, without bringing in all of this confused mythology? The reader's criticism would probably be: the poem is pompous and exaggerated; it rings false. A contemporary reader who has some familiarity with the odes of Malherbe would find in the "**Ode au Comte du Luc**" a somewhat similar tonality, but he would find in it no other beauties, unless he should be willing to devote to the poem the same careful attention that he would give, say to an obscure sonnet of Mallarmé. If he did this, he would at least discover why the poem seemed a masterpiece to the eighteenth century.

First he would find formal perfection. Rousseau was a master at producing the type of harmony or music of verse that classical lyric poets endeavored to produce. Let us note at once that this is not the same type as the music that is to be found in modern verse. When we say that we find "music" in a poem of Mallarmé, we are not referring merely to the effects of the sounds of the words, the rhythm and the rimes. We are also referring to a certain musical effect obtained from the connotations of the poem's images—sense impressions of music, or even other sense impressions which are transposed in our own imaginations (through a tradition built up by poets for a century) so as to become impressions of music. In the poetry of Rousseau the "music" is almost wholly a matter of tone, of sound—the tonal values of the words, the rhythm and the rimes. To appreciate it the reader needs a trained ear, rather than a poetically trained imagination.

In this fairly long poem (thirty-three six-line stanzas) there is not an imperfect rime; more than half are rich, very few are merely *suffisantes* ["sufficient"]. The stanza form is a very flexible one; it is equally well suited to the expression of gravity or lightness. The imposed rhythm of the stanza is a strong, powerful beat, and it is skillfully balanced with the natural rhythm of the discourse in such a way as to prevent monotony. That bugbear of classical versification, unintentional, alliterative repetition of sounds . . . was avoided. What repetition of sounds is to be found is intentional and skillfully spaced.

In the "**Ode au Comte du Luc**" the reader who studies the poem carefully will find that the imagery is almost irreproachable. In a poem literally bristling with figures of speech, severe critics, who have examined it with the greatest attention, have found but one inappropriate metaphor.

What was admired most of all in this poem, however, was the amazing ingenuity of its construction. In producing an ode which should manifest *enthousiasme* or *beau désordre,* Jean-Baptiste wrote a poem which gives an actual demonstration of the effect of *enthousiasme* on a poet, a poem which, furthermore, can be accurately called *sagesse habillée en folie,* or apparent disorder which is in reality logical and reasonable. What to a careless reader might appear to be confusion, extravagant abuse of mythology, or pompous nonsense, turns out, on careful examination, to be a convincing picture of the processes of the mind of a poet who is meditating about his patron and protector to whom he owes a great debt of gratitude. (pp. 238-41)

In this ode the imagery is rich—from the eighteenth-century point of view. And to one who follows carefully and comprehends the poet's thought, the images used appear natural and appropriate. Furthermore, the poem illustrates admirably Rousseau's method of imitation. The reminiscences of Horace and Vergil are numerous, and felicitous. The poet is, to use his own term, ''jousting'' with his predecessors, and is not coming off badly.

There is no need of lingering over the other odes of the third book. They contain, in a less degree, the same qualities that are found in the **"Ode au Comte du Luc."** As much may be said of the odes of the fourth book, which, with one or two exceptions, betray a marked decline in talent.

Before terminating this discussion of the odes, it is necessary to make a few remarks on the stanza form. As in the sacred odes, Rousseau used a wide variety of stanzas, though he kept to the principle of maintaining the same stanza form throughout an ode. In the profane odes he showed greater sureness in his choice of stanzas. The subject matter of the sacred odes being less varied, the variety of stanzas was occasionally a bit arbitrary, and one or two of the stanza forms used were more original than effective or appropriate. In the three books of profane odes, Rousseau's choice of stanzas, while maintaining pleasing variety, was irreproachable in taste. (pp. 242-43)

• • • • •

[Rousseau's cantatas] were most of them products of the most prolific period of the poet's life: 1701-1710. (p. 243)

In developing the form of the cantata, Rousseau was making an intelligent creative effort. The success of the operas of Quinault reveal a definite current of taste. The cantata was Jean-Baptiste's attempt to satisfy that taste in what seemed to him a legitimate way. He had tried his hand at opera, and had come to the conclusion that it was an unsatisfactory form for a poet. It had characteristics of the epic, the tragedy and the ode, but the exigencies of the music hampered the poet to such an extent that he could not produce any real character development or any real lyric swing in an opera libretto. Still Rousseau felt that the union of poetry and music was desirable.

He found a suggestion for a means of accomplishing this in a musical form recently developed in Italy. A type of song, called *cantata,* consisting of a mixture of recitatives and airs for one or more voices, had been enjoying a great vogue in Italy in the last half of the seventeenth century. The Italian cantata was not primarily a poem set to music; it was a musical composition for the voice, using words. (pp. 243-44)

What seems certain is that it was hearing some of the Italian cantatas sung that gave Rousseau the idea of trying to write cantatas in French. He took the Italian cantatas as models, there being no others, but it soon seemed to him that in following the Italian practice of sacrificing the sense to the music, he was not producing a satisfactory result. So he determined to give a definite form to the poem. He decided to give up the method of writing a vaguely idyllic love poem to be set to music, and instead to pick as subject a definite allegory based upon a suitable story from classical mythology. The recitatives then would contain the body of the story, and the airs the ''soul'' or application. The typical Rousseau cantata is thus a story, dealing usually with love, picked from classical mythology, and capable of a simple allegorical application. It is fairly short (fifty to seventy-five verses) and usually consists of three recitatives alternated with two or three airs. The recitatives have about six to twelve verses; the length of the lines and the rime schemes in them are irregular. The airs consist most frequently of three quatrains, with the third a repetition of the first (*aria da capo*). They are almost always *petits vers*—of five or seven syllables. This form became standard, and was soon imitated by other poets.

Was Rousseau justified in claiming to be the creator of the French cantata? There is little doubt that he created it as a poetic form; in fact only one French cantata is known which may have been written before his. . . . Leaving aside the question, which we are not competent to treat, of whether his cantatas, in the musical settings by Morin, Bernier, Batistin and others, are superior as musical compositions, we can state that as poems, it was the consensus of opinion in his time that they were by far the finest examples of the form.

In general, it may be said that the early cantatas are less interesting than the later ones, and that Rousseau did well to suppress **"L'Amant heureux"** and **"L'Amour dévoilé,"** and all but the charming opening lines of **"Sur un baiser."** **"Jupiter et Europe"** was of more significance. It may be that the poet ruled it out because he had decided against using the dialogue form (which is found in that poem) in the cantata. It is hard to understand, however, why he suppressed **"Sur un arbrisseau."** It is a delicate, fragrant little poem, showing the sensibility and grace which Rousseau was often accused of lacking, and which is of course absent from both the sacred odes and the heroic odes. The first few lines are especially charming. . . . (pp. 245-47)

The most admired, and in general the best of Rousseau's cantatas are the ten published as a group in the first edition of his works. They keep a general level of excellence that the poet was not able to attain in his later efforts in the form. The general theme of these cantatas is love. It is neither the heroic passion of the tragedies of Corneille, nor the violent fury of the tragedies of Racine, but it contains . . . the tragic element. . . . Faguet said that Rousseau was a man of his time in lacking feeling, especially feeling for love, and he cited examples to back up his claim, but he could have found other examples to prove the contrary. Watteau's *Embarquement pour Cythère* and Prévost's *Manon Lescaut* show that the eighteenth century in its early period had a feeling for love, and Rousseau's cantatas are far from lacking this feeling. Their theme is this: Love is a tyrant, love is dangerous, love causes suffering, love cannot be resisted, but if it could be resisted, who would want to resist it? (pp. 247-48)

Of Rousseau's cantatas, **"Circé"** is the one that has been most admired. Its theme, with its dramatic presentation of Circe's tragic despair, followed by a return to the half-sentimental, half-sensual wistfulness characteristic of the period and of these cantatas, has variety and power. The versification has great technical virtuosity. . . . (p. 249)

• • • • •

Measured by the modern definition of the essence of poetry, Jean-Baptiste Rousseau's work would certainly seem to be found wanting. It is quite apparent that he was not expressing the inexpressible, that he was not putting into the form of language that which by essence is foreign to that form. Rather his poetry seems most often to be merely an attempt to give a polished expression to the obvious.

Thus it would seem that the eclipse of the vogue of Jean-Baptiste is not arbitrary, but corresponds to a change in poetic taste. (p. 285)

Historically he is a poet of considerable importance. Recent literary historians have been purblind in neglecting this aspect of him. He is the best representative of an important phase in the evolution of French poetry, and his rôle in that evolution has not yet been sufficiently studied.

But is he of interest other than historic? If we examine qualities in his work that the modern reader may admire, we will find that it possesses a certain amount of permanent value.

For the modern reader the language—that is, the versification, the style, the imagery—is an obstacle. We might suggest (although it is risky to make analogies between the arts) that it is primarily this obstacle that has prevented the average man of culture of our day from knowing Jean-Baptiste's work as well as he does that of Watteau or Couperin—to name distinguished contemporaries of Rousseau who were, however, less distinguished at the time in their fields than he was in his. An eighteenth-century painting has an immediate appeal to the modern. Eighteenth-century music, if heard at length, seems monotonous to the inexperienced modern ear, but in small quantities, it has an immediate charm. But such a poem as the cantata **"Circé"** is in a "language" so unattractive to the modern reader that it rebuffs him. Brought up on the fallacious idea that spontaneous sincerity is the earmark of poetry, he finds trite and insincere the conventional embellishments based upon imitation of the Ancients. Furthermore, he has no ear for the harmonious melody of the lines. For him the poetry of Verlaine is the type of musical poetry. Now there is music in the poetry of Verlaine, in addition to the connotative effect of the words, but it is a rather monotonous music, always in the same minor key. The harmonies of Rousseau's verses are rich and varied, but careful reading and rereading is necessary to train the ear to appreciate them.

There is, however, no reason why the modern reader should not learn the "language" in which the poems of Rousseau are written. (pp. 287-88)

In examining Rousseau's work as a whole, with the purpose of discovering what aspects of it should appeal to the modern reader, we can divide it into three general types or manners. First, there is the grand manner, consisting of the poems dealing with religion, patriotism, national feeling, celebration of heroes and high moral problems. Second, is the satirical manner—poems treating satirical and humorous subjects with witty conciseness. Third, and most difficult to define, is the discreet or intimate manner.

It is this third manner of Rousseau, largely ignored by critics in his own day, and which later he was accused of lacking altogether, that has the most appeal to the reader of today. His poems in the grand manner strike no responsive chord in us because we are very critical of that type of poetry and because we accept it only when it presents a certain awe, a certain sense of the mystery of the infinite. (pp. 289-90)

For us, the poetry of Rousseau's second manner, satirical and humorous poetry, is definitely minor, much more so than it was in Rousseau's day. But in those of Rousseau's poems that are in what we call the intimate manner—many of the cantatas, a few odes, a few epigrams, several of the *poésies diverses*—there is to be found a delicate, restrained quality, which runs from gentle wistfulness to plaintive melancholy, and which, to a reader who is sufficiently familiar with the language, conveys a poetic feeling, suggests a mood, a fragrance of the past. It is not the melancholy of the Romantics, breast-beating or querulous, and too often frank and explicit. It is its very reticence and *quasi* unconsciousness that makes it appeal to us, that makes it, if not the expression of the inexpressible, at least the expression of the mystery of a past age. The appreciative reader can find in it the same impression that he gets from the tinkle of a harpsichord or from the misty landscapes

and the quizzical, wistful faces in a Watteau painting. (pp. 290-91)

[Let] us sum up by saying that Jean-Baptiste Rousseau is, historically, a poet of considerable importance, since he is the best representative of a significant, though little-known, phase in the evolution of French poetry. From the absolute point of view, he is a poet who followed an ideal which no longer seems adequate to us, and who was a great master in the use of a technique which is now almost completely forgotten. To appreciate his work, the modern reader must learn his language, not an easy task, but no more difficult than that required to penetrate the obscurity of certain admired modern poets. Those who can comprehend Jean-Baptiste Rousseau's poetic language will find that not infrequently he created discreetly certain moods, ranging from gentle wistfulness to plaintive melancholy, that are still a source of poetic enjoyment. (pp. 293-94)

> *Henry A. Grubbs, in his* Jean-Baptiste Rousseau: His Life and Works, *Princeton University Press, 1941, 300 p.*

ROBERT FINCH   (essay date 1966)

[*Finch is an American-born Canadian poet, literary critic, and educator specializing in French literature. In the following excerpt, he canvasses Rousseau's poetry, discussing his major themes and concerns.*]

Because of the "factional hatred of a brilliant and influential critic [Sainte-Beuve]" [see Additional Bibliography] Jean-Baptiste Rousseau (1671-1741), known throughout his century as "le grand Rousseau," "le grand lyrique français," remained from 1829 to 1940 either condescendingly despised or all but forgotten. Now, thanks to recent scholarship, the way has been opened for objective reconsideration of a poet who was famous as such even before the publication of his immediately successful and oft-reprinted works. (p. 101)

Rousseau's *odes sacrées*, of which there are nineteen, sing the trials and triumphs of the heart. Firmly based on Holy Scripture, they are neither translations nor paraphrases, but the reflection of a modern heart as mirrored in hearts of the past. The heart is, indeed, Rousseau's first concern, the mind coming second. . . . The *odes sacrées* may be said to constitute an *école spirituelle*, a disclosing of the secrets of the human heart in such a way as to reveal the hearts of both poet and reader. The lessons are profound, arising from meditation deeply felt. The poet sings, for example, of the revelation of God in creation, of God's omnipresence, of the strength of God and the weakness of man, of anxiety as to the ways of Providence, of the true nature of prayer, of the true nature of gratitude to God, of the unshakeable peace of those who put their trust in Him, of the truly righteous man, of true greatness in leaders, of the temporal happiness of the wicked, of hypocrites, of slanderers, and of the last judgment.

Two of the finest of these poems, **"Sur l'Aveuglement des Hommes du siècle"** and **"Pour une Personne convalescente,"** are "imitations libres" ["free imitations"] of portions of Scripture in much the same sense . . . as Claudel's ode, **"Magnificat,"** is a free imitation of the Magnificat of the Blessed Virgin Mary. **"Sur l'Aveuglement des Hommes du siècle"** rings with the powerful emotions of the speaker as he faces the follies of his time. . . . (pp. 102-03)

"Pour une Personne convalescente," inspired by the song of Hezekiah, catches the ever-modern crepuscular state of both physical and spiritual convalescence.... (p. 103)

The wide range of tone in the sacred odes is the more impressive in view both of their closely related subject matter and of the fact that the author undoubtedly thought of them as forming a definite series. Yet each poem stands complete and perfect in itself, fully enjoyable without reference to its neighbours. As a sequence the *odes sacrées* provide a striking example of unity in variety and variety in unity.

The same is true of the first twelve *odes en musique* or *odes allégoriques,* a set of poems that sing the vicissitudes of amatory love. The possible sources of inspiration for this new lyric genre were several. Rousseau, having received the classical education of his time, was well-acquainted with mythology. Despite its defects, opera, especially that of Lully, whom he admired, increased his familiarity with the mythological beings who had peopled it since 1671 and were to do so for the next hundred years. In the splendid establishments of his wealthy patrons, similar beings were to be met with in tapestry, painting and sculpture. Beneath their silent but eloquent gaze the poet listened to their stories as recounted in Italian cantatas which, after Lully's death in 1687, came into sudden fashion, along with Italian music as a whole. To a poet who was also a musician, disappointed with the complexities and artificialities of opera, these cantatas made a special appeal. Their brevity and relative simplicity brought them nearer to being purely lyric poetry. He resolved to imitate them.

At first he followed the structure of his Italian models. Their texts, however, entirely subordinate to the music, were primarily a vehicle for the display of vocal virtuosity. Such combinations seemed out of harmony with the spirit of the French language. Rousseau was quick to perceive his mistake.... This led him to a complete revision of form, style and content.... The result was an original series of productions to which he also gave the name of *Nouveautés* ["novelties"].

The term was appropriate. In the first place, the situations are mainly the product of the poet's imagination. Secondly, the mythological characters are not presented as merely such, nor as decorative material, but as figures aptly suggestive of the modern lover's inner life. Moreover, these first twelve *odes allégoriques* constitute a novel and highly poetic *école d'amour* ["school of love"], the lessons of which, prosaically stated, are: (*1*) the uselessness of trying to thwart true love (**"Diane"**); (*2*) the superiority of considerate over inconsiderate affection (**"Adonis"**); (*3*) love is preferable to the poetry it inspires (**"Triomphe de l' Amour"**); (*4*) true union defeats promiscuity (**"L'Hymen"**); (*5*) self-confidence in love may prove dangerous over-credulity (**"Amymone"**); (*6*) a lover's changes of mood are but the growing-pains of love (**"Thétis"**); (*7*) love cannot be had at will (**"Circé"**); (*8*) procrastination wears love out (**"Céphale"**); (*9*) love is a peaceful feast of harmony, beauty and conviviality (**"Bacchus"**); (*10*) love, if let be, would conquer all (**"Les Forges de Lemnos"**); (*11*) jealous vengeance in love rebounds on the vengeful (**"Les Filets de Vulcain"**). The twelfth lesson (**"Les Bains de Thomery"**), that love and loveliness are interdependent now as of old, is addressed to, and presents, a modern woman, the "Vénus nouvelle," as she appeared at Thomery, to this day a popular bathing beach on the Seine.

The true subject of these *cantates* is not the joys and sorrows of mythological characters but the feelings of a poet who perceives embodied in them the joys and sorrows of his own world. They are thus odes in the fullest sense, i.e., poems intended to be sung, by a single person, the poet, who records in them his sensitive reaction to a significant human experience, one in which his poetic genius permits him to be, simultaneously, observer, participant and assessor, both on his own behalf and that of his hearer.

Originality of theme dictated original handling. Since the *cantate* involves a poet's vision of the beginning, development and conclusion of a given matter, together with the affective commentary induced by each of these, its form falls naturally into three twofold sections, Aa, Bb, Cc, the structure of the Italian cantata. Under Rousseau's manipulation the form achieves new force and effectiveness, through the flexibility with which the length and rhythm of a section are governed by its content and by the close weaving of every detail into the texture of the entire poem. This double care in formal presentation ensures the individuality of each *cantate,* an individuality further heightened by a style alternatively expository and affective, finally admonitory, and everywhere suffused with the poet's sensibility.... Even without being sung, Rousseau's twelve *odes en musique* can still find answer in a listening heart. (pp. 105-07)

In addition to *odes sacrées* and *odes allégoriques,* J.-B. Rousseau wrote three other books of odes, thirty-five in all.... The assumption is often made that eighteenth-century odes, even when differing in subject, are practically identical in tone and style. Such could be, and is, true of bad poets, of which this century, too, had its share. It is not so with Rousseau as a brief examination of his thirty-five separate odes makes clear.

These may be divided into four groups, according to subject-matter. Thirteen have to do with people, seven with ideas, nine with events, six with the poet and his art.

I. Four subjects of the first group are contrastedly serious: (1) the effect of a baby's birth, (2) of a woman's life, (3) of a man's life, (4) of a death:

(1) **"Sur la naissance du duc de Bretagne."** Far from being a mere *pièce d'occasion*, this poem sings not only of a particular little prince but of that joyful hope that is felt whenever a man is born into the world....

(2) **"A l'impératrice Amélie."** A woman's goodness, courtesy, piety, studiousness and encouragement of genius prove that "l'éloquence des paroles" ["the eloquence of words"] is not to be compared with a life in action..., the precepts of philosophy are secondary to those of example.... (p. 108)

(3) **"Au comte du Luc."** Were the poet worthy, his prayer would move the fates to spare his friend's life because of what it means to others and take the poet's life instead. Yet the law that rules all lives composes each of good and ill. His friend is no exception, save in the sense that his sole ill is lack of bodily strength. His spirit, transcending this obstacle, and faithful to the task of the true statesman, has by wise conciliation brought about benefits to many, both now and hereafter. Of hereafter the poet is not qualified to speak; of the present he can and does, and of himself as one who, even in the very different sphere of a poet's existence, also benefits by his friend's example, taking from it fresh courage to confront ever greater difficulties in the interest of ever higher achievement.

(4) **"Sur la mort du prince de Conti."** A poem vibrant with affectionate feeling at the loss, in the prime of life, of one universally beloved. But Conti is not dead.... His life informs

even his absence, comforts those who mourn his disappearing, and makes praise, that most dangerous of enemies, superfluous.

It is to be noted that while the tone varies in each of these four odes, the underlying theme, or sustaining harmony, is the same: the significance of an individual human being to his fellows and his responsibility, whether potential, actual or completed, towards them.

The remaining nine odes of the first group are of a more intimate nature and their style is also correspondingly varied. The first two express gratifying solicitude:

(5) "A Zinzindorf." An overworked statesman is gracefully begged to take time off for country enjoyments and (this with a touch of amusement) to moderate his enterprises as even Louis XIV was advised to do by as humble a counsellor.

(6) "A Caumartin." Similar advice to a city-bound business-friend, a new note being that the country is the one place where a man can be fully himself. . . . The next two are light-hearted expressions of a concern that conceals delicate criticism under a wreath of highly literate banter:

(7) "A Courtin." A warning against following the wiseacres Chrysippus, Zeno, Seneca, Epictetus and Diogenes to the exclusion of the poets Homer, Anacreon and Horace and the *bons vivants* Cato, Sonning and J.-B. Rousseau.

(8) "A une jeune veuve." A young widow apparently acquainted with the classics is urged to benefit by examples in them of youthful widows who reasonably forsook their weeds, advice even more piquant if, as might be the case, not intended for the eyes of the widow in question. The next three odes show the poet responding sensitively to critical junctures in the lives of friends:

(9) "Pour Mme la D . . . de N . . . sur le gain d'un procès." Righteous indignation over the long-drawn-out public humiliation of an innocent person turns into rejoicing as justice finally makes the truth clear.

(10) "A d'Ussé." To one in whom misfortune has brought about an "ennui volontaire," the poet recalls the unwisdom of giving way to disappointment, which is temporary, not terminal, less trial than testing.

(11) "A Duché." Unable to join this friend who is in a fever over a real fever, over the rapid approach of the end of summer and over the finishing of a tragedy he is writing, the poet understandingly presents the latter distress as the worst, while prophesying its ultimately successful outcome.

The last two of this group are merry invitations:

(12) "A Chaulieu." The poet forgives a poet for preferring the country in spring, but now that hot summer has come, bids him return to the shady city where welcoming friends await him.

(13) "A de Bonneval." Deftly picturing the delightful occasion, the poet asks this friend to preside, in harvest-time, at a judging of wines.

II. It is hardly surprising that one so sensitive to human relationships should also be moved by ideas arising from their contemplation. Of seven odes thus inspired, the first four have to do with character.

(1) "Sur le devoir et le sort des grands hommes." A leader, by virtue of his calling, is destined to isolation, self-sacrifice, on behalf of others. . . . For the sake of that calling, he must not let himself be lost to sight. . . . Presence is the best publicity. Too long an absence may cause tongues to wag with fearful consequence. . . . But, whether favoured or rejected, the true leader retains his disinterestedness. . . .

There can be, of course, a leader's tragedy:

(2) "Imitée d'Horace." Even a greatly gifted leader may succumb to the charms of a faithless woman, unaware that he is one of a series and destined, in his turn, to be cast off for another. Yet what a man really is outlasts all else:

(3) "A la Fortune." Fortune's fleeting vanities and vagaries may disappear; character is indestructible. . . .

Character is also unforgettable:

(4) "Au prince Eugène de Savoie." Time may obliterate fame but not memory of those who, like Eugène, have preferred truth to trappings.

The last three odes of this group are concerned with collective character, i.e., civilization. The problem of peace:

(5) "A la Paix." Has peace fled earth because of her profaners? Then what of the innocent and their inhuman persecution? Must peace defer to war? Are humans doing expiation? For crimes? For impiety? For imposture? Then may we be granted penitence, new hearts. Indeed, there are signs this prayer is being answered, notably through the influence of Fleury, true peacemaker.

The problem of education:

(6) "A La Fare." To this poet-friend, who nostalgically lamented the golden age, Rousseau replies that the cause of modern ills is the misapplication of *la raison* and (this before 1711) that the sole remaining trace of the golden age still to be found is in the almost purely instinctive life of the North American Indian. . . .

In the face of great general problems, there is but one thing for each separate member of society to do: realize the incomparable value of the moment at hand and function as its master by living it to the full:

(7) "Sur un commencement d'année," for

> Le moment passé n'est plus rien,
> L'avenir peut ne jamais être:
> Le présent est l'unique bien
> Dont l'homme soit vraiment le maître.
>
> [The moment past exists no longer,
> The Future can never be:
> The present—that is the special time
> Of which man is truly the master.]

III. The nine odes inspired by events may, for convenience, be linked with the ode "A la Paix," each being, so to speak, an offshoot of one or another of its implicit notions. Thus civil war among the Swiss is deplored ("Aux Suisses"); Christian monarchs are urged to save Venice from the infidel aggressor ("Aux princes chrétiens"); their departing troops are cheered on by a reminder of previous victories ("A l'ambassadeur de Venise"); and a triumphal battle of the campaign ("Sur la bataille de Peterwaradin") is celebrated. . . . One is on the signing by Germany, France, Great Britain and Holland, of a treaty which promises peace ("A l'empereur, après la conclusion de la quadruple alliance"); one extols (before 1723) British constitutional monarchy ("Au roi de la Grande-Bretagne") and one ("Au roi de Pologne") a constitutional monarch. Finally, whereas "A Philippe de Vendôme" praises a performer of beneficent military exploits, the last ode of this group, **"Au prince Eugène, après la paix de Passarowitz,"** pleads with the prince to forsake war for peace and the arts, and by thus giving fresh impetus to poetry, give the latter new reason to remember him.

It is already evident that, while the subjects of J.-B. Rousseau's separate odes are widely varied, they spring from certain major preoccupations of the poet's mind and feelings: (1) the importance of character and of human relationships, particularly those of an individual toward his friends; (2) the importance of the problems of peace and of education, and the solution of these problems by individuals.

IV. Six odes deal directly with the poet himself and his art. **"A Philomèle"** is an exquisitely modulated song that springs from a secret sorrow too deep for words. **"Palinodie"** is the bitter eloquence of a soul deceived.... **"A de Lannoy"** is inspired by the spiritual effects of physical suffering. Here J.-B. Rousseau, suddenly stricken with paralysis, half alive, half dead, conveys to a faithful friend the resultant inward experience. Longing for death, condemned to linger, the poet hears the voice of Malherbe remind him that the sadness sung by poets is the sadness brought by life, the consoling compensation the hope of life to come. **"Ode à la postérité"** is the poet's last will and testament. Recognizing the faults and failings of his youth, but protesting for the last time against calumnies that have embittered the rest of his life, Rousseau gives and bequeathes his writings as the best witness to what he was and what he tried to be. Finally, **"A Malherbe"** and **"Sur les divinités poétiques"** are part of his defense of himself as artist.... (pp. 109-15)

The themes contained in these last six odes are essentially those which . . . found various developments in all the rest: religion, private and social relationships, and the art of the poetry they kindle. Falsely accused of infamy and banished from France for life, J.-B. Rousseau was forced to lead an existence in which human ties and personal meditation took on a specially heightened emotional significance. Not all the odes through which his feelings found outlet appeal to modern taste. A few, such as **"Sur l'Aveuglement des Hommes du siècle," "Circé," "A Philomèle,"** can stand with the best. Yet most, on careful reading, are alive with a vitality for which Rousseau himself offers the striking explanation:

> Il y a longtemps que j'ai prouvé, en vers, que les trois quarts de l'esprit sont dans le cœur.

> [It has been a long time since I proved, in verse, that three fourths of the spirit is in the heart.]

While J.-B. Rousseau's poetry is everywhere informed by sensibility, not all of it took the form of odes. Twelve *allégories,* ninety *épigrammes,* nine *épîtres* and a few *poésies diverses* make up the considerably smaller portion of his work.

His two books of *allégories,* twelve in all, were regarded, along with his *cantates,* as a genre new to French poetry. Unquestionably experimental, they attempt to express truths of his time, as the poet sees them, by means of a narrative which presents mythological, allegorical and typical personages. A summary of the lessons they embody throws light on the nature of these poems. The first six are satirical in tone. (1) More disastrous than opera itself is the commercialized librettist (**"l'Opéra de Naples"**). (2) Even Laverna, goddess of dishonest persons, who protects such as deceive others, and provides opera-purveyors with the handsome mask of opera itself, refuses to conceal the sort of dishonesty practised behind it (**"Le**

Masque de Laverne"); (3) Parisian society fights shy of a beautiful and discreet nymph until the day she commits her first impropriety by uttering a five-letter word; she then 'belongs' (**"La Liturgie de Cythère"**); (4) for love-birds, Paris is a cage, easier to get into than escape from (**"La Volière"**); (5) the Paris *parvenu,* stupidly cruel to those without money, stupidly indulgent towards those who live on his, learns wisdom, if ever, through reverses (**"Midas"**); (6) Love and Time are always at war—except for thirty years (**"Le Tems"**).

The second six *allégories* are hortatory and monitory. (1) The spirit of hypocrisy, Torticolis (Wryneck), still combats the God-loving spirit, Philothea, though in vain (**"Torticolis"**). (2) Sophronyme (a name possibly suggested by that of the fact-facing poet Sophron), dissatisfied with existence and with himself . . . , pays heed . . . to the voice of divine revelation that declares the nature of the Creator, of creation and of man's spirit which, however it differ from one individual to another, can bridge the gap between man and God. Cheered and encouraged, Sophronyme (who is J.-B. Rousseau and Everyman) prepares to make a fresh start (**"Sophronyme"**). (3) Those responsible for the miscarriage of justice may not suffer in this world, they will in the next (**"Le Jugement de Pluton"**). (4) Human ills are not the result of Pandora's action but of human tampering with imponderables (**"La Morosophie"**); by his substitution of reason for wisdom, modern man forfeits all but occasional glimpses of the latter (**"Minerva"**). (6) That Virtue and her companions, Joy, Freedom and Honour, when attacked by Envy, Fraud, Treachery, Lying, Discord and Calumny, are defended by Truth is as certain today as ever (**"La Vérité"**).

Six *allégories* cover commercialism in art, dishonesty, social veneer, philandering, the irresponsibility of the wealthy, the transience of physical potency; six cover hypocrisy, despair, injustice, misplaced curiosity, the abuse of reason, and the dual nature of man, together with their correctives, seeking after God, heeding of Scripture, awareness of judgment to come, the recognition of human limitations, wisdom's superiority to reason and truth's ultimate triumph. The twelve may be said to constitute a school of ethics, the lessons of which still have pertinency. Their presentation has not. Rousseau could count on having his allegorical symbols interpreted by the contemporary reader in terms of his own times. For the reader of today the truths remain, the times have changed. To all but a specialist in the history of the period, these poems have, inevitably, lost much of their original vividness. Opera is no longer a burning question. Social abuses, still the same wolves, wear other clothing. One thing has not changed; it is for this reason that the three final *allégories* are now the most telling. Even a modern reader has no difficulty in interpreting allegorical symbols in terms of his own heart.

Rousseau's ninety epigrams, instead of being, like those of most of his contemporaries, a few lines of introduction to a stinging conclusion, are little poems in which, from the first, each word contributes to the cumulative effectiveness of the whole. Their subject-matter is as varied as that of the odes, involving anecdote, portrait, criticism, reflection and emotion. Eleven are miniature dramatic scenes, having the brilliant concision of etchings by Callot, whose work Rousseau admired. (pp. 115-16)

J.-B. Rousseau was a modern, in the fullest sense. He admired the poets of old not as monuments but as alive; they inspired not copies but new originals. His *odes sacrées,* instead of recalling the experiences of David, Hezekiah and Solomon, relive them in terms of the present. Overtones of Homer, Virgil,

Pindar, Ovid, Anacreon and Horace linger in many of his other odes but the melody and harmony are Rousseau's own. His two imitations of Horace are transformations. He sought only to make his epigrams worthy of Martial. His poem, **"Contre les détracteurs de l'antiquité,"** by its very beauty, while defending the ancients, defends the moderns. His art is grafted onto the traditions of the past: it bears its own fruit.

He acknowledges three modern masters: Marot, Malherbe, Boileau. Here again, what attracted and influenced him was less technique than character, not letter but spirit. Marot and Malherbe were as close to him as Boileau, whom he knew. (p. 117)

J.-B. Rousseau generously acknowledged his masters, ancient and modern. They indeed taught him much, but their pupil, as a poet, stands on his own merits. Remaining true to the fundamental principles of those from whom he learned them, he established his own directions and emphases, which were in harmony with the newer trends: the importance of personal feeling; the danger of allowing *l'esprit* ["the spirit"] to eclipse *le cœur* ["the heart"]; the necessity for enthusiasm and inspiration; the recommendation of contemporary subject-matter and of its original treatment. To these may be added his recognition of the individuality of the writer, of the plurality of taste, and of the reader's sixth sense of reciprocal aptitude.

His incessant attempts to vary form, tone, manner and rhythm; his invention of new forms toward those ends; his emphasis on a certain *désordre*, conversational communication raised to a level at which discontinuity, ellipsis and digression could perform their highest function; his preference for short, alert metres; his comparative freedom in the matter of vocabulary; his idea of a constantly renewable poetic language of symbols, mythological, allegorical, typical or natural; these identify him as belonging to a fresh orientation. (p. 134)

But J.-B. Rousseau was above all a poet of the new era because of his particular feeling for people. He saw their upward struggle as a matter of intercommunications, less of the mind than of the heart, and his own task, as poet, to make those intercommunications clearer. This he accomplished by concentrating his attention on three relationships, each personal. The relationship of man to himself, on which subject Rousseau's often lively muses offer the up-to-date advice:

> Sois de toi-même un sévère inspecteur.

> [Be to yourself a severe inspector.]

> **["Epître aux muses"]**

The relationship of a man to his associates, estrangement from whom is among life's greatest tragedies. Finally, the relationship of a man to God, especially that of a poet, since Rousseau deems an artist futile who fails to place his creations in the hand of his Creator. Through constant absorption in the changing cross-tensions of this threefold involvement Rousseau determined—and achieved—the central aim of his art: *trouver la clef de l'âme* ["to find the key to the soul"]. (p. 135)

> *Robert Finch, "J.-B. Rousseau: 'Trouver la clef de l'âme'," in his* The Sixth Sense: Individualism in French Poetry, 1686-1760, *University of Toronto Press, 1966, pp. 101-35.*

ADDITIONAL BIBLIOGRAPHY

Davis, James Herbert, Jr. "Jean-Baptiste Rousseau and the Eighteenth-Century *Pièce Restituée*." *Kentucky Romance Quarterly* XVI, No. 3 (1969): 231-41.
   Examines Rousseau's revisions of four original plays: Pierre Corneille's *Le cid*, Paul Scarron's *Don Japhet d'Arménie*, Tristan L'Hermite's *La Mariane*, and Jean La Fontaine's *Le florentin*.

Grubbs, Henry A. "The Vogue of Jean-Baptiste Rousseau." *PMLA* LV, No. 1 (March 1940): 139-66.
   Close examination of the rise and decline of Rousseau's literary reputation, with reference to such French critics of Rousseau's work as Vauvenargues, La Harpe, Voltaire, Lanson, and Sainte-Beuve.

Lewis, Robert G., and Morris, Walter J. "Memoranda and Documents: John Quincy Adams's Verse Translations of Jean-Baptiste Rousseau's 'Ode à la fortune'." *The New England Quarterly* XLIV, No. 3 (September 1971): 444-58.
   Discusses and reprints Adams's metrical translation of Rousseau's best-known ode.

Sainte-Beuve, C. A. "Jean-Baptiste Rousseau." In his *Portraits littéraires*, Vol. I, pp. 128-144. Paris: Garnier Frères, 1862.
   Reprint of Sainte-Beuve's watershed 1829 article in the *Revue de Paris*, in which the critic comments harshly on virtually every aspect of Rousseau's life and work.

(Captain) John Smith

1580?-1631

English historian, autobiographer, and poet.

One of the principal founders of the first permanent English settlement in the New World and an intrepid explorer of colonial America, Smith was a prolific early-American historian and an indefatigable propagandist on behalf of New-World colonization. Ironically, he is enshrined in the popular imagination for his passive role in a single incident which may never have actually taken place: his last-minute rescue from death through the intervention of the Indian maiden Pocahontas. The dramatic tale of how Pocahontas shielded the captured and condemned Captain Smith from the war clubs of his would-be executioners, thereby winning his reprieve from her father Chief Powhatan, is one of the most attractive and enduring of American legends. The source for this romantic story is Smith's own *Generall Historie of Virginia, New-England, and the Summer Isles*, the most comprehensive of his several historical and descriptive accounts of colonial America. Regarded by some as valuable historical testimony from a colonial eyewitness, this work and Smith's others are denounced by other scholars as self-aggrandizing fiction. Nonetheless, critics agree that Smith's works are worthy of study, if only for the light they shed on their author, one of the most interesting and controversial figures of seventeenth-century America.

In any consideration of Smith's life it is important to note that much of our knowledge of his biography derives from Smith's own accounts, the veracity of which is hotly debated. Additional documentary evidence, even where available, is frequently subject to differing scholarly interpretations. Be that as it may, the essentials of Smith's autobiography are usually accepted, though certain of his more exotic adventures are discounted by some. Smith was born to a farming family in Willoughby, Lincolnshire. He left school at fifteen, serving briefly as a merchant's apprentice before embarking on the first of his many adventures: a four-year stint as European traveler and soldier in the Netherlands. Following a short return to England, Smith departed again in 1600; after an adventurous European journey, he served as a mercenary against the Turks of Hungary and Transylvania. During this period, according to his autobiographical relation, *The True Travels, Adventures, and Observations of Captaine John Smith*, he performed one of his most dramatic and daring exploits, including his use of pyrotechnics as a signaling device in battle (for which he was promoted to captain), his slaying of three Turks successively in single combat (which feat prompted Prince Sigismund Bathori of Transylvania to grant him a coat of arms adorned with three Turks' heads), and his escape after capture and enslavement by the enemy.

Back in England, Smith became active in the London Company, joining a group of some 100 colonists who set sail under its auspices for America in December of 1606. Their mission was threefold: to find any trace of Sir Walter Raleigh's "lost colony" of Roanoke, to search for gold, and to establish a permanent settlement. During the long sea voyage, the fiery-tempered, highly outspoken Smith was placed under arrest for reasons not sufficiently clear; though he was apparently charged with complicity in a thwarted mutiny, many biographers sur-

mise that Smith's offense was more likely his inability to get along with other members of the expedition. Shortly after the three ships of the London Company sailed into Chesapeake Bay and up the James River in April 1607, the colonists chose a site on the Virginia Peninsula to build the settlement they called Jamestown. A short time earlier, having landed for a brief time at what is today known as Cape Henry, they had opened, per instructions, a sealed box containing the names of those selected by the Company to govern the settlement. Although Smith (now released from arrest) was one of the seven men chosen, he was not immediately allowed by the others to take his position on the council. Nonetheless, life in the New World agreed with the adventuresome Smith, who during the next months organized and led several exploratory expeditions of the area. Smith's own accounts of his explorations and his encounters with the Indians are set forth in his *A True Relation of Such Occurences and Accidents of Noate As Hath Hapned in Virginia*, as are his largely disapproving opinions of the policies and plans embraced by the Jamestown council.

Although Smith eventually took his place on the council and indeed became its president in September of 1608, he suffered from a chronic inability to relate peaceably to his peers. Characterized by biographers as a self-assured man, competent and efficient but opinionated and even arrogant, he inspired deep dislike in those—and they were many—whose policies he opposed. The settlement's political turmoil was exacerbated by the many other troubles that plagued Jamestown: sickness, lack of food, shiftlessness among the settlers, vulnerability to Indian attack. Smith did what he could to alleviate these problems, trading with the Indians for food, taking charge of Jamestown's fortification and armament, and attempting—through his direction of a rigorous program of building, planting crops, and manufacture of essential products—to make Jamestown a self-sufficient community. But Smith's governance, though effective, was sometimes harsh, and this, together with his undisguised belief that only he could successfully manage the settlement, caused many of his companions to regard him with even greater animosity. (Many historians have remarked, however, that the efficacy of Smith's policies is vindicated by the fact that after his departure the settlement was nearly extinguished due to apparent mismanagement and a series of resultant disasters.)

To the relief of many of his fellow colonists, Smith returned to England in 1609 to recover from wounds sustained when his powder bag caught fire and exploded. In England, he published *A Map of Virginia. With a Description of the Countrey, the Commodities, People, Government and Religion,* a description and history of Virginia combined with a defense of his own activities. No longer welcome with the company that had first sent him to the New World, Smith allied himself with the Plymouth Company and, in 1614, sailed as an explorer to New England. (It was Smith, incidentally, who gave the region its name.) This journey gave rise to his *A Description of New-England* and *New Englands Trials.* The voyage was Smith's last, though not for lack of interest on Smith's part; two subsequent trips were canceled and his offer to accompany the Mayflower pilgrims to New England was declined. Smith lived in England for the remainder of his life, devoting his final ten years to writing about his adventures. Still, he had long since lived what Alan Hamilton described in a 1980 London *Times* article as a "swashbuckling life beside which the screen exploits of Errol Flynn appear as the doings of a temperance tea-dance."

Most of Smith's works deal with some facet of colonial America. The most ambitious and well-known of these is *The Generall Historie of Virginia, New-England, and the Summer Isles.* Divided into six books, *The Generall Historie* is not exclusively the work of Smith, as it incorporates much material from other historians (variously quoted directly, summarized, paraphrased, or condensed), nor are those parts written by Smith entirely original, as he revised many of his earlier writings for inclusion in the *Historie.* Book I is an account, largely culled from Richard Hakluyt's earlier compilation of diverse sources, *The Principall Navigations, Voiages and Discoveries of the English Nation* (1589), of the early voyages to and the settlement of the Virginia colony of Roanoke. Book II is a slight revision of "A Description of Virginia," the first part of the earlier *A Map of Virginia.* In "A Description of Virginia," written exclusively by Smith, minute descriptions of Virginia's geography, climate, flora, fauna, and human inhabitants are coupled with Smith's enthusiastic reports of the opportunities and natural products afforded by the land. A great deal of the work consists of Smith's careful observations of the appearance, characteristics, and customs of the Indians, which many critics claim display an admirable anthropological talent. The third book of the *Historie* is based on the second part of *A Map of Virginia,* of which Smith was but one of several authors and compilers, and which recounts the history of the colony from 1607 to 1609. Nevertheless, this book includes the great-

est amount of Smith's original writing in the *Historie,* as the earlier work is much amended and embellished here. Occurrences not mentioned or only hinted at in *A Map of Virginia* receive full treatment in Book III, and Smith's own part in the adventures he describes is significantly enlarged. Indeed, Book III of *The Generall Historie* is of paramount importance to critics because of its relevance to what has been termed the "Great Debate" in Smith scholarship. Within a section of new material included in the book, written sixteen years after the incident is supposed to have occurred, Smith briefly related the now famous story of how Pocahontas saved him from death. Yet this incident was not included in Smith's earlier telling of his capture by Powhatan, recounted in *A True Relation,* which was written in 1608, right after the events it describes transpired. Book IV extends the history of the Virginia colony from 1609 to 1624; this section is necessarily a compilation of other sources, as Smith was not in Virginia during the period covered. This book, however, does contain much that is original, for it is replete with what Everett H. Emerson has called Smith's "editorializing"—Smith's attempts to establish himself as an authority on colonial matters and to vindicate his own preferred policies and past actions. Book V is a history and description of the Bermudas; as Smith had never been to these "Summer Isles," his account relies wholly on other sources, mainly a manuscript copy of Nathaniel Butler's *The Historye of the Bermudaes* (not published until 1882). The sixth book, "The Generall Historie of New-England," consists of revisions of Smith's *Description of New-England* and *New Englands Trials,* as well as his incorporation of other accounts of the area. Smith's two works about New England are similar in scope to "A Description of Virginia," though they are more obviously propagandist in intent. *A Description of New-England* combines Smith's observations of the area with his remarks on the desirability of colonizing it and his practical suggestions for doing so. *New Englands Trials* is a similar propagandist tract, describing the attributes and possibilities of the region. These works, in common with most of Smith's others, do not lack autobiographical elements; the New England works show touches of Smith's personal bitterness that he was never granted the opportunity to put his colonization plans into action.

A True Relation has the distinction of being the first book written in America. It is both more immediate and more personal than is *The Generall Historie;* whereas even the personal parts of the *Historie* are written in the third person, *A True Relation* is told in the first. Although the work is an account of the establishment of Jamestown, some readers have contended that it is really less historical than autobiographical, as Smith unmistakably emerges as the hero of the piece. Even more forthrightly autobiographical, though written in the third person, is Smith's *True Travels,* the relation of his youthful adventures in Europe. It has been noted that the book, replete as it is with excitement, danger, courageous deeds, and hairbreadth escapes, reads like a particularly action-packed adventure novel. Interspersed with autobiographical elements of *The True Travels* is Smith's incorporation of material from various sources of information on southeast Europe, most notably the otherwise unknown *The Warres of Transilvania, Wallachi, and Moldavia* of Francisco Ferneza and Richard Knolles's *Generall Historie of the Turkes* (1621). Appended to *The True Travels* is a continuation of *The Generall Historie,* which brings the history of English colonization of America down to 1629. In addition to his prose work, three poems are attributed to Smith, though they have rarely been studied. Of these, two are encomiums prefixed to the works of other authors, and one,

''The Sea-Marke,'' appears in Smith's own *Advertisements for the Unexperienced Planters of New England.*

''Racy'' and ''picturesque'' are words frequently used to describe Smith's writing. While critics agree that Smith was by no means a flawless prose stylist, they have praised his enthusiasm and his ability to sustain narrative interest, maintaining that, above all else, Smith was an excellent raconteur. At its best, his prose conveys a sense of immediacy, of ''earnestness,'' according to George S. Hillard, who adds, ''his heart is in every thing he writes.'' Some critics have objected to Smith's emphasis on himself in his works, viewing it as blatant self-aggrandizing and distasteful braggadocio. Others have countered that Smith's focus is but a natural corollary of the kind of books he was writing, that as Smith was an active participant in the events he described, he must inevitably take center stage. These commentators, while acknowledging with Morison that ''whatever subject [Smith] touches leads back very shortly to Captain John Smith, his trials, hairbreadth escapes, bad breaks, and unappreciated virtues,'' find Smith's egotism a part of his charm, or, at the very worst, an unobjectionable peccadillo.

''Was John Smith a liar? Or was his own dramatic story of his life the simple truth? The writer bold enough to put forth an answer would do well to have a sword as well as a typewriter around.'' This assertion, made by Marshall Fishwick in 1958, is an apt testimony to the intensity of the debate that lies at the core of Smith criticism: are Smith's works to be accepted as historical truth or as imaginative tall tales? Smith's accounts of himself, his observations, and his adventures were largely accepted without question throughout his lifetime and for over two hundred years after his death. One atypical skeptic was Thomas Fuller, who wrote in the latter half of the seventeenth century that Smith's ''perils, preservations, dangers, deliverences . . . seem to most men above belief.'' Henry Wharton, however, exemplified the prevailing opinion when he declared in the preface to his enthusiastic 1685 retelling of Smith's adventures: ''I pledge my honor that this entire story is true.'' To most scholars, Smith was the unquestioned authority on Smith and on his historical era; biographers, finding their research already done by their subject, simply rephrased Smith's own narratives, while historians, accepting Smith as one of their number, included his testimony as fact in their own historical works. Further, Smith became a genuine hero, first to his English compatriots—Wharton proclaimed him ''equal to the most celebrated heroes of antiquity''—and soon, and more lastingly, in America, which claimed him for its own. Innumerable novels, plays, poems, and children's stories were written about Smith, all celebrating his courage, his integrity, his exciting adventures—and all based on Smith's own relation of his life and exploits. The Pocahontas episode in particular captured the American imagination, assuming mythical proportions.

Smith's exalted reputation began to falter in 1858, when John Gorham Palfrey remarked, in his *History of New England during the Stuart Dynasty,* that he was ''haunted by incredulity respecting some of the adventures of Smith'' in *The True Travels.* Palfrey's questioning, confined to a footnote in a text otherwise faithful to Smith's account, elicited little attention, nor was much more accorded two years later to Charles Deane's comments (again articulated only in a footnote) on the discrepant versions of the Pocahontas episode in *A True Relation* and *The Generall Historie.* The controversy did not begin in earnest until 1867, when then-novice historian Henry Adams took up Deane's mild observations with a vengeance, publishing a scathing article designed to effect ''nothing less than the entire erasure of one of the most attractive portions of American history.'' Adams placed corresponding passages from *A True Relation* and *The Generall Historie* side by side to emphasize their discrepancies, concluding that such blatant differences as he noted must entirely discredit Smith as a reliable chronicler. Adams's attack launched a furious debate concerning Smith's veracity in general and the truthfulness of the Pocahontas incident in particular. Reviled by some as a braggart and a liar, Smith was just as passionately defended by others as a true— and truthful—American hero. Occurring as it did during the bitter aftermath of the American Civil War, the debate quickly took on an added dimension, becoming a contest between North and South. Many Southern historians accused Northerners (whose criticism, they believed, often evidenced personal animosity toward Smith the man) of attempting to discredit a genuine Southern hero, and, by extension, denigrate the South itself. Most commentators south of the Mason-Dixon line, then, believed that in defending Smith, they were defending nothing less than the cultural and historical honor of the South. For late nineteenth-century critics, the final blow to Smith's reputation for truthfulness was dealt by Lewis L. Kropf, a Hungarian historian. Kropf was the first to systematically compare Smith's descriptions of his early adventures and travels with what was actually known from other sources of southeastern European history and geography: all to the detriment of *The True Travels,* which Kropf dismissed as ''a pseudo-historical romance,'' adding, ''one feels inclined to suspect that [Smith] has not been at all to the south-east of Europe.''

As the nineteenth century gave way to the twentieth, the rancor and acrimony of the controversy lessened. Such ferocity as Edward D. Neill's contemptuous description of Smith as ''a gascon and a beggar'' or Alexander Brown's assertion that Smith's American work ''is in almost every sense a travesty on the true history of the early English colonization of North America'' softened into a more moderate approach. The evidence against Smith's veracity was largely (though in many cases grudgingly) acknowledged sufficiently damning, but still his work did not lack admirers. Though few commentators in the first half of the twentieth century cared (or dared) to defend Smith's truthfulness, favorable criticism existed, peppered with ''ifs'' and ''buts.'' Referring to the adventures related in *The True Travels,* A. G. Bradley wrote that ''even if they were mainly fiction [they] would be fiction of a stimulating kind''; Samuel Eliot Morison admitted: ''John Smith was a liar, if you will, but a thoroughly cheerful and generally harmless liar.'' But the veracity controversy was not ended, only in abeyance. Some recent critics, notably Laura Polanyi Striker, Bradford Smith, and Philip L. Barbour, have argued for the reinstatement of Smith as a reliable historian. Striker and others, doing new comparative research into verifiable history and *The True Travels,* have, they believe, effectively refuted the most damaging of Kropf's charges. In their biographies, Bradford Smith and Barbour have provided both solid evidence and plausible speculation to explain apparent discrepancies or inaccuracies in Smith's works. Bradford Smith has concluded: ''If Smith was an imposter, he was the most successful one in history, for even to this day he cannot be proved one.'' It would seem that the last word has yet to be heard on Smith's accuracy as a chronicler; perhaps the extent of his reliability can never be conclusively established.

Smith's contributions to early American colonization—both in Virginia, through his active role in the settlement of Jamestown, and in New England, via his explorations and the influence he exerted through his propagandist writings—are significant, earning him a unique and important place in American history. But just as important is Smith's place in the American imagination. Mary G. Lockwood, in a 1929 article in the *National Republic*, labeled Smith "the most romantic figure in American history," and in this context, whether or not some of his more remarkable adventures are true becomes, perhaps, almost a moot point. To many, the real importance of Smith lies not in his historical accuracy or his literary merit, but in his value as an American symbol, his nearly mythical status as the first hero of an evolving nation. As Bradford Smith has said of him: "He is our Odysseus, our Siegfried, our Aeneas."

(See also *Dictionary of Literary Biography*, Vol. 24: *American Colonial Writers, 1606-1734*, and Vol. 30: *American Historians, 1607-1865*.)

PRINCIPAL WORKS

A True Relation of Such Occurences and Accidents of Noate As Hath Hapned in Virginia since the First Planting of That Collony, Which is Now Resident in the South Part Thereof, till the Last Returne from There (prose) 1608
A Map of Virginia. With a Description of the Countrey, the Commodities, People, Government, and Religion . . . [with others] (prose) 1612
A Description of New-England; or, The Observations and Discoveries of Captain John Smith, (Admiral of That Country) in the North of America in the Year of Our Lord 1614, with the Successe of Six Ships That Went the Next Yeare 1615; and the Accidents Befell Him among the French Men of Warre: With the Proofe of the Present Benefit This Countrey Affoords: Whither This Present Yeare, 1616, Eight Voluntary Ships Are Gone to Make Further Tryall (prose) 1616
New Englands Trials. Declaring the Successe of 26 Ships Employed Thither within These Six Yeares: With the Benefit of That Countrey by Sea and Land: And How to Build Three-score Sayle of Good Ships, to Make a Little Navie Royall (prose) 1620
The Generall Historie of Virginia, New-England, and the Summer Isles: With the Names of the Adventurers, Planters, and Governours from Their First Beginning, Ano: 1584, to This Present 1624. With the Proceedings of Those Severall Colonies and the Accidents That Befell Them in All Their Journyes and Discoveries. Also the Maps and Descriptions of All Those Countryes, Their Commodities, People, Government, Customes, and Religion Yet Knowne. Divided into Six Bookes [with others] (prose) 1624
An Accidence; or, The Path-Way to Experience. Necessary for All Young Sea-men, or Those That Are Desirous to Goe to Sea, Briefly Shewing the Phrases, Offices, and Words of Command, Belonging to the Building, Ridging, and Sayling, a Man of Warre; and How to Manage a Fight at Sea. Together with the Charge and Duty of Every Officer, and Their Shares: Also the Names, Weight, Charge, Shot, and Powder, of All Sorts of Great Ordnance. With the Use of the Petty Tally (prose) 1626; also published as *A Sea Grammar, with the Plaine Exposition of Smiths Accidence for Young Sea-men . . .* [enlarged edition], 1627
†*The True Travels, Adventures, and Observations of Captaine John Smith, in Europe, Asia, Affrica, and America, from Anno Domini 1593, to 1629. His Accidents and Sea-fights in the Straights; His Service and Strategems of Warre in*

Hungaria, Transilvania, Wallachia, and Moldavia, against the Turks, and Tartars; His Three Single Combats betwixt the Christian Armie and the Turkes. After How He Was Taken Prisoner by the Turks, Sold for a Slave, Sent into Tartaria; His Description of the Tartars, Their Strange Manners and Customes of Religions, Diets, Buildings, Warres, Feasts, Ceremonies, and Living; How Hee Slew the Bashaw of Nalbrits in Cambia, and Escaped from the Turkes and Tartars. Together with a Continuation of His Generall Historie of Virginia, Summer-Iles, New England, and Their Proceedings, since 1624 to This Present 1629; as Also of the New Plantations of the Great River of the Amazons, the Iles of St. Christopher, Mevis, and Barbados in the West Indies . . . [with others] (prose) 1630
Advertisements for the Unexperienced Planters of New England, or Any Where; or, The Path-way to Experience to Erect a Plantation. With the Yearely Proceedings of This Country in Fishing and Planting, since the Yeare 1614, to the Yeare 1630, and Their Present Estate. Also How to Prevent the Greatest Inconveniences, by Their Proceedings in Virginia, and Other Plantations, by Approved Example. With the Countries Armes, a Description of the Coast, Harbours, Habitations, Land-markes, Latitude and Longitude: With the Map, Allowed by Our Royall King Charles (prose and poetry) 1631
Travels and Works of Captain John Smith, President of Virginia and Admiral of New England, 1580-1631. 2 vols. (prose and poetry) 1910
The Complete Works of Captain John Smith: 1580-1631. 3 vols. (prose and poetry) 1986

*This work contains revisions of the earlier *A Map of Virginia*, *A Description of New-England*, and *New Englands Trials*.

†An abridged portion of this work was originally published in *Purchas His Pilgrimes*, by Samuel Purchas, in 1625.

JOHN SMITH   (essay date 1624)

[*In the following excerpt from a prefatory address to the Duchess of Richmond and Lennox, Smith introduces the first edition of* The Generall Historie.]

This History, as for the raritie and varietie of the subject, so much more for the judicious *Eyes* it is like to undergoe, and most of all for that great *Name*, whereof it dareth implore Protection, might and ought to have beene clad in better robes then my rude military hand can cut out in Paper Ornaments. But because, of the most things therein, I am no Compiler by hearsay, but have beene a reall Actor; I take my selfe to have a propertie in them: and therefore have beene bold to challenge them to come under the reach of my owne rough Pen. That, which hath beene indured and passed through with hardship and danger, is thereby sweetned to the *Actor*, when he becometh the *Relator*. I have deeply hazarded my selfe in doing and suffering, and why should I sticke to hazard my reputation in Recording? He that acteth two parts is the more borne withall if he come short, or fayle in one of them. Where shall we looke to find a *Julius Cæsar*, whose atchievments shine as cleare in his owne Commentaries, as they did in the field? I confesse, my hand, though able to weild a weapon among the Barbarous, yet well may tremble in handling a Pen among so many *Judicious:* especially when I am so bold as to call so piercing, and so glorious an *Eye,* as your *Grace,* to view these poore ragged lines. (pp. v-vi)

> *John Smith, in a letter to Lady Francis, in his* The Generall Historie of Virginia, New-England, and the Summer Isles: 1584-1624, *Michael Sparks, 1624, pp. v-vi.*

[JOHN DONNE]   (poem date 1624)

[*Among the several commendatory verses prefacing* The Generall Historie *of 1624 is a poem signed Io: Done. Prevailing tradition, to date unsubstantiated, has it that this poem is the work of John Donne, the great English metaphysical poet. In the following poem, entitled "To His Friend Captaine John Smith, and His Worke," the poet praises "brave Smith."*]

> I Know not how Desert more great can rise,
>   Then out of Danger t' ane for good mens Good;
> Nor who doth better winne th' *Olympian* prize,
>   Than he whose Countryes Honor stirres his bloud;
>   Private respects have private expectation,
>   Publicke designes, should publish reputation.
>
> This Gentleman whose Volumne heere is stoard
>   With strange discoverie of GODS strangest Creatures,
> Gives us full view, how he hath Sayl'd, and Oar'd,
>   And Marcht, full many myles, whose rough defeatures,
>   Hath beene as bold, as puissant, up to binde
>   Their barbarous strength's, to follow him dog-linde.
>
> But wit, nor valour, now adayes payes scores
>   For estimation; all goes now by wealth,
> Or friends; tush! thrust the beggar out of dores
>   That is not Purse-lyn'd; those which live by stealth
>   Shall have their haunts; no matter what's the guest
>   In many places; monies well come best.
>
> But those who well discerne, esteeme not so:
>   Nor I of thee brave *Smith,* that hast beat out
> Thy Iron thus; though I but little know
>   To what t'hast seene; yet I in this am stout:
>   My thoughts, maps to my minde some accidents,
>   That makes mee see thy greater presidents.
>
> (pp. 284-85)

> [*John Donne], "To His Friend Captaine John Smith, and His Work," in* Travels and Works of Captain John Smith: 1580-1631, Vol. I *by John Smith, edited by Edward Arber, revised edition, John Grant, 1910, pp. 284-85.*

THOMAS FULLER   (essay date 1661?)

[*Fuller was an English clergyman, historian, and man of letters. Though all his works were quite popular in his time, he is today best remembered for his collection of brief biographical notices,* The Worthies of England, *published posthumously in 1662. In the following excerpt, he wryly remarks on the incredibility of Smith's adventures in* The True Travels.]

[John Smith] spent the most of his life in foreign parts. First in Hungary, under the emperor, fighting against the Turks, three of which he himself killed in single duels, and therefore was authorized by Sigismund King of Hungary to bear three Turks' heads as an augmentation to his arms. Here he gave intelligence to a besieged city in the night, by significant fire-works formed in the air in legible characters, with many strange performances, the scene whereof is laid at such a distance, they are cheaper credited than confuted.

From the Turks in Europe he passed to the pagans in America, where, towards the latter end of the reign of Queen Elizabeth, such his perils, preservations, dangers, deliverences, they seem to most men above belief, to some beyond truth. Yet have we two witnesses to attest them, the prose and the pictures, both in his own book; and it soundeth much to the diminution of his deeds, that he alone is the herald to publish and proclaim them.

Two captains being at dinner, one of them fell into a large relation of his own achievements, concluding his discourse with this question to his fellow: "And pray, sir," said he, "what service have you done?" To whom he answered, "Other men can tell that." And surely such reports from strangers carry with them the greater reputation. However, moderate men must allow Captain Smith to have been very instrumental in settling the plantation in Virginia, whereof he was governor, as also admiral, of New England. (pp. 75-6)

> *Thomas Fuller, "Cheshire," in his* The Worthies of England, *edited by John Freeman, George Allen & Unwin Ltd., 1952, pp. 61-77.*

GEORGE S. HILLARD   (essay date 1834)

[*Hillard, an American lawyer and author, served at various times as editor of the* Christian Register, *the* Jurist, *and the* Courier. *In the following excerpt from the first full-length biography of Smith, originally published in 1834, Hillard praises Smith's writing style.*]

It is a proof of the versatility of Captain Smith's powers, that, after having passed so many years in stirring and eventful action, he was able to sit quietly down in the autumn of life, and compose book after book, as if he had never gone beyond the walls of his study. It is fortunate, both for us and for his own fame, that he was able to handle the pen as well as the sword, to describe what he had observed and experienced, and to be at once the champion and the herald. (p. 357)

[Smith] writes like a man of sense, observation, and talent, whose acquisitions are by no means contemptible, but who has been trained to the use of the sword and not of the pen. There is a rough vigor and energy in his style characteristic of the man, but it wants the clearness and polish of a practised writer. He betrays in it the irritability of his temperament, and he uses no silken phrases to express his displeasure and disgust. His own unbounded activity made him have no patience with sloth, imbecility, and procrastination. He could not see things going wrong, and be silent. But it is impossible to read any of his works without perceiving that he was largely endowed by nature, a man of lively sensibilities and of easily excited blood, with many of the elements which go to form the poetical character. His writings abound with picturesque and eloquent passages, and with expressions full of a native grace which Quinctilian himself could never have taught.

He was alive to the beautiful and grand in the outward world, as his animated descriptions testify; and, above all, his style is characterized by fervor, earnestness, and enthusiasm. His heart is in every thing which he writes. His mind is warmed and kindled by the contemplation of his subject, and it is impossible to read any of his works (after being accustomed to his antiquated diction) without ourselves catching a portion of their glow. If he has not the smoothness, he has not the monotony of a professed man of letters. His style has the charm of individuality. It has a picture-like vividness arising from the circumstance that he describes, not what he has heard, but what he has seen and experienced.

Reading his tracts, as we do now, with the commentary which the lapse of two centuries has given them, we cannot but wonder at the extent of his knowledge, the accuracy of his observation, and the confidence, amounting almost to inspiration, with which he makes predictions, which, it is needless to say, have been most amply fulfilled. Had he done nothing but write his books, we should have been under the highest obligations to him; and the most impartial judgement would have assigned to him an honorable station among the author's of his age. (pp. 361-62)

> George S. Hillard, *"Account of Captain Smith's Writings,"* in Lives of Eminent Individuals, *William Crosby and H. P. Nichols, 1839, pp. 357-62.*

JOHN GORHAM PALFREY   (essay date 1858)

[*An American clergyman and writer, Palfrey was for many years owner and editor of the* North American Review. *He was the first commentator since Thomas Fuller (see excerpt dated 1661?) to express doubts of Smith's veracity. Although Palfrey's own questions were more tentative than provocative, he was instrumental in encouraging Henry Adams to write the controversial essay that sparked such critical furor over Smith's reliability (see excerpt dated 1867). In the following excerpt, Palfrey considers the credibility of* The True Travels.]

I presume I am not the first reader who has been haunted by incredulity respecting some of the adventures of Smith. How far we have his own authority for statements printed under his name, is a point remaining to be ascertained. I was not able to learn in England that any autograph of his is in existence. Of course this is not a decisive fact as to his having been a writer, for almost the same thing could be said of Shakespeare. But hack-writers abounded in London at the time. Smith was just such a person as, for the salableness of his narratives, would naturally fall into their hands, and into the hands of their masters, the booksellers. They would be disposed to give large room to the element of the marvellous in his stories; and how strictly they would confine themselves to his representations would partly depend on the degree of control which he could exert over them, and the degree of responsibility which he felt for the veracity of what they published. That he was not himself proof against a traveller's temptation to exaggerate, is rendered but too probable by the engravings which illustrate his books, and which it is natural to suppose must, if anything, have passed under his eye. Among their other remarkable representations, those which exhibit him as taking the kings of Pamunkee and Paspahagh prisoners with his own arm show those monarchs as taller than himself by more than a head. He seizes the giants by their long hair, which he is scarcely able to reach. (p. 89n.)

A comparison of Smith's narrative [*The True Travels, Adventures, and Observations of Captain John Smith*] with the authentic history of the Southeast of Europe leads to conclusions on the whole favorable to its credit. (p. 90n.)

On the whole, the reader perhaps inclines to the opinion that John Smith was not the sole author of his books, but that they passed, for embellishment at least, through the hands of some craftsman, who was not perfectly possessed either of Smith's own story, or of the geography or public history to which it related. (p. 92n.)

> John Gorham Palfrey, *in a note from "Early Voyages and Explorations," in his* History of New England during the Stuart Dynasty, Vol. I, *Little, Brown, and Company, 1858, pp. 89-92n.*

CHARLES DEANE   (essay date 1860)

[*An American writer, Deane edited numerous early American works, among them* A True Relation *and Edward Maria Wingfield's* A Discourse of Virginia. *In a footnote to the text of the latter, from which the following excerpt is taken, Deane was the first to question the truth of the Pocahontas story. For a dissenting view of the issue, see the excerpt by William Wirt Henry dated 1882.*]

[Smith's story about being saved by Pocahontas] is an interesting and romantic one. But the critical reader of the accounts of Smith's adventures in Virginia will be struck with the fact, that no mention whatever is made of this incident in his minute personal narrative covering this period [*A True Relation*], written at the time, on the spot, and published in 1608; nor in the narrative of his companions, in the appendix to the tract of 1612 [*A Map of Virginia*]; in neither of which is any attempt made to conceal his valiant exploits and hair-breadth escapes. In his *New England's Trials* (1622) is a brief incidental allusion, in an ambiguous form, to his having been "delivered" by Pocahontas, when taken prisoner. But the current story first appears in the *General Historie,* first published in 1624. This book is compiled chiefly from earlier publications of his own and others; and what relates to Virginia, for this early period, is taken for the most part from the tract of 1612; though there is an occasional variation in the text, and incidents related in the tract of 1608 are sometimes introduced. In the tract last named, written by Smith himself on the spot, it does not appear that he considered his life at all in danger while he was a guest or prisoner of Powhatan. The hazards which he had run when he was first surprised by the Indians, and while in the hands of the King of Pamunkey—who took him prisoner after the slaughter of his only two companions—and of the other minor chiefs, were ended. The whole bearing of the emperor towards him from the first, far from being hostile or even unfriendly, was in every respect kind and hospitable. The emperor, says Smith, "kindly received me with good words, and great platters of sundry victuals; assuring me of his friendship, and my liberty in four days." A conversation then ensued between them, which evidently resulted in inspiring mutual confidence. The savage was curious to know what brought Smith into the country, and appeared satisfied with the answers he received, which were far from the truth. He informed Smith as to the extent of his dominions, the character of the neighboring tribes, &c.; and his guest "requited his discourse" by "describing to him the territories of Europe which were subject to our great king, . . . the innumerable multitude of ships, . . . the terrible manner of fighting" under Capt. Newport, whose "greatness he admired, and not a little feared. He desired me to forsake Paspahegh, and to live with him upon his river. . . . And thus having, with all the kindness he could devise, sought to content me, he sent me home with four men,—one that usually carried my gown and knapsack after me, two others loaded with bread, and one to accompany me.'' This simple story of Smith's interview with Powhatan,—here considerably abridged,—in which the name of the Indian child Pocahontas is not even mentioned, shows quite a different treatment from what is indicated in the following passage, subsequently interpolated in the most abrupt and awkward manner into the account in the *General Historie.* After describing the stately appearance of Powhatan in the midst of his courtiers and women, somewhat as in the former account, the latter narrative proceeds to say, that, on Smith's entrance before the king, the people gave a great shout. The Queen of Appamatuck was deputed to bring him water to wash his hands; and another brought him a bunch of feathers, instead of a towel, to dry them. Then, ''having feasted him after the best barbarous manner they could, a long consultation was held; but the conclusion was, two great stones were brought before Powhatan. Then as many as could laid hands on him, dragged him to them, and thereon laid his head; and, being ready with their clubs to beat out his brains, Pocahontas, the king's dearest daughter, when no entreaty could prevail, got her head in his arms, and laid her own upon his, to save him from death: whereat the emperor was contented he should live to make him hatchets; and her, bells, beads,'' &c. After some days, the emperor came to him, and told him they now were friends, and presently he should go to Jamestown; where, with twelve guides, he soon sent him.

No one can doubt that the earlier narrative contains the truer statement, and that the passage last cited is one of the few or many embellishments with which Smith, with his strong love of the marvellous, was disposed to garnish the stories of his early adventures, and with which he or his editors were tempted to adorn particularly his later works. The name of Pocahontas, afterwards the ''Lady Rebecca,'' had become somewhat famous in the annals of Virginia, since the time Smith knew her there at the age of thirteen or fourteen, when he left the Colony for England. From her position, she had been the means of rendering the Colony some service. Through her, an influence for good had been acquired over Powhatan. As the daughter of an emperor,—possessing, as is said, some personal attractions, and the first convert of her tribe to Christianity,—she had been, on her visit to England with her husband, John Rolfe, in 1616, an object of much curiosity and attention. The temptation, therefore, to bring her on the stage as a heroine in a new character in connection with Smith, always the hero of his chronicles,—and who, in his early adventures in the East, as he subsequently claimed, had inspired the gentle Tragabigzanda with the tenderest emotions towards him,—appears to have been too great for him to withstand, and was not to be resisted by those interested in getting up the *General Historie*; and therefore, in reproducing the account of his imprisonment, this story—the substance of which Smith appears to have intimated to her majesty Queen Anne, in general terms, while the ''Lady Rebecca'' was in England—is introduced for the first time into the narrative of this portion of his adventures.

It should be borne in mind, that Smith makes no claim to have been taken prisoner more than once by the Indians, during his residence of two years and a half in Virginia. All his adventures during this period are related in detail, and there was but one occasion on which the service claimed to have been rendered by Pocahontas could have been performed. This marvellous story finds no proper place in any other adventure; and the introduction of it into the narrative in the *General Historie* is equivalent to setting aside the whole of the earlier account, so far as relates to the manner of his reception and his whole

treatment by Powhatan, when brought before him a prisoner. (pp. 92-4n.)

Without designing to impeach the general trustworthiness of Smith's original narrations, and with no disposition to detract from the *General Historie* (a large part of which is compiled from writings of others) and the *True Travels* . . . , it must be admitted that the tendency to exaggeration and over-statement in his later publications is evident. Referring to what has already been said, it would be curious to trace other variations in the two accounts of Smith's imprisonment especially referred to,—in the *True Relation* and in the *General Historie.* But this note is already too much extended. (p. 95n.)

Charles Deane, in a note from "Wingfield's Discourse of Virginia," in Transactions and Collections of the American Antiquarian Society, *Vol. IV, American Antiquarian Society, 1860, pp. 76-103 n.*

[HENRY ADAMS]   (essay date 1867)

[*Adams was an American autobiographer, historian, essayist, and novelist. His work, considered by many less pertinent to the history of literature than it is to the history of ideas, embodies a particularly modern viewpoint; Adams saw the world becoming less stable and coherent and predicted that this trend would continue unabated. He developed this doctrine most thoroughly in his best-known work, the autobiography* The Education of Henry Adams *(1907), which, according to Robert Regan, "is really the history of an era." As a historian, Adams is chiefly remembered for his* History of the United States of America during the Administrations of Thomas Jefferson and James Madison *(1889-91). This nine-volume work is valued as an insightful analysis of the period and is ranked with the histories of Edward Gibbon and Thomas Macaulay. The following excerpt is taken from Adams's first historical essay, published in the* North American Review, *of which he later became editor. The essay was pivotal in changing the course of critical appraisal of Smith. Although Adams was not the first to cast doubt on the veracity of Smith's writings, it was he who brought the issue to the attention of historians and the general public alike, and it was this essay that provoked the ensuing debate. In* The Education of Henry Adams *(which is written in the third person), Adams described how he came to write his iconoclastic article: "[Dr. John Gorham Palfrey] suggested to Adams, who wanted to make a position for himself, that an article in the* North American Review *on Captain John Smith's relations with Pocahontas would attract as much attention, and probably break as much glass, as any other stone that could be thrown by a beginner. Adams could suggest nothing better. The task seemed likely to be amusing." Here, Adams explains and supports Charles Deane's conclusions regarding Smith's truthfulness (see excerpt dated 1860). For a refutation of Adam's views, see the excerpt by William Wirt Henry dated 1882.*]

If the views advanced by Mr. Deane [see excerpt dated 1860], which it will be our aim to explain, are correct, a very serious change in the received opinions concerning the early history of Virginia will be necessary, and one to which the American people will find it difficult to reconcile themselves.

Stated in its widest bearings, the question raised in this publication is upon the veracity of Captain John Smith; and since the account of the colonization of Virginia has hitherto been almost exclusively drawn from Smith's *Generall Historie,* it is evident that, if the authority of that work is overthrown, it will become necessary to reconsider, not only the statements of fact which rest only on his assertions, but the whole range of opinions which through him have been grafted upon history. These statements and opinions have been received with absolute, unhesitating confidence for more than two hundred years. There are powerful social interests, to say nothing of popular prejudices, greatly concerned in maintaining their credit even at the present day. No object whatever can be gained by their discredit, except the establishment of bald historical truth. It will therefore require that a very strong case indeed should be made out on the part of Mr. Deane and of the party which follows him, before the American public can be induced to listen with attention to an argument which aims at nothing less than the entire erasure of one of the most attractive portions of American history. (pp. 1-2)

[Editor's note: In an unexcerpted section of this essay, Adams places extracts from *A True Relation* and *The Generall Historie* in adjacent columns to highlight perceived factual discrepancies between the two works.]

The first idea that occurs to the mind, in comparing the two narratives . . . , is that the later one is remarkable for a curious air of exaggeration. Eight guards, which had been sufficient in 1608, are multiplied into thirty or forty tall fellows in 1624. What was enough for ten men at the earlier time would feed twenty according to the later version. Four guides were surely an ample escort to conduct Smith to Jamestown, but they are reinforced to the number of twelve sixteen years afterwards. With the best disposition towards Smith, one cannot but remember that this was just the period when Falstaff and his misbegotten knaves in Kendal Green appeared upon the stage. The execution wrought upon the wretched lawyers who wished to try Smith for his life on his return to Jamestown is most prompt and decisive, according to the story of 1624, but in 1608 Smith is happy to accept the aid of Captain Newport to disembarrass him of his too-powerful enemies. With sabre, falcon, and musket-shot he forced the mutinous crew of the pinnace to stay or sink, if we are to believe the *Generall Historie,* while the *True Relation* is quite silent as to any such feat of arms, but simply observes that Captain Newport arrived the same evening.

The same character of exaggeration marks the whole account of the treatment he received among the savages. According to the story written a few months after the event, a people is described, savage it is true, but neither cruel nor bloodthirsty; reckless, perhaps, of life in battle, but kind and even magnanimous towards their captive. It is expressly stated that no such demonstration was made against Smith as that which, in 1624, is affirmed to have taken place within an hour after his capture. Only a few days after he was taken prisoner, he represents himself as giving orders to Opechankanough to take him to Powhatan, and even at this time he knew that he was to be allowed to return to Jamestown. "To him I told him I must go, and so return to Paspahegh." Powhatan received him with the greatest cordiality, and, having sought to content him with all the kindness he could devise, did actually send him with a guard of honor back to his friends. If the *True Relation* is really true, the behavior of these naked barbarians towards Smith was far more humane than that which he would have received at the hands of any civilized nation on the face of the earth. There is not a trace of his having felt any immediate fear for his life, except from a savage whose son he had killed, and from whom Opechankanough protected him. There does indeed occur one line to the effect that they fed him so fat as to make him much doubt they meant to sacrifice him; and this paragraph furnishes the most striking evidence of the kindness of the Indians, and of the fact that he believed himself to have been mistaken in having entertained the suspicion. Yet in 1624 we learn that all this long time of his imprisonment he was still expecting every hour to be put to one death or another.

These variations would be of little consequence to the ordinary reader of the colonial history, if they stopped at trifling inconsistencies. They would merely prove, what is almost self-evident, that the earlier narrative is the safer authority for historians to follow, and that the confidence which has hitherto been felt in the exactness of the *Generall Historie* cannot be altogether maintained. But there is one particular portion of the story where every American who has heretofore had satisfaction in one of the most favorite stories in the early annals of his country will stop with a feeling of surprise and a desire to doubt the evidence of his own senses. When he comes to the paragraph in which the *Generall Historie* relates the touching story of Pocahontas, and her intercession at the moment when no chance appeared to exist that Smith's life could be preserved, and when he casts his eye upon the [corresponding section] . . . of the *True Relation* to find its version of the incident, he will surely be amazed to see that not only does it fail to furnish the remotest allusion to this act, or even by a single word to indicate that Pocahontas so much as existed, but that it expressly states that Powhatan treated his captive throughout with the greatest kindness, assuring him at once of his early liberation.

No American needs to be told that this tale of Pocahontas is probably the most romantic episode in the whole history of his country. . . . One after another, all American historians have

Engraved title page of the first edition of The Generall Historie *(1624).*

contented themselves with repeating the words of the *Generall Historie,* vying with each other in heaping praises which no critics were cynical enough to gainsay, now on the virtues of Pocahontas, and now on the courage and constancy of Smith. (pp. 10-12)

The spirit of Smith has infused itself into the modern historian, as it had already infused itself into the works of his predecessors in the same path. The lights are intensified; the shadows are deepened; the gradations between are softened; the copy surpasses its model. (p. 13)

The quiet investigations of Mr. Deane have . . . now made it absolutely necessary that every historian should hereafter take one side or the other in regard to this serious question. He must either rely upon the testimony of Smith concerning matters of his own personal experience, and upon the prescription of two centuries in favor of his story, or he must reject the authority hitherto considered unquestionable, and must undertake the reconstruction of the history of this whole period out of original material hitherto considered as merely auxiliary to Smith's narrative. Unfortunately, there is no possibility of compromise in the dispute. Cautious as the expressions of Mr. Deane are, and unwilling as he evidently is to treat the reputation of Smith with harshness, it is still perfectly clear that the statements of the *Generall Historie,* if proved to be untrue, are falsehoods of an effrontery seldom equalled in modern times.

It is not, however, to be supposed that the argument against the *Generall Historie* rests merely upon the text of the *True Relation.* (p. 14)

[In 1612 Smith] published at Oxford a short work called *A Map of Virginia. With a Description of the countrey, the Commodities, People, Government, and Religion.* (p. 20)

There is in the text which accompanies the Map only one passage that bears upon the point now principally in dispute. Among the customs which he describes as peculiar to the Indians was the form of execution practised against criminals. Their heads, he says, were placed upon an alter, or sacrificing-stone, while "one with clubbes beates out their braines." During his captivity, he adds, not indeed that he had actually seen this mode of execution, but that an Indian had been beaten in his presence till he fell senseless, without a cry or complaint. Here we have, therefore, the whole idea of the story which he afterwards made public. It may be left to practised lawyers to decide whether, under the ordinary rules of evidence, this passage does not amount to a practical assertion that he had himself not been placed in the position described, and it may perhaps be possible for future students to explain why Smith should have suppressed his own story, supposing it to have been true. The inference is very strong that, if anything of the sort had ever occurred, it would certainly have been mentioned here. . . . (pp. 20-1)

This Oxford tract of 1612 may be considered as decisive of the fact that, down to that date, the story of Pocahontas had not been made public. We are obliged to confess that no explanation whatever, consistent with an assumption of the truth of the later narrative, occurs to the mind to account for Smith's continued silence so long after his connection with the Colony had ceased. (p. 22)

[In 1620 Smith] published another pamphlet, entitled *New England's Trials,* a second and enlarged edition of which appeared in 1622. Here at last, in 1622, we find the long-sought allusion to his captivity, in the following words:—

> For wronging a soldier but the value of a penny I have caused Powhatan send his own men to Jamestowne to receive their punishment at my discretion. It is true in our greatest extremitie they shot me, slue three of my men, and by the folly of them that fled, took me prisoner; yet God made Pocahontas the King's daughter the means to deliver me; and thereby taught me to know their treacheries to preserve the rest.

This in the order of time is the third version given by Smith of his own adventure, the account in the *Generall Historie* being the fourth. Each one of these four stories is more or less inconsistent with all the others; but this one of 1622 is, we are sorry to say it, more certainly mendacious than any of the rest. Read it in whatever light we please, it is creditable neither to Smith's veracity nor to his sense of honor. "By the folly of them that fled," he now states that the Indians succeeded in capturing him. All the other versions agree in this, that at the time Smith was attacked and his two men slain he was quite alone, except for his Indian guide, whom he used as a shield. To throw upon the invented cowardice of companions who were far away, out of sight and out of hearing of the contest, the blame for a disaster which was solely due to his own overboldness, was not an honorable way of dealing with his command. Perhaps it would be better to leave this point unnoticed, in deference to Smith's real merits, but unfortunately this is not the only passage in his works in which the same tendency is apparent.

Nevertheless, the fact remains, that here for the first time the story of Pocahontas appears in print. "God made Pocahontas the means to deliver me." There is a devout form in this statement which is characteristic of the age, and the piety of a man like Smith, if his autobiography gives a true idea of his course of life, must have been a curious subject for study. But to any one who assumes, with Mr. Deane, that this introduction of Pocahontas is a pure invention, this paragraph becomes doubly interesting, as showing to what a degree of quaint dignity the men of this time could rise, even in falsehood.

The date of the first appearance of this famous story can therefore be fixed with sufficient certainty on the five years between 1617 and 1622, although the published account in all its completeness is only to be found in the *Generall Historie,* which was printed in 1624. . . . There remains only one point of difficulty which requires attention to this work.

It is there stated that, when Pocahontas came to England, Smith wrote for her a sort of letter of introduction to the Queen, or, in his own words, "a little booke to this effect to the Queen, an abstract whereof followeth."

> Some ten yeeres agoe, being in Virginia and taken prisoner by the power of Powhatan their chiefe King. . . . I cannot say I felt the least occasion of what that was in the power of those my mortall foes to prevent, notwithstanding al their threats. After some six weeks fatting amongst those Salvage Courtiers, at the minute of my execution, she hazarded the beating out of her owne braines to save mine, and not onely that, but so prevailed with her father, that I was safely conducted to Jamestowne.

It is unquestionable that, if Smith really did write this statement to the Queen, and the Queen received the letter, the case becomes even more complicated than ever. But the fact is, that the letter itself rests on the authority of the *Generall Historie,* and has neither more nor less weight than the other statements in that work. It is by no means necessary to believe that this "abstract of the effect" of the little book contains no interpolations such as those with which the text of the *Generall Historie* overflows. At the time when it was published, in 1624, not only had Pocahontas long been dead, but Queen Anne herself had, in 1619, followed to her grave, and Smith remained alone to tell his own story. The Virginia Company certainly had no interest in denying what was a powerful means of drawing popular sympathy towards the Colony. But even if it be granted that Smith's letter as it stands was really sent to the Queen, the argument against its truth, so far as it is based on the silence of all previous authorities, is left quite untouched; and if it be allowed that there is no conclusive evidence to prove that the story was unknown in 1617, it is at least equally difficult to prove that, if known, it was believed. Smith's character was certainly a matter of warm dispute in his own day, and his enemies seems to have been too numerous and strong for even his energy and perseverance to overcome. (pp. 26-8)

The examination of Smith's works has shown that his final narrative was the result of gradual additions. The influence exercised by Pocahontas on the affairs of the Colony, according to the account given in 1608, was very slight. Her capture and her marriage to Rolfe first gave her importance. Her visit to England, however, made her beyond question the most conspicuous figure in Virginia to the public mind, and it became inevitable that romantic incidents in her life would be created, if they did not already exist, by the mere exercise of the popular imagination, attracted by a wild and vivid picture of savage life.

The history of the emperor's daughter became, as we are led by Smith to suppose, a subject for the stage. Nothing was more natural or more probable. It is not even necessary to suppose that Smith himself invented the additions to his original story. He may have merely accepted them after they had obtained a strong and general hold on the minds of his contemporaries.

In the mean while Smith's own career had turned out a failure, and his ventures ended disastrously, while in most cases he failed to obtain the employment which he continued to seek with unrelaxed energy.... Still, he had the resource left of which he had already made such frequent use, and by publishing the *Generall Historie* he made a direct appeal to the public more ambitious than any he had yet attempted. In this work he embodied everything that could tend to the increase of his own reputation, and drew material from every source which could illustrate the history of English colonization. Pocahontas was made to appear in it as a kind of stage deity on every possible occasion, and his own share in the affairs of the Colony is magnified at the expense of all his companions. None of those whose reputations he treated with so much harshness appeared to vindicate their own characters, far less to assert the facts in regard to Pocahontas. The effort indeed failed of its object, for he remained unemployed and without mark of distinction, and died quietly in his bed, in London, in June, 1631; but in the absence of criticism, due perhaps to the political excitement of the times, his book survived to become the standard authority on Virginian history. The readiness with which it was received is scarcely so remarkable as the credulity which has left it unquestioned almost to the present day. (pp. 29-30)

> [Henry Adams], in a review of "Captain John Smith," in The North American Review, *Vol. CIV, No. CCXIV, January, 1867, pp. 1-30.*

EDWARD D. NEILL   (essay date 1869)

[*Neill was an American clergyman, educator, and author of such colonial history books as* Terra Mariae; or, Threads of Maryland Colonial History (1867) *and* History of the Virginia Company of London (1869). *In the following excerpt from the latter work, Neill succinctly dismisses the worth of Smith's writings.*]

[Captain Smith's] writings are those of a gascon and beggar. He seemed to be always in the attitude of one craving recognition or remuneration for alleged services, and Fuller's description of his writings and character in the *Worthies of England,* is probably not far from the truth [see excerpt dated 1661?]. He is, however, worthy of being remembered, as an early explorer of the Atlantic coast. (p. 211)

> Edward D. Neill, *"First Year of Earl of Southampton's Directorship," in his* History of the Virginia Company of London, *1869. Reprint by Burt Franklin, 1968, pp. 192-212.*

MOSES COIT TYLER   (essay date 1878)

[*An American teacher, minister, and literary historian, Tyler was one of the first critics to examine American literature systematically. His* A History of American Literature (1878) *and* The Literary History of the American Revolution: 1763-1783 (1897) *are examples of his methodical research, authoritative style, and keen insight. While the former work is now considered dated, Tyler's study of the American Revolution remains a valuable sourcebook for modern scholars. In the following excerpt from* A History of American Literature, *Tyler praises Smith as the writer of the earliest American literature.*]

[In the] year 1607, when he first set foot in Virginia, Captain John Smith was only twenty-seven years old; but even then he had made himself somewhat famous in England as a daring traveller in Southern Europe, in Turkey and the East. He was perhaps the last professional knight-errant that the world saw; a free lance, who could not hear a fight going on anywhere in the world without hastening to have a hand in it; a sworn champion of the ladies also, all of whom he loved too ardently to be guilty of the invidious offence of marrying any one of them; a restless, vain, ambitious, overbearing, blustering fellow, who made all men either his hot friends or his hot enemies; a man who down to the present hour has his celebrity in the world chiefly on account of alleged exploits among Turks, Tartars, and Indians, of which exploits he alone has finished the history—never failing to celebrate himself in them all as the one resplendent and invincible hero.

This extremely vivid and resolute man comes before us now for particular study, not because he was the most conspicuous person in the first successful American colony, but because he was the writer of the first book in American literature. It is impossible to doubt that as a story-teller he fell into the traveller's habit of drawing a long bow. In the narration of incidents that had occurred in his own wild life he had an aptitude for being intensely interesting; and it seemed to be his theory that if the original facts were not in themselves quite so interesting as they should have been, so much the worse for the original facts. Yet in spite of this habit, Captain John Smith had many great and magnanimous qualities; and we surely cannot help being drawn to him with affectionate admiration, when we remember his large services in the work of colonizing both Virginia and New England, his sufferings in that cause, and his unquenchable love for it until death. In his later life, after he had been baffled in many of his plans and hopes, he wrote, in London, of the American colonies these words: "By the acquaintance I have with them, I call them my children; for they have been my wife, my hawks, hounds, my cards, my dice, and in total my best content, as indifferent to my heart as my left hand to my right.''

Then, too, as students of literature we shall be drawn to Captain John Smith as belonging to that noble type of manhood of which the Elizabethan period produced so many examples—the man of action who was also a man of letters, the man of letters who was also a man of action: the wholesomest type of manhood anywhere to be found. . . . (pp. 18-19)

Captain John Smith became a somewhat prolific author; but while nearly all of his books have a leading reference to America, only three of them were written during the period of his residence as a colonist in America. Only these three, therefore, can be claimed by us as belonging to the literature of our country.

The first of these books, *A True Relation of Virginia,* is of deep interest to us, not only on account of its graphic style and the strong light it throws upon the very beginning of our national history, but as being unquestionably the earliest book in American literature. It was written during the first thirteen months of the life of the first American colony, and gives a simple and picturesque account of the stirring events which took place there during that time, under his own eye. (pp. 20-1)

[*A True Relation*] is a book that was written, not in lettered ease, nor in ''the still air of delightful studies,'' but under a rotten tent in the wilderness, perhaps by the flickering blaze of a pine knot, in the midst of tree-stumps and the filth and clamor of a pioneer's camp, and within the fragile palisades which alone shielded the little band of colonists from the ever-hovering peril of an Indian massacre. It was not composed as a literary effort. It was meant to be merely a budget of information for the public at home, and especially for the London stockholders of the Virginia Company. Hastily, apparently without revision, it was wrought vehemently by the rough hand of a soldier and an explorer, in the pauses of a toil that was both fatiguing and dangerous, and while the incidents which he records were fresh and clinging in his memory. Probably he thought little of any rules of literary art as he wrote this book: probably he did not think of writing a book at all. Out of the abundance of his materials, glowing with pride over what he had done in the great enterprise, eager to inspire the home-keeping patrons of the colony with his own resolute cheer, and accustomed for years to portray in pithy English the adventures of which his life was fated to be full, the bluff Captain just stabbed his paper with inken words; he composed not a book but a big letter; he folded it up, and tossed it upon the deck of Captain Nelson's departing ship. But though he may have had no expectation of doing such a thing, he wrote a book that is not unworthy to be the beginning of the new English literature in America. It has faults enough, without doubt. Had it not these, it would have been too good for the place it occupies. The composition was extemporaneous; there appears in it some chronic misunderstanding between the nominatives and their verbs; now and then the words and clauses of a sentence are jumbled together in blinding heaps; but in spite of all its crudities, here is racy English, pure English, the sinewy, picturesque and throbbing diction of the navigators and soldiers of the Elizabethan time. And although the materials of this book are not moulded in nice proportion, the story is well told. The man has an eye and a hand for that thing. He sees the essential facts of a situation, and throws the rest away; and the business moves straight forward.

About three months after the departure for England of the ship which carried to the printing-press the book of which an ex-

tended account has just been given, there arrived from England another ship, bringing a new supply of colonists, and bringing likewise a letter of fantastic instructions and of querulous complaints from the London stockholders of the company. It fell to Captain John Smith, as the new president of the colony, to make reply to this document; and he did it in the production which forms the second title in our list of his American writings. This production is brief; but it is a most vigorous, trenchant, and characteristic piece of writing, a transcript of the intense spirit of the man who wrote it, all ablaze with the light it casts into the primal hot-bed of wrangling, indolence, and misery, the village of Jamestown. (pp. 26-7)

Certainly this writing is racy, terse, fearless; a style of sentence carved out by a sword; the incisive speech of a man of action; Hotspur rhetoric, jerking with impatience, truculence, and noble wrath. And it is not without an under-meaning in many ways, that this production, among the very earliest in American literature, should communicate to England a foretaste of what proved to be the incurable American habit of talking back to her. . . . One can easily imagine what a shock this epistolary retort of Captain John Smith must have given to the dignified nerves of those kindly and lordly patrons in London; how its saucy sentences must have made them gasp and stare. Almost the earliest note, then, of American literature is a note of unsubmissiveness. Captain John Smith's letter, in the first decade of the seventeenth century, is a premonitory symptom of the Declaration of Independence.

In the same parcel with this remarkable letter of Captain Smith's was enclosed by him to the adventurers in London another document—a proof of his irrepressible activity and of his versatile talent—a *Map of the Bay and the Rivers, with an annexed Relation of the countries, and nations that inhabit them.* . . . It deals with the climate and topography of Virginia, with its fauna and flora, and particularly with the characteristics of its earlier inhabitants, the Indians. As a whole the work is uncommonly picturesque and even amusing; for though devoted to climatic and topographic descriptions, to matters of natural history, and to the coarse features of savage existence, the genius of the writer quickens and brightens it all, strewing his pages with easy and delightful strokes of imagery, quaint humor, shrewdness, and a sort of rough unconscious grace. (pp. 29-30)

[The author's descriptive manner] is vital with the breath of imagination, and tinted with the very hues of nature. One has not to go far along the sentences . . . in this book without finding all the dull and hard details of his subject made delightful by felicities of phrase that seem to spring up as easily as wild flowers in the woods of his own Virginia. He speaks of ''an infinite number of small rundels and pleasant springs that disperse themselves for the best service as do the veins of a man's body;'' of ''a bay wherein falleth three or four pretty brooks and creeks that half intrench the inhabitants of Warraskoyac;'' of the river Pamaunkee that ''divideth itself into two gallant branches;'' of the river Patawomeke ''fed . . . with many sweet rivers and springs which fall from the bordering hills.'' There is often a quaint flavor in his words—that racy and piquant simplicity which so much charms us in the English descriptive prose of the sixteenth century, and the first third of the seventeenth. (pp. 31-2)

As a writer [Smith's] merits are really great—clearness, force, vividness, picturesque and dramatic energy, a diction racy and crisp. He had the faults of an impulsive, irascible, egotistic, and imaginative nature; he sometimes bought human praise at too high a price; but he had great abilities in word and deed; his nature was upon the whole generous and noble; and during the first two decades of the seventeenth century he did more than any other Englishman to make an American nation and an American literature possible. . . . (p. 38)

> *Moses Coit Tyler, "Virginia: The First Writer," in his* A History of American Literature: 1607-1676, *Vol. I, G. P. Putnam's Sons, 1878, pp. 16-38.*

WILLIAM WIRT HENRY (essay date 1882)

[*An American lawyer and president of the Virginia Historical Society, Henry is best known as the biographer of his famous grandfather, Patrick Henry. In the following excerpt, he refutes the charges made against Smith's veracity, addressing himself particularly to the objections raised by Charles Deane and Henry Adams (see excerpts dated 1860 and 1867).*]

[The] names oftenest mentioned in connection with the Virginia settlement, and which have excited the greatest interest, are those of Captain John Smith, the preserver of the colony, and Pocahontas, the preserver of Smith, and the constant friend of the English. For more than two hundred and fifty years historians have delighted to relate their services, often quoting the quaint, terse language of Smith's *History* in giving his adventures, and especially his rescue from death by Powhatan's "dearest daughter," at the risk of her own life, when as her father's prisoner he was condemned to die.

In all that time no one discredited Smith's account of the colony, if we except Thomas Fuller, whose groundless sneer at Smith in his *Worthies of England* [see excerpt dated 1661?], only demonstrated his ignorance of the sources from which Smith drew the material for his history.

Thus the matter stood till the year 1860, when Mr. Charles Deane, of Massachusetts, edited with notes, for the American Antiquarian Society, of which he was a member, *A Discourse of Virginia,* by Edward Maria Wingfield, the first president of the Colony [see excerpt dated 1860]. . . . (p. 11)

The grounds of Mr. Deane's attack on Smith's veracity may be briefly stated as follows: Smith came to Virginia in 1607 and returned to England in 1609. Accounts of what happened during his stay in the colony were written by himself and others, and many publications concerning the early history of the colony were made, but no mention was made in any publication of Smith's rescue by Pocahontas, as is claimed, till 1622, when Smith published a second edition of a tract entitled *New England Trials,* which contains an allusion to it; and it was only in Smith's *General History of Virginia,* published in 1624, that the full details were given. It is charged that the prominence to which Pocahontas had attained in 1616 induced Smith to invent the story, in order that he might associate her name with his own. Mr. Deane also claimed that the account of Smith's treatment at the hands of the Indians while their prisoner, given at the time in his letter known as the *True Relation,* differs materially from that given in the *General History,* and that all the later accounts given by Smith of his early adventures show considerable embellishment, and are unworthy of belief.

Those who have followed in the wake of Mr. Deane have endeavored to point out many inconsistencies between the accounts given by Smith in his different publications relating to

the same matters, and he has been painted by one at least, (Mr. Neill) [see excerpt dated 1869], as a braggart and a beggar, and unworthy of belief generally. (p. 16)

[The failure of Smith's *True Relation*] to record his rescue by Pocahontas is considered the strongest evidence of the falsity of the account given by him years afterwards. Indeed the force of the attack upon Smith, inaugurated by Mr. Deane, will be found in this alleged omission. But what are we to think of the argument when we learn, what is undoubtedly true, that this letter has never been published as Smith wrote it. Parts of it were suppressed by the person who published it, who, in a preface signed with his initials "J.H.," states that fact. . . . The preface gives an account of how the publisher came by the manuscript, and of a mistake in printing some of the copies under the name of Thomas Watson instead of Captain Smith, the true writer, and then these words follow: "Somwhat more was by him written, which being, as I thought, (fit to be private,) I would not adventure to make it publicke."

What was thus omitted from the letter in its publication has never been known. Until the letter has been reproduced as Smith wrote it, however, it is simply absurd to attempt to build an argument against Smith's veracity upon its alleged omissions. This answer to the main ground of attack would seem to be complete, and yet more may be added. We are not left entirely in the dark as to what was omitted by the publisher. He continues his preface as follows: "What may be expected concerning the scituation of the country, the nature of the clime, number of our people there resident, the manner of their government and living, the commodities to be produced, and the end and effect it may come too, I can say nothing more then is here written. Only what I have learned and gathered from generall consent of all (that I have conversed with all) as well marriners as others which have had employment that way, is that the country is excellent and pleasant, the clime temperate and healthfull, the ground fertill and good, the commodities to be expected (if well followed) many, for our people, the worst being already past, these former having indured the heate of the day, whereby those that shall succeede may at ease labour for their profit in the most sweete, cool, and temperate shade."

Two things are evident from these sentences, one, that what was omitted could only relate to the narrative of what had happened to the colonists, all else had been given fully to the public; another, that the desire of the publisher was to encourage further emigration to Virginia, and therefore what he left out of the narrative was in all probability matters which might tend to discourage emigrants. (pp. 17-18)

Let us now examine the second ground of attack, namely, the alleged inconsistencies between the *True Relation* and the subsequent publications of Smith.

At page 16 of the *True Relation* an account is given of an expedition by Smith to Kegquouhtan, or Kecoughtan (now Hampton) to procure corn by trade with the Indians. No mention is made of an attack on the natives. In the *General History,* in an account of the same expedition, at page 45, it is stated that he fired on the Indians, and captured their idol, called "Okee." In both accounts, it is stated, that at first the Indians treated Smith and his companions scornfully, thinking they were famishing men, but afterwards brought them such provisions as they needed. The reason why the attack was left out of the letter sent to England by Smith in 1608 is evident from the narrative in the *General History* itself. After stating the scornful reception given Smith by the Indians, it continues,

"But, seeing by trade and courtesie there was nothing to be had, he made bold to try such conclusions as necessite inforced, though contrary to his commission, let fly his muskets, ran his boat on shore, whereat they all fled into the woods," &c., &c. We find in the instructions, sent with the Colony by the London Company, this direction, "In all your passages you must have great care not to offend the naturals, if you can eschew it." (p. 28)

This was Smith's first trading expedition, and in order to supply his wants, he found it necessary to disobey instructions. We can well understand why he might not choose to relate his disobedience to orders in his letter to England, and his not doing so should not throw even a suspicion on his statement subsequently given in the *History*. There is an expression in the account of this expedition found in the Oxford Tract [*A Map of Virginia*], however, which is corroborative of the statement of the attack found in the *General History*. The Oxford Tract has the following account: "Being but 6 or 7 in company, he went down the river to Kecoughton, where, at first, they scorned him as a starved man. Yet he so dealt with them, that the next day they loaded his boat with corne." How he dealt with them is explained in the account found in the *General History*. It is apparent that there is no contradiction between Smith's several accounts but a mere omission of the attack in one of them, for which the publisher may have been responsible. (pp. 28-9)

The several accounts given by Smith, of his treatment while a captive, have been claimed to be inconsistent, and so determined has been the effort to show inconsistencies, that some of the passages compared have been made to suffer torture. The first passages so compared are the statements of what occurred immediately on the capture. In the *True Relation* Smith says: "I perceived by the aboundance of fires all over the woods at each place I expected when they would execute me, yet they used me with what kindness they could."

In the *General History*, after describing his gift to their King of his "round ivory double compass Dyall" soon after his capture, and their admiration of it, he continues as follows: "Notwithstanding, within an houre after they tyed him to a tree, and as many as could stand about him prepared to shoot him, but the King holding up the compass in his hand, they all laid downe their Bowes and Arrowes, and in a triumphant manner led him to Orapaks, where he was after their manner kindly feasted and well used." The real difference in these accounts consists in the latter giving the preparation to kill him, and his preservation by Opechankanough's holding up to view the wonderful compass. The kindness of their treatment otherwise is stated in both narratives. When we remember that the *True Relation*, which omits this incident, has never been published as Smith wrote it, we cannot conclude that Smith in that letter made no allusion to it. It may be that he gave it, and his editor included it in the omitted items.

The printed text of the *True Relation* indicates, in fact, that something was omitted from the manuscript just where this incident should have come in. The reader will have noticed doubtless that the sentence quoted from the *True Relation* is ungrammatical and incoherent as it stands. If, however, something was omitted from the manuscript between the words "woods" and "at," we can understand how the want of connection in the sentence was produced.

It is claimed that the accounts of the provisions given Smith, and the guard put over him the first night after his capture, are conflicting, as they appear in the *True Relation,* and the *General History*. Let us compare them. The accounts of his first night's treatment are as follows:

In the *True Relation,* "The Captain conducting me to his lodging, a quarter of Venison and some ten pound of bread I had for supper, what I left was reserved for me, and sent with me to my lodging."	In the *General History,* "Smith they conducted to a long house, where thirtie or fortie tall fellowes did guard him, and ere long more bread and Venison was brought him then would have served twentie men."

There is not the slightest inconsistency in the accounts. A quarter of venison and ten pounds of bread were more than enough to serve twenty men. The careless critics, however, have confounded his subsequent treatment as detailed in the *True Relation,* with what happened on the first night, and thus have created the apparent inconsistency they claim to have discovered. After the passage just given the narrative in the *True Relation* continues: "each morning 3 women presented me three great platters of fine bread, more venison then ten men could devour I had, my goune, points and garters, my compass and a tablet they gave me again, though 8 ordinarily guarded me, I wanted not what they could devise to content me; and still our longer acquaintance increased our better affection." It is apparent from this that as they became better acquainted the guard was reduced from the thirty or forty of the first night to eight ordinarily. There seems to have been but little reduction in his provisions. Three great platters of bread and more venison than ten men could devour might still be more bread and venison than would have served twenty men, and thus, as to the provisions, there would have been no real inconsistency had this referred to the first night.

After his capture, Smith was carried to several places by Opechankanough, and at each found a house of the great Emperor, Powhatan. In the *True Relation* he says, speaking of this Emperor to Opechankanough, "to him I tolde him I must goe, and so return to Paspehigh," (the Indian name for Jamestown.) This statement has been criticised by Mr. Adams. He says: "Only a few days after he (Smith) was taken prisoner, he represents himself as giving orders to Opechankanough to take him to Powhatan, and even at this time he knew he was to be allowed to return to Jamestown" [see excerpt dated 1867]. This, Mr. Adams thinks, is inconsistent with Smith's statement in the *General History,* that he expected all the time of his imprisonment to be put to one death or another.

Wingfield, in his *Discourse,* states that on the 25th of June preceding Smith's capture, the Emperor Powhatan sent a messenger to Jamestown, offering peace and friendship. It was natural for Smith, when the captive of a king who was in subjection to the Emperor, to ask to be carried to Powhatan, with whom the Colony had already entered into articles of friendship, and had he demanded to be carried to him, he would have but claimed a right, which, by boldness, he was endeavoring to make his captor respect. The language of Smith, however, may as well be considered a request as a command.

The treatment which he received when he was carried before Powhatan is differently related in the *True Relation* and the *General History,* and this difference has doubtless given rise to the attacks upon Smith's veracity. Let us compare the two accounts:

From the *True Relation,* "Hee kindly welcomed me with good wordes, and great Platters of Sundrie Victuals, assuring me his friendship, and my libertie within four dayes, hee much delighted in Opechanconough's relation of what I had described to him and oft examined me upon the same."

From the *General History,* "Having feasted him after their best barbarous manner they could, a long consultation was held, but the conclusion was, two great stones were brought before Powhatan, then as many as could layd hands on him, dragged him to them, and thereon laid his head, and being ready with their clubs to beate out his brains, Pocahontas, the King's dearest daughter, when no entreaty could prevaile, got his head in her armes, and laid her owne upon his to save him from death, whereat the Emperor was contented he should live to make him hatchets, and her bells, beads and copper."

We have already seen that the omission of his rescue from the *True Relation* might well have been made by Smith, or by the publisher of that partially printed letter, under the instruction from the London Company, the treacherous conduct of Powhatan towards his prisoner and the colony being calculated to discourage others from coming to Virginia. An examination, however, of the text of the *True Relation* just cited, discloses the fact that the publisher must have left out a part of what Smith wrote in describing his first interview with Powhatan, at which interview his condemnation and rescue occurred. It is apparent that all that is printed up to and including the word "dayes," relates to what happened at the time Smith was brought before Powhatan, while the words which immediately follow, only separated by a comma, namely, "hee much delighted in Opechanconough's relation of what I had described to him, and *oft* examined me upon the same," relate to what happened in subsequent interviews, when some of the wonders of geometry and astronomy, explained to Opechankanough by Smith, were the topic of conversation.

The text, as it is, presents an abrupt transition from the interview of the first day to the interviews of subsequent days, which can be satisfactorily explained only upon the theory of an omission by the publisher of part of the occurrences of the first day, and an effort to conceal the omission by the arrangement of the text presented.

The *True Relation,* in describing Smith's return to Jamestown, says: "Hee sent me home with 4 men, one that usually carried my gowne and knapsack after me, two others loaded with bread and one to accompanie me." The *General History* says: "So to Jamestown with 12 guides, Powhatan sent him." These statements are claimed to be contradictory. It is evident, however, that in the first account Smith merely gave the number of men detailed to wait upon his person, while in the second he meant to enumerate the entire company sent as guides, probably a misprint for guards. (pp. 30-4)

It is asserted by Mr. Adams and others, that Smith contradicts himself by representing in the *True Relation* that the Indians treated him with continual kindness, while, in the *General History,* he says he was all the time of his captivity in continual dread of being put to death. When we remember that he was the captive of a savage people, who had killed his companions, it does not seem strange that no amount of kindness could allay his fears. It does seem strange that his critics should think otherwise, and should read so carelessly the texts they criticise. The passage they refer to in the *General History* is a part of the account of his return to Jamestown, and is in these words:

"That night they quartered in the woods, he still expecting (as he had done all this long time of his imprisonment) every houre to be put to one death or other for all their feasting."

We have seen that in the *True Relation,* soon after his capture, these words occur: "At each place I expected when they would execute me, yet they used me with what kindnesse they could." Afterwards it is related in this book that an Indian attempted to kill him while under guard, and that one of the places he was carried to was called Topahanocke, where it was sought to identify him as one of a party who, some years previously, had slain their King, and captured some of their people. Smith also tells us in this book that their excess of kindness aroused his suspicions. He says: "So fat they fed mee, that I much doubted they intended to have sacrificed mee to the Quiyoughquosicke, which is a superior power they worship." Smith had, before his capture, formed a very correct estimate of the treacherous character of the Indians, and both accounts that he gave of his captivity show that his distrust of them kept him in continual fear of death at their hands. The expression in the *History,* "for all their feasting," indicates the kindness shown him, which is detailed in the *True Relation.* And if we have no details of cruel dispositions recorded in the *True Relation,* such as are recorded in the *General History,* we must remember that the *True Relation,* as we have it, is a mutilated book, and that there was a reason for leaving out of it such incidents. (pp. 34-5)

But we need not pursue this charge of inconsistencies further, as time would fail us to notice every inconsistency charged by the numerous and often ill-informed assailants of Smith. Those not noticed are even more easily disposed of than those we have already exposed. (p. 38)

Turning now to the direct evidence of the truthfulness of Smith as a writer, we shall find it ample and conclusive. (p. 48)

[The] *General History* embodied the "Oxford Tract," with some additions from the pen of Smith, and . . . this tract was carefully compiled out of the writings of the colonists, whose names are given by Dr. Symonds, and is a work of the highest authority. Now a comparison of this book with the *General History* shows that nearly every incident of Smith's stay in Virginia, given in the *History,* is found in the "Tract." Certainly we find in it abundant evidence of "his perils, preservations, dangers, deliverances," which Fuller, through ignorance, or something worse, claimed were published and proclaimed alone by Smith. (p. 49)

When we look to the writings of Smith himself for evidence of the truthfulness of his statement, in regard to the rescue [by Pocahontas], we find it ample to confirm our reliance on his veracity.

It is true that the garbled letter from Virginia, published in 1608, makes no mention of the matter, but it relates an incident very suggestive of the truth of his subsequent statement. Soon after Smith was released from his captivity he determined to arrest some Indians who had been caught thieving in Jamestown. Powhatan was greatly concerned at the arrest, and sent several messengers to obtain their release; finally he sent Pocahontas, who is described as "a child of tenne years old," (she was probably twelve) and Smith delivered to her the prisoners. Why the cunning savage should have trusted his favorite child at such a tender age upon such an errand would be difficult to explain, unless we believe Smith's statement that she had previously saved his life.

In his other writings Smith frequently mentions his rescue, and in such a way as would have led to detection had he made a false statement about it.

In his **General History** he states, that upon the arrival of Pocahontas in England, in 1616, he "to deserve her former courtesies, made her qualities knowne to the Queene's most excellent Majestie and her court, and writ a little book to this effect to the Queene, an abstract whereof followeth." In this abstract he recounts his captivity amongst the Indians while in Virginia, and says: "After some six weeks fatting amongst these salvage courtiers, at the minute of my execution she hazarded the beating out of her owne braines to save mine, & not only that, but so prevailed with her father that I was safely conducted to Jamestowne." He then goes on to relate her coming to him afterwards in the night to apprise him of her father's plot to murder him and his men, her relief of the colonists from want, and her services in keeping peace between them and the Indians. He then adds these words: "Thus, most gracious Lady, I have related to your Majestie what at your best leasure our approved Histories will account you at large."

If this letter was written to the Queen under the circumstances, and at the time stated, we cannot doubt with any reason the truth of its statements. Every statement it contains, except that concerning his rescue, is supported by the writings of others in the "Oxford Tract," who were eye-witnesses. The rescue was only witnessed by the Indians; but an assertion of it in a letter to the Queen on behalf of Pocahontas, when she and her husband and her brother-in-law were in England, would not have been attempted if it had never happened. (pp. 52-3)

The fact that Smith wrote this letter in 1616, if conceded, is conclusive of the rescue, and this was so apparent to Mr. Adams that he attempted to discredit Smith's statement concerning it. If the letter was written as claimed, the members of the court must have known of it, and when Smith published the statement in 1624, there were living many persons who had been members of the court of 1616. The Queen was dead, but the King was alive. There were also surviving, Prince Charles, who named for Smith the localities he had discovered in New England; the celebrated Duchess of Richmond and Lenox, to whom the "General History" was dedicated; the Duchess of Bedford, lady to the Queen's bed chamber, an authoress and a patroness of literary men; the Duchess of Nottingham, lady to the Queen's drawing chamber, famous for her connection with the ring said to have been given by Elizabeth to the unfortunate Earl of Essex, who lost his head; and the Duchess of Suffolk, also of the drawing chamber, and mother of the notorious woman who was divorced from that Earl of Essex, who subsequently led the armies of Parliament against Charles the First.

These, and many others, would have at once detected the falsehood had Smith dared to publish in 1624 a letter purporting to have been written in 1616 to the Queen and her court, about so interesting a person as Pocahontas, which he had in fact never written. (pp. 54-5)

[Smith] was, in fact, a man of high character as well as genius. He was one of the persons selected by the Company to govern the infant colony of Virginia; he was entrusted with the charge of two expeditions to New England, and was appointed Admiral of that country. His maps of the countries he visited, and descriptions of their inhabitants, are acknowledged by all writers to be remarkably accurate, and the estimation in which he was held by those who knew him best, is admirably expressed

by one of the writers in the "Oxford Tract" upon the occasion of his departure from the colony, in these words:

> What shall I saye, but thus we lost him; that in all his proceedings made justice his first guide, and experience his second, ever hating basenesse, sloth, pride and indignitie more than any dangers; that never allowed more for himselfe than for his soldiers with him; that upon no danger would send them where he would not lead them himselfe; that would never see us want what he either had or could by any means get us; that would rather want than borrow, or starve than not pay; that loved action more than wordes, and hated falsehood and coveteousnesse worse than death, whose adventures were our lives, and whose losse our deaths.
>
> (p. 57)

William Wirt Henry, "The Address," in Proceedings of the Virginia Historical Society, *Virginia Historical Society, 1882, 63 p.*

EDWARD ARBER (essay date 1884)

[*An English scholar, Arber is best remembered as the editor of Arber's English Reprints (1868-80), a 39-volume series which made many important works of literature generally accessible and affordable for the first time. In 1884, Arber became the first editor of Smith's complete works. In the following excerpt from his introduction to* Travels and Works of Captain John Smith, *he takes issue with Smith's adverse critics.*]

Mr. J. G. PALFREY, in his famous note on the **True Travels** [see excerpt dated 1858] . . . , is simply laughable for his ignorance of the regulated conditions of publishing books in London during the lifetime of our Author. He states that "hack-writers abounded in London at the time. SMITH was just such a person [!], as, for the saleableness of his narratives, would naturally fall into their hands, and into the hands of their masters, the booksellers. . . . On the whole, the reader perhaps inclines to the opinion that JOHN SMITH was not the sole author of his books."

Mr. PALFREY errs in applying to the lifetime of our Author, the mendacities of the Grub-street era of GEORGE I. and II. Not only were there no "hack-writers," at that time, for books of colonization, &c.; but SMITH manifestly wrote most of his books for nothing, and between 1616 and 1620 "divulged to my great labour, cost, and losse, more than seven thousand Bookes and Maps." . . . Mr. PALFREY's view of our Author is a degrading opinion of one of the most highminded of men, eminently possessing that keen sense of honour which was usual in an English Officer at that time; and whose perspicuous honesty, had we space, could be demonstrated through every line of the present Text. Yet, in spite of his prejudice, in this same note, Mr. PALFREY is compelled to admit the substantial agreement of SMITH's account of his Eastern experiences with the known facts of history.

So far from the following Text having been written by anonymous hack-writers in SMITH's name, it will be seen that no one could have been more scrupulously careful than he was, in naming the authorities for everything he prints. . . . The only exceptions to this, are those bits of verse scattered throughout the **General History** which are intended to "point the moral" of the Story, and which we must attribute to SMITH's deep religious feeling, wide reading, and not very great poetical powers.

For our own part, beginning with doubtfulness and wariness, we have gradually come to the unhesitating conviction, not only of SMITH's truthfulness, but also that, in regard to all personal matters, he systematically understates rather than exaggerates anything he did.

Why New England writers should attack our Author (after the manner of Mr. E. D. NEILL, who says "his writings are those of a gascon and beggar" [see excerpt dated 1869]) is simply amazing: seeing that SMITH preferred New England, as a colony, to Virginia or any other part of the world; that he tried so hard, for years, to go out and end his days there; and that he actually did effect more, by his advocacy and publications, towards its colonization, than ever he was able to accomplish for Virginia, with all his money, personal services, dangers, and magnanimity. (pp. xxiii-xxiv)

[Though] they may offer not a few points which have yet to be cleared up, the general credibility of the *Travels* is beyond question; and in its clear, graphic and condensed style, the narrative is among the very best written English books of travel printed in SMITH's lifetime. (p. xxv)

> *Edward Arber, in an introduction to* Travels and Works of Captain John Smith: 1580-1631 *by John Smith, edited by Edward Arber, John Grant, 1910, pp. xix-xxxii.*

LEWIS L. KROPF (essay date 1890)

[*A Hungarian engineer who spent much of his adult life in England, Kropf was interested in Hungarian and British history. He was able to combine these interests in the study of Smith's* True Travels, *contributing numerous essays on the subject to both Hungarian and English periodicals. In his research, Kropf compared Smith's account of his early adventures with the known history of southeastern Europe. As he reached conclusions almost wholly unfavorable to Smith, Kropf was instrumental in bringing Smith's reputation for historical accuracy, already seriously weakened by the Pocahontas controversy, to its nadir. No systematic attempt was made to refute Kropf's arguments for over forty years, until Laura Polanyi Striker conducted her own research into the subject, reaching very different conclusions (see excerpt dated 1953 and Additional Bibliography). The following excerpt, from a series of articles contributed to* Notes and Queries, *presents part of the evidence Kropf accumulated to discredit* The True Travels.]

Modern research has stripped the *protégé* of Princess Pocahontas of many of his self-conferred laurels and dispelled much of the romance which formerly clung to his name. The truth of a great portion of his wonderful adventures and heroic deeds has lately been questioned, nay, some American writers have even gone so far as to denounce him as a blustering braggadocio and brand his autobiography as a collection of mere traveller's tales and "the gasconades of a beggar" [see excerpt dated 1869].

At the suggestion of a friend, I have lately examined into [Smith's *True Travels*]. . . . (p. 1)

I shall now proceed to lay the captain's case before the reader, to enable him to decide how far Mr. Palfrey, the historian of New England, is correct, when stating that "a comparison of Smith's narrative with the authentic history of the south-east of Europe leads to conclusions on the whole favourable to its credit" [see excerpt dated 1858]. (pp. 1-2)

All that is historically correct in Capt. Smith's narrative may have been borrowed by him from [Knolles's *General Historie of the Turkes*], and all that is new in his book and not to be found in other authors may not be true, but have been invented by the captain to embellish his tale. Indeed, everything seems to point to one conclusion, viz., that the *True Travels and Adventures* is a pseudo-historical romance, with Capt. Smith for its author and principal hero; and one feels inclined to suspect that he has not been at all to the south-east of Europe. (p. 2)

• • • • •

Our author begins the story of his deeds on Hungarian soil by telling his readers that "after the losse of Caniza, the Turkes with twentie thousand besieged the strong Towne of Olumpagh," and continues by relating how the garrison got into sore straits until he appeared on the scene as a *deus ex machinâ*, and came to their rescue with a "strange invention" of torch-signals and the unusual "stratagem" of employing dummy "musketteers" to mislead the unsophisticated Turks. The first device enabled "Kisell, the General of the Archduke's Artillery," to inform Lord Ebersbaught, "the Governour [of the fortress], his worthy friend," that he was about to attack the Turks at a specified time and hour, and to ask him to co-operate with the army of relief. The combined attack and sally of the Christians was successful. The stratagem of dummies confused the Turks, and enabled "Kisell to put 2,000 good soldiers into the town before the morning." Many of the Turks were killed, the rest of them very much scared, and, to cut a long story short, they were obliged to raise the siege and return to Kanizsa. In acknowledgment of the good services rendered by him to the Imperial cause Smith was rewarded and made captain of 250 horsemen under the mysterious "Earle of Meldritch."

Palfrey and Prof. Arber think that by Olumpagh Ober-Limbach (in Hung. Felsö Lendva) is meant. A castle of that name exists in Hungary close to Kanizsa, but it is impossible to find any record of a siege at the period in question. Kanizsa as we know, surrendered on Oct. 22, 1600, to Ibrahim, the Grand Vizier, who, having placed a very strong garrison therein, shortly after recrossed the Save and went into winter quarters at Belgrade. The troops thus left behind often sallied forth on foraging expeditions into the neighbourhood, but they could have hardly spared 20,000 men to lay a regular siege to a fortified place.

Olumpagh was, according to Smith's account, on or near the plain of Hysnaburg—or, according to Purchas, Eysnaburge—and a place in its neighbourhood is named Knousbruck by Smith and Konbrucke by Purchas. A river is said to have divided the Turks, and after the conclusion of the siege and retreat of the enemy Kisell is said to have been received with much honour at Kerment (*i.e.*, Körmend). With the exception of Knousbruck, which I have not been able to identify, all the places named are in the county of Vas; but it is a far cry from Ober-Limbach to Eisenburg, the two places being some thirty-five English miles apart, and as the dummy "musketteers" were placed in the plain of Hysnaburg, and must therefore have been masked by several groups of mountains lying between the two places, it is difficult to understand how they could have influenced the course of the attack, to say nothing of the range at which their sham muskets were called upon to do execution. (pp. 41-2)

The next chapter (chap. v.) treats of the siege of Alba Regalis (or Stuhlweisenburg in German) by the Imperial troops under the Duke of Mercoeur, during which another invention of Capt. Smith was to play an important part, viz., his "fiery dragons," made out of "round-bellied earthenware pots" filled with gun-

Smith's coat of arms, which features the heads of the three Turks Smith killed in single combat.

powder and musket balls and covered with a mixture of pitch, brimstone, turpentine, &c. A full recipe is given of the way in which they were prepared. Though ordinary bombs were known since 1433, when Malatesta, Prince of Rimini, is credited to have invented them, this combination of bombs and stinkpots was, we may presume, entirely new, and we need not be astonished, therefore, at the consternation they produced among both Turks and Christians, according to Smith; though I have consulted several contemporary accounts of the siege and not one of them mentions a word about the "fiery dragons." (p. 42)

· · · · ·

[Let] us, in conclusion, examine the grant of arms which seems to form the *pièce de resistance of* Smith's book. As already stated, there are three transcripts of it extant. The "original," which Sir William Segar, Garter King, saw, and from which he made the official copy preserved at the Heralds' College, is apparently lost, and we are, therefore, unable to examine Prince Sigismund's sign-manual and seal. To all appearance, the draughtsman who copied the latter has largely drawn upon his imagination, as it differs from all other known seals. Should the unexpected happen, and the "original" turn up, we should be able to compare the signature with that on a letter addressed to Lord Keeper Sir John Puckering, dated Alba Julia, Sept. 11, 1593. *En passant*, I wish to direct attention to the fact that although the patent was granted on Dec. 9, 1603, and Capt. Smith reached England in 1604, it was not registered at the College of Arms until Aug. 19, 1625.

With regard to the text of the document, the title of Prince Sigismund is set forth as "Dei Gratia Dux Transilvaniæ, Wallachiæ, et Vandalorum [?], Comes Anchard, Salford, Grow-

enda [?]." We may safely say that this is unique. It is certainly the only known instance in which a Prince of Transylvania assumed the title of the Dukes of Mecklenburg, and described himself as the Duke of the Vandals. In his official documents the prince is generally styled "Dei Gratia Transylvaniæ, Moldaviæ, Wallachiæ Transalpinæ et Sacri Romani Imperii Princeps, Partium Regni Hungariæ Dominus, Aurei Velleris Eques et Siculorum Comes." This, of course, varies according to various dates, but the above represents it in full. Where "Anchard, Salford, and Growenda" may be Smith's commentators do not inform us, and probably no mortal can tell. The mysterious earl's name and full title are given as "Henricus Volda, Comes de Meldri, Salmariæ et Peldoiæ primarius." Salmaria and Peldoia, for all we know, may be very important places or provinces; but we know nothing of them, and probably they are also in cloudland.

The locality from which the patent is dated is given as "Lesprizia in Misnia" in the original Latin text, and in the English translation as "Lipswick in Misenland." Misnia is, as we know, the Marquisate of Meissen; but we search the map in vain for a place named Lesprizia, nor do the gazetteers of Germany help us in the matter.

When Prince Sigismund was secretly negotiating for the transfer of Transylvania to the Austrian dynasty the emperor promised to reinstate him in the possession of the Duchies of Oppeln and Ratibor, in Silesia, formerly owned by him; but the prince at first did not seem inclined to go back to his old home, and would have preferred some quiet nook in the Tyrol, close to his friends in Italy, and far away from all places frequented by Hungarians. . . . And although he subsequently agreed to settle in Silesia, he never went there, but to Libochowitz, which was presented to him by the emperor on Dec. 18, 1602. But Libochowitz is on the river Eger, in Bohemia, close to Prague, and not in the Marquisate of Meissen. So it cannot be meant by "Lipswick"; and we have, therefore, here to face another mystery, this time a geographical blunder in what purports to be an official document, dated from the very place.

I hope I have laid enough evidence before the reader to prove that the patent, as published in Smith's own book, is an exceedingly clumsy piece of forgery. But the captain's audacity is apparently exceeded by the credulity of his dupes. We may find some excuse for a man placed in Sir William Segar's position in the seventeenth century appending his signature and official seal to this precious document, but it is difficult to conceive how any modern author, with all the opportunities of research at his disposal, can be deceived by such a transparent fraud, and undertake the hopeless task of defending the captain's veracity. (pp. 281-82)

Lewis L. Kropf, "Captain John Smith of Virginia," in Notes and Queries, *Vol. 9, Nos. 210, 212 and 224, January 4, January 18 and April 12, 1890, pp. 1-2; 41-3; 281-82.*

ALEXANDER BROWN   (essay date 1890)

[*An American historian, Brown was the author of* New Views of Early Virginia History: 1606-1619 *(1886) and* English Politics in Early Virginia *(1901). In the nineteenth-century debate concerning Smith's veracity, Brown was an anomaly in that he was the only native Virginian critic to attack Smith. Other critics have been taken aback by what they consider the harshness of Brown's views; Philip L. Barbour has commented that "Brown's reason takes wing almost every time John Smith appears." In the fol-*

lowing excerpt, Brown denies Smith a significant role in American history or literature.]

Dozens of biographies have been written of Capt. John Smith; but they are generally based on the accounts furnished by himself. The world has been searching for data regarding him for two hundred years, but has found little beside what he tells us in his own works, and unfortunately his own story of his life cannot be relied on. It is true that the accuracy of all of his statements cannot be tested; but enough can be, to make it evident that all must be, before they can be safely taken for use in accurate history or biography. (p. 1006)

Captain Smith did not carry the first colonists to Virginia; he landed there himself "as a prisoner." He did not support the colony there by his exertions; the colonists were dependent on England for supplies; they were succored by every vessel that arrived during his stay in Virginia, and at no time were they found to be more in need than when Argall arrived in July, 1609, during Smith's own presidency. So long as he stayed, the colony was rent by factions, in which he was an active instrument. Instead of making Jamestown a relief station and plantation, as it was intended to be, he was constantly taking off the men from their duties there, going on voyages to discover mines, the South Sea, etc., all of which, I am sure, can be easily proven. He not only failed to give satisfaction to his employers, but he gave great dissatisfaction, and was never employed by the Council of the Va. Co. again. (p. 1008)

While the vain character of Captain Smith is amply shown in his own compilations, it can be readily understood why he must have been for many years an object of especial interest in England, and why this interest in him should increase to a sympathy which would in the hearts of some get the better of their judgment. The planting of the colonies in America was an all-absorbing topic of the time; their perils and misfortunes were tragedies of the period; and Smith imagined that these colonies were all "pigs of his sow." He tells us himself, in 1630, that "scarce five of those who first went with me to Virginia remain alive." For many years he was probably the only one of those first sent to Virginia under Newport, in December, 1606, living in England; under these circumstances, Smith must have been an object of the greatest interest, and a welcome guest by the hearth of many of the gentry of Old England, where "his twice told tales" afforded amusement and interest, or aroused sympathy; and we can easily forgive him for compiling a romance [*The History of Virginia, The Summer Ilands and newe England*] with himself as his hero, without accepting his story as a trustworthy history of the founding of the first English Protestant colony in America. . . . It was for about 225 years almost the only source of information regarding our beginning. (p. 1009)

Even when compiling from a published narrative he does not hesitate to insert his own name, or a favorable reference to himself, where there was none. For his own purposes, he takes events of several years and bunches them all together, or an event of one year and assigns it to another year. He evidently appropriated to himself incidents in several publications and in the lives of many other men. However, I do not attribute all of his errors to selfish motives. I believe that many are attributable to his lack of knowledge of the facts. He was certainly incapable of writing correct history where he was personally interested, and after he left Virginia he evidently knew no more of the facts than the generality in England.

He was really in no way properly qualified, or properly equipped, for writing a disinterested and accurate history of the great movement.

We are told that Smith was not the author of his *History,* that it consisted of narratives written by others. All histories must be largely compiled from the narratives written by others; but when a man sets to work to collect and publish matter to prove that he is one of the greatest men of his time, and that his peers were mere marplots, and calls his compilation a history, his evidence must be presented in the most straightforward, clear, and distinct way, it must be of the highest character and of the most undoubted accuracy, for a tortuous, vainglorious, and prevaricating compilation must be really the strongest possible evidence against that man; and this is a case in point. Smith's so-called *History of Virginia* is not a history at all; but chiefly an eulogy of Smith and a lampoon of his peers. And it is seldom, indeed, that we can safely turn a man loose in the field of his own biography.

Smith's position in our early history is a remarkable illustration of the maxim, "I care not who fights the battles, so I write the dispatches."

The establishing of an English colony in America was a vast work, requiring the constant support of the king, the purse of the people, and the careful management of the greatest business men of that period for ten long years of "constant and patient resolution." On the other hand, Smith was a mere adventurer; one of the very smallest contributors; an agent of the company in Virginia less than two and half years; in command there about one year; failed to give satisfaction; sent home to answer for his misdemeanors, and was never again even employed by the South Va. Company.

The managers of the enterprise had for their own use ample maps, descriptions, and accounts; but it was against the interest of the colonies to make public their affairs, and no history was compiled from their records. No one who had ever taken the official oath could reveal or publish anything regarding the colonies in Virginia, without authority from the council, unless he broke his oath and betrayed his trust, and Capt. John Smith was probably the only official, or ex-official, who did this. He published "the dispatches;" took possession of the history which others made and turned it to his own service; and it came to pass that for over 200 years these "dispatches" were "almost the only source from which we derived any knowledge of the infancy of our country." I acknowledge that I am anxious to enable the reader to do justice to the real founders of this country, because, as the result of a remarkable chain of circumstances, great injustice has been done them; yet I certainly do not wish to be unjust to Smith. I have weighed well every scrap of evidence within my reach before arriving at the opinions herein given of him and of his so-called *General History.* (pp. 1009-10)

Alexander Brown, "Brief Biographies: Captain John Smith," in The Genesis of the United States, Vol. II, *edited by Alexander Brown, Houghton, Mifflin and Company, 1890, pp. 1006-10.*

JOHN FISKE (essay date 1897)

[*Fiske was one of the leading intellectual figures in the United States during the late nineteenth century. He is best known for his works on early American history and for his philosophical essays, which helped to popularize the theory of evolution de-*

veloped by Charles Darwin and Herbert Spencer. In the following excerpt, Fiske defends Smith's truthfulness.]

The life of Captain John Smith reads like a chapter from *The Cloister and the Hearth*. It abounds in incidents such as we call improbable in novels, although precedents enough for every one of them may be found in real life. The accumulation of romantic adventures in the career of a single individual may sometimes lend an air of exaggeration to the story; yet in the genius for getting into scrapes and coming out of them sound and whole, the differences between people are quite as great as the differences in stature and complexion. John Smith evidently had a genius for adventures, and he lived at a time when one would often meet with things such as nowadays seldom happen in civilized countries. In these days of Pullman cars and organized police we are liable to forget the kind of perils that used to dog men's footsteps through the world. The romance of human life has by no means disappeared, but it has somewhat changed its character since the Elizabethan age, and is apt to consist of different kinds of incidents, so that the present generation has witnessed a tendency to disbelieve many stories of the older time. In the case of John Smith, for whose early life we have little else but his autobiography to go by, much incredulity has been expressed. To set him down as an arrant braggadocio would seem to some critics essential to their reputation for sound sense. Such a judgment, however, may simply show that the critic has failed to realize all the conditions of the case. Queer things could happen in the Tudor times. (pp. 80-1)

[In Smith's] way of telling his tale [in *True Travels*] there is no trace of boastfulness. For freedom from egotistic self-consciousness Smith's writings remind me strongly of such books as the *Memoirs* of General Grant. Inaccuracies that are manifest errors of memory now and then occur, prejudices and errors of judgment here and there confront us, but the stamp of honesty I find on every page. (pp. 87-8)

To this day John Smith is one of the personages about whom writers of history are apt to lose their tempers. In recent days there have been many attempts to belittle him, but the turmoil that has been made is itself a tribute to the potency and incisiveness of his character. Weak men do not call forth such belligerency. (p. 90)

[In Smith's] own writings we have two different accounts [of the Pocahontas incident]. In his tract published under the title, *A True Relation* . . . , Smith simply says that The Powhatan treated him very courteously and sent him back to Jamestown. But in the *General History of Virginia* . . . we get a much fuller story. We are told that after he had been introduced to The Powhatan's long wigwam, as above described, the Indians debated together and presently two big stones were placed before the chief, and Smith was dragged thither and his head laid upon them; but even while warriors were standing, with clubs in hand, to beat his brains out, the chief's young daughter Pocahontas rushed up and embraced him and laid her head upon his to shield him, whereupon her father spared his life.

For two centuries and a half the later and fuller version of this story was universally accepted while the earlier and briefer was ignored. Every schoolboy was taught the story of Pocahontas and John Smith, and for most people I dare say that incident is the only one in the captain's eventful career that is remembered. But in recent times the discrepancy between the earlier and later accounts has attracted attention, and the conclusion has been hastily reached that in the more romantic version

Smith is simply a liar. It is first assumed that if the Pocahontas incident had really occurred, we should be sure to find it in Smith's own narrative written within a year after its occurrence; and then it is assumed that in later years, when Pocahontas visited London and was lionized as a princess, Smith invented the story in order to magnify his own importance by thus linking his name with hers. By such specious logic is the braggadocio theory of Smith's career supported, and underneath the whole of it lies the tacit assumption that the Pocahontas incident is an extraordinary one, something that in an Indian community or anywhere would not have been likely to happen.

As this view of the case has been set forth by writers of high repute for scholarship, it has been generally accepted upon their authority; in many quarters it has become the fashionable view. Yet its utter flimsiness can be exhibited, I think, in very few words.

The first occasion on which Smith mentions his rescue by Pocahontas was the occasion of her arrival in London, in 1616, as the wife of John Rolfe. In an eloquent letter to King James's queen, Anne of Denmark, he bespeaks the royal favour for the strange visitor from Virginia and extols her good qualities and the kindness she had shown to the colony. In the course of the letter he says ''she hazarded the beating out of her own brains to save mine.'' There were then several persons in London, besides Pocahontas herself, who could have challenged this statement if it had been false, but we do not find that anybody did so. [The critic adds in a footnote: ''It is true, this letter of 1616 was first made public in the *General History* in 1624 so that Smith's detractors may urge that the letter is trumped up and was never sent to Queen Anne. If so, the question recurs, Why did not some enemy or hostile critic of Smith in 1624 call attention to so flagrant a fraud?''] In 1624, when Smith published his *General History,* with its minutely circumstantial account of the affair, why do we not find, even on the part of his enemies, any intimation of the falsity of the story? (pp. 102-05)

Why then did Smith refrain from mentioning it in the letter to a friend in England, written in 1608, while the incidents of his captivity were fresh in his mind? Well, we do not know that he did refrain from mentioning it, for we do know that the letter, as published in August, 1608, had been tampered with. Smith was in Virginia, and the editor in London expressly states in his Preface that he has omitted a portion of the manuscript: ''somewhat more was by him written, which being (as I thought) fit to be private, I would not adventure to make it public.'' Nothing could be more explicit. Observe that thus the case of Smith's detractors falls at once to the ground. Their rejection of the Pocahontas story is based upon its absence from the printed text of the *True Relation,* but inasmuch as that printed text is avowedly incomplete no such inference is for a moment admissible. For the omitted portion is as likely as not to have been the passage describing Smith's imminent peril and rescue.

On this supposition, what could have been the editor's motive in suppressing the passage? We need not go far afield for an answer if we bear in mind the instructions with which the first colonists started,—''to suffer no man . . . to write [in] any letter of anything that may discourage others.'' This very necessary and important injunction may have restrained Smith himself from mentioning his deadly peril; if he did mention it, we can well understand why the person who published the letter should have thought it best to keep the matter private. After a few years had elapsed and the success of the colony was assured, there was no longer any reason for such reticence. My own opinion is that Smith, not intending the letter for publication, told the whole story, and that the suppression was the editor's work. It will be remembered that in the fight in which he was captured, Smith slew two Indians. In the circumstantial account given in the *General History* we are told that while Opekankano was taking him up and down the country, a near relative of one of these victims attempted to murder Smith but was prevented by the Indians who were guarding him. The *True Relation* preserves this incident, while it omits all reference to the two occasions when Smith's life was officially and deliberately imperilled, the tying to the tree and the scene in The Powhatan's wigwam. One can easily see why the editor's nerves should not have been disturbed by the first incident, so like what might happen in England, while the more strange and outlandish exhibitions of the Indian's treatment of captives seemed best to be dropped from the narrative.

But, we are told, the difficulty is not merely one of omission. In the *True Relation* Smith not only omits all reference to Pocahontas, but he says that he was kindly and courteously treated by his captors, and this statement is thought to be incompatible with their having decided to beat his brains out. Such an objection shows ignorance of Indian manners. In our own time it has been a common thing for Apaches and Comanches to offer their choicest morsels of food, with their politest bows and smiles, to the doomed captive whose living flesh will in a few moments be hissing under their firebrands. The irony of such a situation is inexpressibly dear to the ferocious hearts of these men of the Stone Age, and American history abounds in examples of it. In his fuller account, indeed, Smith describes himself as kindly treated on his way to the scene of execution and after his rescue. Drop out what happened in the interval and you get the account given in the *True Relation.*

Now that omission creates a gap in the *True Relation* such as to fatally damage its credibility. We are told that Smith, after killing a couple of Indians, is taken captive and carried to the head war-chief's wigwam, and is then forsooth allowed to go scot free with no notice taken of the blood debt that he owes to the tribe! To any one who has studied Indians such a story is well-nigh incredible. As a prisoner of war Smith's life was already forfeited. It is safe to say that no Indian would think of releasing him without some equivalent; such an act might incur the wrath of invisible powers. There were various ways of putting captives to death; torture by slow fire was the favourite mode, but crushing in the skull with tomahawks was quite common, so that when Smith mentions it as decided upon in his case he is evidently telling the plain truth, and we begin to see that the detailed account in the *General History* is more consistent and probable than the abridged account in the *True Relation.*

The consistency and probability of the story are made complete by the rescue at the hands of Pocahontas. That incident is precisely in accordance with Indian usage, but it is not likely that Smith knew enough about such usage to have invented it, and his artless way of telling the story is that of a man who is describing what he does not understand. From the Indian point of view there was nothing romantic or extraordinary in such a rescue; it was simply a not uncommon matter of business. The romance with which white readers have always invested it is the outcome of a misconception no less complete than that which led the fair dames of London to make obeisance to the tawny Pocahontas as to a princess of imperial lineage. Time

and again it used to happen that when a prisoner was about to be slaughtered, some one of the dusky assemblage, moved by pity or admiration or some unexplained freak, would interpose in behalf of the victim; and as a rule such interposition was heeded. Many a poor wretch, already tied to the fatal tree and benumbed with unspeakable terror, while the firebrands were heating for his torment, has been rescued from the jaws of death, and adopted as brother or lover by some laughing young squaw, or as a son by some grave wrinkled warrior. In such cases the new-comer was allowed entire freedom and treated like one of the tribe. As the blood debt was cancelled by the prisoner's violent death, it was also cancelled by securing his services to the tribe; and any member, old or young, had a right to demand the latter method as a substitute for the former. Pocahontas, therefore, did not "hazard the beating out of her own brains," though the rescued stranger, looking with civilized eyes, would naturally see it in that light. Her brains were perfectly safe. This thirteen-year-old squaw liked the handsome prisoner, claimed him, and got him, according to custom. Mark now what happened next. Two days afterward The Powhatan, "having disguised himselfe in the most fearfullest manner he could, caused Captain Smith to be brought forth to a great house in the woods, and there vpon a mat by the fire be left alone. Not long after frome behind a mat that divided the house [*i. e.* a curtain] was made the most dolefullest noyse he ever heard." Then the old chieftain, looking more like the devil than a man, came to Smith and told him that now they were friends and he might go back to Jamestown; then if he would send to The Powhatan a couple of cannon and a grindstone, he should have in exchange a piece of land in the neighbourhood, and that chief would evermore esteem him as his own son. Smith's narrative does not indicate that he understood this to be anything more than a friendly figure of speech, but it seems clear that it was a case of ceremonious adoption. As the natural result of the young girl's intercession the white chieftain was adopted into the tribe. (pp. 105-10)

I have dwelt at some length upon the question of Smith's veracity for three good reasons. First, in the interests of sound historical criticism, it is desirable to show how skepticism, which is commonly supposed to indicate superior sagacity, is quite as likely to result from imperfect understanding. Secondly, justice should be done to the memory of one of the noblest and most lovable characters in American history. Thirdly, the rescue of Smith by Pocahontas was an event of real historic importance. Without it the subsequent relations of the Indian girl with the English colony become incomprehensible. But for her friendly services on more than one occasion, the tiny settlement would probably have perished. (p. 111)

            John Fiske, "The Land of the Powhatans, in his Old
            Virginia and Her Neighbours, *Vol. I,* Houghton Mifflin Company, *1897, pp. 80-118.*

E. KEBLE CHATTERTON   (essay date 1927)

[*Chatterton was an English journalist and author who wrote several books, both fact and fiction, on naval topics, including* The Romance of the Ship *(1910) and* Valiant Sailormen *(1936). In the following excerpt from his biography of Smith, Chatterton briefly appraises Smith as an author.*]

We may count ourselves as fortunate that Smith lived and wrote at a time when the language of England was so full of beauty, containing all the excellence of Elizabethan words and phrases, together with a solemnity of rhythm and quaintness associated

Twenty-one-year-old Pocahontas (or Matoaka) dressed in English attire, in an engraving rendered after her marriage to tobacco planter John Rolfe. Baptized into the Christian faith, her name was changed to Rebecca.

with the Bible's Authorized Version. Smith brought to his task exceptional powers of observation trained by long and diverse travel; clarity of thought developed by the long discipline of organizing and ruling; a sense of humour which is born of familiarity with oft encountered danger; a charm that belongs to a refined mind; an unusual restraint, even when most indignant against injustice and inefficiency; and, finally, an infectious enthusiasm which overflows from a heart that has been filled with patriotic and dutiful longing. The romance of attempting, the joy of beginning for posterity a great and noble task, were to him so real and lovely that all the intrigues of colleagues, all the indifference of superiors were but annoying incidents; and in his narrations, his letters and his criticisms we can almost see the man who writes them. Always we can feel his vigorous, virile personality. (pp. 258-59)

> *E. Keble Chatterton, in his* Captain John Smith, *Harper & Brothers Publishers, 1927, 286 p.*

SAMUEL ELIOT MORISON   (essay date 1930)

[*Morison was a prominent American historian and editor of the* New England Quarterly *whose most important works include the Pulitzer Prize-winning maritime histories* Admiral of the Ocean Sea *(1942) and* John Paul Jones *(1959). In the following excerpt from his history of the Massachusetts Bay Colony, Morison comments on Smith's character and the veracity of* The True Travels.]

Historians have never been able to agree about the veracity of Captain John Smith. Some would have us believe every word

he wrote, others denounce him as a mere lying braggart. The Pocahontas episode, by which he is known to every one in the English-speaking world, may well be true; but very little of his *True Travells* could possibly have happened. The 'siege of Regall,' in which Smith distinguished himself by slaying successively three Turkish champions 'to delight the ladies,' is otherwise unknown to fame. The three Turks' heads, his patent of arms from Prince Sigismund, is a palpable forgery. Nor does authentic history know aught of the bloody field of Rottenton, whence our Captain was led away into Turkish captivity. Of his general the 'Earle of Meldritch, Salmaria and Peldoia,' a tithe of whose exploits as related by Smith would have made him the Roumanian national hero, no vestige can be discovered. Yet one puts down the *True Travells* with the feeling that our Captain had seen plenty of fighting in Transylvania, although he imagined a good deal more than he actually performed; and that after matching stories on long sea voyages and telling tales around Virginia camp-fires, he became unable to distinguish the true from the false. The line between fact and fiction was less sharply drawn in Elizabethan days than in our own, and stretching the long bow was an old English custom which only lately became of ill repute.

John Smith was a liar, if you will; but a thoroughly cheerful and generally harmless liar, and a valiant Christian gentleman withal. A practical adventurer, with a touch of austerity:

> I never knew a Warryer yet, but thee,
> From wine, Tobacco, debts, dice, oaths, so free,

writes one of his old soldiers, in a poetical effusion. A business man with a touch of Don Quixote, common sense and exalted imagination, Christian humility and exaggerated ego. His style, which seemed 'barbarous and uncouth' to the fastidious Thomas Jefferson, is peculiarly irritating to those who like a good plain tale without trimmings; and whatever subject he touches leads back very shortly to Captain John Smith, his trials, hairbreadth escapes, bad breaks, and unappreciated virtues. (pp. 8-9)

> *Samuel Eliot Morison, "Promoters and Precursors," in his* Massachusettensis de Conditoribus; or, The Builders of the Bay Colony, *Houghton Mifflin Company, 1930, pp. 3-20.*

STEPHEN VINCENT BENÉT   (poem date 1943)

[*Benét was an American man of letters whose poetry and fiction is often concerned with examining, understanding, and celebrating American history and culture. The comic short story* "The Devil and Daniel Webster" *and the Pulitzer Prize-winning Civil War epic* John Brown's Body *(1928) are his best-known works. When Benét died in 1943, he left unfinished* Western Star, *an epic poem of the colonization and westward expansion of America. In the following excerpt from this poem, he sketches Smith's character. George Percy, also discussed in the poem, was another member of the London Company.*]

> Young Percy, eighth son of Northumberland,
> Fresh-faced, dark-haired, a very younger son
> Of an old, great, hotheaded, daring name,
> Tempered at twenty-six in Flanders wars
> And now the first of endless younger sons
> To seek a phantom fortune in the West,
> Though soberer than most—George Percy gazed,
> A little dazed, but very courteous,
> At the brisk fellow on the other stool.
>
> Ancients and captains he had seen in Flanders,
> And he was no green boy to gulp the first
> Wild traveler's tale, told with a sober mouth.

He'd heard stage-players rant and noble lords
Rant also, though in different vein from theirs,
And, though he kept his counsel and his peace,
There were some trifling actions of his own—
Aye, a few 'scapes—he'd seen stout fellows slain—
Slain one himself—couched in the Flemish mud—
Taken his chance of shipwreck on the sea—
And, on the whole, not shamed the Percy name,
Or thought not so, at least.
                              But this! But this
Chimera here before him! this bold-eyed,
Talkative, bearded man of twenty-seven
Who had been everywhere, been everything,
(Or so he said) a prisoner of the Turk,
(Or so he said) beggar in Muscovy,
A paladin in Transylvania
(Or so he said), shipwrecked in twenty seas,
Lover of ladies in a dozen lands,
Who, in the midst of some preposterous tale
Would say with such serenity of eye,
Such a bland visage of pure chivalry,
"Here too I found, sir, as I've ever done,
A woman's kindly help my greatest stay
In bitterest misfortune"—that you wondered,
Wondered, believed and wondered yet again,
For, certainly, the fellow was no fool
And had an infinite knowledge of the world,
Its sleights, devices and subtilties,
Ambition huge as his self-confidence
And temper hotter than a beechwood blaze.
What was one to believe? What could one say?
The other men were men predictable
But not this arrant creature with his vast
Mountain of tales, his bright, commanding stare,
His hardy body, his fantastic mind.
("And yet, he knows the sea and men and wars
However he has known them. That is true.
That much is true. I will keep hold of that.
Though, even as he talks, my fingers slip
And I am back in Ariosto's tales.
Am I awake or dreaming? Is this voyage
A voyage at all? I knew before he talked.
But now I've nigh forgotten my own name.
I sail with a chimera to the West.")
So thought George Percy, but he said aloud,
"Nay sir—I pray you—'tis a noble tale—
Continue it—you were about to say—"

"To say?" the other man said briskly. "Aye.
When I had slain the second Turkish champion,
My sword being somewhat hacked, I rested on it
Perhaps the space a bell might toll a knell
And drank a cup of waters, while the Turks
Wailed for their slain most plaintively and loud.
Then there advanced the third—a lusty rogue,
Green-turbaned, their most skillful swordsman he,
And, as he rushed upon me—" said John Smith.

                                        (pp. 42-4)

And now, to Jamestown,
The wildfowl came, and the first cool days of Fall,
And John Smith went exploring.
He is one of the first Americans we know,
And we can claim him, though not by the bond of birth,
For we've always bred chimeras.
                              And he was one,
This bushy-bearded, high-foreheaded, trusting man
Who could turn his hand to anything at a pinch,
Bragging, canny, impatient, durable
And fallen in love with the country at first sight.
For that is something which happens or does not.
It did to him.

You can see the difference in Percy,
Who is always the Englishman among the natives,
And never sheds his skin or his English ways,
A good man, an excellent colonial-governor
But not this skin-changing stepchild of Ulysses,
On fire, yes, fed or fasting, to see new things,
Explore, map out, taste, venture, enjoy, astound
And look, look, look, with a fly's remembering eye,
A child's delight in marvels, a liar's gorgeousness,
And the patient, accurate pen that mapped two great coasts.
This is how they roast corn.
                              This is how their women are painted.
These are the birds, the beasts—oh, look and see!
This is a beast that they call aroughcan,
Much like a badger but useth to live in trees,
This is their beaver, big as a water-dog,
This is the toadfish, swelling in the air,
And here I did—oh, the marvelous things I did!
But the maps that I draw are true, and when I see
Without myself in the picture, I see and know.
This is their language. I will write it down.
"Kekaten pokahuntas—" and the rest,
"Bid Pocahontas bring hither two little baskets
And I will give her white beads to make her a chain."
And, in between, I will get men working again,
Shame the lazy, master the sulky, heave
My shoulder to the sticking wheel of Jamestown
And make it groan and turn till it grinds the corn.
And didn't I do it well? There is not one like me!

No, my chimera—and yet, we'll see you again,
In many shapes, before the long tale is told,
The braggarts who, somehow, carried out the brag,
The stepchildren of Ulysses, many-deviced,
"And it was proved to his face that he begged in Ireland
Like a rogue without a license," says Wingfield angrily.
Well, perhaps he did. I wouldn't doubt it at all.
For such things occur to chimeras—and if he did,
The people he begged from got their money's worth
And goggled, hearing the tale, as we goggle yet.
For this man was always alive to his fingertips.
He would not lie down and die and he will not still.
There were tears on the faces of the men sick for home?
Good God, how could men behave so, in a new world,
With a bay to explore, an aroughcan to see,
An Indian king or a possum to talk about?
How could one weep for the Christmases of England
When we never feasted more or had better fare
Than in the dry smoky houses of Kecoughtan?
How could men be sick at heart,
With a savage chief to visit and beguile,
Or a wild child-princess, bursting out of the woods,
Her train of girls behind her, shouting and screaming,
With deerhorns set on their foreheads—a Bacchant rout,
Led by the nonpareil, the daring child,
Who was to die a Christian and a lady
And leave her slight bones in the English earth
And her son's sons to know Virginia still,
Such being the fate.

                                        (pp. 72-4)

He left the room and never saw her again.
He was outward bound—to chart the New England coast
From Cape Cod to Penobscot.
Two thousand miles of it in an open boat.
And so, by incredible labors, make the map
That drew men's minds to New England—the laborious
Chimera, who could not look at the land and lie,
Only about himself and other men,
Who doubted gentlemen's hearts but never the goal
And, in the end, could say with a flat claim
Superbly boastful and precisely just,

"These colonies being, in some sort, my children."
He had none out of his body, for all the tales.
He had no fortune out of the lands he mapped,
Not even a twelve-pound knighthood—but they came,
Gorged on his books, believing truth and lies,
They settled Massachusetts and Virginia,
And where they settled, he had been before.

You can see why he maddened others and does so still.
But, spent and old, he believed to his last breath
That this was a good country.
We have had others since, and born in the land,
Who blessed it only while they could milk it dry
And, that being done with, cursed it in the street,
Though they were not at Jamestown or the wars
But lived more easily than men at Jamestown,
In fact, lived very well.
                  I may be wrong.
But, thinking of some well-dressed gentlemen
And well-fed ladies I have met at times
Who spent their years despairing of the Republic
And trying ways to beat an income-tax,
I think I can hear the comment of Captain Smith
Clear from St. Sepulchre's, the biting voice,
The huge chimera-scorn.

(pp. 75-6)

Stephen Vincent Benét, in his Western Star, *Farrar*
& Rinehart, Inc., 1943, 181 p.

JAMES BRANCH CABELL   (essay date 1947)

[*Combining extremes of lavish romance and degraded reality,*
idealistic fantasy and jaded disillusionment, Cabell is considered
an outstanding oddity among American writers of fiction. His
most enduring achievement, The Biography of Manuel *(1904-29),*
belongs to a tradition of fantasy literature that includes Edmund
Spenser's The Faerie Queene *(1596) and Jonathan Swift's* Gulliver's Travels *(1726). Beyond Life (1919), an important collec-*
tion of literary criticism which was written to introduce the Bi-
ography, outlines the literary and philosophic concepts which
serve as its foundation. Cabell's most important later criticism
appears in Some of Us *(1930), a defense of several contemporary*
writers—including Elinor Wylie, Ellen Glasgow, and Joseph Her-
gesheimer—against the trend of neo-humanist criticism, which
demanded the subservience of art to moral and social issues. In
the following excerpt from an imaginary dialogue and discourse
on the fictive nature of Virginia's historical legacy, Cabell wryly
investigates the Smith-Pocahontas episode.]

The scene is the Red Drawing Room of Poynton Lodge, in
Northumberland County, Virginia; and Dr. Alonzo Juan Her-
nandez, that noted authority upon Floridian history, has but
now resumed a conversation momentarily disturbed by the need
of preparing two beverages. (p. 45)

HERNANDEZ: . . . [Of] a certainty you cannot put faith in the
absurd hocus-pocus of Pocahontas!

CABELL: As I have granted, even in this manuscript here at my
elbow, it is difficult to understand how, after having been
rescued by Pocahontas in the January of 1608, John Smith
could have forgotten the occurrence before the following May,
when he wrote out the first account of his capture by the
Indians; yet, about fifteen years afterward, he atoned hand-
somely for his negligence, by recollecting as many as three
versions of this rescue. His apparent attack of amnesia has been
accounted for upon several grounds.

HERNANDEZ: It is most easily explained by the fact that, when
John Smith returned to England in 1609, his personal friend,

Richard Hakluyt, had just published a book entitled, *Virginia*
richly valued by the description of the maine land of Florida
her next neighbor; out of four yeeres continuall travell and
discoverie, for above one thousand miles east and west, of Don
Ferdinando de Soto, and sixe hundred able men in his com-
panie. Wherein are truly observed the riches and fertilitie of
those parts abounding with things necessarie, pleasant, and
profitable for the life of man; with the natures and dispositions
of the inhabitants. Written by a Portugall gentleman of Elvas,
emploied in all the action, and translated out of the Portuguese
by Richard Hakluyt. At London, printed by Felix Kingston for
Matthew Lownes, 1609.

CABELL: I am not familiar with this special translation of the
Gentleman of Elvas; yet the title is edifying; and I admire the
powers of a memory which can recall it offhand.

HERNANDEZ: Now, in this book, which after his return to England John Smith most certainly read, one finds the story of
Juan Ortiz, who in 1529 enlisted in an expedition sent into
Florida by the wife of Panfilo de Narváez, in search of her
missing husband. Young Ortiz was captured by the Hirrigua
Indians, near Clear Water Beach; and he was then carried to
the village of the chief called Ucita. There the Indians prepared
to kill the white man, just as the Algonquin Indians are reported
to have made ready to kill John Smith; and there, at what
seemed to be the last moment of his life, Juan Ortiz was rescued
by Ucita's daughter, Ulaheh, in the same manner which was
attributed to Pocahontas about a century later.

CABELL: Yes; but nevertheless—

HERNANDEZ: Ortiz had many other adventures, all in the best
romantic vein, during the nine years he passed among the
Hirriguans: and we can imagine the chagrin with which John
Smith, in reading his friend's spirited translation, observed
with what ease the fine episode of this rescue by an Indian
princess could have been adjusted to some one or other of the
many daughters of Powhatan; but, alas, Smith's own book had
been printed a few months earlier; and he was thus compelled
to wait, for fifteen years, until the death of Pocahontas in
England, as a figure of some casual notoriety, had afforded to
him a chance to reprint selected portions of the story of Juan
Ortiz as being his own story. He did not pretend to any intimacy
with Pocahontas until after she had become celebrated and was
safely dead.

CABELL: You are truly insatiable; for . . . you attempt to convert . . . our prized Pocahontas into a Floridian. And yet what
does it matter?

HERNANDEZ: Were there nothing else, this Pocahontas, even
by Captain John Smith's first account—

CABELL: It so happens, I repeat, that in considering the remarkable Commonwealth of Virginia, I have not failed to appraise the ***True Relation*** with that painstaking completeness
which befits an ethnological study. Yet my remarks are brief;
and should you care to look over this manuscript here, it will
confute, I believe, the still further fault-finding which you now
plan.

HERNANDEZ: I fear that, what with so many interlineations and
your so diminutive handwriting—

CABELL: Very truly I ought not to expect anybody except myself
to decipher the hodgepodge of my manuscripts. Yet you shall
not escape, through the avenue of my cramped penmanship,

from being demolished. I will read aloud to you my comments upon the *True Relation.*

HERNANDEZ: I am suitably grateful.

CABELL: With no less of zeal than is devoted to ignoring the first Virginian, Don Luis de Velasco, do all we Virginians to whom middle-age has become a reminiscence strive to keep hugger-mugger the first book Virginia produced. We reason— through an excess of that same state-loyalty which makes us always complacent and now and then pig-headed—that inasmuch as this volume annihilates the fine tale of Pocahontas, oblivion is its right doom. And yet, to the judgment of the considerate, Captain John Smith's *True Relation* does not in any way affect the ranking of Pocahontas in the official history of Virginia; her legend, the more thanks to Virginia's unfailing good taste in mythology, has been made immortal; and so not any special hurt can arise, nowadays, from considering Virginia's first addition to literature.

One has called it, for the sake of brevity, the *True Relation.* Its birth as a book was accidental, so far as went Smith's part in it. What happened was that, in the May of 1608, Smith wrote, to an unidentified acquaintance in England, a letter as to his experiences in Virginia during the preceding twelve-month. This letter was conveyed oversea, by Captain Francis Nelson, on the *Phœniz,* in June, while Smith remained in Virginia. Of Smith's letter (which ran to the not uncustomary Jacobean length of several thousand words) a number of manuscript copies appear to have been made; and these copies were distributed among persons who shared in common, as to the infant colony, an investor's perturbed interest.

It so followed that an unbackward and thrifty economist (of whom the initials alone survive today), "happening upon this Relation by chance . . . thought good to publish it," during the August of 1608, after having embellished his piracy with a preface. This preface, which is signed "I. H.," admits candidly that the embezzled letter was printed "in the author's absence" and without any thought of obtaining Captain Smith's consent to its publication.

Thus casually got into type the first book to be written in Virginia; and in the orotund fashion of the age, this book was described, upon its title page, as being, *A True Relation of such occurrences and accidents of noate as hath hap'ned in Virginia since the first planting of that Collony which is now resident in the South part thereof, till the last returne from thence. Written by Captaine Smith, Coronell of the said Collony, to a worshipfull friend of his in England. London: Printed for Iohn Tappe, and are to bee solde at the Greyhounde, in Paules-Churchyard, by W. W. 1608.*

In this letter Smith records, for the first time, the now familiar story of how, in the December of 1607, John Smith was captured by a party of Indians and carried before Powhatan; and records also that "with such a grave and Majesticall countenance as drave me into admiration to see such state in a naked Salvage, hee kindly welcomed me with good wordes and great Platters of sundrie Victuals, assuring mee [of] his friendship and my libertie within foure dayes."

Whereafter, it develops, Captain Smith's enforced but uniformly agreeable visit during the first week of 1608, to King Powhatan, "in his house at Werowocomoco," was devoted for the most part to prolonged conferences between the two of them,—during which interviews Powhatan described the polity and customs and geography of his country, and questioned his

hairy outland guest in regard to the tribal habits of Europe. "And thus having, with all the kindness he could devise, sought to content me"—so does Smith round off the primal story of Virginian hospitality,—"hee sent me home [that is, back to the fort at Jamestown] with 4 men—one that usually carried my Gowne and Knapsacke after me, two other[s] loded with bread, and one to accompanie me."

Such is Smith's first, confidential account of his Indian captivity and of its genial aspects. During this four days' stay at Werowocomoco he appears neither to have seen nor heard of Pocahontas. Farther on in the *True Relation,* however, he records that, in the May of 1608—which was the same month wherein Smith completed the letter to his "worshipfull friend,"— "Powhatan, understanding we detained certain Salvages, sent his Daughter, a child of tenne yeares old, which [daughter] not only for feature, coutenance & proportion much exceedeth any of the rest of his people, but for wit and spirit [appears] the only Nonpareil of his Country. This [child] he sent by his most trustie messenger, called Rawhunt . . . [who] with a long circumstance told mee how well Powhatan loved and respected mee, and in [order] that I should not doubt any way of his kindness, he had sent his child, which he most esteemed, to see me—[and] a Deere and bread besides, for a present. . . . His little Daughter hee had taught this lesson also: [she] not taking notice at all of the Indeans that had been prisoners three daies, till that morning that she saw their fathers and friends come, quietly and in good tearmes, to entreate their libertie."

Smith adds that the seven captive Indians "we . . . gave to Pocahuntas, the King's Daughter, in regard to her father's kindness in sending her. . . . Pocahuntas also we requited, with such trifles as contented her, to tel that we had used the Paspaheyans very kindly in so releasing them."

And not anywhere else in the *True Relation* does King Powhatan's "little Daughter," who in the May of 1608 was "a childe of tenne yeares old," figure at all.

Here are the sole mentions of Pocahontas, as Smith put upon paper his first account of his first dealings with Pocahontas— in a private letter, as one needs to remember, wherein, if anywhere, one might suspect him of truth-telling, because there was not anything to be gained by misrepresenting what happened at Werowocomoco. And the wording of the passages which have been quoted, repays, I submit, a consideration which hitherto it has been denied, continuously.

The wording, to my judgment, proclaims in itself, that Captain John Smith had not ever seen or heard of Pocahontas prior to the May of 1608, when the child visited Jamestown. The wording, beyond any possible doubt, shows that she here enters Smith's narrative for the first time; that in his letter she nowhere had been spoken of in any earlier passage which "I.H." omitted; and that at this point Smith is thus led, quite naturally, to explain who Pocahontas was, as well as more or less to describe her endearing small personality. The wording—if aught so obvious needs saying—forbids any least possibility that this "childe of tenne yeares old" could have been during the preceding January "twelve or thirteen yeares of age" (as she becomes in Smith's later romance vending, which requires to have her nubile), or that she had then saved from Powhatan's malignity, "at a hazard of her own life," the life of John Smith.

Pocahontas is introduced, instead, as a sprightly infant whom Smith now encounters, for the first time, at Jamestown, and whom he admires affably. Nor of course can that benign Powhatan, who "with all the kindness he could devise, sought to content me," be very readily reconciled with the improved Powhatan of Smith's heightened and matured fancies concerning a fairy-tale tyrant who was "more like a devill than a man."

The *True Relation*, in short, compels any tolerably intelligent reader to decide whether John Smith lied, quite gratuitously, about Powhatan and Pocahontas in a private letter, when he had nothing to gain by it? or whether Smith lied later, through rather more intelligible motives, during the touching up of a book of travels which he was trying to make salable? There can be, in the present low state of human nature, but one sane answer.

Nor should this answer be modified, I protest, by the fact that in the preface to the *True Relation* "I. H." remarks that "somewhat more was by him [John Smith] written, which being, I thought, fit to be private, I would not attempt to make publicke."

This, says the ever loyal Virginian—and how very often has he repeated his glib *non sequitur,* with an heroic stubbornness!—must of necessity refer to the rescue by Pocahontas; but he does not trouble to explain for what reason "I. H.," in pirating the book for his own private profit, should have chosen to leave out the most striking parts of it; nor above all, does the Virginian pause to reflect that, in any such improbable case, the entire narrative of the *True Relation* must have been rewritten and recolored before it was published.

The impossibility that this episode was left out is shown, in brief, by the impossibility of putting it back in. Nobody, I submit, could do that without contradicting the rest of the story as we here have it. To interject into Smith's high panegyric of a courteous and large-hearted monarch, who displayed unfailingly, throughout four days, "all the kindness he could devise," an account of how the same monarch, upon this or the other of these days, gave orders that the brains of his guest should be dashed out with a bludgeon would border—one somehow feels—upon the discrepant. Nor is it conceivable that Smith could have written anything at all like his portrayal of Pocahontas as it stands today in the *True Relation* if ever, even once, he had mentioned this "childe of tenne yeares old" anywhere earlier in the complete text of his letter.

And in passing, one finds it noteworthy that a wholly credible and unprejudiced witness, who did not suspect Pocahontas of intending to become a heroine of romance, even somewhat lessens those first fatal figures which Smith gave as to the child's age. William Strachey, Secretary of the Colony, records that in the May of 1610, when he arrived at Jamestown, Pocahontas had not yet assumed the leathern loincloth which would have proclaimed her twelfth birthday; and he tells likewise how this "well featured but wanton young girle" then embarrassed the British, by exhibiting to everybody her private parts naked, when Pocahontas was turning handsprings about the fort at Jamestown, with a sportiveness not entirely suited to the great-grandmother of so many leading Virginians.

Even so, it is perhaps my duty to add that this alleged public display of the pudenda of Pocahontas has been afforded a figleaf through the assertion that Powhatan had, "no doubt," two daughters called Pocahontas. I am deterred only by the reflection that neither Powhatan nor anyone of his contemporaries appears to ever have noted this fact; as well as by the yet further reflection that this figleaf was applied, with a chaste deference, by the same native Virginian historian who discovered intrepidly, without needing any mere evidence to abet

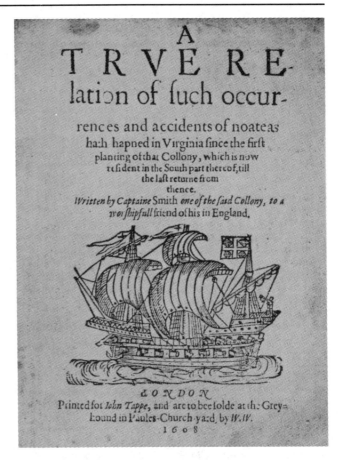

Title page of the first edition of A True Relation *(1608).*

him, that, "no doubt," every one of the jailbirds transported into the Colony of Virginia, during the period of its establishment, had been convicted unjustly. Into the better-thought-of accounts of our commonwealth one does not permit the base intrusions of common-sense.

So then does the *True Relation* demolish faith in the romantic story of Pocahontas as an actual occurrence. It shows that at Werowocomoco this infant did not rescue Captain John Smith from being murdered at her father's orders, or from any other perils. It attests that, later on, John Smith, as a capable and painstaking historian, either invented or else borrowed the entire affair.

—No one of which drab facts, I repeat, can in any way affect the unshakable position of Pocahontas in the official history of Virginia. She at all hazards remains one of its brighter ornaments; she is of a piece with the rest of it, by and large; and through the peculiar favor of Heaven—which has granted to every loyal Virginian "of the old school" an ability to believe neither more nor less by one hair's breadth than that which he elects to believe—her picturesque legend has been made immortal.

And for one, I commend this outcome, without any reservation of any nature, because of my liking for the official history of Virginia as a work of art, "in the more freely interpretative form of fiction."

HERNANDEZ: Your paper, to the best of my knowledge as a professor of history, is both accurate and injudicious. (pp. 51-64)

[CABELL:] It is the fault of you historians—in Florida as well as in all other states except only one state—that you concern yourselves to a suicidal extent (I mean, from art's standpoint) with affairs of fact. How very differently do we shape our history in Virginia, where we accept such facts as we find desirable and dismiss those which are not to our purpose! We have thus enriched the field of American folklore with that stirring epic which is the history of Virginia; nor will any virtuoso of art deny that in its splendor of fancy, in its wealth of heart-warming patriotism, and in its high flights of imagination, it very far excels the history of any other commonwealth. (p. 67)

And of Pocahontas . . . we have need in our epic, if but only because her story figures in all other well-thought-of mythologies. The legend of Pocahontas appears in every known land. That, as seems not improbable, Smith may have founded his special version of it upon an actual occurrence in the life of Juan Ortiz, we may very well concede without argument, inasmuch as Smith could have obtained the tale from hundreds of other sources. He might have borrowed it from the romance of Huon of Bordeaux, or from the fable of Gilbert à Becket (who, with the assistance of a Mohammedan Pocahontas somewhat surprisingly called ''Susy Pye,'' begot St. Thomas of Canterbury), or else from ''The Loving Ballad of Lord Bateman.''

Everywhere in folklore does one find this story, of a young man in the power of a ruthless foreign captor, whose daughter falls in love with and releases the prisoner from the cruelty of her father—with the father appearing, variously, as a gaoler, an emperor, a fiend, a sultan, a god, a giant, or a sorcerer—and with varying sequels. In Andrew Lang's *Custom and Myth* one notes an exceedingly long list of the prototypes of Smith's story, ''ranging from Finland to Japan, from Samoa to Madagascar, from Greece to India.'' The true point is not at all that Smith plagiarized his story, but the fact that in our Virginian mythology Pocahontas has her fit place, and that, howsoever she became enshrined there, the event was praiseworthy.

So Pocahontas remains, as one of our more characteristic Virginian authors has remarked, ''a forest rose, diffusing a sweet odor of the rarest virtues, and forever fragrant in the memory of Virginia.'' Nor does my compatriot omit to prophesy—as to this ''child of the forest, though daughter of an emperor, and scion of a savage race, yet mother of a sterling Christian stock''—that the redolence of her loyal womanhood will forever refresh the pages of history.

He points out that though English royalty claimed Pocahontas as its favorite, and a Briton took her from the wilderness to be his wife, she is nevertheless ''the peculiar heritage and the lasting pridge of Virginia.'' He admits that her mortal remains have mingled with the dust of Albion, far away from the leafy haunts of her dark forebears; but (so does my fellow-Virginian conclude) this Sylvan Maid yet lives in all our memories, throughout the entire state, even from Accomac County to Lee County, as a type of everything which can make her gentle sex most lovable.

That, in Virginia, my dear Hernandez, is considered the correct historical attitude toward the several thousand years old myth of Pocahontas. It defies, I submit, any seriously intended criticism. (pp. 69-71)

James Branch Cabell, ''Myths of the Old Dominion,'' in his Let Me Lie, *Farrar, Straus and Company, 1947, pp. 43-76.*

LAURA POLANYI STRIKER   (essay date 1953)

[*Striker's principal contribution to Smith scholarship has been her attempt to vindicate the historical accuracy of* The True Travels. *The following excerpt contains only a few of the many points on which Striker takes issue with Lewis L. Kropf's unfavorable commentary on* The True Travels *(see excerpt dated 1890). For Striker's further refutations of Kropf's arguments, see Additional Bibliography.*]

[Lewis L. Kropf] concluded that ''*The True Travels* is pseudo-histrical romance with Captain John Smith for its author and principal hero: and one feels inclined to suspect that he has not been at all in South Eastern Europe'' [see excerpt dated 1890]. . . .

Kropf's articles led subsequent historians to regard Smith as an adventurous liar. No American historian dared take issue with a Hungarian expert on his own ground. Consequently it became the habit to shrug off Smith's Hungarian adventures as pure inventions.

Kropf, unfortunately, did not dig deep enough into the contemporary records of that confused epoch of Hungarian history to do justice to Smith's account, or to discover the facts to be presented here, on the basis of which the whole case for Smith's veracity must be reassessed. (p. 312)

The first military event John Smith claims to have been involved in was the siege of Oberlimbach (Smith's Olumpagh). Kropf dismisses this claim by saying that history has no record of such a siege.

It must be admitted that no record of this event has so far been found. Yet the circumstances of the period are such that this proves nothing. After Kanizsa fell to the Turk in 1600, practically all the villages of Zala were at one time or another occupied by Turkish forces. In January, 1601, two thousand Turks had sallied from Kanizsa toward Körmend and, beaten off, had burned Kapronca. In August they took Babocsa. Yet such engagements as these are usually ignored in the history books.

Smith refers to Oberlimbach as a ''strong towne,'' a fact confirmed by Ortelius' illustrated map of 1664 where it is shown as a fortress. . . . The town was strategically located, for it guarded the only route connecting the two main lines for an invasion of Styria from the east—the one by the valley of the Mur and the other by the pass of Szentgotthard. Both were famous in the history of the Turkish wars. The valley, to which the Turks had gained access through their possession of Kanizsa, was blocked by the fortess of Radkersburg. The pass was protected by mountains. On the transverse route linking the two stood the fortress of Oberlimbach.

After the fall of Kanizsa the Turks annually attacked in the direction of Graz—in 1600 and 1602 from the direction of Radkersburg, in 1603 from the direction of Körmend while trying to force Szentgotthard. There is evidence that 1601 was no exception.

On May 15, 1601, Archduke Ferdinand had ordered George von Stubenberg to proceed to Radkersburg with his troops ''in full military readiness'' to resist the Turks. On August ninth a Bernhard von Mundorf petitioned the Archduke to be allowed to send a substitute to the battlefield. It looks as if the annual raid had been attempted in the traditional way, by flanking Radkersburg and Szentgotthard for a surprise attack on Oberlimbach. A good many documents in the archives at Graz could be cited to show that there was military activity in the

Oberlimbach area at this time. It is perhaps enough to add that Lieutenant-Colonel Sigmund Friedrich von Trautmansdorf reported from Szentgotthard on July 31, 1601, that news had just come from Unter-Limbach that ''the enemy is starting in great numbers to undertake something and to attack in this direction from Kanizsa.'' Several years later the Archduke Ferdinand wrote that after the fall of Kanizsa (November 20, 1601) ''the enemy raided daily up to Ober-Limbach and Unter-Limbach even to Olsznitz.'' (pp. 315-16)

In Transylvania John Smith was faced with so impenetrable a situation that only his veracity saves him from making a real mess of the record of his experiences. By his veracity it happens, unexpectedly, that he leads us to otherwise practically unnoticed facts, including a secret agreement which was unknown to his critics and which explains his apparently contradictory statements about the fighting in Transylvania.

This secret agreement explains many up to now puzzling contradictions, not only in his account, but in the confusing picture of the events of these months in Transylvania. It clears up the ''perplexity'' of John Smith's fighting ''Turks'' when the Sultan was the protector of the Prince for whom Smith was fighting, and the reason for his fighting at all during a time of truce.

The western European participants—and these made up four-fifths of the Imperial Army—assumed that the Emperor Rudolph was engaged in a holy war. Nothing could have been further from the truth. The Imperial Army was fighting in Transylvania for the ascendancy of the Germanic Roman Emperor who also had his eye on neighboring Wallachia and Moldavia. Primarily the campaign was directed against the native Hungarian nobility and the hereditary princes.

Transylvania, an independent principality since the breaking up of Hungary in 1541, was a small state with a variety of nationalities, religions and loyalties. At times it was the refuge and home of conflicting Protestant sects.

To remain independent, such a small country needed the good will of its mighty neighbors. Transylvania had to keep the balance between the mightiest powers of the time—the east and the west, the ''High Emperor'' of the Turks and the Holy Roman Emperor. During this period Transylvania paid tribute to the Turks and was protected by them. The residual sovereignty was contested by the Roman Emperor as King of Hungary and the Hereditary Transylvanian princes.

Around 1600 the military and political situation was aggravated by the psychopathic nature of the leading personalities. Emperor Rudolph II, also King of Hungary, had been declared insane in 1598. His raving madness and paroxysms of fury made it impossible for any honest person to remain in his service. He was surrounded by valets in whose hands he was a puppet, and the characteristic of his court was venality. His counterpart was Sigismund Bathory, the hereditary prince of Transylvania—*fluctuantibus undis instabilior,* less stable than the fluctuating waves, says his contemporary Szamoskoezy. These two rulers cynically traded the sovereignty of Transylvania back and forth with an irresponsibility which made the position of their adherents too dangerous to permit any single-minded loyalty. Double-crossing and secrecy were the main features of their dealings with and against each other.

On August 3, 1601, the Imperial Army had defeated Sigismund. The victory seemed so complete that high mass was sung at the cathedral of the Court in Prague, by way of celebration. But the better informed diplomats soon saw that, as

before, nothing was definite where Sigismund was concerned. The victory of Goroszlo had not assured the Emperor's supremacy in Transylvania and soon Sigismund was back—''beyond all beleefe of men,'' as Smith says. He was supported by the Turks and Tartars under the leadership of the Bey of Anatolia and the Basha of Temesvar who supplied about thirty thousand men. Strengthened by Transylvanian faithfuls whose number was enhanced by Rudolph's treatment of them, he was soon ''in possession of the best part of Transilvania.''

Always ready to make a deal, Sigismund was exchanging secret messages with the Emperor and his general, Basta, all through October, November and December. Meanwhile Basta's actions against the Transylvanians, especially against the Hungarian Estates, was becoming more ruthless from day to day. By September, when the main cities had been conquered, the country was scorched and looted. The gates were closed so that no Hungarians could enter, and the captured cities were repopulated with Germans. The estates of the nobles who had aided Sigismund were confiscated and a vast sum in gold turned over to the Emperor. Whole cities, such as the cultural center of Kolozsvar (Cluj), were given to the soldiers as free loot. Nobles who had sided with Sigismund were hanged or beheaded and orders were given to take no prisoners but to cut to pieces any nobles who were caught. At the very time when Hungarians were taking the brunt of the fighting on Rudolph's behalf in Hungary, they were doomed in Transylvania by the same Imperial Army for which they were fighting. And this was the ''policie of Busca'' (Basta), as Smith calls it, which made Henry Volda, the noble Earl of Meldritch, decide not to assist Basta against Sigismund. This is why Volda, and Smith with him, changed sides. (pp. 321-23)

Writing about one's youth and its wonderful adventures could easily lead to coloring and exaggeration, but no literary skill could invent the irrational course of events which actually took place in Hungary at this time. These implausibilities and irrationalities, which troubled Kropf, are far from making John Smith's narrative unlikely. On the contrary, they are the proof that he was really there. (pp. 323)

> *Laura Polanyi Striker, ''Captain John Smith's Hungary and Transylvania,''* in Captain John Smith: His Life & Legend *by Bradford Smith, J. B. Lippincott Company, 1953, pp. 311-42.*

BRADFORD SMITH   (essay date 1953)

[*Smith was an American educator and the author of* Americans from Japan *(1948) and* William Bradford—Pilgrim Boy *(1953), among other books. He was awarded the citation of honor from the Society of Colonial Wars for his study of colonial topics. In the following excerpt from his biography of John Smith, he vindicates* The Generall Historie *as a significant historical document and demonstrates Smith's importance as an American symbol.*]

In the *Generall Historie* [Smith] aimed to tell the whole story of the English settlement of America, beginning with the Cabots in 1497, the year before Columbus (as Smith correctly observes) touched the American mainland. He included the story of the Raleigh settlement, of Jamestown and Plymouth up to 1624 and Bermuda to 1623. Naturally he wrote most fully about his own experiences as a settler and explorer. As a result, John Smith plays a larger part in the story than a disinterested account would warrant—a fact consistently emphasized by Smith's critics, who generally fail to understand what kind of book he was writing. (p. 260)

Smith, with no models to guide him, was trying to do something quite modern. He was trying to connect the living present with the living past. Though he went back to the origins (though not to the creation!) his history was contemporary history. He was trying to look with the perspective of the historian upon recent events. He was trying to fix the record for posterity while it was still freshly in mind. He was trying to bridge the past to the present with his own memory of stirring events. This way of writing, this "I was there" technique, has become so familiar to us that we fail to credit Smith with working it out for himself.

Smith's book is really several things. It is a chronological account of the English settlement of North America. It is a personal narrative of things seen and done. It is a collection of travels and voyages. It is an assemblage of valuable documents. It includes an excellent description of Indian culture, a treatise on the economics of colonizing, and a good proportion of interesting narrative.

To produce this combination, the Captain went through a large amount of material which by his own account came to twelve times as much as he actually printed. He reprinted his own earlier works, making changes here and there or bringing them up to date. He extracted or gave in full the narratives of the men who had made the history he was covering—Thomas Hariot and Ralph Lane of Raleigh's colony, Brereton's account of the Gosnold voyage to New England, Rosier's account of Weymouth's, De la Warr's discourse of 1611, Hamor, Rolfe, Edward Winslow and a great many more. Altogether Smith quoted from or reprinted at least forty-five documents in addition to his own works and the second part of the *Map of Virginia*, which was itself a compilation.

Inevitably, a book so put together must seem like something of a hodgepodge, especially since Smith usually gives up the attempt to alter pronouns after the first few sentences of each quotation from first person narrative. But he names his sources; he gives them credit. Smith's respect for documents has too often been overlooked in judging him as an historian. Well over half of the *Generall Historie* is quoted from first-hand accounts of the new world.

This in itself was essentially the method of compilers like Hakluyt and Purchas. But Smith did more than compile. "I have not spared any diligence to learne the truth of them that have beene actors, or sharers in those voyages," he says. "Had I not discovered and lived in the most of those parts," he wrote in his preface, "I could not possibly have collected the substantiall truth from such a number of variable Relations." It is as one who has taken part in the events described that Smith makes his unique contribution as historian. Though the participant-historian is at least as ancient as Xenophon, it was new in English historical writing. Smith had no handy models to go by and the result is far from polished. But it is also very far from the self-vaunting narrative of his own achievements which some critics have tried to make it. (pp. 261-62)

Far from praising himself and damning everyone else as he has been accused of doing, Smith seems eager to speak well of others. He retains the words of praise for Gosnold, Nelson, Scrivener and others as he finds them in the *Map of Virginia*. He omits any criticism of Argall, who had been accused of scandalously mismanaging the colony during his governorship. He says nothing against Sir Edwin Sandys, Treasurer of the London Company, though he had been one of the few to vote that the charter be surrendered to the King and was thus clearly

against the Sandys administration. In his account of Bermuda he cuts out the bitter criticism of Governor Daniel Tucker which was in the book he clearly used as a source, the anonymous *Historye of the Bermudaes*. He is even kind to the "Brownists"—Pilgrims as we know them—at a time when it was considerd almost as good sport to bait a Brownist or nonconformer as to bait a bear. When one of the sources he quotes imputes evil to a man he knows, Smith rises to the defense. So when Ralph Hamor speaks against Jeffrey Abbot, Smith interpolates a paragraph of defense, concluding: "It seemes he hath beene punished for his offences, that was never rewarded for his deserts."

If the first four books dealing with Virginia are considered as a narrative of events from the 1580's to 1624, it is true that Smith occupies more space on the stage than a just proportion might entitle him to. . . . [The] source of this exaggeration was in a desire to clear himself of accusations he considered grossly unjust. Then as time went on and he was unable to found the colony he dreamed of, it is natural that he should have sought consolation by giving himself a generous space in the record of the past. For Smith was only secondarily a writer. Writing was not his life but a substitute for living. Action was his proper arena. All his writing had been born out of a need to describe what acts he had done, to defend them, to promote new activities. It is ironic that if Smith had been wholly successful in action he might never have turned to writing, in which case we might know so little of him that he would be less regarded as a man of action than is now the case.

It is true that we get no picture of the London Company from Smith's works. We see only what was going on in the colonies themselves. Perhaps Smith did not consider himself sufficiently informed to write of the internal affairs of the two colonizing companies—which is true, since their records would not have been available to him. But more than that, his interest in action rather than administration would have made it difficult, perhaps impossible, to deal with that side of the story. It remained practically untouched until late in the nineteenth century.

The material Smith likes best to deal with is that which has action in it—exploring new rivers, adventuring into Indian villages, sailing along unexplored coasts, escaping from pirates, hacking homes out of the wilderness, surviving Indian massacres, planting crops, or finding a fortune in ambergris.

In view of the fact that the history he knew was chiefly a record of reigns and wars, he deserves some credit for shaping a book in which the positive if not always peaceful activities of men got the emphasis—the building of new communities and industries. Smith does not praise war, though he was a professional soldier. But Faust-like, he finds in strenuous productive activity the most choiceworthy goal of human life. Not a bad point of view for a historian in any age, but quite remarkable in the early seventeenth century. (pp. 262-64)

What, then of his style?

Jefferson found it "barbarous and uncouth." Smith himself was always apologizing for it, excusing himself as one who could handle a weapon better than a pen. Yet the subject he had chosen called more for clarity than eloquence, and compared with other writers of his age, Smith shows a good ability to write directly and clearly. Whenever he touches the subject closest to his heart, the building of a free community in the new world, he can command real eloquence. (pp. 266-67)

Compiling and editing the work of other men does not offer much scope for elegance of style, but whenever Smith takes off on his own, as in the additions he made to Book III, he reveals himself.

When, expecting momentarily to be killed by Indians, he was led to a long house and supplied with enough food for twenty men, he remarks: "I think his [Smith's] stomacke at that time was not very good." When the Indians attack an exploring party, the English "kindly" receive them with a volley of shot. This ironic humor was clearly part of Smith's nature, and it is the leavening quality in his style.

Yet no one would claim that Smith was a great stylist. The significant contribution of his *Historie* is in the matter rather than the manner. A compiler who could test his sources by his own experience, a participant who wrote from personal experience, Smith produced a book quite different from anything that preceded him. He avoided the moralizing of previous histories and concentrated on recording the facts. (p. 267)

The Homeric age of any nation produces heroes somewhat shrouded in mystery, with great deeds clinging to them like Olympian garments and trailing off into the clouded realm of the unverifiable. In most parts of the world these heroes are very ancient, and because they were conceived by men whose problems were very different from ours, the heroes themselves have become unreal and unsatisfying. America is fortunate in having her Homeric age near at hand. We can believe in our heroes because they are culturally close to us. This may be a very important part of our strength as a nation.

The age of Jamestown and Plymouth is still close at hand—documentable, real, a continuing inspiration and a source of optimism and hope. If those first settlers could survive a voyage such as that of the *Mayflower* or sickness like that at Jamestown, we keep telling ourselves by radio, print and movie, surely we can meet our problems. As we retell their stories, their strength becomes ours, and by a sort of mystical infusion they enter into us. This was exactly what the old myths did, and it is what the modern dictator tries desperately to do for himself. We don't have to invent a saga, for we have a real one.

The popular myth of Plymouth or Jamestown is neither fiction nor fact. It is history interpreted through the emotions of those who receive it, it is a history somewhat simplified but essentially true. It is our good fortune to possess a folk myth which corresponds with the facts, to be able to believe a story which not only should have been, but was. We need no imaginary Odysseus or race hero, for our heroes are real and their exploits provable.

This explains the importance of John Smith. He is our Odysseus, our Siegfried, our Aeneas. As Athens had its Pericles but first its Theseus, Rome its Caesar but first its Romulus, England its Elizabeth but first its Arthur—so we need Smith in order to give Washington and Lincoln a proper perspective.

One of the qualities of the folk hero is that a certain mystery surrounds him. Smith gives us even this. Even after we have said all that can be said about his Hungarian exploits, the affair of Pocahontas or the pirates, a touch of the unknown remains. As in the case of the world's great religious leaders, documentation never quite catches up with legend. The size of the person seems to exceed the ability of documents to prove—sure sign of a hero! Here too, Smith satisfies us. He must always remain in part unknowable. This is his good fortune, for while the known is often forgotten, the mysterious lives on.

Smith had many of the qualities we notice in Odysseus—prowess in battle, guile, the ability to stand hard knocks, a love of wandering, and attractiveness to women. But Smith outdid Odysseus by being his own Homer. He wrote his own *Odyssey* in the *True Travels,* his own *Iliad* in the *Generall Historie* and his own *Aeneid* in the *Description of New England.* Here is a feat none of the ancient heroes can match! (pp. 304-05)

Thus he satisfies our need for a folk hero, providing the personality type through which we as a people can look at our history and our leaders, and even at ourselves. This is a great deal for a man to do. We owe as much to John Smith as a legend, a symbol, as we owe to the actual man. And it is very hard to separate them—a sure sign of durability.

Since a people always choose for their national hero the man who comes closest to their picture of what they would be, John Smith can tell us a good deal about ourselves, about our faults as well as our virtues, for he both helped to build the mold and became the first casting. He is flamboyant, expansive, with great faith in the land, scorning the pessimist and the man who holds back. Even his boastfulness can therefore be forgiven; it is an antidote to gloom. He opens the wilderness, tames the savage, brings order out of chaos. He can be both tough and tender. He can laugh and be angry. He punishes the offender with stern justice. It is no accident, or at any rate a happy one, that his very name means to smite. And what could be more appropriate for an American hero, a man symbolic of the people, than the plain name of John Smith? This John Smith, moreover, had won his right to a coat of arms—symbol of ancient class and pedigree—yet preferred the new rough land of America to the ancient culture of Europe. And since all of us, whether recently or ten generations ago, rejected an old culture to become American, we like to see that rejection symbolized, vindicated, made significant.

Perhaps all this explains in part why even one who starts out as a skeptic (as I did) ends by being won over to John Smith. He expresses us; he is us. We cannot reject him without rejecting what we are. (pp. 307-08)

Bradford Smith, in his Captain John Smith: His Life & Legend, *J. B. Lippincott Company, 1953, 375 p.*

EDWIN C. ROZWENC (essay date 1959)

[*Rozwenc was an American educator and historian whose works include* Cooperatives Come to America *(1941) and* The Making of American Society: An Institutional and Intellectual History of the United States *(1972). In the following excerpt, he recognizes the literary and imaginative patterns inherent in* The Generall Historie.]

The interminable debate as to whether the dramatic Pocahontas story can be preserved as part of a true record of the American historical experience has diverted attention from other important questions about Captain John Smith. Those we raise must be concerned with more than the truthfulness of his historical accounts, important—and fascinating—as such questions may be. The redoubtable Captain's accounts of the settlement of Virginia lie athwart the starting point of our history and in one way or another we must come to terms with them. His writings, indeed, are one of the first attempts to make an imaginative reconstruction of the origins and meaning of the American experience.

Every man's vision is directed by the metaphors which rule his mind. We must, therefore, seek to discover how Captain Smith chose to give order and meaning to his experiences in the New World: what models of historical reporting were available to him and what resources could he draw upon out of the imaginative experience of Europeans to construct his own narrative? In the light of these questions, we begin to see how a spirit of knight-errantry and the yearnings of a self-made man are interwoven in his conception of America and its possibilities.

The *Generall Historie,* which contains the fullest account of Smith's experiences in America, adds new dimensions to the literary conventions of the chivalric romance. The third and fourth books, particularly, have a dramatic rhythm and an exciting vividness that charmed Americans for generations until Henry Adams began to throw his stones [see excerpt dated 1867]. Excitement and suspense are at high pitch throughout the *Generall Historie;* surprise attacks and ambuscades, spectacular Indian fights in boats and canoes as well as in the forest, colorful Indian feasts, dances and ceremonies fill its pages. The creation of tension prior to the deliverance by Pocahontas is a little masterpiece of dramatic preparation. Our hero is tied to a tree, and Indian braves dance around him, painted in a fearful manner, shaking rattles and shouting; there are orations, with the chief priest speaking in a "hellish voyce," and the pitting of white man's magic against Indian magic. Throughout the narrative, Captain Smith looms above all other men, matching wits with a wily and resourceful Powhatan, issuing commands, performing acts of individual heroism when personal bravery was the last resource.

The *Generall Historie,* indeed, breathes a spirit that we associate with the popular romances of the Elizabethan Age. (pp. 28-9)

Perhaps if Henry Adams had not been a mere "beginner" when he wrote his essay on Captain John Smith, he might have been able to appreciate that Smith's historical writing was affected by the popular literary attitudes of Elizabethan and Jacobean England.

Yet the influence of popular literary taste alone cannot account for the character of Smith's historical writing. We must remember also that the conceptions of the nature of history and of the office of the historian as it was held in Smith's day differ greatly from our own. When Smith's *Generall Historie* was written, one of the most widely read historians in England was Sir Walter Raleigh. . . . The end and scope of history, Raleigh wrote, was to "teach by example of times past such wisdom as may guide our desires and actions''; the memory and the fame of the great deeds of men were the best examples.

No less was Captain John Smith a child of the Elizabethan Age. In 1630, he wrote, "Seeing honour is our lives ambition, and our ambition after death, to have an honourable memory of our life: and seeing by no meanes we would be abated of the dignitie and glory of our predecessors, let us imitate their vertues to be worthily their successors. . . ." His opening lines in the third book of the *Generall Historie,* which relates the dramatic story of the founding of Virginia, express his desire for the "eternizing of the memory of those that effected it."

Smith's concept of history and his literary imagination gave him the proper dress with which to clothe his image of America. The deeds of Englishmen in Virginia were as worthy of being eternized as those of the Spaniards in Peru and Mexico. Although no gold and silver were discovered in Virginia, Smith saw much that was wonderous in the accomplishments of "those

that the three first yeares began this Plantation; notwithstanding all their factions, mutinies, and miseries, so gently corrected, and well prevented. . . ." He challenged his reader to "peruse the *Spanish Decades,* the Relations of Master *Hackluit,* and tell me how many ever with such small meanes as a Barge of 22 *(or rather two)* tuns, sometimes with seaven, eight, or nine, or but at most, twelve or sixteene men, did ever so discover so many fayre and navigable Rivers, subject so many severall Kings, people, and Nations, to obedience and contribution, with so little bloudshed."

We can understand, therefore, why so much is related about Smith's explorations and Indian fights, and so little is told us of the day-by-day events at Jamestown. Whatever his motives to puff up his personal reputation, history was a matter of the glories and great deeds of men—not their prosaic daily affairs.

Yet we must not be led into a mistaken idea of John Smith's conception of America by the romantic glitter of many of the narrative passages in the *Generall Historie.* America was not simply another field of action for a bold knight. America was a land of opportunity—where men of enterprise might create a flourishing social order. The idea of America that is revealed in other portions of Smith's writing is filled with expectations of great opportunity for the individual even if the society of the New World does not change all of the distinctions of the English social order. John Smith was a self-made gentleman and the impulses that made for social mobility in Elizabethan England are writ large in his estimate of the New World's possibilities.

In the sixth book of the *Generall Historie* dealing with the prospects of New England, Smith asks:

> Who can desire more content that hath small meanes, or but onely his merit to advance his fortunes, than to tread and plant that ground he hath purchased by the hazard of his life; if hee have but the taste of vertue and magnanimity, what to such a minde can bee more pleasant than planting and building a foundation for his posterity, got from rude earth by Gods blessing and his owne industry without prejudice to any. . . .

America is not primarily a place for the soldier-knight; it beckons to the industrious who are willing to build a fortune for themselves and their posterity. But America offers more than a good chance for fortune hunters; it presents the opportunity for creating a happier and more enlightened society. In the same passage, he asks further:

> What so truly sutes with honour and honesty, as the discovering things unknowne, erecting Townes, peopling Countries, informing the ignorant, reforming things unjust, teaching vertue . . . finde imploiment for those that are idle, because they know not what to doe: so farre from wronging any, as to cause posterity to remember thee; and remembering thee, ever honour that remembrance with praise.

This is a magnificent dream of America's possibilities, one which drew thousands of Englishmen to America's shores and is still with us in many respects. (pp. 30-3)

America was more than a land of profit and contentment, even more than a land of honor and virtue; it was a presence of great natural beauty. A tireless explorer and map-maker whose observations in Virginia and New England contributed much to the geographical knowledge of the time, Smith was also a man who felt the power and the charm of Nature in the New World. Often his descriptions have the obvious purpose of advertising the New World to prospective immigrants—the climate is temperate, the soil fertile, the woods abound with wild fruits and game, the waters swim with fish in plenty—but there are also frequent flashes of subjective responses to "glistering tinctures" of water rushing over the rocks in a mountain stream, "sweet brookes and christall springs," the awesome, craggy "clifty rocks" of the Maine coast near Penobscot, the "high sandy clifts" and "large long ledges" along the coast of Massachusetts Bay. By 1616, Smith had become a convinced "northern man" among those in England who were seeking to promote other colonial ventures in America. He speaks of Massachusetts as the "Paradice of all those parts" and declares "of all the foure parts of the world that I have yet seene not inhabited . . . I would rather live here than any where." To be sure, any honest New Englander will grant that Smith often exaggerates the fertility of the soil in New England and the moderateness of the climate, but no one can doubt that the natural beauty of the land had cast a spell on the Captain that exceeded the requirements of seventeenth-century advertising!

Aside from short voyages made to New England, Smith's experience with America was limited to the two years he lived in Virginia; yet to the end of his days his heart and mind were bewitched by America, as it was and as he dreamed it; and Americans in turn have been bewitched by him ever since. (p. 34)

In a very compelling sense, John Smith is an American historian—one who tried to express the meaning of events in the origins of American experience. By the modern canons of history, a man who writes of events in which he is a participant is already suspect, but, when he does so with zestful attention to his personal exploits, we are tempted to dismiss him as a braggart and a liar. Nevertheless, there is an intractable worth in John Smith's historical writings that will not allow us to cast them aside. (p. 35)

By and large, the discrepancies of fact in his historical writing, involving as they often do such questions as the numbers of Indians who guarded him or the quantities of food served to him, are really trivial matters—the peccadillos of an amateur historian over which we need not blush any more than we do for the peccadillos of a historian of any age. The greater amount of data in Smith's historical writings has survived tests of credibility in every generation since they were published. The Pocahontas story may be an invention of Smith's mind, or of many minds in the taverns of seventeenth-century London, but on the basis of recent reexaminations of the evidence, the critical historian can admit the likelihood of Smith's deliverance by "the Indian princess" with fewer doubts than he might have had a generation ago.

Smith's historical imagination is one key to our understanding of the approach of Englishmen to the New World. He wrote of a brief moment only in the minuscule beginnings of Anglo-Saxon culture in North America. But he brought to his relation of events in Virginia the spirit of knight-errantry which still had a hold upon the imaginations of men in Elizabethan and Jacobean England and gave to Englishmen a vision of America as a place in which to achieve personal honor and glory. When we remember W. J. Cash's penetrating analysis of the aristocratic ideals of the South, we can understand readily that the chivalric spirit of the *Generall Historie* makes the defense of John Smith's reputation by Southerners something of an automatic reflex. The *Generall Historie* points to social attitudes and styles of life that actually became fundamental social traits in Virginia and much of the South.

But Captain John Smith is more than a totem in the Southern tradition of chivalry. After his brief trials and encounters in Virginia, he understood well that America was destiny and possibility—that America's history lay in the future. He saw that destiny in terms of opportunity for improvement. America would be a place where men might find economic betterment, not by plunderings of gold and other treasure, but in a balanced society of husbandmen, tradesmen, and merchants. The New World, withal, would be a place where men might teach virtue and establish a morality free of the encumbrances of the Old. John Smith's *Generall Historie* is an important part of the deeper cultural consciousness which has sustained this perennial faith in the promise of American life. (pp. 35-6)

> *Edwin C. Rozwenc, "Captain John Smith's Image of America," in* The William and Mary Quarterly, *third series, Vol. XVI, No. 1, January, 1959, pp. 27-36.*

A. L. ROWSE (essay date 1959)

[*An English historian, poet, and critic, Rowse is the author of numerous studies of Elizabethan history and literature, many of which have been highly controversial for their untraditional approach to conventions of historical and literary scholarship. At the same time, Rowse's works have been praised for their lively prose style and exhaustive knowledge of social and political life in Elizabethan England. In the following excerpt, Rowse lightheartedly considers Smith.*]

There is no more vivid account of [the vanished life of colonial America] than Captain Smith's *General History*. There has been some discussion about how much he is to be believed, but far less appreciation of how much he is to be enjoyed. His was not a Puritan inflexion, and so he has met with some disparagement, in particular from Henry Adams [see excerpt dated 1867]. (Who was it who said that vinegar, not red blood, flowed in the veins of the Adamses; and, anyway, enjoyment was not much in their line.) It is true that Smith's was an assertive personality—in that, truly Elizabethan—with himself well in the centre of action and no doubt making himself out to be more important than he was. But what is the point of an autobiographer suppressing himself? It makes for bad autobiography. I am glad that he passes the test of the strict Miss E.G.R. Taylor, who has a good opinion of him as a geographer; as an historian, where it is possible to test him, he seems pretty reliable. For the rest, he is a writer by nature: the very assertion of personality shows it, against dull dogs; he has an acute sense of others' personalities as well as his own, is racy and humorous, at times funny, at others indignant, but always alive, with a naïve poetry that is endearing. He can turn a good phrase, as with the sainted Pilgrims, 'whose humorous ignorances caused them for more than a year to endure a wonderful deal of misery with an infinite patience'. Or take his delightful description of the mask of Indian ladies. 'Presently they were presented with this antic: thirty young women came naked out of the woods, only covered behind and before with a few green leaves, their bodies all painted, some of one colour, some of another, but all differing. Their leader had a fair pair of buck's horns on her head and an otter's skin at her girdle, a quiver of arrows at her back, a bow and arrows in her hand. The next had in her hand a sword, another a club, another a pot-stick: all horned alike; the rest everyone with their several devices. These fiends with most hellish shouts and cries, rushing from among the trees, cast themselves in a ring about the fire, singing and dancing with most excellent ill variety, oft falling into their infernal passions, and solemnly again to sing and dance; having spent near an hour in this mascarado, as they entered in like manner they departed. Having reaccommodated themselves, they solemnly invited him to their lodgings, where he was no sooner within the house but all these nymphs more tormented him than ever, with crowding, pressing, and hanging about him, most tediously crying, "Love you not me? Love you not me?"

The Captain seems to have preserved his virtue, which, I should have thought, might have recommended him better to virtuous New England. (pp. 207-09)

> A. L. Rowse, "America in Elizabethan Literature, Science and the Arts," in his The Elizabethans and America, *Harper & Brothers Publishers, 1959, pp. 188-216.*

PHILIP L. BARBOUR (essay date 1964)

[*Barbour was an American author who wrote about Russian history and language, medieval and Renaissance studies, and colonial America. Among his works on the latter subject are* The Jamestown Voyages under the First Charter: 1606-1609 *(1969) and* Pocahontas and Her World *(1970). The following excerpt is taken from Barbour's* The Three Worlds of Captain John Smith, *for which he was awarded a citation of honor from the Society of Colonial Wars. Here, Barbour clarifies Smith's historical and personal intentions in* The Generall Historie *and* Advertisements for the Unexperienced Planters of New England.]

[A] designation for Smith's *General History* [as an historical work], it must be quickly explained, is not to be understood in the modern sense. Smith himself, in later years, gave his meaning to the word "history" when he wrote, "History is the memory of time, the life of the dead, and the happiness of the living." This sort of definition, indeed, was "in the air" in those days, for Ben Jonson had penned a similar thought to face the frontispiece of Sir Walter Ralegh's immensely popular *History of the World.* To Ben Jonson, history was

> Time's witness, herald of antiquity,
> The light of truth, and life of memory.

There were of course no professional "standards" for histories in the 1620's, although many books called such existed. Tales and tall tales, and unverified "facts," abounded in practically all. Furthermore, the proper religious or political slant had to be maintained if the author wanted to keep his head and right hand attached to his body. Accuracy was desirable, but variations and digressions did not mar a work provided it was good reading. Much more important was, as the historian John Selden wrote in 1618, "to give other light to the Practice and doubts of the present."

In short, John Smith's work did not purport to be professional history in our sense—indeed, could not. It was merely a thorough, somewhat egocentric compendium of facts as John Smith saw them, elaborated by extensive quotation from other, and usually unacknowledged, sources. Primarily, it was the first attempt to circumscribe historical writing within the geographical limits of the English New World. (p. 355)

Throughout the *General History* there are passages purporting to be verbatim transcripts of speeches or of letters. No one who has read much so-called history of contemporaneous authorship will be misled by this. Smith's history was written with a purpose, as were Bacon's *Henry VII* and Sir Robert Cotton's *Henry III,* for instance. It was also written to be

readable, by Jacobeans, as were the others of the type. Therefore, although the general subject matter of a speech or a conversation is undoubtedly correctly reported, the language is polished, elaborated, tricked out, for readers used to the volcanic vigor of Shakespeare, Ben Jonson, and a dozen lesser lights. Even the astounding letter to Sir Thomas Smythe which John Smith, with a straight face, states he has copied from the original sent to London, can hardly be the sort of copy we should expect of a "serious" historian. For all his frankness, Smith would hardly have written quite such a letter. At the same time, it cannot be doubted that he did write a letter in which the true state of the colony—as he saw it—was reflected without mincing words. He has merely polished the letter for greater effect.

Another side of Smith's *General History* which has been considered, in modern times, to detract from its historical value is his almost total lack of modesty. Again, it is a matter of meaning. The *General History* is not a history; it is not even a journalistic narrative. It is John Smith's Memoirs, his Apologia, and his Defense, rounded out with information from others bearing on what he considered *his* colonies. He knew, or thought he knew, what was right for the colony, how it should behave, how it should be governed, how it could survive—whether the colony was in Virginia or in New England. That characteristic of his mind is spread over the pages of his book. He was not attempting to lie to readers, nor even in a mean way to prejudice them. He had a story to tell, his story. He had a plan to expound, his plan. That was the basis for his book.

Whatever others might think of his purposes, Smith knew that his aim was morally pure—for the tortured ostracism he had suffered from the Company that he had helped form had scourged but not embittered his soul. To rise above these past—and even future—contrarieties became with him a glorified set purpose. He could not but heap scorn on what he considered wrong. But that scorn became as sublimated as his blind loyalty to his ideal. Facts and figures, and even consistency and abstract truth, swam crazily in the tide of his enthusiasm. It was not that he thought foul was fair for being in a good cause. It was that the cause was so fair that there was no foul.

As John Smith wrote on, however, his angered regrets often got the better of him—regrets not for what he had or had not done, but for what others had or had not done. The recollections of his advice ignored or denied, or of his warnings unheeded, surged up far too self-evidently in his story. At times it is impossible to avoid the impression that Smith thought that only *he* could organize, manage, and make a success of a colony in America.

But in part he was right—in the part born of experience. Until he left Virginia, no other Englishman had faced the problem of life there among hostile elements squarely, and, within the bounds of possibility, won out. He knew that pettily squabbling factions would be the literal death of the colony unless somehow a stop was put to them. He knew that scarlet robes belonged in London, not in Jamestown, and that neither Indian nor untamed wilderness knew what bearing gentlemanly rank might have on such things as survival. And yet John Smith was far from "going native," as we say today, in the way Henry Spelman thought he could and should. A true Englishman, Smith sought a compromise. He sought the preservation of what was basically sound in English habits, and a proper "composition" with the needs of a new environment. That fluid principle forms the undercurrent of the *General History.* (pp. 368-69)

[In his last colonial appeal, Smith was once more] determined to place before the reading public what he considered the right idea and the right plan for *any* English colony—even for those already maintaining a more or less precarious existence. He called his book *Advertisements for the unexperienced Planters of New England, or anywhere.* (pp. 387-88)

To the "Reader," Smith addresses [a] . . . significant solicitation. Finding, heaven knows where, a legend that "Appelles by the proportion of a foot, could make the whole proportion of a man," John Smith bitingly begs of his friends not to judge Britain's colonies by what they hear in the gossip forums of London, but by sound knowledge. People who believe all they hear of Virginia and New England could "tell as well what all England is by seeing but Milford Haven," or "what Apelles was by the picture of his great toe." John Smith will give them a true and proportioned picture.

For those who expected in this a reduplication of Smith's righteous indignation and often irritating apologetics, the new volume must have come as a surprise. For all the verbal elaboration of his day, Smith plainly indicates his unsolicited commendation of the Founders of New England. Of their religious quirks, he had no inkling. He only saw what was good in them, and what was good in what they did. And his heart swelled merry in his breast.

"Pardon me," he wrote, "if I offend in loving what I have cherished truly," and, he added, "if it over-glad me to see industry herself adventure now to make use of my aged endeavors." But he deeply hoped, despite all rumors, that that industry was not exercised by "a many of discontented Brownists, Anabaptists, Papists, Puritans, Separatists, and such factious humorists"—such seditious faddists. He admires the Pilgrims for their "wonderful patience," not for their religion; but he trusts that the colonizers of Massachusetts Bay are "good Catholic Protestants according to the Reformed Church of England." Not that he expects them all "to be so good as they should be"—no. "Christ had but twelve apostles, and one was a traitor, and if there be no dissemblers among them [the Puritans], it is more than a wonder." Yet, however they were, Smith seems to foresee that they would be better material than the first colonists in Virginia.

In this he was right. Although he was incapable of understanding the religious principles that motivated the Massachusetts group, he sensed their determination and efficiency. As he puts it: "If they do ill, the loss is but their own; if well, a great glory and exceeding good to this Kingdom, to make good at last what all our former conclusions [experiments] have disgraced."

From there, for thirty pages Smith glows with vicarious pride over the accomplishments of the new settlers of Massachusetts. What they have done, especially in so short a time, is more than praiseworthy. And yet, and yet. Faction in religion can have miserable effects. Smith is no divine, yet he pleads to be heard. He pleads on the side of peace and tolerance. He pleads for at least as much Christian unity as there is unity amongst the Turks. For him, that is strong speech.

The last chapter in this work is John Smith's true testament. He left a will, to be sure, bequeathing paltry things—much of his earlier writings are paltry, too. But his last pages are not only lofty in thought and intention; they are exceptional prose,

in an age of exceptional writing. They lead a reader to wonder how the genuine and far greater genius of William Shakespeare ever could be doubted as his, when so truly ill-educated a man as Captain John Smith could write the peroration to his *Advertisements for the unexperienced.*

Nearly ten years before, Smith had said of New England and Virginia:

> By that acquaintance I have with them, I may call them my children; for they have been my wife, my hawks, my hounds, my cards, my dice, and in total my best content, as indifferent to my heart as my left hand to my right: and notwithstanding all those miracles of disasters [which] have crossed both them and me, yet were there not one Englishman remaining (as God be thanked there is some thousands) I would yet begin again with as small means as I did at first.

Now, in the *Advertisements,* he points out the many errors made in Virginia: that the purses and lives of the planters "were subject to some few here in London who were never there, that consumed all in arguments, projects, and their own conceits, every year trying new conclusions [experiments]," and so on; that material profit was expected in much too short a time; and that London blamed the planters "for not converting the Savages, when those they sent us were little better, if not worse." So, in the end the Company went bankrupt, as we know, and the colony reverted virtually to its status when John Smith first went there.

With New England, it was a different story. They had made, and were still making, great mistakes. But the Puritans (he does not call them such) have voluntarily undertaken a greater plantation, and Smith sees here the opportunity to offer his counsel. Each attempt at settling in America has been made as if no one had done such a thing before. Smith knows that colonists should profit by experience, and so, taking his cue from Ben Jonson's verse opposite the frontispiece of Ralegh's *History of the World,* he writes:

> . . . seeing history is the memory of time, the life of the dead, and the happiness of the living; because I have more plainly discovered, and described, and discoursed of those countries than any as yet I know, I am the bolder to continue the story, and do all men right so near as I can in these new beginnings, which hereafter perhaps may be in better request than a forest of nine-day pamphlets.

A store of sage and practical advice follows, with not a few asides that throw bright light on the weaknesses of the Englishmen of his day as settlers and colonists. It is strange to Smith "that Englishmen should not do as much as any [people]." But no; "upon every slight affront, instead to amend it, we make it worse." Religion is needed in the colonies, and with it law and authority: "the maintainers of good orders and laws is the best preservation next [to] God of a Kingdom." But when these maintainers are "stuffed with hypocrisy and corruption," the results will be "not doubtful but lamentable," especially in a colony which is just begun. "As the laws corrupt, the state consumes," he moralizes.

Perceiving then that he has perhaps written too much, Smith goes on to say that he knows that people do not like advice, but he hopes that intelligent men will excuse him for making his opinion clear. In fact, he has so often been asked for suggestions by honest men that as for the ones who do not want advice, "the more they mislike it, the better I like it myself."

Four or five pages of further exhortation to good government, self-protection, and resolute action follow, after which Smith summarizes his attitude in a few words:

> Lastly, remember as faction, pride and security [over-confidence] produces nothing but confusion, misery, and dissolution; so the contraries well practised will in short time make you happy, and the most admired people of all our plantations for your time in the world.

"John Smith writ this with his own hand," is proudly appended to the book. It was the last public comment that hand ever penned. (pp. 388-91)

Captain John Smith has lived on in legend far more thrillingly than even he could have foreseen. Much has been made—largely by ill-informed people—of trivial inconsequences in his narratives, and controversy has at times raged rather absurdly. Today, passions have died down, except here and there, as more and more evidence of John Smith's basic honesty has been dug out of obscure and widely scattered records. To be sure, much of what John Smith wrote was exaggerated. That was only proper. Rare indeed was the man who wrote in Stuart times without ornament, without exuberance. Let it only be said that nothing John Smith wrote has yet been found to be a lie. (p. 394)

> *Philip L. Barbour, in his* The Three Worlds of Captain John Smith, *Houghton Mifflin Company, 1964, 553 p.*

EVERETT H. EMERSON (essay date 1971)

[*Emerson, an American educator with an interest in early American history and literature, is the author of* John Cotton (1965) *and the editor of* Major Writers of Early American Literature: Introductions to Nine Major Writers (1972). *In the following excerpt from his study of Smith, Emerson surveys the captain's works.*]

A True Relation is the raw material of history, not history itself; for Smith was very close to the events he described. (p. 46)

The first American book is a lively, detailed, personal account of the first permanent English settlement in America. Moses Coit Tyler rightly observed that Smith "wrote a book that is not unworthy to be the beginning of the new English literature in America" [see excerpt dated 1878]. It is valuable not only as a historical document or as a landmark in American history but as a work of literature. Its author was a perceptive man as well as a vigorous one. His work has no real structure, for it was written under pressure; but it is not lacking in organization. Instead of composing a chronicle, as many travelers and explorers did, Smith organized much of his material into large blocks, notably those on his capture by the Indians and his visit to Powhatan with Captain Newport. Certain themes tie the work together: the constant danger of attack by the Indians, the lack of knowledge of the area (Chesapeake Bay was largely unexplored, and the falls of the James River had prevented much exploration inland), the increasing importance of Captain John Smith, the outstanding leader of the colony. (pp. 52-3)

[*A True Relation*] is a thoroughly characteristic piece of seventeenth-century Virginia literature. (p. 53)

[*A Description of the Country, the Commodities, People, Government, and Religion* in *A Map of Virginia*] is perhaps Smith's most permanently interesting work. His biographers have told the story of his life well; the story of the early days of the

Virginia colony are more fully told in modern histories (though, of course, they lack Smith's sense of immediacy); Smith's works on New England seem somewhat dated because of their propaganda approach, which many readers find unattractive. But the *Description* is so consistently entertaining that it is surprising that it has never been republished as a separate work. (p. 55)

Smith began the work with a vocabulary of Indian words and phrases. Besides the Indian words for numbers and other common expressions, Smith demonstrated the Algonkian language with such revealing phrases as "Bid Pocahontas bring hither two little baskets and I will give her white beads to make her a chain," and "Run you to the king Mawmarynough and bid him come hither."

The *Description* proper begins with geography: the climate, the shape of their land, the rivers, a catalogue of the inhabitants. This section is full of interesting observations, some of which reveal an eye sensitive to beauty: "The country is not mountainous nor yet low but such pleasant plain hills and fertile valleys, one prettily crossing another, and watered so conveniently with their sweet brooks and crystal springs as if art itself had devised them."

The next sections of the *Description,* which resemble Hariot's *Brief and True Report,* deal with the useful plants growing naturally and in cultivated fashion, and the products which Virginia could produce for export. This last section is Smith's extended propaganda plea for America, the sort of thing which became his chief concern when he found that he was not able to return to either Virginia or New England. He argued that Virginia could produce the same commodities which bring most wealth to England's competitors: Muscovy, Poland, Sweden, France, Spain, Italy, and Holland. Virginian products were within a hundred miles "to be had, either ready provided by nature or else to be prepared, were there but industrious men to labor."

Despite the unrestrained optimism of this passage and a few others, the tone of most of the work is cautious. . . . (p. 57)

But, more than his optimism or his practicality, what impresses one most about Smith's account is his extensive knowledge. Sometimes it is revealed in minor observations, as when he noted that Indian peas resemble what the Italians call *fagioli* and that Indian beans resemble what the Turks call *garnases.* But chiefly one is impressed by Smith's knowledge of natural phenomena: Indian medicines and herbs, seventeen varieties of animals (including bears "very little in comparison of those of Muscovia and Tartaria"), and twenty kinds of fish.

Smith devoted the second half of his *Description* to the Indians: their appearance, way of life, hunting and fishing, warfare, medicine, religion, and government. . . . Since he made his observations, as he himself noted, mainly as a prisoner of the Indians, the acuteness of his report is all the more remarkable. (p. 58)

Smith was an optimistic, practical, careful observer, working indeed from the assumptions of his time but showing real interest in and rarely condescension towards the Indians. He was surprisingly objective, if tough-minded. (p. 59)

In his comments on Indian religion Smith is perhaps least perceptive, but his account is interesting, comprehensive, full of detail. His reactions to Indian religion occasionally reflect his values (he had definite religious convictions), as when he noted that "before their dinners and suppers, the better sort will take the first bit and cast it into the fire, which is all the grace they are known to use.'' . . . (p. 60)

The last pages of the *Description* demonstrate . . . that *A Map of Virginia* was written to set the record straight. Here Smith attacked in blunt fashion those colonists who pretended to be experts on things Virginian though they ''were scarce ever ten miles from Jamestown.'' These same, he protested, were themselves a ''plague to us in Virginia.'' Nevertheless, all went well ''so long after as I did govern there, until I left the country.''

With this personal note, Smith ended the work. A proud man, Smith chose not to write an extended defense of himself, though he expressed satisfaction that the second part of the *Map* provided a full report. . . . But, instead of writing a personal testament, Smith wrote a precise account of the Virginia he knew so well; packed with information, objective yet far from cold, detailed but not dull, his is the work of an immensely perceptive man whose bold adventures led him to know what a less active man never could have discovered.

The *Description* is highly valued by ethnologists and anthropologists. With the broader view of history which has been adopted in the twentieth century Smith's brief study should be recognized as of great historical importance. Because Smith's later original contributions to the *Generall Historie* in Book III are fragmentary and less objective, the *Description* is really Smith's most important contribution to historical studies. A *True Relation* is also important since, unlike the discussion of his Virginia years in the *Historie*, it is all his own. (pp. 61-2)

Captain John Smith's most famous work is the *Generall Historie of Virginia, New England, and the Summer Isles*. It has been judged worthy to rank with the histories of William Bradford, Edward Johnson, and John Winthrop; indeed, Smith has been called [by Jarvis K. Morse in *American Beginnings* (1952)] ''the father of Anglo-American History.'' The *Generall Historie* is complex, uneven, and controversial. (p. 63)

The *Generall Historie* ends with no grand peroration. Indeed, it is difficult to know where it ends; for the continuation seems to conclude as an ending to the *True Travels* (with an invitation to read more of Smith's adventures in the *Historie*, here described as if it were another portion of the *Travels*). The original six books have no real ending, for the preparation of the *Historie*, especially that of the last pages, was hasty. But Smith did plan a book on an impressive scale, and through the first three books the *Historie* is solid, carefully prepared.

While the book has been called Smith's ''Memoirs, his Apologia, and his Defense'' [see excerpt by Philip L. Barbour dated 1964], it was intended to be something more. The frustration and bitterness of half a lifetime apparently prevented Smith from preparing what he thought he would produce: a memorial collection to promote the colonies with which he felt so closely identified. From the evidence of the rest of the *Historie*, it appears that Book IV became the miscellany it is from personal pressures that Smith could not resist—not from plan. Having departed from his intention, he found it easy under pressure of time to use without much revision his not very appropriate earlier writing in Book VI. *The Generall Historie of Virginia, New England, and the Summer Isles* is not a coherent and satisfying book because it reflects too often the damaged state of Smith's ego, though it should be remembered that the book would never have been written had not Smith been forced by circumstances to turn from the life of a soldier to that of a writer. (pp. 76-7)

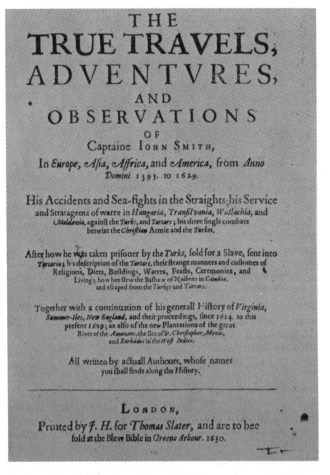

Title page of the first edition of The True Travels, Adventures, and Observations of Captaine John Smith *(1630).*

Having completed the *Generall Historie*, Smith could think of himself as a writer. The work he turned to next, *An Accidence, or The Pathway to Experience, Necessary for Young Sea-men*, was very successful in its time. It was not written from the motives that lie behind most of Smith's other writings; indeed, it seems to have been hack work. . . .

In the preface to Smith's forty-page quarto pamphlet—the first published seamen's manual in English—he explained his motives: since ''many young gentlemen and valiant spirits do desire to try their fortunes at sea, I have been persuaded to print this discourse. . . .'' It was to serve, wrote Smith, ''as an introduction for such as wants experience and are desirous to learn what belongs to a seaman.'' . . .

Smith was not a seaman, but his natural curiosity and practical bent must have led him to learn much from his extensive experiences at sea. . . . (p. 88)

Most of the *Accidence* is little more than a series of lists: sails, winds, ropes, weapons. It is only occasionally that Smith captured the excitement of adventure at sea, as when he described terms of war in a bit of dialogue:

''The ship's on fire. Cut anything to get clear, and smother the fire with wet clothes.''

''We are clear, and the fire is out, God be thanked.''

"The day is spent. Let us consult. Surgeon, look to
the wounded. Wind up the slain, with each a weight
or bullet at his head and feet. Give three pieces for
their funerals."

"Swabber, make clean the ship. Purser, record their
names. Watch, be vigilant to keep your berth to wind-
ward and that we lose him not in the night. Gunners,
sponge your ordnances. Soldiers, scour your pieces.
Carpenters, about your leaks. Boats'n and the rest,
repair the sails and shrouds. Cook, see you observe
against the morning watch." . . .

Though intended to be practical, much of the *Accidence* is so
condensed as to be almost unreadable, except perhaps to provide a vague, general impression of sea matters. (p. 89)

The *Sea Grammar,* a much more impressive work than the
Accidence, is much fuller and more professional. . . . The highly
condensed account in the earlier version of how a ship is built
gave way to a whole chapter that is clear and precise. But its
competence does not increase its literary value. Only a chapter,
an enlargement of the one quoted earlier on how to manage a
sea fight, has much interest now. It is full of lively conversation.

Like several of Smith's other writings, the *Sea Grammar* is
embellished with commendatory verses, seven in all. . . . On
two occasions Smith reciprocated with poems. Since he was
thought to have written only one extant poem, **"The Sea Marke,"**
these two recently discovered poems are of considerable importance; moreover, they show that Smith was a craftsman
with considerable skill.

The earlier of these [**"John Smith of His Friend Master John
Taylor and His Armado"**] appeared in 1627 in *An Armado,
or Navye, of 103 Ships & other Vessels; who have the art to
Sayle by Land, as well as by Sea,* by John Taylor, a popular
writer and famous London character, often known as the "water poet." Taylor's humorous pamphlet concerns such powerful
"ships" as fellowship, courtship, and friendship. Taking his
cue from Taylor, Smith used one dominant image in the poem.
In mock-serious fashion, he warned the world of the danger
occasioned by Taylor's fleet, so powerful that the gods of the
sea, its monsters, and even the famous barriers such as Goodwin Sands off the coast of Kent are threatened. Among other
aspects of Smith's art is his effective use of alliteration and
sea terminology. (p. 91)

[The other poem, **"In the Due Honor of the Author Master
Robert Norton, and His Work"**] is much less striking than the
one he had done the year before: it is full of the commonplaces
of the genre. But the often ungrammatical author of rough-
hewn if vigorous prose did demonstrate with this poem that he
was capable of turning out for a fellow soldier something at
least competent. (p. 92)

Edward Arber, Smith's editor and an authority on sixteenth-
and early seventeenth-century English literature, said of the
True Travels, "in its clear, graphic, and condensed style, the
narrative is among the very best written English books of travel
printed in Smith's lifetime" [see excerpt dated 1884]. . . . To
the reader of contemporary travel writing . . . , this praise seems
somewhat excessive. Smith's style is often far from clear because it is so condensed, and many of the most graphic passages
are borrowed. John Gould Fletcher's comment is more valid:
Smith's "literary style is, at best, the brief campaign-notes of
a blunt soldier." Smith truly did not always tell his story well,
and he lost immediacy by using the third person to refer to
himself. Perhaps he followed the example of Julius Caesar,
whose writings Smith obviously knew. Like Caesar, he told

nothing of his personal reactions to what he saw and did, but
his descriptions are nevertheless vivid enough to permit one
sometimes to picture his actions. (pp. 99-100)

[It] must be said that the borrowings are intelligently made and
that they usually add to the interest of the work. (Since the
Generall Historie is mainly a compilation, Smith was an experienced borrower.) The adventures themselves are frequently
so exciting that the work is interesting despite Smith's failings
as a writer. The book provides a picture of Smith as a dashing
and intrepid adventurer whose ingenuity was a great asset to
his Hungarian colleagues and on occasion saved his life.
(pp. 100-01)

Since Smith was an experienced and on occasion an effective
writer by the time he wrote the story of his youth . . . , it is a
pity that he did not take greater care with his *True Travels.*
Yet the book has remarkable qualities. It is surely striking that
Smith could report with considerable accuracy where he had
been, though he wrote from memory nearly twenty-five years
after the events, without the aid of notes or a journal, without
much knowledge of foreign languages—some Italian, probably
a fair knowledge of French, and a little German—and with
only the typical maps of his day, thoroughly inadequate ones,
to jog his memory. (He does seem, however, to have picked
up some help from books and maps.)

Though the literary quality of the *True Travels* is not consistently high, the adventures themselves still may charm readers
as Othello's "hairbreath 'scapes" charmed Desdemona (and
they have the advantage of being true). (p. 101)

Because everyone knows the story of Pocahontas and because
Smith's *magnum opus* is often referred to as the *Generall His-
torie of Virginia,* Captain John Smith is seldom identified with
New England. Yet he gave it its name. . . .

Smith visited New England only once, in 1614; and he stayed
only three months. He explored the Maine and Massachusetts
coasts; the story of this visit forms the basis of Smith's third
publication, *A Description of New England.* (p. 103)

The framework is basically chronological, but it is loose enough
to permit Smith to include propaganda, specific suggestions
concerning colonization, philosophizing, comments on his map
and his values, and a document providing information about
Smith's unsuccessful voyage of 1615. Some of Smith's best
writing was occasioned by the enthusiasm with which he contemplated the colonization of New England. His frustration at
his inability to be developing a colony there himself led him
to pour his energies into writing.

The prose of the *Description* is often quite different from anything found in Smith's earlier works. For example, in his efforts
to stir his readers to recognize the virtues of colonies, he wrote
the following artful passage of a decidedly philosophical cast.

Consider: what were the beginnings of the monar-
chies of the Chaldeans, the Syrians, the Grecians,
and the Romans, but this one rule—What was it they
would not do for the good of the commonwealth or
their mother city? For example, Rome. What made
her such a monarchess but only the adventures of her
youth, not in riots at home but in dangers abroad,
and the justice and judgment out of their experience
when they grew aged? What was their ruin and hurt
but this: the excess of idleness, the fondness of parents, the want of experience in magistrates, the admiration of their undeserved honors, the contempt of
true merit, their unjust jealousies, their politic incre-

dulities, their hypocritical seeming goodness, and their
deeds of secret lewdness. . . . Then who would live
at home idly (or think in himself any worth to live)
only to eat, drink, sleep, and so die? Or by consuming
that carelessly [which] his friends got worthily? Or
by using that miserably that maintained virtue honestly? . . . Or (to maintain a silly show of bravery)
toil out thy heart, soul, and time basely, by shifts,
tricks, cards, and dice? . . .

Nothing in Smith's earlier writing prepares the reader for the
rhetorical flourishes,—the alliteration, the parallel construc-
tions, the richness—of this passage. (pp. 104-05)

The first edition of *New Englands Trials* is a collection of very
miscellaneous materials. After a brief introduction on New
England's location, geography, and climate, Smith presented
statistics on the profits which have been made from fishing.
Then he noted the advantages of New England for fishing and
cited ten proofs of these advantages in the form of brief factual
reports on successful fishing voyages. Then comes an autobiographical passage. Smith's sense of mistreatment and neglect, reflected in the prefaces and poems of *A Description of
New England,* is in the background of the text of that work;
in *New Englands Trials* it comes to the foreground. (p. 110)

The enlarged *New England Trials* is still very slight; and, except
for the autobiographical passage, its literary value is not great.
Historically, the pamphlet is more important; for it provides a
full record of English voyages to New England from 1616 to
1622. (p. 112)

John Smith's final work on New England was his last book:
*Advertisements For the Unexperienced Planters of New En-
gland, or any where. Or The Path-way to experience to erect a
Plantation.* . . . From the literary point of view, it is doubtless
Smith's best book. (p. 113)

The *Advertisements,* a forty-eight-page quarto pamphlet, provides few facts about Smith which he had not set forth already;
but the personality of the author shines through more attractively than anywhere else. A. L. Rowse has argued that Smith
"is a writer by nature: the very assertion of personality shows
it, against dull dogs" [see excerpt dated 1959]. But elsewhere
Smith's writings are not always *enlivened* by a sense of the
author's personality. Indeed, when Smith injected his personality, he too often marred his work with his tone of the victimized hero. The *Advertisements,* though fuller of braggadocio
than any of Smith's other works, shows much more of the spirit
which was revealed at points in the second part of the *True
Travels*: a sense of his own triumph and success. Here is his
outlook, vigorously expressed:

Having been a slave to the Turks, prisoner amongst
the most barbarous savages, after my deliverance
commonly discovering and ranging those large rivers
and unknown nations with such a handful of ignorant
companions that the wiser sort oft gave me [up] for
lost; always in mutinies, wants, and miseries, blown
up with gunpowder; a long-time prisoner among the
French pirates, from whom escaping in a little boat
by myself and adrift all such a stormy winter night—
when their ships were split, more than a hundred
thousand pound lost they had taken at sea and most
of them drowned upon the isle of Ré, not far from
whence I was driven on shore in my little boat, etc.
And many a score of the worst of winter months
lived in the fields, yet to have lived near thirty-seven
years in the midst of wars, pestilence, and famine,
by which many an hundred thousand have died about
me, and scarce five living of them [that] went first

with me to Virginia, and yet see the fruits of my
labors thus well begin to prosper. Though I have but
my labor for my pains, have I not much reason both
privately and publicly to acknowledge it and give
God thanks, whose omnipotent power only delivered
me, to do the utmost of my best to make his name
known in those remote parts of the world and his
loving mercy to such a miserable sinner.

This passage reveals a great deal about Smith. Once he has
worked his way through the syntax, the reader is struck by the
romanticized or exaggerated view of himself which Smith had
developed in the fifteen years since his last real adventure. The
passage also shows that Smith's imagination offered him considerable consolation and comfort in his pain and bitterness.
It also reveals Smith's new appreciation of the importance of
religion, which also seems to have provided him with consolation. (pp. 113-14)

Smith's newly found piety, if that is what it was, is reflected
in the chapter devoted to religion in the *Advertisements.* Whereas
earlier Smith had disparaged religion as a basis for colonization, or had given only cursory attention to it, he now added
a new ingredient to his formula for a successful colony: the
church. Smith argued that religion was an indispensable instrument of order, a preventer of factionalism: he described at
some length the religious practices of the Jamestown colonists
in his days in Virginia. The most important evidence that religion was now of considerable importance to Smith and helped
him to develop a more philosophic attitude towards his career
is the striking and powerful poem ["The Sea Mark"] which
prefaces the *Advertisements.* (p. 115)

Considerable advances in Smith's literary art are evident to
one who reads the three [New England publications] in the
order of composition (the first edition of *New Englands Trials*
might be omitted), for time and perspective permitted him to
achieve wisdom and philosophic resignation without losing his
excitedly optimistic vision of America, especially New England. Smith's final achievement, and as a writer his greatest,
was the expression of his principles and practice in powerful
language. In the last chapter of the *Advertisements,* his appreciation of the virtues which he believed he had demonstrated
(when given the opportunity) is not obstructed by any petty-
minded bitterness. (p. 118)

Captain John Smith was more than a vivid personality, a historical figure of unquestionable importance, and a propaganda
writer who attracted attention to New England. He was also
the author of works of permanent interest for the picture they
provide of America on the eve of colonization—*The Description of Virginia* and *A Description of New England*—and for
the story that they tell of the Jamestown colonists' struggles—
A True Relation and Book III of the *Generall Historie.*

Smith's most attractive works are the second and third books
of the *Generall Historie,* the former, *A Description of Virginia,*
polished into shape by an editor; the latter, Smith's revision
and amplification of the work of other men. These two works,
however composed, are masterful accounts of *the* place and
the time: the land where England's first permanent American
colony was established, and the first crucial two and a half
years of the colony's life. In Smith's *Description,* as Moses
Coit Tyler has observed, "all the dull and hard details of the
subject [are] made delightful by felicities of phrase that seem
to spring up as easily as wild flowers in the woods of his own
Virginia." The book is truly both *dulce* and *utile*—sweet and
useful. If Smith's contributions in Book III are not of the sort

that entitles him to be considered a historian, nevertheless they do make a very good book even better. (pp. 121-22)

The *Generall Historie* is difficult to evaluate as a whole. The fact that [it] is a large, unusually handsome book, not a thin pamphlet, has given it special importance. As a compilation, it has been long admired and read, especially by historically minded Virginians, of whom there were and are many. But, except for the second and third books and a portion of the sixth, it has no special authority. . . . (p. 123)

A Description of New England, republished as a portion of Book VI of the *Generall Historie,* is also important among Smith's writings. Without the sense of form of Books II and III, it still has much to recommend it, especially a spirit of excitement about the discoveries that Smith had made and the plans they had inspired. Much better, however, is Smith's last pamphlet, *Advertisements For the unexperienced Planters.* It too lacks an adequate organizing principle, but it is not so shapeless as the *Description.* Its special virtue is the quality of its prose.

The prose of Smith's England is among the great glories of literature. In the *Advertisements* Smith gave America some of this inheritance, though his prose . . . is perhaps better described as Elizabethan in its vigor and in its exuberant irregularity. . . . (pp. 123-24)

The most admirable quality of Smith's style is its concreteness. Smith's concern for fact, his acute awareness of the world around him as he moved into unknown lands, gave him great asistance when he turned to writing. Time and again, sometimes unexpectedly, one finds in Smith's prose precise pictures of what he saw in the New World. . . . Smith's acute perceptiveness sometimes reveals itself in a sentence or a phrase, as in his observation on the trees of the New England coast: "Oak is the chief wood, of which there is a great difference in regard to the soil where it groweth."

Captain John Smith is, then, for many reasons a writer of singular importance in the early period of American literature. He was America's first writer, one of whom Americans can be proud. (pp. 124-25)

> *Everett H. Emerson, in his* Captain John Smith, *Twayne Publishers, Inc., 1971, 143 p.*

JOHN SEELYE   (essay date 1977)

[*Seelye is an American novelist whose most notable works include* The True Adventures of Huckleberry Finn (1970), *a rewriting of Mark Twain's classic according to the preferences of modern critics;* Dirty Tricks; or, Nick Noxin's Natural Nobility (1974), *which presents Richard Nixon's rise to power as a Horatio Alger "strive and succeed" story; and the nonfictional* Prophetic Waters: The River in Early American Life and Literature (1977). *Seelye has also published critical studies on the works of Twain, Herman Melville, Booth Tarkington, and other American literary figures. In the following excerpt from* Prophetic Waters, *Seelye approaches* A True Relation *and* The Generall Historie *as picaresque epics.*]

Whatever the authenticity of Captain John Smith's *True Travels, Adventures, and Observations,* the book has a fabulous quality suggesting that the whole cloth of truth had been patched out with colorful fabrications, and the result is a montebank appearance, a sort of clamorous advertisement for the author himself.

Still, the *intended* effect was to certify Captain Smith as a modern knight errant, to provide a pedigree, as it were, of

adventures at martial (and in female) arms which earned him an armorial escutcheon and the cherished title "Gentleman." Though Spenser's epical handbook of courtesy is not listed by Smith among the other moral and military guides he read while practicing as a youth with "lance and ring" in the Lincolnshire woods, he apparently took the pattern of the Red Cross Knight for his own. (pp. 60-1)

The longest of Smith's several versions of his American adventure is a combination of epic and autobiography called *The Generall Historie of Virginia, New England, and the Summer Isles* (1624). An exercise in self-promotion and self-justification, Smith's book was designed to gain him further employment, a strategy revealed by proportions and pitch. Of its six parts, the first four are devoted to the discovery, exploration, and settlement of Virginia, and of these four, the second and third are concerned with Smith's role in founding the colony at Jamestown. The fourth part continues Virginia's history from the year of Smith's departure, 1609, to the Indian massacre of 1622, a chronicle of some dozen years that occupies 125 pages, compared to the 145 taken up by the two and a half years Smith was in Virginia. And these later pages emphasize the stupidity and sloth of the colony's administration after he left, blundering ineptness resulting in the increased boldness of the Indians and their devastating attack.

The *Generall Historie* is informed throughout by Smith's martial spirit and his pragmatic means to an end, his militant utilitarianism. Benefiting from his past experience and plenty of hindsight, Smith's view of Virginia is anything but paradisiac and is designed to dim hopes for quick riches: "There is," he wrote, "no country to pillage as the Romans found: all you expect from thence must be by labor." As for gentle handling of the Indians, Smith takes his text from a prophetic parson, Jonas Stockham, who wrote in 1621 that "fair means" to the end of conversion are rewarded with scorn, that English boys sent among the savages to learn their language (and thus speed the missionary work) "return worse than they went," and that if "Mars and Minerva go hand in hand, they will affect more good in an hour, than those verbal Mercurians in their lives." Instead of inviting the Indians to join the English in cooperative labor, Smith by 1624 was for forcing "the treacherous and rebellious infidels to do all manner of drudgery work and slavery for them," using the once abhorrent Spanish example as his "anvil," beating out "an armor of proof hereafter to defend us . . . and make us more circumspect."

"Smith's forge mends all," wrote Samuel Purchas in a poem affixed to the *Generall Historie,* "makes chains for savage nation," and his was only one of several poetic tributes playing on the conceit latent in the author's name—including some spare lines by the old gold-beater himself, John Donne [see excerpt dated 1624]. But it was Purchas who hit upon the happiest metaphor, comparing the *Generall Historie* to Achilles' shield, "armor 'gainst Time . . . with best arts charged," the book characterized as an instrument with a double-edged intention, a shield against calumny and a weapon of policy. In all his poetic roles, Smith is a Herculean bringer of order through strenuous means, and since his reputation has indeed survived because of his *Generall Historie,* it is ironic that the popular image of the militant author pictures him in the protecting embrace of Pocahontas.

For not only does the pretty story occupy but a single page in Smith's voluminous book, but it is anomalous, the merciful princess related only by blood to Smith's chief antagonist, Powhatan, who is portrayed as a wily, cruel, and unrelenting enemy. Even in the series of illustrations ornamenting the map in his *Generall Historie* the picture of his rescue by Pocahontas is outnumbered by scenes of menace and violence, showing Smith being taken prisoner or wrestling with giant Indian kings, pistol or cutlass in hand. More important, if the story of Pocahontas is not much to the point of Smith's *Generall Historie,* neither does it conform to the actual English experience in the American wilderness, which provided the materials from which Smith's adventure and his book were fashioned—as the map which accompanies it shows the symbolic confluence of the Roanoke and Chowan, not the rivers of Chesapeake Bay. (pp. 61-3)

"The wars in Europe, Asia, and Africa," wrote Smith, "taught me how to subdue the wild savages." Though this sentence appears in one of his last tracts—*Advertisements for the Unexperienced Planters of New England*—we may be reasonably sure that he never did entertain any Golden Age illusions about Indians, that he regarded the red man from the start as just another Turk, a potential enemy, not a possible friend. In sum, before the Hesiodic plan could be affected, a certain amount of heroic action was necessary.

Certainly by the end of Captain Smith's first year in Virginia he had sufficient proof of the wisdom of conducting himself always as if in hostile territory. The *True Relation* which he sent to England from James Fort provides an image of the author and his enemies—white as well as red—which differs little from the one contained in his more ambitious and better-known *Generall Historie*. Founded on facts but shaped to a personal motive, Smith's narrative line is beaten out with an urgency that transforms it into a design, thus contributing to the genesis of the ur-myth of American literature, a myth in which the accommodating savage—as Indian princess—plays a role that is distinctly minor, however prominent. As with other reports coming from James Fort, it has an element of unintended as well as intentional humor, and like earlier captains' narratives it takes its impetus from an inland voyage up a wilderness river.

Smith's *True Relation* belongs to the genre established by Cartier and Lane, and likewise contains the shape of adventure, the heroic line associatd with the epic. But because of the humor in John Smith's story, the line takes a picaresque as well as a heroic road, a lowering level that suits the Captain's reduced stature—both literal and figurative. The *True Relation,* then, belongs to the literature of adventure, a mode in which humorous and heroic elements are mingled, suggesting that at the heart of encounter violence explodes with a sound much like laughter. We can call Smith's accomplishment the "Epic of Virginia" if we wish, and it is certainly the best we have, but let us remember also that his (and our) adventure lacks the high seriousness of classical heroics. Like so many agents of British empire, Smith muddles rather than marches along, slog-slog-slogging through the muck of a wild, wet woods, infested not by Saracen knights but by a sullen, slippery people.

And yet the Captain remains one man in a thousand, a gentleman unafraid who traveled best alone, and if he is given to strong delusion, wholly believing a lie, his faith results in pure, unmitigated act, a fight at the end of which lies an ultimate conclusion, an imperial lesson, wrought on England's anvil from cold iron. In Smith's *True Relation* the nascent aesthetics of adventure are transformed into steel-hard flesh, as the advancing line becomes a sword, symbol of martial technology representing the absolute utilitarian contingency. (pp. 63-6)

Smith's purpose in writing his *True Relation* was similar to that behind Ralph Lane's "Discourse," a desire to explain his conduct in handling the Indians. (p. 67)

The most troublesome of the Indians was the leader of the Paspahegh, who lived near James Fort, but the most problematic was Powhatan, who lived many miles away. Since many of the tribes in the region were under Powhatan's control, gaining his fealty to King James was an important object of the English, but the Indian chief kept away from the fort on the river, preferring to be represented by agents. Powhatan's distance and his power, along with his wilderness seat on the Pamunkey, one of the great rivers of the region, gives him a symbolic stature, and he emerges from Smith's account as a dark force, being enigmatic to the point of mystery. Though hardly an Incan or Aztec prince, Powhatan has a certain grandeur (as Smith has his undoubted courage), and he emerges from the *True Relation* as rather a noble savage, a stern wilderness presence, secretive, moody, even treacherous, yet possessing an undeniable grace. As all rivers led into and out of Powhatan's realm, so the voyage central to Smith's *True Relation* took the Captain into the heart (if not the confidence) of that world, a route which has the ritual and romance of a symbolic quest.

For the sake of literature, it would have been better if Smith's voyage had gained a certain elevation by following the lordly King's River, but exigency dictated a humbler route, in keeping with the picaresque dimension of his adventure. It was up one of the tributaries of the James—the lowly Chickahominy—that the brave Captain sailed, not, like Newport, looking for gold and pearls but, as the name of the river suggests, for supplies of corn. The Chickahominy Indians, unlike many of the tribes in the region, were willing to trade at a reasonable rate, and

Caricature of Smith, by David Levine. Reprinted with permission from The New York Review of Books. *Copyright © 1986 Nyrev, Inc.*

encouraged by their hospitality, Smith decided to explore the headwaters of their river. Having gone as far as he could in his barge, he left it near an Indian town with seven of his men aboard as guard, then, taking two armed companions and two Indian guides, he set off upstream in a canoe, putting himself "upon the adventure: the country only a vast and wild wilderness." In this, the second stage of his journey, Smith stepped off into a great green mystery, disappearing into the interior for a month. Since the two white men with him were killed, we have only his word as to subsequent events. What really happened is of no consequence here, but the story Smith told most certainly is, being an important myth in the process of creation.

Like Cartier on the St. Lawrence and Lane on the Roanoke, Smith went up the Chickahominy in search of a passage to India, and it is typical of his version of the great adventure that his journey ended in a swamp. Hoping to find Hakluyt's lake and Verrazzano's Sea beyond, Smith took an Indian guide with him and went on alone, straight into an ambush, and since his conduct in this affair raised some questions as to his wisdom, he rendered the particulars of ensuing events in minute detail. As usual in Smith's writings, specificity swells with the implications of fiction, and as in a novel by Cooper, Smith's Indians seem to have been extremely obliging to the needs of narrative. Though their marksmanship on the Captain's English companions appears to have been excellent, the "20 or 30" arrows they let fly at the Captain either fell short or inflicted minor wounds. Smith's personal Indian, his "consort," was similarly obliging, allowing himself to be held fast by the Captain as a shield in the line of fire, which permitted Smith to load and fire his pistol "3 or 4 times." His consort then volunteered to serve as translator between him and the hostile savages surrounding them with drawn bows, a delicate conversation during which Smith somehow backed into a quagmire, pulling his *ad hoc* Chingachgook with him. Having become literally bogged down, he surrendered to the inevitable—and to the Indians—but instead of being killed or tortured, Captain Smith was treated by his captors as an officer and gentleman.

This is not to say that Smith's story was a fabrication in the absolute sense, only that it resembles fiction mightily. What happened to Smith at the headwaters of the Chickahominy (and afterward) bears a remarkable similarity not only to earlier accounts of European adventures in America, but to certain romantic nineteenth-century novels, and his narrative acts therefore as a sort of bridge, composed of those coincidences which form a conduit of New World marvels. Thomas Hariot had described the savages' awe of the white man's "instruments," his lodestone and compasses, telling how he took advantage of their superstitious curiosity to explain the mysteries of Christianity, and Rosier likewise brought the Indians "to love and fear us" by tricks with a knife, needle, and lodestone. So Smith with his chief captor, Opechancanough, who "so amazedly admired" his compass that the Captain was able to discourse on "the roundness of the earth, the course of the sun, moon, stars, and planets," leaping high over the barrier of language. For his part, the obliging Opechancanough rivaled Ralph Lane's accommodating Menatonon in describing the country about, including a "great turning of salt water" near the source of the King's River.

Smith's encounter with the Indians of the interior may have begun with some traditional touches, but it soon enough took a turn that adds a completely new dimension. The difference

between the relationship of Smith and Opechancanough, Lane and Menatonon, is indicative, for this time it is the white man who is captive, a condition of enforced passivity which determined Smith's conduct thenceforth, the Captain resorting to his wits in lieu of his missing weapons. In the accounts of Cartier, Rosier, and Lane, the river adventure is a sortie, a tentative probing of mystery, but in Captain Smith's it becomes a captivity narrative, hence a complete immersion, akin to a baptism, the high point of which in one version of events may have been, according to some authorities, an Indian ritual of initiation, but the outcome of which was most certainly a kind of rebirth.

Yet it was an imperfect baptism, for Smith's head stayed above water, and the English Captain in the wilderness became a herald of civilization. The effect of savagery on him was minimal, even nugatory, boding ill for the hoped-for accommodation between red men and white. Like the needle on his magical compass, Captain Smith held steady on his enforced wanderings through the seemingly endless maze of trails, rivers, and villages of Indian America, his gaze always fixed on a farther north. In all his dealings with the Indians—as reported by himself—Smith proved as wily and cunning as his adversaries, pressing always for advantage and information, his eye ever on the main chance. The result is an overflow of the comic spirit, despite the very real hazard involved, for having lost the arms of Mars, Smith develops the head of Minerva: thoroughly middle-class in its set, yet extremely flexible in action, Smith's mind was adaptable to a high degree, a signal virtue for imperial man.

Smith's inland journey culminates in his encounter with Powhatan, a meeting which, like his interview with Opechancanough, compounds what had happened earlier in America with what was yet to be, a mingling of the marvelous and mischievous in a splendidly comic interview, conducted on the banks of yet another imperial stream, not the Powhatan / James but the Pamunkey—soon to be Englished "York." There Captain Smith was led into the presence of the very image of noble savagery, Powhatan "proudly lying upon a bedstead a foot high, upon ten or twelve mats, richly hung with many chains of great pearls about his neck . . . with such a grave and majestical countenance, as drove me into admiration to see such state in a naked savage." (pp. 68-71)

[Though] Smith's *True Relation* was intended as an instrument of policy, as a work of literature it transcends its occasion. Smith's frontier, his point of contact with the red man's world, is a symbolic field of opposing forces, Powhatan's royal residence on the Pamunkey the center of power opposing the imperial outpost on the James. The one man is wilderness incarnate, a personification of deceptive prospects, the other represents the martial, heroic impulse in the New World. Both provide a pattern of encounter, engaged in an antagonistic duet of cross-purposes, linked by outstretched hands of mutual trust and greed as they maneuver to gain the advantage over one another, protestations of friendship mingling with veiled threats of harm. (p. 74)

When the material of Smith's first report from America was adapted to his *Generall Historie* it was considerably shortened, with the result that Powhatan's savagery is simplified, at once Romanized and abbreviated, reduced to a generalized portrait which lacks the psychological complexity of the earlier presentation. By 1624 he had become just another Indian, while the addition of Pocahontas as a Savior Princess provided a dramatic element with great human interest. Small wonder, then, that the story took hold of the popular imagination in later years. (pp. 75-6)

[The] relationship between the Captain and the Indian Princess is strictly avuncular. Though resembling Falstaff in his defensive boastfulness and his large way with facts, Captain John in America lacks Sir John's sensual aspect, his chastity symbolizing the sea change suffered by chivalry when it moved from the Old to the New World. Smith's martial asceticism is more than knightly restraint, but is deeply anchored in Anglo-Saxon attitudes toward savage people, an aversion to relationships other than commercial and military. Powhatan sensed this English reticence and objected to it, hence the hopes attending the Rolfes' marriage. But that fated union was exceptional, and Captain Smith's restraint established the frontier pattern, in literature if not in life: a militant asceticism which necessarily emphasized the male bond, an uneasy alliance between red and white dictated by martial and mercantile considerations that produced misunderstandings often erupting in violence. (p. 77)

Captain Smith's great Powhatan is a more complex portrait of savagery than Captain Newport's Little Powhatan, yet as symbols as well as kin they are related, for in a double sense both Captains found Indians who reflected back their own desires, in specific terms and general, savages who not only told them obliging stories but who mirrored their duplicitous intent. This is the covert burden of Captain Smith's adventure, another version of the imperial experience, lending his story a paradoxical dimension. For Powhatan did nothing to Captain Smith that was not a reversal of what Smith intended for him, the Indian King, like his River, merely reflecting back the Captain's own countenance. Traveling up the devious course of the Chickahominy toward the commodious breadth of the Pamunkey, moving from his island stronghold into "the heart of the country," Captain John Smith found a darkness cast before him on the water, that obscurest of self-images, his shadow. It is . . . a Conradian fable, one in which the tender-hearted Indian maiden plays no part.

Toward the end of Smith's *True Relation* there is a description of Virginia's Nansemond River which can serve to express his expedient, utilitarian, and martial view of the New World and its people:

> This river is a musket-shot broad, each side being shoaled bays, with a narrow channel, but three fathom deep. His course for eighteen miles is almost directly south and by west, where beginneth the first inhabitants; for a mile it turneth directly east, towards the west, where is a great bay, and a white chalky island convenient for a fort. His next course is south, where within a quarter of a mile, the river divideth in two, the neck a plain high corn field, the western bend a high plain likewise, the northeast answerable in all respects. In these plains are planted abundance of houses and people; they may contain 1000 acres of most excellent fertile ground: so sweet, so pleasant, so beautiful, and so strong a prospect, for an invincible strong city, with so many commodities, that I know as yet I have not seen.

The direction of the river's course is described in terms of an upstream voyage, the imperial necessity in America, a male, progenitive, and heroic line which transforms the Nansemond into a masculine presence, providing a setting for that "invincible strong city" which is Smith's favorite figure of orderliness. It is a symbolic landscape much like the Pamunkey region as described by Smith in his account of his departure from

captivity, "a fat, fertile, sandy ground," through which the Pamunkey runs "his course northwest, and westerly."

Captain Smith was a man of many parts, but no more a believer in Arcadia than a lover of Indian maidens, reserving his faith and his passion for other matters. A virgin land for him was no Eden, but a waste of plenty itching for a plow; no sacred vestal, but a fat and fertile presence to be possessed by means of rivers like the male Pamunkey, which "keepeth his course without tarrying some twenty miles" into an interior big with the promise of empire. Smith measured both the Pamunkey, and the Nansemond in terms of a musket shot, a martial unit of measure which did not promise well for the "abundance of people" who already occupied the abundant land, "warlike and tall" and with a concept of territory as fierce as it was primitive. For Captain Smith did not seem to entertain much hope of making pliable Christian sheep out of heathen wolves, and though we hear much concerning the conversion of the land in his *True Relation,* of the conversion of the Indians we hear very little. (pp. 77-9)

If aboriginal possession has priority over subsequent supplantation, then Captain John Smith is the villain of his own story, for his was clearly an imperial errand, however inflated with a darkly comic spirit. Though his advice concerning the handling of the Indians was ignored during the early years of Jamestown, and though his *Generall Historie* and other late writings failed to earn him the employment or reward he most certainly deserved, that single-minded soldier cast a prophetic shadow on the land. What followed in America during the next two centuries bore out, through repetition, Captain Smith's experience, the hard and pointed facts from which his narrative was forged into coarse-hammered steel. There was no compromise, no truce possible between the English and the Indians, and though popular waves of sentimental idealism would succeed waves of frontier hostility, few frontiersmen were able to share that popular mood.

The native American hero who emerged from the wilderness context was to share a number of Captain Smith's traits: his courage, his cunning, his ingenuity, his faith in the future, his utilitarianism, and his generous way with the truth. The American hero's progress would also be inland by waterways, along rivers which were but greater versions of tidewater streams, a course shaped by a mixture of quixotic idealism and expedient means, greed licensed by a sense of destiny. From first to last it would be a picaresque adventure, a mock chivalric romance, yet it is also a tale of arms and the man, linking the American experience to neoclassic precedent, the strategic dimension of imperial design. Shedding clouds of chivalric glory, Captain Smith is a Red Cross Knight with a star-spangled manner, his river voyages putting a seal on the land, yielding both a popular myth and a darker version, too. We can see in his epic a sum of all previous encounters and a determination of the pattern for centuries to come, for as American Aeneas, Captain Smith is father of us all, Captain and Captive, clue to the meaning of our savage heart, primal author of our gigantic tale. (pp. 79-80)

> *John Seelye, "Captain Courageous: Captain John Smith, Father of Us All," in his* Prophetic Waters: The River in Early American Life and Literature, *Oxford University Press, 1977, pp. 57-95.*

PHILIP L. BARBOUR   (essay date 1980)

[*The following excerpt is taken from Barbour's three-volume edition of Smith's complete works, still in preparation when Barbour died in 1980. Here, he discusses Smith's last work,* Advertisements for the Unexperienced Planters of New England, or Any Where, *as "a fitting close to [his] literary career."*]

The *Advertisements,* in addition to being a continuation of the last eight chapters of the *True Travels,* is also a summation of all Smith had to say about the colonization of Virginia and New England. This theme should be no surprise, for everything Smith wrote centered around the subject of colonization, barring his brief excursions into nautical terminology and autobiography.

What is a surprise, perhaps, is that we find in the *Advertisements* a freer hand in writing. At the same time, although he had been publishing books in a steady stream for twenty-two years, his mind seems still to gallop ahead of his pen. Even in this, his last publication, paragraphs of uncommon literary strength and skill alternate with passages of exasperating obscurity for lack of literary finish. Some of the latter may be due to the absence of formal education in his Lincolnshire youth, for he was trained by experience rather than by schooling. Yet the bulk of these unpolished interruptions in lucidity can be attributed primarily to carelessness, a shortcoming that remained with him to the end.

By and large, however, the editor must agree with Everett Emerson, an uncommonly perceptive critic of Smith as a litterateur, that the *Advertisements* is Smith's most attractive work [see excerpt dated 1971]. Despite all, it does read easily. It also has more semblance of organization than his previous works, and the sincerity of his broad aims shines through it. Smith here is a wounded warrior, but a less petulant one; the braggart is less in evidence and we see instead pride of accomplishment. In short, this little book, taken by itself, is convincing. (p. 255)

[The *Advertisements*] is a fitting close to Smith's literary career. In that career, Smith succeeded with somewhat surprising grace, whereas he had repined his failure in the colonial field far too long. (p. 257)

> *Philip L. Barbour, in his introduction to "Advertisements for the Unexperienced Planters of New England, or Any Where (1631),"* in The Complete Works of Captain John Smith (1580-1631): Vol. III, *edited by Philip L. Barbour, The University of North Carolina Press, 1986, pp. 255-57.*

ADDITIONAL BIBLIOGRAPHY

Barbour, Philip L. "Captain John Smith's Observations on Life in Tartary." *The Virginia Magazine of History and Biography* 68, No. 3 (July 1960): 271-83.
Treats Smith's methods in *The True Travels,* concentrating on the use of borrowed material in the work and on Smith's anglicization of foreign words.

————. "Fact and Fiction in Captain John Smith's *True Travels.*" In *Literature As a Mode of Travel: Five Essays and a Postscript,* edited by Warner G. Rice, pp. 101-14. New York: New York Public Library, 1963.
Determines that *The True Travels* is basically true, though containing "a handful of invented or borrowed details."

Bradley, A. G. *Captain John Smith.* London: Macmillan and Co., 1909, 226 p.
Sympathetic biography.

Downs, Robert B. "The First American: Captain John Smith's *The Generall Historie of Virginia, New-England, and the Summer Isles.*" In his *Books That Changed the South,* pp. 3-14. Chapel Hill: University of North Carolina Press, 1977.
Mostly biographical essay, containing short descriptions of Smith's works.

Fishwick, Marshall. "Was John Smith a Liar?" *American Heritage* IX, No. 6 (October 1958): 28-33, 110-11.
Inspects the controversy concerning Smith's accuracy, concentrating on the conflicting conclusions reached by Lewis L. Kropf and Laura Polanyi Striker regarding the truth of *The True Travels.*

Fletcher, John Gould. *John Smith—Also Pocahontas.* 1928. Reprint. New York: Kraus Reprint Co., 1972, 303 p.
Generally favorable biography, which nonetheless takes several of the more astonishing episodes of Smith's life with a grain of salt.

Hart, Albert Bushnell. "American Historical Liars." *Harper's Magazine* CXXXI, No. DCCLXXXV (October 1915): 726-35.
Includes a tongue-in-cheek consideration of the truth of the Smith-Pocahontas episode.

Henry, William W. "A Defense of Captain John Smith." *Magazine of American History* XXV, No. 4 (April 1891): 300-13.
Refutation of Alexander Brown's attacks, scattered throughout his *Genesis of the United States,* against Smith's veracity and character.

Hubbell, Jay B. "The Smith-Pocahontas Literary Legend." In his *South and Southwest: Literary Essays and Reminiscences,* pp. 175-204. Durham, N.C.: Duke University Press, 1965.
Reprint of a 1957 survey of the controversy engendered by the Smith-Pocahontas episode and the fictional retellings it has inspired. The latter focus of the essay is particularly interesting as an illumination of popular attitudes toward Smith.

Jalbert, H. H. "Captain John Smith: Jack of All Trades and Master of Most." *The Mentor* 14, No. 6 (July 1926): 39-40.
Description of Smith's treatise on seamanship, *A Sea-man's Grammar,* which Jalbert characterizes as "a model of its kind."

Kraus, Michael. "The First Settlements." In his *The Writing of American History,* pp. 14-37. Norman: University of Oklahoma Press, 1953.
Includes a brief, favorable commentary on Smith, who "seemed rather a contemporary of Don Quixote than a man of business."

Lewis, Paul. *The Great Rogue: A Biography of Captain John Smith.* New York: David McKay Co., 1966, 306 p.
Biography. Lewis characterizes Smith as a man of great accomplishments, but one whose "imagination and facile pen made him his own worst enemy."

Morse, Jarvis M. "John Smith and His Critics: A Chapter in Colonial Historiography." *The Journal of Southern History* I, No. 2 (May 1935): 123-37.
Lucid review of the work of the principal participants in the controversy over Smith's veracity. Morse's own opinion is that, while Smith's historical accuracy was far from absolute, he has not been "equalled . . . in breadth of interest or comprehension."

Randel, William. "Captain John Smith's Attitudes Toward the Indians." *The Virginia Magazine of History and Biography* XLVIII, No. 3 (July 1939): 218-29.
Asserts that in *A True Relation* and *The Generall Historie* Smith showed himself "a candid, liberal, and fair reporter of the Indians."

Rowland, Kate Mason. "Captain John Smith: Soldier and Historian." *The Conservative Review* I, No. 1 (February 1899): 113-26.
Overview of the veracity controversy, defensive of Smith. Rowland decries what she terms the "anti-Smith crusade."

Scott, Nina M. "Bernal Díaz, Meet John Smith." *Americas* 33, Nos. 6-7 (June-July 1981): 32-9.

Comparison of the historical chronicles of Smith and of sixteenth-century Spanish explorer Bernal Díaz del Castillo.

Smith, Bradford. "Captain Smith of Jamestown." *The National Geographical Magazine* CXI, No. 5 (May 1957): 581-620.

Highly sympathetic and imaginative account of Smith's adventures in America.

Striker, Laura Polanyi. "The Hungarian Historian, Lewis L. Kropf, on Captain John Smith's *True Travels*." *The Virginia Magazine of History and Biography* 66, No. 1 (January 1958): 22-43.

Detailed refutation of Lewis L. Kropf's allegations that *The True Travels* is almost entirely fictional. Striker calls Kropf's own historical accuracy into question, stating of him that he "was not a genuine historian, either by education or avocation."

Striker, Laura Polanyi, and Smith, Bradford. "The Rehabilitation of Captain John Smith." *The Journal of Southern History* XXVIII, No. 3 (August 1962): 474-81.

Recapitulation of the veracity controversy. Striker and Smith review scholarly investigations and documentary evidence to support their conclusion that Smith's writing is accurate and reliable.

Thornton, Willis. "Pocahontas and John Smith." In his *Fable, Fact and History*, pp. 46-54. New York: Greenberg, 1957.

Attempts to determine the validity of the Pocahontas story. Thornton concludes: "This is one of the embellishments of history whose liberal truth is perhaps not a matter of very great importance."

Vaughan, Alden T. *American Genesis: Captain John Smith and the Founding of Virginia*. Edited by Oscar Handlin. Boston: Little, Brown and Co., 1975, 207 p.

Study of Smith's role in the British colonization of America. Vaughan contends that Smith "more than any other man made possible the emergence of British America."

Wecter, Dixon. "Captain John Smith and the Indians." In his *The Hero in America: A Chronicle of Hero-Worship*, pp. 17-30. 1941. Reprint. Ann Arbor: University of Michigan Press, 1963.

Observes treatment of the Pocahontas episode in American folklore via literature, art, and popular culture.

Wharton, Henry. *The Life of John Smith: English Soldier*. 1685. Reprint. Chapel Hill: University of North Carolina Press for the Virginia Historical Society, 1957, 101 p.

First biography of Smith, though only a partial one, ending with Smith's departure from Virginia. Wharton's book is an enthusiastic eulogy of Smith, whom he heralds as "equal to the most celebrated heroes of antiquity."

Woods, Katharine Pearson. *The True Story of Captain John Smith*. New York: Doubleday, Page & Co., 1901, 382 p.

Highly favorable biography; basically a retelling of Smith's own accounts. Woods writes in a preface that her aim "has been to substantiate Smith's account of himself as far as possible by summoning the testimony of contemporary history, enclosing . . . his autobiography in a framework of the manners and customs of the times, and thus demonstrating its thorough credibility."

————. "Captain John Smith and the American Nation." *Harper's Monthly Magazine*, CIV, No. DCXXI (February 1902): 470-75.

Laudatory account of Smith's contributions to the development of colonial America.

Benedictus de Spinoza

1632-1677

(Born Baruch de Spinoza) Dutch philosopher.

Considered a great modern philosopher, Spinoza profoundly influenced generations of Western intellectuals and writers through his two major works: *Tractatus theologico-politicus (Theological-Political Treatise)* and *Ethic ordine geometrico demonstrata (Ethics)*. These treatises propound the author's essentially monistic conception of existence and his deterministic understanding of the relationship between God, humanity, and the cosmos. Within this system individual free will, personal identity, and traditional distinctions between good and evil are ultimately rendered meaningless, for all are part of the divine will which, according to Spinoza, gives purpose to and flows through all of life. His works, divorced as they are from religious dogma but informed by religious faith, have attracted the interest not chiefly of modern philosophers, but of such poets as Samuel Taylor Coleridge and William Wordsworth, and of scientists, including Albert Einstein.

Born in Amsterdam, Spinoza was the son of prosperous Portuguese Jewish parents who, in the midst of the Spanish Inquisition, had emigrated to the Netherlands, then the most religiously tolerant nation in Europe. Raised in comfortable surroundings amidst Amsterdam's thriving Jewish community, he gained early regard at school among his instructors and classmates for his facility with the Old Testament, the Talmud, and the writings of major Jewish theologians and scholars. Through wide reading he familiarized himself as well with the unorthodox views of such liberal Jewish thinkers as Maimonides and Abraham ibn Ezra. Spinoza also acquired a sound education in Latin, mathematics, and the physical sciences. His inquisitive nature and impelling search for a supreme truth underlying all things led him to revaluate Hebrew doctrine and the Bible. He soon acquired a reputation for discoursing with fellow students upon inconsistencies he perceived in the Bible, the possibility that souls are not immortal, and his growing, essentially pantheistic conviction that God and the universe are one in being. Following repeated, unsuccessful attempts by the Jewish religious authorities to silence Spinoza, his views were finally declared anathema in 1656 and he was excommunicated, with his family and all other Jews charged to ostracize him. Due to the extensive influence his coreligionists wielded, Spinoza was for a time banned by Amsterdam's secular authorities from living within the city. Although he returned to Amsterdam a few years later his stay was brief, though during this interim he acquired further classical training under his Latin teacher, the noted classical scholar Francis van den Enden. While maintaining ties with several learned acquaintances, Spinoza organized a discussion group of friends to consider the chief religious, philosophic, and scientific issues of the day. He also assisted van den Enden in instructing schoolchildren and provided for himself by grinding and polishing lenses, a skill he had learned in early life and in which he had become remarkably proficient.

In 1660 Spinoza moved to Rijnsburg, the village that served as headquarters for the Collegiants: a group of philosophers and theologians who embraced the theories of René Descartes,

whose works deeply interested Spinoza. At about the same time he began associating with the Collegiants, he changed his name from the Hebrew Baruch to its Latin equivalent, Benedictus. Having in effect reached a time in his life during which he sought to free himself from past religious strictures, Spinoza began formulating his own philosophic principles and prepared to order them into a coherent system. While continuing to craft lenses and fulfill his various teaching duties, he wrote *Korte Verhandeling (Short Treatise on God, Man, and His Well-Being)* and *De intellectus emendatione (On the Improvement of the Understanding)*, completing both by 1662. Unpublished during Spinoza's lifetime, the two treatises are considered harbingers of the important works that followed. For some time Spinoza had been instructing his students in Cartesian philosophy, and in 1663 he composed a recapitulation and critique of his mentor's *Principia* (1644), supporting Descartes's theorems with parallel demonstrations of geometric principles. In this work, *Renati Descartes principiorum (The Principles of Descartes)*, he articulated reasons for ultimately rejecting the dualistic belief system Descartes had promulgated. Without strong encouragement to the author from his friends in Amsterdam and Rijnsburg, the work would likely not have been printed, for Spinoza increasingly viewed his philosophy as largely understandable by only a small circle of intellectuals rather than the general populace.

Having begun work on *Ethics,* Spinoza removed to Voorburg, near The Hague, late in 1663. In Voorburg, he continued work on *Ethics* but privately questioned the advisability of publishing it, given the constraints of the religious current in even so tolerant a nation as Holland. He thus turned from it to begin work on *Theological-Political Treatise.* This work of biblical criticism and political theory was intended, at least partially, to liberate philosophers from ecclesiastical proscription and by so doing to pave the way for direct philosophic investigation of the existence and practice of religion, as well as the proper relationship between the individual and the state. *Theological-Political Treatise* appeared anonymously in 1670. Its sale was prohibited almost immediately by civil authorities, for many believed that it denies the validity of the Bible as the inerrant record of God's revelation to humankind—which, in fact, it does. However, the work continued to circulate under disguised wrapper and, for its firm grounding in reason and empirical evidence, won many supporters among members of the scientific community.

In 1670 Spinoza moved to The Hague, residing there until his death. In his last years he completed *Ethics* and circulated the manuscript among his friends. He resolved not to publish it, for he knew the censure would be overwhelming; by 1675 it was rumored that in *Ethics* he had attempted to prove the nonexistence of God, a gross misrepresentation of his intent. Spinoza also undertook, but was unable to finish, a Hebrew grammar and a political study presumably meant to expand upon ideas first forwarded in *Theological-Political Treatise.* Following a prolonged, debilitating illness brought on (it is believed) by years of inadvertently inhaling glass dust while grinding lenses, Spinoza died of consumption in 1677.

The main body of Spinoza's philosophy is contained in *Ethics,* which was conceived as the capstone of the earlier *Short Treatise* and *On the Improvement of the Understanding.* Spinoza fashioned his arguments in *Ethics* after the geometrical method originated by Euclid, believing that by constructing his philosophic system upon indisputable mathematic analogues, and then undergirding his propositions with further notes and proofs, he could insure that there could be no doubt as to the intent and soundness of his ideas. The result of Spinoza's labors is a five-part study which addresses the nature of God and of the human mind, the nature and origin of "affections" (emotions), the individual's servitude to the emotions, and the value of nurturing rational understanding in order to free oneself from all such servitude. Spinoza posited an essentially deterministic, monistic universe, though in effect it comprises two main components: God (which Spinoza defines as "Naturing Nature," or the creative and causative power underlying the universe) and the world of mechanical and moral laws ("natured nature," or that subservient to the will of God). The two are linked, according to Spinoza, in that the former completely infuses the latter. Within this pantheistic system, the individual is an integral but infinitesimal component; thus, individuals approach reality *sub specie aeternitatis* ("from the standpoint of eternity"), meaning that the breadth of existence is both utterly holy and unknowable and that therefore one should submit with humble attentiveness to the mysteries of the world. Central to this endeavor, and essential for individual perfection, according to Spinoza, is *amor intellectualis Dei* ("the intellectual love of God"), which, as Henry E. Allison explains, is "equivalent to the delight in the intelligibility of things that accompanies the mind's satisfaction with its own cognitive powers. This

same satisfaction also constitutes human blessedness.'' Within this intellectual love of God lies Spinoza's ethical system. Spinoza asserted that if one disengages oneself from all overt emotion, positive or negative, lives a temperate life, and meditates constantly upon the Divine, one can attain an enlightened state in which complete harmony with God is realized.

Spinoza's reputation as a profound—if controversial—thinker reached far beyond Holland even during his lifetime. He corresponded and conversed with some of the most notable scientists and philosophers of his day, including the German metaphysician and mathematician Gottfried Wilhelm Leibniz. Since then, probably more than any philosopher of the modern world, Spinoza has attracted the attention of the literary and philosophical elite. Coleridge, Immanuel Kant, Johann Wolfgang von Goethe, Matthew Arnold, and numerous others have praised his life and work. To these writers, Spinoza's philosophy represented the most genuinely spiritual, most intellectually viable system to surface in European letters since the beginning of the Renaissance. Spinoza's adherence to one unified reality, in which God is not a distinct, personal divinity but rather an immanent force in the universe, appealed to a great number of poets and literary theorists and led to such bold affirmations as that by Gotthold Ephraim Lessing, as recorded in Friedrich Heinrich Jacobi's "Über die Lehre des Spinoza": "There is no possible view of life but Spinoza's." Spinoza's philosophy, though, provoked harsh denunciations by the religiously orthodox of the author's day, and today the name Spinoza, for some, still connotes such terms as atheist and apostate. This perception was first expressed forcefully by Pierre Bayle, who declared in 1697 that Spinoza's thought is "the most monstrous hypothesis that could be imagined, the most absurd, and most diametrically opposed to the most evident notions of our mind." Conversely, many twentieth-century philosophers reject Spinoza's nonempirical approach to his givens—God, reality, and the human mind—as antiquated and suggest that Spinoza's ethical system is fundamentally irrelevant in modern society. Many others, however, consider *Ethics* a brilliant, if logically problematic, exposition upon the most demanding intellectual problems philosophers have faced. According to Einstein, Spinoza saw in his theory of causality "a remedy for fear, hate and bitterness, the only remedy to which a genuinely spiritual man can have recourse. He demonstrated his justification for this conviction not only by the clear, precise formulation of his thoughts, but also by the exemplary fashioning of his own life." In addition, *Theological-Political Treatise* is now recognized not only as one of the first and most effective pleas for religious toleration but as a pioneering work of modern biblical criticism. In this work, through his emphasis upon the moral essence rather than the historical accuracy of the Scriptures, Spinoza helped prepare the way for the higher criticism of the early nineteenth century and for the Transcendentalists, universalists, and theologically liberal denominations of modern Christianity and Judaism.

As a champion of freedom of thought and as the architect of one of the most complete metaphysical systems yet constructed, Spinoza occupies a secure position in Western intellectual history. Havelock Ellis has written that Spinoza effectively "harmonized the discords that rend us asunder. He combined the rationalist attitude with the religious attitude and put them both on a basis of realism. He achieved a cosmic unity in which a liberated humanity, discarding individual aggressiveness, cooperated in the active vision of things as a whole. There resulted a union of science and mysticism, in a serene and exalted ecstasy disguised in a geometrical shape."

PRINCIPAL WORKS

Renati Des cartes principiorum philosophiae pars I. et II. more geometrico demonstratae per Benedictum de Spinoza (philosophy) 1663
[*The Principles of Descartes,* 1905]

*Tractatus theologico-politicus continens dissertationes all quot, quibus ostenditur libertatem philosophandi non tantum salva pietate, & reipublicae pace posse concedi: sed eandem nisi cum pace reipublicae, ipsaque pletate tolli non posse.... (philosophy) 1670

[*A Treatise Partly Theological, and Partly Political, Containing Some Few Discourses, to Prove That the Liberty of Philosophizing (That is Making Use of Natural Reason) May Be Allow'd Without any Prejudice to Piety, or to the Peace of Any Commonwealth; and That the Loss of Public Peace and Religion it Self Must Necessarily Follow, Where such a Liberty of Reasoning is Taken Away....;* 1689; also published as *Tractatus theologico-politicus: A Critical Inquiry into the History, Purpose, and Authenticity of the Hebrew Scriptures; with the Right to Free Thought and Free Discussion Asserted, and Shown to be Not Only Consistent But Necessarily Bound Up With True Piety and Good Government,* 1862]

†*B. D. S. Opera posthuma* (philosophy, letters, and grammar) 1677

‡*Korte Verhandeling van God, de Mensch und deszelhs Welstand* (philosophy) 1852

[*Short Treatise on God, Man, and His Well-being,* 1910]

The Collected Works of Spinoza. 2 vols. (philosophy, letters, and nonfiction) 1985-

---

*This work is commonly referred to as *Theological-Political Treatise.*

†This work contains *De intellectus emendatione* (*On the Improvement of the Understanding,* 1958) and *Ethic ordine geometrico demonstrata* (*The Ethics of Benedict de Spinoza. Demonstrated after the Manner of Geometers,* 1876), among other works.

‡This work was written between 1660 and 1662.

LUDOVICUS MEYER (essay date 1663)

[*A Dutch poet, dramatist, and scholar, Meyer was a close friend of Spinoza, with whom he shared many philosophical views. In the following excerpt from his introduction, written in 1663, to* The Principles of Descartes—*which he edited for Spinoza—Meyer articulates Spinoza's editorial intentions and philosophical standpoint.*]

Our Author diverges from Descartes very often not only in the formulations and explanations of the Axioms, but even as regards his proofs of the Propositions themselves and the remaining Conclusions, and uses a kind of Demonstration which is very different from that of Descartes. Let no one, however, so interpret this as if the Author wished to correct that most distinguished Man in these matters; let him rather think of the author as doing this for the sole purpose of being able to retain the better the order which he had already adopted, and so as not to increase unduly the number of Axioms. For the same reason he was also compelled to prove many things which Descartes set down without any proof, and to add what he has entirely omitted.

Above all, however, I would remark that in all these, namely, in the First and Second Parts of the Principles, in the fragment of the Third Part, as also in his Metaphysical Thoughts, our Author has set down Descartes's real thoughts and their proofs, as they are found in his writings, or as they ought to be deduced by valid reasoning from the fundamental principles laid down by him. For after he had promised to teach his pupil the philosophy of Descartes it was his sacred duty not to diverge from his thought by a finger's breadth, or to dictate anything that either did not correspond with his doctrines or was opposed to them. On this account, let no one think that he teaches here either his own views or only such as he approves. For although he regards some of them as true, and admits that he has added some views of his own, yet there are many views here which he rejects as false, favouring a view very different from them. (pp. 148-51)

[Mention must] be made of the fact that the expression, found in several places, that *this or that is beyond human comprehension,* ought to be received in the same way, that is, as expressing only the mind of Descartes. For it must not be taken to mean that our Author makes such utterances the expressions of his own thought. For he holds that all those things, and even many others more sublime and subtle, can not only be conceived by us clearly and distinctly, but can even be easily explained, if only the human Intellect be led to the search for truth and the Knowledge of things along another path than that which was cleared and made smooth by Descartes; and the foundations of the sciences as laid by Descartes, and all that he himself has constructed upon them, are not sufficient to disentangle and solve all the difficult questions which are met with in Metaphysics, but others are required if we desire to uplift our intellect to that summit of Knowledge.

Lastly (to bring the preface to an end) we wish the Readers to know that all these treatises are published for no other purpose than that of discovering and spreading the truth, and in order to persuade men to turn to the study of true and genuine Philosophy. (pp. 153-54)

> *Ludovicus Meyer, in an extract in* The Oldest Biography of Spinoza, *by Jean Maximilien Lucas? edited and translated by A. Wolfe, George Allen & Unwin Ltd., 1927, pp. 147-53.*

ALBERT BURGH (letter date 1675)

[*Burgh, who studied philosophy in Leyden, was an early, if not altogether lasting, admirer of Spinoza. In the following excerpt from a letter to Spinoza, he announces his conversion to Roman Catholicism and denounces Spinoza's theology.*]

Many greetings.

When leaving my country, I promised to write to you if anything noteworthy occurred during my journey. Since, now, an occasion has presented itself, and one, indeed, of the greatest importance, I discharge my debt, and write to inform you that, through the infinite Mercy of God, I have been restored to the Catholic Church, and have been made a member thereof. How this came to pass you will be able to learn in greater detail from the letter that I wrote to the most illustrious and experienced Mr. D. Craenen, Professor at Leyden. I will, therefore, now only add some brief remarks, which concern your own advantage.

The more I formerly admired you for your penetration and acuteness of mind, the more do I now weep for you and deplore you; for although you are a very talented man, and have received a mind adorned by God with brilliant gifts, and are a lover of truth, indeed eager for it, yet you suffer yourself to be led astray and deceived by the wretched and most haughty Prince of evil Spirits. For, all your philosophy, what is it but a mere illusion and a Chimera? Yet you stake on it not only your peace of mind in this life, but also the eternal salvation of your soul. See on what a miserable foundation all your interests rest. You presume to have at length discovered the true philosophy. How do you know that your Philosophy is the best among all those which have ever been taught in the world, or are actually taught now, or ever will be taught in the future? And, to say nothing about the thought of the future, have you examined all those philosophies, ancient as well as modern, which are taught here and in India and everywhere throughout the world? And, even if you have duly examined them, how do you know that you have chosen the best? You will say: my philosophy is in accord with right reason, the others are opposed to it. But all the other philosophers except your disciples differ from you, and, with the same right, they declare each about himself and his philosophy what you do about yours, and they accuse you, as you accuse them, of falsity and error. It is clear, therefore, that, in order that the truth of your philosophy may become manifest, you must put forward arguments which are not common to the other philosophies, but which can be applied to yours alone. Otherwise it must be confessed that your philosophy is as uncertain and as worthless as the rest.

However, confining myself now to your book, to which you have given that impious title [*Tractatus Theologico-Politicus*], and taking your Philosophy together with your Theology, for you yourself really blend them, although, with diabolical cunning, you pretend to show that the one is distinct from the other, and that they have different principles, I proceed thus—

Perhaps you will say: Others have not read Holy Scripture as frequently as I have, and it is from Holy Scripture itself, the recognition of whose authority constitutes the difference between Christians and the remaining peoples of the whole world, that I prove my views. But how? I explain Holy Scripture by applying the clear texts to the more obscure, and from this interpretation of mine I form my Doctrines, or confirm those which are already produced in my brain.

But I adjure you seriously to consider what you say. For how do you know that you make the said application correctly, and, next, that the application, even if made correctly, is sufficient for the interpretation of Holy Scripture, and that you are putting the interpretation of Holy Scripture on a sound basis? Especially since Catholics say, and it is very true, that the whole Word of God is not given in writing, so that Holy Scripture cannot be explained through Holy Scripture alone, I will not say, by one man but not even by the Church itself, which is the sole interpreter of Holy Scripture. For the Apostolic traditions must also be consulted. This is proved from Holy Scripture itself, and by the testimony of the Holy Fathers, and it is in accord not only with right reason but also with experience. Since, therefore, your principle is most false, and leads to perdition, where will your whole teaching remain, which is founded and built upon this false foundation?

So then, if you believe in Christ crucified, acknowledge your most evil heresy, recover from the perversion of your nature, and be reconciled with the Church. (pp. 310-13)

Come to your senses, you Philosopher, and realize the folly of your wisdom, the madness of your wisdom; put aside your pride and become humble, and you will be healed. Pray to Christ in the Most Holy Trinity, that he may deign to commiserate your misery, and receive you. Read the Holy Fathers, and the Doctors of the Church, and let them instruct you in what you must do that you may not perish, but have eternal life. Consult Catholics profoundly learned in their faith and living a good life, and they will tell you many things which you have never known and whereat you will be amazed.

I, for my part, have written this letter to you with truly Christian intention, first that you may know the great love that I bear you although a Gentile; and secondly to beg you not to continue to pervert others also.

I will therefore conclude this: God is willing to snatch your soul from eternal damnation, if only you are willing. Do not hesitate to obey the Lord, who has so often called you through others, and now calls you again, and perhaps for the last time, through me, who, having obtained this grace through the ineffable Mercy of God Himself, pray for the same for you with my whole heart. Do not refuse: for if you will not hear God now when He calls you, the anger of the Lord Himself will be kindled against you, and there is the danger that you may be abandoned by His Infinite Mercy, and become the unhappy victim of the divine Justice which consumes all things in its anger. May the omnipotent God avert this fate to the greater glory of His name, and to the salvation of your soul, and also as a salutary and imitable example for your most unfortunate Idolaters, through our Lord and Saviour, Jesus Christ, who with the Eternal Father lives and reigns in the Unity of the Holy Ghost as God for all eternity. Amen. (pp. 323-24)

> *Albert Burgh, in a letter to Benedict de Spinoza on September 3, 1675, in* The Correspondence of Spinoza, *edited and translated by A. Wolf, Lincoln MacVeagh, 1928, pp. 310-24.*

JEAN MAXIMILIEN LUCAS?   (essay date 1677)

[*The supposed author of the first biography of Spinoza (written from 1677 to 1678, but not published until 1719), Lucas was a French publisher and editor of various periodicals. Known as an outspoken opponent of Louis XIV, he spent many years in Holland in an effort to distance himself from governmental interference with his work. In the following excerpt, Lucas esteems the character and philosophy of Spinoza.*]

[Spinoza] said that the more we know God the more are we masters of our passions; that it is quillity of spirit and the true love of God that brings us salvation, which is Blessedness and Freedom.

These are the principal points which according to the teaching of our philosopher are dictated by reason concerning the true life and the supreme good of man. Compare them with the doctrines of the New Testament, and you will see that they are just the same. The Law of Jesus Christ leads us to the love of God and of our neighbour, which is precisely what reason inspires us to do, according to the opinion of Mr. de Spinosa. Whence it is easy to infer that the reason why St. Paul calls the Christian religion a reasonable religion is because reason prescribes it and is its foundation. That which is called a reasonable religion is, according to Origen, whatever is subject to the sovereignty of reason. One may add that one of the ancient Fathers asserts that we ought to live and to act according to the rules of reason.

So the opinions which our philosopher followed are supported by the Fathers and by Scripture; yet he is condemned, but apparently only by those whose interest obliges them to speak against reason, or who have never known it. I make this slight digression in order to arouse the simple to throw off the yoke of envious and false scholars who cannot tolerate the reputation of good people and falsely accuse them of holding opinions little in harmony with the Truth.

To return to Mr. de Spinosa, his conversations had such an air of geniality and his comparisons were so just that he made everybody fall in unconsciously with his views. He was persuasive although he did not affect polished or elegant diction. He made himself so intelligible, and his discourse was so full of good sense, that none listened to him without deriving satisfaction.

These fine talents attracted to him all reasonable people, and whatever time it may have been one always found him in an even and agreeable humour. (pp. 69-71)

Our Philosopher is . . . very fortunate, not only in the glory of his [life], but in the circumstances of his death, which he faced with an intrepid eye, as we have learned from those who were present, as if it had been easy for him to sacrifice himself for the sake of his enemies, so that their memory should not be stained by parricide. It is we that are left who are to be pitied: that is, all those whom his writings have improved, and to whom his presence was moreover of great assistance on the road to Truth.

But since he could not escape the lot of all that has life, let us strive to walk in his footsteps, or at least to revere him with admiration and with praise, if we cannot imitate him. This is what I counsel to steadfast souls: to follow his maxims and his lights in such a way as to have them always before their eyes to serve as a rule for their actions.

That which we love and revere in great men lives still and will live through all the ages. The greater part of those who have lived in obscurity and without glory will remain buried in darkness and in oblivion. BARUCH DE SPINOSA will live in the remembrance of true scholars and in their writings, which are the temple of Immortality. (pp. 74-5)

> *Jean Maximilien Lucas? in his* The Oldest Biography of Spinoza, *edited and translated by A. Wolf, George Allen & Unwin Ltd., 1927, 196 p.*

GOTTFRIED WILHELM LEIBNIZ (essay date 1678)

[*A chief force of the German Enlightenment, Leibniz contributed significantly to the fields of mathematics and philosophy. In the former discipline, he discovered differential and integral calculus at virtually the same time as did Sir Isaac Newton. As a philosopher, he propounded the metaphysical system of matter as a conglomeration of monadic forces united by the supreme monad, God. Leibniz, who met and corresponded with Spinoza, was a decided, yet philosophically cautious, admirer of Spinoza's work. In the following excerpt from an essay written in 1678, Leibniz provides a point-by-point analysis of* Ethics, Book I.]

Definition 1. Cause of itself is that whose essence involves existence.

Definition 2. To say that a thing is finite if it can be limited by another thing of the same nature involves obscurity. For what does it mean to say that a thought is limited by another thought? Does this mean that the other one is greater, in the

sense that [Spinoza] says that a body is limited because another can be conceived which is greater than it? See Proposition 8, below.

Definition 3. Substance is that which is in itself and is conceived through itself. This definition too is obscure. For what does "to be in itself" mean? Then we must ask: Does he relate "to be in itself" and "to be conceived through itself" cumulatively or disjunctively? That is, does he mean that substance is what is in itself and also that substance is what is conceived through itself? Or does he mean that substance is that in which both occur together, that is, that substance is both in itself and conceived through itself? But then it would be necessary for him to prove that whatever has one property also has the other, while the contrary seems rather to be true, that there are some things which are in themselves though they are not conceived through themselves. And this is how men commonly conceive of substance. He continues: substance is that whose concept does not need the concept of any other thing upon which it must rest. But there is also a difficulty in this, for he says in the next definition that an *attribute* is perceived by the understanding as belonging to substance and as constituting its essence. Therefore the concept of the attribute is necessary to form the concept of the substance. If you reply that an attribute is not a thing and that you merely mean that a substance does not need the concept of any other thing, I answer that it is then necessary to explain what "thing" means, in order to understand the definition and see why an attribute is not a thing.

Definition 4. It is also obscure to say that an attribute is that which the understanding perceives about substance as constituting its essence. For the question arises whether he understands by attribute every reciprocal predicate, or every essential predicate whether reciprocal or not, or, finally, every primary essential or indemonstrable predicate of substance. See Definition 5.

Definition 5. A mode is that which is in something else and is conceived through something else. It seems therefore to differ from an attribute in this—that an attribute is indeed in a substance but is conceived through itself. And with the added explanation here the obscurity of Definition 4 disappears.

Definition 6. He says: I define God as the absolute infinite being, or as the substance which consists of infinite attributes, each of which expresses an eternal and infinite essence. He ought to show that these two definitions are equipollent; otherwise the one cannot be substituted for the other. They will be equipollent if it is shown that there is a plurality of attributes or predicates in the nature of things which are conceived through themselves; but also that the several predicates are compatible with each other. Besides, every definition is imperfect, however true and clear it may be, which permits some doubt, even when it is understood, about whether the thing defined is possible. Now this is such a definition, for it still can be doubted whether a being having infinite attributes does not imply a contradiction. Furthermore, it can be doubted whether the same simple essence can be expressed through many different attributes. There are in fact many definitions of composite things, but only one of a simple thing, and its essence can be expressed, it seems, only in one way.

Definition 7. A being is *free* which exists and is determined to action by the necessity of its own nature; a being is *coerced* whose existence and action are determined by another.

Definition 8. By *eternity* I mean existence itself insofar as it is conceived to follow from the essence of a thing. I approve of both of these definitions. (pp. 300-02)

Proposition 1. Substance is by nature prior to its affections, that is, to its modes, for he has said in Definition 5 that by the affections of a substance he means the modes. But he has not explained what the term "prior by nature" means, and so this proposition cannot be demonstrated from what precedes it. But it seems that by "something prior to another thing by nature" he means that through which the other thing is conceived. Yet I confess that I find some difficulty in this too, for it seems that what is posterior cannot only be conceived through what is prior, but also the prior through the posterior. "To be prior by nature" can be defined in this way, however: as that which can be conceived without the other being conceived, while the other thing cannot, on the contrary, be conceived without the concept of the former. But, to tell the truth, to be prior by nature is a little more general even than this. For example, the property of the number 10 to be 6 + 4 is posterior to that of being 6 + 3 + 1, because this latter property is closer to the first property of all; ten is 1 + 1 + 1 + 1 + 1 + 1 + 1 + 1 + 1 + 1. Still it can be conceived without the second property, and, what is more, it can be proved without it. I add another example. In a triangle the property that the three internal angles equal two right angles is posterior in nature to the property that two internal angles are equal to the exterior angle of the third. Yet the former can be understood without the latter and, indeed, can be demonstrated without it, though not as easily. (pp. 302-03)

Proposition 5. In the nature of things there cannot be two or more substances with the same nature or attribute.

Here I point out that what is meant by "in the nature of things" seems obscure. Does he mean in the whole of existing things or in the region of ideas or of possible essences? Then it is not clear whether he meant to say that there are not many essences with the same common attribute or that there are not many individuals with the same essence. I also wonder why he here takes the word "nature" and the word "attribute" as equivalent, unless he means by attribute that which contains the whole nature. If this is assumed, I do not see how there can be many attributes of the same substance which are conceived through themselves.

His proof of the proposition is as follows. If the substances were distinct, they would be distinguished either by affections or by attributes; if by affections, then, since a substance is by nature prior to its affections, by Proposition 1, they must also be distinguished apart from their affections, and therefore they are distinguished by their attributes. If by their attributes, then there are no two substances with the same attribute. I reply that there seems to be a concealed fallacy here. For two substances can be distinguished by their attributes and still have some common attribute, provided they also have others peculiar to themselves in addition. For example, *A* may have the attributes *c* and *d,* and *B* the attributes *d* and *e.* I note further that Proposition 1 is useless except for proving this proposition. It might have been omitted, for it is enough that substance can be conceived without its affections, whether it be prior to them by nature or not. (pp. 304-05)

Proposition 7. *To exist pertains to the nature of substance.* One substance cannot be produced by another, by Proposition 6. Therefore it is the cause of itself, that is, by Definition 1, its essence involves existence. Here he is rightly to be criticized

for using the term "cause of itself" sometimes in the special sense which he has given it in Definition 1 and sometimes in its common and popular meaning. Yet it is easy to remedy this, if he transforms Definition 1 into an axiom and says: Whatever is not from something else is from itself, or from its own essence. But then there remain other difficulties here. For the reasoning is valid only on the assumption that substance can exist. For, since it cannot be produced by something else, it must exist by itself, and hence exist necessarily. But it must be demonstrated that substance is possible, that is, that it can be conceived. This, I think, can be demonstrated: for, if nothing can be conceived through itself, nothing will be conceivable through something else either, and therefore nothing will be conceivable at all. To show this more distinctly, we must consider that, if *a* is assumed to be conceived through *b,* the concept of *b* must be contained in the concept of *a.* And, again, if *b* is conceived through *c,* the concept of *c* must be contained in the concept of *b,* and thus the concept of *c* will be contained in the concept of *a;* and so on, to the last concept. If someone answers that there is no last concept, I reply that then there is no first one either, and I prove it as follows. Since there is nothing except alien elements in the concept of that which is conceived through something else, then proceeding by stages through many concepts, it will have either nothing whatever in it or nothing except what is conceived through itself. I believe that, although this demonstration is new, it is infallible. With its aid it can be proved that what is conceived through itself is possible. Yet we can still doubt whether it is possible in the sense in which it is here assumed to be possible, namely, not merely for that which is conceivable, but for that of which some cause can be conceived which is eventually reducible to a first cause. For not everything which is conceivable by us can therefore be produced, because of other more important things with which it may be incompatible. Thus, to prove that a being conceived through itself actually exists, we must resort to experience, because, since things exist which are conceived through other things, a thing exists through which they are conceived. So you see that an entirely different kind of reasoning is necessary to prove accurately that there is a thing which exists through itself. But perhaps there is no need of this extreme caution.

Proposition 8. Every substance is necessarily infinite, because otherwise it would be limited by another substance of the same nature, by Definition 2, and there would be two substances of the same nature, which contradicts Proposition 5. This proposition must be understood as follows. A thing which is conceived through itself is infinite within its own kind; this must be admitted. But the demonstration suffers from obscurity as to the term "to be limited" and also from uncertainty, by reason of Proposition 5. In the scholium he gives an elegant proof that there is only one thing that is conceived through itself (within its own kind, that is), because, assuming that there is a plurality of individuals, there must be some reason in nature why there should be just so many and no more. But the reason for there being exactly so many is the same that for there being this one and that one, and therefore the same as the reason for there being this particular one. But this reason is not to be found in one of them rather than another; therefore the reason is outside all of them. One objection is possible, namely, that the number of individuals is unlimited or no number at all, or that it exceeds any number. But this could be avoided if we take only some of them and ask why these exist, or if we take several of them having a common property, such as existence in the same place, and ask why they exist in this place.

Proposition 9. The more reality or being a thing possesses, the more attributes belong to it. (He should have explained what is meant by reality or being, for these terms are subject to equivocation.) His demonstration: it follows from Definition 4. Thus our author. But it does not seem to me to follow from it. For one thing can have more reality than another for the reason that it is greater in its own kind or has a greater share in some attribute. For example, the circle has more extension than the inscribed square. And it can still be doubted that several attributes may belong to the same substance, in the sense in which the author understands attributes. Meanwhile I admit that, if his meaning of attributes is accepted and attributes are supposed to be compatible, a substance is the more perfect, the more attributes it has.

Proposition 10. Each attribute of the same substance must be conceived through itself, by Definitions 4 and 3. But then it follows, as I have several times objected, that one substance can have only one attribute if this attribute expresses its whole essence.

Proposition 11. God, or the substance which consists of infinite attributes, each of which expresses an eternal and infinite essence, necessarily exists. He gives three demonstrations. *First,* because God is a substance and therefore exists, by Proposition 7. But this assumes that a substance necessarily exists, which was not sufficiently proved in Proposition 7, and that God is a possible substance, which is not so easy to prove. The *second* proof is that there must always be a cause for the being of a thing as well as for its nonbeing. But there can be no reason why God should not exist—not in his own nature, for this implies no contradiction; not in anything else, for that something else would either be of the same nature and attribute, and therefore would be God, or it would not, in which case it would have nothing in common with God and so could neither support nor prevent his existence. To this I reply (1) that he has not yet proved that God's nature does not imply contradiction, even though the author says without proof that it is absurd to say that it does, and (2) that another being could have the same nature as God in some things but not in all. His *third* argument: finite beings exist, by experience. Therefore, if an infinite being did not exist, the finite beings would be more potent than the infinite being. To this I reply: If the infinite being implies a contradiction, it will have no power at all; not to mention that the capacity to exist cannot properly be called a power.

Propositions 12 and 13. No attribute of substance can truly be conceived from which it would follow that substance is divisible; or, taken absolutely, substance is indivisible. For it will be destroyed by division; the parts will not be infinite and therefore not substances. Or else there would be several substances of the same nature. I grant this argument for a thing existing through itself. Hence the *corollary* follows that no substance is divisible, and therefore the corporeal substance, too, is indivisible.

Proposition 14. There is no substance besides God, and none can be conceived. Because all attributes pertain to God and there is no plurality of substances with the same attribute, there are no substances besides God. All this presupposes the definition of substance as a being which is conceived through itself, as well as many other propositions, already noted, which cannot be granted. (It does not yet seem certain to me that bodies are substances; with minds the case is different.) (pp. 305-09)

Proposition 33. The world could not have been produced by God in any other way than it has been produced, for it follows from the immutable nature of God. This proposition may be true or false, depending on how it is explained. On the hypothesis that the divine will chooses the best or works in the most perfect way, certainly only this world could have been produced; but, if the nature of the world is considered in itself, a different world could have been produced. Thus we say that confirmed angels cannot sin, in spite of their freedom. They could if they willed, but they do not will. Speaking absolutely, they can will to sin, but in this existing state of things they no longer can so will. In his scholium the author rightly recognizes that something may be rendered impossible for two different reasons—either because it implies contradiction or because there is no external cause apt to produce it. He denies, in his second scholium, that God does all things in view of the good. He has already denied God a will, it is true, and he thinks that those who disagree make God subject to fate, though he himself admits that God does all things according to the principle of perfection.

Proposition 34. The power of God is his essence itself, because it follows from his essence that he is the cause of himself and of the other things.

Proposition 35. Whatever is in God's power exists necessarily, that is, it follows from his essence.

Proposition 36. Nothing exists from whose nature some effect does not follow, because it expresses the nature of God, that is, his power, in a certain and determined way, by Proposition 34. This proposition does not follow, but it is nonetheless true.

He adds an appendix [to *Ethics*] in which he attacks those who believe that God acts according to purposes. The appendix is a mixture of truth and falsehood. Even though it is true that not everything happens for the sake of men, it does not follow that God acts without will or knowledge of the good. (pp. 315-16)

> *Gottfried Wilhelm Leibniz, "On the Ethics of Benedict de Spinoza," in his* Philosophical Papers and Letters, Vol. I, *edited and translated by Leroy E. Loemker, The University of Chicago Press, 1956, pp. 300-16.*

PIERRE BAYLE (essay date 1697)

[*Bayle was a prominent French scholar and philosopher who is remembered chiefly for his monumental* Dictionnaire historique et critique *(1697;* A General Dictionary, Historical and Critical, *1734-38), a sourcebook of Enlightenment thought containing biographical and historical discussions of important personages and events from classical to modern times. Bayle was noted in this work for displaying a contentious, highly critical attitude toward those with whom he differed. In the following excerpt from the* Dictionary, *Bayle discusses what he considers the follies of Spinoza's thought.*]

Those who were acquainted with [Spinoza], and the peasants of the villages where he had lived in retirement for some time, all agree in saying that he was sociable, affable, honest, obliging, and of a well-ordered morality. This is strange; but, after all, we should not be more surprised by this than to see people who live very bad lives even though they are completely convinced of the Gospel. Some people claim that he followed the maxim, "Nobody grows very bad suddenly," and that he only fell into atheism gradually and that he was far from it when he published [*The Principles of Descartes*]. He is as orthodox in this work about the nature of God as Descartes himself; but it must be said that he did not speak thus on account of his own convictions. It is not wrong to think that the ill use he made of some of this philosopher's maxims led him to the precipice. . . . All those who have refuted the **Tractatus theologico-politicus** have found in it the seeds of atheism, but nobody has developed this point as clearly as Johannes Bredenbourg. It is not as easy to deal with all the difficulties contained in that work as to demolish completely the system [contained in **Ethics**] that appeared in his **Opera posthuma;** for this is the most monstrous hypothesis that could be imagined, the most absurd, and the most diametrically opposed to the most evident notions of our mind. (pp. 295-97)

[Editor's note: Bayle's remaining remarks in this excerpt are taken from a lengthy explanatory footnote (one of many which accompany this, as well as other essays in Bayle's *Dictionary*) stemming directly from the above assertion. The gap in paging is due to the format of Popkin's edition.]

[Spinoza] supposes that there is only one substance in nature, and that this unique substance is endowed with an infinity of attributes—thought and extension among others. In consequence of this, he asserts that all the bodies that exist in the universe are modifications of this substance in so far as it is extended, and that, for example, the souls of men are modifications of this same substance in so far as it thinks; so that God, the necessary and infinitely perfect being, is indeed the cause of all things that exist, but he does not differ from them. There is only one being, and only one nature; and this nature produces in itself by an immanent action all that we call creatures. It is at the same time both agent and patient, efficient cause, and subject. It produces nothing that is not its own modification. There is a hypothesis that surpasses all the heap of all the extravagances that can be said. The most infamous things the pagan poets have dared to sing against Venus and Jupiter do not approach the horrible idea that Spinoza gives us of God, for at least the poets did not attribute to the gods all the crimes that are committed and all the infirmities of the world. But according to Spinoza there is no other agent and no other recipient than God, with respect to everything we call evil of punishment and evil of guilt, physical evil and moral evil. Let us touch on some of the absurdities of his system.

That according to Spinoza God and extension are the same thing. I. It is impossible that the universe be one single substance; for everything that is extended necessarily has parts, and everything that has parts is composite; and since the parts of extension do not subsist in one another, it must be the case either that extension in general is not one substance, or that each part of extension is a particular substance distinct from all the others. Now, according to Spinoza extension in general is the attribute of one substance. He admits, along with all other philosophers, that the attribute of a substance does not differ actually from that substance. Therefore he must acknowledge that extension in general is a substance. From which it necessarily follows that each part of extension is a particular substance, which destroys the foundations of the entire system of this author. He cannot say that extension in general is distinct from the substance of God; for if he said that, he would teach that this substance in itself is not extended. Then, it could never be able to acquire the three dimensions except by creating them, for it is obvious that extension can never arise or emanate from an unextended subject except by way of creation. Now Spinoza did not believe that nothing could be made from nothing. It is even more obvious that an unextended substance by its nature can never become the subject of three dimensions,

for how would it be possible to place them on a mathematical point? They would therefore subsist without a subject. They would then be a substance; so that, if this author admitted a real distinction between the substance of God and extension in general, he would be obliged to say that God would be composed of two substances distinct from one another, namely his unextended being and extension. We see him thus obliged to recognize that extension and God are only the same thing; and since, in addition, he maintains that there is only one substance in the universe, he has to teach that extension is a simple being, as exempt from composition as the mathematical points. But is it not a joke to maintain this? Is this not to fight against the most distinct ideas we have in our minds? Is it not more evident that the thousandth number is composed of a thousand unities than even that a body of a hundred inches is composed of a hundred parts actually distinct from one another, each having one inch of extension?

That extension is composed of parts which are each a particular substance. Let no one come and urge objections to us against the imagination and the prejudices of the senses; for the most intellectual notions, and the most immaterial ones, make us see with complete evidence that there is a very real distinction between things, one of which possesses a quality and the other of which does not. The Scholastics have perfectly well succeeded in showing us the characteristics and the infallible signs of distinction. When one can affirm of a thing, they tell us, what one cannot affirm of another, they are distinct; things that can be separated from one another with regard to time or place are distinct. Applying these characteristics to the twelve inches of a foot of extension, we will find a real distinction between them. I can affirm of the fifth that it is contiguous to the sixth, and I deny this of the first, the second, and so on. I can transpose the sixth to the place of the twelfth. It can then be separated from the fifth. Observe that Spinoza cannot deny that the characteristics of distinction employed by the Scholastics are very just; for it is by these marks that he recognizes that stones and animals are not the same modality of infinite being. He admits then, I will be told, that there is some difference between things. It is most necessary that he admit it since he was not enough of a madman to believe there was no difference between himself and the Jew who struck him with a knife, or to dare to say that in all respects his bed and his room were the same being as the emperor of China. What then did he say? You are about to see. He taught not that two trees were two parts of extension, but two modifications. You will be surprised that he worked so many years constructing a new system, since one of its principal pillars was the alleged difference between the word ''part'' and the word ''modification.'' Could he promise himself any advantage from this change of words? Let him avoid as much as he wants the word ''part''; let him substitute as much as he wants the word ''modality'' or ''modification''; what does this accomplish? Will the ideas attached to the word ''part'' vanish? Will they not be applied to the word ''modification''? Are the signs and characteristics of difference less real or less evident when matter is divided into modifications than when it is divided into parts? Poppycock! The idea of matter still continues to be that of a composite being, that of a collection of several substances. Here follows what will prove this.

Incompatible modalities require distinct subjects. Modalities are beings that cannot exist without the substance they modify. It is therefore necessary that there be substance everywhere for modalities to exist. It is also necessary that it multiply itself in proportion as incompatible modifications are multiplied among themselves, so that wherever there are five or six of these modifications, there are also five or six substances. It is evident, and no Spinozist can deny it, that a square shape and a round one are incompatible in the same piece of wax. It must necessarily then be the case that the substance modified by a square shape is not the same substance as that modified by a round one. Thus, when I see a round table and a square one in a room, I can assert that the extension that is the subject of the round table is a substance distinct from the extension that is the subject of the other table; for otherwise it would be certain that a square shape and a round one would be at the same time in one and the same subject. Now this is impossible. Iron and water, wine and wood, are incompatible. Therefore they require subjects distinct in number.... All this shows that extension is composed of as many distinct substances as there are modifications. (n., pp. 300-07)

If I did not remember that I am not writing a book against this man, but merely a few brief remarks in passing, I would show many other absurdities in his system. Let us finish with this one. He has embarked on a hypothesis that would make all his work ridiculous, and I am very sure that on each page of his *Ethics* one could find some pitiful nonsense. First, I would like to know what he means when he rejects certain doctrines and sets forth others. Does he intend to teach truths? Does he wish to refute errors? But has he any right to say that there are errors? The thoughts of ordinary philosophers, those of Jews, and those of Christians, are they not modes of the infinite being, as much as those of his *Ethics*? Are they not realities that are as necessary to the perfection of the universe as all his speculations? Do they not emanate from the necessary cause? How then can he dare to claim that there is something to rectify? In the second place, does he not claim that the being of which they are modalities acts necessarily, that it always goes on its course, that it cannot turn aside, cannot stop, nor, since it is the sole entity in the universe, can any external cause ever stop it or correct it? Then, there is nothing more useless than the lectures of this philosopher. Is it right for him, being only a modification of substance, to prescribe to the infinite being what he must do? Will this being hear him? And if he hears, could he profit from this? Does he not always act according to the entire extent of his powers, without knowing either where he is going or what he is doing? A man like Spinoza would sit absolutely still if he reasoned logically. "If it is possible," he would say, "that such a doctrine might be established, the necessity of nature would establish it without my book. If it is not possible, all of my writings would accomplish nothing." (n., pp. 313-14)

> *Pierre Bayle, "Spinoza," in his* Historical and Critical Dictionary: Selections, *translated by Richard H. Popkin with Craig Brush, The Bobbs-Merrill Company, Inc., 1965, pp. 288-338.*

JOHN COLERUS   (essay date 1706)

[*Colerus served for a time as minister of the Lutheran church in The Hague. In the following excerpt, originally published in 1706 in his* Life of Benedict de Spinoza, *he denounces Spinoza as an atheist and propounder of abominable beliefs.*]

[Of] *Spinosa* and his *Tractatus Theologico-Politicus,* I shall say what I think of it, after I have set down the judgment, which two famous Authors made of it, one whereof was of the *Confession of Ausburg,* and the other *Reformed.* The first is *Spitzelius,* who speaks of it thus, in his Treatise entituled *Infelix Litera-*

tor.... "That impious author (*Spinosa*) blinded by a prodigious presumption, was so impudent and so full of Impiety, as to maintain that Prophecies were only grounded upon the fancy of the Prophets; and that the Prophets and the Apostles wrote naturally according to their own light and knowledge, without any Revelation or Order from God: That they accommodated Religion, as well as they cou'd, to the Genius of those who lived at that time, and established it upon such Principles as were then well known, and commonly received." ... *Spinosa* pretends in his *Tractatus Theologico-Politicus,* that the same Method may and ought to be observed still for explaining the Holy Scripture; for he maintains, amongst other things, that, *as the Scripture, when it was first published, was fitted to the established opinions, and to the capacity of the People, so every Body is free to expound it according to his Knowledge, and make it agree with his own opinions.*

If this was true, good Lord! What respect cou'd we have for the Scripture? How cou'd we maintain that it is Divinely inspired? That it is a sure and firm Prophecy; that the holy Men, who are the Authors of it, spoke and wrote by God's order, and by the inspiration of the Holy Spirit; that the same Scripture is most certainly true, and that it gives a certain Testimony of its Truth to our Consciences; and lastly, that it is a Judge, whose Decision ought to be the constant and unvariable Rule of our Thoughts, of our Faith, and of our Lives. If what *Spinosa* affirms were true, one might indeed very well say, that the Bible is a Wax-Nose, which may be turned and shaped at one's will; a Glass, thro' which every Body may exactly see what pleases his fancy; a Fool's Cap, which may be turned and fitted at one's pleasure a hundred several ways. The Lord confound thee, Satan, and stop thy mouth!

Spitzelius is not contented to say what he thinks of that pernicious Book; but he adds to the judgment he made of it, that of Mr *de Manseveld* heretofore Professor at *Utrecht,* who speaks of it thus, in a Book Printed at *Amsterdam,* in 1674. *My opinion is, that that Treatise ought to be buried for ever in an æternal oblivion: Tractatum hunc aa æternas damnandum tenebras,* &c. Which is very judiciously said; seeing that Wicked Book does altogether overthrow the Christian Religion, by depriving the Sacred Writings of the Authority, on which it is solely grounded and established.

The second Testimony I shall produce is, that of Mr. *William van Blyenburg* of *Dordrect,* who kept a long correspondence with *Spinosa,* and who in his 31st Letter to him, ... says, speaking of himself, that he had embraced no Profession, and that he lived by an honest Trade, *Liber sum nulli adstrictus professioni, honestis mercaturis me alo.* That Merchant, who is a learned Man, in the Preface of a Book entituled, *The truth of the Christian Religion,* Printed at *Leyden,* in 1674, gives his judgment about the Treatise of *Spinosa* in these words. *It is a Book,* says he, *full of curious, but abominable discoveries, the Learning and Inquiries whereof must needs have been fetched from Hell. Every Christian, nay, every Man of Sense, ought to abhor such a Book. The Author endeavours to overthrow the Christian Religion, and baffle all our hopes, which are grounded upon it: In the room whereof he introduces Atheism, or at most, a Natural Religion forged according to the humour or interests of the Soveraigns. The wicked shall be restrained only by the fear of Punishment; but a Man of no Conscience, who neither fears the Executioner nor the Laws, may attempt anything to satisfy himself,* &c.

I must add, that I have read that book of *Spinosa* with application from the beginning to the end; but I protest at the same time before God, that I have found no solid arguments in it, nor anything that cou'd shake, in the least, my belief of the Gospel. Instead of solid reasons, it contains meer suppositions, and what we call in the School, *petitiones principii*. The things which the Author advances, are given for Proofs, which being denied and rejected, the remaining part of his Treatise will be found to contain nothing but Lies and Blasphemies. Did he think that the World wou'd believe him blindly upon his word, and that he was not obliged to give good reasons and good proofs for what he advanced? (pp. 401-03)

Several Learned Men have already sufficiently discovered the impious Doctrines contained in [Spinoza's] Posthumous Works, and have given notice to every Body to beware of 'em. I shall only add some few things to what has been said by them. The Treatise of Morals [*Ethic ordine geometrico demonstrata*] begins with some Difinitions or Descriptions of the Deity. Who would not think at first, considering so fine a beginning, that he is reading a Christian Philosopher? All those Difinitions are fine, especially the sixth, wherein *Spinosa* says, that *God is an infinite Being; that is, a Substance, which contains in it self an infinity of Attributes, every one whereof represents and expresses an Eternal and infinite Substance.* But when we enquire more narrowly into his Opinions, we find that the God of *Spinosa* is a meer Phantom, an imaginary God, who is nothing less than God. And therefore the words of the Apostle, *Tit.* 1. 16, concerning impious Men, may be very well applied to that Philosopher: *They profess that they know God, but in Works they deny him.* What *David* says of ungodly Men *Psalm* 14. 1. does likewise suit him: *The Fool has said in his Heart, there is no God.* This is the true Opinion of *Spinosa*, whatever he might say. He takes the liberty to use the word *God*, and to take it in a sense unknown to all Christians. This he confesses himself in his 21st Letter to Mr. *Oldenburg: I acknowledge,* says he, *that I have a notion of God and Nature, very different from that of the Modern Christians. I believe that God is the* Immanent, *and not the* Transient *Cause of all things: Deum rerum omnium Causam immanentem, non vero transeuntem statuo.* And to confirm his Opinion, he alledges these Words of St *Paul; In him we live, and move, and have our Being.* Act. 17. 28.

In order to understand him, we must consider that a *Transient Cause* is, that the Productions whereof are external, or out of it self; as a Man, who throws a Stone into the Air, or a Carpenter, who builds a House: Whereas the *Immanent Cause* acts inwardly, and is confined within itself, without acting outwardly. Thus when a Man's Soul thinks of, or desires something, it is or remains in that thought or desire, without going out of it, and is the immanent Cause thereof. In the same manner, the God of *Spinosa* is the Cause of the Universe wherein he is, and he is not beyond it. But because the Universe has some bounds, it wou'd follow that God is a limited and finite Being. And tho he says that God is infinite, and comprehends an infinity of Perfections; he must needs play with the words *Eternal* and *Infinite*, seeing he cannot understand by them a Being, which did subsist before Time was, and before any other Being was created, but he calls that infinite, wherein the Humane Understanding can neither find an End, nor any Bounds: For he thinks the Productions of God are so numerous, that Man, with all the strength of his Mind, cannot conceive any Bounds in them. Besides, they are so solid, and so well settled and connected one with another, that they shall last for ever. (pp. 404-05)

As far as I am able to understand *Spinosa*, the dispute between us Christians and him runs upon this, *viz*. Whether the true

God be an Eternal Substance, different and distinct from the Universe, and from the whole Nature, and whether by a free Act of his Will he produc'd the World, and all Creatures out of nothing; or whether the Universe, and all the Beings it comprehends, do essensually belong to the Nature of God, being considered as a Substance, whose Thought and Extension are infinite? *Spinosa* maintains the last proposition. The *Antispinosa* of *Ch. Wittichius*, may be consulted. Thus he owns indeed, that God is the general Cause of all things; but he pretends, that God produces 'em necessarily without freedom and choice, and without consulting his Will. In like manner, everything that happens in the World, Good or Evil, Virtue or Vice, Sin or good Works, does necessarily proceed from him; and consequently there ought to be no Judgment, no Punishment, no Resurrection, no Salvation, no Damnation. For if it were so, that imaginary God wou'd Punish and Reward his own Work, as a Child does his Baby. Is it not the most pernicious Atheism that ever was seen in the World? And therefore Mr. *Burmanus*, a Reformed Minister, at *Enkhuysen* calls *Spinosa*, with great Reason, the most impious Atheist, that ever liv'd upon the Face of the Earth.

I don't design to examine here all the impious and absurd Doctrines of *Spinosa;* I have mention'd some of the most important, only to inspire the Christian Reader with the aversion and horror he ought to have for such pernicious Opinions. But I must not forget to say, that it does plainly appear by the second part of his *Ethicks,* that he makes the Soul and Body but one Being, the Properties whereof are, as he expresses it, Thinking and Extension. . . . As for the Soul, which is and acts in the Body, it is only another Modification or manner of being, produced by Nature, or manifested by Thought: It is not a Spirit, or a particular Substance no more than the Body, but a Modification, which expresses the Essence of God, as he manifests himself, Acts and Works by Thought. Did ever any Body hear any such abominations among Christians! At that rate God cou'd neither Punish the Soul nor the Body, unless he would Punish and Destroy himself. (pp. 405-07)

> John Colerus, ''The Life of Benedict de Spinosa,'' in Spinoza: His Life and Philosophy *by Sir Fredrick Pollock, Bart., second edition, The Macmillan Company, 1899, pp. 383-418.*

IMMANUEL KANT (essay date 1790)

[*A highly influential German philosopher, Kant posited—in his* Kritik der reinen Vernunft *(1781;* Critique of Pure Reason, *1929) and other works—that knowledge is derived from both the senses and the understanding and that one cannot arrive at absolute truth through reason alone. Kant allowed that reason serves principally in the construction of our moral laws and works toward an ultimate good, one which must be predicated on faith in a moral author of the world. In the following excerpt from a study originally published in 1790, Kant condemns Spinoza's conception of the world and its resulting moral implications.*]

The *idealism* of finality (I am here all along referring to objective finality) is either that of the *accidentality* or *fatality* of the determination of nature in the final form of its products. The former principle fixes on the relation of matter to the physical basis of its form, namely dynamical laws; the latter on its relation to the hyperphysical basis of matter and entire nature. The system of *accidentality*, which is attributed to Epicurus or Democritus, is, in its literal interpretation, so manifestly absurd that it need not detain us. On the other hand, the system of *fatality*, of which Spinoza is the accredited author, although it is to all appearances much older, rests upon something supersensible, into which our insight, accordingly, is unable to penetrate. It is not so easy to refute: the reason being that its conception of the original being is quite unintelligible. But this much is clear, that on this system the final nexus in the world must be regarded as undesigned. For, while it is derived from an original being, it is not derived from its intelligence, and consequently not from any design on its part, but from the necessity of the nature of this being and the world-unity flowing from that nature. Hence it is clear, too, that the fatalism of finality is also an idealism of finality.

2. The *realism* of the finality of nature is also either physical or hyperphysical. The *former* bases natural ends on the analogue of a faculty acting designedly, that is, on the *life of matter*—this life being either inherent in it or else bestowed upon it by an inner animating principle or world-soul. This is called *hylozoism*. The *latter* derives such ends from the original source of the universe. This source it regards as an intelligent Being producing with design—or essentially and fundamentally living. It is *theism*. (p. 43)

What is the aim and object of all the above systems? It is to explain our teleological judgements about nature. To do so they adopt one or other of two courses. One side denies their truth, and consequently describes them as an idealism of nature (represented as art). The other side recognizes their truth, and promises to demonstrate the possibility of a nature according to the idea of final causes.

The systems that contend for the idealism of the final causes in nature fall into two classes. One class does certainly concede to the principle of these causes a causality according to dynamical laws (to which causality the natural things owe their final existence). But it denies to it *intentionality*—that is, it denies that this causality is determined designedly to this its final production, or, in other words, that an end is the cause. This is the explanation adopted by Epicurus. It completely denies and abolishes the distinction between a technic of nature and its mere mechanism. Blind chance is accepted as the explanation, not alone of the agreement of the generated products with our conception, and, consequently, of the technic of nature, but even of the determination of the causes of this development on dynamical laws, and, consequently, of its mechanism. Hence nothing is explained, not even the illusion in our teleological judgements, so that the alleged idealism in them is left altogether unsubstantiated.

Spinoza, as the representative of the other class, seeks to release us from any inquiry into the ground of the possibility of ends of nature, and to deprive this idea of all reality, by refusing to allow that such ends are to be regarded as products at all. They are, rather, accidents inhering in an original being. This being, he says, is the substrate of the natural things, and, as such, he does not ascribe to it causality in respect of them, but simply subsistence. Thanks, then, to the unconditional necessity both of this being and of all the things of nature, as its inherent accidents, he assures to the natural forms, it is true, that unity of ground necessary for all finality, but he does so at the expense of their contingency, apart from which no *unity of end* is thinkable. In eliminating this unity he eliminates all *trace of design,* and leaves the original ground of the things of nature divested of all intelligence.

But Spinozism does not effect what it intends. It intends to furnish an explanation of the final nexus of natural things, which it does not deny, and it refers us simply to the unity of the subject in which they all inhere. But suppose we grant it this mode of existence for its beings of the world, such ontological unity is not then and there a *unity of end* and does not make it in any way intelligible. The latter is, in fact, quite a special kind of unity. It does not follow from the nexus of things in one subject, or of the beings of the world in an original being. On the contrary, it implies emphatically relation to a *cause* possessed of intelligence. Even if all the things were to be united in one *simple* subject, yet such unity would never exhibit a final relation unless these things were understood to be, first, inner *effects* of the substance as a *cause,* and, secondly, effects of it as cause by *virtue of its intelligence.* Apart from these formal conditions all unity is mere necessity of nature. . . . (pp. 44-5)

[Suppose] that a man, influenced partly by the weakness of all the speculative arguments that are thought so much of, and partly by the number of irregularities he finds in nature and the moral world, becomes persuaded of the proposition: There is no God; nevertheless in his own eyes he would be a worthless creature if he chose on that account to regard the laws of duty as simply fanciful, invalid, and inobligatory, and resolved boldly to transgress them. Again, let us suppose that such a man were able subsequently to convince himself of the truth of what he had at first doubted; he would still remain worthless if he held to the above way of thinking. This is so, were he even to fulfil his duty as punctiliously as could be desired, so far as actual actions are concerned, but were to do so from fear or with a view to reward, and without an inward reverence for duty. Conversely, if, as a believer in God, he observes his duty according to his conscience, uprightly and disinterestedly, yet if whenever, to try himself, he puts before himself the case of his haply being able to convince himself that there is no God, he straightway believes himself free from all moral obligation, the state of his inner moral disposition could then only be bad.

Let us then, as we may, take the case of a righteous man, such, say, as Spinoza, who considers himself firmly persuaded that there is no God and—since in respect of the Object of morality a similar result ensues—no future life either. How will he estimate his individual intrinsic finality that is derived from the moral law which he reveres in practice? He does not require that its pursuit should bring him any personal benefit either in this or any other world. On the contrary his will is disinterestedly to establish only that good to which the holy law directs all his energies. But he is circumscribed in his endeavour. He may, it is true, expect to find a chance concurrence now and again, but he can never expect to find in nature a uniform agreement—a consistent agreement according to fixed rules, answering to what his maxims are and must be subjectively, with that end which yet he feels himself obliged and urged to realize. Deceit, violence, and envy will always be rife around him, although he himself is honest, peaceable, and benevolent; and the other righteous men that he meets in the world, no matter how deserving they may be of happiness, will be subjected by nature, which takes no heed of such deserts, to all the evils of want, disease, and untimely death, just as are the other animals on the earth. And so it will continue to be until one wide grave engulfs them all—just and unjust, there is no distinction in the grave—and hurls them back into the abyss of the aimless chaos of matter from which they were taken—they that were able to believe themselves the final end of creation.—Thus the end which this right-minded man would have, and ought to have, in view in his pursuit of the moral law, would certainly have to be abandoned by him as impossible. But perhaps he resolves to remain faithful to the call of his inner moral vocation and would fain not let the respect with which he is immediately inspired to obedience by the moral law be weakened owing to the nullity of the one ideal final end that answers to its high demand—which could not happen without doing injury to moral sentiment. If so he must assume the existence of a *moral* author of the world, that is, of a God. As this assumption at least involves nothing intrinsically self-contradictory he may quite readily make it from a practical point of view, that is to say, at least for the purpose of framing a conception of the possibility of the final end morally prescribed to him. (pp. 120-21)

> Immanuel Kant, *"Critique of Teleological Judgement: Dialectic of Teleological Judgement"* and *"Critique of Teleological Judgement: Theory of the Method of Applying the Teleological Judgement,"* in his The Critique of Judgement, *translated by James Creed Meredith, Oxford at the Clarendon Press, Oxford, 1952, pp. 35-74, 75-149.*

FRIEDRICH SCHLEIERMACHER   (speech date 1799)

[*Schleiermacher was a German Protestant theologian who postulated in his theoretical work that religion is an essentially personal experience, one in which Christian doctrine is subordinate to individual spiritual awareness. In the following excerpt from a work first published in 1799, Schleiermacher—though professedly a nonSpinozist—defends Spinoza against those who consider him impious.*]

Offer with me reverently a tribute to the manes of the holy, rejected Spinoza. The high World-Spirit pervaded him; the Infinite was his beginning and his end; the Universe was his only and his everlasting love. In holy innocence and in deep humility he beheld himself mirrored in the eternal world, and perceived how he also was its most worthy mirror. He was full of religion, full of the Holy Spirit. Wherefore, he stands there alone and unequalled; master in his art, yet without disciples and without citizenship, sublime above the profane tribe. (p. 40)

> Friedrich Schleiermacher, *"Second Speech—The Nature of Religion,"* in his On Religion: Speeches to Its Cultured Despisers, *translated by John Oman, 1893. Reprint by Harper & Brothers, Publishers, 1958, pp. 26-118.*

JOHANN GOTTFRIED HERDER   (essay date 1800)

[*Herder was an influential German literary critic best known as a primary theoretician of the* Sturm und Drang *("storm and stress") and Romantic movements. His essays on religion, history, and the development of language and literature helped shape later studies on evolution and the development of the social sciences. In the following excerpt from a work first published in 1800, he upholds the rudiments of Spinoza's philosophy through a dialectical discussion between "Philolaus" and "Theophron."*]

PHILOLAUS: My friend, observe the refreshing hour which has followed the frightful thunderstorm. Sulphurous clouds were piled up which hid the sun from our view, and made it difficult to breathe on earth. Now they are dispersed, and once again everything breathes easily and happily. Such, I imagine, was the state of wisdom when Spinoza and his like sought to rob the world of the sight of God with their heavy mists. These too piled themselves up to heaven and overcast the skies. But a sounder philosophy overthrew them like the giant of old, and the reflective mind once more beholds the radiant sun.

THEOPHRON: Have you read Spinoza, dear friend?

PHILOLAUS: No, I have not read him. And who would want to read every obscure book a madman might write? But I have heard from many who have read him, that he was an atheist and pantheist, a teacher of blind necessity, an enemy of revelation, a mocker of religion, and withal, a destroyer of the state and of all civil society. In short, he was an enemy of the human race, and as such he died. He therefore deserves the hatred and aversion of all friends of humanity and of true philosophers.

THEOPHRON: The thundercloud with which you have just compared him, does not however suit him, for it too belongs to the order of nature, and is salutary and good. But to dispense with comparisons, my friend, have you read nothing more specific and definite about Spinoza which we might discuss?

PHILOLAUS: A good deal. For instance, the article about him in Bayle [see excerpt dated 1697].

THEOPHRON: In this instance Bayle is not your best authority. He, to whom all systems were alike indifferent because fundamentally he had no system himself, did not remain impartial towards Spinoza. He zealously took sides against him, encouraged undoubtedly by the circumstances of his time and place. Perhaps he lived too close to the dead Spinoza. The doctrine, even the very name of Spinoza was at that time a term of invective, just as for the most part, they still are. Everything preposterous and godless was, and to a certain extent is still, called Spinozistic. Then, too, it was not the forte of Bayle, the keen dialectician, to get to the bottom of a system as such, or to consider it with the deepest feeling for truth. He skimmed over all systems, and keenly noted their discrepancies insofar as they served his skepticism. Now one view was important to him, now another. But of what can be called inner philosophical conviction, his superficial mind had scarcely any conception, as his *Dictionary* almost incontestably shows. (pp. 76-7)

Even during his lifetime Bayle was reproached for not having rightly grasped Spinoza's system, and had to defend himself against this accusation in one of his letters.

PHILOLAUS: That was unfortunate for Spinoza. For after all, the conception which is now held of him was established for the mass of the people by Bayle. How few read the obscure works of Spinoza, while all the world reads the manifoldly useful, varied and pleasant Bayle!

THEOPHRON: Just so, my friend! Bayle has fixed the conception of Spinoza for the light troop of readers, while for the heavy phalanx, it has been done mainly by militant philosophers and theologians. And with them it befell him even worse. He fared as in the Gospel: his closest relations, the Cartesians, immediately became his bitterest enemies. They wanted and were obligated to separate their philosophy, from which he proceeded and whose language he spoke, from his, so that they too would not come under the suspicion of Spinozism. Naturally this philosophical caution spread from the Cartesian school to every following one. Then the theologians of almost all confessions set upon him even more bitterly, for he had not only expressed very free opinions on Judaism and the books of the Old Testament, but, what must have seemed much worse to them, he had in the first instance lifted his pen against them particularly. To their quarrelsome nature and continual wrangling, he attributed in great part the decline of Christianity, and the inefficacy of its finest teachings. And, though he did all this without any bitterness, you can easily imagine how his book was received.

PHILOLAUS: I can imagine it very vividly. A peacemaker without authority has but to step between two heated factions, and he has both against him.

THEOPHRON: Spinoza had no other authority than that which he believed he had received from the hand of justice and truth. To be sure, he did not make use of it in a worldly-wise manner. He made known his religious politics in a work whose theology inevitably aroused both Jews and Christians [*Tractatus theologico-politicus*]. And his political doctrines were so severe and stringent, that they certainly could not have been acceptable in those times. He granted the state full power to regulate public worship. Yet, at the same time, he retained unlimited freedom in the exercise of reason. This seemed to most people as excessive as if he had wanted to mix fire and water. Thus his theory was an inevitable failure, for in a good many respects it is even now too severe for us, and as it were, too Hobbesian, even though we have advanced a great deal in tolerance and statecraft. (pp. 78-9)

In the criticism of the Old Testament writings much, which already stood more soundly in Spinoza, has since been advanced as new discovery, yet less adequately stated. In the matter of tolerance, our states have been disposed to take almost no other direction than that which Spinoza in his day anticipated to the hatred of all. To be sure, everything in this work, as in all his other writings, is put in a severe manner, and much is extreme. He had, for example, only a metaphysical sense of the poetry of the Prophets; and in the whole composition of his works, he is a solitary thinker, to whom the graces of the social world and an ingratiating manner are entirely unknown.

PHILOLAUS: I marvel, Theophron, that you attribute it solely to that. On what subject could a person without healthy principles, an atheist, a pantheist and the like, write so that it would find a reception among reasonable people? He is even said to have attempted a proof of atheism and pantheism! What could be more preposterous?

THEOPHRON: So it was atheism and pantheism, then? But how are both possible in one and the same system? After all, the pantheist has always a God, although he is mistaken about His nature. On the other hand, the atheist, who absolutely denies God, can be neither a pantheist nor a polytheist, unless one trifles with the names. And, moreover, my friend, how can one demonstrate atheism, which is a negation?

PHILOLAUS: Why not, if one found, or thought one had found, a self-contradiction in the nature of God?

THEOPHRON: A self-contradiction in a simple idea, the highest possible to humanity? I must confess, I do not understand that.

PHILOLAUS: That is exactly why he was a fool, who sought to demonstrate what could not be demonstrated. For our new philosophy says distinctly: "Neither that a God exists, nor that he does not, can be proved. One must believe the former."

THEOPHRON: Wherefore, I, at least, should think it follows that one or the other must be believed, that we are free to be atheists, deists, or theists according to our belief. But let us not touch on this point just yet.

Spinoza is supposed to have been an atheist, pantheist, or a monstrous hybrid of the two. It grieves me to hear these appellations, which you give to one unknown to you. In philosophy we have passed the times of the honorifics with which

Spinoza was still being dubbed by Korthold, Brucker and others. The first thought himself witty when he perverted the *Benedictus* into a *Maledictus,* and the word "Spinoza" into "spiny thornbush." With others, the usual epithets by means of which they conjure him up out of the realm of spirits are, "insolent, godless, preposterous, shameless, blasphemous, pestilential, execrable." One of the elect has even found the mark of eternal banishment on his face, and others have heard him whine for mercy on his deathbed. I am no Spinozist, and shall never become one, but I confess, friend Philolaus, that it is intolerable to me that people in our time still wish to repeat against this departed and silent sage, the judgments of the past century, that century of most deplorable controversy. Here you have a booklet of but eight sheets [John Colerus's *Life of Benedict de Spinoza;* see excerpt dated 1706], in which, moreover, the most part is a miscellany of comments which you may skip entirely. It is nothing but the life of Spinoza, very prosaically told, but with historical accuracy. For one can see that the author was careful about every detail. It is written by an impartial man who was no Spinozist, but a Lutheran pastor who "takes God to witness that he has found nothing well grounded in Spinoza's *Tractatus theologico-politicus,* or anything which was in the least capable of disturbing him in the confession of faith, wherein he followed the Gospel word, because instead of well-grounded proofs, one finds therein nothing but pre-determined conclusions, and what in the Schools are called *petitiones principii.*" You can surely trust yourself to such a cautious guide, if you wish to know the man better.

My affairs call me away now, but we shall soon see each other again. In case you should like to look into them, I am also leaving you some of the works of the atheist himself. Unfortunately there are only two small volumes. (pp. 80-2)

[PHILOLAUS, later]: Am I dreaming, or have I really been reading? I thought that I should find an insolent atheist, and here I discover [in *On the Improvement of the Understanding*] virtually a metaphysical and moral enthusiast. What an ideal of humanity, of science, and of the knowlege of nature, there is in his soul! And he approaches it with such a considered, deliberate pace and style as few have who enter the cloister to transform their lives. This essay plainly belongs to the man's younger years, when he left Judaism and chose his philosophical way of life. He followed this way until the end of his days. What did he achieve in it? But look, here comes Theophron.

THEOPHRON: Still busy? Philolaus, you did not foretell the weather entirely correctly. Your Spinozistic rain clouds have rained themselves out and caused a spell of cold, which one should not have expected from your analogy.

PHILOLAUS: Forget my analogy, and give me this volume to take with me. I see that I have been mistaken about Spinoza. What do you think I should read first?

THEOPHRON: First and almost exclusively his *Ethics.* What remains is fragmentary, and the *Tractatus theologico-politicus* was merely a tract for the times. But take a few rules with you on your journey.

I. Before you read Spinoza, you must necessarily read Descartes, if only as a dictionary. In the latter, you will see the source of Spinoza's words and thoughts, and also the source of his extraordinary, difficult expressions. . . . Then go on to the *Principles of Descartes' Philosophy* by Spinoza himself, which he drew up for one of his students. In it you will find the transition to his own system. One should learn about a tree from its beginning, not only in its parts, but also in the conditions of its origin and growth, even though it is known to be a poisonous Upas tree. For if you read this philosopher of the last century in the language of contemporary philosophy, then he must needs appear a monster to you.

II. Pay very careful attention to his geometrical method. Do not allow yourself to be misled by it, but notice also where it misleads him. He took it from Descartes, only he made the bolder attempt of applying this form to everything, even to the most involved moral matters, and just this attempt should have warned his followers in the geometrical method of metaphysics.

III. Never confine yourself to him, but rather at every one of his paradoxical statements call modern philosophy to your aid, so that you ask yourself how the latter cleared up this or a similar statement, or expressed it more easily, more happily and less objectionably. It will immediately strike you why their author could not have expressed them equally felicitously, and you will perceive both the source of his error, and the progressive advance of the truth. For this purpose use his few letters side by side with his *Ethics*. In many places they are very illuminating. In the margin of my copy you will find references to the *Ethics* written by an old hand, and in the *Ethics* references back to them. If these letters served no other purpose, they would show how very much in earnest Spinoza was about this philosophy, how completely he was convinced by it, and how happy he felt himself in it. (pp. 90-2)

PHILOLAUS: Here I am with my Spinoza, but almost more in the dark than I was before. It is plain on every page that he is no atheist. For him the idea of God is the first and last, yes, I might even say the only idea of all, for on it he bases knowledge of the world and of nature, consciousness of self and of all things around him, his ethics and his politics. Without the idea of God, his mind has no power, not even to conceive of itself. For him it is well nigh inconceivable, how men can, as it were, turn God into a mere consequence of other truths, or even of sensuous perceptions, since all truth, like all existence, follows only from eternal truth, from the eternal, infinite existence of God. This conception became so present, so immediate and intimate to him, that I certainly would rather have taken him to be an enthusiast concerning the existence of God, than a doubter or denier of it. He places all mankind's perfection, virtue and blessedness in the knowledge and love of God. And that this is not some sort of mask which he has assumed, but rather his deepest feeling, is shown by his letters, yes, I might even say, by every part of his philosophical system, by every line of his writings. Spinoza may have erred in a thousand ways about the idea of God, but how readers of his works could ever say that he denied the idea of God and proved atheism, is incomprehensible to me.

THEOPHRON: I am glad my friend, that you have found the same thing that I found. For I too scarcely trusted myself when I read this author and compared my impression with what others had said of him. This feeling was the more intense for me, since I did not read him as a novice in philosophy, or with some subsidiary interest in mind, but entirely dispassionately, and if anything, with hostile prejudice, after I had not only read but studied the works of Baumgarten, Leibniz, Shaftesbury, and Berkeley, in addition to the ancient philosophers. However, let us not linger in this astonishment which will clear up of itself when we examine his system. What criticisms have you to make of it?

PHILOLAUS: Where shall I begin? Where end? The whole system is a paradox to me. "There is but one Substance, and that is God. All things are but modifications of it."

THEOPHRON: Do not be mistaken about the word "Substance." Spinoza took it in its purest meaning, and had to take it in that way if he wanted to proceed geometrically and set down a primitive notion as a basis. What is Substance but a thing which is self-dependent, which has the cause of its existence in itself? I wish that this pure meaning of the word could have been introduced into our philosophy. In the strictest sense, nothing in the world is a Substance, because everything depends on everything else, and finally on God, who therefore is the highest and only Substance. This geometrical conception could not have become generally adopted in a philosophy which must preserve its popular character, for we, in all our dependence yet consider ourselves independent, and in a certain sense, as we shall soon see, we may so consider ourselves.

PHILOLAUS. But we are not mere modifications, are we?

THEOPHRON: The word offends us and will therefore never win a place in our philosophy. However, if the Leibnizian school dared to call matter an "appearance of substances," why should not Spinoza be allowed his more drastic expression? The substances of the world are all maintained by divine power, just as they derived their existence from it alone. Therefore they constitute, if you will, appearances of divine powers, each modified according to the place, the time, and the organs in, and with which, they appear. In his single Substance, Spinoza thus employed a short formula which certainly gives his system much coherence, but which sounds strange to our ears. Nevertheless, it was better than the "occasional causes" of the Cartesians, from whom Spinoza started, and according to whom God is supposed to effect all things, but only on occasion. A far more awkward expression, yet how long it was current! Even the Leibnizian philosophy could only do away with it by means of another hypothesis, which indeed sounds more pleasant, but which also has its difficulties. (pp. 95-7)

PHILOLAUS: . . . Theophron, the knot is not yet unravelled. How drastically [Spinoza] speaks against all God's purposes in creation! How definitely he denies reason and will to God, and derives everything that exists simply and solely from His infinite power which he not only sets above reason and purposes, but also completely separates from them. You know, my friend, how those doctrines brought our philosopher the bitterest opponents. Even Leibniz, who esteemed Spinoza highly, declared himself most definitely against them in his *Theodicy*. If you can reconcile these offensive doctrines with sound reason, or with Spinoza's very fine system, I could wish myself to be the Nemesis who hands you the branch. [The speaker refers here to a discussion of the goddess Nemesis at the beginning of the Third Conversation.]

THEOPHRON: I wish it from the hand of truth alone. For I can clearly prove on the one hand, that Spinoza did not fully understand himself in these doctrines because they are consequences of the pernicious Cartesian explanations which he took, and in those times was compelled to take into his system. On the other hand, I can show that misunderstandings of him have been much greater than were warranted even by his own obscurities of expression. Once we clear away these Cartesian errors and explain the doctrines of Spinoza solely in the light of the fundamental idea on which he built his own system, then they become luminous, the mists clear away, and Spinoza, it seems to me, gains a move even on Leibniz who followed him cautiously but perhaps too cautiously, on this point.

PHILOLAUS: I am very curious.

THEOPHRON: First, I completely deny that Spinoza turned God into an unthinking being. There could scarcely be an error more contrary to his system than this. For him, the nature of God is reality through and through, and Spinoza was too much of a thinker himself not to feel and esteem profoundly the reality of perfection in thought, the highest that we know. Thus his highest Being which possesses all perfection in the most perfect manner, cannot lack thought, the most excellent of these perfections; for how else could there be thoughts and perceptions in finite thinking creatures which are all, according to Spinoza's system, only representations and real consequences of that most real Being, who, as he explains, alone deserves the name self-dependent? As he plainly says, among infinite attributes in God there is also the perfection of infinite thought which Spinoza only distinguishes from the reason and imagination of finite beings in order to designate the former as unique in its kind, and entirely incomparable with the latter. You must have noticed his comparison, that the thought of God could no more resemble human thought than the star in the heavens called the Dog Star, could resemble a dog on earth.

PHILOLAUS: The comparison was more impressive than instructive to me.

THEOPHRON: Nor should it instruct you! And we shall soon see that it really lacks the resemblance necessary to a comparison. However, it shows this much, that Spinoza here again preferred the sharper attack and expressed himself too drastically rather than suffer that he, who strove zealously for the worthiest and highest conception of God, should allow it to be degraded by any weak comparison with individual things in creation. But that all pure, true, complete knowledge in our soul is nothing but an expression of the divine knowledge, no one, I dare say, has maintained more strongly than Spinoza, who placed the divine essence in man solely in this pure, living knowledge of God, of His attributes and effects.

PHILOLAUS. Precisely so, my friend! And, therefore, is not his infinite thinking Being simply a collective name for all the powers of understanding and thought which are real and active solely in individual creatures?

THEOPHRON: So God is a collective name, the most real Being a nonentity, a shadow of the images of individual people, or rather a mere word, the echo of a name? That which is most vital then, is dead? That which is universally efficient is the latest feeblest activity of human powers? Philolaus, if you ascribe this to Spinoza from your own convictions, and can thus make his system into its complete opposite, then I am sorry that I gave you his book and ever exchanged a single word with you about him. Forgive my frankness, for I cannot imagine how this could apply to you, since it is not possible that, page after page, and from beginning to end, you could have so misunderstood this philosopher who even in his errors is at least consistent. You probably voiced the opinions of one of his opponents of the past century, although you should not even have done that.

PHILOLAUS: Don't fly into a passion! In a discussion one sometimes introduces an alien opinion if it helps the matter on, and makes it clear by means of contrasts. As for myself, since reading his *Ethics* I was not at all doubtful of Spinoza's meaning in this matter. How he inveighs against those who want to make God into an abstract, lifeless deduction from the world, when, according to him, this unique nature is the cause of all being, hence also of our reason, of every truth and every relation between truths! How highly he esteems a complete and

perfect idea! For him it is knowledge of the eternal, divine Being, knowledge which also is divine in that it conceives things not as contingent but as necessary under the aspect of eternity, and just because of this inner necessity is as sure of itself as only God can be.

No moral has exalted more highly than Spinoza the essence of the human soul, which in virtue of its nature recognizes truth, and loves it as truth. And he is supposed to have portrayed his God, the source, object and essence of all knowledge, to be as blind as a Polyphemus? I become almost ashamed before the spirit of this man for bringing against him this charge which is as remote as the Antipodes.

THEOPHRON: Well then! An infinite, original power of thought, the source of all thoughts, is, according to Spinoza, of the essence of God. And in this system we cannot doubt His infinitely efficient power.

PHILOLAUS: No, because in Spinoza, reason and will are one and the same thing. That is, in our more moderate language, a reason which conceives the best, must also will the best, and if it has the power, it must effect the best. But there is no doubt as to the infinite power of his God, since he subordinates everything to this power, and derives everything from it.

THEOPHRON: Then what did he lack, that he did not unite the infinite powers of thought and action, and in their union, did not express more clearly what he must necessarily have found in them, namely that the highest Power must necessarily also be the wisest, that is to say an infinite goodness ordered according to inherent, eternal laws? For an unorganized lawless, blind power is never the highest. It can never be the prototype and summation of all the order, wisdom and regularity which we, although finite beings, perceive in creation as eternal laws, if it does not itself know these laws, and exercise them according to its eternal intrinsic nature. A blind power must necessarily have been surpassed by an ordered one, and thus could not be God. Why did Spinoza remain in such darkness at this point, and not recognize the integral strength of his own system?

PHILOLAUS: I understand now, Theophron, and I thank you for helping me on the way. It is still that false Cartesian explanation, which again shut off his own light from him. Thought and extension for him stand opposed as two isolated things. Thought cannot be delimited by extension, nor extension by thought. Now, since he adopted both as attributes of God, an indivisible Being, and could not explain one through the other, he had to adopt a third in which both were included, and this he called power. Had he developed the conception of power as he did that of matter, then he would necessarily, and as a consequence of his own system, have come to the conception of forces which are active in matter, as well as in organs of thought. Then, in that conception, he would furthermore have regarded power and thought as forces, that is, as identical in nature. Thought is also a power, and indeed the most perfect, absolutely infinite power, just because it is and has everything which pertains to the infinite self-established power. Thus the knot is loosed, and the gold it contained lies before us. The eternal, primal power, the force of all forces, is but one, and in every attribute, however our frail reason may divide it up, it is still infinite and the same. According to the eternal laws of His nature, God thinks, acts, and is the most perfect, in every way conceivable to Him, that is to say, in the most perfect way. His thoughts are not wise, but wisdom. His acts are not good alone, but goodness. And all this is not through compulsion or arbitrariness, as if the opposite were possible, but rather through His eternal, essential inner nature, through the most perfect primal goodness and truth. (pp. 118-24)

> *Johann Gottfried Herder, in his* God: Some Conversations, *translated by Frederick H. Burkhardt, Veritas Press, 1940, 247 p.*

JOHANN WOLFGANG VON GOETHE   (essay date 1811)

[*Goethe was a German writer who is considered one of the greatest figures in world literature. A genius of the highest order, he distinguished himself as a botanist, physicist, and biologist; he was an artist, musician, and philosopher; and he had successful careers as a theater director and court administrator. Above all, he contributed richly to his nation's literature. Excelling in all genres, Goethe was a shaping force in the major literary movements of the late eighteenth and early nineteenth centuries in Germany. In the following excerpt from his autobiography (published from 1811-12), he attests to the highly personal influence of Spinoza's philosophy upon him.*]

I had not thought of Spinoza for a long time, and now I was driven to him by an attack upon him. In our library I found a little book, the author of which railed violently against that original thinker, and, to go the more effectually to work, had inserted for a frontispiece a picture of Spinoza himself, with the inscription, "*Signum reprobationis in vultu gerens,*" bearing on his face the stamp of reprobation. This there was no gainsaying, indeed, so long as one looked at the picture; for the engraving was wretchedly bad, a perfect caricature: so that I could not help thinking of those adversaries who, when they conceive a dislike to any one, first of all misrepresent him, and then assail the monster of their own creation.

This little book, however, made no impression upon me; since generally I did not like controversial works, but preferred always to learn from the author himself how he did think, than to hear from another how he ought to have thought. Still, curiosity led me to the article "Spinoza" in Bayle's *Dictionary* [see excerpt dated 1697], a work as valuable for its learning and acuteness as it is ridiculous and pernicious by its gossiping and scandal.

The article "Spinoza" excited in me displeasure and mistrust. In the first place, the philosopher is represented as an atheist, and his opinions as most abominable; but, immediately afterwards, it is confessed that he was a calmly reflecting man, devoted to his studies, a good citizen, a sympathizing neighbor, and a peaceable individual. The writer seemed to me to have quite forgotten the words of the gospel, "*By their fruits ye shall know them;*" for how could a life pleasing in the sight of God and man spring from corrupt principles?

I well remembered what peace of mind and clearness of ideas came over me when I first turned over the posthumous works of that remarkable man. The effect itself was still quite distinct to my mind, though I could not recall the particulars: I therefore speedily had recourse again to the works to which I had owed so much, and again the same calm air breathed over me. I gave myself up to this reading, and thought, while I looked into myself, that I had never before so clearly seen through the world.

As on this subject there always has been, and still is even in these later times, so much controversy, I would not wish to be misunderstood; and therefore I make here a few remarks upon these so much feared, nay, abhorred, views.

Our physical as well as our social life, manners, customs, worldly wisdom, philosophy, religion, and many an accidental event, all call upon us *to deny ourselves.* Much that is most inwardly peculiar to us we are not allowed to develop; much that we need from without for the completion of our character is withheld; while, on the other hand, so much is forced upon us which is as alien to us as it is burdensome. We are robbed of all we have laboriously acquired for ourselves, or friendly circumstances have bestowed upon us; and, before we can see clearly what we are, we find ourselves compelled to part with our personality, piece by piece, till at last it is gone altogether. Indeed, the case is so universal, that it seems a law of society to despise a man who shows himself surly on that account. On the contrary, the bitterer the cup we have to drink, the more pleasant face we must put on, in order that composed lookers-on may not be offended by the least grimace.

To solve this painful problem, however, nature has endowed man with ample power, activity, and endurance. But especially is he aided therein by his volatility (*Leichtsinn*), a boon to man which nothing can take away. By means of it he is able to renounce the cherished object of the moment, provided the next present him something new to reach at; and thus he goes on unconsciously remodelling his whole life. We are continually putting one passion in the place of another: employments, inclinations, tastes, hobbies,—we try them all, and end by exclaiming, *All is vanity!* No one is shocked by this false and murmuring speech; nay, every one thinks, while he says it, that he is uttering a wise and indisputable maxim. A few men there are, and only a few, who anticipate this insupportable feeling, and avoid all calls to such partial resignation by one grand act of total self-renunciation.

Such men convince themselves of the Eternal, the Necessary, and of Immutable Law, and seek to form to themselves ideas which are incorruptible, nay, which observation of the Perishable does not shake, but rather confirms. But, since in this there is something superhuman, such persons are commonly esteemed *in*-human (monsters), without a God and without a World. People hardly know what sort of horns and claws to give them.

My confidence in Spinoza rested on the serene effect he wrought in me; and it only increased when I found my worthy mystics were accused of Spinozism, and learned that even Leibnitz himself could not escape the charge. . . . (pp. 233-35)

> *Johann Wolfgang von Goethe, "Seventh Book," in his* The Autobiography of Goethe: Truth and Fiction, Relating to My Life, Vol. I, *translated by John Oxenford, Belford, Clarke & Company, Publishers, 1882, pp. 214-55.*

SAMUEL TAYLOR COLERIDGE   (lecture date 1819)

[*Coleridge was the intellectual center of the English Romantic movement and is considered one of the greatest literary critics in the English language. He was also the first prominent spokesman for German idealistic metaphysics in England and the forerunner of modern psychological critics, specifically in his conception of the organic nature of literary form. For modern critics, Coleridge's most important achievement was his attempt to fuse such variant ideas as fancy and imagination, talent and genius, mechanical and organic form, taste and judgment, symbol and allegory, even though they believe that his efforts to create a "graceful and intelligent whole" were self-defeating and poor criteria for the actual study of literature. In the following excerpt from a*] lecture originally delivered in 1819, Coleridge sympathetically discusses Spinoza's life and writings.]

[Great] impressions has Spinoza made on the minds of the learned and an impression on the theologians. And the theologic hatred of his name is one of the most incomprehensible parts of philosophic researches. For Spinoza was originally a Jew, and he held the opinions of the most learned Jews, particularly the Cabalistic philosophers. Next he was of the most pure and exemplary life and it has been said of him, if he did not think as a Christian, he felt and acted like one. Thirdly, so far from proselytizing, this man published not a system (it was a posthumous work published against his will) but what is still more strong, he was offered by a German prince a high salary with perfect permission to preach his doctrines without the least danger. Instead of accepting this he wrote to the prince to reprimand him for his neglect of his duty, and asked him what right he had, to abuse the confidence the Fathers of Germans had placed in him, opposite to their wish. And if we come at last to the man's own professions and service, I have no doubt they were ⟨SEVERELY ORTHODOX⟩. I have seen many questions [raised as to the compatibility of Spinozism with religion, natural and revealed, and now am persuaded] to believe that not only the immediate publishers of Spinoza's writings but that Spinoza *did* think that his system was identical ⟨not⟩ with atheism but ⟨with⟩ that of Christianity, on so subtle a point that at least it was pantheism, but in the most religious form in which it could appear. For making the deity that which is independent, which is certain in and of itself and needs no argument, but which is implied in all other truth, and by making all other truths dependent upon that, beyond any other system of pantheism, it divided the deity from the creature. On the other hand I am far from hiding the inevitable consequences of pantheism in all cases, whether the pantheism of India or the solitary cases ⟨like that⟩ of Spinoza. He erred, however, where thousands had erred before him, in Christian charity, communicating his opinions to those only from whom he expected information. And to end all, the quiet family in which he lived, when he was too ill to attend services publicly, he still kept regularly to their duty, and when they came home, as regularly examined them and made them repeat the sermon and comment upon it according to their impressions. A character like that, so unlike an infidel, scarcely exists and I cannot understand the cause ["why then", as Lessing observes, "is no man to speak of Spinoza but] as a dead dog". (pp. 384-85)

> *Samuel Taylor Coleridge, "Descartes, Spinosa, Leibnitz, Locke, Kant, Schelling," in his* The Philosophical Lectures of Samuel Taylor Coleridge, *edited by Kathleen Coburn, The Pilot Press Limited, 1949, pp. 368-91.*

GEORG WILHELM FRIEDRICH HEGEL (lecture date 1840)

[*Hegel was a highly influential German philosopher and lecturer of the early nineteenth century. In opposition to Immanuel Kant, he theorized a unified, rather than dualistic, world, one in which the natural world, the body and soul, and the human spheres of art, religion, philosophy, and government, are subsumed in an absolute spiritual force, or Geist. His entire system, presented in numerous lectures and in such works as* Die Phänomenologie des Geistes *(1807;* The Phenomenology of Mind, *1961), may be characterized by the belief that from each moral, social, or philosophic problem there first arises a positive solution (thesis), which is then countered by a negative proposition (antithesis), from which finally emerges a balanced, reasoned compromise, or synthesis. This unity-through-opposition approach, termed Hegelian dialec-*

tics, shaped the practical and aesthetic theories of several important European intellectuals, including Karl Marx's socioeconomic theory of dialectical materialism. In the following excerpt from a lecture given in 1840, Hegel discusses the essence and flaws of Spinoza's philosophy.]

[In] Benedict Spinoza a direct successor to [René Descartes] may be found, and one who carried on the Cartesian principle to its furthest logical conclusions. For him soul and body, thought and Being, cease to have separate independent existence. The dualism of the Cartesian system Spinoza, as a Jew, altogether set aside. For the profound unity of his philosophy as it found expression in Europe, his manifestation of Spirit as the identity of the finite and the infinite in God, instead of God's appearing related to these as a Third—all this is an echo from Eastern lands. The Oriental theory of absolute identity was brought by Spinoza much more directly into line, firstly with the current of European thought, and then with the European and Cartesian philosophy, in which it soon found a place. (p. 252)

As regards the philosophy of Spinoza, it is very simple, and on the whole easy to comprehend; the difficulty which it presents is due partly to the limitations of the method in which Spinoza presents his thoughts, and partly to his narrow range of ideas, which causes him in an unsatisfactory way to pass over important points of view and cardinal questions. Spinoza's system is that of Descartes made objective in the form of absolute truth. The simple thought of Spinoza's idealism is this: The true is simply and solely the one substance, whose attributes are thought and extension or nature: and only this absolute unity is reality, it alone is God. It is, as with Descartes, the unity of thought and Being, or that which contains the Notion of its existence in itself. The Cartesian substance, as Idea, has certainly Being included in its Notion; but it is only Being as abstract, not as real Being or as extension. . . . With Descartes corporeality and the thinking 'I' are altogether independent Beings; this independence of the two extremes is done away with in Spinozism by their becoming moments of the one absolute Being. . . . The pure thought of Spinoza is therefore not the simple universal of Plato, for it has likewise come to know the absolute opposition of Notion and Being. (pp. 256-57)

This Idea of Spinoza's we must allow to be in the main true and well-grounded; absolute substance is the truth, but it is not the whole truth; in order to be this it must also be thought of as in itself active and living, and by that very means it must determine itself as mind. But substance with Spinoza is only the universal and consequently the abstract determination of mind; it may undoubtedly be said that this thought is the foundation of all true views—not, however, as their absolutely fixed and permanent basis, but as the abstract unity which mind is in itself. It is therefore worthy of note that thought must begin by placing itself at the standpoint of Spinozism; to be a follower of Spinoza is the essential commencement of all Philosophy. For . . . when man begins to philosophize, the soul must commence by bathing in this ether of the One Substance, in which all that man has held as true has disappeared; this negation of all that is particular, to which every philosopher must have come, is the liberation of the mind and its absolute foundation. The difference between our standpoint and that of the Eleatic philosophy is only this, that through the agency of Christianity concrete individuality is in the modern world present throughout in spirit. But in spite of the infinite demands on the part of the concrete, substance with Spinoza is not yet determined as in itself concrete. As the concrete is thus not present in the content of substance, it is therefore to be found within reflecting thought alone, and it is only from the endless oppositions of this last that the required unity emerges. . . . Spinoza is far from having proved this unity as convincingly as was done by the ancients; but what constitutes the grandeur of Spinoza's manner of thought is that he is able to renounce all that is determinate and particular, and restrict himself to the One, giving heed to this alone. (pp. 257-58)

[There is] no ground for the objection that Spinoza's philosophy gives the death-blow to morality; we even gain from it the great result that all that is sensuous is mere limitation, and that there is only one true substance, and that human liberty consists in keeping in view this one substance, and in regulating all our conduct in accordance with the mind and will of the Eternal One. But in this philosophy it may with justice be objected that God is conceived only as Substance, and not as Spirit, as concrete. The independence of the human soul is therein also denied, while in the Christian religion every individual appears as determined to salvation. Here, on the contrary, the individual spirit is only a mode, an accident, but not anything substantial. This brings us to a general criticism of the philosophy of Spinoza. . . . (pp. 279-80)

[As] Spinoza has set up the great proposition, all determination implies negation, and as of everything, even of thought in contrast to extension, it may be shown that it is determined and finite, what is essential in it rests upon negation. Therefore God alone is the positive, the affirmative, and consequently the one substance; all other things, on the contrary, are only modifications of this substance, and are nothing in and for themselves. (pp. 285-86)

Because negation was thus conceived by Spinoza in one-sided fashion merely, there is . . . in his system, an utter blotting out of the principle of subjectivity, individuality, personality, the moment of self-consciousness in Being. Thought has only the signification of the universal, not of self-consciousness. It is this lack which has, on the one side, brought the conception of the liberty of the subject into such vehement antagonism to the system of Spinoza, because it set aside the independence of the human consciousness, the so-called liberty which is merely the empty abstraction of independence, and in so doing set aside God, as distinguished from nature and the human consciousness—that is as implicit or in Himself, in the Absolute; for man has the consciousness of freedom, of the spiritual, which is the negative of the corporeal, and man has also the consciousness that his true Being lies in what is opposed to the corporeal. This has been firmly maintained by religion, theology, and the sound common sense of the common consciousness, and this form of opposition to Spinoza appears first of all in the assertion that freedom is real, and that evil exists. But because for Spinoza, on the other hand, there exists only absolute universal substance as the non-particularized, the truly real—all that is particular and individual, my subjectivity and spirituality, has, on the other hand, as a limited modification whose Notion depends on another, no absolute existence. Thus the soul, the Spirit, in so far as it is an individual Being, is for Spinoza a mere negation, like everything in general that is determined. As all differences and determinations of things and of consciousness simply go back into the One substance, one may say that in the system of Spinoza all things are merely cast down into this abyss of annihilation. But from this abyss nothing comes out. . . . This is what we find philosophically inadequate with Spinoza; distinctions are externally present, it is true, but they remain external, since even the negative is

not known in itself. Thought is the absolutely abstract, and for that very reason the absolutely negative; it is so in truth, but with Spinoza it is not asserted to be the absolutely negative. But if in opposition to Spinozism we hold fast to the assertion that Spirit, as distinguishing itself from the corporeal, is substantial, actual, true, and in the same way that freedom is not something merely privative, then this actuality in formal thought is doubtless correct, yet it rests only upon feeling; but the further step is that the Idea essentially includes within itself motion and vitality, and that it consequently has in itself the principle of spiritual freedom. On the one hand, therefore, the defect of Spinozism is conceived as consisting in its want of correspondence with actuality; but on the other side it is to be apprehended in a higher sense, I mean in the sense that substance with Spinoza is only the Idea taken altogether abstractly, not in its vitality.

If, in conclusion, we sum up this criticism that we have offered, we would say that on the one hand with Spinoza negation or privation is distinct from substance; for he merely assumes individual determinations, and does not deduce them from substance. On the other hand the negation is present only as Nothing, for in the absolute there is no mode; the negative is not there, but only its dissolution, its return: we do not find its movement, its Becoming and Being. The negative is conceived altogether as a vanishing moment—not in itself, but only as individual self-consciousness. . . . Self-consciousness is born from this ocean, dripping with the water thereof, *i.e.* never coming to absolute self-hood; the heart, the independence is transfixed—the vital fire is wanting. This lack has to be supplied, the moment of self-consciousness has to be added. (pp. 287-89)

> *Georg Wilhelm Friedrich Hegel, "The Metaphysics of the Understanding," in his* Lectures on the History of Philosophy, Vol. 3, *translated by E. S. Haldane and Frances H. Simson, 1896. Reprint by The Humanities Press, 1963, pp. 220-359.*

HEINRICH HEINE (essay date 1852)

[*One of the most prominent literary figures in nineteenth-century Europe and in the history of his native Germany, Heine is remembered for his poetry as well as for his distinctive commentaries on politics, art, literature, and society. Among his foremost writings are* Buch der Leider (1827; Heinrich Heine's Book of Songs, 1856) *and* Zur Geschichte in Deutschland (1835; Religion and Philosophy in Germany, 1882). *In the following excerpt from a work first written in 1852, Heine characterizes and praises Spinoza's synthetic philosophy of God and the world.*]

One great genius forms itself from another less by assimilation than by friction. One diamond polishes another. Thus the philosophy of Descartes in no sense originated, it merely advanced that of Spinoza. Hence we find in the disciple the method of the master; this is a great gain. We also find in Spinoza, as in Descartes, a mode of demonstration borrowed from mathematics; this is a grievous fault. The mathematical form gives to Spinoza's writings a harsh exterior. But this is like the hard shell of the almond; the kernel is all the more agreeable. In reading Spinoza's works we become conscious of a feeling such as pervades us at the sight of great Nature in her most life-like state of repose; we behold a forest of heaven-reaching thoughts whose blossoming topmost boughs are tossing like waves of the sea, whilst their immovable stems are rooted in the eternal earth. There is a peculiar, indescribable fragrance about the writings of Spinoza. We seem to breathe in them the air of the future. Perhaps the spirit of the Hebrew prophets still hovered over their late-born descendant. There is, withal, an earnestness in him, a self-conscious bearing, a solemn grandeur of thought that certainly seems as though it were inherited; for Spinoza belonged to one of those martyr-families driven into exile by the most Catholic kings of Spain. Added to this was the patience of the Dutchman, which never belies itself either in the life or in the writings of the man.

It is beyond a doubt that the whole course of Spinoza's life was free from blame, and pure and spotless as the life of his divine cousin, Jesus Christ. Like him, too, he suffered for his doctrine; like him he wore the crown of thorns. Wherever a great spirit utters its thought, *there* is Golgotha. (pp. 69-70)

[Spinoza] was trained not merely in the lessons of the school, but also in those of life. Herein is he distinguished from most philosophers, and in his writings we recognise the indirect influence of his life-training. (p. 71)

The philosophy of Spinoza, third son of René Descartes, as he enunciates it in his principal work, the *Ethics*, is as widely different from the materialism of his brother Locke as from the idealism of his brother Leibnitz. Spinoza does not torment himself with analytical inquiry into the ultimate grounds of our cognitions. He gives us his grand synthesis, his explanation of Deity.

Benedict Spinoza teaches: there is but one substance, which is God. This one substance is infinite; it is absolute: all finite subtances emanate from it, are contained in it, emerge out of it, are submerged in it; they have only a relative, transient, accidental existence. The absolute substance reveals itself to us as clearly in the form of infinite thought as in the form of infinite extension. These two, infinite thought and infinite extension, are the two attributes of the absolute substance. We recognise only these two attributes; but God, the absolute substance, has perhaps many other attributes that we do not know. (pp. 71-2)

Nothing but sheer unreason and malice could bestow on such a doctrine the qualification of "atheism." No one has ever spoken more sublimely of Deity than Spinoza. Instead of saying that he denied God, one might say that he denied man. All finite things are to him but modes of the infinite substance; all finite substances are contained in God; the human mind is but a luminous ray of infinite thought; the human body but an atom of infinite extension: God is the infinite cause of both, of mind and of body, *natura naturans* ["naturing nature"]. (p. 72)

> Heinrich Heine, "Part Second: From Luther to Kant," in his Religion and Philosophy in Germany: A Fragment, *translated by John Snodgrass, Houghton, Mifflin and Company, 1882, pp. 59-104.*

MATTHEW ARNOLD (essay date 1863)

[*Arnold was one of the most important English critics of the nineteenth century. Although he was also a poet and, more significantly, a commentator on the social and moral life in England, Arnold was essentially an apologist for literary criticism. He argued that the major purpose of the critic was to inform and liberate the public at large and to prepare the way—through the fostering of ideas and information—for his or her country's next creative epoch. Arnold was a forceful advocate of the doctrine of "disinterestedness" in all critical activities—the need for flexibility, curiosity, and a non-utilitarian approach to culture and art. He was severely critical of what he considered the spiritual death of Victorian England; nonetheless, he was confident that*

art, which he considered classless and universal, could save modern society from materialism. Arnold's critical methodology called for the rejection of both the personal estimate and the historical estimate of art. In their place he advocated the "real estimate" of the created object, which demands that the critic judge a work of art according to its own qualities, in and of itself, apart from the influence of history and the limitations of subjective experience. In the following excerpt from an essay originally published in Macmillan's Magazine *in 1863, Arnold presents a generally favorable discussion of Spinoza's* Theological-Political Treatise.]

[Spinoza's *Tractatus Theologico-Politicus*] is a work on the interpretation of Scripture,—it treats of the Bible. What was it exactly which Spinoza thought about the Bible and its inspiration? That will be, at the present moment, the central point of interest for the English readers of his Treatise. Now I wish to observe . . . that just on this very point the Treatise, interesting and remarkable as it is, will fail to satisfy the reader. It is important to seize this notion quite firmly, and not to quit hold of it while one is reading Spinoza's work. The scope of that work is this. Spinoza sees that the life and practice of Christian nations professing the religion of the Bible, are not the due fruits of the religion of the Bible; he sees only hatred, bitterness, and strife, where he might have expected to see love, joy, and peace in believing; and he asks himself the reason of this. The reason is, he says, that these people misunderstand their Bible. Well, then, is his conclusion, I will write a *Tractatus Theologico-Politicus*. I will show these people, that, taking the Bible for granted, taking it to be all which it asserts itself to be, taking it to have all the authority which it claims, it is not what they imagine it to be, it does not say what they imagine it to say. I will show them what it really does say, and I will show them that they will do well to accept this real teaching of the Bible, instead of the phantom with which they have so long been cheated. I will show their Governments that they will do well to remodel the National Churches, to make of them institutions informed with the spirit of the true Bible, instead of institutions informed with the spirit of this false phantom.

Such is really the scope of Spinoza's work. He pursues a great object, and pursues it with signal ability; but it is important to observe that he does not give us his own opinion about the Bible's fundamental character. He takes the Bible as it stands, as he might take the phenomena of nature, and he discusses it as he finds it. Revelation differs from natural knowledge, he says, not by being more divine or more certain than natural knowledge, but by being conveyed in a different way; it differs from it because it is a knowledge "of which the laws of human nature considered in themselves alone cannot be the cause." What is really its cause, he says, we need not here inquire (*verum nec nobis jam opus est propheticæ cognitionis causam scire*), for we take Scripture, which contains this revelation, as it stands, and do not ask how it arose (*documentorum causas nihil curamus*).

Proceeding on this principle, Spinoza leaves the attentive reader somewhat baffled and disappointed, clear as is his way of treating his subject, and remarkable as are the conclusions with which he presents us. He starts, we feel, from what is to him a hypothesis, and we want to know what he really thinks about this hypothesis. His greatest novelties are all within limits fixed for him by this hypothesis. He says that the voice which called Samuel was an imaginary voice; he says that the waters of the Red Sea retreated before a strong wind; he says that the Shunammite's son was revived by the natural heat of Elisha's body; he says that the rainbow which was made a sign to Noah appeared in the ordinary course of nature. Scripture itself, rightly interpreted, says, he affirms, all this. But he asserts that the Voice which uttered the commandments on Mount Sinai was a real voice, a *vera vox*. He says, indeed, that this voice could not really give to the Israelites that proof which they imagined it gave to them of the existence of God, and that God on Sinai was dealing with the Israelites only according to their imperfect knowledge. Still he asserts the voice to have been a real one; and for this reason, that we do violence to Scripture if we do not admit it to have been a real one *(nisi Scripture vim inferre velimus, omnino concedendum est, Israëlitas veram vocem audivisse)*. The attentive reader wants to know what Spinoza himself thought about this *vera vox* and its possibility; he is much more interested in knowing this than in knowing what Spinoza considered Scripture to affirm about the matter.

The feeling of perplexity thus caused is not diminished by the language of the chapter on miracles. In this chapter Spinoza broadly affirms a miracle to be an impossibility. But he himself contrasts the method of demonstration *à priori,* by which he claims to have established this proposition, with the method which he has pursued in treating of prophetic revelation. ''This revelation,'' he says, ''is a matter out of human reach, and therefore I was bound to take it as I found it.'' . . .

The reader feels that Spinoza, proceeding on a hypothesis, has presented him with the assertion of a miracle, and afterwards, proceeding *à priori,* has presented him with the assertion that a miracle is impossible. He feels that Spinoza does not adequately reconcile these two assertions by declaring that any event really miraculous, if found recorded in Scripture, must be ''a spurious addition made to Scripture by sacrilegious men.'' Is, then, he asks, the *vera vox* of Mount Sinai in Spinoza's opinion a spurious addition made to Scripture by sacrilegious men; or, if not, how is it not miraculous?

Spinoza, in his own mind, regarded the Bible as a vast collection of miscellaneous documents, many of them quite disparate and not at all to be harmonised with others; documents of unequal value and of varying applicability, some of them conveying ideas salutary for one time, others for another. But in the ***Tractatus Theologico-Politicus*** he by no means always deals in this free spirit with the Bible. Sometimes he chooses to deal with it in the spirit of the veriest worshipper of the letter; sometimes he chooses to treat the Bible as if all its parts were (so to speak) equipollent; to snatch an isolated text which suits his purpose, without caring whether it is annulled by the context, by the general drift of Scripture, or by other passages of more weight and authority. The great critic thus voluntarily becomes as uncritical as Exeter Hall. The epicurean Solomon, whose *Ecclesiastes* the Hebrew doctors, even after they had received it into the canon, forbade the young and weak-minded among their community to read, Spinoza quotes as of the same authority with the severe Moses; he uses promiscuously, as documents of identical force, without discriminating between their essentially different character, the softened cosmopolitan teaching of the prophets of the captivity and the rigid national teaching of the instructors of Israel's youth. He is capable of extracting, from a chance expression of Jeremiah, the assertion of a speculative idea which Jeremiah certainly never entertained, and from which he would have recoiled in dismay,— the idea, namely, that miracles are impossible; just as the ordinary Englishman can extract from God's words to Noah, *Be fruitful and multiply,* an exhortation to himself to have a large family. Spinoza, I repeat, knew perfectly well what this

verbal mode of dealing with the Bible was worth: but he sometimes uses it because of the hypothesis from which he set out; because of his having agreed ''to take Scripture as it stands, and not to ask how it arose.''

No doubt the sagacity of Spinoza's rules for biblical interpretation, the power of his analysis of the contents of the Bible, the interest of his reflections on Jewish history, are, in spite of this, very great, and have an absolute worth of their own, independent of the silence or ambiguity of their author upon a point of cardinal importance. Few candid people will read his rules of interpretation without exclaiming that they are the very dictates of good sense, that they have always believed in them; and without adding, after a moment's reflection, that they have passed their lives in violating them. And what can be more interesting, than to find that perhaps the main cause of the decay of the Jewish polity was one of which from our English Bible, which entirely mistranslates the 26th verse of the 20th chapter of Ezekiel, we hear nothing,—the perpetual reproach of impurity and rejection cast upon the mass of the Hebrew nation by the exclusive priesthood of the tribe of Levi? What can be more suggestive, after Mr Mill and Dr Stanley have been telling us how great an element of strength to the Hebrew nation was the institution of prophets, than to hear from the ablest of Hebrews how this institution seems to him to have been to his nation one of her main elements of weakness? No intelligent man can read the ***Tractatus Theologico-Politicus*** without being profoundly instructed by it: but neither can he read it without feeling that, as a speculative work, it is, to use a French military expression, *in the air;* that, in a certain sense, it is in want of a base and in want of supports; that this base and these supports are, at any rate, not to be found in the work itself, and, if they exist, must be sought for in other works of the author. (pp. 176-80)

[Spinoza's] denial of final causes is essentially alien to the spirit of the Old Testatment, and his cheerful and self-sufficing stoicism is essentially alien to the spirit of the New. The doctrine that ''God directs nature, not according as the particular laws of human nature, but according as the universal laws of nature require,'' is at utter variance with that Hebrew mode of representing God's dealings, which makes the locusts visit Egypt to punish Pharaoh's hardness of heart, and the falling dew avert itself from the fleece of Gideon. The doctrine that ''all sorrow is a passage to a lesser perfection'' is at utter variance with the Christian recognition of the blessedness of sorrow, working ''repentance to salvation not to be repented of;'' of sorrow, which, in Dante's words, ''remarries us to God.'' Spinoza's repeated and earnest assertions that the love of God is man's *summum bonum* do not remove the fundamental diversity between his doctrine and the Hebrew and Christian doctrines. By the love of God he does not mean the same thing as the Hebrew and Christian religions mean by the love of God. He makes the love of God to consist in the knowledge of God; and, as we know God only through his manifestation of himself in the laws of all nature, it is by knowing these laws that we love God, and the more we know them the more we love him. This may be true, but this is not what the Christian means by the love of God. Spinoza's ideal is the intellectual life; the Christian's ideal is the religious life. Between the two states there is all the difference which there is between the being in love, and the following, with delighted comprehension, a demonstration of Euclid. For Spinoza, undoubtedly, the crown of the intellectual life is a transport, as for the saint the crown of the religious life is a transport; but the two transports are not the same.

This is true; yet it is true, also, that by thus crowning the intellectual life with a sacred transport, by thus retaining in philosophy, amid the discontented murmurs of all the army of atheism, the name of God, Spinoza maintains a profound affinity with that which is truest in religion, and inspires an indestructible interest. "It is true," one may say to the wise and devout Christian, "Spinoza's conception of beatitude is not yours, and cannot satisfy you, but whose conception of beatitude would you accept as satisfying? Not even that of the devoutest of your fellow-Christians. Fra Angelico, the sweetest and most inspired of devout souls, has given us, in his great picture of the Last Judgment, his conception of beatitude. The elect are going round in a ring on long grass under laden fruit-trees; two of them, more restless than the others, are flying up a battlemented street,—a street blank with all the ennui of the Middle Ages. Across a gulf is visible, for the delectation of the saints, a blazing caldron in which Beelzebub is sousing the damned. This is hardly more your conception of beatitude than Spinoza's is. But 'in my Father's house are many mansions;' only, to reach any one of these mansions, are needed the wings of a genuine sacred transport, of an 'immortal longing.'" These wings Spinoza had; and, because he had them he horrifies a certain school of his admirers by talking of "God" where they talk of "forces," and by talking of "the love of God" where they talk of "a rational curiosity."

One of his admirers, M. Van Vloten, has recently published at Amsterdam a supplementary volume to Spinoza's works, containing the interesting document of Spinoza's sentence of excommunication . . . , and containing, besides, several lately found works alleged to be Spinoza's, which seem to me to be of doubtful authenticity, and, even if authentic, of no great importance. M. Van Vloten (who, let me be permitted to say in passing, writes a Latin which would make one think that the art of writing Latin must be now a lost art in the country of Lipsius) is very anxious that Spinoza's unscientific retention of the name of God should not afflict his readers with any doubts as to his perfect scientific orthodoxy:—

"It is a great mistake," he cries, "to disparage Spinoza as merely one of the dogmatists before Kant. By keeping the name of God, while he did away with his person and character, he has done himself injustice. Those who look to the bottom of things will see, that, long ago as he lived, he had even then reached the point to which the post-Hegelian philosophy and the study of natural science has only just brought our own times. Leibnitz expressed his apprehension lest those who did away with final causes should do away with God at the same time. But it is in his having done away with final causes, *and with God along with them,* that Spinoza's true merit consists."

Now it must be remarked that to use Spinoza's denial of final causes in order to identify him with the Coryphæi of atheism, is to make a false use of Spinoza's denial of final causes, just as to use his assertion of the all-importance of loving God to identify him with the saints would be to make false use of his assertion of the all-importance of loving God. He is no more to be identified with the post-Hegelian philosophers than he is to be identified with St Augustine. Nay, when M. Van Vloten violently presses the parallel with the post-Hegelians, one feels that the parallel with St Augustine is the far truer one. Compared with the soldier of irreligion M. Van Vloten would have him to be, Spinoza is religious. His own language about himself, about his aspirations and his course, are true; his foot is in the *vera vita,* his eye on the beatific vision. (pp. 183-85)

Matthew Arnold, "A Word More About Spinoza," in his Essays: Literary & Critical, *J. M. Dent & Co., 1906, pp. 174-85.*

JOHN DEWEY (essay date 1882)

[*Dewey is considered a major American thinker and the leading philosopher of pragmatism after William James. Dewey gave his pragmatic philosophy the name "instrumentalism." Like James's pragmatism, Dewey's instrumentalism was an action-oriented mode of speculation which judged ideas by their practical results, especially in furthering human adaptation to change. Dewey criticized the detached pursuit of truth for its own sake and advocated a philosophy with the specific aim of seeking improvements in various spheres of human life. Much of Dewey's influence has been felt in the fields of education and political theory. In the following excerpt, Dewey discourses on weaknesses in Spinoza's concept of God.*]

The problem of philosophy is to determine the meaning of things as we find them, or of the actual. Since these things may be gathered under three heads, the problem becomes: to determine the meaning of Thought, Nature, and God, and the relations of one to another. The first stage of thought being Dogmatism, the first philosophy will be that of the common uneducated mind—Natural Realism. God, self, and the world are three independent realities, and the meaning of each is just what it seems to be. If, however, they are independent realities, how can they relate to each other? This question gives rise to the second stage of Dogmatic Philosophy, which, according to the mind of the holder, takes either the direction of Dogmatic Idealism or a Dualism with God as the *Deus ex Machina,* like that of Descartes. The reconciliation of the elements here involved leads to the third stage, where God becomes the Absolute, and Nature and Self are but his manifestations. This is Pantheism, and the view-point of Spinoza. Thought and being become one; the order of thought is the order of existence. Now a final unity seems obtained, and real knowledge possible. (p. 249)

In truth, Spinoza is a juggler who keeps in stock two Gods— one the perfect infinite and absolute being, the other the mere sum of the universe with all its defects as they appear to us. When he wishes to show God as the adequate cause of all, to explain truth, inculcate morality, his *legerdemain* brings the First before us; when finite things, change, error, etc., are to be accounted for, his Second appears—the God who does things not in so far as he is Infinite, and who is affected with the idea of finite things.

We might have known, *a priori,* that such contradictions must occur in a pantheistic system like Spinoza's. It rests upon the basis that the only real knowledge is immediate knowledge. In this case the Absolute becomes mere Being, an Abstract Universal, possessed with no determinations whatever, for determinations are negations. Such, when Spinoza is truly logical, is his God. But, in this case, he cannot account for particular concrete objects. The two elements are necessarily irreconcilable from such a standpoint as Spinoza's regarding knowledge.

Two logical pantheistic systems are possible. One must start with the conception of an Absolute Perfect Being in whom are all things, but this theory cannot account for things as we find them. It must deny that they are what they seem to be, and elevate them into the Divine. But the rock on which every such theory must split is the problem: If, then, all things are divine, how, then, do they appear to us otherwise? Here is where Spinoza failed. The other theory must start from the conception of things as they seem to be, and produce its Pantheism, not by elevating them into God, but by bringing God down to them. Such a theory, of course, can never arrive at the conception of the Absolute, the Perfect, and the Infinite. Strictly speaking, it is not *Pantheism* at all; it is Pancosmism. But this is not a solution; it is merely an assumption of all that is to be explained. (p. 257)

John Dewey, ''The Pantheism of Spinoza,'' in The Journal of Speculative Philosophy, *Vol. XVI, No. 3, July, 1882, pp. 249-58.*

GEORGE SANTAYANA   (essay date 1886)

[*Santayana was a Spanish-born philosopher, poet, novelist, and literary critic who was educated for the most part in the United States, taking his undergraduate and graduate degrees at Harvard, where he later taught philosophy. Santayana's major philosophical work of his early career is the five-volume* Life of Reason *(1905-06), in which a materialist viewpoint is applied to society, religion, art, and science. Here, and in other works, the author put forth the view that while reason undermines belief in anything whatever, an irrational animal faith suggests the existence of a ''realm of essences'' leading to the human search for knowledge. Late in life Santayana stated that ''reason and ideals arise in doing something that at bottom there is no reason for doing.'' In the following excerpt from an essay originally published in the* Harvard Monthly *in June 1886, Santayana articulates, critiques, and finally rejects the underlying theories of Spinoza's religious philosophy.*]

Spinoza as a moralist holds a peculiar position. He does not belong to that class of writers whose purpose is rather to eulogize virtue than to explain it; nor to that other class which takes delight in pointing out the weaknesses of human nature, and loves wit and piquancy better than complete truth. Both these schools writes for effect, although in different ways; one is pre-occupied with the practical tendencies and the other with the brilliancy of its writings; neither is satisfied with a plain statement of the facts of life. In disinterestedness, in the absence of an ulterior practical motive to color his inquiry, Spinoza resembles the Epicurean moralists; and in fact in its homely, week-day application, his doctrine might pass for that of a cautious Epicurean. But the source of Spinoza's inspiration, his master thought, is the complete negation of the Epicurean ideal. The Epicurean lays all the stress on his surroundings and manner of life; for him a beautiful and comfortable environment is what makes life worth living. But Spinoza makes no mention of such things; it is the significance of the world and not its pleasantness that makes life worth living to him.

There is not, however, in Spinoza any native insensibility to aesthetic and intellectual pleasures; one does not feel that Spinoza is a Philistine; for, strangely enough, Philistines when they try to philosophize, are apt to become Epicureans, although ideally this system is the most contrary to their nature, since it consists in treating life as a fine art. Spinoza's ability to appreciate the finer things of life is what makes his subordination of them impressive. Any fanatic can abuse the Epicurean ideal and declare that there is but one thing needful; but the earnestness of such a man is apt to lose its force when we consider that he is incapable of appreciating more than one ideal. Spinoza, to be sure, was not a broad-minded man, he was not a man of intelligent sympathies, on the contrary, his thinking all turns in very narrow circles about its center. But at the same time his master-thought is of such a nature that it makes anything like fanaticism impossible. For this master-thought is nothing less than the divine right of the real, before which all ideas alike lose their authority. The sum of reality, the one terrible unavoidable presence, was alone to be reverenced; respect for the fact, worship of the inevitable is the fundamental thought of Spinoza.

We hear much about a possible religion of science; Spinoza has one ready for us. The scientific spirit—allegiance to the fact—becomes in Spinoza one with the spirit of worship. That all things happen by a uniform law, that a thing can be understood only by knowing its cause, that the highest good is the unification of knowledge, that reason desires only what is necessary and acquiesces only in what is true—these are principles as essential to Spinoza's religion as they are to science. It is strange, indeed, that Spinoza is not more generally hailed as the prophet of the new dispensation; perhaps the cause of this neglect of him is that the scientific spirit has not yet penetrated into all the thought of scientific men; when they sigh for the religion of science, they are dreaming of a religion founded on facts, which shall retain all the Christian ideals. When Spinoza therefore proposes to them to dethrone the Christian ideals, to give the facts not only labor and love but acquiescence and worship, they think it is a hard saying, and walk no more with him.

After all, it is a great sacrifice that Spinoza asks us to make when he would have us confess that our approvals and disapprovals are nothing but personal equations; or at most, indications of the needs and interests of the human race. Somehow it gives a man a sense of dignity and self-satisfaction to believe that his interests are those of the universe and his likes and dislikes those of God; but this faith Spinoza would have us abandon. A doctrine which bids us lay down our lives and gives us, meantime, the assurance that our cause is absolutely just and our adversary's cause absolutely unjust, demands a smaller sacrifice than a doctrine that bids us keep our lives and give up that assurance. We have, indeed, according to Spinoza, a right or even a duty to live and fight against those who have an equal right to fight against us; for thus we all serve the great power that keeps the world in motion; but we must give up the idea that one man rather than another is doing the will of heaven; that one thing rather than another is pleasing to God.

Spinoza's ethical doctrine consists of two distinct parts; he distinguishes them himself, yet without pointing out the very different footing on which they stand, doubtless because in his mind the subordination of one to the other was obvious enough. The first part is a description of the way thoughts and passions arise in the mind. Here we learn that by the eternal necessity of things, a great diversity of opinions and passions arise in men, which are divided by Spinoza into two classes, called adequate and inadequate ideas. An idea with Spinoza is equivalent to what we call a state of consciousness; it is not confined to the mere perception, but includes judgments and emotions, as well as acts of the will. Spinoza, indeed, has good reason to use one word for all these processes, for he believed them to be identical in their nature. Every perception, according to him, involves an act of judgment, nay, is an act of judgment. Our mind is governed by a system of checks; every perception left to itself is a hallucination; every suggestion of an act, left to itself, is the performance of that act. A man has an adequate idea of any object when his consciousness includes the explanation of that object in so far as that object is represented in his idea, for an idea to be adequate need not represent all the details of its object. What it must include is the immediate cause or explanation of what it does represent. To have an adequate idea of a ship I need not have in mind everything the ship contains, it is enough I perceive nothing in it of which I do not understand the construction. There need be no doubt that such is in fact Spinoza's meaning; for no man could have an adequate idea of a triangle if he first had to know all that is involved in its nature. Much less could anyone have an adequate idea of God, who is absolutely all-inclusive. The adequate idea of God which Spinoza claims to have is adequate in so far as it perceives perfectly that God's existence is involved in the existence of anything, and the existence of everything is involved in God's; for adequacy consists in the clearness, not in the fullness of ideas. A man, on the other hand, has an inadequate idea when the proximate cause or explanation of that idea is not in his consciousness. Both adequate and inadequate ideas may involve emotions; if the idea is adequate, Spinoza calls the emotion an activity of the soul, if the idea is inadequate, he calls the emotion a passion.

Here the second part of Spinoza's ethical doctrine begins to appear; he eulogizes one set of emotions by calling them activities, and casts a reproach on others by giving them the name of passions; whereas, in the ordinary use of words, his activities are also passions and his passions are also activities. Spinoza calls the love of knowledge an activity, because it is awakened by something we comprehend, and fear he calls a passion, because it is produced by what we do not understand, and it is significant that he already begins to condemn all emotions which spring from inadequate ideas; description begins to give place to praise and blame. Nevertheless, there is a certain propriety in calling an emotion springing from inadequate ideas a passion, because such an emotion arises partly from causes foreign to the consciousness of the man who feels it; he therefore thinks it more arbitrary and tyrannical than if he were aware of all its causes. On the other hand, if he saw within himself the sufficient reason of that emotion, he would regard himself (and justly, according to Spinoza) as free in regard to that emotion; not, of course, that it was possible he should not have felt it, but that nothing outside his consciousness was required to produce it.

The first part of Spinoza's ethical doctrine consists, as I have said, in a description of the causes of men's emotions and actions. The psychological side of the question does not concern us here, but the great underlying conception is this: All things are equally necessary, and therefore equally reasonable. What men do from inadequate ideas seems to them irrational, because the causes of it lie outside themselves; but in God all ideas are adequate and for him all things are rational. Good and bad are not to be applied to things absolutely. The good is what is favorable to some end, but God acts for no end; the bad is what threatens the survival of some particular thing, but the flux of things is the life of God. We form a certain ideal of human life, and whatever conforms to it we call right, whatever contradicts it we call wrong. There is nothing in things to make them better or worse; the difference is in their relation to us. Our essence is will to live, and on this will alone depends for us the worth of all things.

Here we pass into the second part of Spinoza's moral system— the discussion of the highest good. Nothing can be good for us but what tends to preserve our nature; our nature is preserved only in so far as our adequate ideas have free scope; therefore the only good for us is the possession of adequate ideas. The highest good, the only good for man is to understand.

By means of the conception of the essence of man as consisting of a man's adequate ideas, Spinoza seems to have intended to connect this second part with the first. It is a plausible thing to say that our own survival can be our only good; that the instinct of self-preservation is the source of all our desires. But such a statement is plausible only when we mean by our preservation something very different from the preservation of our essence in Spinoza's sense of the word; when we mean by instinct of self-preservation an instinct to preserve much more than our adequate ideas. Spinoza's presentation of this second part of his doctrine shows that he knew it rested on very different grounds from the purely descriptive part of his system. The claim of adequate ideas to be the highest good consists mainly in the fact that they tend to destroy the passions; but this consideration would appeal only to those who already felt that the passions should be destroyed. Another claim is the intrinsic value of adequate ideas as satisfying our desire for knowledge; but then the desire for knowledge is not always strong. Other arguments in favor of the chosen standard are found in its probable effect on the state and on the character; that is, in its coincidence with other standards already recognized by men. All these arguments in favor of adequate ideas are so many admissions that adequate ideas stand on the same ground as any other thing men are wont to desire, and have no special right to be regarded as the chief good. In fact, I cannot think that Spinoza meant to present in this second portion of his work more than one of those ideals of human life which may become the standards of good and evil; he cannot have pretended that his choice of understanding as the chief good would commend itself to everyone. He explains the arbitrary character of all ideals too plainly and forcibly to assert that his own ideal is not arbitrary. All that he means to do is to describe a type which to him was the most attractive—the type of the man overwhelmed with a sense of the unity and reality of things, the sense of unity contributing a mystical, the sense of reality a scientific element, in short, the man of adequate ideas. The tendency of a man's mind commonly determines what ideal he shall adopt; and if he is strenuous and single-minded, as Spinoza was, he will do much towards realizing that ideal in his own person; therefore we need not be surprised at the strong likeness between Spinoza's ideal and himself. His strenuous and single-minded nature, indeed, makes him present his ideal in a dogmatic way; and it is not impossible that he convinced himself that it followed necessarily from the first part of his system. In fact, his system was worked out to satisfy the demand for adequate ideas and for a single absorbing object of thought. The dependence of the system on this ideal in his own mental history may have been vaguely felt afterwards as a dependence of the ideal on the system. A man worried by a theorizing spirit might take satisfaction in constructing a theory of happiness; but only by a singular limitation of view could he pronounce happiness to consist in the construction of theories.

All that Spinoza advances in support of his ideal is interesting and true so far as it goes. To acquire clear and distinct ideas is often to remove the causes of fear, of hate, and of love. The knowledge that all the suffering in the world is necessary is apt to make a brave man braver, but it also makes a hard-hearted man more hard-hearted. The conviction that right and wrong vary with personal feeling and with the interests of the race must tend to promote tolerance of others' faults; but as it may also promote tolerance of our own, we may doubt whether the interests of the race can make it right to believe a doctrine with such a tendency. Adequate ideas may make me blessed, but I may prefer to be rich; they may even make me immortal, but I may prefer to be merry and to die. Spinoza can, indeed, assure me that the intellectual love of God is a good that affects the mind to the exclusion of all else; I may believe what he says and yet dislike a state of mind which too much resembles monomania. In the end Spinoza must admit that blessedness, like everything else, is not desired because it is good, but is only good when it is desired; and I must be allowed to retain my conviction that adequate ideas are inadequate for life.

Nevertheless, the demand of science and of the whole intellectual side of our nature is for adequate ideas. In his search for them Spinoza arrived at a conception of the world which is unrivaled for sublimity. Nothing can express the feeling of insignificance, of helplessness, which assails one in the presence of Spinoza's God, from the necessity of whose nature infinite things follow in infinite ways. All thoughts of beautiful and ugly, of late and early, of good and bad, fall away from us. We cannot judge the reality that remains; we cannot love it; we can scarcely think it at all. What we bring away is the feeling that all things are equally sacred; that what we love is no better than what we hate, what we blame no worse than what we admire. No system of morals can follow from this insight; we cannot even say that to gain this insight is the moral aim, for those who have it are no better than those who are without it. (pp. 74-83)

[Spinoza's ideal] seems to us too narrow. In so far as it calls for adequate ideas we share it, for we also like clear thinking and curious knowledge; in so far as it excludes inadequate ideas we reject it, for we are not willing to renounce faith and love, pleasure and ambition.

Aesthetic and social demands must be satisfied as well as intellectual; these call for greater spontaneity and audacity, for greater variety in the objects of pursuit. What is the use of calling one's self free, if one is to do nothing? We prefer to be a little more subject to the influences of the weather, and to enter with more zeal into the life of the day; we prefer to be jostled a little in the crowd to walking alone in the desert. On the other hand, for truth's sake, we would not have the sad things of life ignored any more than we would have the gay things of life despised. To say nothing of more tangible causes of woe, this absolute point of view which Spinoza would have us attain, what does it do but reduce all ideas to hallucinations and all this hurricane of being to an aimless gust? It is very easy to say that in so far as men are rational they desire nothing but what is necessary and acquiesce in nothing but what is true; but this rationality is built on the ruins of our vitality; it means the abandoning of all we love and the dethroning of all we reverence; it is that complete self-surrender which involves death. After all, Spinoza did agree with Plato that wisdom is a meditation of death, for the life which he would have us consider involves the extinction of our separate being. So long as we have anything to live for, so long as we have any concern for what happens to us and to our fellowmen, we cannot acquiesce in what is true and we must desire what is in fact impossible. I believe that the absolute point of view which Spinoza has so impressively, so overpoweringly enforced cannot be avoided; it is the ocean in which every stream of thought is lost; and for that very reason Spinoza's apparent optimism seems to me deceptive. The final word must always be a contradiction of our ideals, of those ideals which alone make things good or bad. The world becomes one oppressive, tyrannous fact, eternally and inexplicably present. It may be possible to lose one's self in this eternal reality, so as no longer to feel its weight: but why should one wish to do so? It is much easier and much saner to confess once for all what seems to be the truth, and then to go about one's other business, guided by the ideal of one's country and of one's heart. (pp. 84-6)

George Santayana, "The Ethical Doctrine of Spinoza," in his The Idler and His Works and Other Essays, *edited by Daniel Cory, George Braziller, Inc., 1957, pp. 74-86.*

JOHN CAIRD (essay date 1888)

[*In the following excerpt, Caird discusses how Spinoza reconciles infinite and finite matter in his philosophical system.*]

The starting-point of Spinoza's system is the idea of "Substance," which he defines as "that which is in itself and is conceived through itself—*i.e.*, that, the conception of which does not need the conception of another thing in order to its formation." This substance he characterises as infinite, indivisible, unique, free, eternal, as the cause of itself and of all things, and as consisting of an infinite number of infinite attributes, two only of which, thought and extension, are cognisable by human intelligence; and he expressly identifies this substance with God, whom he defines as "a Being absolutely infinite—that is, substance consisting of infinite attributes, of which each expresses an eternal and infinite essence."

In beginning with this idea Spinoza is attempting to realise his own theory of knowledge—viz, that "in order that our mind may correspond to the exemplar of nature, it must develop all its ideas from the idea which represents the origin and sum of nature, so that that idea may appear as the source of all other ideas." Philosophy, according to this view, begins with the universal, not the particular; it does not proceed by induction or generalisation from the facts of observation and experience, but it seeks to grasp the ultimate unity, the highest principle of things, and to derive or develop from it all particular existences. Its method is, not to reach the universal from the particular, but to know the particular through the universal. (pp. 130-31)

The problem for Spinoza, by his own showing, was to find a first principle which would explain the universe, after the analogy of mathematical science, according to the simplest of categories. The problem which modern philosophy has had to face is that of finding a final interpretation of nature which must presuppose the previous interpretations of it by the whole range of the physical and biological sciences, and which must supply a principle of criticism of the categories on which these sciences are based, and itself at once comprehend and transcend them.

Spinoza's starting-point, the idea which is to be "the source of all other ideas," that which explains all else but needs no other idea to explain it, is "Substance," which, as already said, he defines as "that which is in itself and is conceived through itself." When we ask what Spinoza means by substance, we seem precluded by the very terms of the definition from all ordinary methods of explanation. The question what it is, seems to be answered simply by the affirmation *that* it is; the question how we are to conceive of it, by what other ideas we are to be enabled to apprehend its meaning, seems to be met by the affirmation that it is that which can be conceived only through itself: we may understand all other ideas by means of it, not it by means of them.

But whilst thus we seem debarred from any direct explanation of the nature of substance, we may come at the answer indirectly if we consider, in the light of Spinoza's theory of knowledge, what is the point of view which this term is intended to express. We can understand the world, or bring our thoughts "into correspondence with the exemplar of nature," he tells us, as we have seen, only by "developing all our ideas from the idea which represents the origin and source of nature;" and the idea which constitutes the "origin of nature," he elsewhere defines as that of "a Being, single, infinite, which is the totality of being, and beyond which there is no being." From this we gather that, according to Spinoza's conception of it, true or adequate knowledge is that which starts from *the idea of the whole,* and for which all other ideas have a meaning and reality only as they are determined by or seen in the light of the idea of the whole. (pp. 133-35)

Rightly viewed, each so-called individual is only a transition-point in a movement of thought that stretches back through the interminable past and onwards through the interminable future. Thus the substantial reality of individual existences vanishes, and we can apply the designation "substance" only to the whole, the totality of being which includes and determines them. That whole is the only true individual, the only being which "is in itself and is conceived through itself." (p. 136)

Infinite intelligence is for [Spinoza] not merely the aggregate of an indefinite number of finite minds, it is infinite in a truer sense. For . . . the conception of "the absolutely infinite intellect," as one of what Spinoza terms "infinite modes," is simply a device by which he is unconsciously seeking to introduce into the idea of God that element of activity which neither his abstract substance nor even its attributes contain. The gulf between the moveless infinite and the finite world is thus bridged over by an expedient which, ostensibly without affecting the indeterminateness of the absolute substance, makes it quick with the life of creative thought—introduces into it, in other words, what is virtually the principle of self-consciousness and self-determination. (p. 302)

The last word of Spinoza's philosophy seems to be the contradiction of the first. Not only does he often fluctuate between principles radically irreconcilable, but he seems to reassert at the close of his speculations what he had denied at the beginning. The indeterminate infinite, which is the negation of the finite, becomes the infinite, which necessarily expresses itself in the finite, and which contains in it, as an essential element, the idea of the human mind under the form of eternity. The all-absorbing, lifeless substance becomes the God who knows and loves Himself and man with an infinite "intellectual love." On the other hand, the conception of the human mind as but an evanescent mode of the infinite substance, whose independent existence is an illusion, and which can become one with God only by ceasing to be distinguishable from God, yields to that of a nature endowed with indestructible individuality, capable of knowing both itself and God, and which, in becoming one with God, attains to its own conscious perfection and blessedness. The freedom of man, which is at first rejected as but the illusion of a being who is unconscious of the conditions under which, in body and mind, he is fast bound in the toils of an inevitable necessity, is reasserted as the essential prerogative of a nature which, as knowing itself through the infinite, is no longer subjected to finite limitations. The doctrine of a final cause or ideal end of existence, which was excluded as impossible in a world in which all that is, and as it is, is given along with the necessary existence of God, is restored in the conception of the human mind as having in it, in its rudest experience, the implicit consciousness of an infinite ideal, which, through reason and intuitive knowledge, it is capable of realising, and of the realisation of which its actual life is the process. At the outset, in one word, we seem to have a pantheistic unity in which nature and man, all the man-

ifold existences of the finite world, are swallowed up; at the close, an infinite self-conscious mind, in which all finite thought and being find their reality and explanation.

Is it possible to harmonise these opposite aspects of Spinoza's system, and to free it from the inherent weakness which they seem to involve? Can we make him self-consistent, as many of his interpreters have done, only by emphasising one side or aspect of his teaching, and ignoring or explaining away all that seems to conflict with it—by clearing it of all individualistic elements, so as to reduce it to an uncompromising pantheism, or by eliminating the pantheistic element as mere scholastic surplusage, in order to find in it an anticipation of modern individualism and empiricism?

The answer is, that though Spinoza's philosophy cannot, in the form in which he presents it, be freed from inconsistency, yet much of that inconsistency is due to the limitations of an imperfect logic, and that the philosophy of a later time has taught us how it is possible to embrace in one system ideas which in him seem to be antagonistic. There is a point of view which he at most only vaguely foreshadowed, in which it is possible to maintain (1) at once the nothingness of the finite world before God and its reality in and through God, and (2) the idea of an infinite unity transcending all differences, which nevertheless expresses itself in nature and man, in all the manifold differences of finite thought and being.

The negation of the finite by which Spinoza rises to the idea of God is, in one sense, an element which enters into the essence of all spiritual life. But when we consider the twofold aspect in which Spinoza himself represents this negative movement,—that, on the one hand, which is involved in the principle

Facsimile of a letter written by Spinoza.

that all determination is negation; and that, on the other hand, which is involved in the rise of the human mind from the lower to the higher stages of knowledge,—we can discern in his teaching an approximation to the idea of a negation which is only a step to a higher affirmation—in other words, of that *self*-negation or self-renunciation which is the condition of self-realisation in the intellectual, the moral, and the religious life. It is the condition of the intellectual life. Scientific knowledge is the revelation to or in my consciousness of a system of unalterable relations, a world of objective realities which I can neither make nor unmake, and which only he who abnegates his individual fancies and opinions can apprehend; and all knowledge rests on the tacit presupposition of an absolute truth or reason, which is the measure of individual opinion, which cannot be questioned without self-contradiction, which in our very doubts and uncertainties we assume, and to which in its every movement the finite intelligence must surrender itself. The intellectual life is one which I can live only by ceasing to assert myself or to think my own thoughts, by quelling and suppressing all thought that pertains to me as this particular self, and identifying myself with an intelligence that is universal and absolute. Yet the negation of which we thus speak is not an absolute negation. The finite intelligence is not absorbed or lost in the infinite to which it surrenders itself. Surrender or subjection to absolute truth is not the extinction of the finite mind, but the realisation of its true life. The life of absolute truth or reason is not a life that is foreign to us, but one in which we come to our own. The annulling of any life that is separate from or opposed to it, is the quickening, the liberation, the reassertion of our own intelligence. (pp. 303-06)

[Knowing this we discern] a profound meaning in those apparently mystical utterances in which [Spinoza] seems to gather up the final result of his speculation—"God loves Himself with an infinite intellectual love;" "God in so far as He loves Himself loves man;" "the intellectual love of the mind to God is part of the infinite love wherewith God loves Himself;" "the love of God to man and the intellectual love of man to God are one and the same." (p. 315)

> *John Caird, in his* Spinoza, *J. B. Lippincott Company, 1888, 315 p.*

SIR FREDERICK POLLOCK, BART. (essay date 1899)

[*Pollock was a distinguished English scholar of jurisprudence who is also remembered for his* Spinoza: His Life and Philosophy. *In the following excerpt from this work, he examines Spinoza's concept of the eternal mind as well as the general philosophy of the* Ethics, *summarizing Spinoza's achievement as a philosopher.*]

[In the fourth part of the *Ethics,* Spinoza] has laid bare the constituents of human motives and passions; he has explained the working of these passions in the various circumstances of life; he has contrasted the slave of passion with the reasonable or free man, and has declared the precepts of righteousness and goodwill. But he esteems his work only half done, and goes on to that which remains as to something he has been longing to take in hand.

> At length (he says in the Preface to Part V.), I pass on to the other division of my *Ethics,* concerning the method or path which leads us to freedom. And in this I shall treat of the power of reason, and show what is its native strength against the emotions, and thence what is the freedom or blessedness of the mind. Whence we shall see in how much better case is the wise man than the ignorant. But by what means

> and method the understanding is to be perfected, and by what skill the body is to be tended that it may truly do its office, pertains not to this inquiry; for the latter of these is the concern of medicine, the former of logic.

The fact is that Spinoza's aim has throughout been practical. He has undertaken the scientific analysis of the passions, not without the pure curiosity of the man of science, but mainly to the end of showing how they may be mastered, and the conditions of man's happiness assured. In this he is at one with the Greeks, and particularly . . . with the Stoics. But Spinoza explicitly denies the Stoic assumption that the will has an absolute power over the emotions; a denial which, on comparison of his express contradictions of Descartes, might be taken to imply an admission that in other ways the Stoic doctrine appeared to him profitable and worthy of respect. In the same passage he goes on to controvert the Cartesian theory of a connexion between the mind and the body through the pineal gland, by which Descartes endeavoured to show "that there is no soul so feeble but that, being rightly trained, it may acquire an absolute dominion over its passions." Spinoza points out that the hypothesis of the pineal gland being the seat of consciousness, transmitting impressions to the mind from without, and receiving orders from the mind which are sent on to the nerves of motion by means of the animal spirits, is contrary to Descartes' own principles of scientific work; introducing as it does assumptions more baseless and occult than any of the scholastic occult qualities which Descartes rejected. He also remarks that Descartes did not and could not assign any mechanical measure of the alleged power of the mind to initiate or control the motions of this gland: "in truth, will and motion being incommensurable, there is no comparison betwixt the power or force of the mind and the body: and therefore the force of the latter can in no wise be determined by that of the former." The physiological difficulties of the hypothesis are lightly touched on, but so as to show that Spinoza did not overlook them. In its actual form this preliminary discussion is now chiefly interesting as a monument of the extraordinary hold the Cartesian philosophy must have acquired on that generation to make Spinoza thus go out of his way to refute the most fantastic and untenable point of it. But the substance of Spinoza's argument remains applicable to the various quasi-materialist attempts that from time to time have been made, in the supposed interest of spiritual truth, to establish or make plausible some kind of physical communication between the mind and the brain.

When we examine in detail what Spinoza has to say "of the power of the understanding, or of Man's freedom," we find that it consists of two independent parts. The first (Part V. of *Ethics* to Prop. 20) is a consistent following out of the psychological method we have already become familiar with. The condition of mastering the emotions is shown to be a clear and distinct understanding of their nature and causes; and the love of God—which is nothing else than the rational contemplation of the order of the world, and of human nature as part thereof—is described as the greatest happiness of man in this life, and the surest way of establishing the rule of the understanding over the passions. Here again one might suppose, and with more reason than before, that nothing more remained to be set forth. But it is not so: Spinoza proceeds to lay before us a theory of intellectual immortality, or rather eternity, the perfection whereof consists in an intellectual love of God which is likewise eternal, and "is part of the infinite love wherewith God loves himself." This exposition, which takes up the fifth Part of the *Ethics* from Prop. 21 onwards, presents great difficulties. It is by no means obvious in the first place, what is Spinoza's real meaning; nor can we feel sure that any explanation is the right one until we have some probable account of the manner in which Spinoza reconciled the doctrine, as we may propose to read it, with the rest of his own philosophy. And this latter problem is a yet harder one.

The question has been evaded, as it seems to me, by most of those who have written on Spinoza. Critics who regard him as a transcendental dogmatist naturally feel no particular difficulty at this point: why should not Spinoza dogmatize about the eternity of the mind as well as about Substance and Attributes? So they are content to give some abridgment or paraphrase of Spinoza's argument which in truth explains nothing. Others, led by their own prepossessions to disregard all the rules of historical and critical probability, have sought, in the face of Spinoza's express and repeated warnings, to make out that his theory is a doctrine of personal immortality in the ordinary sense or some sense practically equivalent to it, only stated in an unusual way and supported by artificial reasoning. Some few, taking a view of the general meaning of Spinoza's philosophy similar to that which has been maintained in the foregoing chapters, have manfully striven to reduce this apparently eccentric part into scientific conformity to the main body. But they are forced to say either that Spinoza did not clearly know his own meaning, or that he did not succeed in saying what he meant, or that he deliberately said things he did not mean: none of which suppositions can be entertained by any serious and impartial reader of the *Ethics* except as a desperate remedy. For my part, I would rather confess myself baffled than help myself out by any one of them, especially the last: and in fact I long thought the obscurity of the last portion of the *Ethics* all but hopeless.

The explanation I shall now put forward with the hope of throwing some light upon the historical affinities of this speculation, and its logical connexion with Spinoza's psychology, is one that has occurred to me almost at the last moment, and after repeated consideration.

It may be observed here, as a matter independent of any particular interpretation of Spinoza's thought, that there is some reason to believe that he was himself conscious of not standing on the firmest ground in this place. The propositions concerning the eternity of the mind seem to be carefully isolated from the rest: the love of God arising from clear and distinct self-knowledge (Prop. 15) is kept apart from the intellectual love which is the privilege of the mind in its eternal quality (Prop. 33), though on almost any possible reading of Spinoza's theory the two must coincide; and at the end Spinoza guards himself by showing that the validity of ethical motives and precepts is independent of the exalted doctrine he has just been setting forth (Prop. 41). In a writer so careful and subtle indications of this kind are not to be neglected. I believe that Spinoza's argument was to himself satisfactory; but it hangs, as I read it, on a very special point in his theory of knowledge, and it may well be that he saw the danger of its not being satisfactory to other people. Moreover I am inclined to think that Spinoza wished emphatically to disclaim any intention of relying on a supernatural or supersensible world for the foundations of ordinary virtue and morality. He puts his eternity of the mind as a kind of supplemental speculation; if we accept it, so much the better; if not, the rest of his work will not be impaired. (pp. 260-64)

Spinoza affirms that the mind in every act of knowledge also knows its own body; though so long as it perceives things "after the common order of nature" its knowledge of itself and the body is not adequate. Now when the mind is in the act of rational or scientific knowledge of anything whatever—in other words, when it perceives things "under the form of eternity,"—Spinoza says, transferring to the relation between the mind and its own body what belongs to the relation between the mind and the object of knowledge, that the mind knows its own body "under the form of eternity." So knowing its own body and consequently itself, it is eternal, and depends only on its own activity for this eternity. As Spinoza says farther on, "the mind conceives nothing under the form of eternity, save so far as it conceives the being of its own body under the form of eternity, that is, save so far as it is eternal." The verbal confusion involved in Spinoza's way of stating his doctrine is no doubt surprising at the present day.... [But] when we remember that in Spinoza's time psychology was really in its infancy, and hardly any serious attempt had been made to work out the theory of perception, our surprise may be considerably abated.

Apart from the peculiar form of his argument, Spinoza has here to meet a metaphysical difficulty of which he was so far aware that he made a distinct effort to escape it. The eternity of which the mind is conscious in the act of rational knowledge is wholly out of relation to time. Also it is distinctly stated to be a kind of existence. Here, then, we have existence out of time, and a knowledge or perception of it in consciousness. Now it is at least a serious question whether existence out of time is conceivable. We cannot think of existence except in terms of actual or possible experience. But experience involves consciousness or at least feeling. And it is not a metaphysical speculation, but an established fact of science, that change of some kind is the necessary condition of all feeling and experience. Every feeling of which we know anything or can form a notion is a feeling of transition, of an event, of something happening: which on the physical side is motion of some kind in the sentient organism.

Even an apparently continuous sensation is a series of many rapidly succeeding nervous shocks. The more we analyse feeling, the more we find change and motion to be its constant form: and these involve time. It would seem therefore, that without making any transcendental or universal affirmation, but as a matter of human experience as far as it has gone, we must say that existence out of time is a combination of words to which we can attach no real meaning. The position involves more consequences than can be here discussed; as for instance the total rejection of all attempts, however powerful and ingenious, to set up an Absolute, Unconditioned, Unknowable, or any form of unapproachable reality supposed to be somehow more real than the things we feel and know. For the present it is enough to beg the reader to believe that such a position is philosophically tenable, notwithstanding that (as he can see for himself) it is in no way repugnant to common sense. If, being valiant in speculation and disregarding objections of this kind, we begin to talk about something alleged to exist without relation to time, the objection will be forced upon us in a practical shape by the extreme difficulty we shall soon find in pursuing our discourse without manifest contradictions. Probably the objection did not occur to Spinoza in the shape in which it is here put: for that shape is the result of modern inquiries. But he felt the logical difficulty of discussing eternity in the language of time; and he endeavoured to secure himself by the following characteristic remark.

> We shall here note that, although we be now certain
> that the mind, so far as it doth conceive things under

the form of eternity, is eternal; yet, in order that our ensuing exposition may be the easier and the better understood, we shall consider the mind (like as we have done thus far) as if at a given moment it began to be, and to understand things under the form of eternity; and this we may safely do without any risk of error, so that we use care to conclude nothing except from evident premisses.

Perhaps we may think, on reflexion, that the objections are less formidable than they appear at first sight. What Spinoza is really maintaining in an artificial form is that the necessary and universal character of exact knowledge is not affected either by this and that particular act of knowledge being associated, as a fact occurring in the sensible world, with a transitory condition of a bodily organism, or by the act, as a particular human act, being subject to the conditions of our finite human consciousness. And this seems a sound position in substance. The second branch of the difficulty disappears for those who accept time as an ultimate reality.

Spinoza proceeds to set forth the ''intellectual love of God'' which is the crown of the mind's perfection. It has already been stated that the most perfect activity and excellence of the mind is to understand things with the third or intuitive kind of knowledge; and that this begets the highest degree of contentment attainable by human nature. Again, this knowledge implies the knowledge of God; hence the delight of the highest intellectual activity is a pleasure accompanied with the idea of God as its cause. That is, it is love of God; ''not in that we conceive him,'' adds Spinoza, ''as now present, but in that we understand God as eternal, and this is what I call the intellectual love of God.'' Like the knowledge from which it springs, it is eternal; on which there is another curious remark.

> Although this love toward God hath had no beginning, yet it hath all the perfections of love in the same manner as if it had arisen in time, as we feigned in the corollary to the foregoing proposition. And herein there is no difference but that the mind hath eternally had the same perfections which (as we feigned) accrued to it at a particular time, and that accompanied by the idea of God as the eternal cause thereof. And since pleasure consisteth in a passage to greater perfection, 'tis plain blessedness must consist in this, that the mind hath perfection in full possession.

Here, the reader will observe, we are required to form the idea of an eternal causation; and this lands us in an impossibility if we regard the cause as an antecedent of the effect, as in that case we have to conceive a relation which is in time and out of time at once. But this difficulty would probably not touch Spinoza. There is nothing to show that he conceived cause and effect as being necessarily antecedent and consequent; on the contrary, it is pretty clear from the First Part of the *Ethics* that he did not. God, as the absolute first cause, is the immediate cause of motion and matter, and they of all material things; and similar relations hold in the other Attributes. But there is here no question of priority in time.

Freedom from the passions, though not itself perfection, is a condition of perfection: hence the mind, so far as it partakes of eternity, must enjoy this freedom, and Spinoza naturally proceeds to show that ''the mind is not exposed, except while the body endures, to those emotions which are reckoned as passions.'' Whence it follows that none but the intellectual love is eternal. And here for the first time Spinoza takes distinct notice of the common opinion of immortality.

''If we consider the general opinion of mankind, we shall find that they are indeed aware of the eternity of their own mind; but confound the same with duration, and ascribe it to the imagination or memory, which they suppose to remain after death.'' This explains why Spinoza throughout this part of his work avoids the use of the term *immortality,* and it exposes more fully than any comment could do the hopelessness of attempting to represent him as maintaining the immortality of the soul in the ordinary sense: yet the attempt has been made.

One more surprise remains: the philosopher is determined to outdo the theologians with their own vocabulary. ''God loves himself with an infinite and intellectual love'': the intellectual love of human minds towards God is part of this infinite love, and in it God may be said to love men; in which there is no contradiction of the foregoing statement that God neither loves nor hates any one, since this intellectual love is not an emotion. It is perhaps difficult to remember that the substance of the propositions thus expressed is still purely and simply the human mind's contemplation of itself and its own certain knowledge as a part of the infinite and necessary order of the universe; that for Spinoza the divine love is nothing else than conscious acceptance of universal law, the ''welcoming every event'' of the Stoics; and that the secret of blessedness and glory (for those titles are expressly claimed and justified) is none other than a mind steadfastly bent on the truth.

It seems a poor and barren conclusion to bear up the solemnity of language: so strong is the prejudice bred of our inveterate custom of hungering after dreams and neglecting the realities under our hands. After all, if we turn Spinoza's thought into a guide for action, if we translate his speculative propositions into a practical imperative, what is the outcome? Even that which true and fearless men have preached through all the generations to unheeding ears. Seek the truth, fear not and spare not: this first, this for its own sake, this only; and the truth itself is your reward, a reward not measured by length of days nor by any reckoning of men. This lesson assuredly is not an idle one, or unworthy to be set forth with fervent and solemn words. And if any man ever had a special title so to repeat the lesson, that man was Spinoza, whose whole life was an example of it.

On the strength of these passages Spinoza has been called a mystic (not that it is a bad name to be called, for some of the mystical doctors of the middle ages were men of great speculative power) and, while the passages in question have perplexed philosophical inquirers, they have exercised a sort of fascination on many readers. As to the actual contents of them, their author is no more a mystic than Aristotle, if . . . the groundwork of his doctrine is the Aristotelian theory that contemplative knowledge is the highest and most proper function of the mind, in respect of which alone it can be said to partake of eternity. Moreover the form chosen by Spinoza may be partly due, as I have already hinted, to the desire of encountering theologians with their own weapons. But there is unquestionably something of an exalted and mystical temper in his expressions; and it seems possible enough that, but for his scientific training in the school of Descartes, he might have gone the way of those mystics who have thought to take the kingdom of heaven by force. If this be so, Descartes has one claim the more to the gratitude of mankind.

But these seemingly transcendental propositions are not left without practical application. The intellectual love, being a quality of the mind ''inasmuch as it is regarded as an eternal truth depending on the nature of God,'' is indestructible. And the greater is the activity in a particular mind of the clear understanding described as the second and third kinds of knowledge, the more does the man partake of eternity, the less is he exposed to evil passions, and the less does he fear death. And then there is a sudden return to the physical aspect of things, as if to show that it has never been forgotten. "He that hath a body of most various capacities hath also a mind whose greatest part is eternal." For the "power of ordering and connecting the affections of the body according to the intellectual order" is a perfection of the body. Naturally the body includes the special organs of thought and reflexion; the outward and apparent excellence of the human body is not asserted to be the necessary index of contemplative power. At the same time Spinoza would no doubt have said that, other things being equal, the commonly recognized qualities of health, strength, comeliness, activity, and the like, are all in themselves good and desirable; and that whatever makes for the health of the body must in some degree make for the health of the mind. (pp. 278-84)

[Spinoza's] doctrine of the eternity of the mind must remain one of the most brilliant endeavours of speculative philosophy, and it throws a sort of poetical glow over the formality of his exposition. We have already said that it has a sufficiently certain practical lesson. But still we linger over it, seeking for some expression which may so give us the central idea that we can accept and use it for ourselves, some concentration of the commanding thought without the precarious dialectical form in which it is clothed. If the task were still to attempt, it might be a hard one; but there is no need for any such attempt. The essence of Spinoza's thought is already secured for us by a master who combines delicacy of perception and the intellectual tact which is the flower of criticism with consummate power over language. M. Renan has expressed it in the perfectly chosen words . . . :*Reason leads Death in triumph, and the work done for Reason is done for eternity.*(p. 288)

We who have thus far endeavoured, however imperfectly, to follow the working of Spinoza's mind, and to explain his thoughts in the language of our own time, honour him even more for that which he suggested, seeing the far-off dawn of new truths as in a vision, than for that which his hands made perfect. Not even from those whom we most reverence can we accept any system as final. A speculative system is a work of art; it is an attempt to fix an ideal, and in the very act of thought which marks it off with individual form the ideal is transformed and drawn up into a still unexplored region. Experience and science combine to warn us against putting our faith in symbols which should be but aids to thought. The word that lived on the master's lips becomes a dead catchword in the mouth of scholars who have learnt only half his lesson. And therefore it will still be in time to come that when men of impatient mind cry out for systems and formulas, demanding to possess the secret of all wisdom once for all, there will be no better answer for them than was given long ago by the son of Sirach: *The first man knew her not perfectly; no more shall the last find her out. For her thoughts are more than the sea, and her counsels profounder than the great deep.* (pp. 381-82)

> *Sir Frederick Pollock, Bart., in his* Spinoza: His Life and Philosophy, *second edition, The Macmillan Company, 1899, 427 p.*

V. T. THAYER (essay date 1922)

[*Thayer was an American educator and active participant in the Ethical Culture Movement, a movement which stressed secularism*

and humanistic progressiveness. In the following excerpt, he differentiates the political philosophies of Spinoza and Thomas Hobbes.]

A suggestive approach to a study of the differences and similarities in the ethics of Hobbes and Spinoza is found in their opinions regarding the function of the state. According to Hobbes, *one* motive prompts men to institute a state—*fear.* The state of nature is a condition of war. Each man seeks to realize his desires, to enhance his power, and in so doing conflicts with others bent upon a like object, and the liberty *(Jus Naturale),* which he has "to use his own power, as he will himself, for the preservation of his own Nature" and thus to appropriate the goods and services of other men is scant compensation for the dangers thus entailed.

> In such condition, there is no place for Industry; because the fruit thereof is uncertain: and consequently no Culture of the Earth, no Navigation, nor use of the commodities that may be imported by Sea; no commodious Building; no Instruments of moving, and removing such things as require much force; no Knowledge of the face of the Earth; no account of Time; no Arts; no Letters; no Society; and which is worst of all, continual fear, and danger of violent death: and the life of man, solitary, poor, nasty, brutish, and short.

Fear prompts reason to devise a condition of peace.

> As long as this naturall Right of every man to every thing endureth, there can be no security to any man (how strong or wise soever he be), of living out the time, which Nature ordinarily alloweth men to live. And consequently it is a precept, or generall rule of Reason, *That every man, ought to endeavor Peace, as farre as he has hope of obtaining it; and when he cannot obtain it, that he may seek, and use, all helps, and advantages of Warre.* The first branch of which Rule, containeth the first and Fundamentall Law of Nature; which is, *to seek Peace and follow it.* The Second, the summe of the Right of Nature: which is, *By all means we can, to defend our selves.*
>
> (pp. 554-55)

If man could live an ideal life, it would be, for Hobbes, a state of absolute subjection of others and absence of impediments to the desires of self. The absolute ruler most nearly embodies this ideal, for he alone enjoys the services of others without obligation to repay in kind. The average citizen, however, endures the state as a necessary evil. He assisted in its origin and helps to sustain it in order to avoid the worst possible calamity, a relapse into the state of nature. (p. 555)

Spinoza conceives the state otherwise. It is true there is a semblance of Hobbes in his account of its origin, for release from fear is one of the motives he mentions. But whereas Spinoza insists that at best fear is a poor motive, a passion in the individual, and a constant danger to the security of the state, Hobbes believes that life is never without fear, and "the terrour of some Power" is the permanent basis of the commonwealth. Hobbes, to be sure, realizes the advantages of co-operative endeavor, but for Spinoza mutual aid is the ultimate justification for social organizations and the indispensable means of realizing man's true happiness. Thus he writes in the **Theologico-Political Treatise:**

> The formation of society serves not only for defensive purpose, but is also very useful, and, indeed, absolutely necessary, as rendering possible the division of labor. If men did not render mutual assistance to

each other, no one would have either the skill or the time to provide for his own sustenance and preservation: for all men are not equally apt for all work, and no one would be capable of preparing all that he individually stood in need of. Strength and time, I repeat, would fail, if every one had in person to plough, to sow, to reap, to grind corn, to cook, to weave, to stitch, and perform the numerous functions required to keep life going: to say nothing of the arts and sciences which are also entirely necessary to the perfection and blessedness of human nature.

(pp. 556-57)

Spinoza saw clearly wherein he differed from Hobbes, and he states in a note to Chapter 16 of the *Theologico-Political Treatise:* "Now reason (though Hobbes thinks otherwise) is always on the side of peace, which cannot be attained unless the general laws of the state be respected." And in Part IV of the *Ethics,* he writes, "Now, if men lived under the guidance of reason, everyone would remain in possession of this his right (his natural right) without any injury to his neighbour." That is, whereas Hobbes considers the desires and wants of men inevitably bring them into conflict, Spinoza insists that it is only passion, the irrational and ill-informed opinions of their wants, which lead men to disagree. The true needs of men are in harmony and are realizable most fully in society. The state, for Spinoza, as for Hobbes, is a necessary evil; but it is a necessary evil, according to Spinoza, only because and in so far as it must resort to means which are a poor substitute for rational behavior. (p. 558)

The best state then would be one which governs rationally; that is, one which establishes laws enabling men to develop and expand the potentialities of their nature. Consequently Spinoza opposes an absolutism and favors a democracy. "In a democracy, irrational commands are still less feared: for it is impossible that the majority of a people, especially if it be a large one, should agree in an irrational design: and, moreover, the basis and aim of a democracy is to avoid the desires as irrational, and to bring men as far as possible under the control of reason, so that they may live in peace and harmony: if this basis be removed the whole fabric falls to ruin." As a necessary means to rational legislation, Spinoza pleads for the utmost freedom of thought and speech, distinguishing sharply between obedience to law and the expression of opinions regarding the wisdom of particular legislation. "No," he exclaims passionately, "the object of government is not to change men from rational beings into beasts or puppets, but to enable them to develop their minds and bodies in security, and to employ their reason unshackled: neither showing hatred, anger, deceit, nor watched with the eyes of jealousy and injustice. In fact, the true aim of government is liberty."

A difference in conception as to the function of the state carries with it a corresponding disagreement as to the nature and purpose of the individual. But here again, on first reading, Spinoza seems to repeat Hobbes. Reason, says Hobbes, "is nothing but Reckoning." And it is no more than a reckoning of consequences in terms of personal self-preservation, enhancement of vital motion and increase in power. Spinoza seems essentially to repeat Hobbes when he writes, "it is the sovereign law and right of nature that each individual should endeavor to preserve itself as it is, without regard to anything but itself." And again, ". . . in no case do we strive for, wish for, long for, or desire anything, because we deem it to be good, but on the other hand we deem a thing to be good, because we strive for it, wish for it, long for it, or desire it."

But it is no mere repetition of Hobbes, for Spinoza does not mean the same thing by reason, nor is his individual an insulated atom. Hobbes considers that reason recognizes little in common between men, nor does it seek to ascertain their mutual welfare. It serves rather to gratify the possessive impulses and to obtain individual advantage. When contrasting man with the bees and ants whose "Common good differeth not from the Private," Hobbes points out that "man, whose Joy consisteth in comparing himself with other men, can relish nothing but what is eminent." Spinoza, however, believes that reason frees man from an isolated and miserable condition and in operating according to notions common to all men, it contributes to their mutual welfare. The rational life unites man to man. In the state of nature man has a natural right to gratify any and all desires, but this state of nature is not something actually prior to and apart from a social medium. The state of nature is merely a condition of subjection to passion and ignorance. Natural right means no more than a natural tendency to act under certain conditions. Consequently, to say, "the ignorant and foolish man has sovereign right to do all that desire dictates, or to live according to desire," just as "the wise man has sovereign right to do all that reason dictates," is not to undermine sound morality; it is merely to say that if one lacks reason and is ruled by passion, he can act only in accordance with passion. Reason frees man from this hopeless state. It enables him neither to exploit another, nor to realize his desires at the expense of others—as it can very well do for Hobbes. As Spinoza conceives it, "men, in so far as they live in obedience to reason, necessarily do only such things as are necessarily good for human nature, and consequently for each individual man." Reason thus supplies us with a criterion by means of which we can select those activities which at once aid us and assist others. Reason breaks down man's isolation; Hobbes' individual remains forever apart from others. In short, that deplorable state which Spinoza calls passion, the bondage of man, from which reason frees him, is for Hobbes the permanent condition of man. Human reason may, according to Spinoza, succeed in inaugurating an era of good will. Life, for Hobbes, is always a pugilistic encounter, and the best reason can do is to substitute gloves, a referee, and Queensbury rules for bare fists and go it as you please until the first man drops. (pp. 559-61)

[The relation between Hobbes and Spinoza] is not that of master and disciple. If we may take an illustration from industrial life, we might say that Spinoza's relation to Hobbes is that of a manufacturer to the producer of his raw materials. Hobbes supplies the raw produce, Spinoza makes it over into a new and original article.

Their disagreements find an explanation in the metaphysical backgrounds of the two men. Hobbes is a mechanical empiricist, Spinoza is a rationalist. Spinoza cannot admit that the individual is other than an expression of a deeper and more fundamental reality. Each individual, as he sees it, testifies in a unique way to the boundless and infinite possibilities of Substance; but Substance is an immanent Energy. Man is Substance and Substance is man. In God and in God alone man lives and moves and has his being. Consequently, in identifying his personal ends with the highest good of his fellows, man approaches to the supreme ethical ideal, "a knowledge of the union existing between the mind and the whole of nature." Hence, the fragmentary and short-sighted character, as Spinoza must see it, of Hobbes' individualism. It is true only as a description of man's condition of bondage; and it has value only as it enables him to escape into the life of reason. Its truth is merely the truth of Imaginative Knowledge. Hence, it lacks ultimate validity both as a description of human relations as they *really* are, and as a program for attaining to a state of blessedness. (pp. 567-68)

V. T. Thayer, "A Comparison of the Ethical Philosophies of Spinoza and Hobbes," in The Monist, Vol. XXXII, No. 4, October, 1922, pp. 553-68.

BENJAMIN DE CASSERES (essay date 1926)

[*De Casseres was an American poet and critic whose writings militantly celebrated individualism. He considered critical writing an art, and his work is characterized by a verbally lush rhetorical style. De Casseres held "logic to be one of the lowest forms of mental activity and imagination the highest"; hence, his critical judgments are usually founded on spontaneous intuition. "I think in images, flashes, epigrams. Creators should spurn Reason as an eagle would spurn a ladder." In the following excerpt, De Casseres offers a paean to Spinoza for his wisdom and sublime conception of the infinite.*]

I partake of the blood and brain and apocalyptic vision of Spinoza. Our ancestor-souls were twin-born. We were an inviolate One before chaos. We were root of the tree Ygdrasil and shoot from its highermost branches. We were a single undimensional atom in the eye of Brahma. We looked into the face of the I Am from Horeb with Moses. We were nailed to the Cross on Calvary, and feasted on our Dream at Weimar. And maybe we were a part of that ghostly world-apparition who ended his days at Saint Helena.

For where the Infinite is, there is Spinoza.

God and the Infinite are not the same things. Spinoza and the Infinite are interchangeable terms. No one can utter the one word without thinking the other. The Infinite may be only an attribute of God. We do not know. Or God may be only an attribute of the Infinite.

But the Infinite was an attribute of Spinoza.

He was born a god of Comprehension. The timeless was in him. He was called the God-intoxicated. But, rather, a god had become intoxicated in him, and through him—a god with eyes against whose glance faded all horizons, a god to whom Olympus was no more than Mont Blanc, a god who swooned in visions.

Spinoza was not of the race of prophets. He was of the race of seers and supermen. He was brother to Æschylus, Shakespeare, Victor Hugo. He was these and more. He was an artist emancipated from the thralldom of sensibility. He had purged himself of objects as objects.

All objects are aspects of God. All movement is foam and spray of a super-phenomenal sea. Character is the illusion of relations. Matter is the blackened bulkhead against which the seas of change swirl and beat and gnash—and finally shall carry away. Evil is a dam that raises the level of the cosmic spectacle. The illusion of freewill is the crowning triumph of Maya.

All these conceptions are in Æschylus, Shakespeare, Balzac. All these things are in Spinoza.

Spinoza was a defiant and impenitent Orestes; a Hamlet who built his house on the back of the Sphinx; a Cain with a jeweled brand on his brow.

His conception of God was the sublimest that has yet come into the world. God is "evil" as well as "good." It was the daring thought of Pantheism. There is only one Substance, and everything is of that Substance. God is a reveler; God is wicked; God is a murderer; God is a traitor; God is cruel. He was Christ, Borgia, Cleopatra and Saint Francis of Assisi; Shelley and the Marquis de Sade; Attila and Tolstoy. God is Ormuzd and Ahriman, Belial and Jehovah. God is earthquake, pestilence, famine, love and hate.

Blasphemer! thou who dost divide thy God into halves. Blasphemer! thou who does say God is not All. Blasphemer! thou who dost not worship evil as well as good. There is only one God, and He reigns undivided and equal in the atoms of Sirius as well as in the atoms of the body of Messalina.

Spinoza was the supreme pontiff of Understanding. Humans judge. Gods understand. Humans divide the Infinite, naming this good, that ill; this big, that little. Gods see processes only. Their visions span the constellations and solve the atoms.

That mighty flambeau in the brain of Spinoza lighted up the world around him. He might have used it to fire a cosmos, but he was not a Nihilist. He might have used it to torch courts and kingdoms, but he was not an Anarchist. He might have set in flames the rotting sanctuaries of greed and priestcraft, but he was not a propagandist.

It was a torch of ether. Each atom in the flame was a sun without heat. It lighted up the abysses of Being. Its beams were scalpels. He brought into the world neither peace nor a sword. He brought Comprehension.

And across that flame, as across a mighty screen, there was played for him the comedy of Time—Time unfolding its worlds; Time folding them up again; Time with its witcheries of change; Time with its revels and masques; Time with its orchestra of atoms; Time with its ironic enormities.

His brain was the caravansary of the Infinite. It was the Mecca of all pilgrim thoughts from strange cities. All streams, springs, brooks, came to that ocean to be absorbed and eternized. All facts came there to be sublimated. All emotions and griefs sought the transports of euthanasia in that temple. All matter, impregnated with the instinct for the Infinite, dissolved in that menstruum. (pp. 51-4)

He was guilty of the strange heresy of impersonality. Monstrous heresy in a world of personal interests! His business lay with the Infinite. He often forgot that he was living. He often forgot to eat. Number was real. Ideas were real. But his clothes, his porridge-bowl, his body were illusions. Was he a body or an orb? Was he a personality or an absolute? Was he the transitory phenomenon called Benedict de Spinoza or a Consciousness with a million million facets?

He was absolute, orb and Consciousness. He was the sublime race-renegade. He abandoned life in order to live. He rubbed the breath of his personality off of his crystal Vision. He hanged himself with a cord that fell from etheric heights. He looked into the ocean within and plunged with hosannas.

Jason went forth to find the golden fleece. Spinoza stayed at home and found it. He quaffed from the Holy Grail each day. That monstrous vegetation that we call the emotional nature bent and broke under the colossal step of this Titan. It was his passage to power. Freedom was to him the sublimation of his emotions. He put an eye in his heart. He laid down for the world the mathematics of liberty. He gave us the sublime algebraic formulas of the way to godhood. His *Ethics* is the

Baedeker of the human soul. It is the Marseillaise of spiritual liberty.

Fate is God. Man is a wisp in the sirocco of God's breath. All life is a predestination. To weep, to regret, to pray, to hope, are weaknesses, blasphemies. Can you change the order of the Everlasting? Can you suborn the Eternal? Can you bribe the Inexorable? Can you add a personal, private link to a Chain that is of infinite length? Can you cozen the Mystical Will?

Man, the tragic comedian, less than a sun-midge, a little more than a nothing, passes through the brain of this serene god, and to him all the world is become a phantasmagoric shadow-play, mathematically precise, stamped with a rigid fatality.

"Merely a spot, an illusory play of shadow and light on the breast of the Transcendent One," sighs Spinoza as he turns with majestic calm toward the Infinite and merges his soul with the Immanent Will. (pp. 55-6)

> Benjamin De Casseres, "Spinoza," in his Forty Immortals, *Joseph Lawren, Publisher, 1926, pp. 51-6.*

WILL DURANT   (essay date 1926)

[*Durant was an American journalist, educator, and historian. He is best known for his eleven-volume nonscholarly series,* The Story of Civilization *(1935-75), a collaborative effort shared with his wife, Ariel. In a* Publishers Weekly *interview in 1975, Durant defended this monumental undertaking, declaring, "I reject the notion that only university professors can write history. There's room for an integral view, which looks at every aspect of an age—its art, its manners and morals, its philosophy, even its architecture—and shows how they all interrelate." The series was immensely popular, as was Durant's collection of revised lectures,* The Story of Philosophy. *In the following excerpt from the latter work, Durant surveys Spinoza's reception and influence among European thinkers.*]

"Blessedness," reads the last proposition of Spinoza's [*Ethics*], "is not the reward of virtue, but virtue itself." And perhaps in the like manner, immortality is not the reward of clear thinking, it is clear thought itself, as it carries up the past into the present and reaches out into the future, so overcoming the limits and narrowness of time, and catching the perspective that remains eternally behind the kaleidoscope of change; such thought is immortal because every truth is a permanent creation, part of the eternal acquisition of man, influencing him endlessly.

With this solemn and hopeful note the *Ethics* ends. Seldom has one book enclosed so much thought, and fathered so much commentary, while yet remaining so bloody a battleground for hostile interpretations. Its metaphysic may be faulty, its psychology imperfect, its theology unsatisfactory and obscure; but of the soul of the book, its spirit and essence, no man who has read it will speak otherwise than reverently. (p. 207)

"Spinoza did not seek to found a sect, and he founded none" [wrote Frederick Pollock; see excerpt dated 1899]; yet all philosophy after him is permeated with his thought. During the generation that followed his death, his name was held in abhorrence; even Hume spoke of his "hideous hypothesis"; "people talked of Spinoza," said Lessing, "as if he were a dead dog."

It was Lessing who restored him to repute. The great critic surprised Jacobi, in their famous conversation in 1784, by saying that he had been a Spinozist throughout his mature life, and affirming that "there is no other philosophy than that of Spinoza." His love of Spinoza had strengthened his friendship

with Moses Mendelssohn; and in his great play, *Nathan der Weise,* he poured into one mould that conception of the ideal Jew which had come to him from the living merchant and the dead philosopher. A few years later Herder's *Einige Gespräche über Spinoza's System* turned the attention of liberal theologians to the *Ethics;* Schleiermacher, leader of this school, wrote of "the holy and excommunicated Spinoza," while the Catholic poet, Novalis, called him "the god-intoxicated man."

Meanwhile Jacobi had brought Spinoza to the attention of Goethe; the great poet was converted, he tells us, at the first reading of the *Ethics;* it was precisely the philosophy for which his deepening soul had yearned; henceforth it pervaded his poetry and his prose. It was here that he found the lesson *dass wir entsagen sollen*—that we must accept the limitations which nature puts upon us; and it was partly by breathing the calm air of Spinoza that he rose out of the wild romanticism of *Götz* and *Werther* to the classic poise of his later life.

It was by combining Spinoza with Kant's epistemology that Fichte, Schelling and Hegel reached their varied pantheisms; it was from the *conatus sese preservandi*, the effort to preserve one's self, that Fichte's *Ich* was born, and Schopenhauer's "will to live," and Nietzsche's "will to power," and Bergson's *élan vital*. Hegel objected that Spinoza's system was too lifeless and rigid; he was forgetting this dynamic element of it and remembering only that majestic conception of God as law which he appropriated for his "Absolute Reason." But he was honest enough when he said, "To be a philosopher one must first be a Spinozist."

In England the influence of Spinoza rose on the tide of the Revolutionary movement; and young rebels like Coleridge and Wordsworth talked about "Spy-nosa" (which the spy set by the government to watch them took as a reference to his own nasal facilities) with the same ardor that animated the conversation of Russian intellectuals in the halcyon days of *Y Narod*. Coleridge filled his guests with Spinozist table-talk; and Wordsworth caught something of the philosopher's thought in his famous lines about

> Something
> Whose dwelling is the light of setting suns,
> And the round ocean, and the living air,
> And the blue sky, and in the mind of man;—
> A motion and a spirit, which impels
> All thinking things, all objects of all thought,
> And rolls through all things.

Shelley quoted the *Treatise on Religion and the State* in the original notes to *Queen Mab,* and began a translation of it for which Byron promised a preface. A fragment of this MS. came into the hands of C. S. Middleton, who took it for a work of Shelley's own, and called it "school-boy speculation . . . too crude for publication entire." In a later and tamer age George Eliot translated the *Ethics,* though she never published the translation; and one may suspect that Spencer's conception of the Unknowable owes something to Spinoza through his intimacy with the novelist. "There are not wanting men of eminence of the present day," says Belfort Bax, "who declare that in Spinoza is contained the fulness of modern science."

Perhaps so many were influenced by Spinoza because he lends himself to so many interpretations, and yields new riches at every reading. All profound utterances have varied facets for diverse minds. One may say of Spinoza what Ecclesiastes said of Wisdom: "The first man knew him not perfectly, no more shall the last find him out. For his thoughts are more than the sea, and his counsels profounder than the great deep."

On the second centenary of Spinoza's death subscriptions were collected for the erection of a statue to him at the Hague. Contributions came from every corner of the educated world; never did a monument rise upon so wide a pedestal of love. At the unveiling in 1882 Ernest Renan concluded his address with words which may fitly conclude also our chapter: "Woe to him who in passing should hurl an insult at this gentle and pensive head. He would be punished, as all vulgar souls are punished, by his very vulgarity, and by his incapacity to conceive what is divine. This man, from his granite pedestal, will point out to all men the way of blessedness which he found; and ages hence, the cultivated traveler, passing by this spot, will say in his heart, 'The truest vision ever had of God came, perhaps, here.'" (pp. 215-17)

> *Will Durant, "Spinoza," in his* The Story of Philosophy: The Lives and Opinions of the Greater Philosophers, *1926. Reprint by Garden City Publishing Co., Inc., 1930, pp. 161-217.*

A. WOLF   (essay date 1928)

[*Abraham Wolf is a highly regarded Spinoza scholar. In the following excerpt, he discusses the importance of the* Correspondence *to an understanding of Spinoza's other writings.*]

The correspondence of Spinoza is deeply interesting in many ways. It presents a pageant of the leading types of seventeenth-century mentality. It affords contemporary glimpses of important scientific researches and discoveries. It brings us into touch with some of the social and political events and tendencies of the period. It throws a flood of light on the pains and vicissitudes which accompanied the birth of the modern spirit and the emancipation of Western thought from the chains of authority and tradition, to which it had grown so accustomed as almost to dread to venture on the uncharted sea of Freedom. The letters contain things of first-rate importance for the correct interpretation of the philosophy of Spinoza; and, above all, they help one to realize something of the greatness and strength of his character—one of the greatest in the whole history of mankind. (p. 23)

[They] reveal, not only his wisdom and tact and unselfish devotion to the pursuit of knowledge, but also his amazing patience with the most trying bores, his calm indifference to the tactlessness of vulgarity of others, his painstaking endeavours to enlighten some of his superstitious correspondents, his constant readiness to help all who avowed an interest in the search for Truth, and withal his outspoken candour and his dislike of all prevarication, even at the risk of estranging some of his oldest friends. (p. 24)

The importance of Spinoza's correspondence for the adequate understanding of his philosophy is very great. Not only does it give us a more homely and less formidable account of various philosophical conceptions (such as Freedom, Duration and Time, Infinity, the Unity of Nature, etc.) than is to be found in his other writings, but some of his fundamental ideas are explained more adequately in his letters than elsewhere, at least in the sense that they are presented in a manner less liable to misinterpretation, if one studies them with an open mind and does not approach them with a mind already steeped in prejudice. It is not too much to say that some of the most mischievous misinterpretations of the philosophy of Spinoza are mainly due to an insufficient study of his letters, or at least to an insufficiently impartial study of them. (p. 58)

> *A. Wolf, in an introduction to* The Correspondence of Spinoza, *edited and translated by A. Wolf, 1928. Reprint by Russell & Russell, Inc., 1966, pp. 23-70.*

RICHARD McKEON   (essay date 1928)

[*McKeon was a highly regarded American scholar of philosophy. In the following excerpt, he discusses the unity of Spinoza's thought.*]

Spinoza, perhaps more than any other great philosopher, directed all his work to a single unvarying aim. The question of how man shall live to realize his best potentialities is never far from any problem on which he embarks. Politics, theology as it enters in the governance of man and as it affects his freedom, man's beatitude and the correction of his understanding, all these are indicated in the titles of his major works; the book which contains his fullest reflections was called an ethics and his other writings build out only practical ramifications to his central doctrine; problems which he promised to take up in his "philosophy" are treated in the *Ethics*. In its general outlines the unity of Spinoza's thought is obvious; it is not difficult to state the system of his philosophy within the limits of a thousand words, but when the investigation becomes more precise the single aim is lost among the confusion of the detailed problems through which it threads. It is clear that ethics must be based on metaphysics and physics, but since Spinoza did not trouble to treat metaphysical, mechanical, methodological problems separately, but only as they are the necessary preparation to ethics, the complications which have come out of this introduction to ethics have attracted rather more attention than has the incidental elucidation. Questions of method, science, or ontology seem to have interested Spinoza chiefly as they were relevant to ethics and he treated them only in such detail as that interest warranted; that it warranted considerable detail followed from the nature of the problem which required such sciences as introduction. Nevertheless these preparations do not always seem to have been sufficient to make his view clear, since there has been no paucity of readers who find in them only a misapprehension of the nature of God, or of the exigencies of the mathematical method, or of the efficacy of the laws of nature, the relation of body and mind, the psychology of the passions and of thinking, or the niceties of any of the dozens of philosophic or technical disciplines in which one reader or another might presume to expertness.

The work of Spinoza, consequently, so far as it needs supplement, calls for the service of disentangling this aim from all the contradictions and confusions in which it has been involved. Even that service involves at first sight a contradiction: that the salient characteristic of a work should be its unity and that the unity of it should have been most frequently overlooked. The contradiction is only in seeming. The unity which is most obvious in Spinoza's work is in the preoccupation which runs through the whole body of his thought. But no great philosophic importance could be attached to a unity of purpose, if the mass of materials and problems through which the investigation proceeded did not form itself in such wise that ethics becomes a selective compendium of all knowledge as it contributes to the knowledge of man. Beside the unity which a single purpose gives the philosophy of Spinoza there is the basis of a logical unity. The system of his philosophy is indicated at every important point, but nowhere in his works is it stated in itself and without the bias of its moral tendencies. What is apparent is a perspicacious philosophic awareness of the diverse layers of implication that can be found in any philosophic problem. But the very acuteness of the perception betrays the exposition, since Spinoza usually sees more than he can induce his reader, even with a scholium and a cross-reference, to see; perhaps if he had finished the physics he had planned, the frequent logical reservations and provisions which he introduced with a *quatenus* in all statements of actual things would be clearer. But they would be clearer only by introducing further aspects of that one distinction between the existence and essence of things, between imagination and knowledge, passion and action, duration and eternity, mode and substance, in a word, between the thing as it exists and changes and the thing as it is and persists in being.

This logical unity, more than the persistent unity of purpose, is of philosophic interest in Spinoza's work. It deserves emphasis because it is a unity evolved rather by philosophic vision than by organization or argument. It is not the unity of an outlined presentation, but rather the peripatetic unity of a conversation which progresses and in which the interlocutor remembers what was last said. The logical unity of this doctrine, therefore, fits nicely to the single purpose; not only is ethics based on physics and metaphysics but that basis is constantly in mind and its principles do not change. Eventually, as the exposition proceeds, that very changelessness becomes so directly relevant to the solution of the problems of ethics that the unity of the doctrine no longer appears as an accidental characteristic; man's best possibility of happiness is in the recognition of essences involved in and implicated in the existence of things.

It is no contradiction that this man in whom the unity and system of thought is so striking, should never have completed a single work. Of the two books he published in his lifetime, one, the **Principles of Descartes's Philosophy,** contains a fragmentary Third Part which is frankly uncompleted because the Second Part does not include the necessary proposition on fluidity; the other, the **Theologico-Political Treatise,** though it is a finished work, is poorly planned if it was to be (as its subtitle, introduction and concluding chapters seem to indicate) a work on the relation of reason and faith with particular practical application to religion and state, and not primarily a work on biblical criticism. The **Short Treatise,** at least as it comes to us, is a fragment; the **Political Treatise** and the **Correction of the Understanding** are incomplete. Moreover the latter ends abruptly in what seems a colossal logical derangement: beginning with a beautiful statement of its problem, it proceeds, with the interposition from time to time of statements of what has been done up to that point, of what does not fall in the province of this treatment and what remains to do, to so indiscriminate an interest in the bypaths that open along the road to the correction of the understanding that one could enumerate, at the point where it does stop, a dozen subjects which might conceivably have followed the last one. And with the spectacle of the dilemmas of all these works, one may be emboldened to the suggestion that even the **Ethics,** though Spinoza was ready to publish it and though by its scope and its method it is the most systematic and elaborately organized of his writings, is an incomplete work; certainly Books IV and V are open to criticism from the point of view of both organization and comprehensiveness. Spinoza's seems to have been a mind of remarkable logical sagacity, not for the architectonic presentation of ideas, but for profound and detailed analysis. The unity of his thought is properly in the principles to which he appealed unceasingly and in the systematic background of his thoughts.

In the moral application which interested Spinoza so persistently, this systematic unity appeared in the reiteration of his insistence that the life of man proceeds simultaneously along two ethical planes. Good action and intelligent action are impossible without enough understanding of God and of bodies and of the mind to make clear what is implicated in the existence of anything and in the continuance of anything, idea or essence, through change. Here are the distinct ways of knowledge, the classification of the emotions, and the relation of passion and intellect on the background of an intelligible universe in which every occurrence results from necessary causes operating according to unchanging principles. The most important philosophic convictions of Spinoza are these, and even in the **Short Treatise,** where the doctrine of the attributes is a little uncertain still, and the distinction of body and mind and their identity is not quite decisive, where the psychology of the passions is detailed shortly in a mere cartesian enumeration, and where the intuitive culmination to the rational ethics is not developed, there is a statement of this relation of God to the universe which is an explicit and as definitely crucial as any statement of it in the later works. God is ubiquitous in the writings of Spinoza because the world is intelligible, and that he should be necessary to the understanding of any part of it follows from any explanation of his nature.

Place man in the universe of contrasted things that depend on and illustrate the rationality of God, and there is the inevitable sequence of passions. The ethical problems follow as a consequence involved in them. Seen in this light the problems are clearer: the real evils of the world are not poverty, neglect, pain or any of the unavoidable accidents of life, but the perturbations of the mind. These are so set by the nature of man and of things that the whole philosophic background must be reviewed to know how they may be removed: in no way other than by understanding the nature of things could one know that the endeavor by which the mind asserts the continued existence of the body, its endeavor to understand, and its endeavor to know God are not only precisely the same, but further, are the mind's one virtue and its one effort toward perfection. Man's perfection, his freedom, and his salvation are one; all three include only the precept to act as reason dictates, and reason's dictates are according to the rational principles on which the universe is set; no one of the three could be contrary to any other. It would be a little sardonic nevertheless if that were all, if this organizing of all the sciences that they may lead to one single end found no more illuminating theoretic pronouncements than that only the good is good, not pleasure, riches, or fame, that the beginning of virtue is self-interest, that our end in action should be so to act that our actions depend as largely as possible on ourselves alone, and that our only secure happiness is one which has its formal cause in our own mind. But there is more; not in the plan of social reform nor in the catalogue of the passions to which it is joined, but precisely in the depth of philosophic implication on which they are founded; virtue significantly is most complete when such things as these are understood best and most completely. Since there is this system which must lie behind Spinoza's conclusions to his moral problems, on even ethical grounds the fundamental unity of it deserves to have been restated and reëxamined, for this is the very knowledge of the union the mind has with all nature and therefore it not only contains the possibility and safeguard of that which is supremely good, but is itself the supreme good. (pp. 313-17)

Richard McKeon, in his The Philosophy of Spinoza: The Unity of His Thought, *Longmans, Green and Co., 1928, 345 p.*

PAUL ELMER MORE   (lecture date 1934)

[*More was an American critic who, along with Irving Babbitt, formulated the doctrines of New Humanism in early twentieth-century American thought. He is especially esteemed for the philosophical and literary erudition of his multi-volume* Shelburne Essays *(1904-21). In the following excerpt from the text of a lecture originally delivered in 1934, More attempts to summarize Spinoza's thought, judging Spinoza's efficacy as an explicator of metaphysics and religion.*]

No one can read the works and letters of Spinoza without being impressed by the depth and sincerity of his religious conviction or without seeing that his whole philosophy is a search for the peace of God which is not of this world. His treatise on the **Emendation of the Intellect** begins with a confession of the vanity and futility of all earthly goods which hitherto he had desired, and with a statement of his determination to look for that true and communicable Good which, being found and acquired, will lead to the eternity of perfect joy. And that Good is nothing less than God. "For this," he declares in the **Tractatus,** "is involved in the very idea of God, that God is our *summum bonum,* and that the knowledge and love of God is the ultimate end to which all our actions should be directed." The words are little more than a paraphrase of St. Augustine's famous sentence, *Inquietum est cor nostrum donec requiescat in te* ["The heart of man is restless until it finds its rest in Thee"]; and to this goal of divine rest the whole argument of the *Ethics* is pointed. It is not without reason that Spinoza has been called "the God-intoxicated," and that he is reckoned among the saints of philosophy.

But if the goal of Spinoza is religious, his chosen way thereto is profoundly and radically irreligious. And there lies the ambush of defeat. He will not be content to start with the first faint glimmering of spiritual light, and to follow its guidance, if perchance it may lead step by step to ever clearer knowledge and deeper love; at once he must *know,* must know in such wise that the object of knowledge shall be identical with the knowing of it, a something defined in the strictest terms of logic, tucked comfortably into a pure theorem of reason, with no frayed edges of conjecture or inference, with no penumbra about it of half-knowledge wherein the imagination may set up its dance of indecent shadows. To this end his theology will purge itself utterly, at a bound, of every taint of anthropomorphism; he will sweep clean. Our human distinctions of good and evil are mere prejudices; we think ourselves free because we hug the delusions of consciousness rather than look at external facts; we imagine a purpose where there is only fatality. And so, if we are deceived about ourselves, how doubly are we deceived when we transfer these anthropomorphic illusions to God. To Spinoza a God, the only God commensurate with a syllogism, can have nothing to do with any ultimate distinctions of right and wrong, can be endowed with nothing corresponding to our supposed human liberty, and above all cannot act for a purpose—above all, for our saint of philosophy fairly grinds his teeth at the bare mention of a cosmic teleology as "doing away with God's perfection." Having thus rejected the very method of faith, with its inference of a Being transcendent yet analogous to our human intuition of conscience, he will turn to the observation of nature for his formula. There he sees a number of things of each of which we say that it is: hence he will abstract the notion of pure Being, not a being which is what it is, but just *Is;* seeing a cause why each thing acts as it acts, he will abstract the notion of pure causality, not a cause of these different actions, but the necessity that being can be only being; seeing that each thing is

a unit amidst other units, he will abstract the notion of pure Unity, not the one supreme thing above all others, but the identity of being with itself as a predicate without any subject or, if you prefer, a subject without any predicate. Hence a God who can be handed about in a single word as absolute Being or Causality or Unity, all of which terms are interchangeable since they are equally without content, and no one of which implies any brute facts to account for.

A more neatly expurgated Deity could not be devised for the comfort of human reason. It defies the atheist, for who shall be bold enough to question the being of Being—if only such a Being could be cured of the prestidigitator's trick of suddenly disappearing and as suddenly reappearing as Not-Being. Indeed the more honest of the metaphysical idealists and their still more honest cousins, the mystics, have not shrunk from this confluence of the *via positiva* and the *via negativa* in the capacious ocean of the Absolute. It was of them that a witty President of Princeton University used to say: "When you take from anything that which makes it something, what you have left is nothing."

Nor could the human brain demand a more tightly formulated idea of God as an axiom from which the whole universe shall be unfolded in a series of logical propositions, just as the properties of a triangle, to use Spinoza's favourite illustration, flow from its definition. The only difficulty is that this world of our actual experience has properties quite different from those of a triangle and refuses to be netted in a mathematical formula. And so the central part of Spinoza's *Ethics* strives desperately to deal logically with a perfectly illogical and arbitrary hypothesis. That absolute Being from which all being things are to be taken out, like rabbits from a magician's hat, is at once the negation of all attributes and the affirmation of all attributes. Now that sounds a bit paradoxical; but not, the metaphysician will say, if you approach it in the right spirit. He will tell you that absolute Being is "a substance consisting of infinite attributes, each one of which expresses eternal and infinite essence." You see how deftly the paradox is resolved; if your Absolute includes an infinite number of attributes, it will be all-inclusive, and, if each of these attributes is infinite no one of them will imply anything finite and the sum of them is all-exclusive of limitations. To be sure only two of this infinite number of attributes are known to the human brain, viz. space and thought; but neither of these need bother you. The attribute of infinite space is perfectly innocuous, since it has nothing in it, no material bodies, no forms, no limitations of any sort; and infinite thought is equally harmless, since it is not a mind thinking about something nor a something about which a mind is thinking, but just thought without any limiting content. No one can accuse you of inconsistency in attributing to your Absolute infinite attributes that attribute nothing. If only the world would submit to your logic! If only you could burke the question of actual experience! What are you going to do with these horrid material bodies that appear to move about in space and with these finite thoughts that seem to be jostling about in our brains? Enter the convenient devil of the imagination. These bodies do not really exist, we only imagine them; we are not really thinking about anything concrete, we only imagine we are doing so. But you must not ask how this cunning serpent of the imagination crept into the Paradise of pure Reason; or, if you do ask, you will get no answer. (pp. 101-04)

If any one thing is certain it is that the quasi-religious metaphysics of Spinoza and Kant simply crumples up under the acid test of scepticism. If any one lesson can be surely learnt from Kant as well as from Spinoza, it is that the endeavour to escape the human condition of intellectual impotence ends invariably in a denial of human responsibility. The sceptic and the man of faith, though they may not understand each other, can live together in mutual respect. Nor is there anything unreasonable in the mental attitude of the sceptic who, seeing the fruits of religion in the enrichment of human life, sets out upon the great experiment of faith. But between religion and metaphysics there is a deep gulf fixed and an irreconcilable feud. The bottom of that severing abyss is strewn with the wrecks of noble efforts to throw a bridge over the broken trail, from the great scholastics of the Middle Ages to such more recent champions of rationalized religion as Bradley and Pringle-Pattison and James Ward and our esteemed contemporaries, Professors Whitehead and Hocking. (pp. 115-116)

Paul Elmer More, "Illusions of Reason," in his The Sceptical Approach to Religion, *Princeton University Press, 1934, pp. 95-117.*

BERTRAND RUSSELL (essay date 1945)

[*A respected and prolific author, Russell was an English philosopher and mathematician known for his support of humanistic concerns. Two of his early works,* Principles of Mathematics *(1903) and* Principia Mathematica *(1910-1913), written with Alfred North Whitehead, are considered classics of mathematical logic. His philosophical approach to all his endeavors discounts idealism or emotionalism and asserts a progressive application of his "logical atomism," a process whereby individual facts are logically analyzed. Russell's humanistic beliefs often centered around support of unorthodox social concerns, including free love, undisciplined education, and the eradication of nuclear weapons. Regarding Russell, biographer Alan Wood states: "He started by asking questions about mathematics and religion and philosophy, and went on to question accepted ideas about war and politics and sex and education, setting the minds of men on the march, so that the world could never be quite the same as if he had not lived." In recognition of his contributions in a number of literary genres, Russell was awarded the Nobel Prize in literature in 1950. In the following excerpt, Russell explicates the main theses of* Ethics *and critically evaluates its worth and relevance in the twentieth century.*]

Spinoza . . . is the noblest and most lovable of the great philosophers. Intellectually, some others have surpassed him, but ethically he is supreme. As a natural consequence, he was considered, during his lifetime and for a century after his death, a man of appalling wickedness. He was born a Jew, but the Jews excommunicated him. Christians abhorred him equally; although his whole philosophy is dominated by the idea of God, the orthodox accused him of atheism. Leibniz, who owed much to him, concealed his debt, and carefully abstained from saying a word in his praise; he even went so far as to lie about the extent of his personal acquaintance with the heretic Jew. (p. 569)

Spinoza's chief work, the *Ethics,* was published posthumously. Before considering it, a few words must be said about two of his other books, the *Tractatus Theologico-Politicus* and the *Tractatus Politicus.* The former is a curious combination of biblical criticism and political theory; the latter deals with political theory only. In biblical criticism Spinoza partially anticipates modern views, particularly in assigning much later dates to various books of the Old Testament than those assigned by tradition. He endeavours throughout to show that the Scrip-

tures can be interpreted so as to be compatible with a liberal theology.

Spinoza's political theory is, in the main, derived from Hobbes, in spite of the enormous temperamental difference between the two men. He holds that in a state of nature there is no right or wrong, for wrong consists in disobeying the law. He holds that the sovereign can do no wrong, and agrees with Hobbes that the Church should be entirely subordinate to the State. He is opposed to all rebellion, even against a bad government, and instances the troubles in England as a proof of the harm that comes of forcible resistance to authority. But he disagrees with Hobbes in thinking democracy the "most natural" form of government. He disagrees also in holding that subjects should not sacrifice *all* their rights to the sovereign. In particular, he holds freedom of opinion important. I do not quite know how he reconciles this with the opinion that religious questions should be decided by the State. I think when he says this he means that they should be decided by the State rather than the Church; in Holland the State was much more tolerant than the Church.

Spinoza's *Ethics* deals with three distinct matters. It begins with metaphysics; it then goes on to the psychology of the passions and the will; and finally it sets forth an ethic based on the preceding metaphysics and psychology. The metaphysic is a modification of Descartes, the psychology is reminiscent of Hobbes, but the ethic is original, and is what is of most value in the book. The relation of Spinoza to Descartes is in some ways not unlike the relation of Plotinus to Plato. Descartes was a many-sided man, full of intellectual curiosity, but not much burdened with moral earnestness. Although he invented "proofs" intended to support orthodox beliefs, he could have been used by sceptics as Carneades used Plato. Spinoza, although he was not without scientific interests, and even wrote a treatise on the rainbow, was in the main concerned with religion and virtue. He accepted from Descartes and his contemporaries a materialistic and deterministic physics, and sought, within this framework, to find room for reverence and a life devoted to the Good. His attempt was magnificent, and rouses admiration even in those who do not think it successful.

The metaphysical system of Spinoza is of the type inaugurated by Parmenides. There is only one substance, "God or Nature"; nothing finite is self-subsistent. Descartes admitted three substances, God and mind and matter; it is true that, even for him, God was, in a sense, *more* substantial than mind and matter, since He had created them, and could, if He chose, annihilate them. But except in relation to God's omnipotence, mind and matter were two independent substances, defined, respectively, by the attributes of thought and extension. Spinoza would have none of this. For him, thought and extension were both attributes of God. God has also an infinite number of other attributes, since He must be in every respect infinite; but these others are unknown to us. Individual souls and separate pieces of matter are, for Spinoza, adjectival; they are not *things*, but merely aspects of the divine Being. There can be no such personal immortality as Christians believe in, but only that impersonal sort that consists in becoming more and more one with God. Finite things are defined by their boundaries, physical or logical, that is to say, by what they are *not*: "all determination is negation." There can be only one Being who is wholly positive, and He must be absolutely infinite. Hence Spinoza is led to a complete and undiluted pantheism.

Everything, according to Spinoza, is ruled by an absolute logical necessity. There is no such thing as free will in the mental sphere or chance in the physical world. Everything that happens is a manifestation of God's inscrutable nature, and it is logically impossible that events should be other than they are. This leads to difficulties in regard to sin, which critics were not slow to point out. One of them, observing that, according to Spinoza, everything is decreed by God and is therefore good, asks indignantly: Was it good that Nero should kill his mother? Was it good that Adam ate the apple? Spinoza answers that what was positive in these acts was good, and only what was negative was bad; but negation exists only from the point of view of finite creatures. In God, who alone is completely real, there is no negation, and therefore the evil in what to us seem sins does not exist when they are viewed as parts of the whole. This doctrine, though, in one form or another, it has been held by most mystics, cannot, obviously, be reconciled with the orthodox doctrine of sin and damnation. It is bound up with Spinoza's complete rejection of free will. Although not at all polemical, Spinoza was too honest to conceal his opinions, however shocking to contemporaries; the abhorrence of his teaching is therefore not surprising.

The *Ethics* is set forth in the style of Euclid, with definitions, axioms, and theorems; everything after the axioms is supposed to be rigorously demonstrated by deductive argument. This makes him difficult reading. A modern student, who cannot suppose that there are rigorous "proofs" of such things as he professes to establish, is bound to grow impatient with the detail of the demonstrations, which is, in fact, not worth mastering. It is enough to read the enunciations of the propositions, and to study the scholia, which contain much of what is best in the *Ethics.* But it would show a lack of understanding to blame Spinoza for his geometrical method. It was of the essence of his system, ethically as well as metaphysically, to maintain that everything *could* be demonstrated, and it was therefore essential to produce demonstrations. *We* cannot accept his method, but that is because we cannot accept his metaphysic. We cannot believe that the interconnections of the parts of the universe are *logical,* because we hold that scientific laws are to be discovered by observation, not by reasoning alone. But for Spinoza the geometrical method was necessary, and was bound up with the most essential parts of his doctrine. (pp. 569-72)

The last two books of the *Ethics,* entitled respectively "Of human bondage, or the strength of the emotions" and "Of the power of the understanding, or of human freedom," are the most interesting. We are in bondage in proportion as what happens to us is determined by outside causes, and we are free in proportion as we are self-determined. Spinoza, like Socrates and Plato, believes that all wrong action is due to intellectual error: the man who adequately understands his own circumstances will act wisely, and will even be happy in the face of what to another would be misfortune. He makes no appeal to unselfishness; he holds that self-seeking, in some sense, and more particularly self-preservation, govern all human behaviour. "No virtue can be conceived as prior to this endeavour to preserve one's own being." But his conception of what a wise man will choose as the goal of his self-seeking is different from that of the ordinary egoist: "The mind's highest good is the knowledge of God, and the mind's highest virtue is to know God." Emotions are called "passions" when they spring from inadequate ideas; passions in different men may conflict, but men who live in obedience to reason will agree together. Pleasure in itself is good, but hope and fear are bad, and so are humility and repentance: "he who repents of an action is doubly wretched or infirm." Spinoza regards time as unreal, and there-

fore all emotions which have to do essentially with an event as future or as past are contrary to reason. "In so far as the mind conceives a thing under the dictate of reason, it is affected equally, whether the idea be of a thing present, past, or future."

This is a hard saying, but it is of the essence of Spinoza's system, and we shall do well to dwell upon it for a moment. In popular estimation, "all's well that ends well"; if the universe is gradually improving, we think, better of it than if it is gradually deteriorating, even if the sum of good and evil be the same in the two cases. We are more concerned about a disaster in our own time than in the time of Genghis Khan. According to Spinoza, this is irrational. Whatever happens is part of the eternal timeless world as God sees it; to Him, the date is irrelevant. The wise man, so far as human finitude allows, endeavours to see the world as God sees it, *sub specie æternitatis,* under the aspect of eternity. But, you may retort, we are surely right in being more concerned about future misfortunes, which may possibly be averted, than about past calamities about which we can do nothing. To this argument Spinoza's determinism supplies the answer. Only ignorance makes us think that we can alter the future; what will be will be, and the future is as unalterably fixed as the past. That is why hope and fear are condemned: both depend upon viewing the future as uncertain, and therefore spring from lack of wisdom.

When we acquire, in so far as we can, a vision of the world which is analogous to God's, we see everything as part of the whole, and as necessary to the goodness of the whole. Therefore "the knowledge of evil is an inadequate knowledge." God has no knowledge of evil, because there is no evil to be known; the appearance of evil only arises through regarding parts of the universe as if they were self-subsistent.

Spinoza's outlook is intended to liberate men from the tyranny of fear. "A free man thinks of nothing less than of death; and his wisdom is a meditation not of death, but of life." Spinoza lived up to this precept very completely. On the last day of his life he was entirely calm, not exalted, like Socrates in the *Phaedo,* but conversing, as he would on any other day, about matters of interest to his interlocutor. Unlike some other philosophers, he not only believed his own doctrines, but practised them; I do not know of any occasion, in spite of great provocation, in which he was betrayed into the kind of heat or anger that his ethic condemned. In controversy he was courteous and reasonable, never denouncing, but doing his utmost to persuade. (pp. 573-74)

The *Ethics* ends with these words:

> The wise man, in so far as he is regarded as such, is scarcely at all disturbed in spirit, but being conscious of himself, and of God, and of things, by a certain eternal necessity, never ceases to be, but always possesses true acquiescence of his spirit. If the way which I have pointed out as leading to this result seems exceedingly hard, it may nevertheless be discovered. Needs must it be hard, since it is so seldom found. How would it be possible, if salvation were ready to our hand, and could without great labour be found, that it should be by almost all men neglected? But all excellent things are as difficult as they are rare.

In forming a critical estimate of Spinoza's importance as a philosopher, it is necessary to distinguish his ethics from his metaphysics, and to consider how much of the former can survive the rejection of the latter.

Spinoza's metaphysic is the best example of what may be called "logical monism"—the doctrine, namely, that the world as a whole is a single substance, none of whose parts are logically capable of existing alone. The ultimate basis for this view is the belief that every proposition has a single subject and a single predicate, which leads us to the conclusion that relations and plurality must be illusory. Spinoza thought that the nature of the world and of human life could be logically deduced from self-evident axioms; we ought to be as resigned to events as to the fact that 2 and 2 are 4, since they are equally the outcome of logical necessity. The whole of this metaphysic is impossible to accept; it is incompatible with modern logic and with scientific method. *Facts* have to be discovered by observation, not by reasoning; when we successfully infer the future, we do so by means of principles which are not logically necessary, but are suggested by empirical data. And the concept of substance, upon which Spinoza relies, is one which neither science nor philosophy can nowadays accept.

But when we come to Spinoza's ethics, we feel—or at least I feel—that something, though not everything, can be accepted even when the metaphysical foundation has been rejected. Broadly speaking, Spinoza is concerned to show how it is possible to live nobly even when we recognize the limits of human power. He himself, by his doctrine of necessity, makes these limits narrower than they are; but when they indubitably exist, Spinoza's maxims are probably the best possible. Take, for instance, death: nothing that a man can do will make him immortal, and it is therefore futile to spend time in fears and lamentations over the fact that we must die. To be obsessed by the fear of death is a kind of slavery; Spinoza is right in saying that "the free man thinks of nothing less than of death." But even in this case, it is only death in general that should be so treated; death of any particular disease should, if possible, be averted by submitting to medical care. What should, even in this case, be avoided, is a certain kind of anxiety or terror; the necessary measures should be taken calmly, and our thoughts should, as far as possible, be then directed to other matters. The same considerations apply to all other purely personal misfortunes.

But how about misfortunes to people whom you love? Let us think of some of the things that are likely to happen in our time to inhabitants of Europe or China. Suppose you are a Jew, and your family has been massacred. Suppose you are an underground worker against the Nazis, and your wife has been shot because you could not be caught. Suppose your husband, for some purely imaginary crime, has been sent to forced labour in the Arctic, and has died of cruelty and starvation. Suppose your daughter has been raped and then killed by enemy soldiers. Ought you, in these circumstances, to preserve a philosophic calm?

If you follow Christ's teaching, you will say "Father, forgive them, for they know not what they do." I have known Quakers who could have said this sincerely and profoundly, and whom I admired because they could. But before giving admiration one must be very sure that the misfortune is felt as deeply as it should be. One cannot accept the attitude of some among the Stoics, who said, "What does it matter to me if my family suffer? I can still be virtuous." The Christian principle, "Love your enemies," is good, but the Stoic principle, "Be indifferent to your friends," is bad. And the Christian principle does not inculcate calm, but an ardent love even towards the worst of men. There is nothing to be said against it except that it is too difficult for most of us to practise sincerely.

The primitive reaction to such disasters is revenge. When Macduff learns that his wife and children have been killed by Macbeth, he resolves to kill the tyrant himself. This reaction is still admired by most people, when the injury is great, and such as to arouse moral horror in disinterested people. Nor can it be wholly condemned, for it is one of the forces generating punishment, and punishment is sometimes necessary. Moreover, from the point of view of mental health, the impulse to revenge is likely to be so strong that, if it is allowed no outlet, a man's whole outlook on life may become distorted and more or less insane. This is not true universally, but it is true in a large percentage of cases. But on the other side it must be said that revenge is a very dangerous motive. In so far as society admits it, it allows a man to be the judge in his own case, which is exactly what the law tries to prevent. Moreover it is usually an excessive motive; it seeks to inflict more punishment than is desirable. Torture, for example, should not be punished by torture, but the man maddened by lust for vengeance will think a painless death too good for the object of his hate. Moreover—and it is here that Spinoza is in the right—a life dominated by a single passion is a narrow life, incompatible with every kind of wisdom. Revenge as such is therefore not the best reaction to injury.

Spinoza would say what the Christian says, and also something more. For him, all sin is due to ignorance; he would "forgive them, for they know not what they do." But he would have you avoid the limited purview from which, in his opinion, sin springs, and would urge you, even under the greatest misfortunes, to avoid being shut up in the world of your sorrow; he would have you understand it by seeing it in relation to its causes and as a part of the whole order of nature. As we saw, he believes that hatred can be overcome by love: "Hatred is increased by being reciprocated, and can on the other hand be destroyed by love. Hatred which is completely vanquished by love, passes into love; and love is thereupon greater, than if hatred had not preceded it." I wish I could believe this, but I cannot, except in exceptional cases where the person hating is completely in the power of the person who refuses to hate in return. In such cases, surprise at being not punished may have a reforming effect. But so long as the wicked have power, it is not much use assuring them that you do not hate them, since they will attribute your words to the wrong motive. And you cannot deprive them of power by non-resistance.

The problem for Spinoza is easier than it is for one who has no belief in the ultimate goodness of the universe. Spinoza thinks that, if you see your misfortunes as they are in reality, as part of the concatenation of causes stretching from the beginning of time to the end, you will see that they are only misfortunes to you, not to the universe, to which they are merely passing discords heightening an ultimate harmony. I cannot accept this; I think that particular events are what they are, and do not become different by absorption into a whole. Each act of cruelty is eternally a part of the universe; nothing that happens later can make that act good rather than bad, or can confer perfection on the whole of which it is a part.

Nevertheless, when it is your lot to have to endure something that is (or seems to you) worse than the ordinary lot of mankind, Spinoza's principle of thinking about the whole, or at any rate about larger matters than your own grief, is a useful one. There are even times when it is comforting to reflect that human life, with all that it contains of evil and suffering, is an infinitesimal part of the life of the universe. Such reflections may not suffice to constitute a religion, but in a painful world they are a help towards sanity and an antidote to the paralysis of utter despair. (pp. 577-80)

Bertrand Russell, *"Modern Philosophy: Spinoza,"* in his A History of Western Philosophy, and Its Connection with Political and Social Circumstances from the Earliest Times to the Present Day, *Simon & Schuster, 1945, pp. 569-80.*

ALBERT EINSTEIN (essay date 1946)

[*Einstein was a German-born mathematician, physicist, and astronomer whose theory of relativity (based on the equation $E = mc^2$) greatly revolutionized scientific conceptions of time, space, and gravitational force. In the following excerpt, he considers Spinoza as an exemplary, enlightened philosopher.*]

Although he lived three hundred years before our time, the spiritual situation with which Spinoza had to cope peculiarly resembles our own. The reason for this is that he was utterly convinced of the causal dependence of all phenomena, at a time when the success accompanying the efforts to achieve a knowledge of the causal relationship of natural phenomena was still quite modest. Spinoza's conviction extended not only to inanimate nature but also to human feelings and actions. He had no doubt that our notion of possessing a free will (i.e. independent of causality) was an illusion resulting from our ignorance of the causes operative within us. In the study of this causal relationship he saw a remedy for fear, hate and bitterness, the only remedy to which a genuinely spiritual man can have recourse. He demonstrated his justification for this conviction not only by the clear, precise formulation of his thoughts, but also by the exemplary fashioning of his own life. (p. xi)

Albert Einstein, in an introduction to Spinoza: Portrait of a Spiritual Hero *by Rudolf Kayser, translated by Amy Allen and Maxim Newmark, Philosophical Library, 1946, pp. ix-xi.*

KARL JASPERS (essay date 1957)

[*Jaspers was a German psychiatrist and philosopher noted for his existentialist theories, particularly his belief that existence is equivalent to time and transcendence (a state attained through the perseverance of reason) analogous to eternity. In the following excerpt from a study originally published in German in 1957, he discusses the philosophical character and essential beliefs of Spinoza.*]

Spinoza appears to be the most thoroughgoing of rationalists. But it is a strange fact that although in Spinoza compelling logical thought expresses the absolute and is itself authentic reality, this thought is *amor intellectualis dei* ["the intellectual love of God"] and as such beatitude. This thought is freedom from passions which, when elucidated by it, cease to be passions. It is not, like finite thinking, content to apprehend objects which are modes, but finds its completion as reason in the third class of knowledge, in the free speculation of loving intuition. Such thinking was bound to be more than the compelling logical thought which on the surface it always remained. Spinoza transcended thought, insofar as thought is taken as a universally valid operation with fixed concepts. His thinking is a new form of the age-old philosophical contemplation which is an inner action and shapes the whole man.

Let us recapitulate in Spinoza's own words: "Once I am in possession of a reliable proof, I cannot fall back into such ideas

as ever to make me doubt this proof. Consequently I am perfectly satisfied with what my understanding shows me, without the least anxiety that I might have been mistaken in it. . . . And even if I should once mistakenly invent the fruit that I have gained from my natural understanding, it would still make me happy, because I strive to spend my life not in sorrow and grief, but in peace, joy, and serenity, and so rise up by degrees. In so doing I recognize (and this is what gives me the greatest satisfaction and peace of mind) that everything so happens through the power of the most perfect being and of His immutable decision."

Spinoza lived and thought on the basis of the fundamental certainty for which God's reality is present in the third class of knowledge as the one all-embracing reality. Starting from this reality, Spinoza takes three courses in the world: to metaphysical knowledge, to personal existence, to the political order. In the language of the second class of knowledge, he develops the communicable knowledge of the totality of Being, of God, the world, and man. By investigating man's affects he finds the way to liberation from them, the happiness and salvation of man through pure insight. In viewing the reality of human society, he investigates the state and revealed religion, in order to set forth an ideal frame in which all human potentialities may unfold in accordance with reason. (p. 378)

This self-conscious rational thinking was Spinoza's life. He was the only one among the great philosophers of the seventeenth century to build his whole life on philosophy without the security of authority and revealed faith, without any misleading concessions to the powers of the time. He was the great, truly independent thinker representative of the Occident, who found in philosophy what churchgoers called their faith. In him was renewed the independence of philosophy, which has no need of ecclesiastical faith, because it is itself faith.

Such philosophy has been called "philosophical religion" in contrast to ecclesiastical religion. In this sense the great philosophy of antiquity was religion, and in this sense all metaphysics is religion. But in using this word we must not forget that philosophical religion has neither cult, nor prayer, nor institutions, nor Church. Like "philosophical faith," "philosophical religion" refers to a thinking with which and by which philosophical man lives, so that everything he does, everything that happens to him, everything he knows, is brought into this area, is illumined, assimilated, and judged from this source. (p. 379)

From the very beginning Spinoza's philosophy was ethos. This is attested by the explanation that he gave in his youth for his decision to take up philosophy, and by the title of his main work, the ***Ethics***. . . . [This ethos] includes features that do not spring from Spinoza's innate being but are a consequence of Spinoza's contact with the world.

Caution: Despite the love of God that was present in Spinoza's whole view of the world, despite the benevolence he felt toward every man he met, Spinoza also felt keen distrust; for he knew the reality of the world. Hence his caution without defiance or blame.

Spinoza gave freely of himself but did not squander his strength: he was on his guard against negligence, and reasonably so, for he knew the harm that can spring from it.

He renounced all idea of fame. Even academic activity involved too much danger in those days, and so he declined it. He delayed publication of his works, but he wrote them—without haste—in the hope of broadening the scope of reason in the world.

Not a recluse, but solitary: Spinoza was formerly regarded as a recluse. The studies of the last half-century have exploded this legend. Not only was Spinoza in touch, through friends and acquaintances, with the whole cultural world of Europe, but he also took part in political activity. There was nothing of the eccentric about him; wherever he went his bearing was easy, natural, noble; he was not only respected, but loved as well.

It is a different matter to say that Spinoza was a solitary man. In his philosophizing he gained a "standpoint outside," in God, and he did not relate his philosophy to worldly affairs. On the one hand he was perfectly independent thanks to his certainty of God, on the other hand he had many human contacts which sufficed him, but did not take away his solitude. The consequence is that for us Spinoza seems to lack the love which unites men in their uniqueness, which through companionship and community of destiny leads to unconditional historical commitment. Spinoza was always himself. And what he thought and set forth was the universal, the cool but utterly satisfying realm of thought, the *amor intellectualis dei,* which was his life itself in its highest aspect, in reason. In conversation Spinoza must have been very different from Kant or Max Weber, for example. His almost superhuman calm would elate us. Imperturbable in all situations, he would speak from the standpoint of eternal truth. He would not concern himself seriously with actual realities, but pass them over as nonessential. We should sit in silence, increasingly aware of our own rebelliousness against fate. (p. 380)

Did Spinoza wish to be a model and prototype? We have no reason to suppose so. Did he wish to show future generations the way? He did not think in historical, reformist perspectives. He wished to live and work in reason, uncertain as to what would come of it.

Or did he regard himself as an exception, condemned by the conflict between his own nature and the existing order to suffer a repugnant fate? No, this too was not the case. He was confident of the natural and appropriate character of his living and thinking. In his work as in his life, he was a healthy, normal man, free from psychological upheavals and crises, free from the endless reflection that drains the mind, never touched by despair in the presence of the void (his illness, tuberculosis, was purely physical; it was able to carry him off at any early age, but not to affect his nature). He must have incurred eclipses of reason, he must have experienced the affects, of which he spoke so knowingly, but only as passing states that vanish once they are understood. (p. 381)

Spinoza has been called a naturalistic, atheistic, amoral philosopher and a precursor of Marxism. But nature in Spinoza is neither the nature of a modern, mechanical, mathematical physics, nor an organic, teleologically structured nature, nor a demonic, sympathetic world; it is the nature of God, conceived as *natura naturans;* in Spinoza's *"deus sive natura,"* the accent is on God. Spinoza's thinking is so far from atheism that Hegel preferred to call it acosmism, because everything is in God, so that no independent, created world, separate from God, is left. His sober view of the natural realities and of God's reality as beyond good and evil has been misinterpreted as amoralism. Acutally his life and work are unswervingly sustained by the living morality of natural reason.

It has been said that as a political thinker Spinoza was interested only in the security of philosophers, in the question: How must state and religion be conceived and actually constructed in order that the wise man may be unmolested in his private life? Epicureans and skeptics may have looked at the state in this light, but neither Plato nor Spinoza. They did not seek to guarantee the security of the philosopher by showing that philosophy and politics are incommensurable and advising philosophers to withdraw from the world (except in particular times and under particular circumstances). They are concerned, rather, with philosophical politics over against blind politics; they have in mind all men and aspire to a state in which all will obtain their proper place and right according to their gifts, insight, and affectivity. The impulse which has been mistaken as a striving for the philosopher's security (which can be safeguarded only by private caution) is rather the impulse to promote reason in the world.

Another criticism is that Spinoza's "Being" is geometrical and static, that time is dismissed as mere appearance. Consequently nature is conceived in timeless mathematical formulas, process is denied and with it history. In the opposite direction a "dynamic" view has been imputed to Spinoza: striving, power, perseverance-in-being and self-assertion, all involved in everlasting change in the realm of modes. These criticisms cancel each other out. Both are right to a certain degree, but they apply only to certain elements in the philosophy, not to its substance. The fallacy of such criticism is to take mere figures of thought for the whole instead of understanding their function for the philosopher's fundamental thought. Although Spinoza's thinking is systematic, it cannot adequately be set forth as a system. It is a simple matter to "refute" it by picking out one systematic view and neglecting the rest. This is to treat philosophy as statement of fact and absolute assertion, as objective and finite knowledge. (pp. 382-83)

Spinoza's limits are the limits of reason. Because Spinoza does not seem to see the limits of reason, perhaps reality as a whole is closed to him. This is where the profoundest criticism of Spinoza sets in.

The limits of reason can be seen by reason itself. Spinoza seems to have an inkling of this when, in speaking of the infinity of the modes, he says that our ignorance of the endlessness of finite relationships is everlasting and that so many—in fact, nearly all—particulars are incomprehensible to us. But this ignorance is only a consequence of finiteness. In principle, knowledge of these matters is possible, because everything comes from God and is rational.

Spinoza seems to see beyond reason still more clearly when he considers that all our reason is encompassed in divine necessity and represents our human reason as helplessly at the mercy of the necessity of all nature, which it is powerless to understand. But Spinoza seems to take it for granted that this necessity is also divinely rational. The irrational only appears to be irrational to our finite understanding. The encompassing God is not a dark abyss. He is not accessible by any obscure ways, but only through the light of reason itself, which if it could overcome its bond with the limited mode would understand everything as reason. Our human reason is itself divine reason, but in a limited form. Our reason is itself natural, an element in *natura naturata,* but not encompassed and not threatened and not limited by something that is more than reason, by a god that is above and before reason, source of reason but also of everything else. God in Spinoza is reason itself. His consciousness of God does not transcend reason.

Thus convinced of the absoluteness of reason, Spinoza anticipated a day when all men would necessarily unite in reason—a grandiose assumption, but only in reference to practical endeavor, not as an insight into the universe and mankind as a whole.

Another aspect of Spinoza's belief in the absoluteness of reason was the pure, passionless joy of his awareness of God. To him freedom was freedom from affects, pure unclouded clarity, beatitude. Freedom is not decision, not the basis of destiny.

Finally, Spinoza's rationalism made him despise all feelings of wonderment. A reasoning man tries to understand the things of nature "with wisdom," "not to gape at them like a fool." "If ignorance is removed, amazement is also taken away." Amazement becomes harmful when it induces blind subjection to authority, miracles, and supernatural forces. (pp. 383-84)

He found no answer to the question: Why are there individuals? For to say that all things "follow" eternally from God (as the sum of the angles of a triangle follows from the essence of a triangle) is not an answer, but a mere statement of the fact that individual things are connected with their source. It is only a metaphor pointing to something that thought cannot fathom, a leap from *logos* to reality. Conceived from the standpoint of eternity, the individual—a mere mode—loses all importance and vanishes.

The statement that *omnis determinatio est negatio* expresses the truth as to the insignificance of individuals, but it also makes possible the error of denying that Existenz derives eternal importance from the irreplaceable character of its embodiment.

Does the renunciation of individuality bring with it blindness to the irreplaceable character of Existenz (though not to the reality of Spinoza's own Existenz)? Liberation from the bonds of individuality might mislead one into sacrificing Existenz in its historicity, into sacrificing that which is eternal in human destiny. As Spinoza states it, eternal immortality of the soul is not very different from the immortality of impersonal reason as such (the *intellectus agens* of Averroës). . . . (p. 384)

By negating time, Spinoza destroys historicity. The world ceases to be fragmented by the riddle of time, the depth of historicity, the opaque ground of all things. No longer is it incumbent on us to attain to transcendence in time, through historical Existenz. History loses its meaning as a temporal process that can never be completed, because the weight of Existenz is absorbed by God. There seems to be only eternity, not time, only God and no world.

The weight of action rooted in our situation is lost; there remains only the inner action of loving ascent to God. Spinoza knows necessity, but he does not know uncertainty, hope, and failure in the active historicity of Existenz. Time is effaced, but it should also be preserved, because without it there can be no true consciousness of eternity. There can be no historicity in a life which moves from metaphysics to metaphysics without striking meaningful roots in temporal reality. Historicity is absent when activity is limited to reasonable thinking without a driving will, when the great venture of reason is not experienced as historical destiny. Consequently Spinoza is not attracted by the depth and grandeur which (as in the Jewish Prophets) are still obscure and demand that a man venture all and sacrifice all. Wholly taken up by pure reason as the type of human being and of all being, he is blind to the passions

of the night, which to him are mere irrational affects. He is blind to evil.

Spinoza rejected not only the anticipation of an actual Messiah and the corresponding expectation of a second coming of Christ as religious imaginations incompatible with philosophical reason, but also the cipher of Messianic thinking. He had no passion to work actively for the transformation of the world. He knew no hope of a better world grounded in human responsibility. A man who lives in eternity cannot live in the future. God is immutable and His actions are themselves eternal. Immutable is the existence of the infinite modes, though within the unchanging whole all the finite modes are subject to perpetual change. (pp. 384-85)

He lived in the truth of God's reality and the consequence was a reliable selfhood, but this selfhood was not conscious of itself. In opposition to Spinoza it may be asked: Is all the anguish to which man is subjected grounded only in the finiteness of modal being and in inadequate ideas? Or is there a very different anguish relating to the reality of the eternal amid the historicity of our existence? Did Spinoza gain his perfect peace at the expense of the God-related anguish of temporal existence, at the expense of the eternal decision in time? Is there not in this philosophy of necessity an impersonality which is at once moving and dangerous?

Because Spinoza was without consciousness of historicity, he was also unaware of the historicity of his own figures of thought. Because he believed that he had conceived the one absolute, compelling truth in a form universally valid for all time, he was a dogmatist. For us the truth of Spinoza does not lie in his dogmatized figures of thought. They themselves are historical symbols; uniquely illuminating, they have become indispensable to us, but they are not objectively absolute.

What carries conviction is not the abstract thought, but the reality lived with this thought. What appeals to us in Spinoza's work is not his solution of so-called objective problems, but the power of philosophical striving for certainty. Men's reactions to Spinoza, as to no other philosopher of modern times, were determined by the philosopher he really was. No other aroused so much warm affection and so much bitter hatred. The name of no other has so unique a ring, no other has been so despised and so loved by Christians and Jews alike. He became almost a mythical figure. No one who knows him can remain indifferent to him, for in connection with Spinoza even expressions of indifference mask a self-protective aggressiveness. (pp. 385-86)

Karl Jaspers, "Spinoza," in his The Great Philosophers: The Original Thinkers, *edited by Hannah Arendt, translated by Ralph Manheim, Harcourt Brace Jovanovich, 1966, pp. 273-387.*

LEO STRAUSS (essay date 1965)

[*A well-known German-born American scholar, philosopher, and political theorist, Strauss is noted for his lucid and insightful interpretations of standard political theories. Credited by one observer with "keeping the study of the political classics alive," he has attempted to demonstrate the abiding value of the works of such thinkers as Plato, Niccolò Machiavelli, Thomas Hobbes, and John Locke. Strauss is perhaps best known for* Die religionskritik Spinozas als grundlage seiner Bibelwissenschaft *(1930; Spinoza's Critique of Religion, 1965), Thoughts on Machiavelli* (1959), *and* What is Political Philosophy? and Other Studies *(1959). In the following excerpt from* Spinoza's Critique of Religion, *a work revised somewhat before its translation into English, he summarizes his commentary on* Theological-Political Treatise.]

[In the ***Theological-Political Treatise***] Spinoza starts from premises which are granted to him by the believers in revelation; he attempts to refute them on the bases of Scripture, of theologoumena formulated by traditional authorities, and of what one may call common sense. For in the ***Treatise*** Spinoza addresses men who are still believers and whom he intends to liberate from their "prejudices" so that they can begin to philosophize; the ***Treatise*** is Spinoza's introduction to philosophy. (p. 254)

If orthodoxy claims to know that the Bible is divinely revealed, that every word of the Bible is divinely inspired, that Moses was the writer of the Pentateuch, that the miracles recorded in the Bible have happened and similar things, Spinoza has refuted orthodoxy. But the case is entirely different if orthodoxy limits itself to asserting that it believes the aforementioned things, that is, that they cannot claim to possess the binding power peculiar to the known. For all assertions of orthodoxy rest on the irrefutable premise that the omnipotent God, whose will is unfathomable, whose ways are not our ways, who has decided to dwell in the thick darkness, may exist. Given this premise, miracles and revelations in general, and hence all biblical miracles and revelations in particular, are possible. Spinoza has not succeeded in showing that this premise is contradicted by anything we know. For what we are said to know, for example, regarding the age of the solar system, has been established on the basis of the assumption that the solar system has come into being naturally; miraculously it could have come into being in the way described by the Bible. It is only naturally or humanly impossible that the "first" Isaiah should have known the name of the founder of the Persian empire; it was not impossible for the omnipotent God to reveal to him that name. The orthodox premise cannot be refuted by experience nor by recourse to the principle of contradiction. An indirect proof of this is the fact that Spinoza and his like owed such success as they had in their fight against orthodoxy to laughter and mockery. By means of mockery they attempted to laugh orthodoxy out of its position from which it could not be dislodged by any proofs supplied by Scripture or by reason. One is tempted to say that mockery does not succeed the refutation of the orthodox tenets, but is itself the refutation. The genuine refutation of orthodoxy would require the proof that the world and human life are perfectly intelligible without the assumption of a mysterious God; it would require at least the success of the philosophic system: man has to show himself theoretically and practically as the master of the world and the master of his life; the merely given world must be replaced by the world created by man theoretically and practically. Spinoza's ***Ethics*** attempts to be the system, but it does not succeed; the clear and distinct account of everything which it presents remains fundamentally hypothetical. As a consequence, its cognitive status is not different from that of the orthodox account. Certain it is that Spinoza cannot legitimately deny the possibility of revelation. But to grant that revelation is possible means to grant that the philosophic account and the philosophic way of life are not necessarily, not evidently, the true account and the right way of life: philosophy, the quest for evident and necessary knowledge, rests itself on an unevident decision, on an act of the will, just as faith. Hence the antagonism between Spinoza and Judaism, between unbelief and belief, is ultimately not theoretical, but moral. (pp. 254-55)

Leo Strauss, "Preface to Spinoza's Critique of Religion," in his Liberalism: Ancient and Modern, *Basic Books, Inc., Publishers, 1968, pp. 224-59.*

E. M. CURLEY (essay date 1969)

[*In the following excerpt, Curley explores the Spinozistic conception of thought and extension, comparing it to that formulated by Descartes.*]

[Spinoza] built on the possibility of a unified science of extended objects. There are certain fundamental laws of nature governing the behavior of all extended objects. The various changes in the objects can all ultimately be understood in terms of these laws. Analogously, we might suppose that he recognized as well the existence of nonextended objects, thoughts, volitions, sensations, and the like, and that he envisaged the possibility of a unified science of nonextended objects, a universal psychology, strictly parallel to the universal physics we have been imagining, with fundamental laws of psychic events, derived laws, and nomological explanations of individual psychical phenomena.

We might be struck by the fact that when, in the ***Theological-Political Treatise,*** Spinoza wants to give examples of laws which depend on natural necessity, he gives one example from physics, a law of impact, and one example from psychology, a law of association. And we might argue that part III of the ***Ethics,*** which discusses the origin and nature of the human emotions, is an attempt to work out the rudiments of this universal psychology.

Confronted with Spinoza's notion that the mode of extension and the idea of that mode are one and the same thing, expressed in two different ways, we might appeal to the currently popular view that mental events are contingently identical with brain events, that a description of what goes on in us in psychological terms has a different sense than, but the same reference as, the corresponding description in physiological terms. And clearly, there are many passages in Spinoza—particularly those in which he connects the vitality of the mind with the vitality of the body—which would tend to support this sort of approach.

But although the approach described might take us a certain distance, I don't believe that we can get very far with it. It attributes to Spinoza a view which is, perhaps, attractive and plausible, probably more plausible than the one I shall argue for, but it is in many respects a misleading model for interpreting him. To mention only one of its most prominent defects, nothing in this line of interpretation would suggest that for Spinoza there should be a mode of thought for each mode of extension. In fact, this line would suggest rather the opposite.

The view that sensations, thoughts, and so forth are brain processes implies that where you do not find the appropriate physiological structures, you cannot expect to find any mental processes either. Even though my watch is a fairly complicated piece of machinery, you would not expect it to have any sensations. But plainly, Spinoza does think that *every* mode of extension has its corresponding mode of thought, or rather, *is* its corresponding mode of thought:

> The order and connection of ideas is the same as the order and connection of things . . . Let us here recall what has been proved above, viz., that whatever can be perceived by the infinite intellect as constituting the essence of substance pertains to one substance only. Therefore, thinking substance and extended substance are one and the same substance, which is now grasped under the one attribute and now under the other. So also a mode of extension and the idea of that mode are one and the same thing, but expressed in two ways . . . For example, a circle existing in nature and the idea which is in God of an

existing circle are one and the same thing, but explained through different attributes.

If my watch, or as I should prefer to say, the fact that my watch has such and such a character, is a mode of extension, then there is a mode of thought which is a different expression of the same thing.

This is, to say the least, puzzling. It is almost enough to make one despair of making sense of Spinoza. But before we despair, let us try another tack. We have to face the fact that Spinoza intends his terms "idea" and "mode of thought" to be understood in a way for which Descartes and Locke have not prepared us. (pp. 119-21)

In defining the term "idea" as a "concept of the mind, which the mind forms because it is a thinking thing," he explains that he uses the term "concept" rather than "perception" because the latter term suggests wrongly that the mind is passive in relation to its object, not active. Later he enlarges on this when he warns his readers to distinguish carefully between an idea and an image. Those, he says,

> who think that ideas consist in images which are formed in us through contact with [NS: external] bodies, persuade themselves that those ideas of things [NS: which can make no trace on our brains, or] of which we can form no similar images, are not ideas, but only inventions, which we feign from a free choice of the will; so they think of ideas as of mute pictures on a tablet, and preoccupied with this prejudice, they do not see that an idea, insofar as it is an idea, involves affirmation or negation.

So ideas, for Spinoza, involve an activity of the mind, an activity of affirmation or negation. Hence, it would be appropriate in most contexts in Spinoza to substitute the term "proposition" or "assertion" for the term "idea." By contrast, this would not be appropriate in most contexts in Descartes or Locke. Spinoza's ideas are the sort of thing that can follow from and entail one another, that can be true or false in the traditional sense of agreeing with their object.

It is customary, of course, to attribute to Spinoza a coherence theory of truth. But the reader who feels that I am placing more weight on [the abovementioned theory of coherence] than that axiom can comfortably bear may find it worthwhile to reflect on the passage in the **Metaphysical Thoughts** in which Spinoza discusses the meaning of the terms "true" and "false." The passage not only supports a correspondence theory of truth, but also is curiously contemporary in its methodology. Spinoza begins by remarking that

> Since the multitude first invent words, which are afterward taken over (usurpantur) by the philosophers, it seems appropriate for one who seeks the original signification of any word to ask what it first denoted among the multitude—particularly where there is a lack of any other explanations which, from the nature of the language, could be brought forward for investigating the signification.

We might note in passing that Spinoza works on the same methodological principle in the preface to part IV of the **Ethics,** where he undertakes to give an account of the meaning of the terms "perfect" and "imperfect" and "good" and "evil." Spinoza continues:

> The original signification of "true" and "false" seems to have arisen from narratives: they called a narrative true which was of a deed which had really happened (quae erat facti quod revera contigerat), and false

when it was of a deed which had not happened. And this signification the philosophers afterward took over to denote the agreement between an idea and its object (ideatum), and the opposite.

As a piece of amateur lexicography, this is remarkably suggestive. People who wonder about the meaning of some word are often counseled to consider how they would teach a child to use it. And it seems to me that it is generally in the context of stories that children are first introduced to the concept of truth. In any case, Spinoza concludes that "an idea is true if it shows us the thing as it is in itself and false if it shows us the thing as other than it really is. For ideas are nothing but mental narratives or histories of nature." I have rendered the term *factum* in this passage as "deed." "Fact," which H. H. Britan uses, strikes me as anachronistic. For as far as I have been able to discover, the Latin term never had the technical sense that its English cognate has. Perhaps this is why Spinoza had to coin the term *"ideatum"* for that with which a true idea agrees.

Earlier I used the assertional character of Spinoza's ideas to argue that their correlates in the attribute of extension, the *ideata* with which true ideas are said to agree, ought to be construed as facts rather than as things. Now I want to suggest that we can do reasonable justice to Spinoza's concept of the relation between thought and extension if we think of the relation between thought and extension as an identity of true proposition and fact. It is misleading to say, even though Spinoza himself says it, that a true idea agrees with the object (read "a true proposition agrees with the fact"), because the mode of extension and the idea of that mode are one and the same thing expressed in two different ways. The fact and the true proposition are the same thing, expressed or viewed in two different ways. To talk about a mode as a proposition or idea, bearing logical relations to other propositions, is to conceive the mode under the attribute of thought. To talk about it as a fact, having causal relations with other facts, is to conceive it under the attribute of extension. But the propositions which make up the set that gives a complete and accurate description of the world are identical with the facts they describe, and the causal relations between the facts have their counterpart in the logical relations between propositions.

This is how I propose to read Spinoza's doctrine that "the order and connection of ideas is the same as the order and connection of things." (pp. 121-24)

In interpreting Spinoza's doctrine that the mode of extension and its idea are one as equivalent to the claim that facts and true propositions are one, in the sense described, I am saying, in effect, that on this point Wolfson is right [see Additional Bibliography]. Wolfson recommends that we understand Spinoza's theory of the mind-body relationship as differing only in terminology from the Aristotelian view that the soul is the form of the body. And I think that this is substantially correct. It is not quite right, because we have to extend the notion of form and matter in the way done above in order to allow for Spinoza's emphasis on the assertional element in ideas. And we have to make further adjustments to allow for the relation's being one-to-one. But only in a way like this can we account for Spinoza's notion that there is a mode of thought for every mode of extension. Spinoza's statement that "all things are animate, though in different degrees," that "there must be in God an idea of everything," does not imply that my watch has thoughts and sensations, any more than Aristotle's doctrine that plants have souls implies that flowers feel pain. (p. 126)

For all that Spinoza owed Descartes—and he owed him much—the points of difference between the two philosophers offer the best opportunity for reconstructing the development of the Spinozistic system. There are, of course, many points of difference. But the most fundamental one, in my view, was that for Spinoza the world was thoroughly intelligible. As Spinoza had Meyer point out in his preface to the **Principles of Descartes' Philosophy** [see excerpt dated 1663], when we read in that work that

> "this or that exceeds human grasp," we must not suppose that the author [Spinoza] is putting this forward as his own opinion. For he thinks that all these things, and many others even more sublime and subtle, not only can be conceived by us clearly and distinctly, but can be explained very easily, provided that, in the search for truth and the knowledge of things, the human intellect is led by a path different from that opened up by Descartes.

If rationalism consists in having this optimistic view of man's ability to comprehend the world around him, then Spinoza was plainly and unequivocally a rationalist.

But Descartes was not. In at least two crucial respects he made the world a mystery—first by exempting man from the domain of law and setting him up as "a kingdom within a kingdom" whose actions could only be given a verbal explanation by appeal to the obscure notion of the human will, and second by maintaining that the eternal truths, the laws of nature, had been set up by God as a king establishes the laws in his kingdom. Descartes had felt compelled to deny that these eternal truths could hold independently of the will of God. To do so would be to cast God as "a Jupiter or Saturn, making him subject to Styx and the Fates."

With this denial Spinoza agreed. But he could not accept the anthropomorphic Cartesian alternative for quite a number of reasons. To begin with, since acts of will are the sort of thing that take place at a particular time, it applied a temporal concept to the explanation of something supposed to be eternal. But more important, it did not offer a genuine explanation. It postulated God's will as a cause in one breath, and in the next admitted that this cause could just as easily have had a contrary effect. To do this is to cloak ignorance in specious verbiage. A cause from which the effect cannot be inferred is not a cause. Furthermore, since it was conceded that God could have willed a different set of laws, there was no good reason to think that he would not change his mind and alter the eternal order. . . . Descartes argued that this could not happen, on the ground that God's will was immutable. But as Descartes also denied that there was any necessary connection between God's nature or essence and his will as exemplified in the nature of the world he created, it was difficult to see why his will should not change. As Spinoza remarked,

> if it is permitted to attribute to God another intellect and another will without any change in his essence and perfection, what is the reason why he cannot now change his decrees about created things and nevertheless remain equally perfect? His intellect and will regarding created things and their order would remain the same in relation to his essence and perfection no matter how it be conceived.

The specter of Hume rises before us and we contemplate the possibility of a world in which nothing is stable and enduring.

Spinoza's way out of this dilemma was to identify the will or intellect of God, the universal laws of nature, with the essence of God. God is neither the slave nor the master of eternal truth, he is eternal truth. The laws of nature neither require nor admit explanation in terms of anything more ultimate, they could not have been otherwise. This is the first of the two main tenets of Spinozism; and the second, that man is a part of nature, following her laws in all his actions, is propounded in the same spirit. Both doctrines arise from the fundamental demand for absolute intelligibility. (pp. 156-58)

> *E. M. Curley, in his* Spinoza's Metaphysics: An Essay in Interpretation, *Cambridge, Mass.: Harvard University Press, 1969, 174 p.*

ARNE NAESS (lecture date 1973)

[*In the following excerpt from a lecture first presented in 1973, Naess explores the inherent difficulties of Spinoza's system with regard to free will and determinism.*]

Spinoza has been charged with inconsistency in proclaiming both determinism and freedom. Some have put forth weighty arguments against the charge, but the matter is still controversial. Many historians of philosophy of this century have upheld the charge.

In one of the most widely read histories of philosophy it is simply said that Spinoza denies human freedom. But he is also said to try to 'have it both ways': to maintain both an extreme determinism and an ethics presupposing freedom (Copleston).

In what follows I shall argue against the thesis on inconsistency and also try to clarify in what sense Spinoza is determinist, in what sense he is not,—and *in what sense he did not take a definite stand.* (p. 6)

Spinoza says freedom presupposes necessary relations and therefore the absence of contingency. When a free agent choses act A in preference to B, the difference in preference must follow with necessity from the nature and striving of the agent, and the insight into the situation. But otherwise what *is* freedom? There are more or less complete extensional, if not intensional, equivalances between the term 'free' and certain other expressions.

In a number of contexts Spinoza says that to be free *is* to follow or be led by reason, which *is*, again, the same as to act out of virtue. To be unfree *is* to submit to passive emotions (affects), to be the slave of (passive) passions. By implication, the free acts from active emotions.

Other extensional equivalences . . . [in Parts III and IV of the **Ethics**]:

> to act freely is
> to act in accordance with one's essence
> to act in accordance with one's nature
> to act from the laws of one's own nature
> to do what follows with necessity from one's nature
> to act, and not from contingency or indifference
> to effect what can be understood from the laws of one's nature
> to act from power
> to live according to the dictate of reason
> to conserve one's being according to reason
> to base one's actions on the fundament of seeking what is really useful

In order to find out exactly what *kind* of relation of equivalence does hold at the particular places in the text, one would have to go deeply into the doctrine of definition, essence and method as suggested, but not elaborated, by Spinoza in **On the Im-**

provement of the Intellect and in other writings. Here it suffices to remind oneself of the inner relations between the term free and other terms in his system. It does not work to try to isolate a problem of freedom from the problems of essence, nature, power, reason, active emotion and adequate ideas. The study of Spinoza is an exercise in systems thinking on the fundamental level.

There is in the *Ethics* nothing hypothetical about free men. The equivalences broadens the relevant places. When Spinoza . . . says that *we* strive when led by reason to prefer a greater future good to a lesser present when, *we* are to that extent free. In the demonstration he uses an analogous expression—'to the extent that we take notice of reason itself'. When Spinoza in the note to the 'pessimistic' stresses that he *does* reckon with the difference between those who have and those who have not insight, he by implication points to the moderate or relative difference in level of freedom. The equivalences give the 'road to freedom' a richer and more earthbound sense. It is a path we all struggle along, with minor or major lapses. The occurrences of explicit grading of 'free' are rare, but the occurrences of gradings of the equivalent expressions are many. They support our conclusion that the freedom envisaged by Spinoza and applied to humans is one that is proportional to the extent to which we act from necessity of our own nature. Like in common sense, he does not find the question relevant whether our nature 'ultimately' is causally fully determined by something else. He does not, because the relevance of 'ultimateness' only gives sense when we are thinking about time: our nature did not exist before we were born or conceived. If, therefore, we conceive of complete determination as one in time, our nature is not ours but a nature prefabricated by something else. Such reflections are not made by Spinoza because the determination he talks about is a mutual one, an interdependence. It is only the timedimension that is onedimensional and gives raise to the thought: 'I am completely prefabricated'.

Equating 'from necessity' with 'not from contingency or indifference', the necessity postulated by Spinoza does not say more than that there is an inner relation between the nature or essence and the acts performed. The acts are manifestations of the nature or essence, and without the acts the essence would be a mere word or fiction. This reveals the dynamic character of the notion of essence (closely related to *conatus*).

Men act from a mixture of causes or determinants, *only some* of which are internal, that is, follow necessarily from their nature. They *tend to* be unaware of the non-internal determinants, the 'external causes'. They all tend to believe that they act so and so for *no other reason* that they want to act so and so. With this in mind let us inspect a famous passage in Letter 58:

> . . . a stone receives from an external cause, which impels it a certain quantity of motion, with which it will afterwards necessarily continue to move . . . Surely this stone, inasmuch as it is conscious only of its own effort (*conatus*), and is far from indifferent, will believe that it is maximally (completely) free (*liberrimus*), and that it continues in motion for no other reason than because it wants to (*vult*). And such is the human freedom which all men boast that they possess . . .

Absolutely all men? Or all men who boast? Or what?—In this letter Spinoza seems in his rhetorical mood to forget for a moment his free men alluded to in Part four. They have been said to understand their own actions, and at least some of them

have presumably read and accepted what Spinoza says in his *Ethics*! They, at least clearly did not boast of their so-called *liber arbitrium*!

What humans *boast of* is, in accordance with the above quotation, complete freedom defined not by necessary action from internal determinants, but by uncaused volitions—falsely defined by certain philosophers as free will (*liber arbitrium*).

If, however, we are spontaneously conscious only of our own effort in the sense of our own *conatus,* this explains that we all are *liable to* take internal determinants to be the only determinants of an action. The mistake is, however, one of analysis, and it does not disqualify the spontaneous consciousness of freedom. This consciousness is not a registration of free *will* or of *all* determinants. If we decide to put up the umbrella, there is a spontaneous feeling of free decision which governs the act, and we have good grounds for taking this freedom at its face value. That the rain caused us externally is irrelevant.

If we have the inclination and interest of analysis, we may take our time and try to list determinants, *including* the external ones. We shall then avoid neglecting the rain, our clothing, our bad health, our cultural determinants, perhaps our conscious vanity, our distaste for polluted sulfuric acid, a slight joy using our new umbrella, and what else. None of these determinants need furnish any arguments against (non-absolute) freedom of our action. If we, however, later find that the use of the umbrella was due to hypnosis or passive affects, we shall arrive at a low estimate of freedom, perhaps a high degree of slavery under passions or of a kind of automatism in that partiuclar situation.

Etching of Spinoza from B.D.S. Opera posthuma *(1677).*

The *illusion of freedom* from false analysis is not universal and constant. Otherwise Spinoza's examples would not single out people with weaknesses or those not yet ripe for making a correct causal analysis:

> So the infant believes that it freely wants revenge; the timid that he wants to escape. Then too the drunkard believes that, by free decision of his mind, he says those things which afterwards when sober he would prefer to have left unsaid.

If sober we may freely decide not to say certain things. But this freedom does not reveal *liber arbitrium*, it reflects in action our nature or essence as an integrated personality.

> So the delirious, the garrulous and many others of the same sort, believe that they are acting according to the free decision of their mind, and not that they are carried away by impulse.

'Others of *the same sort*', that is, subgroup of people at a low level of freedom. 'Carried away'—another way of describing slavery under passive emotions.

The *illusion* of freedom is, in other words, characteristic of uncritical people, in uncritical moments, it is not characteristic of humans as such. Some people have *insight into* their own freedom, an adequate idea of own freedom. The illusion of freedom is not a necessary consequence of human nature or essence, but neither is its absence. (pp. 18-21)

We can as our conclusion subscribe to that of the master himself in his letter to Schuller: '. . . if you will attentively examine my view, you will see that it is entirely consistent. . .' We subscribe, but add a qualification: we cannot *see* this consistency but we can work out a consistent reconstruction on the basis of a set of plausible interpretations. At least this is what I have tried to do.

SUMMARY CONCERNING FREEDOM OF DECISION

1. The immediate and spontaneous feeling of free choice and decision is a consciousness of own *conatus*, our basic dynamics and expressive of our own particular essence or nature. There is nothing illusory about this feeling.

2. The feeling of free choice is sometimes taken to be an indicator of the complete set of determinants of an action. From this stems the illusion of complete or absolute freedom, in the sense of absolute self-causedness or total absence of causes.

3. The feeling of free choice is a genuine indicator of internal, not external determinants.

4. The extent to which we are determined ('internally') by our nature or essence, is a matter of degree, never total, never zero.

5. The way towards increased level of freedom, that is internal determination, is through clarification of our affects, by which means they are converted passive to active emotions.

GENERAL SUMMARY

6. The thesis that Spinoza does not predicate freedom of human beings, and the thesis that if he did, it would result in an inconsistency with his determinism, are both false.

7. 'Freedom' and 'determinism' are loose words with a variety of meanings some of which are such that '*x* is free and *x* is determined' expresses or implies a contradiction, whereas others do not. Among the latter we find those best adapted to the text of the *Ethics*. These meanings have deep roots both in

every day thinking and in that of philosophers before and after Spinoza.

8. Spinoza judges men to be more or less free and therefore also more or less unfree. There is no definite upper limit to human freedom, but it cannot ever be absolute as in God.

9. The freedom whch Spinoza proclaims to be realizable is one that is widely held in every day life to be realizable: to be determined in one's decisions from *own* nature, from the depth of one's soul, from the integrated action of one's personality, and not from pressures, external circumstances or passions which overrun oneself. And of course not to act unintelligibly, unmotivated, chaotic, unaccountably, blindly, randomly, designless. When we judge ourselves free in this sense or these senses we have not yet asserted anything about how we (since birth?) have developed into what we are: We are not speaking about remote causes *in time*. Neither does Spinoza in his judgment. But he stresses that external determinants always are in operation at any definite time, therefore also at the time of our birth—and before that.

10. The determinism of Spinoza is one of essence, *complete determination of essential relations between things*. It is not a determination of particulars, dated or undated, it is not a doctrine of antedetermination. Spinoza does not defend any such doctrine nor does he criticize any. He was not seriously engaged by the problem. What I have tried is therefore only to help a fly to get out of a bottle. (pp. 21-2)

> *Arne Naess, "Is Freedom Consistent with Spinoza's Determinism?" in* Spinoza on Knowing, Being and Freedom, *edited by J. G. Van Der Bend, Van Gorcum & Comp. B.V., 1974, pp. 6-23.*

PAUL WIENPAHL   (essay date 1979)

[*In the following excerpt, Winepahl discusses the metaphysical implications of Spinoza's theories, particularly that of the unity of substance and being, and concludes with comments on the present-day significance of Spinoza's works. (Throughout this excerpt—and throughout the book from which it is extracted— Spinoza is referred to as BdS or Sp.)*]

All of Spinoza's thinking centers about the notion of unity and his life was one of atonement or at-one-ment. When his editors went through the correspondence he left, they apparently omitted for publication letters that would be of purely biographical interest. At last we have very few statements from his own hand which inform us directly about himself. . . . Fortunately there is one, and it provides one of the many possible ways of expressing the notion of unity. It occurs in the opening four pages of the little unfinished essay [*On the Improvement of the Understanding*]. These pages are wholly autobiographical, the only such in all of BdS, and the expression of unity occurs at their end.

Having examined the three traditional goals that have been taken as the highest good by humankind: riches, fame or honor, and the satisfaction of our libidos, or basic drives, and having found from experience that they finally serve only to distract us, BdS expresses his view of the highest good. However he prefaces this by noting that "good" and "ill," and "perfect" and "imperfect" are said of things only relatively. That is, the same thing can be said to be good and ill under different circumstances. Thus music is good for him that is melancholy, ill for him that mourns, and neither good nor ill for him that is deaf. The same is true for "perfect" and "imperfect"; and no thing looked at in itself, without comparison with others, will be said to be perfect or imperfect, "especially as soon as we shall have known that all things that happen, happen according to an eternal order, and according to Nature's certain laws."

BdS is now ready for his statement about the highest good. Since in our weakness we do not attain to this eternal order in our thinking, we conceive a nature far firmer than our own. Then, seeing that there are no impediments to acquiring this nature, we seek means for arriving at such perfection. All these may be called "true goods." "The highest good however is to arrive" at such a nature so that we enjoy it "with other individuals, if it can be done." What exactly this nature is, says BdS, we shall show elsewhere. Briefly, "it is knowledge of the union, which the mind has with total Nature." (pp. 54-5)

There are two common misunderstandings of BdS. The first is that the basis and starting point of his thinking was Cartesian and that his philosophy is an attempt to solve the problems of dualism. The second is that Sp's conception of God differed radically from that in the Christian-Hebraic tradition. Of the first it may be said that, although BdS couched his thinking in terms of the "new philosophy," it was not the starting point of his own. The misunderstanding may have arisen because it is also the case that the problems of dualism do not appear in Sp's work. This, we will see, is because they are typically human problems and not because they are peculiarly the result of Descartes' way of thinking.

The second misunderstanding arises from failure to take proper account of the influence of the Hebraic tradition on BdS, including the language of that tradition, and of BdS himself. If we can trust Lucas' biography of BdS, he was voicing views that express the germ of his philosophical work long before he read Descartes. These in turn led to his excommunication which was the occasion that resulted in a thorough examination of his tradition that finally produced the *TTP* [*Theological-Political Treatise*], a book on which he worked longer and more assiduously than he did on the *Ethic*. The starting point of Sp's thinking was the idea of God, the central idea of the tradition from which he came. Further . . . in his meditations with this idea BdS did not depart from it nor radically change *it*. He profoundly deepened his *understanding* of it. The God of BdS was the God of his fathers. Any change that he made was in himself. He so came to understand God that he, as we might say, experienced God. The expression of this experience, together with the life which it formed, occurs in statements about unity, for there is unification in the experience and the life. The experience of God is the experience of unity. Thus Sp's definition of "God" in the *Ethic* is *Jehova*, that is, "*Being*," with some modifications which signify his deeper understanding of God. Here is that definition . . . :

"By means of *God* I understand *Being* absolutely infinitely, that is, substance being established in infinite attributes, of which each expresses being eternally, & infinitely." In Sp's terms this runs: *Per Deum intelligo Ens absolute infinitum, hoc est, substantiam constantem infinitis attributis, quorum unumquodque aeternam, & infinitam essentiam exprimit.* Of the Latin terms only one requires special notice at this point: *constantem* (being established). It is the present participle of the verb *consto*, which is formed from the verb *sto* (I stand) and the preposition *con*. It therefore differs only in the preposition from the verb for "I exist" which is *exsto* (*ex* and *sto*), and one of the definitions of *consto* is "exist." Thus, we might read in the definition of "God" that he is "substance existing

in infinite attributes." *Consto* can also mean to become clear or manifest, so that we might think of God as becoming clear or made manifest in infinite attributes. Finally, BdS himself defines the verb in the *TTP* . . . as meaning "rising up."

Posed before our eyes now are two statements of the notion of unity: this definition, and that nature which is the knowledge of the union of the mind with total Nature. At first or at the outset they seem neither clear nor related to each other; much less equivalent, as they must be if each is a statement of the notion of unity. Furthermore, by this time you may be asking yourself, the notion of the unity of what? To reply, the unity of God, and to refer you to Letter 34 is an answer but an unhelpful one. Therefore, as a starter let us see how BdS proceeded in the *Ethic* by first clarifying the notions of substance and attribute, the only two main new terms in the definition of "God." ("*Being*" for BdS is simply God's *proper* name.)

Definition 3 of Part I is: "By means of *substance* I understand that which is in itself, & is conceived by means of itself." This was a definition of the term current in Sp's day and was the one stated by Descartes in *Principles* I, 51: "By means of *substance* we can understand nothing other than a thing which so exists that it needs no other thing for existing." Definition 3 was the only definition of "substance" employed by BdS. Descartes, in contrast, always had in mind a second. This was a version of the common notion or axiom that no property or attribute is of nothing . . . : a substance is that to which properties or attributes are attached, or which is the agent of actions. . . . One of the ways of seeing the basic difference between BdS and Descartes is by realizing that BdS abandoned this definition of "substance."

From Letter 2 of 1661 we know that in an early version of the *Ethic* the present first four propositions were among the definitions and axioms. The present Prop. 5 was Prop. 1, the first proposition of the *Ethic*, and Pierre Bayle in his entry on Spinoza in his *Dictionary* took it as the central proposition in the work [see excerpt dated 1697]. It is difficult to get into English, and in various demonstrations and scholia in Part I it is stated in various ways. When the thing is finally reasonably clear, you appreciate the difficulty of stating it in any language. The most commonly accepted translation of Prop. 5 runs: "In the nature of things there cannot be given two, or plural substances of the same nature or attribute." A simpler version of the proposition occurs, for example, in the demonstration of Prop. 13: It is absurd that there be given plural substances of the same nature. "Plural" in both cases has its strict meaning of "more than one." It gradually becomes apparent that the proposition is difficult to state because it comes to abandoning the traditional notion of identity. (pp. 56-9)

The traditional notion of identity is that a thing has an identity when there is something in or about it so that we can say absolutely or without qualification that it is the same thing today that it was yesterday. I am speaking of identity in its sense in the dictionary (the state of being identical or absolutely the same), not any particular notion of identity held by some philosopher. If we regard a thing as composed of a substance which does not change, to which properties which may and do change somehow adhere, we can understand a thing's identity. . . . In Prop. 5 BdS is abandoning this notion of identity because he is saying in effect that there are not substances. So-called "things," therefore, are just collections of properties.

The principle of the identity of indiscernibles (and, therefore, Prop. 5) comes to stating that no thing is ever identical with another. For if two things have the same properties, that is, are identical, we could not distinguish between them because we distinguish things by differences in properties. That is, according to the principle a thing is simply a collection of changeable properties (it has no substance).

There is, however, a double aspect to the principle. It involves seeing that if it be accepted, no thing is identical with any other thing, and no thing is identical with itself, that is, has an identity. It is primarily with the second aspect that we are concerned when we say that Prop. 5, in saying in effect that there are not substances (in the plural), comes to abandoning the traditional or definitional notion of identity. However, this also involves the first aspect. There cannot be plural identical substances. Thus of any one thing it cannot be the case that it retains its identity or sameness over a period of time (that is, it has no identity). Nor are there any plural identical things. (We can allow that there may be plural identical things in a weak or relative sense of "identity," such as strong resemblance.) This in turn comes to realizing, or trying to, that each thing is unique, *and that all things are constantly changing*. Indeed, to see each thing as unique is to see all things as constantly changing. The two insights come to the same thing (that is the relative sense of "same," for their expressions are clearly different).

Lest this seem impossible, let me say that we can *think* that a thing has an identity. For practical purposes we can *assign* an identity, as we do with proper names. Or we can take some property which changes imperceptibly and treat it as constituting a thing's identity (as we do with fingerprints). You can, that is, take it that BdS is changing our *minds,* not saying something new about reality. (pp. 60-1)

Saying that there are not plural substances or that there is not more than one is not equivalent to saying that there is only one or that there is one substance. This may be seen by considering the other version of "there are not plural substances": namely, "there are not substances." For if there were one, it would be true that there are substances, but as it happens only one. Thus BdS says in Letter 50 that either he does not understand God or he speaks of him improperly who says that God is one or unique (remember that God is defined as substance). To say that there is one or only one substance, therefore, is either to speak improperly or to fail to understand the idea of substance.

For this reason BdS cannot, except improperly or without understanding him, be called a monist. Hobbes is a monist. He said that all is made of matter. Hegel is a monist: All is mind, or everything is spiritual. But beyond saying that God is *Being,* BdS attributes no properties to him. (pp. 62-3)

• • • • •

Some studies of historical figures are significant mainly for the history of philosophy and for persons who want to know about philosophers. Occasionally, however, a study . . . , because of its subject, bears not only in these ways. It may also, and perhaps more importantly, have vital significance for our own times. This is the case with Spinoza. It will . . . assist with understanding him . . . if I develop some of the implications of the thinking of BdS for our times.

1. With some understanding of unity our view of *what is* changes drastically. Instead of seeing our world as made up of discrete things existing independently of each other, we see unity. In the language BdS provided, it is a unity of modes of being.

There are not, properly speaking, entities. There is *Being* and modes of being. A tree is an arboreal mode of being. You and I are modes of being, or, more simply human beings. What we have taken to be the real distinctions between things dissolve, and with them the conceptual distinctions between "thing," properties, and actions. Loving, for example, which we commonly take to be an action that some one or thing performs can itself be seen as a mode of being.—This is easy to say, but with time potent in effect. Implications are as follows.

2. There is identity. There is also identifying with. We can identify things or say *what* they are. We can also identify with another mode of being, when what it is is of no moment.

3. There is a kind of knowing that is loving. It is not of universals. In it we know Individuals. There are, then, levels of awareness: imagination and understanding. Imagination is indirect awareness and always involves images or representations of things. It includes seeing, hearing, and ratiocinative thinking. Understanding is direct awareness. We can move from images of things to direct awareness, from universals to particulars. In thinking that knowledge is of universals we mistake means of knowing for the objects of knowledge. The objects of knowing or awareness are always particular modes of being; but at first we see them through the cloud of representations of them.

4. The so-called inanimate is no longer inanimate, except for certain purposes. All modes of being are animate. Like us they are mental as well as physical; though, of course, each in its manner or mode: human, equine, lapidary.

5. And so they are all capable of Affections. A sailboat, a navicular being can be joyful—more clearly, can be joyfully.

6. There is a way of humanly being that is active instead of passive, or rather more active than passive.

7. It involves understanding God. In easy parlance this is to see that every mode of being is divine. Thus, to be humanly we are diligent toward every thing, respect, love it. God ceases to be an object and becomes an experience.

God is not dead. The *image* of God is vanishing from some Minds. This is neither lamentable nor a reason for despair. On the contrary, it is preparatory for understanding. The same is true for the dismantling of metaphysics. To have an image of God is to see *Being* through a cloud. With understanding religion and philosophy are found to be not really distinct. (pp. 155-56)

[When] we have a true idea of unity, that is, when we are unified (and it is important to note that it is a matter of degrees), we are detached from any particular mode of thinking, and such detachment is, of course, itself a mode of being. We are neither Aristotelian, a Spinozist, a Buddhist, a Christian, nor even one who sees a dog as a dog. We attain to no-mind. Truth, meaning, substance, identity, all the categories lose their hold on us and we can be with each mode of being simply as *it is.*

Except for its ending that last sentence might have a familiar ring. Hannah Arendt wrote: "I have clearly joined the ranks of those who have for some time been attempting to dismantle metaphysics, and philosophy with all its categories." . . . She went on, however, to say, "What you are left with, then, is still the past, but a fragmented past, which has lost its certainty of evaluation." Nevertheless, she warns at the last, there are things there that are "''rich and strange,'" "'coral,'" and "''pearls'" that are not to be destroyed (she has been quoting Shakespeare). And she concludes in Auden's words: "Some books are undeservedly forgotten; none are undeservedly remembered." (p. 162)

We are thus left with the pearls of the past *and* the possibility of a new way of thinking and knowing. One of the pearls is "know thyself." Another is "Love thy fellow beings." It is a way of thinking and knowing that is not of the universal but of the particular. "If now the way, which I have shown conducts to this, seem extremely arduous, it can nevertheless be come upon." The more so today, may be added to Sp's observation at the end of the *Ethic*. For more of us have broken with the tradition of representational thinking to become aware of the other. (p. 163)

> *Paul Wienpahl, in his* The Radical Spinoza, *New York University Press, 1979, 281 p.*

JAMES COLLINS　(essay date 1984)

[*An American scholar of philosophy, Collins is the author of such works as* God in Modern Philosophy *(1959) and* Descartes's Philosophy of Nature *(1971). In the following excerpt, he discusses Spinoza's philosophy in terms of humanity's relationship to nature, religion, and God.*]

During the intellectually crowded years 1665-70, Spinoza took time from his revision and expansion of the *Ethics* to write a separate study of religion. His *Theological-Political Treatise* . . . was published anonymously, but its authorship became known in a few weeks. He distributed copies of it to Oldenburg and Boyle in England, clarified its meaning to numerous correspondents, and was only mildly discomfited by having it banned at home along with Hobbes's *Leviathan* and his friend Meyer's *Philosophy the Interpreter of Holy Scripture*. The book hit its mark squarely by disturbing the ecclesiastical authorities and those civil authorities who felt obliged to defend some form of church orthodoxy.

Although the compound term *theological-political* has an odd ring to it today, it was the most succinct adjective to convey one of Spinoza's major concerns in writing his treatise. Among the reasons he gave for composing it was the condition of the times, further specified as the impudence or undue influence of preachers and theological considerations upon the use of political power. In this sense, the *Theological-Political Treatise* was a tract for the times, showing a historical sensitivity toward particular situations which was never suppressed by Spinoza's criticism of temporal imagery and his dedication to nature's eternal order. (p. 201)

[The] *Theological-Political Treatise* is a many-faceted work. It can be read as a theory of religion, as a guide to biblical criticism, and as part of a larger political theory. But what unifies these aspects and also sets limits on their independent development is their common bearing on the freedom of philosophizing. This convergence of purpose is made clear in the book's subtitle: "Containing several discussions whereby it is shown that freedom of philosophizing not only can be granted without harm to piety and public peace; but that it cannot be abolished without also abolishing public peace and piety itself." In conducting these discussions, therefore, Spinoza does not feel that he is wandering away from his main activity of philosophizing. Rather, his arguments seek to prevent any blockage of that activity made in the name of religion and the

state. He is intent upon showing that his general view of nature has implications sufficiently determinate to safeguard the freedom of himself and others to reflect upon socially sensitive questions and publicly report their findings. (pp. 202-03)

Given the careful treatment of religion in the *Ethics*, there would seem to be no need to devote a separate treatise to it. But the very definitions of religion and piety contain some criterial conditions not always met by people claiming to live in accord with these virtues. Religion and piety concern actions of which we are the cause, insofar as we have the idea of God, follow the lead of reason, and associate with others in an honorable, friendly way. In each respect, one can readily fall short of the measure. That is, one's conduct may be governed by an inadequate idea of God, at odds with the one proposed by Spinoza; and it may lead to social relations of a servile and oppressive quality, manifesting the superstitious rather than the genuinely religious origin of the bond and of its political ramifications. Hence, the analysis of religion can go just so far in the *Ethics*, leaving its more detailed pursuit to the *Theological-Political Treatise* and some of the *Correspondence*. (p. 211)

Spinoza did not equate religion with biblical religion, but he gave the latter chief attention because of its personal impact upon himself as well as its deep cultural penetration and involvement in the political life of his times. Along with the Old Testament and traditions of the ancient Hebrews, he included the New Testament (especially Paul's epistles) and the writings of such medieval Jewish thinkers as Maimonides and Crescas.

The Bible is a *purifier* because, when properly understood, it prepares the human mind for acceptance of the view of nature proposed in Spinoza's philosophy. Its imagery and stories dispose us to view our world and every individual entity as components of one encompassing whole, so that we are not entirely at sea when Spinoza discusses natured nature as a totality. Moreover, this reality is not a chaos but an orderly pattern, whose events are governed by divine laws and rules—an anticipation of the idea of nature's order and causal unity. And however distinctive it is, the human soul or spirit is also included within the world order and regulated by God's law. There is life within natured nature, just as there is law governing the desires of man.

Another contribution of the biblical outlook is to regard the universe as God's handiwork. The religiously described universe owes its origin to God and remains open to his creative act. This is a veiled recognition of naturing nature and its productive power, regardless of confusions over the precise relationship of naturing with natured nature. The Bible also fosters the conviction that man is a God-seeker, that man needs help from God's spirit or son, and that in his love for God man finds a new life and salvation, freedom and lasting blessedness. Spinoza's deliberate use of this religious language is something more than cultural accommodation. The images thus verbally stated are dim perceptions of the truth about the human modes of naturing nature, that is, about man's enhancement through union with the whole of nature. The Bible is a chaste and purgative influence, urging men not to be sense-centered and anarchic but to direct their minds to what is real and divine. (pp. 211-12)

It serves ordinary people by communicating at the level of human imagery or imaginative perception, and for the sole purpose of fostering pious and mutually helpful conduct among them. Only a pastoral, purely practical theology can result.

One cannot draw from biblical sources any speculative truths about God, the universe, and man, since these sources convey no method for emending the imagery or guiding our philosophical reasoning and intuitive understanding. Nor can there be anything philosophically decisive about an appeal to a particular view of reality as being presupposed or implied by the biblical stories. Such presuppositions would carry no special evidence coercing assent in matters of philosophical controversy, but would be suggestions that must still submit to methodological reform by our own understanding and its intrinsic grasp of the real. Hence, Spinoza finds no grounds in biblically oriented thought for making a correction of his philosophical theory of nature as naturing and natured.

He spelled out for Blyenbergh [a correspondent of his] the main consequences of the principle that Scripture *"constantly speaks in a human manner."* It means that the biblical writers think and write in the language of commandment and parable, perdition and salvation. "They have adapted all their words closely to this parable [of lawgiving-reward-punishment] rather than closely to truth, and have represented God everywhere as a man. . . . Theology has everywhere, and that not without reason, represented God as a perfect man." Spinoza was careful not to add that, from the internal viewpoint of the Bible and its proper theology, this anthropomorphism is merely childish or an arbitrary departure from the pastoral intent. The biblical way of representing God is "not without reason," insofar as it fulfills the practical aim of making most people responsive to precepts about their neighbors, and of helping them to become affectively related to God. The thought and language of Scripture do serve to counter lawless and godless behavior by representing moral life and God in imagery that builds up men of probity and piety.

Dangerous nonsense creeps in only when such law-and-parable talk is translated into a speculative doctrine, a theology making ontological truth-claims to which philosophy must submit. Spinoza recommends that philosophy disengage itself as much as possible from the integral parable situation. He takes three steps toward achieving this disengagement, without discounting the factual influence of his own close study of Scripture and of a long tradition of Scripture-formed thinkers.

First, he describes the procedure whereby God and human nature become confused. The parable mentality uses a method of substitution. It thinks about causes in the images and language of law, and it thinks about effects in the images and language of saving and losing one's soul. Within this schema of law-salvation-perdition, the divine becomes confused with human nature, and God is imagined as a perfect man or a just law-giver. Spinoza's philosophical reform is to make a systematic reversal of this procedure. He rethinks lawgiving within the theory of causes and rethinks the saving or losing of one's soul within the theory of effects. Thus the primary analogate is the relationship between causes and effects, which reduces the tendency to confuse God with the world of human ideals.

Second, Spinoza is very guarded in the use of his century's favorite phrase: "the laws and rules of nature." It appears more frequently in his theological-political writings than elsewhere. Although he cannot avoid this phrase entirely, he interprets it as a way of describing what happens in the modal world as a consequence of naturing nature's productive power and necessary causation. The accent falls upon the active power and causality of naturing nature, rather than upon the descriptive laws and rules of natured nature.

To sharpen our awareness of this reversed emphasis, Spinoza draws a capital distinction between the causal *per* and the descriptive *secundum*, between "through" and "in accordance with." Modal things and events come about strictly *through* the active power and causality of God or naturing nature. The course of natured nature is described as coming about *in accordance with* the mechanical laws of science and the moral laws of biblical theology. Within the total order of nature, mechanical and moral laws are patterns necessarily determined by and expressive of God's causal immanence. If this clarification is kept in mind, it prevents the confused representation of God either as a perfect man or as an absentee owner.

Spinoza's third countermove is to refrain from the religious naming of God as king and judge. Philosophical criticism of the theory of will as a divine attribute is expressed in the religious field as a denial of a separate legislative will of God and his commandments as the basis of moral law and obligation. Similarly, criticism of the separation of virtue and beatitude stands in the way of any religious image of God as judge, doling out rewards and punishments for our deeds. In order to remove the anthropomorphic elements from this picture, Spinoza has recourse to two points in his theory of nature: conatus and virtue. The human conatus, which expresses the immanent activity of naturing nature in us, provides the direct foundation of our moral actions. And virtue is itself the realization of what is humanly desirable and felicific, without waiting for the approbation or disapprobation of someone else as a rewarder.

As a lagniappe in his correspondence with Blyenbergh, Spinoza gives us a concise statement of the religious response made possible by his critical removal of obstacles. "Our understanding offers mind and body to God without any superstition." This is a good rephrasing of the *Ethics'* theme of love toward God, but now enriched by the act of purifying biblical religion. The proper aim is not to teach the truth of a speculative theology but to arouse people to present their whole being to God, and to do so as conscious and obedient agents rather than as unthinking tools. (pp. 213-15)

[All] of Spinoza's study and experience convinced him of the need to keep faith and philosophy apart. Their separation was not to be based upon ignorance but upon a close inspection of the internal foundation, intent, and scope of each. Any attempt to synthesize faith and philosophy could only result in deforming the cognitive structure of each, as well as in hopelessly confusing any mind trying to learn the truth about God and modal nature. Only in the weak meaning of "philosophy," as a meditative thinking about religious teachings, could there be a scriptural philosophy (whether Hebrew or Christian or Islamic) not ascribing a series of disasters to nature. But this would be different in principle from a philosophical interpretation of nature based on nature itself, with its own method, aim, and evidential reasoning.

In the ***Theological-Political Treatise,*** Spinoza addressed himself primarily to the convention of visualizing the relationship between philosophical reason and theology as that between a handmaid (*ancilla*) and her queen. There was an elaborate spread of diverse interpretations of this metaphor. Most of them held that philosophy performs an honorable and valuable service of methodology, conceptual analysis, and argumentation favoring theology and that, in return, philosophical reason somehow receives strength from the orientation and themes and assurance of theology.

The Spinozan strategy is not to pursue every particular explanation of a handmaid relationship but to reject them all. (pp. 223-24)

Spinoza has no quarrel with a *practical* theology, in the sense of a reflective grasp of the fundamental religious model of upright, caring, and devout conduct. But he opposes any expansion and speculative transformation of it with the help of an ancillated philosophy. This is the gravamen of his critique against all theories viewing philosophic reason as a handmaid to theology. (pp. 224-25)

To prevent any integration and intrinsic connection of the two, Spinoza states flatly that "between faith or theology and philosophy there is no intercourse and no affinity." People of faith and practical theology should not adopt philosophical concepts and arguments as means of explanation and defense. And although philosophers should carefully study scriptural history, language, and credal convictions, they must keep their own assent disengaged as far as truth claims are concerned. The judgment about the moral certitude of prophetic faith is neither identical with, nor derived from, that certitude of speculative truth which belongs only to philosophy. It is best for all parties concerned to disown the confusing dreams and figments generated by ancillation from either side.

Yet Spinoza does not, and indeed cannot, permit his last word on revelational religion to be negative. His critical objective is to show that the elements of biblical religion—its miracle narrative, prophecies, laws, and scriptural expression—do not breach the unity of nature or the philosophically established account of naturing and natured nature. Once this is accomplished, he must reckon with the fact that his own freedom of philosophizing does not ignore religion but finds a function for it (as distinct from scriptural faith and its theology) within his conception of man in nature. . . . This philosophical affirmation of a religious attitude does not water down the principle of "no intercourse and no affinity" between philosophy and scriptural faith or theology, but it does rule out an essential hostility between sage and saint.

Spinoza therefore avoids the dilemma of either handmaid service or hostility as characterizing the relation between revealed faith's practical theology and philosophical reason. Instead, he encourages "each to maintain its domain with supreme harmony [*concordia*]." What keeps this from being just a trite irenic declaration is the threefold way in which Spinoza specifies their concord which is yet no accommodation.

First, the revelational-theological domain has a cognitive structure of its own that does not dissolve under rational inspection. Prophetic faith has a hardiness and rightness about the goals of human living that Spinoza cannot deny. Hence, he often speaks conjunctively about philosophers-and-others, to indicate that the prophets and Christ have a conception of God and man irreducible to, yet in harmony with, the reasoned truth and intellectual intuition of philosophers.

A case in point is the assurance of revealed religion that men can be saved and made blessed solely through obedience to God's word, that is, through acts of faith and piety not dependent upon an understanding of natural things. Since philosophical reason does depend upon the latter understanding and proportions all our knowledge of God and our beatitude to it, Spinoza observes that philosophy cannot strictly show the truth of this religious conviction. Prophets have a singular power above the ordinary, insofar as they proclaim something not perceived by them from the definition of human nature.

Spinoza does not hesitate to comment: "But if there were someone who had another means of perceiving and other foundations of cognition, he might indeed transcend the limits of human nature." Such a cognition would not be an absolute transcendence of nature as a whole, however, or even of the infinite modes constitutive of human nature. It would be precisely an unusually strong influx from the infinite mode of understanding, yet an influx that would remain clouded and distinct from the philosopher's knowledge of God and modal nature.

The second consideration is that the revealed word has the power to illuminate minds which remain impervious to philosophical reasoning. Most people cannot develop the habit of virtue, the pattern of true living, through the guidance of reason alone. But they can listen to the message of faith, grasp and obey it, and thus attain human salvation. This leads Spinoza to affirm explicitly the necessity and usefulness of Sacred Scripture, which brings "a very great consolation to mortals." Scripture cannot make philosophers out of the mass of mankind. But it does remove the doubt of philosophers about whether people lacking a philosophical method of inquiry can nevertheless attain salvation and blessedness. Spinoza's own sympathetic respect for the religious practices of ordinary people is grounded in such considerations rather than in a convenient hypocrisy.

Last, he pinpoints one revelational topic that readily provokes a different sort of reflection, adumbrating his own philosophical view of nature's power and the blessed life. In a remarkable Note added to the *Theological-Political Treatise,* Spinoza draws out the following consequence of his analysis of biblical commandments.

> We have shown that divine commandments appear to us as commandments or statutes only as long as we are ignorant of their cause. But when this is known, they cease thereupon to be commandments, and we embrace them as eternal truths, not as commandments. That is, obedience is thereupon transformed [*transit;* French: *se convertit*] into love, which springs from true cognition just as necessarily as light from the sun.

This text is a masterly compression of Spinoza's thoughts on revelational religion and philosophy.

Within the revelational context, God's will is the central reality. He is viewed as a king issuing laws as commandments for us to obey. But those who share Spinoza's philosophical doctrine on naturing nature, or the divine substance and attributes, do not ascribe will to God. They know philosophically that God acts from the necessity of his nature and that the patterns of being and action in natured nature are eternal truths, expressive of the necessary divine power. Such knowledge of the true causal relation between naturing and natured nature gives rise necessarily to our love toward God.

In the ethical order, this involves a transformational process. What were regarded by veiled revelational faith as commandments for our obedience are now clearly known as eternal truths for our love. The transvaluation does not come from revealed religion but from philosophical understanding of total nature. Hence there is no real ancillation or exchange, but there is a harmony between the two cognitions. And the entire relationship constitutes a specific instance of Spinoza's philosophical meaning for rebirth as a human loving response to the truth about the mind's union with nature in its fullness. (pp. 227-29)

James Collins, in his Spinoza on Nature, *Southern Illinois University Press, 1984, 333 p.*

RALPH C. S. WALKER (essay date 1985)

[In the following excerpt, Walker discusses the coherence theory of truth that undergirds Spinoza's entire metaphysical system.]

Why should one study Spinoza? This question lacks an obvious answer. By tradition Spinoza's name appears in the lists of the great philosophers, and he is catalogued with Descartes and Leibniz as one of the three principal Rationalists. But while Descartes and Leibniz have much to say that is interesting and still of philosophical importance, it is not so evident that Spinoza does. He is often credited with being more consistent than they are; this may or may not be just, but a consistency which is purchased by grounding one's system in a set of unappealing metaphysical axioms is not of very great value. Descartes and Leibniz are of interest because their problems are genuine problems, and their efforts to deal with them are worthwhile attempts even when they are unsuccessful. Spinoza may present some conclusions that one may find attractive, and they may have been sufficiently attractive to other past thinkers to earn him a place in the history of ideas. But since he apparently reaches these conclusions from premises that few people feel much inclination to accept it is natural to doubt whether there is much in his work that is of serious interest to the philosopher; a doubt that may be indirectly strengthened when one observes the great dearth of recent philosophical literature on Spinoza, in contrast with the superabundance of writing on the other philosophers traditionally accounted great.

Spinoza was not always so neglected; and it is my contention that he should not be so neglected now. He was not so neglected by the absolute idealists, who saw him as providing an early, but well worked out, version of the coherence theory of truth. It has now become fairly common to repudiate this interpretation, and to regard Spinoza as a correspondence theorist of a rather conventional kind. I shall try to show that that is a mistake, and that he is not only a coherence theorist, but finds himself constrained to be one by epistemological pressures which retain their force today and have a very similar effect on a number of present-day philosophers. I want also to suggest that this account of truth is far more important to his system as a whole than even the idealists claimed. For if one sees him as *starting* from these epistemological concerns and formulating his coherence theory in response to them, one can then see his principal metaphysical doctrines as following naturally from it. This makes far more sense of his system than the more usual view, which derives his epistemology from his metaphysics and grounds the whole upon a set of disparate and unconvincing assumptions.

That he is a coherence theorist at all requires to be established. That his coherence theory is motivated epistemologically, rather than adopted as a consequence of metaphysical axioms he took to be obvious, must also be shown. And if I am right in suggesting that it is from epistemological considerations that his system starts, rather than grounding itself in the metaphysical axioms of the *Ethics,* it must certainly be explained why he does not make that clear; for I cannot deny that at least in the *Ethics* he gives quite the contrary impression. But before dealing with these issues there is an anterior question which must be got out of the way, if the whole discussion is not to be bedevilled by unnecessary confusion. That is the question what a coherence theory of truth is.

A coherence theory of truth is a theory about the nature of truth; a theory about what truth consists in. It is not simply a theory about how we find out what is true; that we often make use of coherence as a test of truth, and reject as false a belief that fails to cohere with the rest of the things that we believe, is not very controversial. The coherence theory is not the theory that coherence is a likely guide to truth, but rather the view that coherence is all there is to truth, all that truth amounts to.

As such it is not, of course, to be confused with the coherence theory of knowledge. The coherence theory of knowledge is a theory about justification, which the coherence theory of truth is not. The coherence theory of knowledge holds that knowledge claims require justification, but also that no belief can be justified except by reference to other beliefs. Since these other beliefs require justification likewise, and since no infinite regress from belief to belief is possible for infinite creatures like ourselves, claims to knowledge must ultimately be justified by their coherence with the whole system of our beliefs. (They cannot, for example, be grounded in Russellian knowledge by acquaintance, or founded on epistemologically basic beliefs that require no further justification; such possibilities are ruled out.)

One can get from the coherence theory of knowledge to the coherence theory of truth if one takes a verificationistic step, and argues that truth cannot be unknowable: it would not be possible for our beliefs to form a fully justified, coherent set and yet be false of the world. But one can hold the coherence theory of knowledge without the coherence theory of truth if one is prepared to deny that, and admit the sceptical possibility that however good our justifications for our knowledge claims might be, those claims might yet be false. However, many of those who find the coherence theory of knowledge attractive do also find the verificationistic step attractive, and so come to adopt the coherence theory of truth. . . . [It] is worth observing the appeal that the coherence theory of truth continues to have on epistemological grounds.

Indeed, the appeal is not confined to those who are drawn to the coherence theory of knowledge. Quite independently of that, one may be worried by the problems raised by scepticism; and to such problems the coherence theory of truth has a dramatic solution to offer. The sceptic draws attention to the gap that seems to exist between the world, or the facts, on the one hand, and the judgements that we make about them on the other. Our judgements may be justified by all the standards of justification or of rationality that we ordinarily consider satisfactory, but the sceptic asks what right we have to be satisfied with these. Our standards of rationality and justification are *our* standards, after all, and what assures us that our standards are such as to lead us to the truth about the world, and not just reflections of our psychological habits? When the question is posed in so radical a form, many contemporary philosophers are inclined to follow Hume in thinking it unanswerable. But the coherence theorist does have an answer to offer, and for this reason deserves to be taken seriously even though his answer may be at first sight a strange one. For he holds that the truth is not independent of these standards at all: it is what these standards make it, and nothing else. Thus the sceptical gap between our judgements and the world acutally does not exist—or at any rate, does not exist when the judgements in question are as fully rational as we can make them. Again, much needs to be said by way of elaboration and assessment of this suggestion, but this is not the place for it. As we shall see, though, this was the line of argument that made the coherence theory attractive to Spinoza. (pp. 1-3)

The coherence theory of truth is sometimes contrasted with the correspondence theory, but this contrast is at the least misleading. The coherence theory holds that truth consists in nothing more than a relationship of coherence between beliefs; it contrasts with any theory which denies that. It is not however clear that someone who says 'Truth is correspondence with fact' need be denying it at all. The coherence theorist can accept that there are facts, and that true beliefs correspond with them, provided he can give his own account of what the facts and the correspondence ultimately consist in: they ultimately consist in coherence. For the coherence theorist no more seeks to reject what we ordinarily believe than Berkeley sought to reject our ordinary beliefs about the objects around us; what he does is to offer an account, and no doubt a surprising account, of what such beliefs amount to. He does deny that the truth of a belief can ever consist in its corresponding to some reality which is metaphysically independent in the sense that its nature is not determined by the coherent system of beliefs, for if it did then the coherence of the belief system could at best be a guide to truth and not what truth consisted in. But he can perfectly well accept that true propositions 'correspond with the facts' or 'say how things are in the world' if these phrases are understood in the ordinary and commonplace way, not as making a claim about a metaphysically independent reality but as virtual synonyms for 'are true'. (p. 4)

It is therefore by no means possible to establish that Spinoza did not hold a coherence theory of truth simply by pointing out that he sometimes makes remarks one might expect from a correspondence theorist. Most clearly and conspicuously, the sixth axiom of the first part of the *Ethics* says that 'a true idea must agree with that of which it is the idea (*cum suo ideato*)'. But this would show Spinoza not to be a coherence theorist only if it could also be shown that he took the objects of ideas—their *ideata*—to constitute a reality metaphysically independent of beliefs, in the sense that its character is not determined by the coherent system of beliefs. And this cannot be shown, because it is false.

It is false because 'the order and connection of ideas is the same as the order and connection of things', and because this is no mere external parallelism between two distinct orders (such as might have been effected by the will of Descartes' benevolent God) but an essential identity.

> Thinking substance and extended substance are one and the same substance, comprehended now under this attribute, now under that. So, too, a mode of Extension and the idea of that mode are one and the same thing, expressed in two ways. This truth seems to have been glimpsed by some of the Hebrews, who hold that God, God's intellect and the things understood by God are one and the same.

That 'the order and connection of ideas' is such as to constitute a rational and coherent system no reader of Spinoza can seriously doubt. It raises, of course, the question of the relation between the ideas in that rational system and the seemingly confused and incoherent ideas that most of us usually have, but that is a question Spinoza recognizes and to which, as we shall shortly see, he has an answer of some interest. What he is here saying is that the material world, the typical object of thought, is equally a rational order, because it is actually identical with the rational order of thought. The material world is to be equated with coherent thought about it; or in other words, for *p* to be the case in the material world is for the idea that *p* to belong in the coherent system. 'Idea that *p*' is not a mistake: Spinoza is very firm in regarding all 'ideas' as propositional

in form, and so as being in effect beliefs. 'An idea, insofar as it is an idea, involves affirmation or negation'.... (pp. 4-5)

Of course, not all truths are truths about the material world. Spinoza seems to have found the existence of truths of other kinds puzzling, and there are unclarities in his handling of them. What he is consistently clear about, however, is that the relation between the true idea and its object must be of just the same kind in these cases too. This is made entirely explicit in the case of ideas of ideas: the idea of an object is firmly identified with the (rationally coherent) idea of the idea of that object, despite the obvious difficulties that this entails. And truths about things that are merely possible are said to bear the same relation to potentialities that truths about actual things bear to actualities; mathematical truths are included in this class, being taken to be truths about potentialities contained within the attribute of extension. So one is entitled to conclude quite generally that for all values of *p*, the truth of *p* consists in the idea—that—*p* belonging to the coherent system.

Thus a true idea needs nothing outside itself to guarantee its truth or to constitute its correspondence with reality. 'Truth is its own standard'; or again, 'just as light makes manifest both itself and darkness, so truth is the standard both of itself and falsity.' These statements, from the scholium to Prop. 43 of Part II, make so clear a commitment to the coherence theory that it seems hardly necessary to protract the case for ascribing it to Spinoza. Writers like Curley [see excerpt dated 1969]—with whose interpretation I am otherwise, as will be clear, in considerable sympathy—consider that he cannot be a coherence theorist because of his axiom that a true idea must agree with its *ideatum*, and they must therefore interpret statements like these as saying something very different from their clear and obvious sense. I hope I have made it clear that there is no difficulty in holding to a coherence theory while subscribing to that axiom, or to any of the other familiar things we might be inclined to say about true propositions corresponding with facts. What the coherence theory of truth cannot allow is that truth consists in a relationship between a proposition and a reality whose character is not determined by the coherent system of beliefs. But Spinoza does not hold that, and none of his remarks commit him to it; quite the contrary.

However I do not want the case for calling Spinoza a coherence theorist to rest here. For all that has been said so far, the coherence theory might have been comparatively unimportant to him, of interest only as one consequence among others drawn from his metaphysical premises. He might not have considered it particularly interesting in its own right, or thought its ramifications through. If that had been so, the fact that Spinoza was a coherence theorist might still be worth noting, but it would be a point of rather minor significance in the history of ideas. (pp. 5-6)

That the work of Descartes was of great importance to Spinoza can hardly be denied, but it is sometimes thought that all he took from him on philosophical method was the geometrical style of laying out proofs, and that Spinoza was quite insensitive to the worries of Cartesian doubt. This is clearly untrue. His earliest work, *The Principles of Descartes' Philosophy*, begins with a prolegomenon devoted to the method of doubt and to the Cartesian Circle; and his later, unfinished *Treatise on the Improvement of the Understanding* is wholly concerned with the problems of method and of how to secure certainty in the face of sceptical doubt.

It is true that in many respects *The Principles of Descartes' Philosophy* is a presentation of Descartes' views rather than

Spinoza's own. But on the Cartesian Circle he explicitly criticizes Descartes, and attempts to improve on him. Like Arnauld, Gassendi, and many others since, he thinks that Descartes is caught by the accusation of circular reasoning, and can prove that every clear and distinct idea is true only by relying on the truth of his clear and distinct ideas. Spinoza's own argument seeks not so much to prove that our clear and distinct ideas are true as to show that once one has a clear and distinct idea of God one cannot reasonably doubt them. The clear and distinct idea of a triangle, he says, 'compels us to conclude that its three angles equal two right angles'; similarly once we have the clear and distinct idea of God that idea 'compels us to affirm that God is in the highest degree truthful'. But there is a difference between the two cases. In the case of the triangles it is possible to stand back from the proof and raise a doubt whether we may not be deceived, even in so evident a matter, by a malevolent deity. With the idea of God, however, no such standing back is possible. For to possess the clear and distinct idea of God is already to see that the hypothesis of the malevolent deity is ruled out.

This may not be adequate to resolve the difficulty, but it is a serious attempt to tackle it—not a set of offhand remarks by someone for whom the problems of sceptical doubt had no significance. There are, however, two reasons why it will not do. In the first place the sceptic will say that the same kind of standing back *is* possible with the idea of God: for although when I attend to the content of the idea I must find myself convinced of God's benevolence, I can also turn my attention away from that content and raise a doubt as to whether I may not be deceived even in those things that seem to me immediately self-evident, as this did. In the second place, and more fundamentally, Spinoza's argument would at best show that our clear and distinct ideas could not rationally be doubted. But it is one thing to show this, and another and very different thing to show that they are actually true. Any *malin génie* [wicked genius] who was doing his job properly would presumably make sure that we were not only mistaken, but incapable of recognizing the fact.

Spinoza may have a reply to the first of these points, for he regards it as important that, once one has the clear and distinct idea of God, it should simply be self-evident that he is no deceiver. In contrast, it is not immediately self-evident, but only known by demonstration, that the internal angles of a triangle equal two right angles. He apparently thinks that it is only in the case of what is clearly and distinctly known *as a result of demonstration* that a guarantee of truth is needed, and that Descartes went wrong in trying to provide this guarantee by a proof of God which was itself demonstrative and not immediately self-evident. But if this is how he thinks of the matter one can only reply that sceptical doubt can arise over what seems self-evident as much as over what seems to have been demonstrated. For why should the fact that something seems to us obvious, even very immediately obvious, be a sign of its truth? In a world arranged by a *malin génie*, it would not be.

Descartes was aware of this. And if Spinoza was not aware of it here, he was aware of it when he wrote the ***Treatise on the Improvement of the Understanding***. In the ***Treatise*** he is also well aware of the difference between showing that something cannot be doubted and showing that it is true. And it is in the ***Treatise*** that he works towards the coherence theory of truth as providing his own answer to these difficulties.

He still holds that the key to philosophical method lies in possessing the clear and distinct idea of God. But it is no longer offered as sufficient by itself for avoiding the circle and providing a guarantee of truth. It is recognized that it is not, and three separate—though complementary—moves are made in response to that recognition. All of them are remarkably modern in character, and are of types that have come in for much recent discussion.

The first is to suggest that no guarantee of truth is necessary in order to possess knowledge (though Spinoza obscures his argument here by using the word 'certainty'—*certitudo*—where he should have stuck consistently to 'knowledge'). His point is that one possesses knowledge if one's 'idea' is true, and captures the relevant essence. It is not necessary that one be able to *show that* one's idea has this status; it is enough that it should simply have it. It may be necessary to show that it has it if one is to know that one knows, but that is a different matter; to know, one does not have to know that one knows. The sceptic's argument may perhaps show that we do not know that we know; but it does not show that we do not know; and it is therefore less worrying than he makes it appear.

Evidently this is disputable. Many (including myself) would still think that one must standardly be able to justify a belief before one can be said to know it. But theories of knowledge such as Goldman's or Nozick's, which dispense with any such condition of justification, allow their adherents to make very much the same point against the sceptic.

The second move takes the form of a transcendental argument—an argument of the kind much used by Kant or Strawson. Spinoza has started by assuming that we do have some grasp of the truth: we possess 'a true idea', which provides us with a tool for the discovery of more and more truth. But what if some sceptic calls this assumption into question? The reply is that he could not mean it, or he could not even be self-conscious.

> Such persons are not conscious of themselves. If they affirm or doubt anything, they know not that they affirm or doubt: they say that they know nothing, and they say that they are ignorant of the very fact of their knowing nothing . . . In fact, they ought to remain dumb, for fear of haply supposing something which should smack of truth . . . If they deny, grant, or gainsay, they know not that they deny, grant, or gainsay, so that they ought to be regarded automata, utterly devoid of intelligence.

Again this is not immediately convincing as it stands; Spinoza is apparently overlooking the fact that someone might possess some knowledge, e.g. about his own mental states, without having the kind of 'true idea' that he is really arguing for, one that is capable of giving its possessor the key to the whole rational system of knowledge. Again, though, he has provided a form of argument against the sceptic which is much used nowadays (though whether with greater success is another matter).

If the argument were successful it would not, of course, show that we do possess 'a true idea'. What it would show would be that we could not doubt it. If we attempted seriously to doubt it we should lapse into an incoherence which could not even constitute a doubt. This would not show that the idea was actually true: independent reality might fail to correspond, however impossible it was for us to entertain that suggestion seriously. Some epistemologists feel that at this point the argument against scepticism can go no further, and they may be right; but Spinoza was not among them. For he has a third move to make.

The third move consists in giving an account of truth: the coherence theory. This is the most radical of the three moves, and it is not fully worked out in the *Treatise*. It is also the most effective, for if truth consists in coherence the problem is solved: there is no question of our ideas or our beliefs having to match an independent reality about which a malevolent god could deceive us. Truth is now an internal relationship within the rational system of beliefs. There may be problems about determining which of our beliefs belong to the rational system; indeed there undoubtedly are, and it is one of the things Spinoza is most concerned about. But they are problems of a quite different kind from the intractable problem of match with an independent reality. They are to be resolved by the rational examination of our ideas themselves; and this exercise of rational examination will be sufficient to give us the truth, without the need to rely on God to ensure a harmony between the rational order of thought and the order of facts in the world.

Spinoza is explicit about this being an account of the nature (*forma*) of truth.

> It is certain that a true idea is distinguished from a false one, not so much by its extrinsic object as by its intrinsic nature . . . Thus that which constitutes the nature of a true thought must be sought in the thought itself, and deduced from the nature (*natura*) of the understanding . . . Thus *falsity* consists only in this, that something is affirmed of a thing, which is not contained in the conception we have formed of that thing.

He supports it by an argument his opponents might not find convincing, to the effect that there are truths to which nothing in the world corresponds, so that there is nothing their truth can consist in except coherence. Thus, he says, an architect's plan can be 'a true idea' though the building in the plan is never built; or again the geometrical conception of a sphere as produced by a revolving semicircle, 'although we know that no sphere in nature has ever actually been so formed'. This is not the view of the *Ethics,* where, to maintain the identity between the order and connection of ideas and the order and connection of things, he holds rather obscurely that mathematical truths and truths about unactualized possibilities have as their counterparts potentialities in the attribute of extension. But it is not, perhaps, a thought to be dismissed out of hand, since puzzlement over the character of mathematical truth has often led people to think that in that area, at least, truth must consist in something like coherence.

These three moves having been made, Spinoza has given his answer to the problem of the Cartesian Circle. He can now repeat the argument about the clear and distinct idea of God, from *The Principles of Descartes' Philosophy*. But that argument now only purports to show the impossibility of rational doubt, once one has that idea. The gap between what we cannot rationally doubt and what is actually the case has already been bridged, by the coherence theory. (pp. 7-11)

Spinoza differs from Descartes on the usefulness of the synthetic method in philosophy. That much is clear from his having taken the trouble to write a book presenting Descartes' system synthetically, for that is what *The Principles of Descartes' Philosophy* is: the epistemological considerations which we have discussed do not come in the main body of that work, but in the Prolegomenon. His reason, no doubt, is the one given in Meyer's Preface and indeed hinted at by Descartes himself,

that many people found Descartes' analytical arguments unconvincing and hard to follow. This may have been because they were accustomed to systems laid out synthetically, and perhaps because of an undue respect for Euclid's geometry as the model for *scientia;* but whatever the reason it is clearly the synthetic method that he chose to adopt himself in setting his own views out in the *Ethics*. By doing so he committed himself to the view that the axioms and postulates that he uses have the status Descartes claimed for his: they are 'in their own nature intelligible', but not necessarily immediately obvious. Nothing in the account that I have suggested of Spinoza's thought is inconsistent with that. But because they are not immediately obvious we need an argument to persuade us of their truth, and to show us why Spinoza should have been convinced of them. It is just such an argument that we should have been given if Spinoza had provided us with another treatise set out as Descartes' *Meditations* are set out, following the analytic method.

Why did Spinoza not write such another treatise? It is arguable that he did, or rather that he began it. The *Treatise on the Improvement of the Understanding* sets out in the Cartesian style to tackle the problems of epistemology and of philosophical method, and we have seen how seriously it takes these problems and how it ultimately develops the coherence theory of truth in response to them. It then breaks off. But it was intended to go much further than this. It was intended to lead on to a complete account of his philosophy. Since it presents us with the coherence theory, and since the coherence theory does naturally lead on to the rest of Spinoza's metaphysics—some of the key steps, and in particular the recognition that our minds must be part of God's, occurring in the *Treatise* itself—it seems difficult to doubt that the completed work would have taken the lines I have been suggesting, and developed his metaphysics from his epistemological concerns.

The *Treatise* is a relatively early work, in which the coherence theory has not yet been fully assimilated. It seems reasonable to conjecture that he wrote it in the process of developing his views, but postponed the completion of it once his metaphysical position was formed, preferring instead to organize his results in the synthetic form of a Euclidean deductive system. But it also seems clear that he never abandoned the project of rewriting and completing his earlier work. If he had lived long enough to do so, we should have had from Spinoza a work analogous to Descartes' *Meditations;* and perhaps Spinoza would have had a juster appreciation from his philosophical successors. (pp. 17-18)

> *Ralph C. S. Walker, "Spinoza and the Coherence Theory of Truth," in* Mind, *Vol. XCIV, No. 373, January, 1985, pp. 1-18.*

HENRY E. ALLISON   (essay date 1987)

[*Allison is an American philosopher and educator. In the following excerpt, he examines the last three parts of the* Ethics *to illumine Spinoza's thoughts on the human mind and emotions and the concepts of moral perfection and eternity.*]

The last three parts of the *Ethics* form a unity, and together they contain what, broadly speaking, can be characterized as Spinoza's moral philosophy. This comprises an analysis of the human emotions and how human beings are subject to them (part 3); an account of the nature of human virtue, or *ethics* in the narrow sense of the term, which includes both the presentation of rational rules for living and an analysis of the ''good life'' (part 4); and a theory of human blessedness, which provides a philosophical alternative to the traditional religious doctrine of salvation (part 5). These are the main consequences that Spinoza derives from the argument of the first two parts. . . .

Despite its agreement on many points of detail with previous treatments of the subject, most notably that of Descartes, Spinoza's analysis of the human emotions is one of the more interesting and original aspects of his philosophy. This originality consists largely in the thoroughgoing naturalism of his approach. (p. 124)

[Spinoza holds] that the human mind is capable of feeling love or hatred toward any number of things, and much the same can be said in regard to two other key derivative emotions, hope and fear. The former is defined as *''an inconstant pleasure which has arisen from the image of a future or past thing whose outcome we doubt,''* and the latter as *''an inconstant pain, which has also arisen from the image of a doubtful thing.''* These emotions, like everything else in nature, do not arise capriciously, but in accordance with universal and necessary laws. In the context of his analysis, Spinoza presents two such laws. . . . The first has been called the ''law of the association of emotions.'' According to this law, an object that has never been itself a cause of pleasure, pain, or desire may become such by being associated with one that has. This association can be based on similarity, contrast, or contiguity. For instance, the mind necessarily tends to love objects resembling those that it already loves, hate those that contrast sharply with them, and love and hate in turn those things which it commonly finds together with the objects that it loves and hates. The second basic law can be called the ''law of the imitation of the emotions.'' This law explains how an object that is neither an essential nor an accidental (through association) cause of pleasure, pain, or desire may become such if it happens to cause them in other human beings whose emotions we naturally tend to imitate. Here Spinoza deals for the first time with the social nature of human beings and explains emotions such as sympathy, pity, and joy in the well-being of others.

But these laws deal with the mind only insofar as it is passive—that is, only insofar as it is the inadequate, or partial, cause of its affections. To the extent that it is passive, it is subject primarily to external causes, as a result of which ''we are driven about in many ways . . . and . . . like waves on the sea, driven by contrary winds, we toss about, not knowing our outcome and fate.'' Nevertheless, although Spinoza repudiates the Cartesian conception of the power of the mind in terms of a free will, he no more believes that the above account tells the whole story of the emotive life of the mind than that the analysis of sense perception and imagination tells the whole story of the mind's cognitive life.

Accordingly, at the end of his long analysis of the passive emotions, or passions, Spinoza briefly introduces and describes the active emotions: *''Apart from Pleasure and Desire that are passions,''* he notes, *''there are other affects of Pleasure and Desire that are related to us insofar as we act.''* These affects are grounded in the mind's adequate ideas. When the mind conceives anything adequately, it is necessarily also aware of itself. It is thus aware of its power or activity, and this gives rise to an active emotion of pleasure. This emotion is basically what other philosophers have described as ''intellectual pleasure,'' although Spinoza is careful to point out that the source of the pleasure is the mind's sense of its own activity, not the nature of the object. Similarly, desire as an active emotion is simply rational desire, or the endeavor to preserve one's being

insofar as that endeavor is guided by adequate ideas (scientific knowledge). However there is no active analogy to pain, the third primary emotion. This emotion reflects a diminution in the mind's power or activity which, as we have seen, can never be the result of the mind's activity, or adequate ideas, but merely of its being determined by external forces and its possession of inadequate understanding.

This account closes with the suggestion that all a person's actions stemming from active emotions can be ascribed to *''strength of character (fortitudo).''* This, in turn, is divided into *''courage (animositas)''* and *''nobility (generositas).''* Courage is defined as ''the Desire by which each one strives, solely from the dictates of reason, to preserve his being.'' . . . [Courage] construed in this broad sense is equivalent to virtue as a whole, although it is here referred solely to actions concerned with the good of the agent. As such, it is contrasted with nobility, which is defined as ''the Desire by which each one strives, solely from the dictates of the reason, to aid other men and join them to him in friendship.'' This governs our actions when we are concerned with the well-being of others and provides the basis of the social virtues. Within the confines of part 3 and the *Ethics*, however, Spinoza does little more than describe and affirm the possibility of these active emotions through which the mind can escape being a slave to its passions. The actual demonstration of this claim and the development of its implications for the understanding of the moral life are the aims of part 4 of the *Ethics*, which deals with the nature of virtue.

The full and revolutionary implications of Spinoza's naturalistic-rationalistic program emerge with his analysis of virtue. Traditionally, most moral philosophers, as well as the proverbial man in the street, have viewed ''moral perfection'' and ''goodness'' as absolute values that one ought to and can realize. Within the Judeo-Christian tradition, this view has often been linked with the conception of a human being as created wth a free will by a personal deity who requires obedience to a set of commandments that define the morally good. The eternal destiny of the individual is then linked to the fulfillment of these commandments (the ''Divine Law''). For the past three hundred years, this religious ethic has competed with a secular, ''humanistic'' ethic, in which the theological trimmings have been removed but the belief that human beings have free wills and are obligated to perform certain duties quite independently of their interests and desires, remains. The conscientious performance of these duties is called ''virtue'' and is deemed worthy of praise, whereas the failure to perform them is considered morally blameworthy. (pp. 138-41)

Spinoza had little sympathy for this moral outlook in either its religious or secular form. For him, the entire outlook, as well as the conception of human nature that it entails, is a product of the imagination, rather than of reason. As such, it is based on inadequate ideas—specifically, on a failure to recognize that human beings, as finite modes, are parts of nature, and that their particular desires and values, as well as their actions, are necessary consequences of the endeavor to preserve their being. Spinoza succinctly expresses this view at the conclusion of his account of the conatus doctrine in part 3: ''From all this, then, it is clear that we neither strive for, nor will, neither want, nor desire anything because we judge it to be good; on the contrary, we judge something to be good because we strive for it, will it, want it, desire it.''

Spinoza develops his critique of traditional morality further in the preface to part 4. After providing a nonevaluative definition of *perfection* in terms of the completed, or finished, and noting that, so construed, it applies only to artifacts, he attempts to explain how the notion and its opposite came to acquire an evaluative sense and to be applied to natural things (including human beings). This is traced to mankind's tendency, under the domination of the imagination, to form universal ideas (which are, of course, highly confused) and to regard them as norms, or models (*exemplaria*) in terms of which things and their actions are to be judged. Given such models, perfection and imperfection are now understood evaluatively in terms of conformity or lack thereof to the model—for example, the ''perfect'' human being is the one who realizes or comes closest to realizing the ''ideal'' of what it is to be a human being. The specifically moral notions of *good* and *evil* are likewise defined in terms of these models. Not surprisingly, Spinoza connects the development of this way of thinking with the belief in final causes. The basic idea here seems to be that belief in a norm or model reflects belief in a purpose for which a thing has been created. For Spinoza, however, these ''purposes,'' together with the associated models, are really nothing more than projections of human desires. He thus concludes that perfection and imperfection, good and evil, are not intrinsic properties of things, but merely ''modes of thinking''—fictions that we attribute to things insofar as we consider them in light of our desire-based model. (pp. 141-42)

In common with many moralists, Spinoza thus maintains that the virtuous, good, happy, or free life (these terms being used more or less interchangeably) is the life of reason. In opposition to most traditional moralists, however, Spinoza also claims that the possibility of reason governing the passions is not to be explained in terms of some mysterious power of the will (in the manner of Descartes). . . . [Only] a stronger and contrary emotion can destroy or control a given emotion, and hence, that the possibility of reason controlling the passions depends on reason itself, or adequate ideas, possessing an emotive force.

We still have not learned, however, either the specific means for the attainment of victory over the passions or the nature of the human condition in which the victory is attained. These are the subject matter of the last part of the *Ethics,* which falls into two distinct portions. The first twenty propositions present some quite specific guidelines, practical precepts, or (to use Spinoza's term) ''remedies'' by means of which the intellect can maximize its control over the passions. The last twenty-two propositions deal mainly with the nature of blessedness (the state of victory). They contain Spinoza's discussion of the sense in which a part of the human mind can be said to be eternal and his account of the ''intellectual love of God'' (*amor intellectualis Dei*) in which this blessedness consists. A central theme running through both parts is the superior efficacy of the third kind of knowledge.

Spinoza begins by laying down the basic principle in terms of which the entire discussion is to proceed: *''In just the same way as thoughts and ideas of things are ordered and connected in the Mind, so the affections or the body, or images of things are ordered and connected in the body.''* This follows immediately from the identity of the order and connection of things. It has been aptly called the ''metaphysics of the remedy,'' because it allows Spinoza to claim that the mind can have control over the modifications of the body, even though they do not interact. As the proposition makes clear, the modifications or affections in question are the images of the external things that affect the body and determine its appetites. According to the above principle, it follows that insofar as the

ideas in the mind are ordered in the mamner of the ''order of the intellect,'' the images and appetites, which are their physical correlates, will be similarly ordered.

The practical problem is how to produce the desired condition, and its resolution actually requires nothing more than explicitly focusing on a number of points that have already been established. In his general approach Spinoza follows Descartes in affirming that the key lies in the mind's ability to break established patterns of association and replace them with new ones. Unlike Descartes, however, he views these associations as holding between ideas, and not between ideas and corporeal states—for example, Descartes's ''animal spirits.'' His analysis of the remedies for excessive love or hate is a case in point. These emotions . . . were defined respectively as pleasure and pain accompanied by the idea of an external cause. The imagined external cause of one's pleasure or pain is the object of the emotion, and the way to overcome the emotion is to sever it from *this* idea of the external cause. This can be accomplished by uniting it to the thought of another cause. For example, hate toward a particular individual who has done one some harm can be overcome, or at least be diminished, by thinking of the harmful action as only a contributing factor in one's pain and as itself conditioned by a prior cause, and this, in turn, by a prior cause, and so on. In short, rather than focusing one's attention entirely on the unique object of hatred, one comes to see it as merely a link in a causal chain. Since doing this is equivalent to forming a clear and distinct idea of the emotion, Spinoza claims that *''an affect which is a passion ceases to be a passion as soon as we form a clear and distinct idea of it.''*

Furthermore, since *''there is no affection of the Body of which we cannot form a clear and distinct concept''*—that is, none which we cannot understand in terms of general laws, or ''common notions''—and since an emotion is an idea of an affection, or modification, of the body, it follows that there is no emotion of which we cannot form a clear and distinct idea. This, of course, means that our emotions are capable of being understood scientifically; and this possibility provides a basis for Spinoza's recommendation that we endeavor to cultivate a detached, objective attitude toward our own emotional life. Although he naturally recognizes that there are limits to our ability to do this, he also insists that, to the extent to which we can attain such an attitude, we can gain control not only of our loves and hates, but also of our desires and appetites. (pp. 159-61)

[To] have an adequate idea of something is to conceive it under a species of eternity, and this is equivalent to participating in the infinite intellect of God. This, however, is a matter of epistemological accomplishment, not of ontological identification. In other words, on the epistemological interpretation, the identification of the idea in the human mind with the idea in God concerns only the content, or ''objective reality,'' of the idea, not its actual or ''formal reality'' as a mental occurrence. Moreover, if this is how the identity is understood, then the eternity of the human mind turns out to be equivalent to the mind's capacity to conceive itself and the essence of its body as eternally necessitated—that is, to understand itself by the third kind of knowledge. So construed, *eternity* refers to an actual capacity of the human mind, not simply a feature of certain propositions about its object. Nevertheless, the mind retains this capacity only as long as it endures, which is, of course, no longer than the duration of the body of which it is an idea. (pp. 171-72)

[Spinoza's] account culminates in the claim that *"the third kind of knowledge depends on the Mind, as on a formal cause, insofar as the Mind itself is eternal."* Indeed, in a scholium to this proposition, Spinoza suggests not merely that the mind's ability to know things by the third kind of knowledge depends on part of it being eternal, but also that "the Mind is eternal insofar as it conceives things under a species of eternity." If it does not actually require it, this remark certainly supports the epistemological interpretation of the mind's eternity.

We should further expect that Spinoza would not only equate the mind's capacity to conceive things, including itself and the essence of the body, by means of the third kind of knowledge with its eternity, but also with its blessedness, or perfection. Once again, this is precisely what Spinoza attempts to do. This equation, which constitutes the culmination of his philosophy, is reached by showing how the third kind of knowledge gives rise to the intellectual love of God. Since Spinoza has already emphasized the importance of the love of God as the supreme remedy against the passions, it might appear strange to find him reintroducing it in the present context. This can be understood, however, in terms of the twofold function of part 5. The love of God in the previous account was certainly "intellectual," even though Spinoza does not characterize it as such (recall that he connects it with the third kind of knowledge). But, as a force against the passions, as a weapon in the moral struggle, such love is "this-worldly" in the religious sense. In this respect at least, it is analogous to the Christian conception of divine grace as an aid in the struggle with sin. But now, having completed his analysis of that struggle and, with it, "everything which concerns the present life," it is perfectly appropriate for Spinoza to return to the topic of the love of God, this time with the intention of showing that it constitutes human blessedness. Viewed from this perspective, it provides the Spinozistic alternative to the beatific vision.

The connection between the third kind of knowledge, the intellectual love of God, and human blessedness is quite direct. Once again, the main point is that the understanding of anything in this matter is intrinsically satisfying, and since this understanding involves comprehending the thing in question in relation to God, this satisfaction is accompanied by the idea of God as its cause. The equation of the satisfaction connected with such a cognitive state with the love of God depends, of course, on Spinoza's rather peculiar conception of love as pleasure accompanied by the idea of an external cause. Given this conception, anything that can serve as a cause of pleasure can be an object of love. The pleasure—or, better, mental satisfaction—associated with the third kind of knowledge is the pure joy of understanding. God is the cause of this joy in the sense that he is both the ultimate object of knowledge and the source of the very intelligibility of things. In the last analysis, then, the intellectual love of God turns out to be equivalent to the delight in the intelligibility of things that accompanies the mind's satisfaction with its own cognitive powers. This same satisfaction also constitutes human blessedness.

Given this conception of intellectual love, we can also understand Spinoza's mystical-sounding and paradoxical claims that *"God loves himself with an infinite intellectual love,"* and that *"The Mind's intellectual Love of God is the very Love of God by which God loves himself, not insofar as he is infinite, but insofar as he can be explained by the human Mind's essence, considered under a species of eternity; i.e., the Mind's intellectual Love of God is part of the infinite Love by which God loves himself."* Having been told previously that, "strictly speaking, God loves no one," one is taken aback by these propositions. In reality, however, there is no contradiction or change of doctrine, but merely another example of Spinoza's tendency to express his rationalistic thought in traditional religious terms. Since the human mind has been shown to be a finite modification expressed in the attribute of thought and, with regard to its adequate ideas, part of the infinite intellect of God, the mind's love of God is equivalent to God's love of himself so modified. Spinoza's claim, in other words, reduces to an elaborately expressed tautology; and there is no reason to believe that he intended it to be construed otherwise. By expressing himself in this convoluted and paradoxical manner, Spinoza is, in effect, saying to theologians that this is the only way one can understand their central contention that God loves mankind.

Finally, since the mind both acts and is eternal precisely to the degree to which it possesses adequate ideas, and since minds obviously differ on this score, they also differ in the degree to which they are eternal. In fact, since the capacity of the mind has been shown to be functionally (but not causally) related to the capacity of the body, Spinoza can even claim that *"he who has a Body capable of a great many things has a Mind whose greatest part is eternal."* And presumably, although Spinoza is hardly clear on this point, since every human mind has an adequate idea of God and therefore some degree of insight into the rational order of things, every human mind must have some vestige of the satisfaction or blessedness (intellectual love) which necessarily accompanies that insight. Unfortunately, for most of us, this is far outweighed by our imaginatively based ideas and their concomitant passions—hope, fear, and so on. For the fortunate few who are capable of attaining the third kind of knowledge, however, this satisfaction is far greater. Thus, with respect to such minds, Spinoza remarks that the part which perishes with the body "is of no moment in relation to what remains." What perishes, of course, is the imagination and its associated passions; whereas what remains—that is, what constitutes the actuality of such minds—is rational thought.

Spinoza's whole philosophy is epitomized in the final proposition: *"Blessedness is not the reward of virtue, but virtue itself; nor do we enjoy it because we restrain our lusts; on the contrary, because we enjoy it, we are able to restrain them."* In order to understand this proposition, we need only keep in mind the connection between blessedness and knowledge on the one hand and knowledge and power on the other. Spinoza's point is simply that we do not acquire this knowledge by first controlling our lusts or passions, but that we have the power to control them only to the extent to which we already possess adequate knowledge. Thus, whereas the ignorant are perpetually tormented by their passions and seldom attain peace of mind, "the wise man, insofar as he is considered as such, is hardly troubled in spirit but being, by a certain eternal necessity, conscious of himself, and of God, and of things, he never ceases to be, but always possesses true peace of mind." Such, then, is the good, the particular form of human existence to which the *Ethics* attempts to point the way. It is certainly hard to achieve, but as Spinoza remarks in his famous closing words: "What is found so rarely must be hard. For if salvation were at hand, and could be found without great effort, how could nearly everyone neglect it? But all things excellent are as difficult as they are rare." (pp. 172-75)

Henry E. Allison, in his Benedict de Spinoza: An Introduction, *revised edition, Yale University Press, 1987, 254 p.*

ADDITIONAL BIBLIOGRAPHY

Atkins, Dorothy. *George Eliot and Spinoza.* Edited by James Hogg. Salzburg Studies in English Literature, no. 78. Salzburg, Austria: Institut für Englische Sprache und Literatur Universität Salzburg, 1978, 188 p.
> Noncritical exposition of *Ethics,* discussion of the yet unpublished George Eliot translation, and examination of Spinoza's influence on Eliot and her novels.

Bennett, Jonathan. *A Study of Spinoza's "Ethics."* Indianapolis: Hackett Publishing Co., 1984, 396 p.
> In-depth study of *Ethics,* which Bennett considers "Spinoza's one indisputable masterpiece."

Cairns, Huntington. "Spinoza." In his *Legal Philosophy from Plato to Hegel,* pp. 272-94. Baltimore: Johns Hopkins Press, 1949.
> Examines Spinoza's thought regarding divine law, human law, and the role of the State.

Delahunty, R. J. *Spinoza.* London: Routledge & Kegan Paul, 1985, 317 p.
> Analysis of Spinoza's epistemology, metaphysics, theory of the mind, psychology, ethics, and conception of immortality.

Duff, Robert A. *Spinoza's Political and Ethical Philosophy.* Glasgow: James Maclehose and Sons, 1903, 516 p.
> Explores Spinoza's views regarding humanity and society.

Ellis, Havelock. "Spinoza." In his *My Confessional: Questions of Our Day,* pp. 181-83. Boston: Houghton Mifflin, 1934.
> Considers Spinoza's critical reputation.

Feuer, Lewis Samuel. *Spinoza and the Rise of Liberalism.* Boston: Beacon Press, 1958, 323 p.
> Study of Spinoza as a reactionary thinker. Feuer gives particular attention to the political and intellectual milieu that fostered Spinoza's thought.

Freeman, Eugene, and Mandelbaum, Maurice, eds. *Spinoza: Essays in Interpretation.* LaSalle, Ill.: Open Court, 1975, 323 p.
> Collection of fourteen essays, many of which focus on Spinoza's philosophy of the mind. Essayists include E. M. Curley and Stuart Hampshire.

Grene, Marjorie, ed. *Spinoza: A Collection of Critical Essays.* Garden City, New York: Anchor Books/Doubleday, 1973, 390 p.
> Contains essays organized under three major topics: Spinoza's geometric method, his metaphysics, and his conception of humanity and society. Essayists include H. A. Wolfson and William A. Earle.

Hallett, H. F. *Creation, Emanation, and Salvation: A Spinozistic Study.* The Hague: Martinus Nijhoff, 1962, 234 p.
> Speculative study of Spinoza's thought that attempts to clarify his views on nature, morality, humanity, and God.

Hessing, Siegfried, ed. *Speculum Spinozanum 1677-1977.* London: Routledge & Kegan Paul, 1977, 590 p.
> Tricentennial collection of essays by scholars from around the world. Essays include: "Psychotherapeutic Principles in Spinoza's *Ethics,*" by Walter Bernard; "Spinoza and Christian Thought: A Challenge," by Robert Misrahi; and "Individuality and Society in Spinoza's Mind," by Joaquim Cerqueira Goncalves.

Inquiry 12, No. 1 (1969): 1-65.
> Special Spinoza issue contains Ruth L. Saw's "Personal Identity in Spinoza"; G. H. R. Parkinson's "Language and Knowledge in Spinoza"; and Guttorm Floistad's "Spinoza's Theory of Knowledge Applied to the *Ethics.*"

Joachim, Harold H. *A Study of the Ethics of Spinoza.* Oxford: Oxford University Press, Clarendon Press, 1901, 316 p.
> Step-by-step elucidation of *Ethics.*

Kashap, S. Paul, ed. *Studies in Spinoza: Critical and Interpretive Essays.* Berkeley and Los Angeles: University of California Press, 1972, 355 p.
> Includes such articles as "Spinoza and Time," by S. Alexander; "Spinoza and Language," by David Savan; and "Spinoza and the Idea of Freedom," by Stuart Hampshire.

Kennington, Richard, ed. *The Philosophy of Baruch Spinoza.* Studies in Philosophy and the History of Philosophy, edited by Jude P. Dougherty, vol. 7. Catholic University of America Press, 1980, 323 p.
> Presents several contemporary views of Spinoza. Essays include "Spinozistic Anomalies," by Jose Bernardete; "Analytic and Synthetic Methods in Spinoza's *Ethics,*" by Richard Kennington; and "The Deductive Character of Spinoza's Metaphysics," by Michael Hooker.

McEachran, F. "Nietzsche, Spinoza, and Human Pity." *The Contemporary Review* CLIV (December 1938): 707-15.
> Asserts that the "human success" philosophies of Friedrich Nietzsche and Spinoza fail to accommodate humankind's essentially flawed nature, which, McEachran holds, best explains the need for divine salvation.

McShea, Robert J. *The Political Philosophy of Spinoza.* New York: Columbia University Press, 1968, 214 p.
> Examines Spinoza's writings as they pertain to the interconnections between government, society, and the individual.

Martineau, James. *A Study of Spinoza.* London: Macmillan and Co., 1883, 393 p.
> Balanced appraisal of Spinoza's life and philosophy.

Mellone, S. H. "Spinoza." In his *The Dawn of Modern Thought: Descartes, Spinoza, and Leibniz,* pp. 47-86. London: Oxford University Press, 1930.
> Overview of Spinoza's life and the basic tenets of his philosophy.

Mintz, Samuel I. "Spinoza and Spinozism in Singer's Shorter Fiction." *Studies in American Jewish Literature,* No. 1 (1981): 75-82.
> Compares the world views of Isaac Bashevis Singer and Spinoza through an examination of Singer's story "The Spinoza of Market Street."

Oko, Adolph S. *The Spinoza Bibliography.* Boston: G. K. Hall & Co., 1964, 700 p.
> Extensive bibliography of works by and about Spinoza through 1942.

Osgood, Samuel. "The Centenary of Spinoza." *The North American Review* CCLV (March-April 1877): 265-88.
> Essay commemorating Spinoza's philosophical career.

Parkinson, G. H. R. *Spinoza's Theory of Knowledge.* Oxford: Oxford University Press, Clarendon Press, 1954, 194 p.
> Treats Spinoza's views on epistemology. Parkinson draws largely upon *Ethics* in his examination, though he makes frequent comparisons with Spinoza's other works, including the *Theological-Political Treatise* and *On the Improvement of the Understanding.*

Pitts, Edward I. "Spinoza on Freedom of Expression." *Journal of the History of Ideas* XLVII, No. 1 (January-March 1986): 21-35.
> Critiques Spinoza's understanding of free expression.

Scruton, Roger. *Spinoza.* Oxford and New York: Oxford University Press, 1986, 122 p.
> Discussion of Spinoza's life, intellectual background, and complex thought aimed at a broad readership.

Strauss, Leo. *Spinoza's Critique of Religion.* New York: Schocken Books, 1965, 146 p.
> Comprehensive examination of the *Theological-Political Treatise* which includes a general introduction to the tradition of religious critique. Much of this work was written in 1930.

Wetlesen, Jon. *Spinoza's Philosophy of Man: Proceedings of the Scandinavian Spinoza Symposium 1977.* Oslo: Universitetsforlaget, 1978, 224 p.

Collection of addresses focusing on Spinoza's relevance to modern society. Essayists include H. L. Parsons, David Savan, and E. M. Curley.

Wilbur, James B. *Spinoza's Metaphysics: Essays in Critical Appreciation*. Amsterdam: Van Gorcum & Co., 1976, 163 p.

Includes such essays as ''Decartes and Spinoza,'' by Stanley Rosen; ''The Attribute of Thought,'' by Robert N. Beck; and ''Is Spinoza's God Self-Conscious?'' by James B. Wilbur. The collection also contains a selected bibliography of works by and about Spinoza.

Wolfson, Harry Austryn. *The Philosophy of Spinoza: Unfolding the Latent Processes of His Reasoning*. Cambridge, Mass.: Harvard University Press, 1934, 440 p.

Detailed examination of Spinoza's philosophical system by a prominent Spinoza scholar.

Zweig. Arnold. *The Living Thoughts of Spinoza*. New York: Longmans, Green and Co., 1939, 162 p.

Biographical and critical discussion of Spinoza and his works, followed by selections from *On the Improvement of the Understanding* and *Ethics*.

Appendix

The following is a listing of all sources used in Volume 9 of *Literature Criticism from 1400 to 1800*. Included in this list are all copyright and reprint rights and acknowledgments for those essays for which permission was obtained. Every effort has been made to trace copyright, but if omissions have been made, please let us know.

THE EXCERPTS IN LC, VOLUME 9, WERE REPRINTED FROM THE FOLLOWING PERIODICALS:

The Academy, v. XXI, February 18, 1882; v. LI, September 15, 1900.

The Asiatic Review, v. XLIII, October, 1947.

The Atlantic Monthly, v. CII, July, 1908.

Blackwood's Edinburgh Magazine, v. 56, July, 1844.

The Catholic World, v. LXXVIII, February, 1904; v. CIV, January, 1917.

Christianity Today, v. XXVII, October 21, 1983. © 1983 by Christianity Today, Inc. Reprinted by permission of the publisher.

Contemporary Review, v. 54, September, 1888.

The Edinburgh Review, v. II, July, 1803; v. XLII, August, 1825.

English Literary Renaissance, v. 14, Spring, 1984. Copyright © 1984 by *English Literary Renaissance.* Reprinted by permission of the publisher.

The Essex Gazette, May 24, 1828.

Feminist Studies, v. 3, Spring-Summer, 1976. Copyright © 1976 by Feminist Studies, Inc. Reprinted by permission of the publisher, c/o Women's Studies Program, University of Maryland, College Park, MD 20742.

The Harvard Monthly, v. II, June, 1886.

Harvard Theological Review, v. 41, April, 1948.

The Huntington Library Quarterly, v. XX, May, 1957.

Journal of Near Eastern Studies, v. 30, April, 1971; v. 40, October, 1981. © 1971, 1981 by The University of Chicago. All rights reserved. Both reprinted by permission of the publisher.

The Journal of Speculative Philosophy, v. XVI, July, 1882.

THE EXCERPTS IN LC, VOLUME 9, WERE REPRINTED FROM THE FOLLOWING BOOKS:

Adams, John. From *Defence of the Constitutions of Government of the United States of America, Vol. I*. Hall & Sellers, 1787.

Al-Lari, 'Abd al-Ghafur. From "The Translation of al-Lari's 'Commentary' on 'al Durrah al-Fakhirah'," in *The Precious Pearl: Al-Jami's al-Durrah al-Fakhirah*. By al-Jami, edited and translated by Nicholas Heer. State University of New York Press, 1979. Translation © 1979 State University of New York. All rights reserved. Reprinted by permission of the publisher.

Allison, Henry E. From *Benedict de Spinoza: An Introduction*. Revised edition. Yale University Press, 1987. Copyright © 1987 by Yale University. All rights reserved. Reprinted by permission of the publisher.

Althaus, Paul. From *The Theology of Martin Luther*. Translated by Robert C. Schultz. Fortress Press, 1966. © 1966 by Fortress Press. Reprinted by permission of the publisher.

Altman, Leslie. From "Christine de Pisan: First Professional Woman of Letters (French, 1364-1430?)," in *Female Scholars: A Tradition of Learned Women before 1800*. Edited by J. R. Brink. Eden Press Women's Publications, 1980. © 1980 Eden Press Women's Publications. Reprinted by permission of the publisher.

Arber, Edward. From an introduction to *Works: 1608-1631*. By John Smith, edited by Edward Arber. Edward Arber, 1884.

Arberry, A. J. From *Classical Persian Literature*. George Allen & Unwin Ltd., 1958.

Arnold, Matthew. From *Essays in Criticism*. Second series. Macmillan and Co., 1889.

Astell, Mary. From a preface to *The Embassy Letters, 2 Vols*. By Lady Mary Worley Montagu. N.p., 1763.

Atkinson, James. From *Martin Luther and the Birth of Protestantism*. Penguin Books, 1968. Copyright © James Atkinson, 1968. Reprinted by permission of the author.

Aubin, Penelope. From *The Strange Adventures of the Count de Vinevil and His Family*. E. Bell, 1721.

Babur Padshah Ghazi, Zahiru'din Muhammad. From *The Babur-nama in English (Memoirs of Babur), Vol. I*. Translated by Annette Susannah Beveridge. Luzac & Co., 1922.

Bainton, Roland H. From *Here I Stand: A Life of Martin Luther*. Abingdon-Cokesbury Press, 1950. Copyright 1950 by Pierce and Smith. Renewed 1977 by Roland H. Bainton. All rights reserved. Reprinted by permission of the publisher, Abingdon Press.

Barbour, Philip L. From an introduction to "Advertisements for the Unexperienced Planters of New England, or Any Where (1631)," in *The Complete Works of Captain John Smith (1580-1631): Vol. III*. Edited by Philip L. Barbour. University of North Carolina Press, 1986. © 1986 The University of North Carolina Press. All rights reserved. Reprinted by permission of the publisher.

Barbour, Philip L. From *The Three Worlds of Captain John Smith*. Houghton Mifflin, 1964. Copyright © 1964 by Philip L. Barbour. All rights reserved. Reprinted by permission of Houghton Mifflin Company.

Bayle, Pierre. From *Historical and Critical Dictionary: Selections*. Translated by Richard H. Popkin with Craig Brush. The Bobbs-Merrill Company, Inc., 1965. Copyright © 1965 Macmillan Publishing Company. All rights reserved. Reprinted by permission of Richard H. Popkin.

Beasley, Jerry C. From "Politics and Moral Idealism: The Achievement of Some Early Women Novelists," in *Fetter'd or Free?: British Women Novelists, 1670-1815*. Edited by Mary Anne Schofield and Cecilia Macheski. Ohio University Press, 1986. Copyright © 1986 by Ohio University Press. All rights reserved. Reprinted by permission of the publisher.

Benét, Stephen Vincent. From *Western Star*. Farrar & Rinehart, 1943. Copyright, 1943, by Farrar & Rinehart, Inc. Renewed 1971 by Holt, Rinehart & Winston, Inc. All rights reserved. Reprinted by permission of the author.

Brooks, Cleanth. From *The Well Wrought Urn: Studies in the Structure of Poetry*. Reynal & Hitchcock, 1947. Copyright 1947, renewed 1975 by Cleanth Brooks. Reprinted by permission of Harcourt Brace Jovanovich, Inc.

Brown, Alexander, ed. From "Brief Biographies: Captain John Smith," in *The Genesis of the United States, Vol. II*. Houghton, Mifflin and Company, 1890.

Browne, Edward G. From *A History of Persian Literature under Tartar Dominion: (1265-1502)*. Cambridge at the University Press, 1920.

Bunyan, John. From *Grace Abounding to the Chief of Sinners*. Sixth edition. Nathaniel Ponder, 1688.

Burgh, Albert. From a letter in *The Correspondence of Spinoza*. Edited and translated by A. Wolf. Lincoln MacVeagh, 1928.

Bush, Douglas. From *John Milton: A Sketch of His Life and Writings*. The Macmillan Company, 1964. Copyright © Macmillan Publishing Company, 1964. All rights reserved. Reprinted with permission of Macmillan Publishing Company.

Byles, A. T. P. From an introduction to *The Book of Fayttes of Armes and of Chyvalrye*. By Christine de Pisan, edited by A. T. P. Byles, translated by William Caxton. Oxford University Press, 1932.

Cabell, James Branch. From *Let Me Lie*. Farrar, Straus and Company, 1947. Copyright, 1947 by James Branch Cabell. Renewed 1974 by Margaret Freeman Cabell. All rights reserved. Reprinted by permission of the Literary Estate of James Branch Cabell.

Caird, John. From *Spinoza*. J. B. Lippincott Company, 1888.

Cairns, Huntington, Allen Tate, and Mark Van Doren. From *Invitation to Learning*. Random House, 1941. Copyright, 1941, by The Columbia Broadcasting System, Inc. Renewed 1968 by Huntington Cairns. Reprinted by permission of the Literary Estates of Allen Tate and Mark Van Doren.

Calvin, John. From a letter in *Letters of John Calvin, Vol. I*. Edited by Jules Bonnet, translated by David Constable. T. Constable & Co., 1855.

Carlyle, Thomas. From "Lady Mary Worley Montagu," in *The Edinburgh Encyclopaedia, Vol. XIV*. Edited by David Brewater. William Blackwood, 1830.

From *The Censure of the Rota upon Mr. Miltons Book*. Paul Giddy, 1660.

Chatterton, E. Keble. From *Captain John Smith*. Harper & Brothers, 1927. Copyright, 1927 by Harper & Row, Publishers, Inc. Renewed 1955 by Robert Errington Gibbs. Reprinted by permission of Harper & Row, Publishers, Inc.

Chesterton, G. K. From *Saint Thomas Aquinas*. Sheed & Ward, Inc. 1933.

Coleridge, S. T. From *The Complete Works of Samuel Taylor Coleridge*. Edited by W. G. T. Shedd. Harper & Brothers, 1853.

Coleridge, Samuel Taylor. From *Coleridge on the Seventeenth Century*. Edited by Roberta Florence Brinkley. Duke University Press, 1955.

Coleridge, Samuel Taylor. From *The Philosophical Lectures of Samuel Taylor Coleridge*. Edited by Kathleen Coburn. The Pilot Press Limited, 1949.

Colerus, John. From *The Life of Benedict de Spinoza*. Benjamin Bragg, 1706.

Collins, James. From *Spinoza on Nature*. Southern Illinois University Press, 1984. Copyright © 1984 by the Board of Trustees of Southern Illinois University. All rights reserved. Reprinted by permission of the publisher.

Costello, Louisa Stuart. From *The Rose Garden of Persia*. Longman, Brown, Green, & Longmans, 1845.

Curley, E. M. From *Spinoza's Metaphysics: An Essay in Interpretation*. Cambridge, Mass.: Harvard University Press, 1969. Copyright © 1969 by the President and Fellows of Harvard College. All rights reserved. Excerpted by permission of the publishers.

Davis, F. Hadland. From *The Persian Mystics: Jami*. John Murray, 1908.

Deane, Charles. From a note from "Wingfield's Discourse of Virginia," in *Transactions and Collections of the American Antiquarian Society, Vol. IV*. American Antiquarian Society, 1860.

De Casseres, Benjamin. From *Forty Immortals*. Joseph Lawren, Publisher, 1926. Copyright, 1926, by Benjamin De Casseres. Renewed 1953 by Mrs. Benjamin De Casseres.

Dennis, John. From a preface to *The Passion of Byblis*. By Ovid. R. Parker, 1692.

DePorte, M. V. From an introduction to *Enthusiasmus Triumphatus (1662)*. By Henry More. William Andrews Clark Memorial Library, 1966. Reprinted by permission of the publisher.

Donne, John. From "To His Friend Captaine John Smith, and His Work," in *The Generall Historie of Virginia, New-England, and the Summer Illes*. By John Smith. Michael Sparks, 1624.

Dryden, John. From "Epigram on Milton," in *Paradise Lost*. Fourth edition. By John Milton. Richard Bentley & Jacob Tonson, 1688.

Dryden, John. From "A Discourse Concerning the Original and Progress of Satire," in *The Satires of D. J. Juvenalis*. Translated by John Dryden. N.p., 1693.

Dryden, John. From "Dedication of the Aeneis," in *The Works of Virgil*. Translated by John Dryden. N.p., 1697.

Durant, Will. From *The Story of Philosophy: The Lives and Opinions of the Greater Philosophers*. Simon & Schuster, 1926. Copyright 1926 by Simon & Schuster, Inc. and E. Haldeman-Julius. Renewed 1953 by Will Durant. Reprinted by permission of the publisher.

Einstein, Albert. From an introduction to *Spinoza: Portrait of a Spiritual Hero*. By Rudolf Kayser, translated by Amy Allen and Maxim Newmark. Philosophical Library, 1946.

Eliot, T. S. From "Milton I," in *On Poetry and Poets*. Farrar, Straus and Cudahy, 1957, Faber & Faber, 1957. Copyright 1936 by T. S. Eliot. Renewed 1985 by Valerie Eliot. Reprinted by permission of Farrar, Straus and Giroux, Inc. In Canada by Faber and Faber Limited.

Emerson, Everett H. From *Captain John Smith*. Twayne, 1971. Copyright 1971 by Twayne Publishers. All rights reserved. Reprinted with the permission of Twayne Publishers, a division of G. K. Hall & Co., Boston.

Emerson, Ralph Waldo. From *The Early Lectures of Ralph Waldo Emerson: 1833-1836, Vol. I*. Edited by Stephen E. Whicher and Robert E. Spiller. Cambridge, Mass.: Harvard University Press, 1959. Copyright © 1959 by the President and Fellows of Harvard College. Copyright renewed © 1987 by Elizabeth T. Whicher. Excerpted by permission of the publishers.

Engels, Friedrich. From *The Peasant War in Germany*. Edited and translated by Vic Schneierson. Second revised edition. Progress Publishers, 1965.

Erasmus, Desiderius. From a letter in *Christian Humanism and the Reformation: Selected Writings*. Edited by John C. Olin. Harper & Row, 1965. Copyright © 1965 by John C. Olin. All rights reserved. Excerpted by permission of Harper & Row, Publishers, Inc.

Erasmus, Desiderius. From *The Correspondence of Erasmus: Letters 842 to 992, 1518 to 1519*. Translated by R. A. B. Mynors and D. F. S. Thomson. University of Toronto Press, 1982. © University of Toronto Press 1982. Reprinted by permission of the publisher.

Filmer, Sir Robert. From *Observations Concerning the Originall of Government*. R. Royston, 1652.

Finch, Robert. From *The Sixth Sense: Individualism in French Poetry, 1686-1760*. University of Toronto Press, 1966. © University of Toronto Press, 1966. Reprinted by permission of the publisher.

Fiske, John. From *Old Virginia and Her Neighbours, Vol. I*. Houghton Mifflin Company, 1897.

FitzGerald, Edward. From "Letter to Professor Cowell," in *Salaman and Absal: An Allegory*. By Jami, edited by Nathan Haskell Dole, translated by Edward FitzGerald. L. C. Page and Company, Incorporated, 1899.

Forster, E. M. From *Two Cheers for Democracy*. Harcourt Brace Jovanovich, 1951, Edward Arnold, 1951. Copyright 1951 by E. M. Forster. Renewed 1979 by Donald Parry. Reprinted by permission of Harcourt Brace Jovanovich, Inc. In Canada by Edward Arnold (Publishers) Ltd.

Frye, Northrop. From an introduction to *"Paradise Lost" and Selected Poetry and Prose*. By John Milton, edited by Northrop Frye. Holt, Rinehart and Winston, 1951. Introduction copyright, 1951, renewed 1979, by Northrop Frye. Reprinted by permission of Holt, Rinehart and Winston, Inc.

Fuller, Thomas. From *The History of the Worthies of England*. J. G. W. L. and W. G., 1662.

George, Edward Augustus. From *Seventeenth Century Men of Latitude: Forerunners of the New Theology*. Charles Scribner's Sons, 1908.

Gibbbs, Lewis. From *The Admirable Lady Mary: The Life and Times of Lady Mary Wortley Montagu (1689-1762)*. William Morrow and Company, 1949.

Gilfillan, Rev. George. From *Specimens with Memoirs of the Less-Known British Poets, Vol. II*. James Nichol, 1860.

Goethe, Johann Wolfgang von. From *The Autobiography of Goethe: Truth and Fiction, Relating to My Life, Vol. I*. Translated by John Oxenford. Belford, Clarke & Company, Publishers, 1882.

Grieder, Josephine. From an introduction to *The Life of Madam de Beaumount, a French Lady* and *The Strange Adventures of the Count de Vinevil and His Family*. By Penelope Aubin. Garland, 1973. Introduction copyright © 1973, by Garland Publishing, Inc. All rights reserved. Reprinted by permission of the publisher.

Grieder, Josephine. From an introduction to *The Rash Resolve* by Eliza Haywood and *The Life and Adventures of the Lady Lucy* by Penelope Aubin. Garland Publishing, Inc., 1973. Introduction copyright © 1973, by Garland Publishing, Inc. All rights reserved. Reprinted by permission of the publisher.

Grisar, Hartmann, S.J. From *Luther, Vol. II*. Edited by Luigi Cappadelta, translated by E. M. Lamond. Kegan Paul, Trench, Trübner & Co., Ltd., 1916.

Grosart, Rev. Alexander B. From "Memorial-Introduction: Critical," in *The Complete Poems of Dr. Henry More (1614- 1687)*. Edited by Alexander B. Grosart. T. and A. Constable, 1878.

Grubbs, Henry A. From *Jean-Baptiste Rousseau: His Life and Works*. Princeton University Press, 1941. Copyright 1941, renewed 1969 by Princeton University Press. Reprinted with permission of the publisher.

Grundtvig, N. F. S. From "Sermons: All Saint's Day," translated by Enok Mortensen, in *Selected Writings*. Edited by Johannes Knudsen, translated by Johannes Knudsen, Enok Mortensen, and Ernest D. Nielsen. Fortress Press, 1976. Copyright © 1976 by Fortress Press. All rights reserved. Reprinted by permission of the publisher.

Haile, H. G. From "Luther as Renaissance Writer," in *The Renaissance and Reformation in Germany: An Introduction.* Edited by Gerhart Hoffmeister. Frederick Ungar, 1977. Copyright © 1977 by The Ungar Publishing Company. Reprinted by permission of the publisher.

Halsband, Robert. From "'Condemned to Petticoats': Lady Mary Wortley Montagu as Feminist and Writer," in *The Dress of Words: Essays on Restoration and Eighteenth Century Literature in Honor of Richmond P. Bond.* Edited by Robert B. White, Jr. University of Kansas Libraries, 1978. © 1978 by Robert Halsband. Reprinted by permission of the author.

Heer, Nicholas. From an introduction to *The Precious Pearl: Al-Jami's al-Durrah al-Fakhirah.* By al-Jami, edited and translated by Nicholas Heer. State University of New York Press, 1979. Translation © 1979 State University of New York. All rights reserved. Reprinted by permission of the publisher.

Hegel, Georg Wilhelm Friedrich. From *Lectures on the History of Philosophy, Vol. 3.* Translated by E. S. Haldane and Frances H. Simson. Kegan Paul, Trench, Trübner & Co. Ltd., 1896.

Heine, Heinrich. From *Germany, Vol. I.* Translated by Charles Godfrey Leland. William Heinemann, 1892.

Heine, Heinrich. From *Religion and Philosophy in Germany: A Fragment.* Translated by John Snodgrass. Houghton, Mifflin and Company, 1882.

Henry VIII. From *Miscellaneous Writings of Henry the Eighth.* Edited by Francis Macnamara. The Golden Cockerel Press, 1924.

Henry, William Wirt. From "The Address," in *Proceedings of the Virginia Historical Society.* Virginia Historical Society, 1882.

Herder, Johann Gottfried. From *God: Some Conversations.* Translated by Frederick H. Burkhardt. Veritas Press, 1940.

Hill, Christopher. From *Milton and the English Revolution.* Faber, 1977. © 1977 by Christopher Hill. All rights reserved. Reprinted by permission of Brandt & Brandt Literary Agents, Inc. In Canada by Faber & Faber Ltd.

Hillard, George S. From "Account of Captain Smith's Writings," in *The Library of American Biography.* By J. Sparks. Hilliard, Gray & Co., 1834.

Howard, M. F. From an introduction to *The Life of the Learned and Pious Dr. Henry More.* By Richard Ward, edited by M. F. Howard. The Theosophical Publishing Society, 1911.

Hoyles, John. From *The Waning of the Renaissance, 1640-1740: Studies in the Thought and Poetry of Henry More, John Norris and Isaac Watts.* Martinus Nijhoff, 1971. © 1971 by Martinus Nijhoff. All rights reserved. Reprinted by permission of the publisher.

Jami, Mulla Nuru d-Din 'Abdu' r-Rahman. From an extract in *A History of Persian Literature under Tartar Dominion (A.D. 1265- 1502).* By Edward G. Browne. Cambridge at the University Press, 1920.

Jaspers, Karl. From *The Great Philosophers: The Original Thinkers.* Edited by Hannah Arendt, translated by Ralph Manheim. Harcourt Brace Jovanovich, 1966. English translation copyright © 1962 by Harcourt Brace Jovanovich, Inc. Reprinted by permission of the publisher.

Johnson, Samuel. From *Lives of the English Poets; and a Criticism on Their Works, Vol. I.* Whitestone, Williams, Colles, Wilson, 1779.

Kant, Immanuel. From *The Critique of Judgement.* Translated by James Creed Meredith. Oxford at the Clarendon Press, 1952.

Keats, John. From *The Complete Poetical Works and Letters of John Keats.* Edited by H. E. Scudder. Houghton Mifflin Company, 1899.

Keats, John. From *The Complete Works of John Keats, Vol. III.* Edited by H. Buxton Forman. Gowans & Gray, 1901.

Kemp-Welch, Alice. From *Of Six Mediaeval Women.* Macmillan and Co., Limited, 1913.

Lancaster, Henry Carrington. From *A History of French Dramatic Literature in the Seventeenth Century, Part IV: The Period of Racine, 1673-1700, Vol. II.* The Johns Hopkins University Press, 1940. Copyright 1940, The Johns Hopkins Press. Renewed 1967 by Mrs. H. Carrington Lancaster. Reprinted by permission of the publisher.

Lang, Andrew. From *History of English Literature: From "Beowulf" to Swinburne.* Longmans, Green and Co. 1912.

Leibniz, Gottfried Wilhelm. From *Philosophical Papers and Letters, Vol. I.* Edited and translated by Leroy E. Loemker. The University of Chicago Press, 1956.

L'Estrange, Sir Roger. From *No Blinde Guides.* Henry Broome, 1660.

Levy, Reuben. From *Persian Literature: An Introduction.* Oxford University Press, London, 1923.

Lewis, C. S. From *A Preface to Paradise Lost.* Revised edition. Oxford University Press, London, 1942.

Lichtenstein, Aharon. From *Henry More: The Rational Theology of a Cambridge Platonist*. Cambridge, Mass.: Harvard University Press, 1962. Copyright © 1962 by the President and Fellows of Harvard College. All rights reserved. Excerpted by permission of the publishers.

Loewenich, Walther von. From *Martin Luther: The Man and His Work*. Translated by Lawrence W. Denef. Augsburg, 1986. English translation copyright © 1986 Augsburg Publishing House. All rights reserved. Reprinted by permission of the publisher.

London, April. From "Placing the Female: The Metonymic Garden in Amatory and Pious Narrative, 1700-1740," in *Fetter'd or Free?: British Women Novelists, 1670-1815*. Edited by Mary Anne Schofield and Cecilia Macheski. Ohio University Press, 1986. Copyright © 1986 by Ohio University Press. All rights reserved. Reprinted by permission of the publisher.

Lucas, Jean Maximilien? From *The Oldest Biography of Spinoza*. Edited and translated by A. Wolf. George Allen & Unwin Ltd., 1927.

Luther, Martin. From "Preface to the Complete Edition of Luther's Latin Writings, 1545," translated by Lewis W. Spitz, Sr., in *Luther's Works: Career of the Reformer IV, Vol. 34*. Edited by Lewis W. Spitz. Muhlenberg Press, 1960. © 1960 by Muhlenberg Press. Reprinted by permission of the publisher.

MacCarthy, B. G. From *Women Writers: Their Contribution to the English Novel, 1621-1744*. Cork University Press, 1944.

MacDonald, George. From *England's Antiphon*. Macmillan & Co., 1868.

Maritain, Jacques. From *Three Reformers: Luther—Descartes— Rousseau*. Charles Scribner's Sons, 1955.

Marvell, Andrew. From "On Paradise Lost," in *Paradise Lost: A Poem in Twelve Books*. By John Milton. Second edition. S. Simmons, 1674.

McKeon, Richard. From *The Philosophy of Spinoza: The Unity of His Thought*. Longmans, Green and Co., 1928.

McLeod, Enid. From *The Order of the Rose: The Life and Ideas of Christine de Pizan*. Rowman and Littlefield, 1976, Chatto & Windus, 1976. © Enid McLeod 1976. All rights reserved. Reprinted by permission of Rowman and Littlefield. In Canada by the Literary Estate of Enid McLeod and Chatto & Windus.

Melanchthon, Philip. From "Appendix: Funeral Oration over Luther," in *Philip Melanchthon: The Protestant Preceptor of Germany, 1497-1560*. By James William Richard. G. P. Putnam's Sons, 1898.

Melanchthon, Philip. From "Luther and the Paris Theologians," in *Selected Writings*. Edited by Elmer Ellsworth Flack and Lowell J. Satre. Translated by Charles Leander Hill. Augsburg Publishing House, 1962. Copyright © 1962 Augsburg Publishing House. All rights reserved. Reprinted by permission of the publisher.

Melville, Lewis. From *Lady Mary Wortley Montagu: Her Life and Letters (1689-1762)*. Houghton Mifflin Company, 1925.

Meyer, Ludovicus. From an extract in *The Oldest Biography of Spinoza*. By Jean Maximilien Lucas? Edited and translated by A. Wolf. George Allen & Unwin Ltd., 1927.

Milton, John. From *Paradise Lost: A Poem in Twelve Books*. Second edition. S. Simmons, 1674.

Miner, Earl. From *The Restoration Mode from Milton to Dryden*. Princeton University Press, 1974. Copyright © 1974 by Princeton University Press. All rights reserved. Reprinted with permission of the publisher.

More, Paul Elmer. From *On Being Human: New Shelburne Essays, Vol. III*. Princeton University Press, 1936. Copyright, 1936, renewed 1964 by Princeton University Press. Reprinted with permission of the publisher.

More, Paul Elmer. From *The Sceptical Approach to Religion*. Princeton University Press, 1934. Copyright 1934, renewed 1962 by Princeton University Press. All rights reserved. Reprinted with permission of the publisher.

More, Thomas. From *The Complete Works of St. Thomas More, Vol. 5, Part I*. Edited by John M. Headley, translated by Sister Scholastica Mandeville. Yale University Press, 1969. Copyright © 1969 by Yale University. All rights reserved. Reprinted by permission of the publisher.

Morison, Samuel Eliot. From *Massachusettensis de Conditoribus; or, The Builders of the Bay Colony*. Houghton Mifflin, 1930. Copyright, 1930, renewed 1958, by Samuel Eliot Morison. All rights reserved. Reprinted by permission of Houghton Mifflin Company.

Naess, Arne. From "Is Freedom Consistent with Spinoza's Determinism?" in *Spinoza on Knowing, Being and Freedom*. Edited by J. G. Van Der Bend. Van Gorcum, 1974. © 1974. Koninklijke Van Gorcum & Comp. B.V., Assen, The Netherlands. Reprinted by permission of the publisher.

Neill, Edward D. From *History of the Virginia Company of London*. J. Munsell, 1869.

Nicholson, Reynold A. From *The Mystics of Islam*. George Bell & Sons Ltd., 1914.

Nicolson, Marjorie Hope. From *Mountain Gloom and Mountain Glory: The Development of the Aesthetics of the Infinite.* Cornell University Press, 1959. © 1959 by Cornell University. Renewed 1987 by Marjorie Hope Nicolson. Used by permission of the publisher, Cornell University Press.

Niebuhr, H. Richard. From "Martin Luther," in *Christian Ethics: Sources of the Living Tradition.* Edited by Waldo Beach and H. Richard Niebuhr. Ronald Press, 1955. Copyright, 1955, by The Ronald Press Company. Renewed 1983 by Waldo Beach and Florence Niebuhr. All rights reserved. Reprinted by permission of the publisher.

Niebuhr, Reinhold. From *The Nature and Destiny of Man, a Christian Interpretation: Human Destiny, Vol. II.* Charles Scribner's Sons, 1943. Copyright, 1943, by Charles Scribner's Sons. Renewed 1971 by Reinhold Niebuhr. All rights reserved. Reprinted with the permission of Charles Scribner's Sons, an imprint of Macmillan Publishing Company.

Nietzsche, Friedrich. From *The Joyful Wisdom.* Translated by Thomas Common. Second edition. The Macmillan Company, 1910.

Norris, John. From *A Collection of Miscellanies, Consisting of Poems, Essays, Discourses, and Letters.* Oxford, 1687.

Palfrey, John Gorham. From *History of New England during the Stuart Dynasty, Vol. I.* Little, Brown, and Company, 1858.

Panichas, George A. From *The Reverent Discipline: Essays in Literary Criticism and Culture.* University of Tennessee Press, 1974. Copyright © 1974 by The University of Tennessee Press, Knoxville. All rights reserved. Reprinted by permission of the publisher.

Paston, George. From *Lady Mary Wortley Montagu and Her Times.* G. P. Putnam's Sons, 1907.

Pelikan, Jaroslav. From *Luther the Expositor: Introduction to the Reformer's Exegetical Writings.* Concordia Publishing House, 1959. Copyright 1959, renewed 1987 by Concordia Publishing House. Reprinted by permission of the publisher.

Pollock, Sir Frederick, Bart. From *Spinoza: His Life and Philosophy.* Second edition. The Macmillan Company, 1899.

Pope, Alexander. From "Postscript," in *The Odyssey of Homer, 5 Vols.* Translated by Alexander Pope. Bernard Lintot, 1725-26.

Pope, Alexander. From *Of the Characters of Women: An Epistle to a Lady.* Lawton Gilliver, 1735.

Price, Paola Malpezzi. From "Masculine and Feminine Personae in the Love Poetry of Christine de Pisan," in *Gender and Literary Voice.* Edited by Janet Todd. Women & Literature, new series, Vol. 1. Holmes & Meier, 1980. Copyright © 1980 by Holmes & Meier Publishers, Inc. All rights reserved. Reprinted by permission of Holmes & Meier Publishers, Inc., 30 Irving Place, New York, NY 10003.

Rehatsek, E. From an introduction and preface to *The Beharistan (Abode of Spring).* By Jami, translated by E. Rehatsek. Benares, 1887.

Richardson, Jonathan. From "The Life of Milton, and a Discourse on 'Paradise Lost'," in *Explanatory Notes and Remarks on Milton's "Paradise Lost."* By Jonathan Richardson and Jonathan Richardson, Jr. James, John, and Paul Knapton, 1734.

Richetti, John J. From *Popular Fiction before Richardson: Narrative Patterns, 1700-1739.* Oxford at the Clarendon Press, 1969. © Oxford University Press, 1969. Reprinted by permission of Oxford University Press.

Rowse, A. L. From *The Elizabethans and America.* Harper & Brothers, 1959. Copyright © 1959, renewed 1987 by A. L. Rowse. All rights reserved. Reprinted by permission of Curtis Brown, Ltd. for A. L. Rowse.

Russell, Bertrand. From *A History of Western Philosophy, and Its Connection with Political and Social Circumstances from the Earliest Times to the Present Day.* G. Allen and Unwin Ltd., 1946. Copyright 1945, renewed 1972 by Bertrand Russell. All rights reserved. Reprinted by permission of Unwin Hyman Ltd.

Rypka, Jan, with Otakar Klima and others. From *History of Iranian Literature.* Edited by Karl Jahn. D. Reidel Publishing, 1968. © 1968, D. Reidel Publishing Company. Reprinted by permission of the publisher.

Saarnivaara, Uuras. From *Luther Discovers the Gospel: New Light upon Luther's Way from Medieval Catholicism to Evangelical Faith.* Concordia Publishing House, 1951. Copyright 1951, renewed 1980, by Concordia Publishing House. Reprinted by permission of the publisher.

Saintsbury, George. From *The Peace of the Augustans: A Survey of Eighteenth Century Literature as a Place of Rest and Refreshment.* G. Bell and Sons, Ltd., 1916.

Schleiermacher, Friedrich. From *On Religion: Speeches to Its Cultured Despisers.* Translated by John Oman. K. Paul, Trench, Trübner & Co., Ltd., 1893.

Seelye, John. From *Prophetic Waters: The River in Early American Life and Literature.* Oxford University Press, 1977. Copyright © 1977 by John Seelye. Reprinted by permission of Oxford University Press, Inc.

Shah, Idries. From *The Sufis.* The Octagon Press, 1964. All rights reserved. Reprinted by permission of the publisher.

Shawcross, John T. From "The Style and Genre of 'Paradise Lost'," in *New Essays on "Paradise Lost."* Edited by Thomas Kranidas. University of California Press, 1969. Copyright © 1969 by The Regents of the University of California. Reprinted by permission of the publisher.

Shelley, Percy Bysshe. From *The Prose Works of Percy Bysshe Shelley*. Edited by Harry Buxton Forman. Reeves and Turner, 1876?

Smith, Bradford. From *Captain John Smith: His Life & Legend*. J. B. Lippincott Company. Copyright, 1953 by Bradford Smith. Renewed 1981 by Alan B. Smith. Reprinted by permission of Harper & Row, Publishers, Inc.

Smith, John. From *The Generall Historie of Virginia, New England, and the Summer Illes: 1584-1624*. Michael Sparks, 1624.

Southey, Robert. From "Henry More's Song of the Soul," in *Omniana, or Horae Otiosiores*. By Robert Southey and S. T. Coleridge. Longman, Hurst, Rees, Orme, and Brown, 1812.

Spencer, Jane. From *The Rise of the Woman Novelist from Aphra Behn to Jane Austen*. Blackwell, 1986. © Jane Spencer, 1986. All rights reserved. Reprinted by permission of Basil Blackwell Limited.

Strachey, Lytton. From *Characters and Commentaries*. Harcourt Brace Jovanovich, 1933. Copyright, 1933, renewed 1961, by James Strachey. Reprinted by permission of Harcourt Brace Jovanovich, Inc.

Strauss, Leo. From *Spinoza's Critique of Religion*. Schocken Books, 1965. Reprinted by permission of the Literary Estate of Leo Strauss.

Striker, Laura Polanyi. From "Captain John Smith's Hungary and Transylvania," in *Captain John Smith: His Life & Legend*. By Brandford Smith. J. B. Lippincott, 1953. Copyright, 1953 by Bradford Smith. Renewed 1981 by Alan B. Smith. Reprinted by permission of Harper & Row, Publishers, Inc.

Stuart, Lady Louisa. From "Introductory Anecdotes," in *The Letters and Works of Lady Mary Wortley Montagu, 3 Vols*. Edited by Lord Wharncliffe. R. Bentley, 1837.

Tashkubrizadah, Isam al-Din Ahmad ibn Mustafa. From an extract in an introduction to *The Precious Pearl: Al-Jami's al-Durrah al-Fakhirah*. By al-Jami, edited and translated by Nicholas Heer. State University of New York Press, 1979. Translation © 1979 State University of New York. All rights reserved. Reprinted by permission of the publisher.

Tillich, Paul. From *A History of Christian Thought*. Edited by Carl E. Braaten. Revised second edition. Harper & Row, 1968. Copyright © 1968 by Hannah Tillich. All rights reserved. Reprinted by permission of Harper & Row, Publishers, Inc.

Tillyard, E. M. W. From *Milton*. Chatto & Windus, 1930.

Trilling, Lionel. From *Prefaces to The Experience of Literature*. Harcourt Brace Jovanovich, 1979. Copyright © 1967 by Lionel Trilling. Copyright © 1979 by Diana Trilling and James Trilling. Reprinted by permission of Harcourt Brace Jovanovich, Inc.

Troeltsch, Ernst. From *Protestantism and Progress: A Historical Study of the Relation of Protestantism to the Modern World*. Translated by W. Montgomery. G. P. Putnam's Sons, 1912.

Tulloch, John. From *Rational Theology and Christian Philosophy in England in the Seventeenth Century, Vol. II*. Second edition. William Blackwood and Sons, 1874.

Tuve, Rosemond. From *Allegorical Imagery: Some Mediaeval Books and Their Posterity*. Princeton University Press, 1966. Copyright © 1966 by Princeton University Press. All rights reserved. Reprinted with permission of the publisher.

Tyler, Moses Coit. From *A History of American Literature: 1607-1676, Vol. I*. G. P. Putnam's Sons, 1878.

Voltaire. From *An Essay upon the Civil Wars of France, and also upon the Epick Poetry of the European Nations: From Homer Down to Milton*. Samuel Jallasson, 1727.

Voltaire, François Marie Arouet de. From *The Works of Voltaire: A Contemporary Version*. Edited by Tobias Smollett, translated by William F. Fleming. Revised edition. E. R. DuMont, 1901.

Ward, Richard. From *The Life of the Learned and Pious Dr. Henry More*. Joseph Downing, 1710.

Warner, Marina. From a foreword to *The Book of the City Ladies*. By Christine de Pisan, translated by Earl Jeffrey Richards. Persea Books, 1982. Foreword copyright © 1982 by Marina Warner. All rights reserved. Reprinted by permission of the publisher.

Whinfield, E. H. From a preface to *Lawa'ih: A Treatise on Sufism*. By Nur-Ud-Din 'Abd-Ur-Rahman Jami. Translated by E. H. Whinfield. Oriental Translation Fund, 1906.

Wienpahl, Paul. From *The Radical Spinoza*. New York University Press, 1979. Copyright © 1979 by New York University. Reprinted by permission of the publisher.

Willard, Charity Cannon. From *Christine de Pizan: Her Life and Works*. Persea Books, 1984. Copyright © 1984 by Charity Cannon Willard. All rights reserved. Reprinted by permission of the publisher.

Willey, Basil. From *The Seventeenth Century Background: Studies in the Thought of the Age in Relation to Poetry and Religion*. Chatto & Windus, 1934.

Williams, Charles. From an introduction to *The English Poems of John Milton*. Oxford University Press, London, 1940.

Wolf, A. From an introduction to *The Correspondence of Spinoza*. Edited and translated by A. Wolf. George Allen & Unwin, Ltd., 1928.

Wordsworth, William. From *Poems, 2 Vols.* Longman, 1807.

Yenal, Edith. From *Christine de Pizan: Second Edition.* To be published by Scarecrow Press, Inc., Metuchen, N.J., 1989. Appears here by permission of the publisher and the author.

Zwingli, Huldrych. From "Tribute to Luther: 'A Friendly Explanation'," translated by G. R. Potter, in *Huldrych Zwingli*. Edited by G. R. Potter. St. Martin's Press, 1978. Copyright © G. R. Potter 1977. All rights reserved. Used by permission of St. Martin's Press, Inc.

ISBN 0-8103-6108-6

90000

9 780810 361089